The which?
Good Food
Guide 2007

The which?
Good Food
Guide 2007

Edited by
Andrew
Turvil

which

Which? books are commissioned by
Consumers' Association and published by
Which? Ltd, 2 Marylebone Road, London NW1 4DF
Email: *books@which.co.uk*

Distributed by Littlehampton Book Services Ltd
Faraday Close, Durrington, Worthing, West Sussex
BN13 3RB

British Library Cataloguing in Publication Data
A catalogue record for this book is available from the
British Library

ISBN 13: 978 1 84490 027 5
ISBN 10: 1 84490 027 4

Contributing writers: Elizabeth Carter, David Kenning, Lisa Marks and Stuart Walton

Sub-editors and proofreaders: David Kenning, Hugh Morgan, Katherine Servant

Editorial and production: Elizabeth Bowden, Ian Robinson and Angela Newton
Cover design: Adrian Morris, Ian Ascott and Suzanne Taylor
Cover photographs: Getty images/ABPL

Typeset by Saxon Graphics Ltd, Derby
Printed and bound by Bookprint S L, Barcelona

The Which? Good Food Guide makes every effort to be as accurate and up-to-date as
possible. However, readers should check details at the time of booking, particularly if they
have any special requirements.

For a full list of Which books, please call 01903 828557, access our website at www.which.co.uk, or
write to Littlehampton Book Services. For other enquiries call 0800 252100.

To submit a report on any restaurant, please visit *www.which.co.uk/gfgfeedback*

Contents

Choosing the best

The Good Food Guide is celebrating its 55th edition. Over the years our aims and guiding principles have remained constant, to help readers choose the best – and avoid the worst, while continual re-inspection and rewriting have ensured that we remain up-to-date and reflect the contemporary scene. In common with all Which? publications, *The Good Food Guide* is entirely independent and accepts no sponsorship, advertising or payment for inclusion. All restaurants are visited anonymously by our inspectors, who order and pay for their meals in exactly the same way as other diners. In compiling each new edition, we draw on an extensive database of recent reports, and keep a close watch on standards, chef changes and closures. We also inspect new establishments and welcome a select number of these to each year's guide.

Scores on the doors

Environmental health officers inspect food businesses for safety and hygiene. But although all UK local authorities have to inspect food outlets, they're under no obligation to proactively publish the results - and very few councils have done so.

Which? is campaigning for the hygiene score (as well as more detailed information) to be available on the web and the score itself to be displayed on the doors of food outlets. International evidence shows that this will help drive up hygiene standards through competition as well as help consumers make an informed choice.

What's more, this is very popular with consumers: Which? research from 2006 has revealed that almost everybody (97 per cent) feels that they're entitled to know how their local restaurants score for hygiene. Seven out of eight (87 per cent) people want to see this information before they enter a restaurant - so called 'scores on doors' - and nine out of ten (90 per cent) think scores should be available online. There is some progress – the Food Standards Agency is piloting scores on the doors schemes in parts of Scotland and the East Midlands.

A few Councils across the UK do publish information so it is worth checking your council's website to find out if information is available – and asking them why not if they don't.

Using The Good Food Guide

Entries in *The Good Food Guide* are arranged in six sections: London, the rest of England, Scotland, Wales, Channel Islands and Northern Ireland. For London entries, restaurants are listed alphabetically *by name*; in all other sections, they are listed *by locality* (usually the name of the town or village).

- If you already know the name of the restaurant you want: go to the *index* at the back of the book.
- To search for restaurants in a particular area: go to the *maps* at the front of the book, just after page 32. Once you know the location (or, for London, the restaurant's name), go to the relevant section of the book to find the entry for the restaurants shown.
- For details of this year's award-winning restaurants: see the *lists* starting on page 25.

How to read a Good Food Guide entry

The Good Food Guide 2007 is designed to provide a range of information on each establishment. At the top of each entry is the restaurant's name, map reference and location, address, telephone number, its email or website address, as well as any symbols that may apply to the establishment. A description of the cuisine style is also given; this is not a comprehensive assessment of cooking style, but should act as a helpful pointer. At the top of entries you will also find the cooking mark, from 1 to 10 (see below) and the cost for one person having a three-course dinner including wine. The long middle section of the entry describes food, wines, atmosphere and setting, while the final section gives some additional details you might find useful.

Establishments that have not been rated for cooking are marked AR (Also Recommended). The name of the restaurant appears in italic and there is no cooking mark, cuisine style or price given. The description is shorter than a main entry and there are no additional details listed after this. In some cases an AR rating has been given because the chef is too new for us to have carried out a full assessment. Where subsequent reports and inspections merit it, such establishments may have a full entry devoted to them in future years.

The following pages show a sample entry and give a brief guide to the cooking marks and various symbols used throughout the book:

Cooking marks

Each restaurant allocated a mark out of ten has been endorsed by readers and our own independent inspectors. These scores are meant as an indication of the level of skill demonstrated in the cooking, and **every** restaurant assessed in this way is among the best in the UK.

1–2   **competent cooking** Sound, capable cooking

3–4   **competent to good cooking** Fine ingredients cooked appropriately, although there may be occasional inconsistencies

5–6   **good to very good cooking** High-quality ingredients, consistently good results

7–8   **very good to excellent cooking** High level of ambition, finest ingredients consistently treated with skill and imagination

9–10   **the best** The top restaurants in the country, highly individual and displaying impressive artistry

Symbols

The following symbols are used throughout this guide:

| NEW ENTRY | New main entry 2007 (may have been 'also recommended' in previous edition) |

AR   Not a full entry but provisionally recommended

🍾   Wine list well above the average (see page 30)

⊘   Smoking not permitted

£   Budget dining possible (£30 or less per person for three-course dinner, including coffee, a half-bottle of wine and service charge)

£5   Participating restaurant in *The Good Food Guide* £5 voucher scheme (see below for details)

🏠   Accommodation available

Cost

The price given is based on the cost of a typical three-course dinner for one person, including coffee, house wine and service, according to information supplied by the restaurant.

This sample entry shows how information is presented for each restaurant featured in the book.

map reference and restaurant locality

name of establishment

address, telephone number (and website if known)

cooking mark, type of cuisine and average per-person cost for a three course dinner including wine and service

symbols can denote above average wine, smoking prohibited, new chef, budget dining and participation in the £5 voucher scheme. See page 8 and the inside front cover for a full list

other details can include opening time, prices, service, seating, disabled facilities

---

MAP 3 BRIGHTON – East Sussex

Le Poulet Nouvelle

1 High Street, Brighton, BN1 3FG
Tel: (01000) 818181
Website: www.pouletnouvelle.co.uk

| Cooking 1 | Modern French | £68 |

This is what we call the narrative part of the entry, where we give you the low-down on each establishment. We will tell you whether it is a smart country house hotel standing in splendid isolation, a lively city Italian restaurant, or a seafood café overlooking the sea.

The food references come from readers' reports, official inspections, or from menus sent in by the restaurant. Specific dishes mentioned in the entries are not guaranteed to be on the menu at the time of a visit, rather they are intended as an indication of what the restaurant has delivered over the previous year, and are good examples of the style of food you can expect. Comments appearing in 'quotation marks' are generally verbatim comments from readers or inspectors that we considered suitably appropriate to quote in full.

We also write about the kind of service you can expect, again based on the experiences of the readers and inspectors, and most entries finish with details on the drinks available.

Chef: Fred Smith **Proprietors:** John and Josephine **Open:** Sun L 12.30 to 1.30, Mon to Sat D 7.30 to 9 **Closed:** 25 and 26 Dec **Meals:** alc (main courses £16.50 to £19.50). Set L Sun £23.50, Set D £39.50 **Service:** not inc **Cards:** Amex, Delta, Diners, MasterCard, Maestro, Visa **Details:** 80 seats. Car park. Vegetarian meals. Children's helpings. No smoking. Wheelchair access (not WC). No music. No mobile phones **Accommodation:** 16 rooms

---

Meals

At the bottom of each entry information on the types of meals is given, with any variations for lunch (L) and dinner (D), and details of availability. An à la carte menu is signified by the letters *alc*. This is followed by a range of prices for main courses, rounded up to the nearest 50p. *Set L* denotes a set-price lunch; *Set D* means set-price dinner. Set meals usually consist of three courses, but can include many more. If a set meal has fewer than three courses, this is stated. If there is a cover charge, this is also indicated. Brief details of other menus, such as light lunch or bar snacks, are also given.

Service

Net prices means that prices of food and wine are inclusive of service charge, and this is indicated clearly on the menu and bill; *not inc*, that service is not included and is left to the customer's discretion; *10%* that a fixed service charge of 10 per cent is automatically added to the bill; *10% (optional)*, that 10 per cent is added to the bill along with the word 'optional' or similar qualifier; and *none*, that no service charge is made or expected and that any money offered is refused.

Other details

Information is also given on *seating* and *outside seating* . We say *car park* if the restaurant provides free parking facilities for patrons (*small car park* if it has only a few spaces), and say *vegetarian meals* only if menus list at least one vegetarian option as a starter and one as a main course (if this is not noted, a restaurant may still be able to offer vegetarian options with prior notice – it is worth phoning to check).

Any restrictions on children are given, such as *no children* or *no children under 6 after 8pm*; otherwise, it can be assumed that children are welcome. In addition *children's helpings* are noted if smaller portions are available at a reduced price; *jacket and tie* if it is compulsory for men to wear a jacket and tie to the restaurant. *No smoking* means just that; smoking is not permitted on the premises. *Wheelchair access* means the proprietor has confirmed that the entrance is at least 80cm wide and passages at least 120cm wide in accordance with the Royal Association for Disability and Rehabilitation (RADAR) recommendations. *Also WC* means that the proprietor has assured us that toilet facilities are suitable for disabled people (*not WC* that these are not available or the proprietor is not sure). *Music* indicates that live or recorded music is usually played in the dining-room; *occasional music* that it sometimes is; *no music* that it never is. *No mobile phones* means the restaurant requests that these are switched off. At the end of London entries the nearest Underground station is given, where appropriate.

Accommodation

Where establishments offer overnight accommodation, the number of rooms is given. For further details and to check availability contact the restaurant directly.

Good Food Guide £5 voucher scheme

Restaurants that have elected to participate in *The Good Food Guide* £5 voucher scheme are indicated by a £5 symbol. Each voucher is redeemable against a pre-booked meal for a minimum of two people, **provided the customer highlights the intention to use the voucher at the time of booking**. Only one voucher may be used per table booked. For further details please see the reverse side of the vouchers themselves.

Good Food Guide Online

An online version of *The Good Food Guide* is available on the Internet to Which? Online subscribers; for details see www.which.co.uk.

Sending us your feedback

The Which? Good Food Guide receives thousands of reader reports, throughout the year. year. All these forms, emails and letters are recorded and logged, helping to provide a picture of where the good restaurants really are – and where standards may have fallen. This feedback also helps us to identify new establishments that have recently opened. Our anonymous inspectors are sent to restaurants only after places have been recommended. We have a special website dedicated to reader feedback. To log on to this, please go to: www.which.co.uk/gfgfeedback

When you visit our site, you'll be asked a number of questions about your dining experience. These will cover all aspects of the meal, including the quality of the food and drink, the service you received and the general setting. In particular, please consider the following points:

- **Setting:** can include views from the restaurant, as well as the ambience inside. How the restaurant is decorated, how it feels and what the general atmosphere is like.
- **Menus:** the kind of food that is served and any specific influences on the menu. In particular, what did you and others in your party eat? Were you impressed by the range of choice, and the ingredients used? Was the food well-prepared and well-presented?
- **Drinks:** the range of drinks available. Is the wine list extensive? Is it well-priced? Are there plenty of wines available by the glass, as well as by the bottle?
- **Service:** tell us about the efficiency and friendliness of the service you received and how it contributed to your meal.
- **Other points of interest**: In particular, if a restaurant has changed hands and/or acquired a new chef. If other services, such as children's meals, disabled facilities, seating arrangements or dining policy are worthy of note, then please let us know.

In addition to these categories, we'd like to know whether you would recommend the restaurant and if you would return for another meal.

If you do not have computer access, please write to us at *The Which? Good Food Guide*, Which? FREEPOST, 2 Marylebone Road, London, NW1 4DF
We look forward to reading your comments!

One further note
The overwhelming majority of reader's reports we receive are genuine and unsolicited. On very rare occasions we receive a report that has obviously been orchestrated by a restaurateur and, needless this to say, this is of no benefit to anybody. When you submit your feedback, we shall ask you to confirm that you have no connection with the restaurant management or proprietors, and that you have not been asked by them to contact us. It is only through maintaining these strict rules that we can confirm our status and integrity as truly independent.

Introduction

This is the 55th edition of The Good Food Guide, and our mission has remained pretty much the same since 1952: to seek out and review the best restaurants in the UK based on recommendations from thousands of enthusiastic eaters. We don't just take your word for it, though, and all restaurants are regularly visited by our team of inspectors. We're entirely independent, have no axe to grind, and don't take a penny from any restaurants or advertisers. You'll find all kinds of places within these pages, with only one common theme: good, fresh food. What this constitutes varies enormously, and reflects the diversity of restaurants that exist in this country. So, whether you want a curry in Bradford, a place with a bit of a buzz in Leeds, or some straight-up sushi in London, we can tell you what our research has turned up.

Consistently, over the last few years, market research companies and statisticians have told us that we're eating out more and more in the UK, and spending record amounts in restaurants. With the Good Food Guide you can make sure you're not disappointed, or ripped off, and within these pages you will get a taste of what to expect as you plan your next meal out. If you haven't already, please log on to our website (www.which.co.uk/gfgfeedback) and tell us about good meals you've enjoyed, and vent your frustrations at any disappointments.

Are you being served?

The quality of cooking in UK restaurants has undoubtedly improved over the life of the Good Food Guide, but has the quality of service? More and more restaurants vie for our attention (and our money), and, for the customer, food is only part of the equation when choosing where to go. Most people who write to us do so about positive experiences in restaurants, describing great meals they have had, and praising the output of the chefs working in the UK. Our website is not simply a whinging forum. But to eat out in this country is to know that let-downs are only just around the corner (often on the high street), and mediocrity (and worse) is available in abundance. The service in restaurants is a constant cause of frustration among readers.

Some commentators have lamented that we don't view service as a career in this country. Well, I don't think the answer to issues on poor service necessarily depends on the creation of a 'National Waiting School'. Fair pay, good working conditions, and sensitive staff relations may well help keep staff in place for longer, but it is on-the-spot training that matters, ensuring staff understand the tone and pace of the restaurant. It's no good being all chummy in a posh place, and no fun for the customer when staff are distant and uncommunicative in a lively brasserie. Good service is mostly about engagement: eye contact, listening, and good organisation, of course. If staff enjoy their jobs they're more likely to stay longer at the establishment, and shouldn't feel guilty about not wanting to make a career of it. A job as a waiter is a great grounding for a working life, and whether you want to rise through the ranks and eventually displace Jean-Claude Breton as maitre d' at Gordon Ramsay's flagship restaurant, or simply save up some money to go surfing at Waikeikei, that's all right with me, but please do the job with a smile, and don't forget my bleedin' glass of water (for the third time of asking). Restaurateurs spend a great deal of their time dealing with staffing issues, or so they keep on telling me, so issues around the maintenance of good standards in service is a headache for us all.

When the food side is under control, it is the service and atmosphere that distinguishes one restaurant from another. When it comes to deciding where to eat next time, customers will return to the one where they had the better time, and service is likely to be a key consideration. A good atmosphere and setting is a little harder to pin down, but would restaurateurs spend all this money on refurbishments, refits and interior designers if it didn't work? Let's face it, most of us are suckers for an aesthetically pleasing space; just ask Mr Conran.

Look, there goes another bandwagon

Some fads and fashions bring about frustration and despair (low-slung trousers, perhaps), but others seem perfect for the times. Such is the 'Bistrot de Luxe'. The time is right for these unpretentious and lively places, where the food is not overly worked or messed about. No pre-starters, pre-desserts, and myriad of tasters, but rather simple stuff, fair prices, and devotion to good quality produce. And they're not just popping up in London (see J Baker's in York). These restaurants might not be doing anything new, but they are making a virtue of straightforward cooking at a time when there seems an ever-increasing demand for it. The 'Luxe' (or 'Moderne') part might be reassurance to some that these are still comfortable, civilised places. See the pages of the Guide for entries for Arbutus, Galvin, Racine, and La Brasserie in Twickenham, as good examples of the genre.

Another trend is for small, 'tapas-style' dishes. The multiple-course tasting menu has long been a way for a chef to showcase their very best dishes, and by the virtue of the fact that there are so many courses, portion sizes are small. Too often, though, readers' report frustration at the difficulty in getting to grips with a dish that is gone in one or two mouthfuls. Rather like enjoying a good wine, a dish can grow in impact as you work your way through, with layers of flavour and texture revealed, but there is no chance of that with a wee taster portion. It helps if you're lucky enough to be served by waiting staff who can explain exactly what it is you're about to eat, but the pleasure can be over in an instant: pop it in your mouth and it's gone. Now you get it, and want another go, but it's too late, as here comes something else.

Getting hotter

What makes a restaurant hot-spot? What came first: the chicken or the creamy risotto of smoked chicken with Parmesan, sweet corn, tarragon and poached egg? Ludlow was the boom town of the 1990s, but it might be losing its crown since the departure of Shaun Hill and the closure of his Merchant House. Marlow in Buckinghamshire goes from strength to strength, with the arrival of Aiden Byrne at Danesfield House. It has been called the Padstow effect. Rick Stein's success in that town has brought him competition from other restaurateurs, who have arrived confident in the knowledge that there is a demand for good food, and enough customers to go around. And now Paul Ainsworth's No. 6 can claim to be the hottest ticket in that particular town. Padstow was an intelligent choice for a landmark seafood restaurant in the first place (being a fishing town and all), and Stein's Seafood Restaurant can claim to have helped grow the reputation of the area (and probably even the whole county) as a holiday destination. Food tourism is now big business.

A seriously good restaurant, or a headline-grabbing chef, can put a town or village on the map, there's no doubt about that, but it did take Rick Stein years of hard work before the 'effect' took off. There are hundreds of places listed in the Guide that aren't in locations that could remotely be called hot-spots (Winteringham in North Lincolnshire for a start), and for many of them such an influx of customers must be the stuff of dreams.

Independence of mind

To keep the Guide up-to-date, well informed and on the ball, we need you to tell us about your experiences in UK restaurants. This feedback on good lunches or indifferent dinners is the foundation of the book. Every main entry receives regular inspections from our team, and the best of the new recommendations are investigated, thus ensuring the Good Food Guide includes the very best restaurants in the country. The rating system – scoring from 1 to 10 – is an indication of the level kitchen's skill as reported to us by readers and inspectors, but it is important to remember that every entry in the Guide is being recommended, thus a restaurant rated 1/10 is worth a visit.

So, next time you eat out, get on the web and drop us a line at www.which.co.uk/gfgfeedback and have your say.

Andrew Turvil,
Editor

On running a restaurant

Gordon Ramsay, the top-rated chef, is also the architect of a thriving restaurant group – which combines culinary excellence with sound business sense. Here he reveals his recipe for success.

My answer to anyone remotely interested in how we run restaurants is that any new restaurant concept must always start with the chef. Not with the location, not with the restaurant designer and not with the smooth talking front-of-house manager. The passion, the focus and drive of the chef is what will make the restaurant work. Ultimately, we believe it will be his menu that people come to taste.

This presents two problems.

The first is that we need to surround our chosen chef with a solar system of staff that lends support and whose players have an insatiable need to be part of a successful team.

The second is to bring our chef into the real world and not allow him to isolate himself within the kitchen. The world is bigger than that and his remit must include financial percentages, brigade control and the ability to converse with intrigued guests.

At Gordon Ramsay Holdings it was long understood that if we were going to operate a number of establishments, each with its own individuality, then they should have all operational activities centralized. In doing this the front-of-house in each restaurant is able to do the one thing that matters and that is to look after the guest. Hiring and firing, maintenance, menu printing, account reconciliation, cleaning, rotas, reservations and re-silvering, are all taken away to a central control where everything can be done clinically and professionally throughout the day. This has brought an end to situations where such tasks are slotted in with staff desperately trying to set the stage for evening service when the reservation computer has gone down, the carpet has absorbed a glass of the reddest Burgundy and the menus are falling apart.

Our restaurants have become a three ring circus with a kitchen, a dining room and a central control. The trick is to educate everyone to concentrate on their own skills and seek support for anything else. Mutual respect for all colleagues is the cement that makes this work. The plate is carried from the kitchen to the table by a hundred unseen hands and the wine is poured with the bending of a troop of elbows invisible to any guest.

The modern kitchen has advanced in many ways. The introduction of a Chef's Table has brought immaculate working practices, clinical working surfaces and vibrant working chefs. No longer is the kitchen beyond the diners' reach; it is there on display. Temperature control and air extraction makes life in the ship's bowels bearable and lighting has lost the yellow glow from grease filtered bulbs. Chefs and their brigade have become today's theatre and in many cases are taking to the actor's stage like seasoned professionals. Nowadays, chefs and their brigade must understand everything about their kitchen and not just the contents of the cooking pot. How to choose and install a new stove, the effective positioning of work lights, of the types of non-slip floor surfaces available and an awareness of price changes between new and old lamb are all required knowledge for the modern chef. 'Expand your horizons and join the team' is the call, and those that listen and learn will become tomorrow's Chefs de Cuisine.

The dining room staff are the front line. There are a hundred housekeeping rules to consider including the basic disciplines of hair, nails, shoes, whiteness of anything white, personal hygiene and above all the importance of a smiling face. For an understanding of what it is like to be a guest, we invite staff to their own restaurant so that they can sit through dinner and see first hand what it is that their guests are expecting. It is an exercise guaranteed to open their eyes and at the same time they can taste the chef's offerings, which previously they have only served. It is explained as a credo that when Mr. and Mrs. Average Guest enter the restaurant they want to be reassured and welcomed. It is not a place to display arrogance or attitude, to look puzzled or appear distracted. The guest before you is the sole reason for you being there and your purpose is to make that person content. Diners come because they are known and looked after by the restaurant manager, their very best friend who is always pleased to see them, to share a gentle joke or offer a tour through the kitchen. It is the art of making people feel special. As with everything to do with running a restaurant, the science stems from common sense and observation, understanding and reaction. There is nothing overly complicated.

Central control is the orchestral conductor where all the skills needed to make a restaurant successful are brought together to make the right sound. At our restaurants, requests for table bookings come in via a seamless rerouting of the phone line to one of twenty-five reservationists armed with a screen that tells all. There is a record of the caller's previous restaurant experience including the dinner held a year ago for granny's 80th, the present availability of covers and, in the event of a full house, alternative restaurants within the group. Why lose a guest who requests a table in a fully booked restaurant when a simple cross-sale keeps everyone happy?

In head office there is the weekly operations meeting for each restaurant where the sins of the previous week are revisited. It is here that all is laid bare as part of the constant striving to get it right with kitchen and dining room alike. If disappearing napkins is the issue of the day an audit trail will consider the possibility of theft, negligence, bad practice or lost paperwork until the real reason is identified and the problem is rectified.

Correct HR procedures and training are, without doubt, the cornerstone of the business. Selection of staff and the shaping of their inherent abilities ensure a continuation of accomplished talent that is the life blood of sustained standards and growth. Ignore this area at your peril. Likewise, be slow to generate the monthly figures and you risk losing your most valuable indicators. Figures need to be available to your staff within two weeks of month-end and the staff, in turn, need to know how to read them. Go back to the price of lamb and we know at once if the chef has forgotten that when availability is weak, prices soar.

Our way of doing things is not necessarily the golden route to success but it covers all the bases and ignores very few. And one day we shall get it right.

Gordon Ramsay

Restaurants and reporting

John Simpson is a much travelled journalist who has reported from some of the world's most dangerous troublespots for over forty years. Here, he reflects on some memorable restaurant experiences.

Reporting for television news is a social activity. Newspaper and radio journalism requires loners; television needs people who can get on with others.

Think about it: you turn up at the airport to fly to somewhere inhospitable, and you meet your cameraman or -woman, sometimes for the first time. You are going to live cheek-by-jowl with him or her for days or even weeks, under difficult, sometimes even dangerous conditions. You may not like each other much, but you have to get on or the whole enterprise will be wrecked.

And so, over the years, I have come to regard restaurants as the places where an assignment really starts. Nowadays, when I go to Iraq (the journey involves going to Kuwait and being flown into Baghdad on an RAF Hercules) we always stay in the same featureless, impersonally comfortable hotel, and eat at its overblown restaurant.

Although it is invariably empty, the head waiter always asks if you have a reservation. I order steak (flavourless but tender) and lobster (tough but good). It's not a real meal, though, because the most exciting thing you can drink with your meal is fresh orange juice; not what you need the night before you fly into Baghdad.

But the awfulness of Kuwait and the lack of alcohol gives you something to talk about, at least; and by the end of the meal you've begun to get each other's measure. You might even start liking each other.

In the past, television reporting was much more convivial. The teams were bigger, there were more of them, and we used to descend in some numbers on places where things were happening. In the evenings someone would ring a good restaurant and book a table for twenty. The word would go round, and everyone would arrive after their news bulletins had gone out, yell at each other amicably across the table, and divide up the bill with the usual bickering at the end.

But that's all over now. There are fewer television teams around, and in the wonderful new world of twenty-four-hour broadcasting you're never really finished with the day's news. Instead, someone orders pizza, and you finally eat a couple of cold, greasy slices alone in the cutting-room; and, if you're me, you drip the juice down the only tie you have to broadcast in.

Yet when I look back over forty years of travelling the world as a correspondent, restaurants small and large, good and bad, have played a big part in the story. What, I wonder, was the name of the wonderful place in Zimbabwe (only it was called Rhodesia then) where we stopped for lightly-fried lake perch after being ambushed near the Mozambique border? Or the unforgettable restaurant in the ugly, jerry-built city of Shen Zhen in China, where I had perhaps the best meal of my entire life?

Once in Chile, in the days of General Pinochet, a restaurant saved me from a broken arm or a cracked skull. We were covering a particularly fierce political crisis, and filmed the build-up to that night's demonstration in Santiago. The riot police whacked their rubber truncheons on the palms of their hands, anxious to get at us and smash our gear. Then the sound recordist, a friend of mine called Bob Prabhu – a talented chef himself – suggested that we should spend the intervening hours at a restaurant he had heard of, a little way out of town.

A little way was actually a long way, and we got lost at least once. The restaurant was empty, because sensible Chileans don't turn up for dinner till after eleven, but we had an excellent meal – fish, and some superb steaks, and a good deal of excellent Chilean red – and tried to forget the beating we were likely to get at the demonstration that night. The driver got lost again on the way back; and by the time we reached the city centre the demonstration was over. There was just the stench of tear gas, and little pools of sewage from the police water-cannons.

Our hotel, the magnificent *Carrera*, looked like a frontline dressing-station. Cameramen and photographers lay on the chairs in the lobby, blood running down their faces, some with arms or collar-bones broken. The riot police had had a busy night.

The pictures of the demonstration were spectacular; and the next day I got a message of congratulation from my office (they didn't understand we'd used other people's pictures), warning us not to put ourselves in danger. I had to stop them putting us in for a television news award. But at least our skulls and collar-bones were intact.

Another time, I travelled through Communist Afghanistan in the winter, trudging over the snowy mountains for days on end. Being the oldest and least fit, I was slowly left behind by the others – even by the tough, charming Afghan bodyguard who had sworn to protect my life at the cost, if necessary, of his own. He just couldn't walk that slowly. Eventually I found myself alone in the darkness, scarcely able to work out the path through the snow in the starlight, hoping there were no anti-personnel mines around. I was cold, scared, and very hungry.

If I get out of this, I told myself, I'm going to have the best meal ever, at the *Savoy Grill* in London; and, struggling through the snow, I worked out the entire menu: lobster bisque, grilled sole, carré d'agneau, crêpes suzette, and cod roes on toast to end with. I chose the wines, too. It kept me going rather well; in fact I spotted our camp and staggered into it to rejoin the others before I had worked out whether to have Tokay or Beaumes de Venise with the crêpes.

Did I eventually eat the meal? I certainly did, and it was just as good as I thought it would be, that dark night in the Hindu Kush. As I say, the best accompaniment to television reporting is a good restaurant. Even if you have to wait a little for the food.

John Simpson

Beer with food

Food writer David Kenning, author of Beers of the World *, explains why the next time you eat out you should pass on the wines and ask to see the beer list.*

When, in March 2006, Michel Roux Jr announced that he was introducing a beer list to sit alongside the wines at his renowned London restaurant, Le Gavroche, it signalled a seismic shift in the world of gastronomy. For the first time in its 40 year history, this most French of restaurants was acknowledging that the favourite drink of the British had its place alongside fine food.

Admittedly, the list of just eight beers looks less impressive next to the weighty tome detailing the several hundred fine wines that are stocked in Le Gavroche's cellar but it is still eight more than you will find at most other restaurants of this calibre.

Most, but not all. Aubergine, also in London, has recently made strides in the same direction, while at Anthony's in Leeds, the eponymous Anthony Flinn offers cooking that is innovative and often surprising, so perhaps it is to be expected that he should do likewise on the drinks front. Here you will find a list of a dozen beers from around the world, carefully chosen to accompany the exciting food.

Of course, there is nothing particularly new about the idea of drinking beer with food. It's just that until recently the kind of food that was deemed suitable to serve with beer would not be expected to grace the pages of *The Good Food Guide*

So how is it that someone as illustrious as Michel Roux has started to take beer seriously? The truth is that it's the culmination of a trend that has gradually built up a head of steam over the past 15 years or so. And there are three principle factors behind it.

The first of these is fairly obvious: the rise of the gastropub. The Eagle, which opened in 1991 on Farringdon Road in London was among the first of a new breed that retained the more informal aspects of the pub setting while serving meals that were a cut above the usual pub grub. There are now many similar establishments across Britain – places such as the Hoste Arms in Burnham Market, Norfolk, and the Blue Lion in East Witton, North Yorkshire. Both are delightful old coaching inns with flagstone floors, real fires, handpumps on the bar dispensing real ale, and menus of inventive modern cooking that wouldn't look out of place in a cosmopolitan city-centre restaurant.

Michel Roux Sr, uncle of the Gavroche chef, and proprietor of the Waterside Inn, Bray, recognised the significance of the gastropub phenomenon a few years ago when he took over the White Hart in Nayland, Suffolk. His compatriot Jean-Christophe Novelli has also got in on the act, recently taking over the White Horse in Harpenden.

These are some of the more notable examples of the genre, though they are but a handful of the many representatives you will find in this edition of *The Good Food Guide* – far too many to list them all here.

One place that deserves special mention, however, is the Drunken Duck Inn just outside the Lakeland town of Ambleside. As home of the Barngates Brewery, this charming old stone inn always has a range of three or four top-quality real ales lining up alongside its ambitious menu featuring the likes of pigeon marinated with liquorice on Agen prune and Parmesan risotto, and venison fillet with chestnut polenta, caramelised figs and espresso pistachio nuts.

Unfortunately, though, the rise of the gastropub has not been all good news for ale lovers who like to eat well, since the trend has seen many fine traditional public houses taken over by new owners who have concentrated their efforts exclusively on the 'gastro' element, losing the 'pub' part of their identity almost entirely.

It would be great to see more of these establishments taking a leaf out of the Drunken Duck's book, though it is also worth remembering that pubs are not the only establishments where you can expect to find beer and food together. The traditional definition of a brasserie is a restaurant that serves alcoholic drinks, especially beer – indeed, the term comes from the French for 'to brew'. These days, there are few true brasseries in this sense, but one that stands out is Mash in London, whose name has nothing to do with potatoes but in fact refers to a stage of the brewing process – aptly enough for a restaurant where huge working brewing vessels are visible behind a glass screen at one end of the dining room.

The second part of the beer-with-food equation is perhaps less obvious but certainly has equal significance. A trend that has developed almost in parallel to the rise of the gastropub is the major change in our attitudes to sourcing of food: we have all become zealous devotees of organic farming, and fastidious seekers of local produce.

Brewing has benefited from this greatly. Although the vast bulk of brewing still rests in the hands of a tiny number of giant global companies, the past few years have seen a surge in the numbers of small, independent breweries – around 50-80 new openings each year, in fact – as our demand for traditionally crafted, local produce grows and grows.

It should come as no surprise, then, to find that beer figures prominently on the menu of the Goods Shed in Canterbury, Kent. As Britain's first daily farmers' market, the Goods Shed has been a pioneer of local produce since it opened in 2002, which goes as much for its in-house restaurant as the market stalls alongside. So, on its list of drinks you will find a selection of excellent beers from the HopDaemon brewery, which is just a few miles away.

The third factor in the increasing prominence of beer is a better general understanding of the complexities and depths it has to offer.

Consider that beer is made from four ingredients – malt, hops, yeast and water – while wine is made from just grapes. Consider further that malt alone is produced in a huge variety of styles. Malt, to put it simply, is barley that has been partially germinated then heated in a kiln; varying the temperature and duration of heating produces many different types of malt, ranging from the pale crystal malt used to make golden pilsners to the 'chocolate' malt that goes into rich, dark porters and stouts (most beers in fact contain a blend of different malts, just as the best wines usually contain a blend of grapes). Add to this the many different extra ingredients used in brewing – wheat, herbs, spices and fruit, for example – and you'll begin to understand why there is so much more to beer than the simple choice of lager or bitter on offer in most pubs.

With such a huge range of styles to choose from, there is undoubtedly a beer match for any dish. But how on earth do we find it?

There is enough to say on the subject to fill a whole book, but as with matching food and wine, a few general principles will go a long way. Here are some simple pointers:

Classic English bitters are characterised by a well-rounded, slightly sweet, malty flavour balanced by the bitterness of hops. These beers are ideal with roast meats, pies, hearty soups and cheese dishes.

Pilsners are lighter in colour but have a refreshing sharpness that stands up well to moderately spicy food such as a Thai chicken curry. But while lager may be the traditional curry house drink, Indian food is best partnered with something a bit more robust such as an IPA with its potent floral hop aromas An IPA is also an excellent choice with cheese at the end of a meal, particularly a mature cheddar.

Refreshing Belgian wheat beers, pale, aromatic and citrussy go extremely well with a bowl of moules marinière, or indeed any other fish or shellfish. Hoegaarden is perhaps the best known example of this style.

Rich, dark porters with their smoky, coffee-like aromas are the perfect accompaniment to chocolate-based desserts. But try matching fruit-based desserts with a fruit beer, such as raspberry-infused kriek from Belgium, which should provide a complementary sweetness.

Fruit beers also offer interesting possibilities with foie gras (in the same way as a sweet wine such as Sauternes), while at Le Gavroche, Michel Roux recommends Liefmann's cherry kriek with a dish of rare peppered tuna with ginger and sesame dressing.

Beyond this, the possibilities are endless, and perhaps the most important rule of thumb is that above all else, it often pays to experiment. Even if you don't consider yourself a beer drinker, you may be pleasantly surprised if you take a few chances. Of course, there will be some occasions when wine will still be the better choice, but next time you go out to a restaurant, why not at least ask to see the beer list? It might be the first step on the road to ale enlightenment.

David Kenning

The top-rated restaurants 2007

(See inside front cover for explanation of marking system)

Mark 9 for cooking

London
Gordon Ramsay, SW3

England
Fat Duck, Bray
Le Manoir aux Quat' Saisons, Great Milton
Winteringham Fields, Winteringham

Mark 8 for cooking

London
The Capital, SW3
Pétrus, SW1
Pied-à-Terre, W1
Square, W1
Tom Aikens, SW3

Scotland
Restaurant Martin Wishart, Edinburgh

England
Le Champignon Sauvage, Cheltenham
L'Enclume, Cartmel
Hibiscus, Ludlow
Waterside Inn, Bray

Wales
Ynyshir Hall, Eglwysfach

Mark 7 for cooking

London
Le Gavroche, W1
Ledbury, W11

England
Anthony's Restaurant, Leeds
Castle Hotel, Taunton
Chester Grosvenor, Arkle, Chester
Danesfield House, Marlow
Fischer's Baslow Hall, Baslow
Hambleton Hall Hambleton
Harry's Place, Great Gonerby
Holbeck Ghyll, Windermere
Juniper, Altrincham

Midsummer House, Cambridge
Mr Underhill's, Ludlow
Old Vicarage, Ridgeway
Restaurant Sat Bains, Nottingham
St Ervan Manor, St Ervan
Vineyard at Stockcross, Stockcross

Scotland
Andrew Fairlie at Gleneagles, Auchterarder
The Creel, St Margaret's Hope

Wales
Tyddyn Llan, Llandrillo

Channel Islands
Bohemia, St Helier

Special awards 2007

These awards do not necessarily go to the restaurants with the highest mark for cooking, but rather to the ones which have shown particular merit or achievement during the year. It may go to an old favourite or to a new entry, but in either case the places listed below have been singled out because they have made an impact in some special way.

London
St John, EC1 — *London Restaurant of the Year*
Arbutus, W1 — *London Newcomer of the Year*
Bentley's, W1 — *London commended*
Galvin Bistrot de Luxe, W1 — *London commended*
Mint Leaf, SW1 — *London commended*

Rest of England
Black Boys, Hurley — *Berkshire Newcomer of the Year*
Black Door, Newcastle upon Tyne — *Tyne & Wear Restaurant of the Year*
Box Tree, Ilkley — *Yorkshire Restaurant of the Year*
College Arms, Lower Quinton — *Warwickshire Newcomer of the year*
Danesfield House, Marlow — *Buckinghamshire Restaurant of Year*
Fox & Hounds, Goldsborough — *Yorkshire Newcomer of the Year*
Garrick's Head, Bath — *Bath Restaurant of the Year*
Gurnard's Head, Treen — *Cornwall Newcomer of the Year*
Holbeck Ghyll, Windermere — *Cumbria Restaurant of the Year*
Hole in the Wall, Little Wilbraham — *Cambridgeshire Newcomer of the Year*
Horn of Plenty, Tavistock — *Devon Restaurant of the Year*
Montagu Arms, Beaulieu — *Hampshire Restaurant of the Year*
No 6, Padstow — *Cornwall Restaurant of the Year*
Plough, Bolnhurst — *Bedfordshire Newcomer of Year*
Read's, Faversham — *Kent Restaurant of Year*
St Martin's Hotel, St Martin's — *Isle of Scilly Restaurant of the Year*

Scotland
Glenapp Castle, Ballantrae — *Scotland Restaurant of the Year*
Cringletie House, Peebles — *Scotland Newcomer of the Year*
Edenwater House, Ednam — *Scotland commended*

Wales
Tyddyn Llan, Llandrillo — *Wales Restaurant of the Year*
The Hardwick, Abergavenny — *Wales Newcomer of the Year*

Channel Islands
Bohemia, St Helier — *Channel Islands Restaurant of the Year*

New entries

These restaurants are new main entries in the Guide this year, although some may have appeared in previous years, or as 'Also Recommended' entries in the previous edition.

London
Addendum, EC3
Amici, SW17
Arbutus, W1
Awana, SW3
Bar Shu, W1
Bentley's, W1
Brown's Hotel, W1
The Bull, N6
Canteen, E1
Comptoir Gascon, EC1
11 Abingdon Road, W8
Galvin at Windows, W1
Galvin Bistrot de Luxe, W1
Green & Red, E1
Guinea Grill, W1
Latium, W1
Lock Dining Bar, N17
Luciano, SW1
Nobu Berkeley Street, W1
Origin Bar and Dining Room, WC2
Pig's Ear Dining Room, SW3
Roast, SE1
Salt Yard, W1
Sam's Brasserie and Bar, W4
Tamesa @ Oxo, SE1
Tapas Brindisa, SE1
Wizzy, SW6

Rest of England
Baslow, Rowley's
Bath, Dukes Hotel, Cavendish Restaurant
Bath, Garrick's Head
Beaulieu, Montagu Arms, Terrace
Birmingham, Opus
Bolnhurst, Plough
Bournemouth, Barings Restaurant
Bourton on the Hill, Horse & Groom
Bradford, Prashad
Brancaster Staithe, White Horse
Brighton, Real Eating Company
Bristol, Café Maitreya
Broadway, G Russell's

Cheltenham, Brosh
Chester, Locus
Christmas Common, Fox & Hounds
Cleeve Hill, Malvern View Hotel
Crosthwaite, Punch Bowl Inn
Danehill, Coach & Horses
Ely, Boathouse
Exeter, Effings
Exeter, Hotel Barcelona, Café Paradiso
Frilsham, Pot Kiln
Goldsborough, Fox and Hounds
Harpenden, A Touch of Novelli at the White Horse
Hayling Island, Marina Jaks
Hessle, Artisan
Hoghton, Thyme at the Sirloin
Hurley, Black Boys Inn
Kew, Ma Cuisine
Knowstone, Mason's Arms
Leeds, Anthony's at Flannels
Little Wilbraham, Hole in the Wall
Lower Quinton, College Arms
Lyme Regis, Broad Street Restaurant
Manchester, Midland Hotel, French
Manchester, Red Chilli
Masham, Vennell's
Midsomer Norton, Moody Goose at the Old Priory
Milton Abbot, Hotel Endsleigh
Newcastle upon Tyne, Black Door
Newcastle upon Tyne, Brasserie Black Door
Newcastle upon Tyne, Jesmond Dene House
Newmarket, Steven Saunders in Newmarket
Padstow, No. 6
Reading, Forbury's
Richmond, La Buvette
Richmond, Petersham Nurseries Café

Ripponden, Junction
Rishworth, Old Bore
South Dalton, Pipe and Glass Inn
Speldhurst, George & Dragon
Stoke Prior, Epicurean Restaurant
Stow-on-the-Wold, Old Butchers
Stratford-upon-Avon, Malbec
Treen, Gurnard's Head
Truro, Tabb's
Ventnor, Hambrough Hotel
Walberswick, Anchor Hotel
Walberton, Oaks Restaurant
Whitby, Greens
Whitway, Carnarvon Arms
Willian, Fox
Windermere, Kwela's
Wrea Green, Ribby Hall
Yarpole, Bell Inn
York, J. Baker's
York, Tasting Room

Scotland
Carradale, Dunvalanree Hotel
Colonsay, Isle of Colonsay Hotel
Dumfries, Linen Room
Edinburgh, Valvona & Crolla Vincaffè
Glasgow, Michael Caines at ABode Glasgow
Glasgow, Urban Grill
Milngavie, Wild Bergamot
Peebles, Cringletie House
Udny Green, Eat on the Green

Wales
Abergavenny, The Hardwick
Llanwrtyd Wells, Lasswade Country House
Mold, 56 High Street
Newport, Celtic Manor, Owens
Pendolyn, Red Lion
St David's, Lawtons at No 16

Channel Isalnds
Bohemia, St Helier

London restaurants by cuisine

Boundaries between national cuisines can be blurred, so the restaurants listed below are classified by the predominant influence, although there may be some crossover. The headings are in many cases more generalised than the brief cuisine descriptions given at the tops of the entries themselves, and restaurants without a single overriding influence are not included on the list at all.

British
Canteen, E1
Franklins, SE22
Medcalf, EC1
Rhodes Twenty Four, EC2
Roast, SE1
Rules, WC2
St John, EC1
Smiths of Smithfield: Top Floor, EC1
Tate Britain Restaurant, SW1
Wiltons, SW1

Chinese
Bar Shu, W1
Chinese Experience, W1
ECapital, W1
Four Seasons, W2
Fung Shing, WC2
Golden Dragon, W1
Hakkasan, W1
Hunan, SW1
Mandarin Kitchen, W2
Mr Kong, WC2
New World, W1
Nyonya, W11
Phoenix Palace, NW1
Royal China, E14, NW8, W1, W2
Yauatcha, W1

Danish
Lundum's, SW7

East European/Eurasian
Baltic, SE1
Gay Hussar, W1
Potemkin, EC1

French
Admiralty, WC2
Almeida, N1
L'Auberge, SW15
Aubergine, SW10
Bellamy's, W1

Berkeley Square, W1
Bleeding Heart, EC1
Bonds, EC2
Brasserie St Quentin, SW3
The Bull, N6
The Capital, SW3
Le Cercle, SW1
Le Chardon, SE22
Chez Kristof, W6
Club Gascon, EC1
Le Colombier, SW3
Comptoir Gascon, EC1
Le Coq d'Argent, EC2
Drones, SW1
L'Escargot, Ground Floor, W1
L'Escargot, Picasso Room, W1
L'Etranger, SW7
Food Room, SW8
Galvin at Windows, W1
Galvin Bistrot de Luxe, W1
Le Gavroche, W1
Gordon Ramsay, SW3
Gordon Ramsay at Claridge's, W1
Incognico, WC2
Maze, W1
Mirabelle, W1
Mon Plaisir, WC2
Morgan M, N7
Orrery, W1
Patterson's, W1
Pearl, WC1
Pétrus, SW1
Pied-à-Terre, W1
Plateau, E14
La Poule au Pot, SW1
Racine, SW3
Roussillon, SW1
RSJ, SE1
Savoy Grill, WC2
Sketch, Gallery, W1
Sketch, Lecture Room and Library, W1
Square, W1

Swissôtel The Howard, Jaan, WC2
Tom Aikens, SW3
Les Trois Garçons, E1
La Trompette, W4
La Trouvaille, W1
Le Vacherin, W4

Fusion/pan-Asian
e&o, W11
Eight Over Eight, SW3
Great Eastern Dining Room, EC2
Providores, W1

Greek
Real Greek, N1
Real Greek Souvlaki and Bar, EC1

Indian/Pakistani/Bangladeshi
Amaya, SW1
Babur Brasserie, SE23
Benares, W1
Café Spice Namaste, E1
Calcutta Notebook, SW18
Chor Bizarre, W1
Chowki, W1
Chutney Mary, SW10
Cinnamon Club, SW1
Deya, W1
Ginger, W2
Great Nepalese, NW1
Haandi, SW3
Kasturi, EC3
Lahore Kebab House, E1
Masala Zone, W1
Mehek, EC2
Mela, WC2
Mint Leaf, SW1
Mirch Masala, SW16
Painted Heron, SW10
Parsee, N19
Porte des Indes, W1

Radha Krishna Bhavan, SW17
Rasa Samudra, W1
Rasa Travancore, N16
Rasa W1, W1
Rasoi Vineet Bhatia, SW3
Red Fort, W1
Salloos, SW1
Sarkhel's, SW18
Tamarind, W1
Tandoor, NW9
Vama, SW1
Veeraswamy, W1
Yatra, W1
Zaika, SW7

Indian vegetarian
Diwana Bhel Poori, NW1
Kastoori, SW17
Rani, N3
Rasa, N16
Sabras, NW10

Indonesian/Straits/Malaysian
Awana, SW3
Champor-Champor, SE1
Singapore Garden, NW6

Italian
Al Duca, SW1
Alloro, W1
Amici, SW17
Arancia, SE16
Ark, W8
Assaggi, W2
Camerino, W1
Carluccio's Caffe, W1
Cecconi's, W1
Cipriani, W1
Il Convivio, SW1
Enoteca Turi, SW15
Giardinetto, W1
Latium, W1
Locanda Locatelli, W1
Luciano, SW1
Metrogusto, N1
Neal Street Restaurant, WC2
Olivo, SW1
Passione, W1
Philpott's Mezzaluna, NW2

Phoenix, SW15
Quo Vadis, W1
Refettorio, EC4
River Café, W6
Salusbury, NW6
Sardo, W1
Sardo Canale, NW1
Tentazioni, SE1
Timo, W8
Vasco & Piero's Pavilion, W1
Zafferano, SW1

Japanese
Café Japan, NW11
Chisou, W1
Ikkyu, W1
Itsu, SW3, W1
Kiku, W1
K10, EC2
Kulu Kulu Sushi, W1
Matsuri High Holborn, WC1
Moshi Moshi, EC2
Miyama, W1
Nobu Berkeley Street, W1
Nobu London, W1
Roka, W1
Sumosan, W1
Sushi-Hiro, W5
Sushi-Say, NW2
Tokyo Diner, WC2
Tsunami, SW4
Ubon by Nobu, E14
Umu, W1
Yoshino, W1
Zuma, SW7

Korean
Wizzy, SW6

North African/Middle Eastern
Adams Café, W12
Al Hamra, W1
Momo, W1
Noura Brasserie, SW1
Numidie, SE19

Seafood
Bentley's, W1
Chez Liline, N4

Deep, SW6
fish!, SE1
Fish Hook, W4
Fish Shop, EC1
FishWorks, W1
J. Sheekey, WC2
Lobster Pot, SE11
Lou Pescadou, SW5
Manzi's, WC2
One-O-One, SW1
Two Brothers, N3

South/Central American
Armadillo, E8
Cantaloupe, EC2
Green & Red, E1

Spanish/Tapas
Cambio de Tercio, SW5
Cigala, WC1
Fino, W1
Moro, EC1
Olé, SW6
Rebato's, SW8
Salt Yard, W1
Tapas Brindisa, SE1

Swedish
Glas, SE1

Thai
Blue Elephant, SW6
Mango Tree, SW1
Nahm, SW1
Patara, W1
Thai Garden, E2

Turkish
Istanbul Iskembecisi, N16
Iznik, N5
Sofra, WC2
Tas, SE1

Vegetarian
Gate, W6
Manna, SW1

Vietnamese
Huong-Viet, N1

Restaurants with a notable wine list

Marked in the text with a 🍾

London
Almeida, N1
Aubergine, SW10
Bentley's, W1
Bibendum, SW3
Bleeding Heart, EC1
Bonds, EC2
Bradleys, NW3
Café du Jardin, WC2
Cambio de Tercio, SW5
The Capital, SW3
Le Cercle, SW1
Chez Bruce, SW17
Club Gascon, EC1
Connaught, Angela Hartnett, W1
The Don, EC4
Enoteca Turi, SW15
L'Etranger, SW7
Fifth Floor, SW1
Le Gavroche, W1
Gordon Ramsay, SW3
Gordon Ramsay at Claridges, W1
Great Eastern Hotel, Aurora, EC2
Greenhouse, W1
Greyhound, SW11
Hakkasan, W1
Kensington Place, W8
Ledbury, W11
Locanda Locatelli, W1
Lola's, N1
Mandarin Oriental Hyde Park, Foliage, SW1
Maze, W1
Metrogusto, N1
Millennium Knightsbridge, Mju, SW1
1 Lombard Street, EC3
Orrery, W1
Oxo Tower, SE1
Pearl, WC1
Pétrus, SW1
Pied-à-Terre, W1
Providores, W1
Ransome's Dock, SW11
Rasoi Vineet Bhatia, SW3
Redmond's, SW14
Roussillon, SW1
RSJ, SE1
Smiths of Smithfield, Top Floor, EC1
Square, W1
Tate Britain Restaurant, SW1

Tom Aikens, SW3
La Trompette, W4
Umu, W1
Villandry, W1
Wolseley, W1
Zaika, W8
Zuma, SW7

Rest of England
Ambleside, Rothay Manor
Ashbourne, Callow Hall
Barwick, Little Barwick House
Baslow, Fisher's Baslow Hall
Bath, Bath Priory
Bath, Queensbury Hotel, Olive Tree
Bath, Royal Crescent, Pimpernel's
Beaulieu, Montagu Arms
Birmingham, Bank
Birmingham, Hotel du Vin & Bistro
Birmingham, Simpsons
Bolnhurst, Plough
Bowness-on-Windermere, Linthwaite House
Brampton, Grange Hotel
Bray, Fat Duck
Brighton & Hove, Hotel du Vin & Bistro
Bristol, Hotel du Vin & Bistro
Bristol, Riverstation
Brockenhurst, Le Poussin at Whitley Ridge
Bolton Abbey, Devonshire Arms
Cambridge, Midsummer House
Cheltenham, Le Champignon Sauvage
Cheltenham, Lumière
Chester, Chester Grovenor, Arkle
Chettle, Castleman Hotel
Chinnor, Sir Charles Napier
Clipsham, Olive Branch
Corse Lawn, Corse Lawn House
Dartmouth, New Angel
Dinton, La Chouette
East Grinstead, Gravetye Manor
Eastbourne, Grand Hotel Mirabelle
Easton Grey, Whatley Manor
Elland, La Cachette
Emsworth, 36 On The Quay
Faversham, Read's
Fawsley, Fawsley Hall
Fletching, Griffin Inn
Fotheringhay, Falcon
Gittisham, Combe House

Golcar, Weavers Shed
Grasmere, White Moss House
Great Milton, Le Manoir aux Quat' Saisons
Hambleton, Hambleton Hall
Harrogate, Hotel du Vin & Bistro
Henley-on-Thames, Hotel du Vin & Bistro
Hereford, Castle House, La Rive,
Hetton, Angel Inn
Horncastle, Magpies
Huntington, Old Bridge Hotel
Ilkley, Box Tree
Kew, Glasshouse
Keyston, Pheasant
Kibworth Beauchamp, Firenze
Langho, Northcote Manor
Leeds, Anthony's Restaurant
Leeds, Fourth Floor
Lewdown, Lewtrenchard Manor
Lifton, Arundell Arms
Little Shelford, Sycamore House
Liverpool, Hope Street Hotel, London Carriage
   Works
Liverpool, 60 Hope Street
Liverpool, Ziba at The Raquet Club
Long Crendon, Angel Restaurant
Lower Quinton, College Arms
Ludlow, Hibiscus
Ludlow, Mr Underhill's
Lund, Wellington Inn
Madingley, Three Horseshoes
Maidencombe, Orestone Manor
Manchester, Lime Tree
Manchester, Second Floor
Marlow, Danesfield House
Melbourn, Pink Geranium
Morston, Morston Hall
Nayland, White Hart
Newton Longville, Crooked Billet
Norwich, Adlard's
Nottingham, Restaurant Sat Bains
Oakham, Lord Nelson's House
Oxford, Cherwell Boathouse
Oxton, Fraiche
Padstow, No 6
Petersfield, JSW
Poole, Mansion House
Ramsbottom, Ramsons
Ramsgill, Yorke Arms
Ridgeway, Old Vicarage
Salford, Lowry Hotel, River Restaurant
Seaham, Seaham Hall, White Room
Sheffield, Artisan and Catch
Shepton Mallet, Charlton House Hotel
Southwold, Crown Hotel
St Ervan, St Ervan Manor
Stockbridge, Greyhound
Stockcross, Vineyard
Stockton, Three Lions
Stoke Holy Cross, Wildebeast Arms
Taunton, Castle Hotel
Titley, Stagg Inn

Tunbridge Wells, Hotel du Vin & Bistro
Ullswater, Ramsbeck Country House
Ullswater, Shallow Bay
Winchester, Hotel du Vin & Bistro
Windemere, Holbeck Ghyll

Scotland
Achiltibuie, Summer Isles Hotel
Anstruther, Cellar
Ardeonaig, Ardeonaig Hotel
Ballater, Darroch Learg
Blairgowrie, Kinloch House Hotel
Dalry, Braidwoods
Dumfries, Linen Room
Dunvegan, Three Chimneys
Edinburgh, Balmoral
Edinburgh, Forth Floor
Edinburgh, Haldanes
Edinburgh, Restaurant Michael Wishart
Edinburgh, Valvona & Crolla Caffè Bar
Edinburgh, Vintners Rooms
Elie, Sangster's
Glasgow, Brian Maule at Chardon d'Or
Glasgow, Stravaigin
Glasgow, Ubiquitous Chip
Killiecrankie, Killiecrankie House Hotel
Kingussie, The Cross
Lochinver, Albannach
Perth, 63 Tay Street
Port Appin, Airds Hotel
Portpatrick, Knockinaam Lodge
St Andrews, Inn at Lathones
St Andrews, Seafood Restaurant
St Monans, Seafood Restaurant

Wales
Aberdovey, Penhelig Arms Hotel
Beaumaris, Ye Olde Bulls Head
Capel Garmon, Tan-y-Foel
Clytha, Clytha Arms
Crickhowell, Nantyffin Cider Mill Inn
Dolgellau, Dylanwad Da
Eglwysfach, Ynyshir Hall
Harlech, Maes-y-Neuadd
Llandrillo, Tyddyn Llan
Llandudno, Bodysgallen Hall
Llandudno, St Tudno Hotel
Llangammarch Wells, Lake Country House
Penmaenpool, Penmaenuchaf Hall
Pwllheli, Plas Bodegroes
Reynoldston, Fairyhill
Skenfrith, Bell at Skenfrith

Channel Islands
St Saviour, Longueville Manor

Northern Ireland
Belfast, Aldens
Belfast, Cayenne
Belfast, Restaurant Michael Deane

Long serving restaurants

The Guide has seen many restaurants come and go. Some, however, have stayed the course with tenacity. (Qualification for this list is that the restaurant has been in each edition of the Guide subsequent to its first entry.)

Connaught, London W1	54 years
Gay Hussar, London W1	50 years
Gravetye Manor, East Grinstead	50 years
Porth Tocyn Hotel, Abersoch	50 years
Sharrow Bay, Ullswater	46 years
Walnut Tree Inn, Llandewi Skirrid	42 years
Rothay Manor, Ambleside	38 years
Le Gavroche, London W1	37 years
Summer Isles Hotel, Achiltibuie	37 years
The Capital, London SW3	36 years
Miller Howe, Windermere	36 years
Ubiquitous Chip, Glasgow	35 years
Druidstone, Broad Haven	34 years
Plumber Manor, Sturminster Newton	34 years
Waterside Inn, Bray	34 years
White Moss House, Grasmere	34 years
Isle of Eriska, Eriska	33 years
Airds, Port Appin	31 years
Farlam Hall, Brampton	30 years
Corse Lawn House, Corse Lawn	29 years
Hambleton Hall, Hambleton	28 years
Pier Hotel, Harbourside Restaurant, Harwich	28 years
Sabras, London NW10	28 years
Grafton Manor, Bromsgrove	27 years
Magpie Café, Whitby	27 years
Drum and Monkey, Harrogate	26 years
Royal Crescent, Pimpernel's, Bath	26 years
RSJ, London SE1	26 years
Seafood Restaurant, Padstow	26 years
Sir Charles Napier, Chinnor	26 years
Y Bistro, Llanberis	26 years
Le Caprice, London SW3	25 years
Kalpna, Edinburgh	25 years
Little Barwick House, Little Barwick	25 years
Moss Nook, Manchester	25 years
Neal Street Restaurant, London WC2	25 years

To submit a report on any restaurant please visit *www.which.co.uk/gfgfeedback*

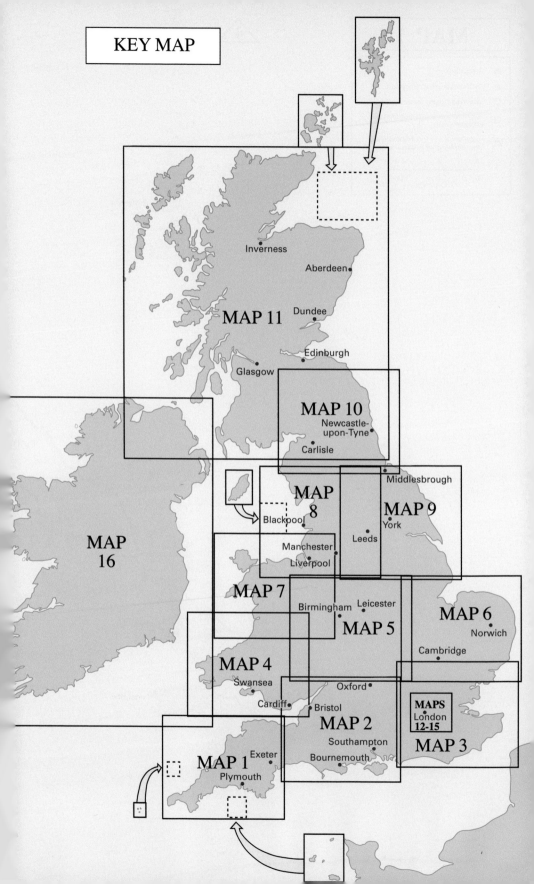

MAP 1

Lundy Island

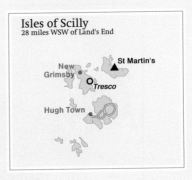

Isles of Scilly
28 miles WSW of Land's End

New Grimsby

▲ St Martin's

○ *Tresco*

Hugh Town

B u d e Bay

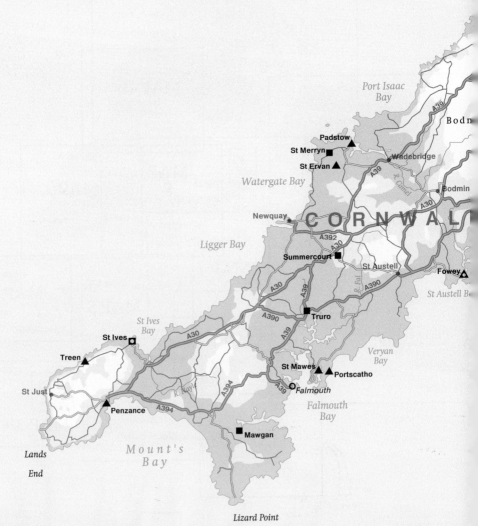

Port Isaac Bay

B o d n

Padstow ▲

St Merryn ■

St Ervan △

Wadebridge

Watergate Bay

● Bodmin

Newquay ●

C O R N W A L

A392

A30

Ligger Bay

Summercourt ■

St Austell

● Fowey △

St Austell B

A390

R. Fal

Truro ■

Veryan Bay

St Ives ⬓

St Ives Bay

A30

St Mawes ▲ ▲ Portscatho

Treen ▲

St Just ●

○ *Falmouth*

Falmouth Bay

Penzance △

A394

Lands

Mawgan ■

Mount's Bay

End

Lizard Point

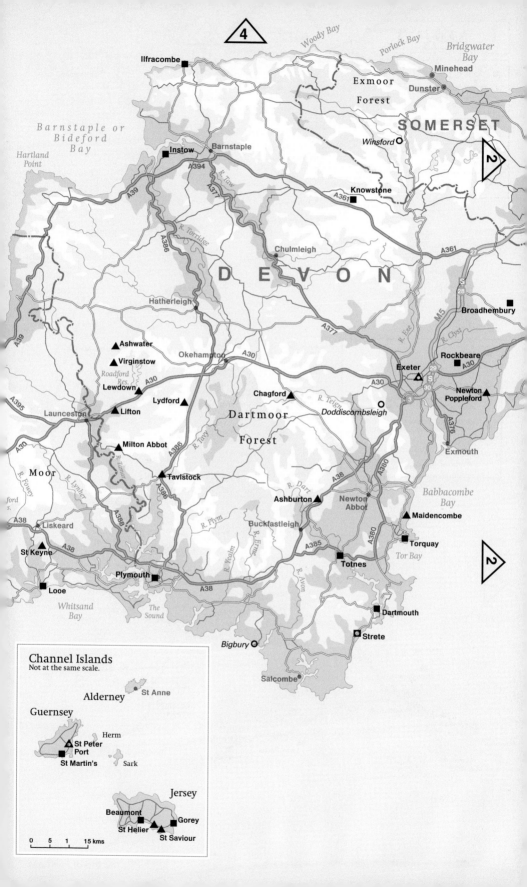

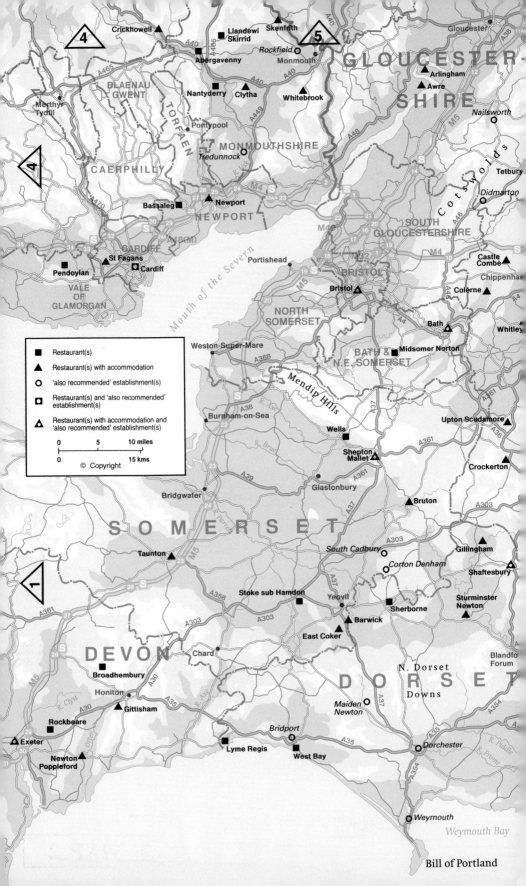

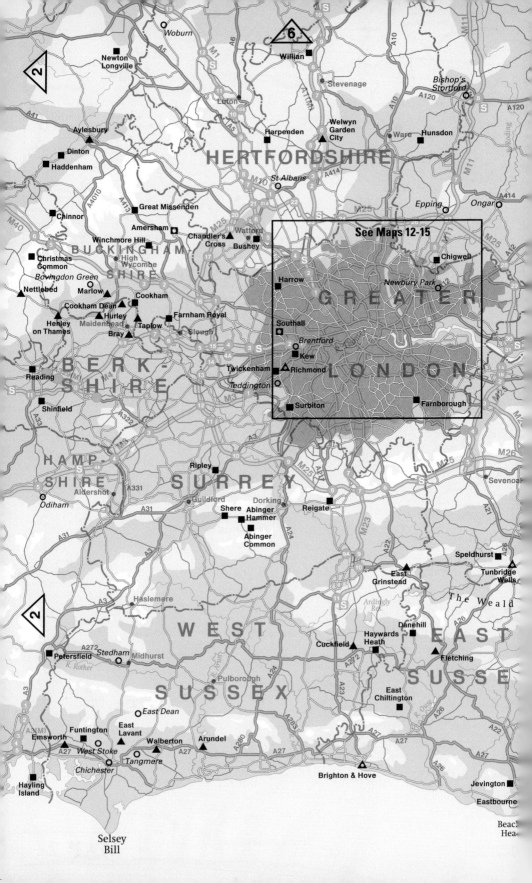

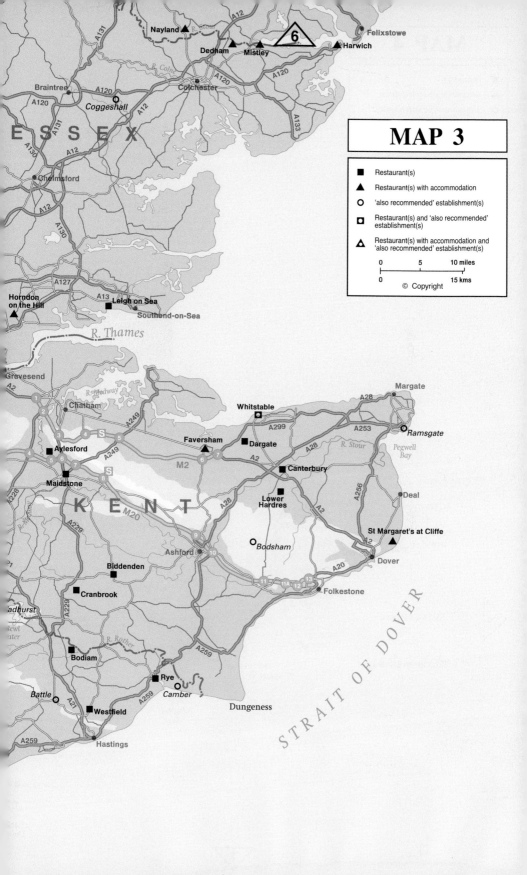

MAP 3

■ Restaurant(s)

▲ Restaurant(s) with accommodation

○ 'also recommended' establishment(s)

◨ Restaurant(s) and 'also recommended'
establishment(s)

△ Restaurant(s) with accommodation and
'also recommended' establishment(s)

0   5   10 miles

0   15 kms

© Copyright

Nayland
Dedham
Mistley
6
Felixstowe
Harwich
Braintree
A131
A12
A120
A120
Coggeshall
Colchester
A120
A12
A133
E S S E X
A131
A130
Chelmsford
A12
A130
A127
Horndon
on the Hill
A13
Leigh on Sea
Southend-on-Sea

R. Thames

Gravesend
A2
R. Medway
Chatham
A249
1
2
3
4
S
5
Aylesford
5
6
7
A249
Maidstone
S
8
A228
A229
M20
K E N T
A28
Faversham
6
7
Dargate
A299
Whitstable
Margate
A28
A253
Ramsgate
Pegwell
Bay
R. Stour
A2
Canterbury
A2
A256
Deal
Lower
Hardres
9
10
Ashford
Bodsham
St Margaret's at Cliffe
A2
Dover
A20
Folkestone
11
11A
12
13
Biddenden
A229
Cranbrook
A229
Bodiam
R. Rother
A259
Rye
Camber
Battle
A21
Westfield
A259
Hastings
Dungeness

STRAIT OF DOVER

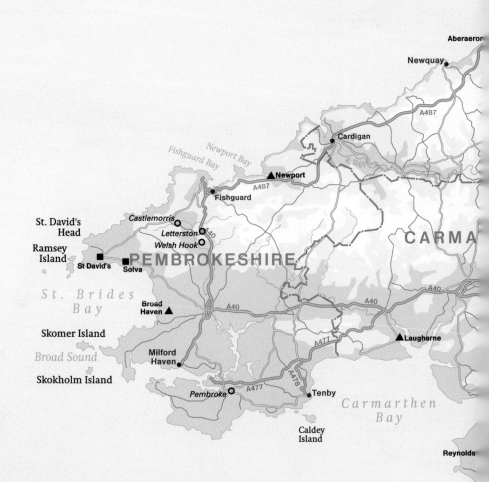

MAP 4

- ■ Restaurant(s)
- ▲ Restaurant(s) with accommodation
- ○ 'also recommended' establishment(s)
- ◻ Restaurant(s) and 'also recommended' establishment(s)
- △ Restaurant(s) with accommodation and 'also recommended' establishment(s)

```
0        5        10 miles
0                 15 kms
      © Copyright
```

CARDIGAN

BAY

Aberaeron

Newquay

A487

Cardigan

R. Teifi

Newport Bay

Fishguard Bay

▲ Newport

A487

Fishguard

Castlemorris ○

Letterston ◻ A40

Welsh Hook ○

St. David's Head

Ramsey Island

■ St David's

Solva ■

PEMBROKESHIRE

CARMA

A40

St. Brides Bay

Broad Haven ▲

A40

Skomer Island

Broad Sound

Milford Haven ■

Laugharne ▲

A477

Skokholm Island

Pembroke ○ A477

Tenby

A478

Carmarthen Bay

Caldey Island

Reynolds

BRISTOL

MAP 5

■ Restaurant(s)
▲ Restaurant(s) with accommodation
○ 'also recommended' establishment(s)
◨ Restaurant(s) and 'also recommended' establishment(s)
△ Restaurant(s) with accommodation and 'also recommended' establishment(s)

0   5   10 miles
0   15 kms
© Copyright

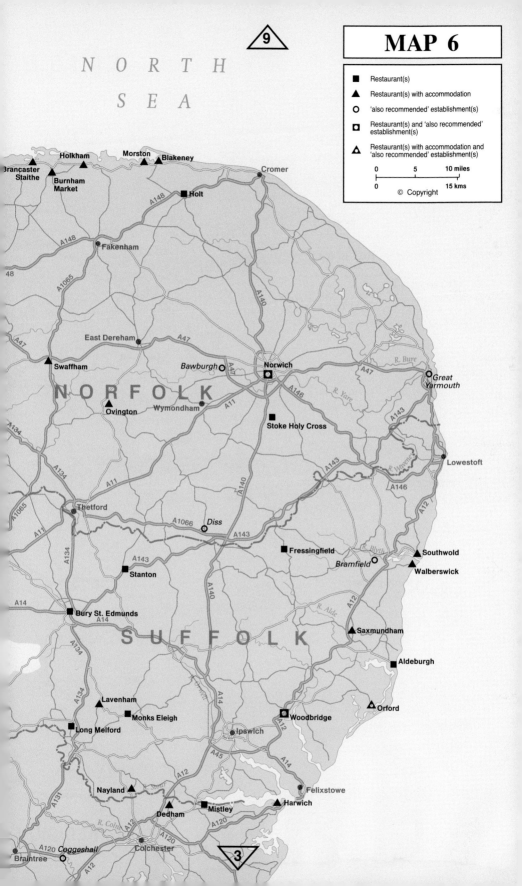

9

MAP 6

NORTH SEA

Legend:
- ■ Restaurant(s)
- ▲ Restaurant(s) with accommodation
- ○ 'also recommended' establishment(s)
- ▣ Restaurant(s) and 'also recommended' establishment(s)
- △ Restaurant(s) with accommodation and 'also recommended' establishment(s)

```
0          5          10 miles
0                     15 kms
© Copyright
```

Holkham
Morston
Blakeney
Brancaster Staithe
Burnham Market
Cromer
Holt
A148
A148
A1065
48
Fakenham
A47
East Dereham
A47
Swaffham
A146
A140
Norwich
Bawburgh
R. Bure
A47
Great Yarmouth
NORFOLK
A134
Ovington
Wymondham
A11
R. Yare
Stoke Holy Cross
A143
R. Waveney
Lowestoft
A146
A1065
A11
A134
Thetford
A1066
Diss
A143
A12
Fressingfield
R. Blyth
Southwold
A143
Stanton
Bramfield
Walberswick
A14
A140
A12
Bury St. Edmunds
A14
R. Alde
A12
SUFFOLK
A134
Saxmundham
Aldeburgh
A134
Lavenham
Monks Eleigh
Woodbridge
Orford
Long Melford
Ipswich
A14
A12
A45
A14
A131
Nayland
Felixstowe
A12
Harwich
Dedham
Mistley
A120
Coggeshall
A120
A120
Braintree
Colchester
R. Colne
R. Stour

NORTH SEA

A140
A11
A134

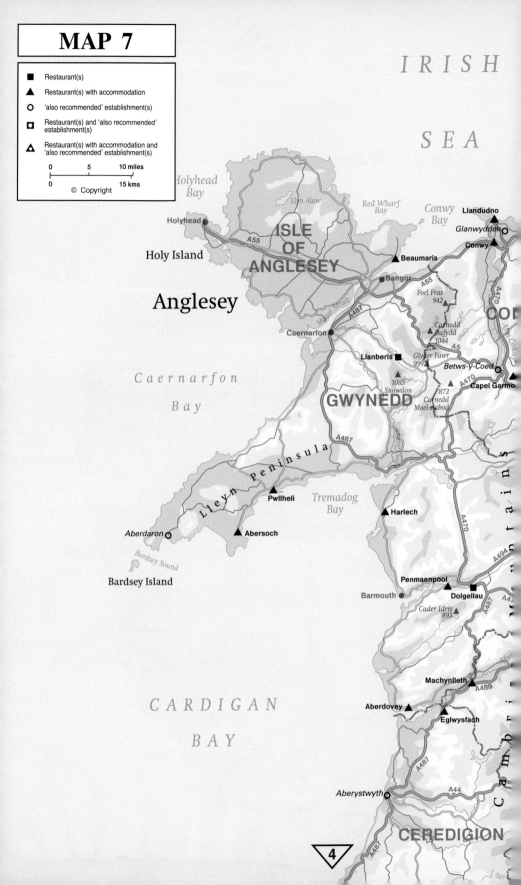

MAP 7

Legend:
- ■ Restaurant(s)
- ▲ Restaurant(s) with accommodation
- ○ 'also recommended' establishment(s)
- ◨ Restaurant(s) and 'also recommended' establishment(s)
- △ Restaurant(s) with accommodation and 'also recommended' establishment(s)

0   5   10 miles
0   15 kms
© Copyright

IRISH

SEA

Holyhead Bay

Llyn Alaw

Red Wharf Bay

Conwy Bay

Llandudno ▲

Glanwydden ○

Holyhead ◨

ISLE OF ANGLESEY

Holy Island

Conwy ▲

Beaumaris ▲

Bangor ◨

Anglesey

Foel Fras 942

A55

CO

Menai Strait

A487

Caernarfon ◨

Carnedd Dafydd 1044 ▲

A5

A470

Afon Conwy

Caernarfon Bay

Llanberis ■

Glyder Fawr 9992

Betws-y-Coed ◨ ▲

A470

Capel Garmo ■

1085 Snowdon

GWYNEDD

872 Carnedd Moel-siabod

A487

Lleyn Peninsula

Afon Glaslyn

Pwllheli ▲

Tremadog Bay

Harlech ▲

Aberdaron ○

Abersoch ▲

Bardsey Sound

Bardsey Island

Penmaenpool ▲

A470

A494

Barmouth ●

Dolgellau ■

A487

A4

Cader Idris 893 ▲

CARDIGAN

Machynlleth ▲

A489

BAY

Aberdovey ▲

Eglwysfach ▲

A487

Afon

Cambrian Mountains

Aberystwyth ○

A44

CEREDIGION

A487

▽4

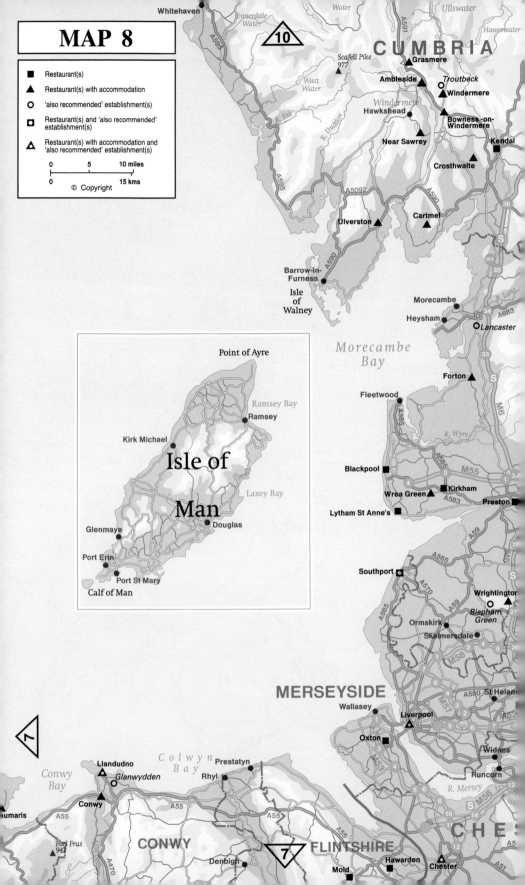

MAP 8

Legend:
- ■ Restaurant(s)
- ▲ Restaurant(s) with accommodation
- ○ 'also recommended' establishment(s)
- ▢ Restaurant(s) and 'also recommended' establishment(s)
- △ Restaurant(s) with accommodation and 'also recommended' establishment(s)

0   5   10 miles
0   15 kms
© Copyright

CUMBRIA

Whitehaven

Ennerdale Water
Ullswater
Water
Haweswater

△10

Scafell Pike 977

Grasmere
Ambleside
Troutbeck
Windermere
Hawkshead
Windermere
Bowness-on-Windermere
Near Sawrey
Kendal
Crosthwaite
36

Wast Water

R. Esk
R. Duddon
A595
A595
A5092
A590
A590

Ulverston
Cartmel

S
35A
35

Barrow-in-Furness
Isle of Walney

Morecambe
Heysham
Lancaster
34
A683
R. Lune

Morecambe Bay
33

Forton
S

Fleetwood
M6

A585
R. Wyre

Blackpool
Kirkham
Wrea Green
A583
Lytham St Anne's
Preston
3
M55
A59

Isle of Man

Point of Ayre
Ramsey Bay
Ramsey
Kirk Michael
Laxey Bay
Douglas
Glenmaye
Port Erin
Port St Mary
Calf of Man

Southport
A565
A570

Wrightington
Bispham Green
Ormskirk
Skelmersdale
A565
M58

MERSEYSIDE
A580
St Helens

Wallasey
Liverpool
Oxton
Widnes
M57

Runcorn
R. Mersey
M56

Conwy Bay
Llandudno
Glanwydden
Conwy
Beaumaris
A55
Foel Fras 942

Colwyn Bay
Prestatyn
Rhyl

△7
◁7

CONWY
A470
Denbigh
FLINTSHIRE
Mold
▽7
Hawarden
Chester
CHE
A51

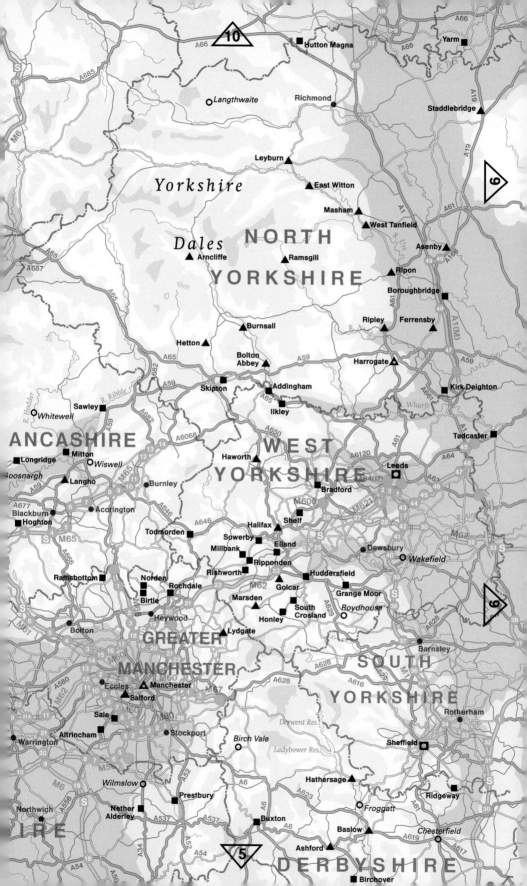

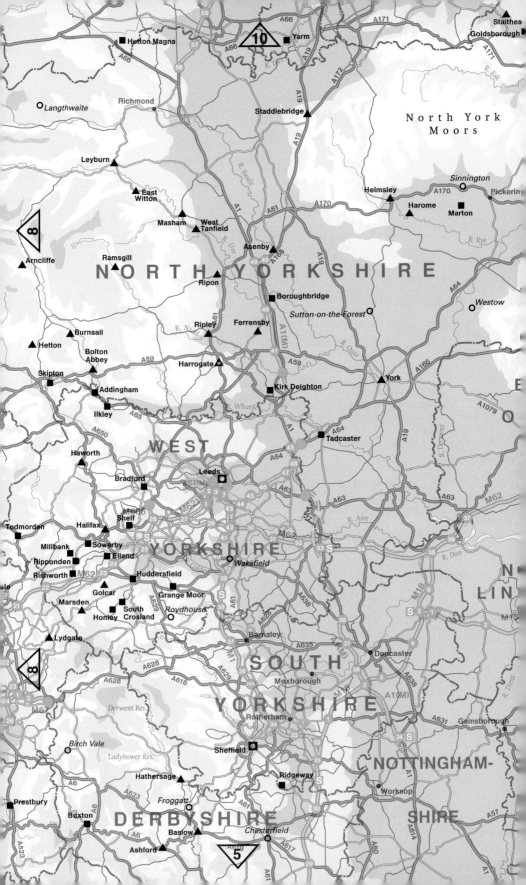

MAP 9

- ■ Restaurant(s)
- ▲ Restaurant(s) with accommodation
- ○ 'also recommended' establishment(s)
- ◻ Restaurant(s) and 'also recommended' establishment(s)
- △ Restaurant(s) with accommodation and 'also recommended' establishment(s)

0		5		10 miles
0			15 kms

© Copyright

Whitby

Scarborough

Flamborough Head

Bridlington

Bridlington Bay

Yorkshire Wolds

ST RIDING

YORKSHIRE

Lund

South Dalton

Walkington

○ Beverley

KINGSTON-UPON HULL

Hessle ■ Hull

R. Humber

Winteringham

○ Barton-upon-Humber

TH

LNSHIRE

Scunthorpe

Grimsby

Cleethorpes

Spurn Head

N.E. LINCOLNSHIRE

The Wolds

Louth

A1103

LINCOLNSHIRE

○ *Lincoln*

Horncastle

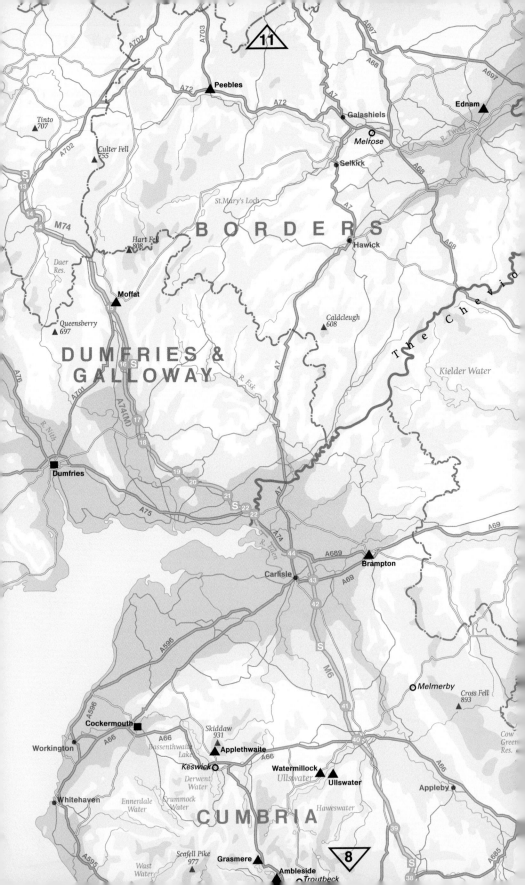

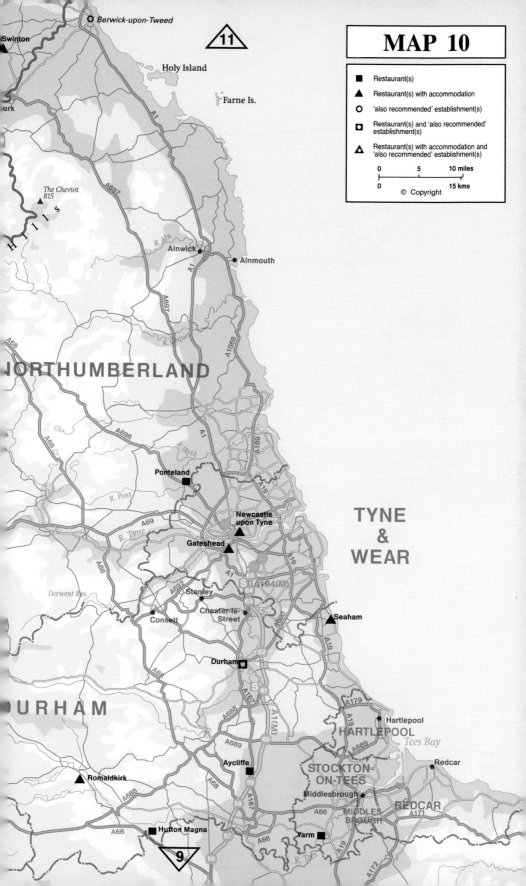

MAP 10

Berwick-upon-Tweed
Swinton
Holy Island
Farne Is.

■ Restaurant(s)

▲ Restaurant(s) with accommodation

○ 'also recommended' establishment(s)

▱ Restaurant(s) and 'also recommended' establishment(s)

△ Restaurant(s) with accommodation and 'also recommended' establishment(s)

0		5		10 miles
0			15 kms

© Copyright

The Cheviot 815

R. Aln

Alnwick
Alnmouth

NORTHUMBERLAND

R. Coquet

A1068

A68

A697

A696

R. Blyth

A189

Ponteland

R. Pont

Newcastle upon Tyne

A69

R. Tyne

Gateshead

A19

TYNE & WEAR

A692

Stanley

65
S 64
A194(M)
63

Consett

Chester-le-Street

A690

Seaham

A19

A68

62

Durham

S 61

DURHAM

A688

A167

A1(M)

A179

60

A689

HARTLEPOOL

Hartlepool

Tees Bay

Romaldkirk

A688

Aycliffe

59

STOCKTON-ON-TEES

Redcar

A66

58

A167

Middlesbrough

REDCAR

A171

A66

Hutton Magna

57

A66

Yarm

MIDDLESBROUGH

A66

56

R. Tees

A19

A172

11

9

MAP 11

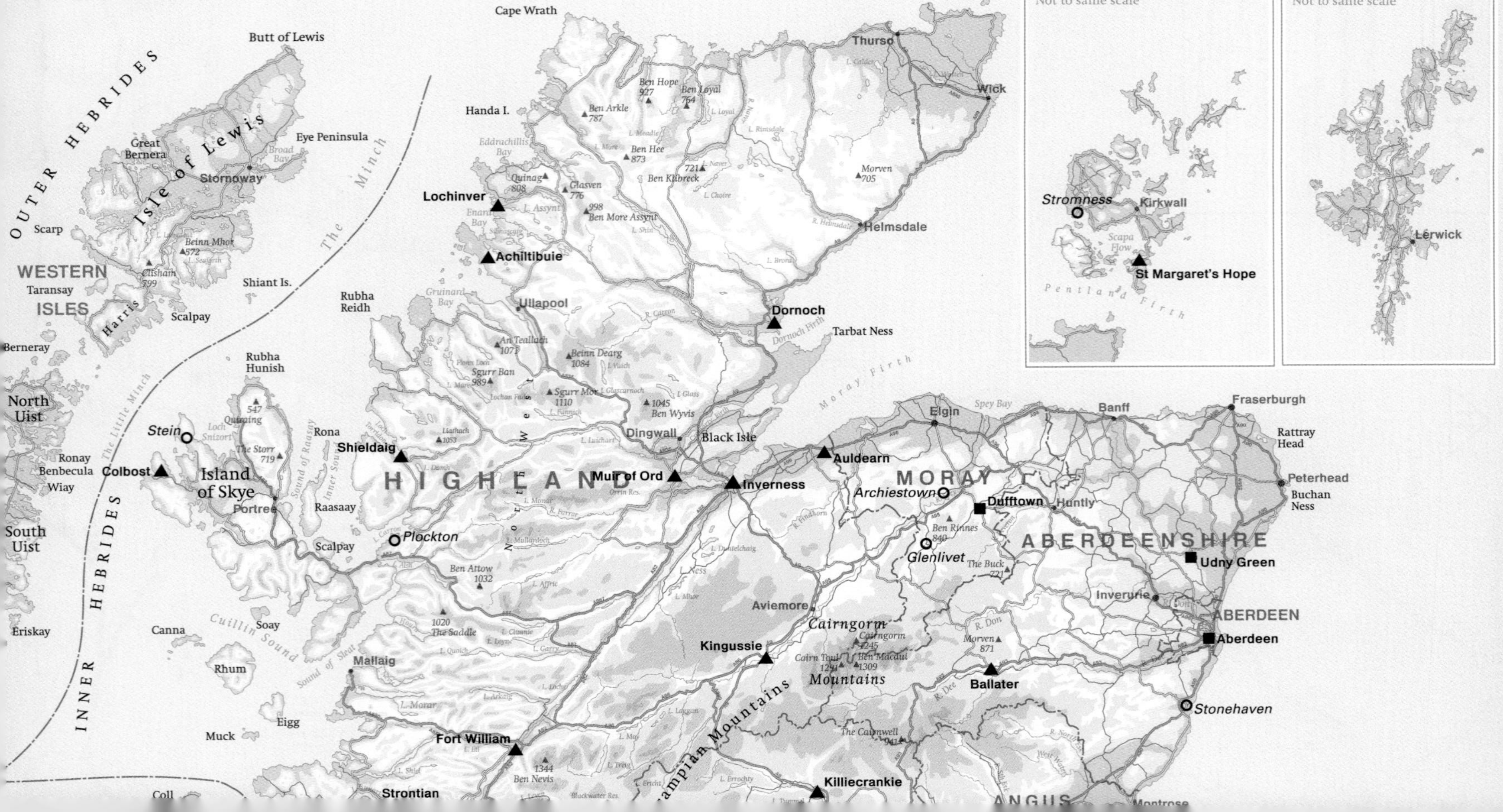

Lerwick

Kirkwall
St Margaret's Hope
Stromness
Scapa Flow
Pentland Firth

Stroma
Wick
Thurso
Cape Wrath
Helmsdale
Handa I.
Morven 705
Ben Hope 927
Ben Loyal 764
Ben Arkle 787
Ben Hee
Ben Klibreck
Ben More Assynt 998
Quinag 808
Oykel
Dornoch
Tarbat Ness
Lochinver
Achiltibuie
Ullapool
Eddrachillis Bay
Enard Bay
Rubha Reidh
Moray Firth
Spey Bay
Elgin
Auldearn
Inverness
Black Isle
Dingwall
Muir of Ord
Ben Wyvis
An Teallach
Slioch
Beinn Eighe 1010
Sgurr Mor 1110
Ben Dearg 1084
Sgurr Ban 989
Beinn Dearg 1084
Shieldaig
Plockton
Scalpay
Raasay
Rona
Sound of Raasay
Inner Sound
Stein
Colbost
Island of Skye
Portree
The Storr 719
Loch Snizort
Quiraing 543
Rubha Hunish
Cuillin Sound
Canna
Rhum
Eigg
Muck
Soay
Mallaig
Fort William
Ben Nevis 1344
The Saddle
Ben Attow 1032
Cairngorm Mountains
Cairn Toul 1291
Cairn Gorm 1245
Ben Macdui 1309
Aviemore
Kingussie
Grampian Mountains
Killiecrankie
Ballater
Morven 871
Glenlivet
Archiestown
Ben Rinnes 840
The Buck
Dufftown
MORAY
Huntly
Banff
Fraserburgh
Rattray Head
Peterhead
Buchan Ness
Udny Green
ABERDEENSHIRE
ABERDEEN
Aberdeen
Stonehaven
Inverurie
Strontian
HIGHLAND
WEST
West Loch Tarbert
Strathconon
Loch Mullardoch
Loch Monar
The Minch
The Little Minch
Butt of Lewis
Eye Peninsula
Stornoway
Broad Bay
ISLE OF LEWIS
Beinn Mhor 572
Beinn Tarsuinn
Scalpay
Shiant Is.
HARRIS
Taransay
Scarp
Great Bernera
WESTERN ISLES
OUTER HEBRIDES
Berneray
North Uist
Benbecula
Ronay
Wiay
South Uist
Eriskay
Canna
INNER HEBRIDES
Coll
ANGUS
Montrose

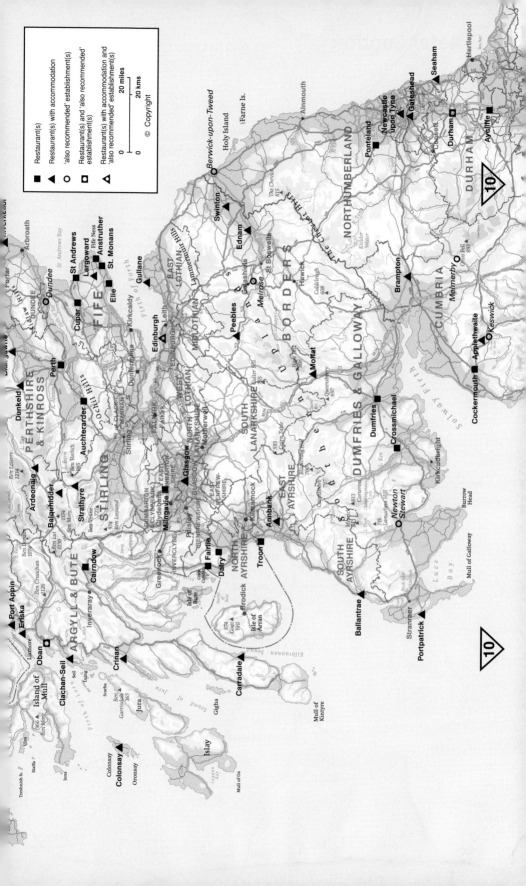

Restaurant(s)

Restaurant(s) with accommodation

'also recommended' establishment(s)

Restaurant(s) and 'also recommended'
establishment(s)

Restaurant(s) with accommodation and
'also recommended' establishment(s)

20 miles

20 kms

Greater London

BARNET

Stanmore

Finchley
Rani

Wood Green

Two Brothers

Mosaica @ the Factory

M1

Hendon

The Bull

HARROW

Parsee

Chez Liline

Café Japan

Philpott's Mezzaluna

WEMBLEY

Willesden

Hampstead

See Map 13

CAMDEN

Sushi-Say

ISL

Sabras

BRENT

A40(M)

See Map 15

Sushi-Hiro

William IV

HAMMERSMITH AND FULHAM

CITY OF WEST-MINSTER

Ealing

Acton

Anglesea Arms

FishWorks

KENSINGTON AND CHELSEA

See Map 14

Ealing Park Tavern

Adams Café

Brackenbury

Popeseye

Le Vacherin

Fish Hook

Chez Kristof

Snows on the Green

Rebato

Ole Tapas

Blue Elephant

Ransome's Dock

Brentford

La Trompette

HAMMERSMITH

Gate

Wizzy

Chutney Mary

Greyhound

Sam's Brasserie & Bar

Sonny's

River Café

Deep

Food Room

Fulham

Emile's

Tsunami

Redmonds

Phoenix

L'Auberge

The Victoria

Enoteca Turi

RICHMOND

WANDSWORTH

Earl Spencer

Amici

Chez Bruce

Balham Bar & Kitche

Twickenham

Calcutta Notebook

Sarkhel's

Kastoori

Radha Krishna Bhavan

Streatham

Wimbledon

Light House

Merton

Kingston upon Thames

Morden

Mitcham

Mirch Masala

KINGSTON UPON THAMES

Malden

MERTON

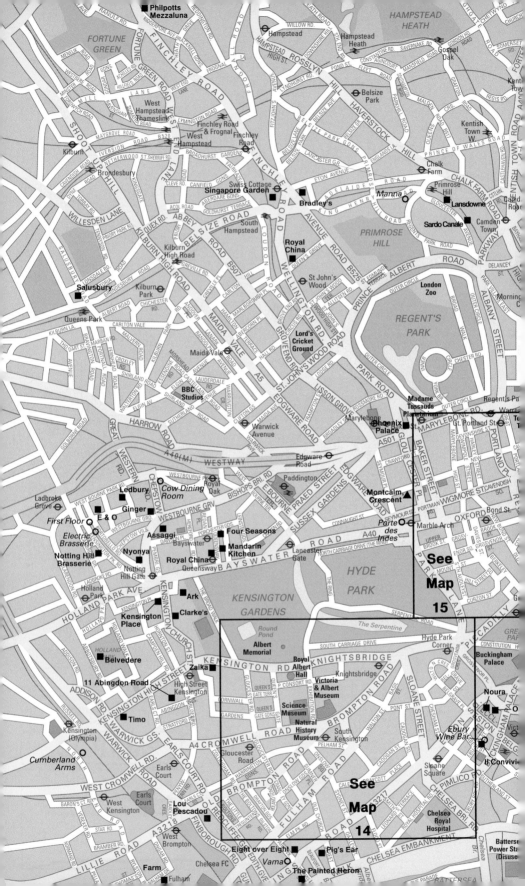

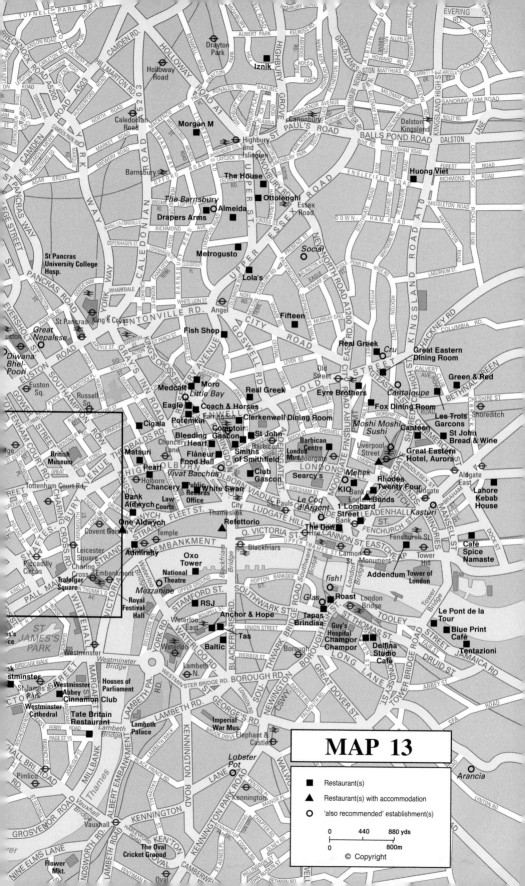

MAP 13

- Restaurant(s)
- ▲ Restaurant(s) with accommodation
- ○ 'also recommended' establishment(s)

0   440   880 yds
0   800m

© Copyright

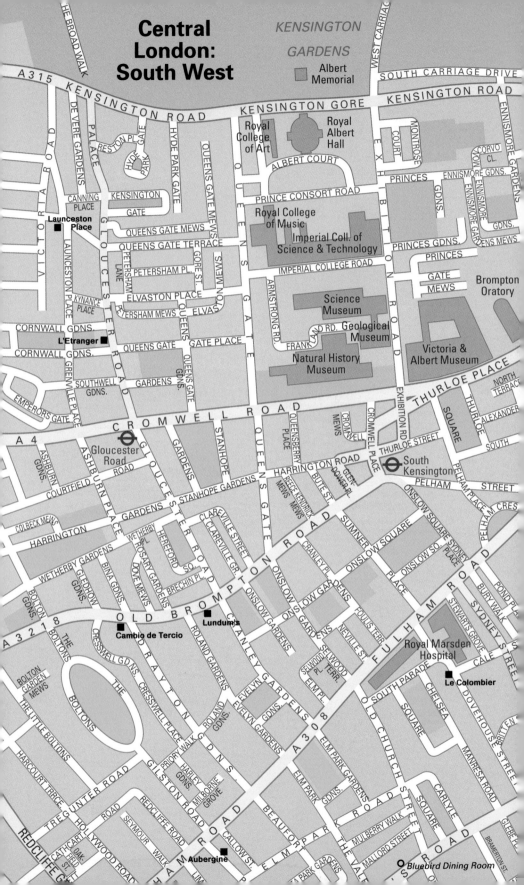

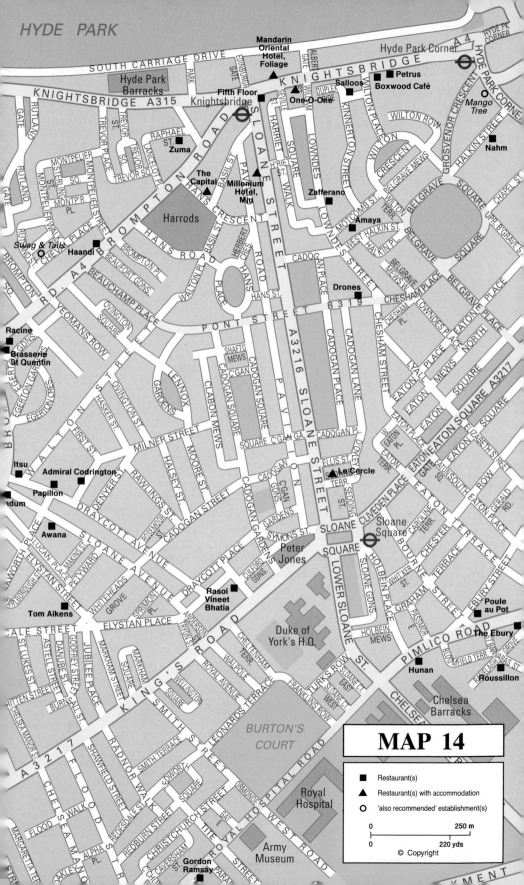

HYDE PARK

SOUTH CARRIAGE DRIVE

KNIGHTSBRIDGE A315

Hyde Park Barracks

Mandarin Oriental Hotel, Foliage

KNIGHTSBRIDGE

Hyde Park Corner

Salloos

Petrus

Boxwood Café

Mango Tree

Fifth Floor

Knightsbridge

One-O-One

WILTON ROW

Nahm

Zuma

The Capital

Millenium Hotel, Miu

Zafferano

Harrods

Amaya

Drones

Racine

Brasserie St Quentin

Le Cercle

Itsu

Admiral Codrington

Papillon

dum

Sloane Square

Poule au Pot

Awana

Peter Jones

The Ebury

Rasoi Vineet Bhatia

Tom Aikens

Duke of York's H.Q.

Hunan

Roussillon

Swag & Tails

Haandi

Royal Hospital

Army Museum

BURTON'S COURT

MAP 14

■ Restaurant(s)

▲ Restaurant(s) with accommodation

○ 'also recommended' establishment(s)

0   250 m

0   220 yds

© Copyright

Gordon Ramsay

Chelsea Barracks

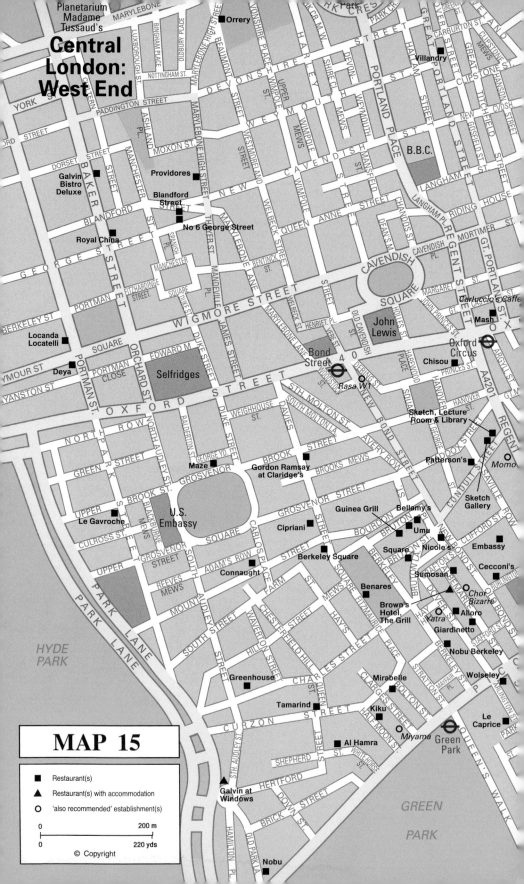

MAP 16

- ■ Restaurant(s)
- ▲ Restaurant(s) with accommodation
- ○ 'also recommended' establishment(s)
- ▣ Restaurant(s) and 'also recommended' establishment(s)
- △ Restaurant(s) with accommodation and 'also recommended' establishment(s)

0	40		80 miles
0	40	80	120 Kms

© Copyright

ATLANTIC

OCEAN

Rathlin I.

Rosapenna

Coleraine

LONDONDERRY

DONEGAL

ANTRIM

Strabane

Carrickfergus

TYRONE

Antrim

Lough Neagh

Belfast

Kircubbin

Lurgan

Donegal Bay

FERMANAGH

Portadown

DOWN

Enniskillen

Armagh

Downpatrick

ARMAGH

Sligo

Monaghan

Crossmolina

MONAGHAN

IRISH

SLIGO

Fenagh

Cavan

SEA

MAYO

Carrick-on-Shannon

LEITRIM

CAVAN

LOUTH

ROSCOMMON

Drogheda

LONGFORD

MEATH

I R E L A N D

Dunshauglin

Athlone

WESTMEATH

GALWAY

Grand Canal

Dublin

KILDARE

DUBLIN

OFFALY

M7

Birr

Portlaoise

Kildare

Shannon

WICKLOW

Wicklow

LAOIS

CLARE

Arklow

TIPPERARY

KILKENNY

CARLOW

Shannon

LIMERICK

Tipperary

Kilmaganny

WEXFORD

Listowel

LIMERICK

Clonmel

Tralee

Kilmallock

WATERFORD

KERRY

CORK

Killorglin

Cobh

ATLANTIC

ST. GEORGE'S CHANNEL

OCEAN

London

MAP 12

Adams Café

77 Askew Road, W12 9AH
Tel: (020) 8743 0572

Cooking 3 | North African | £24

Adams Café has been serving the denizens of
Shepherd's Bush since 1990, providing simple sustenance during the day in the shape of eggs and
bacon, grills and suchlike, then assuming a somewhat more exotic second identity by night with a
good-value set-price menu of authentic, traditional north African cooking. Complimentary
spicy nibbles set the ball rolling in fine fashion –
perhaps mini lamb balls with harissa and pickled
vegetables – followed by a choice of starters that
encompasses grilled sardines, chorba (spicy
Tunisian lamb soup), and various briks (filo pastry
parcels) with fillings such as tuna, egg and herbs.
Main courses include eight ways with couscous
(the 'royal' comes with merguez, chicken and
lamb) and half a dozen tagines (chicken with apricots and almonds, for example) as well as a range
of grilled meat and fish served with rice and vegetables. Finish perhaps with Berber pancakes with
honey sauce, washed down with Moroccan mint
tea with pine kernels. The short wine list runs
from simple house French red and white at £9 a
bottle, £2.50 a glass, to Ch. Musar 1996 at a
princely £19.

Chef: Sofiene Chahed Proprietors: Abdel and Frances
Boukraa Open: Mon to Sat D only 7 to 11 Closed: Christmas
to New Year, bank hol Mon Meals: Set D £10.50 (1 course) to
£15.50 Service: 12.5% Cards: Amex, Delta, Maestro,
MasterCard, Visa Details: 60 seats. Vegetarian meals.
Wheelchair access (not WC). Music Tube: Ravenscourt Park

 This symbol means that the restaurant has
elected to participate in *The Good Food Guide's*
£5 voucher scheme (see 'Using The Good Food
Guide' for details).

MAP 13

Addendum `NEW ENTRY`

Apex City of London Hotel, 1 Seething Lane,
EC3N 4AX
Tel: (020) 7977 9500
Website: www.addendumrestaurant.co.uk

Cooking 3 | Modern European | £64

Addendum was certainly no afterthought in the
design of the new Apex City of London Hotel, but
it does suffer from a surfeit of contemporary
touches so beloved of corporate hotels: dark
wooden floors, panelling and muted colours. What
the dining room lacks in warmth it makes up for
with Tom Ilic's cooking. With a fondness for meat,
especially offal, and a general inclination for gutsi-
ness, Ilic brings an edginess to the food. At inspection Cornish crab came with fennel, basil and,
unusually, Granny Smith gazpacho (the highlight
of the meal), and sea bass teamed with lentils and
wild garlic cream with bone marrow brioche.
Apples were more classically utilised as a tart to
accompany an assiette of pork – belly, fillet, trotter
and black pudding – alongside pickled white
cabbage, while dessert produced an expertly made
ginger brûlée with a lime and rhubarb tart, as well
as a well-made banana tarte Tatin accompanied by
a dense, rich chocolate ganache. Service is polite
and helpful. On the short wine list, prices start at
£18 but move up quickly.

Chef: Tom Ilic Open: Mon to Fri 12 to 2.30, 6 to 9.30
Closed: 22 Dec to 3 Jan, bank hols Meals: alc (main courses
£18.50 to £24.50) Service: 12.5% (optional) Cards: Amex,
Delta, Diners, Maestro, MasterCard, Visa Details: 60 seats.
Vegetarian meals. No smoking. Wheelchair access (also WC).
Music. Air-conditioned Accommodation: 130 rooms
Tube: Tower Hill

The price given next to the cooking score is based on
the cost of a typical three-course dinner for one
person, including coffee, house wine and service.

MAP 14

Admiral Codrington

17 Mossop Street, SW3 2LY
Tel: (020) 7581 0005
Website: www.theadmiralcodrington.com

Cooking 3 | **Modern European** | **£44**

Outside this looks like a classic Victorian pub, and while drinkers still crowd the bar, food is also a big attraction, served in the long, narrow dining area with well-padded banquette seating and a retractable glass roof. The single-sheet menu hasn't changed much over the years, although there are daily specials to ponder. Starters have included herb-crusted goats' cheese with caramelised baby peppers, and diver-caught scallops with minted pea purée, 'bursting with fresh flavour'. Main-course penne with Gorgonzola, baby beets and sprouting broccoli has featured the freshest ingredients, while tender slow-roast Gloucester Old Spot belly pork is served on a bed of Puy lentils with prunes under a crunchy crackling lid, accompanied by a side order of champ. Desserts display a high comfort factor: honeycomb ice cream with Valrhona chocolate sauce, say, or vanilla rice pudding with honey-glazed apricots. Service is impressive, thanks to a well-drilled team, and the compact wine list has been intelligently put together, with around 20 options by the glass (from £3.50), with prices from £13.

Chef: Jon Rotheram **Proprietor:** Longshot plc **Open:** all week 12 to 2.30 (3.30 Sat, 4.30 Sun), 6.30 to 11 (7 to 10 Sun) **Closed:** Christmas **Meals:** alc (main courses £11 to £15). Cover £1 at D. Bar L menu available **Service:** 12.5% (optional) **Cards:** Amex, Delta, Maestro, MasterCard, Visa **Details:** 50 seats. 25 seats outside. Vegetarian meals. Wheelchair access (not WC). Music. Air-conditioned **Tube:** South Kensington

MAP 13

Admiralty

Somerset House, Strand, WC2R 1LA
Tel: (020) 7845 4646

Cooking 5 | **Modern European** | **£59**

There is no doubting the splendour of Somerset House, although once inside there are some drab corridors to negotiate before you reach the high-ceilinged elegance of the dining rooms. The décor is a feast for the eyes: turquoise leather banquettes, a full-size crocodile mounted on the wall and a display case of baby sea horses all command attention. Daniel Groom is at the helm in the kitchen, and his modern European menu offers a contemporary take on some classic dishes. Oxtail ravioli with honey-glazed duck breast is accompanied by Savoy cabbage and a cinnamon jus to start, while crab tortellini accompanies hand-dived scallops along with pickled cucumber salad and lobster velouté. Cornish rump of lamb is paired with flageolet purée and gratin dauphinois, and roast sea bass with razor clams and steamed mussels in a saffron sauce. Other interesting combinations have included white and green asparagus with a quail's egg, goats' cheese and truffle lasagne, while classic ideas are found in the half-dozen desserts: perhaps rhubarb crumble, or chocolate tart with Armagnac cream and pistachio ice cream. The pricey wine list is a mostly European affair, starting at £18.

Chef: Daniel Groom **Proprietor:** Leith's **Open:** all week L 12 to 2.15, Mon to Sat D 6 to 10.15 **Closed:** 23 to 26 Dec, 1 Jan, bank hol Mon D in May and Aug **Meals:** Set L £17.50 to £29 (2 courses), Set D £29.50 (2 courses) to £49.50 **Service:** 12.5% (optional) **Cards:** Amex, Delta, Diners, MasterCard, Visa **Details:** 55 seats. Vegetarian meals. No smoking in 1 dining room. Wheelchair access (also WC). Music **Tube:** Temple, Covent Garden

MAP 15

Alastair Little

49 Frith Street, W1D 4SG
Tel: (020) 7734 5183

Cooking 4 | **Modern European** | **£55**

Alastair Little may no longer be associated with the restaurant that bears his name, but it still carries the hallmarks of his straightforward, no-nonsense style. The dining room has an uncluttered simplicity – cream walls hung with abstract paintings, bright lighting, plain white tablecloths and crockery and so on – that matches the food produced by Sue Lewis and Juliet Peston. A generous choice of starters might include oysters with shallot vinegar and spicy sausages, butternut squash ravioli with butter and sage, and spice-scented scallops with soy, pickled ginger and cucumber. To follow might be a capably made pea and mushroom risotto with a crisp green side salad, cod with smoked haddock, Puy lentils and mustard sauce, or glazed belly of Berkshire pork with mash and Bramley apple sauce. Meals could finish with pannacotta with rhubarb, chocolate fondant with coconut sorbet and bananas, or vanilla ice cream with Pedro Ximénez sherry. A short, uncomplicated wine list opens with a French white and a Spanish red at £17.50.

Chefs: Sue Lewis and Juliet Peston Proprietors: Mercedes André-Vega and Kirsten Tormod Pedersen Open: Mon to Fri L 12 to 3, Mon to Sat D 6 to 11.30 Closed: bank hols Meals: Set L £33, Set D £38 Service: not inc Cards: Amex, Delta, Diners, Maestro, MasterCard, Visa Details: 60 seats. Vegetarian meals. Children's helpings. No cigars/pipes in dining room. No music. Air-conditioned Tube: Tottenham Court Road

Chefs: Mahir Abboud and A. Batah Proprietor: A.H. Fansa Open: all week 12 to 11.30 Closed: 10 days Christmas Meals: alc (main courses £13 to £22.50). Set L £20 to £25, Set D £25 to £30. Cover £2.50 Service: not inc Cards: Amex, Delta, Diners, Maestro, MasterCard, Visa Details: 65 seats. 24 seats outside. Vegetarian meals. Children's helpings. No-smoking area. Wheelchair access (not WC). Music. Air-conditioned Tube: Green Park

MAP 15

Al Duca AR

4–5 Duke of York Street, SW1Y 6LA
Tel: (020) 7839 3090

Modern Italian cuisine is served with panache at this unfussy restaurant, which is just a stone's throw from Fortnum and Mason. The fixed-priced menus range from £18.50 to £29, and might kick off with mille-feuille of red peppers, aubergines, goats' cheese and chard, or carpaccio, and follow with linguine with clams, garlic and chilli oil, or braised rabbit with grilled polenta. Finish with caramelised hazelnut semifreddo with cherries. A good selection of Italian wines from £16. Closed Sun.

MAP 15

Al Hamra

31–33 Shepherd Market, W1J 7PT
Tel: (020) 7493 1954

Cooking 2 | Lebanese | £45

For more than 20 years, Al Hamra has been providing classic Lebanese cooking in a plush dining room with copious plants, quality linen on the tables and a cheerful, relaxed atmosphere. The long menu sticks mainly to the staples of the repertoire, with almost 60 starters (mostly vegetarian) ranging from chargrilled aubergine with garlic, spring onions, parsley and walnuts to Lebanese-style 'pizza' topped with minced lamb, onion, parsley and pine nuts. Chargrilled meats form the bulk of main courses: skewered chunks of tender lamb and mushrooms, or whole boneless baby chicken with garlic sauce, for example. Finish with traditional Lebanese sweets chosen from the display. House French wine is £15, house Lebanese £21.50. The smaller Brasserie Al Hamra offshoot had yet to open at the time the Guide went to press but was due 'shortly';52 Shepherd Market, W1J 7QU, tel: (020) 7493 1068.

MAP 15

Alloro

19–20 Dover Street, W1S 4LU
Tel: (020) 7495 4768

NEW CHEF | Italian | £52

This contemporary Italian restaurant occupies a smart location just off Piccadilly, near the Ritz, and over the years it seems to have settled into an easy familiarity within its surroundings – and when a place works this well, that's no bad thing. There is a new chef but things continue unabated; menus, which are set for two, three or four courses, are a manageable size, with straightforward descriptions. There are few surprises in terms of combinations: pan-fried duck egg with asparagus and Parmesan for a starter, for example, while fresh taglierini is served with girolles sauce and black summer truffle, and a main course of roasted rump of lamb comes with lentils and potato gratin. For dessert, there's perhaps peach and amaretti biscuit tart. Prices kick off at £15 on the all-Italian wine list, but rise quickly. More reports please.

Chef: Daniele Camera Proprietor: A to Z Restaurants Ltd Open: Mon to Fri L 12 to 2.30, Mon to Sat D 7 to 10.30 Closed: Bank hols, 1 week Christmas Meals: Set L £26 (2 courses) to £29, Set D £28.50 (2 courses) to £36 Service: 12.5% (optional) Cards: Amex, Delta, Diners, Maestro, MasterCard, Visa Details: 70 seats. No cigars/pipes. No music. Air-conditioned Tube: Green Park

MAP 13

Almeida

30 Almeida Street, N1 1AD
Tel: (020) 7354 4777
Website: www.conran.com

Cooking 4 | French Bistro | £51

Smart, with clean lines, minimalist décor and convenient for the Almeida Theatre opposite, the cooking at this Conran restaurant is rather more

conservative than the surroundings. The menus stick to a tried and tested repertoire, but, while these include a sprinkling of dressed-up classics, not all dishes are as French in their outlook as salade périgourdine, coquilles St Jacques, or dorade royale en papillote. It is possible to have roast cod with chorizo and Basque pepper ragoût, for example. The principal orientation, though, is French, and you may feel that you are taking a lightning tour of *Larousse Gastronomique* before concluding with profiteroles with sauce au chocolat, a selection of tarts from the famed trolley, or a plateau de fromages. The extensive wine list opens with some 30 wines by the glass, including champagne and pudding wines, pot lyonnais (46cl) or bottle (from £14.95).

Chef: Ian Wood **Proprietor:** Conran Restaurants **Open:** Mon to Sat 12 to 2.30, 5.30 to 10.45, Sun 1 to 9 **Closed:** Christmas, Easter Mon **Meals:** alc (main courses £12.50 to £25). Set L and D 5.30 to 7 £14.50 (2 courses) to £17.50. Bar tapas menu available **Service:** 12.5% (optional) **Cards:** Amex, Delta, Diners, Maestro, MasterCard, Visa **Details:** 100 seats. No-smoking area. Wheelchair access (also WC). No music. Air-conditioned **Tube:** Angel, Highbury & Islington

MAP 14

Amaya

15 Halkin Arcade, Motcomb Street, SW1X 8JT
Tel: (020) 7823 1166
Website: www.realindianfood.com

Cooking 3 | Indian | £57

Amaya manages to be formal and informal by turns: 'one is greeted formally, as if one is entering a seriously swish restaurant' but then faced with lots of plain tables set quite close together, a centrally located grill and much of the preparation area open to view. The menu is divided into tandoor, sigri (charcoal grill) and tawa (skillet), and the idea is to choose several dishes from each and finish with a curry. Bombay masala chicken biryani is a must, but also impressive are lamb chops grilled with ginger, lime and coriander, and duck with tandoori spices and a tamarind glaze. The kitchen also produces commendable seafood: witness a lobster stir-fried in light spices, and a 'light and refreshing' seafood platter of scallop, oyster and tiger prawn. For dessert, lemon and lime tart has impressed, and bread-and-butter pudding with bananas and chocolate proved to be a hit. The wine list is a good match for both the food and the Belgravia location, starting with house vin de pays at £17.05. Under the same ownership as Chutney Mary (see entry).

Chef: Karunesh Khanna **Proprietors:** Ranjit Mathrani, and Namita and Camellia Panjabi **Open:** all week 12 to 2.30 (2.15 Sat and Sun), 6.30 to 11.15 (10.15 Sun) **Closed:** 25 Dec **Meals:** alc (main courses £8.50 to £25). Set L £14.50 to £26.75, Set D £34 to £56.50 **Service:** 12.5% (optional) **Cards:** Amex, Delta, Diners, Maestro, MasterCard, Visa **Details:** 90 seats. Vegetarian meals. No-smoking area. Wheelchair access (also WC). Music. Air-conditioned **Tube:** Knightsbridge

MAP 12

Amici   NEW ENTRY

35 Bellevue Road, SW17 7EF
Tel: (020) 8672 5888
Website: www.amiciitalian.co.uk

Cooking 2 | Italian | £40

Invariably crowded, Amici positively buzzes, and with its close-packed tables and casual atmosphere, it is an appropriate setting for the kind of Italian food – 'authentic and delicious' – long associated with the doyenne of Italian cookery books, Valentina Harris. She is acting as consultant here. A large open-plan kitchen, lots of dark wood and paper napery help crank up the volume and lend an informal air to proceedings. The cooking is bright, modern and not liable to startle, with buffalo mozzarella with roast beetroot, risotto with asparagus and Parmesan, and spaghetti with baby clams and white wine typical starters. 'Spot-on' lamb cutlets with baby onions and rosemary-baked potatoes was a palpable hit at inspection, as was fillet of sea bass with Sicilian almond pesto and roast peppers. Desserts include examples from the standard Italian repertoire, delivering a well-made pannacotta with strawberry coulis, and good home-made sorbets. Cocktails take up almost as much page space as the patriotic wine list, the latter kicking off at £12.50.

Chef: Paolo Zanca **Proprietor:** Christopher Gilmour **Open:** Mon to Fri 12 to 3, 6 to 10.30, Sat and Sun 11 to 4, 6 to 10.30 (9.30 Sun) **Closed:** 25 and 26 Dec **Meals:** alc (main courses £8.50 to £15) **Service:** 12.5% (optional) **Cards:** Amex, Delta, Diners, Maestro, MasterCard, Visa **Details:** 80 seats. 40 seats outside. Vegetarian meals. Children's helpings. No smoking. Music. Air-conditioned

NEW ENTRY	This appears after the restaurant's name if the establishment was not a main entry in last year's Guide. Please note, however, it may have been 'also recommended' in the previous edition.

MAP 13

Anchor & Hope

36 The Cut, SE1 8LP
Tel: (020) 7928 9898

Cooking 5 | Traditional European | £40

The setting is pleasingly rough and ready. Dark aubergine walls, rustic furniture, chrome light fittings and a big theatrical curtain to divide the eating area from the bar set a take-us-as-you-find-us tone. It's all rollickingly informal, with no booking system, but nonetheless runs like a well-oiled machine, thanks to excellent staff and a kitchen that knows what it's doing, from buying to cooking. Plaudits pour in, with many reporters wondering how such quality is achieved with such apparent economy of means. Start with a heap of watercress, throw in quartered beetroot, toss in some creamy horseradish, and top the lot with a halved, runny-yolked, cold boiled egg. How can that be so great? Yet it is. A whole black bream is roasted for a main course and served with purple-sprouting broccoli in a thin white anchovy sauce to make another triumph. Old Spot gammon is almost evanescently smoked but eloquently flavourful, served with a generous portion of creamy champ.

Others have commended such dishes as a mushroom risotto that was 'sort of perfect', a slow-cooked leg of lamb that served a lunch party until they could eat no more and carried the rest of it home wrapped in foil, 'second-to-none' dauphinois, and fine, thick-crusted mirabelle tart with smooth vanilla ice cream. Wines from the short but imaginative list, with prices from £10, are served in little chunky glasses, as is the espresso.

Chefs: Jonathon Jones and Harry Lester Proprietors: Robert Shaw, Jonathon Jones and Harry Lester Open: Tue to Sat L 12 to 2.30, Mon to Sat D 6 to 10.30 Closed: Christmas, bank hols Meals: alc (main courses £10 to £20). Bar menu available Service: not inc Cards: Delta, Maestro, MasterCard, Visa Details: 80 seats. 23 seats outside. Wheelchair access (not WC). Occasional music Tube: Waterloo, Southwark

MAP 12

Anglesea Arms

35 Wingate Road, W6 0UR
Tel: (020) 8749 1291
Website: www.angleseaarms.co.uk

Cooking 2 | Modern European | £45

A neighbourhood favourite, this stylish gastro-pub ticks all the right boxes: they make their own bread, use first-rate raw materials, spark up the fire in winter and open out the terrace in summer. The food is nicely presented and well timed, and the blackboard menu, which changes at each session, is a compilation of bright, modern and straightforward dishes. Duck liver parfait with onion marmalade and Poilâne toast is as likely to be among starters as squid sautéed with chickpeas, chorizo, chilli, parsley and olive oil, while main courses might be fillet of gilthead bream with rosemary and hazelnut couscous and a Bloody Mary sauce, or morcilla with mash and apple sauce. Desserts tend to be familiar: treacle tart with Chantilly cream, for instance. Plenty of wines are served by the glass, from £3, from a short but varied list; bottle prices start at £12.50.

Chef: Henrik Ritzen Proprietor: Jill O'Sullivan Open: all week 12.30 to 2.45 (3 Sat, 3.30 Sun), 7 to 10.30 (9.30 Sun, 10 Mon) Closed: 22 to L 31 Dec Meals: alc (main courses L £8.50 to £13, D £12 to £23.50). Set L Mon to Fri £9.95 (2 courses) to £12.95 Service: not inc Cards: MasterCard, Visa Details: 38 seats. 20 seats outside. Vegetarian meals. Children's helpings. No smoking in 1 dining room. Occasional music Tube: Ravenscourt Park

MAP 13

Arancia   AR

52 Southwark Park Road, SE16 3RS
Tel: (020) 7394 1751

A popular neighbourhood Italian restaurant, Arancia has a bright décor, a lively atmosphere and a short menu offering big, bold flavours. Starters of leek and fava bean soup (£3.50) or fried lambs' kidneys with mustard dressing (£4.50) could be followed by whole roast poussin with honey and rosemary (£9.50) or slow-roast belly pork with parsnip mash and braised leeks (£9.75). Pasta dishes might include linguine with razor clams, parsley and garlic (£4.50/£8.50), and to finish there's chocolate semifreddo (£3) or Italian cheeses (£4.75). Italian wines from £10.50. Closed Sun and Mon.

AR	Not a full entry but provisionally recommended. These 'also recommended' establishments are integrated throughout the book.

MAP 15

Arbutus

63–64 Frith Street,
W1D 3JW
Tel: (020) 7734 4545
Website: www.arbutusrestaurant.co.uk

LONDON
OF THE
YEAR
NEWCOMER

Cooking 6 | Modern European | £40

Anthony Demetre and Will Smith's new Soho venture opened in the early summer of 2006 and was immediately the talk of the town. Named after the arbutus (strawberry tree) that used to stand in nearby Soho Square, it's in the premises that once housed Bruno Loubet's Bistrot Bruno and is a short way along from another landmark address, Alastair Little (see entry). These are cultural as well as geographical markers, because Arbutus looks set fair to do for London cooking something of the job that Little did in the dying days of nouvelle cuisine. To those whose palates have wearied of violent juxtapositions, amuse-bouches and pre-desserts, here will be manna from heaven.

The place is simple enough: an L-shaped dining room with big box tables and high chairs at the front, as well as seating along the bar, a 'bistro moderne', in the words of the proprietors. Demetre, who used to cook at Putney Bridge, brings a heartily unvarnished style of mostly European comfort food to the streets of Soho, at prices that initially defied belief. A slice of braised pig's-head terrine is clagged together with fruity chutney, served with puréed potato and a tangle of caramelised onions, delivering a world of savoury power at less than £6. Squid and mackerel burger is like a Thai fishcake, chunky, moist and full of coriander, and served with a ribbon of exquisite barbecue sauce.

Main courses bring on some interesting ingredients – pieds et paquets are trotters and tripe parcels – as well as showing amazing attention to detail. An early star was a rabbit dish that combined slices of the saddle stuffed with liver and spinach, with the shoulder meat made into a cottage pie, with a serving of sweet hispi cabbage and a stock reduction strewn with mustard seeds. To finish, vanilla cheesecake with strawberries in syrup will take some beating, but there are also floating islands with pink pralines, or raspberry trifle. Cheeses are from La Fromagerie. Service hiccups marred too many early meals (the staircase that descends to the lavatories is shared by waiting staff running up from the kitchen, and tempers can seem close to fraying), but essentially this will be, for many, the venue that Soho has sorely needed

for a long time. A two-page list of wines has been imaginatively chosen and, even more imaginatively, is offered as well by the 250ml carafe for those in the mood to experiment. Prices start at £12.50 (or £4.25 the carafe) for southern French blends.

Chef: Anthony Demetre   Proprietors: Will Smith and Anthony Demetre Open: Mon to Sat 12 to 2.30, 5 to 11, Sun 12.30 to 3.30, 6 to 9.30 Closed: 25 and 26 Dec, 1 Jan Meals: alc (main courses £12.50 to £15.50). Set L and D Mon to Sat 5 to 7 £13.50 (2 courses) to £15.50 Service: 12.5% (optional) Cards: Amex, Delta, Maestro, MasterCard, Visa Details: 75 seats. Vegetarian meals. Children's helpings. No smoking. Wheelchair access (not WC). No music. Air-conditioned Tube: Tottenham Court Road

MAP 13

Ark

122 Palace Gardens Terrace, W8 4RT
Tel: (020) 7229 4024
Website: www.thearkrestaurant.co.uk

Cooking 1 | Italian | £48
£5

A short stroll from Notting Hill Gate tube, the Ark is easily spotted by its nicely fitted out front terrace. Inside, the décor is mostly taupe, with white paper table covers over linen cloths and flowers adding splashes of colour. Bread, ice cream and pasta are all made in-house, and white truffles are a speciality in autumn. Antipasti vary from a salad of crab and bitter leaves to deep-fried artichokes with preserved lemon and capers, while the selection of pasta includes linguine with clams poached in white wine with chilli and garlic. The main event might be lamb cutlets with braised aubergine and olives with mint salsa, or swordfish with caper berries and tomato jus. Desserts fly the flag in the form of tiramisù, or fruits of the forest in a warm Marsala sabayon. A map of the regions is printed on the all-Italian, annotated wine list. A decent choice is served by the glass, with Sicilian red opening proceedings at £13.50.

Chef: Steve Moran   Proprietor: Louise Mayo   Open: Tue to Sat L 12 to 3, Mon to Sat D 6.30 to 11 Closed: bank hols Meals: alc (main courses £10.50 to £18.50). Set L £15 (2 courses) to £17.50 Service: 12.5% (optional) Cards: Amex, Delta, Diners, Maestro, MasterCard, Visa Details: 60 seats. 12 seats outside. Vegetarian meals. Wheelchair access (not WC). Occasional music. Air-conditioned Tube: Notting Hill Gate

To submit a report on any restaurant, please visit *www.which.co.uk/gfgfeedback*.

MAP 12

Armadillo

AR

41 Broadway Market, E8 4PH
Tel: (020) 7249 3633

South America comes to Hackney at this little restaurant. The décor and music are Latin American, service is friendly, and tapas-style dishes might include Cuban pumpkin fritters with goats' cheese crema (£4.70), salt fishcakes with avocado and shrimp salsa (£5), or Ecuadorian potato and cheese cakes (£7.50). Alternatively, go for something more substantial like grilled Argentinian fillet steak with horseradish and avocado cream (£16). Finish with chocolate and chilli truffles (£3). The mainly South American wine list, which takes in some Iberian bottles, starts at £12. Open Mon to Sat D only.

MAP 13

Assaggi

The Chepstow, 39 Chepstow Place, W2 4TS
Tel: (020) 7792 5501

Cooking 4 | Italian | £58

Situated above a pub in Notting Hill Gate, the presence of Assaggi is not obvious at first glance, but it is a real gem. The décor is minimal but not cold, as the bare walls are covered in boldly coloured rectangles of cloth, which do the job of absorbing noise and doubling up as artworks. The atmosphere soon becomes lively as the place fills up, which is often, and booking in advance is essential. Service has been praised, with staff quick to react and cheerful with it. The menu, in Italian, is compact and easy to digest. Buffalo mozzarella, stewed octopus, or sweetbreads in Vernaccia might start, while pasta options include ravioli with butter and sage, and crab tagliolini. Simple main courses might be roast leg of lamb, calf's liver, or griddled fillet of beef. Finish with flourless chocolate cake, or ricotta cheesecake. The all-Italian wine list is fairly pricey, starting at £19.95, or £4.95 a glass.

Chef: Nino Sassu **Proprietors:** G. Fraccari and Nino Sassu **Open:** Mon to Sat 12.30 (1 Sat) to 2.30, 7.30 to 11 **Meals:** alc (main courses £17.50 to £20) **Service:** not inc **Cards:** Delta, Diners, Maestro, MasterCard, Visa **Details:** 35 seats. No music. Air-conditioned **Tube:** Notting Hill Gate

MAP 12

L'Auberge

AR

22 Upper Richmond Road, SW15 2RX
Tel: (020) 8874 3593

This intimate Putney restaurant serves up classic French dishes paying much attention to detail. Owner and chef Pascal Ardilly is an expert in desserts so make room for the moelleux au chocolat amer, sauce miellée and fleur d'oranger (£5.90) to finish your meal. Start with snails and mushroom cassolette (£6.25), and move on to guinea fowl with a pork and apricot stuffing (£12.75) or fillet of zander with a vermouth sauce (£14.95). French wines from £12. Open Tue to Sat D only.

MAP 14

Aubergine

11 Park Walk, SW10 0AJ
Tel: (020) 7352 3449
Website: www.auberginerestaurant.co.uk

Cooking 5 | Modern French | £87

The frontage of this discreet Chelsea venue retains its aubergine-coloured canopy for identification purposes. Inside is a small, comfortable bar area leading to a convivial, relaxing dining room, with natural daylight from a skylight at the back. With a well-drilled team to front it up, this is the setting for William Drabble's self-assured, contemporary French cooking. There are opulent ingredients aplenty, from poached lobster tail with lobster butter sauce, with which you might choose to start, to a main-course assiette of veal with artichokes, watercress and confit lemon. Foie gras crops up reliably, perhaps seared and served with caramelised onions and a warm salad of bacon and apple, and truffle butter is the medium for a main dish of roast monkfish with dill-laced mash. The standard of execution is high, with all dishes looking very well honed, reflected by the fairly ambitious pricing of the three-course dinner menu (at least there are no supplements).

Desserts may sound surprisingly trad – they lead with tarte Tatin, or prune and Armagnac parfait – but here, too, the attention to detail is persuasive. A less familiar way to finish might be with mint mousse and sorbet partnered by chocolate jelly. A quality beer selection leads off the drinking options, which soon get in among the garlanded pantheon of French stars, where the prices may well bring tears to the eyes. New-wave Italian wines and some seriously good Californian stuff add variety but hardly price relief, when Peter Michael's admittedly fine Les Pavots Cabernet Sauvignon 2001 is £223. Prices open at £18 for Chilean Sauvignon Blanc.

Chef: William Drabble Proprietor: A to Z Restaurants Open: Mon to Fri L 12 to 2.15, Mon to Sat D 7 to 11 Meals: Set L £34 (inc wine), Set D £64 to £77 Service: 12.5% (optional) Cards: Amex, Delta, Diners, Maestro, MasterCard, Visa Details: 60 seats. Vegetarian meals. No smoking. No music. Air-conditioned Tube: South Kensington

MAP 15

Avenue AR

7-9 St James's Street, SW1A 1EE
Tel: (020) 7321 2111

The Avenue continues to present brasserie-style dishes from an internationally inspired menu, starting, perhaps, with cream of celeriac soup with spiced apple and walnuts, or Parma ham with figs. Main courses (£14 to £22.50) take in Parmesan chicken escalope with cherry vine tomatoes, and roast sea bream with artichokes. Rich desserts include sticky toffee pudding with vanilla ice cream, or chocolate marquise with custard (£5 to £6.50). Set-price lunches are £19.95/£21.95. Wines from £18. Closed Sat L and Sun.

MAP 14

Awana NEW ENTRY

85 Sloane Avenue, SW3 3DX
Tel: (020) 7584 8880
Website: www.awana.co.uk

Cooking 1 | Malaysian | £62

The name is Malay, meaning 'in the clouds', hinting at the lofty aspirations of this new restaurant from the owner of the Mango Tree (see entry). The décor in the long rectangular dining room is 'all teak, glass and leather', with a purple cloud motif on the wallpaper and plasma screens showing Malaysian TV. The menus stick to the standard Malaysian repertoire. An appetiser of excellent roti canai with dhal or red curry sauce precedes starters of satay, with either tender chicken or carefully cooked scallops, or perhaps deep-fried organic tofu in a feather-light tempura batter with chilli vinaigrette. High-quality ingredi-

ents are a strength, as has been particularly evident in a main course of beef rendang, featuring 'meltingly tender' slow-cooked rib in coconut milk curry. As well as curried dishes, there are grills – perhaps butterfish wrapped in a banana leaf with lemongrass, coriander and chilli – and various stir-fries. The wine list has some exciting bottles, although mark-ups are a touch on the high side, with prices starting at £19.

Chef: Lee Chin Soon Proprietor: Eddie Lim Open: all week 12 to 3, 6 to 11.30 Meals: alc (main courses £9.50 to £24). Set L £12.80 (2 courses) to £15, Set D £36. Bar menu available Service: 12.5% (optional) Cards: Amex, Delta, Diners, Maestro, MasterCard, Visa Details: 80 seats. Vegetarian meals. Children's helpings. Jacket and tie. No smoking. Wheelchair access (not WC). Music. Air-conditioned

MAP 12

Babur Brasserie

119 Brockley Rise, SE23 1JP
Tel: (020) 8291 2400
Website: www.babur.info

Cooking 2 | Indian | £39

A life-size Bengal tiger prowling on the roof marks this south London stalwart as no ordinary restaurant. It has been serving superior Indian cooking for over 20 years and is going as strong as ever, recently given a thorough refurbishment too, with traditional Indian materials and artworks. The menu, changed and updated frequently, blends old and new ideas in vibrant style, with starters of Bengali beetroot cutlets, murgh pattice (a Delhi street snack of minced chicken, potato and sev), spicy crab cakes, or lamb takatin (tender cutlets tossed with peppers on a tawa). Main courses range from familiar favourites such as rogan josh to more unusual beef xacutti (tandoor-roast ribs simmered with Goan spices), Old Delhi-style khargosh (curried rabbit), or gilthead bream Malabar, served with upma (Indian-style couscous). Side dishes include Gujarati pumpkin, and green bean fogath. Wines are priced from £12.75.

Chefs: Enam Rahman and Jiwan Lal Proprietor: Babur 1998 Ltd Open: all week 12.15 to 2.15, 6.15 to 10.30 Closed: 25 and 26 Dec Meals: alc exc Sun L (main courses £8 to £17). Sun buffet L £10.95 Service: not inc Cards: Amex, Delta, Diners, Maestro, MasterCard, Visa Details: 72 seats. Vegetarian meals. Children's helpings. No smoking. Wheelchair access (not WC). Music. Air-conditioned

MAP 12

Balham Bar & Kitchen [AR]

15–19 Bedford Hill, SW12 9EX
Tel: (020) 8675 6900

Five years ago Bedford Hill was hardly the place to site a modern trendy bar, but with a now 'desirable suburban status and a vibrant population' to please, this large corner site fits in a treat. It succeeds with a no-frills brasserie-style menu that ranges from breakfast (all day brunch on Sunday) via squid with a 'zingy' chilli dipping sauce (£4.50) and mussels with cider and parsley (£6.50), to ribeye with béarnaise and chips (£15.50) or whole baked bream. Finish with textbook crème brûlée. Fun drinking too, with cocktails supplementing a lengthy global wine list which kicks off at £12.95. Open all week.

MAP 13

Baltic

74 Blackfriars Road, SE1 8HA
Tel: (020) 7928 1111
Website: www.balticrestaurant.co.uk

Cooking 3 | **East/North European** | **£39**

The huge doors signal a restaurant that has big ideas in a minimalist setting. Enter via the 'dark and swish' bar, where a hlebnaya sour rye vodka might be just the ticket (choose from a list of over thirty vodkas). The dining room is an expansive space, with ceilings opened up to the rafters, and the colour provided by modern art and mood lighting. The menu covers the stretch of Eastern Europe from the Baltic to the Black Sea. There are over 15 starters and about the same number of main courses, with a good-value set lunch and a pre-theatre deal too. Potato latkes, marinated herring and blinis with caviar are small-plate staples, while an inspector was impressed with the barszcz clear beetroot soup with krokiecik. Roast suckling pig with wild mushrooms is as hearty as you might expect, while rump of lamb comes with aubergine in an authentically Georgian walnut sauce. Desserts are also native, with nalesniki – crêpes filled with sweet cheese, nuts and raisins – a delightful way to end. House vins de pays at £13 kick off the wine list, but prices soon ascend above £20.

Chef: Peter Repinski Proprietor: Jan Woroniecki Open: all week 12 to 3, 6 to 11.15 Closed: 1 Jan Meals: alc (main courses £10.50 to £18.50). Set L and D 6 to 7 £11.50 (2 courses) to £13.50 Service: 12.5% (optional) Cards: Amex, Delta, Diners, Maestro, MasterCard, Visa Details: 100 seats. 20 seats outside. Vegetarian meals. Children's helpings. Wheelchair access (also WC). Music Tube: Southwark

MAP 13

Bank Aldwych/Bank Westminster

1 Kingsway, WC2B 6X Buckingham Gate, SW1E 6BS
Tel: (020) 7379 9797 (centralised number)
Website: www.bankrestaurants.com

Cooking 3 | **Modern European** | **£57**

The two Bank branches in London offer pretty much the same experience, with just subtle differences. They are both popular venues for business lunches and City types, as well as with a more casual crowd, and at busy times you can strain to hear yourself talk. The Aldwych branch was the first to open, in 1996 (the third in the chain is in Birmingham; see entry), and they all offer modern brasserie dishes via a good-value set-price lunch and early- and late-evening dinner menus. Service is brisk and professional at both, while the food is suitably cosmopolitan. Among starters might be Baltic herrings with new potatoes and mustard dressing, or grilled asparagus with a fried duck egg and hollandaise. Follow with crab linguine, seared tuna in a miso dressing, or perhaps roast rump of lamb with rocket, walnut and pesto mash and rosemary jus. Finish with something like pistachio parfait with grenadine-infused pineapple. The Aldwych branch is also home to Bankcafé, where there's a lively Sunday jazz brunch. The lengthy international wine lists, each annotated, are strong in Bordeaux and Burgundy, but other regions show up well too. Own-label Merlot and Chardonnay are £15.

Chef: Damien Pondevie (Aldwych), Stuart Dring (Westminster) Proprietor: Bank Restaurant Group plc Open: Mon to Fri L 12 to 2.45, Mon to Sat D 5.30 to 11; Aldwych also open Sat L 12 to 2.45 and Sun brunch 11.30 to 5 Meals: alc (main courses £11 to £25). Set L £13.50 (2 courses) to £16, Set D 5.30 to 7 and 10 to 11 £13.50 (2 courses) to £16 (Aldwych), £15.95 (2 courses) to £17.95 (Westminster). Bar and (Aldwych only) breakfast menus available Service: 12.5% (optional) Cards: Amex, Delta, Diners, Maestro, MasterCard, Visa Details: 230 seats (Aldwych), 180 seats (Westminster). Vegetarian meals. Children's helpings. Wheelchair access (also WC). No music (Westminster), occasional music (Aldwych). Air-conditioned Tube: Holborn, St James's Park

MAP 13

The Barnsbury

NEW ENTRY

209–211 Liverpool Road, N1 1LX
Tel: (020) 7607 5519
Website: www.thebarnsbury.co.uk

Cooking 1 | Modern European/Italian | **£36**

Just off Upper Street, the Barnsbury is a gastro-pub with good intent. The bar is buzzy while the dining room is little more than a back alcove, so benefits from the lively atmosphere. Décor is as fashion conscious as the customers, including chandeliers made of upside-down wine glasses, gilt mirrors and ever-changing for-sale art on the walls. John O' Riordan's menu draws from Italy and is put together with imagination. Chilli-pickled oranges with feta cheese and olive oil start with great invention, while a main course of paprika roast haddock with chives, crème fraîche and spinach is fresh and succulent. A 'light and refreshing' banana and raspberry en papillote is another nice idea to end. The global wine list offers some good choices under £20; house options start at £13.50.

Chef: John O'Riordan Proprietor: Jeremy Gough Open: all week 12 to 3, 6 to 10 Meals: alc (main courses £10 to £15) Service: 12.5% (optional) Cards: Amex, Delta, Maestro, MasterCard, Visa Details: 70 seats. 25 seats outside. Vegetarian meals. Children's helpings. No smoking in 1 dining room. Wheelchair access (also WC). Music

MAP 15

Bar Shu

NEW ENTRY

28 Frith Street, W1D 5LF
Tel: (020) 7287 8822

Cooking 4 | Szechuan | **£39**

Bar Shu exploded on to the London scene in the late spring of 2006, with the owners bringing over five chefs from China, including Fu Wenhong, a master from Chengdu; 'aspirations are sky high'. The classy three-tiered restaurant is not for the squeamish, or for those who aren't keen on the heat of the chilli, but it is the real Szechuan deal. Silvered pig's tripe in chilli oil sauce says it all: nothing has been dumbed down, everything from the kitchen is authentic. At inspection, spare rib stewed with kelp soup, and delicately flavoured duck rolls with duck egg yolk gave way to numbing and hot-dried beef – a 'sexy chilli-hot undertone' setting the scene for the rest of the meal.

'Utterly delicious' baby cuttlefish, which arrived packed full of short, stout red pickled chillies, and melting dongpo pork knuckle, its richness offset by a little vinegar, were both outstanding, and pock-marked old woman bean curd (usually spotted on menus as ma po tofu) was 'earthy comfort food at its very best'. Desserts of pearly glutinous rice balls with sweet black sesame, or deep-fried sweet potato ingots filled with sweet bean paste are fairly pedestrian given what goes before. A long list of wines from £12 is almost incidental, given the fiery nature of the cooking: best to drink Tiger or Tsingtao beer.

Chef: Fu Wenhong Proprietor: Shao Wei Open: all week 12 to 11.30 Closed: 25 and 26 Dec Meals: alc (main courses £7 to £68). Set L £19.50 to £22.50, Set D £22.50 to £24.50 (all min 2) Service: 12.5% Cards: Amex, Delta, Maestro, MasterCard, Visa Details: 150 seats. Vegetarian meals. Wheelchair access (also WC). Music. Air-conditioned Tube: Leicester Square

MAP 15

Bellamy's

18–18A Bruton Place, W1J 6LY
Tel: (020) 7491 2727

Cooking 5 | Brasserie | **£59**

A French deli-brasserie just off Berkeley Square, Bellamy's offers informal eating in a thoroughly *sympathique* atmosphere, with comfortable leather seating and framed art exhibition posters. The clientele might be Mayfair-smart, but the tone is more unbuttoned than that implies. As the Guide went to press, an eight-seat oyster bar was due to open. Seasonally changing menus deal in high-class comfort food. Expect brown shrimp cro-quettes, smoked eel mousse, or truffled scrambled eggs to start, followed by veal with morels, grilled red mullet with tapenade, or liver and bacon. It all sounds as simple as can be, but enjoyably so. Dishes are properly seasoned, satisfying and generous, and are cooked with immense attention to detail. Most of the classic Gallic desserts seem present and correct too, with îles flottantes, peach melba, tarte aux framboises, and crème caramel all given an outing. Service is polished and professional, unob-trusive without being overly distant. A short, entirely French wine list starts at £21, and heads steeply upwards to Cheval Blanc 1982 for £750. Glass prices start at a gentler £5.50.

Chef: Stéphane Pacoud Proprietor: Gavin Rankin Open: Mon to Fri L 12 to 2.30, Mon to Sat D 7 to 10.15 Closed: Christmas, Easter, bank hols Meals: alc (main courses £18 to £27). Set L and D £24 (2 courses) to £28.50. Oyster bar menu available Service: 12.5% (optional) Cards: Amex, Delta, Maestro, MasterCard, Visa Details: 75 seats. Vegetarian meals. Children's helpings. Wheelchair access (not WC). No music. Air-conditioned

MAP 13

Belvedere

Off Abbotsbury Road, Holland Park, W8 6LU
Tel: (020) 7602 1238
Website: www.belvedererestaurant.co.uk

Cooking 4 | Anglo-French | £50

The setting in Holland Park is 'simply stunning', the restaurant itself a 'slice of affordable glamour, romantic and engaging'. The dining room has vaulted ceilings, high, arched, stained-glass windows and a marble staircase, and most of the well-spaced tables have views over the manicured gardens. Evening meals are accompanied by a pianist. The menu is straightforward modern brasserie, with a fine backbone of classics including eggs Benedict, sausage and mash, and rillettes of pork. Parfait of foie gras and chicken livers was a 'simple classic done well', and main courses include the likes of monkfish with red wine and shallot jus, or daube of beef with a well-textured horseradish mash. Generous portions of Amaretto parfait, or pear and cinnamon crumble finish. The mostly French wine list has few options under £25, although there are a handful of half-bottles, and wines by the glass start at £4.

Chef: Billy Reid Proprietor: Jimmy Lahoud Open: all week L 12 to 2.15 (3.30 Sun), Mon to Sat D 6 to 10.30 Meals: alc (main courses £11.50 to £20). Set L £18 to £24.95, Set D 6 to 7 £18 Service: 12.5% Cards: Amex, Delta, Diners, Maestro, MasterCard, Visa Details: 144 seats. 20 seats outside. Vegetarian meals. Music. Air-conditioned Tube: Holland Park, High Street Kensington

NEW ENTRY	This appears after the restaurant's name if the establishment was not a main entry in last year's Guide. Please note, however, it may have been 'also recommended' in the previous edition.

MAP 15

Benares

12A Berkeley Square House, Berkeley Square, W1J 6BS
Tel: (020) 7629 8886
Website: www.benaresrestaurant.com

Cooking 3 | Modern Indian | £48

The auspicious Mayfair address is an appropriate setting for Atul Kochhar's stylishly appointed restaurant. The menu takes a broad sweep, from a traditional rogan josh to a contemporary tamarind-glazed turbot with sauté mushrooms and spring onions, while from several imaginative set menus there could be South Indian chicken korma, Syrian Christian lamb curry, or pan-fried sea bass in a coconut and tamarind sauce. Tandoori smoked salmon mousse with lime and coriander is an interesting starter, and there could be Indian cheesecake with blueberries, strawberry sorbet and caramelised strawberries for dessert. Prices on the wine list are in tune with the Mayfair location with house selections kicking off at £25.

Chef: Atul Kochhar Proprietor: Atul Kochhar and Vikas Nath Open: Sun to Fri L 12 to 2.30, all week D 5.30 to 11 (6 to 10.30 Sun) Meals: alc (main courses £16 to £38). Set L and D £20. Bar menu available Service: 12.5% Cards: Amex, Delta, Diners, Maestro, MasterCard, Visa Details: 160 seats. 15 seats outside. Vegetarian meals. Children's helpings. No children after 7pm. Smoking in bar only. Music. Air-conditioned Tube: Green Park

MAP 14

Bentley's

NEW ENTRY

LONDON GFG 2007 COMMENDED

11-15 Swallow Street,
W1R 7HD
Tel: (020) 7734 4756
Website: www.bentleysoysterbarandgrill.co.uk

Cooking 5 | Modern British/Fish | £46

Richard Corrigan's latest venture (see also Lindsay House) is a restoration and rejuvenation of this venerable old Piccadilly fish restaurant. On the ground floor is a handsome bar with a small informal dining room, while the full-dress dining goes on upstairs. The atmosphere is clubby, but in a friendly way. High-backed chairs and banquettes in electric blue look good, the crockery is Limoges and there is crisp white linen. Fishy prints adorn the walls, indicating that seafood is still very much the order of the day. The small menu card is peppered with fine ingredients, from Clare Island salmon to native oysters, and the preparations make culinary sense. Macaroni with Dublin Bay prawns features fine home-made pasta and fresh, tender shellfish, in a little crustacean stock, while crab brûlée is richly textured, positively flavoured, and comes with a fine take on sesame prawn toast.

Inventive main-courses pair red mullet with roast pumpkin and spinach, or monkfish with cep duxelles wrapped in pastry, while the grilled Dover sole with home-made tartare sauce is an utterly simple treat. Meat-eaters might opt for the well-flavoured Goosnargh duck with caramelised apple and puréed celeriac. Round things off in equally old-school fashion with excellent fruity trifle generously laced with sherry, or a more up-to-date chocolate tart with Seville orange marmalade. With home-baked breads and friendly, capable service, this should prove a popular new central London magnet. A user-friendly list of wines by the glass (from £4.45) opens an expansive list of quality bottles from around the globe, encompassing such star names as California's Au Bon Climat, Henri Pellé in the Loire, and Yves Cuilleron in the Rhône. Bottles start at £15.95.

Chef: Brendan Fyldes Proprietor: Richard Corrigan Open: Sun to Fri 12 to 2.45, all week D 6 to 11 Meals: alc (main courses £11 to £29) Service: 12.5% (optional) Cards: Amex, Delta, Diners, Maestro, MasterCard, Visa Details: 120 seats. Vegetarian meals. Children's helpings. Smoking in bar only. Wheelchair access (also WC). No music. Air-conditioned Tube: Piccadilly

MAP 15

Berkeley Square

7 Davies Street, W1K 3DD
Tel: (020) 7629 6993
Website: www.theberkeleysquare.com

Cooking 6 | Modern French | £73

Not quite on the square itself, the restaurant sits on a prime corner plot with a small decked terrace. Frosted windows ensure plenty of natural light, while a muted mauve and aubergine palette has been brought to bear on the 'elegant and sophisticated' interior. Service has been variable, a little distracted even at quieter sessions.

Steven Black comes to London by way of Michel Guérard in Provence and brings a formidable level of accomplishment to the impeccably contemporary dishes the menus deal in. Seared

scallops, 'sweet and fleshy', are paired with flash-fried duck foie gras as a signature starter, with well-judged accompaniments of ceps and parsnip purée. Earthier still is a 'beautifully creamy and flavourful' morel risotto with white asparagus, the latter giving crunch to the appetising mulch of the rice. Raw materials are top drawer, as is the case with a main course of caramelised Gressingham duck breast with a quince spring roll and an effective dressing of figs, Madeira and honey. At the end, dessert comes as a technical *tour de force*, a citrus plate encompassing lemon tart, orange sorbet and an unimprovable lime pannacotta scoring especially highly at inspection. A note on the front of the wine list states that if any wine over 20 years old turns out to be ruined, the house accepts no responsibility. Best avoid them then. Instead, there are plenty of younger and good French classics, and more restricted selections from the New World. Wines by the glass start at £6 for a Côtes de Duras Sauvignon Blanc.

Chef: Steven Black Proprietor: John de Stefano Open: Mon to Fri 12 to 2.30, 6 to 10 Closed: Christmas, last 2 weeks Aug, bank hols Meals: Set L £17.95 (2 courses) to £55, Set D £42.95 (2 courses) to £55 Service: 12.5% (optional) Cards: Amex, Delta, Diners, Maestro, MasterCard, Visa Details: 70 seats. 14 seats outside. Vegetarian meals. Children's helpings. No smoking in dining room. Music. Air-conditioned

MAP 14

Bibendum

Michelin House, 81 Fulham Road, SW3 6RD
Tel: (020) 7581 5817
Website: www.bibendum.co.uk

Cooking 3 | Modern British | £66

The now twenty-year-old conversion of Michelin House still looks fresh, with the first-floor Bibendum exciting a period feel as if it is timeless and impervious to fashion. Not so the menu, which bobs along on the current that sweeps through many a modern kitchen, taking in a warm salad of ham hock and black pudding with mustard lentils and frisée salad, leek and brown shrimp risotto, and main courses like confit of duck with glazed endive, golden sultanas and Madeira. Other dishes aim for the comfort zone in the shape of slow-cooked belly pork with garlic mash and chorizo with sherry and sage, and deep-fried haddock with chips and tartare sauce, while desserts run to hot chocolate fondant with pistachio ice cream or spiced pineapple carpaccio with basil sorbet. The wine list is a buff's delight, packed full of interesting bottles, with Old World classics alongside rising stars from the New World. Mark-ups are on the steep side, but there's no shortage of options in the £20 to £30 range. House French is £17.95.

On the ground floor is the Oyster Bar, where a pair of reporters were transported south by vitello tonnato rich with garlic-infused mayonnaise, and a fine salad of artichoke hearts, green beans and black olives.

Chef: Matthew Harris   Proprietors: Sir Terence Conran, Simon Hopkinson and Michael Hamlyn   Open: all week 12 to 2.30 (12.30 to 3 Sat and Sun), 7 to 11 (10.30 Sun)   Closed: D 24 Dec to 26 Dec   Meals: alc D (main courses £16.50 to £26). Set L £24 (2 courses) to £28.50   Service: 12.5% (optional) Cards: Amex, Delta, Diners, Maestro, MasterCard, Visa Details: 80 seats. Children's helpings. Wheelchair access (not WC). No music. Air-conditioned

MAP 15

Blandford Street

5–7 Blandford Street, W1U 3DB
Tel: (020) 7486 9696
Website: www.blandford-street.co.uk

Cooking 3 | Modern European | £48

Situated in a quiet street off Marylebone High Street, Blandford Street has an air of understated exclusivity, thanks to its widely spaced, linen-clothed tables, big mirrors and abstracts. Cooking is typically modern European in that it blends old ideas with new and takes inspiration from here, there and everywhere. Expect starters ranging from traditional Russian borscht to crisp-fried sea bream with spiced fishcake, Vietnamese herb salad and mango and lime vinaigrette. To follow, there may be loin of wild rabbit with Suffolk bacon and a pudding made from the legs, or slow-roasted pork belly with a faggot of Savoy cabbage and chorizo, spring onion mash and Bramley apple sauce. To finish, old-fashioned treacle tart or rum and raisin cheesecake with citrus fruit salad. A passable choice of wines by the glass opens an extensive selection that's almost evenly divided between France and the rest of the world. House French is £16.

Chef: Martin Moore   Proprietor: Nicholas Lambert   Open: Mon to Fri L 12 to 2.30, Mon to Sat D 6.30 to 10.30   Closed: Christmas, bank hols   Meals: alc D (main courses £11 to £22). Set L £19.95 (2 courses) to £22.95   Service: 12.5% (optional)   Cards: Amex, Delta, Maestro, MasterCard, Visa Details: 50 seats. 10 seats outside. Vegetarian meals. Children's helpings. No-smoking area. Wheelchair access (not WC). Music. Air-conditioned   Tube: Bond Street, Baker Street

MAP 13

Bleeding Heart

The Cellars, Bleeding Heart Yard, Greville St, EC1N 8SJ
Tel: (020) 7242 8238
Website: www.bleedingheart.co.uk

Cooking 2 | French | £48

Taking its name from the grisly legend of Lady Elisabeth Hatton, this popular City dining venue stands on a quiet courtyard of the same name. There are three parts to the operation: a bistro and a tavern, either ideal for informal occasions, and a charming basement restaurant providing sophisti-cated French cooking. Barbary duck terrine en croûte with red onion marmalade, and Scottish scallops baked in the shell with caramelised shallots are typical starters, while main courses take in grilled sea bass on fennel ratatouille with pastis sauce, and roasted suckling pig 'four ways' with thyme jus and pommes gratin. To finish, there might be marinated pineapple with lime sorbet and crisp coconut tuile. The hefty wine list will appeal to fans of Burgundy and Bordeaux, with many significant vintages represented, but the highlight is the New Zealand section, featuring excellent wines from the owners' vineyard, Trinity Hill, priced from £19.95.

Chef: Pascal Even   Proprietors: Robert and Robyn Wilson Open: Mon to Fri 12 to 2.30, 6 to 10.30   Closed: 1 week Christmas to New Year, bank hols   Meals: alc (main courses £12 to £21.50)   Service: 12.5% (optional)   Cards: Amex, Diners, MasterCard, Visa   Details: 100 seats. 30 seats outside. Vegetarian meals. No smoking in 1 dining room. No music. Air-conditioned   Tube: Farringdon

MAP 14

Bluebird Dining Room   AR

350 King's Road, SW3 5UU
Tel: (020) 7559 1129

Conran's gastrodome is spread over two levels of an impressive building on the King's Road. Downstairs you can get a coffee and a pastry, or a light meal (porcini lasagne, perhaps; £9.50), while upstairs the Dining Room offers a set-price menu (£30 for three courses) featuring the likes of casse-role of lamb sweetbreads, followed by fillets of West Coast gurnard with marsh samphire, or crackled Middle White pork with roast potatoes and red amaranth. End with raspberry knicker-bocker glory, or perhaps Goosnargh iced yoghurt. Over 200 wines from £16. Closed Sun.

MAP 12

Blue Elephant

3–6 Fulham Broadway, SW6 1AA
Tel: (020) 7385 6595
Website: www.blueelephant.com

| Cooking 1 | Thai | £45 |

Visiting the Blue Elephant is an experience that 'dazzles all the senses', the dining room recreating the ambience of a tropical jungle with lush plants, trickling fountains and the scent of exotic flowers mingling with the aromas of herbs and spices emanating from the kitchen. Extensive menus delve into every corner of Thai cooking, starters ranging from chicken satay to prawns in rice paper with plum sauce, and som tam (a spicy salad of shredded green papaya with dried shrimps). To follow, try homok talay, a chilli-hot seafood stew with ginger and garlic; duck breast on seaweed with a sweet-sour tamarind sauce; or perhaps paneng nua, a curry of beef and coconut milk with basil. Wines are chosen to complement the rich and spicy flavours, and bottle prices start at £21.

Chef: Somphong Sae-Jew   Proprietor: Blue Elephant International plc   Open: Mon to Fri L 12 to 2.30, Sun brunch 12 to 3.30, all week D 7 to 12 (10.30 Sun)   Closed: 25 to 28 Dec   Meals: alc (main courses £10 to £22). Set L Mon to Fri £10 (2 courses) to £15, Set D £35 to £53   Service: 12.5% (optional)   Cards: Amex, Delta, Diners, MasterCard, Maestro, Visa   Details: 350 seats. Vegetarian meals. Wheelchair access (also WC). Music. Air-conditioned   Tube: Fulham Broadway

MAP 13

Blueprint Café

Design Museum, 28 Shad Thames, SE1 2YD
Tel: (020) 7378 7031
Website: www.conran.com

| Cooking 2 | Modern European | £58 |

Making the most of stunning views over the Thames, the restaurant on the first floor of the Design Museum now has a summer terrace and a barbecue menu. Décor remains tongue-in-cheek retro, with Formica tables and functional china, while the food is straightforward with a few modern twists. Start with razor clams in a parsley crust, or crisp asparagus rolls, then move on to whole grilled bream with cucumber salad, or ox tongue with little turnips and peas. Imaginative desserts might include greengage trifle, or mille-feuille of apples and vanilla cream. The wine list is global with some interesting house selections at £15 but climbing steeply after that.

Chef: Jeremy Lee   Proprietor: Conran Restaurants Ltd   Open: all week L 12 to 3 (4 Sun), Mon to Sat D 6 to 11   Meals: alc (main courses £12.50 to £20). Set L and D £35   Service: 12.5% (optional)   Cards: Amex, Delta, Diners, Maestro, MasterCard, Visa   Details: 110 seats. 20 seats outside. Vegetarian meals. Children's helpings. Wheelchair access (not WC). Occasional music   Tube: Tower Hill, London Bridge

MAP 13

Bonds

Threadneedle Hotel, 5 Threadneedle Street, EC2R 8AY
Tel: (020) 7657 8088
Website: www.theetoncollection.com

| Cooking 6 | Modern European | £63 |

Beneath a high vaulted ceiling, amid tall pillars, Bonds is fully at home in its surroundings, which – as if you needed to be told – are a former bank building a mere halfpenny's toss from the Bank of England. At once grandly imposing, yet plush and comfortable, it's a thoroughly stylish conversion, and a fit backdrop to Barry Tonks's modern Francophile cooking. That translates as roasting scallops and serving them with chorizo and squid-ink polenta, or kitting out wild Scottish halibut with gem lettuce, caramelised baby onions, girolles and a sauce of Sauternes. Dishes are headlined with their main ingredient, allowing a quick flick through the menu on first perusal while you tick possible boxes, with many items subjected to caramelising. Tarte Tatin might arrest the eye among the main courses, but it's topped with red onions and goats' cheese as a vegetarian option. Steak tartare continues its restaurant comeback, served here with a soft-boiled egg, celeriac rémoulade and horseradish cream, while main course meats run to slow-cooked Baillet mountain pork with caramelised shallots and apple purée. French farmhouse cheeses should be good, if the likes of peanut butter parfait with caramelised banana and Tanzanian chocolate sorbet sounds like too much of a challenge.

A deftly assembled wine list offers generous breadth of choice, with good vintage selections among the European bottles and a nose for subtle, food-friendly styles in the New World. Prices are on the high side, but there is some relief below £25, and a page of well-chosen wines by the glass starts at £5.50.

Chef: Barry Tonks Proprietor: Peter Tyrie Open: Mon to Fri 12 to 2.30, 6 to 10 Closed: 2 weeks Christmas, bank hols Meals: alc (main courses £15.50 to £23.50). Set L £15 (2 courses) to £20, Set D £55. Bar menu available all week Service: 12.5% (optional) Cards: Amex, Delta, MasterCard, Visa Details: 80 seats. Vegetarian meals. No smoking. Wheelchair access (also WC). Music. Air-conditioned Accommodation: 59 rooms Tube: Bank

MAP 14

Boxwood Café

Berkeley Hotel, Wilton Place, SW1X 7RL
Tel: (020) 7235 1010
Website: www.gordonramsay.com

Cooking 3 | Modern British | £59

The cheerful, informative and relaxed staff contribute greatly to the atmosphere at this 'extremely swish café' that forms part of Gordon Ramsay's empire. The cooking is typically modern British in that it blends old ideas with new and takes inspiration from here, there and everywhere. An inspection meal found a few dishes requiring more attention to detail, but hits included a fine glazed pea and leek tart with a poached egg and herb salad, red mullet with mussels in a 'delightfully light and fishy' seafood broth, and an impressive red wine-braised shoulder of beef with black truffle mash, while an indulgent banana sticky toffee pudding with coconut sorbet made a fine finish. Apart from the house Bordeaux blanc at £19, there's nothing on the wine list below £20, and not a lot under £30, although 10 by the glass start at £5.

Chef: Stuart Gillies Proprietor: Gordon Ramsay Holdings Ltd Open: all week 12 to 3 (4 Sat and Sun), 6 to 11 Meals: alc (main courses £9 to £25). Set L £21, Set D £55 Service: 12.5% Cards: Amex, Delta, Diners, Maestro, MasterCard, Visa Details: 140 seats. Vegetarian meals. Children's helpings. No smoking. Wheelchair access (not WC). Music. No mobile phones. Air-conditioned Tube: Knightsbridge

 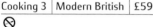

This symbol means that the restaurant has elected to participate in *The Good Food Guide's* £5 voucher scheme (see 'Using The Good Food Guide' for details).

MAP 12

Brackenbury

129–131 Brackenbury Road, W6 0BQ
Tel: (020) 8748 0107

Cooking 4 | Modern European | £42

'A cosy neighbourhood restaurant with good food at good prices' is how the owners describe the Brackenbury, and it's a fair summary of this smart venue in a row of small shops in a quiet residential area. Inside, it is decorated in calm, neutral colours and furnished with smartly varnished wood tables, tall-backed upholstered chairs and plush banquettes with extra cushions. The cooking is French at heart, taking in wider influences to create attractive dishes with a contemporary feel, starters ranging from Thai-spiced butternut squash soup to roast quail and confit leg with foie gras, green beans and sherry raisin salad. Among eight main course options might be roast haddock with salsify, spinach, poached oyster and oyster cream sauce, and roast rump of lamb with flageolet bean purée, braised shallots, tomato and mint jus, as well as simpler options such as Gruyère omelette with chips. To finish, try a classic chocolate tart or perhaps a more fashionable Yorkshire champagne rhubarb fool. New World wines make up the bulk of the short, varied list, though a pair of French vins de pays open proceedings at £12 a bottle, £3.30 a glass.

Chef: Noel Capp Proprietor: Lisa Inglis Open: Sun to Fri L 12.30 to 2.45 (3.30 Sun), Mon to Sat D 7 to 10.45 Closed: 25 and 26 Dec, 1 Jan Meals: alc (main courses £9 to £15). Set L Mon to Fri £12.50 (2 courses) to £14.50 Service: 12.5% (optional) Cards: Amex, Delta, Maestro, MasterCard, Visa Details: 65 seats. 20 seats outside. Vegetarian meals. Children's helpings. Smoking in bar only. No music Tube: Hammersmith

MAP 13

Bradleys

25 Winchester Road, NW3 3NR
Tel: (020) 7722 3457

Cooking 3 | Modern French | £46

Near the Hampstead Theatre in upmarket Swiss Cottage, this modish, elegant dining room is decorated in cream tones, and windows at the back look on to greenery; staff are courteous and in

47

control. The menu might seem at first glance conservative, but there are some interesting combinations and, as a diner has commented, everything is done in style. Feuilleté of rabbit with an oyster mushroom and grain mustard sauce, or hot and cold foie gras with onion confit, roast pear and brioche are typical starters. Main courses might take in rack of Dales lamb with potato dauphinois and minted flageolets, or roast cod with leeks, samphire and a clam beurre blanc. Among six or so desserts could be rhubarb and vanilla soufflé with crème anglaise, or pear Belle Hélène. The lengthy wine list is arranged by style and has terse tasting notes; around a dozen are served by the glass, from £3.20, and there's a decent run of half-bottles. Bottle prices start at £12.90 but soon jump over £20.

> Chef: Simon Bradley   Proprietors: Simon and Jolanta Bradley
> Open: Tue to Fri and Sun L 12 to 3, Tue to Sat D 6 to 11
> Closed: Christmas, bank hols   Meals: alc exc Sun L (main
> courses £11.50 to £17). Set L Tue to Fri and D Tue to Sat 6 to
> 7 £9.95 (2 courses) to £13.95, Set L Sun £18 (2 courses) to
> £22, Set D £19.50   Service: 12.5% (optional)   Cards: Amex,
> Delta, Maestro, MasterCard, Visa   Details: 60 seats.
> Vegetarian meals. Children's helpings. No cigars/pipes in
> dining room. Wheelchair access (not WC). Music. No mobile
> phones. Air-conditioned   Tube: Swiss Cottage

MAP 14

Brasserie St Quentin

243 Brompton Road, SW3 2EP
Tel: (020) 7589 8005
Website: www.brasseriestquentin.co.uk

Cooking 3 | Modern French | £49

The Brompton Road brasserie has been given a makeover: dark blue and ivory dominate the outside, while, inside, the Art Nouveau mirrors, red banquettes and bentwood chairs have been given a bit of a face-lift. Gary Durrant sources exemplary produce from UK suppliers – eels, crab and organic salmon from Northern Ireland, salt-marsh lamb from the Holker Estate in Cumbria and pork from Dorset – and his menus might start with crisp belly pork with apple and frisée salad, or crab ravioli with sauce américaine. Among main courses, traditional things such as grilled ribeye of Buccleuch beef with béarnaise and pommes frites are found alongside organic Shetland salmon with a sweet chilli and ginger dressing. Well-made desserts include coffee brûlée and vanilla cheesecake with blackberry and blueberry compote. The extensive wine list is strongest in France. Ten are offered by the glass from £4.25, and bottle prices start at £14.50.

> Chef: Gary Durrant   Proprietor: Hugh O'Neill   Open: all week
> 12 to 3, 6 to 10.30 (10 Sun)   Closed: 23 to 30 Dec   Meals:
> alc (main courses £10.50 to £25). Set L and D 6 to 7.30
> £15.50 (2 courses) to £17.50   Service: 12.5% (optional)
> Cards: Amex, Delta, Diners, Maestro, MasterCard, Visa
> Details: 55 seats. Vegetarian meals. No cigars/pipes in dining
> room. Wheelchair access (not WC). No music. Air-conditioned
> Tube: Knightsbridge, South Kensington

MAP 15

Brown's Hotel   [NEW ENTRY]

30 Albemarle Street, W1S 4BP
Tel: (020) 7518 4060
Website: www.roccofortehotels.com

Cooking 4 | Modern British | £65

The renovation of Brown's Hotel by Rocco Forte has been a 'wonderful success', writes a reporter. The Grill Room represents 'serious hotel formal dining', capturing something of a 1930s vibe with its panelling, oak pillars, banquette booths and army of old-school waiters beavering away with carving trolleys.

As for the cooking, there is nothing here to frighten the horses, and yet it is not formulaic, delivering simple but expertly cooked British dishes. While some may wonder what the likes of seared bluefin tuna with oriental vegetable salad and soy dressing is doing in the repertoire, traditionalists will appreciate dressed Cornish crab, terrine of duck foie gras, and English lamb cutlets. Such dishes form the centrepiece of a menu that might offer loin of venison roasted with mace and pumpkin polenta – a hit at inspection – or lobster Newburg with spinach and basmati rice. Desserts are a high point, with exemplary treacle and molasses tart with custard ice cream at inspection. Service is charming and hospitable, but deep wallets will be needed to get any joy from the French-leaning wine list (prices start at £25), though 14 are offered by the glass.

> Chef: Laurence Glayzer   Proprietor: Rocco Forte Hotels   Open:
> all week 12 to 2.30, 7 to 10   Meals: alc (main courses £13 to
> £28). Set L Mon to Sat £25 (2 courses) to £30, Set L Sun £27
> (2 courses) to £35, Set D £45   Service: not inc   Cards: Amex,
> Delta, Diners, Maestro, MasterCard, Visa   Details: 80 seats.
> Vegetarian meals. Children's helpings. No cigars or pipes.
> Wheelchair access (also WC). No music. Air-conditioned
> Accommodation: 117 rooms   Tube: Green Park

 This symbol means that the wine list is well above the average.

The Bull

NEW ENTRY

13 North Hill, Highgate, N6 4AB
Tel: (0845) 456 5033
Website: www.inthebull.biz

Cooking 2 | **French** | **£46**

'Bright, on-the-ball' is how one reader described this pub near Highgate village. Housed in a two-storey Victorian building with lots of warmly decorated rooms, it positively throbs with activity and is popular with a young crowd. The informal, unobtrusive service and French-influenced cooking are a big part of its appeal. Everything is home-made and the menu changes seasonally, starting, perhaps, with creamy celeriac soup with croûtons and chives, or moules marinière. The kitchen confidently pairs seared tuna with coriander mash, or keeps things simple with a generous portion of shepherd's pie, topped with cheese and served with green beans. A Bramley apple tart to finish comes with creamy custard, or the alternative cheese plate comes with oatcakes, grapes and celery. The global wine list starts at £13 for their house French, with a dozen by the glass from £3.25.

Chef: Jeremy Hollingsworth **Proprietor:** Barnaby Meredith **Open:** Tue to Sun L 12 to 2.30, all week D 6 to 10.30 **Meals:** alc (main courses £13.50 to £24.50). Set L £14.95 (2 courses) to £17.95 **Service:** 12.5% (optional) **Cards:** Delta, Diners, Maestro, MasterCard, Visa **Details:** 150 seats. 70 seats outside. Car park. Children's helpings. No smoking. Wheelchair access (also WC). Music. Air-conditioned **Tube:** Highgate

Café du Jardin

28 Wellington Street, WC2E 7BD
Tel: (020) 7836 8769 and 8760
Website: www.lecafedujardin.com

Cooking 2 | **Modern British** | **£43**

Tony Howorth has been behind this mainstay of the central London scene for 15 years, and he continues to deliver good brasserie cooking in the heart of Covent Garden. The place to sit is the ground-floor dining room – people-watching is optional – although you might notice the traffic noise outside. The menu includes staples such as Caesar salad and chargrilled ribeye and chips with

béarnaise, but digs deeper for tempura of frogs' legs with garlic mayonnaise or twice-baked soufflé of courgettes and goats' cheese. Sautéed shrimps and monkfish with chickpeas, served with a sweet chill sauce and basmati rice, might follow, and brown bread parfait with mocha cream rounds things off. As at the related Le Deuxième (see entry), the optional service charge is 15 per cent. There are some good wines for those looking for something special, particularly the French bins, while house vins de pays start at the reasonable price of £11.50.

Chef: Tony Howorth **Proprietors:** Robert Seigler and Tony Howorth **Open:** all week 12 to 3, 5.30 to 12 (noon to 11 Sun) **Closed:** 24 and 25 Dec **Meals:** alc (main courses £10 to £17). Set L £10.95 (2 courses) to £14.50, Set D Mon to Sat 5.30 to 7.30, 10 to 12, Sun noon to 11 £10.95 (2 courses) to £14.50 **Service:** 15% (optional) **Cards:** Amex, Delta, Diners, Maestro, MasterCard, Visa **Details:** 105 seats. 20 seats outside. Vegetarian meals. Wheelchair access (not WC). Occasional music. Air-conditioned **Tube:** Covent Garden

Café Japan

626 Finchley Road, NW11 7RR
Tel: (020) 8455 6854

Cooking 4 | **Japanese** | **£30**

There's usually an eager queue of diners at the entrance of this simple café, so there's no lingering over your meal here. 'Quite simply, this is some of the best quality Japanese food I've had in London', as one reader put it, impressed by the quality of the raw materials. The menu is short, and sushi is the thing. An impressive inspection meal included a nigiri sushi selection of 'perfectly fresh' fish including salmon, scallops, mackerel, tuna and sea urchin eggs, and unagi sushi – two pieces of grilled eel brushed with a tart, delicate sauce and scattered with sesame seeds. Other successes have included grilled king crab 'split open, slightly charred and blackened', and perfectly matched with a light, lemony ponzu sauce, and grilled miso-marinated black cod. Ice creams come in green tea, red bean and chestnut flavours and are viable dessert options. Wines are limited to white or red at £8.50, otherwise drink saké or green tea. Note that it's cash only at lunch.

Chef/Proprietor: Koichi Konnai **Open:** Sat and Sun L 12 to 2, Wed to Sun D 6 to 10 (9.30 Sun) **Closed:** 3 weeks Aug **Meals:** alc (main courses £4.50 to £20). Set L £8.50 (2 courses), Set D £12 (2 courses) to £18 **Service:** not inc **Cards:** Maestro, MasterCard, Visa **Details:** 39 seats. No smoking. Music. Air-conditioned **Tube:** Golders Green

MAP 13

Café Spice Namaste

16 Prescot Street, E1 8AZ
Tel: (020) 7488 9242
Website: www.cafespice.co.uk

Cooking 2 | **Indian** | **£45**

Cyrus Todiwala continues to impress after more than 10 years at his bright Whitechapel restaurant, where the spacious, high-ceilinged dining room is decorated in warm, exotic colours, setting an appropriate tone for the vibrant, modern Indian cooking. The extensive menu draws in influences from across the Subcontinent. Among starters, 'squid dynamite' is a fiery dish of grilled squid in Goan peri-peri masala, while cholya prawn chapati consists of chopped prawns tossed with shallots, ginger, chilli and tomato, then wrapped in a chapati coated with date and tamarind chutney. Main courses range from Barbary duck breast marinated in ginger and garlic with yoghurt and chilli, or tandoor-cooked salmon fillet in Parsee-style green chutney, to patra ni machchi (whole pomfret stuffed with green coconut chutney, rolled in a banana leaf and steamed), or lamb dhansak prepared in the time-honoured authentic Parsee way. Wines are chosen to complement the food, prices starting at £14.50.

Chefs: Cyrus Todiwala and Angelo Collaco Proprietor: Cyrus Todiwala Open: Mon to Fri L 12 to 3, Mon to Sat D 6.15 to 10.15 Closed: 25 Dec to 1 Jan, bank hols Meals: alc (main courses £10.50 to £18.50). Set L and D £30 to £60 Service: 12.5% (optional) Cards: Amex, Delta, Diners, Maestro, MasterCard, Visa Details: 120 seats. 40 seats outside. Vegetarian meals. Children's helpings. Music. Air-conditioned Tube: Tower Hill

MAP 12

Calcutta Notebook

201 Replingham Road, SW18 5LY
Tel: (020) 8874 6603
Website: www.sarkhels.com

Cooking 3 | **Bengali** | **£35**

While the long-established Sarkhel's (see entry) has a menu that covers all the regions of India, this tiny offshoot next door specialises in the regional cooking of Bengal, home of owner Udit Sarkhel's family. Starters are inspired by the snacks sold by

vendors on the streets of Calcutta, including ghugni (spiced peas topped with a tart date chutney and roasted cumin), mocha chop (potato croquettes filled with banana flowers) and kakrar chop (a white crabmeat patti spiked with green chilli and topped with beetroot and cucumber relish). Main courses, meanwhile, reflect the kind of dishes you would be served as a guest in a Bengali home: potoler dolma (wax gourd stuffed with cottage cheese and raisins, cooked in a cumin-flavoured tomato sauce), chingri maacher malai (prawns in coconut milk), and panther jhol (tender young goat meat curry). Finish the meal in proper Bengali style with poppadums and chutney. House wine £10.90.

Chef: Udit Sarkhel Proprietors: Udit and Veronica Sarkhel Open: Tue to Sun 12 to 2.30, 6 to 10.30 (11 Fri and Sat) Meals: alc (main courses £7.50 to £10). Set L and D £18 Service: not inc Cards: Maestro, MasterCard, Visa Details: 28 seats. Private parties: 36 main room. Vegetarian meals. Children's helpings. No smoking. Music. Air-conditioned Tube: Southfields

MAP 14

Cambio de Tercio

163 Old Brompton Road, SW5 0LJ
Tel: (020) 7244 8970
Website: www.cambiodetercio.com

Cooking 3 | **Modern Spanish** | **£43**

'A confident performance, vibrant with colour, energy and style,' reported back one inspector, after a visit to this modern Spanish restaurant. Red brick walls, yellow paintwork, dark wood flooring and large modern paintings from the bullring set the scene. The authentic food packs a punch and the bold décor matches the statements on the plate. The tables are packed together, but are set with white linen, rolled napkins and all have oil burning lamps adding to the colourful effect. The all-male waiting staff are highly efficient, and able to talk through the menu, which might start with richly flavoured croquettes of Serrano ham or octopus on a light potato purée. Wild rabbit is slow-cooked and comes with a 'wonderfully sticky and intense' sherry reduction, while monkfish is sautéed with Iberian ham fat and presented with a 'well-balanced and brilliantly orange romescu sauce'. An excess of fashionable 'foam' is a slight distraction for some on desserts of smooth chocolate ice cream with a bitter coffee sauce. The wine list, broken up by regions, is Spanish from beginning to end, opening with an impressive range of sherries. Old and new vintages abound with reasonable mark-ups. Prices start at £17.

Chef: Alberto Criado **Proprietor:** Abel Lusa **Open:** all week 12.15 to 2.30, 6.45 to 11.30 **Closed:** 2 weeks at Christmas **Meals:** alc (main courses £14 to £17) **Service:** not inc **Cards:** Amex, Delta, MasterCard, Maestro, Visa **Details:** 45 seats. 8 seats outside. Music. Air-conditioned **Tube:** Gloucester Road

 MAP 15

Camerino

16 Percy Street, W1T 1DT
Tel: (020) 7637 9900
Website: www.camerinorestaurant.com

Cooking 3 | **Italian** | **£50**

£5

The location may be central London, but the Italian heart of this restaurant shines through. The décor is still a talking point – the red drapes around the walls, particularly – and skylights let in valuable light to the back of the room. Chef Valerio Daros's trademark pasta has drawn praise once again this year, while Billingsgate fish, Smithfield meat and Covent Garden produce all add merit. Starters of thinly sliced veal with tuna sauce or buffalo mozzarella with baked aubergine ensure pasta doesn't take all the plaudits, while roast fillet of cod with lentils and parsley sauce, and braised neck of lamb with red onions, crushed potatoes and Chianti sauce are impressive main courses. Desserts are true to form, with tiramisù and apple tart with nougat ice cream, or there is a selection of Italian cheeses. There are over 100 Italian wines, from £14.50, to choose from, plus a fine selection of grappa.

Chef: Valerio Daros **Proprietor:** Paolo Boschi **Open:** Mon to Fri L 12 to 3, Mon to Sat D 6 to 11 **Meals:** alc (main courses £18.50 to £20.50). Set L and D 6 to 7 £19.50 (2 courses) to £23.50 **Service:** 12.5% (optional) **Cards:** Amex, Delta, Diners, Maestro, MasterCard, Visa **Details:** 70 seats. 8 seats outside. Vegetarian meals. Children's helpings. No cigars/pipes in dining room. Wheelchair access (not WC). Music. Air-conditioned **Tube:** Tottenham Court Road, Goodge Street

MAP 13

Cantaloupe [AR]

35–42 Charlotte Road, EC2A 3PD
Tel: (020) 7613 4411

This lively bar/restaurant is a stalwart of the trendy Shoreditch scene, with eclectic menus taking in

Mediterranean, Spanish and South American influences. Starters of salted Serrano ham croquettes (£5) or cod and salmon ceviche with chilli, lime and coriander (£5.50) might be followed by fillet steak (priced according to weight) with fries and a choice of sauces, or perhaps chicken breast roasted with rosemary and thyme and served with cumin-spiced roast root vegetables and salsa verde (£12). The drinks list offers various beers, cocktails and wines from £11.90, and DJs provide music from Thursday evening to Sunday brunch. Restaurant open Thur to Sat L and Mon to Sat D.

MAP 13

Canteen NEW ENTRY

2 Crispin Place, E1 6DW
Tel: (0845) 686 1122

Cooking 3 | **Modern British** | **£36**

The surroundings – on the ground floor of a modern office block next to Spitalfields Market – may be no gastrodrome, but part of the appeal of this spartan glass box is its commitment to plainness and its lack of pretension. The resolutely unflashy surroundings are matched by equally unshowy food, with the all-day menu centring on dishes in which fine ingredients are treated simply. Best described as 'classic British caff food' (they even serve Horlicks), the kitchen makes a virtue of, for example, a simple hot buttered Arbroath smokie, and potted duck with piccalilli. First-class materials have included fried cod 'coated in breadcrumbs rather than the traditional batter, and all the better for it', served with good chips, and a 'beautifully cooked' ribeye steak with caramelised shallots and horseradish butter. Desserts continue the high standard of delivery if apple crumble and custard is anything to go by. Excellent value for money extends to the global wine list, which offers house bottles from £12 and 17 by the glass from £3.25.

Chef: Cass Titcombe **Proprietors:** Patrick Clayton-Malone, Dom Lake and Cass Titcombe **Open:** all week 11 (9 Sat and Sun) to 11 **Closed:** 25 and 26 Dec **Meals:** alc (main courses £7 to £12.50) **Service:** 12.5% (optional) **Cards:** Amex, Delta, Maestro, MasterCard, Visa **Details:** 80 seats. 50 seats outside. Vegetarian meals. Children's helpings. No smoking. Wheelchair access (also WC). No music. Air-conditioned

 | This symbol means that smoking is not permitted.

MAP 14

The Capital

22–26 Basil Street, SW3 1AT
Tel: (020) 7591 1202
Website: www.capitalhotel.co.uk

| Cooking 8 | French | £70 |

The Capital has always been good at impressing without making a show of itself. Even its location, tucked away down a Knightsbridge back street around the back of Harrods, is less flashy than many five-star addresses in London, but the tone and style are appreciated nonetheless. Muted hues of coffee and taupe create the kind of dining room ambience that befits the status of the place – 'calm class, unfussy elegance, understated luxury' was how one reporter summarised it. The menus have gone bilingual again, as though to make the point that the cooking here is in the hands of a French master, and don't you forget it. Or should that be trilingual? A first course at inspection offered 'lasagne de crabe, cappuccino de langoustine', but was a delight, whatever its mother tongue. Richly flavoured and featuring freshly made pasta, its sauce was subtly spiced, the whole construction topped off by its bonne bouche of a single, impeccably timed scallop.

Fine ingredients are allowed to shine for themselves rather than being weighted down with luxuries, so that saddle of rabbit provençale is accompanied by a cassoulet-like concentrated stew of white beans and tomato, served at the table, only the seared squid with which it was garnished seeming an extraneous addition. Honey-roast duck made another great main course, if an enthusiastically garlicked one, which diverted the attention momentarily with a 'sparklingly accomplished' pear jelly. High-scoring dishes from other reports have included celeriac velouté with smoked chicken ravioli, roast veal cutlet with a fricassee of mushrooms in balsamic jus, and the illustrious – and well-presented – French cheeses. An oddball dessert has been an odd ball (literally) of praline, coconut and lemon in crunchy meringue, and among others might be warm Jivara chocolate sponge with star anise velouté and chocolate sauce.

Irreproachably professional French staff make things all happen as intended, right down to helping to choose wines for those on unfeasibly limited budgets. Otherwise, splash the cash anywhere on the encyclopedic list, which is terrific in Burgundy, Bordeaux, Champagne and the Rhône, but pretty nifty in Italy and Australia too. Wines by the glass don't trust you to cope with more than 125ml at a time, their prices starting at £6.

Chef: Eric Chavot **Proprietor:** David Levin **Open:** all week 12 to 2.30, 6.45 to 10.30 **Meals:** Set L £29.50 to £68, Set D £55 to £68 **Service:** 12.5% (optional) **Cards:** Amex, Delta, Diners, Maestro, MasterCard, Visa **Details:** 34 seats. Vegetarian meals. No smoking in dining room. Occasional music. No mobile phones. Air-conditioned **Accommodation:** 49 rooms **Tube:** Knightsbridge

MAP 15

Le Caprice

Arlington House, Arlington Street, SW1A 1RT
Tel: (020) 7629 2239
Website: www.le-caprice.co.uk

| NEW CHEF | Modern British | £59 |

Age cannot wither this ever-fashionable spot in the heart of St James's, which remains popular for its glamorous, cosmopolitan aura and bustling Parisian brasserie-style atmosphere. Kevin Gratton, listed as chef in last year's Guide, has moved on to high-profile new opening Scotts (under the same ownership at 20 Mount Street, W1, tel: (020) 7629 5248), while Paul Brown has arrived to take over the kitchen here. Unfortunately, these changes happened too late for inspection of either to be possible, but the menu at Le Caprice looks set to continue in the same modern British vein, starters encompassing crispy duck and watercress salad, and seared scallops with carrot and pea shoots, main courses ranging from roast cod fillet with lobster mash and chervil to grilled calf's liver with champ and crispy bacon, plus up-to-the-minute seasonal specials such as roast spring deer with salsify and mousserons. Dessert might be peach and Prosecco jelly, or mochaccino brûlée. Wines are well chosen, although prices are not the cheapest, starting at around £16 a bottle and rising sharply thereafter; 16 are served by the glass from £4.50.

Chef: Paul Brown **Proprietor:** Caprice Holdings Ltd **Open:** all week 12 to 3 (5 Sun), 5.30 to 12 **Closed:** 25 and 26 Dec, 1 Jan, Aug bank hol **Meals:** alc (main courses £13.25 to £26.50). Cover £2 **Service:** not inc **Cards:** Amex, Delta, Diners, Maestro, MasterCard, Visa **Details:** 90 seats. Vegetarian meals. Children's helpings. Wheelchair access (not WC). Occasional music. No mobile phones. Air-conditioned **Tube:** Green Park

The price given next to the cooking score is based on the cost of a typical three-course dinner for one person, including coffee, house wine and service.

MAP 15

Carluccio's Caffé

AR

8 Market Place, W1W 8AG
Tel: (020) 7636 2228

Antonio Carluccio's chain continues to thrive, delivering simple, traditional Italian cuisine in a fashionable and lively environment. The kitchen works at speed, and the friendly waiting staff are eager. Breads and pastries (from £1.20) head up the short menu, while a pasta dish might be traditional lasagne (£6.95), or spaghetti with clams (£7.25). Chargrilled tuna with a courgette 'jam' (£11.25) might be among main courses, and you can finish with something like pannacotta (£4.50), or lemon tart (£3.25). The compact Italian wine list starts at £10.95. Open all week. See www.carluccios.com for other addresses across the country.

MAP 15

Cecconi's

5A Burlington Gardens, W1S 3AZ
Tel: (020) 7434 1500
Website: www.cecconis.co.uk

Cooking 4 | Italian | £57

Cecconi's reopened in September 2005 with a new chef, a glamorous new look – all marble floors, smoked mirrors, emerald green leather, well-spaced tables and soft lighting – and service that's charming and well timed. A feature of the new set-up is that food is served all day (there's a brunch menu on Saturdays) with a selection of cichetti – Venetian-style tapas – no doubt aimed at the area's well-heeled shoppers. This new approach to the menu signals a somewhat less elaborate style. Certainly at inspection dishes were simple in their composition and execution, the highlight being starters of baked courgette flower (with tiny fingers of young courgette) stuffed with ewes' ricotta and set in a pool of quite delicate tomato sauce, spring lamb carpaccio with broad beans and pecorino, and a dessert of a 'suitably gooey' chocolate fondant with pistachio ice cream. Among main courses might be an intensely flavoured dish of slow-cooked rabbit with olives and pappardelle flecked with thyme, and 'moist, succulent' turbot baked in a sea salt crust. The wine list is expensive but well put together (and not just from Italy) with 14 or so interesting options by the glass. House wine is £18.

Chef: Andrea Cavaliere **Proprietors:** Soho House Ltd **Open:** all week noon to midnight **Meals:** alc (main courses £12.50 to £24) **Service:** 12.5% **Cards:** Amex, Delta, Diners, Maestro, MasterCard, Visa **Details:** 90 seats. Vegetarian meals. Wheelchair access (also WC). Music. Air-conditioned **Tube:** Green Park, Piccadilly Circus

MAP 14

Le Cercle

1 Wilbraham Place, SW1X 9AE
Tel: (020) 7901 9999
Email: info@lecercle.co.uk

Cooking 5 | French | £52

Making the most of its elegant marble-floored basement setting – high ceilings, neutral colours and careful lighting create a feeling of space – Le Cercle is an offshoot of Club Gascon (see entry). The food has genuine roots in South-west France (from where many of the ingredients are sourced), but regional dishes from around France are given a twist and portions are deliberately small: 'tapas-style', as is the vogue right now. Some 35 savoury dishes are divided into sections covering vegetables (cassolette of chanterelles), seafood (warm salmon fondant with kohlrabi purée and mussel vinaigrette), the farm (braised veal shank cannelloni), 'terroir' (tartiflette au lardons), and 'plaisirs' (foie gras, caviar, and black truffles). Praise has been heaped on ravioli of Royan cheese with an emulsion of ceps, 'subtle and balanced' pumpkin cream velouté, onglet with a potato and bacon cake and Choron sauce, and the 'mini tour de France' afforded by the selection of cheeses. Desserts continue the high-quality cooking with the likes of chocolate fondant with mandarin sorbet, or pear parfait with salted soft caramel. Not surprisingly, the wine list is exclusively French, but it is not restricted to the classic regions, giving equal coverage to oft-neglected Languedoc-Roussillon, the South-west, Jura, Alsace and Savoie. Over a dozen come by the glass from £4 to £8.50, with bottle prices starting at £14.

Chef: Thierry Beyris **Proprietors:** Vincent Labeyrie and Pascal Aussignac **Open:** Tue to Sat 12 to 3, 6 to 11 **Meals:** alc (main courses £4.50 to £35). Set L £15 to £19.50, Set D 6 to 7 and 10 to 11 £17.50 to £21.50. Bar menu available **Service:** 12.5% (optional) **Cards:** Amex, Delta, Maestro, MasterCard, Visa **Details:** 65 seats. Vegetarian meals. No-smoking area. Wheelchair access (also WC). Music. Air-conditioned **Tube:** Sloane Square

MAP 13

Champor-Champor

62–64 Weston Street, SE1 3QJ
Tel: (020) 7403 4600
Website: www.champor-champor.com

Cooking 3 | Malaysian/Asian | £43

'Creative modern Malaysian' is how they describe
their food at this bright and busily decorated
restaurant by London Bridge, the name of which
roughly translates as 'mix and match'. Chef Adu
Amran Hassan certainly offers food like none you
will find elsewhere, taking traditional Malaysian
village cooking as his starting point and mixing it
up with ideas plucked from across the vast spectrum of Asian cuisine. Thus, starters include butternut squash red curry with beef sirloin won
tons, water buffalo rendang with Japanese pickled
ginger and dhal curry, and a hotpot of loofah and
fried shallot with cassava croûtons. To follow,
Indian-style oxtail and star anise stew with
steamed rice and apple chutney lines up alongside ostrich fillet with peanut sauce, and slow-
cooked rabbit in masala oil with pesto rice and
kerisik sauce. Desserts are no less inventive:
smoked banana, yoghurt and cream brûlée, for
example. Drinks include a wide choice of Asian
beers, saké and a short list of wines from £14.

Chef: Adu Amran Hassan Proprietors: Adu Amran Hassan and
Charles Tyler Open: Mon to Sat D only 6.15 to 10.15; L by
appointment for groups Closed: 1 week Christmas, 4 days
Easter, some bank hols Meals: Set D £23 (2 courses) to £41
Service: 15% (optional) Cards: Amex, Delta, Maestro,
MasterCard, Visa Details: 46 seats. Vegetarian meals.
No-smoking area. Wheelchair access (not WC). Music.
Air-conditioned Tube: London Bridge

MAP 13

Chancery

9 Cursitor Street, EC4A 1LL
Tel: (020) 7831 4000
Website: www.thechancery.co.uk

Cooking 4 | Modern European | £44

Located in the heart of the legal community and
just visible from Chancery Lane, it is hard to tell
whether this nineteenth-century building was formerly a pub or a 'lawyers' cabinet', but there's no
missing the fact that it is now a restaurant. High
ceilings and large windows give a feeling of space
and light in the split dining room, which is decked

out in a subdued colour scheme with white walls
hung with modern art and close-set tables laid
with crisp linen. The sensibly compact, regularly
changing, Mediterranean-influenced menu hits
just the right note, and deserves praise for good
value – one reporter was pleased to see that amuse-
bouche and petits fours were provided even for the
less expensive lunch option. The cooking is generally light, utilizing sound ingredients, appealing
presentation and little pretension. Expect the likes
of 'correctly executed' grilled baby squid, tat soi,
lime and coriander, and roast rump of beef with
fondant potatoes, baby onions and red wine at
lunch, confit foie gras with Earl Grey tea jelly and
honey-glazed cippolini onions, then peppered
monkfish tail with sweetcorn chowder and crisp
radicchio at dinner. Hot chocolate torte with
Baileys ice cream might head up the repertoire of
puddings, while the wine list is a suitably modern
global affair with house vins du pays £14.50.

Chef: Andrew Thompson Proprietors: Andrew Thompson and
Zak Jones Open: Mon to Fri 12 to 2.30, 6 to 10.30 Closed:
22 Dec to 2 Jan, bank hols Meals: Set L and D £15.50 (2
courses) to £20.50, Set D £32 Service: 12.5% (optional)
Cards: Amex, Delta, Diners, Maestro, MasterCard, Visa
Details: 50 seats. Vegetarian meals. Wheelchair access (not
WC). Music. Air-conditioned Tube: Chancery Lane

MAP 12

Chapter Two

43–45 Montpelier Vale, SE3 0TJ
Tel: (020) 8333 2666
Website: www.chaptersrestaurants.co.uk

Cooking 4 | Modern European | £38

Enjoying a prime spot by the heath, this restaurant is spread over two floors, both with distinct
character. The upstairs room is light and airy
while the basement is cloaked in more of a dramatic darkness. Chef Trevor Tobin is now into his
fifth year offering a menu that is European in
influence, comforting and seasonally changing,
although there are some surprising elements.
Cock-a-leekie of wood pigeon and pressed
terrine of duck are typical starters, while mains
could be anything from linguine with young vegetables and a coriander emulsion, to braised shin
of beef with pommes mousseline and honey-
roast root vegetables. Fish might be roast sea trout
with a shellfish lasagne or perhaps poached
Torbay sole with a saffron and lobster brandade.
Desserts are equally well thought out and might
include coconut parfait with cherry soup and an

oatmeal flapjack, or vanilla rice pudding with braised pineapple. Wines happily globetrot but start at a reasonable £16 for house French, with many decent choices under £30. Related to Chapter One, Farnborough (see entry).

Chef: Trevor Tobin Proprietor: Selective Restaurants Open: all week 12 to 2.30, 6.30 to 10.30 Closed: 2 to 5 Jan Meals: Set L £15.95 (2 courses) to £19.95, Set D Sun to Thur £18.45 (2 courses) to £23.50, Set D Fri and Sat £24.50 Service: 12.5% (optional) Cards: Amex, Delta, Diners, Maestro, MasterCard, Visa Details: 75 seats. Vegetarian meals. No smoking. Wheelchair access (also WC). No music. Air-conditioned

MAP 12

Le Chardon AR

65 Lordship Lane, SE22 8EP
Tel: (020) 8299 1921

Chef Didier Dixneuf makes every effort to bring the essence of French cooking to this corner of London via his lively bistro. Moules marinière (£5.65) or foie gras with red onion marmalade and a toasted brioche (£8.45) could start, while coq au vin (£10.50) or pan-fried fillet of salmon in a creamy mushroom and white wine sauce (£10.95) could follow. Breakfast is served at weekends, and there is a large patio area for a touch of the al frescos. French house wines from £10.95. Open all week. Related to the Green (see entry).

MAP 12

Chez Bruce

2 Bellevue Road, SW17 7EG
Tel: (020) 8672 0114
Website: www.chezbruce.co.uk

Cooking 6 | **Modern British** | **£55**

This is a true neighbourhood restaurant, as is evident in its service to the community at lunch and dinner seven days a week, and it is regarded with notable affection by the denizens of Wandsworth and beyond. Bruce Poole's style has always been easy on the palate. Dishes mix well-tried ideas with original but unforced marriages, and 'the urge to over-refine,' according to a regular reporter, 'is consistently rejected'. Innards of lamb – tongue, kidney and sweetbread – make up a fine opening dish, all precisely cooked and served with creamy onion purée. Similarly, tuna ceviche with

king prawn tempura, avocado and coriander combines firmness of texture and strongly defined flavours.

Classic French modes may well bring on main courses such as navarin of lamb, or chateaubriand (for two) with hand-cut chips and béarnaise. Accuracy of cooking hardly ever seems to fail the kitchen, so that a piece of grilled halibut is flawlessly timed, and comes with scallops, their flavour brought out by roasting, Bayonne ham and unstodgy gnocchi. Good pastry work distinguishes desserts such as cherry frangipane tart, which comes with Kirsch crème anglaise and wonderful Jersey cream, or there could be crème brûlée with crisp caramel, creamy custard and a good throb of vanilla, 'a classic done superbly with no silly extras'. Service is nicely judged and properly skilled without being given to fuss.

A thoroughly commendable wine list has been assembled, which mixes and matches the good to very good from all the principal countries. Selections from regional France are a joy, there is a torrent of fine German Riesling, Australia is well-served, and half-bottles are plentiful. One could regret the mark-ups and the niggardly 125ml single-glass size, but this is undoubtedly one of the great lists. Prices start at £16.50.

Chefs: Bruce Poole and Matthew Christmas Proprietors: Bruce Poole and Nigel Platts-Martin Open: Mon to Fri 12 to 2, 6.30 to 10.30, Sat 12.30 to 2.30, 6.30 to 10.30, Sun 12.30 to 3, 7 to 10 Closed: 24 to 26 Dec, 1 Jan Meals: Set L Mon to Fri £23.50, Set L Sat £27.50, Set L Sun £32.50, Set D £37.50 Service: 12.5% (optional) Cards: Amex, Delta, Diners, Maestro, MasterCard, Visa Details: 75 seats. Vegetarian meals. No children under 7 at D. Children's helpings. No smoking. Wheelchair access (not WC). No music. Air-conditioned Tube: Balham

MAP 12

Chez Kristof

111 Hammersmith Grove, W6 0NQ
Tel: (020) 8741 1177
Website: www.chezkristof.co.uk

Cooking 3 | **French** | **£45**

The light grey canopies can be seen clearly along the long residential road. Tables outside provide excellent al fresco opportunities, while inside floor to ceiling windows ensure that natural light is not a problem (and can be opened to provide greater access to the outside area). The kitchen continues to keep customers satisfied with flexible menus packed with robust and gutsy dishes, so Jan Woroneicki's neighbourhood restaurant is fast becoming a local institution. The owner of the

Baltic (see entry) has eschewed Eastern European cuisine in favour of French regional dishes, but while an inspection meal found a few dishes requiring more attention to detail, hits included a 'really fine' sauté of prawns with garlic and parsley, French onion soup with foie gras, and a decent whole sea bream en papillotte with leeks and fennel. Youthful service has been praised, and the Francophile wine list opens modestly at £13.50 before blossoming into something more ambitious.

Chef: Richard Mclellan **Proprietor:** Jan Woroniecki **Open:** all week 12 to 3 (4 Sat/Sun), 6 to 11.15 (10.30 Sun) **Meals:** alc (main courses £12.50 to £16.50). Set L and D before 7pm £12 (2 courses) to £15 **Service:** 12.5% **Cards:** Amex, Delta, Maestro, MasterCard, Visa **Details:** 85 seats. 35 seats outside. Vegetarian meals. Children's helpings. No-smoking area. Wheelchair access (also WC). Music **Tube:** Hammersmith

---

MAP 12

Chez Liline

NEW ENTRY

101 Stroud Green Road, N4 3PX
Tel: (020) 7263 6550

Cooking 1 | Mauritian Seafood | £37

'Not what you might expect in this neck of the woods', commented a reporter on this Mauritian fish restaurant wedged behind a bus stop in an unprepossessing high street of take-aways, a betting shop and Tesco. The cooking combines the Indian-influenced style with that of France, the cultural resonance of which is also deep-rooted. Scallops, for example, are served with a little roe with mushrooms in garlic and black bean sauce, and the kitchen does its own variation of soupe de poisson. Fricassée des Iles is a selection of grilled fish (snapper, swordfish and grouper) with ginger, fresh chilli and herbs, while a fillet of grouper arrives sitting on a very spicy mix of chopped, shredded vegetables with lots of black beans. House wines are £11.75.

Chef: Pascal Doudrich **Proprietor:** Thierry Doudrich **Open:** Tue to Sat L, all week D 12.30 to 2.30, 6.30 to 10 **Meals:** alc (main courses £10.95 to £22.75) **Service:** not inc **Cards:** Amex, Maestro, MasterCard, Visa **Details:** 40 seats. Vegetarian meals. Children's helpings. Music. Air-conditioning **Tube:** Finsbury Park

---

 This symbol means that it is possible to have a three-course dinner, including coffee, half a bottle of house wine and service, for £30 or less per person.

MAP 15

Chinese Experience

118 Shaftesbury Avenue, W1
Tel: (020) 7437 0377
Website: www.chineseexperience.com

Cooking 2 | Chinese | £37

The décor avoids the red, gold and dragon themes of the nearby Soho palaces, concentrating on a sleek, minimalist look, but the draw is classy Chinese food. The menu is not as extensive as most Cantonese restaurants, and when the kitchen is on target what you get on the plate can be leagues ahead of the norm. Dim sum, stir-fried prawns with cashew nuts, salt and chilli squid, Mongolian crispy lamb, and steamed Dover sole with ginger and spring onions cover most bases. The menu also boasts a challenging selection of chef's specials: spare ribs with strawberry sauce evokes mixed feelings, but there's also deep-fried prawns with salted egg yolk or grilled ice fish with lotus. Wines are basic, starting at £12.

Chef: Gun Leung **Proprietor:** Tony Tang **Open:** all week 12 to 11 **Meals:** alc (main courses L £8 to £10, D £10 to £15). Set L £19.90 to £23 (all min 2) **Service:** 10% **Cards:** Amex, Delta, MasterCard, Maestro, Visa **Details:** 130 seats. Vegetarian meals. No smoking. Music. Air-conditioned **Tube:** Leicester Square

---

MAP 15

Chisou

4 Princes Street, W1B 2LE
Tel: (020) 7629 3931

Cooking 4 | Japanese | £47

An authentic slice of Japan, in a quiet back street not far from Oxford Circus, where its ongoing popularity with London's expat Japanese community tells its own story. The plainly decorated dining room is not the only aspect of Chisou to inspire fond recollections of a Tokyo eating house – there is also the extensive menu, highlight of which is the list of chef's special recommendations (dinner only). This changes every two weeks but might include salted king crab legs, thinly sliced grilled beef tongue with mizuna leaves and yuzu dressing, simmered mooli with dark miso paste, and spicy grilled salmon belly. The rest of the menu is divided into starters (deep-fried soft-shell crab, stir-fried belly pork, and marinated seafood, for example), salads, grilled and fried dishes (among them teriyaki mackerel, and deep-fried bread-crumbed oysters), tempura, noodles and so on. And, of course, there is a good choice of traditional sushi and sashimi, priced per piece or for a selection. Finish perhaps with green tea mousse, or Japanese chestnut ice cream, and drink saké or wine, the latter priced from £13.50 a bottle.

> **Chef:** Mr T. Funakoshi **Proprietor:** David Leroy **Open:** Mon to Sat 12 to 2.30, 6 to 10.15 **Closed:** bank hols **Meals:** alc (main courses £6 to £22.50). Set L £13.80 **Service:** not inc L, 12.5% D **Cards:** Amex, Delta, Maestro, MasterCard, Visa **Details:** 60 seats. Vegetarian meals. No-smoking area. Occasional music **Tube:** Oxford Circus

MAP 15

Chor Bizarre
AR

16 Albemarle Street, W1H 4HW
Tel: (020) 7629 9802

The décor of this Mayfair Indian restaurant goes beyond the exotic, with its romantic jumble of ethnic artefacts. The adventurous menu opens with a wide selection of street snacks (grazing and sharing small dishes are encouraged) such as tak-a-tak chicken livers in coriander masala (£6.50), or peppered scallops (£7.50), while main courses include refined versions of curry-house favourites such as Kashmiri rogan josh (£13) and methi chicken (£13), along with lesser-spotted regional specialities such as Tamil-style chicken chettinad with pepper, aniseed and curry leaves (£13). Well-chosen wines from £16. Downstairs is Chai Bazaar, an Indian tea bar. Closed Sun L.

MAP 15

Chowki
AR

2–3 Denman Street, W1D 7HA
Tel: (020) 7439 1330

Good-value Indian home cooking in an informal setting is Chowki's modus operandi, with a monthly-changing menu focusing on the specialities of three different regions. A recent example has featured dishes from Rajasthan, among them tender griddled marinated quail (£4.25), and 'red-hot' lamb with chillies and garlic cooked in a sealed pot with yoghurt (£10.95), from Hyderabad – for example, fried minced chicken in pastry with tamarind chutney (£3.95), and sour lamb stew with lentils (£10.50) – and from Mangalore: mackerel poached in a thick masala

paste (£9.95). Six house wines from £10.95. Open all week. Under the same ownership as Mela (see entry).

MAP 15

Christopher's
AR

18 Wellington Street, WC2E 7DD
Tel: (020) 7240 4222

This respected bar and grill has recently undergone extensive renovation, reopening with an updated menu and Martini bar. Reworked classics might see a Cobb salad with Maine lobster, pancetta, avocado and blue cheese (£9.50), while mains could be Mid-western veal meatloaf with roast salsify, mash and a truffle jus (£15), or baked halibut with Gorgonzola and watercress crushed potatoes (£19). The grill offers 28-day aged steaks from 10oz up to 14 oz (from £16 to £27). House wines from the Napa Valley from £14. Open all week.

MAP 15

Chuen Cheng Ku
AR

17 Wardour Street, W1V 3HD
Tel: (020) 7734 3281

Over a hundred types of dim sum are dispensed from the trolleys at this long-established Chinatown restaurant, which sprawls over three storeys. Crispy aromatic duck (£8 to £28), or grilled pork dumplings (£4.50) to start, perhaps, followed by crabmeat egg fu-yung (£8), sautéed beef steak with lemon grass (£8.50) and stuffed bamboo shoots with minced pork and prawns (£8.90). There are various set meals (£8.80 to £14), with plenty of rice and noodles dishes, too. Wines from £9.95. Open all week.

MAP 12

Chutney Mary

535 King's Road, SW10 0SZ
Tel: (020) 7351 3113
Website: www.realindianfood.com

| Cooking 1 | Indian | £60 |

'An extremely pleasant space' is how one reporter summed up the conservatory dining room at this chic, upmarket Indian restaurant. Here, diners are seated on comfortable curved green sofas at bare wooden tables, surrounded by large plants, while a pianist may be tinkling away at the centre of the restaurant. The kitchen aims to provide refined, modern Indian cooking. Starters of crab and ginger soup, pan-fried lamb kebab, and angara murgh (spiced corn-fed chicken thigh) might be followed by Goan green chicken curry, lobster makhani (in a tomato and brandy sauce), or lamb rack ghazala (cooked with coriander seeds, turmeric and green chillies, served on cracked wheat and raisin pilau), with side dishes such as dhal masoor or broad beans in creamy fenugreek sauce. To finish, try an Indian take on sticky toffee pudding or something more traditional such as date and walnut kulfi. White vin de pays at £16.25 opens an extensive list.

Chef: Nagarajan Rubinath Proprietors: Ranjit Mathrani, and Namita and Camellia Panjabi Open: Sat and Sun L 12.30 to 2.30 (3 Sun), all week D 6.30 to 11.30 (10.30 Sun) Closed: D 25 Dec Meals: alc D (main courses £16 to £26.50). Set L £17 Service: 12.5% (optional) Cards: Amex, Delta, Diners, Maestro, MasterCard, Visa Details: 110 seats. Vegetarian meals. No-smoking area. Wheelchair access (not WC). Occasional music. Air-conditioned Tube: Fulham Broadway

MAP 13

Cigala

54 Lamb's Conduit Street, WC1N 3LW
Tel: (020) 7405 1717
Website: www.cigala.co.uk

Cooking 2 | Spanish | £39

A spacious corner site with full-height picture windows gives views of the daily hustle and bustle of the street. Plain white walls and simple white-clad tables add to the light and spacious feel. The daily-changing menu is overtly Spanish, taking in classics like sardinas à la plancha and pinchitos de cerdo (pork kebab) among starters, and main courses of monkfish, prawns, halibut and clams stewed in romesco sauce. But this is not the heavy, unsubtle cooking of the Spanish old school – dishes are light, well balanced and based on first-rate raw materials. The kitchen has roasted rabbit with ratte potatoes, white wine and garlic, and served grilled lamb chops with pisto manchego, while paella is reworked with pork fillet, chorizo and spinach. Tapas such as patatas bravas and Spanish charcuterie are served in the bar downstairs, or at pavement tables in fine weather. Leche frita (fried milk infused with cinnamon, lemon and anis dulce) is an interesting way in which to finish.

Chef/Proprietor: Jake Hodges Open: all week 12 to 10.45 (9.45 Sun) Closed: D 24 Dec, 25 and 26 Dec, 1 Jan, Easter Sun Meals: alc (main courses £10 to £21). Set L Mon to Sat £15 (2 courses) to £18, Set L and D Sun £10.50 (1 course). Tapas menu available Service: 12.5% (optional) Cards: Amex, Delta, Diners, Maestro, MasterCard, Visa Details: 60 seats. 20 seats outside. Vegetarian meals. Children's helpings. Wheelchair access (not WC). No music. Air-conditioned Tube: Holborn

MAP 13

Cinnamon Club

Old Westminster Library, Great Smith Street, SW1P 3BU
Tel: (020) 7222 2555
Website: www.cinnamonclub.com

Cooking 4 | Modern Indian | £59

The dining room of Iqbal Wahhab's modern Indian restaurant evokes the building's past as an esteemed library. Proximity to the Houses of Parliament means the clientele is likely to include huddles of men in suits, and you won't find regular curry house dishes on the menu. Tandoori swordfish with king prawn and Rajasthani spiced lamb escalope with garlic show the ambition among first courses. Follow with Parsee curry with braised black chicken and prunes, or maybe tandoori breast of Anjou squab pigeon with black lentils. Laal maas, a fiery curry, is made with aged Herdwick mutton from Cumbria, while the roast saddle of Oisin red deer comes with pickling spices. Finish with ginger toffee pudding. The restaurant is open for breakfast, too, and you can have a full English or uttapam (rice pancake with a choice of toppings). The international wine list complements the food, starting at £16 for house selections.

Chef: Vivek Singh Proprietor: Iqbal Wahhab Open: Mon to Fri L 12 to 2.45, Mon to Sat D 6 to 10.45. Breakfast available 7.30 to 9.45 Closed: 26 Dec, 1 Jan, bank hols Meals: alc (main courses £11 to £29). Set L and D before 7 £19 (2 courses) to £22 Service: 12.5% Cards: Amex, Delta, Diners, Maestro, MasterCard, Visa Details: 150 seats. Vegetarian meals. Cigars in bar only. No music. Air-conditioned Tube: Westminster

To submit a report on any restaurant, please visit *www.which.co.uk/gfgfeedback*.

MAP 15

Cipriani

25 Davies Street, W1K 3DE
Tel: (020) 7399 0500
Website: www.cipriani.com

Cooking 4 | Italian | £76

Modelled on Harry's Bar in Venice, the opulent London version, just north of Berkeley Square, has Venetian chandeliers, chequered white marble floor, teak panelling and an Art Deco-style mural depicting biplanes, airships, and the like. A bar runs down one part of the dining area, giving a 'very clubby ambience' as diners take in the buzz from the bar, and vice versa. Giuseppe Marangi's menu includes a list of classics from Harry's Bar, dishes such as carpaccio, pasta e fagioli, veal milanese, and scampi alla thermidor, and these underline the Cipriani's basic principle – namely, the serving of top-quality ingredients cooked in a tried and trusted manner. Prices, though, are high. At inspection, thin slices of octopus terrine and borlotti bean terrine made for a good start, followed by a main course osso buco, 'almost falling off the bone', served with 'perfect' risotto. Or you might choose to start with tuna tartare, and follow it up with roast duck alla Cipriani. The dessert trolley yielded a classic tiramisù, or try lemon meringue pie. Service has impressed this year, too, while the patriotic wine list reflects its Mayfair location by opening at £26.

Chef: Giuseppe Marangi Proprietors: the Cipriani family Open: all week 12 to 3, 6 to 11.45 (11 Sun) Meals: alc (main courses £15 to £36). Set L £28 to £35, Set D £35 to £40 Service: 12.5% (optional) Cards: Amex, Delta, Maestro, MasterCard, Visa Details: 120 seats. Vegetarian meals. Children's helpings. Wheelchair access (also WC). No music. Air-conditioned Tube: Bond Street

MAP 15

Circus

1 Upper James Street, W1F 9DF
Tel: (020) 7534 4000
Website: www.circusbar.co.uk

Cooking 3 | Modern European | £48

Almost a decade after opening, Circus's formula has changed. The expansive, contemporary space has undergone major refurbishment, which has meant not only throwing out the old floor, furniture and lighting, but also the menu, and jumping onto the bistro de luxe bandwagon that's trundling

through the capital at the moment. Richard Lee remains in charge of the kitchen, but now he's delivering classic French bistro dishes like duck rillettes, salt cod brandade and charcuterie among starters. These could be followed by boudin blanc with roast apple and Meaux mustard sauce, leg of lamb steak with flageolets, or roast organic salmon with beurre blanc. Set lunch is good value, offering marinated chicken salad with French beans and tarragon, strips of beef fillet lyonnaise, and blackberry cheesecake for £12.50, while snacks like steak baguette, croque-madame and omelette parmentier are available from 5.30 to 8pm. House selections on the all-French list open at £14. Reports please.

Chef: Richard Lee Proprietor: Mirror Image Group Open: Mon to Fri L 12 to 3, Mon to Sat D 5.45 to 12 Meals: alc (main courses £9 to £16). Set L £12.50. Bar menu available Service: 12.5% (optional) Cards: Amex, Delta, Diners, Maestro, MasterCard, Visa Details: 140 seats. Vegetarian meals. Children's helpings. Wheelchair access (not WC). Air-conditioned Tube: Piccadilly Circus

MAP 13

Clarke's

124 Kensington Church Street, W8 4BH
Tel: (020) 7221 9225
Website: www.sallyclarke.com

Cooking 4 | Modern British | £52

If you start with the best possible ingredients, don't complicate matters, but maintain balance and seasonal sensitively, then you can hardly go wrong. Sally Clarke has been doing this in her 'very restrained' two-tier restaurant for 23 years. She now offers a choice of dishes in the evening, and it is no longer necessary to have all four courses, but the dedication to sourcing fine seasonal ingredients clearly remains the driving force. We have good reports of a lunch that opened with mussels – simple and perfect – and a 'spot-on' mushroom soup, before a generous portion of well-timed cod and an 'upmarket' beef burger. An inspection dinner turned up a loin of Norfolk roe deer that was beautifully cooked and served simply with sage, orange and red wine glaze, honey roasted parsnip and celeriac with watercress and hazelnuts. Finish with Kent strawberry ice cream with rosemary shortbread, or warm bitter chocolate pudding with raspberry sauce. Incidentals like a 'really diverse selection' of flavoured rolls and cafetière coffee are as sound as a bell. Service is diligent. The wine list is a pick and mix of good and prestigious bottles with brief contributions from all over. Prices climb steeply from the £15 starting point.

> **Chef/Proprietor:** Sally Clarke **Open:** all week L 12.30 (11 Sat brunch) to 2, Tue to Sat D 7 to 10 **Closed:** 10 days at Christmas, bank hols **Meals:** alc L (main courses £14 to £16). Set D £39.75 to £49.50 **Service:** net prices **Cards:** Amex, Diners, MasterCard, Visa **Details:** 80 seats. No smoking. Wheelchair access (not WC). No music. No mobile phones. Air-conditioned **Tube:** Notting Hill Gate

MAP 13

Clerkenwell Dining Room

69–73 St John Street, EC1M 4AN
Tel: (020) 7253 9000
Website: www.theclerkenwell.com

Cooking 3 | Modern European | £47

This trendy corner of London is home to many restaurants but the Clerkenwell is blossoming thanks to its modern British cuisine served up in a lively, split level setting. Andrew Thompson's menu is all about the confident handling of great raw materials, and flavours that stand out from the crowd. Expect terrine of foie gras and goose confit, or maybe tiger prawn and sesame-toasted salmon. Dorset crab with avocado and toasted Poilâne, or ravioli of ham hock with Savoy cabbage and mustard start, while well-constructed main courses might be roast cannon of lamb with taglioni of peas and mint, or perhaps fillet of smoked haddock accompanied by asparagus and a poached egg. Half a dozen desserts include a savarin of fresh fruit compote or a rich hot chocolate fondant served with malt ice cream. A selection of British and French cheeses comes with toasted hazelnut and raisin bread. The wine list is predominantly European with a few interesting New World choices, starting at £14 for house French.

> **Chef:** Andrew Thompson **Proprietors:** Zak Jones and Andrew Thompson **Open:** Sun to Fri L 12 to 2.30, Mon to Sat D 6 (7 Sat) to 10.30 **Closed:** Christmas **Meals:** alc (main courses £14.50 to £16.50). Set L £14.50 (2 courses) to £19.50 **Service:** 12.5% (optional) **Cards:** Amex, Delta, Diners, Maestro, MasterCard, Visa **Details:** 110 seats. Vegetarian meals. Children's helpings. Wheelchair access (not WC). Music. Air-conditioned **Tube:** Farringdon

MAP 13

Club Gascon

57 West Smithfield, EC1A 9DS
Tel: (020) 7796 0600

Cooking 5 | French | £57

Advertising its jewel-like interior by means of a huge plate-glass frontage, Club Gascon (elder sibling of Le Cercle, and Comptoir Gascon; see entries) is a smartly turned-out venue, with more than a hint of Japanese in the creative juxtaposition of black steel and floral displays. Its chef, Pascal Aussignac, was one of the first to catch the modern mood for eating a multiplicity of small courses, effectively tasting menu portions but without the no-choice factor.

The initial inspiration is South-west France, but dishes go off on their own tangents from there. Foie gras might come with popcorn, grilled langoustines with smoked violet tea, and veal sweetbread with bergamot and artichokes. There are definite hits: cappuccino of black pudding, crab claws and asparagus is full of properly complementary flavours, and a sweet dish of foie gras and apple pudding made an impression at a summer lunch. More mainstream dishes include new season's lamb partnered with goats' cheese ravioli in a jus of black olives and anchovy. A parfait made with the Basque liqueur Izarra, served with strawberries and a herb syrup, makes a suitably regional way to finish. Good service, particularly from the sommelier, receives due plaudits. Wines from Roussillon, Provence and Gascony make for fascinating exploration on the French list, although there are Bordeaux and champagnes for the classicists. It seems a shame to stay in the Médoc, though, when you have a choice of not one but three wines from the mountainous appellation of Irouléguy: hardly anyone sells those. The starting price for ten wines by the glass is £4.50; expect to spend at least £20 for a bottle.

> **Chef:** Pascal Aussignac **Proprietors:** Vincent Labeyrie and Pascal Aussignac **Open:** Mon to Fri L 12 to 2, Mon to Sat D 7 to 10.30 **Closed:** 22 Dec to 8 Jan, bank hols **Meals:** alc (main courses £4.50 to £42). Set L £35 to £39, Set D £39 **Service:** 12.5% (optional) **Cards:** Amex, Maestro, MasterCard, Visa **Details:** 45 seats. Vegetarian meals. Children's helpings. No smoking. Wheelchair access (not WC). Music. Air-conditioned **Tube:** Barbican, Farringdon

MAP 13

Coach and Horses

26–28 Ray Street, EC1R 3DJ
Tel: (020) 7278 8990
Website: www.thecoachandhorses.com

NEW CHEF | Modern British | £35

The Coach and Horses looks every inch the old-fashioned hostelry but the menu posted up outside is testimony that this is very much a gastro-pub with a serious commitment to good food. A chef change is due as we go to press. The menu takes traditional ingredients and gives them an interesting spin. There's nothing extraneous; this is not the sort of place where you'll see unnecessary garnishes. Brandade comes with a parsley salad and ciabatta, while grilled ox tongue is served as a starter with tartare sauce and a soft-boiled egg. Main courses are equally straightforward, with Highland blade steak coming with chips, watercress and garlic mushrooms, and cod with pesto, Jersey Royals and piquillo peppers. End with ewes' milk yoghurt ice cream with honey and pistachios. There's a bar menu as well. House wine is £11.95.

Proprietor: Giles Webster Open: Sun to Fri L 12 to 3, Mon to Sat D 6 to 10 Closed: 24 Dec to 2 Jan, bank hols Meals: alc (main courses £10 to £14.50). Bar menu available Service: 12.5% (optional) Cards: Amex, Delta, Maestro, MasterCard, Visa Details: 60 seats. 36 seats outside. Vegetarian meals. Wheelchair access (not WC). Occasional music

MAP 14

Le Colombier

145 Dovehouse Street, SW3 6LB
Tel: (020) 7351 1155

Cooking 2 | French | £41

Didier Garnier's straightforward French bistro is a Chelsea stalwart. The menu offers traditional stuff, with the occasional nod to the Mediterranean. There's a blue and white theme throughout with plenty of light from the windows, while the well-drilled staff are smartly turned out. The extensive carte offers good value, opening with a classic combination of chicory, walnut and Roquefort salad, with accurately cooked fillet of beef with béarnaise to follow, or well-flavoured calf's liver with bacon. Finish with well-made tarte Tatin. A full-bodied French-only wine list starts at £13.90.

Chef/Proprietor: Didier Garnier Open: all week 12 to 3 (3.30 Sun), 6.30 to 10.30 (10 Sun) Meals: alc (main courses £13.50 to £20). Set L £16.50 (2 courses), Set L Sun £19 Service: 12.5% (optional) Cards: Amex, Delta, Maestro, MasterCard, Visa Details: 50 seats. 30 seats outside. Vegetarian meals. No children under 10. Wheelchair access (not WC). No music Tube: South Kensington

MAP 13

Comptoir Gascon   NEW ENTRY

61–63 Charterhouse Street, EC1M 6HJ
Tel: (020) 7608 0851

Cooking 4 | South-West French | £39

It started life as a deli, but this offshoot of Club Gascon (see entry) has added nine or so plain wooden tables and some blue velour chairs and now a bistro is part of the operation. It's a great asset in this trendy area of bars, nightclubs and casual eateries. The food, chosen from a short menu supplemented by blackboard specials, is simple. Some are first-rate assembly jobs – for example, the sharing platter of 'piggy treats' tried at inspection, which took in Bayonne ham, garlicky salami, boudin noir, spicy chorizo, a chunk of rillettes, and a spicy slab of brawn – while others show real skill and timing, as in tender beef onglet served with a good sauce bordelaise. Praise, too, has been heaped on specials like foie gras interleaved with spicy apple, and Gascony pie (hot duck mousse on a wild mushroom base), and the kitchen is not above turning out duck à l'orange, which 'takes the clichéd 1970s bistro staple to another, elevated, plain'. French fries cooked in duck fat put most chips to shame. Portions tend to be generous, so you may need to pace yourself if you are going to order dessert from a selection on display: say, ewes' milk yoghurt with black truffle honey, or a small chocolate tart. Service is 'exemplary', and the short wine list has some great choices from the French south-west, with prices starting at £14.

Chef: Laurent Sanchis Proprietors: Vincent Labeyrie and Pascal Aussignac Open: Tue to Sat 12 to 2, 7 to 10 Closed: Christmas to New Year Meals: alc (main courses £7.50 to £13.50) Service: 12.5% (optional) Cards: Amex, Delta, Maestro, MasterCard, Visa Details: 40 seats. 8 seats outside. Vegetarian meals. No smoking. Wheelchair access (also WC). Music. Air-conditioned Tube: Farringdon, Barbican

MAP 15

Connaught, Angela Hartnett

16 Carlos Place, W1K 2AL
Tel: (020) 7592 1222
Website: www.angelahartnett.com

Cooking 6 | Modern European | £78

The redesign of the Connaught dining rooms that took place a few years ago brought a welcome touch of humanity to the Edwardian austerity of earlier days without losing the aura of classical dining that the environs seem to dictate. With its dark panelling and carpet in windowpane check, the main room now exudes a welcoming sense of community, an air accentuated by the genuinely amiable and pleasingly relaxed service. Concise lunch menus of three choices at each stage broaden to a wealth of options at dinner, and the culinary style has become a little more robust than in Angela Hartnett's early days here. That said, there is a concerted effort to keep dishes looking light and simple, so that a row of belly pork slices braised in honey appears on a scant underlay of pearl barley, while a modest fillet of red mullet has excellent, oily aubergine purée, tiny shrimps and cracked hazelnuts for company.

The timing of fish is demonstrably fine, as has been the case with a tranche of herb-coated, roast but still opalescent halibut, successfully paired with a gamey oxtail raviolo. A chunk of unsliced Pyrenean lamb has been gently but positively flavoured (although the knife provided wasn't up to the task of cutting the meat) and comes with tiny baby morels bursting with earthy richness. Some have found the lunchtime main courses a little short on horsepower, but desserts come to the rescue, with confit quince, crème Catalan, pain d'épice, coffee oil and liquorice ice cream adding up to a heavenly assemblage for one reporter. The pre-dessert serving of variously-flavoured ice creams and sorbets is reckoned by one old hand to be 'the best in the business'. A very suave collection of pedigree wines at grand-hotel prices is offered. Choices are sound throughout, and there is a welcome feeling of pains taken in the newer countries as well as in classical France. Wines by the glass start at £5.

	This symbol means that the wine list is well above the average.

Chef: Angela Hartnett **Proprietor:** Gordon Ramsay Holdings Ltd **Open:** all week 12 to 3, 5.45 to 11 **Meals:** Set L £30 to £70, Set D £55 to £70. Bar menu available **Service:** 12.5% (optional) **Cards:** Amex, Delta, Diners, Maestro, MasterCard, Visa **Details:** 70 seats. Vegetarian meals. Children's helpings. No smoking. Wheelchair access (not WC). No music. No mobile phones. Air-conditioned **Tube:** Bond Street, Green Park

MAP 13

Il Convivio

143 Ebury Street, SW1W 9QN
Tel: (020) 7730 4099
Website: www.etruscarestaurants.com

Cooking 2 | Modern Italian | £47

This elegant Georgian house in the heart of Belgravia offers a split-level dining experience; the limestone and cedarwood theme runs through to the conservatory, which also features cedarwood decking. The walls are vibrant red, and dotted with quotes from Dante, giving the space a theatrical feel. Chef Lukas Pfaff accents flavour and style in his modern Italian menu. Antipasti includes burrata cheese with grilled vegetables and basil pesto while a pasta dish puts together spaghetti with cured pork cheek. Among fish dishes may be fillet of John Dory with rice polenta, and breast of mallard duck with a celeriac and parsnip purée might be a meat option. Desserts include cinnamon and quince semifreddo with a mandarin and rum sauce. The wine list is pricey but offers a wide range of Italian and French choices with house selections starting at £13.50.

Chef: Lukas Pfaff **Proprietor:** Enzo and Piero Quaradeghini **Open:** Mon to Sat 12 to 2.45, 7 to 10.45 **Closed:** bank hols **Meals:** alc L (main courses £8 to £19). Set L £15.50 (2 courses) to £19.50, Set D £26.50 (2 courses) to £38.50 **Service:** 12.5% (optional) **Cards:** Amex, Delta, Diners, Maestro, MasterCard, Visa **Details:** 65 seats. Vegetarian meals. No cigars. Music. Air-conditioned **Tube:** Victoria, Sloane Square

MAP 13

Le Coq d'Argent

No. 1 Poultry, EC2R 8EJ
Tel: (020) 7395 5000

Bearing all the hallmarks of a contemporary Conran concern, this well-appointed brasserie boasts great views from its rooftop garden.

Breakfast and bar snacks are available as well as a set-price menu (£23/£27) and the full carte, which plunders the regions of France. Start with caviar (from £43), snails in garlic and tomato butter (£10.75), or marbled foie gras and confit duck terrine (£14.75), then go on to niçoise-style saddle of rabbit with mash and red wine and vinegar jus (£17.50), or roast peppered cod with artichoke casserole (£18.75). End with passion-fruit tart (£7). The hefty wine list is pricey, starting at £15. Closed Sat L and Sun D.

MAP 13

Cow Dining Room   AR

89 Westbourne Park Road, W2 5QH
Tel: (020) 7221 0021

Expect a packed house in the Saloon Bar of this seminal west London boozer, with customers here not just for drinks but for well-received bar food like sausages braised in beer and onions (£9.25) and the house special – a pint of Guinness and half a dozen oysters. Upstairs, the dining room turns out a short menu dealing in foie gras, lentil and French bean salad (£7.50), onglet, ceps, parsley and garlic (£15.50), or goats' cheese, artichoke and onion pastry (£13). Alternatively, there are seafood platters (£27) and a popular Saturday brunch. Wines from £13.75. Dining room open Sat and Sun L and all week D.

MAP 13

Cru   AR

2–4 Rufus Street, N1 6PE
Tel: (020) 7729 5252

Located just off Hoxton Square, this bar/restaurant feels perfectly at ease in its warehouse setting, which is also home to the White Cube Gallery. The menu might deliver Iberian ham with roast vegetables (£6.75) and lobster salad (£9.25) among starters, followed by fried whiting in a Parmesan crust (£14.75), or maybe spaghetti with clams, vermouth, chilli and parsley. Shared platters (from £14) combine cured meats, potato croquettes, deep fried halloumi and chorizo. End with Eton mess or fudge brownie (both £5). Wines from £13. Closed Mon.

MAP 13

Cumberland Arms   AR

29 North End Road, W14 8SZ
Tel: (020) 7371 6806

Understated décor and a daily-changing menu help this friendly gastro-pub pull in the punters. The imaginative cooking puts an emphasis on Mediterranean flavours, so among starters could be mushroom and pancetta risotto with oregano and Parmesan (£6.50), while a main course could be grilled Italian sausages with roast garlic mash, mixed herbs and salsa verde (£9.50), or grilled trout with couscous salad (£11.50). Finish with lemon tart with honeyed yoghurt (£4.50). Wines from £11. Open all week.

MAP 12

Deep

The Boulevard, Imperial Wharf, SW6 2UB
Tel: (020) 7736 3337
Website: www.deeplondon.co.uk

| Cooking 4 | Seafood/Mod. British | £49 |

'Gorgeously stylish', this ultra-cool restaurant is part of a waterside development between Fulham and Chelsea. It may be slightly tricky to find but once inside it's hard not to be impressed with the clean lines, cream upholstery and attractive setting, with a large terrace that overlooks the Thames. The owners also have a policy of not using endangered fish, so forego cod for zander and John Dory on this mostly fish menu, which offers just the occasional nod to carnivores. Scandinavian chefs Christian and Kerstin Sandefeldt start with the likes of mussels, seared gravad lax and assiette of yellowfin tuna, while main courses could include escalope of salmon with an egg yolk and seafood ravioli, grilled Dover sole, and, for the meat eaters, seared brisket with summer greens and a grain mustard velouté. End with Neal's Yard cheeses, or pannacotta with vanilla and black pepper rhubarb. As well as a fine selection of aquavit, the wine list is a

---

| | Not a full entry but provisionally recommended. These 'also recommended' establishments are integrated throughout the book. |

predominately French affair, with a few New World choices thrown in, and starts at £14.50.

> **Chefs:** Christian and Kerstin Sandefeldt **Proprietors:** Christian Sandefeldt and Fredrik Bolin **Open:** Tue to Fri and Sun L 12 to 3, Tue to Sat D 7 to 11 **Meals:** alc (main courses £13 to £22). Set L £15.50 (2 courses) to £19.50. Cover £1. Bar menu available **Service:** 12.5% (optional) **Cards:** Amex, Delta, Maestro, MasterCard, Visa **Details:** 80 seats. 40 seats outside. No smoking. Wheelchair access (also WC). Music. Air-conditioned

MAP 13

Delfina

50 Bermondsey Street, SE1 3UD
Tel: (020) 7357 0244
Website: www.delfina.org.uk

Cooking 4 | Global | £41

Tucked down a narrow street near London Bridge, this converted chocolate factory is now home to artists' studios (the restaurant was originally conceived as a canteen for those who worked here). Nowadays this large ground-floor space, with green tables and plenty of light from the windows and a skylight, is open at lunchtimes and on Friday evenings. Chicken liver pâté on bruschetta with pancetta chips and caper berries impressed for its ingenuity, while olive tarte Tatin with a bitter chocolate syrup and Parmesan shavings worked a treat, getting this potentially tricky balance just right. Soy-glazed sea bass comes with jasmine rice, Asian salad and lime and coriander dressing as a main course, alongside perhaps roast venison with shaved foie gras and caramelised quince, an 'inspired marriage' of components. At dessert, the rhubarb selection, including pannacotta and jelly, scores highly, particularly the crumble. The base price on the international wine list is £12.50, and a number of interesting bottles, including one from Greece, come in under £20.

> **Chef:** Maria Elia **Proprietors:** Digby Squires and Bruce Watson **Open:** Mon to Fri L 12 to 3, Fri D 7 to 10 **Closed:** 23 Dec to 2 Jan **Meals:** alc (main courses £10 to £14) **Service:** 12.5% (optional) **Cards:** Amex, Delta, Diners, Maestro, MasterCard, Visa **Details:** 140 seats. Vegetarian meals. No-smoking area. No cigars in dining room. Wheelchair access (also WC). Occasional music **Tube:** London Bridge

> The price given next to the cooking score is based on the cost of a typical three-course dinner for one person, including coffee, house wine and service.

MAP 15

Le Deuxième

65A Long Acre, WC2E 9JH
Tel: (020) 7379 0033
Website: www.ledeuxieme.com

Cooking 2 | Modern European | £45

This operation (like its sibling, Café du Jardin; see entry) successfully caters for the demanding central London crowd. Front-of-house staff work hard to keep things ticking along, and the food sits comfortably with the simply decorated dining room. Extras such as separately charged vegetables and the 15 per cent service charge will hike up the bill, but for that you get a tour of Europe: Bayonne ham and grilled radicchio on toasted olive bread with red onion jam to start, then pan-fried fillet of sea bass with Jerusalem artichoke purée and gazpacho sauce, or osso buco. Dessert might be baked orange cake with crème anglaise. The wine list offers some interesting choices, mostly French, and opens at £12.50.

> **Chef:** Geoffrey Adams **Proprietors:** Robert Seigler and Tony Howorth **Open:** Mon to Fri 12 to 3, 5 to 12, Sat 12 to 12, Sun 12 to 11 **Closed:** 24 and 25 Dec **Meals:** alc (main courses £13 to £17.50). Set L and D Mon to Fri 5 to 7 and 10 to 12 £10.95 (2 courses) to £14.50, Set L and D Sat 12 to 7, 10 to 12 £10.95 (2 courses) to £14.50, Set L and D Sun 12 to 11 £10.95 (2 courses) to £14.50 **Service:** 15% (optional) **Cards:** Amex, Delta, Maestro, MasterCard, Visa **Details:** 60 seats. Vegetarian meals. Wheelchair access (not WC). No music. Air-conditioned **Tube:** Covent Garden

MAP 15

Deya

34 Portman Square, W1H 7BY
Tel: (020) 7224 0028
Website: www.deya-restaurant.co.uk

Cooking 4 | Modern Indian | £48

Deya can still show a clean pair of heels to most of its rivals. The grand, high-ceilinged Georgian dining room is stylishly restrained, lighting subdued, with murals of Indian figures to divert the eye. While some familiar dishes figure on the menu – rogan josh, for example, or a biryani, correctly cooked in a dish sealed with pastry – the kitchen has made its mark with an eagerness for modern influences and by using prime raw materials. Tuna cooked in the tandoor and served topped with a little blob of mustard on a bed on shredded cabbage and mustard seeds, alongside a salad of spinach, shredded carrot and beetroot, makes an outstanding starter, while spicy sea bass served on a bed of couscous with a rich, lightly spiced tomato sauce is a fine main course. It is all presented with an eye for detail, whether a distinctive version of black lentils, delicately spiced stir-fried vegetables, or a dessert of rose water and vanilla crème brûlée. Equally impressive details such as 'superb' chutneys, good naan bread, and 'excellent' service, round it off nicely. The ambitious wine list is a global selection of classic and contemporary names with eleven by the glass starting at £5.50.

Chef: Sanjay Dwivedi Proprietors: Sir Michael Caine, Claudio Pulze and Raj Sharma Open: Mon to Fri L 12 to 2.45, Mon to Sat D 6 to 11 Closed: Christmas and New Year Meals: alc (main courses £10.50 to £15). Set L £14.95 (2 courses), Set D £25.50 to £38.50. Bar menu available Service: 12.5% (optional) Cards: Amex, Delta, Diners, Maestro, MasterCard, Visa Details: 70 seats. Vegetarian meals. Children's helpings. No cigars/pipes in dining room. Music. Air-conditioned

MAP 13

Diwana Bhel Poori   AR

121 Drummond Street, NW1 2HL
Tel: (020) 7387 5556

Still the pick of the bunch in the enclave of Indian restaurants behind Euston Station, Diwana has been drawing a loyal following for over 30 years. The menus evolve slowly, the focal point being various Bombay-style snacks – aloo papri chaat, bhel puri, and dahi vada, for example (all £3) – and a range of substantial main-course dosai pancakes served with chutney and sambhar, perhaps filled with paneer and spinach (£5.95), or a crisp paper-thin version with mixed vegetables (£5.95). Value for money is 'almost absurdly good'. The restaurant is unlicensed, so drink lassi. Open all week.

MAP 13

The Don

The Courtyard, 20 St Swithin's Lane, EC4N 8AD
Tel: (020) 7626 2606
Website: www.thedonrestaurant.co.uk

Cooking 2 | Modern European | £49

In late 2005 a new dining room was added to this ever-busy City restaurant (under the same ownership as Bleeding Heart; see entry), which should make it easier to get a booking. The cooking is refined without being too elaborate, and makes equally good use of luxury ingredients and humbler cuts, so starters may well feature pressed foie gras, sweetbreads and morels served with Sauternes jelly and toasted brioche alongside rustic Mediterranean fish soup with croûtons, rouille and Gruyère. Main courses likewise range from grilled calf's liver with sage polenta and curly kale to seared sea bass with lobster risotto and watercress sauce. Dark chocolate fondant with Seville-orange ice cream rounds things off on a suitably rich note. There is also a basement bistro with its own menu. Wines are given star treatment here, with big names peppered throughout the vast list – not only from the Old World but from Argentina and Chile too. There are also plenty of more modest bottles, with eight house selections from the owners' vineyard in New Zealand, prices starting at £16.95 a bottle, £4.25 a glass.

Chef: Matt Burns Proprietor: Robert Wilson Open: Mon to Fri 12 to 2.30, 6.30 to 10 Closed: Christmas to New Year, bank hols Meals: alc (main courses £13 to £24) Service: 12.5% (optional) Cards: Amex, Diners, MasterCard, Visa Details: 70 seats. Vegetarian meals. No smoking in 1 dining room. Wheelchair access (also WC). No music. Air-conditioned Tube: Bank

MAP 13

Drapers Arms

44 Barnsbury Street, Islington, N1 1ER
Tel: (020) 7619 0348
Website: www.thedrapersarms.co.uk

Cooking 3 | Modern British-Plus | £39

The contrast between the lively ground-floor bar – overflowing with north London life and pulsating music – and the upstairs dining room is noticeable, if not extreme. Those choosing the relative tranquillity of the restaurant needn't worry that the atmosphere will be sterile, as it is a pleasant space with a life of its own. The tables are well spaced, and the waitresses are a friendly bunch, if not always in a hurry. The menu has found its groove, offering a range of traditional gastro-pub dishes, so start with black pudding bubble, smoked eel, poached egg and hollandaise, or perhaps parfait of chicken livers and foie gras with sourdough toast. Mains might be pan-fried sea bream with crab mash and caper butter or even spiced rump of lamb, pepper and fennel tarte Tatin. End with a bitter chocolate and ginger tart. The compact wine list starts with house selections at £12 and half a dozen by the glass from £3.60.

Chef: Mark Emberton and Lisa Rees Proprietors: Mark Emberton and Paul McElhinney Open: Sun L 12 to 3, Mon to Sat D 7 to 10.30 Closed: 24 to 27 Dec, 1 and 2 Jan Meals: alc (main courses £13.50 to £15). Bar menu available Service: 12.5% (optional) Cards: Amex, Delta, Maestro, MasterCard, Visa Details: 85 seats. 50 seats outside. Vegetarian meals. Children's helpings. Smoking in bar only. Music Tube: Highbury & Islington

MAP 14

Drones

1 Pont Street, SW1X 9EJ
Tel: (020) 7235 9555
Website: www.whitestarline.org.uk

Cooking 4 | Anglo-French | £54

Another star in the Marco Pierre White firmament, this established Belgravia restaurant emits an air of reserved confidence, while the menu walks an expertly balanced line between classic English and French cuisine. The menu du jour might feature parfait de foie gras with toasted Poilâne bread, followed by grilled calf's liver with sauce diable. The carte opens with more than a dozen options, from terrine of duck à la Richelieu, to a tian of Cornish crab, via asparagus in truffle vinaigrette. The style continues in main courses of grilled lobster with sauce Choron, rump of lamb with clams and jus persillé, and tranche of Scottish salmon viennoise. Ten side plates of vegetables – among them celeriac purée and sautéed mushrooms – are charged separately. Finish with rice pudding accompanied by compote of red fruits, or prune and Armagnac tart with crème anglaise. The two-page global wine list encompasses some interesting bins, albeit with few choices under £25. Base prices are £18 (white) and £22 (red).

Chef: Joseph Croan Proprietors: Jimmy Lahoud and Marco Pierre White Open: all week L 12 to 2 (3 Sun), Mon to Sat D 6 to 11 Meals: alc (main courses £13.50 to £24.50). Set L Mon to Sat £14.95 (2 courses) to £17.95, Set L Sun £22.50 Service: 12.5% Cards: Amex, Delta, Diners, Maestro, MasterCard, Visa Details: 96 seats. Vegetarian meals. No pipes in dining room. Wheelchair access (not WC). Music. Air-conditioned

£ | This symbol means that it is possible to have a three-course dinner, including coffee, half a bottle of house wine and service, for £30 or less per person.

MAP 13

e&o

14 Blenheim Crescent, W11 1NN
Tel: (020) 7229 5454
Website: www.eando.nu

Cooking 3 | Asian/Fusion | £46

Ultra-smart Notting Hill eatery with a sparely decorated dining room, all slate, dark wood and glass, with perky young waiting staff who are as stylish as the trendy crowd they serve. The kitchen dips in and out of every Asian cuisine to produce a menu constructed around a number of small dishes and divided into several sections, the idea being to select a range of dishes for grazing. Dim sum turn up prawn and chive dumplings, chicken and coriander gyozas, and chilli-salt squid, while salads include Thai rare beef, or 'excellent' tuna with oriental dressing. Among curries are Malaysian lamb rendang, or green aubergine and pumpkin, and barbecue dishes take in shredded duck with plum sauce, and black cod with sweet miso. 'Very tender' lobster with noodles is a popular choice among house specials. If it all looks a bit baffling, there's a helpful glossary on the back of the menu. A compact, varied selection of wines ranges from modest vins de pays at £13.50 to a 1988 Penfolds Grange red at £200.

Chef: Simon Treadway Proprietor: Will Ricker Open: all week 12.15 to 3 (4 Sat and Sun), 6.15 to 11 (10.30 Sun) Meals: alc (main courses £9.50 to £21.50) Service: 12.5% (optional) Cards: Amex, Delta, Diners, Maestro, MasterCard, Visa Details: 84 seats. 20 seats outside. Vegetarian meals. No smoking in dining room. Wheelchair access (not WC). No music. Air-conditioned Tube: Ladbroke Grove

MAP 13

Eagle

159 Farringdon Road, EC1R 3AL
Tel: (020) 7837 1353

Cooking 2 | Mediterranean | £26

£

This popular East London pub puts all its energies into a short menu, and it is all the better for this focus. The mood is relaxed – specials are chalked up on the wall high above the open kitchen and narrow bar, furniture is a mish-mash of wooden tables and chairs, food is served on odd plates and there is lots of green foliage to match the outside awning. The food charts a path between

Mediterranean and English cuisine – think slow-braised Old Spot belly with cinnamon, ginger and chilli, or grilled Romney Marsh lamb chops served with coriander, aubergines and hummus. Paella and grilled mackerel with tabbouleh and chilli jam also feature. There's a short selection of tapas, too, including chorizo, pimentos and cockles in garlic. The wine list is short, starting at £11, and there is a selection of bottled and draught beers including Hoegaarden and Kirin.

Chef: Ed Mottershaw Proprietor: Michael Belben Open: all week L 12.30 to 3 (3.30 Sat/Sun), Mon to Sat D 6.30 to 10.30 Closed: 1 week Christmas, bank hols (exc Good Fri D) Meals: alc (main courses £5 to £15) Service: not inc Cards: Delta, Maestro, MasterCard, Visa Details: 60 seats. 24 seats outside. Vegetarian meals. Children's helpings. Wheelchair access (not WC). Occasional music Tube: Farringdon

MAP 12

Ealing Park Tavern

222 South Ealing Road, W5 4RL
Tel: (020) 8758 1879

Cooking 2 | Modern British | £34

'The more I think about this place, the more it has grown on me,' writes a satisfied reporter of this finely tuned gastro-pub. Much extolled is the balance between the 'baronial' bar, with its buzzy atmosphere, and a more intimate wood-panelled room. The food is simply prepared but with 'enough invention and skill in presentation to lift it above merely good pub food'. The menu changes daily, and you can expect seared scallops with pancetta, a classic combination given 'a pleasing zip' with spicy coulis, or fresh and flavoursome pan-fried sardines. Beef bourguignonne is a tried and tested main course, and fish is handled well, as in roast fillet of cod in saffron velouté. To finish, chocolate nemesis gets the thumbs-up. Service is discreet and swift, while a compact European wine list offers plenty of variety from £11.50.

Chef: Vince Morse Proprietor: Nic Sharpe Open: Tue to Sun L 12 to 3 (3.45 Sun), all week D 6 to 10.15 (9.15 Sun) Closed: 25 and 26 Dec, 1 Jan Meals: alc (main courses £9 to £16). Bar tapas menu available Thur to Sat D Service: not inc Cards: Amex, MasterCard, Visa Details: 72 seats. 50 seats outside. Vegetarian meals. No children in dining room after 8.30pm. No smoking in dining room. No music Tube: South Ealing

To submit a report on any restaurant, please visit *www.which.co.uk/gfgfeedback.*

MAP 12

Earl Spencer

AR

260–262 Merton Road, SW18 5JL
Tel: (020) 8870 9244

A lively gastro-pub, the Earl Spencer has the expected relaxed atmosphere, with food ordered and paid for at the bar. The daily-changing menus feature some eclectic European dishes that are a fair nudge above the pub norm: crispy-fried belly pork with salsa verde (£6.50), slow-cooked lamb shoulder with butter beans and kale (£11.50), or chargrilled sardines with a sauce of red pepper, almond and garlic (£6.50), followed by caramel and banana rice pudding (£4.50). There is a good range of wines from £10.50, plus four real ales. Open all week.

MAP 14

The Ebury

11 Pimlico Road, SW1W 8NA
Tel: (020) 7730 6784
Website: www.theebury.co.uk

Cooking 5 | Modern European | £40

A gastro-pub at the top of its game, this impressive building at the end of Pimlico Road is hard to miss. There's a choice of two dining rooms – one in the busy bar area and the other a quieter affair upstairs. Chef James Holah came in at the end of 2005 from Gordon Ramsay at Claridge's (see entry), and he seemingly sources with great care and displays a keen eye for timing. At inspection, a pair of Cornish oysters were 'as fresh as though just pulled from Porth Navas waters', while seared tuna had great colour and was perfectly cooked. A simple dressed crab with aïoli garnered high praise, as did the young, friendly waiting staff who delivered a requested bowl of plain mayonnaise 'with a cheery smile'. Main courses of sea trout and rack of lamb didn't disappoint either; the former rosy-pink inside, served with English asparagus and white quail's eggs, while the lamb from Devon had been rested for just the right length of time. Tarte fine aux pommes has been described as 'plate-licking good'. The wine list makes bold French statements, with some great names from Burgundy, plus a considered selection from Languedoc, Lubéron, Toro and Tuscany; house starts at £13.95, or £3.50 by the glass for their Tempranillo.

Chef: James Holah **Proprietor:** Tom Etridge **Open:** all week 12 to 3.30 (4 Sat and Sun), 6 to 10.30 (10 Sun). Dining Room: Mon to Sat D only 6 to 10.30 **Closed:** 25 and 26 Dec **Meals:** alc (main courses £9.50 to £16) **Service:** 12.5% (optional) **Cards:** Amex, Delta, Maestro, MasterCard, Visa **Details:** 65 seats (60 Brasserie). Vegetarian meals. Wheelchair access (also WC). Music. Air-conditioned **Tube:** Sloane Square

MAP 13

Ebury Wine Bar `AR`

139 Ebury Street, SW1W 9QU
Tel: (020) 7730 5447

Describing itself as a 'global restaurant with roots', this well-established wine bar is now approaching its half-century. The menu continues to embrace everything from home-made gravad lax with honey and dill sauce (£6.25) to quail and oyster mushroom pithiviers (£9.75) to start, with main courses ranging from braised rabbit with tarragon and cream linguine (£13.50) to grilled sea bass fillet with spring vegetables and caprese sauce (£16.75). Finish with passion-fruit profiteroles in toffee sauce (£5.45). The superior wine list starts at £12.70. Closed Sun L.

MAP 15

ECapital `AR`

8 Gerrard Street, W1D 5PJ
Tel: (020) 7434 3838

The cooking of Shanghai is the speciality of this smart, bright Chinatown restaurant, and the diverse culinary influences of the bustling port, 'China's melting pot', are evident in a varied menu with some highly unusual dishes: a starter 'cold combination' platter (£6.50 per person), for example, comprising marinated meats, smoked fish, vegetarian 'goose' (Chinese mushroom wrapped in crisp tofu layers), and pigs' ears. Main courses range from shredded five-spice-marinated roast chicken in a dark vinaigrette (£9.80) to light and simple whole sea bass 'West Lake style' (£16.80). House wines are £10.90. Open all week.

 This symbol means that the restaurant has elected to participate in *The Good Food Guide's* £5 voucher scheme (see 'Using The Good Food Guide' for details).

MAP 13

Eight Over Eight

392 King's Road, SW3 5UZ
Tel: (020) 7349 9934
Website: www.eightovereight.nu

Cooking 2 | **Asian/Fusion** | **£48**

Will Ricker's slick and stylised restaurant on the King's Road is part of his successful group of Pan-Asian restaurants (see entries for the Great Eastern Dining Room and e&o). It's a very trendy space, divided into bar and restaurant, with dark wooden floors and white-clothed tables ensuring it isn't overly sterile. There's a selection of dim sum, sushi/sashimi, salads, roasts, curries and house specials. Salt and pepper squid and tuna tartare with wasabi is a straightforward dish that makes a big impact due to the quality of its ingredients, as is 'crisp and sizzling' rock shrimp tempura served with jalapeño and tempura dipping sauces. A rich, creamy, perfectly timed black cod with big blobs of miso sauce and green fried rice is a 'wow' of a dish. However, the two-hour time slot allocated to one party on a Saturday evening meant no time for puddings such as chocolate honeycomb mochi. Contemporary cocktails feature and wine drinkers can choose from 11 by the glass; few bottles come in at under £20, although prices start at £14.

Chef: Richard Francis **Proprietor:** Will Ricker **Open:** Mon to Sat L 12 to 3 (4 Sat), all week D 6 to 11 **Meals:** alc (main courses £10 to £26). Set L £15 (2 courses). Bar menu available **Service:** 12.5% (optional) **Cards:** Amex, Delta, Diners, Maestro, MasterCard, Visa **Details:** 95 seats. Smoking in bar only. No music. Air-conditioned **Tube:** Sloane Square

MAP 13

Electric Brasserie `AR`

191 Portobello Road, W11 2ED
Tel: (020) 7908 9696

Part of the Electric Cinema complex, this trendy bar/brasserie is a lively place. Breakfast starts the day, while the carte brings a flexible approach, with 'small plates' of crispy squid or chipolatas with mustard mayonnaise (both £6) as well as starters (perhaps spinach and ricotta ravioli; £7), and main courses of lamb cutlets with caponata (£17.50), or chicken and mushroom pie (£13). Seafood is a speciality: dressed crab (£11), half a lobster (£16), and oysters (£3 a pair) all feature. A varied, international wine list starts at £13.75 and offers a decent choice by the glass (from £3.75). Open all week.

MAP 13

11 Abingdon Road

11–13 Abingdon Road, W8 6AH   **NEW ENTRY**
Tel: (020) 7937 0120

Cooking 3 | **Modern European** | **£43**

Rebecca Mascarenhas, who also owns Sonny's and the Phoenix (see entries), has spread her wings further still with this new neighbourhood restaurant, which seems perfectly pitched for the area in both pricing and atmosphere. An imminent redesign will see the front section become the bar area, while a skylight adds welcome daylight to the simply decorated dining room. Three kinds of excellent bread, including cinnamon, are delivered swiftly to the table by friendly young staff, while interesting combinations have intrigued reporters. Risotto with peas, brown shrimps and clams sounds a busy starter but works well, and steamed asparagus with romescu sauce has been another simple success. Main course pot-roast rabbit with artichoke, broad beans and pancetta was a 'good, gentle seasonal dish' at inspection. To finish, there might be properly textured vanilla pannacotta with cherries marinated in brandy. The global wine list is compact but well thought out, and starts at £12.75 for French house selections.

Chef: David Stafford   Proprietor: Rebecca Mascarenhas   Open: all week 12 to 2.30, 6.30 to 11   Closed: bank hols   Meals: alc (main courses £11.50 to £17.50). Set L £13.50, Set D £17.50. Bar menu available   Service: 12.5% (optional)   Cards: Amex, Delta, Maestro, MasterCard, Visa   Details: 80 seats. Vegetarian meals. Children's helpings. No smoking in dining room. Wheelchair access (also WC). No music. Air-conditioned   Tube: High Street Kensington

MAP 15

Embassy

29 Old Burlington Street, W1S 3AN
Tel: (020) 7851 0956
Website: www.embassylondon.com

Cooking 4 | **Modern British** | **£57**

Named after the infamous 80s Embassy Club, this twenty-first-century version houses a nightclub with a glass-fronted VIP lounge above the dance floor, and there's an outside terrace, a cocktail bar, and a light and airy dining room. Garry Hollihead's kitchen brigade turns out suitably modern food for such a setting, starting perhaps with carpaccio of beef fillet or white bean soup with a fried quail's egg. Main courses can be as hearty as braised beef in Guinness with runner and broad beans, while roast rump of lamb is paired with sweet and sour aubergines. Ideas are sound and execution is good, as in sautéed lemon sole, clams and brown shrimps, served with crushed potatoes. You might choose to dance off the calories from a steamed orange sponge with a brown sugar parfait in the basement nightclub. The wine list starts at £16.50, with six choices by the glass from £4.50, and rising steeply after that.

Chef: Garry Hollihead   Proprietors: Mark Fuller and Garry Hollihead   Open: Tue to Sat D 6 to 11.30   Meals: alc (main courses £14 to £28). Set D £17 (2 courses) to £20   Service: 12.5% (optional)   Cards: Amex, Delta, Maestro, MasterCard, Visa   Details: 120 seats. 20 seats outside. Vegetarian meals. Wheelchair access (not WC). Music. Air-conditioned   Tube: Green Park, Piccadilly Circus

MAP 12

Emile's

96–98 Felsham Road, SW15 1DQ
Tel: (020) 8789 3323
Website: www.emilesrestaurant.co.uk

Cooking 2 | **Modern European** | **£34**

The décor is conservative at this popular neighbourhood restaurant near Putney High Street, but owners Emil Fahmy and Andrew Sherlock infuse the atmosphere with their enthusiasm and efficiency. Changing monthly, there's a choice of a two- or three-course set-price menu (with supplements). The popular individual fillet of beef Wellington appears consistently throughout the year, but if you can resist that you might start with pigeon terrine with apricot and sultana mustard chutney or tuna ceviche with avocado quenelle, before 'carefully crafted' main courses such as pork tenderloin medallions with a broad bean and Parmesan risotto, or fillet of sea bass on saffron couscous with a vanilla butter sauce. A broad range of desserts might include white chocolate and passion-fruit mousse. The succinct but wide-ranging wine list opens at £10.95, and prices throughout are fair.

Chef: Andrew Sherlock   Proprietors: Emil Fahmy and Andrew Sherlock   Open: Mon to Sat D only 7.30 to 11   Closed: 24 to 30 Dec, 2 Jan, Easter Sat, bank hols   Meals: Set D £19.50 (2 courses) to £22.50   Service: not inc   Cards: Delta, Maestro, MasterCard, Visa   Details: 100 seats. Vegetarian meals. Wheelchair access (not WC). Music   Tube: Putney Bridge

Enoteca Turi

28 Putney High Street, SW15 1SQ
Tel: (020) 8785 4449

Cooking 3 | Italian | £47

Proprietor Guiseppe Turi has a passion for traditional country Italian cooking, and he has a likeminded chef in Brian Fantoni. The dining room itself is informal, with pictures of Italian country scenes, a terracotta wash on the walls and large, well-spaced tables covered in white linen tablecloths. A starter ravioli filled with beetroot and ricotta, with butter and poppy seed sauce, was an excellent combination of flavours at inspection, followed by 'top-class' spinach and ricotta gnocchi in a roasted tomato sauce, and veal wrapped in pancetta, set on a bed of spring greens, and served with a 'nicely judged' veal jus. Standards don't drop in side dishes such as a simple green salad. Prune and almond crostata, accompanied by zabaglione ice cream, made for a strong finish. The wine list takes some reading, having been styled 'with love and enthusiasm', and is mainly Italian with some New World choices, with house options starting at £13.

Chef: Brian Fantoni Proprietors: Mr and Mrs G. Turi Open: Mon to Sat 12 to 2.30, 7 to 11 Closed: 25 and 26 Dec, 1 Jan, bank hols L Meals: alc (main courses L £8.50 to £12, D £10.50 to £17.50). Set L £13.50 (2 courses) to £16.50 Service: 12.5% (optional) Cards: Amex, Delta, Diners, Maestro, MasterCard, Visa Details: 80 seats. Vegetarian meals. Children's helpings. No smoking. Wheelchair access (also WC). Music. Air-conditioned Tube: Putney Bridge

MAP 15

L'Escargot, Ground Floor

48 Greek Street, W1D 4EF
Tel: (020) 7439 7474
Website: www.lescargotrestaurant.co.uk

Cooking 3 | Modern French | £46

The ground floor dining room is almost a mini art gallery, with the works of Miró lining the walls and a Hockney in the front hall. However, it retains a well-lived-in period feel, with splendid Art Nouveau lamps, wood floors and ornate ceilings the backdrop to well-spaced white-clothed tables. Brasserie cooking is the order of the day, and results are straightforward with no illusions of grandeur. Ham hock and foie gras terrine with sauce gribiche, or escabèche of mackerel with a petit salad of herbs might be curtain-raisers to fillet of smoked haddock with colcannon, poached egg and grain mustard sauce, or Welsh lamb navarin with pommes dauphinoise, while dessert could be something like lemon tart or coconut crème brûlée. The pre-theatre menu has been appreciated for its reasonable price. House wine is £16.

Chefs: Dominic Teague Proprietor: Jimmy Lahoud Open: Mon to Fri L 12 to 2.15, Mon to Sat D 6 (5.30 Sat) to 11.15 Closed: D 25 and 26 Dec, 1 Jan Meals: alc (main courses £12.50 to £15). Set L and D (not after 7) £15 (2 courses) to £18 Service: 12.5% Cards: Amex, Delta, Diners, Maestro, MasterCard, Visa Details: 70 seats. Vegetarian meals. No pipes; cigars at management's discretion. Music. Air-conditioned Tube: Tottenham Court Road, Leicester Square

MAP 15

L'Escargot, Picasso Room

48 Greek Street, W1D 4EF
Tel: (020) 7439 7474
Website: www.lescargotrestaurant.co.uk

Cooking 4 | Modern French | £62

This landmark Soho building is divided into a smart, lively brasserie on the ground floor (see above), and a first-floor dining room that has traditionally dealt in more elaborate cooking at rather higher prices. Here dishes are complex and ally French technique to modern British sensibility, as in a beignet of Cornish scallops served with lardons of smoked salmon, sautéed langoustines, confit tomatoes and chive butter sauce, and a fillet of herb-crusted monkfish with a mussel and Alsace bacon chowder. There could be breast of guinea fowl with Bayonne ham, tart fine of roasted endive and sauce albufera, or rump of Charolais beef with cromesquis of oxtail and foie gras. Desserts are where the kitchen excels if a first-rate mini coffee crème brûlée pre-dessert and a blood orange soufflé and blood orange sorbet are anything to go by. Service is polite and efficient and house wine is £16.

Chef: Warren Geraghty Proprietor: Jimmy Lahoud Open: Tue to Fri L 12 to 2, Tue to Sat D 7 to 11 Closed: 25 and 26 Dec, 1 Jan, Aug Meals: Set L £20.50 (2 courses) to £42, Set D £42 Service: 15% Cards: Amex, Delta, Diners, Maestro, MasterCard, Visa Details: 30 seats. Children's helpings. No pipes; cigars at management's discretion. Occasional music. Air-conditioned Tube: Leicester Square, Tottenham Court Road

 This symbol means that the wine list is well above the average.

L'Etranger

36 Gloucester Road, SW7 4QT
Tel: (020) 7584 1118
Website: www.circagroupltd.co.uk

Cooking 2 | **Modern French-Plus** | **£56**

Like the hero of Camus's novel of the same name, this popular South Kensington restaurant has something of an identity crisis. Is it French? Is it Asian? Something else? There's salmon sashimi with seaweed salad among starters, and confit lamb shoulder with grilled aubergine among main courses, but things get really complicated when you come to pan-fried foie gras with beetroot jus, tempura and tamarind sauce, and steamed scallops with black truffles and wasabi. The lunch menu even features fish and chips with tartare sauce. By and large, though, the kitchen manages to make a success of its ambitious approach. All the wines on the extensive list (which includes a page of saké) can also be bought in the adjacent wine shop. A dozen house selections are priced from £14.50.

Chef: Jerome Tauvron **Proprietor:** Ibi Issolah **Open:** Mon to Fri L 12 to 3, Mon to Sat D 6 to 11 **Meals:** alc (main courses L £12 to £20, D £16.50 to £45). Set L £16.50 (2 courses) to £18.50, set D £65 **Service:** 12.5% (optional) **Cards:** Amex, Delta, Diners, Maestro, MasterCard, Visa **Details:** 60 seats. Children's helpings. No-smoking area. No music. Air-conditioned **Tube:** Gloucester Road

Eyre Brothers

70 Leonard Street, EC2A 4QX
Tel: (020) 7613 5346
Website: www.eyrebrothers.co.uk

Cooking 2 | **Iberian** | **£49**

Handy for both City slickers and the trendy Hoxton set, this style-conscious Shoreditch dining room is as comfortable as it is good looking, with black walnut and leather banquettes and white-clothed tables. Traditional Spanish and Portuguese cooking forms the backbone of the menu. Starters range from grilled chorizo on Puy lentils to pressed duck foie gras marinated in Madeira and port, while main courses typically feature dry-fried king scallops on braised shallots, morcilla and minted peas, with raw fennel with lemon, or perhaps caldeirada, a Portuguese fish and shellfish stew with potatoes, red peppers and saffron. And to finish there might be baked pistachio cheesecake with prune and red wine syrup, or a platter of Spanish cheeses with membrillo and raisin and walnut bread. The wine list is brief but eclectic, focusing appropriately on good Iberian choices. Prices start at £14.95.

Chefs: David Eyre and João Cleto **Proprietors:** David and Robert Eyre **Open:** Mon to Fri L 12 to 3, Mon to Sat D 6 to 11 **Meals:** alc (main courses £10 to £21) **Service:** 12.5% (optional) **Cards:** Amex, Delta, Diners, Maestro, MasterCard, Visa **Details:** 75 seats. Vegetarian meals. No-smoking area. Wheelchair access (also WC). Music. Air-conditioned **Tube:** Old Street

Fifteen

15 Westland Place, N1 7LP
Tel: (0871) 330 1515
Website: www.fifteenrestaurant.com

Cooking 3 | **Modern European** | **£81**

'It seems easier to get a table here than it was when Fifteen first opened', notes a reporter of Jamie O's basement restaurant, an 'achingly Shoreditch' amalgamation of warehouse-style wood floors spiced up with black and white Verner Panton chairs, graffiti-esque murals and lipstick-pink banquettes. Five years on, the approach to food remains consistent – namely, vibrant Italianate dishes based on fresh seasonal ingredients, delivered by confident staff. Dinner brings a six-course tasting menu and hits at inspection included tagliatelle with venison ragù and scented citrus zest, pan-fried halibut with tomatoes, agretti, braised artichokes and taggiasca olive sauce, and vanilla pannacotta with poached rhubarb and biscotti. The trattoria on the ground floor successfully combines rustic Italian touches (strings of chillies, jars of antipasti) with modern design. There's an open kitchen, a buzzy bar, and some closely packed wood tables – half of which are available on a first-come basis – where you can tuck into the likes of linguine vongole with chilli, garlic, parsley and pangrattato, and roasted spatchcock poussin with butternut squash caponata and olive sauce. The restaurant's extensive wine list is organised by grape variety and kicks off at a more-Mayfair-than-Shoreditch £21; the trattoria offers a shorter all-Italian list.

Chef: Andrew Parkinson Proprietor The Fifteen Foundation
Open: trattoria all week L 12 to 3, D 6 to 10 (5.30 to 9.30 Sun); restaurant all week L 12 to 2.30, D 6.30 to 9.30 **Meals:** trattoria alc (main courses £15 to £18); restaurant alc L (main courses £17.50 to £23.50). Set D £60 **Service:** 12.5% (optional) **Cards:** Amex, Delta, Maestro, MasterCard, Visa **Details:** trattoria 65 seats; restaurant 68 seats. Vegetarian meals. Children's helpings. No smoking. Wheelchair access to trattoria (also WC). Music. Air-conditioned **Tube:** Old Street

MAP 14

Fifth Floor

Harvey Nichols, 109–125 Knightsbridge,
SW1X 7RJ
Tel: (020) 7235 5250
Website: www.harveynichols.com

Cooking 4 | Modern British | £54

This is the place that set the standard for in-store restaurants and remains an obvious meeting place for ladies who lunch. Our inspector thought it was like being cocooned inside a pod in a sixties' science fiction film, such is the retro style of the room, enhanced by the fact that the skylight is designed to mimic the weather outside. Helena Puolakka has put together a short and focused menu that uses exemplary ingredients. Start with white Cornish crab meat with avocado and baby leaf salad, or tartare of hand-dived scallops served with Sevruga, capers and lemon oil. Move on to caramelised sweetbreads with a fricassee of young turnips, broad beans, truffle and Grelot onions, or perhaps Anjou baby pork 'miroton' with Camargue red rice. Desserts include caramelised banana with vanilla parfait or pineapple cannelloni with a passion-fruit mousse and French meringue. Their own label house wine starts at £12.50.

Chef: Helena Puolakka **Proprietor:** Dickson Poon **Open:** all week L 12 to 3 (3.30 Fri, 4 Sat/Sun), Mon to Sat D 6 to 11 **Meals:** alc (main courses £14.50 to £19.50). Set L £19.50 (2 courses) to £24.50. Set D £19.50 (2 courses) to £39.50. Bar menu available **Service:** 12.5% (optional) **Cards:** Amex, Delta, Diners, Maestro, MasterCard, Visa **Details:** 120 seats. 45 seats outside. Vegetarian meals. Children's helpings. No-smoking area. Wheelchair access (also WC). Music. Air-conditioned **Tube:** Knightsbridge

MAP 15

Fino

33 Charlotte Street (entrance in Rathbone Street),
W1T 1RR
Tel: (020) 7813 8010
Website: www.finorestaurant.com

Cooking 2 | Spanish | £47

As you descend into the sleek, table-packed basement, neither the décor nor the international slant to the staff give any impression that this is a tapas bar. But brothers Sam and Eddie Hart deliver a fair interpretation of the genre, taking a classic approach with variations of croquetas and tortillas, as well as pulpo a la gallega, buñuelos de bacalao, pimientos de pardon and pinchos morunos being typical of the offerings on the lengthy menu. Results can be patchy, but among highlights at inspection were tender grilled squid, a gutsy, rustic dish of white beans, chorizo and spinach, and a simple plate of broad beans with jamon. Chocolate fondant may not be typically Spanish but proves to be a very good example, and sherry is one of the stars on an all-Spanish wine list, which includes around nine by the glass. Prices start at £16.

Chef: Jean Philippe Patruno **Proprietors:** Sam and Eddie Hart
Open: Mon to Sat 12 to 2.30, 6 to 10.30 **Meals:** alc (main courses £7 to £16.50). Set L £17.95 to £30 (inc wine; all min 2 or more), Set D £17.95 to £28 (min 2) **Service:** 12.5% (optional) **Cards:** Amex, Maestro, MasterCard, Visa **Details:** 80 seats. Vegetarian meals. No cigars/pipes in dining room. Wheelchair access (also WC). No music. Air-conditioned **Tube:** Goodge Street, Tottenham Court Road

MAP 13

First Floor   AR

186 Portobello Road, W11 1LA
Tel: (020) 7243 0072

On lively Portobello Road, First Floor has a decidedly boho feel. The food is modern and imaginative: start with home-smoked duck with Puy lentils (£7.50), and go on to marinated poussin with a gratin of sweet potatoes and yellow beetroot (£13.50), before ending with chocolate tart and orange cream (£5). The interesting wine list opens with house Sicilian at £12, and six come by the glass. Open all week.

MAP 13

fish!

AR

Cathedral Street, SE1 9AL
Tel: (020) 7407 3803

This glass-roofed building next to Southwark Cathedral is, on Fridays and Saturdays at least, right in the heart of Borough Market. Fish is prepared daily at the long-established fishmonger, Jarvis of Kingston. Start with calamari with rocket and lemon mayonnaise (£5.95), or rock oysters with shallot vinegar (£1.50 each), and follow with a swordfish club sandwich with chips (£10.95), or steamed monkfish with red wine sauce (£15.95). End with bread-and-butter pudding with custard (£4.95). A short wine list starts at £13.95. Open all week.

MAP 12

Fish Hook

6–8 Elliott Road, W4 1PE
Tel: (020) 8742 0766
Website: www.fishhook.co.uk

Cooking 2 | Seafood | £46

'A good example of a smart, unpretentious, local restaurant', said one reporter of this well-run, lively venue, formerly Fish Hoek. Located in a tall Victorian house at the end of a small line of shops, the dining room has a relaxed seaside feel to it, while chef/proprietor Michael Nadra imaginatively uses seasonal ingredients in his daily-changing menu. Typical starters might include a 'lovely combination' of hand-dived scallops with sweet potato mash, followed by crisp sea bass with buttered courgettes, crab ravioli and bisque sauce, which has boasted excellent raw materials. Sea bream with asparagus was another success, with an excellent side order of roast salsify with Alsace bacon. Finish with chocolate fondant with caramel and vanilla ice cream. France gets the biggest look-in on this wine list, with house selections starting at £12.50.

Chef/Proprietor: Michael Nadra **Open:** Tue to Sun 12 (12.30 Sun) to 2.30 (3.30 Sat and Sun), 6 to 10.30 (6.30 to 10 Sun) **Meals:** alc (main courses £12 to £24). Set L and D (before 7) £12.50 (1 course) to £18.50 **Service:** 12.5% (optional) **Cards:** Amex, Delta, Maestro, MasterCard, Visa **Details:** 52 seats. Children's helpings. No smoking. Wheelchair access (not WC). Music. Air-conditioned **Tube:** Turnham Green

MAP 13

Fish Shop

360–362 St John Street, EC1V 4NR
Tel: (020) 7837 1199
Website: www.thefishshop.net

Cooking 2 | Seafood | £46

Unambiguously named, the Fish Shop is ideally placed for supper before the show at Sadler's Wells. The pre-theatre menu offers about two choices per course: perhaps smoked haddock brandade or prawns with garlic mayonnaise, followed by fish-cake with a delicate ginger sauce or deep-fried haddock and chips. The latter is also a highlight of the regular menu, featuring perfectly cooked fish in crisp, non-greasy batter. Otherwise, starters take in everything from potted shrimps to seared scallops with cauliflower purée and sauce vierge, main courses typically ranging from roast cod with braised celery, broad beans, peas, lardons and thyme sauce to grilled swordfish with baked tomato, crisp parsnips and basil mascarpone sauce. Finish perhaps with treacle tart with whisky clotted cream. Wines are mostly white, of course, but comprise an imaginative and varied selection priced from £13.95, with up to 30 by the glass.

Chef: Kamel Bouakkaz **Proprietor:** John Moyle **Open:** Tue to Sat 12 to 3, 5.30 to 11, Sun 12 to 8 **Meals:** alc (main courses £10 to £24). Set L Tue to Sun £13.50 (2 courses) to £17, Set D Tue to Sat 5.30 to 7 £13.50 (2 courses) to £17 **Service:** 12.5% (optional) **Cards:** Amex, Delta, Diners, Maestro, MasterCard, Visa **Details:** 80 seats. 20 seats outside. Vegetarian meals. Children's helpings. No smoking in 1 dining room. Wheelchair access (also WC). No music **Tube:** Angel

MAP 15

Fishworks

6 Turnham Green Terrace, W4 1QP
Tel: (020) 8994 0086
Website: www.fishworks.co.uk

Cooking 2 | Seafood | £45

The Fishworks brand is popping up all over London, with Parsons Green, Battersea, Islington and Richmond joining Marylebone High Street and this one, which was the first in the Capital (others are in Bath, Bristol and Christchurch; see entries). Mitchell Tonks has shown there is a demand for fresh fish, simply delivered, and his formula of wet fish sales at the front, and a modern, lively dining area at the back, is a winner. The fish is the star of the show. Smoked salmon with capers and red onion is a simple starter, the slices thickly cut, and Dartmouth crab is 'very fresh and bursting with flavour'. Sea bass gets the foil treatment, with garlic, rosemary and chilli oil at inspection. Baked chocolate pudding made a satisfying finish. Fish-friendly European whites (from £18) dominate the wine list.

> **Chef:** Jack Scarterfield **Proprietor:** Fishworks plc **Open:** Tue to Sun L 12 to 2.30, Tue to Sat D 6 to 10.30 **Closed:** 24 Dec to early Jan, day after bank hols **Meals:** alc (main courses £12 to £25) **Service:** not inc **Cards:** Amex, Delta, Maestro, MasterCard, Visa **Details:** 48 seats, 22 seats outside. Vegetarian meals. Children's helpings. No smoking. Music. Air-conditioned **Tube:** Turnham Green

MAP 13

Flâneur

41 Farringdon Road, EC1M 3JB
Tel: (020) 7404 4422
Website: www.flaneur.com

| Cooking 2 | Modern European | £41 |

Large windows offer views from the street of the industrial-scale displays of food at this deli-cum-restaurant in a former warehouse. Venture in to bag a table and you'll find yourself surrounded by a veritable take-away feast, but the kitchen shows its mettle on the plate too, with a brasserie repertoire that has a strong Italian accent. Starters like smoked eel with pea and bacon fritters, watercress and crème fraîche, and main courses of risotto of courgette, goats' cheese and basil, or steak with blue cheese, chips and béarnaise exemplify the straightforward approach. Desserts are mainly cakes and tarts, but there's also rhubarb fool and panettone bread-and-butter pudding. The wine list tends to favour France and starts at £11.55, with 28 by the glass (from £3.60 to £7).

> **Chef:** Simon Phelan **Proprietors:** Mike Metcalfe and Chris Fraser **Open:** all week L 12 to 3, Mon to Sat D 6 to 10 **Closed:** 25 Dec to 2 Jan **Meals:** alc (main courses £11 to £18) **Service:** 12.5% (optional) **Cards:** Amex, Delta, Maestro, MasterCard, Visa **Details:** 60 seats. Vegetarian meals. No smoking. Wheelchair access (not WC). No music **Tube:** Farringdon

> ⓔ This symbol means that it is possible to have a three-course dinner, including coffee, half a bottle of house wine and service, for £30 or less per person.

MAP 12

Food Room

123 Queenstown Road, SW8 3RH
Tel: (020) 7622 0555
Website: www.thefoodroom.co.uk

| Cooking 3 | French/Mediterranean | £44 |

Bringing a touch of Gallic sophistication to an unglamorous corner of London, the Food Room is the second venture of Eric and Sarah Guignard, owners of the French Table in Surbiton (see entry). The two dining rooms create the right impression, with a restful beige colour scheme, subtle lighting, and white tablecloths and candles on the tables, as does the efficient service. The menus imaginatively reinvent the classic provincial French repertoire to come up with starters of lobster bisque with spinach and smoked salmon ravioli, pan-fried foie gras with tarte Tatin and balsamic vinegar, and rabbit with goats' cheese on cocoa bean purée and chorizo sauce. For main course, choices might include rump of Welsh lamb with tartiflette, tian provençale and olive jus, crisp sea bass with sautéed spinach and vanilla sauce, or venison with celeriac timbale, cranberries and chocolate sauce. Classics such as crème brûlée or dark chocolate parfait could be among desserts. Wines range from house red and white vins de pays at £12.50 to a Condrieu at £49, with a varied choice from around the world in between.

> **Chef:** Eric Guignard **Proprietors:** Eric and Sarah Guignard **Open:** Tue to Fri and Sun L 12 to 2.30, Tue to Sat D 7 to 10.30 **Meals:** alc D (main courses £12 to £16). Set L Tue to Fri £13.50 (2 courses) to £16.50, Set L Sun £19.50, Set D £19.50 (2 courses) to £24.50 **Service:** 12.5% (optional) **Cards:** Amex, Delta, Maestro, MasterCard, Visa **Details:** 60 seats. Vegetarian meals. Children's helpings. No smoking in dining room. Wheelchair access (also men's WC). Music. No mobile phones. Air-conditioned

MAP 13

Four Seasons

84 Queensway, W2 3RL
Tel: (020) 7229 4320

| Cooking 2 | Cantonese | £30 |

Roast duck, crispy roast pork and char sui pork fillet are the reasons why legions of regulars and newcomers queue up early in the evening to secure a table. In response, the Queensway restaurant squeezes tables into the cramped surroundings, but given the expectant customers blocking the entrance and the frenzied pace in the dining room, don't expect too much of the service. If you choose to eschew the roast meats, the long main menu promises everything from sizzling chicken with orange peel to stir-fried squid with green peppers in black bean sauce and grilled sea bass. The long list of chef's specialities is worth exploring for things like fish lips and duck webs, pot dishes like stewed brisket of lamb with dry bean curd and many seafood dishes.

> **Chef:** Mr Tong **Proprietor:** Paul Chung **Open:** all week 12 to 11.15 **Closed:** 24 to 26 Dec **Meals:** alc (main courses £6 to £20). Set L and D £13.50 to £18 (all min 2 or more) **Service:** 12.5% **Cards:** Delta, Maestro, MasterCard, Visa **Details:** 60 seats. Vegetarian meals. Music. Air-conditioned **Tube:** Bayswater, Queensway

---

MAP 13

Fox Dining Room

28 Paul Street, EC2A 4LB
Tel: (020) 7729 5708
Email: fox.ph@virgin.net

Cooking 3 | Modern European | £32

This unpretentious pub puts the food front and centre stage with a menu that lets quality ingredients and well-teamed flavours speak for themselves. The upstairs dining room (the bar takes up the ground floor) is dark by most standards, with a wall of Victorian mirrors, old chairs and dining tables, plus a few standard lamps. The food is European but rustic with it, and the menu cuts the descriptions back to the bone. Starters might be confit of guinea fowl with trevisse and blood orange, or scallops with chilli, lemon and garlic. Main courses are similarly pared down: lamb is served simply with celeriac mash, while skate comes with purple-sprouting broccoli and anchovies. A vegetarian option might include pumpkin and ricotta ravioli, while desserts also reflect the simplicity of approach: try crème caramel or steamed rhubarb sponge pudding. A simple sheet of wines, mostly European, starts at £11.

> **Chef:** Trish Hilferty **Proprietor:** Michael Belben **Open:** Mon to Fri 12.30 to 3, 6.30 to 10.30 **Meals:** Set L and D £16.50 (2 courses) to £21.50. Bar L menu available **Service:** not inc **Cards:** Delta, Maestro, MasterCard, Visa **Details:** 34 seats. 20 seats outside. Vegetarian meals. No music **Tube:** Old Street, Liverpool Street

---

MAP 12

Franklins

157 Lordship Lane, SE22 8HX
Tel: (020) 8299 9598
Website: www.franklinsrestaurant.com

Cooking 2 | British | £38

The presence of this bistro isn't immediately apparent to the casual observer, as you have to weave your way through the well-populated bar to get to the dining room. The emphasis is on traditional British food that is well sourced and delivered with a refreshing honesty. The menu is written with brevity, but that merely serves to place more importance on the food. Curried parsnip soup, devilled kidneys and kipper pâté are among first-course options, while calf's liver with onions and bacon, ribeye steak with horseradish or Oxford Down lamb with aubergine and anchovy could be main courses. Finish with something traditional like spotted dick or rhubarb crumble. A page-long wine list, predominantly French, opens at £12.

> **Chef:** Tim Sheehan **Proprietors:** Rodney Franklin and Tim Sheehan **Open:** Mon to Sat 12 to 10.30, Sun 1 to 10 **Closed:** 25, 26 and 31 Dec, 1 Jan **Meals:** alc (main courses £10.50 to £18.50). Set L £9 (2 courses) to £12. Bar menu available **Service:** not inc **Cards:** Amex, Delta, Maestro, MasterCard, Visa **Details:** 66 seats. Vegetarian meals. Children's helpings. No smoking in 1 dining room. Wheelchair access (also WC). No music. Air-conditioned

---

MAP 15

Fung Shing

15 Lisle Street, WC2H 7BE
Tel: (020) 7437 1539
Website: www.fungshing.co.uk

Cooking 2 | Chinese | £46

Fung Shing has been plying its trade on the edges of Chinatown for more than three decades and it stays with the tried-and-true formula. Like many of its neighbours, it deals in broadly based Cantonese cooking, with some of the exotica now seen in other establishments (venison with spiced yellow bean sauce, ostrich with ginger and spring onion). Some reporters have been well satisfied with the 'pungent punch' of a hot and sour soup, steamed sea bass with black bean sauce, sizzling prawns, and egg fried rice, otherwise the list of chef's specials might run to asparagus with crab meat sauce, braised suckling pig, lobsters – which come four ways – and hot-pots like braised eel with roasted belly pork. Service is polite. The wine list is a decent selection and opens at £14.50.

Chef: Chun-Fat Cheung   Proprietor: Fung Shing Partnership   Open: all week 12 (6 bank hols) to 11.10   Closed: 24 to 26 Dec, bank hol L   Meals: alc (main courses £8 to £30). Set L and D £17 to £30 (all min 2 or more)   Service: 10%   Cards: Amex, Delta, Diners, Maestro, MasterCard, Visa   Details: 100 seats. Vegetarian meals. Music. Air-conditioned   Tube: Leicester Square

MAP 15

Galvin at Windows [NEW ENTRY]

Hilton Hotel, 22 Park Lane, W1Y 4BE
Tel: (020) 7208 4021
Website: www.hilton.co.uk/londonparklane

| Cooking 6 | French | £68 |

The brothers Galvin, Chris and Jeff, hit the ground running when they opened their joint venture, Galvin Bistrot de Luxe (see entry, below), and now Chris is again making waves on the London dining scene with this project on the twenty-eighth floor of the Hilton Hotel. It has had the sleekest of makeovers; the colour scheme is subdued, with subtle browns and golds, and by raising the central area of the room 'some of the best views of London' have been maximised.

Installing André Garrett from Orrery as head chef was a smart move. He combines sure-handed technique with confident, clear flavours, and dishes are always well balanced: 'plump and succulent' langoustine tails, for example, are paired with slow-cooked belly pork, and the accompanying cauliflower purée 'could not be bettered'. Equally impressive are main courses of risotto of morels, peas and broad beans, with watercress topping it off, and Anjou pigeon that had been cooked in a bag with a little pigeon stock and Madeira, then quickly grilled before serving with petits pois and pomme cocotte. Other high points have included oak-smoked salmon served with a rémoulade of crab and crème fraîche, and perfectly timed wild halibut. To finish, there is an excellent cheeseboard from Philippe Olivier across the Channel, although more serious temptation might come from a Valrhona palet d'or oozing with dark chocolate, topped with gold leaf and nicely contrasted by the coldness of milk ice cream. Prices are as sky high as the location, and with a wine list aimed squarely at the corpo-

rate diner, with the starting price £22 and just a handful under £30, this is a place 'more geared towards a special occasion'.

Chefs: Chris Galvin and André Garrett   Open: Sun to Fri L 12 to 2.30, Mon to Sat D 6 to 10.30   Meals: alc (main courses £15 to £29.50). Set L £28, Set D £65   Service: 12.5% (optional)   Cards: Amex, Diners, Maestro, MasterCard, Visa   Details: 108 seats. Vegetarian meals. No smoking. Wheelchair access (also women's WC). No music. Air-conditioned   Accommodation: 453 rooms   Tube: Hyde Park Corner, Green Park

MAP 15

Galvin Bistrot de Luxe [NEW ENTRY]

LONDON GFG 2007 COMMENDED

66 Baker Street, W1V 7DH
Tel: (020) 7935 4007
Website: www.galvinbistrotdeluxe.co.uk

| Cooking 5 | French | £42 |

The Galvin brothers' 'Bistrot de Luxe' is surely a restaurant to reflect the times: the pricing is designed to soothe, not shock, the vibrant French brasserie-inspired food appeals to an egalitarian crowd, while the 'luxe' reassures us that it is all going to be jolly civilised. And it delivers. The converted shop on Baker Street looks the part: dark wooden panelling, green leather banquettes, and Jeff and Chris Galvin have a pedigree on the London dining scene between them that suggests they were born to run a joint like this.

The menu is not intended to challenge, but it has plenty of interest. Due diligence is taken in the sourcing of materials – 'universally good-quality ingredients,' as one reader put it – and the choice is of a sizeable carte or an early-evening prix fixe. Lasagne of Dorset crab is enriched with a silky shellfish sauce as a comforting and stylish starter, or there might be classic soupe de poissons, or steak tartare. Although many dishes are familiar, reassuringly so you might say, the delivery is first class, as in pot-roast Landaise chicken with Jerusalem artichoke and Alsace bacon. Marsala sauce accompanies braised veal cheeks with macaroni, and a fish main course might see whole roast bream with watercress and fennel salad. Desserts keep up the pace with tarte au citron, or apricot and chocolate soufflé. Service seems to have settled in to a good rhythm. The wine list is firmly rooted in France but does offer some interesting bottles from elsewhere. House wine is £13.75 a bottle, and a dozen are available by the glass.

Chefs: Jeff and Chris Galvin **Proprietors:** Jeff and Chris Galvin, and Ken Sanker **Open:** all week 12 to 2.30 (3 Sun), 6 to 11 (10.30 Sun) **Closed:** 25 and 26 Dec, 1 Jan **Meals:** alc (main courses £9.50 to £18.50). Set L £15.50, Set D 6 to 7 £17.50 **Service:** 12.5% (optional) **Cards:** Amex, Delta, Maestro, MasterCard, Visa **Details:** 90 seats. Vegetarian meals. Children's helpings. No-smoking area. Wheelchair access (also WC). No music. No mobile phones. Air-conditioned **Tube:** Baker Street

MAP 12

Gate

51 Queen Caroline Street, W6 9QL
Tel: (020) 8748 6932
Website: www.thegate.tv

Cooking 2 | Vegetarian | £34

A million miles away from the cliché of sandal-wearing vegetarianism, this modern restaurant oozes friendly charm. Located in a renovated church, the light and airy dining room may contain a few too many tables, but there's a happy buzz about the place. Jo Tyrell's food could turn the head of even the staunchest carnivore as she brings vegetarian cooking to life with wasabi potato cakes stuffed with roast shiitake mushrooms, ginger and chilli, or feta and broccoli tart. Among interesting main courses, aubergine is served as a schnitzel layered with mozzarella, pesto and roast red peppers, while butternut, basil and goats' cheese go into ravioli accompanied by cherry tomato compote, rocket and Parmesan shavings. Desserts include rhubarb and ginger crumble, and, like everything else on the menu, are labelled vegan or gluten-free. The wine list is a muted affair but reasonably priced, with prices starting at £11.95, £3.25 a glass.

Chef: Jo Tyrell **Proprietors:** Adrian and Michael Daniel **Open:** Mon to Fri L 12 to 2.45, Mon to Sat D 6 to 10.45 **Meals:** alc (main courses £7.50 to £13.50) **Service:** 12.5% (optional) **Cards:** Amex, Delta, Maestro, MasterCard, Visa **Details:** 60 seats. 20 seats outside. Vegetarian meals. No smoking. Music. Air-conditioned **Tube:** Hammersmith

NEW ENTRY This appears after the restaurant's name if the establishment was not a main entry in last year's Guide. Please note, however, it may have been 'also recommended' in the previous edition.

MAP 15

Le Gavroche

43 Upper Brook Street, W1K 7QR
Tel: (020) 7408 0881
Website: www.le-gavroche.co.uk

Cooking 7 | French | £122

The basement dining room off Park Lane has been feeding the Mayfair glitterati, as well as lovers of classical French cuisine, since 1967, when the Roux brothers' dynasty began. It still has the feel of a refuge, sepulchrally lit, where the vulgarity of daylight doesn't penetrate, and hung about with photographs of the culinary stars, as well as Matisse prints. 'The first thought when dining here is that we are not alone', commented a reporter, noting the innumerable staff and the way they manage to be at tableside just when needed. Indeed, the place has always felt most comfortable with an old-school tone – silver domes, unpriced ladies' menus, the insistence on jackets for gentlemen.

Michel Roux Jnr naturally inherited his father's ways of doing things, and much of the bilingual menus still deal in the richnesses of yesteryear, at prices that may well bring tears to the eyes. The famous lobster mousse with caviar in a champagne butter sauce is now £52.40. Altogether gentler on the pocket is a first course of langoustine paired with a mousse of Dover sole, served with a delicately scented sauce of mushrooms and basil. Main courses that have impressed have included superb veal cutlets, carved from the roast rib at the table, enhanced with a 'beautifully perfumed' sauce of morels and cream and served with mashed potato, and full-flavoured pork fillet stuffed with prunes, on a mini risotto surrounded by seasonal broad beans. A touch of innovation might creep in to fish dishes such as turbot served on the 'T-bone', with a gratin of cauliflower and a lemon and herb butter, but desserts revert to the textbook for tarte Tatin, omelette Rothschild, and passion-fruit soufflé with ivory (white chocolate) ice cream. For the unsweet of tooth, a handsome cheeseboard is served with knowledge and generosity.

The wine list specialises, as it always has, in the leading regions of France, lingering for page after page over the great names, many of them offered in successive vintages. Will it be the 1996 Lynch-Bages or the 1995? Decisions. Italy is accorded some dignity too, with runs of Sassicaia and Tignanello to delight initiates. There are plenty of half-bottles, but basically everything is expensive. If you're having to count the pounds, house wines are £4 a glass, and the mineral water list includes Badoit at the same price a bottle.

Chef: Michel Roux Proprietor: Le Gavroche Ltd Open: Mon to Fri L 12 to 2, Mon to Sat D 6.30 to 11 Closed: Christmas and New Year, bank hols Meals: alc (main courses £26.50 to £46.50). Set L £46 (inc wine), Set D £86 Service: 12.5% (optional) Cards: Amex, Delta, Diners, Maestro, MasterCard, Visa Details: 70 seats. Vegetarian meals. Jacket. No smoking in 1 dining room. No music. Air-conditioned Tube: Marble Arch

MAP 15

Gay Hussar

2 Greek Street, W1D 4NB
Tel: (020) 7437 0973
Website: www.simplyrestaurants.com

Cooking 1 | Hungarian | £36

For 55 years this Hungarian warrior hasn't shown any inclination to embrace anything outside the culinary tradition of its native country. And why should it, when it yields the legendary chilled wild cherry soup and marinated fillet of herring with soured cream among starters? Main courses are equally traditional: chicken palacsinta (pancakes) with paprika sauce, fish dumplings in creamy dill and mushroom sauce, stuffed cabbage with sauerkraut, smoked bacon and sausage, and, of course, goulash. Consider sweet cheese pancakes to finish, or poppy seed strudel with vanilla ice cream. The 30-strong wine list naturally lists Bull's Blood and Tokaji, but also gives a decent picture of what's happening in Hungarian viticulture nowadays. House wine is £13.95.

Chef: Carlos Mendoca Proprietor: Restaurant Partnership plc Open: Mon to Sat 12.15 to 2.30, 5.30 to 10.45 Closed: 25 to 28 Dec, 1 to 3 Jan Meals: alc D (main courses £9.50 to £16.50). Set L £16.50 (2 courses) to £18.50 Service: 12.5% (optional) Cards: Amex, Delta, Diners, Maestro, MasterCard, Visa Details: 82 seats. Vegetarian meals. No cigars/pipes in dining room. Music. Air-conditioned Tube: Tottenham Court Road

This symbol means that the restaurant has elected to participate in *The Good Food Guide's* £5 voucher scheme (see 'Using The Good Food Guide' for details).

MAP 15

Giardinetto

39–40 Albemarle Street, W1S 4TE
Tel: (020) 7493 7091
Website: www.giardinetto.co.uk

Cooking 3 | Italian | £66

You have to press two buzzers to be let in and, once inside, you might think you've been transported to Milan: white linen covers over coffee-coloured tablecloths, copper and terracotta walls, and lighting 'a little too bright'. The trendy black-covered menu reveals lasagne with beef fillet and sausage ragoût with cocoa powder, and scallops paired with a purée of lentils and vegetable foam. This is adventurous stuff, and all dishes are served with great drama on different-shaped plates. Main-course choices at inspection included a pink breast of guinea fowl with red peppers and olives, and pan-fried turbot with Parmesan-encrusted baked chicory and red wine sauce, plus interesting vegetables such as spinach dressed with pine nuts and raisins. Finish with chocolate sponge with a pair of light and dark chocolate mousses, or apricot tart 'perfectly made to the Italian recipe'. Over 20 wines by the glass enable you to pick and choose. The rest of the Italian list is extensive and expensive, although a Puglian white starts proceedings at £15.

Chef/Proprietor: Maurizio Vilona Open: Mon to Fri L 12 to 3, Mon to Sat D 7 to 11 Meals: alc (main courses £18 to £27.50). Set L £22 Service: 12.5% (optional) Cards: Amex, Delta, Diners, Maestro, MasterCard, Visa Details: 54 seats. Vegetarian meals. Wheelchair access (also WC). Music. Air-conditioned Tube: Green Park

MAP 13

Ginger

115 Westbourne Grove, W2 4UP
Tel: (020) 7908 1990
Website: www.gingerrestaurant.co.uk

Cooking 2 | Bangladeshi | £36

Beyond the bright turquoise exterior is a relatively calm dining room in a cream and white colour scheme set off with arrangements of eucalyptus branches and flowers. The effect is suitably contemporary and informal for a restaurant that aims to re-create traditional Bangladeshi home cooking. The menus offer a good range of bright, lively dishes, with starters of masumbi paneer (roast cheese cubes stuffed with sweet lime pickle), duck and mango sticks, and squid stuffed with crab and Indian mushrooms, served with mint and coriander chutney. To follow, main courses include spicy wok-fried lamb, and macher jhol (mustard-flavoured fish curry), while the 'chef's selection' features king prawn balchao (sun-dried prawns with pickled peppers and tomatoes), and chicken cafereal (a Portuguese dish with green spices and roast potatoes). To accompany these, try side dishes of green banana curry, or spinach kofta. The simple and sensible wine list starts at £11.95.

Chef: Cruz Gomes **Proprietor:** W. Rahman **Open:** Mon to Thur 5 to 10.45, Fri 5 to 12, Sat 12 to 12, Sun 12 to 11 **Meals:** alc (main courses £7.50 to £13). Set L and D noon (5 Mon to Fri) to 7.30 £9.95 **Service:** 12.5% (optional) **Cards:** Amex, Delta, Maestro, MasterCard, Visa **Details:** 130 seats. Vegetarian meals. No-smoking area. Music. Air-conditioned **Tube:** Notting Hill Gate

MAP 13

Glas

NEW ENTRY

3 Park Street, SE1 9AB
Tel: (020) 7357 6060
Website: www.glasrestaurant.com

Cooking 1 | Swedish | £38

Glas is a few paces from the main hub of bustling Borough Market. Swedish minimalism is perhaps expected, and the understated premises don't disappoint: blond laminate flooring, grey panelling, and stainless steel framed chairs. It's all understated, yet stylish, and light and airy. The place can get quite lively, especially if there are large parties in sampling the delights of their native aquavit, but the staff keep smiling. There is a 'grazing menu' – two or three dishes per person is the recommendation – featuring Swedish mainstays such as herring, which one diner praised as 'extremely good in whatever combination they are served'. Beef tartare with beetroot and capers is 'not for the faint-hearted', served with a raw egg, while the smoked pork belly in a blackcurrant reduction is an example of 'real peasant cuisine'. Rhubarb compote was a 'deliciously sharp' way to end. The short wine list matches the style of the food, and starts at £15.95.

Chefs: Anna Mosesson, Andrea Aberg, Mikael Brobert and Klas Nyrinder **Proprietor:** Glas Restaurants **Open:** Mon to Sat 12 to 2.30, 6.30 to 9.30 **Service:** 12.5% (optional) **Cards:** Amex, Delta, Maestro, MasterCard, Visa **Details:** 40 seats. Vegetarian meals. Children's helpings. No smoking. Wheelchair access (also WC). No music. No mobile phones. Air-conditioned **Tube:** London Bridge

MAP 15

Golden Dragon

28–29 Gerrard Street, W1V 7LP
Tel: (020) 7734 2763

Cooking 2 | Chinese | £36

Chinese screens on the walls and a red-and-gold-patterned dragon display set an appropriate tone in this large, bustling, brightly lit restaurant spread over two levels. Straightforward Cantonese cooking is what to expect, the vast menu comprehensively covering the standard repertoire, from barbecued spare ribs to braised lamb belly hotpot with bean curd. Crabmeat and sweetcorn soup, made with a carefully seasoned, flavoursome broth, has been a well-received starter; likewise fresh-tasting deep-fried soft-shell crab sprinkled with plenty of salt and pepper. Among main courses to receive praise have been steamed sea bass, served partially filleted, with black-bean sauce and coriander, spicy Szechuan prawns, and Singapore noodles. Lunchtime dim sum are also a popular option, including deep-fried lobster dumplings, 'first-rate' steamed half-moon prawn dumplings, and 'superb' cheung fun. Own-label wines at £9 open the straightforward list.

Chef: Mr Man **Proprietor:** Mr Lam **Open:** all week 12 (11 Sun) to 11.15 (11.45 Fri and Sat, 10.45 Sun) **Meals:** alc (main courses £7 to £18). Set L and D £12.50 (2 courses, min 2) to £23.50 (min 5) **Service:** 10% **Cards:** Amex, Delta, Diners, Maestro, MasterCard, Visa **Details:** 150 seats. Vegetarian meals. Music. Air-conditioned **Tube:** Leicester Square, Piccadilly Circus

MAP 14

Gordon Ramsay

68–69 Royal Hospital Road, SW3 4HP
Tel: (020) 7352 4441
Website: www.gordonramsay.com

Cooking 9 | French | £93

May we presume you've heard of Gordon Ramsay? You'll have seen him on *Top Gear* or *Soccer Aid* perhaps, or bought one of his books. He also runs restaurants, all over London and the world, and this one, in the heart of Chelsea, near the Royal Hospital and the National Army Museum, is where the world wants to come and eat. That being said, trying to get a booking is a test of wills, a character-building challenge in which you will likely be held in a phone queue, until someone answers and tells you they're full. They don't book up more than a month ahead, so every morning at 9am a fresh telephone stampede begins. Try faxing if you can.

Is it worth the hassle? Yes, it is. Once you're in you will find the service approach exactly the opposite of all that, the courtesies flowing and the slick professionalism and knowledge of every last member of staff a tribute to the dedication with which the place is run. First-timers will note the relatively restricted dimensions of the dining room (hence those phone queues). It's fairly comfortable and fairly stylish, although not excessively either. The chairs have no arms, and the wall shelving with its clunking great pieces of Murano glass evoked the set of *Abigail's Party* for one unkind soul. Still, you're here to eat, so let's look at the menu.

Eight choices each of starter or main are offered, along with one or two specials. The range is wide and deep, with no need to settle on one central protein, as different ones combine in many dishes. Take a main course of roast fillet of pork, thickly sliced, strongly flavoured and lightly fatty, alongside a section of the belly, which has been braised for 48 hours to a state of splendid tenderness. Bedded on smooth apple purée, it is topped with a couple of sea-fresh langoustines. Meats are indeed breathtaking throughout: best end of Cornish lamb is terrific, even better a little pepper-wrapped portion of the confit shoulder that comes with it, along with pin-fresh ratatouille vegetables and a sauce of creamed morels. A fine balance is maintained between dishes that push at the boundaries of what ingredients can do but stop short of wacky combinations. Lobster tails appear with aubergine gratin and truffle and – like most other dishes – have their sauce, in this case a sublime crab and coriander bisque, poured over them at the table.

With so many elements close to perfect, one perhaps notices the near-misses the more obtrusively. A first course of steak tartare, half-topped with oscietra caviar, doesn't quite come off, the meat very shyly seasoned, so as not to overwhelm one of the more delicately flavoured of caviars, so that the whole seems more a thing of texture than of taste. Breads are not quite what one might expect from the best restaurant in the capital. Come desserts, however, admiration flows forth again. A glass of pannacotta on prune and Armagnac compote is topped with vanilla foam. You get to watch the chocolate sauce the waiter pours sink through it before setting about it. The majestic wine list is not for the faint of heart. Our inspector asked the sommelier whether a youngish Crozes-Hermitage would be drinking well yet, and was directed without a murmur to a wine at

£30 (plus 12.5 per cent service charge) more. If money doesn't have to matter, there are mature clarets and Burgundies in battalions, together with some very clever stuff from Italy, Australia and California. Other sections are distinctly lighter on allure. Prices do, however, start at a little under £20, and there are good wines by the glass from a mere fiver.

Chef: Gordon Ramsay **Proprietor:** Gordon Ramsay Holdings Ltd **Open:** Mon to Fri 12 to 2.30, 6.45 to 11 **Meals:** Set L £40 to £90, Set D £70 to £90 **Service:** 12.5% (optional) **Cards:** Amex, Delta, Diners, Maestro, MasterCard, Visa **Details:** 44 seats. Vegetarian meals. Children's helpings. No smoking. Wheelchair access (not WC). No music. No mobile phones. Air-conditioned **Tube:** Sloane Square

---

MAP 15

Gordon Ramsay at Claridge's

Brook Street, W1A 2JQ
Tel: (020) 7499 0099
Website: www.gordonramsay.com

| Cooking 6 | French | £83 |

It's worth lingering a while as you pass through the hotel lobby. Claridge's is an exquisite Art Deco treasure. By common assent, though, it's hard to love what they've done in the main dining room, which is a predominantly brown and orange job with massive, ungainly, cylindrical lanterns hanging over the scene. Lighting tends to the sepulchral, and one has to say – despite the excellent, polished service – that it isn't a scene that's guaranteed to lift the spirits.

For that, we turn gratefully to Mark Sargeant's cooking, which has taken on the lineaments of the GR house style and brings off successive dishes with convincing panache. 'There is no lack of nibbles,' commented our inspector, proceeding with gay abandon from truffled cream cheese and pâté de foie gras, to a salmon fishcake, a chicken dumpling and a little serving of watercress velouté. After that lot, it's time to look at the menu. There is perhaps less of the urge to complexity demonstrated, say, by Marcus Wareing at Pétrus (see entry), but nevertheless the same confidence in making dishes work. A square of bluefin tuna carpaccio is top-drawer, dressed in citrus and soy, and is accompanied by three tuna rolls in black sesame seeds, a stunning opener. Sea bass on a layer of wilted gem lettuce makes a refreshing main course, especially with the bracing asparagus velouté poured over it at the table, and the crushed Jersey Royals just coming triumphantly into season. Cheeses have been uneven in quality, but a dessert plate that musters proper crème brûlée, a good sablé biscuit, a disc of chocolate, poached pear and star anise ice cream showed nerveless execution throughout. Superb wines comprise a long list that does justice to a grand hotel. Sweet wines alone are astonishing, a fine selection of food-friendly Alsace wines gives cheer, and there are some fabulous Spanish reds. Even if you can make it only up to £30, there is a pretty decent spread of choice.

Chef: Mark Sargeant Proprietor: Gordon Ramsay Holdings Ltd Open: all week 12 to 3, 5.45 to 11 Meals: Set L £30 to £70, Set D £60 to £70 Service: 12.5% (optional) Cards: Amex, Delta, Diners, Maestro, MasterCard, Visa Details: 100 seats. Vegetarian meals. Children's helpings. No smoking. Wheelchair access (not WC). No music. No mobile phones. Air-conditioned Tube: Bond Street

MAP 13

Great Eastern Dining Room

54–56 Great Eastern Street, EC2A 3QR
Tel: (020) 7613 4545
Website: www.greateasterndining.co.uk

Cooking 3 | Pan-Asian | £41

The cool, contemporary warehouse conversion wows first-time visitors, and the refreshingly informal, laid-back atmosphere is matched by a menu that bypasses starters and main courses in favour of a flexible assortment of pan-Asian favourites. There is an air of excitement about a repertoire that offers chicken and snowpea gyozas, prawn dumplings, soft-shell crab salad with sweet tamarind and lotus root, barramundi and physalis jungle curry, and black cod with sweet miso, and finishes with warm chocolate pudding and green tea ice cream. If you're uncertain about a dish, flip over the carte and there's a useful glossary on the back. The popular bar next door adds to the vibrant atmosphere generated by close-packed tables, and wines on a short, contemporary global list open with house Italian at £13 with eleven offered by the glass. The style is similar to Will Ricker's other restaurants (see e&o and Eight Over Eight).

Proprietor: Will Ricker Open: Mon to Fri L 12 to 3, Mon to Sat D 6.30 to 11 Meals: alc (main courses £7 to £19.50). Set L and D £22.50 (2 courses) to £45. Bar menu available Service: 12.5% (optional) Cards: Amex, Delta, Diners, Maestro, MasterCard, Visa Details: 65 seats. Vegetarian meals. No smoking in 1 dining room. No music. Air-conditioned Tube: Old Street

MAP 13

Great Eastern Hotel, Aurora

Liverpool Street, EC2M 7QN
Tel: (020) 7618 7000
Website: www.aurora-restaurant.co.uk

Cooking 4 | Modern European | £59

Although no longer a part of the Conran group, one visitor described the Aurora dining room of this large hotel as 'classic Conran'. The new management have kept the suite of restaurants at the hotel – Miyabi's Japanese and Fishmarket's seafood options, via Terminus (an all-day brasserie) to the pubby, oak-panelled George – and Aurora is the jewel in the crown. Allan Pickett is still in charge of the kitchen, and his menu kicks off with tian of crab with chilli, coriander and crab bonbons, or a risotto of parsley with sautéed snails and crispy pancetta. Dishes show sound technique, including well-made squeaky-fresh fillet of sea bass with truffled celeriac purée and a Burgundy jus, and a slow-braised daube of beef. Fine presentation has characterised desserts such as chocolate fondant with five-spice ice cream. The wine list is full of the big names, but doesn't ignore the lower end of the spectrum. Prices start at £15, with an impressive 20 or so available by the glass.

Chef: Allan Pickett Proprietor: Hyatt International Open: Mon to Fri 12 to 2.30, 6.45 to 10 Closed: 22 Dec to 2 Jan, bank hols Meals: alc (main courses £16.50 to £24). Set L £23.50 (2 courses) to £28, Set L 12 to 2 and D 6.45 to 9 £50 to £75 (inc wine). Bar menu available Service: 12.5% (optional) Cards: Amex, Delta, Diners, Maestro, MasterCard, Visa Details: 100 seats. Vegetarian meals. Wheelchair access (also WC). Music. No mobile phones Accommodation: 267 rooms Tube: Liverpool Street

MAP 13

Great Nepalese ▢AR

48 Eversholt Street, NW1 1DA
Tel: (020) 7388 6737

Anyone feeling hungry while waiting for a train from Euston could do a lot worse than a meal at this long-running family restaurant just a couple of minutes' walk away. As well as the usual curry house staples, the menu features a range of more interesting Nepalese specialities, with starters including masco-bara (deep-fried lentil pancakes with curry sauce; £3.95) and haku choyala (spicy barbecued mutton; £4.25), and main courses including hariyo hash (duck breast with mint, coconut and cream sauce; £11.95) and pork bhutuwa (with spices and green herbs; £6.95). Drink Nepalese Gurkha beer, lassi or house wine (£9.50). Open all week.

MAP 12

The Green

58–60 East Dulwich Road, SE22 9AX
Tel: (020) 7732 7575
Website: www.greenbar.co.uk

Cooking 2 | Modern European | £39

The Green ticks all the right boxes when it comes to the brasserie experience, with bare wooden tables, spotlighting, and Rothko-inspired block-colour art; regular jazz and art evenings help keep the attention of locals. Chicken liver terrine, or salmon, ginger and coriander fishcakes will start things off, followed by whole roast sea bass with olives, peppers, aubergines and courgettes, or roast ostrich fillet with sauce bordelaise. Breakfast is served from 10 to noon, and all-day bar snacks are also available. The fairly priced wine list is arranged by style, starting at £10.95, and around 20 are offered by the glass.

Chef: Damien Gillespie **Proprietor:** Robert Benyayer **Open:** all week 12 to 3.30, 6 to 11 **Closed:** 30 Dec, 1 and 2 Jan **Meals:** alc (main courses £10 to £17.50). Set L £8.50 (2 courses) to £11.50 **Service:** 10% (optional) **Cards:** Amex, Delta, Maestro, MasterCard, Visa **Details:** 110 seats. 30 seats outside. Vegetarian meals. Children's helpings. No smoking in 1 dining room. Wheelchair access (also WC). Music

MAP 13

Green & Red
NEW ENTRY

51 Bethnal Green Road, E1 6LA
Tel: (020) 7749 9670
Website: www.greenred.co.uk

Cooking 3 | Mexican | £35

The cooking at Green & Red (the colours of the Mexican flag) is inspired by the cantinas and restaurants of Jalisco, the home of tequila. The dining room has a relaxed feel, with plank flooring and heavy wooden tables, and linen drapes over the floor-to-ceiling windows softening the overall effect. Bar snacks include corn tortilla chips, gua-

camole, albondigas (pork and beef meatballs in tomato and chilli sauce) and chorizo pan-fried with shallots and coriander, while the main menu has antojitos (small dishes), platos fuertes (mains) and algo mas (sides). Among starters, served in earthenware pots, have been chargrilled shrimps with a roast cherry tomato and haberno salsa, and ceviche of sea bass with pomegranate seeds, Serrano chilli and coriander. Succulent whole gilt-head bream is baked in a banana leaf, which is then opened and a tomato and chilli salsa poured on, while roast belly pork with crackling is 'deliciously flavoured' with chilli and orange salt and served with avocado salsa and wedges of lime. Churros come with a deep bowl of creamy chocolate dipping sauce to finish. Young staff are 'jolly', and South American wines start at £12.50, and there's a great range of cocktails and beers too.

Chef: Alberto Figueroa **Proprietors:** Will Beckett, Henry Besant, Huw Gott and Dre Masso **Open:** Sat and Sun L 12 to 5, all week D 6 to 11 **Closed:** 25 to 30 Dec **Meals:** alc (main courses L £4.50 to £6.50, D £9.50 to £14.50). Bar menu available **Service:** 12.5% (optional) **Cards:** Amex, Delta, Maestro, MasterCard, Visa **Details:** 65 seats. 15 seats outside. Vegetarian meals. Wheelchair access (also WC). Music. Air-conditioned **Tube:** Liverpool Street

MAP 15

Greenhouse

27A Hays Mews, W1J 5NY
Tel: (020) 7499 3331
Website: www.greenhouserestaurant.co.uk

Cooking 6 | Modern European | £88

The Greenhouse has undergone a fair number of transformations and makeovers in recent years, both in the kitchen and out front. It is still reached by means of a walkway from a Mayfair mews, and the dining room is looking as smart as it has ever done, with stylish modern furniture by Philippe Hurel, and well-dressed, expert staff. Antonin Bonnet is the latest incumbent at the stoves. He is a Lyonnais with a CV to impress, having done stints at three-star Michelin addresses in France. Given evident carte blanche to source what he wants, the auspices look good, and first impressions have certainly not lacked for excitement. A brace of excellent Scottish scallops with sweet onion and apple was a great curtain-raiser at a spring dinner, and a main course of sea bass delivered a top-quality raw material served with good tapenade and a smear of vanilla sauce.

The seven-course tasting menu may be a good way to test the new boy's skills. It began one evening with a sublime sea urchin and mussel soup, served in a vivid Thai red curry broth poured on at the table, and made its way eventually on to Limousin veal assertively partnered by a gratin of bitter praline and salsify and an intriguing dressing of star anise and hazelnut. Pre-desserts involving chocolate, caramel and salt are very much the mood of the moment, here as elsewhere, and the oddball ice creams that accompany many desserts may equally well be flavoured with peppercorns or basil as with rum and raisin. Or you might have a go with pain d'épice, served with an 'essence' of quince, lemon and liquorice. The vast and impressive wine list seems to go on forever, and there is plenty to catch the eye along the way, particularly among the top-end Bordeaux and Burgundy. It all starts at £26, and then it is onwards and upwards.

Chef: Antonin Bonnet **Proprietor:** Marc Group **Open:** Mon to Fri L 12 to 2.30, Mon to Sat D 6.45 to 11 **Closed:** Christmas, 31 Dec, bank hols **Meals:** Set L £30 (2 courses) to £85, Set D £60 to £85 **Service:** 12.5% (optional) **Cards:** Amex, Delta, Diners, Maestro, MasterCard, Visa **Details:** 60 seats. Vegetarian meals. Wheelchair access (also WC). No music. Air-conditioned **Tube:** Green Park

MAP 12

Greyhound

136 Battersea High Street, SW11 3JR
Tel: (020) 7978 7021
Website: www.thegreyhoundatbattersea.co.uk

Cooking 3 | Modern British-Plus | £44

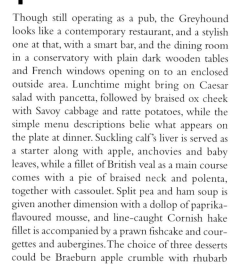

Though still operating as a pub, the Greyhound looks like a contemporary restaurant, and a stylish one at that, with a smart bar, and the dining room in a conservatory with plain dark wooden tables and French windows opening on to an enclosed outside area. Lunchtime might bring on Caesar salad with pancetta, followed by braised ox cheek with Savoy cabbage and ratte potatoes, while the simple menu descriptions belie what appears on the plate at dinner. Suckling calf's liver is served as a starter along with apple, anchovies and baby leaves, while a fillet of British veal as a main course comes with a pie of braised neck and polenta, together with cassoulet. Split pea and ham soup is given another dimension with a dollop of paprika-flavoured mousse, and line-caught Cornish hake fillet is accompanied by a prawn fishcake and cour-gettes and aubergines. The choice of three desserts could be Braeburn apple crumble with rhubarb

and lemon-curd ice cream, with Neal's Yard cheeses a savoury alternative.

The pub strives to make wine accessible ('at the end of the day it's only grape juice,' proclaims the list) and runs a wine club for buffs (membership free). In light of this, the inspired list caters for every price bracket, with house selections starting at £13.

Chef: Marco Tori **Proprietors:** Mark and Sharlyn van der Goot **Open:** Tue to Sun L 12 to 2.45 (3.30 Sun), Tue to Sat D 7 to 10 **Closed:** Christmas and New Year **Meals:** alc L (main courses £7 to £12). Set D £27 (2 courses) to £31. Bar menu available **Service:** 12.5% **Cards:** Amex, Delta, Maestro, MasterCard, Visa **Details:** 55 seats. 30 seats outside. Vegetarian meals. No children under 13 at D. Children's helpings. No smoking in dining room. Wheelchair access (also WC). Music. No mobile phones

MAP 15

Guinea Grill **NEW ENTRY**

30 Bruton Place, W1J 6NL
Tel: (020) 7409 1728
Website: www.theguinea.co.uk

Cooking 2 | Modern British | £65

Situated in a traditional-looking pub in a moneyed Mayfair street, the Grill has a separate entrance, and you are led through a narrow corridor, past the kitchen to a low-ceilinged room. The décor pays no concession to modernity, but there are interesting paintings and the tables are set with quality linen. The menu is a mixture of pub grub and gentleman's club dishes, with sections headed 'pies' and 'grills'. Sourdough bread and pitted olives are an encouraging start, followed perhaps by grilled goats' cheese with a tomato and pine-nut salad, an assertive combination of tastes and textures, or Cornish crab tart. At main-course stage, traditional dishes of pink and tender chump of lamb, accompanied by garlic, roast aubergine and a rich Madeira sauce, or steak and mushroom pie in suet pastry 'robustly flavoured' with herbs and spinach may share the billing with something more modern such as pan-fried red mullet with saffron-braised fennel and Jersey Royals. Puddings were a disappointment at inspection. Prices on the wine list, starting at £15, reflect the West End location, with wines by the glass costing £3.50 to £9.50.

Chef: Mark Newbury **Proprietor:** Young's Brewery **Open:** Mon to Fri L 12.30 to 2.30, Mon to Sat D 6 to 10.30 **Closed:** 24 to 26 and 31 Dec, 1 Jan **Meals:** alc (main courses £12.50 to £34). Bar menu available **Service:** 12.5% **Cards:** Amex, Delta, Diners, Maestro, MasterCard, Visa **Details:** 28 seats. Vegetarian meals. No children. No smoking in 1 dining room. No music. Air-conditioned

MAP 12

Gun

27 Coldharbour, E14 9NS
Tel: (020) 7515 5222
Website: www.thegundocklands.com

Cooking 3 | Modern British | £53

With excellent views from the terrace across the Thames to the Millennium Dome, this early-eighteenth-century pub, originally used by dockers and boatmen, has had a sympathetic makeover, creating a quietly stylish venue which places food at the top of the agenda. The dining room is bright, with white walls and tablecloths, a smattering of maritime artefacts, and dark wooden floors to match the splendid bar. The food aims high, highlighting chef Scott Wade's interesting combinations and above-par presentations. Potted duck with pear chutney and sage brioche, roast halibut steak with curly kale, pancetta and oyster sauce, then Sharrow Bay sticky toffee pudding with vanilla ice cream come together on the dinner menu. Neal's Yard British cheeses with green tomato chutney make a good savoury ending. The wine list, arranged stylistically, is comprehensive but pricey, although Spanish red and Argentinian white kick off at £12.50. Under the same ownership as the White Swan (see entry).

Chef: Scott Wade Proprietors: Tom and Ed Martin Open: Mon to Fri 12 to 3, 6 to 10.30, Sat and Sun 10.30 to 4.30, 6 to 10.30 (9.30 Sun) Closed: 26 Dec Meals: alc (main courses £11 to £21). Bar menu available Service: 12.5% (optional) Cards: Amex, Delta, Maestro, MasterCard, Visa Details: 85 seats. 30 seats outside. Vegetarian meals. Children's helpings. Wheelchair access (also WC). Music. Air-conditioned Tube: Canary Wharf DLR

MAP 14

Haandi

136 Brompton Road, SW3 1HY
Tel: (020) 7823 7373
Website: www.haandi-restaurants.com

Cooking 4 | Indian | £33

Part of a chain with branches in Edgware, Nairobi and Kampala, this upmarket Kensington restaurant gets its name from a type of Indian cooking vessel with a concave bottom. These vessels are much in evidence here, used in theatrical style in the kitchen – all the stirring and flambéing can be viewed

through 'an ingenious curved window' – and in miniature form as serving dishes. Of more interest is the food itself, a mix of traditional and contemporary dishes executed with flair by an experienced and accomplished kitchen. To start there are dakshin vadas (crisp fried lentil cakes with coconut chutney) and bhindi and onion bhajis, while among main courses, tandoori dishes are to the fore, including grilled lobster served in the shell with garlic tomato chutney, minced chicken breast kebab with mint and spices, or lamb chops in a ginger-flavoured yoghurt marinade. Non-tandoori dishes feature Goan-style haddock, and roast chicken in a rich, spicy tomato gravy, while vegetarian options include baked potatoes stuffed with cashews, paneer and sultanas. Finish perhaps with carrot halva or gulab jamun. House wine £12.95. The second London branch is at 301–303 Hale Lane, Edgware; tel: (020) 8905 4433.

Chef: Ratan Singh Proprietor: Haandi Restaurants Ltd Open: all week 12 to 3, 5.30 to 11 (11.30 Fri and Sat) Closed: 25 Dec Meals: alc (main courses £6 to £13). Set L £5.95 to £13.95 (all 1 course). Light lunch menu available Service: 12.5% (optional) Cards: Amex, Delta, Diners, Maestro, MasterCard, Visa Details: 94 seats. 4 seats outside. Vegetarian meals. No-smoking area. Music. Air-conditioned Tube: Knightsbridge

MAP 15

Hakkasan

8 Hanway Place, W1T 1HD
Tel: (020) 7927 7000
Email: mail@hakkasan.com

Cooking 5 | Chinese | £102

The elder of Alan Yau's two siblings (see Yauatcha) opened in 2001, immediately setting a radical new tone for Eastern dining in London. Against a slinky backdrop of dark panelling, with interrogation spotlights hovering over each table, and as many as four door staff to look you up and down, the cooking is nominally Cantonese, although a distant cry from the Wardour Street formula.

A full dim sum menu is offered at lunchtime, but the dim sum platters on the carte are reliably superb, the dumplings of scallops, mixed vegetables and prawns all verging on perfection. Among other dishes, a single scallop in black-bean sauce is achingly tender, the various ways with silver cod (fried with XO sauce or roasted with champagne and Chinese honey) can be revelatory, and nor are vegetable dishes mere makeweights but instead explode with flavour, as in steamed pak choi with garlic, or choi sum with mushrooms and chilli. While not exactly pan-Asian, the food does make the occasional Japanese or Thai foray, and the star of one visit was Assam prawns, cooked with okra and aubergine in a 'beautifully judged' sauce of tamarind and chilli. If you're in for a splash and give 24 hours' notice, a whole new world opens up, including Peking duck with beluga caviar and a dish called 'Monk Jumps over the Wall', which has probably gained rather than lost in translation. Culturally indeterminate desserts – fennel crème brûlée with jelly, grapefruit and a sesame tuile – add the final grace notes. Drinking is expensive, but expansive too, with cocktails, single malts and Japanese whiskies to go at, as well as a thoroughly opulent wine list opening at around £25 before heading for the stars.

Chef: Tong Chee Hwee Proprietor: Alan Yau Open: all week 12 to 3.30 (4.45 Sat and Sun), 6 to 11.30 (12 Wed to Sat) Closed: 24 and 25 Dec Meals: alc (main courses £12.50 to £68). Set L £30 to £50, Set D £50 to £70 Service: 13% Cards: Amex, Delta, Maestro, MasterCard, Visa Details: 200 seats. Vegetarian meals. Wheelchair access (also WC). Music. Air-conditioned Tube: Tottenham Court Road

MAP 13

The House

63–69 Canonbury Road, N1 2DG
Tel: (020) 7704 7410
Website: www.inthehouse.biz

Cooking 2 | Modern European | £46

A mainly young, local crowd frequent this red-brick pub, which offers good food in appropriately chilled-out surroundings. Go through the semi-circular bar area into the main dining room, which will probably be packed pretty tightly. The House is a popular weekend brunch destination, and the evening menu continues to gain approval from GFG readers: crab hash cakes with wilted rocket and lemon or red onion and goats' cheese tarte Tatin preceding well-crafted main courses like pan-fried brill with braised chickpeas, or roast corn-fed chicken served with potato confit, baby leeks and wild mushroom cream. Check out the blackboard for daily specials, and there is also an 'express' lunch menu. Finish with vanilla-poached pear with hot chocolate sauce and roast cardamom shortbread. Staff are friendly, and the wine list, arranged by style, opens at £13. Related to The Bull, 13 North Hill, Highgate, N6 4AB; tel: (0845) 456 5033.

Chef: Rob Arnott Proprietor: Barnaby Meredith Open: Tue to Sun L 12 to 2.30 (3.30 Sat and Sun), all week D 6 (6.30 Sat and Sun) to 10.30 Closed: Christmas Meals: alc (main courses £9.50 to £22.50). Set L Tue to Fri £14.95 (2 courses) to £17.95 Service: 12.5% (optional) Cards: Delta, Maestro, MasterCard, Visa Details: 80 seats. 40 seats outside. Vegetarian meals. Children's helpings. No-smoking area. Wheelchair access (also WC). Music Tube: Highbury & Islington

MAP 14

Hunan

51 Pimlico Road, SW1W 8NE
Tel: (020) 7730 5712
Email: hunan.peng@btopenworld.com

Cooking 3 | Chinese | £49

There's a distinctly modest air about this intimate family-run restaurant, set among chic furniture shops on an affluent main road. Exterior décor is plain; inside it is neutral (some would say nondescript), livened up slightly with pictures of ancient Chinese people in ceremonial dress. The aim of the kitchen is to serve rustic home-cooked dishes, and the preferred mode of eating here is the tasting menu, in which a long succession of small dishes (perhaps as many as 20, with the price of the meal a mystery until the bill is presented) are brought to the table one after the other. If you prefer to know what to expect (both financially and gastronomically), opt for the carte, which typically offers pan-fried spicy frogs' legs ('plump' and 'cooked to perfection') topped with diced water chestnut, camphor tea-smoked duck with pancakes, spicy braised aubergine, griddled stuffed prawns in ginger and onion sauce, and steamed whole sea bass in toasted sesame oil dressing. Finish perhaps with glazed toffee bananas. House wine is £14.

Chef/Proprietor: Michael Peng Open: Mon to Sat 12.30 to 2, 6.30 to 11 Closed: 25 Dec, bank hols Meals: alc L (main courses £7 to £32). Set L £29.80, Set D from £32.80. Cover 80p Service: 12.5% (optional) Cards: Amex, Delta, Diners, Maestro, MasterCard, Visa Details: 44 seats. Vegetarian meals. No smoking in 1 dining room. Music. Air-conditioned Tube: Sloane Square

The price given next to the cooking score is based on the cost of a typical three-course dinner for one person, including coffee, house wine and service.

MAP 13

Huong Viet

An-Viet House, 12–14 Englefield Road, N1 4LS
Tel: (020) 7249 0877

Cooking 1 | Vietnamese | £24

This unassuming venue is essentially the canteen for the Vietnamese community centre in which it is housed. It is a popular spot, both with Vietnamese and others, who come for authentic cooking at exceptionally fair prices. For starters, the wide-ranging menu offers numerous variations on the traditional hot-and-sour canh and noodle-based pho soups, along with Vietnamese pancakes filled with chicken and prawns or tofu, and items like fish cakes or squid stuffed with prawn and pork. Among main courses, options include charcoal-grilled specialities such as pork cutlets with rice and pickles, or lamb with galangal, as well as plenty of other meat and fish dishes ranging from chicken with cashew nuts to kingfish with mango. Finish perhaps with banana fritters. Wines from £7.45.

Chef: Thanh Vu Proprietor: Diep Bui Open: Mon to Sat 12 to 3.30 (4 Sat), 5.30 to 11 Closed: Christmas, New Year Meals: alc (main courses £4 to £7). Set L £6 (2 courses) Service: 10% Cards: MasterCard, Visa Details: 60 seats. Vegetarian meals. Wheelchair access (also WC). Music. Air-conditioned Tube: Angel, Liverpool Street

MAP 15

Ikkyu

67A Tottenham Court Road, W1P 9PA
Tel: (020) 7636 9280

Near Goodge Street, this basement café offers good-value Japanese food, with sushi and sashimi a big draw. Sushi see the likes of mackerel oshi (£5.70) and conger oshi (£7.50), while sashimi take in a multitude of fish, from octopus (£6.60) through to cuttlefish with fermented soya beans (£6.30). Other plates include tofu steak (£3.70), grilled aubergine (£3.40), and salmon roe with grated white radish (£4.50). You can hand-roll your own sushi set for £35. Set lunches come with rice and miso soup (from £4.90). Closed Sat and Sun L.

MAP 15

Incognico

117 Shaftesbury Avenue, WC2H 8AD
Tel: (020) 7836 8866
Website: www.incognico.com

Cooking 4 | Modern European | £51

The sombre brown tones of this easy-to-walk-past restaurant effectively recreate the look of a classic French brasserie, and the well-practised menu soothes with a combination of the familiar (salt cod with aïoli), the modern (home-made tagliolini with fresh crab and chilli) and luxuries (foie gras with orange). Main courses offer plenty of choice, from roast sea bass served with braised endive and citrus fruit, and organic salmon fillet with asparagus and tarragon butter, to honey-roasted breast of duck with pomme fondant, and veal Milanese. Desserts such as chocolate pannacotta with griottines or pear and almond tart provide a comforting finish. The general consensus is that the kitchen delivers food that is 'reliable' and 'well done', though reporters have been disappointed by indifferent service this year. Wines can help bump up the bill: prices start at £16.50 for house vins de pays, although most bottles are over £25, and there are nine by the glass from £4.50.

Chef: Dafydd Watkin Proprietor: Chez Nico Restaurants Ltd Open: Mon to Sat 12 to 3, 5.30 to 11 Meals: alc (main courses £12.50 to £18.50) Service: 12.5% (optional) Cards: Amex, Delta, Diners, Maestro, MasterCard, Visa Details: 85 seats. Vegetarian meals. No smoking. Music. Air-conditioned Tube: Leicester Square

MAP 15

Inn the Park

St James's Park, SW1A 2BJ
Tel: (020) 7451 9999
Website: www.innthepark.com

NEW CHEF | Modern British | £47

Overlooking the lake at St James's Park, the contemporary décor and uncomplicated menu are a breath of fresh air for this particular London park. Eating on the terrace is a bonus. There's been a change of chef but the place is still open from breakfast (think eggs Florentine, cinnamon pancakes) through to the dinner carte, which is only slightly different from their set lunch menu. Start with a poached pear, walnut and Garstang Blue salad, or classic prawn cocktail, followed by wild halibut steak with broad beans, peas and herbs or even warm grilled Goosnargh chicken with spring greens and a tomato dressing. Desserts might be plum crumble or rice pudding with Seville orange marmalade. The short global wine list starts at £14.50 for house Shiraz. Reports please.

Chef: Scott Wade **Proprietor:** Gruppo Ltd **Open:** all week L 12 to 3 (4 Sat and Sun), D 5 to 10.30 **Meals:** alc (main courses £10.50 to £22.50). Set L Sat and Sun £19.50 (2 courses) to £24.50. Bar menu available 5pm onwards **Service:** 10% (optional) **Cards:** Amex, Delta, Diners, Maestro, MasterCard, Visa **Details:** 100 seats. 70 seats outside. Vegetarian meals. Children's helpings. No smoking. Wheelchair access (also WC). Occasional music. **Tube:** St James's Park

MAP 12

Inside

19 Greenwich South Street, SE10 8NW
Tel: (020) 8265 5060
Website: www.insiderestaurant.co.uk

Cooking 1 | Modern British | **£38**

This friendly neighbourhood restaurant has a well-chosen bistro menu and a relaxed atmosphere. Those looking for a decent Saturday brunch are well catered for, while the carte might kick off with sautéed calves' sweetbreads with pea and mint purée, or morel and wild garlic leaf risotto. Main courses deliver pan-fried sea bass with crème fraîche mash, baked aubergine and a basil and tomato coulis, or roast breast of guinea fowl with a sausage and thyme jus. There are plenty of vegetarian choices, and desserts can be as comforting as apple crumble with custard or as modern as cardamom crème brûlée with coconut biscotti. France and the New World dominate the wine list, which opens at £11.95.

Chefs: Guy Awford and Brian Sargeant **Proprietors:** Guy Awford, Pavlin Petrov and Brian Sargeant **Open:** Tue to Sun L 12 (11 Sat) to 2.30 (3 Sun), Tue to Sat D 6.30 to 11 **Meals:** alc exc Sun L (main courses £11 to £17). Set L Tue to Fri £11.95 (2 courses) to £19.95, Set L Sat £15.95 (2 courses) to £19.95, Set L Sun £16.95 (2 courses) to £19.95, Set D 6.30 to 8 £15.95 (2 courses) to £19.95. Sat brunch menu available **Service:** not inc **Cards:** Amex, Delta, Maestro, MasterCard, Visa **Details:** 40 seats. Vegetarian meals. Children's helpings. No smoking. Wheelchair access (also WC). Music. Air-conditioned **Tube:** Greenwich DLR

MAP 12

Istanbul Iskembecisi

9 Stoke Newington Road, N16 8BH
Tel: (020) 7254 7291

This is an authentic and traditional family-run Turkish restaurant. The long menu opens with a wide choice of meze, both vegetarian and meat, ranging from imam bayaldi (£3.75) to arnavut cigeri sicak (Albanian-style liver and onion; £3.50). Soups include the eponymous iskembe (tripe; £3), while main courses encompass a range of chargrilled meats and kebabs (chicken shish £8.50; lamb chops £9.50), served with rice and salad, as well as dishes such as kuzu tandir (roast lamb with potatoes, mushrooms and herbs; £9.50) and vegetarian options including moussaka (£8). House French is £10. Open all week.

MAP 14

Itsu

118 Draycott Avenue, SW3 3AE
Tel: (020) 7590 2400
103 Wardour Street, W1F 0UQ
Tel: (020) 7479 4790
Website: www.itsu.co.uk

Cooking 2 | Japanese | **£28**

The Itsu brand continues to grow, and it is possible to get their modern blend of traditional and contemporary sushi delivered all over London. There are shops, too, as well as three restaurants. Sitting at the kaiten is now a familiar activity for Londoners, and the combination of cool design and fresh, healthy food is a winning one. Press the buzzer when you need to attract the staff for drinks or cooked dishes such as grilled eel sushi, spicy dumplings, or a prawn Asian pesto hand roll, otherwise it's a case of grabbing whatever takes your fancy as it passes by. The seafood is first-rate, chilli salmon nigiri, for example, or tuna sashimi, while desserts are a limited range including coconut chocolate shot. Drink green tea and Asahi beer, or choose from the modest selection of wines from £15.95.

Proprietors: Julian Metcalfe and Clive Schlee **Open:** Mon to Sat 12 to 11 (Sun 10) **Closed:** 25 Dec **Meals:** alc (main courses £3.50 to £20) **Service:** not inc **Cards:** Amex, Delta, Maestro, MasterCard, Visa **Details:** 80 seats. Vegetarian meals. No smoking. Music. Air-conditioned **Tube:** Piccadilly Circus (Soho), South Kensington (Chelsea)

MAP 15

Ivy

1–5 West Street, WC2H 9NQ
Tel: (020) 7836 4751

Cooking 4 | Modern British | £56

Queues for mere mortals to get in to this celeb hangout are longer than ever. 'A call in mid-February evinced an offer of a mid-evening table on 13 September at the earliest. We settled for a late Saturday lunch', ran one report of a meal taken in early April. That visitor found it quite gratifying to find a restaurant that brings serious kitchen resources to bear upon such dishes as shepherd's pie and fish and chips, and concluded that, on the whole, results are good. Eggs Benedict are declared 'as classy as ever', a hamburger uses top-quality beef, and the same praise extends to tender tempura squid, and slow-roast pork belly with black pudding, caramelised apple, grain mustard sauce and parsnip mash. The service is as slick and unintrusive as you would expect. You will struggle to find much under £25 worth drinking, despite a good range. A Maipo Valley Sauvignon Blanc kicks off at £15.25, followed by a Bardolino at £19.75.

Chef: Alan Bird   Proprietor: Caprice Holdings Ltd   Open: all week 12 to 3.30 (4 Sun), 5 to 12   Closed: 25 and 26 Dec, 1 Jan, Aug bank hol   Meals: alc (main courses £12 to £35). Set L Sat and Sun £21.50. Cover £2   Service: not inc   Cards: Amex, Delta, Diners, Maestro, MasterCard, Visa   Details: 100 seats. Vegetarian meals. Children's helpings. Wheelchair access (not WC). No music. No mobile phones. Air-conditioned   Tube: Leicester Square

MAP 13

Iznik

19 Highbury Park, N5 1QJ
Tel: (020) 7704 8099

Cooking 2 | Turkish | £25

The décor at this friendly Turkish restaurant – glass lamps, decorative tiling and a plethora of candles – sets the tone and it fits well into this corner of north London. The menu runs the gamut of Turkish cuisine, with plenty of vegetarian options; hummus, falafel, kofta and kebabs are naturally covered, but step off the beaten track and starters could be lightly spiced meatballs with onions, or even courgette and feta cheese fritters. Main course options might be Turkish dumplings (manti) or vine leaves stuffed with ground lamb, rice and onions, or maybe lamb knuckles baked in tomato sauce with vermicelli. Desserts are a wonderfully sweet and sticky affair, so go for baklava or perhaps a traditional 'asure', a dried fruit compote with pomegranates and pears. Alongside Turkish tea the wine list is short but good value, starting at £9.95 for house selections.

Chefs/Proprietors: Adem and Pirlanta Oner   Open: all week 10am to midnight   Closed: 25 and 26 Dec, 1 Jan   Meals: alc (main courses £6 to £12.50)   Service: 10%   Cards: Delta, Maestro, MasterCard, Visa   Details: 80 seats. Vegetarian meals. Music. Air-conditioned   Tube: Highbury & Islington

MAP 15

J. Sheekey

28–32 St Martin's Court, WC2N 4AL
Tel: (020) 7240 2565
Website: www.j-sheekey.co.uk

Cooking 4 | British Seafood | £53

This long-established London restaurant has been through a few owners since it first opened over one hundred years ago, but the ethos remains the same: fresh seafood, served in an approachable, comforting manner. Traditional dishes such as jellied eels and steamed Devon cockles make an appearance, but you can take a more adventurous journey if you like: chargrilled razor clams to start, perhaps, or endive salad with Arbroath smokies and soft-boiled quail's eggs. Main courses run to roasted whole gilthead bream, or grilled monkfish and tiger prawns served with Sardinian couscous and a spicy tomato sauce. Daily specials see the likes of grilled Loch Linnhe salmon with spring vegetables. Griddled tiger prawns, Mersea pearl oysters and dressed crab demonstrate that simplicity plays its part, including the three different types of caviar served with blinis and sour cream. End with double chocolate pudding soufflé or spotted dick. The wine list is a rangy global affair, starting at £15, with prices rising steeply after that, although there are 19 choices by the glass from £4.

Chef: Martin Dickinson   Proprietor: Caprice Holdings   Open: all week 12 to 3 (3.30 Sun), 5.30 (6 Sun) to 12   Closed: 25 and 26 Dec, 1 Jan, Aug bank hol   Meals: alc (main courses £11 to £35). Set L Sat and Sun £21.50   Service: not inc   Cards: Amex, Delta, Diners, Maestro, MasterCard, Visa   Details: 106 seats. Vegetarian meals. Children's helpings. No cigars/pipes. Wheelchair access (not WC). No music. No mobile phones. Air-conditioned   Tube: Leicester Square

MAP 13

K10

20 Copthall Avenue, EC2R 7DN
Tel: (020) 7562 8511
Website: www.K10.net

Cooking 2 | Japanese | £28

This simply decorated basement dining room gets exceptionally busy at lunchtimes, when it serves hordes of hungry City workers who know a good deal when they see one. The kaiten from which the restaurant gets its punning name snakes around the room bearing plates of sushi and sashimi, colour-coded for price, which are frequently replenished by a team of busy chefs. Salmon, fatty tuna and swordfish are typical, but there are also cooked dishes such as miso soup, chicken teriyaki, peppered tuna tataki and Japanese pork curry, and desserts of green tea crème with plum coulis or chocolate and coconut mousse. Drink Japanese beer, warm or cold saké, or wines from £12.95.

> **Proprietor:** K10 Ltd **Open:** Mon to Fri L only 12 to 3 **Closed:** 22 Dec to 3 Jan, bank hols **Meals:** plate prices £1.50 to £6 **Service:** not inc **Cards:** Amex, Delta, Diners, Maestro, MasterCard, Visa **Details:** 70 seats. Vegetarian meals. No smoking. Music. Air-conditioned **Tube:** Moorgate, Liverpool Street, Bank

MAP 12

Kastoori

188 Upper Tooting Road, SW17 7EJ
Tel: (020) 8767 7027

Cooking 3 | Gujarati Vegetarian | £21

Still one of the best vegetarian restaurants in London, this long-running family business continues to provide excellent Gujurati-style home cooking from one year to the next. Décor is plain and simple but the same cannot be said of the food, which is bright and lively. Long-standing favourites among starters include paneer cheese in a rich chilli sauce, and dahi puri, a crisp, fried pastry ball filled with diced potatoes, chickpeas, puffed rice, onions and sweet and sour sauce, and topped with yoghurt sauce. To follow, there are various curries, including cobi bateta (a sweet and spicy dish of cabbage and potato), and speciality dishes inspired by the Thanki family's time in Uganda,

ranging from chilli banana to kasodi (an African variety of corn in coconut milk with peanut sauce). Parathas and chapatis are always fresh and well made, and traditional desserts include ras malai and shrikand. House wine is £8.95.

> **Chef:** Manoj Thanki **Proprietor:** Dinesh Thanki **Open:** Wed to Sun L 12.30 to 2.30, all week D 6 to 10.30 **Closed:** 25 and 26 Dec **Meals:** alc (main courses £4.50 to £6.50) **Service:** not inc **Cards:** MasterCard, Visa **Details:** 82 seats. Vegetarian meals. Children's helpings. Wheelchair access (not WC). Music. Air-conditioned **Tube:** Tooting Broadway

MAP 13

Kasturi   AR

57 Aldgate High Street, EC3N 1AL
Tel: (020) 7480 7402

Indian cooking from the North-West Frontier region is the speciality of this smart restaurant on the fringe of the City. Kebabs and grilled meats are at the heart of the menu, with starters including chargrilled lamb chops with ginger (£5.50) or a vegetarian option such as shikampuri kebab (mashed sweet potato and banana with spices and dill; £3.95), followed perhaps by dahi machli (tilapia fillets with chilli sauce and yoghurt; £8.95) or patiala shahi gosht (£8.95), a lamb dish originally prepared for the Punjabi royal family. House Chilean is £13.95. Closed Sun.

MAP 13

Kensington Place

201–209 Kensington Church Street, W8 7LX
Tel: (020) 7727 3184
Website: www.egami.co.uk

Cooking 5 | Modern British | £53

'Well-oiled and well-established', as one reporter put it, KP continues to turn out good food in a lively (to put it mildly) atmosphere. The large room with its slightly industrial feel, bare tables, close packed, and huge glass windows is hardly cutting edge any more, such have times changed since it opened in 1987. The customers are a loyal bunch, drawn back time and again by an enticing menu and wine list as well as 'extremely efficient' service. Rowley Leigh's menu shows the eternal triangle of France, Italy and Britain as the main influences, is heavy on fish (the restaurant has opened a wet fish shop next door), and has the confidence not to over-describe dishes; the cooking stays just as simple, with the focus on careful preparations. At its best the food achieves crisp, clean flavours, as in a dish of thinly sliced raw tuna topped with wafer-thin discs of turnip and served with soy sauce, fiery wasabi and a sprinkling of chopped chives, and 'succulent and tender' wild boar chop. Timing and seasoning is spot-on, witness black bream served with a gentle marjoram, garlic and olive oil sauce. Among desserts, crème caramel with chocolate financières and rice pudding come in for praise, the latter served with a delicately caramelised top and with soft young rhubarb poached with ginger strips in syrup on the side. Four densely printed pages of wines pack in an inspired international mix at good prices (from £16.50). Twenty-two of them come by the glass.

> **Chef:** Rowley Leigh   **Proprietor:** Place Restaurants Ltd   **Open:** all week 12 to 3.30, 6.30 to 11.15 (11.45 Fri and Sat, 10.15 Sun)   **Meals:** alc (main courses £15.50 to £24.50). Set L Mon to Sat £19.50, Set L Sun £24.50, Set D Mon to Fri £24.50 to £39.50 (with glass of wine)   **Service:** 12.5% (optional)   **Cards:** Amex, Delta, Diners, Maestro, MasterCard, Visa   **Details:** 140 seats. Vegetarian meals. Children's helpings. Wheelchair access (also WC). No music. Air-conditioned   **Tube:** Notting Hill Gate

MAP 15

Kiku

17 Half Moon Street, W1J 7BE
Tel: (020) 7499 4208/4209

Cooking 4 | Japanese | £46

Traditional values are at the core of this long-running Japanese restaurant in Mayfair. A serene atmosphere prevails in the dining room, where natural materials are used – bamboo blinds, stone floors, pale beech furniture and panelling – though it can be busy and is popular with Japanese families. Menus are neatly arranged into sections covering every area of traditional Japanese cooking. Marinated grilled eel and squid might be among cold appetisers, while hot options include deep-fried aubergine with miso. The 'grilled, casseroled and fried' section takes in everything from grilled cod marinated in saké and miso to mackerel casserole with grated white radish; another section comprises sunomono and salads – perhaps sliced jellyfish in light vinaigrette – tofu dishes, soups and hotpots, perhaps thinly sliced beef and vegetables in stock with dipping sauce. Those after a light meal can choose from the assortment of noodle and rice dishes. And there is, of course, a good choice of sushi and sashimi, as well as various all-in-one set meals. House wines are £14.50 but prices rise steeply thereafter.

> **Chefs:** H. Shiraishi, Y. Hattori and T. Nishimura   **Proprietors:** Hisashi and Mariko Taoka   **Open:** Mon to Sat L 12 to 2.30, all week D 6 to 10.15 (5.30 to 9.45 Sun and bank hols)   **Closed:** 25 and 26 Dec, 1 Jan   **Meals:** alc (main courses L £10 to £30, D £14 to £40). Set L £13.50 to £23, Set D £42 to £60   **Service:** 12.5% (optional)   **Cards:** Amex, Delta, Diners, Maestro, MasterCard, Visa   **Details:** 95 seats. Vegetarian meals. Wheelchair access (also WC). Music. Air-conditioned   **Tube:** Green Park

MAP 15

Kulu Kulu Sushi

76 Brewer Street, W1F 9TX
Tel: (020) 7734 7316

Cooking 2 | Japanese | £26

One of the pioneers of kaiten dining in the UK, this tiny Japanese diner has established a strong reputation that attracts large crowds at all times, the clientele ranging from Japanese families to tourists from all over. (Be prepared to sit closer to your neighbour than seems polite and expect a time limit at especially busy periods.) The format is simple: grab plates as they pass by on the conveyor belt loaded with a wide range of sushi and sashimi, typically including sweet shrimp, eel, horse mackerel, whelks and California or salmon and avocado rolls. There are also hot dishes such as agedashi tofu, chicken teriyaki, tempura udon and salmon oroshimi with radish sauce. Help yourself to complimentary green tea or order Japanese beer, saké, or house wine at £12. Branches at 39 Thurloe Place, SW7, tel: (020) 7589 2225, and 51–53 Shelton Street, WC2, tel: (020) 7240 5687.

> **Chef/Proprietor:** K. Toyama   **Open:** Mon to Sat 12 to 2.30 (3.30 Sat), 5 to 10   **Closed:** bank hols   **Meals:** alc (main courses £8.50 to £13)   **Service:** not inc   **Cards:** MasterCard, Visa   **Details:** 30 seats. No smoking. Music. No mobile phones. Air-conditioned   **Tube:** Piccadilly Circus

> This symbol means that it is possible to have a three-course dinner, including coffee, half a bottle of house wine and service, for £30 or less per person.

MAP 13

Lahore Kebab House

2–10 Umberston Street, E1 1PY
Tel: (020) 7488 2551

Cooking 1 | Punjabi | £18

Prizes for decorative style will always elude this basic Punjabi cafeteria, which is spread over two floors on a site just off the busy Commercial Road – conspicuous neon signs mean you can't miss it. White-tiled floors, bare tables and a jolly and relaxed atmosphere are what to expect, along with simple, good-value cooking from a short menu. Seekh kebab, mutton tikka, chicken wings and samosas open proceedings, followed perhaps by karahi chicken, keema curry, or bhindi gosht. Meat dishes are the kitchen's strength, though there are a few vegetarian options including chana masala and sag aloo. Unlicensed, so drink lassi or bring your own. There are branches at King's Cross Holiday Inn, 56 Calthorpe Street, WC1, tel: (020) 7833 9787, and 148–150 Brent Street, NW4, tel: (020) 8203 6904.

> **Chefs:** Mohammad Azeem and Naeem Hussain **Proprietor:** Mohammad Siddique **Open:** all week 12 to 12 **Meals:** alc (main courses £5 to £6.50). **Service:** not inc **Cards:** MasterCard, Visa **Details:** 350 seats. Vegetarian meals. Wheelchair access (not WC). Music. Air-conditioned **Tube:** Aldgate East, Whitechapel

MAP 13

Lansdowne

90 Gloucester Avenue, NW1 8HX
Tel: (020) 7483 0409

Cooking 2 | Modern British | £39

The double act of Amanda Pritchett and Isabel Davies pays dividends at this buzzy north London pub, which offers honest British food with Mediterranean influences. Walk through the lively bar to get to the first-floor restaurant; a relaxed ambience awaits, plus an unfussy and contemporary menu. Organic ribeye steak with chips and béarnaise is a favourite by all accounts, while typical starters are steamed razor clams with chorizo, sherry and braised bean shallots, followed, perhaps, by pan-fried mackerel with warm tahini and walnut dressing, or chargrilled poussin with spiced lentils and basmati rice. Finish with home-made ice cream, or chocolate biscuit cake with

fresh cream. The short but carefully chosen wine list starts at £13.90 for Chilean house, with 14 options by the glass from £3.70.

> **Chef:** Isabel Davies **Proprietor:** Amanda Pritchett **Open:** all week 12.30 to 3, 7 to 10 **Meals:** alc (main courses £9 to £16.50). Set D £20 (2 courses) to £25. Bar snacks available **Service:** 12.5% (optional) **Cards:** Delta, Maestro, MasterCard, Visa **Details:** 160 seats. 30 seats outside. Vegetarian meals. Children's helpings. Occasional music. No mobile phones. Air-conditioned **Tube:** Chalk Farm

MAP 15

Latium   NEW ENTRY

21 Berners Street, W1T 3LP
Tel: (020) 7323 9123
Website: www.latiumrestaurant.com

Cooking 2 | Italian | £42

Opposite the hip Sanderson Hotel, this Italian restaurant is easily identifiable by its blue neon light. The L-shaped dining room is brightened up by some colourful artwork on its white walls, tables are neatly dressed in white linen, chairs are of black wood, and banquettes are black leather. Chef/patron Maurizio Morelli has a good track record, having previously worked at Zafferano (see entry), and here he produces a long menu, including a special page of ravioli dishes. 'Rusticity' marked out a winter dish of curls of Dover sole with earthy lentils and baby leeks, or you could start with tuna carpaccio with puntarelle and blood orange before proceeding to pasta. Those ravioli might come with oxtail and celery sauce, or with mixed mushrooms in a sauce of tomatoes and snails. Generous main courses have included squid stuffed with mussels and prawns, and 'quite delicious' best end of lamb roasted with thyme and served with chicory and mash. Lime parfait encased in a thin film of pineapple is a refreshing finale. Italian wines start at £12, and around half a dozen are served by the glass from £4.

> **Chef:** Maurizio Morelli **Proprietors:** Maurizio Morelli and Claudio Pulze **Open:** Mon to Fri L 12 to 2.45, Mon to Sat D 6 to 10.30 (11 Sat) **Closed:** bank hols **Meals:** Set L and D £24.50 (2 courses) to £32.50 **Service:** 12.5% (optional) **Cards:** Amex, Delta, Diners, Maestro, MasterCard, Visa **Details:** Vegetarian meals. No cigars/pipes in dining room. Wheelchair access (also WC). Music. Air-conditioned

MAP 14

Launceston Place

1A Launceston Place, W8 5RL
Tel: (020) 7937 6912
Website: www.egami.co.uk

Cooking 2 | **Modern British** | **£50**

Launceston Place provides a welcome break from the whirl of activity outside. The décor is classic English dining room, with plenty of space between the tables making it easy to talk without being overheard by your neighbour. The restaurant is celebrating its twentieth birthday this year and presenting the best of modern British cuisine is still a priority. Set lunches and Sunday dinners are available but the à la carte menu pulls together the best of everything. Twice-baked goats' cheese soufflé continues to win praise, or try seared foie gras with mushroom pancake for starters. Main courses could be seared scallops with pea purée and mint vinaigrette or grilled calf's liver with pancetta and crispy onion rings. Desserts are simple but effective with sticky toffee pudding and raspberry panna-cotta leading the charge. The wine list offers a good selection by the glass from £4.50.

Chef: Phillip Reed **Proprietor:** Image Restaurants Plc **Open:** Sun to Fri L 12.30 to 2.30, all week D 6 to 11 (10 Sun) **Closed:** 24 Dec to 4 Jan, 14 to 18 Apr, Aug bank hol weekend **Meals:** alc (not Sun or 14 Feb; main courses £14.50 to £18). Set L £16.50 (2 courses) to £18.50, Set L Sun £24.50, Set D (Mon to Fri 6 to 7) £15.50 (2 courses) to £18.50 (2 courses) **Service:** 12.5% (optional) **Cards:** Amex, Delta, Diners, Maestro, MasterCard, Visa **Details:** 75 seats. Wheelchair access (not WC). No music. Air-conditioned **Tube:** Gloucester Road

MAP 13

Ledbury

127 Ledbury Road, W11 2AQ
Tel: (020) 7792 9090
Website: www.theledbury.com

Cooking 7 | **Modern European** | **£64**

The residents of Notting Hill may have to pay one hell of a premium for their houses, but at least they can walk to this gem of a restaurant, the newest in the stable that includes the Square, Chez Bruce, La Trompette (see entries, London), and the Glasshouse (see entry, Kew). The frontage is hidden away behind a wall of shrubbery, beyond which lurks a surprisingly sizeable outdoor eating space.

Inside, the room achieves an easy balance of sophistication and unpretentious urban chic, with smartly set (and well-spaced) tables in an airy, high-ceilinged room with large windows.

Brett Graham shows his colours early on with impressive bread – bacon and onion brioche, for example – and an amuse-bouche of brandade with cauliflower purée laced with a few shavings of white truffle. Loin of tuna with radish and soy might come as a pre-starter for those not choosing it as a first course, and it's not one to miss out on either way, the fish, seared on the outside, with perfect colour within, given a South-east Asian flavour by judicious use of soy and sprouting shoots. Raviolo of crab is 'bursting at the seams' with white meat, razor clams adding texture, the flavour of lemongrass permeating the velvety sauce with an understated ease; 'superbly judged,' summed up one recipient. Combinations are uniformly successful and inventive: scallops with pumpkin purée or roasted in liquorice, for example.

A main-course squab is roasted with juniper, orange and pepper (the legs given the extra time they require), accompanied by a smear of carrot and verjus purée – 'a lesson in balance' – and joined by a tarte fine of endive, glistening with caramelisation. Fish seems to elicit fewer raptures than meat dishes, but John Dory has been as fresh as can be and comes with a fine combination of caramelised onions and sautéed potatoes in a wine reduction. The kitchen delivers acute technical skills in so many areas it is no surprise that chocolate soufflé with malted milk ice cream should prove a 'perfect' version, served with a small jug of chocolate sauce to pour, self-service, into the centre. Sauternes cream with apricots and vanilla cream was summed up by one diner as 'utterly stupendous and hugely refreshing'.

Service receives plaudits again this year, for its ease, its charm, and general professionalism from top to bottom. The good range of wines by the glass and half-bottle is useful, given that bottle prices start at around £16 and then head upwards at a pace. It's a serious list, though, big on Burgundy and Bordeaux, California showing strongly, and plenty of red Tuscans.

Chef: Brett Graham **Proprietors:** Nigel Platts-Martin and Philip Howard **Open:** all week 12 to 2.45, 6.30 to 10.30 **Closed:** 24 and 25 Dec, 1 Jan, Aug bank hol **Meals:** Set L Mon to Sat £24.50 (2 courses) to £55, Set L Sun £30 to £55, Set D £45 to £55 **Service:** 12.5% (optional) **Cards:** Amex, Delta, Maestro, MasterCard, Visa **Details:** 64 seats. 32 seats outside. Vegetarian meals. No smoking. Wheelchair access (also WC). No music. No mobile phones. Air-conditioned **Tube:** Westbourne Park

MAP 12

Light House Restaurant

75–77 Ridgway, Wimbledon, SW19 4ST
Tel: (020) 8944 6338
Website: www.lighthousewimbledon.com

Cooking 3 | Modern European | £45

True to its name, the Light House projects a 'light, airy and cheerful' ambience via a spacious, contemporary-styled room, the walls adorned with large, colourful modern art. A modern vein also runs through the menus with flavour combinations as forthright as the décor. A starter of well-timed scallops is teamed successfully with a Savoy cabbage and crème fraîche flan, while chicken liver pâté is complemented by 'pungent, sweet' apricot jelly. Confident and accomplished handling of ingredients is evident also in such main courses as pan-fried bream with warm potato salad, samphire, poached egg and salsa verde, or in the token vegetarian option – home-made fettucine with mousserons, pea shoots, garlic leaves, Parmesan cream and crispy herbs. Elsewhere, there might be cassoulet of duck with Toulouse sausage, or slow-roast pork belly with garlic mash. Meals are rounded off with the likes of chocolate St Emilion, or blackcurrant jelly 'with the right degree of wobble' served with clotted cream and madeleine. Service is friendly and accommodating, and the wine list (house starts at £12.50) has a good selection by the glass and is well judged if not great value.

Chef: Chris Casey   Proprietors: Ian Taylor and Bob Finch
Open: all week L 12 to 2.45, Mon to Sat D 6.30 to 10.30
Closed: 25 and 26 Dec, Easter Day   Meals: alc (main courses
£11.50 to £17.50). Set L £14 (2 courses) to £16.50, Set L
Sun £18 (2 courses) to £23   Service: 12.5% (optional)
Cards: Amex, Delta, Maestro, MasterCard, Visa   Details: 75
seats. 15 seats outside. Vegetarian meals. Children's helpings.
No-smoking area. Wheelchair access (also WC). Music   Tube:
Wimbledon

MAP 15

Lindsay House

21 Romilly Street, W1D 5AF
Tel: (020) 7439 0450
Website: www.lindsayhouse.co.uk

Cooking 6 | Modern British | £85

The pleasing ambience of a private dining club (which of course it isn't) contrasts with the hubbub of the Soho grid, in the midst of which Lindsay House sits. Ground-floor and first-floor dining takes place amid glass-fronted cupboards and high mantelpieces, with bare varnished floors strewn with thin rugs, and pastoral paintings in the naïve style adding to the idiosyncratic tone. This is one of the longer central London tenures. Richard Corrigan is approaching his first decade here, and the cooking has changed over the years, the rustic Irish mode of yesteryear now largely supplanted by a touch of refinement. Appetisers appear on spoons, there are foamy sauces and a pre-dessert, and very posh petits fours, but there is still rabbit stuffed with black pudding for those who hanker after the old modes.

An inspection evening started well in fine style with the previously praised roasted scallops on oily chickpea purée, and an appealing Spanish-themed dish of roasted veal sweetbreads with chorizo and shaved Manchego, dressed in sherry vinegar. Fish cookery remains sound as a bell, as was evidenced by the poached turbot that came with cockles and mussels in the shells, with some shredded spring cabbage. A little pan of machine-smooth mashed potato added to the delight. Rhubarb crumble is a very restauranty version, presented in a round timbale on a pool of crème anglaise. Service is almost entirely French, and not always as confident with its *anglais* as is required. We weren't supplied with a wine list this year.

Chef/Proprietor: Richard Corrigan   Open: Mon to Fri L 12 to
2.30, Mon to Sat D 6 to 11   Closed: bank hols L   Meals: Set
L £27 to £56, Set D £56 to £66   Service: 12.5% (optional)
Cards: Amex, Delta, Diners, Maestro, MasterCard, Visa
Details: 50 seats. Vegetarian meals. Children's helpings. No
smoking. No music. Air-conditioned   Tube: Leicester Square

MAP 13

Little Bay

171 Farringdon Road, EC1R 3AL
Tel: (020) 7278 1234

Always buzzing, this restaurant does a roaring trade in good-value food, with starters and puddings £1.95 and main courses £5.95; add £1 to starters and puddings after 7pm and £2 to mains. The modern European menu takes in choux de crab with citrus hollandaise, fillet of salmon with spicy coconut potatoes and a Thai sauce, or chicken breast stuffed with mozzarella and sun-dried tomatoes served with mash, then warm chocolate fondant. Wines from £10.90. Open all week. See www.little-bay.co.uk" for details on the other branches throughout London.

MAP 13

Lobster Pot AR

3 Kennington Lane, SE11 4RG
Tel: (020) 7582 5556

The nautical décor of Hervé Régent's long-running traditional French restaurant is by now as familiar as the house specialities of bouillabaisse (£16.50) and plateau de fruits de mer (£11.50/£22.50). Elsewhere on the menu, expect simple starters such as marinated salmon with cucumber (£8.50), while a generous choice of main courses typically ranges from roast monkfish fillet with Pernod sauce (£16.50) to duck stew with sweet-and-sour sauce and flageolet beans (£15.50). To finish, there might be profiteroles (£5.30). The set lunch menu (£14.50) looks excellent value. Short French wine list from £12.50. Open Tue to Fri L and Tue to Sat D.

MAP 15

Locanda Locatelli

8 Seymour Street, W1H 7JZ
Tel: (020) 7935 9088
Website: www.locandalocatelli.com

Cooking 6 | **Italian** | **£56**

Although accessible through the Churchill Inter-Continental Hotel, this is a quite separate operation. Blinds over the expansive windows shield clients from external view, the place can seem softly lit even at lunchtime, but all are agreed that it is a chic and soothing place. Seating is designed so as to provide seclusion too (try to bag one of the central booth tables), while staff are well versed in both the menus and the niceties of first-class service.

Giorgio Locatelli needs no introduction either to TV cookery watchers or to supporters of modern Italian cuisine. The menus may read quite plainly, but the emphasis is on the ingredients, as is apparent from the initial service of mixed breads with olive oil. Start maybe with thinly sliced veal brawn with lampascioni (Puglian wild onions), parsley and capers for a forthright and generous introductory salvo. Pasta is always well considered, as when garganelli are served lightly sauced with flaked red mullet and black olives, while main-course fish might deliver a stunningly fresh, whopping great chargrilled mackerel with heaps of rocket. Meats include roast rabbit leg with Parma

ham, polenta and radicchio, or perhaps roast pigeon with lentils and garlic purée. With vegetable side orders, the bill can mount up, but save space for desserts such as the formidably labour-intensive chocolate-coated Amaretto mousse on a sponge base, served with a scoop of intense espresso sorbet.

The Italian wine list offers fine testament to those who would doubt the quality of wine-making in that country, with Tuscany and Piedmont particularly outstanding. Prices are not giveaway, but nor are they as terrifying as the location might suggest. House wines are only £12, or £3.50 a glass.

> Chef: Giorgio Locatelli **Proprietors:** Giorgio and Plaxy Locatelli **Open:** all week 12 to 3 (3.15 Sun), 6.45 to 11 (11.30 Fri and Sat, 9.45 Sun) **Closed:** Christmas, New Year, bank hols **Meals:** alc (main courses £12 to £29.50) **Service:** not inc **Cards:** Amex, Delta, Maestro, MasterCard, Visa **Details:** 70 seats. Vegetarian meals. Children's helpings. Wheelchair access (also WC). Music. Air-conditioned **Tube:** Marble Arch

MAP 12

Lock Dining Bar NEW ENTRY

Heron House, Hale Wharf, Ferry Lane, N17 9NF
Tel: (020) 8885 2829
Website: www.thelock-diningbar.com

Cooking 5 | **Modern European** | **£36**

After a slowish start in the gastronomic stakes, the north London district of Tottenham Hale is suddenly off and running. This exciting new venue opened in January 2006, in a site near the Lea Valley reservoirs, between a river lock and the flood relief channel, on the ground floor of a building owned by the College of North East London. It has a bright, open warehouse feel, with white walls and a wood floor, tile-topped tables, and a bar area with huge leather sofas.

The minimal menu descriptions serve notice that Adebola Adeshina's cooking is not about pretension, but about sound ingredients cooked and presented with self-confidence and panache. A bowl of foamed white bean soup swirled with truffle oil is satisfyingly textured and seasoned. Scallops are carefully timed, surmounted on slices of fried plantain, and dressed in a frothy sauce of the corals. Flavours are clean and clear, and dishes know what they are about, as when a generous tranche of halibut is served with braised cabbage and mushy peas, and garnished cleverly with wontons of salmon. Breathtaking depth of flavour is conjured out of pork belly by caramelising it, adding some discs of the crisped skin, and accompanying it with oily mash and creamed leeks. A truffle oil emulsion and deep-fried chives add the final grace notes.

A trio of crème brûlée variations – vanilla, lemongrass and ginger – are flawlessly executed, with thin crusts, and tiny doughnuts to add textural variety. Breads and pasta are made in-house, while service – led by one of the partners, Fabrizio Russo – never misses a beat. Get that Tube map out. N17 is happening. The single-page wine list is divided into Italians, French, 'and the rest'. Prices are peachy-keen throughout, and the selections just on the bright side of serviceable. Sicilian house wines are £13.50.

Chef: Adebola Adeshina **Proprietor:** Black Olive Restaurants Ltd **Open:** Sun to Fri L 12 to 2, Mon to Sat D 6 to 10 **Closed:** 1 and 2 Jan, 1 to 10 Jun **Meals:** alc exc Sun L (main courses £7 to £16). Set L £12 (2 courses). Set L Sun £10. Bar menu available **Service:** 10% (optional) **Cards:** Delta, Maestro, MasterCard, Visa **Details:** 60 seats. 30 seats outside. Car park. Vegetarian meals. Children's helpings. No-smoking area. Wheelchair access (not WC). Music **Tube:** Tottenham Hale

MAP 13

Lola's

The Mall, 359 Upper Street, N1 0PD
Tel: (020) 7359 1932
Website: www.lolas.co.uk

| Cooking 3 | Modern European | £39 |

On the first floor of an old tram shed, with enough glass and daylight to create a conservatory feel, Lola's rates highly for atmosphere – though after a decade the décor is beginning to look a little frayed round the edges. A new chef is at the helm, but the modern European cooking continues in the same vein. The menu revels in Mediterranean materials from aïoli to harissa, and the care in cooking is firmly bolstered by formidable buying skills. A delicate ratatouille, for example, teamed with a strongly flavoured St Tola goats' cheese and a light balsamic reduction makes a good start, or there might be sizzling prawns with parsley, chilli and garlic. Main courses tread a path between tagine of spring lamb well matched with citrus couscous and grilled vegetables, and sea bass served with wilted stinging nettle ('quite similar in texture to spinach') and spicy tomato and basil fondue. Finish with Eton mess, or a plate of British cheeses. Service generally gets the thumbs-up for friendliness and the wine list still looks groundbreaking, from the opening page of eight 'current

house favourites', a dozen wines by the glass and a handful of sherries. The main range offers bottles from both classic and modern regions. Prices, starting at £14.25, are not outlandish.

Chef: John Taylor **Proprietor:** Morfudd Richards **Open:** all week L 12 to 2.30 (3 Sat and Sun), Mon to Sat D 5.30 to 11 **Closed:** 25 and 26 Dec, 1 Jan, Easter Mon **Meals:** alc (main courses £12.50 to £18.50). Set L £16.75, Set D Mon to Thur £19.75. Cover £1.50 **Service:** not inc **Cards:** Amex, Delta, Diners, Maestro, MasterCard, Visa **Details:** 80 seats. Vegetarian meals. Children's helpings. Occasional music. Air-conditioned **Tube:** Angel

MAP 13

Lou Pescadou

241 Old Brompton Road, SW5 9HP
Tel: (020) 7370 1057

| Cooking 3 | Seafood | £45 |

A smattering of tables on the pavement in warm weather brings a bit of bustle to the stretch of Old Brompton Road outside this French seafood restaurant. The interior is adorned with seafaring knick-knacks, such as paintings of French ports and models of boats. Shellfish and mixed seafood platters take centre stage. Starters might be king prawns sautéed with garlic and fennel seeds, or white crabmeat salad, while the main-course fish of the day could be poached smoked haddock with beurre blanc, or roast monkfish with mustard sauce. Meat eaters will be pleased to see corn-fed chicken and rib of beef on the menu. Dessert could be chocolate moelleux with matching ice cream, or apple tart flambé with Calvados. Service is friendly, and the French wine list has been chosen to complement the seafood and is a reasonably priced affair, starting at £11.80.

Chef: Laurent David **Proprietors:** Daniel Chobert and Laurent David **Open:** all week 12 to 3, 7 (6.30 Sat and Sun) to 12 **Meals:** alc (main courses £13.50 to £18). Set L Mon to Fri £10.90, Set L Sat and Sun £14.50, Set D Sat 6.30 to 7.45 and Sun £14.50 **Service:** 15% (optional) **Cards:** Amex, Diners, Maestro, MasterCard, Visa **Details:** 55 seats. 15 seats outside. Vegetarian meals. Children's helpings. No-smoking area. Wheelchair access (not WC). No music **Tube:** Earls Court

 This symbol means that the restaurant has elected to participate in *The Good Food Guide's* £5 voucher scheme (see 'Using The Good Food Guide' for details).

MAP 15

Luciano

NEW ENTRY

72–73 St James's Street, SW1A 1PH
Tel: (020) 7408 1440
Website: www.lucianorestaurant.co.uk

Cooking 4 | Italian | £60

This Marco Pierre White venture, which opened at the end of 2005, is on the site of Madame Prunier's fish restaurant, a notorious London haunt during the first half of the twentieth century. The dining room has a traditional feel in true MPW style, with panelled walls, slate pillars and copious paintings, while crisp white tablecloths, tealights and flowers add to the elegance of it all. The efficient waiting staff are formally attired, while the menu scans the regions of Italy. Chef Marco Corsica shows a light touch, as in a first-course Cornish crab, served in two discrete piles, white meat with basil, brown with mayonnaise, separated by a cone of crisp carta da musica. Tagliatelle with wild boar ragù has been another authentic and enjoyable starter, followed, perhaps, by fillet of beef with caramelised baby onions and ceps, or grilled tuna with cannellini beans and salsa verde. Good timing and excellent raw materials are very much in evidence throughout. Typical Italian desserts include tiramisù. The wine list is mostly Italian. Prices start at £14.95 and rise to three figures for great vintages from great houses.

Chef: Marco Corsica **Proprietor:** Marco Pierre White **Open:** Mon to Sat 12 to 2.45, 5.30 to 11.15 **Closed:** 25 and 26 Dec **Meals:** alc (main courses £12.50 to £26). Set L and D £42 to £45 **Service:** 12.5% **Cards:** Amex, Delta, Diners, Maestro, MasterCard, Visa **Details:** 120 seats. 50 seats outside. Vegetarian meals. Children's helpings. Occasional music. Air-conditioned **Tube:** Green Park

MAP 14

Lundum's

119 Old Brompton Road, SW7 3RN
Tel: (020) 7373 7774
Website: www.lundums.com

Cooking 3 | Danish | £55

Once through the heavy doors, this restaurant 'transports you to another world', which must be Denmark, I suppose. The small sitting area is surrounded by walls of books and the main restaurant itself is impressive, with deep-blue ceilings and large Danish seascapes and landscapes on the walls.

The lunch menu offers herring with egg and caviar, and home-made pork meatballs, plus a selection of open sandwiches (gravad lax and mustard dill sauce, or pan-fried fillet of plaice with rémoulade, for example). Dinner might start with a blue-cheese soufflé on white wine poached pears, or king prawn ravioli, while main courses take in haddock in a crisp potato parcel, or perhaps sundried tomato-crusted fillet of pork on a spinach and potato timbale. Desserts are a high point: try vanilla baked lemon tart with raspberry sorbet, or dark chocolate and caramel truffle. The impressive wine list features around 300 bins, from £16.50, with a primary focus on classic white Burgundy and red Bordeaux.

Chefs: Kay Lundum and Torben Lining **Proprietors:** the Lundum family **Open:** all week L 12 to 4, Mon to Sat D 6 to 11 **Closed:** 22 Dec to 4 Jan **Meals:** alc Mon to Sat (main courses L £13 to £18.50, D £14.50 to £28). Set L Mon to Sat £13.50 (2 courses) to £16.50, Sun buffet brunch £21.50, Set D £19.50 (2 courses) to £24.50 **Service:** 13.5% (optional) **Cards:** Amex, Delta, Diners, Maestro, MasterCard, Visa **Details:** 60 seats. 20 seats outside. Vegetarian meals. No-smoking area. Wheelchair access (also WC). Music. Air-conditioned **Tube:** Gloucester Road, South Kensington

MAP 13

Mandarin Kitchen

14–16 Queensway, W2 3RX
Tel: (020) 7727 9012

Cooking 1 | Chinese | £38

Chinese seafood restaurants are not ten-a-penny in London, which makes Mandarin Kitchen all the more interesting. This stalwart Queensway place has been serving fish and shellfish since 1980, and continues at a pace. Most readers tell of plates of lobster and noodles, with the crustacean appearing as sashimi or plainly steamed, and enlivened with ginger and spring onions, or black bean and green pepper chilli sauce. Otherwise, try baked whole tiger prawns with crispy crushed garlic, or braised sea cucumber with sliced abalone. There are meat dishes such as steamed lotus chicken with eight treasures, or fillet steak in Mandarin sauce. Service mostly copes with the crowds. Wine prices start at £13.50.

Chef: De De Ly **Proprietor:** Steven Cheung **Open:** all week 12 to 11.30 **Meals:** alc (main courses £5.90 to £28). Set L and D £10.90 (2 courses) to £20 **Service:** not inc **Cards:** Amex, Delta, Diners, Maestro, MasterCard, Visa **Details:** 120 seats. Vegetarian meals. Wheelchair access (not WC). No music. Air-conditioned **Tube:** Queensway

MAP 14

Mandarin Oriental Hyde Park, Foliage

66 Knightsbridge, SW1X 7LA
Tel: (020) 7201 3723
Website: www.mandarinoriental.com/london

| Cooking 5 | Modern European | £70 |

The restaurant is reached via a hall of mirrors within this Knightsbridge hotel, which has Harvey Nichols in front of it and Hyde Park behind. All is sleek designer chic, with a leafy theme reflecting the park's visible proximity echoed in the walls and at each *mise en place*. You will need a fair amount of time to read through the à la carte menu, which extends to around nine choices at starter and main, with lengthy descriptions attached. Chris Staines's cooking ticks all the right boxes, pairing meats and fish in the same dish, herbs and vegetables in the desserts, and with veloutés, purées and caramelising all present and correct. A tendency to combine too many elements in a dish risks taking the edge off it, as when fillets of John Dory share a plate with spiced lentils, carrot and cardamom purée, and a cider and green apple mousseline.

When dishes pull together, the results can be impressive, as was the case with an inspection main course of herb-crusted cannon of lamb served with cannelloni of sweetbreads and morels and a jus gras, a well-executed and resonant dish. Desserts, too, up the ante with properly oozy hot chocolate fondant alongside delicate Amaretto parfait, or bitter Valrhona tart with a sorbet of blood orange and cardamom. Although mark-ups are as hard as you would expect in this part of town, the wine list has strength in depth. Fine Italians and Australasians supplement the roll-call of illustrious French names, and the listing of dessert wines will bring out the sybarite in you. Prices start at around £16.

Chef: Chris Staines **Proprietor:** Mandarin Oriental Hotel Group **Open:** all week 12 to 2.30, 7 to 10 **Closed:** 25 Dec, D 26 Dec, 31 Dec, 1 Jan **Meals:** Set L £25 to £70, Set D £50 to £70 **Service:** 12.5% (optional) **Cards:** Amex, Delta, Diners, Maestro, MasterCard, Visa **Details:** 46 seats. Vegetarian meals. No cigars in dining room. Wheelchair access (also WC). Music. Air-conditioned **Accommodation:** 200 rooms **Tube:** Knightsbridge

 This symbol means that accommodation is available at this establishment.

MAP 14

Mango Tree
AR

46 Grosvenor Place, SW1X 7EQ
Tel: (020) 7823 1888

Decidedly upmarket, the Mango Tree serves traditional Thai food in an elegant, minimalist dining room. Among starters might be green papaya salad with snake beans, cherry tomatoes, peanuts, shrimps and spicy lime sauce (£6), seared tuna salad with chilli and lemongrass (£6.80), or spicy fishcakes with curry and kaffir lime leaves (£5.50), while main courses take in classic pad thai (£12.80), slow-roast belly pork with Chinese kale, chilli and orange (£15.50), and stir-fried chicken with cashew nuts (£12.75). A pricey wine list opens at £19. Closed Sat L. Awana in Sloane Street (see entry) is under the same ownership.

MAP 13

Manna
AR

4 Erskine Road, NW3 3AJ
Tel: (020) 7722 8028

Established in 1995, Manna is something of an institution. Vegetarian and vegan cooking is its stock in trade, with a menu that changes seasonally, and might start with filo triangles filled with paprika cream cheese and potato on tabbouleh (£6.50), go on to nettle and ricotta ravioli with wild garlic leaf pesto (£12.95), and end with organic lemon and tofu cheesecake with blueberry sauce (£6.75). Wines from £11.50. Open Sun L and all week D.

MAP 15

Manzi's
AR

1–2 Leicester Street, WC2H 7BL
Tel: (020) 7734 0224

An esteemed and long-established seafood restaurant in the midst of theatreland. Fresh fish is served simply in a room that harks back to the Paris of the 1930s. Smoked eel (£9.25), potted shrimps (£6.50) or fried devilled whitebait (£4.50) will start, while grilled plaice on the bone (£12.50) or scallops Mornay (£16.95) follow, with fillet steak (£19.95) available for meat eaters. Dover sole (£21.95) is an ever-popular favourite. Wines from £12.50. Seventeen guest rooms available. Closed Sun.

MAP 15

Masala Zone AR

9 Marshall Street, W1F 7ER
Tel: (020) 7287 9966

The straightforward menu at this informal Indian diner, part of a small chain, offers good-value eating. For a starter or just a snack, there are small plates of 'street food', such as puris, samosas and bhajis (from £3.50). Main courses might be masala burgers (£5.50 to £6.50), one-pot meals such as chicken Madras noodles (£6.55), or 'curry and rice plates': perhaps lamb korma (£7.45) or prawn malai (£7.65). For a full meal there are also various thali options (from £7). Wines from £10.10. Open all week. Branches at 80 Upper Street, N1 0NU, tel: (020) 7359 3399, and 147 Earls Court Road, SW5 9RQ, tel: (020) 7373 0220.

MAP 15

Mash

19–21 Great Portland Street, W1W 8QB
Tel: (020) 7637 5555
Website: www.mashbarandrestaurant.co.uk

Cooking 2 | Modern European | £39

There is style and substance at Oliver Peyton's café, bar, restaurant and microbrewery, just a few steps from Oxford Street. The signature orange sign points the way into the downstairs bar/café, with its small booths and tables, while the main restaurant is upstairs, decked out in olive and electric green, with the kitchen in full view. The short, well-sourced menu is easy to navigate: start, perhaps with wild rabbit terrine with onion marmalade and melba toast, and follow on with wood-roasted sea bass with mussels and mixed beans, or rack of lamb with grilled asparagus. Burgers are also staples of the menu, as are imaginative pizzas (Asian spiced duck with plum sauce, for example). End with dark chocolate tart with crème fraîche. The compact global wine list starts at £12.50, with eight choices by the glass from £4.

Chef: Simon Wadham **Proprietors:** Gruppo Ltd **Open:** Mon to Sat 12 to 3, 6 to 10.30 **Closed:** bank hols **Meals:** alc (main courses £9 to £17.50). Set L £9.50 (1 course), Set D £26. Bar menu available **Service:** 12.5% (optional) **Cards:** Amex, Delta, Maestro, MasterCard, Visa **Details:** 120 seats. 20 seats outside. Vegetarian meals. Children's helpings. No-smoking area. Wheelchair access (also WC). Music. Air-conditioned **Tube:** Oxford Circus

MAP 13

Matsuri High Holborn

Mid City Place, 71 High Holborn, WC1V 6EA
Tel: (020) 7430 1970
Website: www.matsuri-restaurant.com

Cooking 3 | Japanese | £61

Simplicity bordering on austerity is the style at this spacious corner-sited Japanese restaurant on bustling High Holborn. Expect lots of glass and plain white walls, and service that is willing and ready to guide diners around the menu. The focus is on set meals at lunchtime but covers a broader range in the evenings. The dinner menu lists a wide selection of sushi as well as sashimi, grilled and fried dishes and soups, plus teppanyaki and set dinners of eight or so courses. From the carte, start with agedashi tofu (deep-fried cubes of bean curd in a sweet soy-based sauce, and dobinmushi (clear soup with chicken, shrimp and vegetables), before moving on to lobster tail tempura, and duck teriyaki. Overall standards are high, and the restaurant is dedicated to demystifying Japanese cuisine for the benefit of Westerners. Drinks include hot and cold sakés as well as a decent selection of wines, priced from £16. The original branch of Matsuri is at 15 Bury Street, SW1, tel: (020) 7839 1101.

Chef: Hiroshi Sudo **Proprietor:** JRK (UK) Ltd **Open:** Mon to Sat 12 to 2.30, 6 to 10 **Closed:** Christmas, bank hols **Meals:** alc (main courses L £12 to £28, D £15 to £35). Set L £8.50 (2 courses) to £22, Set D 6 to 7 £20 to £70, Set D 6 to 10 £35 to £70 **Service:** 12.5% (optional) **Cards:** Amex, Delta, Diners, Maestro, MasterCard, Visa **Details:** 117 seats. Vegetarian meals. Wheelchair access (also WC). Music. Air-conditioned **Tube:** Holborn

MAP 15

Maze

10–13 Grosvenor Square, W1K 6JP
Tel: (020) 7107 0000
Website: www.gordonramsay.com

Cooking 6 | Modern French | £55

Grosvenor Square is closely associated with the US Embassy that dominates it, and judging from the number of American accents in Maze it's a useful source of customers to Gordon Ramsay's trend-setting restaurant. The large, somewhat imposing square has an authoritarian austerity about it, so what lies through the door of numbers 10–13 is even more of a surprise. It's hard to tell if it is even a restaurant from street level. Once inside, though, the work of designer David Rockwell is revealed. It must have cost a few bob, and it is certainly glamorous, with 'something of a James Bond set about it', as one reporter put it. If you don't have time for a full meal, prop up the rosewood bar and choose just a couple of the tapas-style dishes. A brown and tan theme runs through the large L-shaped room; it is all very chic, but not formal – tables are clothless and the staff relaxed.

Jason Atherton's menu is based on small dishes of Asian-influenced but primarily French-driven food, which arrives as a multitude of courses (they recommend between six and eight per person). They're not ideally suited to sharing, either too small or too intricate for division. A salad of Scottish lobster with white radish, aigre-doux dressing and ginger salt got the prize for the smallest dish at inspection, but it certainly packed a punch: the lobster firm and full of flavour and wrapped in pickled radish. Pressed foie gras and smoked duck with spiced pineapple and sweet-and-sour onions is a plate of strong flavours, the wafer-thin piece of pineapple perfectly cutting the richness of the foie gras. Dishes keep coming – the waiting staff have to deliver twice the number of a regular meal and manage the task with aplomb – and cutlery is changed periodically. Loch Duart salmon comes with 'perfectly soft and melting' belly pork, choucroute and a smoked raisin reduction, while wood-fired oven-baked squab, pink and tender, is paired with a rich and silky parsnip purée, vanilla shallots and sherry vinegar.

Intricate constructions and powerful flavours continue into puddings such as 'texture of pear' with chocolate mille-feuille ('a textbook version'), and what appears to be the signature dessert, the humorously named peanut butter and cherry jam sandwich with salted nuts and cherry sorbet. It isn't easy matching wine to the myriad of flavours, so the ten or so available by the glass (from £5 to £15.50) are a good bet. Otherwise it is a strong list, with a decent global reach. Bottle prices start at £18.

Chef: Jason Atherton **Proprietor:** Gordon Ramsay Holdings Ltd **Open:** all week 12 to 2.45, 6 to 11 **Meals:** alc (main courses £16.50 to £18.50, tasting menu dishes £6 to £9). Set L and D £37 to £60 **Service:** 12.5% (optional) **Cards:** Amex, Delta, Diners, Maestro, MasterCard, Visa **Details:** 90 seats. Vegetarian meals. Children's helpings. No smoking in dining room. Wheelchair access (also WC). Music. No mobile phones. Air-conditioned **Tube:** Bond Street

AR	Not a full entry but provisionally recommended. These 'also recommended' establishments are integrated throughout the book.

MAP 13

Medcalf

40 Exmouth Market, EC1R 4QE
Tel: (020) 7833 3533
Website: www.medcalfbar.co.uk

Cooking 4 | **Modern British** | **£37**

An asset to Exmouth Market, this relaxed restaurant takes its name from a butcher's shop that occupied the site at the turn of the last century. Inside, the sparse yet contemporary décor (scruffy painted garden tables and rickety old metal and wooden chairs) is the setting for simple dishes that never overreach themselves yet consistently please. The food is staunchly British (meat comes from Chesterton Farm in Gloucestershire), with some European influences at work, as in a main course of gilthead bream with ratatouille and herb oil. Friendly staff are on hand to serve Welsh rarebit or smoked and soused mackerel terrine with pickled cucumber for starters, followed by rump of lamb with mushy courgettes and dauphinois potatoes, herb-crusted cod with peas and tarragon, or grilled pork chop with apple mash and smoked black pudding. The chunky chips are also worth a punt. Finish with a selection of British cheeses and chutney, or blackberry and apple crumble with vanilla ice cream. The wine list is compact (fewer than 20 bins), with most bottles under £20. The house selections start at £13, or £3.75 a glass.

Chef: Tim Wilson **Proprietors:** Justin Unsworth and Simon Lee **Open:** all week L 12 to 3 (4 Sat and Sun), Mon to Thur and Sat D 6 to 10 (10.30 Sat) **Closed:** bank hols **Meals:** alc (main courses £9.50 to £16.50) **Service:** not inc **Cards:** Maestro, MasterCard, Visa **Details:** 50 seats. 20 seats outside. Vegetarian meals. No cigars/pipes in dining room. Wheelchair access (also WC). Music **Tube:** Farringdon

MAP 13

Mehek   AR

45 London Wall, EC2M 5TE
Tel: (020) 7588 5043

The lavish interior of this modern Indian restaurant was designed by renowned Bollywood film-set designer Vimlesh Lal. The menus incorporate regional specialities from across the Subcontinent, with starters including chicken chaat (£3.70), malai chops (£5.90), spicy whitebait (£3.90) and haash tikka (chargrilled marinated duck breast; £3.90). Main courses take in everything from Goan chicken (with coconut milk, pepper and lime; £7.90) to raan-e-jalfraize (roast leg of lamb with fresh green chilli, red pepper and onions; £7.90). Well-chosen wines from £12.90. Open Mon to Fri.

MAP 15

Mela AR

152–156 Shaftesbury Avenue, WC2H 8HL
Tel: (020) 7836 8635

'Creative yet uncompromisingly indigenous' is how chef Uday Seth describes his cooking style, which takes in dishes from across the Subcontinent in a celebration of the wholesome quality of Indian food. This means robust aromas and earthy flavours in starters ranging from scallops and squid tossed in mustard, garlic and cumin (£6.25) to pot-roast quail marinated in ginger and garlic with mango (£5.25), and main courses such as Hyderabadi crab curry (£14.95), chargrilled marinated duck breast and vegetable skewers (£11.25), and coconut chicken curry with fennel and tamarind (£8.95). There are plenty of vegetarian options too. Wines from £10.95. Open all week.

MAP 13

Metrogusto

13 Theberton Street, N1 0QY
Tel: (020) 7226 9400
Website: www.metrogusto.co.uk

| Cooking 3 | Modern Italian | £42 |

Much of the artwork covering the walls of Metrogusto is surreal and darkly humorous, as are some of the artefacts sprinkled about the place, including a wine bottle filled with cigarettes with a no-smoking label on it. The large but intimately arranged space is convivial; service is courteous and the food is described as 'progressive Italian cooking'. This amounts to starters such as Sicilian mussel soup, or salted veal tonnato with anchovies. Among main courses have been a first-rate, generous portion of halibut in a white wine, rosemary, mint and garlic sauce, and lamb cutlets with artichoke sauce. Parmesan ice cream accompanies a 'nicely zingy' thin apple tart. The whole of Italy is covered by the wine list, which features some good producers. Around a dozen are served by the glass from £3.50, with bottles starting at £13.50.

Chef: Antonio Di Salvo Proprietors: Susi and Ambro Ianeselli Open: Fri to Sun L 12 to 2.30 (Sun and bank hols 12.30 to 4.30), Mon to Sat D 6.30 to 10.30 (11 Fri and Sat) Closed: 25 and 26 Dec, Easter Sun and Mon Meals: alc (main courses £11.50 to £17.50) Service: 12.5% (optional) Cards: Amex, Delta, Maestro, MasterCard, Visa Details: 65 seats. 10 seats outside. Vegetarian meals. Children's helpings. No smoking in 1 dining room. Wheelchair access (not WC). Music. Air-conditioned Tube: Angel

---

MAP 13

Mezzanine AR

National Theatre, SE1 9PX
Tel: (020) 7452 3600

For stunning views of the River Thames arrive early to bag the best seats. Pre-theatre two or three course deals (£19.50/£21.95), and a dinner menu might see goats' cheese risotto with red peppers (£6.50) as a possible starter, followed by roasted duck breast accompanied by sauté spinach and roasted squash (£12.50), or perhaps grilled tuna loin on ciabatta with Thai basil mayonnaise (£12.75). Finish with passion-fruit tart (£4.95). Wines from £12.95. Open Mon to Sat D and Sat L only.

MAP 14

Millennium Knightsbridge, Mju

17–19 Sloane Street, SW1X 9NU
Tel: (020) 7201 6330
Website: www.millenniumhotels.com

| Cooking 5 | Modern European-Plus | £60 |

Being located on the first floor of the Millennium Hotel hardly makes Mju an instant choice as a destination restaurant, but Sloane Street is not well blessed with places to eat, and Tom Thomsen has settled into his stride. His innovative modern European cooking blends up-to-date concepts with careful restraint and proper technique. This is the sort of place where you eat duo of duck foie gras – terrine and crème brûlée – with yuzu jelly and Granny Smith mousse and white chocolate, then perhaps organic herb-cured cod served with a shallot tart, pork confit and raisin sauce. The culinary idiom is essentially modern French with Asian undertones, and one way to try the style is via the nine-course tasting menu, where a succession of little dishes might bring lobster salad with pickled daikon, aigre-doux and crispy lobster won ton, slow-cooked wild salmon with basil and tomato fondue, melted leeks and spring vegetables, and new season lamb with Japanese eggplant, cauliflower couscous and sorrel nage. Desserts range from a tart rhubarb parfait with rosewater and lemon pannacotta and lemon shortbread, via a rich chocolate and hazelnut mousse with ginger milk foam, caramel ice cream and praline anglaise, to mango soufflé with green tea ice cream.

Masterful wine service is on hand to guide diners through the global list, whether matching a series of glasses (from £6.50) to your meal or helping to navigate the pricier bottles. There are no budget options; prices start at £21.

Chef: Tom Thomsen Proprietor: Millennium Copthorne Open: Fri L 12 to 2.30, Mon to Sat D 6.30 to 10.30 Meals: alc (main courses £22 to £35). Set L £36 (2 courses) to £46, Set D £39 to £62 Service: 12.5% (optional) Cards: Amex, Delta, Maestro, MasterCard, Visa Details: 80 seats. Vegetarian meals. Children's helpings. No smoking. Music. Air-conditioned Accommodation: 222 rooms Tube: Knightsbridge

MAP 15

Mint Leaf

LONDON GFG 2007 COMMENDED

Suffolk Place, SW1Y 4HX
Tel: (020) 7930 9020
Website: www.mintleafrestaurant.com

Cooking 4 | Indian | £66

'Stunning' décor creates a big first impression as you enter this basement dining room just off the bottom end of Haymarket, and traversing the catwalk adds quite a glamorous touch. And the food lives up to the setting, the modern Indian cooking redolent of delicate blends of distinctly fresh spices. Minced rabbit rolls with cardamom, and lamb chops with ginger have been among starters to receive praise this year. Main courses are divided into grilled, roasted and steamed on the one hand, and curries on the other (with various platters if you want to sample a range). From the former, marinated sea bass steamed in a banana leaf has been well received, while the delicate spicing and tender meat of a mild chicken curry have flown the flag for the curries. Other options might be lotus stem dumplings with cottage cheese, dried figs and cashew nuts, jumbo prawns in chilli and garlic, and tandoor-roast rack of lamb marinated in spicy yoghurt. Side dishes, bread and rice are all of an excellent standard. The wine list includes some big French names with three-figure price tags,

although some of the less complex and cheaper options would be a better match for the food. Prices start at £17.

Chef: K.K. Anand Proprietor: Dinesh Bhattessa Open: Mon to Fri L 12 to 3, all week D 5.30 to 11 Meals: alc (main courses £9 to £32). Set L £15 (2 courses). Bar menu available Service: 12.5% (optional) Cards: Amex, Delta, Diners, Maestro, MasterCard, Visa Details: 200 seats. Vegetarian meals. Wheelchair access (also WC). Music. Air-conditioned Tube: Charing Cross

MAP 15

Mirabelle

56 Curzon Street, W1J 8PA
Tel: (020) 7499 4636
Website: www.whitestarline.org.uk

Cooking 4 | French | £69

The entrance is not obvious, and the doorman of old was missing during our inspection visit, but this is a basement dining room that does not feel starved of light or space. The MPW trademark of dramatic flower arrangements remains a focal point, and this restaurant is pretty clear where it's coming from. The repertoire continues to deliver well-rehearsed dishes in which prime ingredients (parfait of foie gras with truffles en gelée, or grilled lobster with sauce béarnaise) produce seductive results. The classical French background also delivers humbler items such as Bayonne ham with celeriac rémoulade, omelette Arnold Bennett, and braised pig's trotter with morels. The kitchen can turn out some fine dishes – in particular the tarte Tatin of endive and scallops with beurre à l'orange was a notable hit at inspection, and first-class ingredients made roast venison à la forestière and duck à l'orange stand out. Tarte Tatin of pears aux vanilla was a good version at inspection, but a prune and Armagnac soufflé was disappointing. Service is described as 'generally plentiful but hardly hospitable'. The set-price lunch is considered extremely good value, and a dozen wines on the concise wine list are served by the glass.

Chef: Igor Timchishin Proprietors: Marco Pierre White and Jimmy Lahoud Open: all week 12 to 2.30, 6 to 11.30 (10.30 Sun) Meals: alc (main courses £16.50 to £27.50). Set L £17.50 (2 courses) to £21, Set L Sun £23.95 Service: 12.5% (optional) Cards: Amex, Delta, Diners, Maestro, MasterCard, Visa Details: 120 seats. Children's helpings. Music. Air-conditioned Tube: Green Park

To submit a report on any restaurant, please visit *www.which.co.uk/gfgfeedback*.

MAP 12

Mirch Masala   [AR]

1416 London Road, SW16 4BZ
Tel: (020) 8679 1828

'Food extraordinaire halal' is the promise emblazoned on the menu at this flagship branch of a small chain of uncomplicated Indian diners. Meat-eaters and vegetarians are served equally well by the comprehensive menus, starters ranging from mushroom bhajia (£2.50) to chicken tikka (£3) and garlic mussels (£4). Karahi dishes are the main-course speciality, the wide choice on offer including ginger chicken (£5.50). Choose accompaniments from a wide range of rice and breads, plus assorted chutneys, raita and so on. Unlicensed so bring your own, or drink plain or flavoured lassi. Branches at 213 Upper Tooting Road, SW17, tel: (020) 8672 7500; 171–173 The Broadway, Southall, tel: (020) 8867 9222; and 111–113 Commercial Road, E1, tel: (020) 7377 0155.

MAP 15

Mr Kong

21 Lisle Street, WC2H 7BA
Tel: (020) 7437 7341

Cooking 2 | Chinese | £33

This long-standing Cantonese restaurant offers a wide-ranging menu that takes in scores of stir-fries, hotpots, barbecued meats and adventurous combinations of flavour and texture, such as spicy pig's knuckle with jellyfish, and steamed minced pork with salted egg. Although the menu lists its share of Westernised dishes, it pays to focus on the chef's specials, which feature the likes of steamed stuffed prawns with prawn paste in garlic sauce, and fried cuttlefish cake with garlic sprouts. And Mr Kong's cooking continues to delight those who like to dive deeply into its authentic ingredients and try such things as fish lips, pig's intestine, and duck's web. Dining takes place in two rooms, the simply decorated ground floor having the edge over the basement. House French is £8.50.

Chefs: K. Kong and Y.W. Lo   Proprietor: Mr Kong Chinese Restaurant Ltd   Open: all week 12 to 2.45am (1.45am Sun)   Meals: alc (main courses £6 to £16). Set L and D £9.30 (2 courses) to £22 (all min 2 to 8)   Service: 10%   Cards: Amex, Delta, Diners, Maestro, MasterCard, Visa   Details: 110 seats. Vegetarian meals. No cigars/pipes in dining room. Occasional music. Air-conditioned   Tube: Leicester Square

MAP 15

Miyama   [AR]

38 Clarges Street, W1Y 7PJ
Tel: (020) 7499 2443

This stalwart Mayfair Japanese restaurant offers reliable and authentic traditional cooking. Extensive menus offer everything from simple noodle dishes (perhaps soba with grated yam, £8.20, or udon with crab and wild vegetables, £9.20) to meat (chicken teriyaki, £9) and fish (grilled black cod with miso, £16), as well as assorted sushi (from £2 a piece) and platters of sashimi. Prices are reasonable for this part of town, including on the wine list, which opens around the £16 mark.

MAP 15

Momo   [AR]

25 Heddon Street, W1R 7LG
Tel: (020) 7434 4040

Entering Momo is like stepping through a portal that transports you to the kasbah, the ornate Moroccan décor and evocative north African music providing a fitting atmosphere for the kitchen's creations. The cooking is mostly traditional, with starters including briouats (pastries stuffed with fish, cheese and potato; £9.50) and sweet-and-spicy pigeon pastilla (£10), to be followed perhaps by chicken tagine (£14.50) or lamb couscous (£15.50). There are also a few 'modern Maghrebin' dishes, such as pan-roast guinea fowl with braised red cabbage, cumin and roast parsnips (£17.50). House wines are £18. Closed Sun L.

MAP 15

Mon Plaisir   [AR]

19–21 Monmouth Street, WC2H 9DD
Tel: (020) 7836 7243

For the full-on French experience consider this long-established, family-run restaurant. Good value pre-theatre menus are useful given the location. Snails and morels with pigs' trotters in puff pastry (£8.95), or perhaps carpaccio of Scottish beef with pickled onions and herb salad (£9.95), could be followed by fricassee of rabbit with prune and Armagnac sauce (£14.95). The staunchly French wine list starts at £12.75. Closed Sat L and Sun.

MAP 15

Montcalm Hotel, Crescent Restaurant

34–40 Great Cumberland Place, W1H 7TW
Tel: (020) 7402 4288
Website: www.montcalm.co.uk

NEW CHEF | Modern British | **£39**

Although attached to the Montcalm Hotel, The Crescent has a separate entrance, and the elegantly decorated restaurant features high ceilings, tall windows and green and gold drapes; tables are well spaced and covered in white linen cloths and napkins. The set menu includes half a bottle of wine per person, and might start with tartare of lightly cured salmon with a salad of pickled fennel, followed by roast pavé of cod accompanied by mushy peas and pont neuf potatoes, or confit leg of duck with a cassoulet of white beans, braised pork and chorizo. Side orders, incurring an extra charge, could include Parmesan polenta chips with aïoli. Finish off with chocolate fondant with crème fraîche, or passion-fruit mousse with a berry sorbet. The wine list offers some choice around the £20 mark, and then rises steeply; twelve are available by the glass from £4.20.

Chef: Cesar Varricchio **Proprietor:** Nikko Hotels (UK) Ltd **Open:** Mon to Fri L 12.30 to 2.30, all week D 6.30 to 10.30 **Closed:** D 25 Dec, L 26 Dec, bank hols **Meals:** Set L (inc ½-bot wine) £21 (2 courses) to £26, Set D (inc ½-bot wine) £24.50 (2 courses) to £29.50. Bar/lounge menu available **Service:** 10% (optional) **Cards:** Amex, Delta, Maestro, MasterCard, Visa **Details:** 60 seats. Vegetarian meals. Children's helpings. No-smoking area. Wheelchair access (also WC). Music. No mobile phones. Air-conditioned **Accommodation:** 120 rooms **Tube:** Marble Arch

---

MAP 13

Morgan M

489 Liverpool Road, N7 8NS
Tel: (020) 7609 3560
Website: www.morganm.com

Cooking 5 | Modern French | **£52**

Morgan Meunier's restaurant occupies a corner site on a Barnsbury main road, not far from an attractive park with a church at the far end. It's a single room, done mainly in cream, benefiting from plenty of natural light, the walls hung with colourful abstract paintings. Smart table settings set off the relatively humble feel. Pasta is often the vehicle for starters and might appear as cannelloni rolled around crabmeat and cockles, in a shellfish cappuccino broth studded with lots of tiny clams and mussels, all topped with an excellent scallop. Main courses might offer venison from the Iken Valley, Suffolk, pot-roasted and served with a purée of braised apple and chestnuts, in a classical sauce grand veneur. An inspection dish of roast confit duck with caramelised onions looked a treat and delivered upstanding, orange-glazed meat and a kind of linear potato galette dusted with cracked pepper. Soufflés are the exhibition dishes they should be, a passion-fruit version more than passing muster at a spring dinner, anointed with crème anglaise and set beside an intense sorbet of the same fruit. Service is a little Franco-florid but ultra-professional with it. Prices on the France-orientated wine list tend to be on the wrong side of £20. Around a dozen by the glass start at £4.50, with house white £15 a bottle, red £16.

Chefs: Morgan Meunier and Sylvain Soulard **Proprietor:** Morgan Meunier **Open:** Wed to Fri and Sun L 12 to 2.15, Tue to Sat D 7 to 10.30 **Closed:** 24 to 30 Dec **Meals:** Set L £19.50 (2 courses) to £39, Set D £32 to £39 **Service:** 12.5% (optional) **Cards:** Delta, Maestro, MasterCard, Visa **Details:** 48 seats. Vegetarian meals. Children's helpings. No smoking. Wheelchair access (not WC). Occasional music. No mobile phones. Air-conditioned **Tube:** Highbury & Islington

---

MAP 13

Moro

34–36 Exmouth Market, EC1R 4QE
Tel: (020) 7833 8336
Website: www.moro.co.uk

Cooking 5 | Spanish/North African | **£39**

The busy, bustling ambience and continued popularity of this innovative venue specialising in Moorish (Spanish and North African) cooking are a credit to the partnership that runs the kitchen. The food struck an instant chord when the place opened a decade ago, and the unbuttoned atmosphere suits it down to the ground.

Ingredients are all, and are given centre-stage prominence in starters such as calves' kidneys and jamon in an oloroso sauce with toast, or warm cuttlefish, yellow from its cooking liquor, served with a salad of preserved lemon and celery. Move on to main courses of 'fantastically fresh' wood-roasted skate with braised spinach and white beans in paprika and garlic, or Iberico pork loin cooked in milk, served with silky-smooth mashed potato. Desserts are quite as stimulating as the rest of the menu, with Seville orange tart, yoghurt and pistachio cake, and 'stunningly good' rosewater and cardamom ice cream, not to be missed. A useful list of sherries by the glass proudly heads up a largely Spanish wine list, which takes in some of the undiscovered delights of that country, such as the Basque dry white, Txakoli, as well as a rare white Irouléguy, made just over the border in South-west France. Bottle prices open at £12.50.

Chefs: Sam and Sam Clark   Proprietors: Mark Sainsbury, and Sam and Sam Clark   Open: Mon to Sat 12.30 to 2.30, 7 to 10.30   Closed: Christmas to New Year, bank hols   Meals: alc (main courses £14.50 to £17). Tapas menu available   Service: not inc   Cards: Amex, Delta, Diners, Maestro, MasterCard, Visa   Details: 90 seats. 12 seats outside. Vegetarian meals. Children's helpings. No smoking. Wheelchair access (also WC). No music. Air-conditioned   Tube: Farringdon

---

MAP 12

Mosaica @ the factory

Chocolate Factory, Clarendon Road, N22 6XJ
Tel: (020) 8889 2400
Website: www.mosaicarestaurants.com

Cooking 3 | Modern European | £38

This large, cavernous restaurant is part of an old factory complex which is now used to house studios for artists, potters and the like. The restaurant is found through a reception area and by passing various offices, but, once inside, there is no lack of life and vibrancy. The menu is imaginative with some classy elements, while service is enthusiastic, and the kitchen is open to view. Arancini with a tomato and basil sauce is a delicately flavoured starter, followed, perhaps, by main course sea bass with vanilla crushed potatoes and confit tomatoes – 'full of flavour'. Ribeye steak with garlic mash came well-seared, but tender within, topped off with a good, rich gravy. Tiramisù is a strong finish, while the rhubarb crème brûlée has also received good reports. The wine list is a good-value affair, with plenty of choice under £20, starting with Italian house at £12.

Chef: Jon Ashby   Proprietor: John Mountain   Open: Tue to Fri and Sun L 12 to 2.30, Tue to Sat D 7 to 9.30   Closed: 2 weeks Christmas   Meals: alc (main courses L £5 to £15, D £10 to £16)   Service: 10% (optional)   Cards: Amex, Delta, Maestro, MasterCard, Visa   Details: 100 seats. Car park. Vegetarian meals. Children's helpings. Wheelchair access (also WC). Occasional music. Air-conditioned   Tube: Wood Green

---

MAP 13

Moshi Moshi

Unit 24, Liverpool Street Station, Broadgate, EC2M 7QH
Tel: (020) 7247 3227

With what can only be described as unique views across Liverpool Street Station, this long-established sushi restaurant has some strong political ideals to serve up alongside its food, including a statement that they no longer serve endangered bluefin tuna. Also well signalled is the way in which their fish arrives from Cornwall fresh every day, so look out for sushi sets (£7 to £13), the most basic of which consists of salmon and tuna nigiri, and California rolls of avocado and crab. Hot seasonal dishes include Loch Duart salmon teriyaki (£9). Sashimi platters are from £9.50, saké £4.80 a flask, and house wine is £11.50. Closed Sat and Sun.

MAP 14

Nahm

Halkin Hotel, 5 Halkin Street, SW1X 7DJ
Tel: (020) 7333 1234
Website: www.nahm.como.bz

Cooking 3 | Thai | £66

The dining room of the chic Halkin Hotel is a sleek, minimalist space with wooden screens, teak furniture and honey-coloured walls, and it makes an elegant yet surprisingly unpretentious setting for David Thompson's Thai-inspired cuisine. Staff do their best at making recommendations, but it might be easier to follow the nahm arharn set meal (basically, two people share five dishes from the carte). Choose from a long list that includes salad of foie gras, oysters and heart of coconut with red shallots and mint, spicy oxtail soup, steamed red curry of Scottish scallops with Thai basil and kaffir lime leaves, chiang mai-style curry with Middle White pork, ginger and pickled garlic, and smoky curry of grilled venison and 'bai yar'. The wine list is well chosen, though sadly its prices make depressing reading. Around a dozen wines are offered by the glass from £7.50.

Chefs: David Thompson and Matthew Albert **Proprietor:** Como Hotels & Resorts **Open:** Mon to Fri L 12 to 2.15, all week D 7 to 10.45 (10.30 Sun) **Closed:** bank hols **Meals:** alc (main courses £8.50 to £16.50). Set L £26, Set D £49.50. Bar menu available **Service:** 12.5% (optional) **Cards:** Amex, Delta, Diners, MasterCard, Visa **Details:** 90 seats. Vegetarian meals. Children's helpings. No smoking. Wheelchair access (also WC). Music. Air-conditioned **Accommodation:** 41 rooms **Tube:** Hyde Park Corner

MAP 15

Neal Street Restaurant

26 Neal Street, WC2H 9QW
Tel: (020) 7836 8368
Website: www.carluccios.com

Cooking 3 | **Italian** | **£63**

On the left is the Carluccio shop, giving diners a chance to get acquainted with some of the ingredients, and the entrance to the restaurant is made more appealing by a basket of Antonio Carluccio's trademark wild mushrooms. The restaurant certainly catches the eye, with its bright red paint, red banquettes, bright paintings and white cloths, diverting attention from the fact that tables are squeezed together. Dishes can be as straightforward as a generous signature dish of mixed sautéed mushrooms of the day, enlivened with garlic and chilli, and as accomplished as Sicilian-style rabbit casseroled with peppers and tomatoes. Desserts take in an 'elegant' tiramisù, an 'authentically Italian' crostate (jam tart) that 'demanded a glass of Vin Santo', and an intensely rich, creamy crème brûlée with Barolo jam. A fixed-price lunch offers respite from largish bills, and prices on the in-depth, patriotic wine list are not exactly competitive either, starting at £18.50 and rising quickly.

Chef: Maurilio Molteni **Proprietors:** Antonio and Priscilla Carluccio **Open:** Mon to Sat 12 to 2.30, 6 to 11 **Closed:** Christmas to New Year, bank hols **Meals:** alc (main courses £16 to £27). Set L and D 6 to 7 and 10 to 11 £21 (2 courses) to £25 **Service:** 12.5% (optional) **Cards:** Amex, Delta, Diners, Maestro, MasterCard, Visa **Details:** 60 seats. Vegetarian meals. No smoking. No music. No mobile phones. Air-conditioned **Tube:** Covent Garden

 This symbol means that smoking is not permitted.

MAP 15

New World AR

1 Gerrard Place, W1D 5PA
Tel: (020) 7434 2508

This vast Cantonese 700-seater is always busy, particularly for lunchtime dim sum (£2.20 to £2.60), which arrive by perambulating trolleys pushed by legions of staff, who tour the tables dispensing all manner of delightful morsels, including steamed and deep-fried dumplings and big bowls of soup. Elsewhere, the long menu is gentle on those not too familiar with Cantonese cooking – there is everything from steamed lobster (market price) to quick-fried lamb with ginger and spring onion (£6.80). Good value, great fun. House wine £11. Open all week.

MAP 15

Nicole's

158 New Bond Street, W1Y 9PA
Tel: (020) 7499 8408
Website: www.nicolefarhi.com

Cooking 3 | **Modern European** | **£61**

Nicole's runs with the fashion crowd and is generally packed with ladies tucking into lobster Caesar salad and glasses of Pinot Grigio. The décor remains simple and elegant, with classic oak flooring and subtle lighting. Start with a simple salad of prosciutto, spiced sweet potato, and pecorino with a lemon crème fraîche dressing, or crispy artichokes with lemon aïoli. Fish is given separate space on the menu, offering grilled Indian-spiced swordfish with basmati rice and chickpea salad, or roast sea bass with winter vegetable bagna cauda. A meaty main course might be Moroccan-spiced chicken with saffron onions, couscous and date relish. If you're not worried about squeezing into the latest Bond Street creation, finish with crème brûlée with a citrus salad, or vanilla cheesecake with rhubarb compote. Afternoon tea is served from 4 to 6. The wine menu has a strong accent on France with a wide choice by the glass. House Spanish red and Argentinian white are £15.25.

Chefs: Annie Wayte and Christophe Lafontaine **Proprietor:** Stephen Marks **Open:** Mon to Sat 12 to 3.30 (4 Sat) **Closed:** bank hols **Meals:** alc (main courses £18 to £24). Cover £1. Bar L and tea menus available **Service:** 15% (optional) **Cards:** Amex, Delta, Diners, Maestro, MasterCard, Visa **Details:** 87 seats. Vegetarian meals. No smoking in dining room. Wheelchair access (not WC). Music. Air-conditioned **Tube:** Green Park, Bond Street

MAP 15

Nobu Berkeley Street

15 Berkeley Street, W1J 8DY **NEW ENTRY**
Tel: (020) 7290 9222
Website: www.noburestaurants.com

Cooking 5 | Modern Japanese | £71

Nobu's latest branch lurks in a street of smart car showrooms. Behind an acid-etched glass frontage guarded by men in black with earpieces, the interior is like an enchanted forest theatre set. Designed by the ubiquitous David Collins on an organic binge, it features a bar counter fashioned from a gigantic tree trunk, with tree branch chandeliers overhead, the light diffused in fragments of mirror and wavy stainless steel. The dining goes on upstairs, where the sylvan theme continues, but is rather lost amid the sheer size of the two interlinked rooms. Service, 'maddeningly erratic' at inspection, begins with the traditional welcoming screech of 'Irashimasa!'

The food, overseen as at Nobu London and Ubon by Nobu (see entries) by the tirelessly peripatetic Mark Edwards, plies the house formula of cutting-edge modern Japanese cuisine, spiked with South American spicing and technique. Palpable freshness means the seafood dishes score highly, as in yellowtail sashimi pointed up with the sharp attack of jalapeño pepper and the acidity of ponzu sauce. Nigiri sushi are exemplary, incorporating marine-scented sea urchin, and perfect, grainy salmon. Star of the show at inspection was the toro steak, a fatty collar of tuna looking like a lump of T-bone, a magisterial cut that spans the textural range from firmly fatty to soft and gelatinous. Once again, the chocolate bento box comes up trumps, matching unctuous chocolate fondant with acerbic green tea ice cream inside a red-lacquered box. With so many menu options, execution is almost bound to be patchy, but, when on song, dishes will amaze. As will the final bill, particularly if you've had a drop of wine, which kicks off at £26 per bottle, or there's saké of course.

Chef: Mark Edwards Proprietor: Nobuyuki Matsuhisa Open: Mon to Sat L 12 to 2.15, all week D 6 to 12.30 (10 Sun) Meals: alc (main courses £9.50 to £29.50). Set D £60. Bar menu available Service: 15% Cards: Amex, Delta, Diners, Maestro, MasterCard, Visa Details: 180 seats. Vegetarian meals. No smoking. Wheelchair access (also WC). Occasional music. Air-conditioned Tube: Green Park

MAP 15

Nobu London

19 Old Park Lane, W1K 1LB
Tel: (020) 7447 4747
Website: www.noburestaurants.com

Cooking 5 | Modern Japanese | £71

In a big white first-floor room overlooking the hurly-burly of Hyde Park Corner, the original London branch of Nobuyuki Matsuhisa's mini empire continues doing its Japanese fusion thing. The atmosphere is lively, pleasingly informal even, and as long as you understand upfront that you are given ninety minutes for lunch and two hours for dinner, strictly enforced, the experience is an enjoyable one.

The menu is long and fascinating. At lunchtime you could abdicate choice and pay £25 for a bento box meal, which includes sashimi salad, rock shrimp tempura with ponzu, the famous black cod with miso, assorted sushi, and a cup of miso soup. Elsewhere on the menu there is much to catch the eye, the absorption of non-Japanese ingredients being almost seamlessly achieved. Seared toro comes with jalapeño dressing, or there may be steamed Irish abalone, confit duck roll with cashew sauce, or the beguiling tea-smoked lamb with grilled tomato relish. Classic sushi, sashimi and harumaki rolls, meanwhile, remain the benchmarks by which Japanese kitchens are judged, and New Zealander Mark Edwards knows what he's doing in those departments too. It's also worth allowing time for the electrifying desserts, such as slow-cooked nashi pear with star anise ice cream, almond 'cloud', candied yuzu and peanut 'soil' (sic). Drinking virtually anything apart from tea will inflate the bill considerably, but if cash is no object there is a fine, stylistically arranged wine list, opening at £26, and naturally a roll-call of pedigree saké.

Chef: Mark Edwards Proprietor: Nobuyuki Matsuhisa Open: Mon to Fri 12 to 2.15, 6 to 10.15 (11 Fri), Sat 12.30 to 2.30, 6 to 11, Sun 12.30 to 2.30, 6 to 9.30 Meals: alc (main courses £9.50 to £29.50). Set L £25 to £60, Set D £70 to £90 Service: 15% (optional) Cards: Amex, Diners, Maestro, MasterCard, Visa Details: 150 seats. Vegetarian meals. No smoking in 1 dining room. Wheelchair access (also WC). No music. Air-conditioned Tube: Hyde Park Corner

 This symbol means that the restaurant has elected to participate in *The Good Food Guide's* £5 voucher scheme (see 'Using The Good Food Guide' for details).

MAP 13

Notting Hill Brasserie

92 Kensington Park Road, W11 2PN
Tel: (020) 7229 4481
Email: enquiries@nottinghillbrasserie.com

Cooking 4 | Modern European | £59

A pianist playing smooth jazz adds to the atmosphere every evening and Sunday lunchtimes at this strikingly elegant restaurant, which is more upmarket than the 'brasserie' designation might suggest. Mark Jankel's cooking, however, fits the description well. Dishes are listed in the fashionable style of a heading naming the main component followed by a fuller description, as in starters of lobster (in a cannelloni with prawns, cep purée and shellfish velouté) or rabbit (ballottine of rabbit and roast pepper with tiger prawn tortellini and pesto minestrone), which might be followed by pork (roast shoulder and confit belly with lentils and cassoulet), halibut (pan-fried and served with baby artichokes, pancetta and jus) or duck (roast magret accompanied by caramelised onion purée, crisp potato and warm salad of confit). Among desserts, 'apple' is a tarte Tatin with crème fraîche, while 'banana' is a parfait with milk chocolate and peanut praline ice cream. Wines are a varied international bunch, with more from France than elsewhere, opening with a couple of vins de pays at £14 a bottle, £3.50 a glass.

Chef: Mark Jankel   Proprietor: Carlo Spetale   Open: all week L 12 to 3.30, Mon to Sat D 7 to 11   Closed: Christmas   Meals: alc D (main courses £19 to £24.50). Set L Mon to Sat £14.50 (2 courses) to £19.50, Set L Sun £25 (2 courses) to £30. Bar menu available   Service: 12.5% (optional)   Cards: Amex, Delta, Maestro, MasterCard, Visa   Details: 110 seats. Vegetarian meals. Children's helpings. No smoking in dining room. Wheelchair access (not WC). Music. Air-conditioned   Tube: Notting Hill Gate

MAP 13

Noura Brasserie

16 Hobart Place, SW1W 0HH
Tel: (020) 7235 9444
Website: www.noura.co.uk

Cooking 3 | Lebanese | £50

The Belgravia branch was the first in London of this smart mini chain imported from Paris by the Bou-Antoun brothers. A simple formula is the key

to its success: all-day opening and a comprehensive menu of mostly traditional Lebanese cooking. Hot and cold meze – either individually priced dishes or mixed platters – take in everything from tabbouleh, falafel, and shankleesh (aged cheese with thyme, tomatoes, onions and green peppers), to sojok (spicy sausages) with eggs, foul medames (broad beans in tomatoes, garlic and olive oil), and chicken livers marinated in lemon and garlic. The charcoal grill turns out main dishes of quail seasoned with coriander, and sea bass with tarator sauce, and vegetarians also have plenty of choice. The compact wine list has no space for anything under £20, with big-name French and Lebanese wines dominating. House selections start at £20. See the website for a list of other branches.

Chef: Badih Asmar   Proprietor: Nader Bou-Antoun   Open: all week 11.30 to 11.45   Meals: alc (main courses £10 to £19). Set L £14.50 (2 courses), Set D £25 to £34 (all min 2). Cover £2. Bar menu available   Service: not inc   Cards: Amex, Delta, Diners, Maestro, MasterCard, Visa   Details: 125 seats. Vegetarian meals. Wheelchair access (also WC). Music. Air-conditioned   Tube: Victoria

MAP 15

No. 6 George Street

6 George Street, W1U 3QX
Tel: (020) 7935 1910

Cooking 2 | Modern British | £38

The window of Emma Miller's restaurant and shop is full of enticing things to buy, but if you can't wait until you get home, walk on through to the dining room at the back and take a seat. From midday until 3pm the restaurant serves a daily-changing menu, which might start with carrot, cumin and coriander soup, before a main course of grilled scallops with spiced red lentils and baby spinach. Desserts are a highlight: pear and cranberry tart, for example, or apple and rhubarb crumble with ginger ice cream. Note the minimum charge is £14 per head, which amounts to a couple of courses, or perhaps just a main course and a drink. House wines kick off at £14.50.

Chef: Emma Miller   Proprietors: the Miller family   Open: Mon to Fri L 12 to 3   Closed: bank hols, 2 weeks Aug   Meals: alc L (main courses £10.50 to £15.50)   Service: not inc   Cards: Maestro, MasterCard, Visa   Details: 32 seats. Private parties: 32 main room. Vegetarian meals. Children's helpings. No smoking. No music. Air-conditioned   Tube: Bond Street

MAP 12

Numidie

48 Westow Hill, SE19 1RX
Tel: (020) 8766 6166
Website: www.numidie.co.uk

Cooking 2 | North African | £34

🚫 £

Crystal Palace may not be the trendiest of London suburbs, but it has a real gem in Numidie. The dining room has a laid-back, informal feel, with décor incorporating lots of mirrors in decorative frames, and there is an appealing menu of lively, modern dishes with a Mediterranean and North African slant. To start, there might be tiger prawns in pastis sauce, salt-beef on toasted bagel with horseradish and cornichons, or a mosaic of fish with pomegranate and olive oil, which could be followed by grilled duck breast on chard gratin, baked John Dory with lemon confit and globe artichoke, or classic dishes such as merguez frites or vegetable tagine with couscous. Finish with chocolate tart or pear stuffed with almonds and pistachios. Prices on the straightforward wine list start at £10.50, and around a dozen are served by the glass.

Chef: Serge Ismail **Proprietors:** Serge Ismail and Ashleigh Hope **Open:** Thur to Sun L 12 to 2, Tue to Sun D 6 to 10.30 **Meals:** alc (main courses L £6.50 to £12.50, D £9.50 to £15). Set L £8.50 (2 courses), Set D Tue to Thur £13.50 (2 courses) **Service:** not inc **Cards:** Maestro, MasterCard, Visa **Details:** 35 seats. Vegetarian meals. Children's helpings. No smoking. Music. Air-conditioned

MAP 13

Nyonya

2A Kensington Park Road, W11 3BU
Tel: (020) 7243 1800
Website: www.nyonya.co.uk

Cooking 2 | Malay/Chinese | £35

🚫 £

Honest, enthusiastic and genuine in its intentions, this modestly appointed little restaurant deals in the 'Nyonya' tradition of Malaysian home cooking. The style is a gutsy amalgamation of dishes from the Malay-Chinese community, with the cooking noted for flavours that are subtle and intricate. There's no décor to speak of, and service is casual and smiling. The short menu breaks down

into appetisers (pork dumplings, sliced fish wrapped in banana leaves and steamed with coconut milk, herbs and spices), stir-fries and stews like cashew nuts and prawns in a mildly spiced coconut sauce, curries and 'hawker' dishes based on soups and noodles like Singapore laksa and char mee (fried yellow noodles with prawns, fishcake and vegetables in a thick gravy). Save room for freshly baked kuih, traditional Nyonya desserts. While there are a few wines from £13.50, there's also Asian beer or jasmine tea.

Chefs: Mary Chong and Teng Chye Yeoh **Proprietor:** Nyonya Ltd **Open:** Mon to Fri 11.30 to 2.45, 6 to 10.30 (10.45 Fri), Sat and Sun 11.30 to 10.30 (10.45 Sat) **Meals:** alc (main courses £5.50 to £8.50). Set L Mon to Fri £8 (2 courses) **Service:** not inc **Cards:** Amex, Delta, Diners, Maestro, MasterCard, Visa **Details:** 48 seats. Vegetarian meals. No smoking. Music. Air-conditioned **Tube:** Notting Hill Gate

MAP 12

Olé

240 Upper Richmond Road, SW15 6TG
Tel: (020) 8788 8009

Authentic tapas served all day is the main draw at this Spanish restaurant/bar, which has relocated from its former site on Fulham Broadway since the last edition of the Guide. Everything, from patatas bravas and boquerones to mussels in white wine, is included (dishes priced from £1.75 to £5.55). There is also a full menu, with starters of king prawns (£6.45), or deep-fried goats' cheese with a compote of honey, pears and thyme (£5.50), followed by, for example, zarzuela (seafood casserole; £11.75), or roast breast and confit leg of duck with peach and pepitoria sauce (£12.25). Wines from £10.75 on the all-Spanish list. Open all week.

MAP 13

Olivo

21 Eccleston Street, SW1W 9LX
Tel: (020) 7730 2505
Email: maurosanna@oliveto.fsnet.co.uk

Cooking 2 | Italian/Sardinian | £45

With tightly packed tables and wooden floor-boards, and a lively throng of customers, Olivo can generate a fair bit of noise. But that's all part of its charm. The traditional Italian and Sardinian fish specialities are worth seeking out: octopus salad with rocket, perhaps, or chargrilled stuffed baby squid and linguine with fresh crab. Iced raw sea urchins with crostini certainly catches the eye. Pasta might take in fresh pasta ribbons with rocket and a broad bean purée, or maybe spaghetti and grey mullet roe, while meat dishes see the likes of chargrilled beef with juniper berries or veal escalope with sautéed spinach. End with mixed Sardinian cheeses, or perhaps lemon and mascarpone cake. The all-Italian wine list opens at £15 for the house Sardinian.

Chef: Marco Melis   Proprietor: Mauro Sanna   Open: Mon to Fri L 12 to 2.30, all week D 7 to 11 (10 Sun)   Closed: bank hols   Meals: alc (main courses £13.50 to £15.50). Set L £17.50 (2 courses) to £19.50. Cover £1.50   Service: not inc   Cards: Amex, Delta, Diners, MasterCard, Maestro, Visa   Details: 42 seats. Vegetarian meals. No music. Air-conditioned   Tube: Victoria

MAP 13

One Aldwych, Axis

Aldwych, WC2B 4RH
Tel: (020)7300 0300
Website: www.onealdwych.com

Cooking 3 │ Modern European │ £62

Though part of One Aldwych hotel, Axis has its own entrance at street level, stairs leading down to a large, high-ceilinged basement dining room done out in kitsch retro style. Menus are long enough to ensure that most tastes are catered for, showing occasional inventive touches but generally playing it safe with a repertoire of broadly contemporary dishes. Crispy duck noodle salad is a fixture among starters, while other options range from cauliflower and ginger soup to seared beef carpaccio with shiitake mushrooms, shaved Parmesan and wild rocket.

Main courses feature a choice of meat and fish 'from the grill' – perhaps yellowfin tuna, or Scottish ribeye steak – paired with a choice of sauces ranging from tartare to tomato and chilli. Otherwise there might be roast pheasant with creamed chestnut, roast parsnip and Savoy cabbage, or roast halibut provençale with saffron potatoes and Mediterranean vegetables, and to finish perhaps toffee profiteroles with roast peach and vanilla sauce, or baked chocolate pot with Black Forest cherry compote. The well-chosen international wine list offers a good selection by the glass but few bottles under £20.

Chef: Mark Gregory   Proprietor: Gordon Campbell Gray   Open: Mon to Fri L 12 to 2.45, Mon to Sat D 5.45 to 10.45 (11.30 Sat)   Closed: Christmas, New Year   Meals: alc (main courses £14 to £28). Set L and D (before 7.15pm and after 10pm) £16.75 (2 courses) to £19.75   Service: 12.5% (optional)   Cards: Amex, Delta, Diners, Maestro, Visa   Details: 120 seats. Vegetarian meals. Children's helpings. No cigars/pipes. Wheelchair access (also WC). Occasional music. Air-conditioned   Accommodation: 105 rooms   Tube: Covent Garden

MAP 13

1 Lombard Street

1 Lombard Street, EC3V 9AA
Tel: (020) 7929 6611
Website: www.1lombardstreet.com

Cooking 6 │ Modern European │ £62

There are two eating areas here, each with its own entrance. The restaurant (unlike the brasserie) is a smoke-free haven of white-clothed tables, with a large reproduction of Titian's *Rape of Europa* on one wall. Suits are very much in evidence, unsurprisingly in the heart of the City, but the atmosphere is smooth and inviting, with well-drilled service. The cooking, under Herbert Berger, keeps in tune with the times by offering novel combinations, but in a gentle, toned-down style. The nine-course dégustation dinner menu gives some indication of the range, extending on a June evening from the elegant simplicity of tuna carpaccio with ginger and lime vinaigrette and black radish, to the unabashed opulence of seared foie gras with parsnip cream and white truffle oil, and a pair of meat courses. Noisette of lamb with celeriac confit and carrot fondant was tender and flavourful, and even better was a pavé of Angus beef with morels in a vin jaune cream sauce. The show-stopping main course might be a whole salt-crusted sea bass for two.

Desserts generally lack firepower, although feuillantine of caramelised Granny Smith apple has hit the spot. Wines are a serious bunch, with bottles 'from the Lombard vault' going up to £1500 for a 1950 Pétrus with a damaged label. Prices are stiff all round, but the house selection opens at £16.50 for a decent Montepulciano d'Abruzzo, while glasses start at £4.75.

Chef: Herbert Berger   Proprietor: Soren Jessen   Open: Mon to Fri 11.30 to 10   Closed: 24 and 25 Dec, bank hols   Meals: alc (main courses £14.50 to £27.50)   Service: 12.5% (optional)   Cards: Amex, Delta, Diners, Maestro, MasterCard, Visa   Details: 170 seats. No children under 15. Wheelchair access (also WC). Music. Air-conditioned   Tube: Bank

MAP 14

One-O-One

Sheraton Park Tower, 101 Knightsbridge,
SW1X 7RN
Tel: (020) 7290 7101
Website: luxurycollection.com/parktowerlondon

Cooking 4 | Seafood | £81

The Sheraton Park Tower, in which this restaurant is found, holds Bedroom Boudoir evenings once a month, in which guests take dinner while reclining on beds. Food is laid out on a petal-strewn buffet table, with slippers provided for padding to and fro. Main courses are served at bedside, and dropped into your mouth by semi-naked waiting staff (we made the last bit up).

Our inspectors haven't yet made it to the Boudoir, but we can report that the more conventional way of taking Pascal Proyart's cooking, seated at tables in a dining room, is quite satisfying. Quality seafood is the draw: red king crab is freighted here from the Barents Sea, while Marennes oysters are served in five different ways. It all comes burnished to a sleek, contemporary sheen, scallops sharing a plate with foie gras, tiger prawns à la plancha served with paella and chorizo, and even the odd dish for the mammalians among you (perhaps beef fillet au poivre with green peppercorn sauce). Finish luxuriously with warm chocolate fondant offset by mandarin sorbet. Wines are arranged by style. Prices are high, from around £25, and the axis is tilted firmly towards France.

Chef: Pascal Proyart **Proprietor:** Starwood Hotels and Resorts **Open:** all week 12 (12.30 Sun) to 2.30, 7 to 10.30 **Meals:** alc (main courses £21 to £28). Set L £21 (2 courses) to £25, Set D (7 to 9 or 9.30, whole table only) £48 to £79 **Service:** not inc **Cards:** Amex, Delta, Diners, MasterCard, Visa **Details:** 60 seats. Children's helpings. No smoking in dining room. Wheelchair access (also WC). Music. No mobile phones. Air-conditioned **Accommodation:** 280 rooms **Tube:** Knightsbridge

	This appears after the restaurant's name if the establishment was not a
NEW ENTRY	main entry in last year's Guide. Please note, however, it may have been 'also recommended' in the previous edition.

MAP 15

Origin Bar and Dining Room

NEW ENTRY

24 Endell Street, WC2H 9HQ
Tel: (020) 7170 9200
Website: www.origin-restaurant.com

Cooking 4 | Modern British-Plus | £52

An office-style entrance lobby serves the whole building. It doesn't feel like arriving at a restaurant at all, until you head upstairs and happen upon a chic, modern dining room. Wood floors, white leather seating, embedded ceiling spots and prints of abstract art announce that this is a twenty-first-century eaterie, and the menus certainly reinforce the impression.

Adam Byatt means to make his mark with dishes that are presented simply, with every option turning on a central partnership of two main ingredients. Crab with tarragon partners Cornish crab ravioli with a frothy broth containing plenty of the herb, plus a few leaves of tender pak choi, while risotto with spring vegetables takes the pairing theme punctiliously enough to present the veg on top of the firm-textured rice. Enjoyable main courses at inspection included turbot cooked on the bone with ricotta gnocchi and broad beans, and another tarragon-based dish that presented sliced ballottine with tortellini of chicken, tarragon and foie gras, and a little chicken consommé as a sauce. Light, fluffy texture and powerful flavour marked out a chocolate soufflé as a dessert of class, while blood orange posset was pleasantly textured, and served with a Campari-laced sorbet of the same and pain d'épice. Service is on the ball, steadily paced and knowledgeable. A compactly presented wine list is arranged by style, from fresh and aromatic to bold and spicy; prices are fairly forbidding, but a bit of foraging turns up bottles from as little as £15.50.

Chef/Proprietor: Adam Byatt **Open:** Mon to Fri L 12 to 2.30, Mon to Sat D 6 to 10.30 (5 to 11 Sat) **Meals:** alc (main courses £15 to £25). Set L £18 (2 courses) to £24, Set D (not after 7) £15 (2 courses) to £20. Bar menu available **Service:** 12.5% (optional) **Cards:** Amex, Delta, Diners, Maestro, MasterCard, Visa **Details:** 84 seats. Vegetarian meals. Wheelchair access (also WC). Music. Air-conditioned **Tube:** Covent Garden

MAP 15

Orrery

55 Marylebone High Street, W1M 3AE
Tel: (020) 7616 8000
Website: www.orrery.co.uk

Cooking 5 | **French** | **£68**

Take your pick between the staircase and lift to ascend to the first-floor dining room above the Conran shop in Marylebone. It's a long, narrow room with arched windows looking out over a small park, and angled mirrors allowing those facing the wall to keep an eye on goings-on behind them. A changing of the guard in the kitchen took place when André Garrett departed to cook at Galvin at Windows (see entry), but the Conran house style of populist brasserie cooking is maintained. The bracing freshness of crab salad is enhanced by a layer of grapefruit jelly, subtly dressed leaves and basil, while a pair of scallops on peas and broad beans are accurately timed and served with frothy lemon butter.

At inspection, the star main course was Telmara duck breast, sliced around a central slab of foie gras, on robustly textured lentils, while a dessert of rich chocolate fondant made with Toscano, and served with pink praline ice cream also impressed, and a benchmark apple tart featured fine pastry, caramelised fruit, and pertinent accompaniments of vanilla ice cream and caramel sauce. The impressively comprehensive wine list opens with 15 extensively annotated 'sommelier's choices' by the bottle (from £15) or by the glass (from £4).

Chef: Allan Pickett **Proprietor:** Conran Restaurants **Open:** all week 12 to 2.30, 6.30 to 10.30 **Closed:** Christmas, 1 Jan, 17 April **Meals:** alc (main courses £18 to £28). Set L £23.50 to £55, Set D £55 **Service:** 12.5% (optional) **Cards:** Amex, Diners, Maestro, MasterCard, Visa **Details:** 80 seats. Vegetarian meals. No-smoking area. Wheelchair access (also WC). No music. Air-conditioned **Tube:** Baker Street, Regent's Park

The price given next to the cooking score is based on the cost of a typical three-course dinner for one person, including coffee, house wine and service.

MAP 13

Ottolenghi

287 Upper Street, N1 2TZ
Tel: (020) 7288 1454
Website: www.ottolenghi.co.uk

Cooking 2 | **Global** | **£36**

The displays of food on shiny white shelves at the deli part of Ottelenghi are extremely alluringly set out: salads, tarts, breads and cakes are placed with an interior designer's eye for impact. The bar area bustles with customers, while at the back, the dining room is a functional, minimalist space. The format is to choose two or three small plates, and many and various global influences are on display. 'Delicious' breads are served with fruity olive oil while 'from the counter' dishes include grilled aubergines with yoghurt and pine nuts, and figs and grilled manouri cheese with basil and rocket. 'From the kitchen' brings poppy seed tart with carrot jam, butternut squash and goats' cheese, and well-seasoned rack of lamb. Fondant cake to end is 'heaven for the real chocolate lover'. The short wine list starts at £13.50. Branches at 63 Ledbury Road, W11, and 1 Holland Street, W8.

Chef: Tricia Jadoonanan and Ramael Scully **Proprietors:** Yotam Ottolenghi and Noam Bar **Open:** all week 11.30 to 5, 6 (7 Sat) to 10.30 **Meals:** alc D (main courses £5.50 to £8.50). Set L £7.50 to £11.50 **Service:** not inc **Cards:** Delta, Maestro, MasterCard, Visa **Details:** 54 seats. 4 seats outside. Vegetarian meals. No smoking. Wheelchair access (not WC). Music. Air-conditioned **Tube:** Angel, Highbury & Islington

MAP 13

Oxo Tower

Oxo Tower Wharf, Barge House Street, SE1 9PH
Tel: (020) 7803 3888

Cooking 4 | **Modern British** | **£64**

This familiar South Bank landmark, close to Waterloo Bridge, is even easier to spot at night when lit up. It gives fine views of other London sights from its eighth floor dining room, a stylishly attired space with wide expanses of glass, neon lights and bare wooden floors. Inventive modern British cooking is the kitchen's modus operandi, with starters taking in mackerel escabèche with cauliflower and crisp garlic alongside seared foie gras with apple cake and beetroot, or lobster with daikon salad, mango and basil. Main courses range from Barbary duck breast with pistachio and five-spice to turbot fillet with spiced crab and grapefruit, or sea bass with asparagus and grilled chorizo, and to finish there might be coconut and lime parfait with roasted pineapple and pistachio baklava, or pumpkin cheesecake with hazelnut foam and gingerbread ice cream. Meals in the bar/brasserie are a little simpler but no less inventive or appealing.

The wine list is loaded with fine and interesting bottles, with France particularly well represented. There is little under £20 but there are no quibbles over value, with mark-ups reasonable throughout. Prices start at £15.50 for red and white vins de pays.

Chef: Jeremy Bloor Proprietor: Harvey Nichols Open: Restaurant Mon to Sat 12 to 2.30, 6 to 11, Sun 12 to 3, 6.30 to 10; Brasserie all week 12 to 3.15 (2.45 Sun), 5.30 to 11 (6 to 10.30 Sun) Meals: Restaurant alc D (main courses £16.50 to £25). Set L £33.50 to £35, Set D £33.50 to £70; Brasserie alc (main courses £14 to £18). Set pre-theatre D £16.50 (2 courses) to £21.50 Service: 12.5% (optional) Cards: Amex, Delta, Diners, Maestro, MasterCard, Visa Details: 150 seats. 80 seats outside. Vegetarian meals. Children's helpings. No-smoking area. Wheelchair access (also WC). Music. No mobile phones. Air-conditioned Tube: Blackfriars, Waterloo

MAP 13

Painted Heron

112 Cheyne Walk, SW10 0DJ
Tel: (020) 7351 5232
Website: www.thepaintedheron.com

Cooking 3 | Modern Indian | £41

Since it opened in 2002, the Painted Heron has been following a steady upward trajectory, building on a foundation of unshowy but accomplished modern Indian cooking, with a menu that, aside from the occasional use of the word 'tandoori' or 'tikka', uses the language of European menus: calf's liver in green chillies marinade, roasted in the tandoor, for example. Pre-meal nibbles with inimitable home-made pickles and chutneys start things off in familiar style, but what follows is an intriguing blend of the modern and the classic. Rack of lamb, for example, comes in a Kashmiri rogan josh with rose petals and sweet red chilli, but the menu also lists roasted duck breast in green-herbs chutney sauce with coconut; you might even find Alaskan black cod steamed in a banana leaf and served with Keralan boatmen's curry and pork

vindaloo. Exotic fruit salad with milk jam ice cream is a good way to finish. Wines start at £15.

Chef: Yogesh Datta Proprietors: Charles Hill and Yogesh Datta Open: Sun to Fri L 12 to 2.30, all week D 6.30 to 10.30 Closed: 25 and 26 Dec, 1 Jan Meals: alc (main courses £11 to £20). Set menu £27.50 Service: 12.5% (optional) Cards: Amex, Delta, Diners, Maestro, MasterCard, Visa Details: 75 seats. 20 seats outside. Vegetarian meals. No smoking in 1 dining room. Music. Air-conditioned Tube: Sloane Square

MAP 14

Papillon

96 Draycott Avenue,
Tel: (020) 7225 2555 SW3 3AD

This oenophile's paradise has more than 600 wines on its impressive list, with fair mark-ups and bottles priced from £19.50. The straightforward food is also worth investigating. Grilled cuttlefish with baby spinach salad (£6.50) is a typical starter, while main courses feature 'delicious and harmonious' Scottish lobster with steamed vegetables and shell cream (£19.50). End with refreshing melon soup with basil sorbet and Parmentier biscuit (£6). Open all week.

MAP 12

Parsee

34 Highgate Hill, N19 5NL
Tel: (020) 7272 9091
Website: www.the-parsee.com

Cooking 2 | Parsee | £37

This informal bistro-style establishment – wood floor, bright lighting, eclectic music and bare tables – between Highgate village and Archway specialises in the Parsee style of Indian cooking. Exotic starters include akoori on toast, a Zoroastrian dish of sweet, sour and hot-spiced scrambled eggs that proved a hit at inspection, and Papeta na pattice, two crunchy, light-textured fried potato cakes with peas, coconut, cashews and spices, served with a thick tomato gravy flavoured with chilli and cardamom. Main course specialities include murghi ni curry nay papeto, a mild chicken dish with chilli, almonds, cashews, roasted chickpeas and peanuts – 'like a korma with a bit of bite' – and roast marinated shank of lamb with ginger, garlic, cumin and green chillies. To finish there might be warm baked custard with nuts and spices. Drinks range from smooth mango lassi, through Indian beers, to wines starting at £13.90 a bottle. Related to Café Spice Namaste (see entry).

Chef/Proprietor: Cyrus Todiwala Open: Mon to Sat D only 6 to 10.40 Closed: 25 Dec to 1 Jan, bank hols Meals: alc (main courses £10 to £13). Set D £25 to £30 Service: 10% (optional) Cards: Amex, Delta, Diners, Maestro, MasterCard, Visa Details: 50 seats. Vegetarian meals. No-smoking area. Wheelchair access (not WC). Music. Air-conditioned Tube: Archway

MAP 15

Passione

10 Charlotte Street, W1T 2LT
Tel: (020) 7636 2833
Website: www.passione.co.uk

Cooking 4 | Modern Italian | £55

Gennaro Contaldo's restaurant on Charlotte Street has built up a loyal following who keep returning for the simple, modern Italian food. The dining room is split into two areas, neither particularly large, and the staff can set a steady pace at busy times; there's also a small number of tables outside perched on a raised terrace. That simplicity, along with careful sourcing, can be seen in smoked rainbow trout with artichoke salad, fennel and pea shoots, which makes a clean and fresh beginning to a meal. A pasta dish might be pappardelle with pork sausage in a tomato sauce, or a Venetian spaghetti dish with clams and bottarga. Rabbit is served on the bone as a main course with rosemary and garlic and sauté potatoes, and king prawns with garlic, chilli, blood orange and green cauliflower. Flavours are paramount throughout, and the robust and hearty nature of the food is the main attraction. Desserts include a rhubarb semifreddo with a rhubarb sauce, or go for pecorino cheese with chestnuts, honey and carta da musica. The Italian wine list start at £13.50 for Sicilian house wines, with little choice by the glass.

Chef: Mario Magli Proprietors: Gennaro Contaldo and Gennaro D'Urso Open: Mon to Fri L 12.30 to 2.15, Mon to Sat D 7 to 10.15 Meals: alc (main courses £21 to £26) Service: 12.5% (optional) Cards: Amex, Delta, Diners, Maestro, MasterCard, Visa Details: 42 seats. 6 seats outside. Vegetarian meals. No pipes/cigars. No music Tube: Goodge Street

 This symbol means that the restaurant has elected to participate in *The Good Food Guide's* £5 voucher scheme (see 'Using The Good Food Guide' for details).

MAP 15

Patara

15 Greek Street, W1D 4DP
Tel: (020) 7437 1071

Cooking 3 | Thai | £51

An upmarket modern Thai restaurant, Patara is part of an international chain, with branches in Singapore, Taipei, Geneva and Bangkok, as well as three other London sites (see below). Wooden Thai figures inlaid with glass mosaic tiles line the walls, and there is a miniature (but still several feet tall) wooden Thai house, all set against a simple colour scheme to create a smart effect. Stylish presentation extends to the food, including traditional Thai-style vegetable carving. But above all it is the quality of the ingredients that stands out, whether in starters of chicken, prawn and beef satay, fish and prawn cakes with cucumber salsa, traditional hot-and-sour tom yum goong soup, or a salad of thinly sliced raw tuna in spicy lemongrass and mint vinaigrette. Main courses show the same commitment to good sourcing, from grilled Aberdeen Angus sirloin in green basil curry sauce to spiced crispy duck leg confit in a piquant tamarind sauce with roast pineapple. Meat and fish dishes are plentiful, and there is also a wide choice of vegetarian options. A short but well-chosen wine list opens with house selections at £13.50. The other London branches are at 9 Beauchamp Place, SW3 1NQ, tel: (020) 7581 8820; 181 Fulham Road, SW3 6JN, tel: (020) 7351 5692; and 3&7 Maddox Street, W1S 2QB, tel: (020) 7499 6008.

Proprietor: S&P Restaurants Ltd Open: Mon to Sat L 12 to 2.30, all week D 6.30 to 10.30 Closed: 25 Dec Meals: alc (main courses £12.50 to £20). Set L £11.95 (2 courses) to £14.95 Service: 12.5% Cards: Amex, Delta, Diners, Maestro, MasterCard, Visa Details: 110 seats. Vegetarian meals. No smoking in dining room. Wheelchair access (also WC). Music. Air-conditioned Tube: Tottenham Court Road

MAP 15

Patterson's

4 Mill Street, W1S 2AX
Tel: (020) 7499 1308
Website: www.pattersonsrestaurant.com

Cooking 4 | Modern French | £57

This intimate restaurant located on a tiny street opposite Saville Row is an appropriately contemporary setting to showcase Raymond Patterson's short but urban and up-to-date menu. All of the dishes have been treated to individual twists, so, to start, you might find tartare of tuna with an anchovy tapenade and egg yolk mousseline, or fried belly of pork on sole with sauerkraut mayonnaise and smoked bacon crumb. Main courses feature the same approach, with steamed cod in a consommé of garden peas, mackerel tortellini, and creamy vegetables, and duck with purée of figs, beetroot with balsamic vinegar, and courgette blossom tempura. To complete your taste sensation, finish off with nougatine torte with poached pineapple, almond cream, and honeycomb, or a Catalan crème brûlée with strawberry infusion. Respondents have commented on enjoying 'charming service and fair prices' in what is, unusually for this part of town, a family-run establishment. France dominates the wine list with house vin de pays at £15 and ten vintages served by the glass from £3.50 to £7.

Chefs/Proprietors: Raymond and Thomas Patterson Open: Mon to Fri L 12 to 3, Mon to Sat D 5 to 11 Closed: bank hols Meals: alc (main courses £10 to £20) Service: 12.5% (optional) Cards: Amex, Delta, Maestro, MasterCard, Visa Details: 80 seats. Vegetarian meals. Children's helpings. Music. Air-conditioned Tube: Oxford Circus

MAP 13

Pearl

252 High Holborn, WC1V 7EN
Tel: (020) 7829 7000
Website: www.pearl-restaurant.com

Cooking 5 | Modern French | £61

The former Pearl Assurance building is the setting for one of the more dramatic hotel conversions of recent years in the Capital, with a striking central courtyard and elegant, capacious public rooms. Pearl has its own entrance and bar, and is a magnificent marble space, divided off from the dining-area by strings of (what else?) pearls. Gently modernised French dishes are Jun Tanaka's forte. His culinary philosophy is all about letting ingredients speak for themselves, so there is a refreshing absence of automatic recourse to luxuries. To start, you might find a Provençal vegetable terrine with aubergine caviar and a mushroom croquette, or a salad of smoked duck from the Landes, served with baby beetroot and walnuts, pickled shallots and goats' cheese. An even balance of fish and meat is in evidence among main courses, which run from sea

bass poached in red wine with oyster beignets and puréed cabbage to olive-crusted Pyrenean lamb with peppers and tomato, white beans and baby artichokes and a pastilla of the shoulder meat. Finish with a cheesecake of Brillat-Savarin with citrus terrine, or rum baba with poached pineapple and coconut ice cream.

A superb wine list includes many opulent French offerings of course, but is also thorough in the United States and the southern hemisphere – there is even a trio of decent German Rieslings. With millions of hand-strung pearls hovering over you, don't expect too many bargains; prices start at £18, and soon hit the roof.

Chef: Jun Tanaka Proprietor: Hotel Property Investors Open: Mon to Fri L 12 to 2.30, Mon to Sat D 6 to 10 Closed: Christmas to New Year, Easter, last 2 weeks Aug Meals: Set L £23.50 (2 courses) to £26.50, Set D £39 (2 courses) to £55 Service: 12.5% (optional) Cards: Amex, Delta, Diners, Maestro, MasterCard, Visa Details: 70 seats. Vegetarian meals. No smoking. Wheelchair access (also WC). Music. No mobile phones. Air-conditioned Accommodation: 356 rooms Tube: Holborn

MAP 14

Pétrus

The Berkeley, Wilton Place, SW1X 7RL
Tel: (020) 7235 1200
Website: www.marcuswareing.com

Cooking 8 | Modern French | £84

Enveloped within the Berkeley Hotel, just off Knightsbridge, Marcus Wareing's restaurant contrasts sharply in visual impact with the light, white hotel foyer. It's a low-lit, sexy, slightly clubby but elegant space, with panels of plum-coloured velvet on the walls and low-backed, red leather chairs. Glass-fronted wine racks overlook the room at one end, while a large display of flowers adds to the tone. Central London feels a world away.

Wareing achieves a rare degree of refinement in what he does, the menus a roll-call of thoroughly original dishes, not just rehashes of ideas found elsewhere. Yes, there's foie gras in a terrine, but paired with tea-smoked mackerel on a carpaccio layer of beetroot. A slip-up at inspection with a mistimed scallop first course was promptly corrected. When properly turned out, the dish involved a trio of tender shellfish on spiced apple purée with a lush celeriac velouté. Culinary fashion still hasn't quite done with purées yet, so another (of white beans) pops up with a brilliantly timed piece of pan-fried halibut, its truffled

Madeira sauce adding to the depth and opulence of the dish.

Ringing endorsements have been received for a starter serving of quail, the breast portions tender and faintly gamey, with deep-fried croquettes of the leg meat, and carrots à la grecque, and also for 'seriously fresh, sweet and moist' braised turbot with butternut squash. Pre-desserts, a bonbon trolley and fine petits fours with coffee mean that you may not necessarily want an actual dessert as well. Then again, consider the opéra coffee gâteau with its coffee mousse and espresso jelly and resist it if you can. Choices lean more towards chocolate, caramel, praline and the ubiquitous tonka beans than fruit, but still exert a powerful pull. All reporters commend the service for flawless attention to detail, combined with genuine charm.

Wines by the glass from £5 lead a list that is high on quality and generously inclusive outside France, which remains, however, its main port of call. There are three vintages from the micro-appellation of Château-Grillet to choose from, for a start, as well as a whole page of Pétrus reaching back to 1924. California is well served too, and definitely worth a look.

Chef/Proprietor: Marcus Wareing **Open:** Mon to Fri L 12 to 2.30, Mon to Sat D 6 to 11 **Closed:** 1 week Christmas **Meals:** Set L £30 to £80, Set D £60 to £80 **Service:** not inc **Cards:** Amex, Delta, Diners, Maestro, MasterCard, Visa **Details:** 70 seats. Vegetarian meals. Children's helpings. No smoking. Wheelchair access (not WC). No music. No mobile phones. Air-conditioned

---

MAP 13

Philpott's Mezzaluna

424 Finchley Road, NW2 2HY
Tel: (020) 7794 0455
Website: www.philpotts-mezzaluna.com

Cooking 3 | **Italian** | **£49**

The long-standing partnership of David Philpott and Alex Ross continues to work its magic, bringing a taste of Italy to Child's Hill. Large windows create a light and airy setting, but the restaurant nevertheless has an intimate feel. The lunch menu changes weekly, the dinner one monthly, and the emphasis on each is clear: this is Italian cooking, produced with imagination and care. Grilled quail with polenta and a caper and raisin salsa, or seared squid with saffron and orange salsa and green bean salad can start off, leading to main courses of stuffed breast of lamb with haggis ravioli, garlic and rosemary, or almond-crusted plaice with roast

potatoes and tomato salsa. Pannacotta with orange and almonds, and chestnut mousse with chocolate filo and espresso jelly are authentic-sounding desserts. Italy forms the bulk of the wine list, which opens in Sicily at £13. Some notable producers shine out, and prices throughout are fair.

Chef: David Philpott **Proprietors:** Alex Ross and David Philpott **Open:** Tue to Fri and Sun L 12 to 2.30 (3 Sun), Tue to Sun D 7 to 11 **Meals:** Set L £17 (2 courses) to £20, Set D £24.50 (2 courses) to £29.50 **Service:** 12.5% (optional) **Cards:** Delta, Maestro, MasterCard, Visa **Details:** 56 seats. 9 seats outside. Vegetarian meals. Children's helpings. Wheelchair access (not WC). Occasional music. Air-conditioned

---

MAP 12

Phoenix

162–164 Lower Richmond Road, SW15 1LY
Tel: (020) 8780 3131
Email: phoenix@sonnys.co.uk

Cooking 4 | **Italian-Plus** | **£42**

'The Phoenix delivers the real deal' says a reporter, commenting on Roger Brooks's one-page menu, which has decidedly Italian leanings. The high quality of ingredients has met with approval, too. The dining room itself is spacious, with lots of framed prints, decent lighting and good-sized tables. Start with grilled lambs' kidneys accompanied by streaky bacon, purple-sprouting broccoli and garlic butter, or perhaps something lighter like grilled English asparagus with Parmesan and balsamic. Specialities such as vincisgrassi maceratesi, truffle lasagne made from an eighteenth-century recipe, remain favourites. Main courses might be whole baked crab with chilli, coriander and ginger, or pot-roast rabbit with garlic and rosemary. The daily-changing set-price menu runs to fettucine, bacon and nettle soup, followed by home-made pork sausages with butter beans and bruschetta. Puddings are plentiful: push the boat out with lemon and polenta cake with fiore di latte, or pineapple and banana pavlova. The wine list is a mixed bag, starting in Sicily at £11.95 but soon climbing above £20.

Chef: Roger Brooks **Proprietor:** Rebecca Mascarenhas **Open:** all week 12.30 to 2.30 (3 Sun), 7 to 11 (10 Sun) **Closed:** 3 days Christmas **Meals:** alc (main courses £11.50 to £17.50). Set L Mon to Sat £13.50 (2 courses) to £15.50, Set L Sun £19.50, Set D Sun to Thur £15.50 (2 courses) to £17.50 **Service:** 12.5% (optional) **Cards:** Amex, Delta, Maestro, MasterCard, Visa **Details:** 100 seats. 30 seats outside. Vegetarian meals. Children's helpings. No-smoking area. Wheelchair access (also WC). Occasional music. Air-conditioned **Tube:** Putney Bridge

---

MAP 13

Phoenix Palace

3–5 Glentworth Street, NW1 5PG
Tel: (020) 7486 3515

| Cooking 2 | Chinese | £33 |

Set below a block of flats not far from Baker Street, this sprawling Chinese restaurant offers predominantly Cantonese cooking on its 200-dish strong menu. It's familiar territory, taking in smoked shredded chicken, ribs and chilli pot stickers (pork dumplings) as appetizers, before baked crab in chilli and garlic, steamed sea bass with ginger and scallion, crispy shredded beef and chicken with cashew nuts. But there's also eel and belly pork casserole, venison and chive udon, and beef brisket noodle. Dim sum have impressed and aromatic crispy duck has been skillfully handled. The minimal wine list kicks off with house French at £10.

Chef/Proprietor: Mr Tan **Open:** all week 12 to 11.30 (10.30 Sun) **Meals:** alc (main courses £6 to £28). Set D £15.80 (2 courses) to £26.80 **Service:** 12.5% **Cards:** Amex, Delta, Maestro, MasterCard, Visa **Details:** 250 seats. Vegetarian meals. No-smoking area. Music. Air-conditioned **Tube:** Baker Street

MAP 15

Pied-à-Terre

34 Charlotte Street, W1T 2NH
Tel: (020) 7636 1178
Website: www.pied-a-terre.co.uk

| Cooking 8 | French | £80 |

After being damaged by fire in 2005, Pied-à-Terre has reopened with a subtly different new look, with small but vivid contemporary paintings to enliven muted design with splotches of primary colour. The place is still run with supreme professionalism, with a bevy of French staff, a good sommelier and even pace throughout.

There has also been subtle modulation in the tone and style of the cooking. Shane Osborn no longer strives for high-wire complexity, but that doesn't reflect any slackening in the kitchen, only an acknowledgement that more straightforward food is fashionable once again. Evidence of the pains taken comes when rabbit is served not just as

the usual saddle, but with ribs too, and a raviolo of the liver. Wispy garnishes are a common feature: pieces of a savoury tuile are set atop John Dory with purple sprouting broccoli, while drifts of sesame filo added lightness to a first course of sliced scallops with a broccoli and crème fraîche purée at inspection. The instinct to let the components of a dish meld together produces a gloriously harmonious main course of roast best end of salt-marsh lamb with minted peas, caramelised sweetbread, crisp bacon, fabulous puréed potato and a garlicky stock reduction.

All stops are pulled out for unmissable desserts, which have included: gin and lime parfait with citrus jelly; and exquisite mango rice pudding squeezed into crisp rolls, and served with an astonishingly rich coconut cream sorbet. Incidentals such as the numerous appetisers, wonderful petits fours and damn fine coffee all impress. One of the best wine lists in London finds room for dry whites from Austria and many diverting wines from Australia and California, in addition to the pick of 1990s burgundy, and clarets stretching back to 1961. Wines by the glass start from £5.

Chef: Shane Osborn **Proprietors:** David Moore and Shane Osborn **Open:** Mon to Fri L 12 to 2.45, Mon to Sat D 6.15 to 10.45 **Meals:** Set L £24 (2 courses) to £60, Set D £49.50 (2 courses) to £75 **Service:** 12.5% (optional) **Cards:** Amex, Delta, Maestro, MasterCard, Visa **Details:** 40 seats. Vegetarian meals. No smoking in 1 dining room. Wheelchair access (not WC). Occasional music. Air-conditioned **Tube:** Goodge Street

MAP 14

Pig's Ear Dining Room

35 Old Church Street, SW3 5BS   NEW ENTRY
Tel: (020) 7352 2908
Website: www.thepigsear.co.uk

| Cooking 2 | Modern European | £41 |

The Pig's Ear is a blueprint for the ideal gastropub: wood panelled, low lit, mirrored. Make your way through the busy bar to find the upstairs dining room, and take a gander at the daily-changing, bistro-style menu while chewing on fresh French sourdough bread sliced at the table. Beetroot and goats' cheese risotto with peas and Parmesan is an impressive starter, with perfectly cooked rice and none of the ingredients getting in each other's way. Following on, pan-fried haddock with mackerel marzipan and roasted fennel is a creative main course, or there might be steak tartare with French fries, served with a side order of French beans and samphire. Lemon and goats' cheesecake with blueberries, Vermouth and mint syrup has impressed among desserts. Service was at times off-hand. The wine list is mainly French, with house choices from £14.

Chef: Ashley Hancill Proprietors: Simon Cherry, Olly Daniaud and Jamie Prudon Open: Sat and Sun L 12.30 to 3, Mon to Sat D 7 to 10.30 Meals: alc (main courses £10 to £19.50) Service: 12.5% (optional) Cards: Amex, Delta, Maestro, MasterCard, Visa Details: 36 seats. Car park. Vegetarian meals. No smoking. Occasional music Tube: Sloane Square

MAP 12

Plateau

Canada Place, Canary Wharf, E14 5ER
Tel: (020) 7715 7100
Website: www.conran.com/eat

| Cooking 3 | Modern French | £64 |

Offering breathtaking views over Canada Square Gardens, this fourth-floor steel and glass restaurant bears all the distinguishing marks of a Conran enterprise: contemporary styling, a semi-open kitchen and smart tablewear to match the immaculately laid marble-topped tables. There is also a separate bar and grill, plus a terrace which offers barbecues during the summer months. The modern French menu changes four times a year. Fish is from Billingsgate, perhaps dressed crab, squid à la plancha, seared tuna and spiced scallops with Jerusalem artichokes for starters, while main courses might be monkfish cooked in black olive oil or Dover sole crusted with rice flour and served with a passion-fruit beurre noisette. Meat eaters might plump for Barbary duck breast with candied almonds. Finish with blood orange soufflé and chocolate sorbet, or praline parfait. The well-constructed wine list is not as pricey as you might expect, with house French opening the list at £18.

Chef: Tim Tolley Proprietor: Conran Restaurants Open: Mon to Fri L 12 to 3, Mon to Sat D 6 to 10.30 Closed: Christmas, Easter, bank hols Meals: alc (main courses £17 to £27.50). Set D £24.75 to £48. Bar and Grill menus available Service: 12.5% (optional) Cards: Amex, Delta, Diners, Maestro, MasterCard, Visa Details: 124 seats. 28 seats outside. Vegetarian meals. Wheelchair access (also WC). No music. Air-conditioned Tube: Canary Wharf

 This symbol means that it is possible to have a three-course dinner, including coffee, half a bottle of house wine and service, for £30 or less per person.

MAP 13

Le Pont de la Tour

36D Shad Thames, SE1 2YE
Tel: (020) 7403 8403
Website: www.conran.com

| Cooking 3 | Modern European | £68 |

Without the spectacular views of Tower Bridge, Pont de la Tour might be hard to distinguish from any one of several Conran-owned venues. Old-fashioned-style prints on the creamy-yellow walls of the low-ceilinged dining room, and smartly laid tables with crisp white cloths, lend a comforting air of familiarity. The style of cooking is essentially traditional French updated with a few modern ideas. Seafood platters are a good choice for anyone after a showpiece starter; otherwise, options run to smoked eel with treacle-cured bacon, beetroot and horseradish, steak tartare, or roast foie gras with a duck egg and Banyuls vinegar. To follow, 'Les Poissons' might feature pike mousse with lobster sauce, or whole Dover sole meunière, while 'Les Viandes' typically encompass goose à la bourguignonne, or chateaubriand (for two to share) with slow-roast tomatoes, pommes châteaux and béarnaise. Desserts might include champagne jelly with lime mascarpone, or chocolate fondant with pistachio ice cream. Fantastic bottles from high-profile producers are scattered liberally throughout the wine list, and the choice by the glass is excellent, though prices are generally unforgiving to those on a budget. House vins de pays are £17.50.

Chef: James Walker Proprietor: Conran Restaurants Open: all week 12 to 3, 6 to 11 Closed: 1 Jan Meals: alc D (main courses £17 to £35). Set L £29.50. Bar/grill menu available Service: 12.5% (optional) Cards: Amex, Delta, Diners, Maestro, MasterCard, Visa Details: 95 seats. 70 seats outside. Vegetarian meals. Children's helpings. Wheelchair access (also WC). Music Tube: Tower Hill, London Bridge

MAP 12

Popeseye

108 Blythe Road, W14 0HD
Tel: (020) 7610 4578

| Cooking 1 | Steaks | £45 |

For honest to goodness steak and chips, look no further than this friendly, straightforward restaurant. The square room is decorated with modern

prints and antique mirrors, while the steak grill sits in the corner deftly churning out the best grass-fed Aberdeen Angus, hung for a minimum of two weeks. The menu gets straight to the main course, which proudly offers sirloin, fillet and popeseye (rump) steak, all with fat crisp chips, and salad if desired. Steak sizes range from a petite 6oz to a giant 30oz, leaving little room for home-made desserts, ice cream or farmhouse cheeses. The wine list is surprisingly comprehensive for such an unpretentious diner, offering a plethora of fine clarets and house selections from £11.50. Their other branch can be found at 277 Upper Richmond Road, SW15; tel: (020) 8788 7733.

Chef/Proprietor: Ian Hutchison Open: Mon to Sat D only 6.45 to 10.30 Meals: alc (main courses £10 to £45.50) Service: 12.5% (optional) Cards: none Details: 34 seats. No cigars. Wheelchair access (not WC). Music Tube: Olympia

MAP 13

Porte des Indes

32 Bryanston Street,
Tel: (020) 7224 0055 W1H 7EG

Waterfalls, giant palms and a bright colour scheme give a theatrical feel to this vast Indian restaurant. Colonial French influences are felt in dishes such as chumude karaikal (rare beef tenderloin with roasted cinnamon, aniseed, cloves and black pepper sauce, £16.90) and policha meen (grilled marinated sea bass in banana leaves with tomato 'rougail' sauce, £19). The long menu also incorporates a wide range of standards, such as Bombay chaat among starters (£6.50) and chicken tandoori for a main course (£11.90), as well as plenty of interesting and unusual vegetarian options. House wines £18. Closed Sat L.

MAP 15

Portrait Restaurant

St Martin's Place, WC2H 0HE
Tel: (020) 7312 2490
Website: www.searcys.co.uk

Cooking 2 | Modern British | £46

Sitting atop the National Portrait Gallery, with fine views over Trafalgar Square and beyond, Portrait is a welcome spot for a bite to eat between viewings, opening for breakfast, afternoon tea and weekend brunch, as well as lunch and dinner. The kitchen's main thrust is a straightforward modern British menu, with starters ranging from potted confit duck and smoked chicken with sweet pickled red cabbage, Cox's apple, caper and cornichon dressing to smoked black pudding with poached egg, spinach and bacon and a wholegrain mustard dressing. Pan-fried wild sea trout with crushed peas and marjoram velouté typifies the simple appeal of main courses, with meat options perhaps including roast corn-fed chicken breast with creamy mash, leeks and bacon with a wild mushroom sauce. Baked peach and apricot clafoutis might round off the meal. Decent wine list with good choice by the glass; prices start at £15.

Chef: Katarina Todosijevic Proprietor: Searcy's Open: all week L 11.45 to 2.45 (3 Sat/Sun), Thur and Fri D 5.30 to 8.30 Closed: 24 and 25 Dec Meals: alc (main courses £12 to £23). Brunch, lounge and pre-theatre (Thur and Fri 5.30 to 6.30) menus available. Service: 12.5% (optional) Cards: Amex, Delta, Maestro, MasterCard, Visa Details: 120 seats. Vegetarian meals. Children's helpings. No smoking. Wheelchair access (also WC). No music. Air-conditioned Tube: Leicester Square, Charing Cross

MAP 13

Potemkin

144 Clerkenwell Road, EC1R 5DP
Tel: (020) 7278 6661
Website: www.potemkin.co.uk

Cooking 3 | Russian | £39

Tucked tidily away beneath the renowned vodka bar, this basement restaurant serves traditional Russian fare from the Baltics and beyond. The décor is arresting, with high-backed red chairs, long white linen tablecloths and large gilt-edged still lifes. All the staples are here, including pickles and rye bread, caviar, and cured herring, but don't expect any seasonal variations. Smoked salmon with blinis, and Kamchatka crab salad, using only meat from the four-inch-long legs of this crab, start the ball rolling, while main courses may include Cossack lamb casserole, lightly spiced pork dumplings, golubcy (cabbage leaves stuffed with chopped pork) and sturgeon, lightly pan-fried and served with asparagus tips. Desserts include the simple, such as berries in sweetened vodka, or luxurious chocolate truffle. The wine list has a Georgian Tamada Saperavi at £18.50, while house choices start at £12.50.

Chef: Elena Makusiyeva **Proprietor:** Burrow Investments Ltd **Open:** Mon to Fri L 12 to 3, Mon to Sat D 6 to 10.30 **Meals:** alc (main courses L £5 to £10, D £9.50 to £18.50). Set L £10 (2 courses) **Service:** 12.5% (optional) **Cards:** Amex, Delta, Diners, Maestro, MasterCard, Visa **Details:** 40 seats. Vegetarian meals. No smoking in dining room. Occasional music. No mobile phones. Air-conditioned

MAP 14

La Poule au Pot

231 Ebury Street, SW1W 8UT
Tel: (020) 7730 7763

Cooking 2 | **French** | **£51**

For a truly French experience, look no further than this fine Parisian-style brasserie. The décor is all clutter, with birdcages, bric-à-brac and large candle chandeliers. The waiters are straight from central casting, and the food is spot-on. Look out for classics such as bouillabaisse, escargots, steak frites and the eponymous poule au pot. Get started with crab salad or perhaps quiche, then try grilled Dover sole, coq au vin or ever-popular cassoulet – or branch out for something like guinea fowl with Calvados sauce. Chocolate mousse or flambé bananas in caramel sauce with ice cream will both tempt at dessert stage. The unashamedly French wine list starts at a reasonable £12.50.

Chefs: Kris Goleblowski and Francisco Reis-Viela **Proprietor:** Peter Frankel **Open:** all week 12.30 to 2.30 (3.30 Sun), 7 to 11 (10 Sun) **Meals:** alc (main courses £14 to £20). Set L £15.50 (2 courses) to £17.50 **Service:** 12.5% (optional) **Cards:** Amex, Delta, Diners, Maestro, MasterCard, Visa **Details:** 70 seats. 40 seats outside. No music. Air-conditioned **Tube:** Sloane Square

MAP 15

Providores

109 Marylebone High Street, W1U 4RX
Tel: (020) 7935 6175
Website: www.theprovidores.co.uk

Cooking 5 | **Fusion** | **£65**

Peter Gordon's Marylebone restaurant is divided into the downstairs Tapa Room and first-floor restaurant. The former is ideal if you want a quick bite to eat and only Gordon's form of fusion food will do; you'll have to sit cheek-by-jowl with like-minded people, but at least you'll have your fix. While, upstairs in the restaurant, the atmosphere is a little more sedate, but only a little. If the setting is

a subdued, monochrome space, the menu is eye-catchingly inventive. Many restaurants have abandoned fusion cooking in favour of a more back-to basics approach, but here the menu may take you from Thai-style soft-shell crab and hot-smoked salmon salad with Cape gooseberries, cucumber, green papaya, young coconut and toasted karengo to roast black pepper and wattle seed-crusted New Zealand venison loin served on umeboshi braised chicory, courgettes and Jersey Royals with pistachio, sultana and caper salsa.

Technique is versatile enough to attempt sashimi of Scottish scallops with watermelon, yuzu, coriander, miso and extra virgin olive oil, and there's gooseberry espresso compote with vanilla cream, wild strawberry sorbet and hazelnut praline with a Sevilla 'torte de aceite' biscuit for dessert. The drinking is fun too, with inventive cocktails supporting a lively wine list noted for its exemplary selection from New Zealand, and a fair choice from 'other world' producers. Prices start at £14.50 and 18 come by the glass.

Chefs: Peter Gordon, Miles Kirby and Christian Hossack **Proprietors:** Peter Gordon, Michael McGrath and Jeremy Leeming **Open:** all week 12 to 2.45, 6 to 10.30 (10 Sun), tapa room all week 9 to 10.30 (10 to 10 Sun) **Meals:** alc (main courses £18 to £24.50) **Service:** 12.5% (optional) **Cards:** Amex, Delta, Maestro, MasterCard, Visa **Details:** 80 seats. 6 seats outside. Vegetarian meals. No smoking. Wheelchair access (also WC). No music. Air-conditioned **Tube:** Baker Street, Bond Street

MAP 15

Quo Vadis

26–29 Dean Street, W1D 3LL
Tel: (020) 7437 9585
Website: www.whitestarline.org.uk

Cooking 4 | **Italian/Mediterranean** | **£58**

The edgy Brit-art may divide people, but at least the imaginative and intriguing menu is as exciting as the surroundings demand. Unusually for a Marco Pierre White owned establishment, the chef, Fernando Coradazzi, doesn't adhere to tried-and-trusted techniques, but seems willing to give unusual combinations a whirl: a main course fillet of turbot, for example, comes with wild rice, thyme and lime and rhubarb soup, while crêpes stuffed with soft cheese and an orange, carrot and vanilla coulis accompany grilled fillet of beef. Bright and lively ideas pop up in starters like Piedmont ravioli with organic soft cheese, broad beans, mint and speck, or salmon marinated in Jamaican coffee and served with a seasonal fruit salad. Desserts are a cut or two above the Italian norm – strawberry soup with balsamic jelly – and service, on the whole, is professional and friendly. Predominantly Italian and French wines aim for the upper end of the market and there is little for modest spenders. House French is £16.

> **Chef:** Fernando Coradazzi **Proprietors:** Marco Pierre White and Jimmy Lahoud **Open:** Mon to Fri L 12 to 3, Mon to Sat D 5.30 to 11.30 **Closed:** 25 and 26 Dec, 1 Jan **Meals:** alc (main courses £9 to £18). Set L £14.95 (2 courses) to £19.95, Set D 5.30 to 6.45 £14.95 (2 courses) to £19.95 **Service:** 12.5% (optional) **Cards:** Amex, Delta, Diners, Maestro, MasterCard, Visa **Details:** 90 seats. No smoking area, no cigars in dining room. Wheelchair access (not WC). No music. Air-conditioned **Tube:** Tottenham Court Road

MAP 14

Racine

239 Brompton Road, SW3 2EP
Tel: (020) 7584 4477

Cooking 4	Rustic French	£50

At a time when the 'bistrot de luxe' is taking the country by storm, Racine can claim to have been ahead of the game; for five years now, Henry Harris has been delivering a traditional French menu in a smart-yet-relaxed setting – the consummate example of the genre. Waiters serve with gusto and a minimum of fuss, and the menu is unassailably Gallic. Start with a soupe de poissons with all the bits and pieces you'd expect, or an even more classic escargot bourguignonne. The quality of the produce shines through, as in a daube of venison, 'tender and full of flavour', served with chestnuts, quince and celeriac purée, and a benchmark grilled calf's liver with sautéed shallots, lardoons and pommes purée. The kitchen is equally adept at handling fish, as in a 'fine' seared monkfish with a risotto of cherry tomatoes, chives and anchovy, or fillet of red mullet with brown shrimps, capers and lemon. Desserts continue in the traditional vein, with tarte au citron, and apricot and chocolate soufflé. The wine list eschews the rest of the world, with bottle prices starting at £16, and 15 available by the glass.

> **Chefs:** Henry Harris and Chris Handley **Proprietors:** Eric Garnier and Henry Harris **Open:** all week 12 to 3 (3.30 Sat and Sun), 6 to 10.30 (10 Sun) **Closed:** 25 Dec **Meals:** alc (main courses £13.25 to £20.75). Set L £16.50 (2 courses) to £18.50, Set D 6 to 7.30 £16.50 (2 courses) to £18.50 **Service:** 14.5% (optional) **Cards:** Amex, Delta, Diners, Maestro, MasterCard, Visa **Details:** 65 seats. Vegetarian meals. Children's helpings. No smoking. No music. Air-conditioned **Tube:** Knightsbridge, South Kensington

MAP 12

Radha Krishna Bhavan

86 Tooting High Street, SW17 0RN
Tel: (020) 8682 0969
Website: www.mcdosa.com

Cooking 1	South Indian	£24

Food from the South Indian region of Kerala is the speciality at this ever-popular Tooting venue. Opening the menu are various dosa pancakes, filled with spiced vegetables and meat and served with sambar and coconut chutney, along with the likes of idli (a steamed cake of rice and black gram), uthappam (Indian-style pizza), and mysore bonda (fried spiced lentil balls). Otherwise there is a wide choice of curry-house standards. Wines start at £9.95.

> **Chefs:** Mr T. Ali and Mr Yusuf **Proprietors:** T. Haridas and family **Open:** all week 12 to 3, 6 to 11 (12 Fri and Sat) **Closed:** 25 and 26 Dec **Meals:** alc (main courses £2.50 to £8) **Service:** 10% **Cards:** Amex, Delta, Maestro, MasterCard, Visa **Details:** 50 seats. Vegetarian meals. Children's helpings. No-smoking area. Wheelchair access (not WC). Occasional music. Air-conditioned **Tube:** Tooting Broadway

MAP 15

Randall & Aubin AR

14–16 Brewer Street, W1R 3FS
Tel: (020) 7287 4447

This lively diner, which also boasts a deli, was once a butcher's shop – hence the white tiling and hooks hanging from the ceiling. Now, however, seafood is as much a feature as the rôtisserie, which turns out spiced chicken (£10.50) and a roast of the day. The menu caters for lighter appetites with the likes of eggs Benedict (£7.25), while main courses range from roast langoustines in garlic butter with chips (£18.50), through fish and chips with tartare sauce (£10.50) to lobster. Wines from £13.50. Closed Sun L. A second branch is at 329–331 Fulham Road, SW10; tel: (020) 7823 3515.

> AR Not a full entry but provisionally recommended. These 'also recommended' establishments are integrated throughout the book.

MAP 12

Rani

7 Long Lane, N3 2PR
Tel: (020) 8349 4386

Reliable, traditional Gujarati vegetarian cooking is what to expect at this long-established family-run restaurant. Chana chat (£3.60) and bhel poori (£3.70) are among cold starters, hot options taking in samosas (£3.30) and akhaa murcha (deep-fried stuffed chillies; £3.50). Main courses, meanwhile, range from matar gobi (mildly spiced cauliflower and peas; £4.60) to akhaa ringal (whole Kenyan aubergines stuffed with spices, peanuts and coriander; £5.40). All-in-one set meals include masala dosa with sambhar and coconut chutney (£7.80). Drink lassi, falooda or wine from £9.70. Open Sun L and all week D.

MAP 12

Ransome's Dock

35–37 Parkgate Road, SW11 4NP
Tel: (020) 7223 1611
Website: www.ransomesdock.co.uk

Cooking 4 | **Modern European** | **£47**

This 'convivial neighbourhood restaurant' has an enviable canalside location, and Martin and Vanessa Lam have built up a solid following over the last 15 years. Bag a place on the terrace when the weather allows, although the unpretentious dining room is pleasant enough, with smartly set, well-spaced tables. The menu is wide-ranging, with daily fish specials of particular interest: monkfish and pea and mint risotto, for example. Deep-fried salt cod in saffron butter was a 'simple but delicious dish', while chargrilled quail with a watercress, ginger and olive salad has also impressed. Meat cookery is also well timed, as in a vast portion of grilled Barrow Gurney lamb, pink and tender, or another large dish of slow-roast belly pork in sherry with an excellent accompaniment of lentils and spinach. Rice pudding with golden plum and blueberry compote is a comforting finish, or go for blood orange jelly with crème fraîche ice cream. The bulky global wine list, starting at £15, attends to all tastes and carries a good number of half-bottles, although only five by the glass (from £4.50).

Chefs/Proprietors: Martin and Vanessa Lam **Open:** all week L 12 to 5 (3.30 Sun), Mon to Sat D 6 to 11 **Closed:** Christmas, Aug bank hol **Meals:** alc (exc Sat and Sun L; main courses £10.50 to £22.50). Set L £14.75 (2 courses). **Service:** 12.5% (optional) **Cards:** Amex, Delta, Diners, Maestro, MasterCard, Visa **Details:** 56 seats. 20 seats outside. Car park (evenings and weekends only). Children's helpings. Vegetarian meals. No smoking in 1 dining room. Wheelchair access (also WC). Music. No mobile phones **Tube:** Sloane Square

MAP 12

Rasa

55 Stoke Newington Church Street, N16 0AR
Tel: (020) 7249 0344
Website: www.rasarestaurants.com

Cooking 2 | **Indian Vegetarian** | **£29**

Das Sreedharan's chain of restaurants has done much to bring awareness of Keralan cooking to London. This Stoke Newington branch is the original, opened thirteen years ago, and the only one in the group that is entirely vegetarian, with cashew nuts, coconuts, green bananas and yoghurt all key ingredients. The trademark poppadom selection is unmissable: they come plain and spiced, together with cake-like snacks made of rice flour and flavoured with cumin and black sesame seeds, and are served with home-made chutneys. When you're done with the poppadoms, move on to starters like rasam (a peppery lentil broth) or masala verdal (crunchy, spicy, deep-fried patties teamed with coconut chutney), before engaging the subtle spicing and rounded flavours that characterise main courses such as rasa kayi (a mixed vegetable curry), or crisp, spicy, potato-filled masala dosa. House wine is £11.95. See below for some of the other restaurants in the group.

Chef: Rajan Karattil **Proprietor:** Sivadas Sreedharan **Open:** Sat and Sun L 12 to 3, all week D 6 to 10.45 (11.45 Fri and Sat) **Closed:** 24 to 26 Dec, 1 Jan **Meals:** alc (main courses £3.50 to £5.95). Set L and D £16 **Service:** 12.5% (optional) **Cards:** Amex, Diners, Maestro, MasterCard, Visa **Details:** 64 seats. Vegetarian meals. No smoking. Wheelchair access (not WC). No music. Air-conditioned **Tube:** Finsbury Park

	This symbol means that it is possible to have a three-course dinner, including coffee, half a bottle of house wine and service, for £30 or less per person.

MAP 15

Rasa Samudra

5 Charlotte Street, W1T 1RE
Tel: (020) 7637 0222
Website: www.rasarestaurants.co.uk

| Cooking 4 | Indian Seafood/Vegetarian | £37 |

As part of Das Sreedharan's Rasa chain (see entries above and below), Samudra offers Keralan seafood specialities and vibrant vegetarian dishes. The décor is as exotic at the food; Indian silks billow from the ceilings, two wooden donkey heads sit above the door and friendly waiters wear flowing robes. The meal starts with a variety of poppadoms, including pappadavadai (poppadoms dipped in a light batter), and home-made chutneys. Starters could be konju varuthathu (king prawns marinated in a chilli paste) or vadais (a South Indian speciality of deep-fried lentils, cashew nuts and spinach patties). Continue with varatha meen masala (lightly fried pieces of king-fish cooked in a thick tomato and chilli sauce), or the chef's speciality, crab varuthathu (a dry dish prepared with chilli and mustard seeds). Breads are plentiful, from parathas to chapatis, while desserts are above average: the kulfi has been praised in the past for its full flavour, as has the kesari, a semolina dish made with mango and cashew nuts. The brief wine list opens at £11.95.

Chef: Prasad Mahadevan Proprietor: Das Sreedharan Open: Mon to Sat L 12 to 2.30, all week D 6 to 10.30 Closed: 24 Dec to 1 Jan Meals: alc (main courses £6.50 to £12.50). Set L and D £22.50 to £30 Service: 12.5% (optional) Cards: Amex, Delta, Maestro, MasterCard, Visa Details: 90 seats. Vegetarian meals. No smoking. Wheelchair access (not WC). Music. Air-conditioned Tube: Tottenham Court Road, Goodge Street

MAP 12

Rasa Travancore

56 Stoke Newington Church Street, N16 0NB
Tel: (020) 7249 1346

Lively Indian restaurant related to the original Rasa (see entry above), which is on the other side of Stoke Newington Church Street. Menus have a similar focus on Kerala but are not exclusively vegetarian. Crab varuthathu (£7.95), flavoured with turmeric and chilli, highlights their love of shellfish, while arachu varatha meen (kingfish with tamarind; £6.50) is a speciality. Mutton muppas

(£5.95) is a traditional curry, while vegetarians might go for potato porichathu (sliced potatoes with coriander; £2.75). End with cardamom and banana pancake (£2.75). Wines from £9.50. Open Sun L and all week D.

MAP 15

Rasa W1

6 Dering Street, W1S 1AD
Tel: (020) 7629 1346

Just off Oxford Street, this outpost of the mini chain of Indian restaurants (see entries above) is a natural choice for lunching shoppers. As at the other branches, the focus is on the cooking of Kerala, although meat as well as vegetarian dishes are on offer here. The menu takes in snacks, including pappadavadai (£4), and idli with sambhar and coconut chutney (£4.50), starters such as banana boli (£4.25) and main courses ranging from malabar erachi chaaru (tender aromatic spiced lamb; £7.95) to kappayum meenum (kingfish cooked in onions, chillies, turmeric and ginger, served with cassava; £12.50). Wines from £10.95. Closed Sun.

MAP 14

Rasoi Vineet Bhatia

10 Lincoln Street, SW3 2TS
Tel: (020) 7225 1881
Website: www.vineetbhatia.com

| Cooking 5 | Modern Indian | £69 |

Less like dining out at a smart restaurant, eating at Vineet Bhatia's very personal restaurant is more like having dinner at a friend's house, albeit a friend who is a highly rated cook living at an exclusive Chelsea address. Ring at the front door to gain admission before being welcomed into a cosy front room on a very domestic scale (tables are necessarily small), where walls painted in exotic shades – coffee and cinnamon, for example – are adorned with many brightly coloured face masks.

Bhatia's cooking style shows great respect for his roots in traditional Indian regional cooking, but brings to it a generous measure of inventiveness and intelligence to create some sophisticated modern dishes. If the nine-course 'gourmand' menu sounds a bit too much, a good way to sample the kitchen's range is the starter platter for two from the carte, which could comprise spiced home-smoked salmon, a skewer of grilled spice-crusted scallops with cucumber and peanut chaat, crispy prawns, malai chicken tikka, lamb seekh kebab and chilli tandoori broccoli. Creativity is given full rein in main courses to produce grilled ginger and chilli lobster tail, served with spiced lobster jus, curry leaf and broccoli khichdi with dried broccoli florets, and spiced cocoa powder. More conventional-sounding alternatives might be lamb biryani with apricots, saffron, almonds and basmati rice baked under a flaky crust. Desserts include rasmalai layered with fresh fruit and cinnamon rabdi, and mango mousse with lemon jelly and strawberry sorbet. The wine list is unusually good by Indian restaurant standards, with many bottles chosen well to accompany the rich, spicy flavours. Prices start at around the £20 mark.

Chef: Vineet Bhatia Proprietors: Vineet and Rashima Bhatia Open: Mon to Fri L 12 to 2.30, Mon to Sat D 6.30 to 10.45 Closed: bank hols Meals: alc (main courses £14 to £27). Set L £19 (2 courses) to £30, Set D £58 to £69 Service: 12.5% (optional) Cards: Amex, Delta, Diners, Maestro, MasterCard, Visa Details: 58 seats. Vegetarian meals. No smoking. No music. Air-conditioned Tube: Sloane Square

MAP 13

Real Greek

14–15 Hoxton Market, N1 6HG
Tel: (020) 7739 8212
Website: www.therealgreek.com

Cooking 4 | Greek | £42

One reader mused that the Real Greek has done for Greek food what Moro (see entry) has done for Spanish/North African cooking. Theodore Kyriakou adopts an individual, unfussy approach, serving up fresh, clean flavours amid unaffected décor – notably plain wooden tables and chairs. Meze combinations are the way to start, say sliced octopus baked in parchment with tzatziki and spiced lentils, or grilled crevettes with mayonnaise, pickled fennel and deep-fried squash, bulgur wheat and herb fritters. The food is wholesome and has an appealing rural edge that seems to elevate the main ingredients; it does not aim to be grand cuisine. Witness venison roasted as a rack and served as two chops with 'deep, mature, rich gaminess' complemented by mushrooms and a rich red-wine sauce, or a 'basic, rustic, country-style' roast pork served carved with prunes and piled on a mound of leeks resting on a whole artichoke. Fish is equally well handled: John Dory, for example, comes with breadcrumbs, moistened with tomatoes and zipped up with spring onions and caper

leaves. Passion-fruit cheesecake and chocolate torte are among desserts to get the thumbs-up and the all-Greek wine list is grouped according to suitability to fish, meat etc., with 11 available by the glass. Prices start at £12.50.

Chef: Alasdair Fraser Proprietor: Theodore Kyriakou and Paloma Campbell Open: Mon to Sat 12 to 3, 5.30 to 10.30 Meals: alc (main courses £8 to £17) Service: 12.5% (optional) Cards: Delta, Maestro, MasterCard, Visa Details: 80 seats. 30 seats outside. Vegetarian meals. No smoking in 1 dining room. Wheelchair access (also WC). No music Tube: Old Street

MAP 13

Real Greek Souvlaki and Bar

140–142 St John Street, EC1V 4UA
Tel: (020) 7253 7234
Website: www.therealgreek.co.uk

Cooking 2 | Greek | £25

£

Quite a different enterprise from the parent restaurant, the Real Greek (see entry above), this lively bar serves a selection of mezedes and souvlaki. These small dishes and marinated meats are served as lots of little plates, all freshly cooked and following the seasons. Souvlaki come with flat bread to wrap or tasty chunks of bread to dip, and you can choose from lamb, chicken or pork. Mezedes see the likes of stuffed vine leaves, feta cheese dressed with olive oil, grilled octopus or charcoal-grilled crevettes. Other notables here include spiced Armenian sausages and their Real Greek burger made with ribeye steak, served with minted Greek yoghurt and chips. End with traditional favourites such as baklava. Greek wines from £11.75. Other branches are at Putney, Bankside, Covent Garden and Marylebone.

Proprietor: Clapham House Group Open: Mon to Sat 12 to 11 Meals: alc (main courses £4 to £6.50). Set L 12 to 7 £8.75 (2 courses), Set D 7 to 11 £9.75 (2 courses). Bar menu available Service: 12.5% (optional) Cards: Delta, Maestro, MasterCard, Visa Details: 120 seats. 24 seats outside. Vegetarian meals. Children's helpings. No-smoking area. Wheelchair access (not WC). Music. Air-conditioned Tube: Farringdon

To submit a report on any restaurant, please visit *www.which.co.uk/gfgfeedback*.

MAP 12

Rebato's

169 South Lambeth Road, SW8 1XW
Tel: (020) 7735 6388

This enduringly popular tapas bar attracts a loyal crowd. Its menu has changed little over the years – indeed, one diner commented that it was 'like stepping back into the seventies', with long-serving Spanish waiters providing an authentic touch. The à la carte features calamares à la romana, and prawns in olive oil and garlic (both £4.75), while daily specials might include 'flavourful' roast suckling pig, or paella Valencia (both £11.95). End with desserts from the trolley such as strawberry flan (£3.75). Spanish house wines from £10.50. Closed Sat L and Sun.

MAP 15

Red Fort

77 Dean Street, W1D 3SH
Tel: (020) 7437 2525/2115
Website: www.redfort.co.uk

| Cooking 3 | Modern Indian | £54 |

A distinctly upmarket feel pervades this smart West End venue. Low lighting gives the dining room a cosy ambience, while a tastefully neutral colour scheme provides the simple backdrop for Indian jars and statues displayed in wall recesses, and white-clothed tables are adorned with tea lights floating in brass dishes among rose petals. Menus focus on the regional cooking of Hyderabad and Lucknow, albeit with ideas and ingredients brought in from elsewhere. Seafood is a strong point, appearing in interesting and unusual starters such as oyster pickle with cucumber in a ginger and star anise dressing, or lightly spiced monkfish with ginger. Main courses could include whole tandoori sea bass, or king prawns in chilli and tomato with coconut milk and Thai lemon leaf, while meat dishes might be grilled Scottish lamb chops in star anise and pomegranate juice, or smoked chicken in ginger, garlic, pickles and chilli, with side dishes such as sautéed spinach with 'tangy spices'. Wines start at £19 for a pair of house French selections.

Proprietor: Amin Ali **Open:** Mon to Fri L 12 to 2.15, all week D 5.45 to 11.15 (5.30 to 10.30 Sun) **Meals:** alc (main courses £12.50 to £30). Set L £12 (2 courses) to £25, Set D 5.45 to 7 £16 (2 courses) to £45 **Service:** 12.5% (optional) **Cards:** Amex, Delta, Maestro, MasterCard, Visa **Details:** 77 seats. Vegetarian meals. No-smoking area. Wheelchair access (also WC). Music. Air-conditioned **Tube:** Tottenham Court Road

MAP 12

Redmond's

170 Upper Richmond Road West, SW14 8AW
Tel: (020) 8878 1922
Website: www.redmonds.org.uk

| Cooking 5 | Modern British | £46 |

Large, plate-glass windows entice the curious into the single, rectangular room that is Redmond's. The space is divided up well, done in today's relaxing, muted colours, and an air of assured professionalism pervades the place, strong testament to Redmond and Pippa Hayward's considerate approach. Redmond takes care to note what dishes garner support among his regulars. Home-salted cod brandade seems a winner, served in a shellfish bisque in winter, with gazpacho in spring and summer. Scallops are ever-popular, done modishly with cauliflower pannacotta, perhaps, or in a lobster broth with bi-coloured pasta and aromatics of ginger and coriander.

An early evening menu with a pair of choices at each stage supplements the principal prix fixe, which might offer main courses of sea bass with smoked salmon and basil risotto, or duck breast with butternut squash, spinach and thyme jus. Appealing desserts have included apple sorbet with apple fritters and cider soup, or caramelised banana tart with an ice cream of lime and cardamom. The already fine wine list has just got finer, with a third of it made up of new listings since last year. These include some Austrian Grüner Veltliner, Chilean Syrah and a great Collioure from southern France, indicating the broad-mindedness that has always typified the approach to wine here. House wines include a Greek rosé, and are priced from £15.25, or £4.95 a glass.

This symbol means that the restaurant has elected to participate in *The Good Food Guide's* £5 voucher scheme (see 'Using The Good Food Guide' for details).

Chefs: Redmond Hayward and Jason D'Orsi   Proprietors: Redmond and Pippa Hayward   Open: Sun L 12 to 2.30, Mon to Sat D 6.30 (7 Fri and Sat) to 10   Closed: 3 days Christmas, bank hols exc Good Friday   Meals: Set L £18.50 (2 courses) to £23, Set D Mon to Thur 6.30 to 7.45 £14.25 (2 courses) to £16.95, Set D Mon to Sat £27.50 (2 courses) to £32   Service: not inc   Cards: Delta, Maestro, MasterCard, Visa   Details: 48 seats. Vegetarian meals. Children's helpings. No smoking. Wheelchair access (not WC). Occasional music. Air-conditioned

MAP 13

Refettorio

Crowne Plaza – the City, 19 New Bridge Street, EC4V 6DB
Tel: (020) 7438 8052
Website: www.tableinthecity.com

Cooking 2 | Italian | £52

Sleek, stylish and smart, in fact everything you'd expect given this hotel restaurant's City location. First you encounter the bar area, before reaching the more formal dining room decked out in crisp, white linens, brown leather and dark chocolate walls. The menu is staunchly traditional Italian, so look out for the varied antipasti, as well as the pastas and main courses. Gnocchi with a tomato and basil sauce was a good version at inspection, while main course pan-fried breast of duck with spelt and honey was well-timed, and pan-fried red mullet has also impressed this year. High praise went to their apple carpaccio which was innovatively accompanied by a brown tea sorbet. The all-Italian wine list climbs steeply but their house Salento starts at £15.

Chef: Mattia Camorani   Proprietor: Crowne Plaza Hotels   Open: Mon to Fri L 12 to 2.30, Mon to Sat D 6 to 10.30 (10 Fri and Sat)   Closed: 24 Dec to 2 Jan, bank hols   Meals: alc (main courses £9 to £22)   Service: 12.5% (optional)   Cards: Amex, Delta, Diners, MasterCard, Visa   Details: 100 seats. Vegetarian meals. Wheelchair access (also WC). No music. Air-conditioned   Accommodation: 203 rooms   Tube: Blackfriars

The price given next to the cooking score is based on the cost of a typical three-course dinner for one person, including coffee, house wine and service.

MAP 13

Rhodes Twenty Four

Tower 42, 25 Old Broad Street, EC2N 1HQ
Tel: (020) 7877 7703
Website: www.rhodes24.co.uk

Cooking 5 | British | £59

The escalators, lifts, security doorways and airport-style check-in desk will make you feel you are about to embark on a transatlantic flight, but the preliminaries are certainly worth it. You are rewarded with a spectacular, eagle's-nest view over London that has cameras flashing all around, while Adam Gray's interpretations of Gary Rhodes' dishes are capable of dazzling in their own way.

An instant highlight at an inspection visit was the starter of glazed lobster thermidor risotto, an opulently rich and accomplished dish that is sure to be a crowd-pleaser. Refined seafood also finds its way into a composition that matches a cream-bound terrine of smoked salmon with quail's egg Benedict, with some further seared smoked salmon in a salad. When it comes to main courses, the kitchen aims for maximum impact, delivering resonant depth of flavour in many dishes. Moist-textured brill with wild mushrooms, and 'beautifully intense' creamed celeriac and onion, was a fine inspection dish, and so was the now terribly unfashionable chicken breast, served here with morels and a rich braise of the leg meat in a risotto.

Childhood memories will come flooding back with the likes of Jaffa cake pudding, or steamed apple and blackberry sponge with custard, while grown-up tastes are catered for by means of tiramisù ice cream with a cognac sabayon. Service is keen, single-mindedly determined to get the job done. A shorter wine list than you might be expecting opens with vins de pays at £17, and stays almost entirely within double figures, which isn't bad for the City of London.

Chef: Adam Gray   Proprietors: Gary Rhodes and Restaurant Associates – Compass Group   Open: Mon to Fri 12 to 2.30, 6 to 9   Closed: Christmas, New Year, bank hols   Meals: alc (main courses £17.50 to £25)   Service: 12.5% (optional)   Cards: Amex, Delta, Diners, Maestro, MasterCard, Visa   Details: 72 seats. Vegetarian meals. No smoking in 1 dining room. Wheelchair access (also WC). Music. Air-conditioned   Tube: Liverpool Street

MAP 12

River Café

Thames Wharf, Rainville Road, W6 9HA
Tel: (020) 7386 4200
Website: www.rivercafe.co.uk

Cooking 6	Italian	£65

Rose Gray and Ruth Rogers have been flying the flag for new-wave Italian cooking for twenty years and, media brouhaha and time restraints on tables notwithstanding, the River Café is as sharp and cosmopolitan as ever. The white dining room feels restrained but not austere, while the flickering wood-burning oven catches the eye. The simple and uncluttered presentation of dishes highlights the care and precision of the cooking and the understated approach. Menus change with each service while seasonality, natural flavours and avoidance of gimmickry are the watchwords. Fish is accurately timed and often lifted by a lightly spicy accompaniment: say antipasti of crab with bruschetta, chilli, fennel seeds, agretti, olive oil and lemon, or a main of chargrilled monkfish with chilli and mint sauce, deep-fried lemon slices and artichoke and mâche salad. Freshness, timing and balance combine to give the food vitality. And meat dishes equally accomplished could include pigeon, T-bone beefsteak, or perhaps osso buco served with saffron risotto. To finish, unerringly applied craftsmanship creates rich pressed chocolate cake with Vin Santo ice cream, or a pannacotta with grappa and champagne rhubarb: accurate treatment and fine judgement turning straightforward into first class. Service is confident and evenly paced, and wine, after tasting, is left on the table for DIY pouring.

The all-Italian list is packed with interesting stuff, and prices that encourage experimentation. Explore the 14 that come by the glass (£4.25-£17.25) to tour the range of flavours; bottles start at £17.50.

Chefs: Rose Gray, Ruth Rogers and Theo Randall **Proprietors:** Rose Gray and Ruth Rogers **Open:** all week L 12.30 to 3 (12 to 3.30 Sun), Mon to Sat D 7 to 9.30 **Closed:** Christmas, bank hols **Meals:** alc (main courses £25 to £31) **Service:** 12.5% (optional) **Cards:** Amex, Delta, Diners, Maestro, MasterCard, Visa **Details:** 105 seats. 70 seats outside. Car park (D and weekends only). Children's helpings. No smoking. Wheelchair access (also WC). No music **Tube:** Hammersmith

MAP 13

Roast

NEW ENTRY

Floral Hall, Borough Market, Stoney Street, SE1 1TL
Tel: (020) 7940 1300
Website: www.roast-restaurant.com

Cooking 4	British	£51

One reader mourned the transformation of the 'touchy-feely character' of the Victorian Borough Market into 'a middle-class foodie destination with aspirational prices to match'. But Iqbal Wahhab of Cinnamon Club fame (see entry) is to be commended for his great British restaurant 'which appears like a glass-fronted mission-control deck in a gigantic James Bond film set', and gives panoramic views of the market. The food is relaxed and unpretentious, and menus focus on showing off good raw materials. A spring inspection meal produced boned and spatchcocked roast Lancashire quail with slices of mulled pear, and a successful partnership of well-timed sea bass with waxy, nutty potatoes and a caper salad. That meal finished in style with Welsh rarebit and an excellent rhubarb crumble with custard. Service is pretty efficient and cheerful, while wine prices reflect the stylish surroundings (house wine is £18), but the succinct, varietally arranged global selection is consistently interesting and 15 are offered by the glass.

Chef: Lawrence Keogh **Proprietor:** Iqbal Wahhab **Open:** Sun to Fri L 12 to 2.30 (4 Sun), Mon to Sat D 5.30 to 10.30 **Meals:** alc (main courses £13.50 to £25). Set L £18 (2 courses) to £21. Set D (exc 6.45 to 9) £18 (2 courses) to £21. Breakfast and bar menus available **Service:** 12.5% (optional) **Cards:** Amex, Delta, Maestro, MasterCard, Visa **Details:** 110 seats. Vegetarian meals. Children's helpings (Sat). No smoking. Wheelchair access (also WC). No music. Air-conditioned **Tube:** London Bridge

MAP 15

Roka

37 Charlotte Street, W1T 1RR
Tel: (020) 7580 6464

Cooking 4	Japanese-Plus	£34

With its sheer-glass frontage and abundance of pale wood and zinc, this ultra-hip Charlotte Street establishment catches the eye. Like Rainer Becker's other restaurant, Zuma (see entry), it attracts a

fashionable crowd, all here for food that is an accessible fusion of new-wave Japanese with pan-Asian undertones. The kitchen's output lives up to the billing, with an enticing variety of sushi, sashimi and maki rolls, salmon cured in brown rice miso and baked on a hoba leaf, and quail marinated in plum wine and red miso. High-quality ingredients are complemented by careful balancing of flavours, but prices can mount up – the sushi set (£15) and robata set (£18) offered as business lunches make good introductions. Tonka-bean ice cream or dark chocolate pudding with pineapple and caramelised marshmallow and vanilla ice cream might finish things off nicely. A compact wine list kicks off with a South African white at £17.50, but saké seems the appropriate accompaniment, with hot or cold carafes offered from £8.

Chefs: Nicholas Watt and Rainer Becker Proprietors: Arjun Waney and Rainer Becker Open: Mon to Sat L 12 to 2.30, all week D 5.30 to 11.15 (10 Sun); summer all week 12 to 11.15 Meals: alc (main courses £7 to £55). Set L £15 to £18, Set D £50 to £75 Service: 12.5% (optional) Cards: Amex, Delta, Diners, MasterCard, Visa Details: 88 seats. 20 seats outside. Vegetarian meals. No smoking. Wheelchair access (also WC). Music. Air-conditioned Tube: Goodge Street

MAP 14

Roussillon

16 St Barnabas Street, SW1W 8PE
Tel: (020) 7730 5550
Website: www.roussillon.co.uk

Cooking 5 | **Modern French** | **£64**

Although Roussillon is a touch unassuming when viewed from the quiet residential Chelsea street, once you're through the door it makes a good impression with its two small, softly coloured dining rooms enlivened by splashes of colour from well-spaced art work. Alexis Gauthier hails from southern France, but he is a keen advocate of seasonal British produce, so the spring menu, for example, may open with a salad of Kentish spring leaves alongside a thin tart of confit rabbit and rosemary, or poached Shetland sea trout served, perhaps, with caramelised young beetroots in their jus and a red wine and pink shallots reduction. There's a wide spread of flavours in appealing main-course options along the lines of crunchy Black Spot Welsh pork with an almond and truffle crust, simmered leeks and parsley and herb mashed potato, or steamed fillet of John Dory with clams, pineapple, grapefruit and curry sauce. Highly pol-

ished desserts take in aromatic rose cream, or mascarpone and lemon sorbet. The set lunch menu offers good choice and good value at £35, (including water, half a bottle of wine and coffee), and children get their own seven-course mini gastronomic menu. Service is generally expertly coordinated and there is no doubting the professionalism.

France is obviously the first love of the wine list and the authoritative selection includes impressive wines and producers. Italy and Spain are well represented, too, but the list turns up interesting bottles from around the globe; prices start at £18. There's a good selection of wines by the glass.

Chef: Alexis Gauthier Proprietors: James and Andrew Palmer, and Alexis Gauthier Open: Mon to Fri L 12 to 2.30, Mon to Sat D 6.30 to 10.30 Closed: Christmas, New Year, Easter, bank hols, last 2 weeks Aug Meals: Set L £35 (inc ½ bot wine), Set D £48. Tasting menus £55 to £65 Service: 12.5% (optional) Cards: Amex, Delta, Maestro, MasterCard, Visa Details: 42 seats. Vegetarian meals. No children under 12. No smoking. Wheelchair access (not WC). No music. Air-conditioned Tube: Sloane Square

MAPS 12, 13, 15

Royal China

24–26 Baker Street, W1M 7AB
Tel: (020) 7487 4688
68 Queen's Grove, NW8 6ER
Tel: (020) 7586 4280
13 Queensway, W2 4QJ
Tel: (020) 7221 2535
30 West Ferry Circus, E14 8RR
Tel: (020) 7719 0888
Website: www.royalchinagroup.co.uk

Cooking 3 | **Chinese** | **£40**

Defined by their décor of back and gold lacquered walls, golden birds and mirrored ceilings, the four Royal China restaurants offer virtually identical menus, too. Front-runner is the original branch in Queensway, where 'excellent' dim sum prove 'that the cooking here remains on the ball' – among them may be deep-fried prawn dumplings, vegetarian steamed dumplings, roast pork puff, and roast pork cheung fun. The main carte is just as dependable. Seafood is a high point, perhaps whole steamed sea bass with black bean sauce, filleted at the table, or 'carefully cooked and tasty' Szechuan prawns, while 'chef's favourites' produce roasted chicken with monk bean flavour, and stewed pork belly with preserved cabbage. Gai lan (Chinese broccoli) continues to draw praise, and you might like to try milk and egg tarts, coconut cream cake, or sago pudding with yam for dessert. It's all dispensed by loads of staff who are 'bustling, knowledgeable, unflappable and courteous'. House wine is £15.

> **Chef:** Man Yuk Leung (executive chef) **Proprietor:** Royal China Restaurant Group **Open:** all week 12 (11 Sun) to 10.45 (11.15 Fri and Sat, 9.45 Sun) **Meals:** alc (main courses L £8 to £15, D £10 to £25). Set L £12 (2 courses) to £13, Set D £28 **Service:** 15% (optional) **Cards:** Amex, Delta, Maestro, MasterCard, Visa **Details:** (for Baker Street; may vary at other branches) 200 seats. Vegetarian meals. No-smoking area. Wheelchair access (also WC). Music. Air-conditioned **Tube:** Baker Street, St John's Wood, Bayswater, Queensway, Westferry DLR

MAP 13

RSJ

33 Coin Street, SE1 9NR
Tel: (020) 7928 4554
Website: www.rsj.uk.com

| Cooking 3 | Modern French | £43 |

This old building, dating back to the nineteenth century, was once stables but had to be reinforced with several rolled steel joists – hence the name – but there's more to this civilised dining room than architecture. The venue is widely known for its Loire valley wines and also for its lack of pretension and its quiet assurance. It's also good value for money. The mainly French carte could start with steamed green and white asparagus with hollandaise, or seared roulade of duck and foie gras with an apple and walnut salad. Move on to poached wild sea trout with caviar and beurre blanc or maybe pan-fried Dutch calf's livers with crushed potatoes in a thyme jus. Vegetarians are well catered for: potato gnocchi with peas, broad beans and pecorino shavings, for example. End with something indulgent such as loquats in white wine with mascarpone sorbet, or flourless chocolate and almond cake with whipped cream and orange sauce. Other than the 'divine' selection of wines from the Loire, the list comes mainly from the rest of France, with only a handful of bottles from elsewhere; prices start at £14.95.

> **Chef:** Ian Stabler **Proprietor:** Nigel Wilkinson **Open:** Mon to Fri L 12 to 2.30, Mon to Sat D 5.30 to 11 **Meals:** alc (main courses £13 to £18). Set L and D £15.95 (2 courses) to £17.95 **Service:** 12.5% (optional) **Cards:** Amex, Delta, Diners, Maestro, MasterCard, Visa **Details:** 90 seats. 10 seats outside. Vegetarian meals. Children's helpings. No smoking. No music. Air-conditioned **Tube:** Waterloo

MAP 15

Rules

35 Maiden Lane, WC2E 7LB
Tel: (020) 7836 5314
Website: www.rules.co.uk

| Cooking 3 | British | £57 |

Established in 1798 by Thomas Rule, London's oldest restaurant remains a haven of decorum. Waiters are impeccably well mannered, the décor would make Edward VIII feel at home, and food mixes stiff-upper-lip restraint with well-sourced produce and a classic ideology. A glance at the menu reveals a number of traditional dishes, including plenty of game and some rarely seen treats such as Eccles cakes and damson relish. Lobster bisque or potted Morecambe Bay shrimps with melba toast might start, followed by roast loin of Wiltshire rabbit (served with bacon, leeks and creamed sweetcorn), Irish grass-fed beef (in the shape of sirloin steak with béarnaise and chips), and Gloucestershire Old Spot pork (as a chop with crackling and Barnstaple chutney). Steak and kidney pudding and fish and chips are also popular, while side dishes include macaroni cheese, and samphire with shallots and mushrooms. Finish with treacle sponge pudding with custard. Wines from Burgundy and the Rhône Valley are a speciality. House French is £16.95.

> **Chef:** Richard Sawyer **Proprietor:** John Mayhew **Open:** all week 12 to 11.45 (10.45 Sun) **Closed:** 4 days Christmas **Meals:** alc (main courses £16 to £20). Set D 10 to 11.45 Mon to Thur £18.95 (2 courses) **Service:** 12.5% (optional) **Cards:** Amex, Delta, Maestro, MasterCard, Visa **Details:** 93 seats. Vegetarian meals. Children's helpings. No smoking. Wheelchair access (not WC). No music. No mobile phones. Air-conditioned **Tube:** Covent Garden

MAP 12

Sabras

263 High Road, Willesden Green, NW10 2RX
Tel: (020) 8459 0340/0541

| Cooking 4 | Indian Vegetarian | £23 |

In an unassuming spot next to Willesden bus garage, Hemant Desai's restaurant is a family-run business specialising in traditional vegetarian dishes from Gujarat, Punjab, Kashmir and southern India. Four blue-and-white china elephants greet you on the way in and the covered tables are well spaced, with Bombay mix provided. Starters run to dhal dahi vada or pastry filled with garden peas, coconut and pomegranate pearls (ghughara kachori). Dhosas come with a variety of fillings such as masala with onions and potatoes, while other dishes include quick-fried okra and stuffed baby aubergine, or patra (stripped yam leaves baked as a cake with a mixture of spices including tamarind and sesame seeds). Home-made desserts include kulfi, and shiro, a sweet semolina with almonds. Wines start at £9.50 but there is also a selection of Indian beers and lassi.

Chef: Nalinee Desai Proprietor: Hemant Desai Open: Tue to Sun D only 6.15 to 10 (10.30 Fri and Sat) Meals: alc (main courses £4.50 to £7.50). Set D 6.15 to 8.30 £6.50 to £9.50 Service: 10% (optional) Cards: Maestro, MasterCard, Visa Details: 32 seats. Vegetarian meals. No smoking. Wheelchair access (not WC). Music Tube: Dollis Hill

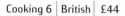

MAP 13

St John

LONDON OF THE YEAR RESTAURANT

26 St John Street, EC1M 4AY
Tel: (020) 7251 0848
Website: www.stjohnrestaurant.com

Cooking 6 | British | £44

Fergus Henderson's cooking celebrates a British earthiness – the food is plain, unadulterated – and it does not go unnoticed that physically the restaurant has the same attributes. Formerly a smoke-house, St John has been turned into a series of plain, whitewashed rooms with the barest of fittings and little attempt at decoration. 'Food and architecture are in perfect symbiosis', thought one visitor. True to form, the menu writing is terse, but promises a host of unusual ingredients in 'clean, almost austere combinations' – a plate of brawn, or the signature roast bone marrow and parsley salad, perhaps, or tripe, bacon and white beans. While the cooking can appear deceptively simple, it works because of the quality of the raw materials.

At inspection, grilled razor clams were exactly that, extremely fresh and served with lemon, butter and parsley sauce, while crisp pig's ear and dandelions was a 'simple yet amazing' textural salad. Guinea fowl can often be a disappointment, but here it was a hit with a hint of gaminess and crisp skin, served with a mound of sliced fennel and a side dish of fresh, buttered spring greens. Desserts range from the traditional jam roly poly – 'no school version has ever tasted like this one' – to the appealing blood orange sorbet and Russian vodka,

followed, perhaps, by freshly baked madeleines. The all-French wine list opens at £14.50.

Chefs: Fergus Henderson and Chris Gillard Proprietors: Fergus Henderson and Trevor Gulliver Open: Mon to Fri L 12 to 3, Mon to Sat D 6 to 11 Closed: Christmas, New Year, bank hols Meals: alc (main courses £12.50 to £21.50) Service: not inc Cards: Amex, Delta, Maestro, MasterCard, Visa Details: 100 seats. Vegetarian meals. No-smoking area. No music. No mobile phones. Air-conditioned Tube: Farringdon

MAP 13

St John Bread & Wine

94–96 Commercial Street, E1 6LZ
Tel: (020) 7251 0848
Website: www.stjohnbreadandwine.com

Cooking 3 | British | £39

Housed in a former bank opposite Spitalfields Market, this rather spartan restaurant, which doubles as a bakery and deli, has an almost schoolroom feel with its evenly spaced tables and pegs on the walls. As an offshoot of the original Clerkenwell St John (see entry above), it's no surprise to see that 'we also sell offal'. With its easygoing atmosphere, it's a place where you could happily take breakfast – expect a brace of Lowestoft kippers, or Old Spot bacon sandwich – then stay for lunch and dinner, especially as the meals make no distinction between courses and plates are small to encourage sharing. You'll always find laverbread and bacon, Stinking Bishop (cheese) and potatoes, or beetroot, sorrel and boiled egg to get stuck into, but there are also fish and meat choices. Needless to say, robust flavours and friendly, expert service are hallmarks. Wines are available retail, but if you're eating in, expect to pay £14.50 for house vin de pays.

Chef: Tom Pemberton Proprietors: Fergus Henderson and Trevor Gulliver Open: all week L 12 to 5.45, Mon to Sat D 6 to 10.15 Closed: 24 to 30 Dec Meals: alc (main courses £10 to £15) Service: not inc, 12.5% (optional) Cards: Amex, Delta, Maestro, MasterCard, Visa Details: 60 seats. Vegetarian meals. No music. Air-conditioned Tube: Liverpool Street

£ This symbol means that it is possible to have a three-course dinner, including coffee, half a bottle of house wine and service, for £30 or less per person.

MAP 14

Salloos

62–64 Kinnerton Street, SW1X 8ER
Tel: (020) 7235 4444
Website: www.salloos.co.uk

Cooking 3 | Pakistani | £51

In a 'village-like' back street off Knightsbridge, the recently renovated upstairs dining room has an elegant but cosy feel, although the tables are a good size and well spaced. This is a beacon of traditional but refined Pakistani cooking – many of the recipes have been handed down from owner Muhammad Salahuddin's mother. Grilled dishes are a highlight, thanks to the real charcoal tandoor, with succulent chicken tikka, tandoori prawns, and seekh kebab among starters. To follow, specialities include a cheese soufflé containing pieces of roast chicken in a gooey cheese sauce, as well as slow-roast whole leg of lamb marinated in mild spices (order a day ahead if you want this). There might also be palak gosht (lamb with spinach, fenugreek and ginger), gurda masala (stir-fried hot-spiced kidneys), and karahi-cooked king prawns in spicy tomato gravy. Breads are consistently excellent, and, to finish, desserts include kulfi and carrot halva. House wines at £12.50 (£3.50 a glass) open a well-chosen list.

> **Chef:** Abdul Aziz **Proprietor:** Muhammad Salahuddin **Open:** Mon to Sat 12 to 2.15, 7 to 11 **Closed:** 25 and 26 Dec **Meals:** alc (main courses £12.50 to £16.50). Cover £1.50 **Service:** 12.5% (optional) **Cards:** Amex, Delta, Diners, Maestro, MasterCard, Visa **Details:** 65 seats. Vegetarian meals. No children under 8. No cigars/pipes in dining room. No music. Air-conditioned **Tube:** Knightsbridge

MAP 15

Salt Yard | NEW ENTRY

54 Goodge Street, W1T 4NA
Tel: (020) 7637 0657
Website: www.saltyard.co.uk

Cooking 2 | Tapas-Plus | £37

Lost among a parade of Goodge Street shop fronts, it's easy to miss the Salt Yard. At street level, the bar dispenses platters of cheese and charcuterie alongside nibbles like caperberries, almonds and more substantial marinated sardinillas on ciabatta. Downstairs in the basement, with the kitchen exposed to view, the tapas menu delivers a fusion of Italian antipasti and Spanish tapas. Chargrilled

salmon comes with a with a cavalo nero sauce, 'wonderfully tender' braised beef cheeks are well matched by parsnip purée, and full-flavoured sautéed chicken livers served with pickled figs. The 'undoubted stars' of one meal were the courgette flowers stuffed with Monte Enebro cheese and drizzled with honey, which were simply 'bursting with flavour'. Service is brisk and efficient and the wine list offers a reasonably priced mix of modern Spanish and Italian bottles. House wine is £14.50.

> **Chef:** Benjamin Tish **Proprietors:** Simon Mullins and Sanja Morris **Open:** Mon to Fri L 12 to 3, Mon to Sat D 6 to 11 (Sat 5 to 11) **Meals:** alc (tapas £3 to £8.50, charcuterie £7.50 to £13) **Service:** 10% (optional) **Cards:** Amex, Delta, Maestro, MasterCard, Visa **Details:** 70 seats. 12 seats outside. Vegetarian meals.

MAP 13

Salusbury

50–52 Salusbury Road, Queens Park, NW6 6NN
Tel: (020) 7328 3286
Email: info@thesalusbury.com

Cooking 1 | Italian | £41

This gastro-pub serving the denizens of Queens Park delivers both as a pub and as a venue for good food. The cooking has an Italian bent, with borlotti bean and pasta soup or grilled ewe's milk ricotta with blossom honey and chestnut bread to start, and a choice of pasta dishes including porcini ravioli, and linguine with clams and chilli. Slow-roasted pork belly with braised Savoy cabbage and mash, or pan-fried veal chop with sauté spinach are among main-course options. End perhaps with peach tarte Tatin. The wine list is short but offers some interesting global choices, starting at £11 for house Italian.

> **Chef:** Germano Novati **Proprietors:** Nick Mash and Robert Claassen **Open:** Tue to Sun L 12.30 to 3.30, all week D 7 to 10.15 **Closed:** 25 and 26 Dec, 1 Jan **Meals:** alc (main courses £10.50 to £16.50) **Service:** 12.5% (optional) **Cards:** Delta, MasterCard, Maestro, Visa **Details:** 45 seats. 20 seats outside. Vegetarian meals. No children under 5 at D. No smoking. Wheelchair access (not WC). Music **Tube:** Queens Park

NEW ENTRY	This appears after the restaurant's name if the establishment was not a main entry in last year's Guide. Please note, however, it may have been 'also recommended' in the previous edition.

MAP 12

Sam's Brasserie and Bar

NEW ENTRY

11 Barley Mow Passage, Chiswick, W4 4PH
Tel: (020) 8987 0555
Website: www.samsbrasserie.co.uk

Cooking 4 | Modern British-Plus | £41

Owner Sam Harrison's lively brasserie has hit the ground running, which is perhaps not surprising given the pedigree of those involved; Sam was Rick Stein's general manager in Padstow, while chef Rufus Wickham has worked at Kensington Place and the Crown Hotel at Southwold (see entries). Small blond-wood tables are tightly packed together ('one almost has to talk to one's neighbours'), but there's a slightly more spacious mezzanine floor, and a view into the kitchen. Start with grilled goats' cheese with endive and watercress salad, or ballottine of rabbit stuffed with persillade. Main courses run to crisp sea bass – a 'beautifully fresh, meaty piece of tail fillet' at inspection – accompanied by sautéed potatoes and horseradish cream. Good desserts, including a chocolate and Amaretti torte and apple crumble and custard, hit the spot. The good-value wine list starts at £12.50, and there's a good choice by the glass (from £3.25) or 50cl carafe (from £8.50).

Chef: Rufus Wickham Proprietor: Sam Harrison Open: all week 12 to 3 (4 Sat and Sun), 6.30 to 10.30 Meals: alc (main courses £7 to £16.50). Set L Mon to Fri £11.50 (2 courses) to £15. Bar menu available Service: 12.5% (optional) Cards: Amex, Delta, Maestro, MasterCard, Visa Details: 100 seats. Vegetarian meals. Children's helpings. No smoking in 1 dining room. Wheelchair access (also WC). Music. Air-conditioned Tube: Chiswick Park, Turnham Green

MAP 15

Sardo

45 Grafton Way, W1T 5DQ
Tel: (020) 7387 2521
Website: www.sardo-restaurant.com

Cooking 4 | Sardinian | £48

There's nothing stuffy about this Sardinian restaurant just off Tottenham Court Road. It is quite stylish in an understated way, and presents a sunny face to the world. Staff are an attentive bunch, and there is a nice buzz about the place, even at lunchtimes. Beef carpaccio, grilled baby squid or tuna bresaola start things off on the right foot. Pasta dishes include the popular spaghetti bottarga (dried mullet roe) or home-made pasta parcels filled with pecorino cheese and potatoes. Among traditional meat main courses might be calf's liver in balsamic vinegar, or grilled veal steak with fresh spinach and sauté potatoes, while fish options include grilled swordfish, or tuna steak, both accompanied simply by rocket and fresh tomatoes. Desserts naturally include pannacotta and tiramisù. The Italian wine list favours Sardinian bottles and offers plenty of choice in all price brackets, starting at £14 for a Sardinian Colle Moresco. Related to Sardo Canale (see entry below).

Chef: Roberto Sardu Proprietor: Romolo Mudu Open: Mon to Fri L 12 to 3, Mon to Sat D 6 to 11 Closed: 25 Dec, bank hols Meals: alc (main courses £12 to £16.50) Service: 12.5% (optional) Cards: Amex, Delta, Diners, Maestro, MasterCard, Visa Details: 55 seats. 9 seats outside. Vegetarian meals. No smoking in 1 dining room. Wheelchair access (not WC). Occasional music. Air-conditioned Tube: Warren Street

MAP 13

Sardo Canale

42 Gloucester Avenue, NW1 8JD
Tel: (020) 7722 2800
Website: www.sardocanale.com

Cooking 4 | Sardinian | £43

The large brick building on the Regent's Canal is divided into four distinct eating areas, with an outside space for al fresco dining. The décor is contemporary, with funky ceiling lights, exposed-stone walls and low-backed chairs. Like its sibling Sardo (see entry above), the Sardinian dishes are well prepared, using high-quality ingredients. There are daily specials, announced by staff, for both starters and mains, but you could start on the printed menu with anchovies marinated in apple vinegar served with grilled courgettes, or traditional Sardinian pasta with an aromatic sausage and tomato sauce. Grilled swordfish with orange-infused oil and asparagus, or lamb fillet marinated in olive oil and herbs might follow. Finish with panettone cake with champagne sauce or a selection of Sardinian cheeses. The wine list is split

 This symbol means that smoking is not permitted.

between Sardinia and the rest of Italy, with some good-value bottles starting at £14.

> **Chefs:** Roberto Sardu and Massimo Soddu **Proprietors:** Romolo and Bianca Mudu **Open:** Tue to Sun L 12 to 3, all week D 6 to 10 **Meals:** alc (main courses £12 to £17.50). Set L Mon to Fri £13 (2 courses), Set L Sun £23. Cover £1.50 **Service:** 12.5% (optional) **Cards:** Amex, Delta, Maestro, MasterCard, Visa **Details:** 100 seats. 25 seats outside. Vegetarian meals. Children's helpings. No smoking in 1 dining room. Wheelchair access (also WC). Music. Air-conditioned **Tube:** Camden Town, Chalk Farm

---

MAP 12

Sarkhel's

199 Replingham Road, SW18 5LY
Tel: (020) 8870 1483
Website: www.sarkhels.com

Cooking 3 | Indian | £37

Udit Sarkhel's Southfields restaurant is into its tenth year in 2007. A large mural of a Bombay street scene dominating one wall helps to set the scene, while paper tablecloths, and terracotta-coloured lino on the floor show that this is an unpretentious place, with the focus very much on the cooking. Sev puri made an impressive start to an inspection dinner, served with both tamarind and tomato sauces, mung beans and chilli. Among vegetarian dishes are shahi paneer and vegetable shashlik, or dhal makhani, the latter among the highlights of that inspection. Galinha cafreal is a main course dish of chicken, on the bone, marinated in a masala paste, and there is Mangalorean fish or prawn curry. The nan bread receives notices: 'the best I have had for years', according to one seasoned traveller. Express lunches, Sunday buffets and thalis are also available, and offer good value. Drink lassi, beer, or wine from £10.90. A second branch is now open at 119 Upper Richmond Road West, SW14, tel: (020) 8876 6220.

> **Chef/Proprietor:** Udit Sarkhel **Open:** Tue to Sun 12 to 2.30, 6 to 10.30 (11 Fri and Sat) **Meals:** alc (main courses £7.25 to £10.50). Set L Tue to Sat £5 (2 courses), Set L Sun £9.95, Set D 6 to 8 £9.95 **Service:** not inc **Cards:** Maestro, MasterCard, Visa **Details:** 88 seats. Vegetarian meals. Children's helpings. No smoking in 1 dining room. Wheelchair access (also WC). Music. Air-conditioned **Tube:** Southfields

---

MAP 15

Savoy Grill

The Strand, WC2R 0EU
Tel: 020 7592 1600
Website: www.marcuswareing.com

Cooking 6 | Modern French-Plus | £89

The dear old Savoy Grill, stalwart of many a Guide gone by, has been under the aegis of Marcus Wareing since 2003. Its ambience retains enough of the formality expected in the circumstances, with wood panelling and lowering brown light fittings throwing out a strangely fake-tan sort of glow, but the atmosphere is palpably more relaxed than in the old days. There are black-jacketed French waiters still, but the tone is cheery rather than reverential.

In the talented and creative Lee Scott, the old place also has a major new asset. The emphasis is on British ingredients and seasonality, and produces some fine dishes. A single plump raviolo is filled with a prawn mousse textured with slivers of roasted king prawn, while its accompanying foamy bisque, scented with ginger and coriander, is what lifts the dish into another dimension. Rack of lamb comes as three thick, succulent, pink cutlets around a serving of meltingly braised shoulder. New season's broad beans and cherry tomatoes, together with a rich, not over-reduced jus, complete a refreshingly straightforward main course. Fish is well handled too, as witness a crisp-skinned, well-timed fillet of sea bass on an underlay of faintly smoky potato purée, with glazed baby beetroots, cabbage ribbons and a perfectly judged red wine dressing.

After a properly palate-cleansing pre-dessert, you might fall headlong into the richness of warm Valrhona chocolate truffle rolled in a finely crumbled pastry crust and sauced with a vivid green sweet basil potion. Wines are still a matter of expensive famous names. If you're more Pinot Grigio than Bâtard-Montrachet, there is one (albeit at £39). Otherwise, it's a *tour d'horizon* of the great and good of France, with classic rather than new-wave Italians and Spaniards, and a handful from the southern hemisphere. Halves are nearly all bigwigs again.

Chef: Lee Scott Proprietor: Marcus Wareing and Gordon Ramsay Group Open: all week 12 to 3, 5.45 to 11 (Sun 12 to 11) Meals: Set L £30 to £65, Set L Sat and all day Sun £18 (2 courses) to £25, Set D £55 to £65 Service: 12.5% (optional) Cards: Amex, Delta, Diners, Maestro, Visa Details: 100 seats. Vegetarian meals. Children's helpings. No smoking. Wheelchair access (not WC). Music. No mobile phones. Air-conditioned Tube: Charing Cross, Covent Garden, Embankment

---

MAP 13

Searcy's

Level 2, Barbican Centre, Silk Street, EC2Y 8DS
Tel: (020) 7588 3008
Website: www.barbican.org.uk

| Cooking 2 | Modern British | £42 |

The L-shaped room is narrow, the view of St Giles Cripplegate Church large, and the Level 2 Barbican location couldn't be handier for theatre- and concert-goers. In the kitchen, Jane Collins keeps an eye on London fashion and throws together a starter of carpaccio with foie gras tortellini and chorizo oil, and a main course of organic salmon with spinach, lemon and chive spätzli. Bouillabaisse contains bream, mussels, clams, prawns, scallop, split green beans and rouille, and ribeye is coupled with mushroom brûlée, while poached rhubarb with vanilla ice cream and jelly is one way to finish, or there's citrus soufflé with lemongrass anglaise. The short, modern wine list is businesslike rather than inspired and prices are on the high side, with house South African £17.50.

Chef: Jane Collins Proprietor: Searcy Tansley & Co. Ltd Open: Mon to Fri L 12 to 2.30, Mon to Sat D 5 to 10.30 Closed: 24 to 26 Dec, Aug to mid-Sept Meals: Set L and D £22.50 (2 courses) to £26.50, Set D pre- and post-performance £21.50 (2 courses) to £25.50. Bar snack menu available Service: 12.5% (optional) Cards: Amex, Delta, Diners, Maestro, MasterCard, Visa Details: 80 seats. Vegetarian meals. No smoking in dining room. Wheelchair access (also WC). Music Tube: Barbican, Moorgate

---

This symbol means that the restaurant has elected to participate in *The Good Food Guide's* £5 voucher scheme (see 'Using The Good Food Guide' for details).

MAP 13

Singapore Garden

83–83A Fairfax Road, NW6 4DY
Tel: (020) 7328 5314

| Cooking 2 | Singaporean | £45 |

After two decades of continuous operation, Singapore Garden closed for refurbishment at the start of 2006, reopening with an elegant, contemporary look. There have also been changes behind the scenes, as former chef/proprietor Mrs Lim has retired, handing the restaurant over to her daughter. But staff are otherwise unchanged, and service continues to be friendly and efficient. Most important, the food is as good as ever. One long-time fan proclaimed prawn noodle soup with pork scratchings and hollow-stalk spinach up to 'its usual standard', also praising deep-fried bean curd with sesame and red-bean paste, and 'tender and delicious' pork satay. Alongside the extensive regular menu of Singaporean and Malay standards is a list of specials such as fried soft-shell crab with garlic and chillies, and monkfish curry with okra, while desserts include soya bean curd with palm sugar. House wines are £15 from a short list.

Proprietor: Hibiscus Restaurants Ltd Open: Mon to Sat 12 to 3, 6 to 11, Sun 12 to 11 Closed: 4 days Christmas Meals: alc (main courses £7.50 to £20). Set D £23.50 to £38.50 (all min 2 or more) Service: 12.5% (optional) Cards: Amex, Delta, Maestro, MasterCard, Visa Details: 85 seats. 12 seats outside. Vegetarian meals. No smoking in dining room. Wheelchair access (also WC). Music. Air-conditioned Tube: Swiss Cottage

---

MAP 15

Sketch, Gallery

9 Conduit Street, W1S 2XG
Tel: (0870) 777 4488
Website: www.sketch.uk.com

| Cooking 5 | Modern French | £65 |

Those hankering after a piece of the Pierre Gagnaire action but lacking the means to go for the full package in the Lecture Room and Library (see entry below) have a more gently priced option within this shrine to aesthetic gastronomy just off Bond Street. The Gallery is on the ground floor, just past the pâtisserie. Beneath a mile-high ceiling, a light show plays on plain white walls, with seating a mixture of white leather sofas and low-slung chairs, and riotously decorated screens divide up the space.

Minimal use of oil, dairy fats and carbohydrate will appeal to the diet-conscious, while the restless exuberance of the cooking style makes its own statement. A spin on croque-monsieur involves dyeing the bread black with squid ink and piling it up with Paris ham, buffalo mozzarella, tomatoes and courgette. Organic salmon could be a starter or main, with its accompaniment of fruit escabèche, Japanese noodles, endive and an apple tuile. In the context, some things sound positively traditional, such as Bresse chicken roasted with thyme and lemon and served with macaroni in Gorgonzola cream, but then the side orders might include an almond tart with leek and wasabi. Finish Mexican-style in the shape of coffee parfait with a candied morel and tequila coffee syrup, and then spend the next few days telling friends all about it. This is food for dining out on, as well as dining on. Wines are stylistically bunched, according to whether you're in the market for a 'crispy' or 'generous' bottle. Prices start at £21 for a Sardinian Vermentino or a Rhône vin de pays.

Chef: Pierre Gagnaire Proprietor: Mourad Mazouz Open: Mon to Sat D only 7 to 11 Closed: bank hols Meals: alc (main courses £11.50 to £28) Service: 12.5% (optional) Cards: Amex, Diners, Maestro, MasterCard, Visa Details: 140 seats. Vegetarian meals. Music. Air-conditioned Tube: Oxford Circus

MAP 15

Sketch, Lecture Room and Library

9 Conduit Street, W1S 2XG
Tel: (0870) 777 4488
Website: www.sketch.uk.com

Cooking 5 | Modern French | £124

'The menu is a culinary journey and each dish is an adventure of tastes ... each menu delves into the very essence of each exquisite, sensational ingredient.' That's what the menu says. And our inspector responded thus: 'Indeed, it was a journey, an adventure even, but whether we delved into the essence of anything was less easy to say. I'm not big on delving – as opposed to just eating, say.' That's the thing about Sketch, it brings out strong feelings. Since the last edition of the Guide the Lecture Room and Library and Gallery (see entry above) have been joined by Glade, a daytime dining room.

The first task is getting past the doormen and getting to table; staff seem keen to give first-timers a mini-guided tour. The Lecture Room and Library is the main dining room, reached via a marble staircase, and essentially one large, high-ceilinged space with ostentatious décor. The menu is at the very peak of the cost spectrum. Waiting staff do their best to explain the nature of the dishes, but they've been set a difficult task. If you had not already gathered this was going to be an unusual experience, the appearance of the appetiser trolley is a clear indication: plates are arranged around each diner with clear instructions to eat the dishes in a specific order – Guinness and liquorice jelly sandwiched between thin squares of chocolate sponge, and a crisp ginger biscuit shell topped with cuttlefish and pine nuts to name but two.

Menu descriptions are enigmatic. Langoustines are 'addressed in four ways': roasted in a spice mixture described as 'Terre de Sienne', tartare, a kind of carpaccio, and a quenelle of mousse seasoned with cardamom and surrounded by a strongly flavoured jelly. 'Taste of Spring' includes a piece of steamed cod on a red pepper coulis, a plate of young octopus festooned with dill, and warm smoked duck in a reduced veal stock that was decidedly old school (and much enjoyed for it). The Spring expedition continued with a shot glass of apple granita topped with smoked bacon foam, and finally a salad of various bits of spring veg which must be spooned out of a martini glass.

The vision of Pierre Gagnaire and Mourad Mazouz gets a mixed response from GFG readers. The ideas and experimentations thrill some, while others find the whole thing rather too much in every sense. As might be expected in the context, the wine list is a decidedly upmarket tome, featuring several bottles with four-figure price tags (such as a 1999 Romanée-Conti at £5,490) but quality is high throughout and perhaps more surprising is the fact that there are even a few bottles under £30, with house selections at £21.

Chef: Pierre Gagnaire Proprietor: Mourad Mazouz Open: Lecture Room/Library Tue to Fri L 12 to 2.30, Tue to Sat D 7 to 10.30; Glade Mon to Fri L 12 to 3 Closed: bank hols Meals: Lecture Room/ Library alc (main courses L £25 to £35, D £46 to £56). Set L £35, Set D £65 to £90; Glade alc (main courses £6.50 to £24). Set L £18 (2 courses) to £21 Service: 12.5% (optional) Cards: Amex, Delta, Diners, Maestro, MasterCard, Visa Details: 50 seats. Vegetarian meals. Music. Air-conditioned Tube: Oxford Circus

The price given next to the cooking score is based on the cost of a typical three-course dinner for one person, including coffee, house wine and service.

MAP 13

Smiths of Smithfield, Top Floor

67–77 Charterhouse Street, EC1M 6HJ
Tel: (020) 7251 7950
Website: www.smithsofsmithfield.co.uk

| Cooking 4 | Modern European | £56 |

Opposite Smithfield Market, this Victorian warehouse is a multi-level operation. On the ground floor is a bustling café/bar, floors one and two house a quieter cocktail bar and informal brasserie respectively, and topping it all is the spare, urban-edged fine dining option with a panorama of City rooftops forming a backdrop. There's a bullish Brit-inspired menu interspersed with the occasional foray into the Mediterranean and beyond (perhaps Thai-style omelette with tiger prawns, ginger and basil to start), and emphasis is placed on organic/additive-free ingredients. Given its location, meat is understandably a strength, perhaps featuring braised shoulder of Oxford down lamb, but the menu's big draw is a section devoted to 'Fine Meat', which deals in breeds like Chesterton Farm longhorn rump or fillet, properly hung then simply grilled or fried and served with béarnaise, red wine butter or creamed horseradish. There is a good fish selection too, perhaps roast halibut with lobster mash and parsley sauce. Among desserts might be iced brown sugar and ginger parfait with roast fig and port syrup. The wine list offers lots of robust red to go with the steaks, as well a substantial choice by the glass (16 at the last count). Prices start at £15 for red or white Rioja.

Chef/Proprietor: John Torode   Open: Sun to Fri L 12 to 2.30, all week D 6.30 to 10.45   Closed: 25 and 26 Dec, 1 Jan   Meals: alc (main courses £14 to £29)   Service: 12.5% (optional)   Cards: Amex, Delta, Diners, Maestro, MasterCard, Visa   Details: 84 seats. 32 seats outside. Vegetarian meals. Children's helpings. No smoking. Wheelchair access (also WC). No music. No mobile phones. Air-conditioned   Tube: Farringdon

 Not a full entry but provisionally recommended. These 'also recommended' establishments are integrated throughout the book.

MAP 12

Snows on the Green

166 Shepherd's Bush Road, W6 7PB
Tel: (020) 7603 2142
Website: www.snowsonthegreen.co.uk

| Cooking 4 | Modern British | £41 |

'This has been (and continues to be) a highly like-able and well-regarded neighbourhood restaurant' writes a reporter of this 'worthy gastro beacon'. For the past 16 years Sebastian Snow has pitched his efforts appropriately and makes a success of providing sensibly unfussy dishes in a modern British style. In this he takes a fairly broad approach: foie gras with a fried egg and balsamic vinegar, or char-grilled squid with chorizo, clams, vegetable fritters and rocket. The food deserves credit for its lack of ostentation, with the kitchen often using modest ingredients and simple treatments in dishes like roast saddle of rabbit en croûte with prunes and honey-glazed roast vegetables, or crisp confit of pork with a fricassee of artichokes, ratte potatoes and field mushrooms. Equally well-handled desserts have included chocolate fondant pudding with malt chocolate ice cream, and a vacherin of meringue with passion fruit, kiwi fruit and Chantilly cream. The wide-ranging modern wine list is designed to encourage experimentation, with 14 wines by the glass. House French is £11.95. Sebastian Snow has opened a second place, Parmigiano, 238 Blythe Road, W8, (020) 7603 1122, which is a family-friendly Italian restaurant.

Chefs/Proprietors: Sebastian and Lana Snow   Open: Mon to Fri L 12 to 3, Mon to Sat D 6 to 11   Closed: 4 days Christmas, bank hol Mon   Meals: alc (main courses £14 to £17). Set L and D £13.50 (2 courses) to £17.50. Cover 95p   Service: not inc   Cards: Amex, Delta, Diners, Maestro, MasterCard, Visa   Details: 70 seats. 10 seats outside. Vegetarian meals. Children's helpings. No-smoking area. Wheelchair access (not WC). Music. Air-conditioned   Tube: Hammersmith

MAP 13

Social

33 Linton Street, N1 7DU
Tel: (020) 7354 5809

This laid-back establishment has a 'lounge lizard' bar with a pool table for those who want to hang out, as well as some comforting favourites from the compact menu: salmon, prawn and crab fishcakes (£4.50) might start, followed by roast pork belly with apple sauce, streaky bacon and swede and carrot mash (£13.50), or balsamic chargrilled lamb cutlets with minted mash peas, pak choi and yoghurt sauce (£13). Chocolate brownie with cream (£4.50) ends. Wines from £12.50. Closed Mon to Fri L.

MAP 15

Sofra

36 Tavistock Street, WC2E 7PB
Tel: (020) 7240 3773

A fixture on the scene in Covent Garden for more than 25 years, this Turkish dining room (part of a mini-chain), values the simple approach, drawing on an eclectic mix of Mediterranean, Middle Eastern and Oriental styles. Sautéed lamb's liver (£4.95) starts, or you might choose assorted meze (tabbouleh, falafel; £3.95 each), before moving on to grill dishes such as kofte (£9.95), or lamb shish (£11.95). Fish might be monkfish casserole (£12.95), while specials include beef goulash (£11.95). Wines from £11.65. Open all week. Branches at 18 Shepherd Market, tel: (020) 7493 3320, and 1 St Christopher Place, tel: (020) 7224 4080, both in W1.

MAP 12

Sonny's

94 Church Road, SW13 0DQ
Tel: (020) 8748 0393
Website: www.sonnys.co.uk

NEW CHEF | Modern European | £43

Ed Wilson arrived to take over the stoves just days after our inspector's visit. Sonny's is a 20-year fixture on the Barnes scene and it remains an archetypal neighbourhood restaurant – simple, well-executed food in relaxed surroundings. Eclectic modern art hangs on the walls, while tables are well spaced and covered in white linen. Expect to start with something like sea trout rillettes, or artichoke, chicken liver and mâche salad, and follow with roast squab with braised lettuce and peas, or poached halibut with Puy lentils and a salsa verde. Desserts include nougatine parfait and mille-feuille of fromage blanc and cherries. The compact wine list offers 22 options by the glass (from £3.50), with a good choice of bottles under £20, starting at £11.95 for house selections.

MAP 15

Square

6–10 Bruton Street, W1J 6PU
Tel: (020) 7495 7100
Website: www.squarerestaurant.com

Cooking 8 | Modern French | £82
🍷 ⊘

The Square has had a bit of a makeover since last year's Guide, but a very subtle one. Regulars will breathe a sigh of relief that the place still looks familiar, but the plainer beige hues of yore have given way to a shimmering burgundy wall at the back, and there is a classy mixture of designer mirrors and bold abstract paintings. Service is as impeccable as always, on the crisp side of formal, but expertly choreographed. The sheer size of the room, however, invites a certain amount of babble when the place fills up, ensuring that the atmosphere is anything but staidly reverential.

Philip Howard's cooking achieved a rarefied pitch here several years ago and has, most impressively, sustained it. Dishes are elaborately worked and yet emerge from the kitchen with that deceptive feeling of effortlessness about them. A case in point might be the 'sublime and fragrant' mushroom consommé that comes garnished with a morel topped with delicately potent pigeon mousse. Roast scallop is gently partnered with a purée of new season's garlic, a fondue of shallots, a little chive oil and a gram-flour blini to make another preliminary course.

Main courses teaming roast halibut with boulangère potatoes and pancetta, and roast duck with a tarte fine of caramelised endive, glazed carrots and raisin purée, both exhibit stunning technique and a sound understanding of what works with what, and why. A pair of winter diners departed from the main menu to try a daily special that paired woodcock and mallard, individually bedded on creamed cabbage and butternut squash, the woodcock liver set on a croûte, with a separate raised pie of the leg meat of both birds, in which the pastry was as much a delight as the filling.

Stratospheric standards are maintained through to desserts that might favour chocolate – mocha soufflé with vanilla chocolate chip ice cream has been an emphatic triumph – or might aim to dazzle with fruity fireworks, as when a cheesecake of Brillat-Savarin and passion fruit is accompanied by citrus terrine and banana ice cream.

If you had a nigh on unlimited budget and a global travel permit, you might very well come up with something like the Square wine list – but only after many years of assiduous labour. It is astonishing in every department, according the same dignity to the regions of California as it does to the districts of Bordeaux. Not everything costs an arm and a leg either. If you wish to start modestly before working up a head of steam, a glass of Touraine Sauvignon is £4.95.

> **Chef:** Philip Howard **Proprietors:** Nigel Platts-Martin and Philip Howard **Open:** Mon to Fri L 12 to 2.45, all week D 6.30 to 10.45 (10 Sun) **Closed:** 25 Dec, 1 Jan, L bank hols **Meals:** Set L £25 (2 courses) to £30, Set D £60 to £80 **Service:** 12.5% (optional) **Cards:** Amex, Delta, Diners, Maestro, MasterCard, Visa **Details:** 75 seats. No smoking. Wheelchair access (also WC). No music. No mobile phones. Air-conditioned **Tube:** Green Park

MAP 15

Sumosan

26 Albemarle Street, W1S 4HY
Tel: (020) 7495 5999
Website: www.sumosan.com

Cooking 4 | Modern Japanese | £58

Sleek, elegant and ultra-fashionable, Sumosan makes the most of the ongoing popularity of Japanese food and does so in some style. Behind a vast expanse of glass, the dining room is on show, full of 'the beautiful people', and the entrance through a mock-Japanese garden of raked sand and rock is suitably spectacular. The space is divided into several bars (including a sushi bar) and dining areas, both on the ground floor and in the basement. Unsurprisingly, this is not the place to come for authentic traditional Japanese food. Although the list of sushi and sashimi includes salmon roe, squid, yellowtail, toro (tuna belly) and so on, there are also things like Peking duck and creamy spicy scallops. The full menu offers starters such as poached oysters with foie gras and sea urchin, seared tuna in a sesame and almond crust, and tartare of tuna, avocado, quail's egg and sevruga with truffle oil. Among main courses, roast leg of rabbit in girolle sauce appears alongside more traditional chicken yakitori, while fish options typi-

cally include yellowtail teriyaki, spicy lobster somen with baby asparagus, and, of course, black cod with miso. Desserts are only superficially Japanese: perhaps a spectacularly presented wild berry dorayaki with almond and plum sauce. Wines include some hugely expensive classic French bottles, but prices start at a relatively modest £15.

> **Chef:** Bubker Belkheit **Proprietor:** Janina Wolkow **Open:** Mon to Fri L 12 to 3, all week D 6 to 11.30 (10.30 Sun) **Closed:** bank hols **Meals:** alc (main courses £8 to £55). Set L £19.50 **Service:** 12.5% (optional) **Cards:** Amex, Delta, Diners, Maestro, MasterCard, Visa **Details:** 140 seats. Vegetarian meals. Children's helpings. No-smoking area. Wheelchair access (also WC). Music. Air-conditioned **Tube:** Green Park

MAP 12

Sushi-Hiro

1 Station Parade, Uxbridge Road, W5 3LD
Tel: (020) 8896 3175

Cooking 2 | Japanese | £19

The presence of plastic models of the food on offer points up the lack of pretension about this practical Japanese eatery. Bright lights, pine tables and Western pop music go down well with the Japanese clientele who are here for the sushi – it is all they do here. Nor is there any wine (other than a single plum wine), but there is a choice of six sakés and either Budweiser, Asahi or Kirin beers. Overall standards are high, with good-quality traditional sushi including sea urchin, eel, mackerel, tuna belly, yellowtail, organic salmon, turbot and salmon roe, plus a few maki rolls, and an accompanying miso soup. Prices are modest and payment is by cash only.

> **Chef/Proprietor:** H. Shimakage **Open:** Tue to Sun 11 to 1.30, 4.30 to 9 **Meals:** alc (main courses £1.50 to £9). Set L and D £5 to £14 **Service:** not inc **Cards:** none **Details:** 21 seats. Music. Air-conditioned **Tube:** Ealing Common

---

> This symbol means that it is possible to have a three-course dinner, including coffee, half a bottle of house wine and service, for £30 or less per person.

MAP 12

Sushi-Say

33B Walm Lane, NW2 5SH
Tel: (020) 8459 2971 and 7512

| Cooking 3 | Japanese | £45 |

Inconspicuously located among a row of shops in the centre of Willesden, this is an unpretentious family-run restaurant. The kitchen's performance far outshines the dining room's modest appearance: the décor in the sushi bar at the front and small tatami room to the rear tends towards the spartan, with pale wood-veneer tables, a parquet floor and light green wallpaper lined with Japanese prints. The long menu features around a dozen set-lunch options comprising a main dish (perhaps deep-fried pork cutlet, or a selection of sashimi) with rice, pickles and miso soup, alongside an extensive choice of other dishes. Starters vary from grilled chicken wings, or gyoza dumplings with minced pork, to squid grilled with salt, or grilled aubergine with dried bonito flakes. Main courses are divided into grilled dishes (among them salted horse mackerel, and chicken teriyaki), fried dishes (including deep-fried oysters and cuttlefish, soft-shell crab tempura, and crispy-battered king prawns), as well as noodles, rice dishes and a wide choice of sushi and sashimi. Courteous service is 'helpful, willing and able', and a straightforward, compact wine list opens with house choices at £10.50, as well as hot saké by the small or large flask and nine varieties of cold saké.

Chef: Katsuharu Shimizu Proprietors: Katsuharu and Yuko Shimizu Open: Tue to Fri L 12 to 2.15, Sat and Sun L 1 to 3.15, Tue to Fri D 6.30 to 10.30, Sat D 6 to 11, Sun D 6 to 10 Closed: 25 and 26 Dec, 1 Jan, mid-Jan to mid-Feb Meals: alc (main courses £8 to £20.50). Set L £8.80 to £13.50 (all 1 or 2 courses), Set D £19.50 to £30.30 Service: not inc Cards: Delta, Maestro, MasterCard, Visa Details: 36 seats. Vegetarian meals. No smoking. Wheelchair access (also WC). No music. Air-conditioned Tube: Willesden Green

MAP 14

Swag & Tails

10–11 Fairholt Street, SW7 1EG
Tel: (020) 7584 6926

Just a short stroll from Harrods and Harvey Nichols, this pub and restaurant is a quiet oasis away from the shops. Flowers adorn the exterior, while the décor inside is equally well presented: cream half-panelled walls, contemporary artwork and wooden tables. The menu casts its net wide: sautéed squid with coriander and lime served with stir-fried vegetables (£8.25), braised lamb shank with Castilian chickpeas, buttered spinach and crispy Serrano ham (£14.95), and citrus crème brûlée with raspberries and shortbread (£6) are typical. Wines from £12.95. Closed Sat and Sun.

MAP 15

Tamarind

20 Queen Street, W1J 5PR
Tel: (020) 7629 3561
Website: www.tamarindrestaurant.com

| Cooking 4 | Modern Indian | £63 |

Tradition and innovation combine to outstanding effect in this smart Mayfair restaurant. The former appears in the shape of a genuine tandoor and familiar-sounding dishes such as rogan josh, but these are merely starting points for a creative kitchen that provides authentic modern Indian cooking. Lamb cutlets marinated with papaya, garlic, paprika and star anise, chicken breast marinated in mint, coriander, green chillies and pomegranate seeds, and broccoli marinated in cinnamon, green chillies and garlic with spiced potato and dried-fruit-filled paneer are given the clay-oven treatment, while curry dishes include pan-fried sea bass on crisp spinach with garlic and coconut sauce, and chicken with a mint, coriander and green chilli chutney. Meals are rounded out with snacky starters such as aloo tikka and bhalla papdi chaat, and side dishes of sautéed mushrooms and spinach with garlic and cumin, or spiced okra with chickpeas and pickled onions, as well as the usual rice and breads. To finish, try tandoor-grilled pineapple with fennel and star anise served with rose-petal ice cream. Eleven house wines from £16.50 open a varied list chosen to suit the food.

Chef: Alfred Prasad Proprietor: Indian Cuisine Ltd Open: Sun to Fri L 12 to 2.45, all week D 6 to 11.15 (10.30 Sun) Closed: 25 and 26 Dec, 1 Jan Meals: alc (main courses £13 to £28). Set L £16.50 (2 courses) to £24.50, Set D £48 to £65 Service: 12.5% (optional) Cards: Amex, Delta, Diners, Maestro, MasterCard, Visa Details: 92 seats. Vegetarian meals. No children under 6. No-smoking area. Music. Air-conditioned Tube: Green Park

MAP 13

Tamesa @ Oxo   `NEW ENTRY`

Second Floor, Oxo Tower Wharf, Barge House
Street, SE1 9PH
Tel: (020) 7633 0088

Cooking 2 | Modern European | £39

With floor-to-ceiling windows and a second-floor
location, Tamesa makes the most of views of the
Thames. It's the latest incarnation on a site that has
seen few ventures last long, yet with its bright,
contemporary feel and menu that is simple and
reasonably priced, this one could last the course. A
June dinner for one party provided satisfaction in
the form of half a grilled lobster with garlic butter,
watercress and lemon, three generous slices of new
season's lamb chump accompanied by beetroot
relish and minted peas, and crisp-skinned oriental-
glazed duck with stir-fried greens, and the accompanying sweet potato chips enlivened with a chilli
salt. Finish with hazelnut and chocolate tart with
milk chocolate sorbet and a rich, buttery butterscotch sauce. Service is on the ball, and the global
wine list offers reasonably priced drinking, with
prices from £13.50.

Chef: David Schofield Proprietor: Dominic Ford Open: all
week 12 to 3.30, 5.30 to 11.30 (10.30 Sun) Closed: 25
and 26 Dec, 1 Jan Meals: alc (main courses £9 to £14). Set L
and D 5.30 to 7 and 10 to 11.30 £12.50 (2 courses) to
£15.50. Bar menu available Service: 12.5% (optional)
Cards: Amex, Delta, Maestro, MasterCard, Visa Details: 120
seats. Vegetarian meals. Children's helpings. No smoking.
Wheelchair access (also WC). Music. Air-conditioned Tube:
Waterloo, Blackfriars

MAP 12

Tandoor   `AR`

232 Kingsbury Road, NW9 0BH
Tel: (020) 8205 1450

An up-to-date Indian restaurant housed in a large
north London pub that draws the crowds for its
prepared-to-order, delicately spiced dishes.
Tandoori-cooked options are a good bet: mahi
(fish) tikka and chicken makhni, for example,
while the rest of the extensive menu trips around
the Subcontinent for main dishes such as Goan fish
curry, or Kashmiri rogan josh. Good selection of
vegetarian dishes, rice and breads. Open all week.

MAP 13

Tapas Brindisa   `NEW ENTRY`

18–20 Southwark Street, SE1 1TJ
Tel: (020) 7357 8880

Cooking 2 | Tapas | £34

Invariably crowded, bustling and cheery, Tapas
Brindisa, with its authentic Spanish atmosphere,
tightly packed tables and all-day opening, can be
counted on to produce convincing modern tapas.
A concrete floor, mirrored walls scrawled with in-
house promotions, and table mats that double as
menus help crank up the volume and lend an
informal air to proceedings. There are plenty of
interesting Spanish specialities, ranging from cold
assemblies of first-rate Iberian hams, regional charcuterie and cheeses in perfect condition, via
quality tinned sardines, tuna, smoked mackerel and
anchovies (cold tapas are served all day) to hot
tapas (served at lunch and dinner) like classic
patatas bravas and tortilla, or the more evolved,
starter-sized plates of pisto Manchego with a fried
duck egg and Teruel Serrano ham, or black
pudding sautéed with apples, roast red peppers and
almonds. In between there are exceptional grilled
chorizo and tender squid with aïoli. Desserts are
missable, but not the concise, all-Spanish wine list,
which includes a good selection of sherries. House
red is £13.20, white £15.50.

Chef: José Manuel Pizarro Proprietor: Brindisa Retail Ltd
Open: Mon to Sat 12 to 3 (4 Fri and Sat), 5.30 to 11 Closed:
Christmas, bank hol Mon Meals: alc (tapas £3 to £8)
Service: 12.5% (optional) Cards: Delta, Maestro, MasterCard,
Visa Details: 44 seats. 12 seats outside. Vegetarian meals.
No smoking. Wheelchair access (also women's WC). Music.
Air-conditioned

MAP 13

Tas

33 The Cut, SE1 8LF
Tel: (020) 7928 1444
Website: www.tasrestaurant.com

Cooking 2 | Turkish | £34

Authentic meze and Turkish specialities are the
draw at this lively venue just a stone's throw from
the South Bank. A light wooden floor, white walls
and modern wooden chairs at tightly packed tables
all help create the atmosphere of a brasserie.

Casseroles figure prominently among main courses (a tas is a traditional Anatolian cooking pot): chicken with almonds, green peppers and tomatoes, say, or diced lamb with vegetables and herbs. Other main courses range from barbecued mixed grill to squid with lentils, chickpeas and orange peel, or grilled mackerel with salad, and could be book-ended by hot or cold starters (among them hummus, and falafel with tahini) and puddings of yoghurt with home-made grape molasses and walnuts, or sun-dried apricots with cream, almonds and pistachios. Turkish house wines are £12.15. See the website for the addresses of the other branches, in SE1, WC1 and EC1.

> **Chef/Proprietor:** Onder Sahan **Open:** all week 12 to 11.30 **Closed:** 25 Dec **Meals:** alc (main courses £6 to £14.50). Set L and D £8.25 (2 courses) to £18.50 **Service:** 12.5% **Cards:** Amex, Delta, Maestro, MasterCard, Visa **Details:** 140 seats. 4 seats outside. Vegetarian meals. No-smoking area. No cigars/pipes in dining room. Wheelchair access (also WC). Music. Air-conditioned **Tube:** Southwark

MAP 13

Tate Britain Restaurant

Millbank, SW1P 4RG
Tel: (020) 7887 8825
Website: www.tate.org.uk

Cooking 3 | Modern British | £45

The 'bright and convivial' restaurant in the basement of Tate Britain has its confirmed supporters among both wine lovers and devotees of modern British cooking, with the famous Rex Whistler mural providing an unparalleled background. Richard Oxley's contemporary repertoire offers a short carte that features plenty of seasonal choice and appealing combinations: Highland venison carpaccio with apple crackling and beetroot rémoulade, for example, or artichoke and salsify salad with lemon and herb dressing, while main courses might include pot-roast spring poussin with a broad bean, pea and lettuce velouté, or boiled smoked gammon with pease pudding, braised red cabbage and a grain mustard sauce. Among desserts might be a chocolate brownie with hazelnut parfait and hot chocolate sauce, or pear and ginger financier with Poire William custard. Wines are a fundamental part of a meal here, and there is plenty on the list to tempt, including an impressive 60 or so by the half-bottle. Well-chosen bottles from throughout France and Europe, with a decent selection from the New

World, are backed up by fair pricing. The sommelier's suggestions start at £15.

> **Chef:** Richard Oxley **Proprietor:** Tate Catering **Open:** all week L only 11.30 to 3 (10 to 5 Sat and Sun) **Closed:** 24 to 26 Dec **Meals:** alc (main courses £15 to £18.50) **Service:** 12.5% (optional) **Cards:** Amex, Delta, Maestro, MasterCard, Visa **Details:** 80 seats. 20 seats outside. Vegetarian meals. Children's helpings. No smoking. Wheelchair access (also WC). No music. Air-conditioned **Tube:** Pimlico

MAP 13

Tentazioni

Lloyds Wharf, 2 Mill Street, SE1 2BD
Tel: (020) 7237 1100
Website: www.tentazioni.co.uk

Cooking 3 | Modern Italian | £49

Situated among the throng of developed former warehouses close to Tower Bridge, including the Butler's Wharf development, Tentazioni (which means 'temptation' in Italian) is an amiable place. The narrow dining room has the happy air of a picture gallery, thanks to colourful art on the walls. There are as many menus as there are paintings, the à la carte version offering, say, marinated salmon carpaccio with a spider crab salad, followed by grilled fillet of monkfish with spinach, raisins and pine nuts, and strawberry gelatine with prosecco sorbet to finish. The five-course 'degustazione' menu, meanwhile, offers home-made agnolotti stuffed with ricotta and porcini, followed by grilled monkfish with spinach, raisins and pine nuts, then pistachio-crusted rack of lamb with artichoke mille-feuille, and Williams pear tart with cinnamon ice cream to finish. There is also a vegetarian menu and a short but appealing traditional one offering simple classics such as home-made fettucine with amatriciana sauce and polenta cake. The reasonable Italian wine list opens with house selections at £15, and many more appealing choices under £30.

> **Chef:** Riccardo Giacomini **Proprietors:** Anna Perra and Riccardo Giacomini **Open:** Tue to Fri L 12 to 2.45, Mon to Sat D 6.45 to 10.45 **Closed:** 23 Dec to 2 Jan **Meals:** alc (main courses £12.50 to £19). Set L and D £28 to £38 **Service:** 12.5% **Cards:** Amex, Delta, Maestro, MasterCard, Visa **Details:** 60 seats. Vegetarian meals. Children's helpings. No-smoking area. Wheelchair access (not WC). Music **Tube:** London Bridge

MAP 12

Thai Garden

249 Globe Road, E2 0JD
Tel: (020) 8981 5748

Long-standing East-End Thai diner where the menu focuses on fish and vegetarian dishes. Som tum salad (£5), shiitake mushroom satay (£4.50) and deep-fried tofu with hot and sour sauce (£4.50) are among vegetarian starters, with mains including fried cucumbers, pineapples, peppers and tomatoes in sweet-and-sour sauce (£5). Fish options open with steamed mussels with garlic, lemongrass, lime leaf and basil (£5), or hot and sour prawn salad (£5.50), followed by prawn and aubergine green curry (£6), or rice with prawns, crab claws, fish balls and vegetables (£6.25). House wine £8.50. Closed Sat L and Sun L.

MAP 13

Timo

343 Kensington High Street, W8 6NW
Tel: (020) 7603 3888

Cooking 2 | Italian | £52

A long, thin dining room, with a wooden floor, pale-coloured walls hung with two attractive paintings of London parks, and funky modern lights, forms the backdrop for some authentic Italian cooking. There are few surprises on the menu, with the kitchen dealing with the likes of tagliatelle with calamari, peas and spicy tomatoes ('delicious'), and pan-fried cod in a basil crust served with courgettes and cherry tomatoes. But it can also turn out more original dishes: lamb carpaccio or a courgette flower stuffed with sea bass and cod on a bed of tomato coulis, followed by roast leg of duck with pomegranate sauce. Vanilla bavarese with chocolate sauce, or tiramisù fly the flag at dessert stage. The wine list is equally patriotic; prices rise sharply from a base price of around £15.

Chef: Franco Gatti   Proprietor: Piero Amodio   Open: Sun to Fri
L 12 to 2.30, all week D 7 to 11   Meals: alc D (main courses
£13.50 to £19.50). Set L £14.50 (2 courses) to £21.50
Service: 12.5% (optional)   Cards: Amex, Delta, Maestro,
MasterCard, Visa   Details: 52 seats. Vegetarian meals.
Children's helpings. No smoking in dining room. Wheelchair
access (also WC). Occasional music. Air-conditioned   Tube:
High Street Kensington

MAP 15

Tokyo Diner

2 Newport Place, WC2H 7JJ
Tel: (020) 7287 8777

Informal all-day eating house (open noon to mid-night, 365 days a year) such as you might find in the Japanese capital (hence the name), offering everyday food at affordable prices. Excellent-value all-in-one lunches (available noon to 6.30) include udon noodles with two pieces of salmon nigiri (£7.60), or chicken teriyaki with a small side dish, pickles, rice and miso soup (£8.60). The full menu offers an extended range of donburi (perhaps salmon sashimi with rice, cucumber and omelette; £7.90) and bento box meals, curries, noodle soups and sushi. House wine is £6.90.

MAP 14

Tom Aikens

43 Elystan Street, SW3 3NT
Tel: (020) 7584 2003
Website: www.tomaikens.co.uk

Cooking 8 | Modern French | £84

The corner site on a Chelsea side street is discreet and even slightly forbidding. Topiaried box bushes front the windows, which are screened in dark bamboo as though to prevent anyone from peering in. Browns, creams and black are the decorative hues inside, while the subdued, angled lighting is of the complexion-flattering type. It all feels very understated, perhaps a little anonymous, but emphasis is thereby thrown on the proprietor's signature style of cookery.

Since opening here in 2003, Aikens has established a reputation as one of the more characterful among London's high-end chefs. His creations somehow couldn't belong to anybody else, and his ways with combinations and adventures in texture don't just rehash what's going on elsewhere. Obliged with the tasting menu at an inauspiciously late hour, a lone diner began with a roast scallop with scallop tartare, which came with tiny pickled carrots and the signature lemon purée, a substance of ineffable richness and tang. Sourness is in, so after the pickled carrots, pickled mushrooms turned up in the next course with a slice of cured foie gras terrine. Vegetables are celebrated for the often overlooked colour and intensity they can bring to a dish, so that a superb piece of John Dory with anchovy beignets comes with fennel 'gazpacho', broad beans and a carrot sauce. One inspector felt that salt is used with unfashionable vigour.

The French cheeses are in flawless nick, and diners are given a nibble of anything unfamiliar to see if they want a full portion of it, and the desserts look spectacular. A strawberry plate involving a mousse, a tuile and some poached whole fruit is garnished with an eight-inch-long strip of brilliant shortbread, while a martini glass is layered with passion fruit in the bracing forms of tart mousse, crystal-clear jelly and some pulp, with a bowl of anglaise and passion-fruit syrup sitting alongside it.

Meals, be it noted, proceed at a pace that suits the kitchen. You may still be lingering over the copious canapés before you've even seen a menu. That said, 'service is quite excellent, totally professional, while making the diner feel completely at ease'. A list of Very Important Wines has been assembled. Prices are, of course, top end throughout, but you're hardly expecting anything else in SW3, are you? By-the-glass selections are a stimulating bunch (from £8), and then it's into the main list, where Rhônes and Burgundy take some beating, California is top notch, and even the shorter listings from Australasia all look great. Uruguay and Greece have walk-on parts, like lucky qualifiers at a World Cup. Good halves bring up the rear.

Chef/Proprietor: Tom Aikens **Open:** Mon to Fri 12 to 2.30, 6.45 to 11 **Closed:** 2 weeks Christmas to New Year, last 2 weeks Aug, bank hols **Meals:** Set L £29, Set D £60 to £75 **Service:** 12.5% (optional) **Cards:** Amex, Delta, Maestro, MasterCard, Visa **Details:** 60 seats. Vegetarian meals. Children's helpings. Jacket and tie. No smoking. Wheelchair access (also WC). No music. No mobile phones. Air-conditioned **Tube:** South Kensington

MAP 13

Les Trois Garçons

1 Club Row, E1 6JX
Tel: (020) 7613 1924
Website: www.lestroisgarcons.com

Cooking 3 | Modern French | £64

In the hinterland between Liverpool Street and Bethnal Green, this former pub stands out. Wrought-iron torches are lit, throwing impressive flames into the air to welcome guests, who are then mesmerised by the array of stuffed animals and by the jewellery, baubles and trinkets dripping from the walls and ceiling; 'it's camper than Christmas', and its popularity ensures a permanent buzz. The kitchen steers a modern French course

(rather unevenly sometimes), and there are good things to be had, notably oxtail ravioli with crispy sweetbreads, broad beans and braising jus, and 'a lovely springtime dish' of Orchard Farm lamb with pea and morel fricassee, pommes savoyarde and minted jus. For dessert, you can't beat les trois chocolats: a white chocolate soup, a milk chocolate wafer tart, and a tiny dark chocolate sponge pudding. The wine list is almost entirely French, and prices are mostly stiff, starting at £19.

Chef: Daniel Phippard **Proprietors:** Hassan Abdullah, Stefan Karlson and Michel Lasserre **Open:** Mon to Fri L 12 to 2, Mon to Sat D 7 to 10 (10.30 Fri and Sat) **Closed:** 23 Dec to 8 Jan, bank hol Mon **Meals:** alc (main courses £18 to £24). Set L £22 (2 courses) to £26, Set D Mon to Wed £22 (2 courses) to £45, Set D Thur to Sat £45 **Service:** 12.5% (optional) **Cards:** Amex, Delta, Diners, Maestro, MasterCard, Visa **Details:** 78 seats. Vegetarian meals. Wheelchair access (also WC). Music. Air-conditioned **Tube:** Liverpool Street

MAP 12

La Trompette

5–7 Devonshire Road, W4 2EU
Tel: (020) 8747 1836
Website: www.latrompette.co.uk

Cooking 6 | French | £52

With its expansive glass frontage, this wildly popular neighbourhood restaurant is certainly not afraid to blow its own trompette. A muted interior colour scheme riffs on dullish mushroom, but is hardly the main point. Tables are not packed too close, for all the press of custom means they could be, and the comfortable, high-backed banquette seating is made for relaxing into.

Contemporary French finesse with the odd Iberian flourish is what the menus are about, and everything sounds enticing. A warm salad of duck and root vegetables with a wobbly poached egg and red wine jus produces 'good synergy' on the plate, while 'sublime delicacy and precision' marked out a near-flawless dish of steamed plaice with scallop mousseline, samphire, buttered mussels and chives. The eponymous fungi might find their way into a main course of guinea fowl breast, served with crêpe Parmentier, salsify and a velouté founded on foie gras, an array of 'distinctive and intriguing combinations', while a lighter dish of rosy-pink veal rump and sweetbreads, with endive, spinach and a crunchy potato galette, managed to be both 'accomplished and satisfying'.

Finish with a selection of Valrhona desserts, including a slice of crisp-shelled bitter chocolate tart, or an unashamedly dainty meringue-topped rhubarb torte, teamed with rhubarb and orange compote and 'freshly delectable' orange and crème fraîche sorbet. Staff are on the ball, laid-back but efficient, and the wine service in particular is highly knowledgeable. This is just as well, as a treasure-trove of a wine list is on hand. By-the-glass options alone are great, starting at £4.50 for a Portuguese pair, but the main list hoves into view with pedigree selections from the French regions, a decent list of Germans and central Europeans, and some very sexy stuff from California and Australasia. Bottle prices open at £16.

> **Chef:** James Bennington **Proprietors:** Bruce Poole and Nigel Platts-Martin **Open:** Mon to Sat 12 to 2.30, 6.30 to 10.30, Sun 12.30 to 3, 7 to 10 **Closed:** 24 to 26 Dec, 1 Jan **Meals:** Set L Mon to Fri £23.50, Set L Sat £25, Set L Sun £29.50, Set D £35 **Service:** 12.5% (optional) **Cards:** Amex, Delta, Maestro, MasterCard, Visa **Details:** 75 seats. 16 seats outside. Vegetarian meals. Children's helpings. No smoking. Wheelchair access (also WC). No music. Air-conditioned **Tube:** Turnham Green

MAP 15

La Trouvaille [AR]

12A Newburgh Street, W1F 7RR
Tel: (020) 7287 8488

The French bistro cooking at this Soho restaurant, just behind Carnaby Street, delivers terrine of rabbit, snails in filo parcels or quail ravioli preceding main dishes including a hearty cassolette of river fish in a red wine reduction or confit of duck in a light harissa sauce. Desserts come with wine recommendations and could be pumpkin roulade with orange blossom water or chocolate fondant. Set D menus are £27.50 (2 courses) to £33. Wines from £13. Closed Sat L and all Sun.

MAP 12

Tsunami

5–7 Voltaire Road, SW4 6DQ
Tel: (020) 7978 1610
Website: www.tsunamijapaneserestaurant.co.uk

Cooking 2 | **Japanese** | **£34**

Exotic flowers add a splash of colour to the otherwise minimalist décor at this popular south London choice for upmarket Japanese cooking. Chef-proprietor Ken Sam's repertoire features his own versions of several dishes reminiscent of those

made famous by Nobu, with whom he trained. Take your pick from a long list of small plates designed for sharing, and brought to the table as they are prepared. Make your way from such appetizers as steamed snow crab and prawn dumplings, or Korean kimchi lamb skewers, to tempura of oysters or sea urchin, followed by main courses of steamed sea bass with saké and soy, or beef fillet with sea urchin and foie-gras butter. Particularly recommended are the house speciality clay-pot dishes. Finish in traditional Japanese fashion with a selection of sushi and sashimi. The drinks list includes a handful of hot or cold sakés and wines from £12 a bottle.

> **Chef/Proprietor:** Ken Sam **Open:** Mon to Fri 6 to 11, Sat 12.30 to 11, Sun 1 to 9 **Closed:** 3 days Christmas, 31 Dec, 1 Jan **Meals:** alc (main courses £6.50 to £16.50) **Service:** 12.5% (optional) **Cards:** Amex, Delta, Diners, Maestro, MasterCard, Visa **Details:** 100 seats. 10 seats outside. Vegetarian meals. Children's helpings. No-smoking area. No Music. Air-conditioned **Tube:** Clapham North

MAP 12

Two Brothers

297–303 Regents Park Road, N3 1DP
Tel: (020) 8346 0469

Cooking 1 | **Fish and Chips** | **£29**

The fish and chips at this bustling family-run restaurant continue to prove so popular that you could find yourself queuing for a table (the Manzi brothers don't take reservations). Waiters, who congregate at the entrance, are helpful, and daily specials are highlighted on the blackboards. Kick off with jellied eels, rock oysters, or cod's roe in batter before making a selection from an extensive array of fresh fish, including cod, rock, haddock, skate, halibut and sea bass. All mains are served with chips, a roll with butter, and home-made tartare sauce. Polish it all off with apple and almond tart or a traditional knickerbocker glory. House wines start at £10.55 with a Côte de Duras from the proprietors' own vineyard.

> **Chefs/Proprietors:** Leon and Tony Manzi **Open:** Tue to Sat 12 to 2.30, 5.30 to 10.15 **Closed:** bank hol Mon and succeeding Tue, 2 weeks Aug **Meals:** alc (main courses £9 to £18.50) **Service:** not inc **Cards:** Amex, Delta, Maestro, MasterCard, Visa **Details:** 90 seats. Children's helpings. No smoking in evenings. Wheelchair access (not WC). Music. Air-conditioned **Tube:** Finchley Central

MAP 12

Ubon by Nobu

34 Westferry Circus, Canary Wharf, E14 8RR
Tel: (020) 7719 7800
Website: www.noburestaurants.com

| Cooking 5 | Modern Japanese | £73 |

Once valet-parked and admitted by doorbell through the forbidding iron gates, you will find the sister restaurant of Nobu London and Nobu Berkeley Street (see entries) behind the Four Seasons Hotel, on the Canary Wharf riverside. A spectacular riparian view brings you the Swiss Re building and the twinkling of Tower Bridge, while the décor in the room itself, with its huge, jaw-dropping light fittings, exercises its own fascination.

Mark Edwards is listed as head chef here and at Hyde Park Corner as well as Nobu Berkeley Street (see entry), so one assumes he has a fair amount of shuttling back and forth to do, presumably not within the same service. Anti-Cucho Peruvian dishes, such as spicy chicken or salmon skewers, or spicy ribeye (served with miso soup and rice), mingle with the finely wrought traditional Japanese offerings. Among the menu highlights are tomato rock shrimp ceviche, inaniwa pasta salad with lobster, scallops with wasabi pepper, beef tenderloin teriyaki, and the ever-reliable tempura vegetables, which extend from Japanese aubergine to enoki mushrooms. Head-turning desserts end things with a flourish, perhaps with apricot and jasmine soup with peanut crumble and Nobu beer ice cream. Speciality sakés with evocative tasting notes head up a list of expensive quality wines. A small glass of house Italian can be yours for £6, and bottle prices start at £27.

> **Chef:** Mark Edwards **Proprietor:** Nobuyuki Matsuhisa **Open:** Mon to Fri L 12 to 2, Mon to Sat D 6 to 10 **Closed:** bank hols **Meals:** alc (main courses £5.50 to £29.50). Set L £45 to £50, Set D £70 to £90 **Service:** 15% (optional) **Cards:** Amex, Delta, Diners, Maestro, MasterCard, Visa **Details:** 120 seats. Car park. Vegetarian meals. No smoking. Wheelchair access (also WC). Music. Air-conditioned **Tube:** Canary Wharf DLR, Westferry DLR

> ▯ This symbol means that the wine list is well above the average.

MAP 15

Umu

14–16 Bruton Place, W1J 6LX
Tel: (020) 7499 8881
Website: www.umurestaurant.com

| Cooking 5 | Japanese | £80 |

So committed to the authentic flavours of his native Kyoto is chef Ichiro Kubota that he has Japanese water shipped over so as to avoid the indignity of having to simmer anything in London tap. This should give some indication of the style of Umu, where a secluded, easily missed Mayfair doorway leads into a design paradise of timber, stone and Venetian glass.

A range of fixed-price kaiseki menus may be taken with pre-selected sakés or wines, or you might just choose to graze through the carte. The extensive sushi options are supplemented by the likes of suppon jitate, a saké-spiked clear soup made with konbu seaweed and fish stock. The fabled wagyu beef is served with its proper garnishes of wasabi and Japanese mustard (at £45), while grilled dishes of note include peppered eel kabayaki, and special rice dishes might involve delicacies such as marinated sea bream with pickled vegetables. Desserts offer ice creams made of tea, both green and brown, or perhaps green tomato sorbet with ume plum. It all comes at a price beyond most mere mortals, with many of the chef's special menus effortlessly galloping into three figures. Service is multi-ethnic and might seem to fall short of the expected level of formality the atmosphere mandates. This is the place to get into saké if you need initiating. There is a huge range, at all levels of age and weight. Wines are something special too, with runs of Sancerre and Pouilly-Fumé as well as magisterial New World selections, carefully matching the food. Prices start at around £25.

> **Chef:** Ichiro Kubota **Proprietor:** Marc Group **Open:** Mon to Fri L 12 to 2.30, Mon to Sat D 6 to 11 **Closed:** Christmas, 30 July to 14 Aug, bank hols **Meals:** alc (main courses £8 to £45). Set L £22 to £44, Set D £60 to £165 (inc wine) **Service:** 12.5% (optional) **Cards:** Amex, Delta, Diners, Maestro, MasterCard, Visa **Details:** 60 seats. Vegetarian meals. No smoking. Wheelchair access (also WC). Music. Air-conditioned

MAP 12

Le Vacherin

76–77 South Parade, W4 5LF
Tel: (020) 8742 2121
Website: www.levacherin.co.uk

Cooking 4 | Modern French | £49

A double-fronted venue on a leafy Chiswick thoroughfare, the Johns' comfortable, welcoming place is a classic neighbourhood restaurant. Hard surfaces ensure a fair amount of hullabaloo when they are busy, but staff are vigilant and the brasserie ambience works well. An unmistakably French tone bears the menus along, producing smoked duck and wild garlic velouté as one possible starter, with a plate of charcuterie, steak tartare, and crispy frogs' legs in attendance. Slow-braised veal shin doesn't crop up that often nowadays but appears here with saffron risotto, and indeed slow cooking is a favoured technique, being employed also for rabbit, calf's tongue and classic bouillabaisse. If you've a hankering for a pig's ear, there's one of those here too, stuffed with morels and choucroute. Finish with îles flottantes, pot au (Valrhona) chocolat, crème brûlée, or French cheeses. The wine list, too, is exclusively French but delves into rarely seen appellations such as Irouléguy and Roussette de Savoie, as well as Bordeaux and Bourgogne. House wines are £13.40, or £3.50 a glass.

Chef: Malcolm John Proprietors: Donna and Malcolm John
Open: Tue to Sun L 12 to 3, all week D 6 to 10.30 Meals: alc (main courses L £10 to £12, D £13 to £19) Service: 12.5% (optional) Cards: Delta, Maestro, MasterCard, Visa Details: 86 seats. 15 seats outside. Vegetarian meals. Children's helpings. No smoking. No music. No mobile phones. Air-conditioned Tube: Turnham Green

MAP 13

Vama | AR

438 King's Road, SW10 0LJ
Tel: (020) 7565 8500

Specialising in north-west Indian cooking, this brightly decorated restaurant makes good use of its charcoal-fired clay oven to produce starters ranging from tandoori phool (spiced broccoli and cauliflower with Indian cheese and herbs; £6.95) to masala crab (£14.50). Among exotic main courses are kala chicken (with roast cumin, black salt, ginger and garlic; £10.95) and sukhi macchi

(grilled sea bass marinated in lemon, chilli oil and coriander; £11.95); non-tandoori dishes include coconut prawn curry (£14.95). Traditional desserts such as gulab jamun and rasmalai to finish. Wines from £15. Open all week.

MAP 15

Vasco & Piero's Pavilion | AR

15 Poland Street, W1F 8QE
Tel: (020) 7437 8774

Ever-popular Italian restaurant focusing on the straightforward cooking of the Umbria region ('just two or three ingredients per dish'). Olive oil, lombetto (cured pork loin), black and white truffles from the Umbrian hills, and balsamic vinegar from Modena are imported, while pasta is made in-house. Dishes such as taglietelle with a richly flavoured meat ragù, or a generous portion of accurately cooked pan-fried sea bass are typical of the set-price dinner menu (three courses £26). To finish, pannacotta is 'deliciously delicate', while the well-rounded all-Italian list starts at £14. Closed Sat L and Sun.

MAP 15

Veeraswamy | AR

99–101 Regent Street, W1R 8RS
Tel: (020) 7734 1401

The sumptuously refurbished décor evokes the luxury of 'royal India in the 1920s', according to the restaurant, which is, incidentally, when Veeraswamy first opened. It continues to enjoy a reputation for fine Indian dining, with menus encompassing starters of mussels in aromatic coconut and ginger sauce (£6.50) or crispy chicken 'lollipops' (£5.25), and main courses ranging from begum bahar (chicken curry with saffron; £13) to sea bream paturi (fish wrapped in banana leaf, steamed in a chilli and mustard sauce; £17.50) or whole tandoori lobster (£25). A serious wine list, with prices from £16.50. Open all week.

AR	Not a full entry but provisionally recommended. These 'also recommended' establishments are integrated throughout the book.

MAP 12

Victoria

10 West Temple Sheen, SW14 7RT
Tel: (020) 8876 4238
Website: www.thevictoria.net

Cooking 2 | **Modern European** | **£45**

Described as a 'restaurant and bar with bedrooms', this delightful south-west London venue may not look especially exciting from the outside, but, once through the door, the L-shaped bar (boasting a beer and juice menu) with its leather armchairs and low tables with tea lights immediately sets a sophisticated tone. The dining room, which leads out on to a small, airy conservatory, is simply decorated, complementing the well-executed, uncomplicated food. Start, perhaps, with asparagus and risotto tart or lamb sweetbreads, followed by monkfish saltimbocca with spiced aubergine and curried lentils, or roast guinea fowl with garlic and mascarpone polenta. Passion-fruit tart or elder-flower sorbet are appealing desserts. The wine list is compact, but there are a great many *digestifs* and half bottles; house options from £12.95.

> **Chef:** Darren Archer **Proprietors:** Mark Chester, Rex Chester and Darren Archer **Open:** all week 12 to 2.30 (3 Sat, 4 Sun), 7 to 10 (9 Sun) **Closed:** 4 days Christmas **Meals:** alc (main courses £9 to £20) **Service:** 12.5% (optional) **Cards:** Amex, Delta, Maestro, MasterCard, Visa **Details:** 75 seats. 40 seats outside. Car park. Vegetarian meals. Children's helpings. No smoking. Wheelchair access (not WC). No music **Accommodation:** 7 rooms **Tube:** Richmond

MAP 15

Villandry

170 Great Portland Street, W1W 5QB
Tel: (020) 7631 3131
Website: www.villandry.com

Cooking 2 | **Modern European** | **£46**

'Although it was my third visit I still found it hard to resist browsing around the deli,' said one visitor to this foodie's paradise, which changed hands in 2005. There's also a small charcuterie counter, which is open all day from breakfast for plates of salame di Milano with fig chutney and the like, plus a large bar which is open for lunch and dinner. The main dining room is large, light and spacious, and is the setting for a modern menu that puts the focus on keenly sourced produce (as you might expect, given the high quality stuff for sale a few steps away). Start with something like French red mullet soup with Gruyère cheese and croûtons, and follow on with smoked haddock with a poached egg on top of a potato cake, or rack of lamb au poivre. Hand-cut chips are good, but you have to pay extra for them. Summer pudding, or lemon tart with orange syrup are typical desserts. Service can lack direction at times. The well-presented wine list favours France, and pithy notes will help with decision-making. House selections start at £13.50, with 19 by the glass from £3.50.

> **Chef:** David Rood **Proprietor:** Jamie Barber **Open:** all week L 12 to 3, Mon to Sat D 6 to 10.30 **Closed:** 25 and 26 Dec, 1 Jan, bank hols **Meals:** alc (main courses £12 to £19.50). Bar menu available **Service:** 12.5% (optional) **Cards:** Amex, Maestro, MasterCard, Visa **Details:** 100 seats. Vegetarian meals. Children's helpings. No smoking. Wheelchair access (not WC). Music. Air-conditioned **Tube:** Great Portland Street

MAP 13

Vivat Bacchus

47 Farringdon Street, EC4A 4LL
Tel: (020) 7353 2648

There are five wine cellars and two cheese storage rooms at this basement restaurant a stone's throw from Smithfield Market. There are set lunches (£15.50/£17.50), and a carte, starting, perhaps, with foie gras terrine with caramelised apples and leaf salad (£10) and progressing to pan-fried whole lemon sole with crayfish and lemon and parsley mayonnaise (£16), or grilled springbok with a biltong crust and sweet potato chips (£17.50). Finish with white chocolate cheesecake with ginger syrup (£5.50). The impressive 25,000-bin cellar starts at £14. Closed Sat and Sun.

MAP 12

Wapping Food

Wapping Hydraulic Power Station, Wapping Wall, E1W 3ST
Tel: (020) 7680 2080
Website: www.thewappingproject.com

Cooking 3 | **Modern European** | **£46**

Housed in the cavernous shell of a former power station, with lots of machinery still *in situ*, this is a wonderfully atmospheric venue for a leisurely

Sunday lunch with the family, or cocktails at any time. The kitchen takes a simple approach, focusing on assembly dishes in which the top-quality ingredients are allowed to shine. The short menu is full of fashionable flavours, starting perhaps with broad bean, mint and buffalo mozzarella bruschetta, or braised octopus with chilli, fennel and capers. To follow, main courses range from classic spaghetti al vongole to roast leg of spring lamb with potato and aubergine gnocchi, raisins and pine nuts, or chargrilled whole lemon sole with chorizo, salted lemon and green olives. Don't miss out on the ever-popular desserts, such as stewed rhubarb pudding with mascarpone, or Valrhona chocolate fondue. Eating options extend to afternoon tea all week and brunch at weekends, and an exclusively Australian wine list offers a good range of bottles, priced from £16.50, with lots of choice by the glass.

Chef: Cameron Emirali **Proprietor:** WPT **Open:** Mon to Fri 12 to 3, 6.30 to 11, Sat 1 to 3.30, 7 to 11, Sun 1 to 4 **Closed:** 24 Dec to 2 Jan **Meals:** alc (main courses £12.50 to £17.50). Brunch menu available Sat and Sun 10 to 12.30 **Service:** 12.5% (optional) **Cards:** Amex, Delta, Maestro, MasterCard, Visa **Details:** 150 seats. 70 seats outside. Car park. Vegetarian meals. Children's helpings. No cigars/pipes in dining room. Wheelchair access (also WC). Music **Tube:** Wapping

MAP 13

White Swan

108 Fetter Lane, EC4A 1ES
Tel: (020) 7242 9696
Website: www.thewhiteswanlondon.com

Cooking 3 | Modern British | £48

Tucked away near Fleet Street, this narrow gastropub is compact but perfectly pieced together. The downstairs bar is lively and as stylish as the upstairs dining room, which features a mirrored ceiling, white-clothed tables and plenty of wood. The short menu lightly skips across Britain and Europe, delivering first courses such as grilled spatchcock of quail with smoked lentils, and truffle-infused mozzarella with rocket and tomato tartare. Whole grilled rainbow trout with a smoked eel and potato cake and braised chicory is a well conceived main course, and roast duck breast with smoked black pudding and apple reveals a flair for apposite combinations. Dessert could be prune and Armagnac crème brûlée, or lemon-curd tart. Service is friendly and welcoming, and the international wine list is pretty extensive, with a dozen good-quality bottles served by the glass from £3.50. Prices open at £15.

Chef: Grant Murray **Proprietors:** Tom and Ed Martin **Open:** Mon to Fri 12 to 3, 6 to 10 **Closed:** Christmas, New Year, bank hols **Meals:** alc D (main courses £13 to £19.50). Set L £20 (2 courses) to £25. Bar menu available **Service:** 12.5% (optional) **Cards:** Amex, Diners, Maestro, MasterCard, Visa **Details:** 40 seats. Vegetarian meals. Children's helpings. Music. Air-conditioned **Tube:** Chancery Lane

MAP 12

William IV `AR`

786 Harrow Road, NW10 5JX
Tel: (020) 8969 5944

A Spanish menu is the main focus of this trendy north London pub, but they also serve a traditional Sunday roast. Small tapas-style dishes form the bulk of the menu. Meat options might be grilled lamb chops (£7.50), albóndigas (£5), or sausage and bean casserole (£6.25), while fish choices run to salt cod croquettes (£4.95) and calamari (£5.75), and vegetarian dishes such as patatas bravas (£4.25), or traditional tortilla (£4.50). There's also seafood paella (£18) to share. Wines from £12.75. Open all week.

MAP 15

Wiltons

55 Jermyn Street, SW1Y 6LX
Tel: (020) 7629 9955
Website: www.wiltons.co.uk

Cooking 4 | Traditional English | £83

As Olaf Hambro was eating oysters alone at Wiltons in 1942 a bomb landed in nearby Piccadilly; when the owner declared the restaurant closed, he immediately asked for it to be added to his bill, and his family still owns the establishment. Immaculately set tables set the tone in the long, narrow dining room, which has the air of a gentleman's club, and staff are quietly attentive. The menu is as staunchly traditional as the surroundings – crab and avocado salad, grilled Dover sole, and braised oxtail, for example – raw materials are first-rate and dishes are well timed. Start with classic lobster bisque, cold beef consommé, or foie gras with toasted brioche. A good selection of poached or grilled fish – maybe halibut or wild turbot – is found among main courses, and meat dishes might include traditional Irish stew, or venison in a red wine and pepper sauce. Finish with an old-school dessert like bread-and-butter pudding or sherry trifle, or a savoury such as Welsh rarebit. Prices on the far-reaching wine list are high even by St James's standards, with little under £30, although ten are served by the glass from £6.50.

Chef: Jerome Ponchelle Proprietors: the Hambro family
Open: Mon to Fri 12 to 2.30, 6 to 10.30 Closed: Christmas, bank hols Meals: alc (main courses £18 to £50). Set D Fri £50 Service: 12.5% (optional) Cards: Amex, Delta, Diners, Maestro, MasterCard, Visa Details: 100 seats. Jacket. Wheelchair access (also WC). No music. No mobile phones. Air-conditioned Tube: Green Park

MAP 12

Wizzy

NEW ENTRY

616 Fulham Road, SW6 5RP
Tel: (020) 7736 9171
Website: www.wizzyrestaurant.co.uk

Cooking 1 | Korean | £34

Hwi Shim Chung (Wizzy) has brought a little taste of Korea to the far end of the Fulham Road. The two small, minimalist dining rooms are decorated in pale greys, creams and greens, while the cooking is 'more akin to Korean home cooking', and perfect for 'Korean food virgins'. The grazing style is bang up-to-date, too, with dishes such as marinated baby crab in rice topped with tobiko caviar, and main courses of beef rib stew or ginseng chicken (served with kim-chee, spinach, marinated cuttlefish and a dollop of mashed potato) displaying quite diverse flavours based around sweet, sour and salt. For dessert, try an unusual organic granita made from pine leaves, or red-bean tiramisù. House wine is £12.50.

Chef/Proprietor: H.S. Chung Open: Mon to Sat 12 to 3, 6.30 to 10.30 Meals: alc (main courses £8.50 to £15) Service: 10% Cards: Amex, Delta, Maestro, MasterCard, Visa Details: 55 seats. No-smoking area. Music. Air-conditioned Tube: Parsons Green

MAP 15

Wolseley

160 Piccadilly, W1J 9EB
Tel: (020) 7499 6996
Website: www.thewolseley.com

Cooking 3 | International | £62

The car showroom on Piccadilly may be long gone, but the building lives on as a grand venue for

Chris Corbin and Jeremy King's all-day brasserie. While there's a real sense of the grandiose to the high-impact décor, there's not too much pomp and circumstance, helped by the fact that the place is usually 'rocking' from the 7am start for breakfast until the doors close at midnight. The carte offers the sort of dishes you can eat every day, ranging from classical British (fish pie) and French (coquelet rôti) right through to dishes with a touch of Vienna (wiener schnitzel). Both Roquefort tart with pear and beet leaves and chicken soup with dumplings impressed at inspection, as did a main course of choucroute garnie à l'alsacienne – served in a portion big enough for two. Desserts are not strong points, judging by a dry and oversweet pavlova with mixed berries. Reporters have singled out the 'impeccable' service, recommend the Sunday roast beef and Yorkshire pudding, and find the wine list exact and well formed, with everything but the reserve selection available by the glass. House Spanish red and French white start the ball rolling at £15.50, or £4.25 the glass.

Chef: Cyrus Cato Proprietors: Chris Corbin and Jeremy King Open: all week 12 to 3, 5.30 to 12 (11 Sun) Meals: alc (main courses £9.50 to £30). Cover £2 Service: 12.5% (optional) Cards: Amex, Delta, Diners, Maestro, MasterCard, Visa Details: 150 seats. Vegetarian meals. Children's helpings. No smoking in 1 dining room. Wheelchair access (also WC). No music. Air-conditioned Tube: Green Park

MAP 15

Yatra

AR

34 Dover Street, W1S 4NF
Tel: (020) 7493 0200

Yatra means 'spiritual journey', we are told. A relaxed, modern dining room is the setting for some interesting Indian food. Start with barwan aloo tikki (crisp-fried mashed potato stuffed with cashew nuts and chickpeas; £5.25), and follow on with main courses such as dum ki nalli (lamb shank braised in cinnamon and lemon; £13.35), or the house speciality platter (£15.25), which includes lamb kebab, chargrilled prawns and paneer tikka. End with shrikhand (£4.75). Wines from £14. Open Tue to Sat D only.

NEW ENTRY	This appears after the restaurant's name if the establishment was not a main entry in last year's Guide. Please note, however, it may have been 'also recommended' in the previous edition.

MAP 15

Yauatcha

15–17 Broadwick Street, W1F 0DL
Tel: (020) 7494 8888
Email: mail@yauatcha.com

Cooking 4 | Chinese | £56

The younger sister of Hakkasan (see entry) aims for a slightly simpler style in its approach to new-wave Chinese cooking, though with the same attention to detail and with scarcely less elegance in the surroundings. A chic basement room with low-slung chairs and Santa's-grotto lighting is the setting for a dim sum menu supplemented by larger dishes, and an afternoon tea menu with a tempting range of pâtisserie.

Steamed dishes show up exceptionally well, the har-gau prawn dumplings an object lesson, and the shumai of scallop or Shanghai sticky rice are usually well reported. Cheung fun preparations avoid sliminess and come filled with anything from prawns to wagyu beef, but oddly the more straightforward Cantonese dishes may not impress (sweet-and-sour pork seemed to hark back to an earlier, oilier generation). The Chinese vegetable gai lan crops up all over the place and should not be missed, whether with Dover sole, ginger and soya, or simply stir-fried with ginger. Desserts represent a final creative flourish, as in Szechuan pepper pannacotta with cocoa sorbet and raspberry sauce. All sorts of stimulating drinks may pass your lips while here, from Taiwanese blue tea through honeydew melon martini to Australian Liqueur Muscat. In between, there is a fine, compact listing of stylistically grouped, expensive wines to consider.

Chef: Mr Wong Proprietor: Alan Yau Open: Mon to Fri 12 to 3, 5.30 to 11.45, Sat and Sun 11.45 to 11.45 (10.30 Sun) Meals: alc (main courses £3.50 to £38) Service: 13% Cards: Amex, Delta, Diners, Maestro, MasterCard, Visa Details: 110 seats. Vegetarian meals. No smoking. Wheelchair access (also WC). Music. Air-conditioned Tube: Tottenham Court Road

MAP 15

Yoshino AR

3 Piccadilly Place, W1V 0DB
Tel: (020) 7287 6622

A 'healthy buzz' pervades this straightforward Japanese restaurant that's usefully located just off Piccadilly. It offers a good selection of bento boxes (from £5.80), while a set dinner (£19.80) is built around tempura, teriyaki and the like. There's a wide selection of sushi and sashimi (from £2.50) on the carte, and a sushi bar downstairs. Wines are not very exciting – best to drink beer or saké. Closed Sunday.

MAP 14

Zafferano

15 Lowndes Street, SW1X 9EY
Tel: (020) 7235 5800
Website: www.zafferanorestaurant.com

Cooking 6 | Italian | £56

Extensive refurbishment in 2005 brought a pleasing sense of space to this Knightsbridge restaurant. There is now a bar upstairs, a private room in the new wine cellar and, within the kitchens, an in-house buttery to supply the dining room. Seasonal specials menus now supplement Andy Needham's carefully crafted take on real Italian cooking.

Don't miss the fabulous breads, including warm onion focaccia, served perhaps with a plate of antipasti to set the ball rolling. A pair of scallops makes a nicely weighted starter, served with a little saffron sauce. Pasta dishes score highly, as was the case with one reporter's pheasant ravioli, its flavour deepened with rosemary, and with another's autumn chestnut tagliatelle with wild mushrooms. Foie gras is cleverly used to add further richness to an already comforting risotto, and nor do main dishes disappoint. Traditional veal cutlet combines positive flavour with simple accompaniments of rösti and mushrooms, or there might be chargrilled monkfish with courgettes and sweet chilli. Clear flavours and simple presentation distinguish desserts such as poached peach with lemon sorbet, or pear and almond tart with mascarpone ice cream. Service, once it got used to the expanded dining room, seems to have settled back to its normal sleek proficiency.

Pages of top-flight Italian wines make a refreshing change from the Francocentrism of many lists, but the mark-ups don't exactly entice the novice. A fine list of dessert wines is a cheering sight,

The price given next to the cooking score is based on the cost of a typical three-course dinner for one person, including coffee, house wine and service.

although only a handful come by the glass. House wines are £14.50.

Chef: Andy Needham **Proprietor:** A to Z Restaurants **Open:** all week 12 to 2.30, 7 to 11 **Closed:** 24 Dec to 2 Jan, bank hol L **Meals:** Set L £25.50 (2 courses) to £34.50, Set D £29.50 (2 courses) to £45 **Service:** 13.5% (optional) **Cards:** Amex, Delta, Diners, Maestro, MasterCard, Visa **Details:** 75 seats. Vegetarian meals. No smoking. Wheelchair access (also WC). Music. No mobile phones. Air-conditioned **Tube:** Knightsbridge

---

MAP 13

Zaika

1 Kensington High Street, W8 5NP
Tel: (020) 7795 6533
Website: www.zaika-restaurant.co.uk

| Cooking 3 | Modern Indian | £54 |

Zaika is an airily modern dining room with sumptuous décor in a rich palette of colours – ivy-green, gold, crimson and purple – evoking colonial-era India. The kitchen aims to combine old and new ideas in a similar fashion, with traditional dishes alongside original creations, all presented in a refined style. So, for example, tandoori lamb chops with ginger and chillies appear among starters alongside a prawn platter comprising red onion and shrimp risotto, crispy tiger prawns and tandoori king prawns marinated in chillies and rosemary with coconut chutney. To follow, main courses feature roast cod with black ink upma (Indian couscous) and a tomato, chilli and yoghurt sauce, and grilled Gressingham duck breast in a rich black lentil sauce with celeriac and parsnip mash, crispy okra and wild mushroom naan, and to finish there might be rose-water and vanilla crème brûlée. For those who wish to sample a wider choice of dishes, the six-course tasting menu and nine-course gourmand menu are tempting options. Wines are expertly chosen with an eye to matching the vibrant flavours of the food. The substantial list covers 17 countries, taking in everything from classic French bottles to fashionable modern producers. Prices are fair, with a good range of house selections in the £16 to £22 bracket and around 15 wines by the glass.

Chef: Sanjay Dwivedi **Proprietor:** Cuisine Collection **Open:** Sun to Fri L 12 to 2.45, all week D 6 to 10.45 (9.45 Sun) **Closed:** 25 and 26 Dec, 1 Jan **Meals:** alc (main courses £14 to £19). Set L £15 (2 courses) to £19, Set D £38 to £88 (inc wine). Bar menu available **Service:** 12.5% (optional) **Cards:** Amex, Diners, Maestro, MasterCard, Visa **Details:** 80 seats. Vegetarian meals. No smoking in dining room. Wheelchair access (not WC). Music. Air-conditioned **Tube:** High Street Kensington

---

MAP 14

Zuma

5 Raphael Street, SW7 1DL
Tel: (020) 7584 1010
Website: www.zumarestaurant.com

| Cooking 5 | Modern Japanese | £67 |

An expansive modern Japanese eatery in the Knightsbridge hinterland, Zuma is less formal than many other such places. Vast pink marble pillars hold up the roof, while the granite bar counters reinforce the chunkiness of the décor, but the place is run with appreciable warmth and charm. The extensive menus anatomise Japanese eating into its various categories, with sushi, maki rolls and small nibbly bits preceding the house specialities, which take in black cod wrapped in hoba leaf, crisp-fried lemon sole in ponzu sauce with green onions, and grilled taraba crab with chilli, garlic and butter. Aficionados of the style have commended eel sushi of 'supreme freshness', miso-marinated lamb chops with pickled onions and myoga ('one of the best dishes'), and wafer-thin slices of rare beef with a citrus and chilli sauce. The more familiar dishes are well rendered too, as evidenced by 'extremely tender' salmon teriyaki. Desserts may not be a high point, but the sorbets, such as melon or strawberry, have impressed.

A lengthy listing of aged sakés will thrill the initiated, and there is also a very fine list of wines, arranged by grape variety, including a few rarities such as a Greek white and a German Spätburgunder (Pinot Noir). Prices are high, starting at around £20, but ten wines by the glass are £5.50 to £13.50.

Chef: Colin Clague **Proprietors:** Rainer Becker and Arjun Waney **Open:** all week 12 to 2.30, 6 to 11 (10.30 Sun) **Meals:** alc (main courses £12 to £30). Set L £21.80, Set D £96 (min 2). Bar menu available **Service:** 13.5% (optional) **Cards:** Amex, Delta, Diners, Maestro, MasterCard, Visa **Details:** 127 seats. Vegetarian meals. No smoking in dining room. Wheelchair access (not WC). Music. Air-conditioned **Tube:** Knightsbridge

---

To submit a report on any restaurant, please visit *www.which.co.uk/gfgfeedback.*

England

MAP 3	ABINGER COMMON – Surrey

Stephan Langton Inn

Friday Street, Abinger Common RH5 6JR
Tel: (01306) 730775

Cooking 3	Modern British	£37

It's well worth seeking out this red-brick and timbered building, named after the Archbishop of Canterbury responsible for drawing up the Magna Carta, tucked away down narrow country lanes. You won't find anyone standing on ceremony here, with its dining room of stripped floorboards, dark wooden tables and contemporary artwork. The menu draws a lot from the Mediterranean and southern Europe, so Serrano ham with guindillas (pickled whole sweet chillies) might crop up among starters along with mussels with harissa and coriander. Hearty main courses have included braised lamb shank with mash, capers and olives, and duck breast with cassoulet, with roast cod with mash and salsa verde a fish option. Finish with blood-orange sorbet with Campari, or buttermilk pudding with poached rhubarb. The southern hemisphere and Europe are the focus of the brief wine list. Prices start at £11.75, and there's a decent showing below £20.

Chef: Jonathan Coomb **Proprietors:** Jonathan and Cynthia Coomb **Open:** Sun L 12.30 to 2.30, Tue to Sat D 7 to 9.30 **Closed:** Tue after bank hols **Meals:** alc (main courses £9.50 to £14.50). Bar L menu available Tue to Sun **Service:** not inc **Cards:** Delta, Maestro, MasterCard, Visa **Details:** 80 seats. 70 seats outside. Car park. Children's helpings. No smoking. Wheelchair access (not WC). No music

(£) This symbol means that it is possible to have a three-course dinner, including coffee, half a bottle of house wine and service, for £30 or less per person.

MAP 3	ABINGER HAMMER – Surrey

Drakes on the Pond

Dorking Road, Abinger Hammer RH5 6SA
Tel: (01306) 731174
Website: www.drakesonthepond.com

Cooking 5	Modern European	£61

This solid-looking red-brick building, resembling a farmhouse, is surrounded by gently rising countryside yet is right on the A25, making it a useful lunch stop if you're passing. It shares an entrance and car park with a trout farm. Its long, narrow and comfortable dining room with primrose-yellow walls and ceilings and floor-length white cloths on the tables may strike rather an exuberant note, but the kitchen has integrity, and for the most part the cooking is highly competent and well presented. Ideas range from a starter of seared duck foie gras with sweetened red cabbage and golden sultana dressing to a diver-caught scallop tarte Tatin with a rocket salad and langoustine sabayon. Attempts to be modern and original may be outshone by more classic ideas, such as a plate of lamb incorporating soft-crusted best end and sweetbreads teamed with sarladaise potatoes, caramelised baby onions and red wine jus, or fillet of beef with a ragoût of wild mushrooms, asparagus tips and baby plum tomatoes, and herb rösti. Texture and flavour contrasts are well managed: for example, in a rhubarb and apple pain d'épice charlotte with yoghurt sorbet. Eleven wines by the glass (house Sauvignon is £18, or £4.75 a glass) introduce a list that balances France against the New World.

Chef: John Morris **Proprietors:** John Morris and Tracey Honeysett **Open:** Tue to Fri L 12 to 1.30, Tue to Sat D 7 to 9.30 **Meals:** alc D (main courses £21 to £25). Set L £18.50 (2 courses) to £23.50 **Service:** not inc **Cards:** Diners, Maestro, MasterCard, Visa **Details:** 32 seats. Car park. No children under 10. No smoking. Wheelchair access (also WC). No music. Air-conditioned

MAP 8 **ADDINGHAM –**
West Yorkshire

Fleece

154 Main Street, Addingham LS29 0LY
Tel: (01943) 830491

Cooking 3 | Modern British | £40

Step back in time at the Fleece, which comes with requisite low ceilings, walls hung with copious prints and pictures, and a separate bar for drinking with a fire on cold days. The kitchen pays attention to the seasons and has built up a network of specialist suppliers – shellfish from Scotland, crab from Dorset, beef from a farm two miles away – to produce a menu that's strong in traditional pub dishes as well as more modern ideas. Choose from the blackboards, which offer roasts and pies, from suckling pig with caramelised apples and gravy to shepherd's pie, alongside starters of grilled goats' cheese with beetroot and walnut salad, or queenie scallops with bacon and rocket, and main courses of Islay king scallops with white crabmeat and lime risotto, or duck confit with saucisson and butter beans. Among desserts might be banana crêpe, and chocolate and walnut tart, or plump for the carefully selected cheeses, including Wensleydale and Dovedale Derbyshire Blue. The wine list offers more than 70 bins, most from France, and a separate list of 20 house wines provides a range of styles at prices from £11.95 to £17.50.

Chef: Matthew Brown Proprietor: Chris Monkman Open: all week 12 to 2.15, 6 to 9.15 (Sun 12 to 8) Meals: alc (main courses £8 to £16) Service: not inc Cards: Delta, Maestro, MasterCard, Visa Details: 60 seats. 50 seats outside. Car park. Vegetarian meals. Children's helpings. No smoking in 1 dining room. Wheelchair access (not WC). No music. Air-conditioned

MAP 6 **ALDEBURGH – Suffolk**

Lighthouse

77 High Street, Aldeburgh IP15 5AU
Tel: (01728) 453377
Website: www.lighthouserestaurant.co.uk

Cooking 3 | Modern British-Plus | £32

On the busy high street of this ever-popular coastal town, this bistro-style restaurant is the hub of a thriving enterprise that includes a cookery school, a wine shop and a fruit and vegetable stall at Aldeburgh market. The cooking offers classic seafood dishes such as starters of potted shrimps with toast, or kedgeree, with non-fish choices including chicken liver parfait with pickled figs, or crispy duck salad with cucumber, spring onions and hoisin sauce. To follow, the varied main-course options range from fish in beer batter with chips, peas and tartare sauce, or pan-fried calf's liver on mash with smoked streaky bacon, to tuna niçoise with a soft-boiled egg, cherry tomatoes, anchovies and new potatoes, or rack of Suffolk spring lamb on fennel and tomato ragoût. Desserts typically take in chocolate nemesis with double cream, or boozy banana pancake with almond and toffee ice cream. Around a dozen wines by the glass open a varied list, with bottle prices from £11.95.

Chefs: Sara Fox, Guy Welsh and Leon Manthorpe Proprietors: Sara Fox and Peter Hill Open: all week 12 to 2 (2.30 Sat and Sun), 6.30 to 10 (later by arrangement) Closed: 1 week Jan, 1 week Oct Meals: alc (main courses £7.50 to £15) Service: not inc Cards: Amex, Delta, Maestro, MasterCard, Visa Details: 95 seats. 12 seats outside. Vegetarian meals. No smoking. Wheelchair access (also WC). No music. No mobile phones. Part air-conditioned

152 Aldeburgh

152 High Street, Aldeburgh IP15 5AX
Tel: (01728) 454594
Website: www.152aldeburgh.co.uk

Cooking 3 | Modern European | £38

With an overall feel and atmosphere that are in keeping with its seaside location, this small, informal bistro looks especially inviting. The look is bright, airy and contemporary: no tablecloths, a stripped wooden floor, and walls hung with simple modern artwork. Seafood looms large on the menu: escabèche of mackerel with new potato salad might be one starter, Thai-style gravad lax with coriander dressing (exemplifying the upbeat approach) another. There are appealing combinations in meat and fish main courses too: rack of spring lamb in a herb crust with dauphinois potatoes, or skate with lemon potato purée and a caper and raisin dressing. The success rate is maintained in desserts of wild plum and crumble fool, or chocolate bread-and-butter pudding with vanilla ice cream. Prices on the short, straightforward wine list (from Adnams of Southwold) start at £12.75 and stay mostly below £25.

Chef: Garry Cook Proprietors: Andrew Lister and Garry Cook
Open: all week 12 to 3, 6 to 10 Meals: alc (main courses
£10.50 to £18). Set L and D (exc Sat D) £14 (2 courses) to
£17.50 Service: not inc Cards: Amex, Delta, Maestro,
MasterCard, Visa Details: 56 seats. 24 seats outside.
Vegetarian meals. Children's helpings. No smoking.
Wheelchair access (not WC). Music. No mobile phones

| MAP 8 | ALTRINCHAM –
Greater Manchester |
|---|---|

Juniper

21 The Downs, Altrincham WA14 2QD
Tel: (0161) 929 4008
Website: www.juniper-restaurant.co.uk

Cooking 7 | Modern French | £56

Juniper is one of a half-dozen restaurants in the
UK at the vanguard of culinary adventurism,
where a solid base of modern French cooking is
built upon and shifted into uncharted territory. Ten
years ago, Juniper was delivering something a little
more classical, but, as the dining room became
more refined, so the food became increasingly
bold, with the arrival of slicks and splashes of
various emulsions replacing the traditional stock
reduction sauces. Paul Kitching's technical expert-
ise remains a feature of even the craziest concepts,
but these have been moderated in recent months.

First impressions are of a low-key neighbourhood restaurant, with large windows and neatly
painted panelling suggesting something a little
more traditional than the reality – a glance at the
menu should put the uninitiated in the picture.
Inside, the basement bar has grown more comfortable over the years, and is the place in which to
become acquainted with the menu. Katie O'Brien
is on hand to explain the dishes, and she leads the
service with the right balance of friendliness and
professionalism. The ground-floor dining room is
lush with plant life, tables are smartly set, and the
imposing *Rout of San Romano* by Uccello dominates one wall.

It wouldn't be a modern culinary adventure
without the full range of inter-course tasters, and
here they come: red pepper gazpacho, a square of
dark chocolate with sea salt, and a tomato jelly. The
menu descriptions remain in the listing style, such
as a starter of 'warm scallops, Welsh rarebit, asparagus, leeks, artichokes', which delivered a single
scallop – lightly cooked – with a frothy leek cream,
two small spears of white asparagus, and the rarebit

in the form of a 'yellow gunge'. Dishes won't necessarily appear as you anticipate, so expect the
unexpected and don't bother trying to second-
guess this particular chef.

Next, a small cup of creamy carrot soup, lifted
out of the ordinary by the addition of cinnamon,
lemon and sage. Among main courses, one
reporter was dazzled by the matching of trout
fillets with the salty contrast of caviar and a smoky
kipper glaze. Best end of lamb has come with
saffron noodles, pineapple, a basil, tomato and
pimento gâteau, brazil nuts, white chocolate drops
and blue cheese dressing, and, although the list of
ingredients is long, what appears on the plate has
purpose and vigour.

A shooter of wheat milk might precede a hot
cross bun soufflé, which certainly delivers the
expected thoughts of Easter and is accompanied by
an impressive chocolate and sea-salt ice cream.
'Excellent' espresso comes with dense chocolate
truffles and a slice of the trademark custard tart.
The wine list is Franco-centric, strong in
Bordeaux and Burgundy, and limited in South
America. There is not a great deal under £20.

Chef/Proprietor: Paul Kitching Open: Fri and Sat L 12 to 2,
Tue to Sat D 7 to 10 Closed: Christmas, 1 week Feb, 2 weeks
Aug Meals: alc L (main courses £17 to £20). Set L £20 to
£45, Set D £40 to £60 Service: not inc Cards: Amex, Delta,
Maestro, MasterCard, Visa Details: 32 seats. No smoking.
Occasional music. Air-conditioned

MAP 8	AMBLESIDE – Cumbria

Drunken Duck Inn

Barngates, Ambleside LA22 0NG
Tel: (015394) 36347
Website: www.drunkenduckinn.co.uk

Cooking 3 | Modern British | £46

You can see why this place is popular. A country
pub with unusual flair, it combines informal eating
with food that would not look out of place in a
classier establishment. It can be thought of as a
gentrified pub in two parts: a bar where drinkers
are welcome and soup and sandwiches are served
at lunchtime, and several smart dining areas delivering a menu of contemporary brasserie-style
dishes. Basic materials are well sourced (many
locally) and well handled. Equally, the kitchen's
feeling for comfort food is finely tuned, coming up
with some interesting combinations as it teams
pan-fried crab and chive cake with a warm green

bean and sun-blush tomato salad, and grilled crumpet with Keldthwaite Gold Brie, crispy smoked bacon and raspberry vinegar dressing. Main courses offer pork fillet with grilled black pudding and apple and rosemary tarte Tatin, and roast wild sea bass with a crab and spring onion sauce, while for dessert there might be warm rhubarb and custard tart with gingerbread ice cream. The approachable wine list offers plenty of decent drinking at keen prices, including plenty of choice by the glass and house wine from France and Italy at £11.80 and £14 respectively.

Chef: Nick Foster Proprietors: Stephanie Barton and Paul Spencer Open: all week 12 to 2.30, 6 to 9 Closed: 25 Dec Meals: alc (main courses L £9.50 to £25, D £14.50 to £25). Bar L menu available Service: not inc Cards: Amex, Delta, Maestro, MasterCard, Visa Details: 60 seats. Car park. Vegetarian meals. Children's helpings. No smoking. Wheelchair access (also WC). No music Accommodation: 16 rooms

Rothay Manor

Rothay Bridge, Ambleside LA22 0EH
Tel: (015394) 33605
Website: www.rothaymanor.co.uk

Cooking 3 | Modern British | £46

A peaceful spot in which to unwind, Rothay Manor is well cared for, inside and out. It feels like a family home, with its relaxed air of smart informality and comfortable rather than luxurious furnishings. It does its best to accommodate everyone, offering light lunches, afternoon teas and children's high teas. The four-course dinner combines traditional and more up-to-date ideas, producing the likes of grilled goats' cheese with baby onion confit, or a rose of melon with a compote of berries and blackcurrant sorbet (not a dessert but a starter). A second course (such as cream of parsnip and Stilton soup) might be followed by fillet of red mullet with couscous, red pepper coulis and fried basil leaves. Finish with lemon tart, champagne jelly, or crêpes suzette. Lunch is particularly good value, producing cream of mushroom soup, then shank of fell-bred lamb with braised root vegetables, and bread-and-butter pudding to finish. Wines cover a wide range of styles and nationalities, starting at £14 for a soft-fruited Chilean Merlot and reaching into three figures for Ch. Palmer *grand cru classé*.

Chefs: Jane Binns and Colette Nixon Proprietors: Nigel and Stephen Nixon Open: all week 12.30 to 1.45, 7.15 to 9 Closed: 3 to 26 Jan Meals: alc exc Sun (main courses £7 to £10). Set L Mon to Sat £17.50, Set L Sun £19.50, Set D £35 to £39. Light L menu available Mon to Sat Service: not inc Cards: Amex, Delta, Diners, Maestro, MasterCard, Visa Details: 65 seats. Car park. Vegetarian meals. No children under 7 at D. Children's helpings. No smoking. Wheelchair access (also WC). No music. No mobile phones. Air-conditioned Accommodation: 19 rooms

MAP 3 AMERSHAM –
Buckinghamshire

Artichoke

9 Market Square, Amersham HP7 0DF
Tel: (01494) 726611
Website: www.theartichokerestaurant.co.uk

Cooking 4 | Modern French | £53

Laurie Gear's conscientious, quality-first approach to sourcing and cooking wins this smart, intimate restaurant many fans. A salad of quail breast with a ravioli of the confit leg and sage beurre noisette makes an opulent starter, that's if new season's asparagus or scallops don't catch your eye. Duck foie gras comes with spiced pear tarte Tatin, chicory and celery leaves and Chinese five-spice sauce, and might precede fillet of veal on herb gnocchi with sweetbreads, root vegetables and black truffle sauce. The overtly French style adds grapes and raisins soaked in Muscat to a fillet of Dover sole, and figs glazed with Banyuls to a saddle of venison, and when it comes to desserts chocolate bavarois is paired with chocolate ganache and warm griottine cherry doughnuts, or blueberry compote with iced peanut parfait. A French-dominated wine list parades its share of prestige bottles, although there is some relief for the price-conscious, including a South African Pinotage for £15.50 and a Viognier Vin de Pays de l'Ardèche for £16.

Chef: Laurie Gear Proprietors: Laurie and Jacqueline Gear Open: Tue to Sat 12 to 2, 6.30 to 9.30 (9.45 Fri and Sat) Closed: 1 week Christmas, 1 week Easter, 2 weeks from Aug bank hol Meals: alc L (main courses £12 to £18). Set L £18.50 (2 courses) to £22.50, Set D £28 (2 courses) to £49 (whole table only) Service: 12.5% (optional) Cards: Delta, Maestro, MasterCard, Visa Details: 25 seats. 4 seats outside. Vegetarian meals. Children's helpings. No smoking. Music

Gilbey's [AR]

1 Market Square, Amersham HP7 0DF
Tel: (01494) 727242

Occupying a converted school building dating from 1642, Gilbey's is a busy neighbourhood restaurant with a pleasant, informal atmosphere and cheerful, helpful staff. Reports suggest that the kitchen is on the up, turning out consistently satisfying results from an appealing modern British menu. Parma ham with roast fig salad (£5.75) and smoked tuna with wasabi-marinated crab and green beans (£6.50) might be among starters, main courses taking in pan-fried guinea fowl breast with wild mushrooms (£13.95). Lemon tart with coconut sorbet has been a popular dessert. Wines from £11.25. Open all week.

MAP 10   APPLETHWAITE – Cumbria

Underscar Manor

Applethwaite CA12 4PH
Tel: (01768) 775000

Cooking 5 | Anglo-French | **£63**

Set in 40 acres of grounds on the lower slopes of Skiddaw, Underscar Manor has everything you'd expect from a Lakeland country house. Awe-inspiring views of Derwent Water and the fells are the backdrop for the almost-as-spectacular drawing room, with its ornate decorative plaster-work and impressive candelabra. The views are shared by the conservatory dining room, which has a formal feel, with lace tablecloths, reserved but friendly staff, and menus presented in oversized decorative folders. All this is of a piece with the elaborate cooking produced by an accomplished kitchen brigade headed by Robert Thornton. The main menu covers plenty of ground, with six choices per course plus daily market specials, starters ranging from goats' cheese soufflé with spiced cauliflower fritters and tomato relish to pan-fried calf's liver with celeriac, dauphinois potatoes, caramelised apple and shallot sauce. Main courses raise the game further, taking in pan-fried Angus beef fillet on an oxtail medallion filled with mushroom mousse, served with roast root vegetables, spinach and parsnip crisps, creamed potato and red wine sauce, or perhaps saddle of local venison with a liquorice-scented game sauce, pumpkin ravioli, Savoy cabbage with bacon, cocotte potatoes and cranberries in port. To finish, options might include creamed rice pudding with orange and cardamom, and nutmeg ice cream. Wine prices start at £18.50 and mark-ups remain fair throughout the list.

> **Chef:** Robert Thornton **Proprietors:** Pauline and Derek Harrison, and Gordon Evans **Open:** all week 12 to 1, 7 to 8.30 **Meals:** alc (main courses L £16 to £17, D £22 to £23). Set L £28, Set D £38 **Service:** not inc **Cards:** Amex, Maestro, MasterCard, Visa **Details:** 55 seats. 12 seats outside. Car park. Vegetarian meals. No smoking in dining room. Occasional music. No mobile phones **Accommodation:** 11 rooms

---

MAP 2   ARDINGTON – Oxfordshire

Boar's Head

Church Street, Ardington OX12 8QA
Tel: (01235) 833254
Website: www.boarsheadardington.co.uk

Cooking 4 | Modern European | **£50**

There's much to like about this 150-year-old vibrant village pub. The bar is a haven for locals, while the restaurant, which overlooks a small patio, is warmly decorated with simple drapes, bare tables and tea lights. Bruce Buchan's menu is short but focused on seasonal produce; game comes from the Lockinge Estate and lamb and pork from local farms. The broad British brush-strokes are augmented by flavours from Europe, so deep-fried goats' cheese in filo with a tomato compote might start, arriving on a white rectangular plate and drizzled with chilli oil. Cannelloni of scallops with artichoke velouté features 'fat, meaty, fabulous' bivalves, while a main course of roast Gressingham duck has also been a success, perched on top of some good rösti and 'sitting in a fabulous deep-flavoured sauce' of morels. Toffee banana crumble with vanilla ice cream, reminiscent of banoffi pie, is a hit among desserts. House Côtes du Rhône red and Chilean Sauvignon Blanc are £12.50.

> **Chef:** Bruce Buchan **Proprietors:** Bruce Buchan, Terry Chipperfield and Richard Douglas **Open:** all week 12 to 2.15, 7 to 9.30 (10 Fri and Sat) **Meals:** alc exc Sun (main courses £14.50 to £19.50). Set L Mon to Sat £14.50 (2 courses) to £17.50, Set L Sun £22 (3 courses). Bar menu available **Service:** not inc **Cards:** Amex, Delta, Maestro, MasterCard, Visa **Details:** 40 seats. 20 seats outside. Car park. Children's helpings. No smoking in 1 dining room. Occasional music. No mobile phones **Accommodation:** 3 rooms

MAP 2 | **ARLINGHAM** – Gloucestershire

Old Passage Inn

Passage Road, Arlingham GL2 7JR
Tel: (01452) 740547
Website: www.fishattheoldpassageinn.co.uk

| Cooking 3 | Seafood | £47 |

A secluded riverside spot west of Arlingham, with little but meadows and the Severn to gaze at, provides an enviable setting for this simple and amenable family-run brasserie-style inn. Raoul Moore now heads the kitchen; his six years working beside Patrick Le Mesurier means little has changed. The menus continue to revolve around a regular supply of seafood, and there is an appealing mix of traditional simplicity and the influence of foreign climes, in particular the Mediterranean. Thus, provençale fish soup or potted shrimps might preface a main course such as beer-battered cod with hand-cut chips and tartare sauce or chargrilled fillets of John Dory with sun-blanched tomatoes, asparagus, black olives, capers, sliced new potatoes and rosemary and lemon olive oil, while token meat dishes include jambon persillé and ribeye steak with sauce bordelaise. 'Good service' adds to the enjoyment, and the wine list includes a decent range under £20. House French is £12.40.

Chef: Raoul Moore **Proprietors:** the Moore family **Open:** Tue to Sun L 12 to 2, Tue to Sat D 6.30 to 9 **Closed:** 24 to 31 Dec **Meals:** alc (main courses £12 to £36.50) **Service:** not inc **Cards:** Amex, Delta, Maestro, MasterCard, Visa **Details:** 65 seats. 22 seats outside. Car park. Vegetarian meals. Children's helpings. No smoking. Wheelchair access (also WC). Occasional music. No mobile phones. Air-conditioned **Accommodation:** 3 rooms

This symbol means that the restaurant has elected to participate in *The Good Food Guide's* £5 voucher scheme (see 'Using The Good Food Guide' for details).

MAP 8 | **ARNCLIFFE** – North Yorkshire

Amerdale House

Arncliffe, Littondale BD23 5QE
Tel: (01756) 770250
Website: www.amerdalehouse.co.uk

| Cooking 4 | Modern European | £46 |

Wend your way along a 'twisting, narrow and seemingly never-ending' road to this country hotel, which has a distinctly homely feel. Guests take drinks in the drawing room before being escorted across the hall to the dining room, which features polished mahogany tables, pretty oil-burning lamps and hunting prints. Nigel Crapper's menu is short; three starters, a middle course, a choice of fish or meat, two desserts and local cheeses. Inspection found this uncomplicated approach reflected in the style of cooking and presentation. Grilled Somerset goats' cheese and cherry tomato and basil tart were both very simple but carefully prepared dishes, while the main of tender pan-roasted loin of Dales lamb on minted couscous with a sweet and light redcurrant jus also hit the spot. Poached pear with warm butterscotch and vanilla ice cream rounded things off well. 'If I'd been staying there, I'd have gone to bed quite content.' The wine list is a mostly French affair with a few New World choices, starting at £14.75.

Chef: Nigel Crapper **Proprietors:** Paula and Nigel Crapper **Open:** all week D only 7.30 to 8 **Closed:** Nov to mid-Mar **Meals:** Set D £34.50 **Service:** not inc **Cards:** MasterCard, Visa **Details:** 27 seats. Car park. Children's helpings. No smoking. No music **Accommodation:** 11 rooms

MAP 3 | **ARUNDEL** – West Sussex

Arundel House

11 High Street, Arundel BN18 9AD
Tel: (01903) 882136
Website: www.arundelhouseonline.co.uk

| Cooking 3 | Modern British | £48 |

Carved from what was once a run-down B&B, Arundel House has a modern, sleek yet comfortable look and service that is friendly and professional. The menu aims to catch the attention too, with some assured modern cooking and impeccable sourcing, much of it local. Crab and smoked haddock fishcake on a bed of creamed leeks and topped with a poached egg might kick things off, to be succeeded by the old-school pleasure of oxtail with grain mustard mash and roast winter root vegetables. Slightly less traditional are fillet of roe deer with curly kale and a savoury fig tart, or roast breast and braised leg of Barbary duck on glazed pear and red onion marmalade with a creamy nutmeg reduction, with maybe rhubarb and Pernod clafoutis with rhubarb-scented cream for dessert. Wines are a modern mixture arranged by style, with a good balance of budget and smarter bottles. Prices start at £14 and a handful come by the glass at £3.50.

> **Chef:** Luke Hackman **Proprietors:** Billy Lewis-Bowker and Luke Hackman **Open:** Sat L 12.30 to 2.30, Mon to Sat D 6.30 to 9.30 **Closed:** 24 to 27 Dec, 19 Feb to 4 Mar **Meals:** Set L £22 (2 courses) to £28, Set D Mon to Thur £22 (2 courses) to £28, Set D Fri and Sat £28 (2 courses) to £34 **Service:** not inc **Cards:** Amex, Delta, Maestro, MasterCard, Visa **Details:** 34 seats. Vegetarian meals. No children under 12. No smoking. Music **Accommodation:** 5 rooms

MAP 9   ASENBY – North Yorkshire

Crab & Lobster

Dishforth Road, Asenby YO7 3QL
Tel: (01845) 577286
Website: www.crabandlobster.co.uk

Cooking 3	Fish/Modern European	£50

The Crab & Lobster restaurant 'does exactly what it says on the tin' but in a most fanciful style: a marine theme runs throughout the lively dining room, which boasts yellow linen tablecloths, models of yachts, billowing blinds that resemble sails and even a diver's outfit suspended from the ceiling. Naturally, seafood is the main event, with lobster a favourite. Scallops, both king and queenie, mussels with Yorkshire ale, and Loch Fyne oysters might be among starters, while roast local cod comes with slow-roast belly pork and duck fat-roast potatoes as a main course. Also popular is garlic lobster with scallops and king prawns, while meatier options could include calf's liver, or honeyed breast of Goosnargh duck. Finish with something like baked cherry Alaska with berry compote. The bread has been commended, while service is friendly and efficient. The spirited wine list runs to around 60 bins, starting at £16 for

Georges Duboeuf. Accommodation is in nearby Crab Manor.

> **Chef:** Steve Dean **Proprietor:** Vimac Leisure Ltd **Open:** all week 12 to 2.30, 7 to 9 (6.30 to 9.30 Sat) **Meals:** alc (main courses £13.50 to £37). Set L £14.50 (2 courses) to £17.50, Set D £29.50. Afternoon menu available 3 to 6 **Service:** not inc **Cards:** Amex, Delta, Maestro, MasterCard, Visa **Details:** 140 seats. 70 seats outside. Car park. Vegetarian meals. Children's helpings. No smoking. Wheelchair access (also WC). Music. No mobile phones. Air-conditioned **Accommodation:** 14 rooms

MAP 5   ASHBOURNE – Derbyshire

Callow Hall

Mappleton Road, Ashbourne DE6 2AA
Tel: (01335) 300900
Website: www.callowhall.co.uk

Cooking 3	Modern British-Plus	£54

Callow Hall is a Victorian country-house hotel with a human touch, with the emphasis on comfort amid lovely rural surroundings. The Spencers' approach is relaxed and friendly, while maintaining professionalism, and, as one reporter remarked, 'the food isn't bad either'. Dinner, a four-course affair at a fixed price, furnishes generous breadth of choice. A summer evening began with a salad of very fresh king prawns and scallops in a sharp herb vinaigrette, and featured an impressive main course of rack and loin of lamb with a red onion and feta tartlet and rosemary jus. In between comes a choice of either fish or sorbet, and it all ends with either an international cheese selection or perhaps a brandy-snap basket of prune and brandy ice cream. France is the anchor of the carefully constructed wine list, with New Zealand and Australia offering good back-up. Plenty of halves and a list of fine wines complete the picture. Prices open at £12.50.

> **Chefs:** David and Anthony Spencer **Proprietors:** David, Dorothy, Anthony and Emma Spencer **Open:** Sun L 12.30 to 1.30, Mon to Sat D 7.30 to 9 **Closed:** 25 and 26 Dec **Meals:** alc (main courses £17.50 to £21). Set L £25, Set D £42 **Service:** not inc **Cards:** Amex, Diners, MasterCard, Visa **Details:** 80 seats. Car park. Vegetarian meals. Children's helpings. No smoking. Wheelchair access (also WC). No music. No mobile phones **Accommodation:** 16 rooms

The Dining Room

33 St John Street, Ashbourne DE6 1GP
Tel: (01335) 300666
Website: www.thediningroomashbourne.co.uk

Cooking 4 | Modern British-Plus | £51

A pale cream and green exterior gives a modest air to this tiny building dating from 1604. Past a small courtyard is the dining room, which has dark wooden ceiling beams, limestone lintels, and a cast-iron range on a dark-tiled hearth. The setting may be old-worldly but Peter Dale's cooking is ardently cosmopolitan and highly inventive. Dishes are meticulously described on the short menu of three choices per course: for example, 'home-smoked organic salmon, pea and basil pannacotta, lemon sorbet, fennel, buckwheat pancake, spice of angels, lemon oil, chives', which sounds like a five-course meal but is in fact just a starter. Among main courses might be a duo of Ellastone beef (braised and roasted) with buttered Savoy cabbage and leeks, roast onion tart, mustard foam and a thyme jus, and to finish perhaps Victoria plum upside-down cake with ginger beer jelly, Tahitian vanilla brûlée, honey ice cream, shortbread and pollen. A note on the menu states: 'If you would like simpler cuisine then please do not hesitate to ask.' But to do so would surely be churlish, given Peter Dale's efforts – and would be to deny yourself a treat, for his skill matches his ambition. Wines are well chosen and fairly priced, from £15.95.

Chef: Peter Dale Proprietors: Peter and Laura Dale Open: Tue to Sat 12 to 1.30, 7 to 8.30 Closed: 2 weeks after 25 Dec, 1 week Mar, 1 week Sept Meals: alc (main courses L £13, D £20). Set L £22. Set D (needs booking) £40 Service: not inc Cards: Delta, Maestro, MasterCard, Visa Details: 16 seats. No children under 12. Children's helpings. No smoking. Wheelchair access (also WC). Music. No mobile phones

---

MAP 1 **ASHBURTON – Devon**

Agaric

30 North Street, Ashburton TQ13 7QD
Tel: (01364) 654478
Website: www.agaricrestaurant.co.uk

Cooking 4 | Modern British-Plus | £46

This charming restaurant is a real home-from-home; there's nothing pretentious about the Coileys' set up, which is popular for its honest presentation of well-chosen, locally-sourced produce, served with a smile. Simplicity is key here; the décor is reminiscent of a domestic dining room with no sign of stuffy formality; a big dresser is loaded with preserves and other provisions, a couple of Persian rugs hang on the wall and the furniture is rustic. Sophie tends to the front-of-house, while Nick works on his seasonally aware menu, which uses produce from his kitchen garden (he also cures his own ham and roe). Smoked mutton ham and rillettes of venison come with an onion and chilli marmalade for starters, while roasted best end of Moroccan-marinated Devon lamb or perhaps grilled turbot steak served with a fennel and sorrel Hollandaise might follow. Dessert could be rhubarb and ginger oaty crumble with clotted cream, while local Ticklemore cheeses include Sharpham Elmhirst, Ticklemore Button and Denhay Cheddar. There are around 30 bins on the global wine list, which favours France and starts at £13.50.

Chef: Nick Coiley Proprietors: Nick and Sophie Coiley Open: Wed to Fri L 12 to 2, Wed to Sat D 7 to 9 Closed: 2 weeks at Christmas, 1 week Jan, 2 weeks Aug Meals: alc (main courses £11 to £17.50). Set L £14.95 (2 courses) Service: not inc Cards: Delta, Maestro, MasterCard, Visa Details: 28 seats. 15 seats outside. Vegetarian meals. Children's helpings. No smoking. Wheelchair access (also WC). No music Accommodation: 5 rooms

---

MAP 9 **ASHFORD – Derbyshire**

Riverside House

Ashford in the Water DE45 1QF
Tel: (01629) 814275
Website: www.riversidehousehotel.co.uk

Cooking 4 | French-Plus | £60

Ashford is 'surely one of the most picturesque villages in Derbyshire' state the owners of Riverside House: a bold claim indeed, but not far from the truth. This fine Georgian country house fits in well, and the dining room makes the most of the setting, overlooking peaceful gardens towards the River Wye, although your gaze is as likely to be drawn towards the artistically presented food. Indeed, meticulous attention to detail is evident in every aspect of the creative, modern cooking, from the sourcing of high-quality ingredients to precise timing of fish and meat. The dinner menus run to six choices per course, starters ranging from soused sea bass with orange and olive oil to a warm rabbit spring roll with pepper and olive salad, to be followed perhaps by roast rack of lamb with fondant potato, pan-fried turbot fillet with pasta and mussel sauce, or slow-roast belly pork with smoked bacon potatoes and wild mushrooms. For dessert, try a grown-up version of jelly and ice cream with vanilla and black pepper syrup. A heavyweight list of over 150 wines opens with around a dozen house selections from £16.95, all available by the glass from £3.40.

> Chef: John Whelan Proprietor: Penelope Thornton Open: all week 12 to 2, 7 to 9.30 Meals: alc L exc Sun (main courses £10.50 to £19). Set L Sun £28.95, Set D £45.95 Service: not inc Cards: Amex, Delta, Diners, Maestro, MasterCard, Visa Details: 40 seats. 10 seats outside. Car park. Vegetarian meals. No children under 16. No smoking. Wheelchair access (also WC). No music. No mobile phones Accommodation: 14 rooms

---

MAP 1 | ASHWATER – Devon

Blagdon Manor

Ashwater EX21 5DF
Tel: (01409) 211224
Website: www.blagdon.com

Cooking 2 | English/Mediterranean | £49

The Moreys' chocolate-brown Labradors stretch out on the living-room floor of this family-run hotel, setting an informal tone. The Grade II listed manor enjoys great views over the Devonshire countryside, and the dining room is run with hands-on efficiency by Liz Morey. Reports have noted a move towards a less fussy approach in Steve Morey's menus, allowing fresh ingredients, good combinations and well-timed cooking to show to their best advantage, as in a starter of 'light and wobbly' smoked haddock and leek mousse with a warm salad of smoked haddock, eel and salmon. To follow, roasted rump of new season lamb is partnered with ham hock, buttered Savoy cabbage and a mustard froth, and for one June diner, a Pimms jelly with poached strawberries and mint ice cream was a simple, well-made and thoroughly seasonal way to end. The wine list is fairly compact, with French house selections starting at £13.50.

> Chef: Steve Morey Proprietors: Liz and Steve Morey Open: Wed to Sun L 12 to 2, Tue to Sat D 7 to 9 (residents only Sun D and Mon D) Closed: 2 weeks Jan, 2 weeks Oct Meals: Set L Wed to Sat £17 (2 courses) to £21, Set L Sun £23.50, Set D £32 (2 courses) to £35 Service: not inc Cards: Delta, Maestro, MasterCard, Visa Details: 24 seats. Car park. No children under 12. No smoking. Wheelchair access (also WC). No music. No mobile phones Accommodation: 7 rooms

---

MAP 2 | AWRE – Gloucestershire

Red Hart Inn

Awre GL14 1EW
Tel: (01594) 510220

Cooking 2 | Modern British | £32

Proprietors Marcia Griffiths and Martin Coupe have done a fine job of restoring this Grade II listed fifteenth-century village pub on the bank of the River Severn. There's a list on each table of the local suppliers and growers, and seasonal organic vegetables come from nearby Oaklands Park. Specialities include Severn salmon, game from Lydney Park Estate and Awre wild rabbit, to name but a few. Home-cured gravad lax with mustard dressing, or deep-fried local Camembert with redcurrant dressing might start, followed by slow-roast shank of lamb with cassoulet, or pan-fried loin of Awre pork in a 'Severn Sider' cider sauce with honey-glazed apples. Steamed syrup sponge pudding with custard gives a meal a traditional finish. A page of wines by the glass opens the short wine list, where bottle prices start at £11.95.

> Chef: Andrew Palmer Proprietors: Marcia Griffiths and Martin Coupe Open: all week 12 to 2.30 (2 winter), 6 to 9.30 (6.30 to 9 winter) Closed: Sun D, Mon L and Tue L winter Meals: alc (main courses £7.50 to £15) Service: not inc Cards: Delta, Diners, Maestro, MasterCard, Visa Details: 72 seats. 40 seats outside. Car park. Vegetarian meals. Children's helpings. No smoking in dining room. Wheelchair access (not WC). Music. No mobile phones Accommodation: 2 rooms

---

MAP 10 | AYCLIFFE – Co Durham

County

13 The Green, Aycliffe DL5 6LX
Tel: (01325) 312273
Website: www.the-county.co.uk

Cooking 2 | Modern European | £37

On a corner of the village green, this attractive cream-painted inn has retained a distinctly pub-like décor and atmosphere, though the blackboard menu reveals loftier ambitions. Changing two or three times a week, it offers inventive modern European cooking, with starters of pan-fried king scallops with crispy bacon and croûton salad, or risotto of red onion, roast peppers and goats' cheese, followed by duck breast with poached figs, parsnip purée, fondant potatoes and a port reduction, or slow-roast belly pork with creamed cabbage, smoked bacon and mashed potato. Portions are generous, but try to save room for sophisticated desserts such as warm bitter chocolate tart with confit oranges and Chantilly cream. Lunchtime visitors have found simpler food on offer. Wines start at £11.95 a bottle, or £3.10 and £4.10 per glass.

Chef: John McCerery   Proprietor: Andrew Brown   Open: Mon to Sat 12 to 2, 6 (6.45 Sat) to 9.15   Closed: 25 and 26 Dec, 1 Jan   Meals: alc (main courses £9 to £18.50). Express L menu available   Service: not inc   Cards: Amex, Delta, Diners, MasterCard, Visa   Details: 75 seats. Car park. Vegetarian meals. Children's helpings. No smoking in dining room. Music

MAP 3 | AYLESBURY – Buckinghamshire

Hartwell House

Oxford Road, Aylesbury HP17 8NL
Tel: (01296) 747444
Website: www.hartwell-house.com

Cooking 4 | Modern European | £55

Jacobean and Georgian decorative features are in abundance at this grand stately home surrounded by parkland. Despite its gentrified air and a degree of formality, there is nothing solemn or stuffy about the friendly service in the dining room. Chef Daniel Richardson shares this lack of pomposity in his approach, with an elaborate but unpretentious cooking style that makes excellent use of the vegetables and herbs supplied by the hotel's own kitchen gardens, backed up by diligently sourced produce from local suppliers. Galantine of Aylesbury duck and foie gras, served on toasted brioche with spiced pears, has been among 'professionally executed' starters, and other options might include a 'mosaic' of sole, monkfish, sea bass and langoustine accompanied by lime crème fraîche and pickled cucumber. To follow, there might be pan-fried sea bass fillet on dauphinois potato with buttered spinach and an accomplished sauce that 'somehow incorporated port and truffles without dominating the dish'. A first-rate selection of British cheeses makes an appealing alternative to desserts of feather-light pear mousse with a refreshing raspberry jelly. The choice of wines by the glass has increased this year, and the list also sees the welcome addition of a selection of 'value wines', with prices starting at £17.50.

Chef: Daniel Richardson   Proprietor: Historic House Hotels Ltd   Open: all week 12.30 to 1.45, 7.30 to 9.45   Meals: Set L Mon to Sat £22 (2 courses) to £29, Set L Sun £31, Set D £46 to £65. Buttery L menu available   Service: net prices   Cards: Amex, Maestro, MasterCard, Visa   Details: 60 seats. 25 seats outside. Car park. Vegetarian meals. No children under 6. No smoking. Wheelchair access (also WC). Occasional music. No mobile phones   Accommodation: 46 rooms

MAP 3 | AYLESFORD – Kent

Hengist

7–9 High Street, Aylesford ME20 7AX
Tel: (01622) 719273
Website: www.hengist-restaurant.co.uk

Cooking 3 | Modern French | £51

The village of Aylesford is steeped in history – its name comes from 'Angle's Ford', the place where the county's first invaders crossed the river Medway. The 'coolly modern' restaurant is entered by glass doors into a smoked-glass lobby with walls of brown suede, while the dining room itself is set around a central brick chimney; tables are large and smartly set, and smoked-glass screens cover the Georgian windows. Chef Jean-Marc Zanetti has ably taken over the kitchen, and brings modern twists to a basically French menu. Ham hock confit and shallot terrine comes with strongly mustardy home-made piccalilli, contrasting sweetness provided by 'delicious' walnut and raisin bread. Intensity of flavour has also been the hallmark of another starter of creamy squid risotto. Artful presentation gives a modern look to grilled calf's liver and bubble and squeak, carrot purée and sauce diable, while well-timed roast cod comes with roast winter vegetables, marinated cherry tomatoes, braised gem lettuce and bouillabaisse sauce. Another fine marriage has been Kentish apple tart glazed with vanilla and star anise served with apple compote and cinnamon ice cream. France is at the heart of the wine list, with around a dozen served by the glass (from £3.50), with bottle prices starting at £12.95.

Chef: Jean-Marc Zanetti   Proprietors: Paul Smith, Richard Phillips and Kevin James   Open: Tue to Sun L 12 to 2.30, Tue to Sat D 6.30 to 10.30   Closed: 25 to 27 Dec, 1 Jan   Meals: alc exc Sun L (main courses £14 to £18). Set L Tue to Sat £10.95 (2 courses) to £12.95, Set L Sun £16.50 (2 courses) to £18.50, Set D Tue to Thur £19.95, Set D Tue to Sat £42.50   Service: 11% (optional)   Cards: Amex, Maestro, MasterCard, Visa   Details: 73 seats. Vegetarian meals. Children's helpings. No smoking in dining room. Wheelchair access (also WC). Music. Air-conditioned

MAP 2   **BARNSLEY –**
Gloucestershire

Barnsley House

Barnsley GL7 5EE
Tel: (01285) 740000
Website: www.barnsleyhouse.com

Cooking 5	Modern European	£59

Built from the lighter shade of Cotswold stone that predominates in these parts, Barnsley House sits in acres of gardens designed by landscapist Rosemary Verey. From the first entrance through a stone-flagged hall, it's clear that the place is going to be fairly grand, but it's a modern version of grand, with shiny new fittings and plenty of up-to-the-minute amenities. A restful green to match the gardens is the predominant hue.

The gardens also supply Graham Grafton's menus with vegetables, fruit and herbs, and there is an appealing freshness about much of the cooking, especially at the height of the seasons. A salad of crab and Jersey Royals with herbs, lemon and chives is just the sort of first course one wants to see in May. Local spring lamb might make an appearance among main courses, served with braised vegetables, or there might be poached salmon with asparagus and lemon butter. An Italian undertow informs the output: vincisgrassi, a luxurious lasagne-style pasta dish containing porcini and truffles, is a house speciality, and there is also wild boar bresaola with rocket and Parmesan, and pannacotta with strawberries and passion fruit to finish. The wine list kicks off at £24, and there is a good selection by the glass. The nearby Village Pub is under the same ownership.

Chef: Graham Grafton   **Proprietors:** Tim Haigh and Rupert Pendered   **Open:** all week 12 to 2, 7 to 9.30   **Meals:** Set L £19.50 (2 courses) to £25.50, Set D £39.50 to £46   **Service:** 12.5% (optional)   **Cards:** Delta, Maestro, MasterCard, Visa   **Details:** 50 seats. 24 seats outside. Car park. No children under 12 at D. Children's helpings. No smoking. Wheelchair access (also men's WC). Occasional music. No mobile phones   **Accommodation:** 18 rooms

MAP 2   **BARTON ON SEA –**
Hampshire

Pebble Beach

Marine Drive, Barton on Sea BH25 7DZ
Tel: (01425) 627777
Website: www.pebblebeach-uk.com

Cooking 3	Modern European/Seafood	£45

Seen from the road, Pebble Beach is 'a rather unremarkable, modern yellow building set to seaward', its strongest suit being its commanding position over Christchurch Bay, giving virtually uninterrupted sea views from its amply proportioned terrace to the white chalk of the Needles on the Isle of Wight. They may serve sandwiches alongside a serious-sounding carte, as well as specials and 'lighter options' menus, but it's 'seriously posh' inside, a bit 'glitzy' with a gleaming white baby grand, expensive uplighters, wrought-iron railings and freestanding chrome ice buckets. The cooking hits all the fashionable buttons, with globe artichoke served with Serrano ham, rocket salad and a creamy truffle dressing, pot-au-feu with a 'textbook' sauce gribiche, and 'a fantastic piece' of fillet steak simply accompanied by mushrooms, fat chips and mixed leaves, all components of an April inspection meal. Fish dominates the list of specials, and desserts are impeccably crafted: witness iced nougat coated in chocolate and flavoured with praline and griottine cherries, and vanilla pannacotta with poached pears, rhubarb and strawberries. Service is well drilled, and the French-led wine list is shortish but to the point. Most bottles are north of £20, but house wines start at £11.95.

Chef: Pierre Chevillard   **Proprietor:** Mike Caddy   **Open:** all week 12 to 2 (2.30 Sun), 6.30 to 9.30 (10 Fri and Sat)   **Closed:** D 25 Dec, D 1 Jan   **Meals:** alc (main courses £10 to £25). Light menu available exc Sat D   **Service:** not inc   **Cards:** Amex, Delta, Maestro, MasterCard, Visa   **Details:** 70 seats. 40 seats outside. Car park. Vegetarian meals. Children's helpings. No smoking. Wheelchair access (also WC). Music. No mobile phones. Air-conditioned   **Accommodation:** 3 rooms

This symbol means that accommodation is available at this establishment.

The price given next to the cooking score is based on the cost of a typical three-course dinner for one person, including coffee, house wine and service.

MAP 9 | BARTON-UPON-HUMBER – North Lincolnshire

Elio's

AR

11 Market Place, Barton-upon-Humber
DN18 5DA
Tel: (01652) 635147

The 'speciality board' features the catch of the day – perhaps Dover sole (£24.50), or chargrilled tuna steak with roast peppers (£15.50) – at this congenial Italian restaurant. The pizza menu features all the usual suspects (from £8.75), while antipasti include pâté (£5.95) and grilled sardines (£6.50). Pasta dishes range from lasagne verde (£5.50) to seafood tagliolini (£6.50), and among main courses may be lambs' kidneys sautéed with shallots and mushrooms (£13.95), and saltimbocca alla romana (£16.95). The all-Italian wine list starts at £12.95. Open Tue to Fri L and Mon to Sat D.

MAP 2 | BARWICK – Somerset

Little Barwick House

Barwick BA22 9TD
Tel: (01935) 423902
Website: www.littlebarwickhouse.co.uk

Cooking 6 | Modern English | £51

The white Georgian house stands on a steep hillside a little proud of the rest of the village. It's in a serenely rural setting, despite being only a stone's throw from Yeovil. Enjoyable views down the handsome garden divert the eye from the understated dining room, which Emma Ford runs with brisk professionalism.

Great pains are taken with dishes that typically combine a number of counterpointing elements, such as vividly colourful carrot and orange 'escabèche' and salsa verde that come with grilled Cornish mackerel. Risottos as accompaniments are a feature, so a main course of saddle of wild rabbit might be teamed with a cep version as well as roast butternut squash. Crumbed lamb sweetbreads as a robust starter have been a little overwhelmed by their intensely sweet and over-copious sauce of sherry and raisins, but the black pepper reduction supporting medallions of beef fillet and whole roast shallots has displayed fine judgement. Fish as a main course might pair pan-fried sea bass with a langoustine sauce. Desserts end things on a high,

such as a tripartite apple dish that combines a cone of Calvados parfait with a crumble served in a sherry glass and a stunning sorbet in a brandy-snap.

A splendid wine list will provide scope for much happy perusal by aficionados. Grouped by style, it is an honour roll of the very best growers in many regions and, while prices are not low, there is certainly enough choice below £25 for those on a budget. House selections start at £15.95.

Chefs: Tim Ford, Chris Hale, Faye Ridler and Lee Watson **Proprietors:** Tim and Emma Ford **Open:** Wed to Sun L 12 to 2, Tue to Sat D 7 to 9 (9.30 Sat) **Meals:** alc L (main courses £15 to £25), Set L Wed to Sat £18.95 (2 courses) to £20.95, Set L Sun £23.95, Set D £34.95 **Service:** not inc **Cards:** Maestro, MasterCard, Visa **Details:** 40 seats. 10 seats outside. Car park. Vegetarian meals. No children under 5. No smoking. No music. No mobile phones. Air-conditioned **Accommodation:** 6 rooms

MAP 9 | BASLOW – Derbyshire

Cavendish Hotel, Gallery Restaurant

Baslow DE45 1SP
Tel: (01246) 582311
Website: www.cavendish-hotel.net

Cooking 3 | Modern European | £50

This country-house hotel has views overlooking the Chatsworth Estate. The sight can be enjoyed from the Gallery Restaurant, but it was the 'beautiful new décor' that drew one visitor's attention: 'very drawing room rather than dining room' was the verdict. The Mediterranean-inspired food of, say, pan-seared scallops with Parma ham crisps, butternut squash purée and threads of garlic and rosemary oil dressing may be the foundation, but the kitchen is perfectly at home with a dish of Asian flavouring in whole roast monkfish tail with a creamy shellfish and potato curry served with onion and cumin fritters. Materials are of top quality: note a simple dish of pan-roast breast and braised leg of guinea fowl that has impressed, the meat perfectly paired with creamed potato mixed with Savoy cabbage and a Madeira and thyme jus. Among desserts might be hot steamed praline pudding with caramel and balsamic ice cream and plum and port compote. Plenty of thought has gone into the wine list, which begins at £13.95. In addition, a good-value, all-day menu ensures that the Garden Room is altogether less formal.

Chefs: Ben Handley and Chris Allison Proprietor: Eric Marsh
Open: all week 12 to 2.30, 6.30 to 10 Closed: 25 Dec
Meals: Set L and D £29.50 (2 courses) to £43.95 Service:
5% Cards: Amex, Delta, Diners, Maestro, MasterCard, Visa
Details: 50 seats. Car park. Vegetarian meals. No smoking.
Wheelchair access (also WC). Music. No mobile phones
Accommodation: 24 rooms

Fischer's Baslow Hall

Calver Road, Baslow DE45 1RR
Tel: (01246) 583259
Website: www.fischers-baslowhall.co.uk

| Cooking 7 | Modern European | £54 |

The hall is a fine manor house on the edge of the Chatsworth estate. Deeply traditional in design and approach, it's the kind of place that reflects its owners' taste, being crammed with antiques and *objets* of one sort or another. Swagged drapes hang at the dining room windows, the tables are set with white china, silver, good glassware and candles, and the lighting is discreet. Our postbag for Fischer's bulges reliably at the seams most years, the overwhelming consensus being of satisfaction, indeed excitement. Canapés and appetisers never fail to impress, and multifarious breads are readily forthcoming. The fixed-price menus read well, furnishing a generous range of culinary styles and techniques. Caramelised ballottine of pork with roast spiced John Dory and white beans comprise one eventful starter, while the expected luxuries of truffles and foie gras might accompany squab pigeon ravioli (without a supplement). The shooting season might bring on a show-stopping treatment of grouse with red cabbage and wild mushrooms, lavishly sauced with red wine and port. That sense that main ingredients are handled with the utmost respect was also evident in a lunchtime main course of pink sea bream with Mediterranean vegetables, crushed new potatoes and a sauce of tomato and olive oil, in which the fish was flawlessly timed. At the end come the kinds of desserts that stick in the memory for all the right reasons, textbook cheesecakes and gâteaux doing their bit, as does passion-fruit soufflé with a matching sorbet.

Note that the six-course, no-choice Prestige Menu costs a little less than the main menu – a rather neat way of enticing you to let the kitchen show what it can do. The wine list exudes quality. Strongest in the classic French regions, it also finds room for decent selections from Australia and California. Five house wines are around the £20 mark. The Fischers and chef Rupert Rowley now run a second venue in the form of a renovated pub a little way along the road from the hall (see entry, Rowley's, below).

Chefs: Max Fischer and Rupert Rowley Proprietors: Max and
Susan Fischer Open: Tue to Sun L 12 to 2, Mon to Sat D 7 to
9 (residents only Sun D) Closed: 25, 26 and 31 Dec Meals:
Set L Tue to Sat £20 (2 courses) to £24, Set L Sun £35, Set D
Mon to Fri £30 (2 courses) to £65, Set D Sat £60 to £65
Service: not inc Cards: Amex, Delta, Diners, Maestro,
MasterCard, Visa Details: 70 seats. Car park. Vegetarian
meals. No children under 12. Children's helpings. No smoking.
Wheelchair access (not WC). No music. No mobile phones
Accommodation: 11 rooms

Rowley's

NEW ENTRY

Church Lane, Baslow DE45 1RY
Tel: (01246) 583880
Website: www.rowleysrestaurant.co.uk

| Cooking 3 | Modern European | £40 |

This new venture from Max Fischer of Baslow Hall (see entry above) and chef Rupert Rowley is a vibrant, modern space next to the church in the centre of town, with a ground-floor bar and first-floor dining room. Well-drilled staff are attired in purple – the themed colour throughout – and walls are hung with the work of a local artist. Local suppliers are used wherever possible and the menus change with the seasons as you would expect with the pedigree behind this operation. Chargrilled asparagus with rocket and Parmesan is a simple and successful first course, or there might be smoked salmon and Cornish crab roll with a buckwheat blini. Peak District beef, traditionally reared and suitably aged, is a speciality, and a 'deep rosy pink' fillet was a hit at inspection, coming with an excellent fondant potato. Crisp-skinned sea bream is paired with crab and lime couscous as a successful fish course. Ice cream sorbets – mandarin and mixed berry, perhaps – are served with 'excellent paper-thin brandy-snap tuiles' to finish. Wines start at £14.50, with six by the glass from £3.70.

Chef: Robert Allison Proprietors: Max and Susan Fischer, and
Rupert Rowley Open: Tue to Sun L 12 to 2.30, Tue to Sat D 6
to 10 Meals: alc (main courses L £6.40 to £16, D £9 to £18,
L £6.40 to £16). Sun L £12 (2 courses) to £16 Service: not
inc Cards: Maestro, MasterCard, Visa Details: 60 seats. 14
seats outside. Car park. Vegetarian meals. No toddlers after
7pm. Children's helpings. No smoking. Wheelchair access (inc
WC).

MAP 2 **BATH –**
Bath & N.E. Somerset

Bath Priory

Weston Road, Bath BA1 2XT
Tel: (01225) 331922
Website: www.thebathpriory.co.uk

| Cooking 6 | Modern French | £76 |

The hotel is so named as the land on which it stands was once owned by the Priory of Bath Abbey. Built as a private residence in 1835, about a mile from the city centre, it is fashioned from familiar honey-hued stone and has four acres of lush gardens. It all looks the part inside too, with sofas piled high with cushions and walls adorned with Edwardian sporting portraits, while the dining room seating brings whole new dimensions to the concept of squishy.

Chris Horridge writes his menus in the contemporary idiom, with crisps, foams, powders and pencils as much in evidence as Gressingham duck and foie gras. Close liaison with head gardener Jane Moore also brings in such delicacies as sycamore sap and St John's wort. When dishes arrive, all this makes sense, as in an inspection opener of chicken, garlic and chive boudin on haricots, accompanied by pleasingly sharp apple purée. The cooking is not without a sense of humour, as when a mignon of beef comes tricked out with a tiny Yorkshire pudding, in among banana shallot, a rectangular roast potato and smoky horseradish cream. Purées are the thing with fish – perhaps pea with salmon, fennel with turbot – and cooking methods can be eyebrow-raising, as witness the fondness for poaching red meats such as lamb and venison. To finish, you might opt for an array of shot glasses variously charged with fruity purées, ice creams and sorbets, the flavours embracing camomile, lime, apple, cherry, chocolate and raspberry in one vibrant sweep. Well-attuned staff experience the sense of discovery vicariously with you. The wine list evinces imagination and care on every page, with plenty from Italy and shorter but fine New World selections, while the focus remains on classical France. Prices are high, the house recommendations starting at £20.50 (or £5 a glass) for an Argentinian Sauvignon Blanc.

Chef: Chris Horridge **Proprietors:** Andrew and Christina Brownsword **Open:** all week 12 to 1.45, 7 to 9.30 **Meals:** Set L Mon to Sat £20 (2 courses) to £25, Set L Sun £30, Set D £55 to £70 **Service:** not inc **Cards:** Amex, Delta, Diners, Maestro, MasterCard, Visa **Details:** 64 seats. 20 seats outside. Car park. Vegetarian meals. No children under 8 at D. Children's helpings. No smoking. Wheelchair access (not WC). Occasional music. No mobile phones **Accommodation:** 31 rooms

Dukes Hotel, Cavendish Restaurant

NEW ENTRY

Great Pulteney Street, Bath BA2 4DN
Tel: (01225) 787963
Website: www.dukesbath.co.uk

| Cooking 3 | Modern British | £49 |

On one of Bath's showpiece streets, where numerous Jane Austen adaptations (and *Vanity Fair*) have been shot, Dukes Hotel looks the part. While it is architecturally distinguished outside, the décor inside is more cautious, with 'numerous shades of beige' in the dining room. Menus are quite cosmopolitan and the cooking is inventive, with some combinations working better than others. Terrine of confit rabbit, for example, was enhanced at inspection by the addition of pistachios and smoked bacon, providing contrasts of texture and flavour, but was served with a pastilla of the leg and a superfluous Caesar salad. A main course of wild Devonshire sea bass was praised for its crisp skin and succulent flesh, and accompaniment of pink fir potato and mussel chowder. Desserts are a strength: witness a caramelised citrus tart with rumtopf fruit, rum sabayon and 'startlingly intense' basil sorbet, or griottine cherry clafoutis with cinnamon ice cream and orange shortbread. Service is formal but pleasant and the short global wine list offers fair value, with house recommendations at £16 and eight wines by the glass from £3.75.

Chef: Richard Allen **Proprietors:** Alan Brookes and Michael Bokenham **Open:** all week 12 (12.30 Sun) to 1.45, 6.30 to 9.45 (9.30 Sun) **Meals:** alc D (main courses £13 to £20). Set L £12.95 (2 courses) to £15.95 **Service:** not inc **Cards:** Amex, Delta, Diners, Maestro, MasterCard, Visa **Details:** 36 seats. 36 seats outside. Vegetarian meals. Children's helpings. Smoking in bar only. Music **Accommodation:** 17 rooms

Firehouse Rotisserie

2 John Street, Bath BA1 2JL
Tel: (01225) 482070

Watch the chefs at work at this buzzy rôtisserie and grill, which puts locally sourced produce at the top of its agenda. Among 'small plates' might be a Brie and grape quesadilla with jalapeño salsa fresca (£5.75), pizzas from the brick-fired oven are a speciality, and main courses range from half a rôtisserie free-range Texas-spiced chicken served with jalapeño coleslaw and hickory-smoked barbecue dip (£11.50) to baked fillets of sea bass with oregano and lemon and olive butter (£14.95). A short wine list starts at £12.95. Closed Sun. There's a branch at Anchor Square, Bristol, tel: (0117) 915 7323.

FishWorks

6 Green Street, Bath BA1 2JY
Tel: (01225) 448707
Website: www.fishworks.co.uk

Cooking 2 | Seafood | £58

The original restaurant and fishmonger in this small chain, including Bristol, Christchurch and London (see entries), is a force to be reckoned with when it comes to serving simply cooked fresh fish. There are lunchtime and pre-theatre dishes as well as a carte, plus blackboard specials. Classic dishes include Dartmouth crab, potted shrimps, mussels steamed with wine and parsley, and whole sea bream baked in sea salt. Fisherman's stew might also tempt, or maybe the shellfish, which includes rock oysters, cockles, clams and impressive shellfish platters. Wines are pricey, starting at £17.90 and rising steeply after that. Seven choices are available by the glass from £4.50.

> Chef: Neil Roach   Proprietor: FishWorks plc   Open: Tue to Sat 12 to 2.30, 6 to 10.30   Closed: bank hols and day after bank hols   Meals: alc (main courses £13 to £50)   Service: not inc   Cards: Amex, Delta, Maestro, MasterCard, Visa   Details: 50 seats. 12 seats outside. Vegetarian meals. Children's helpings. No smoking. Music. Air-conditioned

Garrick's Head

NEW ENTRY

8 St John's Place,
Bath BA1 1ET
Tel: (01225) 318368
Email: info@garrickshead.wanadoo.co.uk

BATH OF THE YEAR RESTAURANT

Cooking 4 | Modern British | £38

£5

The Digneys have stayed faithful to the ideals they established at the King William (see entry below) – food with integrity in unpretentious surroundings – but here everything has moved up a gear. Both the cooking and the décor are slightly sharper, more in tune with the city-centre setting and the faster-moving crowd at the Theatre Royal next door. Perhaps it's down to his fondness for pork, but Charlie Digney manages to get the richest of flavours out of the thriftiest cuts, one reporter noting his style as a real tribute to slow cooking. Pea and ham soup, 'simply the most comforting bowlful imaginable', might start, while English asparagus makes an appearance in season, accompanied by a poached egg and hollandaise. Rarely seen Bath chaps – thinly sliced tongue on one side of the plate, richly fatty cheek on the other, separated by a generous heap of piquant green lentils – and boiled bacon with blackeye beans are sublimely tender and flavoursome, the former balanced by a 'bracing' lemony caper dressing with a pungent mint sauce for the latter. Traditional English desserts of rice pudding, apple pie with cream, or trifle bring things to an impressive finale. Plenty of wines by the glass will encourage mixing and matching with the food. France gets the lion's share of the list, but Italy, Spain and the southern hemisphere get a look in too. Prices open at £11.50.

> Chefs: Hugh Dennis-Jones and Darren Littlewood   Proprietors: Charlie and Amanda Digney   Open: all week L 12 to 3, Mon to Sat D 6 to 10.30   Closed: 25 and 26 Dec   Meals: alc (main courses L £8.50 to £15, D £10 to £18). Bar menu available   Service: not inc   Cards: Amex, Delta, Diners, Maestro, MasterCard, Visa   Details: 60 seats. 30 seats outside. Vegetarian meals. No smoking in 1 dining room. Music

> This symbol means that the wine list is well above the average.

King William

36 Thomas Street, Bath BA1 5NN
Tel: (01225) 428096
Website: www.kingwilliampub.com

Cooking 2 | **English** | **£36**

Charlie and Amanda Digney, having given this once-derelict pub a new lease of life, have repeated the feat at the Garrick's Head (see entry above). The King William is a re-energised city watering hole, which is now primarily noted for its food. The weekly-changing menu is short and slightly tersely written ('there's no mistaking their London gastro-pub roots'), but it has been composed with the seasons in mind and its integrity is not in doubt. The kitchen buys carefully and draws inspiration from English traditions, delivering game terrine, ham hock braised in cider served with mash and carrots, and steak and kidney pudding. Desserts can vary from homespun apple crumble to a molten-centred chocolate pot. Service is knowledgeable and keen to please (they are 'currently serving the best cappuccino and espresso in Bath'), and wines number around 20 bottles, with prices starting at £11 and most less than £20.

Chefs: Charlie Digney and Hugh Dennis-Jones Proprietors: Charlie and Amanda Digney Open: all week L 12 to 2.30, Wed to Sat D 6.30 to 10 Closed: 25 and 26 Dec Meals: alc (main courses £9 to £18). Set D £20 (2 courses) to £25. Bar snack D menu available Mon to Sat Service: not inc Cards: Delta, Maestro, MasterCard, Visa Details: 70 seats. Vegetarian meals. No smoking in dining room. No music. No mobile phones

Queensberry Hotel, Olive Tree Restaurant

4–7 Russel Street, Bath BA1 2QF
Tel: (01225) 447928
Website: www.thequeensberry.co.uk

Cooking 3 | **Modern British** | **£54**

There's a comforting warmth to the décor of the Queensberry Hotel's dining room, thanks to soothing neutral colours, subtle lighting and generously sized tables laid with white cloths, candles and small potted plants. In such a setting, Marc Salmon's upmarket but unpretentious modern British cooking matches the mood perfectly, with starters of ham hock ravioli in winter vegetable broth, or Gressingham duck and wood pigeon

terrine with cranberry and Muscat dressing, followed by main courses of baked cod with champ, pancetta, green beans and a parsley and red wine dressing, or poussin with seared foie gras and lentil cassoulet. Dessert choices typically include white chocolate and griottine cherry crème brûlée, and rhubarb, coconut and mascarpone cheesecake. Wines are a cleverly chosen bunch, arranged by style with serious classics lining up next to fashionable bottles; the list opens with a mixed bunch of 22 wines available by the bottle (from £14.25) or by the large or small glass (from £4.75 and £3.75).

Chef: Marc Salmon Proprietors: Laurence and Helen Beere Open: Tue to Sun L 12 to 2, all week D 7 to 10 Meals: alc (main courses L £13.50 to £14, D £15.50 to £23). Set L £14.50 (2 courses) to £16.50 Service: not inc Cards: Amex, Delta, Maestro, MasterCard, Visa Details: 55 seats. Vegetarian meals. Children's helpings. No smoking. Music. Air-conditioned Accommodation: 29 rooms

Royal Crescent, Pimpernel's

16 Royal Crescent, Bath BA1 2LS
Tel: (01225) 823333
Website: www.royalcrescent.co.uk

Cooking 4 | **Modern British** | **£76**

The elegant Georgian splendour of the Royal Crescent is rightly renowned for its views over Bath, and the eponymous hotel stands right at its centre, although the restaurant is in a grey-stone building to the rear (originally the dower house) overlooking immaculate gardens. A mural depicting a classical landscape is the dominant decorative feature. As might be expected in the setting, Steven Blake's cooking is refined, luxurious and slightly conservative, although modern culinary ideas also make their presence felt in starters ranging from terrine of foie gras with Parma ham and truffle dressing to stuffed langoustines with a shellfish and balsamic froth. Main courses might feature braised beef cheek with sliced fillet, wild mushrooms, vanilla squash purée and roast shallots, alongside red mullet, scallops and foie gras with spiced carrot, red wine sauce and froth. Invention is given full rein in desserts of Cassis pannacotta with balsamic ice cream and blackberry compote, or citrus cheesecake with spiced pear won tons and pomegranate sorbet. Many great names from the wine world are assembled in an undeniably classy list, with suitably exclusive prices, although there are also plentiful options in the £20 to £30 range from regional France, Chile, Argentina and South Africa.

Chef: Steven Blake Proprietor: Von Essen Hotels Open: all week 12.30 to 2, 7 to 10 Meals: Set L £18 (2 courses) to £25, Set D £45 (2 courses) to £55. Light L and bar menus available Service: not inc Cards: Amex, Delta, Diners, Maestro, MasterCard, Visa Details: 60 seats. 45 seats outside. Car park. Children's helpings. No smoking. Music. Air-conditioned Accommodation: 45 rooms

Yak Yeti Yak

AR

12A Argyle Street, Bath BA2 4BQ
Tel: (01225) 442299

Whether you choose to sit on traditional floor cushions or conventional chairs and tables, you will be served authentic Nepalese cooking at Yak Yeti Yak. Crispy-fried cheese balls with tomato and chilli dipping sauce, or spiced potato and sesame salad (both £3.50) get things started, followed by the likes of chicken stir-fried on the bone (£5.90), or the vegetarian Kathmandu speciality of aloo tamar (fermented stir-fried bamboo shoots, new potatoes and black-eyed peas; £3.50). Freak Street apples (£2.90), a speciality spiced apple tart, ends. House wines are £11.50. Open all week.

MAP 3   BATTLE – East Sussex

Pilgrims

AR

1 High Street, Battle TN33 0AE
Tel: (01424) 772314

Opposite the entrance to Battle Abbey, Pilgrims dates back to 1360, so look out for ancient timber window frames and the like. Modern bistro dishes are what to expect: carpaccio of local Limousin beef with shaved Parmesan and rocket (£7), leg steak of Romney Marsh spring lamb with a minted potato cake and garlic butter (£14.95), and black cherry and Kirsch cheesecake (£4.95). House vins de pays are £10.95. Closed Sun D

AR Not a full entry but provisionally recommended. These 'also recommended' establishments are integrated throughout the book.

MAP 6   BAWBURGH – Norfolk

Kings Head

AR

Harts Lane, Bawburgh NR9 3LS
Tel: (01603) 744977

The Kings Head is a 'welcoming country pub of character', rustic and minimalist in style, with a menu that puts an environmentally sensitive stamp on the food. Caramelised red onion, thyme and goats' cheese tart with rocket pesto and walnut oil (£7), or escabèche of whitebait (£7.50) might start. Roast sirloin of beef with 'properly light and airy' Yorkshire pudding could be a main-course choice, while roast lemon and thyme free-range chicken breast has been declared 'excellent' (both £11). Lime posset, or apple and winter berry crumble might end. House Chilean is £13.50. Open all week L and Tue to Sat D.

MAP 2   BEAULIEU – Hampshire

Montagu Arms, Terrace

NEW ENTRY

Palace Lane, Beaulieu SO42 7ZL
Tel: (01590) 612324
Website: www.montaguarmshotel.co.uk

Cooking 5	Modern British	£56

The Montagu Arms is situated within the Beaulieu Estate on the edge of the New Forest, in the distinguished company of the abbey, a great stately home and the ever-popular Motor Museum. It's a 200-year-old building of red brick set in mature gardens, with a restaurant terrace looking out over the tranquil view. Its kitchen is in the executive hands of Shaun Hill (ex-Merchant House, Ludlow), who favours a classical style of cooking, with combinations that work and presentations that look delightfully straightforward. Take a first course of roast monkfish. It doesn't arrive in a row of other constructions on an oblong plate, but sits simply in a puddle of bright red sauce, an intense tomato concoction spiked with chilli and ginger – 'a terrific, perfectly balanced, highly subtle dish'.

Great pains are taken to get the obvious things up to a dizzying standard, so rack of lamb impresses for the resonance of its flavour, its fine crust of breadcrumbs and herbs, and the impeccably made aubergine charlotte it comes with. A copybook, sticky, stocky red wine sauce adds depth. Menu billings are no-nonsense in their brevity, offering roast quail with parsley risotto, followed maybe by steamed fillet of turbot with creamed leeks in champagne sauce. Finish with peach and almond tart with pistachio ice cream. Service is from a large, variously abled team. A commendable wine list, arranged by style, displays evidence of imaginative buying, bringing lighter wines such as German Riesling and Italian Dolcetto in among the blockbusters. Prices are fair; the bidding opens at £17, or £4 a glass.

Chefs: Shaun Hill and Scott Foy Proprietor: Mr Leach Open: all week 12 to 2.30, 7 to 9.30 Meals: Set L Mon to Sat £19 (2 courses) to £22, Set L Sun £25, Set D £39 Service: not inc Cards: Amex, Delta, Diners, MasterCard, Visa Details: 70 seats. 30 seats outside. Car park. Vegetarian meals. No children under 8 at D. No smoking. Wheelchair access (also WC). Occasional music. No mobile phones Accommodation: 23 rooms

MAP 11 BERWICK-UPON-TWEED – Northumberland

No. 1 Sallyport `AR`

1 Sallyport, off Bridge Steet,
Berwick-upon-Tweed TD15 1EZ
Tel: (01289) 308827

Elizabeth Middlemiss is the warm hostess at this smart B&B on a quiet cobbled lane. The interior is thoroughly modern, with a wood-burner in an inglenook a feature of the dining room, where dinner (£35) is taken communally at the large oak table: maybe scallops with bacon in a garlicky mushroom sauce, followed by leg steaks of Lammermuir lamb cooked with ginger and Bramley apples, rounded off with tangy lemon tart in coconut pastry. Bring your own wines – no corkage charge. Five letting rooms.

MAP 9 BEVERLEY – East Riding of Yorkshire

Cerutti 2 `AR`

Station Square, Beverley HU17 0AS
Tel: (01482) 866700

Run by Tina Cerutti this restaurant in Beverley's railway station, with its black and white tiles and subtle spotlights, offers an extensive, mostly seafood menu, with daily-changing blackboard specials. You could open with king scallops wrapped in Parma ham with garlic mushrooms (£9.95) or spinach and smoked haddock roulade (£5.25), and proceed to lightly curried monkfish medallions (£16.95) or breadcrumbed fillets of lemon sole (£15.75). Meat eaters could go for fillet steak with rösti, crispy shallots and mustard hollandaise (£18.95). End with a traditional pudding such as treacle sponge. Wines from £10.95. Closed Sun.

MAP 3 BIDDENDEN – Kent

West House

28 High Street, Biddenden TN27 8AH
Tel: (01580) 291341

| Cooking 5 | Modern British | £44 |

Housed in an ancient tile-hung village house, West House is not short of character, sporting a dining room marked by cream walls, beams, floorboards, a wood-burner, simply laid wooden tables and a myriad of candles. Respondents continue in their enthusiasm for Graham Garrett's cuisine: 'great intensity of flavours, fabulous textures,' as one reader put it. What power the kitchen are local materials, which are woven into an ever-changing menu. The dedication to eclectic ideas remains, flavours are accurately gauged and the results are harmonious. Pea soup with foie gras and truffle cream, or smoked haddock carpaccio with leek and bacon dressing and pea shoots might open proceedings, followed perhaps by cumin-spiced shank of lamb served with pilaff rice and purple-sprouting broccoli, or fillet of wild sea bass with spring greens, kipper cream and an anchovy beignet. Desserts might take in blood-orange sponge pudding with buttermilk sorbet, or caramel-poached banana with a warm banana cake and mincemeat ice cream. A good-value wine list opens at £13.95.

Chef: Graham Garrett Proprietors: Graham Garrett and Jackie Hewitt Open: Tue to Fri and Sun L 12 to 1.45 (2.30 Sun), Tue to Sat D 7 to 9.30 Closed: Christmas to New Year, 2 weeks Aug Meals: Set L £21 (2 courses) to £24, Set D £29.50 Service: 12.5% (optional) Cards: Delta, Maestro, MasterCard, Visa Details: 32 seats. Car park. Children's helpings. No smoking. Wheelchair access (not WC). Occasional music

MAP 1 · BIGBURY-ON-SEA – Devon

Oyster Shack   `AR`

Milburn Orchard Farm, Stakes Hill,
Bigbury-on-Sea TQ7 4BE
Tel: (01548) 810876

Oysters farmed in the River Avon are the speciality here, coming au naturel (£1 each) or in a variety of ways, including with spicy sausage (£7.95 for six) or garlic butter and Parmesan (£6.95 for six). Or sit under their giant orange sail on the deck and enjoy roast gurnard with white chilli beans and Parma ham (£14.75) or local moules marinière (£8.95). House wine £12.50. Breakfast 9 to 10.30am. Open all week; closed Mon Nov to June.

MAP 5 · BIRCHOVER – Derbyshire

Druid Inn

Main Street, Birchover DE4 2BL
Tel: (01629) 650302
Website: www.thymeforfood.co.uk

Cooking 3 | Modern European | £38

This renovated country inn makes the most of its 200-year-old building; there is a bar and snug with all the appeal of a traditional village pub, where you can enjoy bar lunches (roast Bakewell black pudding with bacon, blue cheese and brown sauce onions), or eat in one of the two contemporary dining rooms: the lower room has an open kitchen, while the upper room is more intimate and has a wine cave where buffs can peruse the shelves for fine vintages. The menus are essentially the same throughout, and Michael Thompson delivers good flavours from well-sourced local ingredients. Confit chicken leg and duck leg terrine with home-made chutney, or white crab-meat and apple salad may be among starters, while simple but well-presented main courses include shepherd's pie with morels, or seared fillet of Scottish salmon with garden pea and mint risotto. Apple and pear crumble is a typically traditional dessert. The wine list is a decent selection of bottles from Europe and the southern hemisphere. Around a dozen are served by the glass from £3.75, with bottle prices opening at around £14. Part of a group including Artisan & Catch in Sheffield (see entry).

Chef: Michael Thompson **Proprietors:** Adrian Cooling, Richard and Victoria Smith, and Michael Thompson **Open:** all week 12 to 2.30, 6 to 9 (9.30 Fri and Sat) **Closed:** Sun D and Mon Oct, Nov and Jan to Mar **Meals:** alc exc Sun L (main courses £8 to £16). Set L Mon to Sat and D 6 to 7 £12 (2 courses) to £17.50, Set L Sun £19.50 **Service:** not inc **Cards:** Maestro, MasterCard, Visa **Details:** 80 seats. 40 seats outside. Car park. Vegetarian meals. Children's helpings. No smoking in dining room. Wheelchair access (not WC). Music

MAP 8 · BIRCH VALE – Derbyshire

Waltzing Weasel   `AR`

New Mills Road, Birch Vale SK22 1BT
Tel: (01663) 743402

Another reason, if needed, to visit the Peak District, this stone-built inn offers a hearty welcome and while there have been a few changes both in ownership and at the stoves, simple, old-fashioned cooking remains the order of the day. Button mushrooms cooked with Hartington Stilton (£4.95) start, followed by game and vegetable casserole (£12.50), or seared loin of tuna in a provençale sauce with olives (£11.75). The fixed-price menu (£14.50) offers rare Derbyshire beef cottage pie. A short but considered wine list starts at £10.25. Accommodation. Open all week.

MAP 5 · BIRMINGHAM – West Midlands

Bank

4 Brindley Place, Birmingham B1 2JB
Tel: (0121) 633 4466
Website: www.bankrestaurants.com

Cooking 2 | Modern European | £45

This lively brasserie, the Birmingham outpost of a small chain (see entry, London), serves breakfast, lunch and dinner. The menu offers contemporary twists on traditional dishes served in an atmosphere that is lively and unashamedly cosmopolitan. The dining room is cavernous, with a long granite bar and two covered terraces, great for dining al fresco. One diner commented that the 'menu is as contemporary as you can get without breaking into experimental or fusion food', so look out for a salad of prosciutto, dolcelatte, pear and pine nuts to start, followed by rock oysters or perhaps confit belly pork with buttered cabbage and carrot purée. Among fish options might be seared peppered tuna with chorizo and sautéed leeks and potatoes with aïoli. Around ten desserts could run to peanut butter and jelly cheesecake with chocolate and banana ice cream. The lengthy wine list, arranged by style, covers a lot of ground, with France and the southern hemisphere covered particularly well. There's a decent choice of styles below £25, starting with own-label Vins de Pays d'Oc at £12.95.

> **Chef:** Steven Woods **Proprietor:** Bank Restaurant Group plc **Open:** all week 12 (11.30 Sat and Sun) to 3 (3.30 Sun), 5.30 (5 Sun) to 11 (11.30 Sat, 10 Sun) **Meals:** alc (main courses £12 to £19). Set L and D (exc 7 to 10pm) £12.50 (2 courses) to £15. Bar menu available **Service:** 12.5% (optional) **Cards:** Amex, Delta, Diners, Maestro, MasterCard, Visa **Details:** 260 seats. 60 seats outside. Vegetarian meals. Children's helpings. No-smoking area. Wheelchair access (also WC). Occasional music. Air-conditioned

Brasserie Blanc `AR`

9 Brindley Place, Birmingham B1 2HS
Tel: (0121) 633 7333

Fashionable foodie buzzwords abound at Raymond Blanc's brasserie chain – sustainable, free-range and wild produce, for example. They sit happily with the ethos of providing modern French food in a convivial setting, where children are actively welcomed and have their own sophisticated but accessible menu. Grown-up meals might open with grilled Alsace bacon on warm potato salad with a poached egg (£6.50), before grilled sea trout with herb purée and Riesling sauce (£14.50) or roast Barbary duck breast with butternut squash and Madeira dressing (£17.50). Good-value set lunches are £12 for two courses. Wines from £12.95. Open all week. Branches in Cheltenham, Manchester, Oxford and Tunbridge Wells; see entries.

Chung Ying Garden `AR`

17 Thorp Street, Birmingham B5 4AT
Tel: (0121) 666 6622

Declaring itself one of the largest and most popular Chinese restaurants in the Midlands, Chung Ying Garden celebrates its twentieth anniversary in 2007. It is a brightly decorated dining room in the heart of Chinatown, with space for 380 diners and a menu of around 400 dishes (including 100 varieties of dim sum), mostly from the traditional Cantonese repertoire. Specialities include fried scallops and king prawns in XO sauce served in a bird's nest, sizzling beef in black pepper sauce, deep-fried soft-shell crab in salt and pepper, and steamed chicken with kai-lan vegetables in royal broth. Own-label wines are £10. Open all week.

Hotel du Vin & Bistro

25 Church Street, Birmingham B3 2NR
Tel: (0121) 200 0600
Website: www.hotelduvin.com

| Cooking 3 | Modern European | £48 |

The formula of this ever-burgeoning hotel group (now owned by the Malmaison group) is to convert historical or interesting buildings into contemporary hotels, giving each its own individual character. This revamped old hospital is no exception – and visitors happily testify that the prices continue to be fair, the service hospitable, and the ambience 'hits all the right spots'. A reporter found breakfast 'excellent', but the main focus is on the sensibly short carte that has some Mediterranean undertones, ranging from a lively starter of herb-rubbed tuna carpaccio with chilli syrup, through pan-fried sea bass with baby fennel, asparagus, broad beans, and a chive and cockle velouté, to roast breast of chicken with chorizo and white-bean cassoulet. The wine list is a blockbuster with good drinking right across the range. House wines are £13, and the 20 by the glass look tempting.

> **Chef:** Nick Turner **Proprietor:** MWB Group plc **Open:** all week 12 (12.30 Sun) to 2, 6 (7 Sun) to 10 **Meals:** alc exc Sun L (main courses £12.50 to £22). Set L Mon to Sat £14.50 (2 courses), Set L Sun £32.50 **Service:** not inc **Cards:** Amex, Delta, Maestro, MasterCard, Visa **Details:** 94 seats. 25 seats outside. Vegetarian meals. No smoking in dining room. Wheelchair access (also WC). No music **Accommodation:** 66 rooms

Jessica's

1 Montague Road, Edgbaston, Birmingham
B16 9HN
Tel: (0121) 455 0999
Website: www.jessicasrestaurant.co.uk

| Cooking 5 | Anglo-French | £52 |

The location may be one of Birmingham's leafier suburbs, but the feel of Jessica's is more that of a small cottage in the countryside. A bright white dining room is supplemented by a conservatory extension next to a walled courtyard. Pale wooden floors and simple décor maintain the cool, modern tone. Modernity is also the keynote of Glynn Purnell's cooking, which pushes most of the buttons urban sophisticates will expect to see pushed. Start with cheesecake of goats' cheese with Bramley apple sorbet, hazelnuts and celery jelly, perhaps, or foie gras mousse with carrots, passion fruit and toffee and an accompaniment of parkin. Thus fortified with fruit and sweet things, move on to cod cooked in beetroot and cranberry juice alongside slow-cooked radishes, button onions and wild garlic purée, or a serving of spring lamb styled as a 'baklava', with spiced aubergines, pistachios and almonds, all sauced with coffee syrup.

Sweet wine suggestions come with the dessert offerings, perhaps pairing a glass of De Bortoli botrytised Semillon from Australia with vanilla and lavender tortellini in strawberry soup. Service, sad to say, has been found sorely wanting for some, but willing and welcoming on other occasions. Outside France, the wine list confines itself to one or two choices in each colour from other regions, with a slate of house wines starting at £16.95, or £4.95 a glass.

> **Chef:** Glynn Purnell **Proprietors:** Diane and Keith Stevenson, and Glynn Purnell **Open:** Tue to Fri L 12 to 2, Tue to Sat D 6.45 to 10 **Closed:** 1 week Christmas, 1 week Easter, last 2 weeks July **Meals:** Set L £19.50 (2 courses) to £24.50, Set D £29.50 (2 courses) to £46.95 **Service:** 12.5% (optional) **Cards:** Delta, Maestro, MasterCard, Visa **Details:** 36 seats. Vegetarian meals. No smoking. Wheelchair access (also WC). Music. No mobile phones. Air-conditioned

Lasan [AR]

3–4 Dakota Buildings, James Street, Birmingham B3 1SD
Tel: (0121) 212 3664

Lasan rides the crest of the new wave of Indian cooking, with a starkly 'urban' décor of bare concrete floors, bare wooden tables, and a coffee and chocolate colour scheme. The cooking is inventive, sometimes to a fault, but successful dishes have included khodu gosht (delicately spiced lamb and pumpkin curry; £10.95), and lau chingri (king prawns in exotic marrow curry; £12.95). Start perhaps with aloo Brie tikki (potato cakes with ginger and cashews stuffed with Brie; £3.95) and finish with raspberry shrikand (£4.95). House wine is £14.95. Closed Sat L.

Metro Bar & Grill

73 Cornwall Street, Birmingham B3 2DF
Tel: (0121) 200 1911
Website: www.metrobarandgrill.co.uk

Cooking 2 | Modern European | £41

Only a couple of streets away from the cathedral, the Metro is lively and popular with the business community. The split-level dining room, much quieter than the bar area, boasts wooden floors, an oval skylight and a spit/grill in full view of diners. The blackboard features daily fish specials such as pan-seared scallops with lobster risotto, while 'light plates' might be warm smoked salmon with toasted brioche, asparagus and hollandaise. Among main courses may be toad-in-the-hole with creamy mash and onion gravy, or chargrilled pork T-bone with bubble and squeak and parsley sauce; finish with honeycomb pannacotta with chocolate and ginger twists. Sandwiches and the bar menu are available throughout the day. The short, international wine list opens with Chilean Sauvignon Blanc and Cabernet Sauvignon at £12.95, and eight wines come by the glass from £4.50.

> **Chef:** Andrew Twigg **Proprietors:** Chris Kelly and David Cappendell **Open:** Mon to Fri L 12 to 2.30, Mon to Sat D 6 to 10 **Closed:** 25 Dec to 2 Jan, bank hols **Meals:** alc (main courses £10 to £18). Bar menu available **Service:** not inc **Cards:** Amex, Delta, Maestro, MasterCard, Visa **Details:** 120 seats. Vegetarian meals. Wheelchair access (also WC). Music. Air-conditioned

Opus [NEW ENTRY]

54 Cornwall Street, Birmingham B3 2DE
Tel: (0121) 200 2323
Website: www.opusrestaurant.co.uk

Cooking 2 | Modern British | £51

'You have to be myopic to miss this place,' noted a reporter, commenting on the prominent sign set in concrete. Essentially a brasserie in a large-scale setting, Opus has a handsome crustacean bar and wine racking acting as the centrepiece for the titanic dining room, and floor-to-ceiling windows and skylights provide a bright ambience. The modern British menu runs the full gamut from lobster and mango salad, and terrines (perhaps of ham hock with potato salad and mustard dressing), to pan-fried scallops with braised belly pork and caper berries, grilled steak, and Dover sole with lemon butter. Leek and haddock fishcake, served with a free-range egg and beurre blanc, made a 'balanced and precise' starter at inspection, while pork sausages were of excellent quality, served with 'marvellous fat chips' and onion gravy. For desserts there may be strawberry and rhubarb crunch, served in a martini glass with yoghurt sorbet. Service is accommodating and enthusiastic, and the wide-ranging wine list is helpfully annotated. House vins de pays are £12.95.

> **Chefs:** David Colcombe and Dean Cole **Proprietor:** Opus Restaurant Ltd **Open:** Mon to Fri L 12 to 2.30, Mon to Sat D 5.30 to 10 (7 to 10.30 Sat) **Closed:** 24 Dec to 1 Jan, bank hols **Meals:** alc (main courses £11.50 to £20). Set L and D Mon to Fri £15.50 (2 courses) to £17.50 **Service:** 12.5% (optional) **Cards:** Amex, Maestro, MasterCard, Visa **Details:** 80 seats. Vegetarian meals. Children's helpings. No smoking. Wheelchair access (also WC). No music. Air-conditioned

Paris

109–111 Wharfside, The Mailbox, Birmingham
B1 1RF
Tel: (0121) 632 1488
Website: www.restaurantparis.co.uk

Cooking 4 | **Modern French** | **£73**

The seventh floor of a provincial shopping centre seems an unlikely spot in which to find an upmarket French restaurant, but here it is. The smart dining room – which lets in no natural light despite its elevated position and a high ceiling – has a coffee, brown and cream colour scheme, its walls hung with modern abstract paintings. Service is fittingly formal. Chef Richard Turner cooks with ambition and some verve, an inspection meal getting off to a good start with a 'tantalising' amuse-bouche of pea velouté 'full of the freshness of spring'. Starters might include a terrine of ham hock and foie gras, its richness countered by earthy Puy lentils, or seared scallops with boudin noir, pomme mousseline and truffled chicken jus. Main courses similarly feature multi-layered combinations of flavour and texture, as in sea bass with Jerusalem artichoke purée, roast salsify and cep jus. A pre-dessert treat of bitter chocolate tart topped with gold leaf might precede a prune and Armagnac soufflé. A large, well-constructed wine list has a strong focus on France and not much in the way of bargains, although 12 by the glass aid the budget-conscious. House red is £24, white £22.

> **Chef:** Richard Turner **Proprietor:** Patrick McDonald **Open:** Tue to Sat 12 to 2, 7 to 9 (10 Fri and Sat) **Closed:** 1 week Christmas, 1 week Easter, last 2 weeks Aug **Meals:** alc (main courses £22.50 to £25.50). Set L £16.50 (2 courses) to £21.50, Set D £55 (whole table only) **Service:** 12.5% (optional) **Cards:** Amex, Maestro, MasterCard, Visa **Details:** 40 seats. Vegetarian meals. Children's helpings. No smoking. Wheelchair access (also WC). Music. No mobile phones. Air-conditioned

San Carlo

AR

4 Temple Street, Birmingham
Tel: (0121) 633 0251

The first restaurant in the group that now boasts three others in Bristol, Leicester and Manchester, San Carlo offers authentic Italian cuisine with a modern twist. The menu takes in all manner of pizzas, pastas and antipasti including barbecue spare ribs (£6.70). Follow that with a 'very old Roman connoisseurs' dish, pan-fried breast of chicken with spicy sausage (£10.95) or maybe saltimbocca cooked in white wine and sage (£11.75). Fish specials chalked on the blackboard might feature giant prawns and scallops. Mostly Italian wines from £12.95. Open all week.

Simpsons

20 Highfield Road, Edgbaston, Birmingham
B15 3DU
Tel: (0121) 454 3434
Website: www.simpsonsrestaurant.co.uk

Cooking 6 | **Modern French** | **£64**

Impressed by the look of the elegant Georgian villa that has housed Simpsons since it opened in 2004, one visitor noted that 'no expense appears to have been spared in creating an equally elegant interior'. Of the several dining areas, perhaps the most interesting is the one that allows you to see the chefs at work through 'a glass wall arrangement'. Here, Andreas Antona and Luke Tipping cook in an elegant and luxurious but unfussy modern French style. The menus offer plenty of choice, starters ranging from seared foie gras with black pudding, pomme purée and Madeira sauce to loin of tuna rolled in black sesame seeds served with white radish and cucumber salad and wasabi cream via slow-cooked peanut-crusted belly pork with seared scallops, baby pak choi and sauce orientale. To follow, there might be tronçonnettes of lobster with truffled spaghettini and lobster and pepper sauce, fillet of beef with haggis, snails, garlic and parsley jus and pomme galette, and a duo of lamb with aromatic couscous, apricots, butternut squash and a saffron and cumin sauce. A fine cheeseboard is a tempting alternative to desserts, but praline soufflé has been described as 'well worth the wait', or you could opt for caramelised poached pear with butterscotch ice cream. Service has been found 'quiet and proficient'. An ambitious, food-orientated range of ten wines by the glass opens a list that is long on style if a bit too short on value: from £8 by the glass and precious few bottles under £30.

Chefs: Andreas Antona and Luke Tipping Proprietor: Andreas Antona Open: all week 12 to 2 (2.30 Sun), 7 to 9.30 (10 Fri and Sat) Closed: 24 to 27 and 31 Dec, 1 and 2 Jan, bank hol Mon Meals: alc (main courses £21 to £32.50). Set L £22.50 (2 courses) to £27.50, Set D £30 Service: 12.5% (optional) Cards: Amex, Delta, Maestro, MasterCard, Visa Details: 75 seats. 40 seats outside. Car park. Vegetarian meals. Children's helpings. No smoking. Wheelchair access (also WC). No music. No mobile phones. Air-conditioned Accommodation: 4 rooms

MAP 8 **BIRTLE – Greater Manchester**

Waggon

131 Bury and Rochdale Old Road, Birtle BL9 6UE
Tel: (01706) 622955
Website: www.thewaggonatbirtle.co.uk

Cooking 3 | Modern British | £33

Few traces remain of the Waggon's former identity as a pub, except on the outside. Nowadays it is a restaurant with a 'very bistro' feel, thanks to a simple décor and bare wooden tables. There's also a hint of bistro about the menu, with a range of influences evident in the broadly modern British style. Among starters, scallops with ginger, lime and spring onions have stood out, the shellfish bound in a light, creamy sauce and baked under a short-crust pastry lid. A salad of Lancashire cheese, apple and lardons with mustard vinaigrette topped with slices of black pudding in light, crisp tempura batter has also proved a successful combination. Main courses might be relatively straightforward, as in perfectly timed fillet steak on rich braised beef and oxtail with creamy mash, or slightly more unusual, as in a 'wonderfully savoury plateful' of soft, not-too-fatty belly pork and 'melt-in-the-mouth' ox tongue with lentils. To finish, this year's

fashionable ingredient might appear as rhubarb crème brûlée with rhubarb and cream ice cream. Wines are a fairly priced bunch, with house selections at £10.95.

Chef: David Watson Proprietor: Resolute Ltd Open: Wed to Fri L 12 to 2, Wed to Sat D 6 to 9.30, Sun 12.30 to 7.45 Closed: 10 days from 1 Jan, first 2 weeks Aug Meals: alc (main courses £8 to £15.50). Set L and D Wed to Fri £12.50 (2 courses) to £14.50 Service: not inc Cards: Amex, Delta, Maestro, MasterCard, Visa Details: 60 seats. Car park. Vegetarian meals. Children's helpings. No smoking in dining room. Wheelchair access (also WC). Music

MAP 3 **BISHOP'S STORTFORD – Hertfordshire**

Lemon Tree [AR]

14–16 Water Lane, Bishop's Stortford
Tel: (01279) 757788

Near the centre of the busy market town, the Lemon Tree holds wine tastings and themed evenings. The kitchen takes a wide-ranging approach, with the dinner menu featuring, for example, Thai fishcakes with a marinated bean sprout salad (£6.50), followed by flaked duck and wild mushroom pudding with root vegetables (£13), then coffee pannacotta with crème anglaise (£4.75). The set lunches (£15/£18) might include black pudding with new potatoes, pancetta and a poached egg, followed by grilled calf's liver with bacon. Wines from £11.95. Closed Sun D and Mon.

MAP 5 **BISHOP'S TACHBROOK – Warwickshire**

Mallory Court

Harbury Lane, Bishop's Tachbrook CV33 9QB
Tel: (01926) 330214
Website: www.mallory.co.uk

Cooking 3 | Modern British | £66

A short drive from Leamington Spa, Mallory Court is a picture of charm, especially the view from the handsome wood-panelled dining room over well-tended gardens. The cooking follows the country-house style, showing culinary good sense

by blending modern and traditional ideas intelligently, and revealing a preference for fish and game, typically kicking off with roast scallops with black pudding, potato and apple, or herb-crusted wood pigeon with celeriac and a caper beignet. Main courses range from pan-fried fillet of brill with spinach and Parmesan cannelloni, to roast loin of Oisin Finnebrogue Estate venison with wild garlic and a red wine jus. Vanilla and crème fraîche mousse with a minestrone of fruits is the sort of dessert to expect, although the cheeseboard is an appealing alternative. Wine prices start at £19.50, and around a dozen are served by the glass from £5.50.

> Chef: Simon Haigh Proprietor: Sir Peter Rigby Open: all week 12 to 1.45, 6.30 to 9.30 Meals: alc D (main courses £25). Set L £19.50 (2 courses) to £25, Set D £39.50 to £49.50 Service: not inc Cards: Amex, Delta, Diners, Maestro, MasterCard, Visa Details: 40 seats. 30 seats outside. Car park. Children's helpings. No smoking. Wheelchair access (also WC). Occasional music. No mobile phones Accommodation: 30 rooms

MAP 3 BISPHAM GREEN – Lancashire

Eagle & Child

[AR]

Malt Kiln Lane, Bispham Green L40 3SG
Tel: (01257) 462297

This quintessential country pub in a lovely Lancashire setting offers honest pub grub in the bar and a more refined menu in the restaurant. Meat and vegetables come from the owner's organic farm, with seasons taken into account. Look out for Formby asparagus wrapped in Parma ham (£6), followed by sugar-cured pork fillet in a wild mushroom and port sauce, or baked escalope of cod in pancetta with leek and potato broth (both £13). Sticky toffee pudding (£4) ends. Wines from £11.25, plus six real ales. Open all week.

NEW ENTRY	This appears after the restaurant's name if the establishment was not a main entry in last year's Guide. Please note, however, it may have been 'also recommended' in the previous edition.

MAP 8 BLACKPOOL – Lancashire

Kwizeen

47–49 King Street, Blackpool FY1 3EJ
Tel: (01253) 290045
Website: www.kwizeen.co.uk

Cooking 2 | Modern European | £38

A cheerful bistro with a strong local reputation, Kwizeen adds a splash of colour to King Street. The tables are well spaced and covered in cream cloths, lighting is subdued and jazz flows from the speakers. The two-course set-price lunch is excellent value, while the carte verges on the inventive, taking in Mediterranean black pudding with local ham and mascarpone ravioli, and skewered spiced lamb in a cumin and mango sauce. Another starter might be the regionally focused Lancashire cheese crispy pancakes with roast tomato sauce. Strawberry and pepper sauce gives a new dimension to a traditional main course of roast suckling pig with baked apples, and Fylde pheasant breasts are partnered by a sauce of chocolate and chilli. Strawberry and sweet basil ice cream pavlova is a typically fun dessert. The short but well-chosen wine list is good value, starting at £9.95, or £3.80 a glass, for house French.

> Chef/Proprietor: Marco Callé-Calatayud Open: Mon to Fri L 12 to 1.30, Mon to Sat D 6 to 9 Meals: alc (main courses £12 to £20). Set L £6.50 (2 courses) Service: not inc Cards: Delta, Maestro, MasterCard, Visa Details: 40 seats. Vegetarian meals. Music. No mobile phones

MAP 6 BLAKENEY – Norfolk

White Horse Hotel

4 High Street, Blakeney NR25 7AL
Tel: (01263) 740574
Website: www.blakeneywhitehorse.co.uk

Cooking 1 | Modern British-Plus | £36

Narrow streets of fishermen's cottages define Blakeney, although you'll have to negotiate the abundance of cars to get to this fine old pub/hotel on the pretty high street. Dining takes place in two rooms: the light and airy courtyard conservatory or the relatively staid main dining room in converted stables. Fresh fish is a signature here, coming from King's Lynn, while meat is traceable and small-holders supply vegetables and dairy produce. Start with a simple fresh crab salad, or 'wonderfully salty and smoky' smoked cod's roe from Cley Smokehouse on bruschetta with horseradish cream cheese. To follow, there may be 'pink, succulent and tender' Gressingham duck breast with Asian coleslaw, wasabi oil and sweet potato crisps, or Loch Duart salmon with roasted fennel, cherry tomatoes, olives and cockles. Vanilla crème brûlée and rich chocolate mousse both hit the spot for dessert. The wine list starts at £13.50 for house Chilean.

Chef: Chris Hyde **Proprietors:** Dan Goff and Martin Painter **Open:** all week D only 7 to 9 **Closed:** second week Jan **Meals:** alc (main courses £9 to £17). Bar menu available L and D **Service:** not inc **Cards:** Delta, Maestro, MasterCard, Visa **Details:** 34 seats. Car park. Vegetarian meals. Children's helpings. No smoking. Occasional music. No mobile phones **Accommodation:** 9 rooms

---

MAP 3 BODIAM – East Sussex

Curlew

Junction Road, Bodiam TN32 5UY
Tel: (01580) 861394
Website: www.thecurlewatbodiam.co.uk

Cooking 2 | Modern European | £42

 £5

Surrounded by textbook English rolling countryside on the Kent/Sussex border – with the equally archetypal Bodiam Castle just a mile or so away – the Curlew is a modest-looking white-painted weatherboarded old pub, now plying its trade predominantly as an ambitious country restaurant. The décor in the dining room (a converted outbuilding) is homely in a contemporary way, while the cooking has an inventively cosmopolitan edge. Classic fish soup with chilli rouille and garlic croûtons lines up alongside lobster and salmon sausage with wilted spinach and 'tandoori foam' among starters. Main courses, meanwhile, typically take in pan-fried turbot in a black olive crust, served with braised fennel and olive mash, as well as more conventional options such as extra-mature ribeye steak with hand-cut chips, field mushrooms, spinach and red wine jus. For dessert, try Cox's apple tarte Tatin with toffee ripple ice cream. The long wine list includes some impressively grand names from around the world, with prices to match, although there are also plenty of options at

the lower end of the scale, with house selections from £14.95.

Chefs: Robert Leeper and Tom Clarke **Proprietor:** Rare Inns **Open:** all week L 12 to 2, Tue to Sun D 7 to 9 **Meals:** alc exc Sun and Mon (main courses £13 to £19). Set L Mon to Sat £16.95 (2 courses) to £21.95, Set L Sun £14.95 (2 courses) to £17.95, Set D Tue to Fri £16.95 (2 courses) to £21.95. Light L menu available Mon to Sat **Service:** not inc **Cards:** Delta, Diners, Maestro, MasterCard, Visa **Details:** 60 seats. 20 seats outside. Car park. Vegetarian meals. No smoking in dining room. Wheelchair access (not WC). Music. Air-conditioned

---

MAP 3 BODSHAM – Kent

Froggies at the Timber Batts

School Lane, Bodsham TN25 5JQ
Tel: (01233) 750237

This fifteenth-century inn fuses an English setting with traditional French cuisine. The Gallic team who run it also hold magic evenings and a food market on the last Sunday of every month. Lots of locally sourced produce (lamb from Wincheap butchers in Canterbury, fish from Griggs of Hythe) features, so seared scallops in ventrèche bacon (£9.50) open, followed by cassoulet Toulousain (£14), ending with crêpes suzette (£5.50). The mostly French wine list opens at £14. Closed Sun D and all day Mon.

MAP 6 BOLNHURST – Bedfordshire

Plough   NEW ENTRY

Kimbolton Road, Bolnhurst
MK44 2EX
Tel: (01234) 376274
Website: www.bolnhurst.com

BEDFORDSHIRE OF THE YEAR NEWCOMER

Cooking 5 | Modern British | £37

A sensitively restored medieval building in a long, straggly village not far from Bedford, the Plough has had a chequered history. It was one of only two buildings left after the Great Plague, which explains its slightly aloof distance from the rebuilt village. The history lesson concludes with the arrival in June 2005 of Martin and Jayne Lee, who have re-established the place as a rural pub serving its local community. Martin runs a tight ship, baking bread in-house and buying organic meat and game from renowned suppliers. Tempura-battered tuna contains strong, meaty fish, aptly accoutred with strips of raw mooli, flakes of wasabi and a sesame and soy dipping sauce. An inspection main course of top-notch venison from the Denham Estate in Suffolk was a blue-cooked tournedos steak, bedded on rough spinach and topped with fabulous chopped wild mushrooms. Pains taken are evident in a labour-intensive terrine of duck, pigeon, chicken and pork with home-made piccalilli, while fish could be roast brill with pak choi, served with chargrilled potatoes and a sauce of fennel and olives.

Intensity of flavour once again characterises home-made ice creams, such as a caramel version with thin-crust caramelised apple tart; there might also be classic sticky toffee pudding, and cheeses are impressive. Completing a richly nuanced picture, the wine list is a gem. Grouped by style, it contains many fine international selections at mostly manageable prices. A page of 17 by the glass opens the proceedings, starting at £3.25.

Chef: Martin Lee Proprietors: Martin Lee and Jayne Lee, and Michael Moscrop Open: Tue to Sun L 12 to 2 (2.30 Sun), Tue to Sat D 6.30 to 9.30 Closed: first 2 weeks Jan Meals: alc (main courses £9.50 to £19). Set L Tue to Sat £11 (2 courses) to £15 Service: not inc Cards: Delta, Diners, Maestro, MasterCard, Visa Details: 70 seats. 35 seats outside. Car park. Vegetarian meals. Children's helpings. No smoking. Occasional music

innovative cooking. The menus (there's a ten-course tasting menu, vegetarian alternatives, and a carte) showcase judiciously sourced ingredients – local meats, estate game and produce from the extensive kitchen garden – that are at the heart of the enterprise. Dishes are thoughtfully composed, and skill shines through in bold, confident flavours that could take in cumin-scented yellowfin tuna with langoustine and alfalfa rémoulade, lemongrass pannacotta and soy and ginger dressing. Opulent ingredients appear alongside the more everyday, so a salad of marinated warm foie gras and Jabugo ham supports braised farce of veal served with ham hock and sweetbreads, while more foie gras arrives with a main course of slow-poached fillet of pork scented with lavender, accompanied by black pudding farce, braised cheek and choucroute. To finish, try kaffir lime mousse with caramelised mango, dark chocolate and citrus Banyuls, and coconut ice cream. Service is polite and professional, and the wine list is something to behold (and quite difficult to hold). There is choice under £20, but the real attraction is the sheer number of quality wines, plus the intelligent pricing policy.

Chef: Michael Wignall Proprietor: The Duke of Devonshire Open: Sun L 12 to 2, Tue to Sun D 6.30 to 9.30 Meals: Set L £33, Set D £58 to £118 (inc wine). Snack and brasserie menus available Service: 10% (optional) Cards: Amex, Delta, Diners, Maestro, MasterCard, Visa Details: 70 seats. Car park. Vegetarian meals. Children's helpings. No smoking. Wheelchair access (also WC). No music Accommodation: 40 rooms

MAP 9 BOLTON ABBEY – North Yorkshire

Devonshire Arms, Burlington

Bolton Abbey BD23 6AJ
Tel: (01756) 710441
Website: www.devonshirehotels.co.uk

Cooking 5 | Modern British | £71

The Devonshire Arms makes the most of its countryside surroundings and offers plenty of scope for walks on the Duke of Devonshire's estate. Dining takes place in a period setting of polished wooden tables and ancient landscapes and architectural sketches, a serene backdrop to Michael Wignall's

MAP 9 BOROUGHBRIDGE – North Yorkshire

Dining Room

20 St James Square, Boroughbridge YO51 9AR
Tel: (01423) 326426

Cooking 4 | Modern British | £38

Boroughbridge's attractive Georgian square is the backdrop to this informal yet smart restaurant. Pre-dinner drinks are taken in the first-floor lounge, while dining happens downstairs in the large, off-white dining room, with its wooden beams and friendly waiting staff. The cooking is beguilingly simple yet technically proficient. Lightly curried smoked haddock and saffron chowder, and confit of honey-roast Gressingham duck with an apple and Calvados sauce are typical starters, with main courses of fillet of Cornish halibut with hollandaise, or pan-fried breast of guinea fowl with black pudding and a creamy port sauce. Vegetarians might choose baked feta and spinach in a filo parcel on a sauce of tomato and mascarpone, and proceed to desserts of warm rhubarb and frangipane tart with crème Chantilly or warm chocolate mousse with peanut butter ice cream. The far-reaching wine list has a something-for-everyone appeal and is good value too, with a number of bottles under £20. Chilean house wines are £13.95.

Chef: Christopher Astley **Proprietors:** Christopher and Lisa Astley **Open:** Sun L 12 to 2, Tue to Sat D 7 to 9.15 **Closed:** 25 and 26 Dec, 1 Jan, bank hol Mon **Meals:** alc L (main courses £13.50). Set D £21.95 (2 courses) to £30 **Service:** not inc **Cards:** Delta, Maestro, MasterCard, Visa **Details:** 32 seats. Car park. Vegetarian meals. No children under 3. Children's helpings. No smoking. Wheelchair access (not WC). Music. No mobile phones

---

MAP 2 BOURNEMOUTH – Dorset

Barings Restaurant NEW ENTRY

324 Wimborne Road, Winton Banks,
Bournemouth BH9 2HH
Tel: (01202) 515105
Website: www.baringsrestaurant.co.uk

Cooking 4 | **Modern European** | **£40**

Once a bank, this corner site has been given a sympathetic makeover to create a red-carpeted dining room with a burgundy and cream décor and neatly set tables, and two cosier eating areas, one raised and surrounded by banisters, the second darker and more intimate. Chef and co-proprietor Matt Appleton has come here from the Three Tuns in Romsey, and his sensibly short menu shows some clever ideas which are well executed. A meal might kick off with 'excellent' Dorset crab gazpacho or a generous slab of chicken and wood pigeon terrine with celeriac rémoulade. Sauces are exemplary, as in a light tapenade accompanying crisp-skinned sea bass with mash and spinach, and a rich foie gras jus with perfectly cooked calf's liver with braised Savoy cabbage and mash. Lemon parfait topped with an 'excellent' strawberry sorbet makes a refreshing finale, and for heartier appetites there may be sticky toffee pudding. Service is friendly, and the wine list has a good choice under £20. Eight house wines are £12.95 to £17.95 a bottle, £3.25 to £6.45 a glass.

Chefs: Matt Appleton and Mark Emery **Proprietors:** Matt Appleton and David Tugwell **Open:** Tue to Sat 12 to 2, 7 (6.30 Sat) to 9.30 **Closed:** 25 Dec, 1 Jan **Meals:** alc (main courses £13 to £20). Set L £12.95 (2 courses) to £15.95, Set D Tue to Thur £12.95 (2 courses) to £15.95 **Service:** not inc **Cards:** Amex, Delta, Maestro, MasterCard, Visa **Details:** 52 seats. 12 seats outside. Vegetarian meals. No-smoking area. Wheelchair access (also WC). Music

---

Chef Hong Kong AR

150–152 Old Christchurch Road, Bournemouth
BH1 1NL
Tel: (01202) 316996

Proof that you don't have to go to the Chinatown district of some big city for decent Cantonese cooking, Chef Hong Kong keeps Bournemouth folk happy with a long menu of capably rendered authentic dishes. As well as familiar items such as sliced beef in oyster sauce (£5.25) and pork with cashew nuts (£5.25), there are more esoteric options, including an appetiser of soft-shell crab with garlic salt and chilli (£4.95), and, at lunchtime, a wide range of dim sum ranging from king prawn cheung fun (£3) to spicy chicken feet (£3.50). Open all week.

MAP 5 BOURTON ON THE HILL – Gloucestershire

Horse & Groom NEW ENTRY

Bourton on the Hill GL56 9AQ
Tel: (01386) 700413
Website: www.horseandgroom.info

Cooking 2 | **Modern British** | **£37**

Brothers Tom and Will Greenstock left their parents' pub, the Howard Arms in Ilmington (see entry), to launch their first stand-alone venture in 2005. The interior of the old Cotswold-stone building, on the busy A44, has been revamped with style: it's all very open and done out in natural colours and materials, with board floors, subtle lighting and wooden tables. 'Simple dishes but no pub clichés' are on offer, as an inspector put it. The blackboard menu changes regularly, even during service, and might start with breaded fillets of 'very fresh' flounder with lightly dressed wild rocket salad and salsa verde, or Scotch quail's eggs with mustard sauce, and go on to thick, pink slices of roast lamb rump on a bed of first-class celeriac purée with a subtle rosemary jus. Accompanying vegetables are 'perfectly timed', and the momentum continues into puddings such as vanilla pannacotta served with rhubarb compote. Hardworking staff are friendly and open, and the page-long wine list opens at £11.

Chef: Will Greenstock Proprietors: Tom and Will Greenstock Open: Tue to Sun L 12 to 2 (2.30 Sun), Mon to Sat D 7 to 9 (9.30 Fri and Sat) Closed: 25 Dec Meals: alc (main courses £9.50 to £15) Service: not inc Cards: Delta, Maestro, MasterCard, Visa Details: 75 seats. 50 seats outside. Car park. Vegetarian meals. Children's helpings. No smoking. Wheelchair access (not WC). No music Accommodation: 5 rooms

---

MAP 2 **BOURTON-ON-THE WATER – Gloucestershire**

Dial House   AR

High Street, Bourton-on-the-Water GL54 2AN
Tel: (01451) 822244

Found in the lovely town of Bourton-on-the-Water, this Cotswold-stone hotel manages to blend the old and the new. The décor may be period but the food is contemporary and stylish. Roast beetroot and local cheese tart (£6) could start, followed by lemon sole fillet with a salmon and fennel mousse, accompanied by mousseline potatoes and a lemon and chive beurre blanc (£16.50). End with a selection of cheeses (£8) including Stinking Bishop and Cerny, or rhubarb cheesecake (£6.50). Wines from £13.95. Open all week.

MAP 3 **BOVINGDON GREEN – Buckinghamshire**

Royal Oak   AR

Frieth Road, Bovingdon Green SL7 2JF
Tel: (01628) 488611

Imaginative gastro-pub food is the order of the day at this inn far enough away from the M40 to bring blessed relief from modern life. A varied menu offers lunchtime specials such as cauliflower and blue cheese soup (£4), and plenty of 'small plates' include pine-nut-crusted goats' cheese on rocket with pesto (£5.75). Main courses could be cod fillet on colcannon with pea purée (£13.75) or

slow-roast belly pork with a port-based gravy. Finish with banana pudding with chocolate sauce (£4.75). Most bottles on the compact wine list are under £20, with £11.50 the base price. Open all week.

MAP 8 **BOWNESS-ON-WINDERMERE – Cumbria**

Linthwaite House

Crook Road, Bowness-on-Windermere LA23 3JA
Tel: (015394) 88600
Website: www.linthwaite.com

Cooking 4 | Modern British | £61

Linthwaite House offers 'traditional country-house cooking with polished, efficient service to match', according to one contented diner. The hotel is in 15 acres with commanding views over Lake Windermere, although the dining room looks on to wooded hills. It's 'a totally unfussy set-up', with comfortable sofas and chairs in the drawing room and an appealing, old-fashioned dining room with deep red carpets, mahogany tables and a shelf of collectables. The menu nudges a modern European approach but keeps well within the restraints of 'almost homely simplicity'. Cauliflower soup and twice-baked goats' cheese and pistachio soufflé vie for attention with other starters of 'chunky yet tender' ham hock pressed with Parma ham. Old Spot pork three ways (confit belly, seared fillet and a sage and onion sausage), and honey-glazed Goosnargh duck breast with a Madeira and raisin jus are typical main courses, while roast cod fillet on a bed of peas with diced pancetta has impressed. Desserts don't disappoint, judging by 'excellent' plum crumble. Staff are smiling and chatty. The intelligently annotated wine list, arranged by style, is a global affair, starting at £18.50.

Chef: Simon Bolsover Proprietor: Mike Bevans Open: all week 12.30 to 2, 7 to 9 Meals: alc L (main courses £8 to £16). Set L Mon to Sat £13.95 (2 courses) to £16.95, Set L Sun £18.95, Set D £46. Bar menu available Service: not inc Cards: Amex, Delta, Diners, Maestro, MasterCard, Visa Details: 60 seats. 20 seats outside. Car park. Vegetarian meals. No children under 7 at D. Children's helpings. No smoking. Wheelchair access (also WC). Music. No mobile phones Accommodation: 27 rooms

MAP 8 | **BRADFORD –**
West Yorkshire

Mumtaz

386–400 Great Horton Road, Bradford BD7 3HS
Tel: (01274) 571861
Website: www.mumtaz.co.uk

| Cooking 1 | Kashmiri | £24 |

Just outside the city centre, this vast restaurant occupies a converted stone terrace, made over in ultra-modern style with expanses of glass and external neon lights. A take-away counter offers jars of produce – pickles, sweets and ready meals – but the experience is best enjoyed in-house, in the plushly decorated dining rooms, spread over two levels. The extensive menus major in Kashmiri dishes, with chargrilled marinated lamb chops, chicken wings, or shami kebab to start, followed by karahi main courses such as chicken with fenugreek or okra, lamb on the bone in a rich and spicy tomato-based sauce, grilled prawns with pistachios and almonds, or cod with pomegranate. Value is excellent. Note that alcohol is not served and is not even allowed on the premises, but several flavours of lassi and fruit juice are offered.

Proprietor Mumtaz Khan **Open:** all week 11 to 12 (1am Fri and Sat) **Meals:** alc (main courses £6 to £14.50) **Service:** not inc **Cards:** Amex, Delta, Diners, Maestro, MasterCard, Visa **Details:** 500 seats. Car park. Children's helpings. No-smoking area. Wheelchair access (also WC). Music. Air-conditioned

Prashad

NEW ENTRY

86 Horton Grange Road, Bradford BD7 2DW
Tel: (01274) 575893
Website: www.prashad.co.uk

| Cooking 2 | Indian Vegetarian | £26 |

Occupying a modest corner site on the busy Bradford ring road, this two-part operation has a shop at the front selling prepared food and take-aways, while a side entrance leads to the small restaurant. The décor is basic, with a tiled floor, metal tables and plastic chairs, but a mirrored wall gives a sense of space and light. Chef Kaushy Patel cooks the every-day vegetarian dishes of her native Gujarat. Poppadoms served with home-made pickles and chutneys get things off to a promising start, paving the way for impressive street snack-style starters such as dhokra – steamed squares of light savoury sponge

topped with black mustard seeds and served with a coriander and yoghurt dipping sauce. Simpler main courses might be chickpeas in spicy tomato sauce, while specialities include various pancakes filled with mixed spiced vegetables, and hara bara burger with masala chips: a mashed pea and cauliflower 'burger' in a bun with spicy chips. Dessert might be hot carrot halva with ice cream. Alcohol is not served, so drink lassi or faluda.

Chef: Kaushy Patel **Proprietors:** Mohanbhai and Bobby Patel **Open:** Tue to Sun 11 to 2.30, 6 to 9.30 (10 Sat) **Meals:** alc (main courses £7 to £12). Set L £7.50 (2 courses), Set D £10 **Service:** not inc **Cards:** Delta, Maestro, MasterCard, Visa **Details:** 30 seats. Vegetarian meals. Children's helpings. No smoking. Occasional music. Air-conditioned

MAP 6 | **BRAMFIELD – Suffolk**

Queen's Head

AR

The Street, Bramfield IP19 9HT
Tel: (01986) 784214

Bramfield is notable for its unusual thatched church, and, as you'd expect of an ancient village pub, the Queen's Head has an open fire, exposed beams and scrubbed pine tables. The daily-changing menu reflects the seasons, and the kitchen sources as many ingredients as possible from local organic farms. Chicken wings marinated in lemon, garlic and chilli (£3.95) could start, followed by baked cured pork shoulder stuffed with parsley (£10.90), or fillet of cod topped with cheese and garlic served on tomato salad (£10.95), then apple crumble with custard (£4.35). Wines from £11.50. Open all week.

MAP 6 | **BRAMPTON –**
Cambridgeshire

Grange Hotel

115 High Street, Brampton PE28 4RA
Tel: (01480) 459516
Website: www.grangehotelbrampton.co.uk

| Cooking 2 | Modern European | £37 |

There's been a paring down of ideas at this elegant Georgian hotel and restaurant, thanks to Nick Steiger's simplification of the menu, which now typically runs to just 12 dishes. There remains a

modern twist to most combinations, plus some old favourites, and sourcing is everything: Friday night is fish night, while meat, such as sausages, bacon, pork and venison, is bought from the Denham Estate. Steamed mussels with white wine, tomato passata and garlic, or pea, ham and mint risotto might start, followed by seared red mullet with orange-scented couscous, or braised lamb shank with a basil jus accompanied by peas, broad beans and crushed potatoes. Ginger cake with crème fraîche and ginger syrup, or banoffi pie with toffee ice cream might finish. The menu may be shorter, but wines, arranged by style, are plentiful. Prices start at £13.50 for Australian house, and most bottles are under £30, including a Cloudy Bay Sauvignon Blanc 2004 for £26.

Chef: Nick Steiger **Proprietors:** Nick and Susanna Steiger **Open:** Mon to Sat 12 to 2.30, 6.30 to 9.30 **Meals:** alc (main courses £7.50 to £18.50). Bar menu available **Service:** not inc **Cards:** Amex, Delta, Maestro, MasterCard, Visa **Details:** 40 seats. Car park. Vegetarian meals. Children's helpings. No smoking in dining room. Wheelchair access (also WC). Music. No mobile phones **Accommodation:** 7 rooms

MAP 10   BRAMPTON – Cumbria

Farlam Hall

Brampton CA8 2NG
Tel: (016977) 46234
Website: www.farlamhall.co.uk

Cooking 3 | **Modern English** | **£53**

A 'comfortable, old-fashioned ambience' hangs about Farlam Hall, a sixteenth-century manor house in rolling countryside. In the dining room, waitresses wear long skirts, plates are patterned or flowered, and damask tablecloths hark back to a gentler age. But the style of cooking is in the modern English country-house idiom, and most raw materials are sourced locally. The set-price menu runs to five courses, including coffee. Cream of watercress and pear soup might be one of the three starters alongside a terrine of pheasant, herbs and pistachios with plum chutney. Cumbrian beef and lamb and Lancashire duck all make appearances among main courses, the last perhaps turning up as pan-fried breast on ginger risotto with a red wine sauce. Grilled fillet of sea bass with herbs could represent fish, accompanied by Mediterranean-style vegetables and pesto sauce, while hazelnut meringue with banana ice cream and caramel sauce will please the sweet of tooth. A separate vegetarian menu is available by arrange-

ment. Four New World bottles and one Chablis, priced from £19.95 to £22, open the international wine list.

Chefs: Barry Quinion and Martin Langford **Proprietors:** the Quinion and Stevenson families **Open:** all week D only 8 to 8.30 **Closed:** 25 to 30 Dec **Meals:** Set D Sun to Fri £38, Set D Sat £39.50 **Service:** not inc **Cards:** Amex, Maestro, MasterCard, Visa **Details:** 45 seats. Car park. No children under 5. No smoking. Wheelchair access (not WC). No music. No mobile phones **Accommodation:** 12 rooms

MAP 6   BRANCASTER STAITHE – Norfolk

White Horse   NEW ENTRY

Main Road, Brancaster Staithe PE31 8BW
Tel: (01485) 210262
Website: www.whitehorsebrancaster.co.uk

Cooking 2 | **Modern British** | **£36**

Overlooking the Norfolk coastal path with views of Scolt Head Island, a table on the terrace in summer is a real treat; as one visitor remarked it's a great place 'to unwind as the sun sets over the marsh'. Inside Cliff Nye's contemporary renovation the conservatory dining room is light and airy; he's also taken over The Fox in Willian, Hertfordshire – see entry. Locally available seafood figures large on the menu, particularly oysters from the 'beds' at the bottom of the garden. Cream of spinach soup was 'well-balanced and generous' at inspection, while grilled fillets of red mullet with pomme purée was a successful main course. Roast rump of English lamb with sweet potato gnocchi, spinach and thyme jus is a typical meat main course. Finish with Amaretto parfait, or rhubarb and custard. The concise international wine list is arranged by style, opening at £11.20 for their house Duboeuf.

Chef: Nicholas Parker **Proprietor:** Cliff Nye **Open:** all week; 12 to 2, 6.45 to 9 **Service:** not inc **Cards:** Delta, Diners, Maestro, MasterCard, Visa **Details:** 90 seats. 90 seats outside. Car park. Vegetarian meals. Children's helpings. No smoking. Wheelchair access (also WC). Music. No mobile phones **Accommodation:** 15 rooms

£	This symbol means that it is possible to have a three-course dinner, including coffee, half a bottle of house wine and service, for £30 or less per person.

MAP 3 BRAY – Berkshire

Fat Duck

1 High Street, Bray SL6 2AQ
Tel: (01628) 580333
Website: www.fatduck.co.uk

| Cooking 9 | Modern European | £112 |

It all seems so obvious now: to question the rules of cooking based on scientific evidence, and to investigate the folklore of the kitchen with reasoning and curiosity. Heston Blumenthal may not have been the first to ponder why we do what we do in the kitchen, but he was the first to put such application into proving that we are not at the end of the journey as far as culinary discovery is concerned. And now he's got letters after his name: OBE, from Her Majesty, and PhD, from the University of Reading.

The Fat Duck is considered one of the top few restaurants in the world by many of those who have eaten in the others, and it is no surprise that it tops the GFG's poll once again. But it is just a restaurant, and we have to spend our hard-earned money to eat there. The menu du jour has fallen by the wayside, which leaves the choice of the carte at £80 for three courses or the tasting menu at £97.75 (to be precise). At inspection, most customers seemed to be going for the latter, suggesting that once they've managed to secure a table (a perpetual cause of frustration for readers) they're jolly well going to make the most of the experience.

The former pub hard on the road through the village has been gently cajoled into becoming a suitable venue for such culinary fireworks, and it now possesses an understated charm that seems a wholly appropriate setting. The low-ceilinged room is smart and light and is brightened further by large gold and purple canvases specially commissioned for the restaurant. The tables are smartly – and expensively – set, and the space between them is generous. There is no bar or lounge area, so it is straight to table and the menus. The champagne trolley is the first arrival, but no prices are indicated, so beware the sting in the tail. Service seems to be getting rather more formal nowadays, but the mostly French staff remain friendly and not overly stiff. Bread is simply old-fashioned artisan white and brown, and all the better for it: 'just what bread used to be like.'

Guests ordering the tasting menu each get a souvenir copy of the menu placed on the table in an envelope, and the full theatre of the chef's signature dishes. The nitro-green tea and lime mousse usually gets a gasp when the trolley containing the liquid nitrogen rolls into view, and the drama continues to impress each first-time visitor. The snail porridge is here, plus the sardine on toast sorbet and the smoked bacon and egg ice cream. Eight courses in all, plus an array of tasters and teasers.

The à la carte menu is more inclined to evolution, combining new dishes with a few old favourites. A range of inter-courses here, too, mean that recipients still get a sense of adventure: rock oyster, for example, in the half-shell with passion-fruit jelly, horseradish cream and lavender is a tantalising combination. Among starters, the crab biscuit with roast foie gras is a lesson in taste and texture, with crystallised seaweed, sharp rhubarb and oyster vinaigrette supporting the 'perfect piece of foie gras, perfectly cooked'. Grilled scallops come with a fashionable pairing of cauliflower purée as well as small cubes of oloroso sherry jelly and a marinated cep. Ingredients are uniformly excellent: main-course venison, for example, each rare slice topped with a marron glacé and accompanied by a rich civet, and celeriac as purée, roast and rémoulade; finally, the waiter delivers a cup of venison and frankincense tea, richly gamey and aromatic. Roast turbot manages to incur a £6.50 supplement, but that is probably down to the accompanying turbot and langoustine royale.

Among desserts, tarte Tatin is a reminder of the chef's interest in the tastes of childhood and the importance of memory in the dining experience. The Tatin, so rich and sticky, took one recipient back to the toffee-apples of childhood. Macerated strawberries are dusted in grated cheese and come with black olive and leather purée – a sort of S&M tapenade – and pistachio scrambled egg (a glorious custard). Coffee and petits fours are first class, with the violet tartlets better than any jam tart deserves to be. The wine list leaves no stone unturned, apart from the bargain one, of course, and delivers a fine selection from all over France. There are also plenty of German Rieslings and an impressive collection from California. Nothing by the bottle is under £30.

Chef/Proprietor: Heston Blumenthal **Open:** Tue to Sun L 12 to 1.45 (2.30 Sun), Tue to Sat D 7 to 9 **Closed:** 2 weeks Christmas **Meals:** Set L and D £80 to £97.75 **Service:** 12.5% (optional) **Cards:** Amex, Delta, Maestro, MasterCard, Visa **Details:** 46 seats. Children's helpings. No smoking. No music. No mobile phones. Air-conditioned

Hinds Head Hotel

High Street, Bray SL6 2AB
Tel: (01628) 626151

Cooking 4 | **British** | **£44**

You can 'almost smell the history' at the Hinds Head, a big old inn with a buzzing bar, oak beams, panelling, open fires and numerous dining areas. It's unstuffy, and the food is as traditional as the surroundings, with dishes like pork chop and pease pudding, and a fried duck egg with ham and Cheddar on the short, simple menu – which may come as quite a surprise to fans of Heston Blumenthal, who owns the place. His Fat Duck (see entry above) is practically next door, but this is not an extension of the restaurant. What animates the whole operation is Blumenthal's commitment to maintain the Hinds Head as the village pub and to offer traditional British tavern cuisine. There is much to commend, from pea and ham soup and Lancashire hotpot to the now-legendary oxtail and kidney pudding, and reporters are unanimous in their approval. Otherwise the occasional contemporary note is struck, via goats' cheese, onion and red pepper tart, say, soused herrings with chopped beetroot, yoghurt, and grated horseradish to 'give it some added kick', or sea bream with fennel. Posh lunchtime sandwiches (including smoked salmon with cucumber and cream cheese) and snacks are available at the bar. Desserts, meanwhile, run from an unusual apple and blackberry crumble with custard to Eton mess. Service hits the spot, and more than 60 wines are featured on a well-chosen wine list, where prices start at £13 and around a dozen come by the glass from £3.35.

Chef: Dominic Chapman Proprietors: Heston Blumenthal and James Lee Open: all week L 12 to 2.30 (3 Sun), Mon to Sat D 6.30 to 9.30 Closed: 25 and 26 Dec Service: not inc Cards: Amex, Delta, Maestro, MasterCard, Visa Details: 150 seats. Car park. Children's helpings. No smoking. No music

Riverside Brasserie

Bray Marina, Monkey Island Lane, Bray SL6 2EB
Tel: (01628) 780553
Website: www.riversidebrasserie.co.uk

Cooking 3 | **Modern European** | **£46**

An area of decking in front of this small, café-like wood and glass building right by the Thames makes it a popular choice for al fresco lunches in summer.

But even when the weather is not so good, the river views can be enjoyed from inside the no-frills, minimalist dining room, which has a relaxed, informal, brasserie-type atmosphere, although evening visitors should note the necessity to book in advance (marina security allows you in only if your name is on the guest list). The informal feel extends to the straightforward menu, with starters of gazpacho, pig's-head terrine with apple chutney, or Parma ham and mozzarella spring rolls with Gewürztraminer dressing. To follow, choices include ribeye with bone-marrow sauce and triple-cooked chips (made to Heston Blumenthal's famous method, although he is no longer a co-owner), alongside pan-fried sea bream with vinaigrette potatoes. There is also a superior children's menu, and the likes of chocolate tart or pannacotta to finish. The wine list is brief but still covers a good range of interesting bottles, opening with red and white Vins de Pays d'Oc at £14 a bottle, £4 a glass.

Chef: Garrey Dawson Proprietors: Garrey Dawson, Lee Dixon, Bob Angus and Alfie Hitchcock Open: all week 12 to 2.30, 7 to 9.30 Meals: alc (main courses £11 to £17) Service: 12.5% (optional) Cards: Amex, Delta, Maestro, MasterCard, Visa Details: 40 seats. 80 seats outside. Car park. Children's helpings. Wheelchair access (not WC). Music

Waterside Inn

Ferry Road, Bray SL6 2AT
Tel: (01628) 620691
Website: www.waterside-inn.co.uk

Cooking 8 | **French** | **£148**

Reporters never fail to comment on the setting. Although Bray has become Gastronomy Central in recent years, it is still the picture of an unruffled thirteenth-century English village, and the Waterside Inn was where it all started. Perched on a bank of the Thames, the scene in balmy weather is an unfailing delight, although some have felt that the dining room itself – expansive though it is – could stand a little updating.

The tone of the cuisine under the father and son Roux partnership at the helm barely alters from one year to another. Occasionally the lightest touch of innovation is brought to bear, so that the five-course Menu Exceptionel might begin with a tartare of scallops in Granny Smith velouté with shavings of truffle. The opulent ingredients one expects might be subjected to unexpectedly demotic treatments, a lobe of foie gras turning up with wild mushrooms and white beans, which complemented it rather well. Otherwise, poached fillets of sole with smoked salmon mousse, brown shrimps and champagne sauce, or milk-fed lamb with sauce paloise are the classical order of the day.

There is just too noticeable a hint of trouble in paradise in this year's reports for comfort, but then again, when expectations are raised so high by price and reputation, we might come away having a lower opinion of perfectly sound cooking if it didn't have the 'gosh' factor the menu seems to promise. When the kitchen is on song, though, it can compete. Creamy mussel soup with diamonds of sole has been a lush-textured accomplishment, and desserts always seem to impress. Textbook crème brûlée is among the best, and soufflés such as the spring rhubarb version, into which a raspberry coulis is poured by the waiter, are the business. Cheeses are also reliably fine, as are coffee and petits fours.

As to wine, if you've just discovered Argentinian Malbec, you're in for a disappointment. Francophiles, on the other hand, will romp through pages of pedigree vintages. That said, a South African interloper, Hamilton Russell Chardonnay (£50, or £10 a glass), has inveigled its way among the house whites, perhaps inevitably misspelled. Prices start at 'ouch!'.

Chef: Alain Roux Proprietors: Michel and Alain Roux Open: Wed to Sun 12 to 2 (2.30 Sun), 7 to 10; also Tue D 1 June to 31 Aug Closed: 26 Dec to 1 Feb Meals: alc (main courses £38 to £52). Set L Wed to Sat £40 to £89.50, Set L Sun £56 to £89.50, Set D £89.50 Service: 12.5% (optional) Cards: Amex, Delta, Diners, Maestro, MasterCard, Visa Details: 75 seats. Car park. Vegetarian meals. No children under 12. Children's helpings. No smoking in dining room. Wheelchair access (not WC). No music. No mobile phones Accommodation: 11 rooms

---

MAP 12 BRENTFORD – Greater London

Pappadums AR

Ferry Quays, Ferry Lane, Brentford TW8 0BT
Tel: (020) 8847 1123

Views of Kew Gardens are one of the draws at this bright, modern Indian restaurant by the Thames. The cooking of northern India is the main focus of the menu, with dishes such as spicy spring chicken on the bone (£8.95) and haandi gosht (lamb chops and seasonal vegetables; £9.90). Occasionally, the kitchen stretches its wings to bring in southern specialities such as masala dosai (£7.25) and goes even further afield for Thai green chicken curry with aubergines (£9.20). Wines from £12.90. Open all week.

MAP 2 BRIDPORT – Dorset

Chez Cuddy AR

47 East Street, Bridport DT6 3JX
Tel: (01308) 458770

This smart bistro-style venue is a useful lunch stop in Bridport. Expect Greek salad (£6.50), lamb's liver and bacon with mash and mustard and wine sauce (£6.50) and fishcakes with salad and lemon mayonnaise (£7.25). The more ambitious evening menu (Sat night only) could open with roast red mullet on celeriac rémoulade (£6) or duck liver pâté with spicy tomato relish (£6), followed perhaps by roast cod fillet bourguignonne (£12.75), with pistachio crème brûlée (£5) to finish. The wine list opens at £11.75. Open Tue to Sat L and Sat D.

MAP 3 BRIGHTON AND HOVE – East Sussex

Due South NEW ENTRY

139 Kings Road Arches, Brighton & Hove BN1 2FN
Tel: (01273) 821218
Website: www.duesouthrestaurant.co.uk

Cooking 2 | Modern British | £45

'You couldn't get any more Brighton than this,' noted an impressed visitor of Due South's seafront location, tucked away as it is in one of the arches under the promenade. The décor is simple and unfussy – basic wooden tables and chairs, a boarded floor – with the sweeping views of the sea and beach taking the plaudits. James Jenkins runs a well-organised kitchen, which thrives on fresh ingredients and good combinations, and much is made of local provenance. Fish soup, 'a wonderfully overcrowded dish', is more like bouillabaisse, while fried scallops in garlicky parsley butter have been declared 'dead simple but very good'. The fish of the day might be grilled Dover sole with garlic, lemon and thyme, contrasting with a heartier main course of slow-roast belly pork with crisp crackling, sage and apple mash, Savoy cabbage and mustard sauce. Reports on puddings are enthusiastic too, from warm chocolate brownie with vanilla ice cream to cappuccino parfait. Around ten are served by the glass from £3.80, with bottles priced from £12.95.

Chef: James Jenkins Proprietor: Rob Shenton Open: all week 12 to 4, 6 to 9.30 Meals: alc (main courses £11.50 to £19) Service: 10% (optional) Cards: Amex, Maestro, MasterCard, Visa Details: 50 seats. 25 seats outside. Vegetarian meals. Children's helpings. No smoking. Wheelchair access (not WC). Music

---

La Fourchette

105 Western Road, Brighton & Hove BN1 2AA
Tel: (01273) 722556
Website: www.lafourchette.co.uk

Cooking 2 | French | £39

This aspirational bistro has a corner position on Western Road, giving plenty of scope for people watching. The ground-floor room is bright and airy thanks to large windows, but you never feel exposed. The contemporary décor boasts dark wooden flooring, and a natural, comfortable air pervades throughout. The staff are efficient, sometimes overly so, but the entire experience ticks along nicely. The menu is divided into meat and fish, but the descriptions are in English, with just the odd French word here and there. Poached eggs on toast with spinach and wine butter sauce might precede braised oxtail with mushroom mousse and chive and garlic pomme purée, or roast pavé of sea bass with creamed white-bean purée. A fulsome dessert menu includes red fruit sabayon served with a caramelised sweet champagne egg cream. The wine list opens at £11.

Chef/Proprietor: Pascal Madjoudj Open: Sun to Fri L 12 to 2.30, Mon to Fri D 7 to 10.30, Sat 12 to 10.30 Meals: alc (main courses L £6 to £15, D £15). Set L £10 (2 courses), Set D £22 (2 courses) Service: 10% Cards: Amex, Delta, Diners, Maestro, MasterCard, Visa Details: 75 seats. Children's helpings. No smoking in 1 dining room. Wheelchair access (also WC). Music. Air-conditioned

---

Gingerman

21A Norfolk Square, Brighton & Hove BN1 2PD
Tel: (01273) 326688
Website: www.gingermanrestaurants.com

Cooking 2 | Modern European | £39

The original incarnation of Ben McKellar's South Coast restaurants (see also Gingerman at Drakes, below) remains a popular venue. In the muted,

smallish room, the feel is hang-loose Brighton, with a fair old hubbub of relaxed enjoyment at busy sessions. Start with Jerusalem artichoke and sautéed cep risotto, or herring beignet with avocado and tomato before going on to well-sourced meat and fish main courses. The latter might be roast monkfish tail with steamed leeks and a creamy mussel broth, while South Downs lamb is favoured for a dish involving grilled aubergine, roast garlic purée, balsamic vinegar and thyme. Banish that diet with desserts such as sticky banana cake with pecans and honeycomb ice cream. A short wine list of well-chosen bottles opens with house Chilean and Italian at £12.50, or £3.50 a glass.

Chef: David Keates Proprietors: Ben and Pamela McKellar Open: Tue to Sun 12.30 to 1.45, 7 to 9.45 Meals: Set L £13.95 (2 courses) to £16.95, Set D £24 (2 courses) to £27 Service: not inc Cards: Amex, Delta, Maestro, MasterCard, Visa Details: 36 seats. Vegetarian meals. Children's helpings. No smoking. Music. Air-conditioned

---

Gingerman at Drakes

44 Marine Parade, Brighton & Hove BN2 1PE
Tel: (01273) 696934
Website: www.gingermanrestaurants.com

Cooking 6 | Seafood | £45

Local boy Ben McKellar opened a second front in Brighton, right on the seafront, in 2004, in the basement room of a swish contemporary hotel. Despite being underground, the room is light and airy by day, with a cool ambience and great staff.

The kitchen doesn't mind sourcing ingredients from further afield than locally when the quality justifies it, so beef is Scottish and poultry is from France, although local scallops and fish from Newhaven strongly feature too. Devilled calves' brains with deep-fried parsley is the kind of starter to make an impression, while those scallops might turn up on open ravioli with carrot purée, baby leeks and cumin as a main course. A reporter who had his first restaurant outing of the year here enjoyed celeriac and apple soup with chestnut dumplings, sea bass on a powerful lobster risotto, and a finely balanced dessert that matched plum and date crumble with light custard and decent vanilla ice cream. A pair of diners might get into the seaside mood by sharing dark chocolate and Amaretto fondue, served with honeycomb, baby bananas and marshmallows. Vegetarians have their own menu, with a pair of options at starter and main. The same wine list operates here as at the original Gingerman (see entry above).

> **Chefs:** Ben McKellar and Andrew McKenzie **Proprietors:** Ben and Pamela McKellar **Open:** all week 12.30 to 2 (2.30 Sun), 7 to 10 **Meals:** Set L £15 (2 courses) to £18, Set D £27 (2 courses) to £32 **Service:** not inc **Cards:** Amex, Delta, Diners, Maestro, MasterCard, Visa **Details:** 50 seats. Vegetarian meals. No smoking. Music. Air-conditioned **Accommodation:** 20 rooms

Hotel du Vin & Bistro

2–6 Ship Street, Brighton & Hove BN1 1AD
Tel: (01273) 718588
Website: www.hotelduvin.com

Cooking 2 | Modern European | £46

Sharing a successful formula with its sibling operations (see entries in Birmingham, Bristol, Harrogate, Henley-on-Thames, Tunbridge Wells and Winchester), this informal bistro within a Gothic-looking building close to the seafront serves some classy comfort food. The menu is as pan-European as the name implies, offering gravad lax, a plate of Serrano ham and Manchego cheese, or foie gras and chicken liver parfait, but it also includes a selection of 'simple classics', which appeals to reporters: say, coq au vin with buttered mash. Elsewhere, combinations are generally mainstream modern, whether in a seared fillet of sea bass with pipérade and aged balsamic or confit duck leg with braised red cabbage and pommes dauphinois. The classical undercurrent breaks surface at dessert stage, producing zabaglione with roast plums, crème brûlée, and chocolate tart with pistachio ice cream. Wines are taken seriously, with all regions brimming with good choices over a options price range. Prices start at £14, with decent options under £20 and 16 or so by the glass from £3.75.

> **Chef:** Rob Carr **Proprietor:** MWB Group plc **Open:** all week 12.30 to 1.45 (2.30 Sun), 7 to 9.45 **Closed:** L 31 Dec **Meals:** alc exc Sun L (main courses £12.50 to £20). Set L Mon to Fri £14.50 (2 courses) to £19.95, Set L Sun £23.50 **Service:** not inc **Cards:** Amex, Delta, Maestro, MasterCard, Visa **Details:** 80 seats. Vegetarian meals. Children's helpings. No smoking in dining room. Wheelchair access (also WC). No music **Accommodation:** 37 rooms

La Marinade

77 St George's Road, Kemp Town, Brighton & Hove BN2 1EF
Tel: (01273) 600992
Website: www.lamarinade.co.uk

Cooking 1 | Modern European | £41

Honesty is Nick Lang's watchword, a virtue much in evidence at this welcoming neighbourhood restaurant. His southern-European inspired dishes are attractive, bolstered by good-value set menus for both lunch and dinner. The à la carte menu also embraces the international theme; pan-fried baby squid with white wine, garlic and butter is spiced up with paprika, while Bahamian lobster tail is roasted and served with Parmesan on an avocado and mango salsa. A meat dish might be 28-day hung Scottish beef with fresh sautéed wild mushrooms and crisp French fries. End with lemon and lime posset. The fairly priced wine list is a nicely balanced global affair with house options from £11.95.

> **Chef/Proprietor:** Nick Lang **Open:** Thur to Sat L 12 to 2, Tue to Sat D 6 to 9.30 (10 Sat) **Meals:** alc (main courses £15.50 to £16.50). Set L and D (not Sat) £15 **Service:** 12.5% for Set L and D **Cards:** Delta, Maestro, MasterCard, Visa **Details:** 40 seats. No cigars/pipes. Music. Air-conditioned

Moshi Moshi Sushi

Bartholomew Square, Brighton & Hove BN1 1JS
Tel: (01273) 719195

The cleverly designed glass box of a building is home to the kaiten (conveyor belt) that carries plates of sushi, sashimi, and salads tantalisingly alongside the customers. Take whatever catches your eye as it passes by on colour-coded plates, priced from £1.20 to £3.50, or order from the menu. There are sushi sets like the 'clear conscience set' (£7.50) and a hot seasonal dish might include teriyaki ribeye steak with fried sweet potato (£10.50), and desserts run to yuzu rice with mango and orange (£3). Drink, beer, saké or wine. Closed Mon.

> **AR** Not a full entry but provisionally recommended. These 'also recommended' establishments are integrated throughout the book.

The price given next to the cooking score is based on the cost of a typical three-course dinner for one person, including coffee, house wine and service.

One Paston Place

1 Paston Place, Brighton & Hove BN2 1HA
Tel: (01273) 606933
Website: www.onepastonplace.co.uk

| Cooking 4 | Modern European | £56 |

Paston Place is in a part of town full of Regency splendour, and the road on which it stands leads down to the seafront. Parking is always likely to prove a challenge. The dining room is adorned with a large collection of gilt-framed mirrors, and with tables covered in crisp white cloths and the high-backed chairs upholstered in deep red there is an air of the baroque about the place. Service is suitably sharp and professional.

Francesco Furriello, now into his third year, continues to make adjustments to his menu structure. An 'everyday' menu has been introduced for lunch and dinner, offering less complex, but equally interesting, dishes such as linguine with sautéed squid and mussels to start, followed by roast loin of pork with potato gratin, and a selection of organic ice creams to finish. The carte and tasting menu are where his true colours are shown, with starters like Sauternes-poached foie gras with pan-fried duck suprême and summer berries, followed by pan-fried brill with braised gem lettuce, sautéed girolles and a Sauternes sauce. The highlight of a winter meal was the pear and chocolate dessert, with a fruit of 'magnificent pedigree' combined with 'top-notch' chocolate and amaretti cake. The wine list is a straight fight between Italy and France, starting at £18.

Chef: Francesco Furriello Proprietor: Gusto Ltd Open: Tue to Sat 12 to 2, 7 to 9.30 Meals: alc (main courses £19 to £21). Set L £16 (2 courses) to £59, Set D £23 (2 courses) to £59 Service: not inc Cards: Amex, Delta, Maestro, MasterCard, Visa Details: 42 seats. No smoking. Wheelchair access (not WC). Music. No mobile phones. Air-conditioned

Real Eating Company

NEW ENTRY

86–87 Western Road, Brighton & Hove BN3 1JB
Tel: (01273) 221444
Website: www.real-eating.co.uk

| Cooking 2 | Modern European | £42 |

At the Hove end of Western Road, this hybrid deli/restaurant/all-day brasserie offers simple, basic surroundings and a relaxed and informal atmos-

phere matched by informed, friendly service. The daytime menu mixes assemblages – charcuterie, British cheeses – with the likes of fishcakes and chargrilled chicken breast (with hummus, piquillo pepper, asparagus and capers), while a lunchtime blackboard lists daily fish and other specials. The results are fresh, exuberant even, with the focus more on tried and trusted treatments than on pushing culinary boundaries. But in the evening the kitchen is not above turning out accurately cooked salmon with 'extremely well-balanced' hollandaise, 'pink and well-flavoured' lamb chops with horseradish dauphinois, and warm chocolate and pear pithiviers with Poire William ice cream and chocolate sauce. The wine list is clear, sensibly short and fairly priced, with house white starting proceedings at £12.75.

Chef: Chris O'Brien Proprietor: Helena Hudson Open: all week L 12 to 4, Wed to Sat and bank hol Sun D 6.30 to 9.30 Closed: 25 and 26 Dec, 1 Jan Service: not inc Cards: Amex, Delta, Maestro, MasterCard, Visa Details: 40 seats. 12 seats outside. Vegetarian meals. Children's helpings. No smoking. Wheelchair access (also WC). Music. Air-conditioned

Sevendials

1 Buckingham Place, Brighton & Hove BN1 3TD
Tel: (01273) 885555
Website: www.sevendialsrestaurant.co.uk

| Cooking 3 | Modern European | £44 |

Now in its sixth year, Sam Metcalfe's restaurant is an established part of the Brighton dining scene. The premises, a former bank on the corner of the Sevendials roundabout, have high ceilings and large windows and were ripe for conversion to a restaurant. The atmosphere is relaxed and informal, tables are clothless, you pour your own wine, and the staff are efficient and confident. The menu features some brasserie classics such as fish soup with rouille and croûtons and extends as far as pan-fried quail breast with crispy foie gras-filled leg on sautéed baby spinach with shallot foam and beetroot crisps. Steak and kidney pie is considered a speciality among main courses, while roast rack of young venison might come with a juniper, herb and Dijon mustard crust partnered by roast sweet potato, braised red cabbage and a port jus. An inspector's hot Valrhona chocolate fondant didn't deliver due to overcooking, but the accompanying pistachio ice cream was just-so. There are cocktails – as Brighton demands – and a decent wine list kicking off at £12.

Chef/Proprietor: Sam Metcalfe   Open: all week L 12 to 2.30, Mon to Sat D 7 (6.30 Fri and Sat) to 10   Closed: Christmas to New Year, bank hol Mon D   Meals: alc (main courses £10 to £20), Set L Mon to Sat £10 (2 courses)   Service: 12% (optional)   Cards: Amex, Diners, Maestro, MasterCard, Visa   Details: 55 seats. 50 seats outside. Vegetarian meals. Children's helpings. No smoking before 10pm at D. No cigars/pipes in dining room. Wheelchair access (also WC). Occasional music

Terre à Terre

71 East Street, Brighton & Hove BN1 1HQ
Tel: (01273) 729051
Website: www.terreaterre.co.uk

| Cooking 3 | Global Vegetarian | £47 |

'Neither of us is vegetarian but more meals like this could convert us' is a typical response to this highly original meat-free restaurant. The cooking takes in European, South-east Asian and Indian influences, and myriad ingredients combine in complex creations – fortunately, staff know the dishes and are 'helpful and attentive'. To start, savour the aromatic kick of a truffle-laden risotto served with a set cep consommé, fresh chestnut Parmesan milk foam, virgin oil and balsamic green tops, toasted barley and 'scrunched' fried sage. To follow might be fragrantly curried cauliflower and coconut masala tandoori spice sausage served with okra channa panch phoran, and a hot onion and mustard-seed muffin splashed with tamarind jelly, accompanied by banana-wrap lemon rice, spice-dust poori and mango 'stinger'. Home-made brown-bread ice cream was a 'truly memorable' part of one meal. Wines, organised by style, are all organic or biodynamic, and kick off with house Italian and French at £16.25.

Chef: Glen Lester   Proprietors: Philip Taylor and Amanda Powley   Open: Wed to Fri L 12 to 3.30, Tue to Fri D 6.30 to 10.30, Sat and Sun 12 to 10.30   Closed: 25 and 26 Dec, 1 Jan   Meals: alc (main courses £12.50 to £14)   Service: not inc   Cards: Amex, Delta, Diners, Maestro, MasterCard, Visa   Details: 100 seats. 12 seats outside. Vegetarian meals. Children's helpings. No smoking. Wheelchair access (also WC). Music. Air-conditioned

 This symbol means that the restaurant has elected to participate in *The Good Food Guide's* £5 voucher scheme (see 'Using The Good Food Guide' for details).

MAP 2   BRISTOL – Bristol

Bell's Diner

1–3 York Road, Montpelier, Bristol BS6 5QB
Tel: (0117) 924 0357
Website: www.bellsdiner.com

| Cooking 5 | Modern European-Plus | £44 |

A low-key exterior on a corner site conceals Chris Wicks's ambitious, high-achieving restaurant. Cosy up to the real fire on chilly days in a sitting-out area from where you can see the chefs at work. The long windows on two sides of the dining room retain the feel of shopfronts from a generation ago. In fact, it was once where Smiles beer was brewed, as locals remember.

Inspiration comes from the molecular school of gastronomy that has taken the country by storm. There are foams and dusts, sweet starters and spicy desserts, and the ice cream might be vindaloo flavour. Oysters in strawberry gazpacho with a dust of Serrano ham is an adventurous way to start, and might lead you on to rump of lamb with sweet potato, beetroot, onion soubise and a liquorice jus. Not everything is quite so eccentric: braised pork comes with Savoy cabbage, a juniper jus and truffled macaroni cheese. An eight-course tasting menu, with optional wine flight, is probably the best way to test the range, from potato foam to coconut délice with a poppadom. Wines begin well in the posh regions of France, before marching out into the big wide world. Prices start at £13.

Chefs: Christopher Wicks and Johnny Hazel   Proprietor: Christopher Wicks   Open: Tue to Fri L 12 to 2.15, Mon to Sat D 6.30 to 10.30   Closed: 24 to 30 Dec   Meals: alc (main courses £14.50 to £19.50). Set D £45 (Mon to Thur, whole table only, max 6)   Service: 10% (optional)   Cards: Amex, Delta, Maestro, MasterCard, Visa   Details: 50 seats. Vegetarian meals. Children's helpings. No smoking. Wheelchair access (not WC). Music. No mobile phones

Café Maitreya   NEW ENTRY

89 St Mark's Road, Easton, Bristol BS5 6HY
Tel: (0117) 951 0100
Website: www.cafemaitreya.co.uk

| Cooking 4 | Vegetarian | £30 |

'What I love about this place is that it treats vegetables, fruits and nuts as the main component and gives them a starring role,' said one happy visitor, while also praising Mark Evans's light touch and imagination. Café Maitreya (Sanskrit for 'universal love'), with its cream-tiled floors, pine tables and benches, abstract paintings on the walls and an open-to-view kitchen, makes good use of less commonly used produce such as rosehip, wild garlic, lovage, samphire and sorrel. Combinations are well considered, as in a starter of pink mushroom and Parmesan gnocchi with sage cream and quince preserve, and grilled vegetable and balsamic ballottine with pesto. Main-course walnut, Gruyère and radicchio ravioli with garlic butter and pickled walnuts is a dish packed with complementary flavours and contrasting textures. Among imaginative and successful desserts have been a cocotte of summer berries in rosehip syrup accompanied by lemon-balm and yoghurt ice cream, and nougatine ('utterly delicious'). A key on the menu flags dishes that are vegan, gluten-free or dairy-free, and all the wines on the short list are organic, with house French and Sicilian at £10.95 a bottle, £3.75 a glass.

Chef: Mark Evans **Proprietor:** Rob Booth **Open:** Tue to Sat D only 6.45 to 9.45 **Closed:** 24 Dec to 2 Jan **Meals:** Set D £16.50 (2 courses) to £20.25 **Service:** not inc **Cards:** Delta, Maestro, MasterCard, Visa **Details:** 50 seats. Vegetarian meals. No smoking. Wheelchair access (also WC). Music

Culinaria

1 Chandos Road, Bristol BS6 6PG
Tel: (0117) 973 7999
Website: www.culinariabristol.co.uk

| Cooking 3 | Bistro | £38 |

'Our deli/takeaway section is now very popular,' writes Judy Markwick, adding: 'It gives an added dimension to the restaurant.' Since the Markwicks opened Culinaria in May 2004, they have unfailingly treated customers with happy, unforced politeness, made them feel at home, and fed them good food and wine at reasonable prices. Using first-class raw materials, Stephen Markwick produces the likes of bruschetta of lambs' sweetbreads with mushrooms and Madeira, and smoked eel with beetroot, horseradish and a potato pancake. Underpinning all is a culinary intelligence, and, with weekly-changing menus keeping up interest for regular visitors, main-course choices range from scallops with sun-dried tomato risotto, via sautéed chicken with sherry vinegar, to vegetable tagine with couscous. Desserts include classic French items like petit pot au chocolat, but panna-cotta with passion fruit may show up too. A compact wine list opens at £12.50.

Chef: Stephen Markwick **Proprietors:** Stephen and Judy Markwick **Open:** Fri and Sat L 12 to 2, Wed to Sat D 6.30 to 9.30 **Meals:** alc (main courses £11.50 to £14.50) **Service:** not inc **Cards:** Maestro, MasterCard, Visa **Details:** 30 seats. Vegetarian meals. Children's helpings. No smoking. Wheelchair access (also WC). No music

FishWorks

128 Whiteladies Road, Clifton, Bristol BS8 2RS
Tel: (0117) 974 4433
Website: www.fishworks.co.uk

| Cooking 2 | Seafood | £58 |

There are now ten restaurants in this ever-growing seafood chain (see entries in Bath, Christchurch and London), so the combination of fishmonger and restaurant is clearly a winning one. As one diner commented, 'You cannot but notice the whiff of fish when you first enter', but that adds to the easy-going ambience. Blackboards list daily specials, ranging from 'superb' roast cod to 'devastatingly fresh', accurately timed yellowfin tuna steak, while the menu offers the likes of Brixham scallops grilled in the half-shelf to start, then roast skate with black butter and capers, and spaghetti with langoustines, tomatoes, garlic and parsley. Prices are on the high side, but the quality of the fish is excellent: 'what it is all about' as far as one reporter was concerned. Lemon tart or chocolate pudding may round things off. The wines have been selected to complement the food. Prices start at £17.90 for a Vinho Verde.

Chef: Romero Costas **Proprietor:** FishWorks plc **Open:** Tue to Sat 12 to 2.30, 6 to 10.30 **Closed:** bank hols and day after bank hols **Meals:** alc (main courses £13 to £50) **Service:** not inc **Cards:** Amex, Delta, Maestro, MasterCard, Visa **Details:** 54 seats. Vegetarian meals. Children's helpings. No smoking. Music. Air-conditioned

Hotel du Vin & Bistro

The Sugar House, Narrow Lewins Mead, Bristol BS1 2NU
Tel: (0117) 925 5577
Website: www.hotelduvin.com

| Cooking 3 | Modern European | £46 |

The Bristol branch of the chain (see entries in Birmingham, Brighton, Harrogate, Henley-on-Thames, Tunbridge Wells and Winchester), a listed

building, dates from the eighteenth century, when it was a sugar warehouse. The menu is infused with the flavours of France, and also gives a nod to Italy, embracing classic brasserie fare such as trout almondine and chargrilled ribeye with chips and béarnaise. Start with chicken liver parfait with shallot marmalade, or devilled lambs' kidneys with toasted brioche, following perhaps with roast belly pork with crushed Jersey Royals and Madeira sauce, or fillet of sea bass with pimentos and spinach. Vegetarians are well catered for too, with options including roast butternut squash with herb couscous. Lime cheesecake with a scoop of chocolate ice cream makes an unusual but satisfying way to end. The extensive wine list covers most regions of France in some depth. The rest of Europe is well presented too, and there are particularly good showings from Australia and California in the New World listings, where Canada and even Thailand get a look in. The house selection of a dozen bottles runs from £13, or £3.50 a glass.

Chef: Marcus Lang **Proprietor:** MWB Group plc **Open:** all week 12 to 2 (2.30 Sun), 6 to 10 **Meals:** alc exc Sun L (main courses £12.50 to £20). Set L Mon to Sat £15 (2 courses), Set L Sun £22.50. Bar menu available 2 to 5 **Service:** 10% **Cards:** Amex, Delta, Diners, Maestro, MasterCard, Visa **Details:** 80 seats. Vegetarian meals. Children's helpings. No smoking in dining room. Wheelchair access (also WC). Occasional music **Accommodation:** 40 rooms

One30

130–132 Cheltenham Road, Bristol BS6 5RW
Tel: (0117) 944 2442
Website: www.one30.co.uk

Cooking 2 | Modern European/Tapas | £39

A no-nonsense interior features timber floors, exposed steel piping and brick walls at this tapas restaurant, an offshoot of Bell's Diner (see entry). The menu, which has expanded over the past year, is lively, with plenty of Spanish-inspired dishes that can be eaten while lounging on the leather sofas or at the narrow teak tables. Patatas bravas, spicy mussels, shellfish stew and marinated anchovies are among more traditional dishes, while plantain and polenta fritters with tapenade, fried langoustines with chilli, garlic and parsley, and salt-cod croquettes with dried tomato salad and basil aïoli are for the more adventurous. Meatier options include sticky chicken with a honey and chilli glaze or grilled lamb cutlet with an aubergine, yoghurt and butter sauce. Desserts are a more home-grown affair, so go for rhubarb crumble with hazelnut ice

cream or baked Alaska. A short list of wines from Spain and Portugal starts at £12.50.

Chefs: Johnny Evans and Christopher Wicks **Proprietors:** Christopher Wicks and William Bowen **Open:** Fri to Sun L 12 to 3, Mon to Sat D 6.30 to 11 **Closed:** 24 to 30 Dec **Meals:** alc (tapas £2.50 to £7) **Service:** not inc **Cards:** Delta, Maestro, MasterCard, Visa **Details:** 100 seats. 30 seats outside. Vegetarian meals. Children's helpings. Wheelchair access (also WC). Music

Quartier Vert

85 Whiteladies Road, Clifton, Bristol BS8 2NT
Tel: (0117) 973 4482
Website: www.quartiervert.co.uk

Cooking 4 | Mediterranean | £41

You'd be hard pushed to find anything that isn't organic on Barny Haughton's menu, and the bread baked at his on-site bakery is now certified as such by the Soil Association; he also runs a cookery school. The compact, daily-changing menus are defined by a broadly Mediterranean approach, which could see Serrano ham salad with a soft-boiled egg and Parmesan, or bruschetta with beetroot, radicchio and mozzarella opening proceedings. Main courses might bring on pan-fried sea bream with chorizo, chermoula, couscous and rocket, or something like braised shank of Barrow Gurney lamb with rosemary jus, red cabbage, and truffle-infused mash. Farmhouse cheeses are English, or end on a sweet note with dark chocolate marquise with pistachio crème anglaise and a tuile. The predominantly European wine list, which highlights some organic producers, is arranged by style, ranging from 'light and crisp' whites to 'prestige' reds. Over a dozen are served by the glass, and bottle prices open at £12.95. The café serves cakes, pastries and so on all day, and there's a brunch menu on Sundays.

Chefs: Barny Haughton and Simon Searle **Proprietors:** Barny Haughton and Connemara Coombes **Open:** all week L 12 to 3, Mon to Sat D 6 to 10 (10.30 Fri and Sat) **Closed:** 24 to 26 Dec, 1 Jan **Meals:** alc (main courses £11.50 to £19.50). Set L £16.50 (2 courses) to £19.50. Bar tapas menu available **Service:** 10% (optional) **Cards:** Delta, Maestro, MasterCard, Visa **Details:** 70 seats. 25 seats outside. Vegetarian meals. No smoking. Occasional music

riverstation

The Grove, Bristol BS1 4RB
Tel: (0117) 914 4434
Website: www.riverstation.co.uk

| Cooking 3 | Modern British-Plus | £44 |

This former river-police station is now a stylish café with a dining room upstairs. The décor is contemporary, with great views over the water and a terrace for warmer weather. The brasserie-style menu offers everything you'd expect from this kind of modern diner, and there's a hearty brunch menu on Saturdays. Timings are good, as are combinations, so look out for carpaccio of venison fillet with rocket and truffle oil to start, or maybe griddled scallops with wild rice salad. Rack of spring lamb comes with braised arrocina beans, fennel and pesto, while halibut arrives with peas, steamed new potatoes and a lemon butter sauce. For pudding, try iced rhubarb, ginger and red wine parfait, or warm blueberry frangipane tart with crème fraîche. The international wine list, arranged by style, is fairly priced and has been compiled with an eye on quality. Ten house selections are served by the glass from £3.50, from £13.50 by the bottle.

> **Chefs:** Peter Taylor and Ross Wills **Proprietors:** Peter Taylor and John Payne **Open:** Mon to Fri 12 to 2.30, 6 to 10.30 (11 Fri), Sat 10.30 to 2.30, 6 to 11, Sun 12 to 3, 6 to 9 **Closed:** 24 to 26 Dec, 1 Jan **Meals:** alc (main courses £12 to £20). Set L Mon to Fri £12.50 (2 courses) to £14.75, Set L Sun £15.50 (2 courses) to £18.75. Bar and Sat brunch menus available **Service:** not inc **Cards:** Delta, Diners, Maestro, MasterCard, Visa **Details:** 120 seats. 28 seats outside. Vegetarian meals. Children's helpings. No smoking. No music

Sands [AR]

Queen Street, Bristol BS8 1LW
Tel: (0117) 973 9734

Lebanese food in a lively atmosphere is the name of the game. Tucked away in the cellars of an impressive Georgian building, the modest interior boasts orchid displays, brass lanterns and simply covered tables. Shared meze meals (from £17.50 per person, or £8.95 for lunches) offer the likes of fattoush, hummus, falafel and tabouleh, while main course options include lamb mixed grill (£11.50), shish taouk (boneless chicken marinated in garlic; £9.95) or samaka harra (spiced baked snapper fillet; £11.95). Sweets include 'delicious' mahalabia, a white mousse with rose water (£3.50). Wines from £11.50. Open all week.

| MAP 2 | **BROADHEMBURY** – Devon |

Drewe Arms

Broadhembury EX14 3NF
Tel: (01404) 841267

| Cooking 3 | Seafood | £42 |

The interior of this fine old thatched pub is quite cramped, with historical knick-knacks around every corner, but the atmosphere buzzes. The seafood is mostly from Newlyn in Cornwall, while crab is from Beer in Devon. The emphasis is on taste and simplicity, with two blackboards offering a wide choice of dishes, although you may have to walk between the two dining areas to take it all in. Crab thermidor or seared scallops with mango and chilli sauce may open proceedings, while sea trout with asparagus and herb butter or John Dory with anchovy and capers could follow among main courses. There are also a couple of meat choices, including perhaps fillet of beef with mushroom sauce or rack of lamb with Dijon potatoes and onion marmalade. Finish with one of the fulsome puddings: prune and cognac tart with honeycomb ice cream, say, or spiced pineapple crumble. The bar also offers a variety of open sandwiches. White wines are listed in order from driest to sweetest, while the reds go from lightest to fuller-bodied. Prices open at £13.45 for a Côtes du Roussillon.

> **Chef/Proprietor:** Andrew Burge **Open:** all week L 12 to 2, Mon to Sat D 7 to 9 **Closed:** 25 Dec **Meals:** alc (main courses £18). Bar menu available **Service:** not inc **Cards:** Amex, Delta, Maestro, MasterCard, Visa **Details:** 40 seats. 50 seats outside. Car park. Children's helpings. No smoking in dining room. Wheelchair access (also WC). No music

| MAP 5 | **BROADWAY** – Worcestershire |

Dormy House Hotel

Willersey Hill, Broadway WR12 7LF
Tel: (01386) 852711
Website: www.dormyhouse.co.uk

| Cooking 2 | Modern European | £50 |

This honey-coloured stone building sits on the top of Willersey Hill, next to a golf course. The Dining Room has a separate entrance to the Barn Owl where pub food is served, and once inside, the large medieval tapestry dominates. The à la carte and three-course chef's recommendation menu are thoroughly European affairs, with many influences colliding to create some imaginative dishes. However, pleasant surprises include the curry cured salmon starter with a goat's cheese taco, which was an 'interesting idea that proved to be a huge success'. The cannon of lamb with sweetbreads and Jerusalem artichoke was let down by a poorly butchered cut of meat at inspection, while pineapple and mascarpone paupiette with a Malibu poached pineapple and sorbet ended the meal. A chunky international wine list opens at £15.75 for house choices, with twelve by the glass from £3.95.

Chef: Saleem Ahmed Proprietor: Mrs I.P. Sørensen Open: Sun L 12 to 2, all week D 7 to 9.30 (9 Sun). Bar food available Closed: 25 Dec eve, 26 Dec Meals: alc D (main courses £19.50 to £23). Set L Sun £25, Set D £35 Service: not inc Cards: Amex, Delta, Maestro, MasterCard, Visa Details: 70 seats. 60 seats outside. Car park. Vegetarian meals. Children's helpings. No smoking. Wheelchair access (also WC). No music. Air-conditioned Accommodation: 45 rooms

G Russell's

NEW ENTRY

20 High Street, The Green, Broadway WR12 7DT
Tel: (01386) 853555
Website: www.russellsofbroadway.com

Cooking 4 | Modern British | £50

There is much to praise about this self-styled 'boutique restaurant-with-rooms', not least the location, square in the middle of Broadway village, a real Cotswold gem. The honey-coloured Georgian building was once a furniture factory but tasteful renovation has given it a new lease of life. The L-shaped dining room is dominated by an enormous fireplace, which now stores wines, and although the background music may not be to everyone's taste, the appeal is broad in every possible way. Matthew Laughton's modern European brasserie cooking shows a flair for good flavour combinations and excellent raw materials, as in a starter of 'beautifully crusted and caramelised' scallops with parsnip purée, black pudding and chicory salad, and a citrussy orange and black pepper caramel dressing. Among impressive main courses have been crisp-skinned roast breast of Gressingham duck with apple sauce, sage and onion stuffing, while dessert might be an attractively presented and surprisingly light combination of a pyramid of iced chestnut parfait with fruitcake ice cream, chocolate sauce and a brandy wafer. The globe-trotting wine list offers reasonable value, opening with a dozen house choices at £14.95.

Chef: Matthew Laughton Proprietors: Barry Hancox and Andrew Riley Open: all week L 12 to 2.30, Mon to Sat D 6 to 9.30 Meals: alc D (main courses £13 to £23). Set L and D before 7pm £10.95 (1 course) to £16.95, Set D £17.95 (2 courses) to £22.95 (no set meals after 7pm Fri and Sat) Service: not inc Cards: Amex, Delta, Maestro, MasterCard, Visa Details: 55 seats. 40 seats outside. Vegetarian meals. Children's helpings. No smoking. Wheelchair access (also WC). Music. Air-conditioned Accommodation: 7 rooms

Lygon Arms

Broadway WR12 7DU
Tel: (01386) 852255
Website: www.thelygonarms.com

Cooking 3 | Modern European | £63

Halfway along the attractive broad street that gives the village its name, the Lygon Arms stands out with its weathered-stone frontage and steeply pitched gable fronts. It's an ancient building, and enough remains inside to convey an olde-worlde impression: rough stone everywhere, old fireplaces, carved archways, panelling and doors that 'date from a time when nobody was taller than about five feet'. The Great Hall is suitably impressive and plays the Scottish baronial theme to the hilt. Martin Blunos has departed and Martin Lovell now heads the kitchen. A steamed lobster boudin, impressively light and shot through with a delicate curry flavour, is served atop saffron couscous with a lobster dressing and makes a largely successful first course, as does a 'very accomplished' caramelised duck foie gras cream with macerated cherries and a warm brioche, but a serving of braised shoulder of Light Horn lamb was a disappointment at inspection. Desserts are not a highlight. Service is well paced, and 11 wines come by the glass on the French-led wine list, where prices kick off at £16.25.

Chef: Martin Lovell Proprietor: Paramount Hotel Open: all week 12.30 to 2, 7 to 9.30 Meals: alc D (main courses £20 to £26.50). Set L £15 (2 courses) to £21, Set D £39.50. Bar menu available Service: not inc Cards: Amex, Delta, Maestro, MasterCard, Visa Details: 100 seats. Car park. Vegetarian meals. No children under 10 at D. Children's helpings. No smoking in dining room. Occasional music. No mobile phones Accommodation: 69 rooms

MAP 2 BROCKENHURST – Hampshire

Le Poussin at Whitley Ridge

Beaulieu Road, Brockenhurst SO42 7QL
Tel: (01590) 622354
Website: www.lepoussin.co.uk

Cooking 6 | **Modern British** | **£67**

The original home of Le Poussin at Parkhill in Lyndhurst is still under renovation, as reported last year. One heck of a makeover is clearly going on, but for the time being, home is still this foursquare, wisteria-covered, Georgian hunting lodge. Menus continue to develop along contemporary lines, with lengthy descriptions presaging food of great technical complexity and dramatic impact. A salad of poached lobster with crispy claws is dressed in a pea and truffle cream, while another first course might see well-executed pearl barley 'risotto' spiked with smoked haddock, and served with baby broad beans and a quail's egg.

Lemon sole as a main course seemed as good as Dover to one diner, and was certainly as regally treated, with sauce Nantua and wild mushrooms, but meat cookery is of a high order too. A roundel of rare beef fillet is topped with horseradish butter, and served on a good red wine reduction with roasted mini-vegetables. A diverting semi-dessert has been half a Comice pear, filled with Roquefort and grilled, served with walnut ice cream. For something more mainstream, finish with airy, light passion-fruit soufflé with matching sauce. Staff are both friendly and efficient, attentive perhaps to a fault.

The broad-minded, enterprising wine list that used to serve the previous address is on offer here too, with its lively explorations of both classic and regional France. Selections from elsewhere are much more restricted, but listings from Uruguay and Luxembourg might tempt the curious. Small glasses start at £3.95, large ones at £6.50.

> **Chefs:** Alex Aitken and Shane Hughes **Proprietors:** Alex and Caroline Aitken **Open:** all week 12.30 to 2, 6.30 to 9.30 **Meals:** alc (main courses £25.50 to £27.50). Set L £15 (2 courses) to £20, Set D £39.50 to £55 **Service:** 10% (optional) **Cards:** Amex, Delta, Maestro, MasterCard, Visa **Details:** 40 seats. 15 seats outside. Car park. Children's helpings. No smoking. Wheelchair access (not WC). No music. No mobile phones **Accommodation:** 18 rooms

Simply Poussin

The Courtyard, Brookley Road, Brockenhurst SO42 7RB
Tel: (01590) 623063
Website: www.simplypoussin.co.uk

Cooking 3 | **Modern British** | **£37**

Alex Aitken's popular brasserie in the centre of Brockenhurst is the little brother to Le Poussin (see entry above). It's a welcoming place, with well-spaced bare tables and professional service. Part of the appeal is the set-price two-course menu, and the broadly European repertoire on a carte that takes in a salad of smoked duck breast with fig salad, and whole sea bass en papillote with spicy provençale vegetables. Good raw materials are sympathetically treated, and anyone in search of comfort food will not go away disappointed: the roll-call includes twice-baked cheese soufflé, creamed cauliflower soup with toasted walnuts, braised lamb shank, and a creamy fish pie. House wine is £13.50, and some nine wines are available by the glass from £2.95 to £7.95.

> **Chef:** Steven Styles **Proprietor:** Alex Aitken **Open:** Tue to Sat 12 to 2, 6.30 to 9.45 **Meals:** alc (main courses £10.50 to £16). Set L 12 to 1.30 and Set D Tue to Thur 6.30 to 8.30 £10 (2 courses) **Service:** 10% (optional) **Cards:** Amex, Maestro, MasterCard, Visa **Details:** 32 seats. 6 seats outside. Vegetarian meals. No smoking. Wheelchair access (not WC). Music. No mobile phones

MAP 5 BROMSGROVE – Worcestershire

Grafton Manor

Grafton Lane, Bromsgrove B61 7HA
Tel: (01527) 579007
Website: www.graftonmanorhotel.co.uk

Cooking 3 | **Modern Indian/European** | **£39**

Built in 1567 by the Earl of Shrewsbury, Grafton Manor has played an important part in several historical events, including the Gunpowder Plot. Today, the baronial atmosphere of the ancient red-brick house makes it a popular venue for weddings and a fittingly grand setting for chef Simon Morris to ply his trade. Exotic Indian flavours are built on top of classic French foundations in an inventive style that produces starters taking everything from

Goan crab cakes on an egg, chickpea and peanut salad, or Maharashtran prawns with carrot and dill purée, to steamed lemon sole with a courgette pudding and Parmesan with lemon oil. Main courses have featured pan-fried duck breast with apple, foie gras, fennel and a red wine jus, and pink-cooked loin of lamb with a fennel and morel emulsion and fondant potato, while for dessert there might be lemon and lime posset with short-bread. Prices start at £10.25 on the mostly French wine list, and wines by the glass and half-bottle are plentiful.

Chefs: Simon Morris and Tim Waldren Proprietors: the Morris family Open: all week 12.30 to 2, 7.30 to 9.30 Closed: first week Jan Meals: Set L £18.50 to £20.50, Set D £27.85 to £32.75 Service: not inc Cards: Amex, Diners, MasterCard, Visa Details: 50 seats. Car park. Vegetarian meals. Children's helpings. No smoking. Wheelchair access (also WC). No music. No mobile phones Accommodation: 9 rooms

MAP 2 **BRUTON** – Somerset

Bruton House

2–4 High Street, Bruton BA10 0AA
Tel: (01749) 813395
Website: www.brutonhouse.co.uk

Cooking 6 | British | £48

As you drive through Bruton you can't miss this bright blue restaurant-with-rooms. The elegant dining room – all pale walls, floor-length white tablecloths and fat candles in the fireplace – oper-ates along formal restaurant lines. The food, though, is unmistakably modern. The menus offer a short choice, and conscientious effort is evident in both the sourcing of materials (much of it within a 30-mile radius) and the flair with which they are cooked. The style is appealing without being flamboyant, and results have included foie gras, Portobello mushroom and chicken terrine with grape chutney, as well as a main course of line-caught wild sea bass with potato galette and saffron and fennel sauce vierge. A refreshing lack of over-elaboration, seen in a straightforward dish of sirloin of beef with fondant potato and caramelised shallots, puts the emphasis on sound technical skills and flavour. Indeed, simplicity is one of the keynotes of the good-value lunch menu, with dishes making use of uncomplicated assemblies to produce the likes of mature Cheddar omelette with a tomato and shallot salad, and sirloin steak with chips and béarnaise. To finish, a West Country

cheeseboard is an appealing alternative to desserts such as poached pink rhubarb with nougat glace. The modern wine list is exactly right for the job – unfussy, with a dozen house selections priced from £13.50 to £19.50 also offered by the glass (from £3.50).

Chefs: Scott Eggleton and James Andrews Proprietor: Christie-Miller Andrews Ltd Open: Tue to Sat 12 to 2, 7 to 9 Closed: 26 Dec to 12 Jan Meals: alc L (main courses £11 to £16). Set D £28 (2 courses) to £42 Service: not inc Cards: Amex, Delta, Maestro, MasterCard, Visa Details: 30 seats. Vegetarian meals. No smoking. Wheelchair access (not WC). Music Accommodation: 3 rooms

MAP 3 **BUCKLAND** – Oxfordshire

Lamb at Buckland

Lamb Lane, Buckland SN7 8QN
Tel: (01367) 870484
Website: www.thelambatbuckland.co.uk

Cooking 1 | Modern British | £41

In a tiny village, the restaurant is tucked away but well worth seeking out. Peta and Paul Barnard continue to make the most of their country-pub setting, offering honest-to-goodness English cooking in a friendly atmosphere. Both the bar area and the dining room offer the same menu, which changes according to the season: the autumn months, for example, bring plenty of venison, partridge and other game to the table. A warm three-cheese and red onion tart might start a meal, followed by steak and kidney pie, or roast rack of English lamb with rosemary and garlic. Daily specials are listed on the blackboard too. Desserts tend to be traditional, including treacle tart with custard or perhaps steamed syrup sponge. The four-course Sunday lunch is as impressive as the attentive service. The compact wine list starts at £11.95.

Chef: Paul Barnard Proprietor: Lamb at Buckland Ltd Open: Tue to Sun L 12 to 2 (3 Sun), Tue to Sat D 6.30 to 9.30 (10 Sat) Meals: alc exc Sun L (main courses £8 to £24). Set L Tue to Sat £10 (2 courses) to £15, Set L Sun £19.95 (2 courses) to £23.25, Set D Tue to Fri £10 (2 courses) to £15 Service: not inc Cards: Delta, Maestro, MasterCard, Visa Details: 55 seats. 28 seats outside. Car park. Vegetarian meals. Children's helpings. No smoking. Wheelchair access (not WC). No music Accommodation: 1 room

MAP 2 **BUCKLERS HARD –**
Hampshire

Master Builder's House Hotel, Riverview Restaurant

Bucklers Hard SO42 7XB
Tel: (01590) 616253
Website: www.themasterbuilders.co.uk

Cooking 2 | **Modern European** | **£46**

There is a delightful glimpse of the yachts bobbing about on the Beaulieu River as you reach the car park of this impressive building. Inside, the dining room is just the right side of elegant; sash windows, pale colours and black and white David Bailey prints contrast nicely with the abstract art on the walls. An inspection dinner started with a 'primitive' warm salad of sausage, onion and green beans with mustard dressing and was followed by breast of chicken with 'rather sticky' sweet potato purée, roast parsnips and wild mushroom sauce. Alternatives might be a gratin of scallops with tomato salad, and whole Dover sole with béarnaise. Finish with almond and pear tart with Amaretto ice cream. The wine list, which starts at £14.75 with a dozen house selections, all available by the glass, has some interesting choices from around the world.

Chef: Denis Rhoden **Proprietors:** Jeremy Wilcox and John Illsley **Open:** all week 12 to 3, 7 to 10 **Meals:** alc (main courses £10 to £22). Set L £16.95 (2 courses) to £22.50, Set D £31.50. Bar menu available **Service:** not inc **Cards:** Amex, Maestro, MasterCard, Visa **Details:** 70 seats. 30 seats outside. Car park. Vegetarian meals. Children's helpings. No smoking. Music **Accommodation:** 25 rooms

MAP 5 **BUCKMINSTER –**
Leicestershire

Tollemache Arms

48 Main Street, Buckminster NG33 5SA
Tel: (01476) 860007
Website: www.thetollemachearms.com

Cooking 4 | **Modern British** | **£42**

Close to Melton and Grantham, this impressive nineteenth-century hotel has been transformed by owner and chef Mark Gough. Over the past two

years, Mark has established a minimalist, airy dining room, offering modern British cooking. Sunday lunch, for example, is packed full of game from local estates including hare pithiviers with roasted apples, pot-roasted pheasant, and confit duck leg with nutmeg and apple risotto. However, the daily menu also offers a competent selection of well-constructed, thoughtful dishes, aided by the 'unobtrusive' yet efficient waiting staff. There are some nice touches: deep-fried feta comes with sweet chilli wontons, while Serrano ham and Parmesan salad is served with lightly poached figs. Mains offer braised pork belly with locally sourced roasted root vegetables, or grilled whole sea bass with basil mash and baby chorizo sausages, the latter a perennial favourite. 'Flavoursome' desserts include lemon pannacotta with poached blackberries or a selection of home-made sorbets. There is a comprehensive, mostly-French wine list with long descriptive notes; house choices begin at £12.95, with a handful more under £20.

Chef/Proprietor: Mark Gough **Open:** Tue to Sun L 12 to 2, Tue to Sat D 7 to 9 **Meals:** alc (main courses £9.50 to £18). Set L £10 (2 courses) to £14, Set D Tue to Thurs £10 (2 courses) to £14. Bar menu available **Service:** not inc **Cards:** Amex, Maestro, MasterCard, Visa **Details:** 50 seats. 30 seats outside. Car park. Vegetarian meals. Children's helpings. Smoking in bar only. Music **Accommodation:** 5 rooms

MAP 6 **BURNHAM MARKET –**
Norfolk

Fishes

Market Place, Burnham Market PE31 8HE
Tel: (01328) 738588
Website: www.fishesrestaurant.co.uk

Cooking 4 | **Seafood** | **£53**

Matthew Owsley-Brown is now well established on the north Norfolk coast – into his fifth year – and it is local boats that bring in most of the fish that appear on his lively menus, with oysters, lobsters and mussels from Brancaster and crab from Wells-next-the-Sea getting starring roles. Brown shrimps with home-made linguine, tomato fondue and herbs, fish soup, and an unusual terrine featuring smoked eel, foie gras and peppers with chilli salt and brioche are all appealing starters. Main courses could range from roast halibut with caramelised fennel, oranges and hollandaise to bourride. But look out, too, for some Asian twists:

John Dory in a Thai-style curry with peanuts, aubergines and sticky rice, say, or tandoori porbeagle shark kebab with pilau rice. Tonka bean pannacotta with deep-fried banana and coconut won tons could end a meal. There are a dozen or so wines by the glass (from around £5), and the menu suggests appropriate matches with the food. Bottle prices start at £17 but soon climb above £25.

Chef: Matthew Owsley-Brown Proprietors: Matthew and Caroline Owsley-Brown Open: Tue to Sun L 12 to 2.15, Tue to Sat D 6.45 to 10 Closed: 1 week Christmas, 3 weeks Jan Meals: Set L £19 (2 courses) to £22, Set D £32 (2 courses) to £37 Service: not inc Cards: Delta, Maestro, MasterCard, Visa Details: 42 seats. No children after 8.30pm. Children's helpings. No smoking. Wheelchair access (not WC). Music

Hoste Arms

The Green, Burnham Market PE31 8HD
Tel: (01328) 738777
Website: www.hostearms.co.uk

Cooking 2 | Modern British | £41

Even in winter, visitors' cars are much in evidence in this north Norfolk village. Easily recognisable overlooking the village green is Paul Whittome's hotel and restaurant, with its pubby front bar, various dining rooms mixing ancient and modern trappings, and a light, airy conservatory filled with leather sofas. The menu reads enticingly. Think mixed seafood in cockle and horseradish chowder, confit of duck leg, herb-crusted best end of lamb, and sausage and mash. Singled out at inspection were a 'pink, juicy' 21-day dry-aged New York ribeye from the butcher across the green, and a plate of four small desserts – orange crème caramel, pineapple gratin, passion-fruit tart and sticky toffee pudding. But while materials are first-rate, they sometimes have to struggle to prove it: local oysters, for instance, have been served with an overwhelming, jam-like fennel and vanilla granita. Elsewhere there's good home-made bread, decently paced and attentive service, and a confident, fairly priced wine list, starting with house French at £11.95.

Chef: Rory Whelan Proprietor: Paul Whittome Open: all week 12 to 2, 7 to 9 (9.30 Fri) Meals: alc (main courses £10 to £21.50) Service: not inc Cards: Delta, Maestro, MasterCard, Visa Details: 140 seats. 100 seats outside. Car park. Vegetarian meals. Children's helpings. No smoking in 1 dining room. Wheelchair access (also WC). Occasional music. Air-conditioned Accommodation: 36 rooms

MAP 8 **BURNSALL –** North Yorkshire

Devonshire Fell

Burnsall BD23 6BT
Tel: (01756) 729000
Website: www.devonshirehotels.co.uk

Cooking 3 | Modern British | £38

Panoramic views of the Dales and the River Wharfe are star attractions at this offshoot of the Devonshire Arms at Bolton Abbey (see entry). The building, originally a club for local mill owners, was extensively refurbished when the current owners took over in 1998. Since then it has established a reputation for first-rate modern hospitality, the warm atmosphere of a traditional Dales pub contrasting with contemporary décor majoring in glass and blond wood. The main dining room is in a conservatory extension, which has full benefit of the views, and tables are formally laid. The menus read well in a typically modern British way, starters ranging from classic French onion soup to monkfish carpaccio with aubergine caviar, or rillettes of rabbit with black pudding and apple salad. Main courses take in minted lamb shank with cep dauphinois and parsnip cream as well as breaded chicken breast with pheasant stuffing and roast polenta, or halibut en papillote. To finish, there might be apricot tart with Chantilly cream. An extensive wine list opens with French Chardonnay and Merlot at £11.95.

Chef: Mehdi Boukemach Proprietor: The Duke of Devonshire Open: all week 12 to 2.30, 6.30 to 9.30 Meals: alc (main courses £13 to £17.50). Bistro menu available Service: 10% Cards: Amex, Delta, Diners, Maestro, MasterCard, Visa Details: 60 seats. 18 seats outside. Car park. Vegetarian meals. Children's helpings. No smoking. Wheelchair access (also WC). Occasional music Accommodation: 12 rooms

 This symbol means that the restaurant has elected to participate in *The Good Food Guide's* £5 voucher scheme (see 'Using The Good Food Guide' for details).

MAP 5   **BURTON ON THE WOLDS –**
Leicestershire

Langs

Horse Leys Farm, 147 Melton Road, Burton on
the Wolds LE12 5TQ
Tel: (01509) 880980
Website: www.langsrestaurant.co.uk

| Cooking 3 | Modern European | £39 |

A traditional old farmhouse this might appear
from the outside, but its inner self is a contemporary space with a split-level dining room. The
menus, too, follow modern lines with Italian leanings – roast pepper and goats' cheese tart with
pesto dressing among starters – balanced by a trio
of lamb (best end, shepherd's pie, grilled kidneys),
or beef fillet with creamed wild mushrooms. Meals
end with the likes of banana parfait with bitter
chocolate sorbet, or crème brûlée, and service continues in its own pleasant way. The wine list has
been put together with an eye for interesting
names and good value. House French is £13.50.

> **Chefs:** Gordon Lang, John Duffin and Tom Middleton
> **Proprietors:** Gordon and June Lang **Open:** Tue to Sun L 12 to
> 2.15 (3 Sun), Tue to Sat D 7 to 9.30 (6.30 to 10 Sat) **Meals:**
> alc (main courses £11.50 to £17). Set L Tue to Sat £11.50 (2
> courses) to £15.50, Set D Tue to Fri £17.50 **Service:** not inc
> **Cards:** Maestro, MasterCard, Visa **Details:** 48 seats. 12 seats
> outside. Car park. Vegetarian meals. Children's helpings. No
> smoking. Wheelchair access (also WC). Occasional music. No
> mobile phones

MAP 6   **BURY ST EDMUNDS –**
Suffolk

Maison Bleue

30–31 Churchgate Street, Bury St Edmunds
IP33 1RG
Tel: (01284) 760623
Website: www.maisonbleue.co.uk

| Cooking 2 | Seafood | £39 |

On a grey-stone terraced street a few minutes'
walk from St Edmundsbury Cathedral, this French
seafood restaurant knows what it does best.
Norfolk mussels marinière, whole sardines stuffed
with crayfish served on tomato and coriander salsa,
and Irish rock oysters are just some of the carefully

chosen starters on offer. There are a couple of nods
to meat eaters, including fillet of Scottish beef with
béarnaise, but seafood mostly wins out among
main courses: choose from grilled fillet of turbot
on celery and tomato chutney with spinach sauce,
baked sea bass in fennel and Pernod sauce, or
whole grilled Dover sole with anchovy butter. If
you have room, there's white chocolate mousse
with orange confit and strawberry coulis, or
French cheeses. Staff are smart and attentive, and
France is the focus of the wine list, although the
rest of Europe and the New World get a look in
too. Five house vins de pays are £11.50 or £12.75.

> **Chef:** Pascal Canévet **Proprietor:** Régis Crépy **Open:** Tue to
> Sat 12 to 2.30, 7 to 9.30 (10 Fri and Sat) **Meals:** alc (main
> courses £10.50 to £19). Set L £13.95 (2 courses) to £15.95,
> Set D £24.95 **Service:** not inc **Cards:** Delta, MasterCard,
> Visa **Details:** 65 seats. Children's helpings. No smoking.
> Wheelchair access (not WC). Music

MAP 3   **BUSHEY –** Hertfordshire

St James

30 High Street, Bushey WD23 3HL
Tel: (020) 8950 2480

| Cooking 3 | Modern British | £45 |

Wooden floors, white ceilings, a strategically
placed mirror, globe lights and informal but efficient staff create a good atmosphere at this local
restaurant. The menu is long – around ten starters
and the same number of main courses – but holds
interest without overwhelming. Begin with crispy
chilli beef with an oriental salad, or a terrine of
smoked and grilled mackerel with asparagus and
olive and anchovy tapenade. Main courses also
strike a balance between meat and fish and show
the same imaginative approach: roast fillet of beef
with a smoked mozzarella salsa crust, say, alongside
seared swordfish with a risotto of tomatoes and
grilled vegetables, a creamy chilli sauce, and fried
aubergine and courgette. Along with a selection of
cheeses, desserts include the ever-popular
Toblerone cheesecake, raspberry brûlée with
strawberry ice cream, or panettone bread-and-
butter pudding with crème anglaise. House
Sicilian at £12.95 heads up the short wine list.

MAP 9 | BUXTON – Derbyshire

Columbine

7 Hall Bank, Buxton SK17 6EW
Tel: (01298) 78752
Website: www.buxtononline.net/columbine

Cooking 2 | Modern British | £31

Value for money is what reporters comment on at this bustling restaurant, in a Georgian house a few minutes' walk from Buxton's theatre and gardens. On the carte might be starters of herring fillets marinated in sweet cider and mustard seeds, and classic main courses such as chargrilled sirloin steak with cracked black pepper and cognac sauce, or roast Aylesbury duckling with oranges and Grand Marnier. 'Fish was particularly good,' according to a reporter who enjoyed a selection of tuna, salmon and bream on a bed of creamed spinach, then 'excellent' summer pudding. Portions are generous, vegetarians have their own menu, and service has a 'friendly, relaxed, matter-of-fact style and efficiency'. The wine list is fairly brief but thoughtfully chosen, with most bottles under £15. House Duboeuf is £8.95.

MAP 3 | CAMBER – East Sussex

The Place   AR

New Lydd Road, Camber TN31 7RB
Tel: (01797) 225057

The wide expanses of Camber Sands are just a stone's throw from this small hotel and brasserie, where friendly staff generate a relaxed mood in the light, airy dining room. Seasonally focused menus make good use of fish supplied by the Hastings fleet, and only non-threatened species appear on the menu, perhaps in the shape of classic bouillabaisse (£6.25/£11.75), or grilled mackerel fillets glazed with chilli jam served on wild garlic mash and spring greens (£12.95). Among non-fish dishes might be wild rabbit slow-cooked in Kentish cider and cream (£14.50). Treacle tart with crème anglaise (£4.95) to finish. Wines from £12.50. Accommodation. Open all week.

MAP 6 | CAMBRIDGE – Cambridgeshire

Hotel Felix, Graffiti

Whitehouse Lane, Huntingdon Road, Cambridge CB3 0LX
Tel: (01223) 277977
Website: www.hotelfelix.co.uk

Cooking 4 | Modern British | £49

The low ultra-modern building tacked on to a period structure may not be to everyone's taste, and the corresponding lighting, art and music might not be either, but reports this year indicate that under the new chef the Graffiti restaurant has taken on a new level of culinary ambition. Ian Morgan cooks vivid modern dishes with a few pioneering partnerships – butternut squash with cep risotto and balsamic ice cream – and the emphasis on sound raw materials. Meats appear to be well timed (as in a fine loin of Denham Estate venison with pickled red cabbage and espresso syrup), and fish, delivered from Cornwall, is treated innovatively: grilled fillet of brill with chorizo oil, aubergine caviar, fennel and sun-dried tomato juices, for example. A lightness of touch is evident too, not least when it comes to saucing, as in a sweet pepper dressing to accompany scallop and endive tarte Tatin with Jerusalem artichoke purée. Tonka bean and lemongrass pannacotta didn't exactly raise the rafters at inspection, and service got a definite thumbs-down for the unsmiling attitude of the staff. A reasonable number of bottles on the good-value, roving wine list come in under

£	This symbol means that it is possible to have a three-course dinner, including coffee, half a bottle of house wine and service, for £30 or less per person.

£20, and the house selection kicks off at £12.50, with 14 by the glass (from £3.95).

Chef: Ian Morgan **Proprietor:** Jeremy Cassel **Open:** all week 12 to 2, 6.30 to 10 (10.30 Fri and Sat, 9.30 Sun) **Meals:** alc D (main courses £14 to £22). Set L £12.50 (2 courses) to £16.50. Bar menu available **Service:** not inc **Cards:** Amex, Delta, Diners, Maestro, MasterCard, Visa **Details:** 45 seats. Car park. Vegetarian meals. Children's helpings. No smoking. Wheelchair access (also WC). Music **Accommodation:** 52 rooms

Midsummer House

Midsummer Common, Cambridge CB4 1HA
Tel: (01223) 369299
Website: www.midsummerhouse.co.uk

Cooking 7 | Modern French | £77

This is a rather unassuming-looking Victorian villa on the Cam, with an extended conservatory dining room overlooking a splendid garden, and a first-floor bar with river views. The feel is intimate and gentle, with large tables and good chairs upholstered in cream leather. The menu format is fixed-price, with a higher-priced tasting menu, in the modern way. Daniel Clifford cooks unmistakably contemporary food, full of twists and turns and surprising technique. A meal might begin mesmerisingly with the delivery of a soda siphon, which squirts out a velvet foam of pink grapefruit and champagne. A signature starter is smoked eel, served in a salad with crisp pig's trotter, cured foie gras, Braeburn apple purée, and that currently essential ingredient, wild cress. Apples (this time Granny Smith) also turn up to top another first course, of seared scallops with truffled celeriac purée, a 'beguiling, intelligent and precise' balance of flavours.

Anybody not yet convinced of what the new British cuisine can aspire to will find powerful testimony here. Main courses are extraordinarily complex but successful arrays: perhaps turbot braised with peanuts and pistachios, alongside wilted cos, squash purée and asparagus, adorned at the table with a viscous vanilla essence, or veal kidney cooked in its own fat, with snails, spinach, garlic purée and sauce soubise. Not all is quite so great. Cheeses have been under par, and there are reports again of indifferent service, as though staff are unaware of the calibre of the place. Faith is bolstered anew, though, by the desserts, which end things on the same note of effervescence with which proceedings began. Even tarte Tatin comes frothing under a spume of garlic and bay leaf, while passion-fruit and mango délices with

spearmint ice cream, tea jelly and lavender honey is an 'intoxicating' combination. Then it's on to coffee with beignets and dips before a final chocolate box, which offers all manner of fillings, from Darjeeling to green peppercorn. A brilliant wine list has been assembled, offering a dazzling spectrum of flavours to go with the adventurous cooking. There are German Rieslings, racy Rhônes, aromatic rosés and oodles of lovely claret to consider. Prices, alas, are high, opening with French and Italian house wines at £20.

Chef/Proprietor: Daniel Clifford **Open:** Fri and Sat L 12 to 1.30, Tue to Sat D 7 to 9.30 **Closed:** 2 weeks Christmas, 1 week from Easter, last 2 weeks Aug **Meals:** Set L £30, Set D £55 to £123 (inc wine) **Service:** not inc **Cards:** Amex, Delta, Maestro, MasterCard, Visa **Details:** 64 seats. No smoking. Wheelchair access (not WC). No music

Restaurant 22

22 Chesterton Road, Cambridge CB4 3AX
Tel: (01223) 351880
Website: www.restaurant22.co.uk

Cooking 2 | Modern European | £37

There is nothing Tardis-like about this converted Victorian building; it's as small inside as it looks, but the intimate atmosphere only adds to the 'food is everything' mantra. The set-price three-course menu continues to offer straightforward and well-timed dishes. Mushroom bisque with truffle oil, or smoked pigeon breast on Savoy cabbage with bacon and redcurrant jus are robust starters, and main courses may see grilled plaice fillets with sweet peppers and roast bananas alongside sautéed calf's liver with roast beetroot and a red wine and shallot jus. Cheese can be taken as an extra course or as an alternative to puddings of perhaps steamed lemon sponge with marmalade anglaise. The wine list is strong in France, but bottles from other regions have been chosen with an eye on value and quality too. Four house bottles are £12.95 and £13.95.

Chefs: Martin Cullum and Seb Mansfield **Proprietor:** David Carter **Open:** Tue to Sat D only 7 to 9.45; also open L during Dec **Closed:** 1 week Christmas to New Year **Meals:** Set D £24.95 **Service:** not inc **Cards:** Amex, Delta, Maestro, MasterCard, Visa **Details:** 40 seats. Vegetarian meals. No children under 10. No smoking. Occasional music. No mobile phones. Air-conditioned

MAP 3 **CANTERBURY – Kent**

Goods Shed

Station Road West, Canterbury CT2 8AN
Tel: (01227) 459153

Cooking 1 | Modern British | £39

The setting is a cavernous brick-built Victorian railway shed, most of which is given over to the stalls of a daily farmers' market, appetisingly laden with jars of produce, salamis, breads and so on. Diners occupy a raised platform along one side, with views of trains coming in and out of the station. The kitchen, which admirably uses only produce from the market, offers straightforward, no-frills modern British cooking, with starters such as steamed whole crab with aïoli, or wafer-thin slices of air-dried tuna on an earthy bean purée, liberally scattered with caper berries. Main-course portions are typically generous to a fault, as in a huge hunk of crisp-skinned slow-roast belly pork set on a mound of roast root vegetables. To finish, there might be lemon posset with lemon pie, and drinks include excellent local bottled beers and fruit juices as well as a decent selection of wines from £13.

Chefs: Rafael Lopez, Robin Walker, Nick Packer, Daniel Proud and Jonathon Rodriguez **Proprietor:** Susanna Atkins **Open:** Tue to Sun L 12 to 2.30 (3 Sat and Sun), Tue to Sat D 6 to 9.30 **Closed:** 25 and 26 Dec, 1 Jan **Meals:** alc (main courses £10 to £18) **Service:** not inc **Cards:** Amex, Delta, Diners, Maestro, MasterCard, Visa **Details:** 80 seats. Car park. Vegetarian meals. Children's helpings. No-smoking area. No music

MAP 8 **CARTMEL – Cumbria**

L'Enclume

Cavendish Street, Cartmel LA11 6PZ
Tel: (015395) 36362
Website: www.lenclume.co.uk

Cooking 8 | Modern European | £69

Cartmel is reached via tortuously winding roads after you leave the motorway, a pastoral voyage of discovery that may leave you pleased you invested in that sat-nav system. L'Enclume is on a corner, a long, low, stone building with tiny windows and a neat, well-tended garden at the back, bordered by a tranquil stream. A conservatory extension for pre- and post-prandial business enjoys pleasant views over the greenery. A welter of menus is offered, rising not in stages of opulence so much as in levels of customer proficiency in the new cuisine and its increasingly esoteric terminology. If the idea of a menu dish entitled 'Fried beer, ploughman in pudding form' leaves you slack-jawed in bemusement, best start with the Introduction menu, where pea and cassia cream with almond froth and Jabugo on toast will initiate you gently into the style. This is no flimflam. Simon Rogan is undoubtedly one of the country's foremost practitioners of cutting-edge gastronomy, and the surprises that await on a journey through whichever of his menus you opt for are many. Staff are on hand to interpret the menu prose, in which each dish is given a name from the world of conceptual art.

Highlights at inspection included a serving of squab pigeon breast cooked long and low (less than 60 degrees Celsius, according to the menu), so the meat is meltingly tender, and then juxtaposed sharply with the flavours of blackcurrant and Darjeeling tea. 'Razor shell reversal, multi-coloured organic egg' turned out to be a pale blue egg (courtesy of an Old Cotswold Legbar hen), its top cut off and filled with the meat of razor clams, while the accompanying razor shell was filled with a delicate scrambled egg mixture. That fried beer was an astonishing cubic item of what tasted exactly like bitter ale on the tongue.

The various fixed-price menus are also supplemented by a carte, where some of the same compositions reappear, allowing you to progress in a more familiar rhythm through three courses – perhaps Scottish langoustine cooked in clay with spiny artichokes and spicy butter, through Goosnargh duck breast with confit gizzard, blood orange and juniper, before coming to land on an upside-down coconut soufflé. Cheeses are served in the classical manner from a trolley. If there is any small criticism to be made of the approach of L'Enclume, it is that, with so many courses on offer, and portions naturally very constrained, the overall quantity may be superbly judged, but each individual dish has barely had time to make its point before it has gone. But then there is another excitement just around the corner. The large wine list is surprisingly traditional given everything else, and focuses on France.

Chef: Simon Rogan **Proprietors:** Simon Rogan and Penny Tapsell **Open:** Wed to Sun 12 to 1.45, 7 to 9.30 **Meals:** alc (main courses £23 to £27). Set L £18 (2 courses) to £25, Set D £38 to £100 **Service:** not inc **Cards:** Amex, Delta, Diners, Maestro, MasterCard, Visa **Details:** 40 seats. Car park. Vegetarian meals. No smoking. Wheelchair access (also women's WC). No music. No mobile phones **Accommodation:** 7 rooms

MAP 2 **CASTLE COMBE –**
Wiltshire

Manor House, Bybrook Restaurant

Castle Combe SN14 7HR
Tel: (01249) 782206
Website: www.exclusivehotels.co.uk

Cooking 3 | English | £70

Just 12 miles from Bath, this fine Cotswold-stone manor house ticks all the boxes for its setting: there are carefully tended gardens, a water feature in the shape of the Bybrook, and manicured lawns (and a golf course if that is your thing). Inside, the dining room décor is elegant, and, while service can be 'intermittent', staff are 'friendly and unstuffy'. The food is in the country-house mode, with starters including a scrambled organic hen's egg with Cornish crab, chives, sevruga caviar and melba toast, and a terrine of marbled foie gras with a rhubarb and ginger compote and pepper caramel. Local produce is abundant, including purple curly kale that comes with lamb, while other main courses can be more complex, such as fillets of John Dory roasted in herbs with a fricassee of gnocchi and wild mushrooms infused with white truffle and lemon. Local farm cheeses make a fine alternative to puddings such as iced ginger nut parfait with warm oven-poached rhubarb and rhubarb sorbet. Every bottle on the brief, international wine list is served by the glass. Prices, unfortunately, are high, starting at £20, or £5 a glass.

Chef: David Campbell **Proprietor:** Exclusive Hotels **Open:** Sun to Fri L 12.30 to 2.30, all week D 7 to 10 (10.30 Sat) **Meals:** Set L Mon to Fri £20 (2 courses) to £24, Set L Sun £25, Set D £35.50 (2 courses) to £49.50. Bar menu available **Service:** not inc **Cards:** Amex, Delta, Diners, Maestro, MasterCard, Visa **Details:** 60 seats. 40 seats outside. Car park. Vegetarian meals. Children's helpings. No smoking. Wheelchair access (not WC). No music. No mobile phones **Accommodation:** 48 rooms

 This symbol means that the restaurant has elected to participate in *The Good Food Guide's* £5 voucher scheme (see 'Using The Good Food Guide' for details).

MAP 5 **CAUNTON –**
Nottinghamshire

Caunton Beck

Main Street, Caunton NG23 6AB
Tel: (01636) 636793

Cooking 2 | Modern European | £38

Apart from the odd car, bountiful birdsong and a babbling beck, this is a peaceful rural spot. Like its parent the Wig & Mitre (see entry, Lincoln), this restored and extended cottage is open all day, for drinks and snacks as well as the 'main menu'. The dining room is dotted with fresh flowers, staff are helpful and the food is 'well executed'. A warm salad of goats' cheese, baby beets and orange has been described as 'well balanced and attractive', while devilled lambs' kidneys come 'bursting with flavour'. Main courses could run from tender, moist roast chicken breast wrapped in Parma ham with Stilton and sage mash, to baked sea bass stuffed with chilli, coriander and pickled ginger. Desserts including Turkish delight with chocolate marquise, and lemon posset don't disappoint. The decent wine list offers plenty of good-value choices under £20, starting at £12.45.

Chefs: Andrew and Katie Pickstock **Proprietor:** Wig & Mitre **Open:** all week 8 to 11 **Meals:** alc (main courses £9.50 to £19). Set L Mon to Sat £11 (2 courses) to £13.95, Set D Sun to Fri £11 (2 courses) to £13.95 **Service:** not inc **Cards:** Amex, Delta, Diners, Maestro, MasterCard, Visa **Details:** 90 seats. 40 seats outside. Car park. Vegetarian meals. Children's helpings. No smoking in dining room. Wheelchair access (also WC). No music

MAP 5 **CHADDESLEY CORBETT –**
Worcestershire

Brockencote Hall

Chaddesley Corbett DY10 4PY
Tel: (01562) 777876
Website: www.brockencotehall.com

Cooking 4 | Modern French | £54

In pastoral surroundings, this 'grandish' country house is classical in style, overlooks a duck-strewn lake and sits in 70 acres of parkland. It has lounges, a terrace for sitting, and a dining room with swagged curtains and candelabra. The cooking style tends to gentle opulence, too, so that a

chicken and foie gras boudin with pancetta comes with chilled pea soup, cod fillet is accompanied by smoked haddock and saffron risotto as well as courgette fritters with parsley and caper sauce, and lamb is served as trio of moussaka, chargrilled cutlet and sautéed liver with garlic purée. A June lunch left one visitor with happy memories of accurately timed and crisp-skinned sea bass, and chocolate and griottine cherry clafoutis with pistachio ice cream. Other desserts are equally comforting: rhubarb and vanilla soufflé teamed imaginatively with gingerbread ice cream. Service may seem a little more formal than absolutely necessary, but on the whole it doesn't stand too much on ceremony, so it is 'comparatively welcoming for the genre'. Meals are supported by good bread, and a French-leaning wine list opens at £15.50.

Chef: Colin Layfield **Proprietors:** Alison and Joseph Petitjean **Open:** Sun to Fri L 12.30 to 1.30, all week D 7 to 9.30 **Meals:** alc exc Sun L (main courses £15.50 to £22.50). Set L Mon to Fri £14 (two courses) to £18, Set L Sun £24.50, Set D £32.50 to £48 **Service:** not inc **Cards:** Amex, Delta, Diners, Maestro, MasterCard, Visa **Details:** 75 seats. Car park. Vegetarian meals. Children's helpings. No smoking. Wheelchair access (also WC). Music. No mobile phones **Accommodation:** 17 rooms

MAP 1 **CHAGFORD** – Devon

22 Mill Street

22 Mill Street, Chagford TQ13 8AW
Tel: (01647) 432244

Cooking 5 | Modern European | £47

An unassuming shopfront-style façade on a side street off Chagford's main square does little to prepare you for the ambition of Duncan Walker's pint-sized restaurant-with-rooms. Settle into deep leather armchairs and make friends, if you will, with the golden retriever as you peruse the menu. Modern European is the name of the game, producing dishes such as sautéed calves' sweetbreads with braised lentils, smoked bacon and sherry vinegar to begin, followed by roast cod with crab risotto, red peppers and balsamic. Technique impresses, as in a first-course Mediterranean tart of baby plum tomatoes, pine nuts and basil on a superbly executed puff pastry base.

Main courses favour roasting, whether for guinea fowl with foie gras, or 'very fresh, succulent' monkfish with rosemary and bacon, served with good gnocchi. Timing is all, as when a pairing of poached turbot and sautéed scallops produces

perfect pearly fish and lightly browned shellfish, in cooking juices carefully enriched with a little Madeira. Puddings are simple classics rendered well, the crème caramel properly silky, a pear and almond tart moist and fragile, a hot blackcurrant soufflé nicely offset by cinnamon ice cream. Staff are adept and professional, and there is a straightforward international miscellany of wines from £15.40. Glass prices are around £4.50.

Chefs: Duncan Walker and Raphael Lapin **Proprietor:** Duncan Walker **Open:** Wed to Sat L 12.30 to 1.45, Mon to Sat D 7.30 to 9 **Meals:** Set L £22 (2 courses) to £25.50, Set D £32.50 (2 courses) to £41 **Service:** net prices **Cards:** Delta, Maestro, MasterCard, Visa **Details:** 22 seats. No smoking. Wheelchair access (not WC). Occasional music. No mobile phones **Accommodation:** 2 rooms

MAP 3 **CHANDLER'S CROSS** – Hertfordshire

The Grove, Colette's

Chandler's Cross WD3 4TG
Tel: (01923) 296015
Website: www.thegrove.co.uk

Cooking 5 | Modern European | £70

Billed as 'London's country estate', the Grove is a Grade II listed building, formerly home to the Earls of Clarendon, set in 300 acres of parkland. Facilities include a golf course, a spa, and three restaurants, Colette's being the gastronomic flagship. High ceilings and tall windows give the dining room an airy feel, while distinctive chandeliers and ornate plasterwork add a baroque touch and contribute to the overall impression of luxury.

The cooking is refined and presentation artistic but not overly fussy. A starter of crab, sevruga caviar, coriander-cured tuna and lemon dressing arrives as four mini towers on a rectangular glass plate, the subtle flavours and contrasting textures finding favour at inspection, although surpassed by a simpler dish of hot-smoked salmon with Jerusalem artichoke velouté. At the same meal, complexity prevailed in main courses. Well-timed pan-fried Dover sole with linguine, shellfish and a herb juice was an eye-catching and well-balanced dish, but the star turn was a perfectly judged combination of roast Denham Estate venison with caramelised chicory, celeriac purée, and chocolate and juniper sauce. A blackcurrant mousse topped with apple sorbet precedes desserts such as banana tarte Tatin with hot chocolate fondant and lemon-curd ice cream. An excellent range of top-class

Burgundies is the highlight of the wine list, although there are interesting bottles throughout. Even better, mark-ups have been reduced to improve the value of the more expensive bottles. Prices start at £20.

> **Chef:** Chris Harrod **Proprietor:** The Grove **Open:** Sun L 12.30 to 2.30, Mon to Sat D 7 to 10.30 **Closed:** bank hol Mon **Meals:** Set L £35, Set D £49 (2 courses) to £54 **Service:** not inc **Cards:** Amex, Delta, Diners, Maestro, MasterCard, Visa **Details:** 40 seats. Car park. Vegetarian meals. No-smoking area. Wheelchair access (also WC). Music. Air-conditioned **Accommodation:** 227 rooms

---

> **MAP 2** **CHELTENHAM – Gloucestershire**

Brasserie Blanc `AR`

The Promenade, Cheltenham GL50 1NN
Tel: (01242) 266800

Occupying the former ballroom of the Queens Hotel, the Cheltenham branch of this chain (formerly known as Petit Blanc) of informal, family-friendly brasseries (see entries in Birmingham, Manchester, Oxford and Tunbridge Wells) has a typically lively atmosphere. The menus offer broad-based modern cooking with French leanings, opening with pan-fried gnocchi with wild mushrooms, spinach and Jerusalem artichoke shavings (£7), or hot-smoked salmon with champagne choucroute and crab butter (£6.50), followed perhaps by moules marinière (£11.25), or chargrilled pork escalope with harissa and lemon butter (£14.50). Good-value set menus (£12/£14.50), decent children's meals, and mostly French wines from £12.95 a bottle. Open all week.

Brosh `NEW ENTRY`

8 Suffolk Parade, Cheltenham GL50 2AB
Tel: (01242) 227277
Website: www.broshrestaurant.co.uk

Cooking 2 | **North African-Plus** | **£40**

In a street of shops slightly out of town, Brosh favours simplicity in decoration, but is comfortable and contemporary. 'It certainly provides some exotic interest in Cheltenham,' noted an inspector. The Mediterranean meets North Africa and the Middle East on the menu, with meze served at lunchtimes: a well-flavoured pile of baba ganoush, shakshuka (a variation on ratatouille), hummus,

and 'terrific' sourdough bread among them. The dinner menu might open with brik of chicken and preserved lemons with fried aubergine in harissa, or bazargan (nut, cauliflower and radish salad with pomegranate dressing). Main courses are in similar vein – cod fillet is marinated in chermoula, 'cooked spot on', then served with tomatoes, olives, capers and couscous. Haroset ice cream, sweetly fragrant and lightly floral in character, makes an intriguing dessert, and the less adventurous could opt for cheesecake. The compact wine list starts at £12.95, and four choices by the glass are £4.50 and £5.25.

> **Chef:** Raviv Hadad **Proprietors:** Raviv and Sharon Hadad **Open:** Wed to Sat 12 to 2.30, 7 to 9.30 **Meals:** alc (main courses L £5.50 to £20, D £12 to £20) **Service:** not inc **Cards:** Delta, Maestro, MasterCard, Visa **Details:** 42 seats. 4 seats outside. Vegetarian meals. No smoking. No music

Le Champignon Sauvage

24–26 Suffolk Road, Cheltenham GL50 2AQ
Tel: (01242) 573449
Website: www.lechampignonsauvage.co.uk

Cooking 8 | **French** | **£62**

A refit in 2005 has resulted in a thorough overhaul to the Champignon. It still looks like an ordinary terraced building, on an ordinary busy street on the outskirts of the town centre, but once inside you're now in a different world. Pale maple panelling and cream walls set off the bright modern oil paintings well. Lighting is cleverly relaxing, and there is an unusually generous degree of space between tables, as though the place is enjoying stretching itself out a bit. David Everett-Matthias also rejoices at being able to swing a cat (if he so chooses) in the kitchens nowadays. This has long been one of the premier addresses in the region – in the country, indeed – and standards remain at a rarefied level. 'Admirable consistency', in the words of an inspector, is what it's about. The extraneous menu French has now gone, technical skills are honed to a flawless pitch, and there is a true sense of purpose and profundity to everything you will eat.

Scallops with cauliflower purée may have become something of a cliché elsewhere, but this is how they're done: a trio of perfectly seared specimens on smooth, intense purée, the garnish no more than apple julienne and a few pea shoots, a thin yet intense frothy stock sauce anointing the whole. All this sounds so straightforward, yet the dish is resonant and sublime. Baby squid is the partner for a serving of poached and roast

Gloucester Old Spot belly pork, the dual cooking of the meat producing textural perfection, its crisped fat offset by silky, oily mash, earthiness coming from plenty of wild mushrooms, and further crunch provided by halved water chestnuts.

Interesting ingredients abound but find their places in dishes that show them off well, so cock's kidneys are teamed with langoustines, with tortelloni of the shellfish, as a starter, while Hereford snails and ground elder go into a risotto to accompany a fillet of zander. Desserts may be only deceptively light, as was discovered in the course of an actually rather rich lemon and pine-kernel parfait, paired with fromage frais and pepper sorbet, into which a peppered tuile was stuck. Helen Everett-Matthias runs the front-of-house with assurance and is the best possible ambassador for David's cooking. The wine list is Franco-centric, but not obsessively so, and starts at the remarkable price of £11 for house French.

Chef: David Everitt-Matthias Proprietors: David and Helen Everitt-Matthias Open: Tue to Sat 12.30 to 1.30, 7.30 to 9 Closed: 10 days Christmas, 3 weeks June Meals: Set L £22 (2 courses) to £47, Set D Tue to Fri £22 (2 courses) to £47, Set D Sat £38 (2 courses) to £47 Service: not inc Cards: Amex, Delta, Diners, Maestro, MasterCard, Visa Details: 40 seats. No smoking. Wheelchair access (not WC). No music. No mobile phones

Daffodil

18–20 Suffolk Parade, Montpellier, Cheltenham GL50 2AE
Tel: (01242) 700055
Website: www.thedaffodil.co.uk

Cooking 3 | Modern European | £44

This beautiful Art Deco room (a renovated cinema) provides an ambience harking back to the golden age of movies, and a truly theatrical dining experience. Not one but two sweeping staircases, old film reels and pictures of screen stars from days of yore all add to the unique setting. The food, however, is right up to date, with contemporary, accurately timed dishes that amble around Europe. Warm asparagus and carrot brisé tart with marinated artichokes and crispy leeks, fillet of red snapper with spiced red pepper wild rice, or roast duck breast with wasabi-flavoured mash, and pear and brown sugar cheesecake might all appear on the dinner menu. Lunch brings much of the same: devilled kidneys in puff pastry followed by pan-fried salmon with a dill and mustard sauce, for instance. Service is courteous, with athletic waiters negotiating the stairs, and there's live jazz on Mondays. The reasonable wine list comprises

nearly 40 bins, starting at £13.50 a bottle, with eight by the glass from £4 to £5.50.

Chef: Mark Davidson Proprietor: Marcel Frichot Open: Mon to Sat 12 to 2.30, 6 to 9.30 (10 Sat) Meals: alc D (main courses £12 to £19). Set L £12 (2 courses) to £14.50, Set D Mon £15 (2 courses) to £18.95, Set D Mon to Sat £28 Service: not inc Cards: Amex, Delta, Maestro, MasterCard, Visa Details: 140 seats. Vegetarian meals. Children's helpings. No smoking. Wheelchair access (also WC). Music. Air-conditioned

Lumière

Clarence Parade, Cheltenham GL50 3PA
Tel: (01242) 222200
Website: www.lumiere.cc

Cooking 5 | Global | £51

The restaurant may not be in the loveliest part of lovely Cheltenham, but, once through the door and into the stylish, oyster-hued dining room, people tend to become willing converts. This is thanks in large part to Lin Chapman's 'vivacious, genuinely friendly and caring approach'. Nothing escapes her notice, and she is a great advocate for Geoff's accomplished cooking. A gentle hint of Pacific north-western style to the food reflects the owners' Canadian origins. Sea bass is partnered by sweet chilli tiger prawns and tomato pasta as one possible starter, while a main course of black bream fillet might come with lemon, shrimp and crab bisque.

An inspection dish that teamed a fine smoked haddock cake with giant-sized seared scallops and intense leek sauce was a pretty persuasive opener, and fillet of springbok is a regular, perhaps adorned with sweet onion mash, wild mushrooms and a red wine sauce. Simple dessert constructions are enjoyed, as when a cup with a layer of ginger biscuit crumbs at the bottom is filled with a pair of ices or sorbets (banana and bitter chocolate have particularly impressed), and topped with frothed coffee cream. The wine list is kept in a productive state of flux, with guest wines supplementing the intelligent and tempting core listings. Notes are good and witty (Planeta Chardonnay from Sicily is described as being like 'Meursault on steroids'), and if the mark-ups seem a trifle keen the options by the glass at around £3 to £4 are worth enquiring about.

Chef: Geoff Chapman Proprietors: Lin and Geoff Chapman Open: Tue to Sat D only 7 to 8.45 Closed: first 2 weeks Jan, 2 weeks late summer Meals: Set D Tue to Thur £29.50 (2 courses) to £36, Set D Fri and Sat £36 Service: not inc Cards: Maestro, MasterCard, Visa Details: 28 seats. Unsuitable for very small children. No smoking. No music. No mobile phones. Air-conditioned

Mayflower

32–34 Clarence Street, Cheltenham GL50 3NX
Tel: (01242) 522426

The Mayflower, a 25-year-old family-run Chinese restaurant, now has a second branch in Cirencester. The formula is the same at both, with the long menus sticking to popular tried and tested dishes, with a wide choice of set meals for those who want to make choosing easier. Starters include the likes of crispy fried won tons (£6.50) and minced king prawn wrapped in lettuce (£9.95), while main dishes range from duck with bamboo shoots and Chinese mushrooms (£11.95) to Szechuan seafood hotpot (£13.95). A decent wine list starts at £14.95. Open all week.

MAP 7 **CHESTER – Cheshire**

Brasserie 10/16

Brookdale Place, Chester CH1 3DY
Tel: (01244) 322288

This is a buzzy modern brasserie that explores the globe with starters including an oriental platter to share (£9.50), but is also happy to stay closer to home with potted duck, potato and foie gras with beetroot chutney (£6.25). Signature main courses include fillet of sea bass with crab and tomato risotto and tapenade (£16.75), and rump of lamb niçoise (£15.95), while the extensive dessert menu boasts Cheshire farm ice creams (from £3.95) and profiteroles with hot chocolate sauce (£3.95). There are 'lite' lunches from £2.95. House wines are £9.95. Open all week. Related to the Hawarden Brasserie (see entry, Wales).

Chester Grosvenor, Arkle

Eastgate, Chester CH1 1LT
Tel: (01244) 324024
Website: www.chestergrosvenor.com

Cooking 7 | **European** | **£78**

Slap-bang in the middle of Chester, the Grosvenor has long been one of the city's prize assets. Owned by the Dukes of Westminster, it's a luxy hotel in the old-fashioned manner, full of uniformed, punctilious staff and, at its heart, a grand dining room that does the overall ambience justice. Pictures of the eponymous racehorse adorn the Arkle restaurant, where the expensive, sleek tone is enlivened by modern design features like tall chairs, and the cooking, by Simon Radley, changes with the seasons. An emphasis on seafood invests the starter selection with good value, producing Devon crab with pressed tomatoes, avocado sorbet and basil jelly, or a pairing of snails and scallops in a parsley and garlic coulis. It is expected that we will take meat and fish combinations in our stride by now, so there's a main course of veal blanquette with langoustine tails, accompanied by braised veal cheek and a crisp sweetbread beignet, while turbot, baby squid and sweet clams come with chorizo and what the menu calls a 'whiz' of smoked pimento and saffron.

A lot of cheffy technique is mobilised for the oddball desserts, which take in warm chocolate liquid cake with pistachio cream and pink grapefruit, or vanilla squash blossom fritter with poached rhubarb, a macaroon and beets. If experimentation rules the culinary repertoire, rest assured that the wine list is as old school as can be. Masses of French stuff – including runs of Dom Pérignon and Romanée-Conti – will intimidate the uninitiated, but there are enterprising explorations of Spain and California, and good South African growers too. Prices are generally tough, but there is some relief below £25, and wines by the glass start at £4.95. La Brasserie, also in the hotel, is well worth knowing about, and is open for breakfast, lunch and dinner.

Chef: Simon Radley **Proprietor:** Duke of Westminster Estate
Open: Tue to Sat D only 7 to 9.30 **Meals:** Set D £55 to £65
Service: 12.5% **Cards:** Amex, Delta, Maestro, MasterCard, Visa **Details:** 50 seats. No children under 12. Jacket. No smoking. Wheelchair access (also WC). No music. No mobile phones. Air-conditioned **Accommodation:** 80 rooms

Locus

NEW ENTRY

111 Boughton, Chester CH3 5BH
Tel: (01244) 311112
Website: www.locustheplace.co.uk

Cooking 1 | **Modern British** | **£37**

Locus is a great example of a pub turned modern neighbourhood restaurant. The bar area boasts African slate flooring, while in the dining room dark wooden tables, ambient lighting and large abstract paintings give a pleasant, relaxed effect. Andrew Smyth cooks in the modern idiom, turning out starters of 'well-executed' salmon and haddock fishcakes with lemon mayonnaise, and a well-balanced dish of seared scallops with a white crabmeat and coriander cake and tomato ragoût.

Pork and herb terrine wrapped in bacon with gooseberry compote may be followed by corn-fed chicken in Parma ham on a fricassee of oyster mushrooms and haricots blancs in a light mustard cream. Enjoyable desserts have included 'clever' white chocolate and mango custard topped with mascarpone cheesecake. Service is relaxed but efficient, and the globetrotting wine list holds much of interest, with a good range of styles in the seven house wines, priced at £11.95 and £12.25.

Chef: Andrew Smyth Proprietors: Andrew and Sally Smyth Open: Tue to Sun D only 6 to 10 Closed: 25 and 26 Dec, 1 to 12 Jan, bank hol Mon Meals: alc exc Sun D (main courses £12 to £16). Set D Tue to Thur £11.95 (2 courses), Set D Sun £13.95 (2 courses) to £15.95 Service: not inc Cards: Amex, Delta, Diners, Maestro, MasterCard, Visa Details: 42 seats. Car park. Vegetarian meals. No smoking. Wheelchair access (also WC). Music

MAP 9 CHESTERFIELD – Derbyshire

Old Post AR

43 Holywell Street, Chesterfield S41 7SH
Tel: (01246) 279479

A fifteenth-century town-centre property is the setting for Hugh Cocker's ambitious and fairly complex modern British cooking. Among starters might be crispy duck confit caramelised in crab apple jelly served with watercress and blood orange salad (£5.95), and broad bean and Coulommiers cheese risotto with toasted goats' cheese and watercress oil (£6.25). Follow perhaps with wild sea bass fillet with merguez sausage mash, seared scallops and sauce vierge (£20.95), finish with something like crunchy banana and butterscotch pancakes, and drink house wine at £12.95. Closed Sat L, Sun D and Mon.

MAP 2 CHETTLE – Dorset

Castleman Hotel

Chettle DT11 8DB
Tel: (01258) 830096
Website: www.castlemanhotel.co.uk

Cooking 2 | Modern British | £32

Formerly the dower house of the local manor, the Castleman is a substantial building, partly of rough grey stone, partly plastered. Inside, abundant antiques and an old-fashioned décor give an air of faded gentility, but the mood is relaxed and unstuffy, with affable service overseen by owner Edward Bourke. The cooking is of no fixed gastronomic abode, taking in ideas from far and wide, old and new, to come up with starters ranging from devilled lambs' kidneys on a croûton to pan-fried cod fillet on a warm salad of white beans, chorizo and olives. Among main courses, roast loin of venison with a mushroom and port sauce and rösti appear next to roast guinea fowl breast glazed with chilli jam on Puy lentils with chorizo. Dessert might be chilled creamy rice pudding with poached apricots. The wine list balances quality and value admirably well across the board, from easy-drinking house Chilean red and white at £11 through to a selection of keenly priced vintage clarets.

Chefs: Barbara Garnsworthy and Richard Morris Proprietors: Edward Bourke and Barbara Garnsworthy Open: Sun L 12.30 to 1.30, all week D 7 to 9.30 Closed: 25, 26 and 31 Dec, Feb Meals: alc D (main courses £9 to £17.50). Set L Sun £20 Service: not inc Cards: MasterCard, Visa Details: 40 seats. Car park. Vegetarian meals. Children's helpings. No smoking in dining room. Wheelchair access (also WC). No music Accommodation: 8 rooms

MAP 2 CHICHESTER – West Sussex

Comme Ça AR

67 Broyle Road, Chichester PO19 6BD
Tel: (01243) 788724

The pre- and post-theatre crowd is attracted to this charming establishment just across the road from the Chichester Festival Theatre. The evening carte is Gallic through and through, with a tartlet of Selsey crab (£6.45), followed by roast tenderloin of pork wrapped in Parma ham with a cassoulet-style garnish (£14.55), or grilled fillet of salmon with Noilly Prat and sorrel velouté (£14.55), and Williams pear poached in red wine (£5.95). Wines from £14.75. Open Wed to Sun L and Tue to Sat D.

AR — Not a full entry but provisionally recommended. These 'also recommended' establishments are integrated throughout the book.

MAP 3 **CHIEVELEY – Berkshire**

Crab at Chieveley

Wantage Road, Chieveley RG20 8UE
Tel: (01635) 247550
Website: www.crabatchieveley.com

| Cooking 2 | Seafood | £52 |

You won't hear a gently lapping wave or spot a seagull anywhere near this seafood restaurant, but the Crab manages to draw the crowds with its dedicated seafood menu. Inside, the décor is decidedly nautical, with fishing nets, cork floats and shells hanging from the ceiling. Fish comes in daily from Brixham, Looe and Newlyn, and the restaurant also has a two-acre vegetable garden. Starters could be anything from creamed mussel and saffron soup with wild sorrel to poached Carlingford Lough oysters or sautéed squid with a sweet Tuscan salad. Continue with mustard-crusted turbot with gravad lax sauce and crushed potatoes or roast monkfish with Jerusalem artichokes and a fricassee of wild mushrooms. Meat eaters have Goosnargh chicken breast with Parmesan gnocchi to satisfy their cravings. Vanilla pannacotta with passion-fruit jelly and blackcurrant sorbet makes a refreshing end. House wines are £16, or £3.50 a glass.

Chef: David Horridge **Proprietor:** David Barnard **Open:** all week 12 to 2.30, 6 to 10 **Meals:** alc (main courses £10.50 to £37). Set L and D 6 to 7 £16.50 (2 courses) to £19.50 **Service:** not inc **Cards:** Amex, Delta, Maestro, MasterCard, Visa **Details:** 120 seats. 60 seats outside. Car park. Vegetarian meals. Children's helpings. No smoking. Wheelchair access (also WC). No music. Air-conditioned **Accommodation:** 17 rooms

MAP 3 **CHIGWELL – Essex**

Bluebell

117 High Road, Chigwell IG7 6QQ
Tel: (020) 8500 6282
Website: www.thebluebellrestaurant.co.uk

| Cooking 3 | Modern European | £44 |

Reports have branded the Bluebell a great neighbourhood asset, and indeed there's a good buzz about this place. Inside the 400-year-old walls there are two dining areas just beyond the cosy sofas and bar area. The kitchen takes a tour around Europe and beyond, so you might choose from tandoori-style chicken with mint yoghurt, grilled

herb-crusted fillet of Brixham cod with Chablis sauce, and sea bream with pak choi and a soy and sesame dressing. Start, perhaps, with deep-fried Cromer crab cake with a jalapeño and white onion salsa, and move on to a simple grilled fillet of beef with chips and a brandy and mustard sauce, or the more complex roast boneless guinea fowl stuffed with a tomato and basil mousse. Finish with classic crème brûlée or the flamboyance of caramelised apples flamed with Calvados and accompanied by crisp filo pastry and crème anglaise. The short wine list manages to cover a lot of ground. House French is £12.95, £3.50 a glass.

Chef: Paul Korten **Proprietor:** Gregory Molen **Open:** Tue to Fri and Sun L 12 to 2, Tue to Sat D 6.45 to 10 **Meals:** alc D (main courses £15 to £20). Set L Tue to Fri £12.95 (2 courses), Set L Sun £21.95 **Service:** not inc **Cards:** Amex, Delta, Maestro, MasterCard, Visa **Details:** 95 seats. Vegetarian meals. Children's helpings. No cigars/pipes in dining room. Wheelchair access (not WC). Occasional music. Air-conditioned

MAP 2 **CHINNOR – Oxfordshire**

Sir Charles Napier

Sprigg's Alley, Chinnor OX39 4BX
Tel: (01494) 483011
Website: www.sircharlesnapier.co.uk

| Cooking 4 | Modern European | £49 |

Truly an assault on all senses, this Chilterns' restaurant mixes the old and the new with creativity, imagination and assurance. The terrace is a joy on a warm day, while the eye is entertained by Michael Cooper's sculptures, including a giant snail by the lake. The dining room is a relaxed affair, with green walls, lots of wood and a genteel air, appealing to a wide age group. Richard Burkert's team produces consistently interesting dishes, which push the boundaries just far enough to offer a sensory ride without getting too complicated. The handwritten menus include lots of fish (Julie Griffiths is a champion of Fairford's market in Gloucestershire, where they source their produce), so smoked trout on a potato pancake with mustard and dill dressing, and seared tuna with aubergine caviar jostle for attention among starters, while main courses could feature fillet of sea bream with mussels or perhaps rack of lamb with broad beans, capers and garlic cream. Desserts intrigue: peach soup with champagne sorbet, and espresso crème brûlée with biscotti, for instance. Wines are a diverse, well-chosen bunch, with plenty of choice under £20, and intelligent introductions to the various regions.

Chef: Richard Burkert **Proprietor:** Julie Griffiths **Open:** Tue to Sun L 12 to 2.30 (3.30 Sun), Tue to Sat D 6.30 to 10 **Closed:** 3 days Christmas **Meals:** alc (main courses £15.50 to £21). Set L Tue to Fri £15.50 (2 courses), Set D Tue to Fri £16.50 (2 courses) **Service:** 12.5% (optional) **Cards:** Amex, Delta, Diners, Maestro, MasterCard, Visa **Details:** 70 seats. 70 seats outside. Car park. Vegetarian meals. No children under 6 at D. Children's helpings. No smoking in 1 dining room. Wheelchair access (not WC). Music. Air-conditioned

Chef: Jamie Foreman **Proprietors:** Christa and Ian Taylor **Open:** Sun L 12 to 2.30, all week D 7 to 9.30 **Meals:** Set L £27.50, Set D £35 (2 courses) to £45. Brasserie menu available **Service:** 12.5% **Cards:** Amex, Delta, MasterCard, Visa **Details:** 46 seats. 30 seats outside. Car park. Vegetarian meals. Children's helpings. No smoking. Wheelchair access (also WC). Occasional music. No mobile phones. Air-conditioned **Accommodation:** 29 rooms

---

MAP 5 CHIPPING CAMPDEN – Gloucestershire

Cotswold House, Juliana's

The Square, Chipping Campden GL55 6AN
Tel: (01386) 840330
Website: www.cotswoldhouse.com

Cooking 5 | Modern British | £59

This handsome Georgian-fronted hotel is in the centre of one of the prettiest Cotswolds towns, its smart urban conversion tailor-made for the gentrified affluence of Chipping Campden. This is especially so of the dining room, the cosmopolitan air of which is tempered by starched tablecloths and dark wooden walls. It offers a compact, modern carte incorporating lively ideas and good supplies. The short roll-call of well-sourced ingredients includes Cornish crab (served as a starter with tomato fondue and fennel and cress salad), Buccleuch Estate beef fillet, and line-caught sea bass (with palourde clams, fennel purée and sauce antibiose). A preference for rich earthy flavours is apparent in a terrine of suckling pig and black pudding with apple purée and haricot beans, and in a main course of honey-glazed Gressingham duck with confit leg and baby beetroots, but the scope of the menu is sufficient to take in lighter options, such as nage of seafood with young vegetables, tomatoes and herbs. An impressive selection of British and Irish cheeses provides a savoury alternative to inventive desserts such as citrus soufflé with gin and tonic sorbet, or warm apple samosa with liquorice bavarois. Prices are not the cheapest, and that goes for wine as well as food, the extensive list offering plenty of quality but few bargains. Prices start at £15.

MAP 2 CHRISTCHURCH – Dorset

FishWorks

10 Church Street, Christchurch BH23 1BW
Tel: (01202) 487000
Website: www.fishworks.co.uk

Cooking 3 | Seafood | £48

The combination of fishmonger plus a dining room is proving popular, so much so that Mitchell Tonks now heads a small chain across southern England (see entries for Bath, Bristol and London). This branch, in a pretty pedestrianised street, offers the added charm of being close to Christchurch Priory. Diners can choose a whole fish to share from the counter or go for the carte, where all manner of things piscatorial are delivered in a fashionably modern manner: simple starters of crab with mayonnaise, say, or scallops with lemon and parsley, with main courses of baked sea bass with roast garlic, rosemary, chilli and olive oil, or classic roast skate served with black butter and capers. Deliveries arrive daily, mostly from the catch at Brixham, so the specials board is worth checking, while platters of fruits de mer offer a crash course in marine biology. Desserts are not a highlight. House wines from £17.90.

Chef: Nick Davies **Proprietor:** FishWorks plc **Open:** Tue to Sat 12 to 2.15, 6 to 9.45 **Closed:** bank hols and day after bank hols **Meals:** alc (main courses £13 to £50) **Service:** not inc **Cards:** Amex, Delta, Maestro, MasterCard, Visa **Details:** 44 seats. Vegetarian meals. Children's helpings. No smoking. Music

To submit a report on any restaurant, please visit *www.which.co.uk/gfgfeedback*.

MAP 2 **CHRISTMAS COMMON –**
Oxfordshire

Fox and Hounds   NEW ENTRY

Christmas Common OX49 5HL
Tel: (01491) 612599

Cooking 3 | Modern British | £40

A tiny village in pretty countryside noted for its Christmas tree farms is home to this brick and flint pub. It's good and traditional inside: fireplaces, pictures on the walls, and a mixture of stripped-pine and oak furniture. Kieron Daniels, who also owns the Three Tuns in nearby Henley-on-Thames, works the stoves and creates a classic gastro-pub menu that feature 'wholesome, hearty and unshowy' dishes. Chicken and asparagus soup is a 'beautifully simple' way to start, while Cornish hake, served with chorizo, chunks of boiled potato, green olives and gazpacho dressing, is a well-thought-out combination. Alternatives might be a seasonal starter of griddled asparagus with aged feta and salsa verde, followed by Gressingham duck breast, rare and tender, with an endive, bacon and cheese gratin. Reporters are full of praise for desserts of rhubarb parfait with roast rhubarb, and apple crumble tart with crisp pastry. The wine list is pretty brief, numbering around 25 bottles, but manages to cram in a variety of styles, from Argentinian Malbec (£15) to Pinot Gris from California's Russian River Valley (£38).

> **Chef/Proprietor:** Kieron Daniels **Open:** all week 12 to 2.30, 7 to 9.30 **Closed:** 25 Dec, D 31 Dec **Meals:** alc (main courses £11 to £18) **Service:** not inc **Cards:** Delta, Maestro, MasterCard, Visa **Details:** 60 seats. 45 seats outside. Car park. Vegetarian meals. Children's helpings. No smoking in 1 dining room. Wheelchair access (also WC). Music

MAP 7 **CHURCH STRETTON –**
Shropshire

The Studio   AR

59 High Street, Church Stretton SY6 6BY
Tel: (01694) 722672

The sign outside in the shape of a palette is a reminder that this terraced restaurant was once an artist's studio. Inside, there is an air of domesticity, and the menu takes on reliable bistro favourites: French onion soup with Gruyère (£4.50) or

smoked salmon with lemon crème fraîche (£6.50) to start, followed by breast of Barbary duck with Puy lentils and a red wine and thyme jus (£13.95) or pan-fried fillets of sea bass with a sauce of white wine, saffron and mussels (£14.50). Finish with a duo of coffee and vanilla crème brûlée (£4.50). Wines from £11.95. Open Tue to Sat D only.

MAP 5 **CLEEVE HILL –**
Gloucestershire

Malvern View Hotel

Cleeve Hill GL52 3PR   NEW ENTRY
Tel: (01242) 672017
Website: www.malvern-viewhotel.co.uk

Cooking 3 | Modern British | £47

Paul and Anna Hackett have swapped the rustic Yew Tree Inn at Clifford's Mesne in Gloucestershire for a smart restaurant-with-rooms on the outskirts of Cheltenham. It's comfortably appointed throughout, with the focal point the bright dining room where generous, well-spaced tables look on to the garden, with seasonal views of the Malverns (when the leaves have dropped). Paul's cooking, a well-travelled take on modern British, which emphasises local produce, delivers largely straightforward dishes along the lines of a satay chicken salad with 'good depth of flavour', and an 'extremely light' salmon fishcake gently infused with dill, topped with fried cod and served with a light, creamy sauce dotted with a few cockles and mussels, or pan-fried lambs' liver with braised shoulder and spring onion mash, pearl barley and wine sauce. The chef's assiette of desserts for sharing (baked Malibu cheesecake, lemon tart, spiced ice cream, dark chocolate fondant and white chocolate ice cream) makes for a good finish. Service from Anna Hackett is welcoming and enthusiastic and the wine list offers good variety, excellent value and plenty of choice by the glass.

> **Chef:** Paul Hackett **Proprietors:** Paul and Anna Hackett **Open:** Wed to Sun L 12 to 2, Tue to Sat D 7 to 9 **Meals:** alc (main courses L £10 to £18, D £18 to £22). Set L £15.95 (2 courses), Set D (exc Sat) £25 **Service:** not inc **Cards:** Delta, Maestro, MasterCard **Details:** 35 seats. 16 seats outside. Car park. Vegetarian meals. Children's helpings. No smoking. Wheelchair access (not WC). Music **Accommodation:** 4 rooms

> This symbol means that the wine list is well above the average.

MAP 6   CLIPSHAM – Rutland

Olive Branch

Main Street, Clipsham LE15 7SH
Tel: (01780) 410355
Website: www.theolivebranchpub.com

Cooking 3 | Modern British | £39

Low ceilings coupled with small rooms centred around a bar give a distinctly homely atmosphere to the Olive Branch. The menu, however, has a more contemporary feel. Raw materials are good, and the menu is not so long on ingredients that it loses focus. Starters such as roast scallops with black pudding mash and red wine jus feature 'perfectly cooked' bivalves, while rigatoni with rocket, pine nuts and Parmesan proves to be a 'simple, rustic dish'. Similarly, a main course of roast breast of chicken with fondant potato and a sherry and morel sauce, and chargrilled ribeye with béarnaise and chips have been appreciated precisely for their straightforwardness. These are well-judged dishes, admirable in their restraint and balance, and that sense of perception is sustained into desserts such as steamed ginger sponge with tangerine ripple ice cream. Exemplary value distinguishes the wine list, which darts about the globe in search of interesting flavours, kicking off with house wines from France at £12.50. Around ten are sold by the glass from £3.

Chef: Sean Hope Proprietors: Ben Jones and Sean Hope
Open: all week 12 to 2 (3 Sun), 7 (6 Fri) to 9.30 (9 Sun)
Meals: alc (main courses £7.50 to £19). Set L Mon to Sat £14 (2 courses) to £16.50, Set L Sun £19. Snack L menu available Mon to Sat Service: not inc Cards: Delta, Maestro, MasterCard, Visa Details: 48 seats. 24 seats outside. Car park. Vegetarian meals. Children's helpings. No smoking in 1 dining room. Wheelchair access (also WC). Music Accommodation: 6 rooms

MAP 10   COCKERMOUTH – Cumbria

Quince & Medlar

11–13 Castlegate, Cockermouth CA13 9EU
Tel: (01900) 823579

Cooking 4 | Vegetarian | £36

'Country style on a budget, but that's country without any chintz or dried flowers': a fair description of Colin and Louisa Le Voi's small and very personal enterprise. Run as a restaurant with a mission, it stands out as 'a real one-off'. The food is strictly vegetarian, but any preconceptions have to be left aside. A short, inventive menu takes in Mediterranean, Middle Eastern and Asian influences, and there are no nut rissoles here. Expect dishes such as intensely flavoured broad bean and green olive tapenade with crostini, or a thin, crisp, buttery tartlet filled with fennel, leek, feta and goats' cheese. Main courses might turn up a 'nutty nest' of cashews, grated parsnip and bulgur wheat with red onion marmalade and crème fraîche or Middle Eastern pancakes with sweet potato and oyster mushrooms served with a creamy mustard sauce. Desserts have included a 'light and utterly delightful' date and banana pudding, and layered rhubarb with toasted breadcrumbs, muscovado sugar and cinnamon. 'Calm, attentive, thoughtful and helpful' just about sums up the service, and the wine list has garnered organic wines from all over the world, starting with French house wine at £11.50.

Chef/Proprietors: Colin and Louisa Le Voi Open: Tue to Sat D only 7 to 9.30 Closed: 24 to 26 Dec Meals: alc (main courses £14) Service: not inc Cards: Delta, Maestro, MasterCard, Visa Details: No children under 5. 26 seats. No smoking. Wheelchair access (not WC). Music

MAP 2   CODFORD ST PETER – Wiltshire

George Hotel

High Street, Codford St Peter BA12 0NG
Tel: (01985) 850270

Cooking 4 | Modern British | £36

It still has the air of a true village local, albeit with bar lunches running from posh sandwiches made with home-made bread – roast lamb and mint sauce, say, or bacon and Brie – to a platter of smoked salmon, fish and chips, and a full three-course affair. With an unpretentious, contemporary look, this all adds up to a distinctive yet relaxed atmosphere. Boyd McIntosh's modern menu, showcasing local produce, reveals realistic ambition, and the resulting clear focus is much appreciated, especially in the evening when dinner in the restaurant could bring starters of caramelised scallops with crispy Parma ham and Bloody Mary dressing, or a tian of crayfish with spicy lime mayonnaise, before moving on to roast rack of new season's lamb with roast garlic and a minted jus, or roast fillet of line-caught sea bass with sautéed cucumber, English asparagus, and a chive and scallop cream. Service, led by Joanne Fryer, is 'friendly, eager to help', while the thoroughly accessible wine list kicks off at £12.95.

Chefs: Boyd McIntosh and James King Cole Proprietors: Boyd McIntosh and Joanne Fryer Open: Wed to Mon L 12 to 2, Mon and Wed to Sat D 7 to 9 Meals: alc (main courses £8 to £17) Service: not inc Cards: Delta, Maestro, MasterCard, Visa Details: 50 seats. 24 seats outside. Car park. Children's helpings. No smoking in 1 dining room. Music Accommodation: 3 rooms

---

MAP 3 COGGESHALL – Essex

Baumanns Brasserie `AR`

4-6 Stoneham Street, CO6 1TT
Tel: (01376) 561453

'Like dining in a small art gallery,' wrote one diner of this informal brasserie in the centre of town. The L-shaped dining room is full of mismatched dining chairs, while the tables are covered in white damask cloths. The wide-ranging menu takes inspiration from around the globe. Button mushroom popcorn on toasted ginger bread with lime mayonnaise (£6.95) is typical of starters, and could be followed by Moroccan-style braised lamb shank with harissa and onion mash (£17.50), or more mainstream toad-in-the-hole with a rich red wine gravy (£16.50). Puddings can be as inventive as saké-poached pears with warm chocolate sauce and pistachio ice cream (£6.50). A list of around 40 wines opens with Duboeuf at £11.50. Open Wed to Sun.

MAP 2 COLERNE – Wiltshire

Lucknam Park

Colerne SN14 8AZ
Tel: (01225) 742777
Website: www.lucknampark.co.uk

Cooking 6 | Modern European | £75

The park is comprised of 500 acres of prime Wiltshire, with corporate facilities in profusion. At its centre is a Palladian mansion dating from 1720,

all classical gravitas and majestic enough to have given over its one-time ballroom, with its four chandeliers, to do service as the restaurant. Full-drop windows and Venetian mirrors reinforce the grandeur, although the live guitarist might come as a surprise.

Hywel Jones once cooked at the Foliage restaurant in London's Mandarin Oriental (see entry) and has brought the same level of nerveless panache to the kitchen here. The emphasis, unusually for this sort of setting, is very much on the main menu dishes; such is the confidence in the essential elements that no need is felt to add pre-starters and pre-desserts as well. Organic Devon duck is given star billing among first courses, appearing in a variety of guises, including a ballottine with mushrooms and chutney wrapped in Parma ham, alongside caramelised orange. Even though dishes might involve a number of components, the overall feeling remains one of considered lightness, as in a starter of grilled red mullet, served with a couple of crab fritters, a compote of fennel and peppers, fennel purée and tapenade. A main course that excelled at inspection involved tender local lamb, the loin roasted, the shoulder slowly cooked and wrapped in vertically presented cannelloni, with baby artichokes in a light jus gras. The separate vegetarian menu might offer truffled risotto with a confit of ceps and truffle honey. Desserts keep presentations simple, so that a délices of white chocolate comes topped with a chocolate and pistachio log and segments of blood orange, while a trio of passion-fruit items takes in a mousse, a sorbet and an impeccably delicate soufflé. Staff impress for their lack of hauteur, and France is the backbone of the wine list, which offers little under £20.

Chef: Hywel Jones Proprietor: Lucknam Park Hotels Ltd Open: Sun L 12.30 to 2.30, all week D 7 to 10 Meals: Set L £30, Set D £55. Light menu available Service: not inc Cards: Amex, Delta, Diners, Maestro, MasterCard, Visa Details: 80 seats. Car park. Vegetarian meals. No children under 5. Children's helpings. No smoking. Wheelchair access (also WC). Occasional music. No mobile phones Accommodation: 41 rooms

---

NEW ENTRY	This appears after the restaurant's name if the establishment was not a main entry in last year's Guide. Please note, however, it may have been 'also recommended' in the previous edition.

MAP 5   COLWALL STONE – Herefordshire

Colwall Park

NEW ENTRY

Walwyn Road, Colwall Stone WR13 6QG
Tel: (01684) 540000
Website: www.colwall.com

Cooking 2 | Modern British | £46

Malvern's famous spring water is bottled only 50 metres from this charming hotel, which has great views over the hills. The elegant oak-panelled dining room features two impressive wrought-iron chandeliers, while service is 'highly efficient, bright and watchful'. Chef James Garth puts a great deal of effort into making everything himself, from breads and ice creams through to gravad lax and piccalilli. Raw materials are superb throughout, as in a starter of 'fresh and meaty' pan-seared hand-dived scallops with 'soft, silky' sweet potato purée and crisp Parma ham, a dish that exemplifies the unpretentious modern British cooking style. Similarly, a main course of roast loin of Cotswold venison has featured 'hugely tasty meat with a great texture'. Finish with melting dark chocolate pudding or perhaps the British cheeseboard, typically featuring Hereford red and Old Worcester white. A French-focused wine list starts at £13.50.

> **Chef:** James Garth **Proprietors:** Iain and Sarah Nesbitt **Open:** all week 12 to 2, 7 to 9 (L by reservation only) **Meals:** alc D (main courses £17.50 to £20). Set L £15.95 (2 courses) to £19.95, Set D £19.95 (2 courses) to £24.95 **Service:** not inc **Cards:** Maestro, MasterCard, Visa **Details:** 40 seats. Car park. Vegetarian meals. Children's helpings. Wheelchair access (also WC). Music. Air-conditioned **Accommodation:** 22 rooms

MAP 3   COOKHAM – Berkshire

Manzano's

19–21 Station Hill Parade, Cookham SL6 9BR
Tel: (01628) 525775

Cooking 3 | Spanish/Mediterranean | £47

A white canopy emblazoned with the restaurant's name picks Manzano's out from the other shopfronts near the station, while, inside, the white walls are hung with large mirrors, chairs are uphol-stered and the tables are covered in white cloths. It's unpretentious but welcoming, while the menu is modern Mediterranean with Spanish influences. Look out for king prawns with garlic and saffron mayonnaise, sliced lambs' kidneys in sherry sauce, or the speciality of paella. Otherwise, gazpacho, and a rustic salad of chorizo, plum tomatoes and butter beans with a honey and mustard dressing are typical starters, while main courses could be anything from bouillabaisse to traditional Castilian-style lamb, slowly roasted in a wood-fired oven. Richard serves 'my dad's crème caramel' for dessert as well as chocolate cream truffle with raspberry purée. Spain exerts a heavy influence on the wine list, which also offers some New World and other European bottles. Prices start at £14.95.

> **Chef:** Richard Manzano **Proprietors:** Richard and Deena Manzano **Open:** Mon to Fri L 12.30 to 2, Mon to Sat D 7 to 9.30 **Closed:** 1 week Christmas, 2 weeks Aug, bank hols **Meals:** Set L £13.50 (2 courses), Set D £27.50 (2 courses) to £31.50. Tapas menu available Mon to Fri L and Mon to Thur D **Service:** 12.5% **Cards:** Delta, Maestro, MasterCard, Visa **Details:** 36 seats. 12 seats outside. Car park. Vegetarian meals. Children's helpings. Wheelchair access (not WC). Occasional music. Air-conditioned

MAP 3   COOKHAM DEAN – Berkshire

Inn on the Green

The Old Cricket Common, Cookham Dean SL6 9NZ
Tel: (01628) 482638
Website: www.theinnonthegreen.com

Cooking 4 | Modern British | £54

An ordinary-looking mock-Tudor pub on the outside, it's certainly different inside. The rambling building confounds expectations with a rural-chic blend of rich colours, bare brick, log fires, and leather sofas. Garry Hollihead (see Embassy, London) oversees the menus, offering up-to-the-minute but unpretentious cooking. While there is a perfectly sound classical foundation to the cooking – in the shape of terrine of foie gras with port jelly, fish soup with rouille, or roast fillet of beef with buttered runner beans, potato galette, and foie gras jus – the food is not without a bit of spice: stir-fried vegetables, sesame seeds and sweet chilli sauce accompany pan-fried cod, and sautéed fillet of sea bass comes with sauerkraut. Finish with apple and raisin crumble with custard. Classy

French wines dominate the short list, but prices rise steeply from the £14.50 starting point.

Chef: Garry Hollihead Proprietors: Mark Fuller and Garry Hollihead Open: Sun L 1 to 4, Tue to Sat D 7 to 10 Meals: alc exc Sun L (main courses £12 to £22). Set L Sun £19.95 (2 courses) to £23.50. Set D Tue to Fri £16.95 (2 courses) to £19.95 Service: 12.5% (optional) Cards: Amex, Delta, Maestro, MasterCard, Visa Details: 64 seats. 100 seats outside. Car park. Vegetarian meals. Children's helpings. No smoking. Wheelchair access (also WC). Music. No mobile phones. Air-conditioned Accommodation: 9 rooms

---

MAP 5 **CORSE LAWN –**
Gloucestershire

Corse Lawn House

Corse Lawn GL19 4LZ
Tel: (01452) 780771
Website: www.corselawn.com

| Cooking 3 | Anglo-French | £48 |

After Denis Hine's death in April 2005, his widow Baba has eased herself out of her long-standing kitchen role after 28 years to work front-of-house. Otherwise, this gentrified hotel continues to be run much along the same lines, with Baba's co-chef of nine years, Andrew Poole, now working the stoves. The sedate dining room in the Grade II listed building benefits from Baba's hands-on approach, while uniformed, friendly staff provide good back-up. The menu offers a lot of choice, with around 15 starters and the same number of main courses. A salad of smoked chicken breast with avocado and croûtons is an example of the straightforward approach, or there might be baked queen scallops with pasta stuffed with provençale-style vegetables. Truffled breast of guinea fowl with a wild mushroom and Madeira sauce or char-grilled salmon with crushed peas and chive beurre blanc might be among main courses. Puddings round things off well: perhaps hot passion-fruit soufflé and sorbet with 'gorgeous' shortbread. The exceptional wine list is a weighty tome, with interesting notes. France is the main focus, with some fine vintages from notable producers, but quality is evident throughout. Half-bottles are abundant, and around half a dozen are served by the glass. The short house selection starts at £13.50.

 This symbol means that accommodation is available at this establishment.

Chefs: Andrew Poole and Martin Kinahan Proprietors: Baba and Giles Hine Open: all week 12 to 2, 7 to 9.30 Closed: 24 to 26 Dec Meals: alc (main courses £15 to £23.50). Set L £19.50 (2 courses) to £22.50, Set D £29.50. Bistro menu available Service: not inc Cards: Amex, Diners, Maestro, MasterCard, Visa Details: 80 seats. 40 seats outside. Car park. Vegetarian meals. Children's helpings. No smoking. Wheelchair access (also WC). No music. No mobile phones Accommodation: 19 rooms

---

MAP 2 **CORTON DENHAM –**
Somerset

Queens Arms [AR]

Corton Denham DT9 4LR
Tel: (01963) 220317

'Dogs and muddy boots welcome' proclaims a sign outside the door of this 'cracking' country pub. A log fire, low wooden tables, pews, deep leather armchairs and sofas add up to 'rustic, simple yet quite stylish' surroundings. Locally sourced materials appear as seared pigeon breast with Puy lentil salad and parsnip crisps (£5), followed by 'moist and juicy' Old Spot pork loin cutlet with grain mustard sauce (£9.80), or Corton Denham stinging nettle risotto with Parmesan shavings (£9.20). End on a high note with 'firm, not gooey' treacle tart – 'lovely flavour' – with Dorset clotted cream (£4.20). The wide-ranging wine list opens at £11.20. Accommodation. Open all week.

MAP 3 **CRANBROOK – Kent**

Apicius

23 Stone Street, Cranbrook TN17 3HE
Tel: (01580) 714666

| Cooking 4 | Modern European | £41 |

Apicius, an unassuming double-shopfronted building on the main street of this well-heeled country town, is made up of just one smart but unpretentious dining room. The scale may be domestic – there are only about six tables – but what lifts this beyond the ordinary is the kitchen's attention to detail, a confident mastery of combinations and an awareness of seasonality. Starters of soused mackerel fillet with beetroot and balsamic salad, or smoked duck breast with foie gras velouté and confit leg ballotine give way to pan-fried fillet of turbot with baby leeks, salt-roast potatoes and rocket pesto, or perhaps slow-roast shoulder of pork with creamed potato, Savoy cabbage and caramelised apples. Desserts such as cinnamon-poached apple and chocolate tart have drawn enthusiastic comments, and service from Faith Hawkins is attentive and knowledgeable. All in all, reporters have been impressed by 'this very inventive chef's talents' (Tim Johnson's skills were honed under Nico Ladenis), and by the 'fantastic value'. The short wine list has been put together with an eye for interesting names and good value. Prices start at £16.

Chef: Tim Johnson **Proprietors:** Tim Johnson and Faith Hawkins **Open:** Wed to Fri and Sun L 12 to 2, Tue to Sat D 7 to 9 **Meals:** Set L £18.50 (2 courses) to £22.50, Set D £22.50 (2 courses) to £26.50 **Service:** 10% (optional) **Cards:** Delta, Maestro, MasterCard, Visa **Details:** 22 seats. Vegetarian meals. No children under 8. No smoking. Wheelchair access (also WC). No music. No mobile phones

---

MAP 2 CRAY'S POND – Berkshire

White Lion

Goring Road, Goring Heath, Cray's Pond RG8 7SH
Tel: (01491) 680471
Website: www.whitelioncrayspond.com

NEW CHEF | Modern European | £40

The White Lion deftly combines the qualities of a traditional pub with an ambitious restaurant that fuses British cooking with European influences. Chef Jonathan Clarke has joined from Drakes on the Pond at Abinger Hammer (see entry), and his menu, while compact, is a lively affair. Starters range from pressed ham hock terrine with home-made piccalilli, to a king crab, salmon and potato cake with sauce gribiche. Around eight choices of main course see the likes of chargrilled yellowfin tuna steak with a fine bean, feta and potato salad, or honey-glazed belly pork with smoked bacon and thyme sarladaise. Desserts run from raspberry crème brûlée to Malibu-roasted pineapple with sweet ginger parfait and caramel sauce. Prices on the wine list start at £13.95, with half a dozen options by the glass from £3.40.

Chef: Jonathan Clarke **Proprietor:** Paul Suter **Open:** Tue to Sun L 12 to 2 (2.30 Sun), Tue to Sat D 6 to 9.30 **Closed:** 25 and 26 Dec, 1 Jan **Meals:** alc (main courses £10 to £18). Set L £19.95, Set D £22.95 to £25.95. Bar L menu available **Service:** not inc **Cards:** Delta, Maestro, MasterCard, Visa **Details:** 55 seats. 60 seats outside. Car park. Vegetarian meals. Children's helpings. No smoking in dining room. Wheelchair access (not WC). Occasional music

---

MAP 2 CROCKERTON – Wiltshire

Bath Arms

Crockerton BA12 8AJ
Tel: (01985) 212262

Cooking 3 | Modern British | £33

Visitors to the Longleat Estate will do well to seek out Dean Carr's country pub, where they will be pleasantly surprised to find a chef with a CV that includes stints at some of London's top restaurants. He has done some remodelling this year, and the new Garden Suite overlooking the lawn provides additional seating during busy periods. The menu is straightforward yet wide-ranging, with good quality ingredients used throughout. Pub favourites get their own section and include fish-cakes with Cornish crab and broad beans, Cumberland sausage with champ, and breaded plaice with chips. The menu extends to successful starters such as rabbit terrine with apple chutney, or baked mushroom Welsh rarebit, and main courses like roast cod with red pepper and bran-dade, or chicken breast with tomato, basil and Parmesan. White chocolate cannelloni with mixed berries would hit the spot for dessert. The short wine list is good value, starting at £10.95 for house Australian.

Chefs: Dean Carr and Mark Payne **Proprietor:** Dean Carr **Open:** all week 12 to 2, 6 to 9 **Closed:** D 25 Dec and D 26 Dec **Meals:** alc (main courses £10 to £15) **Service:** not inc **Cards:** Delta, Maestro, MasterCard, Visa **Details:** 64 seats. 80 seats outside. Car park. No children under 14 in bar. Children's helpings. No smoking in dining room. Wheelchair access (also WC). Music **Accommodation:** 2 rooms

---

MAP 8 CROSTHWAITE – Cumbria

Punch Bowl Inn [NEW ENTRY]

Crosthwaite LA8 8HR
Tel: (015395) 68237
Website: www.the-punchbowl.co.uk

Cooking 3 | Modern European | £49

Under new ownership since 2005, the exterior remains largely unchanged, so one visitor was surprised by the transformation inside: 'I didn't recognise any part of it.' The simple, uncluttered décor features floors of slate or polished oak boards, sand-

213

blasted beams and pale walls; polished wooden tables fill the bar but are white-clad and formally laid in the dining room. Here the kitchen works to a menu of complex dishes, but Mathew Waddington and co. are sure of their ground. Good raw materials are well sourced, and many of the main courses follow the contemporary fashion of pairing a prime cut of meat with a slow-cooked version of a more humble one (Herdwick lamb as roast loin and braised neck pie, for instance). Elsewhere, sea bass fillet is teamed with roast salsify, olive potatoes, marinated red peppers, and lemon and sorrel butter. Ambitious starters include an artfully presented foie gras parfait accompanied by fiery ginger beer jelly ('more of a light tingle'), toasted chocolate bread, maple syrup and hazelnuts, while dessert could be vanilla pannacotta with roast rhubarb, and cinnamon and raisin beignets. Care is taken over details – freshly baked breads in particular – service is obliging and efficient, and wines are priced from £13.50.

Chef: Mathew Waddington Proprietor: The Punchbowl Partnership Ltd Open: all week 12 to 2.45, 7 to 8.45 Meals: alc exc Sun L (main courses £15 to £22). Set L Sun £19.95 (2 courses) to £24.95. Bar menu available Service: not inc Cards: Amex, Maestro, MasterCard, Visa Details: 30 seats. Car park. Vegetarian meals. No smoking in dining room. Wheelchair access (also WC). No music Accommodation: 9 rooms

MAP 2 **CRUDWELL – Wiltshire**

Rectory Hotel

Crudwell SN16 9EP
Tel: (01666) 577194
Website: www.therectoryhotel.co.uk

Cooking 3 | Modern British | £43

There is something timeless about this Cotswold-stone Victorian rectory on the road between Cirencester and Chippenham. It's in an absolutely lovely spot, and the view from the wood-panelled dining room of the walled garden, with the church tower behind sounding the hours, is idyllic. Peter Fairclough still heads the kitchen, placing priority on local produce like local Hereford beef and game in season, and delivering 'nicely executed' Cornish crab and avocado with a pink grapefruit dressing then, perhaps, roasted chump of new season Welsh lamb with garden mint-crusted tomatoes and rosemary and sea-salt new potatoes,

or Cornish cod topped with Welsh rarebit served with tomato risotto and basil oil. Among the sweets might be iced orange parfait with a 'very good' liquorice ice cream, or there's a selection of British farmhouse cheeses. Freshly baked bread rolls get an enthusiastic thumbs-up, while service has been described as 'willing'. House wine is £12.

Chef: Peter Fairclough Proprietor: Julian Muggridge Open: all week 12 to 2, 7 to 9 (9.30 Fri and Sat) Meals: alc (main courses £13.50 to £18.50) Service: not inc Cards: Delta, Maestro, MasterCard, Visa Details: 60 seats. 24 seats outside. Car park. Vegetarian meals. Children's helpings. No smoking. Wheelchair access (also WC). Occasional music Accommodation: 12 rooms

MAP 3 **CUCKFIELD – West Sussex**

Mansfields

1 Broad Street, Cuckfield RH17 5LJ
Tel: (01444) 410222

Cooking 2 | Modern European | £40

Son Marc helps dad Günther in the kitchen at this well-established family business, while mum Patricia takes charge in the three small dining rooms. The menus lean towards tried and tested classic French techniques and flavour combinations, perked up with a few more current ideas, typically turning up starters of chicken liver parfait with red onion marmalade, grilled goats' cheese on warm marinated sweet peppers, or spicy oriental duck salad. Among the half-dozen main-course options might be Scottish beef fillet on rösti with red wine sauce, and pan-fried scallops with prawns and dry vermouth sauce, with Belgian chocolate and orange tart, or sticky toffee pudding with butterscotch sauce to finish. A trio of French house wines are £11.95 a bottle, £3.60 a glass, while the rest of the compact wine list is a well-balanced selection.

Chefs: Günther and Marc Schlender Proprietors: Günther and Patricia Schlender Open: Tue to Sat D only 7 to 10 Closed: Christmas to New Year, 2 weeks May to June Meals: alc (main courses £11 to £16) Service: not inc Cards: Amex, Delta, Maestro, MasterCard, Visa Details: 32 seats. Vegetarian meals. No smoking. Music

| | This symbol means that smoking is not permitted. |

Ockenden Manor

Ockenden Lane, Cuckfield RH17 5LD
Tel: (01444) 416111
Website: www.hshotels.co.uk

Cooking 6 | Modern French | £65

Ockenden Manor is on a tiny lane, its surrounding nine acres complete with a terrace overlooking a secluded walled garden. Inside are beautifully appointed drawing rooms, hallways heavy with paintings, and antique furniture. The panelled dining room makes a fitting setting for Steve Crane's well-presented cooking. He offers an attractive range of dishes from set-price menus, and his approach is uniformly straightforward: less is definitely more here. An amuse-bouche in the form of slivers of fried bread with tapenade, then a small cup of tomato soup with basil precede starters of four 'beautifully caramelised' scallops on a delicate crayfish velouté and thinly sliced courgettes, or ballottine of salmon rolled in finely chopped herbs, served with asparagus and a spoonful of unctuous hollandaise. Main-course options follow in a similar vein: thinly sliced honey-roast duck, its richness cut by wilted chicory, comes with a creamy mushroom and mustard sauce, the whole dish demonstrating a light but far from bland touch, or sliced saddle of Ditchling lamb with wild garlic leaves, Parmesan gnocchi and provençale-style French beans. Desserts maintain the momentum: rhubarb and almond tart, its pastry 'nothing less than perfect', with vanilla ice cream. Service could be more knowledgeable. As you'd expect from such an august establishment, the international wine list shows depth, thought and some hefty price tags. The list opens with an enterprising selection of ten bottles, all priced at £18.50, or £4.50 a glass.

Chef: Steve Crane Proprietors: the Goodman and Carminger families Open: all week 12.15 to 2, 7 to 9.30 Meals: Set L £14.50 (2 courses) to £46, Set D £46. Bar menu available Service: not inc Cards: Amex, Delta, Diners, Maestro, MasterCard, Visa Details: 45 seats. 20 seats outside. Car park. Vegetarian meals. Children's helpings. No smoking. Wheelchair access (also WC). Occasional music. No mobile phones Accommodation: 22 rooms

NEW ENTRY	This appears after the restaurant's name if the establishment was not a main entry in last year's Guide. Please note, however, it may have been 'also recommended' in the previous edition.

MAP 3 **DANEHILL** – East Sussex

Coach & Horses   NEW ENTRY

School Lane, Danehill RH17 7JF
Tel: (01825) 740369

Cooking 1 | Modern British | £35

The pub is on a fairly steep hill, with views over fields with sheep and assorted farm buildings. The sloping lawn to the front has trestle tables, while, inside, the dining room is barn-like and unpretentious, with stone walls and bare tables. Catherine Philpots makes various chutneys, pesto, jams and peanut butter, which are on sale, while Jason Tidy works the kitchen stoves. Pickled Newick veal tongue, served with olives and caper berries, and baked goats' cheese with a modish salad of beetroot and orange might be among starters. A main course of slowly braised loin of Ashdown venison has come with 'absolutely excellent' mash and a stack of fine beans, and 'an utterly simple' and very good liquorice pannacotta with poached rhubarb was the high point of an inspection meal. Good-value global wines start at £12.50 for house Vins de Pays d'Oc.

Chef: Jason Tidy Proprietors: Ian and Catherine Philpots Open: all week L 12 to 2 (2.30 Sat and Sun), Mon to Sat D 7 to 9 (9.30 Fri and Sat) Closed: D 24 Dec, 25 and 26 Dec, D 1 Jan Meals: alc (main courses £10 to £15.50) Service: not inc Cards: Delta, Maestro, MasterCard, Visa Details: 66 seats. 70 seats outside. Car park. Vegetarian meals. Children's helpings. No smoking in dining room. Wheelchair access (not WC). Music

MAP 3 **DARGATE** – Kent

Dove

Plum Pudding Lane, Dargate ME13 9HB
Tel: (01227) 751360

Cooking 3 | French | £45

The Dove is an informal, friendly country pub hidden away down narrow lanes, and it's been the focal point of village life since the mid-nineteenth century. It's very simple inside: sepia-tint photographs depicting the history of the pub line the walls, and there's an open fire, bare floorboards and mixed pine furniture. Food is listed on blackboards: a selection of snacks and light meals at lunchtime, and a longer carte with the emphasis firmly on the quality sourcing of ingredients such as local fish and seasonal game, as well as locally grown fruit and vegetables. Sardines are grilled and flavoured simply with garlic and olive oil, while wild sea bass comes with a shallot, garlic and herb dressing. Among meat dishes might be fillet of beef (with mustard, confit shallots, garlic and oyster mushroom jus), or braised shank of lamb (on potato purée with tomato and basil jus flavoured with beetroot). Shepherd Neame ales are on hand-pump, or look to the ten or so wines by the glass from £3.30, as the collection of Old and New World bottles does not dip below £17.

Chef: Nigel Morris Proprietors: Nigel and Bridget Morris Open: Tue to Sun L 12 to 2, Wed to Sat D 7 to 9 Meals: alc (main courses £14 to £22). Bar snack menu available Service: not inc Cards: Delta, Maestro, MasterCard, Visa Details: 24 seats. 20 seats outside. Car park. Children's helpings. No-smoking area. Music

MAP 1 DARTMOUTH – Devon

New Angel

2 South Embankment, Dartmouth TQ6 9BH
Tel: (01803) 839425
Website: www.thenewangel.co.uk

Cooking 4 | **Modern Anglo-French** | **£52**

John Burton-Race pitched his camp at this landmark restaurant in 2004, reworking both the premises and his own cooking style. What he is offering is very much in tune with modern times, at least for those who don't expect three lots of appetisers and a pre-dessert with their dinner. It's on two floors, both of which have been simply decorated, the lower with more atmosphere and views of the open-plan kitchen, and the first-floor with the best views over the harbour. The food makes a virtue of local produce, although results can be hit or miss. Three grilled fillets of mackerel arranged atop a mound of salad dressed with tarragon vinaigrette was a successful starter at inspection, or there might be foie gras and baby leek terrine with summer truffle. Combinations are good: thus, Chinese-style belly pork is teamed with herb-crusted loin and set on a bed of Savoy cabbage with lardons and a potato cake, while fish might be grilled red mullet with garlic potato, summer vegetables and its own cream. Meals end strongly with the likes of pannacotta with exotic diced fruit and passion-fruit sorbet, or chocolate marquise with vanilla ice cream. Italy and Australia look particularly tempting on an international wine list packed with good bottles at fair prices.

France appeals too, with house vins de pays opening at £12.

Chefs: John Burton-Race, Nigel Marriage and Robert Spencer Proprietors: John and Kim Burton-Race Open: Tue to Sun L 12 to 2.30, Tue to Sat D 6.30 to 10; also open bank hol Mon Closed: Jan Meals: alc (main courses £16 to £29) Service: not inc Cards: Amex, Delta, Maestro, MasterCard, Visa Details: 110 seats. Vegetarian meals. Children's helpings. No smoking in dining room. Wheelchair access (not WC). Music. Air-conditioned

MAP 6 DEDHAM – Essex

milsoms

Stratford Road, Dedham CO7 6HW
Tel: (01206) 322795
Website: www.milsomhotels.com

Cooking 1 | **Global** | **£38**

If the prospect of dining in a Georgian house in pretty countryside, with lawns and a terrace for drinks in fine weather, is an enticing one, then milsoms lives up to expectations. Some find the no-booking policy 'quirky', but the kitchen is pretty vigorous, belting out a wide-ranging brasserie menu that is ordered pub-style at the bar and then brought by cheerful staff to your table. The food has broad appeal, with ideas ranging from shredded duck tacos with hoisin, via potted salt-beef, to a retro prawn and crayfish cocktail. Main courses take in Aegean fish and shellfish stew, and slow-roast belly pork with pear and wilted greens, while at dessert stage there might be plum, pistachio and white chocolate trifle, or rich chocolate brownie with vanilla ice cream and pecan fudge sauce. House French is £12.50, and a dozen wines come by the glass.

Chef: Stas Anastasiades Proprietor: Paul Milsom Open: all week 12 to 9.30 (10 Fri and Sat) Meals: alc (main courses £8.50 to £22). Set L Sun £19.50 (2 courses) to £25 Service: not inc Cards: Amex, Delta, Diners, Maestro, MasterCard, Visa Details: 80 seats. 80 seats outside. Car park. Vegetarian meals. Children's helpings. No-smoking area. Wheelchair access (also WC). Music. Air-conditioned Accommodation: 15 rooms

AR	Not a full entry but provisionally recommended. These 'also recommended' establishments are integrated throughout the book.

Sun Inn

High Street, Dedham CO7 6DF
Tel: (01206) 323351
Website: www.thesuninndedham.com

Cooking 2 | Mediterranean | £32

£

Surrounded by the beautiful scenery of Constable country, the Sun is a fifteenth-century village inn with a twenty-first-century soul. The setting is all real fires and exposed timbers, the mood relaxed and informal, and the cooking modern British with Mediterranean influences. Big flavours and a lack of unnecessary frills are what to expect: grilled Tuscan-style sausages with braised lentils and salsa verde, beef casserole with celeriac purée, and roast skate wing with roast potatoes, anchoïade and rocket. To finish, try baked rhubarb with blood-orange sorbet, or walnut flan with lemon ice cream. There is also a bar menu of sandwiches and ploughman's at lunchtime. Four real ales are on tap, along with an adventurous list of over 40 wines (priced from £11), with around a dozen available by the glass.

Chef/Proprietor: Piers Baker Open: all week L 12 to 2.30 (3 Sat and Sun), Mon to Sat D 6.30 to 9.30 (10 Fri and Sat) Closed: 25 to 27 Dec Meals: alc (main courses £8.50 to £15). Bar L menu available Service: not inc Cards: Maestro, MasterCard, Visa Details: 80 seats. 100 seats outside. Car park. Vegetarian meals. Children's helpings. No-smoking area. Music Accommodation: 5 rooms

MAP 5 **DERBY – Derbyshire**

Darleys

Darley Abbey Mills, Haslams Lane, Darley Abbey, Derby DE22 1DZ
Tel: (01332) 364987
Website: www.darleys.com

Cooking 4 | Modern British | £47

There's a relaxed feel to this restaurant in an old cotton mill on the Derwent. Jonathan Hobson is a keen advocate of locally available ingredients, and ventures towards the Mediterranean for culinary ideas but doesn't seek to impress with outlandish fireworks. While his dishes avoid over-elaboration, they are accurately timed and reassuringly consistent. Some are robust combinations like a starter of potato and bacon tartiflette glazed with goats' cheese, and a main course of loin of rabbit

wrapped in Parma ham, stuffed with prunes and served with pearl barley risotto and a thyme jus; others are marked by subtlety and careful balance, as in breast of Gressingham duck with an orange and duck liver ravioli and anise sauce. Puddings such as lemon-curd parfait with pineapple samosa and cinnamon syrup, and milk chocolate and Amaretto truffle with malted milkshake make satisfying ends. The short wine list is a mixed bag from around the world, opening with 'personal recommendations' from £14.

Chef: Jonathan Hobson Proprietors: Jonathan and Kathryn Hobson Open: all week L 12 to 2, Mon to Sat D 7 to 9.30 Closed: bank hols Meals: alc D (main courses £16.50 to £19). Set L £13.95 (2 courses) to £15.95 Service: not inc Cards: Delta, Maestro, MasterCard, Visa Details: 60 seats. 12 seats outside. Car park. Vegetarian meals. Children's helpings. No smoking in 1 dining room. Wheelchair access (not WC). Music. No mobile phones. Air-conditioned

MAP 2 **DIDMARTON – Gloucestershire**

Kings Arms

AR

The Street, Didmarton GL9 1DT
Tel: (01454) 238245

Game from the local Badminton estate is a feature of this characterful seventeenth-century coaching inn, so look out for daily blackboard specials and their Rook Supper in June, when rook pie is served. More typical dishes, though, include Stilton and nutmeg brûlée glazed with Parmesan and red onion marmalade (£5.10), and main courses of an assiette of pork on herb mash with pepper sauce (£12.95), or crisp-skinned sea bass with mustard-infused crushed potatoes and butter sauce (£12.50). Finish with marbled chocolate parfait served with honeycomb and brandied berries (£5.50). The short global wine list starts at £12.40, or £3.30 a glass. Accommodation. Open all week.

| £ | This symbol means that it is possible to have a three-course dinner, including coffee, half a bottle of house wine and service, for £30 or less per person. |

MAP 3 DINTON – Buckinghamshire

La Chouette

Westlington Green, Dinton HP17 8UW
Tel: (01296) 747422

Cooking 4 | Belgian | £48

Don't be fooled by appearances. It may look every inch the quaint old English village inn, but La Chouette is in fact an extension of the personality of its Belgian chef/proprietor, Frederic Desmette. The menus rarely venture beyond the canon of classic French and Belgian cooking: sole fillets with sorrel sauce, skate wing salad, duck breast in green peppercorn sauce, and veal chop served simply with its own jus, for example. But first-rate ingredients and a deft touch in the kitchen prove that when such dishes are done well they can still cause a stir. More innovative creations inspired by Desmette's homeland include a fillet of brill in a sauce made with Duvel, a potent Belgian beer whose well-deserved name means 'devil'. Desserts might include crêpes flambé with mandarin sauce, and dame blanche (vanilla ice cream topped with a fine Belgian chocolate sauce). The hefty wine list is packed with big French names, the Loire and Rhône being particularly well represented. Prices are not outrageous given the quality of the vintages, but there is little choice for those with less than £30 to spend, although house red and white are £13.50.

> **Chef/Proprietor:** Frederic Desmette **Open:** Mon to Fri L 12 to 2, Mon to Sat D 7 to 9 **Meals:** alc (main courses £13 to £17). Set L £13.50 to £39.80, Set D £29.80 to £39.80 **Service:** 12.5% (optional) **Cards:** Delta, Maestro, MasterCard, Visa **Details:** 35 seats. Car park. Children's helpings. No smoking in dining room. Occasional music. No mobile phones

MAP 6 DISS – Norfolk

Weavers Wine Bar AR

Market Hill, Diss IP22 4JZ
Tel: (01379) 642411

In the centre of the busy market town, Weavers is in an ancient timber-framed building. The reliable cooking contrasts with the setting, employing a broad palette of contemporary flavours ranging from gravad lax on crushed potatoes with horseradish cream (£5.25) to roast teal stuffed with

chicken and pistachios served on sweet pickled red cabbage with an apple and whole grain mustard sauce and dumplings (£16.95). Finish perhaps with pear, blackberry and chocolate-chip biscotti trifle. Set-price menus offer excellent value, and 16 wines at £11.95 head up a well-chosen list. Open Tue to Fri L and Mon to Sat D.

MAP 1 DODDISCOMBSLEIGH – Devon

Nobody Inn AR

Doddiscombsleigh EX6 7PS
Tel: (01647) 252394

If you like malt whisky, this thatched fifteenth-century inn must be one of the best places outside Scotland to sample them, with a huge range on offer. The list of over 800 wines is no less spectacular, and prices are modest throughout. Equally appealing is the restaurant menu of modern British cooking, with smoked eel and crispy bacon salad (£5.15) typical among starters, while main courses take in beef fillet with creamy tarragon sauce (£12.75) and pan-fried halibut with a sauce of green peppercorns, tomatoes, coriander and white wine (£12). Bar meals follow similar lines. Restaurant open Tue to Sat D; bar food served L and D all week.

MAP 2 DONHEAD ST ANDREW – Wiltshire

Forester Inn AR

Lower Street, Donhead St Andrew SP7 9EE
Tel: (01747) 828038

Steeped in character, this sixteenth-century inn on the Dorset/Wiltshire border offers unexpectedly contemporary cooking. Chef Tom Shaw may conjure up wok-cooked mussels with Thai spices (£5.75), followed by Scottish chargrilled ribeye steak au poivre with confit tomatoes, wild rocket and pommes frites (£13.95). Livarot and Exmoor Blue may be on the cheeseboard (£6.95), while cappuccino crème brûlée (£4.95) could be one of the desserts. Wines are globally explored, starting at £12.75. Two guest rooms. Open all week.

> To submit a report on any restaurant, please visit *www.which.co.uk/gfgfeedback*.

MAP 2 **DORCHESTER – Dorset**

Sienna

36 High West Street, Dorchester DT1 1UP
Tel: (01305) 250022

Everything is made in-house at Russell and Eléna Brown's restaurant, with the emphasis on the seasons and local produce. Caramelised pear and Beenleigh Blue tartlet with a rocket and walnut salad might precede pan-fried fillet of brill with braised artichoke hearts, salsify, tagliatelle and a red wine and butter sauce. Finish with lemon, sultana and ricotta cheesecake with lemon sorbet. Lunch £15.50/£18.50; dinner £26.50/£32. The lively wine list starts at £12. Closed Sun and Mon.

MAP 5 **DORRIDGE – West Midlands**

The Forest

25 Station Approach, Dorridge B93 8JA
Tel: (01564) 772120
Website: www.forest-hotel.com

Cooking 2 | **Modern French** | **£38**

Once a railway hotel, this large, many-gabled building has the air of a Swiss chalet about it. Inside, there's a conference centre and a restaurant called the Olive Room, with a good-sized terrace for al fresco eating. The daily-changing set-price menu du jour is good value, while the full carte offers a broad range of brasserie-style dishes. 'Stupendous' home-made bread gets things off to a fine start, to be followed perhaps by a simple starter of seared scallops with a blini and caviar, or devilled chicken livers with Caesar salad. Raw materials are exemplary, as shown by thinly sliced roast duck breast, accompanied by Parmentier potatoes, while fish might show up as turbot roasted with pancetta and served with crushed new potatoes and a red wine sauce. Iced nougat glace with orange and Cointreau jelly and orange sorbet could be one of the arty-looking desserts. Most bottles on the short wine list are under £25, starting at £12.95. Around ten are served by the glass from £3.50.

> The price given next to the cooking score is based on the cost of a typical three-course dinner for one person, including coffee, house wine and service.

Chef: Dean Grubb Proprietors: Gary and Tracy Perkins Open: all week L 12 to 2.30, Mon to Sat D 6.30 to 10 Closed: 25 Dec Meals: alc (main courses £8 to £19). Set L and D Mon to Fri £12 (2 courses) to £15, Set L Sun £14.50 (2 courses) to £17.50 Service: 10% Cards: Amex, Delta, Maestro, MasterCard, Visa Details: 70 seats. 60 seats outside. Car park. Vegetarian meals. Children's helpings. No smoking in dining room. Wheelchair access (also WC). Music. Air-conditioned Accommodation: 12 rooms

MAP 10 **DURHAM – Co Durham**

Almshouses

Palace Green, Durham DH1 3RL
Tel: (0191) 386 1054

Next to the cathedral, this long-established café/restaurant offers honest home cooking and baking, with a few global influences thrown in. Smoked cod chowder (£5), or monkfish with rosemary and crème fraîche (£7.25) might start, with main courses along the lines of roast leg of pork with plum sauce and parsnip purée (£11.95), or duck cassoulet with white beans and sage (£15.50). Vegetarian options include lentil and coriander rissole served on butternut squash risotto (£10.25). Wines are priced from around £11. Open all week.

Bistro 21

Aykley Heads House, Aykley Heads, Durham DH1 5TS
Tel: (0191) 384 4354

Cooking 3 | **Mediterranean** | **£43**

Within the pink-washed building in a wooded area you'll find Terry Laybourne's welcoming bistro. The kitchen's roll-call of dishes may not be large, but it spans the globe. Sharp, modern ideas abound: say, Asian-cured salmon with pickled white crabmeat, or tempura of king prawns with a Thai dressing for starters. Among main courses, grilled calf's liver with bacon and onions rubs shoulders with posh fish and chips (roast cod fillet with pea purée, tomato salsa and straw potatoes), or there might be a straightforward whole lemon sole meunière. Desserts tend to be variations on classic themes such as rhubarb strudel with strawberry sorbet, and profiteroles with pistachio ice cream and hot chocolate sauce. Occasional lapses (poor timing, tough pastry) have been highlighted over the past year, and reports suggest that some of the zing in the service appears to have evaporated. A rather compact wine list trots the globe; prices start at £12.50 and stay mostly under £20.

Chef: Paul O'Hara **Proprietor:** Terence Laybourne **Open:** Mon to Sat 12 to 2, 7 to 10.15 **Meals:** alc (main courses £12.50 to £20). Set L £13 (2 courses) to £15.50 **Service:** not inc **Cards:** Amex, Delta, Diners, Maestro, MasterCard, Visa **Details:** 55 seats. 24 seats outside. Car park. Vegetarian meals. Children's helpings. No smoking. Wheelchair access (also WC). Music. No mobile phones

---

MAP 3 **EASTBOURNE –** East Sussex

Grand Hotel, Mirabelle

King Edwards Parade, Eastbourne BN21 4EQ
Tel: (01323) 412345
Website: www.grandeastbourne.com

Cooking 5 | **Modern European** | **£46**

If you're a newcomer, the dimensions of the Grand Hotel may well come as a surprise. It's a fine Victorian sprawl of a place, wedding cake white, dazzling on a bright day, alluringly sexy when floodlit at night. So grand is it that its flagship restaurant, the Mirabelle, even has its own entrance on a side street. This leads into a well-appointed hotel dining room, done in dusky pink, the kind of place where dinner may well be eaten to the strains of the resident pianist.

A series of fixed-price menus is available, at three different prices in the evenings, depending on what sort of protein you want to eat and how many courses' worth. Gerald Röser is an old Sussex hand and cooks well, in an essentially classic style with contemporary flourishes. Scallops are thinly sliced, flash-seared, and alternate on the plate with slices of Spanish morcilla, all embedded in smooth potato purée, within a moat of good parsley pesto. An old-fashioned soufflé made with pike might start the cheaper menu, sauced nonetheless with smoked salmon and dill, before a simple main course of chicken breast with wild mushroom risotto. An inspection dish of new season's salt-marsh lamb produced meat of fabulous flavour (from nearby Pevensey), the best end cooked pink in the middle and appetisingly blackened on the surface. The temptation to gild the lily is hearteningly resisted even at dessert stage, where the simplicity of rhubarb fool is enhanced by only a pair of orange-flavoured, heart-shaped shortbread biscuits.

A youthful service team is led by the professional and hugely knowledgeable Benjamin Warren, who is a credit to the place. The wine list has developed well in recent years and is now quite a tome. France is the fulcrum, the list replete with intelligent tasting notes that explain why you might want to part with, say, £86 for the 1996 Ch. Talbot. A good range of halves, and wines by the glass from £5 (from £18 by the bottle).

Chefs: Keith Mitchell and Gerald Röser **Proprietor:** Elite Hotels **Open:** Tue to Sat 12.30 to 2, 7 to 10 **Closed:** first 2 weeks Jan **Meals:** Set L £17.50 (2 courses) to £20, Set D £36.50 to £55 **Service:** net prices **Cards:** Amex, Delta, Diners, Maestro, MasterCard, Visa **Details:** 48 seats. Car park. Vegetarian meals. Children's helpings. Jacket and tie. No smoking. Wheelchair access (also WC). Music. No mobile phones. Air-conditioned **Accommodation:** 152 rooms

---

MAP 3 **EAST CHILTINGTON –** East Sussex

Jolly Sportsman

Chapel Lane, East Chiltington BN7 3BA
Tel: (01273) 890400
Website: www.thejollysportsman.com

Cooking 3 | **Modern European** | **£39**

Still a pub at first glance, this particularly jolly Sportsman is really all about the food; the small bar area does dispense real ale and all, but people flock from miles around to eat here (Lewes and Brighton are within easy reach). The staff contribute much to the atmosphere: well informed and friendly, they work hard to keep the place running smoothly even at busy times. Sit in one of the series of linked rooms on slightly different floor levels or outside on the fabulous terrace. The kitchen concentrates on clear, strong flavours, using excellent raw materials, and details are not overlooked; praise is heaped on the olive oil, served with good-quality bread, and home-made ice creams and sorbets, and a poly tunnel in the garden provides some vegetables and herbs. Braised ox cheek with shallot purée and red wine sauce makes an 'unusual, simple and delicious' starter, and there might also be pickled fillet of red mullet with salsify salad. A well-balanced combination of flavours and textures shows up in main courses of grilled sea bass with Cornish mussels, samphire and tomatoes, or fillet of Ditchling lamb with haricot beans, tomatoes and tarragon. Seville orange marmalade ice cream with a 'fresh, eggy biscuit' makes a refreshing finish. The lengthy wine list has a decent selection of bottles under £20, starting with house wines at £12.85.

Chef: Richard Willis   Proprietors: Bruce and Gwyneth Wass
Open: Tue to Sun L 12.30 to 2.15 (3 Sun), Tue to Sat D 7 to
9.15 (10 Fri and Sat)   Closed: 4 days Christmas   Meals: alc
(main courses £9 to £17.50)   Set L Tue to Sat £12.50 (2
courses)   Service: not inc   Cards: Delta, Maestro, MasterCard,
Visa   Details: 80 seats. 30 seats outside. Car park. Vegetarian
meals. Children's helpings. No smoking in dining room.
Wheelchair access (also WC). No music. Air-conditioned

MAP 2   EAST COKER – Somerset

Helyar Arms

Moor Lane, East Coker BA22 9JR
Tel: (01935) 862332
Website: www.helyar-arms.co.uk

Cooking 1 | Modern European | £39

T.S. Eliot's ashes are interred in East Coker's churchyard, and those on a pilgrimage will appreciate this typical English village of thatched and Ham stone houses. Dating from the fifteenth century, the Helyar Arms is a traditional country pub that advertises itself as 'a real food inn'. Local supplies include artisan bread from Crabb's in nearby Halstock, pheasants from the Sherborne Estate and lamb from a farm in Melplash. Such ingredients translate into starters of sautéed East Coker garlic mushrooms on grilled country bread, and deep-fried Somerset goats' cheese in 'chocolate' balsamic with a red pepper reduction. Beer-battered Brixham haddock, or braised beef (from a nearby farm) with carrots and watercress mash might follow. Finish with West Country cheeses or a pudding along the lines of lemon cheesecake with sautéed buttered apricots. All the wines on the list are served in two sizes of glass as well as by the bottle (from £12.50).

Chef: Mathieu Eke   Proprietor: Ian McKerracher   Open: Mon
to Sat 12 to 2.30, 6.30 to 9.30, Sun 12 to 4.30, 6.30 to 9
Closed: 25 Dec   Meals: alc (main courses L £7 to £10, D £8
to £16). Bar menu available   Service: not inc   Cards: Amex,
Delta, Maestro, MasterCard, Visa   Details: 95 seats. 40 seats
outside. Car park. Vegetarian meals. Children's helpings. No-
smoking area. Wheelchair access (not WC). Music
Accommodation: 6 rooms

This symbol means that the restaurant has elected to participate in *The Good Food Guide's* £5 voucher scheme (see 'Using The Good Food Guide' for details).

MAP 3   EAST DEAN – West Sussex

Star & Garter

AR

East Dean PO18 0JG
Tel: (01243) 811318

This archetypal village pub, found after navigating a maze of rural lanes, has been given an attractive 'sophisticated rustic' makeover with stripped beams, flintstones and exposed brick. The food is modern gastro-pub and fish is a speciality, listed on a daily-changing blackboard, typically featuring cod in beer batter with chips and tartare sauce (£10.50), and grilled trout with asparagus (£11.50). Non-fish options might home-made steak and kidney pudding (£9.75), with apple and rhubarb crumble (£5) to finish. Wines from £12. Open all week.

MAP 2   EAST END – Hampshire

East End Arms

NEW ENTRY

East End SO41 5SY
Tel: (01590) 626223
Email: joanna@eastendarms.co.uk

Cooking 1 | Modern British | £38

To find the pub, take the ferry road from Lymington and continue towards East End and Bucklers Hard; at East End green, take the left fork over a cattle grid and the pub is half a mile on the right. There are two East Ends in Hampshire, so hopefully that will ensure you get to the right one. Once there, you will find a well-tended garden with topiary and plenty of space for al fresco eating. Inside is a bar and a restaurant with mix-and-match furniture, panelling and cream walls hung with black and white photographs. The straightforward menus see lunches offering baguettes and the likes of salmon fishcakes with chips and tartare sauce. Dinner brings on the full works, so you could start with chicken liver pâté, or mussels in a 'full-flavoured' red wine and shallot sauce, and go on to 'perfectly cooked' (i.e. pink) pan-fried collops of venison with lyonnaise potatoes. Desserts are chalked on a board: perhaps cherry torte with local ice cream. Young staff are 'charming and friendly', and house wines on the short list are £14.

Chef: Stuart Kitcher   Proprietor: John Illsley   Open: Tue to Sun
L 12 to 2.30, Tue to Sat D 7 to 9.30   Meals: alc (main courses
L £6 to £15, D £12 to £17.50)   Service: not inc   Cards:
Delta, Maestro, MasterCard, Visa   Details: 35 seats. 40 seats
outside. Car park. Children's helpings. No smoking in dining
room. Wheelchair access (not WC). Music

MAP 3 | EAST GRINSTEAD – West Sussex

Gravetye Manor

Vowels Lane, East Grinstead RH19 4LJ
Tel: (01342) 810567
Website: www.gravetyemanor.co.uk

Cooking 5 | **Modern British/French** | **£69**

Make sure there's enough petrol in the tank for the drive from the road. Gravetye's grounds meander on and on, through woods and sudden valleys, so that the house itself may seem rather timidly proportioned after such an approach. It's a many-gabled Elizabethan manor, all dark oak panelling and ornate plaster mouldings inside, with a service tone that aims for old-school formality rather than newfangled relaxation. Mark Raffan oversees a fairly classic country-house menu, with all the expected prime ingredients on parade. Smoked salmon and crab come in the form of a pillow, with avocado purée and a dollop of caviar, or you might start with foie gras served whole (sautéed) and in a ballottine with Sauternes jelly. At main course, there could be something as richly traditional as steak pudding, with creamed potato and a red wine and oyster sauce, or then again as modish as a partnering of turbot, clams and oxtail. Chef's night off may see standards wobble, as when a serving of new season's lamb in five ways didn't seem to justify the considerable fiddliness it involved, and an iced dessert that came out still frozen solid. An immense wine list opens with recommendations for the menu dishes before offering 'A Few Ideas' from the redoubtable Bristol merchant Bill Baker. There are half-bottles in battalions before you get into the meat of the list, which is built around solid Burgundy selections and of course plenty of mature claret. Prices open at £17.

Chef: Mark Raffan **Proprietors:** Andrew Russell and Mark Raffan **Open:** all week 12.30 to 1.45, 7.30 to 9.30 **Meals:** Set L £24 to £55, Set D £38 to £55 **Service:** net prices **Cards:** Amex, MasterCard, Visa **Details:** 45 seats. Car park. Vegetarian meals. No children under 8. Jacket and tie. No smoking. Wheelchair access (not WC). No music. No mobile phones **Accommodation:** 18 rooms

---

	This symbol means that it is possible to have a three-course dinner, including coffee, half a bottle of house wine and service, for £30 or less per person.
£	

MAP 3 | EAST LAVANT – West Sussex

Royal Oak

Pook Lane, East Lavant PO18 0AX
Tel: (01243) 527434
Website: www.thesussexpub.co.uk

Cooking 3 | **Modern British** | **£41**

Not far from Goodwood, this gastro-pub can be found off the beaten track in a Downs village. The owners have retained original features – fireplaces, beams, and nooks and crannies – yet have created a smart and simple interior, with a subtly lit, comfortable and well-run dining room. The large menu might see the likes of a trio of Selsey crab cakes with guacamole and herb salad, or baked halloumi wrapped in Serrano ham with radishes, fine beans and cider dressing to start. Main courses offer pub staples such as battered cod and chips with mushy peas alongside confit of twice-cooked belly pork with bubble and squeak, Savoy cabbage and a red wine and shallot sauce, or lamb cutlets with sautéed kidneys and Madeira jus. There are also blackboard specials and classic puddings such as spotted dick, or a mini raspberry pavlova with white chocolate cream. The wine list is reasonably priced, from £12.50, and easy to navigate, with helpful descriptions. Around a dozen are available by the glass from £3.20.

Chefs: Malcolm Goble and Oz Whatson **Proprietors:** Nick and Lisa Sutherland **Open:** all week 12 to 2.30, 6 to 9 **Meals:** alc (main courses £11.50 to £18) **Service:** not inc **Cards:** Amex, Delta, Maestro, MasterCard, Visa **Details:** 50 seats. 30 seats outside. Car park. Vegetarian meals. Children's helpings. No smoking in dining room. Wheelchair access (not WC). Music. Air-conditioned **Accommodation:** 6 rooms

---

MAP 2 | EASTON GREY – Wiltshire

Whatley Manor

Easton Grey SN16 0RB
Tel: (01666) 822888
Website: www.whatleymanor.com

Cooking 6 | **Modern European** | **£80**

A beautifully restored Cotswold manor house under the aegis of one-time international event rider Christian Landolt, Whatley is set in 12 acres of gardens and woodland. If you're lucky enough

to be staying, it's the kind of place where mint-scented water comes out of the showers, but if you're not we'll presume you're here for Martin Burge's supremely confident, pace-setting cooking – which is lucky enough in itself. Within the softly lit, pastel-coloured dining room, some surprising culinary fireworks are in evidence. Complexity is a hallmark of the cooking, as is clear from the menu billings. A starter might see a tiny breast of Anjou quail roasted under a glaze of Pedro Ximénez, served with a stuffed leg and a salad tossed in walnut vinaigrette.

Pasta crops up in a fair few dishes, and some have felt it is offered a little too al dente for its own good, as was the case in one reporter's main course of sea bass with a pasta parcel of oyster and lime, and a tomato- and coriander-based white wine sauce. Otherwise, venison from the Balmoral Estate looks a good bet, served with cauliflower purée and poached pear, in a deglaze of brandy and green peppercorns. After a pause for breath, the cheese trolley will be wheeled forth, its English and French wares all mature and described by the staff, or you might opt for the shameless indulgence of caramelised apple croustade with vanilla cassonade. Service is of the school that evokes the comment: 'Nothing was too much trouble.' An enormous wine list begins with all the smart French stuff before heading off into the Italian regions and then the wider world, which last includes a good Canadian Pinot Noir and a Devon red (and there aren't many of those to the pound). Prices are what are known as 'toppy'. Glasses start at £4.50 for a Californian Merlot. Le Mazot is a less formal brasserie-style restaurant served by the same kitchen.

Chef: Martin Burge **Proprietor:** Christian Landolt **Open:** Wed to Sun D only 7 to 10 **Meals:** Set D £60 to £75 **Service:** 10% **Cards:** Amex, Delta, Maestro, MasterCard, Visa **Details:** 40 seats. Car park. Vegetarian meals. No smoking. Wheelchair access (also WC). Occasional music. No mobile phones **Accommodation:** 23 rooms

MAP 8   EAST WITTON – North Yorkshire

Blue Lion

East Witton DL8 4SN
Tel: (01969) 624273
Website: www.thebluelion.co.uk

Cooking 3 | Modern British | £38

One of those traditional eighteenth-century stone pubs that 'one wishes would be part of every

village throughout the land'. In addition to the comfortable and lived-in décor (mismatched chairs, framed prints and small open fireplaces), the food is imaginative and the staff are 'a really pleasant, friendly bunch'. John Dalby's well-prepared, and fairly extensive, menu is dotted about the place – starters are chalked over the bar, while mains are listed on a large board above the fireplace, with a smaller board displaying the day's specials. Grilled king scallops come with a 'creamy and delicate' lemon and spring onion risotto for starters, perhaps followed by Kiev-style sautéed chicken breast wrapped in Parma ham with tarragon butter oozing out of the middle, or roast cod fillet with chorizo sausage and sautéed potatoes. To finish, apple and rhubarb crumble with a separate sauce boat of custard hits the spot. There's a wide-ranging choice of wines, mostly French, starting at £12.95 for house vins de pays.

Chef: John Dalby **Proprietor:** Paul Klein **Open:** Sun L 12 to 2.15, all week D 7 to 9.30 **Meals:** alc (main courses £10 to £19) **Service:** not inc **Cards:** Delta, Maestro, MasterCard, Visa **Details:** 70 seats. 30 seats outside. Car park. Vegetarian meals. Children's helpings. No smoking in 1 dining room. Wheelchair access (also WC). No music **Accommodation:** 12 rooms

MAP 8   ELLAND – West Yorkshire

La Cachette

31 Huddersfield Road, Elland HX5 9AW
Tel: (01422) 378833

Cooking 3 | Modern European | £36

The atmosphere at this bright and modern French-style bistro and wine bar is generally bustling without being overwhelmingly noisy, and plentiful staff are well trained, friendly and helpful. 'Our motto is don't tweak when it ain't broke!' writes partner David Gault, and the place certainly seems to have established a winning formula. A big attraction is the good value and a brasserie-style menu that pleases all-comers. Alongside standard fare such as fishcake with tartare sauce, calf's liver and bacon, and sirloin steak with peppercorn sauce, there are some interesting options: chicken tempura with Caesar salad, venison and foie gras burger with parsnip chips and caramelised red onions, followed by chargrilled pork steak with buttered cabbage and thyme sauce, or fillets of sea bass with a prawn and caper butter. There are also salad bowls, pasta and risotto options, plus a fish of the day. Finish with poached pear glazed with a

cinnamon sabayon. The wine list includes many good French bottles but does not neglect the rest of Europe or the New World, with house selections starting at £11.95.

Chef: Jonathan Nichols **Proprietor:** CGL Partnership **Open:** Mon to Sat 12 to 2.30, 6 to 9.30 (10 Fri and Sat) **Closed:** 10 days Christmas, last 2 weeks Aug, bank hol Mon **Meals:** alc (main courses £9 to £18). Set L £9.95 (2 courses), Set D Mon to Thur and 6 to 7 Fri and Sat £16.95 (inc wine) **Service:** not inc **Cards:** Delta, Maestro, MasterCard, Visa **Details:** 85 seats. Vegetarian meals. Children's helpings. Wheelchair access (not WC). Music. Air-conditioned

---

MAP 6 | ELY – Cambridgeshire

Boathouse

NEW ENTRY

5–5A Annesdale, Ely CB7 4BN
Tel: (01353) 664388
Website: www.cambscuisine.com

Cooking 1 | Modern British | £37

The Boathouse is on the Great Ouse and has a terrace overlooking the water. Inside are white-painted brick walls, a wooden floor and small, simply set black tables. The kitchen cooks in the modern British idiom, turning out a starter of leek, mushroom and goats' cheese gratin topped with hazelnuts alongside pork, apple and venison terrine cut by tangy sweet-and-sour pickled summer berries. Baked hake with wild mushrooms, pea purée, broad beans and mint is a well-handled main course, or there might be pan-fried duck breast with dauphinois potatoes, caramelised pineapple and ginger sauce. Peach and frangipane tart with basil syrup and Chantilly cream is a summery way in which to end, while strawberry ice cream took one diner back to childhood days. The wine list offers a broad choice, with house French starting at £12; around a dozen come by the glass from the £3 mark. Part of a small group including the Cock at Hemingford Grey and the Crown & Punchbowl in Horningsea (see entries).

Chef: Chris Brading **Proprietors:** Oliver Thain, Richard Bradley and Chris Brading **Open:** all week 12 to 2.30, 6.30 to 9 (9.30 Fri and Sat, 8.30 Sun) **Closed:** 26 to 28 Dec **Meals:** alc (main courses L £5 to £14, D £11 to £19). Set L Mon to Sat £9.95 (2 courses) to £12.95, Set L Sun £11.95 **Service:** not inc **Cards:** Maestro, MasterCard, Visa **Details:** 90 seats. 40 seats outside. Vegetarian meals. No children under 8 at D. Children's helpings. No smoking. Wheelchair access (also WC). No music. No mobile phones. Air-conditioned

---

MAP 3 | EMSWORTH – Hampshire

Fat Olives

30 South Street, Emsworth PO10 7EH
Tel: (01243) 377914
Website: www.fatolives.co.uk

Cooking 3 | Modern British | £37

'I've never seen such fat ones,' exclaimed a diner of the ramekin of enormous green olives on the table. After that, nothing really disappoints, and even though some ideas may be old-fashioned – such as the copious amounts of side vegetables, which are the same for every dish – this converted seventeenth-century cottage, a short distance from the harbour, is a triumph for the double act of Lawrence and Julia Murphy. Front-of-house, Julia efficiently runs things, while Lawrence's modern British menu offers some eclectic twists and precise timings as well as some excellent raw materials, plenty of which are locally sourced. Seared scallops with leek risotto and truffle oil make a 'nicely made and prettily presented' starter, with perhaps a terrine of guinea fowl with peas and mint among alternatives. A scoop of 'classically and perfectly made' tapenade makes a good foil for best end of lamb, along with strips of yellow and red pepper and courgette and a tomato-based sauce, while brill with chorizo is sauced with hazelnut beurre blanc and accompanied by cavolo nero. To end, 'very tasty' cherry summer pudding comes lined up on the plate with bavarois and vanilla ice cream. A concise but far-reaching wine list starts at £12 with Chilean Chardonnay and Cabernet Sauvignon.

Chef: Lawrence Murphy **Proprietors:** Lawrence and Julia Murphy **Open:** Tue to Sat 12 to 2, 7 to 9.15 **Closed:** 2 weeks Christmas, 1 week Oct, Tue after bank hol **Meals:** alc (main courses £13 to £19). Set L £15.25 (2 courses) to £16.95 **Service:** not inc **Cards:** Delta, Maestro, MasterCard, Visa **Details:** 28 seats. 10 seats outside. Vegetarian meals. No children under 8. No smoking. Wheelchair access (also WC). Music

---

36 on the Quay

47 South Street, Emsworth PO10 7EG
Tel: (01243) 375592
Website: www.36onthequay.co.uk

Cooking 6 | Modern European | £59

Refurbishment since last year's Guide has replaced the old-fashioned look of yore with spare, modern

styling, with generously spaced tables and some original local artwork on the walls. Ramon Farthing has a keen eye for current trends and cooks with confidence. That modern classic pairing of scallops and cauliflower is given a twist, with the vegetable appearing as crisp florets and a sauce gribiche giving the dish an edge, while meltingly tender quail sits on a croûton with pancetta, grapes and Gruyère, with a salad of pea-shoots. In this maritime setting, it's good to hear that fish shows up well, as was the case with an inspector's superlative roast turbot, which came with creamed celeriac, lardons of smoked bacon and wild mushrooms, in a cep-based chicken stock reduction. Meat-eaters might consider duck, the breast and a crisp-skinned confit leg, garnished with caramelised pear, and accompanied by vegetables stir-fried with ginger, and a sauce of vanilla and star anise.

The desire to dazzle with many layers continues into desserts that might match a tian of chocolate biscuit and orange bavarois with rhubarb and vermouth sorbet, the plate decorated with 'squiggles and squirts' of syrup, flavoured with caramel and rhubarb. 'Excellent, professional and not over-formal' service gets the nod. Wines are an engagingly serious collection. The grouping is fairly random, being partly stylistic and partly geographical, but the selections are sound; Italy and southern France being especially well-served. Pricing is ambitious, but opens at £13.95 a bottle or £4 a glass.

> **Chef:** Ramon Farthing **Proprietors:** Ramon and Karen Farthing **Open:** Tue to Sat 12 to 2, 7 to 10 **Closed:** Oct half term, 3 weeks Jan **Meals:** Set L £17.95 (2 courses) to £22.95, Set D £42.95 to £60 **Service:** not inc **Cards:** Amex, Delta, Diners, Maestro, MasterCard, Visa **Details:** 50 seats. 10 seats outside. Car park. Vegetarian meals. Children's helpings. No smoking. Wheelchair access (not WC). Occasional music. No mobile phones **Accommodation:** 5 rooms

| MAP 3 | EPPING – Essex |

Clocktower AR

4 Station Road, Epping CM16 4HA
Tel: (01992) 575707

This thriving town-centre bar and restaurant opens for breakfast and continues to serve food all day. The menu has plenty of choice: starters such as fishcake with creamy tarragon sauce (£4.95) or chicken liver terrine (£5.50), various salads (duck breast with apple and mango chutney; starter £5.95, main course £9.50), and main courses of roast cod loin on Mediterranean vegetables with basil dressing (£9.25), and braised lamb shank on mash with rosemary and red wine jus (£11.25). Also baguettes and simpler dishes such as chicken and ham pie (£5.50) at lunchtime. House wines £11.95. Open all week.

| MAP 5 | EVESHAM – Worcestershire |

Evesham Hotel AR

Cooper's Lane, Evesham WR11 1DA
Tel: (01386) 765566

Smart hotel occupying a Tudor farmhouse in two and a half acres of gardens just outside the town centre. The elegant dining room enjoys views that take in a 180-year-old cedar of Lebanon, although there is also plenty to look at on the weekly-changing menu: starters ranging from mushroom pesto strudels (£5.75) to prawns with sizzling halloumi (£8.50), and main courses typically of monkfish in a coconut curry sauce (£14.75), or roast lamb with roast garlic, pearl barley risotto and pepper sauce (£15.25). Spiced sangria jelly (£5) might be among dessert options. Wines from £14.50. Open all week.

| MAP 1 | EXETER – Devon |

Blue Fish AR

44–45 Queen Street, Exeter EX4 3SR
Tel: (01392) 493581

Opposite Exeter Central station, this is a stylish modern brasserie with a Mediterranean edge and is popular with a lively young crowd. Daily caught fish and seafood takes centre stage on an ambitious menu, with scallops wrapped in Parma ham (£7.95), or Devon moules marinière (£9.95) to start, followed by giant butterflied crevettes (£24.95), or grilled cod with asparagus and Hollandaise (£13.95). Seafood platters for two are gargantuan (from £69.95). End with passion-fruit cheesecake (£5.95). Wines from £12.95. Closed Sun L.

> **AR** Not a full entry but provisionally recommended. These 'also recommended' establishments are integrated throughout the book.

Effings

NEW ENTRY

74 Queen Street, Exeter EX4 3RX
Tel: (01392) 211888
Website: www.effings.co.uk

| Cooking 4 | Mediterranean | £38 |

With a 'large and swish' ground-floor deli, an unpretentious mezzanine restaurant, and décor that combines lots of neutral colours with pale wood and glass, this second branch of Effings (see entry, Totnes) is a great asset in central Exeter. The kitchen works in tandem with local producers, but inspiration comes from near and far: homespun English cold meat platters, such as Devon chicken, beef, and honey and mustard ham served with Quickes Cheddar and home-made chutney, sit happily beside deli-derived plates of jamon pata negra, say, or classic European ideas like starters of risotto nero with sautéed calamari that kicked off an inspection meal. The kitchen is sure-handed when it comes to technique, timing and seasoning, sending out main courses of excellent-quality beef Rossini with 'rich and sweet' foie gras and black truffle jus, and red mullet with spinach gnocchi in a saffron cream. The highlight at inspection was a vanilla-flecked pannacotta, or there could be a rich and intense chocolate nemesis served with a dollop of crème fraîche. Excellent service is unobtrusive, and the wine list covers most bases quite affordably, with prices from £10.95.

Chefs: Tony Hetherington and Shaun Davis **Proprietors:** Michael Kann and Jacqueline Williams **Open:** Mon to Sat L 12 to 2.30, Fri and Sat D 7 to 9 **Closed:** bank hols **Meals:** alc (main courses L £9 to £20, D £13 to £20). Light menu available **Service:** not inc **Cards:** Delta, Diners, Maestro, MasterCard, Visa **Details:** 60 seats. Vegetarian meals. Children's helpings. No smoking.

Galley

AR

41 Fore Street, Topsham, Exeter EX3 0HU
Tel: (01392) 876078

Traditional Buddhist values of enjoyment are the driving force behind this eccentric seafood 'restaurant-with-cabins' occupying a seventeenth-century cottage. Daily deliveries of fish from Brixham are used in a highly individual cooking style that takes in starters of crab, avocado and papaya salad with Armagnac seaweed cocktail sauce, followed by turbot in tempura with 'Yorkshire caviar' and chips, or grilled fillets of halibut on seaweed mash with chilli ice cream, seared scallops and herby ginseng butter sauce. Desserts come with names like 'Seductress' and

'Take Me'. Two courses £28.50, wines from £12.95. Closed Sun and Mon.

Hotel Barcelona, Café Paradiso

NEW ENTRY

Magdalen Street, Exeter EX2 4HY
Tel: (01392) 281000
Website: www.aliashotels.com

| Cooking 2 | Modern European | £38 |

This characterful restaurant, part of the striking Hotel Barcelona, has steadily improved over the last couple of years. The Victorian building houses not only an excellent cocktail bar in the basement but the conservatory dining room is also worth seeking out. Waiting staff are in jeans, and the clientele is young and lively. Dishes are imaginatively put together and there's a separate chef working a huge open pizza oven. A terrine of salmon, wild sea bass, red pepper and asparagus made a sound starter at inspection, while a main course of duck breast with confit leg and citrus fruits was also 'spot on', and calf's liver with polenta was served with minted fine beans. Desserts have also impressed, including a 'wonderfully rich' crème brûlée with plum compote. The quirky wine list groups bottles by style, with house options starting at £13.25.

Chef: Christopher Archambault **Proprietors:** Alias Hotels **Open:** all week 12 to 2, 7 to 10 (6.30 to 10.30 Fri and Sat, 7 to 9.30 Sun) **Meals:** alc (main courses £7.50 to £19). Set L Mon to Fri £10 (2 courses) to £15 **Service:** not inc **Cards:** Amex, Delta, Diners, Maestro, MasterCard, Visa **Details:** 60 seats. 35 seats outside. Car park. Vegetarian meals. Children's helpings. Smoking in bar only. Music **Accommodation:** 46 rooms

La Petite Maison

35 Fore Street, Topsham, Exeter EX3 0HR
Tel: (01392) 873660
Website: www.lapetitemaison.co.uk

| Cooking 4 | Modern British | £43 |

La Petite Maison occupies a riverside property that shows signs of great age, with a Dutch brick fireplace in the main dining room. As the name suggests, it is an intimate, family-run operation with a warm, welcoming atmosphere. The name also points up a French influence in the cooking, although dishes are largely shaped by the first-rate West Country produce that is at the heart of everything the kitchen does. Among starters, crab from

Lyme Bay goes into a risotto with tarragon and crab bisque. Locally landed fish appears in a main course of brill and monkfish with spinach bubble and squeak, spaghetti of vegetables and chive beurre blanc, while meat options might offer herb-crusted medallion of outdoor-reared Somerset pork with slow-roast belly pork and black pudding on creamy leeks with dauphinois potatoes and a pork and cider jus. Inventive desserts have included a rhubarb cocktail comprising a jelly, a compote and a rhubarb and ginger ice cream. A plate of West Country cheeses makes a tempting alternative. Approximately half the bottles on the list of around 60 wines are attractively priced under £25, including house French at £13.95.

Chefs: Douglas Pestell and Sara Bright **Proprietors:** Elizabeth and Douglas Pestell **Open:** Tue to Sat 12.30 to 2, 7 to 10 **Meals:** Set L £19.50 (2 courses) to £22.50, Set D £26.50 (2 courses) to £32 **Service:** not inc **Cards:** Maestro, MasterCard, Visa **Details:** 30 seats. Vegetarian meals. No smoking. Music

---

Royal Clarence Hotel, Michael Caines at ABode

Cathedral Yard, Exeter EX1 1HD
Tel: (01392) 223638
Website: www.michaelcaines.com

| Cooking 3 | French | £61 |

The posh façade is pillared and faces one of the towers of Exeter Cathedral across the green. Inside is a smartly appointed restaurant whose kitchen is headed by Simon Dow, with Michael Caines taking an executive role. With ABode Glasgow (see entry) up and running, and Canterbury due to open after we go to press, this is a busy time for Mr Caines; he is also executive chef of Gidleigh Park, Andrew Brownsword's latest acquisition, which is closed for refurbishment as we go to press (hence its absence from the Guide). Here in Exeter, the kitchen makes use of good West Country materials such as local Ark chicken (stuffed with a tarragon mousse and served with white wine sauce), or Devonshire Red Ruby beef (the fillet served with asparagus, roast shallots and wild mushrooms with a red wine jus). At inspection, Dow's contempo-

rary French-inspired cooking delivered an 'excellent' appetiser of white haricot soup, while pan-fried scallops with pea purée, crispy bacon and shallot velouté made an impressive starter. The main course best end of local lamb, however, was somewhat overwhelmed by its accompaniments (onion purée, braised fennel, roast garlic, tomato fondue packed with basil, and a tapenade jus). Raspberry soufflé with raspberry coulis and vanilla ice cream is a typical dessert. Service is smart but could smile more. The varietally arranged wine list opens at £16.50.

Chef: Simon Dow **Proprietors:** Andrew Brownsword and Michael Caines **Open:** Mon to Sat 12 to 2.30, 7 to 10 **Meals:** alc (main courses £19 to £25). Set L £12.50 (2 courses), Set D £20 (2 courses) **Service:** not inc **Cards:** Amex, Delta, Diners, Maestro, MasterCard, Visa **Details:** 80 seats. Vegetarian meals. Children's helpings. No smoking in dining room. Wheelchair access (also WC). No music. No mobile phones. Air-conditioned **Accommodation:** 53 rooms

---

St Olaves Hotel

Mary Arches Street, Exeter EX4 3AZ
Tel: (01392) 217736

A listed Georgian building near the cathedral, this small hotel offers set-price menus (lunch £14.50/£18.95, dinner £27.50/£31.95), with all produce sourced from the West Country. Game terrine with prune chutney and Earl Grey syrup might start, continuing with pan-fried wild sea bass on noodles and prawns with a Thai-style sauce, or peppered sirloin steak with garlic butter, mushrooms and foie gras. End with warm fig turnovers with ginger mascarpone and elderflower syrup. Six house wines start at £13.50. Open all week.

Thai Orchid

Three Gables, 5 Cathedral Yard, Exeter EX1 1HJ
Tel: (01392) 214215

A newly renovated sixteenth-century building hard by the cathedral makes an unusual setting for this authentic Thai restaurant. Nine set-menu options are on offer, designed to provide a balanced and varied meal, but if you prefer you can choose from a comprehensive carte, starting perhaps with north-eastern style sausages with crispy sticky rice, ginger and roast chillies (£6.30), or deep-fried battered prawns with a sweet chilli dip (£6.30), followed by spicy squid salad (£6.30), and dry curried chicken with coconut milk, peanuts, tomatoes and lime leaves (£9.60). House wines are £12.50. Closed Sat L and Sun.

| **NEW ENTRY** | This appears after the restaurant's name if the establishment was not a main entry in last year's Guide. Please note, however, it may have been 'also recommended' in the previous edition. |

MAP 5 **FAIRFORD –**
Gloucestershire

Allium

1 London Street, Fairford GL7 4AH
Tel: (01285) 712200
Website: www.allium.uk.net

Cooking 6 | Modern European | £46

Situated at the bottom of the market square in this pretty Cotswold town, Allium occupies a pair of attractive Grade II listed stone houses. The welcome is warm, the atmosphere relaxed, with soothing background music and service from smartly attired waiting staff who strike a balance between informality and professionalism. Beyond the comfortable bar area is the dining room where décor in light, neutral tones and tables with plenty of elbow room impart a sense of spaciousness, while crisp white tablecloths, oversized wine glasses and tea lights in ceramic holders create an elegant impression.

Chef-proprietor James Graham aims for a similar degree of refinement in his cooking. Menus show modern sensibilities at work, combining fashionable flavours in sometimes unusual but always well-considered ways, as in a starter of pan-fried peppered skate wing, in which the succulent, flaky fish is placed on a nutty-flavoured, slightly crunchy spelt risotto with parsley and porcini mushrooms, and topped with two lemon-infused chicken wings and asparagus. The fact that the cooking doesn't rely on expensive cuts to make an impact is demonstrated amply in a main course of organic hoggett, the flavoursome meat poached to perfect tenderness in olive oil and served with young broad beans and morels, finished with a lamb's kidney and a rich sauce. Fish eaters might be equally impressed with black bream served crisp skin uppermost on top of fennel in a light, fishy sauce redolent with the colour and flavour of saffron. Standards are maintained through to dessert, which might be banana and praline soufflé with a galette of caramelised banana and vanilla ice cream. France dominates on the wine front but no region is neglected and even English wines get a look-in. There is plenty of choice by the glass or carafe, and house selections start at around £16.

> **Chef:** James Graham **Proprietors:** James and Erica Graham, and Nick Bartimote **Open:** Wed to Sun L 12 to 2, Wed to Sat D 7 to 9 **Meals:** Set L £16 (2 courses) to £18.50, Set D Wed to Fri £20 to £50, Set D Fri and Sat £28.50 (2 courses) to £50, Set L Sun £22.50 **Service:** not inc **Cards:** Delta, Maestro, MasterCard, Visa **Details:** 34 seats. Vegetarian meals. Children's helpings. No smoking in 1 dining room. Occasional music. No mobile phones

MAP 1 **FALMOUTH – Cornwall**

Three Mackerel AR

Swanpool Beach, Falmouth TR11 5BG
Tel: (01326) 311886

With its seafront location on Falmouth Bay, this lively café is worth visiting for the eye-popping views alone, and it offers plenty of outdoor seating on the deck. Locally caught fish naturally features on the menu, which could open with pan-seared scallops served with steamed asparagus and garlic butter (£7.95), while whole roast sea bass with crab and tarragon butter (£14.95) could follow, alongside pan-seared steak with spicy lyonnaise potatoes and a thyme jus (£17.95). There is a lighter lunch menu and a separate children's menu. House wines £10.95. Closed Tue D.

MAP 3 **FARNBOROUGH – Kent**

Chapter One

Farnborough Common, Locksbottom,
Farnborough BR6 8NF
Tel: (01689) 854848
Website: www.chaptersrestaurants.co.uk

Cooking 5 | Modern European | £41

A half-timbered building on the common, sister to Chapter Two (see entry, London), this is a spacious, unobtrusively decorated venue with a choice of restaurant or brasserie eating. It's run with enthusiasm and zest by young front-of-house staff, and Andrew McLeish is a chef with an eye for contemporary trends. This may be suburban Kent, but the menu is distinctly metropolitan. Dishes of surprising richness aim for impact: a creamy gratin of Cornish crab with truffled macaroni is quite a hefty, but indubitably successful, way to start, or there might be morel risotto pointed up with wild garlic and Parmesan. Main courses are where the effort pays off most handsomely, as witness a serving of duck that boldly pairs the breast with a portion of stuffed neck, the richness of the meats productively offset by the bitterness of roast endive and a purée of caramelised turnips. Earthy vegetables are favoured accompaniments, so pumpkin and butternut squash might well make an appearance with a pairing of roast salmon and king prawns. Desserts were less convincing at inspection – a thin layer of blood-orange trifle at the bottom of an enormous brandy balloon felt like conceptualism taken too far. The wine list does Western Europe succinctly before heading off around the world. A page of personal sommelier's selections kicks off with Chilean varietals at £16.

Chef: Andrew McLeish Proprietor: Selective Restaurants Group Open: all week 12 to 2.30 (2.45 Sun), 6.30 to 10 (11 Fri and Sat, 9.30 Sun) Closed: first few days Jan Meals: Set L £16.50 (2 courses) to £19.95, Set D £26.95. Brasserie menu available Service: 12.5% (optional) Cards: Amex, Delta, Diners, Maestro, MasterCard, Visa Details: 120 seats. 20 seats outside. Car park. Vegetarian meals. Children's helpings. No smoking. Music. Air-conditioned

MAP 2 | FARNHAM – Dorset

Museum Inn

Farnham DT11 8DE
Tel: (01725) 516261
Website: www.museuminn.co.uk

Cooking 5 | Modern European | £40

Designed by the father of modern archaeology, General Augustus Pitt-Rivers, to accommodate visitors to his nearby museum, this thatched, red-brick slice of history has a traditional bar with a handsome inglenook, flagstone floors and antique furniture, while the separate dining room, the Shed, is, in contrast, bright and barn-like, with Mrs Beeton-style prints on the walls. Chef Daniel Turner has settled in well after taking over the stoves in 2005, and the style continues to be 'straightforward gastro-pub' cooking. Local supplies remain 'a source of strength', with game from nearby estates and fish delivered daily. At inspection, three giant scallops were perfectly seared and accompanied by parsnip purée, and a main course of slow-roast belly pork in cider and apple sauce came with colcannon. Otherwise, go for something like pan-fried pigeon breast with split peas, pancetta and Madeira jus, then steamed monkfish wrapped in Parma ham with a compote of fennel, shallots and dill. Artistic presentation continues in desserts like Neapolitan parfait with a vanilla tuile and strawberry sauce. Attentive waitresses are 'smiley', and the French-led wine list, with some prestigious bottles from Bordeaux, has much of interest from around the world under £25. A page of house selections starts at £12.

To submit a report on any restaurant, please visit *www.which.co.uk/gfgfeedback*.

Chef: Daniel Turner Proprietors: Vicky Elliot and Mark Stephenson Open: all week 12 to 2 (2.30 Sat and Sun), 7 to 9.30 Closed: 25 Dec, D 1 Jan Meals: alc (main courses £13.50 to £17) Service: not inc Cards: Delta, MasterCard, Visa Details: 80 seats. 40 seats outside. Car park. Vegetarian meals. No children under 5. No smoking in dining room. Wheelchair access (also WC). No music. No mobile phones Accommodation: 8 rooms

MAP 3 | FARNHAM ROYAL – Buckinghamshire

King of Prussia

Blackpond Lane, Farnham Royal SL2 3EG
Tel: (01753) 643006
Website: www.thekingofprussia.com

NEW CHEF | British | £44

On a quiet country road, this pretty whitewashed inn takes the spirit of pub food and gives it a modern polish, using influences from around the globe. A salad of smoked haddock, rocket, crispy bacon and a poached egg lines up among starters alongside pork and rabbit rillettes with pickles and toast. Main courses may be roast rump of lamb with shredded celeriac, capers and parsnip crisps, or pan-fried sea bass with pea risotto. End with banoffi pie or lemon posset with sweet basil pesto. The wine list starts at £14.95. Reports please.

Chef: Gary Irving Proprietors: David Gibbs and Chris Boot Open: all week L 12 to 2.15, Mon to Sat D 6.30 (7 Sat) to 10 Meals: alc (main courses £11 to £17.50) Service: not inc Cards: Amex, Delta, Maestro, MasterCard, Visa Details: 80 seats. 40 seats outside. Car park. Vegetarian meals. No children under 5 at D. Children's helpings. No smoking in dining room. Wheelchair access (not WC). Music. Air-conditioned

MAP 3 | FAVERSHAM – Kent

Read's

Macknade Manor,
Canterbury Road, Faversham
ME13 8XE
Tel: (01795) 535344
Website: www.reads.com

Cooking 6 | Modern British | £65

Long service should count for something, and for appreciative returnees to Read's it does: 'David and Rona Pitchford must be one of the longest-running husband-and-wife teams on Guide records, and they have my sincere admiration.' Long-running means 30 years in their case, during which this red-brick Georgian restaurant-with-rooms has weathered the tides of fashion and is still run with consummate Gallic professionalism and considerable charm. David Pitchford knows his suppliers well, but he reports that he is also about 70 per cent self-sufficient for summer produce from Read's own kitchen garden. He is not above having a little retro fun with dishes, as in an inspection starter that combined Cornish crabmeat layered with chopped cucumber and avocado mousse with a textbook paprika-dusted prawn cocktail complete with pink mayonnaise. It worked beautifully. Or you may start more voguishly with Rye Bay scallops, sautéed and served on a purée of Jerusalem artichoke, with smoked bacon powder and a reduction of port.

Menu descriptions are lengthy, with many elements built in to main courses especially, although the final result on the plate is always more straightforward than you might expect. Turbot might be crusted with foie gras and served on spinach with 'melted' leeks, Parmesan gnocchi and a creamed fennel sauce, while Gressingham duck breast comes also with spinach and rösti strongly seasoned with mustard and thyme, as well as an irreproachable stock sauce containing exquisite morello cherries. To finish, there is likely to be the famous lemon tart, or perhaps a stupendous summer fruit soufflé, with first raspberry sauce poured in and then vanilla ice cream, accompanied by wonderful shortbread biscuits. Read's has always had a killer wine list too. Currently encompassing over 300 listings from all over, it has been thoughtfully condensed for you in a prefatory section to a manageable 60 or so of the most representative. Quality throughout is sound, with the likes of d'Arenberg and Plantagenet in the Australian brigade, and Meerlust and Thelema in South Africa. Its heart, though, lies in France, with good Rhônes and Loires backing up the VIP parades of Bordeaux and Burgundy. Prices start at £16.

Chefs: David Pitchford and Ricky Martin **Proprietors:** Rona and David Pitchford **Open:** Tue to Sat 12 to 2, 7 to 9.30 **Closed:** 25 and 26 Dec **Meals:** Set L £21 to £48, Set D £48 to £72 (inc wine) **Service:** not inc **Cards:** Amex, Diners, Maestro, MasterCard, Visa **Details:** 60 seats. 20 seats outside. Car park. Children's helpings. No smoking in dining room. Wheelchair access (also WC). No music **Accommodation:** 6 rooms

---

| MAP 5 | FAWSLEY –
Northamptonshire |

Fawsley Hall, Knightley Restaurant

Fawsley NN11 3BA
Tel: (01327) 892000
Website: www.fawsleyhall.com

Cooking 5 | **Modern European** | **£56**

Fawsley is a grand old pile, its wood-floored dining room big enough to hold medieval banquets. Retire afterwards to the Great Hall, where reproductions of Tudor portraits you might have seen in the National Portrait Gallery keep watch. Service is elegantly formal, ensuring that everybody feels properly looked after. 'Those who think breast of chicken is dull and tasteless,' begins a report, 'should try confit black-leg chicken with sautéed foie gras and spiced pear at Fawsley Hall.' He at least considers this 'the most interesting menu for miles around', and certainly a strong commitment to both inventiveness and quality sourcing is in evidence. Serrano ham might start you off, served with green beans, beetroot and truffle, or perhaps seared bluefin tuna with avocado and coriander. Daring combinations with fish have included John Dory fillets served with thyme and raisin cabbage and an orange and chicken jus, while meats are more traditionally treated, a roast loin of veal appearing with a mousseline of the sweetbreads and rösti. Finish with a trio of chocolate desserts at three different temperatures – hot, cold and frozen. Children have their own menus.

The wine list opens with 'Wines of the Moment', a choice of fine house offerings from £14.50, while the 'Affordable Excess' section rises to £195 for a 2001 Bienvenues-Bâtard-Montrachet, which – believe it or not – isn't over-priced at all. Selections elsewhere are nearly all exciting and helpfully grouped by style.

Chef: Philip Dixon **Proprietor:** Simon Lowe **Open:** Sat and Sun L 12 to 2.30, all week D 7 to 9.30 **Meals:** alc (main courses L £9.50 to £14.50, D £12.50 to £24.50). Set D £35 to £75 (inc wine). Bar menu available **Service:** 12.5% (optional) **Cards:** Amex, Delta, Maestro, MasterCard, Visa **Details:** 70 seats. 30 seats outside. Car park. Vegetarian meals. Children's helpings. No smoking. Wheelchair access (also WC). Music. No mobile phones **Accommodation:** 43 rooms

MAP 9 FERRENSBY – North Yorkshire

General Tarleton

Boroughbridge Road, Ferrensby HG5 0PZ
Tel: (01423) 340284
Website: www.generaltarleton.co.uk

Cooking 4 | **Modern British** | **£42**

While this 250-year-old coaching inn is no longer on the main road to the north, it's close enough to the A1 to be a useful pit stop. It's also a popular destination in its own right, with a smart restaurant and more informal bar/brasserie, where John Topham delivers inventive modern cooking. His admirable policy of sourcing 80 per cent of his supplies from within a 20-mile radius doesn't restrict his culinary thinking, and menus show a broad range of influences, with starters on the restaurant menu taking in Asian-style squid with papaya and a lime and palm sugar dressing alongside home-cured bresaola with rocket and Parmesan, and a terrine of Yorkshire ham and foie gras with red onion jam. To follow, roast ribeye of Birstwith beef with Yorkshire buffalo blue cheese polenta and salsa verde vies for attention with seared wild sea bass fillet on roast fennel and crisp green beans with lemon and herb crème fraîche. For dessert, Yorkshire rhubarb is presented three ways: in a crème brûlée, crumble and compote, all served with strawberry ice cream. Around a dozen house wines from £13.15 open a well-balanced, varied list arranged by style.

Chef: John Topham **Proprietors:** John and Claire Topham **Open:** Sun L 12 to 2.15, Mon to Sat D 6 to 9.30 **Meals:** Set L £18.95, Set D £29.95. Bar/brasserie menu available all week L and D **Service:** not inc **Cards:** Amex, Delta, Maestro, MasterCard, Visa **Details:** 70 seats. 40 seats outside. Car park. Vegetarian meals. Children's helpings. No smoking in dining room. Wheelchair access (not WC). No music **Accommodation:** 14 rooms

---

 This symbol means that the restaurant has elected to participate in *The Good Food Guide's* £5 voucher scheme (see 'Using The Good Food Guide' for details).

MAP 3 FLETCHING – East Sussex

Griffin Inn

Fletching TN22 3SS
Tel: (01825) 722890
Website: www.thegriffininn.co.uk

Cooking 2 | **Modern European** | **£40**

The Griffin Inn, a Grade II listed building with an attractive garden, manages to capitalise on the fact that it offers fine dining in the bar as well as the restaurant, and it's not unusual to find all rooms full. The two bar areas are traditional in appearance, with the restaurant a little smarter – white linen cloths and flowers. The kitchen uses mainly Sussex suppliers and vegetables (some from their own garden). Although this is very much a traditional English pub, the dishes have a European accent, as in a starter of roast boned quail with lemon, sage and mascarpone wrapped in Parma ham. There are around eight main courses to choose from, including perhaps pan-seared Rye Bay turbot with a crab, lobster and saffron risotto, or roast rump of Fletching lamb with ratatouille, sautéed potatoes and tapenade. Those with a sweet craving will enjoy pear tarte Tatin with vanilla ice cream. The wine list, split between Europe and the New World, is notable for its quality producers and some fine vintages. Around a dozen carefully chosen bottles, from Sicilian red and white at £11.50, are served by the quarter-bottle glass from £3.

Chef: Andrew Billings **Proprietors:** Bridget, Nigel and James Pullan **Open:** all week L 12 to 2.30, Mon to Sat D 7 to 9.30 **Closed:** 25 Dec **Meals:** alc exc Sun L (main courses £11 to £19.50). Set L Sun £25. Bar menu available **Service:** not inc **Cards:** Amex, Delta, Diners, Maestro, MasterCard, Visa **Details:** 60 seats. 35 seats outside. Car park. Vegetarian meals. Children's helpings. No smoking in dining room. Wheelchair access (also WC). Music. No mobile phones **Accommodation:** 13 rooms

MAP 8 FORTON – Lancashire

Bay Horse Inn

Bay Horse, Forton LA2 0HR
Tel: (01524) 791204
Website: www.bayhorseinn.com

Cooking 3 | **Modern British** | **£38**

Forton is an isolated rural hamlet, although it's just minutes from the M6. At its heart is this thriving

pub. In the bar, an open fire, local cask ales on tap and dried hops hanging from the ceiling keep up traditional appearances, but then the gastro bit takes over – the 'have you booked?' greeting from the rather formal staff fortunately tempered by the long list of wines available by the glass, and the sign that tells you that raw materials are sourced locally as far as possible. And the results are good, according to a couple who were impressed by hot-smoked salmon with horseradish cream, Andrew Ireland's black pudding served with carrot rémoulade and balsamic vinegar, and roast Goosnargh duck (two legs) teamed with buttery potato purée, figs, and a gentle sauce of elder-flower, honey and balsamic vinegar. The highlight, though, was a 'masterpiece' of a lemon and Garstang Blue cheese crumble cheesecake. House wine is £11.95.

Chef: Craig Wilkinson **Proprietors:** Brian and Mae Wilkinson, Craig Wilkinson and Yvonne Wilkinson-Wright **Open:** Tue to Sun L 12 to 2 (3 Sun), Tue to Sat D 7 to 9.30 **Closed:** 25 Dec, 1 Jan **Meals:** alc exc Sun L (main courses £11.50 to £18.50), Set L Sun £13.95 (2 courses) to £17.90 **Service:** not inc **Cards:** Amex, Delta, Maestro, MasterCard, Visa **Details:** 60 seats. 20 seats outside. Car park. Vegetarian meals. Children's helpings. No smoking in dining room. Wheelchair access (not WC). music **Accommodation:** 4 rooms

MAP 6	FOTHERINGHAY – Northamptonshire

Falcon

Fotheringhay PE8 5HZ
Tel: (01832) 226254
Website: www.huntsbridge.com

Cooking 3 | **Modern European** | **£39**

This informal pub in a pretty country location is part of the Huntsbridge group (see also Old Bridge Hotel, Huntingdon; Three Horseshoes, Madingley; Pheasant, Keyston) and has a similar laid-back approach to its siblings. That's not to say that the food is anything but well-presented, timed and sourced from the best raw materials but the philosophy that you can 'eat whatever you like – no minimum orders' means that a light lunch in the bar or full meals in the restaurant are relaxed affairs. Bar snacks might be fisherman's pie or Suffolk pork sausages, while the dining room has a strong Italian influence in the shape of hand-made pumpkin and ricotta ravioli, or buffalo mozzarella with violetta artichokes. Portland crab with dill, dried chilli, peppered green beans and Jersey Royals

was enjoyed at inspection, as was chargrilled rump of Cornish lamb, which came with 'excellent' olive oil mash with Parmesan, braised fava beans and a very good salsa verde. To end, chocolate almond cake is served with a 'lovely tasting' zabaglione ice cream. The extensive wine list is arranged by style and price, with some short informative notes and John Hoskins advising customers to 'please experiment'; 15 house wines start at £12.95, but there are many good-value bins under £20.

Chefs: Dave Sims and Chris Kipping **Proprietor:** John Hoskins **Open:** all week 12 to 2.15, 6 to 9.30 (10 Sat) **Meals:** alc (main courses £10 to £20). Snack menu available **Service:** not inc **Cards:** Amex, Diners, Maestro, MasterCard, Visa **Details:** 80 seats. 40 seats outside. Car park. Vegetarian meals. Children's helpings. No smoking. Wheelchair access (also WC). No music. No mobile phones

MAP 1	FOWEY – Cornwall

Fowey Hall

AR

Hanson Drive, Fowey PL23 1ET
Tel: (01726) 833866

An impressive hotel with gorgeous views over the estuary and only a ten-minute drive from the Eden Project, Fowey Hall aims high when it comes to cuisine. Glyn Wellington's locally sourced set-price three-course dinner menu (£32.50) runs to seared Cornish scallops with Parmesan mash, followed, perhaps, by saddle of Treesmill lamb served with wilted chard, or an array of shellfish including Fowey river mussels. End with chilled vanilla rice pudding with rhubarb compote. Some excellent wines from £15.50. Open all week.

Marina Villa, Waterside

17 Esplanade, Fowey PL23 1HY
Tel: (01726) 833315
Website: www.themarinahotel.co.uk

Cooking 4 | **Seafood** | **£56**

Although this charming hotel restaurant is found on a tiny back street that is hardly wide enough to drive a car down, the sea views from window tables are enough to forgive the boarding-house façade. It is, unsurprisingly given the setting, a predominantly seafood establishment and chef Chris Eden, who trained at The Square (see entry, London), is clearly determined to make his mark in this corner of the world with an ambitious menu, offering starters of lightly spiced white spider crab with avocado, apple and pink grapefruit salad, or seared Looe scallops with Jerusalem artichokes, bacon crisps, banyuls and raisin purée. The handful of mains continue the theme with Parmesan and thyme-glazed brill on cauliflower purée, hand-rolled macaroni, broccoli and shellfish bisque, or with a pairing of roast rump of Cornish lamb and braised pork belly on creamed potato, caramelized sweetbreads and a rosemary and balsamic jus. Desserts extend to mango and vanilla Arctic roll or hot praline soufflé. The wine list is international with the house sauvignon costing £16.50 a bottle.

> **Chef:** Chris Eden **Proprietor:** Steve Westwell **Open:** all week 12 to 2.30, 6.30 to 9.30 **Meals:** Set L £19.95 (2 courses) to £22.95, Set D £33 to £39 **Service:** not inc **Cards:** Amex, Delta, Maestro, MasterCard, Visa **Details:** 40 seats. 50 seats outside. Vegetarian meals. Children's helpings. Smoking in bar only. Music. No mobile phones **Accommodation:** 18 rooms

Old Quay House

28 Fore Street, Fowey PL23 1AQ
Tel: (01726) 833302
Website: www.theoldquayhouse.com

Cooking 2 | **Modern British** | **£49**

The Old Quay House is contemporary in attitude and operation. The kitchen roams widely in its seasonally changing menus and gives local fish due preference, teaming marinated monkfish with aïoli and fennel, and offering pan-fried skate wing with sautéed potatoes, brown shrimps and beetroot sauce. Occasionally, high-class comfort food makes an appearance, as in main courses of braised shoulder of mutton with flageolet beans and spinach, and roast crown of chicken with sage and pancetta gnocchi. Puddings are generally variations on a traditional theme: apple tart with ginger wafers and vanilla ice cream, and caramel rice pudding with coffee sauce. A short wine list with a fair range opens with house wines at £13.50.

> **Chef:** Ben Bass **Proprietors:** Jane and Roy Carson **Open:** all week 12.30 to 2.30, 7 to 9 **Closed:** L Nov to Apr **Meals:** alc (main courses L £10 to £12, D £12.50 to £21) **Service:** 10% (optional) **Cards:** Amex, Delta, Maestro, MasterCard, Visa **Details:** 38 seats. 38 seats outside. Vegetarian meals. No smoking. Wheelchair access (not WC). Music. No mobile phones **Accommodation:** 12 rooms

---

MAP 2	**FRAMPTON MANSELL –** Gloucestershire

White Horse

Cirencester Road, Frampton Mansell GL6 8HZ
Tel: (01285) 760960

Cooking 2 | **Modern British** | **£38**

The premises have undergone a makeover since the last edition, the once eclectic décor swapped for something more modern, with seagrass flooring, cream and pale-chocolate walls and original Victorian and modern art. The focal-point seafood tank remains, though. Oysters, mussels and clams are popular options, with lobster making an appearance in springtime. The wide-ranging modern British menu also encompasses leek and potato soup or duck leg confit with braised red cabbage to start, while mains feature seared tuna with black olives and tomato, chilli and caper relish, Toulouse sausages with sweet potato mash, or pork fillet stuffed with dates. Puddings might be elderflower and raspberry jelly with vanilla ice cream or spiced steamed pear pudding. The wine list comprises 61 bins with noted recommendations; house choices start at £13.50, with plenty more under £20.

> **Chef:** Howard Matthews **Proprietors:** Emma and Shaun Davis **Open:** all week L 12 to 2.30 (3 Sun), Mon to Sat D 7 to 9.45 **Closed:** 25 to 26 Dec, 1 Jan **Meals:** alc (main courses £11 to £16.50) **Service:** not inc **Cards:** Delta, Maestro, MasterCard, Visa **Details:** 45 seats. 50 seats outside. Car park. Vegetarian meals. Children's helpings. Smoking in bar only. Music

---

MAP 6	**FRESSINGFIELD –** Suffolk

Fox and Goose

Fressingfield IP21 5PB
Tel: (01379) 586247
Website: www.foxandgoose.net

Cooking 3 | **Modern British** | **£38**

'Don't forget to look at the spectacular rear of the building,' writes chef/proprietor Paul Yaxley of his Grade II★ listed property, as it's composed of nogging and herringbone brickwork. The great age of the one-time guildhall is apparent inside too, in the shape of heavy black beams and some ancient framed documents relating to the inn's history. The style of cooking, however, is rooted in the present: sautéed goats' cheese comes as a starter with a couscous crust, pear tarte Tatin and port vinaigrette, and duck breast as a main course with caramelised pineapple, five-spice and spring onion gnocchi, pak choi and red wine sauce. More traditional treatments are handled no less confidently, as in a trio of lamb – loin, neck and kidney – on garlic mash with carrots, minted crème fraîche and lamb jus, or a starter of pan-fried calf's liver and bacon with marmalade mash. Desserts can range from spotted dick with custard to lemon panna-cotta with chocolate mousse. Chile and Australia head up the wine list, at £12.50 for a Sauvignon Blanc and a Merlot/Shiraz respectively, which gives as much weight to the southern hemisphere as to Europe.

Chefs: Paul Yaxley and Mat Wyatt   Proprietor: Paul Yaxley   Open: Tue to Sun 12 to 2, 7 to 9 (6.30 to 8.15 Sun)   Meals: alc exc Sun L (main courses L £8 to £17.50, D £12 to £17.50). Set L Mon to Sat £11.50 (2 courses) to £13.95, Set L Sun £13.50 (2 courses) to £16.95, Set D £35   Service: not inc   Cards: Amex, Delta, Maestro, MasterCard, Visa   Details: 48 seats. 18 seats outside. Car park. Vegetarian meals. No children under 9 at D. Children's helpings. No smoking. Wheelchair access (not WC). Music

MAP 2   **FRILSHAM** – Berkshire

Pot Kiln

NEW ENTRY

Frilsham RG18 0XX
Tel: (01635) 201366
Website: www.potkiln.co.uk

Cooking 3 | Modern European | £43

Despite being taken over by 'TV chef' Mike Robinson, this attractive red-brick country pub doesn't forget its pub roots; on the contrary, the place 'simply oozes unpretentious country atmosphere'. Picnic-style tables are outside, West Berkshire ales are on draught, and hunting, shooting and fishing prints hang on the walls. The menu, crisply scripted with only main components listed, changes regularly to reflect the seasons and availability. Starters of pork and venison terrine, and rillettes of rabbit with celeriac rémoulade sound appropriately rustic, given the location. Game is something of a speciality, so among main courses may be saddle of roebuck with asparagus and mash, or whole roast wood pigeon with sautéed potatoes and beetroot sauce. Sea bream with crushed Jersey Royals and sauce vierge may be the single fish option, and to end there could be chocolate brownie with pears poached in red wine, or pain perdu with strawberries and crème

fraîche. Staff are 'willing and helpful', and the wine list runs to 60-plus bins, opening with Vins de Pays d'Oc at £12.50.

Chef: Duncan Welgemoed   Proprietor: Mike Robinson   Open: all week L 12 to 2, Mon to Sat D 7 to 9   Closed: 25 Dec   Meals: alc (main courses £12 to £17.50). Set L Mon to Fri £13.50 (2 courses) to £16.50, Set L Sun £15.50 (2 courses) to £19.50. Bar menu available   Service: 10% (optional)   Cards: Amex, Delta, Maestro, MasterCard, Visa   Details: 48 seats. 100 seats outside. Car park. Vegetarian meals. Children's helpings. No smoking in dining room. Wheelchair access (not WC). No music. No mobile phones

MAP 9   **FROGGATT** – Derbyshire

Chequers Inn

AR

Froggatt Edge S32 3ZJ
Tel: (01433) 630231

A favourite with Peak District walkers, this lovely old coaching inn is still more defiantly pub than 'gastro' but has an appealing menu: smoked duck with caramelised kumquats and redcurrant dressing (£5.95) could start, followed by local pork sausage with 'Scarborough Fair' mash (£9.25), or roast salmon and coriander brochette with a new potato and chorizo salad (£11.95). Among desserts might be pistachio, honey and mascarpone cheesecake. House wines are £12. Accommodation. Open all week.

MAP 3   **FUNTINGTON** – West Sussex

Hallidays

Watery Lane, Funtington PO18 9LF
Tel: (01243) 575331

Cooking 2 | Modern British | £44

Charmingly located within a thatched terrace of ancient flint cottages, this village restaurant has a very traditional feel. Chef Andy Stephenson is passionate about sourcing locally and his uncomplicated menu moves with the seasons; an added bonus is the plethora of made-on-the-premises goodies, including their own cured or smoked fish and meats, chutneys, ice cream and breads. Twice-baked cheese soufflé or home-cured gravad lax might prelude a main course of Scotch beef fillet with wild mushroom ravioli in a tarragon cream sauce, or possibly roast monkfish with crème fraîche, mustard, apple and cider. Desserts with a twist could be Seville orange buttermilk mousse or warm French chocolate tart with Cointreau cream. The wine list meanders all over the globe offering house selections from £12.50.

Chef: Andy Stephenson **Proprietors:** Andy Stephenson and Peter Creech **Open:** Wed to Fri and Sun L 12 to 1.15, Wed to Sat D 7 to 9.15 **Closed:** 2 weeks early Mar, 1 week late Aug **Meals:** alc L Wed to Fri (main courses £13.75 to £18). Set L Wed to Fri £16 (2 courses) to £18.50, Set L Sun £21, Set D £26 (2 courses) to £30.50 **Service:** not inc **Cards:** Delta, Maestro, MasterCard, Visa **Details:** 26 seats. Car park. No smoking. Wheelchair access (also WC). No music

---

MAP 10   GATESHEAD – Tyne & Wear

Baltic, McCoys Rooftop Restaurant

Centre for Contemporary Arts, South Shore Road, Gateshead NE8 3BA
Tel: (0191) 440 4949
Website: www.mccoysbaltic.com

Cooking 2 | **Modern British** | **£56**

While the enormous silver and glass shell of the Sage music complex now rather dwarfs the Baltic Mill, it is still a 'pretty substantial building'. Security is tight but with a reservation you're soon whisked to the top in a glass lift and taking in the views of the Newcastle skyline. Lots of influences are at work here, so a starter of king scallops with asparagus risotto, blobs of pea purée, ballottine of quail, Parma ham and truffle foam may be followed by loin of pork with apple purée, black pudding, confit pork with mixed herbs, potato fondant, fried polenta and brandy jus. Desserts are equally complex, perhaps a harmonious combination of white chocolate mousse with dark chocolate Arctic roll, milk chocolate ice cream, marinated cherries, milk chocolate beignet and cherry coulis with dark chocolate 'paint' streaked across the plate. Service is well informed and helpful; the wine list opens at £15.95.

Chefs: Marcus Bennett and Simon Wood **Proprietors:** Eugene and Tom McCoy, and Marcus Bennet **Open:** all week L 12 to 2, Mon to Sat D 7 to 9.30 **Meals:** Set L £16.95 (2 courses) to £19.95, Set D £19.95 (before 8pm) to £39.95 **Service:** 10% (optional) **Cards:** Amex, Delta, Diners, Maestro, MasterCard, Visa **Details:** 85 seats. Vegetarian meals. Children's helpings. Smoking in bar only. Wheelchair access (also WC). Music. Air-conditioned

---

Eslington Villa

8 Station Road, Low Fell, Gateshead NE9 6DR
Tel: (0191) 487 6017
Website: www.eslingtonvillaltd.co.uk

Cooking 3 | **Modern European** | **£43**

There's an air of calm about this substantial Edwardian villa set in a leafy suburb, its smart conservatory dining room overlooking attractive, steeply sloped gardens. It's a fitting setting for cooking that doesn't aim to thrill with outlandish ideas but still achieves highly satisfying results, thanks to skilful techniques and well-sourced ingredients. Goats' cheese rarebit with Parma ham and beetroot salad, and ravioli of slow-cooked duck with red onion compote and verjuice are typical of starters, while main-course options might include a casserole of monkfish with spiced mussel broth, roast pheasant with shallots, garlic and salsify, and fondant potato, and saltimbocca with truffle risotto, a Parmesan tuile and rocket. To finish, go for perhaps sticky toffee pudding with hot toffee sauce, or Baileys crème brûlée. Wines are a straightforward selection, with seven house wines from £11.90 a bottle, £3.35 a glass.

Chef: Andrew Moore **Proprietors:** Nick and Melanie Tulip **Open:** Sun to Fri L 12 to 2, Mon to Sat D 7 to 10 **Meals:** alc exc Sun L (main courses £13.50 to £19.50). Set L Mon to Fri £14 (2 courses) to £16, Set D Mon to Fri £20 **Service:** not inc **Cards:** Amex, Delta, Diners, Maestro, MasterCard, Visa **Details:** 80 seats. 20 seats outside. Car park. Vegetarian meals. Children's helpings. No smoking. Wheelchair access (also WC). Music **Accommodation:** 18 rooms

---

MAP 2   GILLINGHAM – Dorset

Stock Hill

Stock Hill, Gillingham SP8 5NR
Tel: (01747) 823626
Website: www.stockhillhouse.co.uk

Cooking 5 | **Modern European** | **£49**

Stock Hill is a late-Victorian mansion set in 11 acres of grounds, a mixture of woodland and beautifully landscaped gardens, which can be enjoyed from the dining room. Traditional country-house elegance is the prevailing style, with well-spaced candlelit tables with starched white linen and sparkling glassware. Peter Hauser's Austrian origins are a strong influence on his cooking, and authentic dishes from his homeland are highlighted on the menu, such as calf's liver pâté with cranberry compote and toasted lemon brioche, or marinated dill herring fillet with poached fennel, red onion and white wine cream, perhaps followed by tapfelspitz (poached H-bone beef with chive cream and 'potato nonsense'). The rest of the menu is more broadly modern European in scope, with starters of dandelion leaves and root salad with baby new potatoes and a poached quail's egg, or marinated king scallops with green peppercorns and pink grapefruit, and similarly inventive main courses such as saddle of rabbit stuffed with its kidney and sage, served with a carrot flan. The Austrian influence shines through particularly in classic desserts of Apfelstrudel, Linzertorte and Esterhazy torte. The wine list is a substantial, well-annotated tome. France is the main focal point, with Bordeaux and Burgundies prominent, but best value is in the 'wines from around the world' section, including some Austrian bottles. Prices start at £17.50.

Chefs: Peter Hauser and Lorna Connor Proprietors: Peter and Nita Hauser Open: Tue to Fri and Sun L 12.15 to 1.45, all week D 7.15 to 8.45 Meals: Set L £26, Set D £36 Service: not inc Cards: Maestro, MasterCard, Visa Details: 36 seats. 8 seats outside. Car park. Vegetarian meals. Children's helpings. No smoking. No music. No mobile phones Accommodation: 8 rooms

MAP 2   GITTISHAM – Devon

Combe House

Gittisham EX14 3AD
Tel: (01404) 540400
Website: www.thishotel.com

Cooking 4 | Modern British | £57

Arab horses roam freely in the 3,500 acres of grounds that surround Combe House; you may see them as you drive first through woodland, then open parkland on the approach to this magnificent Grade I listed, creeper-covered Elizabethan mansion. Despite the grandeur of the setting, service is friendly and relaxed, a mood that runs through to the refined but unpretentious modern British cooking produced by chef Philip Leach, whose devotion to sourcing the best local produce is demonstrated by a page in the menu naming suppliers – which include their own kitchen gardens. The kitchen's output typically runs to starters of warm mutton pie with split pea purée and sherry vinegar jus, or seared Cornish scallops with parsnip purée and caramelised garlic foam,

and main courses including roast wild mallard breast with celeriac fondant, a ragoût of wild mushrooms, smoked bacon and spinach, and truffle sauce. Classic lemon cheesecake might be among desserts, alongside more inventive options such as pumpkin and ginger tart with caramelised ginger ice cream. Around 90 carefully chosen bottles make up the wine list, with France and Australia particularly well represented. Value is good throughout, with prices starting at £17.50.

Chef: Philip Leach Proprietors: Ken and Ruth Hunt Open: all week 12 to 2, 7 to 9.30 Meals: Set L £20 (2 courses) to £26, Set D £39.50 to £49. Bar L menu available Service: not inc Cards: Delta, Maestro, MasterCard, Visa Details: 60 seats. 30 seats outside. Car park. Vegetarian meals. Children's helpings. No smoking. Wheelchair access (also WC). Occasional music. No mobile phones Accommodation: 15 rooms

MAP 8   GOLCAR – West Yorkshire

Weavers Shed

88 Knowl Road, Golcar HD7 4AN
Tel: (01484) 654284
Website: www.weaversshed.co.uk

Cooking 5 | Modern British | £56

The Jacksons have been running this hugely accomplished restaurant-with-rooms on the hills overlooking Huddersfield since 1993. It seems the operation grows a little more self-sufficient with each passing year, as fruit, vegetables, herbs and eggs are all home-produced. Stephen Jackson reports that he makes 'the occasional foray into molecular gastronomy' nowadays, but not enough to startle his customers. Compositions make sense, as witness a homely soup of root vegetables and pearl barley, served with shallot and thyme cream and a piece of brioche. Smoked haddock is worked into a risotto, and finished with parsley and lemon butter and a 'caramel' of roast shellfish. It's the precision that impresses, with meats timed so as to leave them rare, and dishes are put together with healthy appetites in mind. Braised and roast belly of saddleback pork is teamed with a braise of the cheek meat, roots and herbs, some black pudding mash and red cabbage, the whole sauced with a syrup of braising juices and Suffolk cider. Nothing could be more defiantly northern than serving Wensleydale cheese with an Eccles cake hot from the oven, or perhaps less so than gelato affogato – a scoop of vanilla ice cream with a shot of hot espresso to pour over it.

Local wine merchants (plus one or two from further afield) are credited on the list, which is annotated in chatty, unpretentious style, and – more to the point – demonstrates fair pricing and intelligent choosing from top to bottom. Half a dozen house wines are priced uniformly at £13.95, or £3.50 a glass.

Chefs: Stephen Jackson, Ian McGunnigle and Cath Sill **Proprietors:** Stephen and Tracy Jackson **Open:** Tue to Fri L 12 to 1.30, Tue to Sat D 7 to 9 **Closed:** 25 Dec to second week Jan **Meals:** alc (main courses £16 to £26). Set L £13.95 (2 courses) to £16.95 **Service:** not inc **Cards:** Amex, Delta, Diners, Maestro, MasterCard, Visa **Details:** 24 seats. Car park. Vegetarian meals. No smoking in 1 dining room. Music. No mobile phones **Accommodation:** 5 rooms

MAP 9 **GOLDSBOROUGH –
North Yorkshire**

Fox and Hounds NEW ENTRY

Goldsborough
YO21 3RX
Tel: (01947) 893372

Cooking 5 | Modern European | £37

£

Here is a little Yorkshire gem, hidden away all on its own on a narrow twisting country lane off the A174, not far from the bright lights of Whitby. Inside is as simple as can be, with a pair of rooms for eating and drinking, the menus chalked up on a board, and food being ordered from the counter. So far, so country pub, right down to the infectious cheer with which Susan Wren greets those who happen in. The cooking, however, is a revelation. Jason Davies favours a modern European style, based on Whitby seafood, organic local vegetables, and meat from a butcher in Ruswarp, with regional speciality cheeses an added attraction.

The bill of fare changes every day but may well include nettle soup, roast langoustines with chilli, fennel and lemon, cotechino sausage with Puy lentils, Savoy cabbage and salsa verde, or simple ribeye with chips and béarnaise. Fish dishes were hugely impressive at inspection, the high points being a wing of meltingly well-timed skate in a rocket salad zingily dressed with garlic and anchovies, and a main course of golden-seared halibut – 'a sensational piece of fish' – on a layered bed of porcini, sliced potatoes and spinach, moistened with salsa verde. To finish, there is a straight choice of one dessert or cheese, the former perhaps bitter chocolate and almond torte in crisp pastry, served with powerful espresso ice cream. Wines, like the food, are chalked up. Expect an

evenly split bunch of French and New Worlders, with prices from about £12, or £3.20 a glass.

Chef: Jason Davies **Proprietors:** Susan Wren and Jason Davies **Open:** Wed to Sun L 12 to 2, Wed to Sat D 6.30 to 9 **Closed:** Christmas, bank hol Mon **Meals:** alc (main courses £8.50 to £18) **Service:** not inc **Cards:** Delta, Diners, Maestro, MasterCard, Visa **Details:** 30 seats. 16 seats outside. Car park. Vegetarian meals. No smoking in dining room. Music. No mobile phones

MAP 8 **GOOSNARGH –
Lancashire**

Solo AR

Goosnargh Lane, Goosnargh PR3 2BN
Tel: (01772) 865206

This 'delightful' eighteenth-century cottage is long established and proves a popular draw for locals. There is a global flavour to Simon Eastham's five course set-price menu (£29.50). Begin with confit duck with borlotti bean and rocket salad, moving on to a soup or sorbet, followed by pan-fried lamb chops with red onion and rosemary gravy. Three-course Sunday lunch is £16.90. Wines from £12.90. Open Sun L, Tue to Sat D.

MAP 2 **GORING – Oxfordshire**

Leatherne Bottel

The Bridleway, Goring RG8 0HS
Tel: (01491) 872667
Website: www.leathernebottel.co.uk

Cooking 3 | Modern European | £50

It's impossible not to find the location beguiling: the whitewashed house is on the bank of the Thames, with a large terrace the perfect spot for drinks in summer (there is also provision for cooler days, with an open fire in the bar). Chef Julia Storey brings her years of cooking in New Zealand straight to the table, via her own salad and herb garden, proving that she's happy with strong flavours and aromatic spices; her breads are seasonal, with tomato and olive featuring in spring and sweet ginger and coriander in summer. Start with roast horopito-crusted (a herb from NZ) boneless quail served with spring vegetables and a chocolate jus, or grilled squid and melon salad with lemon confit and peppercorn vinaigrette, before moving on to roast tenderloin of veal, accompanied by a turnip tarte Tatin and Puy lentils. A choice of eight puddings might include a triple chocolate Neapolitan mousse torte. The wine list leans towards France and Italy, although the southern hemisphere is represented. Around half a dozen are served by the glass, from £3.50, and bottle prices start at £15.50.

Chef: Julia Storey Proprietor: Croftchase Ltd Open: all week L 12 to 2 (2.30 Sat, 3.30 Sun), Mon to Sat D 7 to 9 (9.30 Sat) Meals: alc (main courses £17.50 to £20). Set D Mon to Thur £24.50. Light L menu available Mon to Thur Service: 10% Cards: Amex, Delta, Maestro, MasterCard, Visa Details: 48 seats. 120 seats outside. Car park. Vegetarian meals. No children under 10. No smoking. No music. No mobile phones

---

MAP 8 **GRANGE MOOR** – West Yorkshire

Kaye Arms

29 Wakefield Road, Grange Moor WF4 4BG
Tel: (01924) 848385

Cooking 3 | Modern British | £42

There's a moment on a Saturday night at the Kaye Arms when all hell breaks loose: our inspector found that, thanks to a no-reservations policy, at precisely 6.30pm there was a dash for tables, with every one full a few minutes later. So, this food-focused pub is clearly as popular as ever. The décor is on the traditional side – some would say old-fashioned – while the carte offers much of interest, supported by daily specials. Start with a mature Cheddar soufflé, or there might be salad of roast pear, Parma ham, Roquefort and rocket. Roast rump of lamb (cooked pink) with its accompaniments of minted Puy lentils, broad beans and gratin dauphinois was a 'well-executed' main course at inspection, while rabbit leg braised in red wine sauce with prunes, pancetta and vegetables has also been a hit. Rhubarb pavlova – 'nice squishy, chewy meringue' – makes a good ending. Service is well paced, and an interesting wine list of about 50 bins represents good value, from around £12.50.

Chef: Adrian Quarmby Proprietors: Adrian and Niccola Quarmby, and Sarah Allott Open: Tue to Sun 12 to 2, 7.15 (7 Fri, 6.30 Sat) to 9.30 (10 Fri and Sat) Closed: 25 Dec to 4 Jan Meals: alc (main courses £8 to £20). Light L menu available Tue to Sat Service: not inc Cards: Maestro, MasterCard, Visa Details: 90 seats. Car park. Vegetarian meals. No children under 14 at D. No smoking in dining room. Wheelchair access (also WC). Music

---

MAP 8 **GRASMERE** – Cumbria

Jumble Room

Langdale Road, Grasmere LA22 9SU
Tel: (015394) 35188
Website: www.thejumbleroom.co.uk

Cooking 2 | Global | £38

There's a cheerful, feel-good atmosphere at Andy and Chrissy Hill's small restaurant, fuelled by their sheer enthusiasm for what they do. Displays of bright, colourful artefacts ensure the dining room lives up to its name, and also reflect the lively flavours on the menu. Spicy Thai tiger prawns with Asian greens and papaya is a typically forthright starter, as is handmade cannelloni stuffed with a mousseline of goose confit and chicken on a mushroom and Madeira jus. To follow, options might include baked halibut fillet with tomatoes, thyme and a sweet lemon sauce, or roast Galloway sirloin steak with dauphinois potatoes, greens, a herb-crusted baked mushroom, and a red wine and Cassis sauce. Organic produce from small, mostly local producers is at the heart of everything. Not surprisingly, the wine list opens with around ten organic bottles. The main list opens at £10.95, and there are also fine beers from well-renowned Lakeland brewers.

Chefs: Chrissy Hill, and David and Trudy Clay Proprietors: Andy and Chrissy Hill Open: Easter to end Nov Wed to Sun 11 to 4, 6 to 10; also open Sat and Sun Jan (phone for times) Closed: 11 to 27 Dec Meals: alc (main courses L £8 to £15, D £11 to £20) Service: not inc Cards: Maestro, MasterCard, Visa Details: 45 seats. 10 seats outside. Vegetarian meals. Children's helpings. No smoking. Wheelchair access (not WC). Music

---

White Moss House

Rydal Water, Grasmere LA22 9SE
Tel: (015394) 35295
Website: www.whitemoss.com

Cooking 5 | British | £52

Once the home of William Wordsworth's son, this relaxed, laid-back family-run hotel makes pleasing first impressions. There are fresh flowers everywhere, the welcoming lounge has an open fire and is furnished with Victorian panache, and tables in the low-ceilinged, cottagey dining room are neatly rather than smartly laid. Uncomplicated cooking of mostly local materials is Peter Dixon's forte.

Dinner, served at 8pm, is a daily changing, five-course menu with no choice until pudding. Simplicity and elegant presentation are hallmarks, meals typically opening with spiced celeriac and chive soup, then going on to trout cured with peat smoke and served on a bed of rocket, radicchio, red chard and edible flowers, or maybe a soufflé of haddock and halibut with Westmorland smoked cheese. Among main courses might be rack of herb-crusted Herdwick lamb accompanied by a blueberry and Bordeaux sauce, or crispy roast mallard with damson, port and Pinot Noir sauce.

It's a well-balanced repertoire that focuses on perfecting the tried-and-true, rather than chasing novelty – which is why you may finish happily with a choice of bread-and-butter pudding, or sticky chocolate hazelnut slice. A page of 'personally selected wines' opens a list with a quality-first approach and with French classics to the fore, but there are good options under £20 from around the world.

Chefs: Peter Dixon Proprietors: Susan and Peter Dixon
Open: Mon to Sat D only 8 (1 sitting) Closed: Dec and Jan
Meals: Set D £39.50 Service: not inc Cards: Maestro, MasterCard, Visa Details: 18 seats. Car park. Vegetarian meals. No toddlers. Children's helpings. No smoking. Wheelchair access (not WC). No music. No mobile phones
Accommodation: 6 rooms

MAP 6 **GREAT GONERBY –** Lincolnshire

Harry's Place

17 High Street, Great Gonerby NG31 8JS
Tel: (01476) 561780

Cooking 7 | **Modern French** | **£69**

Harry's is a unique experience. Located in a tall, blue-and-white Georgian property in a village near Grantham, it is what Americans would call a Mom and Pop operation, entirely run by the two of them, and imbued with the feeling of a private house hosting a special occasion. The small dining room has walls in deep cerise, a bundle of willow twigs garlanded in fairy lights, and the Hallams' family photos to look at. Meals start as they mean to go on, with canapés that kick the tastebuds into action, perhaps warm tartlets of cherry tomato concasse topped with feta. Then you're into the pint-sized menu, which offers just two alternatives at each stage.

What Harry Hallam has always been good at is the kind of cooking that allows the inherent

quality of ingredients to shine. The freshest fish appears in main courses such as gently sautéed wild halibut with diced beetroot, sweetcorn, peas and spring onions in a fine reduction sauce based on Noilly Prat and Sauternes; the meat alternative might see Angus beef fillet seared on the outside, pink and tender within, teamed with a stuffing of onion and green peppercorn, in a first-class jus of red wine, Madeira, thyme, sage and rosemary. First courses are usually either a soup – perhaps spring-fresh, chilled tomato with pistou – or a serving of smoked wild Irish salmon with a vibrant dressing of mango and avocado, vodka crème fraîche and onuga herring 'caviar'. Stimulating, often alcohol-based desserts have included cherry brandy jelly with black pepper and yoghurt, and richly creamy prune and Armagnac ice cream in a pool of passion-fruit juice. The brief wine list extends to just one handwritten page, and opens with Riojas at £20 (white) and £26 (a Reserva red). Despite its compact nature, you will probably find something there to match the day's menu. Glasses are £4.50 for white and £5 for red.

Chef: Harry Hallam Proprietors: Harry and Caroline Hallam
Open: Tue to Sat 12.30 to 2, 7 to 9 Closed: bank hols, 1 week at Christmas Meals: alc (main courses £32 to £35) Service: not inc Cards: Delta, Maestro, MasterCard, Visa Details: 10 seats. Car park. Children's helpings. No children under 5. No smoking. Wheelchair access (not WC). No music

MAP 2 **GREAT MILTON –** Oxfordshire

Le Manoir aux Quat' Saisons

Church Road, Great Milton OX44 7PD
Tel: (01844) 278881
Website: www.manoir.com

Cooking 9 | **Modern French** | **£115**

It is hard indeed not to be drawn in by the spell the Manoir still casts, even in its third decade. A mellow-stone manor house with tall brick chimneys set a little way out of a somnolent Oxfordshire village, it is – if Raymond Blanc doesn't mind our saying so – English to its very core. There are no big, dramatic architectural gestures, but nor is there brutal minimalism. There are, however, extensive gardens, where much of the kitchen's fresh produce is grown organically, and where an unhurried turn in fine weather makes much the best introduction to the place, whether you've been before or not.

Inside, it's much the same. It is all supremely comfortable, impeccably stylish and easy on the eye, and yet somehow avoiding intimidating grandeur. The conservatory dining room is the place to be, especially when sun is dappling the lawns outside. Villeroy & Boch tableware and sumptuous floral arrangements provide a classy ambience, and draped chairs invite relaxation. In a certain sense the food is relaxing too. While it has always had an innovative edge, it evolves slowly and surely. You won't have your senses jarred by oddball collisions, nor does it demand the analysis of every bemusing mouthful. What it does offer is lightness and freshness, a relatively hands-off approach to main ingredients and a keen eye to seasonality. A September reporter was thus enthralled to find breast of grouse cooked to immaculate tenderness, served on a bed of shredded cabbage, in a rich reduced sauce of St-Emilion. Accompaniments were two strips of spinach, topped with blackcurrants and diced apple. This, for all the care lavished on its presentation, is what most people would still recognise as a classic autumn game dish.

Foie gras gets appropriately regal treatment, appearing in a terrine with duck confit, surrounded by green beans, pink grapefruit, shallots and herbs, and a chunk of toasted sourdough bread. A risotto at an inspection lunch veered hazardously close to dead plain, being composed of creamy grains interspersed with garden-fresh spring vegetables and some sweet, grilled Sicilian tomatoes, but impressed for the honesty and authenticity of its flavours. Fish, brought up from Cornwall, seems never less than exquisite, as when a fillet of gilthead bream, crisp-skinned and full-flavoured, is teamed with salty brandade on a slice of potato, and with tiny tomatoes filled with squid; bouillabaisse sauce, vivid with saffron, completes the picture.

Desserts probably make the prettiest impression. A silver oyster-shell dish contains a fan of orange segments, sprinkled with zest, around a perfectly risen Grand Marnier soufflé, the interior as 'fluffy, creamy and moist' as can be. Others might enjoy an inventive spin on tiramisù that comes with cocoa sauce and coffee-bean ice cream. Cheeses are kept in well-nigh-flawless condition, and the coffee is always singled out for praise. Smoothly unobtrusive service holds the line between warmth and formality. There is no stinting on wine, although you might want to see about a loan before you get much beyond base camp with it. Its magnetic north, as it were, is naturally France, where the unexplored byways of the south-west and the east are at least as fascinating as the inevitable roll-calls of classics. Elsewhere, California and Spain are notably good. Bottles start at £21, or order by the glass from £6 for a good Côtes du Rhône blanc.

Chef/Proprietor: Raymond Blanc   Open: all week 12.15 to 2.30, 7.15 to 9.45   Meals: alc (main courses £36 to £38). Set L Mon to Fri £45 to £95, Set L Sat and Sun £95, Set D £95   Service: not inc   Cards: Amex, Delta, Diners, Maestro, MasterCard, Visa   Details: 90 seats. Car park. Vegetarian meals. Children's helpings. No smoking. Wheelchair access (also WC). No music. Air-conditioned   Accommodation: 32 rooms

MAP 3   GREAT MISSENDEN – Buckinghamshire

La Petite Auberge

107 High Street, Great Missenden HP16 0BB
Tel: (01494) 865370

Cooking 3 | French | £42

Consistently serving classical French dishes, this intimate restaurant continues to charm. Chef/patron Hubert Martel offers a tantalising meander through the staples of French cuisine, carefully selecting his ingredients and serving them with flair. Among starters might be foie gras terrine, fish soup, or pan-fried scallops with Xeres vinegar dressing. Fillet of beef with green peppercorn sauce, or breast of guinea fowl with lime could be among the main courses. There's plenty of fish too – perhaps fillet of red mullet with herbs, or medallions of monkfish with prawns – and all are served with seasonal vegetables. Desserts include crème brûlée, lemon tart, and iced nougat with chocolate sauce. Naturally, the wine list is proudly French, with some impressive choices for under £20.

Chef: Hubert Martel   Proprietors: Hubert and Danielle Martel Open: Mon to Sat D only 7.30 to 10   Closed: 2 weeks Christmas, 2 weeks Easter   Meals: alc (main courses £17 to £19)   Service: not inc   Cards: Delta, Maestro, MasterCard, Visa   Details: 30 seats. Children's helpings. No smoking. Wheelchair access (not WC). No music

AR   Not a full entry but provisionally recommended. These 'also recommended' establishments are integrated throughout the book.

MAP 6 | GREAT YARMOUTH – Norfolk

Seafood Restaurant

85 North Quay, Great Yarmouth NR30 1JF
Tel: (01493) 856009

Well-sourced Lowestoft seafood with a distinctly old-school attitude. Start with gravad lax with mustard dill sauce (£8.50), or crab claws in garlic butter (£7.95); move on to scampi provençale with rice (£17.75), or halibut with banana and grapes in a white wine sauce (£17.95). There are also mixed seafood platters (£17.95 to £26.95). The global wine list opens at £11.95. Closed Sat L and Sun.

MAP 9 | GRIMSBY – N.E. Lincolnshire

Granary

Haven Mill, Garth Lane, Grimsby DN31 1RP
Tel: (01472) 346338
Website: www.granarygrimsby.co.uk

Cooking 1 | Seafood/Modern European | £35

Ron and Mary Houghton continue to serve their predominately seafood menu, with fish straight from Grimsby docks, at this friendly restaurant located in a converted waterside grain store. You first climb the stairs to the dining room, where Mary makes sure things run smoothly out front. Ron's daily changing menu is a straightforward affair so look out for seared scallops in a redcurrant reduction for starters, followed by fillet of grouper with a crab vinaigrette or perhaps baked whole baby turbot. Meat-eaters might like the wild boar steak with a sweet Muscat and cep sauce. End with 'off the trolley' desserts, which include home-made ice cream. The short but capable wine list starts at £11.

Chef: Ron Houghton Proprietors: Ron and Mary Houghton Open: Mon to Fri L 12 to 2, Wed to Sat D 7 to 9 Closed: 1 week Christmas to New Year, 2 weeks summer Meals: alc (main courses £9.50 to £22.50) Service: not inc Cards: Amex, Delta, Maestro, MasterCard, Visa Details: 90 seats. Vegetarian meals. No-smoking area. Occasional music

To submit a report on any restaurant, please visit *www.which.co.uk/gfgfeedback.*

MAP 6 | GRIMSTON – Norfolk

Congham Hall, Orangery

Lynn Road, Grimston PE32 1AH
Tel: (01485) 600250
Website: www.conghamhallhotel.co.uk

Cooking 3 | Modern British/French | £64

This Georgian manor, standing in acres of grounds just a few miles from Sandringham, feels very English: it is small-scale, and more comfortable than grand, despite some ambitious work going on in the kitchen. The cooking style is broad-ranging, maybe ham hock and chicken terrine alongside tuna with confit beetroot and spring onion and tomato salsa to begin. Among main courses, fish might take in wild sea bass spiked with lemongrass and served with new potatoes, wilted spinach, sugar snaps and mussel and chive chowder, or a classical treatment of halibut (with noisette potatoes and beurre meunière). Meanwhile, roast chump of lamb is indulgently served with sautéed kidney, confit potatoes, salsify and lamb jus dressing. Desserts aim to be as comforting as the rest, judging by a hot chocolate fondant with fig ice cream, or William pear tarte Tatin with spiced rum ice cream. House wines start at £19.50 and there are 10 wines by the glass.

Chef: Jamie Murch Proprietor: Von Essen Hotels Open: all week 12 to 1.45, 7 to 9.15 Meals: Set L £15.50 (2 courses) to £33, Set L Sun £22.50, Set D £35 (2 courses) to £57.50. Bar L menu available Mon to Sat Service: not inc Cards: Amex, Delta, Diners, Maestro, MasterCard, Visa Details: 40 seats. 24 seats outside. Car park. Vegetarian meals. Children's helpings. No children under 7 at D. No smoking. Wheelchair access (also WC). No music. No mobile phones Accommodation: 14 rooms

MAP 2 | HADDENHAM – Buckinghamshire

Green Dragon

8 Churchway, Haddenham HP17 8AA
Tel: (01844) 291403
Website: www.eatatthedragon.co.uk

Cooking 1 | Modern British | £39

Often used as a backdrop for TV programmes, the village of Haddenham is worth a wander, but be sure to make a bee-line for this 350-year-old pub.

Peter and Sue Moffat oversee the operation carefully and have hit the jackpot by offering seasonal food and regularly changing menus. Fish landed the day before in Devon is a big draw, as is the attentive service and generally happy-to-have-you ambience. Steamed Devon mussels or crab and Lincolnshire Cheddar tart with spicy tomato chutney are both examples of the kitchen's philosophy, while seared sea bass with a tiger prawn confit or shank of local lamb with a vegetable tagine could follow. Desserts range from classic sticky toffee pudding to banana bavarois with caramel ice cream. The wine list concentrates on Europe and the southern hemisphere, with French house wines opening the card at £13.

Chef: Dean Taylor **Proprietors**: Peter and Sue Moffat **Open**: all week L 12 to 2 (3 Sun), Mon to Sat D 6.30 to 9.30 **Closed**: 25 Dec, 1 Jan **Meals**: alc (main courses £8 to £17.50). Set L Sun £19.95, Set D Tue and Thur £12.95 (2 courses) **Service**: 10% (optional) **Cards**: Maestro, MasterCard, Visa **Details**: 65 seats. 30 seats outside. Car park. Vegetarian meals. No children under 7. No smoking. Wheelchair access (not WC). No music

MAP 9   HALIFAX – West Yorkshire

Design House

Dean Clough, North Bridge, Halifax HX3 7NE
Tel: (01422) 383242
Website: www.designhouserestaurant.co.uk

Cooking 2	Modern European	£43

Living up to its name, this stylish restaurant, in an old mill complex, has been refurbished recently and boasts etched-glass windows, lots of chrome, spotlights and a few choice pieces of furniture by designer Philippe Starck. Choose between a fixed-price three-course deal and carte, both offering modern European dishes served with a flourish. Starters like crab and sweetcorn ravioli or chargrilled venison steak with a wild mushroom and green peppercorn sauce might precede lemon-marinated ostrich fillet, or duck shepherd's pie accompanied by truffled polenta chips. Pasta and risottos get their own short space on the menu, while among desserts could be spiced walnut and date cake. The large wine list is categorised by style ('big boys', 'old firm favourites', 'cream and crisp dry whites' and so on) and shows good value, with house selections from £13.50.

Chef/Proprietor: Lee Stevens Marshall **Open**: Mon to Fri L 12 to 2.30, Mon to Sat D 6 to 9.30 **Closed**: 26 Dec to 11 Jan, bank hols **Meals**: alc (main courses £8.50 to £18.50). Set L £10.50 (2 courses), Set D £14.50 **Service**: not inc **Cards**: Amex, Delta, Maestro, MasterCard, Visa **Details**: 100 seats. Car park (D only). Vegetarian meals. No smoking in dining room. Wheelchair access (also WC). Music. No mobile phones. Air-conditioned

Holdsworth House

Holdsworth, Halifax HX2 9TG
Tel: (01422) 240024
Website: www.holdsworthhouse.co.uk

Cooking 3	Modern British	£49

Gail Moss and Kim Pearson took over this beautifully preserved Jacobean manor house three miles north of Halifax way back in 1963, and they have made the very best of the setting: the walled garden and the unique listed gazebo are just two of the gems, and the food is another attraction. With the freshest ingredients, most of which are locally or regionally sourced – think pure-bred Galloway beef from Cumbria, for example – the kitchen cooks in a modern but distinctly British style. Spice Barley Bridge lamb meatballs with coriander, tomato fondue and white truffle spaghetti is an imaginative starter, while main courses could be pan-fried Grizedale venison with honey-roast root vegetables and cider fondant or local game pie with shortcrust pastry. Rum baba or hot chocolate fondant fill any gaps, but the cheeses are something special, among them ewes' cheese from the Shepherds Purse Dairy near Thirsk and Ribblesdale oak-smoked goats' cheese. The easily digestible wine list is split into sections according to style, with reasonable choices under £20. The house selection of 20 bottles starts off at £13.50.

Chef: Gary Saunders **Proprietors**: Gail Moss and Kim Pearson **Open**: Mon to Fri L 12 to 2, Mon to Sat D 7 to 9.30 **Closed**: 24 Dec to 3 Jan exc L 25 and 26 Dec, D 31 Dec **Meals**: alc D (main courses £14.50 to £19.50). Set L £13.95 (2 courses) to £16.95 **Service**: not inc **Cards**: Amex, Delta, Maestro, MasterCard, Visa **Details**: 50 seats. 10 seats outside. Car park. Vegetarian meals. Children's helpings. No smoking in dining room. Wheelchair access (also WC). Music. No mobile phones **Accommodation**: 40 rooms

 This symbol means that the wine list is well above the average.

Shibden Mill Inn

Shibden Mill Fold, Shibden, Halifax HX3 7UL
Tel: (01422) 365840
Website: www.shibdenmillinn.com

Cooking 3 | Modern British | £34

This seventeenth-century inn is hidden within the folds of the Shibden valley, and the sympathetically renovated maze of rooms offers guests a bar and restaurant as well as accommodation. The bar menu offers a variety of choices, from a starter of roast Lincolnshire wood pigeon risotto to more traditional dishes, including home-made chicken pie. A steep narrow staircase leads to the beamed upstairs dining room. Cornish mackerel or lamb shank faggot are typical of starters, while interesting main courses could be Shetland sea trout with lentils, bacon and tapenade butter or calf's liver with figs, vinaigrette and smoked cheese polenta. Anyone with room to spare could go for chocolate three ways: chocolate and pear brûlée, chocolate sorbet and chocolate and Amaretto pie. The wine list, notable for its lengthy annotations, starts with half a dozen house selections, all at £10.50.

> **Chef:** Steve Evans **Proprietor:** Simon Heaton **Open:** Mon to Fri 12 to 2, 6 to 9.30, Sat 6 to 9.30, Sun 12 to 7.30 **Meals:** alc (main courses £10 to £16). Bar menu available **Service:** not inc **Cards:** Amex, Delta, Maestro, MasterCard, Visa **Details:** 100 seats. 60 seats outside. Car park. Vegetarian meals. Children's helpings. No smoking in dining room. Music **Accommodation:** 12 rooms

---

MAP 6 HAMBLETON – Rutland

Hambleton Hall

Hambleton LE15 8TH
Tel: (01572) 756991
Website: www.hambletonhall.com

Cooking 7 | Modern British | £92

The stately house on a promontory overlooking Rutland Water was built in 1881 as a hunting lodge by one Walter Marshall, a bon viveur noted in the locality for the excellence of his table. It's still a peaceful rural retreat, its gardens sloping down towards the lake. Within it seems grand but relaxed, with a marble fireplace in the lounge, soft upholstery and luxuriant flora, and, while the dining room is as smart as can be, they don't make you wear a tie. Aaron Patterson has headed the kitchens since 1994, and the weight of his experience shows in dishes that are carefully composed and vividly presented. Canapés and breads get things off to a fine start. The urge for clarity of flavour might express itself in starters where separate elements are arranged in a neat row, as in a poached plum, a pyramid of Madeira and orange jelly, a piece of pain d'épice redolent of five-spice, a slice of ballottine of foie gras, and a scoop of foie gras ice cream garnished with an orange crisp. This was a bravura opening dish at inspection.

Variations on a theme may well appear among first courses, so a winter menu offered arrays of Périgord truffle, of tomato, and of pea and mint, as well as a more speculative pairing of Thai-spiced Scottish langoustines with mango. Unusually, fish very much plays second fiddle among main-course choices, being limited to just one: perhaps poached sea bass with chorizo tortellini in minestrone. Otherwise, dishes such as the benchmark Aberdeen Angus fillet with shallot and banana tarte Tatin and stuffed cabbage impress in all the right ways – tender, flavourful meat, rich accompaniments, a fine red wine reduction. More of those ingredients-on-parade arrangements may well return at dessert, as when a line-up of citrus creations appears, the star among which has been lemon posset topped with blood-orange zest and crystals of crackling candy. Service is a model of understanding and gentility. The wine list is exceptionally posh, with compact New World selections backing up the quality classic French listings. There are some regional French offerings too, but even here prices quickly leap above £20. A page of 'Wines of the Moment' has many more affordable bottles from around £16.

> **Chef:** Aaron Patterson **Proprietors:** Tim and Stefa Hart **Open:** all week 12 to 1.30, 7 to 9.30 **Meals:** alc (main courses £25 to £39). Set L £18.50 (2 courses) to £35, Set L Sun £37.50 to £50, Set D £40 to £60. Snack menu available **Service:** not inc **Cards:** Amex, Delta, Diners, Maestro, MasterCard, Visa **Details:** 64 seats. 20 seats outside. Car park. Vegetarian meals. Children's helpings. No smoking. Wheelchair access (not WC). No music. No mobile phones **Accommodation:** 17 rooms

---

MAP 5 HANWELL – Oxfordshire

Moon and Sixpence

Hanwell OX17 1HW
Tel: (01295) 730544
Website: www.moonandsixpencehanwell.com

Cooking 3 | Modern British | £37

'What a lovely, relaxed place to spend an evening,' observed a reporter of this large roadside pub in a tiny village. The dining areas are in keeping with a traditional pub ethos, boasting bare wooden tables, panelling and 'a worn pubby carpet'. Specials are chalked on boards (braised belly pork with black pudding, crackling and apple sauce, perhaps); there is also a 'pub favourites' menu featuring ham, egg and chips, Scottish beef and ale pie and the like, plus a separate list of steaks. A timbale of smoked trout and salmon with tomato coulis was considered a good idea among starters, while main-course venison fillet, 'beautifully soft and supple', comes with sweet red cabbage and a bitter chocolate sauce. Pan-fried fillet of wild sea bass with leek fondue and vanilla sauce might be one of the fish options, and tarte Tatin with Calvados sorbet shows fine pastry work at pudding stage. Service is friendly and informal, and there's a choice of real ales and a reasonably priced wine list opening at £11.95.

> **Chef:** Toby Hill **Proprietors:** Rupert and Toby Hill **Open:** all week 12 to 2 (3 Sun), 6 to 9 **Closed:** Sun D and Mon L Oct to Mar **Meals:** alc (main courses £10 to £20). Set L Tue to Sat £7.50 (2 courses) to £9.50, Set D Tue to Fri £7.50 (2 courses) to £9.50 **Service:** not inc **Cards:** Delta, Maestro, MasterCard, Visa **Details:** 70 seats. 30 seats outside. Car park. Vegetarian meals. Children's helpings. No smoking in dining room. Wheelchair access (not WC). Music. No mobile phones

---

MAP 9 **HAROME** – North Yorkshire

Star Inn

High Street, Harome YO62 5JE
Tel: (01439) 770397
Website: www.thestaratharome.co.uk

Cooking 5 | Modern British | £45

'This is one of the few places,' a reporter observed, 'where eating in the bar is at least an equal match to eating in the restaurant – the perfect English country pub.' Such places are all the more treasured for not alienating local custom with pretension, and all are agreed that the Perns have brought off this balancing act with great flair. In the setting of a fourteenth-century thatched inn, all snugness and cheer, some great cooking, built, of course, on local supply lines, is offered. The menus are chalked up on a board as well as printed, and the hits are legion. A slab of chunky game terrine comes with date and apple chutney, a well-dressed salad sprinkled with chopped salt-beef, and an accompanying glass of greengage spritzer just for the tang of the thing. Posh fish pie (so posh, indeed, it's spelled 'pye') is crammed to capacity with various white fish as well as tuna and prawns, under a spare

topping of herb-crusted mash, to make a thoroughly admirable main course, while roe deer steak is carefully timed, bedded on Cheddary kale and sauced with a deeply flavoured red wine and juniper reduction.

Among desserts, the 'Taste of the Star' selection of miniaturised items includes Bramley apple cheesecake, blood-orange tart and gooseberry ice cream. A mighty fine wine list has been assembled. Beginning with two pages of wines by the glass (from £3.50), it stretches out into a thoroughgoing exploration of the French regions before jetting around the rest of the world, finding quality producers and good value everywhere. Prices are commendably fair, the bottle prices starting at £13.50 for Stickleback house blends from Australia. The Star at Scampston (Scampston Hall, Malton; tel: 01944 759000) is also run by the Perns, and is open Tue to Sun, 10am to 5pm, for sandwiches and light lunches.

> **Chef:** Andrew Pern **Proprietors:** Andrew and Jacquie Pern **Open:** Tue to Sat 11.30 to 2, 6.30 to 9.30, Sun 12 to 6 **Meals:** alc (main courses £12.50 to £21.50) **Service:** not inc **Cards:** Delta, Maestro, MasterCard, Visa **Details:** 40 seats. 60 seats outside. Car park. Vegetarian meals. Children's helpings. No smoking in dining room. Wheelchair access (not WC). Music **Accommodation:** 11 rooms

---

MAP 3 **HARPENDEN** – Hertfordshire

A Touch of Novelli at the White Horse   **NEW ENTRY**

Hatching Green, Harpenden AL5 2JP
Tel: (01582) 713428
Website: www.atouchofnovelli.com

Cooking 4 | Modern British | £42

The White Horse may look like a typical country pub from the outside, but once you step through the door it is obvious there is much more to it. The name says it all. Jean-Christophe Novelli (for it is he) is making a good go of this new branded venture, judging by a recent inspection, which saw the place buzzing with atmosphere, the staff smart and enthusiastic, and the kitchen clearly capable of good things. The menu is a flexible carte with a strong emphasis on the use of local suppliers. Highlights have included two jumbo scallops teamed with spiced boudin noir and a mixture of crushed sour potato, horseradish cream and dried Granny Smith, and main courses of chargrilled rib of beef with provençale and wild garlic butter, and double-fried hand-cut chips, as well as roast royal sea bream with chorizo oil, served with 'extremely spicy' baked aubergine, and sage and olive fritters. Nowadays the trademark Novelli desserts are much simpler, more appropriate to the setting, delivering a good plum clafoutis with roast pecan and Armagnac ice cream. A dozen wines by the glass introduce a decent global selection. House wine is £13.

Chef: Wesley Smalley Proprietors: Sweet Medicine Open: all week 12 to 3, 6 to 10 Closed: 24 and 25 Dec, 1 Jan Meals: alc (main courses £9.50 to £16.50) Service: not inc Cards: Amex, Delta, Maestro, MasterCard, Visa Details: 50 seats. 50 seats outside. Car park. Vegetarian meals. No smoking. Wheelchair access (also WC). Music

---

MAP 8 **HARROGATE – North Yorkshire**

Drum and Monkey

5 Montpellier Gardens, Harrogate HG1 2TF
Tel: (01423) 528014

Cooking 2 | Seafood | £47

Year in, year out, this former pub remains a popular choice for reliable fish and seafood. The freshness of daily-delivered supplies is to the fore in predominantly classic treatments, whether it's the simplicity of a hot shellfish platter with garlic butter or a plate of large Mediterranean prawns with mayonnaise, or relatively elaborate dishes such as monkfish with a prawn and brandy sauce, garnished with mushrooms and prawns, or Dover sole 'bonne femme' with crab stuffing and hollandaise. More exotic touches include salmon cakes with ginger and lime dressing, and spicy Malaysian fish brochette. House selections are £11.95 from a short list of mostly white wines.

Chefs: Keith Penny and Matty Barnett Proprietor: Jan Fletcher Open: all week 11.45 to 2.45, 5.45 to 9.45 (7 Sun) Meals: alc (main courses £8 to £26) Service: not inc Cards: Maestro, MasterCard, Visa Details: 63 seats. No smoking. Music. Air-conditioned

---

 This symbol means that accommodation is available at this establishment.

Hotel du Vin & Bistro

Prospect Place, Harrogate HG1 1LB
Tel: (01423) 856800
Website: www.hotelduvin.com

Cooking 3 | Modern European | £45

The Harrogate outpost of this quirky hotel group (see entries in Birmingham, Brighton, Bristol, Henley-on-Thames, Tunbridge Wells and Winchester) is a dynamic place that successfully blends a contemporary setting with a lively, enjoyable atmosphere and a serious approach to food and wine. Straightforward bistro cooking takes in foie gras terrine with rhubarb compote, chicken and leek feuilleté, and soft herring roes on toasted brioche among starters, and main courses such as pan-fried skate wing with capers and brown butter, and roast rump of lamb with aubergine caviar and rosemary jus. The cheese selection shows imagination, extending perhaps to Vignotte and Swaledale, while desserts are firmly in the comfort zone with apple and plum crumble, chocolate brownie with marinated cherries, and sticky toffee pudding. Although France is understandably given much room, the long wine list is underpinned by a well-priced selection of less-often-seen styles from around the globe. House wines start at £13.

Chef: Gareth Longhurst Proprietor: MWB Group plc Open: all week 12 to 2 (12.30 to 2.30 Sun), 7 to 10 Meals: alc (main courses £12.50 to £21.50). Set L Mon to Fri £12.50 (2 courses) to £17.50 (inc wine) Service: not inc Cards: Amex, Delta, Maestro, MasterCard, Visa Details: 85 seats. Vegetarian meals. No smoking in dining room. Wheelchair access (also WC). No music Accommodation: 43 rooms

Quantro   AR

3 Royal Parade, Harrogate HG1 2SZ
Tel: (01423) 503034

This eclectic modern European menu is never dull: crayfish spring rolls with a flat pea salad (£4.60) to start, perhaps, followed by locally sourced venison steak with pancetta potatoes and a juniper and port jus (£13.90). Dessert could be the ever-popular sticky toffee pudding with crème fraîche (£3.25). A light lunch menu offers Thai green vegetable curry with cardamom rice (£5). Wines from £11.95. Closed Sun. A sister restaurant is at 62 Street Lane, Leeds, tel: (0113) 288 8063.

MAP 3 HARROW – Greater London

Golden Palace

146–150 Station Road, Harrow HA1 2RH
Tel: (020) 8863 2333

| Cooking 4 | Chinese | £30 |

The Golden Palace has a long-standing reputation as one of the best Chinese restaurants in Britain, which may seem at odds with its uninspiring setting in a row of shops on a busy main road; inside, however, the two dining areas are comfortably turned out, with Chinese calligraphy hung on golden cloth wall coverings, plush blue carpets throughout and well-spaced tables laid with fine white linen and fresh flowers. Lengthy menus specialise in Cantonese, Szechuan and Peking dishes, supplemented by specials including such esoteric items as stir-fried prawns with thousand-year egg; and goose feet with mushroom hotpot. But the kitchen staff's technical prowess ensures exciting results across the board, even in more mainstream choices, such as 'perfectly sweet and translucent' plump scallops deep-fried in a thin, crisp batter. Don't expect too much refinement, as the cooking tends towards the 'rustic and wholesome'. An inspector's main course of spicy prawn with celery and spring onion showed 'edgy and exotic' flavours; while stuffed beancurd and roast pork with mixed meat hotpot was 'wonderfully delicious and robust'. Desserts are things like red bean pancakes and chilled yam paste with sago cream, and wines are better than might be expected in the context.

> **Chef/Proprietor:** Mr G. Ho **Open:** Mon to Sat 12 (11 bank hols) to 11.30, Sun 11 to 10.30 **Closed:** 25 Dec **Meals:** alc (main courses £5.50 to £30). Set L and D £16.50 to £24 (all min 2) **Service:** 10% **Cards:** Amex, Delta, Diners, Maestro, MasterCard, Visa **Details:** 160 seats. Vegetarian meals. Wheelchair access (also WC). No music. Air-conditioned **Tube:** Harrow-on-the-Hill

---

>
> This symbol means that it is possible to have a three-course dinner, including coffee, half a bottle of house wine and service, for £30 or less per person.

MAP 6 HARWICH – Essex

Pier Hotel, Harbourside Restaurant

The Quay, Harwich CO12 3HH
Tel: (01255) 241212
Website: www.milsomhotels.com

| Cooking 2 | Seafood/English | £50 |

This smart quayside restaurant-with-rooms in the heart of old Harwich is part of an upmarket hotel chain (under the same ownership as milsoms in Dedham; see entry). The first-floor dining room is the ideal place at which to enjoy inventive modern seafood cookery while taking in the views of the Stour estuary. Starters typically include home-smoked halibut with an onion and horseradish tartlet, lobster bisque, and a gâteau of crab claw with mango and cucumber dressing, while main courses range from classic pan-fried skate wing with caper butter to original creations such as walnut-crusted cod with parsnip sauce and glazed carrots. A handful of non-fish options takes in roast stuffed pork fillet with almonds and apricot, and for dessert there may be burnt orange parfait glace with kumquat compote. Downstairs, the brasserie-style Ha'penny Bistro offers a more informal mode of eating. House white wine is £14, red £13.25.

> **Chef:** Chris Oakley **Proprietor:** Paul Milsom **Open:** all week 12 to 2, 6 to 9.30 **Closed:** D 25 Dec **Meals:** alc (main courses £12.50 to £32). Set L £18 (2 courses) to £22 **Service:** 10% **Cards:** Amex, Delta, Diners, Maestro, MasterCard, Visa **Details:** 80 seats. 30 seats outside. Car park. Vegetarian meals. Children's helpings. No-smoking area. Music. Air-conditioned **Accommodation:** 14 rooms

---

MAP 9 HATHERSAGE – Derbyshire

George Hotel

Main Road, Hathersage S32 1BB
Tel: (01433) 650436
Website: www.george-hotel.net

| Cooking 4 | Modern British-Plus | £43 |

The management describes this 500-year-old coaching inn as having been transformed into 'a stylish and modern hotel', and it functions as such, providing an impressive backdrop for Ben

Handley's contemporary cooking. Treatments are straightforward but far from mundane, as in a 'perfect winter warmer' of pumpkin and pine-nut soup (with a muffin of the same ingredients), caramelised onion and goats' cheese risotto with red pepper pesto, or roast fillet of beef with braised shin, horseradish and potato soufflé and red wine sauce. Accurate timing shows in, for example, a whole roast monkfish tail, simply but effectively served with baby roast potatoes and wild mushrooms in a creamy Madeira sauce. Desserts have included a strongly flavoured espresso brûlée, its accompaniment of banana ice cream making a good contrast, and well-made, lightly spiced roast pear and ginger crumble. Breads are worth a mention, and 'very nice staff' get the thumbs-up. Wines, arranged by style, are reasonably priced. House Chilean is £14.95, and eight are served by the glass from £3.75.

Chefs: Ben Handley and Helen Heywood Proprietor: Eric Marsh Open: all week 12 to 2.30, 6.30 to 10 Meals: alc (main courses £12 to £19). Set L 12.30 to 1.30 and D 6.30 to 7.30 Mon to Fri £13.50 (two courses) to £16. Lounge L menu available Service: not inc Cards: Amex, Delta, Diners, Maestro, MasterCard, Visa Details: 50 seats. Car park. Vegetarian meals. Children's helpings. No smoking. Wheelchair access (also WC). Music. No mobile phones Accommodation: 23 rooms

---

MAP 8 **HAWORTH –**
West Yorkshire

Weavers

13–17 West Lane, Haworth BD22 8DU
Tel: (01535) 643822
Website: www.weaverssmallhotel.co.uk

Cooking 3 | Modern British | £38

Just off the main cobbled street of picturesque Haworth, Weavers is a bar and restaurant spread through the ground floor of three knocked-together terraced cottages, giving it a cosy feel. Local ingredients play a prominent role in the modern British cooking. Among starters might be duck and Yorkshire venison terrine with brandied prunes, a drizzle of pomegranate juice and walnut toast, or a plate of thinly sliced smoked ale-cured beef with a salad of watercress and roast beetroot. Main courses, meanwhile, take in homely dishes like meat and potato pie with onion relish, as well as more cosmopolitan options such as spiced duck breast with pak choi, confit potatoes and a cinnamon and orange glaze. Sticky toffee pudding with whipped cream is typical of desserts. Lunches are a

simpler affair, with snacky dishes such as Morecambe Bay potted shrimps on toast, or black pudding, potato and corned-beef hash topped with an egg. House Chilean is £12.50.

Chefs: Tim, Jane and Colin Rushworth Proprietors: the Rushworth family Open: Wed to Fri and Sun L 12 to 2, Tue to Sat D 6 to 9 Closed: 10 days from 25 Dec Meals: alc (main courses L £8 to £14, D £11 to £18). Set L Wed to Fri £9.95 (2 courses), Set L Sun £16.95, Set D Tue to Fri £13.95 (2 courses) to £16.95 Service: not inc Cards: Amex, Delta, Diners, Maestro, MasterCard, Visa Details: 65 seats. Vegetarian meals. Children's helpings. No smoking. Music. No mobile phones. Air-conditioned Accommodation: 3 rooms

---

MAP 2 **HAYLING ISLAND –**
Hampshire

Marina Jaks   [NEW ENTRY]

Sparkes Boatyard, 38 Wittering Road, Hayling Island PO11 9SR
Tel: (02392) 469459
Website: www.marinajaks.co.uk

Cooking 2 | Modern British | £40

'I cannot emphasise too strongly how important it is for first-timers to ask for detailed directions,' writes a reporter on the difficulties of finding this awkwardly located, but classily converted, former chandlery. Views on to yachts and the quay are a big plus, and high ceilings and copious expanses of wood and leather characterise the interior. At dinner, prawns with aïoli have exhibited freshness with a spicy bite, and a salad of pear with bitter leaves and blue cheese dressing has had good depth of flavour. Main courses tend towards hearty dishes such as rack of lamb with dauphinois potatoes and buttered asparagus, or local turbot with 'immaculate' olive oil mash, gremolata and aged balsamic. Desserts are not a strong point. 'Brisk and efficient' service enhances the sense of well-being, and wines are chosen for both interest and value. House wine is £10.95, and around ten wines are offered by the glass.

Chef: Lester Kettleley Proprietors: Mr and Mrs Scutt Open: all week 12.30 to 3, 7 to 10 Closed: Mon Nov to June Meals: alc (main courses £8 to £30). Bar L menu available Mon to Sat Service: not inc Cards: Amex, Delta, Diners, Maestro, MasterCard, Visa Details: 100 seats. 50 seats outside. Car park. Vegetarian meals. Children's helpings. No-smoking area. Wheelchair access (also WC). Music. Air-conditioned

MAP 3 HAYWARDS HEATH – West Sussex

Jeremy's

Borde Hill, Balcombe Road, Haywards Heath
RH16 1XP
Tel: (01444) 441102
Website: www.jeremysrestaurant.com

Cooking 4 | Modern European | £47

Among the attractions of this unpretentious restaurant in the grounds of Borde Hill Gardens is its expanse of terrace overlooking a Victorian walled garden, a prime spot for al fresco dining during the summer. If the weather isn't so good, the dining room is pleasant enough, with a casual atmosphere and simple décor featuring a pitched ceiling, beams and art for sale on its fawn and terracotta walls. The eclectic cooking aims for good value as well as broad appeal, and the kitchen takes pride in making use of some top-notch local produce, notably fish and seafood. While loin of Balcombe venison and chorizo with plum and ginger relish sounds pretty hefty as a starter, it proves to be well judged as to quantity, and 'a nice build-up of flavours'. Main courses have included pan-fried breast of Gressingham duck with creamy mash, roast beetroot and orange sauce. Desserts such as the generous lime and passion-fruit tart served with blueberry and lime compote and lime and mascarpone sorbet are a high point. Service is willing but can be elusive at busy periods. House wines are around £15.

Chef: Jeremy Ashpool **Proprietors:** Jeremy and Vera Ashpool **Open:** Tue to Sun L 12.30 to 2.30, Tue to Sat D 7.30 to 10 **Meals:** alc exc Sun L (main courses £13.50 to £20). Set L Tue to Sat £17.50 (2 courses) to £23, Set L Sun £22 (2 courses) to £26, Set D Tue to Thur £17.50 (2 courses) to £23 **Service:** not inc **Cards:** Amex, Diners, Maestro, MasterCard, Visa **Details:** 55 seats. 35 seats outside. Car park. Vegetarian meals. Children's helpings. No smoking. Wheelchair access (not WC). Music

 This symbol means that the restaurant has elected to participate in *The Good Food Guide's* £5 voucher scheme (see 'Using The Good Food Guide' for details).

To submit a report on any restaurant, please visit *www.which.co.uk/gfgfeedback*.

MAP 9 HELMSLEY – North Yorkshire

Feversham Arms Hotel

Helmsley YO62 5AG
Tel: (01439) 770766
Website: www.fevershamarmshotel.com

Cooking 5 | Modern British | £52

Ideally sited for visiting York, Whitby and tranquil James Herriot country, Helmsley is a pleasing village, once the hub of the local weaving trade. The Feversham Arms is next to the church. Having extended into a handful of adjacent cottages, it is now a full-on tourist venue, with a spacious, tile-floored, modern dining room. The cooking offers a variety of takes on European cookery, with Mediterranean notes to the fore. Bresaola of venison from the carte comes with honey-soused vegetables, gaining sharpness from Dunsyre Blue cheese, while the fixed-price menu might kick off with a sardine and tomato tart with a dressing of confit fennel. Dinner menus might surprise for the complete absence of fish at main course, as was the case with the one sent to the Guide, although lunch may furnish roast haddock with pomme purée and a mussel and onion broth. Pot-roast lamb heart is stuffed with kidneys and orange, while more mainstream tastes might rise to breast of corn-fed chicken with artichoke barigoule and foie gras sauce. Finish with prune and Armagnac soufflé with its own ice cream. A commendable wine list covers a fair amount of ground, giving slight but not undue prominence to the French regions and including a handful of good Argentinian reds. Prices open at £18.50.

Chef: Charlie Lakin **Proprietor:** Simon Rhatigan **Open:** all week 12 to 2 (1 to 3 Sun), 7 to 9.30 **Meals:** alc (main courses L £12 to £14.50, D £17 to £22). Set D £32 **Service:** not inc **Cards:** Amex, Maestro, MasterCard, Visa **Details:** 55 seats. 30 seats outside. Car park. Vegetarian meals. No children after 8pm. Children's helpings. No smoking. Wheelchair access (also WC). Music. No mobile phones **Accommodation:** 20 rooms

 Not a full entry but provisionally recommended. These 'also recommended' establishments are integrated throughout the book.

MAP 6 | HEMINGFORD GREY – Cambridgeshire

Cock `AR`

47 High Street, Hemingford Grey PE28 9BJ
Tel: (01480) 463609

More gastro-pub than restaurant, the Cock, which is the sister of the Crown & Punchbowl at Horningsea and the Boathouse in Ely (see entries), is an informal and comfortable venue. Specialities are their home-made sausages (barbecue pork, or dill and mustard, for example) served with a variety of mashes; or else start with seared scallops with a wild mushroom tart, rocket and truffle oil (£6.95), followed by braised leg of mutton with a parsnip gratin, Puy lentils and chorizo (£14.95). End with fig and Muscat crème brûlée. Wines from £10.80. Open all week.

MAP 2 | HENLEY-ON-THAMES – Oxfordshire

Hotel du Vin & Bistro

New Street, Henley-on-Thames RG9 2BP
Tel: (01491) 848400
Website: www.hotelduvin.com

NEW CHEF | Modern European | £46

The former Brakspear brewery is home to the newest member of this popular mini chain of boutique hotels, which efficiently replicates the successful blueprint created by the other branches in Birmingham, Brighton, Bristol, Harrogate, Tunbridge Wells and Winchester (see entries). Indeed, the formula is so well established by now that the arrival of a new chef shortly before the Guide went to press – too late for inspection – shouldn't rock the boat in any significant way. Expect the lively restaurant to continue in much the same vein as previously, with bright modern bistro cooking taking in starters of braised oxtail en crépinette, or pan-fried mackerel fillet with artichoke salad, followed by confit duck leg with Savoy cabbage and chestnut jus, or 'simple classics' such as salt-cod fishcakes with sorrel beurre blanc, and perhaps rhubarb and orange custard tart to finish. As with the other branches, wines are a strong suit, scoring well both for value and variety, with an excellent range by the glass and very drinkable house selections from £13 a bottle.

Chef: Matt Green-Armitage   Proprietor: MWB Group plc
Open: all week 12.30 to 2.30, 7 to 9.45 (10 Fri and Sat)
Meals: alc (main courses £12.50 to £20). Set L Mon to Fri
£15 (2 courses), Set L Sun £23.50. Bar L menu available
Service: 10%   Cards: Amex, Delta, Maestro, MasterCard, Visa
Details: 85 seats. 16 seats outside. Children's helpings. No
smoking in dining room. Wheelchair access (also WC). No
music   Accommodation: 43 rooms

MAP 5 | HEREFORD – Herefordshire

Castle House, La Rive

Castle Street, Hereford HR1 2NW
Tel: (01432) 356321
Website: www.castlehse.co.uk

Cooking 5 | Anglo-French | £54

A good-looking Regency town house not far from the cathedral, Castle House is home to the Heijns' sympathetically run hotel. La Rive dining room has attractive views over the garden. New chef Claire Nicholls has made her mark already, with some subtly inventive food that sits well with the surroundings. Seared scallops, sweet and fresh, come with an accomplished fennel and tarragon risotto as one way to start. A slice of classic pressed ham hock and foie gras terrine has a dollop of good pear and nutmeg chutney and neatly dressed leaves with pine nuts for company.

Fish shows up well at main-course stage, with a lightly sautéed piece of crisp-skinned halibut getting the nod at inspection. It came with parsnip and sweet potato chips, and a stunning lobster butter sauce. Local beef fillet might be served with creamed spring greens in season, together with a tian of calf's liver and a jus enriched with morels. Main courses come with rather old-fashioned vegetable side dishes. Those who like to be indulged at dessert time will lack for nothing here. Simply and dramatically presented dark chocolate and Grand Marnier parfait with caramelised orange compote and orange ice went 'above and beyond the call of ordinary duty'. Service could be a little more clued-up about the menu but is conscientious nonetheless. An alluring wine list is properly democratic, not according undue prominence to France (other than for the inevitable clarets and Burgundies). The helpful notes are worth consulting, and prices are fairly restrained. Glasses start at £4.20, bottles at £16.95.

Chef: Claire Nicholls Proprietors: Dr and Mrs A. Heijn Open: all week 12.30 to 2, 7 to 10 (9 Sun) Meals: alc exc Sun L (main courses L £14.50 to £15, D £18.50 to £25). Set L Sun £23.95, Set D £54.95 Service: not inc Cards: Amex, Delta, Maestro, MasterCard, Visa Details: 32 seats. 20 seats outside. Car park. Vegetarian meals. Children's helpings. No smoking. Wheelchair access (also WC). Occasional music. No mobile phones. Air-conditioned Accommodation: 15 rooms

---

MAP 9 | HESSLE – East Riding of Yorkshire

Artisan NEW ENTRY

22 The Weir, Hessle HU13 0RU
Tel: (01482) 644906
Website: www.artisanrestaurant.com

| Cooking 4 | Modern British | £48 |

Richard and Lindsey Johns' restaurant near the Humber Bridge is fast making a name for itself. Richard single-handedly produces a compact menu, which makes good use of organic produce. Lindsey's front-of-house service is exemplary, and the dining room has a contemporary feel and, although small, there's no impression of being cramped. Honey-roast duck salad, classic French onion soup, and and cockles marinière have all been well-flavoured starters. At inspection, a fillet of free-range chicken breast was served with a red wine and tarragon sauce, and partnered with tiny wild mushrooms, asparagus tips and crushed potatoes, while pan-fried fillet of Yorkshire-landed sea bass, firmly textured and crisp skinned, comes on champ with spring vegetables and 'perfectly executed' brown butter. Just one or two desserts round things off: perhaps hot passion-fruit soufflé with a matching sorbet. The 20-bottle wine list has around half a dozen served by the glass, from £3.75, with Vins de Pays d'Oc opening proceedings at £14.95.

Chef: Richard Johns Proprietors: Richard and Lindsey Johns Open: Tue to Fri L 12.30 to 2.30, Tue to Sat D 6.30 to 9.30 Meals: Set L £14.50 (2 courses) to £18.95, Set D £29.95 (2 courses) to £33.95 Service: not inc Cards: Amex, Maestro, MasterCard, Visa Details: 18 seats. Car park. No smoking. Wheelchair access (not WC). Occasional music. Air-conditioned

---

MAP 3 | HETTON – North Yorkshire

Angel Inn

Hetton BD23 6LT
Tel: (01756) 730263
Website: www.angelhetton.co.uk

| Cooking 3 | Modern British | £39 |

Food is the main business at this former farm building, parts of which are over 500 years old, and its reputation has spread far beyond its immediate locale. Tables fill up quickly inside the cheerfully pubby and non-bookable bar/brasserie, where the kitchen delivers bistro food with a flexible attitude (wild mushroom risotto, or hog sausages and mash), but you can book tables in the upmarket dining room. While there is a separate menu here, there is some crossover of dishes (the trademark seafood money bags, for example, or home-made black pudding with foie gras) and generally the kitchen succeeds in its efforts. The cooking is reputed for good materials, especially fish – John Dory fillet in a mussel and coriander broth, for instance – and a fairly straightforward approach that takes in the likes of roast loin of mutton with caramelised sweetbreads. Desserts might include rhubarb done three ways – a crumble, brûlée and compote – while cheeses are from Yorkshire. Around a dozen decent wines are available by the glass (£2.37 to £4.46), while the main list reveals a passion for France and Italy at fair prices but stretches to some world-class bottles.

Chef: Bruce Elsworth Proprietor: Juliet Watkins Open: Sun L 12 to 2.15, Mon to Sat D 6 to 9 Meals: alc exc Sat D and Sun L (main courses £11 to £19). Set L Sun £23.95, Set D Mon to Fri 6 to 6.45 £14 (2 courses) to £17, Set D Sat £34.50. Bar menu available Service: not inc Cards: Delta, Maestro, MasterCard, Visa Details: 60 seats. 40 seats outside. Car park. Vegetarian meals. Children's helpings. No smoking in dining room. Wheelchair access (not WC). No music. Air-conditioned Accommodation: 5 rooms

---

MAP 2 | HEYTESBURY – Wiltshire

Angel Coaching Inn AR

High Street, Heytesbury BA12 0ED
Tel: (01985) 840330

Seventeenth-century coaching inn, which has benefited from stylish renovation. The two- or three-course dinner menu (£14.95-£16.95) is compact – only three choices for each course – but is a hearty affair. Start with pan-fried red mullet with orange and sesame dressing, moving on to haunch of venison with braised red cabbage, or seared fillet of salmon with baby beetroot, spinach and crème fraîche. End with lemon posset with sablé biscuit. Wines from £13.50. Open all week. Accommodation.

MAP 2 HIGHCLERE – Hampshire

Marco Pierre White's Yew Tree

Hollington Cross, Andover Road, Highclere RG20 9SE
Tel: (01635) 253360
Email: gareth.mcainsh@theyewtree.net

Cooking 5 | **Modern British/French** | **£52**

If your botanical knowledge is insufficient for you to recognise the yew tree outside, garlanded as it is in white lights, just look for the brooding, black-lettered announcement of the proprietor's name on the low, whitewashed façade. A long way from home Marco may be in these parts, but his influence is stamped all over Neil Thornley's menus, right down to the offer of venison Pierre Koffmann au chocolat amer, which is simmered over two days in red wine and port and has pure chocolate added to the cooking liquor. Despite many ritzy touches, the brasserie-style menu also offers haddock and chips with tartare sauce, and shepherd's pie, in acknowledgement that this is after all a roadside inn, but quality is at a premium throughout. Croustade of quail's eggs Maintenon with hollandaise was on the menu at the Connaught back in the day, and so too were kedgeree and lobster Newburg. Vegetables are charged extra, although they do include such temptations as spinach à la crème. Finish with glace amandine and sauce chocolat, or rice pudding. Sustaining the tone, wines are listed as vins blancs and vins rouges, despite including bottles from Italy, New Zealand, South Africa and so forth. A fair spread of prices kicks off at £13.75 for reliable Norte Chico varietals from Chile. The accommodation could do with upgrading, according to one reporter who stayed overnight.

Chef: Neil Thornley Proprietor: Marco Pierre White Open: all week 12 to 3, 6 to 10 (9 Sun) Meals: alc exc Sun (main courses £10.50 to £27.50). Set L Mon to Sat £13.50 (2 courses) to £16.50, Set L Sun £17.50 (2 courses) to £19.95, Set D Sun £12.50 (2 courses) to £14.50. Cover £2 Service: not inc Cards: Amex, Delta, Maestro, MasterCard, Visa Details: 90 seats. 30 seats outside. Car park. Vegetarian meals. Children's helpings. No-smoking area. Music Accommodation: 6 rooms

MAP 2 HINDON – Wiltshire

Angel Inn [AR]

Angel Lane, Hindon SP3 6DJ
Tel: (01747) 820696

Fairy lights are strung in the trees outside this Georgian coaching inn in a rural village, while, inside, the contemporary renovation is sympathetic and elegant. Grilled goats' cheese on garlic-roast butternut squash with plum and date chutney (£5.95) comes as a starter, while main courses could be mustard-glazed hock of local ham with bubble and squeak, shallots and parsley butter (£10.50). Finish with something like lemon tart with fruit coulis and ice cream (£4.95). Around a dozen wines by the glass, with bottles from £11.50. Accommodation. Closed Sun D.

MAP 9 HOGHTON – Lancashire

Thyme at the Sirloin

Station Road, Hoghton PR2 0DD **NEW ENTRY**
Tel: (01254) 852293
Website: www.thymeatthesirloin.co.uk

Cooking 2 | **Modern European** | **£39**

The Sirloin is a typical Lancashire mill-town pub built of local stone. The ground-floor bar has a homely feel, the restaurant is in the room above, open to the rafters, and thus light and airy. This is the sister to Thyme at Longridge (see entry), offering a similarly ambitious, modern menu. At inspection, a tossed salad of Cajun chicken was attractively presented, while pan-seared scallops with truffled brown butter scored highly for freshness. To follow, a generous portion of tender honey and orange glazed gammon comes with herb crushed potatoes and an 'exceptional' mustard cream sauce, or there might be sea bass with tartare potatoes, scallops and a brandy and tomato velouté. Finish perhaps with iced chocolate and mint torte with crème de menthe sauce. Service is warm and welcoming. Wines start at £10.95, with six options by the glass.

Chefs: Andrew Nuttall and Paul Whalley Proprietors: Alex Coward and Wayne Keogh Open: Tue to Fri L 12 to 2, Tue to Sat D 6 to 9.30 (10 Sat), Sun 12 to 8 Meals: alc (main courses £13 to £17). Set L and D (before 7.30pm) £12.95 (2 courses) to £13.95. Light L menu available Service: not inc Cards: Delta, Diners, Maestro, MasterCard, Visa Details: 65 seats. Car park. Vegetarian meals. Smoking in bar only. Music. No mobile phones. Air-conditioned

MAP 6 | HOLKHAM – Norfolk

Victoria

Park Road, Holkham NR23 1RG
Tel: (01328) 711008
Website: www.victoriaatholkham.co.uk

Cooking 3 | Modern British | £39

The Victoria harks back to yesteryear with its sleepy Georgian setting and Jewel-in-the-Crown-style décor – handsome Rajasthani furniture, hand-carved lattice doors and intriguing knick-knacks add to the bohemian atmosphere. It stands on the impressive Holkham estate, which provides game for the kitchen; roasted guinea fowl, perhaps. Starters might include Thornham oysters in pear salsa, or confit of duck leg with a crisp dandelion, fig and walnut salad. Roasted organic salmon comes with red pepper and date couscous among main courses, or there might be best end of lamb with rösti potato and braised leeks, while 'Vic's favourites' include a 6oz venison burger and Caesar salad. End with rhubarb rice pudding with nutmeg ice cream, or pecan tart with a sweet balsamic glaze. Wines start at £12.95 for house French.

Chef: Neil Dowson **Proprietor:** Tom and Polly Coke **Open:** all week 12 to 2.30, 7 to 9.30 **Meals:** alc (main courses £7 to £16). Bar menu available. BBQ menu available in summer **Service:** not inc **Cards:** Delta, Diners, Maestro, MasterCard, Visa **Details:** 70 seats. 100 seats outside. Car park. Vegetarian meals. Children's helpings. No smoking. Wheelchair access (also women's WC). Music **Accommodation:** 14 rooms

MAP 6 | HOLT – Norfolk

Yetman's

37 Norwich Road, Holt NR25 6SA
Tel: (01263) 713320
Website: www.yetmans.net

Cooking 4 | Modern British | £51

Alison and Peter Yetman run a 'very likeable' restaurant with an 'appealing no-nonsense informality' and a friendly, laid-back atmosphere. Peter, a natural host, takes care of front-of-house in the prettily decorated dining room. Alison cooks in a straightforward domestic style, using a broad palette of contemporary flavours. A starter of home-cured herring with horseradish and red cabbage has been succinctly described as 'generous, wholesome, tasty' by one reporter. Other choices might include chargrilled king prawns with bacon, or Louisiana crab cakes with red capsicum mayonnaise. Main courses offer a good balance of meat and fish dishes, typically encompassing poached brill fillet with a champagne and potted shrimp sauce, roast rack of lamb with provençale herbs and apricot stuffing, or an expertly made steak and kidney pie with a herb and butter crust. Among desserts, a brandy-snap with plum sauce and ginger ice cream has been favourably received, and there might be toasted cinnamon and apple pancakes. The wine list may be short but offers a good choice of interesting bottles. Alternatively, try one of the 'extremely flavoursome' beers from Yetman's brewery.

Chef: Alison Yetman **Proprietors:** Alison and Peter Yetman **Open:** Sun L 12.30 to 2, Wed to Sat and bank hol Sun D 7 to 9.30 **Meals:** Set L and D £28 (2 courses) to £40 **Service:** not inc **Cards:** Amex, Diners, Maestro, MasterCard, Visa **Details:** 32 seats. Vegetarian meals. Children's helpings. No smoking in dining room. Wheelchair access (not WC). No music

MAP 5 | HOLY CROSS – Worcestershire

Bell and Cross   AR

Holy Cross DY9 9QL
Tel: (01562) 730319

At the foot of the Clent Hills, this popular country inn has south-facing gardens making the most of the views on fine days. Modern British and traditional French cooking provide the culinary inspiration. Starters take in roast red pepper and aubergine soup (£4.25), with everything from chargrilled ribeye with fries, sweet-and-sour onions and béarnaise (£13.75) to roast cod with Vichy carrots, mustard mash and parsley sauce (£12.25) to follow, and sticky toffee and banana waffle (£4.95) to finish. Blackboard menus and light lunches extend the choice, and cask ales and French house wines at £13.50 complete the picture. Open all week.

> The price given next to the cooking score is based on the cost of a typical three-course dinner for one person, including coffee, house wine and service.

MAP 8   HONLEY – West Yorkshire

Mustard and Punch

6 Westgate, Honley HD9 6AA
Tel: (01484) 662066
Website: www.mustardandpunch.co.uk

Cooking 3 | Modern European | £36

This quietly confident restaurant in the pretty village of Honley provides a welcome blend of discreet sophistication and relaxed charm. In keeping with the 'home-from-home' feel, bread, ice cream and preserves are also made on the premises. Beer-battered Brie, or roast king scallops with curried apple and parsnip purée may be good ways to start, while the Whitby cod fillet or pork belly braised in cider accentuate the modern European theme. There is a separate grill menu featuring veal, chicken and steaks plus interesting side orders including courgette fritters, herb salads and home-made chips cooked in dripping. If you have room, end with warm chocolate molten cake or roast plums with mulled wine, or the excellent cheese-board, which offers among others, Whitehaven goats' cheese, crumbly Lancashire and Long Clawson blue Stilton. Their re-vamped wine list is split into flavour and style sections, and features many boutique wineries from around the globe. Prices start around £12.

Chefs: Richard Dunn and Wayne Roddis **Proprietor:** Richard Dunn **Open:** Thur and Fri L 12 to 2, Mon to Sat D 6 to 9.30 **Closed:** 26 Dec to 5 Jan, bank hol Mon **Meals:** alc (main courses £12 to £18). Set L £10.50 (2 courses), Set D Mon to Fri and before 6.30 Sat £17.95 (inc wine). **Service:** not inc **Cards:** Amex, Delta, Maestro, MasterCard, Visa **Details:** 55 seats. Vegetarian meals. Children's helpings. No smoking. Music. Air-conditioned

---

MAP 9   HORNCASTLE – Lincolnshire

Magpies

71–75 East Street, Horncastle LN9 6AA
Tel: (01507) 527004
Website: www.eatatthemagpies.co.uk

Cooking 5 | Modern British | £46

Magpies is in a row of traditional terraced cottages, and at the back is a small square courtyard with shrubs and pots – ideal in summer for aperitifs.

Inside, the L-shaped dining room has a wood-burning stove, candles and white linen tablecloths. Andrew Gilbert continues to offer well-structured, good-value menus, which at first glance may seem conservative but the food is stylishly delivered and well thought through. The restaurant is now open for lunch: perhaps a glazed tart of quail's egg and smoked salmon with goats' cheese dressing, followed by pan-fried cod on truffle and wild mushroom risotto with crispy pancetta. After a light appetiser, the four-course evening menu could start with honey- and soy-roast pork fillet with mustard champ and caramelised apples, while main courses could feature fillet of roe deer on parsnip and potato rösti, or corn-fed chicken breast on creamy polenta with baked figs, mozzarella and Serrano ham. Breads, including granary, onion, and cheese and walnut, are baked in-house, and desserts have included an unusual dark chocolate brûlée with a chilli and black pepper chocolate chip cookie and white chocolate ice cream. Cornish Yarg is among the Irish and British cheeses, while handmade petits fours come with coffee. The wine list relies heavily on Bordeaux and Burgundy, although good producers have been selected from other countries too, such as Vavasour's 2004 Sauvignon Blanc from Marlborough, New Zealand (£22.85). Corney & Barrow wines head around a dozen house selections at £11.85.

Chef: Andrew Gilbert **Proprietors:** Caroline Ingall and Andrew Gilbert **Open:** Wed to Sun 12 to 2.30, 7 to 9.30 **Closed:** New Year **Meals:** Set L £21 (2 courses) to £25, Set D £32 to £39.50 **Service:** not inc **Cards:** Maestro, MasterCard, Visa **Details:** 34 seats. 8 seats outside. Vegetarian meals. No smoking. Wheelchair access (also WC). Music. No mobile phones. Air-conditioned

---

MAP 3   HORNDON ON THE HILL – Essex

Bell Inn

High Road, Horndon on the Hill SS17 8LD
Tel: (01375) 642463
Website: www.bell-inn.co.uk

Cooking 2 | Modern European | £38

This ancient coaching inn (building started in the fifteenth century) stands opposite the even more ancient guildhall in the centre of the small village, formerly an important centre for trade thanks to the Thames ferry crossing. The beamed bar and dining room show plenty of character, and so do

the menus, which, by contrast, are full of contemporary ideas. These include starters of spider crab with potato and scallion salad and a honey, mango and pimento dressing, and Parma ham with port-roast figs and a Stilton and red wine vinaigrette, which might be followed by sautéed scallops on pea pancake with nut-brown butter and crisp pancetta, or garlic chump of lamb with chorizo mash and a redcurrant and shallot jus. And for dessert there might be lemon cheesecake with port and plum sorbet and maple syrup. The bar menu offers simpler main dishes and sandwiches. House Australian at £11.50 opens the decent, global wine list.

Chef: Stuart Fay **Proprietors:** John and Christine Vereker **Open:** all week 12 to 1.45 (2.15 Sun), 6.45 to 9.45 **Closed:** 25 and 26 Dec, bank hol Mon **Meals:** alc (main courses £9.50 to £14.50). Sandwich L and bar menus available. **Service:** not inc **Cards:** Amex, Delta, Maestro, MasterCard, Visa **Details:** 80 seats. 36 seats outside. Car park. Vegetarian meals. Children's helpings. No smoking in dining room. No music. No mobile phones **Accommodation:** 15 rooms

---

| MAP 6 | **HORNINGSEA –**
Cambridgeshire |

Crown & Punchbowl

High Street, Horningsea CB5 9JG
Tel: (01223) 860643
Website: www.cambscuisine.com

Cooking 2 | Modern British | **£41**

This village pub is now a restaurant-with-rooms, and the owners (who also run the Cock in Hemingford Grey and the Boathouse in Ely; see entries) have done a good job retaining the character of the seventeenth-century building while lending it a distinctly modern feel. Exposed timbers and bare tables characterise the dining room, where blackboards showcase daily specials and the home-made speciality sausages. Starters might be confit duck leg with a tarragon salad and citrus dressing, or a terrine of smoked chicken and asparagus with diced mango, with main courses of breast of pheasant stuffed with orange couscous accompanied by sweet potato purée, wild mushrooms and a redcurrant jus. Home-made ice creams and sorbets lead the charge for dessert, which might also feature banana meringue with berries. French house bottles open the wine list at £12, and a number are served by the glass from £2.80.

Chef: John Dillow **Proprietors:** Oliver Thain and Richard Bradley **Open:** all week L 12 to 2.30, Mon to Sat D 6.30 to 9 (9.30 Fri and Sat) **Meals:** alc (main courses L £9 to £16, D £10 to £19) **Service:** not inc **Cards:** Maestro, MasterCard, Visa **Details:** 75 seats. 20 seats outside. Car park. Vegetarian meals. No children under 6 at D. Children's helpings. No smoking. Wheelchair access (also WC). No music. No mobile phones **Accommodation:** 5 rooms

---

| MAP 6 | **HOUGHTON CONQUEST –**
Bedfordshire |

Knife & Cleaver

The Grove, Houghton Conquest MK45 3LA
Tel: (01234) 740387

Dating from the seventeenth century, this country inn, now operating more along the lines of a restaurant-with-rooms, is opposite the splendid medieval parish church of All Saints. The food served in the conservatory-style dining room is of cosmopolitan provenance. Crab and shrimp tart with ginger pesto, lime and coriander salad (£6.25), for example, may start, followed by char-grilled hake fillet with warm spiced fruit chutney and potato crisps (£13.25), then frozen banana ice cream parfait (£4.95). Wines from £11.50. Closed Sat L and Sun D.

| MAP 9 | **HUDDERSFIELD –**
West Yorkshire |

Bradley's

84 Fitzwilliam Street, Huddersfield HD1 5BB
Tel: (01484) 516773

Cooking 2 | Mediterranean/Mod. British | **£36**

Energetic owner Andrew Bradley is always looking at ways to liven up the dining experience with the inclusion of themed lunches and dinners at his ever-popular, informal restaurant. A blackboard of specials supports a menu that starts with roast French black pudding with apples and celeriac, or smoked duck and Chinese vegetable spring roll with marinated cucumber and ginger. Main courses could be rack of lamb with 'cured' aubergine and a tomato, thyme and garlic reduction, or grilled fillets of turbot with spicy Puy lentils, fondant potato, and a red wine glaze. Around half a dozen puddings could include malt loaf bread pudding with custard, or strawberry and rhubarb tartlet. Service is buoyant, and the wine list hops around most of the wine-producing world, with £11.95 the bottom line.

Chef: Eric Paxman **Proprietor:** Andrew Bradley **Open:** Mon to Fri L 12 to 2, Mon to Sat D 6 (5.30 Fri and Sat) to 10 **Meals:** alc (main courses £11 to £17). Set L £6.95 (2 courses) to £8.95, Set D £16.95 (inc wine) **Service:** not inc **Cards:** Maestro, MasterCard, Visa **Details:** 120 seats. Car park (D only). Vegetarian meals. Children's helpings. No smoking. Wheelchair access (also WC). Music. Air-conditioned

Dining Rooms @ Strawberry Fair

14–18 Westgate, Huddersfield HD1 1NN
Tel: (01484) 513103

Cooking 2 | **Modern European** | **£27**

It is much lamented that this attractive dining room is open only for breakfast, lunch and afternoon tea but sharing a location with a home-accessories shop means its hours are limited. However, the locals flock here for their midday sustenance, served briskly and efficiently in a comfortable room where large windows give plenty of light on the dullest day and the high-backed brown leather chairs are very relaxing. Smoked Whitby haddock on a plum tomato and watercress salad is typical of their locally sourced dishes, followed by Lishmans of Ilkley sausages on creamy mash with a rich gravy, or perhaps pan-fried calf's liver with crispy bacon and baby onions. Finish with fluffy drop pancakes, layered with baked Bramley apples and sultana caramel sauce. A short wine list opens with Chilean red and white at £10.65.

Chefs: Glenn Varley and Rachel Miller **Proprietor:** Phillip Harrison **Open:** Mon to Sat L only 11.30 to 3 (breakfast 9 to 11.30, afternoon tea 2 to 4) **Closed:** bank hol exc Good Fri **Meals:** alc (main courses £6.50 to £7.50) **Service:** not inc **Cards:** Amex, Delta, Maestro, MasterCard, Visa **Details:** 48 seats. Vegetarian meals. Children's helpings. No smoking. Wheelchair access (also WC). Music. No mobile phones. Air-conditioned

Vanilla

73–75 Lidget Street, Lindley, Huddersfield HD3 3JP
Tel: (01484) 646474

Cooking 2 | **Modern European** | **£34**

A Victorian building in a row of shops is the setting for this first-floor restaurant, with its exposed stonework, original wooden flooring and blond-wood chairs and tables. Chris Dunn's modern bistro menu is fashioned by the seasons and boasts an array of local produce, including Yorkshire lamb, ham and game, but there is also an infusion of European flavours. Thus, starters can vary from a spring roll of Grecian-style lamb with feta, tsatsiki and harissa dressing to a salad of warm black pudding and wild boar sausage with a poached egg. Move on to a trio of pork: fillet stuffed with wild boar, pot-roast cheek and belly, accompanied by braised red Normandy cabbage, sage and lemon stuffing, apple sauce and cider gravy. Lunchtimes bring out lighter alternatives, such as Caesar salad, corned-beef hash, and Asian-spiced fishcakes. Finish with white chocolate tart with bilberry ice cream. The concise wine list, arranged by style, starts at £11.50 for house Merlot and Chardonnay.

Chefs: Chris Dunn and Alex Knott **Proprietor:** Chris Dunn **Open:** Tue to Fri L 12 to 2, Tue to Sat D 5.30 to 9.30 **Meals:** alc (main courses L £7 to £8.50, D £12.50 to £15). Set D 5.30 to 7 (6 Fri and Sat) £16.95 (2 courses) **Service:** not inc **Cards:** Delta, Maestro, MasterCard, Visa **Details:** 50 seats. Vegetarian meals. No smoking. Music

MAP 9 | **HULL – Kingston upon Hull**

Boars Nest

22 Princes Avenue, Hull HU5 3QA
Tel: (01482) 445577
Website: www.theboarsnest.co.uk

Cooking 2 | **British** | **£35**

The building was once a butcher's shop, and chef/proprietor Simon Rogers has carefully preserved all eye-catching detail, like the tiling in the front dining room. The tables are highly polished and laid with gingham napkins, and the kitchen is in full view. Naturally, meat features heavily on both the lunch and dinner menus. Beef and barley broth makes a hearty starter, and the seasonal winter salad stands out, combining roast tomatoes, Bury black pudding, Yorkshire Blue cheese, green beans, crisp bacon and a soft-poached egg. Among robust main courses may be steak and kidney pudding, or slow-roast belly pork with Savoy cabbage purée, mash, and a honey and red wine gravy, with whole roast lemon sole with crawfish tails and lemon butter an alternative. Finish with something traditionally British like spotted dick and custard. Staff are 'friendly and welcoming', and the annotated wine list roams the globe. Prices are virtually all below £20, starting at £12.95.

Chefs: Simon Rogers, Richard Bryan and Andy Young Proprietor: Simon Rogers Open: all week 12 to 2, 6.30 to 10 Meals: alc (main courses L £5 to £10, D £8 to £15) Service: not inc Cards: Delta, Diners, Maestro, MasterCard, Visa Details: 34 seats. Vegetarian meals. Children's helpings. No smoking. Wheelchair access (also WC). Music

MAP 3 | HUNSDON – Hertfordshire

Fox & Hounds

2 High Street, Hunsdon SG12 8NH
Tel: (01279) 843999
Website: www.foxandhounds-hunsdon.co.uk

Cooking 1 | Modern British | £38

Just a few miles from Ware, the Fox & Hounds is a relaxed venue, particularly when the thumping rock music is switched off. Wooden beams, panelling and pale tones all add to the ambience, with the lavatories quirkily hidden behind doors covered in fake books. Sourdough bread is an excellent introduction to a meal, while the daily-changing, seasonal menu delivers good combinations and some nice Mediterranean touches. Start with rabbit, pigeon and foie gras terrine, or moules marinière, and proceed to Aberdeen Angus beef with good chips and béarnaise, or liver and bacon, served with 'satisfying' onions and mash. Fish might be roast monkfish tail with wild mushrooms, and to end there could be raspberry and almond tart. Around 30 wines, most from France, start at £11.

Chef: James Rix Proprietors: James and Bianca Rix, and Gemma Marsh Open: Tue to Sun L 12 to 3 (3.30 Sun), Tue to Sat D 6 to 10 Meals: alc (main courses £9 to £17). Set L Tue to Fri £11 (2 courses), Set L Sun £17.50 (2 courses) to £19.50, Set D Tue to Thur £13.50 (2 courses). Bar menu available Service: 10% (optional) Cards: Delta, Maestro, MasterCard, Visa Details: 70 seats. 40 seats outside. Car park. Vegetarian meals. Children's helpings. No smoking in dining room. Wheelchair access (not WC). Occasional music

NEW ENTRY	This appears after the restaurant's name if the establishment was not a main entry in last year's Guide. Please note, however, it may have been 'also recommended' in the previous edition.

MAP 6 | HUNTINGDON – Cambridgeshire

Old Bridge Hotel

1 High Street, Huntingdon PE29 3TQ
Tel: (01480) 458410
Website: www.huntsbridge.com

Cooking 4 | Modern British | £44

The Old Bridge Hotel is the heart of the Huntsbridge Group, which comprises the Falcon, Fotheringhay; the Pheasant, Keyston and the Three Horseshoes, Madingley (see entries). Overlooking the River Ouse, the hotel has been tastefully extended, with lounges and a bar area, where it's possible to have anything from a coffee or a pint to a sandwich or a full meal. The conservatory dining room is simply decorated, with white-clothed tables. New chef Chris Tabbitt trained at the Three Horseshoes, then spent several years at Bibendum (see entry, London). His menus follow the style of the group, with top-quality ingredients going into modern combinations inspired by British, French and Mediterranean traditions. Veal kidneys are partnered by morel mushrooms in a puff pastry tartlet, served on garlic-flavoured greens and surrounded by a creamy sauce that had 'all the essence of the kidney cooking juices'. Risotto primavera, with broad beans, peas, asparagus, Jersey Royals, tarragon, Parmesan and vermouth, is another successful starter. Among main courses, roast Gressingham duck breast, 'meltingly soft and delicious', comes with a deep, glossy sauce infused with thyme, and green and yellow beans and new potatoes. Excellent farmhouse cheeses make a good alternative to puddings along the lines of cherry pie with vanilla ice cream. The wine list runs to around 300 bins. Prices throughout are fair, with a mark-up policy favouring the more expensive bottles – a 1989 Ch. Palmer is £145, for instance. Two pages are devoted to wines £20 and under, bottle prices start at £12.95, and a commendable number are served by the glass.

Chef: Chris Tabbitt Proprietors: Huntsbridge Ltd Open: all week 12 to 2.15, 6.30 to 10 Meals: alc (main courses £11 to £24). Set L Mon to Sat and D Mon to Fri 6.30 to 7.30 £13.50 (2 courses) to £16.75 Service: not inc Cards: Amex, Delta, Diners, Maestro, MasterCard, Visa Details: 100 seats. 30 seats outside. Car park. Vegetarian meals. Children's helpings. No smoking in dining room. Wheelchair access (also WC). No music. No mobile phones. Air-conditioned Accommodation: 24 rooms

MAP 2　HURLEY – Berkshire

Black Boys Inn

Henley Road, Hurley SL6 5NQ
Tel: (01628) 824212
Website: www.blackboysinn.co.uk

Cooking 5 | Modern British | £39

A carefully restored sixteenth-century inn with rooms just outside the village of Hurley, on the Henley to Maidenhead road, the Black Boys (think urchins up chimneys) is no haven for horse brasses; it feels modern inside, with grey-green, well-upholstered chairs, a varnished wooden floor and plain tables. It's the kind of place that revels in local produce, including game and even crayfish, but there is also fish brought up from Newlyn, salt-marsh lamb from Wales, and bluefin tuna from much further afield. That last might start off a meal in the form of a tartare, teamed with a blob of smoulderingly intense liquorice dressing. Salcombe crab appears as a visually striking cube layered with avocado purée and minted tomato.

An eye to value is always welcome in a country pub, and main courses at inspection were exemplary in this respect. Steamed Cornish monkfish with scallops, a mini serving of Toulouse sausage cassoulet, a beehive of mash with a strip of pancetta stuck in, and a sauce of sherry vinegar added up to an utterly satisfying, three-dimensional dish, while baked rack of local pork with apple and ginger in a well-balanced, gingery jus offered high-octane flavours and sublime meat. To finish, two might enjoy the wafer-thin apple tarte fine, which comes with glorious vanilla ice cream, or there could be that standby of country cooking, sticky toffee pudding, here made with dates and pecans. Helpful service and an overall feeling of smooth relaxation contribute to the success of an exciting Berkshire newcomer. Two pages of wines offer a predominantly European mix with plenty of household names, including LA Cetto's beefy Petite Sirah from Mexico. Prices open at £12.95, or £3.25 a glass.

Chef: Simon Bonwick　Proprietors: Adrian and Helen Bannister　Open: Tue to Sun L 12 to 2, Tue to Sat D 7 to 9　Closed: 2 weeks Christmas, 2 weeks Aug　Meals: alc (main courses £10.50 to £15　Service: not inc　Cards: Delta, Diners, Maestro, MasterCard, Visa　Details: 45 seats. 20 seats outside. Car park. No children under 12. No smoking. Wheelchair access (also WC). Occasional music　Accommodation: 8 rooms

MAP 10　HUTTON MAGNA – Co Durham

Oak Tree Inn

Hutton Magna DH11 7HH
Tel: (01833) 627371

Cooking 2 | Modern European | £37

Alastair and Claire Ross continue to thrive with their modern European style of cooking at their pub/restaurant in a terrace of tiny cottages. Their emphasis is on locally sourced ingredients, with game, for instance, coming from within a two-mile radius and seasonal fruit and vegetables from within half a mile. The personal touch is everything here, with daily specials chalked above the bar and another board brought to the table. Wild mushroom risotto with grilled goats' cheese or onion soup could be followed by roast fillet of halibut with hand-rolled spaghetti, king prawns and basil or ribeye steak accompanied by new season's broccoli and béarnaise. Finish with something like lemongrass pannacotta with mango compote and raspberry sorbet. The compact, reasonably priced wine list opens with French Sauvignon Blanc and Chilean Merlot at £10.90.

Chef: Alastair Ross　Proprietors: Alastair and Claire Ross　Open: Tue to Sun D only 6.30 to 9　Closed: 25 and 26 Dec, 1 Jan　Meals: alc (main courses £14.50 to £17.50)　Service: not inc　Cards: Delta, Maestro, MasterCard, Visa　Details: 20 seats. Car park. No smoking in dining room. Music. No mobile phones

MAP 1　ILFRACOMBE – Devon

Quay

11 The Quay, Ilfracombe EX34 9EQ
Tel: (01271) 868090
Website: www.11thequay.co.uk

NEW CHEF | Modern European | £50

The Quay is a handsome stone and brick building with a bar on the ground floor, and two dining rooms upstairs, each with a different view (one over the harbour and the other over the bay). The main dining room – the Atlantic Room – has an unusual ceiling shaped like an 'upturned boat'. Laurence Hill-Wickham took over in the kitchen as the Guide went to press. The team works to a varied menu that produces everything from bar food ranging from nibbles (crispy fried broad beans) to light snacks (Lundy crab claws with aïoli) and beyond to main courses of meatballs with spaghetti. The restaurant, meanwhile, deals in starters of scallops with black pudding and braised asparagus, and wild mushroom risotto. Main courses take in whole Dover sole with a classic caper butter and new potatoes, and a robust braised oxtail tart with lamb cutlet, crushed peas and mash, and desserts are along the lines of lemon tart with blackberry sorbet. Most bottles on the restaurant wine list are over £20. France is the focus, although a Rioja at £15.50 is the starting line.

> **Chef:** Laurence Hill-Wickham **Proprietors:** Damien Hirst and Simon Browne **Open:** Wed to Sun L 12 to 3, Wed to Sat D 6 to 9.30 **Meals:** alc (main courses £14.50 to £23.50). Set L Wed to Sat £17.50, Set L Sun £19 (2 courses) to £22.50, Set D £17.50 to £80 (inc wine). Bar menu available **Service:** not inc **Cards:** Amex, Delta, Maestro, MasterCard, Visa **Details:** 80 seats. 10 seats outside. Vegetarian meals. Children's helpings. No smoking in dining room. No music. Air-conditioned

---

MAP 8 ILKLEY – West Yorkshire

Box Tree

35–37 Church Street, Ilkley
LS29 9DR
Tel: (01943) 608484
Website: www.theboxtree.co.uk

YORKSHIRE OF THE YEAR RESTAURANT

Cooking 6 | Anglo-French | £67

Simon and Rena Gueller took over the Box Tree in 2004 and have brought a widely appreciated lighter touch to the place, both in terms of décor and approach. Soft creamy browns and mustards make for a relaxed feel, staff are solicitous and considerate, and to draw near the fire on a rainy April day felt like a homecoming for one couple who remembered the place from days gone by. The cooking, in Simon's hands, achieves an impressive degree of refinement, bringing some modern touches to what is essentially classical technique. A mosaic terrine of chicken, ham and foie gras is accompanied by apricot and orange chutney, or there could be lobster risotto, gaining from additions of braised fennel and a seasoning of tarragon. The quality is in the detail, fine fondant potato sprinkled with mustard seeds and coarse salt making a good partner for top-notch roast rump of veal, while an old-fashioned but beautifully rendered chervil cream sauce elevates lightly seared salmon with asparagus into the realms of the memorable.

Presentations are kept refreshingly simple, as when a slice of high-octane Valrhona chocolate tart turns up on a big glass plate with a scoop of vanilla ice cream and a few toasted nuts. Fine chocolates with coffee, as well as good breads, add to the sense of occasion. Thoroughbred Italian wines are one of the high points of a distinguished list, which also finds room for Oregon and Washington as well as a handful of good French regional choices. Half-bottles are plentiful, and the house selections embrace Argentina, France and New Zealand, starting at £19, or £5 a glass.

> **Chef:** Simon Gueller **Proprietor:** Rena Gueller **Open:** Fri to Sun L 12 to 2, Tue to Sat D 7 to 9.30 **Meals:** alc (main courses £25 to £28). Set L £18 (2 courses) to £25, Set D Tue to Thur £28 **Service:** not inc **Cards:** Delta, Maestro, MasterCard, Visa **Details:** 50 seats. No children under 10 at D. Children's helpings. No-smoking area. Wheelchair access (not WC). Music. No mobile phones. Air-conditioned

Farsyde

1–3 New Brook Street, Ilkley LS29 8DQ
Tel: (01943) 602030
Website: www.thefarsyde.co.uk

Cooking 4 | Modern British-Plus | £34

There's plenty of buzz and bustle in this breezy brasserie-style restaurant opposite the parish church. Bare floorboards, polished tables and a peachy colour scheme set the tone, while staff are friendly and efficient, and the menu lays on a display of contemporary ideas. Gavin Beedham's easy-going, straightforward style of cooking suits the materials well, delivering light lunches (seafood salad, fishcakes, cheeseburger) and at dinner offering starters of Thai chicken and shiitake mushroom stir-fry, king prawn and crab cannelloni, and warm mushroom and leek tart. Fillet of beef teamed with creamy Savoy cabbage, oxtail ravioli and red wine sauce might crop up among main courses, alongside fillet of cod wrapped in pak choi, smoked salmon and prosciutto, served on seafood risotto. Straightforward desserts (jam roly-poly or cherry clafoutis) round things off, and a well-chosen list of wines rarely strays over £20, starting with house French at £9.25.

> **Chef/Proprietor:** Gavin Beedham **Open:** Tue to Sat 11.30 to 2, 6 to 10 **Closed:** 25 and 26 Dec, 1 Jan **Meals:** alc (main courses L £5 to £9, D £12.50 to £15.50). Set L £12.95, Set D 6 to 7.15 £13.45 (2 courses) **Service:** not inc **Cards:** Delta, Maestro, MasterCard, Visa **Details:** 82 seats. Vegetarian meals. No smoking in dining room. Wheelchair access (also WC). Music. Air-conditioned

---

MAP 5 | ILMINGTON – Warwickshire

Howard Arms [AR]

Lower Green, Ilmington CV36 4LT
Tel: (01608) 682226

Owners Gill and Rob Greenstock are against 'making pretty pictures on odd-shaped plates', preferring to concentrate on flavours and textures and buying local, seasonal produce. Parsnip fritters with a Stilton and walnut dip (£5.50) make a lively starter, followed perhaps by beef, ale and mustard pie (£9.50), or pan-fried sea bass with herb couscous, sun-blush tomatoes and an olive dressing (£14.50). Desserts have included steamed marmalade pudding with Drambuie custard sauce (£5). Wines from £11.15. Three letting rooms. Open all week.

MAP 1 | INSTOW – Devon

Decks

Hatton Croft House, Marine Parade, Instow
EX39 4JJ
Tel: (01271) 860671
Website: www.decksrestaurant.co.uk

Cooking 2 | Modern European | £41

This two-floor restaurant makes the most of its seaside location, offering diners views over the beach and across the estuary, thanks to the windows that also create a light, airy feel. The white walls are hung with 'amusing and colourful' art. The food matches the vibrant surroundings with plenty of locally sourced seafood and a sprinkling of West Country meat dishes. A starter of Muddiford rainbow trout fillet, served with cauliflower purée and herbs, is typical of a menu that extends to local lamb or beef as well as sea bass fillet with marjoram butter sauce. Desserts include a cheeseboard selection, among them Somerset Brie, while those with a sweet tooth might try the cappuccino brûlée or hot chocolate fondant. There are approaching 50 wines to choose from, covering all corners of the globe, with house selections starting at £9.95.

Chef/Proprietor: Lee Timmins **Open:** Tue to Sat 12 to 2.30, 7 to 9.30 **Closed:** 25 and 26 Dec **Meals:** alc (main courses L £7 to £9, D £16.50 to £17.50). Set L and D £19.50 **Service:** not inc **Cards:** Amex, Delta, Maestro, MasterCard, Visa **Details:** 40 seats. 20 seats outside. Vegetarian meals. Children's helpings. No smoking in 1 dining room. Wheelchair access (also WC). Music. Air-conditioned

---

MAP 5 | IRONBRIDGE – Shropshire

Malthouse [AR]

The Wharfage, Ironbridge TF8 7NH
Tel: (01952) 433712

Overlooking the River Severn, this unexpectedly stylish restaurant has a something-for-everyone menu. Choose from two or three courses (£19/£22), with chicken liver and foie gras parfait with apricot and ginger chutney, or house-cured gravad lax opening the proceedings. Main-course lamb tagine with mint and lemon couscous or smoked haddock and crayfish lasagne could be followed by sticky toffee pudding. Children's dishes are £4.95. House wines from £11. Closed Sun D.

MAP 3 | JEVINGTON – East Sussex

Hungry Monk

Jevington BN26 5QF
Tel: (01323) 482178
Website: www.hungrymonk.co.uk

Cooking 2 | Anglo-French | £46

One of the oldest buildings in the Guide, dating from the fourteenth century, this reassuringly cosy restaurant remains familiar and down to earth. The décor is all comfortable sofas, roaring fires and a cornucopia of knick-knacks. The Anglo-French cuisine remains consistently good. Goats' cheese mousse with beetroot and ginger salad, or sausage in brioche with a Puy lentil salad are typical starters. Medallions of venison with butter-bean and parsnip purée on sloe gin sauce, or monkfish cooked in banana leaves with chilli, ginger and garlic may follow. Aside from its famous banoffi pie, there's chocolate fondant and a golden ginger sponge with custard. France dominates the wine list, although England is represented by a handful of bottles. Four house selections are around £15, and half a dozen come by the glass from £3.50.

Chefs: Gary Fisher and Matt Comben **Proprietors:** Nigel and Sue Mackenzie **Open:** Sun L 12 to 2.30, all week D 6.45 to 9.30 **Closed:** 24 to 26 Dec **Meals:** Set L £29.95, Set D £30.95 **Service:** not inc **Cards:** Amex, Delta, Maestro, MasterCard, Visa **Details:** 38 seats. Car park. Vegetarian meals. No children under 4. Children's helpings. No smoking in dining room. Occasional music. Air-conditioned

MAP 8   KENDAL – Cumbria

Bridge House

1 Bridge Street, Kendal LA9 7DD
Tel: (01539) 738855
Website: www.bridgehousekendal.co.uk

| Cooking 4 | Modern British | £44 |

A 'super restaurant' with an old-fashioned approach, Bridge House occupies a Georgian building and has a small bar with leather sofas and an upstairs dining room decorated in subdued green. Roger Pergl-Wilson, an assured presence in the kitchen, enjoys presenting 'travel collection' menus throughout the year, from northern Italy to Vietnam. Otherwise, his menus deal in home-cured salmon with a shallot, lime and herb dressing, avocado Caesar salad, and main courses of Moroccan-spiced chargrilled chicken breast ('bursting with flavour') on a bed of couscous, or loin of Gloucester Old Spot pork slowly cooked in milk with herbs. A gentle tomato and saffron sauce has been a good complement to grilled fillet of halibut, and desserts are a highlight, from honey and walnut pie ('beautiful pastry') to brown sugar meringue with bananas, ginger cream and chocolate sauce. Service is friendly but unobtrusive, and the well-considered wine list runs to around 80 bins, starting at £12.95, or £3.50 a glass.

Chef: Roger Pergl-Wilson Proprietors: Roger and Alena Pergl-Wilson Open: Tue to Sat 12.30 to 1.30, 6.30 to 9.30 Closed: 25 and 26 Dec, 1 Jan Meals: alc (main courses £12.50 to £20). Set L £14.50 (2 courses) to £18, Set D Tue to Fri £19.95 Service: not inc Cards: Delta, Maestro, MasterCard, Visa Details: 36 seats. Vegetarian meals. Children's helpings. No smoking. Wheelchair access (not WC). Music. No mobile phones

Déjà-vu

124 Stricklandgate, Kendal LA9 4QG
Tel: (01539) 724843
Website: www.dejavukendal.co.uk

| Cooking 2 | French Bistro | £39 |

This unassuming bistro has burgundy walls and simply dressed wooden tables, and presents a relaxed and unpretentious face to the world. A focal point remains the front of the bar, which is covered in corks and picks out the name of the restaurant. Tapas remain popular: well presented and enjoyable, the usual suspects include tortilla,

patatas bravas, calamares, and paella croquettes. The evening carte is more French than Spanish (and both menus are labelled to inform those with specific dietary needs), so a Brie, walnut and rocket tartlet might start, followed by chicken medallions on roast artichoke hearts with a tomato and rosemary sauce. The dessert menu has half a dozen options, among them lemon roulade filled with quince paste cream, and the cheeseboard is a truly European affair. The wine list has a decidedly French accent, and starts at £12.

Chef: Fabien Bellouère Proprietors: Fran and Ian Wood Open: all week D only 5.30 to 9 (9.30 Fri and Sat) Closed: 25 and 26 Dec, 1 Jan, bank hol Mon Meals: alc (main courses £10 to £17). Tapas menu available Mon to Sat L 12 to 2, D 5.30 to 6.30 Service: not inc Cards: Amex, Delta, Maestro, MasterCard, Visa Details: 34 seats. Vegetarian meals. No smoking. Wheelchair access (not WC). Music. No mobile phones

MAP 5   KENILWORTH – Warwickshire

Restaurant Bosquet

97A Warwick Road, Kenilworth CV8 1HP
Tel: (01926) 852463
Website: www.restaurantbosquet.co.uk

| Cooking 4 | French | £50 |

Bernard and Jane Lignier make a formidable double act at their restaurant, which brings a taste of France to Warwickshire. Jane's chatty style out front helps bring in the local custom, and the two dining rooms are smartly decorated in shades of coffee, with good, stiff table linen and high-backed upholstered chairs. There is a three-course set-price menu as well as a carte, which might start with pan-fried duck foie gras served with beetroot and apple, or sweetbreads with wild mushrooms on a pastry base. For main courses, squab pigeon is stuffed with apricots, chestnuts and foie gras, while saddle of venison is paired with a Cassis and chocolate sauce; look out also for the daily fish specials. Desserts might include lemon tart with passion-fruit sorbet. The all-French wine list is divided into regions and starts at £14.80.

Chef: Bernard Lignier Proprietors: Bernard and Jane Lignier Open: Tue to Fri L (bookings only) 12 to 1.15, Tue to Sat D 7 to 9.30 Meals: alc (main courses £19.50). Set L and D Mon to Fri £29.50 Service: not inc Cards: Amex, Delta, Maestro, MasterCard, Visa Details: 30 seats. Children's helpings. No smoking. Wheelchair access (not WC). No music. No mobile phones

Simply Simpsons

101–103 Warwick Road, Kenilworth CV8 1HL
Tel: (01926) 864567

This contemporary brasserie, which is related to Simpsons in Birmingham (see entry), spans the usual repertoire with some imaginative extras, so starters might be traditional Black Country faggot with mushy peas (£5.50), with main courses of pavé of Loch Duart salmon with truffled spaghetti and lobster sauce (£14.50), or breast of Barbary duck with aromatic couscous (£14.25). Finish with warm almond tart with apricots and amaretti mascarpone, or sticky toffee pudding (both £5.95). Interesting wines from £17. Closed Sun and Mon.

MAP 10 KESWICK – Cumbria

Swinside Lodge

Grange Road, Newlands, Keswick CA12 5UE
Tel: (017687) 72948

Standing alone in one of the most untouched areas of the Lake District, just three miles from the market town of Keswick, this Georgian hotel offers set-price four-course dinners (£35), with no choice until pudding. Asian-style fishcakes with sweet chilli and yoghurt dressing might start, followed by a soup – perhaps roast vine tomato and coriander – before a main course of roast breast of Swinside pheasant with chestnut stuffing, root vegetables and kumquat chutney, then warm chocolate mousse with Kirsch cherries. Wines from £14.50. Open all week D only.

MAP 3 KEW – Greater London

Glasshouse

14 Station Parade, Kew TW9 3PZ
Tel: (020) 8940 6777
Website: www.glasshouserestaurant.co.uk

Cooking 5 | **Modern British** | **£52**

Consistency is a watchword at this neighbourhood restaurant close to Kew Gardens. Anthony Boyd continues to treat first-class ingredients skilfully and brings a light touch to imaginative dishes that have a classic base. A British slant to raw materials complements a fairly discreet French flavour, the

enterprising fixed-price menus giving top billing to the likes of Finnebrouge venison, Coln Valley smoked salmon and Middle White pork. Start with grilled skate salad with beetroot, horseradish, shrimps and capers, or foie gras and ham hock pavé, and move on to fillet of cod with creamed white polenta, buttered vegetables, braised fennel and chives, or roast guinea fowl with a ragoût of white beans, wild mushrooms, cauliflower and garlic. Desserts might feature iced griottine cherry and coconut parfait with a chocolate madeleine. Tables are close together, but service is professional and informed. The substantial wine list covers the world with discernment, not overlooking the less mainstream (Germany, Alsace, Loire reds). A couple of pages of Bordeaux and Burgundy add gravitas, while house wines start at £16 and around a dozen good options are available by the glass.

Chef: Anthony Boyd **Proprietors:** Nigel Platts-Martin and Bruce Poole **Open:** Mon to Sat 12 to 2.30, 7 (6.30 Fri and Sat) to 10.30, Sun 12.30 to 3, 7.30 to 10 **Closed:** 24 to 26 Dec, 1 Jan **Meals:** Set L Mon to Sat £23.50, Set L Sun £27.50, Set D £35 to £50 (whole table only) **Service:** 12.5% (optional) **Cards:** Amex, Delta, Maestro, MasterCard, Visa **Details:** 65 seats. Vegetarian meals. Children's helpings. No smoking. Wheelchair access (not WC). No music. Air-conditioned. **Tube:** Kew Gardens

Ma Cuisine [NEW ENTRY]

9 Station Approach, Kew TW9 3QB
Tel: (020) 8332 1923
Website: www.macuisinekew.co.uk

Cooking 3 | **French** | **£35**

'You could well imagine yourself in France,' notes a reporter of John McClements's staunchly Gallic restaurant, the sibling of Ma Cuisine and La Brasserie, Twickenham (see entries). With red and white checked plastic cloths on the close-packed tables, black and white chequered floor, and Toulouse-Lautrec posters covering the pale yellow walls, it conjures up a traditional view of the French bistro, as does the menu, which features black pudding en croûte (three fat little pastry parcels of good-flavoured black pudding with a delicate Dijon mustard sauce), a homely blanquette of rabbit cooked with fennel and white wine and served with 'excellent pomme purée', well-timed John Dory with grilled fennel and Pernod jus, and a textbook poulet Bresse with mushroom sauce and dauphinoise potatoes. Bouillabaisse is classically served with rouille, while fillet steak comes with peppercorn sauce, and pudding pulls out all the stops for 'zesty' lemon tart. Amiable, efficient staff help everyone feel at home and the good-value French wine list should keep all-comers smiling. There's a dozen by the glass and house wine is £12.50

Chef: Tim Francis **Proprietors:** John McClements and Dominique Sejourne **Open:** all week 9 to 3, 6.30 to 10.30 (all day Sat and Sun) **Meals:** alc (main courses £12.50 to £15). Set L £12.95 (2 courses) to £15.50, Set D (exc Sat) £18.50. Light L menu available Sat **Service:** 10% (optional) **Cards:** Delta, Maestro, MasterCard, Visa **Details:** 60 seats. 20 seats outside. Vegetarian meals. Children's helpings No smoking. Wheelchair access (also WC). Music

MAP 6 KEYSTON – Cambridgeshire

Pheasant

Loop Road, Keyston PE28 0RE
Tel: (01832) 710241
Website: www.huntsbridge.com

Cooking 2 | Modern European | £44

Despite a reputation for food, readers are pleased to see that this pretty thatched, whitewashed cottage continues to maintain its pubbiness. Drinkers and diners mingle in the informal bar with its open fire, comfortable armchairs, and flagstone floor. But it's in the various rustic dining rooms where Jay Scrimshaw delivers ultra-modern food: a meal in April, for example, taking in a starter of salt-baked salmon with dandelion, peas, roast tomatoes and chive oil, followed by corn-fed chicken with a potato and sweetcorn pancake, new morels and garlic greens. Elsewhere, there could be snails with garlic and parsley butter, or fillet of red mullet with ratatouille, pommes Anna, bouillabaisse and anchoide crostini, while desserts have included ginger and whisky parfait with poached pears and madeleines. Home-made breads are a bonus, as is professional and pleasant service, and, this being a member of the Huntsbridge Group (see entries: the Old Bridge Hotel at Huntingdon, the Three Horseshoes at Madingley, and the Falcon at Fotheringhay), breadth and a sense of adventure are the keys to the well-thought-out wine list. It opens with 15 characterful house wines by the bottle from £12.95 (£3.50 a glass) and moves to an exciting mixture of classy global bins with moderate mark-ups.

Chef: Jay Scrimshaw **Proprietors:** Huntsbridge Ltd **Open:** all week 12 to 3 (4 Sun), 6.30 to 9.30 **Meals:** alc (main courses £9.50 to £23.50) **Service:** not inc **Cards:** Amex, Delta, Diners, Maestro, MasterCard, Visa **Details:** 87 seats. 30 seats outside. Car park. Vegetarian meals. Children's helpings. No smoking in dining room. Wheelchair access (not WC). No music. No mobile phones

MAP 5 KIBWORTH BEAUCHAMP – Leicestershire

Firenze

9 Station Street, Kibworth Beauchamp LE8 0LN
Tel: (0116) 279 6260
Website: www.firenze.co.uk

Cooking 3 | Modern Italian | £47

As homage to Florence, this modern restaurant does very well, from the plethora of Italian-themed pictures to the Roman head in the dining room, with its wooden lattice-backed chairs with blue-padded seats. Chef/proprietor Lino Poli continues to offer low-fuss traditional Italian cuisine with some lively modern touches: polenta with Taleggio and wild mushrooms, lobster wrapped in pancetta with cannellini beans, and spaghetti with air-dried tuna roe, for example. At inspection, pea soup with slices of 'tender' pink pigeon breast and truffle made an impressive starter, while a main course of griddled fillet of halibut with pennette in a rich, creamy sauce with al dente asparagus spears worked well. To finish, go for Brachetto (a sparkling red wine) jelly with raspberry compote, or 'subtly flavoured' warm mango tart with vanilla ice cream. The completely Italian wine list is extensive, running from lesser-known producers to the blockbusters of Tuscany. Fifteen wines by the glass (plus sparkling and pudding wines) are a good cross-section of the full list, where bottle prices start at £12.75.

Chefs: Lino Poli and Stuart Batey **Proprietors:** Lino and Sarah Poli **Open:** Mon to Sat 12 to 2, 7 to 10 **Closed:** 10 days from 23 Dec **Meals:** alc (main courses £7.50 to £30). Set L £12 (1 course), Set D Tue to Thur £15 (2 courses) to £25 **Service:** not inc **Cards:** Delta, Maestro, MasterCard, Visa **Details:** 60 seats. Vegetarian meals. Children's helpings. No smoking. Wheelchair access (not WC). Music

This symbol means that the wine list is well above the average.

MAP 6   KING'S LYNN – Norfolk

Riverside

AR

27 King Street, King's Lynn PE30 1ET
Tel: (01553) 773134

Outdoor seating on the Great Ouse is a draw at this 500-year-old building on a summer's day. The food is a good mixture of traditional English and modern European ideas, so expect Arbroath smokies (£6.95) or confit chicken and leek terrine with tomato chutney to start (£5.95), then beef fillet medallions on truffle-flavoured mash with roast tomatoes and rocket salad (£19.50) or pan-fried fillet of sea bass with tomato, shallot and pesto sauce (£16.50). Plum and apple crumble with sauce anglaise makes a good finale. Half a dozen bottles at £12.50 kick off the wine list. Closed Sun.

Rococo

11 Saturday Market Place, King's Lynn
PE30 5DQ
Tel: (01553) 771483
Website: www.rococorestaurant.org.uk

Cooking 3 | Modern British | £47

Nick Anderson's white-painted restaurant is situated in King's Lynn old town, near the town hall, conveniently located opposite a car park. The exterior belies the rather unconventional décor of the lounge with its bold colours and brightly patterned rugs, while the dining room is less dramatic with yellow walls and two welcome skylights. The modern British carte has been joined by a simpler bistro menu, which typically offers red onion tart with goats' cheese, tomato and rocket to start, followed by tiger prawns in a 'well-flavoured' creamy chilli sauce with noodles, or crisp duck confit on braised red cabbage with a sweet red wine sauce. The main menu kicks off with a twice-baked Beaufort soufflé with crème fraîche, tomato and chicory, followed by breast of Gressingham duck with roasted parsnip purée and a raspberry vinegar reduction. Finish with caramelised rice pudding with two fruit sauces. Service is pleasant, with Nick happy to chat to guests. The wine list is international, starting at £13.95 for their French house.

Chefs: Nick Anderson and Tim Sandford Proprietors: Nick and Susannah Anderson Open: Tue to Sat 12 to 2, 7 to 9 (6.30 to 10 Sat) Meals: alc (main courses £14.50 to £21). Bistro menu available exc Sat D Service: not inc Cards: Delta, Maestro, MasterCard, Visa Details: 40 seats. Vegetarian meals. Children's helpings. No-smoking area. Wheelchair access (also WC). Occasional music

MAP 5   KINGTON –
Herefordshire

Penrhos Court

Kington HR5 3LH
Tel: (01544) 230720
Website: www.penrhos.co.uk

Cooking 3 | Mediterranean | £50

'Alex Gooch is now the chef at Penrhos', writes Martin Griffiths, noting that 'after 30 years this is a watershed'. Fans of this quirky ancient manor, and its medieval atmosphere, will find little changed as he works under the guidance and influence of Daphne Lambert, whose dedication to sourcing fine seasonal and often local ingredients is clearly a driving obsession. Only organic produce is used, red meat banned (but fish and chicken allowed), and vegetarians are well catered for on the daily-changing dinner menu, which will often begin with a soup like beetroot, followed by a salad such as spiced sprouted lentil and avocado, before moving on to, say, roast root vegetable frittata with sprouted red clover. Otherwise, there's seared sea bass with a mustard and dill dressing, or lemon and thyme chicken with roast sweet potato and caramelised shallots. Desserts have included exotic-sounding chocolate hemp cake as well as brandied plums with brioche and vanilla ice cream. An affordable slate of some 30 organic or biodynamic wines starts at £15.80.

Chefs: Alex Gooch and Daphne Lambert Proprietors: Daphne Lambert and Martin Griffiths Open: all week D only 7.30 to 9 Meals: Set D £37.50 Service: not inc Cards: Delta, Maestro, MasterCard, Visa Details: 50 seats. 20 seats outside. Car park. Vegetarian meals. Children's helpings. No smoking. Wheelchair access (also WC). No music. No mobile phones Accommodation: 15 rooms

MAP 2   KINTBURY – Berkshire

Dundas Arms

AR

53 Station Road, Kintbury RG17 9UT
Tel: (01488) 658263

This inn sits between the River Kennet and the Kennet and Avon Canal, offering either bar food on the river patio or bigger meals in the bright dining room. Dorset crab salad (£6.90) might start, while roast duck breast with cider and apple sauce (£13.50), or baked cod with chips and peas

(£12) could follow. The extensive wine list exploits the best of European and New World choices, with house selections starting at £12. Open Tue to Sat D only; bar meals Mon to Sat L, Tue to Sat D.

MAP 9   KIRK DEIGHTON –
North Yorkshire

Bay Horse

Main Street, Kirk Deighton LS22 4DZ
Tel: (01937) 580058

Cooking 3 │ Modern European │ £35

More cosy than cramped, this rustic pub promotes Yorkshire produce on a menu that is bolstered by seafood specials. Salmon is smoked in-house (and sold in portions for two people for customers to take away) and black pudding is made on the premises. The venue is split into two interconnecting rooms – the smaller is the bar area – while staff are efficient and welcoming. The menu, no longer handwritten, is a large printed sheet of card, with wines listed on the back. Starters could be pork dim sum with pickled ginger, lime and soy, or smoked haddock risotto, followed by main courses such as Gressingham duck, pan-fried with oranges and served with a timbale of Asian vegetables, or pan-fried sea bass accompanied by an avocado, roast tomato and rosemary salsa. Desserts include Wakefield rhubarb on a crisp ginger biscuit base. The short wine list represents good value, with prices from £12.95 and only one bottle above £25.

Chefs: Stephen Ardern, Darren Danby and Phil Barker
Proprietor: Karl Mainey Open: Tue to Sun L 12 to 2.15, Mon
to Sat D 6 to 9.15 Meals: alc (main courses £8 to £14). Set L
and D 6 to 7 £13.95 (2 courses) Service: not inc Cards:
Delta, Maestro, MasterCard, Visa Details: 50 seats. 15 seats
outside. Car park. Vegetarian meals. Children's helpings. No
smoking in dining room. Wheelchair access (not WC).
Occasional music

MAP 8   KIRKHAM – Lancashire

Cromwellian

16 Poulton Street, Kirkham PR4 2AB
Tel: (01772) 685680

Cooking 2 │ Modern British │ £35

This long-running restaurant occupies a cottagey seventeenth-century building in the centre of Kirkham and has a welcoming and friendly atmos-

phere, with Peter Fawcett a calm, good-natured host. The cooking is dependable rather than spectacular, Josie Fawcett turning out a tried and tested repertoire with admirable consistency. A trio of starters usually features a soup, perhaps sweet potato, apple and ginger, while other options might include 'tipsy shrimps' (hot potted Southport shrimps in spiced butter with a dash of cognac). Follow, perhaps, with wild Lune trout fillet on spinach with an orange and ginger sauce; Aberdeen Angus fillet steak is a fixture, and the dauphinoise-style potatoes accompanying main courses are 'legendary'. The platter of local cheeses is an excellent alternative to desserts such as warm marmalade and orange sponge pudding or walnut tart with Armagnac icing. House wines from £12 open a varied list.

Chef: Josie Fawcett Proprietors: Peter and Josie Fawcett
Open: Wed to Sat D only 7 to 9 Closed: first week Jan, first 2
weeks June Meals: Set D £19 (2 courses) to £22.50
Service: not inc Cards: Delta, Maestro, MasterCard, Visa
Details: 28 seats. Vegetarian meals. No smoking in 1 dining
room. Wheelchair access (not WC). No music

MAP 5   KNIGHTWICK –
Worcestershire

The Talbot

Knightwick WR6 5PH
Tel: (01886) 821235
Website: www.the-talbot.co.uk

Cooking 1 │ British │ £40

The Clift family have clocked up almost a quarter of a century at their large, black and white pub overlooking the River Teme. Cooking, like the bare bones village pub décor, keeps things simple to make the best of local and home-grown supplies but makes an impact with some robust flavour combinations: for example, confit wild duck leg with sweet potato purée and walnut dressing, haddock fillet on a laverbread potato cake with chive cream, or lamb cutlets with leek and truffle ravioli and artichoke velouté. Aga-cooked daubes and braises are a speciality: shin of beef in Teme Valley ale, perhaps, or lamb, tomato and olive casserole. If you have room, treacle hollygog – shortcrust pastry rolled with golden syrup and baked in milk – is the dessert to go for. Wines are varied and sensibly priced, starting with house Chilean at £11.25.

Chefs: Annie Clift and Jamie Tarbox Proprietors: the Clift family Open: all week 12 to 2, 6.30 to 9.30 (9 Sun) Closed: D 25 Dec Meals: alc (main courses £13 to £15),Set D £22.95 (2 courses) to £27.95. Set L Sun £17 (2 courses) to £20. Bar menu available L and D Service: not inc Cards: Delta, Maestro, MasterCard, Visa Details: 90 seats. 40 seats outside. Car park. Vegetarian meals. Children's helpings. Wheelchair access (not WC). No music Accommodation: 11 rooms

MAP 5 KNOSSINGTON – Leicestershire

Fox & Hounds

6 Somerby Road, Knossington LE15 8LY
Tel: (01664) 454676
Website: www.foxandhounds.biz

Cooking 2 | Modern British | £33

This rather handsome three-storey building, covered in creepers, is four miles from Oakham, deep in farming and hunting country. Typically buzzing with locals and out-of-towners, the dining room boasts two large tables for groups, while Brian Baker's menu takes account of its geography and the seasons. Look out for chicken liver parfait with balsamic onions, or king scallops and king prawns with crème fraîche for starters, followed by roasted fillet of cod with herb mash and mustard dressing or maybe skate wing with lemon, capers and shallots. Meat eaters might plump for roast rump of lamb with roasted aubergines and artichokes or grilled calf's liver with champ, Parma ham and sweet and sour onions. Dessert sees the likes of white peach tart with vanilla ice cream or Colston Bassett Stilton with oatcakes. The international wine list starts at £10.25 for house French.

Chef/Proprietor: Brian Baker Open: Tue to Sun 12 to 2.30, 7 to 9.30 Meals: alc (main courses £9.50 to £14). Set L £9.95 (2 courses) to £16.95, Set L Sun £15.95 (2 courses) to £17.95. Bar L menu available Service: not inc Cards: Delta, MasterCard, Maestro, Visa Details: 35 seats. 20 seats outside. Car park. Vegetarian meals. Children's helpings. No smoking in 1 dining room. No music

NEW ENTRY — This appears after the restaurant's name if the establishment was not a main entry in last year's Guide. Please note, however, it may have been 'also recommended' in the previous edition.

MAP 1 KNOWSTONE – Devon

Mason's Arms   NEW ENTRY

Knowstone EX36 4RY
Tel: (01398) 341231
Website: www.masonsarmsdevon.co.uk

Cooking 6 | Modern British | £46

Knowstone is a pint-sized village between Tiverton and Barnstaple, signposted off the A361 on a detour that begins with the crossing of a cattle-grid. There is a church, of course, a few houses, a call box, and this long, low thirteenth-century inn, yellow of hue and neatly thatched. To the rear, a good-sized patio and adjacent dining room look out towards Exmoor; silence, other than birdsong, prevails. 'Cliveden comes to the Devon moors,' commented our inspector, indicating just one of Mark Dodson's previous postings (the Waterside Inn at Bray was another; see entries). That gives notice of a certain complexity in the cooking, as well as the kind of portion size that might raise eyebrows in a pub, but the man can surely cook. A trio of fat scallops sits on vanilla crème fraîche, teamed with artfully sliced pear and caramelised yellow pepper, the whole accompanied by trendy saladings dressed in a sweet pear vinaigrette, to make a triumphant opener. Vivid colours distinguished another's starter of roast tuna niçoise, with all the expected components on parade and brilliantly timed tuna to boot.

For main course, lamb might arrive in three preparations – loin, confit neck, and a kind of lasagne of the liver – with tart ratatouille, smooth garlic purée and a tomatoey jus. Fillet of John Dory might be voguishly paired with veal sweetbreads and served with potato pancakes and cep cream, while desserts bring on vibrant assemblies such as chocolate and raspberry mousse with lime syrup and raspberry granita. Readers are wholly impressed. There's a new star in Devon's firmament. An agreeably concise wine list is largely French with a smattering of New Worlders. House wines start at £11.75 for a Loire Chenin, while glass prices are £3.50 for house red and white, £5.50 for Chablis.

Chef: Mark Dodson Proprietors: Mark and Sarah Dodson Open: Tue to Sun L 12 to 2, Tue to Sat D 7 to 9 Closed: first 2 weeks Jan Meals: alc exc Sun L (main courses £10.50 to £16.50). Set L Sun £29.50 Service: not inc Cards: Delta, Maestro, MasterCard, Visa Details: 22 seats. 20 seats outside. Car park. Children's helpings. No smoking in dining room. Wheelchair access (not WC). No music

MAP 8 LANCASTER – Lancashire

Quite Simply French AR

27A St Georges Quay, Lancaster LA1 1RD
Tel: (01524) 843199

A lobster tank is a focal point at this spacious split-level restaurant. A dozen snails stuffed with garlic and Pernod butter (£5.60) will start things off on the right note, while grilled venison cutlets come with a sauce of cracked black pepper, redcurrant and red wine (£14.80). Desserts include a Belgian white and dark chocolate fondue for two (£7). House wines from £11.95. Closed Mon to Fri L.

MAP 5 LANGAR – Nottinghamshire

Langar Hall

Langar NG13 9HG
Tel: (01949) 860559
Website: www.langarhall.com

Cooking 4 | English | £49

Many restaurants tell us that they use local produce 'wherever possible', but few can match Imogen Skirving in that respect. From her substantial Georgian manor house she has built a symbiotic relationship with local supply networks, as well as a sizeable home-produce operation. The well-established kitchen gardens are run by Bill the gardener, who keeps ferrets that help control the rabbits on Belvoir Castle Estate, which also means the restaurant gets first pick of the estate's game in season. Fish and seafood, not being abundant in land-locked Nottinghamshire, is delivered daily from Brixham. The kitchen does its bit to make the best of its bounty, with straightforward cooking to emphasise flavour and freshness. Starters of crab timbale with avocado and tomato or pork and foie gras terrine with home-made chutney might be followed by roast saddle and chargrilled leg of lamb, roast stuffed saddle of Belvoir rabbit with Puy lentils, or wild sea bass with tomato and saffron herb dressing. Finish perhaps with glazed lemon tart or a selection of local cheeses. A selection of fine Bordeaux is the highlight of a varied wine list, which opens with house vins de pays at £14.50.

Chef: Toby Garratt Proprietor: Imogen Skirving Open: all week 12 to 2, 7 to 9.30 Meals: alc D (main courses £13.50 to £20). Set L Mon to Thur £13.50 (2 courses) to £16.50, Set L Fri and Sat £20, Set L Sun £25, Set D £20 (2 courses) to £25 Service: 10% (optional) Cards: Amex, Delta, Maestro, MasterCard, Visa Details: 60 seats. 20 seats outside. Car park. Vegetarian meals. Children's helpings. No smoking in dining room. Wheelchair access (also WC). Occasional music Accommodation: 12 rooms

MAP 8 LANGHO – Lancashire

Northcote Manor

Northcote Road, Langho BB6 8BE
Tel: (01254) 240555
Website: www.northcotemanor.com

Cooking 5 | Modern British | £59

Tall bay windows command views over the Ribble Valley at this handsome manor house. Done in muted tones with some striking artwork, the dining room is a comfortable spot, with well-drilled, attentive service showing its paces. The complicated menu structure, with Tasting and Gourmet options supplementing the dinner and lunchtime cartes, as well as a pair of vegetarian menus, might bear a little streamlining, but the emphasis ultimately is on quality produce.

A bowl of soup is the product of woodland foraging, combining bitter cress, nettles, chervil and wild garlic, together with gnocchi made from local sheep's cheese. Provenances are proudly stated on menus that take in red mullet with Woodall's aged ham, smoked shallots, saffron foam and purple basil oil, as well as potato-wrapped Goosnargh chicken breast, with its wings served steamed, on mushroom purée. The 'market price' for whole Dover sole might turn out to be a little eye-watering, but relief arrives in the form of newly fashionable mutton, a knuckle piece slowly cooked and served surprisingly delicately with pak choi, cucumber and tomato. Finish in northern style with 'melting ginger pudding', kitted out with iced double cream and caramel custard. An encyclopaedic wine list will provide something for just about everyone, as regards style and price, with bottles from Hungary and Austria cropping up among the regulars. Half-bottles are plentiful, and house wines come in at £17.50 or £18.50. See also the Three Fishes in Mitton.

Chefs: Nigel Haworth and Lisa Allen Proprietors: Craig Bancroft and Nigel Haworth Open: all week 12 to 1.30 (2 Sun), 7 to 9.30 (10 Sat) Closed: 25 Dec, 1 Jan, bank hol Mon Meals: alc (main courses £19.50 to £26.50). Set L £20, Set D £50 to £85 Service: not inc Cards: Amex, Delta, Maestro, MasterCard, Visa Details: 80 seats. Car park. Vegetarian meals. Children's helpings. No smoking. Wheelchair access (not WC). Music. No mobile phones Accommodation: 14 rooms

MAP 9 LANGTHWAITE – North Yorkshire

Charles Bathurst Inn [AR]

Langthwaite DL11 6EN
Tel: (01748) 884567

The beautiful moorland setting draws walkers on the Pennine Way to this eighteenth-century inn, where a warm, friendly atmosphere, and well-kept Yorkshire ales are part of the appeal. There's also the ambitious modern cooking, typically asparagus and Wensleydale cheese tartlet with tomato chutney (£4.75) to start, followed by pan-fried halibut fillet with leek and fennel terrine and Bercy sauce (£14.50), then chocolate tart with raspberry coulis (£3.95). House wine is £9.95. Accommodation. Open all week.

MAP 6 LAVENHAM – Suffolk

Great House

Market Place, Lavenham CO10 9QZ
Tel: (01787) 247431

Cooking 2 | French | £46

Owned and run by Regis and Martine Crépy, this restaurant in a prime setting in historical Lavenham oozes Gallic authenticity. Inside, the décor is traditional, with exposed timbers and interesting pieces of carved furniture. While not blazing a revolutionary trail, the menu offers classic dishes, and shows some genuine flair along the way: home-smoked salmon fillet on a bed of warm beetroot makes a promising start, while terrine of foie gras and pork confit comes tender and pink. Simple main courses might include grilled beef fillet with boulangère potatoes and fillet of halibut with pan-fried artichokes in beurre blanc. Desserts end things on a high with hot dark chocolate ganache enjoyably served with crème anglaise and a garnish of berries. Service is 'friendly and profes-

sional', and the extensive wine list starts with around half a dozen house choices from £11.50.

Chef: Regis Crépy Proprietors: Regis and Martine Crépy Open: Tue to Sun L 12 to 2.30, Tue to Sat D 7 to 9.30 (10 Sat) Closed: Jan Meals: alc exc Sun L (main courses L £7.50 to £13.50, D £16 to £18). Set L Tue to Sat £14.95 (2 courses) to £16.95, Set L Sun £24.95, Set D Tue to Fri £24.95 Service: not inc Cards: Delta, Maestro, MasterCard, Visa Details: 45 seats. 30 seats outside. Vegetarian meals. Children's helpings. No smoking in 1 dining room. Music Accommodation: 5 rooms

MAP 5 LEDBURY – Hertfordshire

Malthouse

Church Lane, Ledbury HR8 1DW
Tel: (01531) 634443

Cooking 3 | Modern British | £41

The setting for this ambitious restaurant is engaging; Ledbury is a small market town with a good range of food shops. This split-level restaurant is a tidy affair (and there's a pretty courtyard for warmer days), while the menu has lofty aspirations, which it mostly lives up to. Twice-baked Oxford blue cheese soufflé with red wine pears is accompanied by a walnut and herb salad, while for main courses, chump of lamb is roasted pink with a herb crust and served with potato fondant and a honey and cumin purée. Fish could be sautéed medallions of salmon with a salmon, lobster and lemon cannelloni. Creative desserts include a spiced molasses cake, which shares the plate with a caramel poached apple and apple ice cream. The international wine list won't break the bank; there are a dozen choices by the glass with the house Chilean a reasonable £12.50.

Chef: Ken Wilson Proprietors: Ken Wilson and Jamila Belkoniene Open: Sat L 12 to 1.30, Tue to Sat D 7 to 9.30 Meals: alc (main courses L £9 to £18.50, D £13 to £19). Set D Tue to Thurs £17.25 (2 courses) to £23 Service: not inc Cards: Maestro, MasterCard, Visa Details: 30 seats. 14 seats outside. Vegetarian meals. Children's helpings. No smoking in 1 dining room. Music. No mobile phones

[AR] Not a full entry but provisionally recommended. These 'also recommended' establishments are integrated throughout the book.

MAP 8 **LEEDS** – West Yorkshire

Anthony's at Flannels

68–78 Vicar Lane, Leeds LS1 7JH
Tel: (0113) 242 8732

| NEW ENTRY |

Website: www.anthonysatflannels.co.uk

Cooking 4 | Modern British | £25

£

A new venture from the precocious young Yorkshire star Anthony Flinn (see entry below) is this top-floor restaurant in the Leeds branch of Flannels, an upmarket chain of designer-clothing stores. It's a big, light space with rooftop views and a beamed, pitched ceiling. Leather chairs and well-dressed tables ensure the all-important comfort factor. A whole variety of eating occasions is catered for, depending whether you are in the market for brunch, afternoon tea, a sandwich snack, or indeed full-dress lunch. The cooking is simple, funky, modern to its asparagus tips, with many dishes scoring highly for upstanding flavours. A slice of ham hock terrine, thick and moist, arrives surrounded by a properly piquant gribiche dressing, while another starter, of crisply grilled mackerel fillet, is well served by its accompaniment of oily, home-made hummus. Belly pork with asparagus and spinach, sauced with cider, should prove a main-course hit. Sticky toffee pudding is a 'beautifully light' version, served with smooth banana ice cream. Service ranges from the proficient to the endearingly inept. The compact wine list is a model of intelligent concision, with wines by the glass from around £4.

Chef: Christopher Kelly **Proprietor:** Anthony Flinn **Open:** Tue to Sat 10 to 6, Sun 11 to 5 **Meals:** alc (main courses £6.50 to £10). Set L £12.95 (2 courses) to £15 **Service:** 10% (optional) **Cards:** Maestro, MasterCard, Visa **Details:** 75 seats. Vegetarian meals. Children's helpings. No smoking in 1 dining room. Wheelchair access (also WC). Music. Air-conditioned

Anthony's Restaurant

19 Boar Lane, Leeds LS1 6EA
Tel: (0113) 245 5922
Website: www.anthonysrestaurant.co.uk

Cooking 7 | Modern European | £54

Anthony Flinn's restaurant opened in March 2004 and is already well and truly ensconced at the vanguard of cutting-edge cookery in the UK. The empire has expanded – see Anthony's at Flannels, above – but it is here on the busy shopping street of Boar Lane that Anthony Flinn delivers a menu that, as one reader put it, is 'a revelation at every turn'. His stint at El Bulli near Barcelona, 'the best restaurant in the world' (or thereabouts), has given him the confidence to take his bold and inventive cooking back home to Leeds.

The basement restaurant is every inch the fine dining space, with lots of room between smartly set tables, neutral colours, high-backed leather chairs, and ceilings shimmering with the light from a legion of spotlights. The Spanish connection extends to many of the waiting staff, who do their best to explain what is to follow. Praise is due for the pricing of set lunches, perhaps making the central location even more appealing for some. This is a world of pre-starters, tasters and inter-courses, which this year seem to have made a good impression: a tiny soup plate of saffron velouté with smoked shrimps and a pea stalk, for example. The risotto of white onion, espresso and Parmesan 'air' remains a signature starter ('to eat it is to understand it'), while another starter sees braised pig's cheek, maws and lung, artfully combined, producing an 'outstanding' intensity of flavour. Delivery is uniformly impressive, with swirls of rich emulsions, and every angle on the plate precise to the nearest degree.

Whole roast squab pigeon on artichoke purée with a peanut and cocoa reduction sees the starring bird set off with a rich, glossy cocoa sauce, and the various squiggles and splashes on the plate making their mark without overwhelming the perfectly cooked breasts. Roast silver hake comes on shredded beetroot with a brochette of baby squid, with a garlic cream poured by the waiter as a final touch. A pre-dessert of caramelised pear with a quenelle of ginger ice cream might precede lemon chiboust with barley ice cream and sumac caramel – mentioned in dispatches once again – or there might be chocolate pot. Make sure you order coffee and the excellent petits fours, which include pumpkin oil-flavoured chocolate-coated bonbons, home-made Turkish delight and truffles. The wine list is set out by style, bottle prices start at £13.99, and 16 are available as half-bottles.

Chef: Anthony James Flinn **Proprietors:** Anthony Flinn and Anthony James Flinn **Open:** Tue to Sat 12 to 2, 7 to 9.30 **Meals:** alc (main courses £20 to £25). Set L £18.95 (2 courses) to £55, Set D £55 **Service:** not inc **Cards:** Maestro, MasterCard, Visa **Details:** 36 seats. No smoking in 1 dining room. Wheelchair access (also WC). Music. Air-conditioned

Bibis Criterion

Criterion Place, Swinegate, Leeds LS1 4AG
Tel: (0113) 243 0905
Website: www.bibisrestaurant.com

| Cooking 3 | Italian | £42 |

This long-established Leeds favourite can get busy – Saturdays can see crowds queuing outside. The cavernous Art Deco room is all tiled floors, marble-effect pillars and candelabra, with an open-plan kitchen adding to the buzz. Service is everything here, as is attention to detail and the judicious use of good-quality ingredients imaginatively presented. Antipasti could be anything from smooth goose liver pâté with Sauternes jelly to bresaola with wild rocket and marinated palm hearts. Pastas and pizzas are naturally a draw: for instance, gnocchi with goats' cheese, spaghetti con frutti di mare, and the house pizza, made with mozzarella, dolcelatte and Parma ham. Among a long list of main courses might be pan-fried veal escalope filled with roast ham, cheese and sage, and Tuscan wild boar steak in Chianti served with grilled polenta. Finish with vanilla and ricotta cheesecake. The wide-ranging wine list opens at £15 a bottle, and around ten are available by the glass from £3.75.

Chef: Piero Vinci **Proprietor:** Oliver Teodorani **Open:** all week 12 to 2.15 (3.30 Sun), 6 (5.30 Sat and Sun) to 11 (11.30 Sat, 10.30 Sun) **Closed:** 25 Dec **Meals:** alc (main courses £8 to £20). Bar menu available **Service:** 10% (optional) **Cards:** Amex, Delta, Maestro, MasterCard, Visa **Details:** 325 seats. Vegetarian meals. Children's helpings. No smoking in dining room. Wheelchair access (also WC). Music. Air-conditioned

Brasserie Forty Four

44 The Calls, Leeds LS2 7EW
Tel: (0113) 234 3232
Website: www.brasserie44.com

| Cooking 3 | Modern European | £45 |

There have been changes since the last edition of the Guide. The ambitious sister restaurant, Pool Court, has closed (with the retirement of Michael Gill) and its dining room has been incorporated into Brasserie Forty Four (as the non-smoking option). Jeff Baker, chef at Pool Court, has also departed for pastures new (see J. Baker's, York), but the kitchen continues to deliver reasonably priced food in an 'informal, friendly atmosphere'. Start with spiced Whitby crab, perhaps, or roulade of foie gras served with well-dressed frisée and walnuts, before confit of duck leg with creamed Savoy cabbage and port sauce, or wild boar sausages with onion compote and creamy mustard sauce. Among desserts – including an elegant little treacle sponge served with a dollop of mascarpone – warm plum and frangipane tart proved to be a substantial wedge featuring good short pastry and bags of almond flavour. Service is obliging, and the relatively large globetrotting wine list starts at £14.75.

Chef: David Bukowicki **Proprietor:** Steve Ridealgh **Open:** Mon to Fri L 12 to 2, Mon to Sat D 6 to 10 (10.30 Fri and Sat) **Closed:** bank hols **Meals:** alc (main courses £12.50 to £17.50). Set L £12.50 (2 courses) to £16, Set D 6 to 7.15 £19.95 (inc wine) **Service:** 10% (optional) **Cards:** Amex, Delta, Maestro, MasterCard, Visa **Details:** 130 seats. Vegetarian meals. Children's helpings by arrangement. No smoking in 1 dining room. Wheelchair access (also WC). Music. Air-conditioned

Dough Bistro

293 Spen Lane, West Park, Leeds LS16 5BD
Tel: (0113) 278 7255

Chef/proprietor Abdel Hamzaoui has taken over this local bistro, which once served as a bakery. It's a case of bring your own wine (there's an off-licence opposite) to match the regularly changing set-price menus (four courses £23.95, with three also available Tue to Thur at £18.95). A choice of around half a dozen dishes at each stage might take in starters of sautéed chicken livers with marsala sauce, grapes and pine nuts, or fishcake with sweet chilli sauce, and main courses of fillet of lamb with dauphinois potatoes and a rosemary and port sauce. Round things off with lemon cheesecake with raspberry coulis. Open Tue to Sat D only (phone to check times).

Fourth Floor Café and Bar

Harvey Nichols, 107–111 Briggate, Leeds
LS1 6AZ
Tel: (0113) 204 8000
Website: www.harveynichols.com

| Cooking 4 | Modern British | £42 |

Fashions may come and go, but the Fourth Floor restaurant remains a firm favourite. The modish room has chrome chairs with claret-coloured leather seats, an open-plan kitchen, and views of the rooftops of Leeds from the safety of a glassed-in terrace. The menu is updated every six weeks, with the last year heralding changes to the sourcing of produce: organic flour from Ripon, breads from nearby Garforth, and meat from Yorkshire farms. East meets West on the menu, with everything in between: grilled mackerel fillet with a warm potato salad and radicchio dressing, or seared tuna loin with crisp vegetable salad, mango dressing and spicy cashews could precede sesame-crusted fillet of turbot with tempura pak choi and sweet chilli dressing. Interesting side dishes include butternut squash with chilli and smoked paprika. Finish with a plate of fruit accompanied by blueberry sorbet, or the contrasting dark chocolate mousse cake with brandy-snap semifreddo. The wine list gives lots of choice from around the world, starting with own-label French at £13.50, with plenty by the glass. Oenophiles and footballers' wives should ask to see the 'big list'. (See Fifth Floor, London, and Forth Floor, Edinburgh).

Chef: Richard Walton-Allen **Proprietor:** Harvey Nichols **Open:** all week L 12 to 3 (4 Sat and Sun), Thur to Sat D 5.30 (7 Sat) to 10 **Closed:** 25 and 26 Dec, Easter Sun **Meals:** alc (main courses £10 to £17). Set L and D £15 (2 courses) to £18. Bar menu available Mon to Sat **Service:** 10% (optional) **Cards:** Amex, Delta, Diners, Maestro, MasterCard, Visa **Details:** 85 seats. 14 seats outside. Vegetarian meals. Children's helpings. No smoking in dining room. Wheelchair access (also WC). Music. Air-conditioned

---

Hansa's AR

72–74 North Street, Leeds LS2 7PN
Tel: (0113) 244 4408

An evergreen stalwart in Leeds city centre for 20 years, Hansa's serves reliable Gujarati vegetarian cooking from an all-women kitchen headed by the eponymous Hansa Darbhi. The menus offer a wide range of snacky starters (grazing is encouraged), including 'Hansa's delight' (battered deep-fried tomato stuffed with spicy paneer; £3.75), while among larger dishes are masala dosai with sambhar and coconut chutney (£5.25), and bhagat muthiya (chickpea koftas with potatoes; £6.75). Finish perhaps with pistachio kulfi (£3.25) and refreshing tea with ginger (£1.60). Excellent breads have also been noted. Wines from £11.50. Open Sun L and Mon to Sat D.

Leodis

Victoria Mill, Sovereign Street, Leeds LS1 4BA
Tel: (0113) 242 1010
Website: www.leodis.co.uk

| Cooking 3 | Brasserie/Modern British | £41 |

A stylish warehouse conversion is the setting for this bustling brasserie by a canal. Old iron beams,

---

brick walls and a stone floor remain, contrasting with modern lighting and glass partitions. The food takes its influence from Europe but has a clear British stamp to it. The set lunch and dinner menus are good value, while the carte embraces everything from grilled black pudding with celeriac rémoulade, pancetta and shallots to choucroute garni (smoked sausages, belly pork and bacon). You could start with six Carlingford oysters with shallot vinegar, or perhaps moules marinière, and go on to cod in beer batter with chips, or pan-fried calf's liver with bubble and squeak. The dessert menu includes poached pear in a brandy-snap basket with mascarpone sorbet, and treacle sponge with crème anglaise. The wine list includes a 'fine and rare selection', plus some good options under £20. House wines, from Spain, are £13.95.

Chef: Steven Kendell **Proprietors:** Steven Kendell and Martin Spalding **Open:** Mon to Fri L 12 to 2.30, Mon to Sat D 6 to 10.30 **Closed:** 26 and 27 Dec, 1 and 2 Jan **Meals:** alc (main courses £8.50 to £17.50). Set L £16.95, Set D Mon to Fri and Sat 6 to 7.15 £16.95 **Service:** 10% (optional) **Cards:** Amex, Delta, Diners, Maestro, MasterCard, Visa **Details:** 160 seats. 48 seats outside. Vegetarian meals. Children's helpings. Wheelchair access (also WC). Music

---

Little Tokyo AR

24 Central Road, Leeds LS1 6DE
Tel: (0113) 243 9090

A coal-fired yakitori grill has been installed at this city-centre café, reinforcing its position as the first choice for authentic Japanese food in Leeds. Handmade sycamore and poppy wood tables give the dining room an individual look and set an appropriately informal mood. Good-value bento boxes are at the heart of the extensive menu, each containing a complete meal based around main courses such as spicy mackerel teriyaki (£11.25), chicken ginseng (£12.35) or duck with mango (£15.35). Other options include sushi and sashimi platters (£10.55 for 12 pieces of nigiri) and soup noodles (chicken ramen £6.25). House wines around £12. Closed Sun.

No. 3 York Place

3 York Place, Leeds LS1 2DR
Tel: (0113) 245 9922
Website: www.no3yorkplace.co.uk

| Cooking 5 | Modern European | £53 |

In a quiet street close to the city centre, this modern operation has uncluttered but stylish design, with leather armchairs and a restrained colour scheme of cream and chocolate. A gauzy blind shields an atrium roof, and tables are set with heavy white linen. As we go to press, though, we've heard of changes afoot, with plans to simplify the approach both to the décor and food. This year, combinations have been successful, including a quartet of king scallops bedded on appositely sweet parsnip purée, but counterpointed with five-spice gnocchi dressed in Cabernet Sauvignon vinegar. Barbary duck breast roasted in honey and black pepper is nicely charred on the outside, served alongside a pasta parcel of the shredded leg meat, all sauced not with fruit as per the culinary cliché but with a savoury essence of wild mushrooms. To finish, perhaps, coffee mousse in a chocolate container on warm caramel sauce with a scoop of smooth Baileys ice cream. Regulars confirm that the Anglo-French cheese selection is always worth a whirl. An atmosphere of 'serious endeavour, though not panic' pervades the place at busy sessions. The varietally arranged wine list starts at £15.50 with a Languedoc Sauvignon and displays evidence of imagination throughout. Reports please.

Chef: Martel Smith **Proprietor:** Mardenis Ltd **Open:** Mon to Fri L 12 to 2, Mon to Sat D 6.30 to 10 **Closed:** 25 Dec to 4 Jan **Meals:** alc (main courses £13 to £21). Set L and D 6.30 to 7.30 Mon to Fri £14.50 (2 courses) to £18.50, Set D £45 **Service:** 10% (optional) **Cards:** Amex, Delta, Maestro, MasterCard, Visa **Details:** 46 seats. Vegetarian meals. Children's helpings. No smoking in dining room. Wheelchair access (also WC). Music. Air-conditioned

---

Olive Tree

Oaklands, 55 Rodley Lane, Leeds LS13 1NG
Tel: (0113) 256 9283

Long-established Greek-Cypriot restaurant which places great emphasis on sourcing produce locally – lamb is from Ilkley, for instance. Traditional Greek dishes are what to expect: meze to share (£16.95 per person), starters of kalamari (£6.50), chicken pastries (£5.50) or keftedes (£5.50) or main courses of kleftiko (£12.50) or lamb cutlets marinated in garlic (£11.50). End with baklava (£2.50). Wines from £11.95. Open all week. A sibling can be found at 188–190 Harrogate Road, Chapel Allerton; tel: (0113) 269 8488.

Raja's

186 Roundhay Road, Leeds LS8 5PL
Tel: (0113) 248 0411

Raja's puts its popularity and longevity (it has been going for more than 20 years) down to a policy of

openness: you can watch your meal being freshly prepared in the open kitchen, a sure way to inspire confidence. Low prices are another draw (most main courses are £5.95, most starters under £2). The menu amounts to a list of curry-house standards – rogan josh, chicken korma, et al. – but a handful of more interesting options includes desi chicken (cooked with limes, chillies and coriander) and khas biryani (rice with lamb, chicken, prawns and vegetables). House wines are £10.25. Open Mon to Fri L and all week D.

Simply Heathcotes

Canal Wharf, Water Lane, Leeds LS11 5PS
Tel: (0113) 244 6611
Website: www.heathcotes.co.uk

| NEW CHEF | Modern British | £42 |

Once a grain store, this stone building by the Leeds & Liverpool canal stands out among the modern office developments. The interior has been given a hard-edged, modern makeover, with wooden floors, stone walls hung with abstract paintings and a curved staircase leading up to a mezzanine bar. The menu pays homage to the north-west as well as drawing on influences from mainland Europe to come up with starters of potted kipper pâté with sour cream and Guinness loaf, black pudding hash brown with baked beans, a fried egg and brown sauce, and a risotto of peas, broad beans, mascarpone and herb oil. Typical main courses are citrus-seared fillet of sea bream with pipérade and black olives, or black pudding deep-fried in beer batter and served with chips and mushy peas. Finish with Yorkshire curd tart with rhubarb compote. The international wine list has a something-for-everyone appeal. Two Italian house wines are priced at £13.95, and ten come by the glass from £3.85.

Chef: Luke Cullen **Proprietor:** Paul Heathcote **Open:** all week 12 to 2.30, 6 to 10 (11 Sat, 9 Sun) **Closed:** 25 and 26 Dec, 1 Jan **Meals:** alc (main courses £9.50 to £22). Set L and D 6 to 7 Mon to Sat £12.95 (2 courses), Set D Mon £15 (2 courses, inc wine) **Service:** not inc **Cards:** Amex, Delta, Maestro, MasterCard, Visa **Details:** 80 seats. Vegetarian meals. Children's helpings. No smoking. Wheelchair access (also WC). Music. Air-conditioned

---

 This symbol means that the restaurant has elected to participate in *The Good Food Guide's* £5 voucher scheme (see 'Using The Good Food Guide' for details).

Sous le Nez en Ville

The Basement, Quebec House, Quebec Street,
Leeds LS1 2HA
Tel: (0113) 244 0108

Cooking 4 | **Modern European** | **£38**

Robert Chamberlain and Andrew Carter clearly
have a winning formula on their hands, with little
changing over the years at this busy basement
brasserie. Old favourites such as 'juicy' tempura
king prawns with tomato and chilli jam, and chargrilled ribeye steak with peppercorn sauce remain
on the menu, joined by new arrivals such as
cayenne-spiced crab served with Jersey potato
and chive salad. Chargrilled côte de boeuf with
béarnaise is well timed, and served with crispy
fried onions, and fish is a strength: grilled halibut,
carefully cooked and moist, comes on a smoked
prawn frittata with butternut squash salad. Walnut
brownie with white chocolate ice cream makes a
satisfying way to end, and there might also be traditional crème brûlée. Fifty new bins, including a
page of Châteauneuf-du-Pape and an expanded
South African section, have been added to the
already substantial wine list. France inevitably
shows up strongly, but Italy, Spain and the
New World are well represented too. Useful
descriptions should help selecting a bottle; prices
start at £11.95.

> **Chefs:** Andrew Carter and Andrew Lavender **Proprietors:**
> Robert Chamberlain and Andrew Carter **Open:** Mon to Sat 12
> to 2.30, 6 to 10 (11 Sat) **Closed:** 24 Dec to 3 Jan, bank hols
> **Meals:** alc (main courses £10 to £18.50). Set L Sat £20.95,
> Set D 6 to 7.30 (7 Sat) £20.95 (inc wine). Bar menu available
> **Service:** not inc **Cards:** Delta, Diners, Maestro, MasterCard,
> Visa **Details:** 85 seats. Vegetarian meals. Music. Air-condi-
> tioned

MAP 5 **LEEK – Staffordshire**

Number 64

64 St Edward Street, Leek ST13 5DL
Tel: (01538) 381900
Email: enquiries@number64.com

NEW CHEF | **Modern British** | **£36**

This double-fronted Georgian building is home to
a speciality food shop, a pâtisserie, cellar wine bar
and first-floor restaurant, plus three letting bedrooms. The interior can seem like a labyrinth, but

the restaurant is elegant, done out in shades of
apricot, with plain light wooden furniture. New
chef Chris Rooney seems to be continuing the
style set by his predecessors, with some bright,
modern ideas, as in a May starter of goats' cheese
and asparagus mousse with a beetroot and horseradish salsa. Follow with a main course of duck
breast roasted with honey and balsamic and served
with noodles, shavings of fennel, sugar snaps, lamb's
lettuce, red pepper and a Szechuan-style sauce.
Caramelised blueberries are the partner for mocha
tart. Five house wines are priced £11.95 to
£12.95.

> **Chef:** Chris Rooney **Proprietor:** Nigel Cope **Open:** all week L
> 12 to 2, Mon to Sat D 7 to 9 **Meals:** alc (main courses L £6 to
> £11, D £9 to £17). Bar and snack menus available **Service:**
> not inc **Cards:** Amex, Delta, Maestro, MasterCard, Visa
> **Details:** 42 seats. 26 seats outside. Vegetarian meals.
> Children's helpings. No smoking. Music. Air-conditioned
> **Accommodation:** 3 rooms

MAP 5 **LEICESTER – Leicestershire**

Entropy

3 Dover Street, Leicester LE1 6PW
Tel: (0116) 254 8530
Website: www.entropylife.com

Cooking 6 | **Modern European** | **£57**

Fairly centrally located in the city, not far from the
railway station and on the same street as the Little
Theatre, the Cockerills' restaurant hit the ground
running when it opened in 2004. Within a classically modern-minimalist setting, all Scandinavian
monochrome with floor-to-ceiling windows
affording generous views of office blocks and a
multi-storey car park, it's a hip urban showcase for
some seriously capable cooking.

Ingredients are sourced with pride and care,
bringing Harbourne Blue cheese into a vegetarian
main course of artichoke tart, and Comoros islands
vanilla into an ice cream to accompany lavender-
scented tarte Tatin. There is a refreshing willingness
to use rarely seen components too, as when a lamb
main course includes cured tongue, or when
cocks' combs and pancetta garnish lemon-roasted
monkfish with pea risotto. Once again, the king
scallop starter interleaved with black truffle
receives the thumbs up, this time served with buttered leeks and an intense cauliflower foam. That
lamb composition, built around roast rack and
confit shoulder, gains depth from a spiky sauce
diable and pools of Manni olive oil, while the

monkfish was well timed, the whole dish constituting an array of mild and strong flavours with soft and crisp textures. Orange and passion-fruit soufflé made a pleasingly feather-light inspection dessert, partnered with full-on blood-orange sorbet. A compact, painstakingly annotated wine list keeps prices on a taut leash, opening with vins de pays at £12.50, or £3.25 a glass.

> **Chef:** Tom Cockerill **Proprietors:** Cassandra and Tom Cockerill **Open:** Mon to Sat 12 to 2.30, 6 to 10 **Closed:** 25 Dec, 1 Jan, bank hols **Meals:** alc (main courses £18.50 to £30). Set L £12.95 (2 courses) to £15.95, Set D Mon and Tue £12.95 (2 courses) to £15.95, Set D Wed to Sat 6 to 7.30 (7 Fri and Sat) £12.95 (2 courses) to £15.95. Bar L menu available **Service:** not inc **Cards:** Amex, Delta, Maestro, MasterCard, Visa **Details:** 60 seats. Vegetarian meals. No smoking. Music. Air-conditioned

Opera House

10 Guildhall Lane, Leicester LE1 5FQ
Tel: (0116) 223 6666
Website: www.theoperahouserestaurant.co.uk

| NEW CHEF | Modern European | £45 |

A stone's throw from the cathedral, this grade II-listed fifteenth-century building is a sympathetic cottage conversion. In past incarnations it has been a jail and also an antique shop, now it's a modish hang-out with a labyrinth feel to the restaurant area, which is all brick flooring and cosy nooks giving diners a sense of privacy. Smoked ham hock terrine is served imaginatively with beetroot and pears, while wood pigeon comes with figs and roasted hazelnuts for starters. Steamed monkfish with a Parmesan crust, scallops and beurre blanc, or glazed duck with a sweet potato purée and braised cabbage are typical main courses. Vegetarian options include goats' cheese risotto. The half-dozen desserts include chocolate fondant with pistachio ice cream. The large wine cellar is well-stocked with an appealing international selection; prices start at around £15 with some good-value bins under £20. Reports please.

> **Proprietors:** Noel and Val Weafer **Open:** Mon to Sat 12 to 2, 7 to 10 **Closed:** 24 Dec to 2 Jan, bank hols **Meals:** alc D (main courses £12 to £17.50). Set L £10.95 (2 courses) to £14.50 **Service:** 10% **Cards:** Amex, Delta, Diners, Maestro, MasterCard, Visa **Details:** 60 seats. Vegetarian meals. Children's helpings. No smoking. Wheelchair access (not WC). Music. No mobile phones. Air-conditioned

> To submit a report on any restaurant, please visit *www.which.co.uk/gfgfeedback*.

MAP 3   LEIGH-ON-SEA – Essex

Boatyard

8–13 High Street, Leigh-on-Sea SS9 2EN
Tel: (01702) 475588
Website: www.theboatyardrestaurant.co.uk

| Cooking 1 | Modern European | £47 |

A street on the Thames estuary of weatherboarded cottages is the setting for this impressive glass, steel and wood building. As its name suggests, it's a conversion of a former boatyard, and its position at the edge of the estuary gives it stunning views over the water. The menu offers a mix of European flavours, from chorizo, cannellini bean and squid salad, through shaved Serrano ham with celeriac rémoulade in white truffle oil, to baked sea bass with a provençale-style dressing. There might also be baked Dover sole with parsley sauce, or Thai-spiced pork fillet with cabbage steeped in chilli sauce. Desserts are along the lines of passion-fruit mousse with mango coulis. The international wine list features a 'connoisseur' list for deeper pockets, with Chilean Merlot and French Sauvignon Blanc opening proceedings at £12.95.

> **Chef:** Jonathan Luck **Proprietor:** John Cross **Open:** Wed to Sun L 12 to 3, Tue to Sat D 6.30 to 10.30 **Meals:** alc D (main courses £12 to £20). Set L £11.95 (2 courses) to £15.95 **Service:** not inc **Cards:** Delta, Maestro, MasterCard, Visa **Details:** 200 seats. 60 seats outside. Car park. Vegetarian meals. No children under 11 after 9.30pm. Children's helpings. Wheelchair access (also WC). Music. Air-conditioned

MAP 1   LEWDOWN – Devon

Lewtrenchard Manor

Lewdown EX20 4PN
Tel: (01566) 783222
Website: www.lewtrenchard.co.uk

| Cooking 6 | Modern British | £51 |

Lewtrenchard Manor is the definition of country handsome, all stained-glass windows and armorial crests, and the interiors are a sober vision of dark oak panelling and ornate plaster mouldings. Since last year's Guide, Jason Hornbuckle has been elevated to effective chef/patron. He runs a tight ship, bringing in fish from the Looe and Brixham boats, and harvesting 90 per cent of the kitchen's requirements in fruit and vegetables from the Manor's own walled garden. A range of set-price menus is available, including one with pre-selected wines, and a vibrant, modern style is in evidence throughout. Grilled tiger prawns with cauliflower mousse and vegetables pickled in sweet chilli vie for first-course attention with sautéed sea bass on cassoulet with chorizo and basil oil. Precision in timing and attention to individual detail distinguish main courses such as roast breast of duck with Morteau sausage and artichoke purée. English rose panna-cotta will invoke the kitchen garden, while the toasted coconut that comes with advocaat parfait and Malibu syrup has presumably travelled a little further.

A productive partnership with wine merchants Red & White, headed by Britain's youngest Master of Wine, Liam Stevenson, contributes to a majestic list, surely one of the finest in Devon. Bordeaux and Burgundy are a connoisseur's dream, as is the Rhône, but there are also pedigree selections from Australia and South Africa, and a rather helpful vintage chart. The base price for house wines is a very reasonable £14, or £3.50 a glass.

Chef: Jason Hornbuckle Proprietor: Von Essen Hotels Open: Tue to Sun L 12 to 2, all week D 7 to 9.30 Meals: Set L £20, Set D £39.50 to £99 (inc wine). Bar menu available Service: not inc Cards: Amex, Delta, Maestro, MasterCard, Visa Details: 45 seats. 16 seats outside. Car park. Vegetarian meals. No children under 8 at D. Children's helpings. No smoking. Wheelchair access (not WC). Music. No mobile phones Accommodation: 14 rooms

MAP 8 · LEYBURN – North Yorkshire

Sandpiper Inn

Market Place, Leyburn DL8 5AT
Tel: (01969) 622206

Cooking 3 | Modern European | £38

A stone pub that oozes history, it sits snugly by the road and is neighboured by two churches. Inside, past the entrance hall, with its amusing pictures of the kitchen staff, the décor is restrained, with green walls, bare tables, a boarded floor and shelves of books. Jonathan Harrison's menu takes in all corners of Europe, starting with Mediterranean fish soup with rouille, or a terrine of pressed ham hock, chicken and mushrooms. Imaginative main courses rely heavily on fresh, locally sourced produce: Wensleydale spring lamb with new season's vegetables alongside halibut on a spaghetti of courgettes with lobster sauce, or fillet of pork wrapped in Parma ham with roast peppers. The half-dozen desserts might include warm Valrhona chocolate tart, and sticky toffee pudding. The wine list of 30-plus bins is well considered and good value, with house selections £11.50.

Chef: Jonathan Harrison Proprietors: the Harrison family Open: Tue to Sun 12 to 2.30 (2 Sun), 6.30 (7 Sun) to 9 (9.30 Fri and Sat) Closed: 25 Dec, 1 Jan Meals: alc (main courses £10 to £17). Light L menu available Service: not inc Cards: Delta, Maestro, MasterCard, Visa Details: 40 seats. 20 seats outside. Vegetarian meals. Children's helpings. No smoking. Music. No mobile phones Accommodation: 3 rooms

MAP 5 · LICHFIELD – Staffordshire

Chandlers
AR

Corn Exchange, Conduit Street, Lichfield WS13 6JU
Tel: (01543) 416688

Buzzy city-centre brasserie on the first floor of the former Corn Exchange. The bar menu – tortilla wrap with shredded hoisin duck (£4.50), say, or chicken and bacon Caesar salad (£4.95) – is popular, while the full menu works its way around perennial favourites such as chicken liver parfait with pear and cognac chutney (£4.95), roast rump of lamb in a redcurrant and port sauce (£12.50), and desserts such as baked chocolate tart with pistachio ice cream (£4.50). Wines from £11.75. Open all week.

MAP 6 · LIDGATE – Suffolk

Star Inn
AR

The Street, Lidgate CB8 9PP
Tel: (01638) 500275

Log fires, heavy beams, oak tables – this textbook English pub has the lot, along with the warm air of good patronage from locals and visitors alike. The food attracts compliments too, thanks to its pleasing Mediterranean combinations: clams with artichokes or warm chicken liver salad (both £5.90) precede pan-fried lambs' kidneys with bacon and sherry (£15.50) or medallions of wild boar in a sauce of Muscadelle and strawberries (£16.50). Cod with garlic mousseline and monkfish marinière (both £15.50) are just a couple of the many fish options. Wines from £12.50. Closed Sun D.

MAP 1 LIFTON – Devon

Arundell Arms

Lifton PL16 0AA
Tel: (01566) 784666
Website: www.arundellarms.com

Cooking 5 | Modern British | £48

'For a returning regular it is all reassuringly as it always was,' sighed a contented fan of this rambling old coaching inn, adding that the stone flags, the low ceilings, enormous fireplace in the sitting room, and the immense trees in the garden 'all impress with a great sense of history'. The atmosphere is relaxed, but one is left in no doubt that this is a serious operation, with Anne Voss-Bark still very much at the helm.

The kitchen is now headed by Steven Pidgeon, formerly sous-chef, and his professional touch is totally in keeping with the simple, uncomplicated class of the set-up. Devon beef, English black-faced lamb and organic Duroc pork, fish from Cornwall, and farmhouse cheeses emphasise the West Country connection, flavours are forthright, and sauces are out of the top drawer, whether a béarnaise used to accompany first-class tournedos of beef on a bed of 'fabulous' mashed potato, or a 'silky and delicate' wine sauce accompanying a mixed grill of duck, chicken and guinea fowl ('the chicken tasted nostalgically real'). Starters might include 'visually stunning' coarse pork, duck and chicken liver terrine accompanied by a fruity apricot chutney, and among puddings might be a generous slice of orange and polenta cake ('redolent with oranges') teamed with a compote of kumquats and a scoop of orange and vanilla ice cream. France is the first love of the wine list, but a good global round-up adds to the appeal. Half-bottles are in plentiful supply, and seven come by the glass. House bottles open at £14.50.

Chef: Steven Pidgeon Proprietor: Anne Voss-Bark Open: all week 12.30 to 2, 7.30 to 9.30 Closed: 24 Dec, D 25 Dec Meals: Set L £22 (2 courses) to £26, Set D £36 to £40. Bar menu available Service: not inc Cards: Amex, Delta, Diners, Maestro, MasterCard, Visa Details: 70 seats. 20 seats outside. Car park. Vegetarian meals. Children's helpings. No smoking in dining room. Wheelchair access (also WC). Music Accommodation: 21 rooms

---

This symbol means that the wine list is well above the average.

MAP 9 LINCOLN – Lincolnshire

Wig & Mitre AR

30–32 Steep Hill, Lincoln LN2 1TL
Tel: (01522) 535190

The building dates from the fourteenth century and is near both the cathedral and castle. Food is served all day, from breakfast (full English £9.25), through sandwiches, to lunch and dinner: perhaps smoked haddock and leek risotto (£6.95), followed by herb-crusted rack of lamb with lovage mash (£16.50), finished off with terrine of dark chocolate with cherry ice cream (£4.95). Good-value wines from £12.45. Open all week. The proprietors also own Caunton Beck in Caunton (see entry).

MAP 6 LITTLEPORT – Cambridgeshire

Fen House AR

2 Lynn Road, Littleport CB6 1QG
Tel: (01353) 860645

This small, intimate restaurant has been going for 20 years, suggesting a rare level of reliability and consistency. Unpretentious seasonal cooking is the draw, the set-price dinner menu (four courses £34.75) offering starters of pumpkin soup with nutmeg croûtons, or open raviolo of pigeon breast with Puy lentils, followed perhaps by rack of lamb with provençale vegetables and tarragon sauce. Brioche bread-and-butter pudding or rich chocolate terrine might round off a meal. House wines £14. Open Fri and Sat D only, other times by arrangement.

MAP 6 LITTLE SHELFORD – Cambridgeshire

Sycamore House

1 Church Street, Little Shelford CB2 5HG
Tel: (01223) 843396

Cooking 3 | Modern British | £36

This modest and unpretentious establishment delivers few surprises, but the charm of the place is very much in knowing what's ahead, which is why

the restaurant continues to attract a loyal clientele. The two small, linked rooms are cosy, with a few prints on the walls, white table linen and posies dotted about. Pea and leek tart or smoked mackerel pâté open the restrained fixed-price menu, followed by a salad. Main courses – perhaps roast partridge with port and redcurrants or grilled fillet of Scottish beef with red onion gravy – are accompanied by generous portions of well-timed vegetables. Dessert wines are listed with the puddings, which may include Bakewell tart with vanilla ice cream or chocolate torte. The well-thought-through wine list balances Europe with the New World. Quality producers are to the fore throughout, and the majority of bottles are below £25 – a 2004 Sauvignon Blanc from Thelema in Stellenbosch is £20.50, for instance – with a white Bordeaux and a red Côtes du Rhône opening the list at £13 a bottle, £3.25 a glass.

Chef: Michael Sharpe **Proprietors:** Michael and Susan Sharpe **Open:** Wed to Sat D only 7.30 to 9 **Closed:** Christmas to New Year **Meals:** Set D £25 **Service:** not inc **Cards:** Delta, Maestro, MasterCard, Visa **Details:** 24 seats. Car park. Vegetarian meals. No children under 12. No smoking. No music. No mobile phones

MAP 6 | **LITTLE WILBRAHAM** – Cambridgeshire

Hole in the Wall

NEW ENTRY

2 High Street, Little Wilbraham
CB1 5JY
Tel: (01223) 812282

Cooking 4 | Modern British | £37

Stephen Bull, last seen in the Guide in 2005 at the Lough Pool Inn at Sellack, has bought this country pub with his former management couple, Christopher Leeton (who runs the kitchen) and Jenny Chapman ('the smiling head of house'). The kitchen has been modernised, the furniture changed and piped music banned, but otherwise the timbered interior has been left alone. It still lives up to its title as a freehouse, dispensing real ales and pub hospitality, but elsewhere it pulls out all the stops for customers in search of food. Raw materials are consistently good, and the kitchen shows off its prowess with confidence: caramelised onion tart with 'delicious melting' puff pastry is served with roast garlic, cherry tomatoes and Gruyère, roast guinea fowl comes with wild mushrooms, foie gras, fondant potato and sherry

vinegar, while a generous portion of roast monk-fish fillets married well with shaved fennel and radish salad, chorizo fritters and a tomato, olive and caper dressing. Reporters have also applauded old-fashioned dishes like osso buco with gremolada, 'perfect' saffron risotto, and 'melting' blade of boeuf bourguignonne. While pastry work is considered 'exemplary', at inspection desserts were not a highlight. The promising wine list kicks off at £12.50, with eight by the glass.

Chef: Christopher Leeton **Proprietors:** Stephen Bull, Christopher Leeton and Jenny Chapman **Open:** Tue to Sun and bank hol Mon L 12 to 2, Tue to Sat D 7 to 9 **Meals:** alc (main courses £10 to £15) **Service:** not inc **Cards:** Delta, Maestro, MasterCard, Visa **Details:** 70 seats. 15 seats outside. Car park. Vegetarian meals. Children's helpings. No smoking. No music

MAP 8 | **LIVERPOOL** – Merseyside

Chung Ku

Riverside Drive, Columbus Quay, Liverpool
L3 4DB
Tel: (0151) 726 8191
Website: www.chung-ku.com

Cooking 2 | Chinese | £38

It may not be the best place in which to explore the outer limits of Chinese cuisine, but what Chung Ku does it does very well. The large, stylish dining room occupies two floors of a modern building overlooking the river. Dim sum are served daily until 6pm, while the main menu caters largely for the 'crossover' market with a range of banquets, avoiding more esoteric items and largely sticking to the crowd-pleasing crispy duck and sizzling steak end of the spectrum. At inspection, the kitchen performed consistently well, turning out 'tender, moist' salt and pepper ribs with 'the right amount of bite', 'fresh, juicy, well-flavoured' deep-fried prawns in crisp batter with a mayonnaise dip, and Dover sole with asparagus in a bird's nest. 'Friendly and helpful' service enhances the favourable impression, as do house wines at £10.90.

Chef: Mr Lu **Proprietor:** Esther Ng **Open:** all week 12 to 12 **Closed:** 25 Dec **Meals:** alc (main courses £7.50 to £35). Set L £6.50 (2 courses) to £9.50, Set D £19 (min 2) to £35 (min 4) **Service:** not inc **Cards:** Amex, Delta, Maestro, MasterCard, Visa **Details:** 350 seats. Car park. Vegetarian meals. Wheelchair access (also WC). Music. Air-conditioned

Hope Street Hotel, London Carriage Works

40 Hope Street, Liverpool L1 9DA
Tel: (0151) 705 2222
Website: www.tlcw.co.uk

| Cooking 5 | Modern British | £60 |

Located on one of Liverpool's most famous streets, this classy boutique hotel occupies a splendidly restored Victorian building in Venetian palazzo style. The ground-floor restaurant (which takes its name from the building's original identity) has lots of bare oak and exposed yellow brick, and a series of spectacular glass sculptures provide a dramatic touch. Menus showcase an ambitious but well-conceived cooking style. To start, 'carrot five ways' incorporates the root in a granita topped with honey foam, a cake, a terrine with cumin, a ginger-infused soup, and raw with coriander mayonnaise. Alternatively, there might be a tian of impeccably fresh and succulent lobster bound in coral-coloured mayonnaise, with a vividly coloured but delicately flavoured green basil and turbot jelly. The wow-factor is equally present in main courses such as a three-part lamb dish comprising slow-cooked breast with Moroccan spices, roasted loin with rosemary and garlic, and pan-fried cutlets with braised vegetables. Or there could be juniper and orange marinated Gressingham duck, partnered with 'five-spice ice cream confit leg' and duck crackling. And to finish, there might be a relatively simple but well-made tarte Tatin served with vanilla ice cream.

The 230-bin wine list features a red and white 'cult wine of the month' – typically a French arneis (£16.50) and an Australian barbera (£27) from Gary Crittenden's 'i' range. The rest of the list is cannily chosen with a good balance between price and quality. House selections start at £13.50.

Chefs: Paul Askew **Proprietor:** David Brewitt, Paul Askew, Jane Farreley and Tony Harvey **Open:** Restaurant Sun to Fri L 12 to 3.30, Mon to Sat D 5.30 to 9.30; Brasserie all week L and D **Meals:** Set L £15.50 (2 courses) to £19.50, Set D £35 (2 courses) to £55. Brasserie menu available **Service:** not inc, card slips closed **Cards:** Amex, Delta, Maestro, MasterCard, Visa **Details:** 70 seats. Vegetarian meals. Children's helpings. No smoking in 1 dining room. Wheelchair access (also WC). Music. No mobile phones. Air-conditioned **Accommodation:** 48 rooms

Mei Mei

9 Berry Street, Liverpool L1 9DF
Tel: (0151) 707 2888

Liverpool's Chinatown may be awash with choice, but Mei Mei stands out for its stylish décor and much-praised dim sum. The extensive menu starts with set-price dinners (from £14.50 per head, minimum two people) and longer banquets (from £22.50 per head, minimum two people), while dim sum combinations (£6.50 per head) offer seaweed, prawn and meat dumplings, deep-fried prawn balls and the like. Look out also for the full carte, which offers all the usual suspects, including sweet-and-sour king prawns (£9.50) and ribs in Peking sauce (£6). Wines from £10. Open all week.

Side Door

29A Hope Street, Liverpool L1 9BQ
Tel: (0151) 707 7888

| Cooking 2 | Modern European | £35 |

Despite a change of name (it was previously known as the Other Place Bistro), this contemporary restaurant remains under the same ownership, although a recent makeover has replaced the rather gloomy green interior with a décor of raspberry and taupe. In the kitchen, global influences are brought to a largely modern European approach, and good use is made of well-sourced and high-quality ingredients. Starters hit the mark, with crisp fried haddock with spring onion dressing and gremolada potatoes, described as 'well executed and well balanced', or perhaps confit duck and red onion spring rolls with soy dipping sauce. A daily special might be monkfish in garlic butter with spring onion, herb and chilli risotto, while pan-fried calf's liver and bacon might be found on the menu. End on a high note with warm pear and almond tart. The wine list is modest but offers good value from £11.50.

Chefs: Sean Millar and Alex Navarro **Proprietors:** Sean Millar, Sheila Benson, Philippa Feeney and Mark Benson **Open:** Mon to Sat 11.30 to 2.30, 5.30 to 10 **Closed:** 25 to 28 Dec, 31 Dec to 2 Jan **Meals:** alc (main courses L £7 to £10, D £11 to £15). Set D Mon £15.95 (2 courses, inc wine), Set D Tue to Fri and Sat 5.30 to 6.30 £14.95 (2 courses) to £16.95 **Service:** not inc **Cards:** Delta, Maestro, MasterCard, Visa **Details:** 60 seats. 8 seats outside. Vegetarian meals. No children after 7.30pm. Children's helpings. No smoking. Wheelchair access (not WC). Music. Air-conditioned

Simply Heathcotes

Beetham Plaza, 25 The Strand, Liverpool L2 0XL
Tel: (0151) 236 3536
Website: www.heathcotes.co.uk

Cooking 2 | Modern British | £42

Although one of a group of Simply Heathcotes (the others are in Leeds, Manchester and Wrightington), it doesn't suffer from being part of a chain. Home-made black pudding is a speciality, wittily served as a starter with a hash brown, baked beans, a fried egg and brown sauce, while main courses could be one of what the menu describes as 'Heathcotes comfort', including glazed Pendle lamb shepherd's pie, or John Penny's pork and leek sausages with champ and onion gravy. Field mushroom and malt loaf bruschetta is just one of the four interesting vegetarian choices, and a fish dish could be citrus-seared fillet of sea bream with red pepper pipérade and black olives. Dessert might be something regional like baked Yorkshire curd tart with rhubarb compote and clotted cream, or bread-and-butter pudding. Wines, from £13.95, offer an interesting wander around the major wine-producing countries.

> Chef: Philip Sinclair Proprietor: Paul Heathcote Open: all week 12 to 2.30, 6 to 10 (11 Sat, 9 Sun) Closed: bank hols Meals: alc (main courses £9.50 to £22). Set L Mon to Sat £12.95 (2 courses, inc wine), Set D Mon £15 (inc wine), Set D Mon to Sat 6 to 7 £12.95 (2 courses, inc wine) Service: not inc Cards: Amex, Delta, Maestro, MasterCard, Visa Details: 110 seats. Vegetarian meals. Children's helpings. No smoking. Wheelchair access (also WC). Music. Air-conditioned

60 Hope Street

60 Hope Street, Liverpool L1 9BZ
Tel: (0151) 707 6060
Website: www.60hopestreet.com

Cooking 4 | Modern European | £52

In a 'respectable' Georgian town house, the Manning brothers' modern enterprise consists of a buzzy, colourful basement café/bar and a ground-floor restaurant, its pale wood and white walls offset by large mirrors, period fireplaces and odd spots of colour 'to relieve the minimalism'. A great deal of confidence is evident about the cooking, with both braised mussels in a creamy Madras sauce, with 'plenty of turmeric, cumin, chilli and other spices to give it punch', and pan-fried

halibut with a risotto of clams and herbs singled out for praise at inspection. The kitchen is more than capable with meat too, judging by a first-class pork cutlet 'bursting with flavour' served with excellent rösti, butternut squash purée and pied de mouton mushrooms in a light mushroom foam. Desserts, equally accomplished, include bread-and-butter pudding with vanilla ice cream and a notable lemon cheesecake parfait with honey foam. Service is of the good, no-nonsense but friendly variety. The wine list is refreshingly straightforward; mark-ups are not greedy, giving reasonable choice under £20. House wines from Argentina and Spain are £13.95, and six are available by the glass.

> Chef: Sarah Kershaw Proprietors: Colin and Gary Manning Open: Mon to Fri L 12 to 2.30, Mon to Sat D 6 to 10.30 Closed: bank hols Meals: alc (main courses £10.50 to £26). Set L and D 6 to 7 £13.95 (2 courses) to £16.95 Service: not inc Cards: Amex, Delta, Maestro, MasterCard, Visa Details: 90 seats. 15 seats outside. Vegetarian meals. Children's helpings. No smoking. Music. Air-conditioned

Ziba at the Racquet Club

5 Chapel Street, Liverpool L3 9AG
Tel: (0151) 236 6676
Website: www.racquetclub.org.uk

Cooking 3 | Modern British | £50

Ziba is a seamless fusion of the old and the new, housed in a grand Victorian building with ornate chandeliers set off against blond wood flooring and bare candlelit tables in the spacious dining room. Friendly service sets an informal mood, a good match for creative modern cooking that reveals a kitchen with a sense of fun and adventure. Starters of seared scallops with butternut squash purée and beetroot foam, or pan-fried pigeon with beans on toast might be followed by monkfish steak with what the menu describes as 'black treacle pork two ways' and seared tangerine, or Orkney beef three ways: roast fillet, braised shin and oxtail jus with horseradish mash. Desserts include similarly outré creations such as malt brûlée with Baileys milkshake. A simpler menu of light, snacky dishes, such as bookmaker sandwich or caramelised chorizo in red wine, is available in the bar from lunchtime through to early evening, and the imaginative streak continues into the wine list, a well-chosen and good-value international selection opening with house Australian red and white at £14.

Chef: Neil Dempsey Proprietors: Helen and Martin Ainscough Open: Mon to Fri L 12 to 2.30, Mon to Sat D 6 to 10 (10.30 Sat) Closed: bank hols Meals: alc (main courses L £7 to £20, D £12 to £25). Set L £16 (2 courses) to £19.50. Bar menu available Mon to Sat 12 to 6.30 Service: not inc Cards: Amex, Delta, Maestro, MasterCard, Visa Details: 65 seats. Vegetarian meals. Children's helpings. No smoking in dining room. No music. Air-conditioned Accommodation: 8 rooms

MAP 5   LLANFAIR WATERDINE – Shropshire

Waterdine

Llanfair Waterdine LD7 1TU
Tel: (01547) 528214
Website: www.waterdine.com

Cooking 4 | Modern British | £44

Ken Adams' country restaurant-with-rooms sits on the English side of the border, albeit on the Welsh marshes, between Shropshire and Powys, in a lovely, peaceful setting. The sixteenth-century long house is homely; there's a bar area and a sitting room for pre-meal drinks in the restaurant, which boasts immaculate white linen, fresh flowers and friendly service. 'A nice place to escape and unwind,' said one visitor, who was also impressed by the personal touch. The compact menu is 'accomplished and comforting', and a lot of attention is given to the sourcing of produce, starting, perhaps, with lightly spiced seafood soup with smoked salmon, or grilled red mullet with well-flavoured tapenade sauce. Main courses might be tender pot-roasted fillet of beef with a horseradish relish that 'packed a punch', or carefully cooked Mortimer Forest roe deer on creamed spinach. Strawberry mousse with passion-fruit sauce has proved a 'good, light way to finish', while the home-made chocolate almond squares that come with coffee have also garnered praise. Wines are a global selection starting at £15.50, with a handful by the glass from £2.25.

Chef/Proprietor: Ken Adams Open: Tue to Sun L 12.15 to 1.30, Tue to Sat D 7.15 to 9, bookings only Closed: 1 week autumn, 1 week spring Meals: Set L Tue to Sat £23.50 (2 courses) to £30. Set L Sun £20. Set D £30. Bar L menu available by arrangement Service: not inc Cards: Maestro, MasterCard, Visa Details: 24 seats. Car park. Children's helpings. No children under 8 at D. No smoking. No music Accommodation: 3 rooms

MAP 2   LONG CRENDON – Buckinghamshire

Angel Restaurant

47 Bicester Road, Long Crendon HP18 9EE
Tel: (01844) 208268
Website: www.angelrestaurant.co.uk

Cooking 1 | Modern British | £47

In a sleepy village, this sixteenth-century coaching inn has a wall of wattle and daub on display as a testament to the building's age. Various dining areas, united by laminate flooring, include a large conservatory and a comfortable bar. Trevor Bosch takes classic British dishes and gives them an international twist. Seafood is delivered daily, so you could start with Thai-spiced fishcakes with lime and coriander mayonnaise, or roast scallops with chorizo and tomato and avocado salsa, and proceed to poached fillet of naturally smoked haddock on leek and mustard mash with a soft-poached egg. Meat eaters might go for roast rack of new season's lamb in a herb crust served with ratatouille and a rosemary jus. End with warm chocolate tart, or passion-fruit crème brûlée. The substantial, globe-trotting wine list is categorised by style, from 'elegant and zesty' whites to 'weightier, robust' reds. A dozen by the glass, from £4.50, with bottle prices starting at £14.95.

Chefs: Trevor Bosch and Donny Joyce Proprietors: Trevor and Annie Bosch Open: all week L 12 to 2.30, Mon to Sat D 7 to 10 Closed: 1 and 2 Jan Meals: alc exc Sun L (main courses £14.50 to £25). Set L Mon to Sat £14.95 (2 courses) to £18.50. Set D Mon to Thur £35 Service: not inc Cards: Maestro, MasterCard, Visa Details: 65 seats. 35 seats outside. Car park. Vegetarian meals. Children's helpings. No smoking. Music. Air-conditioned Accommodation: 3 rooms

MAP 6   LONG MELFORD – Suffolk

Scutchers

Westgate Street, Long Melford CO10 9DP
Tel: (01787) 310200
Website: www.scutchers.com

Cooking 2 | Modern British | £45

A large open-plan interior, with old and worn supporting beams and well-spaced tables, is the setting for Nick Barrett's extensive bistro-style

menu. Quality ingredients and generous portions are the order of the day. Seared hand-dived Scottish scallops on celeriac purée with pancetta and a red wine jus, or Cheddar soufflé with a rich langoustine sauce are the sort of modern ideas that crop up among starters. Main courses can be as traditional as grilled fillet of halibut with asparagus and lemon hollandaise, and pan-fried calf's liver with bacon, or as novel as roast fillet of monkfish in a light curry sauce on a bed of prawn risotto. Desserts are an eclectic mix, so end with warm chocolate and pecan tart or steamed syrup sponge with custard. The wine list is a mixture from the New and Old Worlds, starting with a house selection of 11 bottles from £14, by the glass from £2.80.

Chefs: Nick Barrett and Guy Alabaster Proprietors: Nick and Diane Barrett Open: Tue to Sat 12 to 2, 7 to 9.30 Closed: Christmas, 10 days early Mar, 10 days late Aug Meals: alc (main courses £14 to £22). Set L Tue to Fri £15 (2 courses), Set D Tue to Thur £15 (2 courses) Service: not inc Cards: Amex, Delta, Maestro, MasterCard, Visa Details: 60 seats. 30 seats outside. Car park. Vegetarian meals. Children's helpings. No smoking. Wheelchair access (also WC). No music. Air-conditioned

MAP 8 **LONGRIDGE – Lancashire**

Longridge Restaurant

104–106 Higher Road, Longridge PR3 3SY
Tel: (01772) 784969
Website: www.heathcotes.co.uk

Cooking 5 | Modern British | £48

Chris Bell heads the kitchen at Paul Heathcote's flagship restaurant, but the style of food continues in the same vein. Indeed, the repertoire moves along gently, with plenty of original ideas and novel presentations, but the focus is on sound culinary principles and traditional cooking methods, backed up by well-sourced local and regional materials. There are plenty of favourites, and many will ring reassuring bells with those who are fans of the Paul Heathcote chain: 'a wonderful meaty slab' of black pudding topped with a deep-fried hash brown and set in a pool of caramelised apple, or a 'cooked-to-perfection' Goosnargh duck breast with colcannon, smoked bacon, glazed baby onions and asparagus. But the menu has also delivered a starter of twice-baked cauliflower and Garstang Blue cheese soufflé that 'was a good balance of flavours', and a main course of seared scallops topped with lobster and

served with ratte potatoes, chorizo, and fennel broth. Puddings are rather more workaday affairs if the assiette of desserts tried at inspection is anything to go by, but bread-and-butter pudding has come in for praise. Service can be on the cool side of efficient, while the overall effect of the décor is contemporarily sharp and comfortable. The straightforward wine list, divided stylistically, starts with house wines at £13.95 and offers a dozen by the glass.

Chef: Chris Bell Proprietor: Paul Heathcote Open: Tue to Fri and Sun L 12 to 2.30, Tue to Sun D 6 (5 Sat) to 10 (9 Sun) Closed: bank hols Meals: alc (main courses £12.50 to £25) Service: not inc Cards: Amex, Delta, Maestro, MasterCard, Visa Details: 85 seats. Car park. Vegetarian meals. No smoking in dining room. Wheelchair access (also WC). Music. Air-conditioned

Thyme

1–3 Inglewhite Road, Longridge PR3 3JR
Tel: (01772) 786888

Cooking 2 | Modern European | £38

Often crowded, the service at this split-level brasserie remains cheerful and hard working. Portions are generous, and dishes are 'big on flavour', as demonstrated by a starter of pressed confit duck leg layered with spiced chorizo and ham hock with a salad of potato and chives and ginger and redcurrant dressing. Slow-roasting is a favoured technique: crisp duck breast, say, or lamb shoulder with sweet-and-sour red cabbage and a minted potato beignet, its sparse sauce of garlic, lemon and rosemary adding 'to the success of this enjoyable country dish'. Desserts are a plus point, among them hot cross bun bread-and-butter pudding, and St Clement's iced parfait. A short, serviceable wine list starts at £11.95. A second branch is at the Sirloin Inn, Station Road, Hoghton, Preston; tel: (01254) 852293.

Chefs: Mike Law and Alex Coward Proprietors: Alex Coward and Wayne Keough Open: Tue to Sat 12 to 2, 6 to 9.30, Sun 1 to 8 Meals: alc (main courses £13 to £18). Set L Tue to Sat £8.95 (2 courses) to £10.95, Set D 6 to 7.30 £9.95 (2 courses) to £11.95. Light L menu available Tue to Sat Service: not inc Cards: Amex, Maestro, MasterCard, Visa Details: 45 seats. Vegetarian meals. No children after 7.30pm Sat. No smoking. Wheelchair access (also women's WC). Music. No mobile phones. Air-conditioned

MAP 2 · LONGSTOCK – Hampshire

Peat Spade `AR`

Longstock SO20 6DR
Tel: (01264) 810612

New owners Andrew Clark and Lucy Townsend worked together at the Hotel du Vin in Winchester (see entry) and spent some time locating what they call the 'perfect country inn' to run together. Robust English food is the order of the day, so among starters might be ham hock terrine with home-made piccalilli (£5.50), with main courses of pork tenderloin with braised red cabbage and roast pear (£12.90), or braised beef cheeks with parsnip purée (£13). Bread-and-butter pudding (£4.50) could conclude. Wines from £12.50. Open all week.

MAP 1 · LOOE – Cornwall

Trawlers on the Quay

The Quay, East Looe PL13 1AH
Tel: (01503) 263593
Website: www.trawlersrestaurant.co.uk

Cooking 3 | Seafood | £41

Cheerful surroundings and fresh seafood, served simply with the occasional twist sums up this harbourside restaurant. The fish is from Looe market, just down the quayside, and diners can watch as the trawlers moor up with the daily catch. Chef Todd Varnadoe loves his spices and strong flavours, so spicy Creole crab cakes with a cucumber and sweet-and-sour dressing, or seafood gumbo are habitual starters. Roast monkfish with butternut squash or a trio of local fish with a lime and shallot butter may represent the sea, while Cornish lamb in St Austell Tribute ale with tomatoes, peppers and garlic also flies a local flag. Vegetarians have their own menu: perhaps grilled blue cheese with peach and pecan salad, then baked tomatoes stuffed with spicy vegetable couscous. Desserts include bread-and-butter pudding, and cheeses, all from within the county, are worth a look. Wines are from £13.50, but you might want to try the Cornish Camel Valley, a good match for seafood, at £18.95.

Chefs: Todd Varnadoe Proprietors: Nick Love and Mark Napper Open: Tue to Sat D only 6.15 to 10 Closed: 25 and 26 Dec Meals: alc Easter to Nov (main courses £14 to £18). Set D Nov to Easter £23.50 (2 courses) to £28 Service: not inc Cards: Amex, Delta, Maestro, MasterCard, Visa Details: 40 seats. 10 seats outside. Vegetarian meals. No smoking. Wheelchair access (not WC). Music

MAP 3 · LOWER HARDRES – Kent

Granville

Street End, Lower Hardres CT4 7AL
Tel: (01227) 700402

Cooking 4 | Modern European | £37

Although one part of the Granville is a traditional roadside pub serving real ales from Shepherd Neame, this younger sibling of the Sportsman (see entry, Whitstable) is predominantly an eating place and shows high ambitions. The blackboard menu is a shrine to the best of local produce, and meals get off to a good start with 'fabulous, fresh, home-made' focaccia and sourdough bread. Among starters, a generous plate of bresaola marinated in wine and spices has made a favourable impression, not least for managing to be both 'gutsy and delicate', while smoked mackerel served in a heap with potato and bound with horseradish, teamed with a couple of slices of soda bread spread with Boursin cheese (a successful combination), is equally well judged. For main course there might be braised belly pork with apple sauce and crackling, or crispy duck with sour cream and chilli sauce, while desserts eschew soothing familiarity for a final fanfare: tangerine sorbet liberally sprinkled with space dust, a shot glass of lemony jelly and a faultless mini crème brûlée make a mesmerising essay in contrasts. Casual service is eager to please, and the wine list balances value and quality. Bottle prices start at £10.95.

Chefs: Jim Shave, Ezra Gaynor and Natalie Toman Proprietors: Philip and Stephen Harris Open: Tue to Sun L 12 to 2 (2.30 Sun), Tue to Sat D 7 to 9 Closed: 25 and 26 Dec Meals: alc (main courses £11 to £19) Service: not inc Cards: Delta, Maestro, MasterCard, Visa Details: 60 seats. Car park. Vegetarian meals. Children's helpings. No-smoking area. Wheelchair access (also WC). Music. Air-conditioned

 This symbol means that smoking is not permitted.

MAP 5 **LOWER ODDINGTON –**
Gloucestershire

Fox Inn

Lower Oddington GL56 0UR
Tel: (01451) 870555
Website: www.foxinn.net

Cooking 1 | Modern British | £33

Almost totally covered in Virginia creeper, this Cotswolds cottage inn offers a dip in the toe of country life. The décor is all natural colours and exposed stone, while the atmosphere is buzzy and the service friendly and helpful. Chef Ray Pearce has been here for eight years now, which means that his dishes are consistently prepared and well timed, and he makes good use of local produce. Smooth duck liver pâté with French bread might start things off, followed by pan-fried sea bass with stewed red peppers, chorizo and crème fraîche, or slow-cooked lamb shank with garlic and rosemary. Try clementines in cinnamon caramel for dessert. The short wine list spans both Old and New Worlds, with a clutch of house wines from both starting at £11.75.

Chef: Ray Pearce Proprietor: Ian Mackenzie Open: all week 12 to 2 (3 Sun), 6.30 to 10 (9.30 Sun) Closed: 25 Dec Meals: alc (main courses £9.50 to £14) Service: not inc Cards: MasterCard, Visa Details: 80 seats. 80 seats outside. Car park. Vegetarian meals. Children's helpings. No cigars/pipes in dining room. Occasional music Accommodation: 3 rooms

MAP 5 **LOWER QUINTON –**
Warwickshire

College Arms

NEW ENTRY

Lower Quinton CV37 8SG
Tel: (01789) 720342
Website: www.collegearms.co.uk

Cooking 4 | Modern British | £49

After a spell as a grotty local boozer, this classic sixteenth-century pub has been taken over by Steve and Claire Love, who have turned it into a stylish restaurant-with-rooms. The enterprise is split into two main parts: Love's 'fine dining' restaurant and Henry's Bar. It is in the former where Steve produces an elaborate no-choice seven-course tasting menu that bears the hallmarks of his training under Alain Ducasse. Highlights have included a seared scallop with a deep-fried frog's leg in crisp, light batter, and an intense parsley jus, 'perfect' slow-cooked ox cheek with parsnip purée, and banana sorbet with pork scratchings (an entirely successful invention both in conception and execution).

Henry's Bar, named jointly after Henry VIII (a former owner of the building) and the owners' dog, makes the most of its original features of rough-stone walls and low, heavily beamed ceiling. While the menu is certainly simpler than the one in the main dining room, it is anything but a list of trad pub grub. Most impressive at inspection was a starter of rich, luscious home-made corned beef – 'light years away from the stuff in tins' – with spicy, crunchy piccalilli and crisp, sharply dressed salad leaves. A main course of exemplary crisp-skinned confit duck leg comes with the house speciality 'pommes d'amour' (crushed potato with piquant vinegared shallots), creamy Savoy cabbage and a girolle-infused sticky stock reduction, and to finish there might be warm poached pineapple topped with toffee sauce, vanilla ice cream and a delicate sesame seed wafer. Prices are remarkably low for this level of cooking – the 5/5/5 menu (any two courses for £10) is especially good value. The wine list takes a commendably user-friendly approach, grouping wines by style and offering helpful tasting notes, fair prices throughout and even the more modest bottles making good drinking. Prices start at £12.50.

Chef: Steve Love Proprietors: Steve and Claire Love Open: Henry's Bar: Tue to Sun L 12 to 2 (4 Sun), Tue to Sat D 7 to 9 (9.30 Fri and Sat); Love's Restaurant: Thur, Fri and Sat D only 7 to 10 Meals: Henry's Bar: alc (main courses £8.50 to £18). Set L Tue to Sat and D Tue to Fri £10 (2 courses) to £15; Love's Restaurant: Set D £48 Service: not inc Cards: Maestro, MasterCard, Visa Details: Henry's Bar: 75 seats; Love's Restaurant: 14 seats. 40 seats outside. Car park. Vegetarian meals (Henry's Bar). Children's helpings. No smoking. Music Accommodation: 4 rooms

MAP 6 **LOWICK –**
Northamptonshire

Snooty Fox

16 Main Street, Lowick NN14 3BH
Tel: (01832) 733434

Cooking 3 | Modern British | £37

Built in the late sixteenth century as a manor house, nowadays the Snooty Fox is an informal country inn offering real ales, fine wines and superior pub food. At one end of the spectrum are humble-sounding but well-executed bar snacks such as chicken and ham pie, or hot pork sandwich with apple sauce. The main rôtisserie menu makes a feature of Aberdeen Angus steaks, cut to order and priced per 25g. Otherwise there might be carpaccio with rocket and Parmesan, or classic prawn cocktail to start, followed by pork T-bone with potatoes roasted with garlic and rosemary, or salmon and whiting fishcakes with vine tomato sauce. Rhubarb and banana tart with Chantilly cream makes an unusual way to finish. The wine list offers plenty of variety and fair value, with prices starting at £12.95 and around a dozen by the glass.

Chef: Clive Dixon Proprietors: David Hennigan and Clive Dixon Open: all week 12 to 2, 6.30 to 9.30 Closed: D 25 Dec, 1 and 2 Jan Meals: alc (main courses £8 to £15). Set L Mon to Sat £9.95 (2 courses) to £14.50. Bar menu available Service: not inc Cards: Delta, Diners, Maestro, MasterCard, Visa Details: 100 seats. 50 seats outside. Car park. Vegetarian meals. Children's helpings. No smoking in dining room. Music

MAP 5 LUDLOW – Shropshire

Hibiscus

17 Corve Street, Ludlow SY8 1DA
Tel: (01584) 872325
Website: www.hibiscusrestaurant.co.uk

| Cooking 8 | French | £61 |

It may look like an ordinary eatery on the high street of an English market town, but Ludlow stopped being gastronomically ordinary a long time ago, and Hibiscus is part of the reason for that. Three tiny interlinked rooms – a bar and a pair of dining rooms – are all it consists of, but the oak panelling establishes an air of quiet dignity. Quality table settings and knowledgeable, self-assured staff help too. Once settled at your table, you are quite likely to be handed something like a glass of chilled elderflower soda seasoned with black pepper to set the ball rolling. Claude Bosi likes to keep you on your toes. This is fully evident from the menus, which announce forthrightly that the cooking style is very much in the avant-garde idiom of today, with perhaps more of a French emphasis than might be found from other modern masters of the genre. Dishes are fashioned from many components, and, if not all the combinations sound altogether convincing, the proof, as always, is in the eating.

Sautéed lambs' sweetbreads, gently browned and full of flavour, are paired with fat Spanish prawns and offset with a Thai curry purée of lemongrass, lime leaves and chilli. Some might have been tempted to leave it there, but there's more. The plate is dotted with soft, juicy, fresh dates, which have been stuffed with Valencia orange. A final element of confit Staffordshire asparagus adds a just-about-seasonal note and is modishly adorned with a white, peppery foam. Impressively, this adds up to a fine opening course, not least because each element individually does its bit. You want to start more simply? How about five Cornish oysters, poached and served in the shell, garnished merely with an artichoke tuile and the obligatory froth – this time of eucalyptus?

It wouldn't work if the principal ingredients weren't so classy, but they reliably are, as was the case with inspection main courses of Dover sole and roast saddle of Welsh lamb. The former was strewn with button mushrooms and sweet onions, and almost traditionally served with buttered broad beans (as well as a spot of coconut purée), while the lamb was brilliantly supported by vine tomatoes caramelised in Muscavado, as well as baby carrots cooked in orange, both dishes resonant with sound culinary intelligence. The experimentation continues into desserts, although not at the cost of preserving the odd menu fixture, such as tarte au chocolat with Indonesian basil ice cream, which might come with gariguette strawberries in their own jelly and a savoury cream scented with rosemary and pepper.

A formidable wine list has been assembled, expansively spanning the globe to take in all the major producers. Australia is well served for quality, Spain is good, and there are some excellent French country wines, as well as their posher cousins. A page of special recommendations opens at £14.75 for a Languedoc Sauvignon or a mature Côtes du Lubéron red blend.

Chef: Claude Bosi Proprietors: Claire and Claude Bosi Open: Wed to Sat L 12.15 to 1.30, Tue to Sat D 7 to 9.30 Closed: 23 Dec to 10 Jan, 2 weeks summer Meals: Set L £21 (2 courses) to £25, Set D £45 to £67.50 Service: not inc Cards: Delta, Maestro, MasterCard, Visa Details: 36 seats. Car park. Children's helpings. No smoking. Wheelchair access (not WC). No music. No mobile phones

Mr Underhill's

Dinham Weir, Ludlow SY8 1EH
Tel: (01584) 874431
Website: www.mr-underhills.co.uk

| Cooking 7 | Modern European | £57 |

A substantial, yellow-painted house on the edge of the River Teme, close to Dinham Bridge, this

venture represents 25 years of dedicated work by the Bradleys. While it all feels a little grander than the restaurant-with-rooms designation might suggest, the tone is completely relaxed, and the setting a treat. A narrow terrace provides a pleasant spot for aperitifs, and the dining room offers views of the garden through a wall of windows.

Chris Bradley cooks a fixed-price menu of six courses plus coffee, with choice only at dessert stage. It's a formula that regulars understand and appreciate, and it turns up many resounding successes. A soup often starts, making an immediate impact with the likes of roast butternut squash with Parmesan and balsamic, sharpening the appetite for what's to follow. Foie gras custard with sweetcorn cream and sesame glaze has been a favourite second course for many, and might precede a fish course such as lemon sole, given a paper-thin crust of garden herbs and timed to perfection. Red meat is favoured for the main course and has produced such resonant dishes as slow-roast fillet of Marches beef, the first-rate, well-hung meat topped with a cloud of mashed potato and accompanied by an impressive ox cheek cottage pie. Tiny fruit sponges make delightful pre-desserts, and then might come a hot apple strudel with superbly light pastry, replete with sultanas, almonds and pecans. Judy Bradley oversees proceedings with tireless professionalism.

Wines from Western Europe, Australasia and California comprise a list that is the product of much careful selection. A real effort has been made in Italy, and the Special Selection listings are worth perusal. Plenty of halves and dessert wines expand the range. House wines start at £13.

> Chef: Chris Bradley Proprietors: Chris and Judy Bradley Open: Wed to Sun D only 7.15 to 8.15 Closed: Christmas, 1 week summer, 1 week autumn Meals: Set D £45 Service: not inc Cards: Delta, Maestro, MasterCard, Visa Details: 30 seats. 30 seats outside. Car park. No children under 8. No smoking. No music. No mobile phones Accommodation: 9 rooms

Overton Grange

Old Hereford Road, Ludlow SY8 4AD
Tel: (01584) 873500
Website: www.overtongrangehotel.com

| Cooking 3 | Anglo-French | £58 |

About a mile from Ludford Bridge, the Grange is a country manor house with a certain sense of old-school swagger, although the dining room presents a contrastingly modern decorative face to the traditionalism of the rest. Olivier Bossut cooks a modern French menu that has some neat creative touches, while managing to avoid the wilder shores of experimentation. Feuilleté of langoustine comes with buttered spinach and a langoustine coulis as a first course, and might be the prelude to a 'cassoulet' of quail, snails and butter beans, or Gressingham duck breast with celeriac tagliolini and a sauce of Cassis. Finish in classic style with rum baba and fromage frais sorbet, or chocolate pudding with caramel sauce and praline ice cream. House wines start at £19.50.

> Chef: Olivier Bossut Proprietor: Indigo Hotels Ltd Open: all week 12 to 2, 7 to 9 Closed: New Year Meals: Set L £27.50 to £32.50, Set D £39.50 to £55 Service: 10% (optional) Cards: Delta, Maestro, MasterCard, Visa Details: 78 seats. Car park. No smoking. Wheelchair access (not WC). Occasional music. No mobile phones Accommodation: 14 rooms

MAP 9 LUND – East Riding of Yorkshire

Wellington Inn

19 The Green, Lund YO25 9TE
Tel: (01377) 217294

| Cooking 3 | Modern British | £39 |

Although off the beaten track, this country pub is well worth seeking out. It's been tastefully and comfortably refurbished – beams, white walls, polished tables – and Russell and Sarah Jeffery run the place with real dedication; he's front-of-house and she's at the stoves. Her imaginative menu runs from oriental-style slow-roast Gloucester Old Spot belly pork on roast sweet potato to baked salmon fingers crumbed with Parmesan and oats accompanied by pea purée and spicy tomato salsa. Start with a hotpot of devilled lambs' kidneys and mushrooms or warm home-smoked breast of Gressingham duck with grapefruit and lemon balm, and finish with rum and raisin crème caramel. There are half a dozen dessert wines on the intelligently annotated, global wine list, which gives a wide variety of styles. Prices open in Italy and Australia at £11.95.

> Chef: Sarah Jeffery Proprietors: Russell and Sarah Jeffery Open: Tue to Sat D only 7 to 9.30 Meals: alc (main courses £14 to £19). Bar menu available Service: not inc Cards: Delta, Maestro, MasterCard, Visa Details: 42 seats. Car park. Vegetarian meals. No children under 12. No smoking. Music. No mobile phones

MAP 1 **LYDFORD – Devon**

Dartmoor Inn

Lydford EX20 4AY
Tel: (01822) 820221
Website: www.dartmoorinn.com

Cooking 3 | Modern British-Plus | £42

The pebbledash Dartmoor Inn is a constant work-in-progress for Karen and Philip Burgess, who are as community minded as they are food obsessed, founding the Dartmoor Festival and producing the *Dartmoor Inn News*. Inside the maze of rooms there is even a boutique selling jewellery and gifts. The kitchen produces a variety of menus, including the new 'easy dining' menu, which, as one diner noted, makes for 'rather a lot of dishes'. Expect starters along the lines of pan-fried scallops with crispy bacon and wilted rocket salad, or gutsy braised pork cheeks with cracked pepper sauce, and main courses of braised oxtail with a well-balanced prune and stock sauce, or pan-fried hake in red wine sauce with fennel purée and sweet potato crisps. To finish, lemon tart with citrus syrup comes with a 'beautifully flavoured' scoop of herby, lemony sorbet. Karen's service is 'top of the range', while incidentals such as bread are also praiseworthy. Around a dozen house wines, from £12.75, or £3.25 a glass, open the international wine list.

> **Chefs:** Philip Burgess and Andrew Honey **Proprietors:** Karen and Philip Burgess **Open:** Tue to Sun L 12 to 2.15 (2.30 Sun), Tue to Sat D 6.15 to 10 **Meals:** alc (main courses £12 to £22.50). Set L Tue to Sat £16.95, Set D Tue to Thur £16.95. Bar menu available **Service:** not inc **Cards:** Amex, Delta, Maestro, MasterCard, Visa **Details:** 80 seats. 20 seats outside. Car park. Vegetarian meals. No children under 5 Fri and Sat D. Children's helpings. No smoking. Occasional music. No mobile phones **Accommodation:** 3 rooms

MAP 8 **LYDGATE – Greater Manchester**

White Hart Inn

51 Stockport Road, Lydgate OL4 4JJ
Tel: (01457) 872566
Website: www.thewhitehart.co.uk

Cooking 4 | Modern British | £44

Located in a conservation area opposite a church and overlooking the Pennines, this unpretentious

inn blends the old and the new to great effect. There is a bar/brasserie as well as the restaurant, which boasts oak beams, upholstered chairs and great views. Chef John Rudden lets the ingredients speak for themselves; there are no grand works of art but the food is nicely presented and well timed. Tempura chilli squid with a saffron and garlic mayonnaise, or Loch Fyne smoked salmon might start, followed by braised shank of lamb with pickled red cabbage, or perhaps pot-roast pheasant breast with sautéed potatoes. House specialities include Saddleworth sausages, made on the premises, and every Tuesday they offer a fish menu: perhaps champagne-glazed oysters, baked hake fillet with a brochette of prawns, and lobster thermidor. Finish with a classic British dessert such as apple and blackberry crumble. France features heavily on the wine list, which opens at £15 for house Chilean.

> **Chef:** John Rudden **Proprietors:** Charles Brierley and John Rudden **Open:** Mon to Sat 12 to 2.30, 6 to 9.30, Sun and bank hol Mon 1 to 7.30 **Meals:** alc (main courses £14 to £19). Set L Mon to Sat and D Mon to Thur 6 to 6.45 £14.90 (2 courses) to £18.75. Set D £35 **Service:** not inc **Cards:** Amex, Delta, Maestro, MasterCard, Visa **Details:** 130 seats. 30 seats outside. Car park. Children's helpings. No smoking in dining room. Wheelchair access (also WC). Occasional music **Accommodation:** 12 rooms

MAP 2 **LYME REGIS – Dorset**

Broad Street Restaurant   NEW ENTRY

57–58 Broad Street, Lyme Regis DT7 3QF
Tel: (01297) 445792

Cooking 2 | Modern British | £37

A much-welcomed neighbourhood restaurant, this contemporary addition to Lyme Regis has much to praise, including its extensive sourcing of local produce; many suppliers are less than ten miles away, and scallops are advertised as 'landed this evening from Lyme Bay'. Service is 'well informed and unpretentious', while the long basement dining room is lit by arched windows and fat candles. Jake Dodds makes the most of his raw ingredients. Those scallops ('very fresh and really nicely timed') might come as a starter with cauliflower purée and sherry caramel, while main courses might include rack of lamb, accompanied by potato hotpot and sautéed leeks. Alternatives might be wild rabbit and apricot terrine, followed by locally landed sea bass with ratatouille and saffron potatoes, and among puddings could be roast rhubarb with butterscotch sauce and 'crisp yet gorgeous' home-made shortbread. Six wines are served by the glass, with bottle prices opening the short list at £11.50.

Chef: Jake Dodds **Proprietor:** Franny Owen **Open:** Sun L 12.30 to 2.30, Tue to Sat D 7 to 9.15 (9.30 Fri and Sat); phone to check opening hours during low season **Meals:** alc L (main courses £9.50 to £12.50). Set D £25 **Service:** 12.5% (optional) **Cards:** Delta, Diners, Maestro, MasterCard, Visa **Details:** 50 seats. Vegetarian meals. Children's helpings. No smoking. No music. No mobile phones

---

MAP 2 LYMINGTON – Hampshire

Egan's

24 Gosport Street, Lymington SO41 9BE
Tel: (01590) 676165

Cooking 2 | Modern British | £40

John Egan makes admirable used of local produce at his relaxed restaurant, where tables are well-spaced and look out over a pretty plant-filled patio. The daily-changing lunch menu shows seasonality and freshness are to the fore, and evening specials might include breast of guinea fowl with a tarragon topping. All sorts of influences show up among starters: curried monkfish and crab samosa with couscous spiked with coconut and chillies alongside a dome of smoked salmon filled with prawns, cream cheese and chives with avocado and a quail's egg. Main courses take in roast marinated loin of venison with spring cabbage, bacon and mushrooms in a chocolate and redcurrant sauce, and fish is a strong suit (lemon sole meunière topped with seared scallops, perhaps). Finish with something straightforward like raspberry Eton mess. The good-value wine list concentrates on France, Italy and the New World. Six house wines are each £13.95, or £3.75 a glass.

Chef: John Egan **Proprietors:** John and Deborah Egan **Open:** Tue to Sat 12 to 2, 6.30 to 10 **Closed:** 26 Dec to 9 Jan **Meals:** alc D (main courses £12.50 to £18). Set L £10.95 (2 courses) to £13.95 **Service:** not inc **Cards:** Delta, Maestro, MasterCard, Visa **Details:** 50 seats. 20 seats outside. Vegetarian meals. Children's helpings. No smoking. Music

---

 This symbol means that the wine list is well above the average.

MAP 8 LYTHAM ST ANNE'S – Lancashire

Chicory

5–7 Henry Street, Lytham St Anne's FY8 5LE
Tel: (01253) 737111
Website: www.chicorygroup.co.uk

Cooking 3 | Global | £40

In a street just off the conservation area of Lytham Square, the downstairs restaurant shares an entrance with the cocktail lounge (in the same ownership) upstairs; for a pair of reporters the Saturday-night bouncer on the door 'is not a welcoming sight'. However, it is worth getting past him for cooking that is global in scope, taking inspiration from here, there and everywhere. While an inspection meal found a few dishes requiring more attention to detail, hits included a parcel of goats' cheese, Stilton, wild mushrooms and Brie teamed with a spinach and citrus salad as well as home-made salad cream, and king scallops and tiger prawns roasted with garlic and parsley and served with pappardelle and a tarragon and Calvados velouté. The dessert menu may not be a hotbed of inventiveness, but bread-and-butter pudding manages to include caramel sauce and clotted cream. Service has received the thumbs-down of late. House wines start at £12.50.

Chefs: Felix Santoni, Richard Martin and Gary Cartwright **Proprietors:** Bevan Middleton, Felix Santoni, Richard Martin and Gary Cartwright **Open:** all week 12 to 2 (2.30 Sun), 6 to 9.30 (10 Fri and Sat, 9 Sun) **Meals:** alc exc Sun L (main courses L £7 to £12.50, D £13 to £19). Set L Sun £18.95, Set D Sun to Thur £18.95 **Service:** not inc **Cards:** Amex, Maestro, MasterCard, Visa **Details:** 70 seats. Vegetarian meals. Children's helpings. No-smoking area. Wheelchair access (also WC). Music. Air-conditioned

---

MAP 6 MADINGLEY – Cambridgeshire

Three Horseshoes

High Street, Madingley CB3 8AB
Tel: (01954) 210221
Website: www.huntsbridge.com

Cooking 3 | Mediterranean | £50

The pretty little village of Madingley is really on the map thanks to the Three Horseshoes, one of

the Huntsbridge Group's collection of East Anglian pubs/restaurants (see entries at Fotheringhay, Huntingdon and Keyston). Richard Stokes is at the helm, delivering a menu written in Italian with English translations and focusing on dishes in which fine ingredients are treated simply. At inspection, a main course of roast saddle of Denham Estate fallow deer served with verdure miste (leeks, fennel, carrots and vine tomatoes) and a red wine, balsamic and thyme reduction impressed with its impeccable freshness and flavour. Starters may feature the likes of Portland crab with celery, fennel, bottarga and olive oil, or vitello tonnato (cold roast saddle of veal with tuna sauce, capers and lemon). To finish, Italian and English cheeses make an alternative to something sweet like chocolate truffle cake with Vin Santo ice cream. Wines (which open with a sensibly short list of moderately priced house recommendations and bottles under £20) don't stint on quality. The full list is a well-rounded, international selection that's been put together with something like evangelical glee. House Italian and Chilean are £12.95.

Chef: Richard Stokes Proprietor: Huntsbridge Ltd Open: all week L 12 to 2, Mon to Sat D 6.30 to 9.30 Closed: 1 and 2 Jan Meals: alc (main courses £15.50 to £24). Bar/grill menu available Service: not inc Cards: Amex, Delta, Maestro, MasterCard, Visa Details: 115 seats. 50 seats outside. Car park. Children's helpings. No smoking in 1 dining room. Wheelchair access (not WC). No music

---

 MAP 1 | **MAIDENCOMBE – Devon**

Orestone Manor

Rockhouse Lane, Maidencombe TQ1 4SX
Tel: (01803) 328098
Website: www.orestonemanor.com

Cooking 4 | Modern English | £55

For a pair of reporters visiting on a bleak, wintry evening, it was too dark to take in the view over Babbacombe Bay, but an open fire and comfortable sofa were ample compensation, as was the impression that the 'Raffles-like ambience seems to work as well in the winter as in the summer'. Darron Bunn has moved here from the Greyhound at Stockbridge (see entry) and creates an ambitious menu of bright, modern ideas. Top-quality regional produce is at the heart of the cooking, and a lightness of touch distinguishes most dishes. This was certainly the case with an inspector's first course of 'very fresh, fat and very lightly seared' Start Bay scallops with cauliflower

purée and a couple of cauliflower beignets. Star of the show among main courses was aged prime Devon beef fillet, beautifully rare, served with a couple of slices of 'perfectly cooked' foie gras, braised celeriac, and a port jus. Desserts haven't faired so well – a perfectly executed but ultimately bland pear tarte Tatin, for example – so the selection of West Country cheeses continues to be a good bet. A straightforward wine list, arranged by style, is full of good ideas at all price levels from £14.95.

Chef: Darron Bunn Proprietors: Rose and Mark Ashton Open: all week 12 to 2, 7 to 9 Meals: alc (main courses £18 to £24.50). Set L Mon to Sat £14.75 (2 courses) to £17.95, Set L Sun £19.50 Service: 10% (optional) Cards: Amex, Delta, Maestro, MasterCard, Visa Details: 45 seats. Car park. Vegetarian meals. Children's helpings. No smoking. Wheelchair access (also WC). Music. No mobile phones Accommodation: 12 rooms

---

MAP 2 | **MAIDEN NEWTON – Dorset**

Le Petit Canard

Dorchester Road, Maiden Newton DT2 0BE
Tel: (01300) 320536

Cathy and Gerry Craig run a hospitable cottage restaurant, with Gerry constantly developing his modern Anglo-French cooking. Perennial favourites on the set-price dinner menu (two courses £26, three £29) include Dorset crab risotto, seared scallops with Parma ham and sherry butter, roast breast of Gressingham duck with an orange, ginger and port sauce, and sticky toffee pudding. Wines from £14.95. Open Tue to Sat D only; also L first and third Sun in month.

MAP 3 | **MAIDSTONE – Kent**

Souffle

31 The Green, Bearsted, Maidstone ME14 4DN
Tel: (01622) 737065
Website: www.soufflerestaurant.co.uk

Cooking 2 | Modern British | £45

'Utterly charming, so English and so Kent,' noted a diner of Souffle's location; in summer you might catch a game of cricket on the green, while the tiny front garden is packed with plants. The interior is a series of knocked-through rooms, with beams and standing timbers, a large mirror widening out the genteel dining room. The food is interesting without being over-elaborate, with some ideas working better than others. Escabèche of red mullet on a bed of olives, anchovies, aubergine and peppers lacked distinct flavours at inspection, but roast rump of lamb in rosemary sauce came with 'tasty and nicely timed' vegetables, particularly 'lovely fresh peas'. The crowning glory was a hot pistachio soufflé with vanilla ice cream, which had an old-fashioned charm and was exceptionally well flavoured. The wine list favours France and opens at £12.50.

Chef: Nick Evenden Proprietors: Nick and Karen Evenden
Open: Tue to Fri and Sun L 12 to 2, Tue to Sat D 7 to 9.30
Meals: alc exc Sun L (main courses £16 to £18.50). Set L £13.50 (2 courses) to £16.50, Set D £25 Service: 10% (optional) Cards: Amex, Delta, Maestro, MasterCard, Visa
Details: 40 seats. 20 seats outside. Car park. Vegetarian meals. Children's helpings. No smoking. Wheelchair access (also men's WC). Occasional music. No mobile phones

MAP 8 **MANCHESTER – Greater Manchester**

Brasserie Blanc

55 King Street, Manchester M2 4LQ
Tel: (0161) 832 1000

Formerly Le Petit Blanc (with other outlets in Birmingham, Cheltenham, Oxford and Tunbridge Wells; see entries), this remains a firm favourite, particularly with families, thanks to the something-for-everyone brasserie menu (including a separate one for children). Set-price deals are good value at £12/£14.50, and the carte deals in starters of deep-fried goats' cheese with French bean salad and tomato chutney (£6.50), or moules marinière (£7.50), and main courses of roast Barbary duck breast with butternut squash and Madeira dressing (£17.50). Mixed red berry and almond crumble (£5.50) makes for a big finish. Wines from £12.95. Open all week.

Bridge

58 Bridge Street, Deansgate, Manchester M3 3BW
Tel: (0161) 832 0242

'We use only the finest (and where possible) locally sourced, freshest ingredients' proclaims the menu at this central gastro-pub. Original ideas grafted on

to traditional British and regional dishes are what to expect. Start with Manx kipper fillets on toast with a poached egg and hollandaise (£5.50), or watercress and radish salad with salted goats' cheese and lemon butter (£5.50), and followed by rabbit and wild mushroom pie with mash (£10). Chips are fried in duck fat, cheeses are all English or Irish farmhouse, and classic Eccles cake with cream (£4.95) is among puddings. Wines from £10.90. Closed Sun.

Bridgewater Hall, Charles Hallé Room

Lower Mosley Street, Manchester M2 3WS
Tel: (0161) 907 9000

The Charles Hallé restaurant is open concert nights only for pre-performance meals (last orders 6.45pm) at this prestigious arts complex. Set menus (£18.50/£23.50) might see the likes of confit of duck and chicken terrine with an apricot and banana chutney, followed by medallions of pork fillet in a port wine and wild mushroom cream, or even pan-fried leg of lamb steak in a chasseur sauce. End with vanilla pannacotta with aromatic poached fruits. House wines from £12.45.

Cotton House

Ducie Street, Manchester M1 2TP
Tel: (0161) 237 5052

The restaurant is large, with both the atmosphere and décor lending themselves more to a nightclub, and in fact this contemporary space attracts plenty of the city's bright young things. A chef change before we went to press prevented a full inspection, but the ambitious modern European dishes take in chicken and bacon Caesar salad (£6.50) and Scottish smoked salmon with toasted brioche (£7.50), through to roast Castle Mey fillet of beef with a fricassee of oyster mushrooms in a Madeira sauce (£21). Fish might be roast loin of cod with herb mash and parsley sauce (£15), with cappuccino pannacotta (£5) among puddings. Chilean house red is £16, white £14.95. Closed Sun. Reports please.

AR	Not a full entry but provisionally recommended. These 'also recommended' establishments are integrated throughout the book.

Establishment

43–45 Spring Gardens, Manchester M2 2BG
Tel: (0161) 839 6300
Website: www.establishmentrestaurant.com

Cooking 4 | **Modern British** | **£62**

Establishment occupies a Victorian banking hall that was designed to exude the kind of opulence that is too lofty for anything as everyday as decoration. Walls are lavishly marbled, pillars soar, and there's a domed atrium. With a change of chef, however, the burst of fiery enthusiasm that characterised the restaurant's early output seems to have settled down to a gentle simmer, but the kitchen still delivers modish food, and froths, shot glasses and pre-desserts are *de rigueur*. Ambition comes across clearly in combinations like lasagne of wild mushrooms and Goosnargh chicken with caramelised ceps and mushroom velouté, and a reporter was impressed by a pairing of perfectly timed monkfish tail with Iberico ham, queenies, crab tortellini, poached gem lettuce, peas and a sparse Parmesan velouté froth. Those for whom dessert is the highlight of a meal may enjoy consommé of poached winter fruits with frozen yoghurt mousse and 'stunning' spiced madeleines, or a 'perfect' prune and Armagnac soufflé. An international wine list, arranged by country, provides sound support, albeit at fairly steep prices. House wine is £14.50.

> **Chef:** Davey Aspin **Proprietor:** Carl Lewis **Open:** Mon to Fri L 12 to 2.30, Mon to Sat D 6.30 to 10 **Closed:** Christmas, bank hols **Meals:** alc (main courses £21 to £26). Set L £18 (2 courses) to £21.50, Set D £48 to £75 (inc wine) **Service:** not inc **Cards:** Amex, Delta, Diners, Maestro, MasterCard, Visa **Details:** 85 seats. Vegetarian meals. Children's helpings. No smoking in 1 dining room. Wheelchair access (also WC). Music. No mobile phones. Air-conditioned

Glamorous Chinese

Wing Yip Business Centre, Oldham Road, Ancoats, Manchester M4 5HU
Tel: (0161) 839 3312

Cooking 2 | **Chinese** | **£35**

A popular destination for those seeking well-prepared Sunday lunch dim sum; doors open at 11am, with crowds generally arriving before midday. Families provide the atmosphere, while heated trolleys are wheeled around the restaurant showcasing their sweet and savoury wares. Steamed has the edge over fried so look out for dumplings including prawn with chive, scallops, or spicy meat and nuts, while other dim sum might see the like of spare ribs in black bean sauce or won ton with a sweet and sour sauce. The rest of the menu takes in most recognisable Cantonese dishes including deep-fried crab claw, crispy seaweed, and king prawns in black bean sauce. Vegetarian options see the likes of braised tofu and stir fried Chinese mushrooms and seasonal vegetables. Wines from £9.90.

> **Chef:** Piu Hung **Proprietor:** Mr M. Hung **Open:** all week 11.30 (11 Sun) to 10.45 (11.30am to 11.45pm Fri and Sat) **Meals:** alc (main courses £6.50 to £13). Set L £5.95 (2 courses) to £9.95, Set D £15.50 (min 2) to £22 (min 2) **Service:** not inc **Cards:** Amex, Delta, Maestro, MasterCard, Visa **Details:** 400 seats. Car park. Vegetarian meals. No smoking in 1 dining room. Wheelchair access (also WC). Music. Air-conditioned

Greens

43 Lapwing Lane, West Didsbury, Manchester M20 2NT
Tel: (0161) 434 4259

Cooking 2 | **Vegetarian** | **£30**

The bold and eclectic menu at this bistro-like vegetarian could make even the most committed carnivore forget about meat for the evening: at least, that's what one diner thought. A green awning welcomes visitors, while the interior has a buzzy atmosphere, with bentwood chairs, some tables covered in red Perspex, and well-organised staff keeping proceedings ticking over nicely. The carte might start with Thai-spiced potato cake with Asian coleslaw, or Cheshire goats' cheese and pine-nut salad with rocket, spinach and watercress. 'Irish stew' made with aubergines, crispy potatoes and braised cabbage, served with soda bread, is a meat-less take on a stalwart, while pea and mint pesto ravioli comes in a red wine ragoût. Finish with coffee and mascarpone tiramisù, or raspberry crème brûlée. The wine list may not be long but it's well chosen and reasonably priced, starting at £11.

> **Chef:** Simon Rimmer **Proprietors:** Simon Rimmer and Simon Connolly **Open:** Tue to Fri and Sun L 12 to 2 (12.30 to 3.30 Sun), all week D 5.30 to 10.30 **Closed:** 25, 26 and 31 Dec **Meals:** alc (main courses L £6.50 to £8.50, D £10.50). Set L Sun and D Sun to Fri 5.30 to 7 £12.95 (2 courses) **Service:** not inc **Cards:** Delta, Maestro, MasterCard, Visa **Details:** 48 seats. Vegetarian meals. Children's helpings. No smoking. Music

Koh Samui

16 Princess Street, Manchester M1 4NB
Tel: (0161) 237 9511

Now in its eighth year, this colonial-style dining room on the outskirts of Chinatown is peppered with Thai artefacts; service is friendly while the menu runs the gamut of Thai cuisine. Start with duck spring rolls, chicken or prawn satay, or maybe spicy Thai sausage (all £5.95), moving on to staples such as red, green or yellow curry (£7.95), steamed sea bass with lime (£15.95) or pineapple fried rice with chicken, squid and prawns (£9.95). End with mango and coconut sticky rice with coconut ice cream (£3.95). Wines from £13. Closed Sat and Sun L.

Kosmos Taverna

248 Wilmslow Road, Manchester M14 6LD
Tel: (0161) 225 9106

The larger-than-life personality of Loulla Astin is the driving force behind this long-established Greek-Cypriot taverna. An early-bird dinner menu (£14.50) or set-price three-course menu (£18) might tempt, or you can explore the carte. Start perhaps with mini mezethes for two (£12), including hummus, falafel, stuffed vine leaves and tabbouleh, and go on to a traditional main course – moussaka (£10.50), say – or something more unusual like chicken breast stuffed with feta and mushrooms and cooked in a garlic, wine and tomato sauce (£12.90). Greek house wines are £14 a litre. Open all week D only.

Lime Tree

8 Lapwing Lane, West Didsbury, Manchester M20 2WS
Tel: (0161) 445 1217

Cooking 3 | **Global** | **£38**

The Lime Tree, now 21 years of age, is a busy neighbourhood restaurant, although tables are not so close that people feel cramped. Emphasis is placed on sourcing quality local and seasonal ingredients, so starters could easily be grilled asparagus spears with goats' cheese and roast peppers, or whole roast quail with black pudding, leeks and a lentil jus. The kitchen shows its credentials with main courses of fricassee of sea bass, salmon and scallops in a herb sauce, or a full-blooded dish of venison medallion and mallard

breast with balsamic-glazed beetroot, mashed root vegetables and a port jus. Dessert could be apple and frangipane tart with vanilla ice cream, or chocolate torte. It's worth seeking out the ten or so wines of the month for the variety and value they offer. The rest of the list has been assembled with cost and quality in mind, with Burgundy showing up particularly well. Six house wines, from France, Spain and the New World, are each £12.95, or £3.25 a glass.

Chefs: Jason Parker and Jason Dickenson **Proprietor:** Patrick Hannity **Open:** Tue to Fri and Sun L 12 to 2.30, all week D 5.45 to 10.15 **Meals:** alc exc Sun L (main courses £7 to £16.50). Set L Tue to Fri £14.95, Set L Sun £16.95, Set D 5.45 to 6.30 £14.95 **Service:** not inc **Cards:** Amex, Delta, Maestro, MasterCard, Visa **Details:** 90 seats. 24 seats outside. Vegetarian meals. Children's helpings. No smoking. Wheelchair access (not WC). Music

Little Yang Sing

17 George Street, Manchester M1 4HE
Tel: (0161) 228 7722
Website: www.littleyangsing.co.uk

Cooking 1 | **Cantonese** | **£40**

£

A perennially popular choice among those seeking authentic dim sum in Manchester, this large, colourful and ornately decorated dining room always has a buzz. Fried beef buns, shredded duck rolls, scallop dumplings and Shanghai-style steamed pork buns are all in the repertoire, along with less familiar items such as prawn bauble with almond flakes. There is also an extensive menu of traditional Cantonese appetisers and main courses, ranging from crispy duck pancakes and sweet-and-sour pork to salt and pepper soft-shell crab and oyster stew with ginger and spring onions, plus desserts with irresistible names such as 'lemon teardrop' and 'joyful sweetness'. Special banquet menus are an excellent way to sample the range. Wines from £11.50.

Chef: Kui Keung Yeung **Proprietor:** LYS Restaurants Ltd **Open:** all week 12 to 11.30 (12 Fri, 12.30 Sat, 10.45 Sun) **Closed:** 25 Dec **Meals:** alc (main courses £8 to £13). Set L £9 (2 courses) to £11, Set D £17.50 to £27.95 (min 2) **Service:** 10% **Cards:** Amex, Delta, Maestro, MasterCard, Visa **Details:** 240 seats. Vegetarian meals. Children's helpings. No-smoking area. Wheelchair access (also WC). Music. Air-conditioned

Livebait   `AR`

22 Lloyd Street, Manchester M2 5WA
Tel: (0161) 817 4110

A stone's throw from Albert Square, this buzzy bistro is bright and welcoming, with a menu that puts fish at the centre of the picture, with only chargrilled sirloin steak with chips and béarnaise for meat eaters. Among starters, all from £3.95, might be rock oysters, a bowl of whelks or cockles, or half a lobster with potato salad, while main courses, from £9.95, include chargrilled yellowfin tuna with stir-fried vegetables and noodles and a soy and ginger butter, or fillet of sea bass with grilled baby leeks and a mussel and coriander butter. Bitter chocolate and orange tart (£4.50) for dessert. Seafood-sympathetic wines from £12.50. Open all week.

Market Restaurant   `AR`

104 High Street, Manchester M4 1HQ
Tel: (0161) 834 3743

Marching to the beat of its own drum, the Market serves modern British classics and internationally inspired dishes amid 1950s décor. A typical menu starts with twice-baked crab soufflé (£6.45) or Thai-style gravad lax with lime and ginger mayonnaise (£5.95) and goes on to fillet of salmon on green lentils with salsa verde (£14.95) or chestnut and walnut pie (£13.95). Desserts could be lemon meringue pie or marzipan baklava (both £5.25). A fine selection of Belgian beers complements the good-value wines (from £8.95). Open Wed to Fri L and Wed to Sat D.

Midland Hotel, French   `NEW ENTRY`

Peter Street, Manchester M60 2DS
Tel: (0161) 236 3333

Cooking 4 | Modern British | £61

At first glance it is hard to spot if any of the recent millions spent on the refurbishment of this corporate hotel extended to the French restaurant. Closer inspection reveals a slight uplift (new maroon-patterned wallpaper, new carpet), but essentially the room remains the same: high ceilings, chandeliers, panels and doors of mirrored panes or clear glass, and heavily draped tables laid with good glassware and porcelain. The full panoply of formal service – polite, old-school waiters fillet and carve at table, wheel out the bread on a trolley, and brandish silver domes – may seem dated, but the food has a modern, light touch that reporters appreciate. Clever first courses of well-timed red mullet served with a tomato tart of 'refreshingly assertive sharpness', and a warm salad of 'particularly impressive' scallops (served on a pool of cauliflower purée) and langoustines (on a fennel purée) precede a main course of guinea fowl in an upmarket variation of coq au vin that is 'big on flavour'. Desserts are not a highlight. A stylistically arranged wine list is somewhat pricey, although house red is £17 and around 20 are offered by the glass from £4.10.

Chef: Gary Jenkins   Proprietor: Q Hotels   Open: Tue to Sat D only 7 to 10.30 (11 Fri and Sat)   Closed: bank hols   Meals: alc (main courses £20 to £33). Set D Tue to Thur £22 (2 courses) to £38   Service: not inc   Cards: Amex, Delta, Diners, Maestro, MasterCard, Visa   Details: 50 seats. Vegetarian meals. Children's helpings. No smoking. Wheelchair access (also WC). Music. No mobile phones. Air-conditioned   Accommodation: 312 rooms

---

Moss Nook

Ringway Road, Manchester M22 5WD
Tel: (0161) 437 4778

Cooking 4 | Modern British | £58

Moss Nook feels somewhat removed from the fashion-sensitive whims of urban cosmopolitanism, both in its location away from the hubbub of the city centre, close to the airport, and in its old-fashioned elegance, with lace table covers, crystal table lamps and heavy drapes the key decorative notes. Chef Kevin Lofthouse has been here since 1983 and, while some of his dishes wouldn't have looked out of place then, his refined cooking style incorporates plenty of modern ideas, starters ranging from pan-seared scallops with asparagus and a light butter sauce to spiced king prawns with basmati rice and sweet chilli relish, or tuna carpaccio with sun-blush tomatoes and a honey and lime dressing. Likewise, main-course options might include roast breast of duckling on dauphinois potatoes with redcurrant sauce. House specialities at dessert stage include their own version of tiramisù and a 'medley' of small chocolate creations, and meals are padded out with finely crafted amuse-bouche at the beginning and petits fours at the end. The substantial wine list concentrates mostly on France but

---

The price given next to the cooking score is based on the cost of a typical three-course dinner for one person, including coffee, house wine and service.

includes some interesting selections from elsewhere, and prices start at £15.

> Chef: Kevin Lofthouse   Proprietors: Pauline and Derek Harrison   Open: Tue to Fri L 12 to 1.30, Tue to Sat D 7 to 9.30 Closed: 2 weeks Christmas   Meals: alc (main courses £19.50 to £23). Set L £19.50 (whole table only), Set D £37 (whole table only)   Service: not inc   Cards: Amex, Delta, Maestro, MasterCard, Visa   Details: 65 seats. 20 seats outside. Car park. No children under 12. Jacket and tie. No pipes in dining room. No music. No mobile phones. Air-conditioned

Ocean Treasure

Greenside Way, Middleton, Manchester
M24 1SW
Tel: (0161) 653 6688
Website: www.chiyip.co.uk

| Cooking 2 | Chinese | £36 |

Fine cooking at competitive prices is found at this Chinese restaurant on a trading estate on the outskirts of Oldham. It caters to a largely Western clientele without compromising the authenticity of its cooking, offering dishes such as jellyfish with pork shank, prawn-stuffed 'three treasures' with black-bean sauce, Mrs Spotty's hot and spicy tofu, and chow mein of Thai beef with squid. But for those with more conservative tastes, the menu also encompasses a wide range of mainstream dishes, from sweet-and-sour pork to stir-fried duck with plum sauce. Portions are generous, so there is no need to order a huge number of dishes, which helps keep the cost of a meal down. House wine is £10.90.

> Chef: Chi Keung Wong   Proprietors: Stewart Yip and Jack Lui Open: all week 12 to 10.30 (11.30 Fri and Sat)   Meals: alc (main courses £7.50 to £13). Set L £5.30 (2 courses) to £7.80, Set D £18 to £26 (all min 2)   Service: not inc   Cards: Amex, Delta, Diners, Maestro, MasterCard, Visa   Details: 260 seats. Car park. Vegetarian meals. No-smoking area. Wheelchair access (also WC). Music. Air-conditioned

Pacific

58–60 George Street, Manchester M1 4HF
Tel: (0161) 228 6668
Website: www.pacific-restaurant-manchester.co.uk

| Cooking 2 | Chinese/Thai | £39 |

Located in a Victorian terrace in the heart of Chinatown, Pacific is done out with bare wooden flooring and predominantly white walls with splashes of colour to give a stylish, modern feel.

While the restaurant caters principally to a Western clientele, the Chinese menu, served on the first floor, turns up everything from crispy aromatic duck to a wide range of authentic dim sum (steamed minced lobster and bamboo shoots in pastry parcels, deep-fried cuttlefish cake, for example) and main-course specialities such as steamed whole eel with garlic and black-bean sauce, braised bean curd with minced pork and Chinese sausage, and lotus root with carrots, asparagus and straw mushrooms. A separate Thai menu, of similar scope, is offered on the ground floor, with starters taking in crisp minced chicken and prawn tartlets, and oysters with lime and chilli dressing, main courses encompassing deep-fried sea bass with red curry sauce and lime leaves, and roast pork spare ribs. House wines start at £11.50.

> Chef: Tim Wong   Open: Thai: Mon to Sat 12 to 3, 6 to 11, Sun 12 to 10; Chinese: all week 12 to 12 (11.30 Sun)   Meals: alc (main courses £8 to £18). Set L and D £19 to £35.50 (some min 2)   Service: 10%   Cards: Amex, Delta, Diners, Maestro, MasterCard, Visa   Details: 250 seats. Vegetarian meals. No-smoking area. Wheelchair access (also WC). Music. Air-conditioned

Palmiro

197 Upper Chorlton Road, Manchester M16 0BH
Tel: (0161) 860 7330

Family-run restaurant that features classic Italian dishes, most notably those from Venice, with proprietor Stefano Bagnoli's passion shining through. Grilled mushrooms with caciocavallo (£4.95), or smoked haddock, spinach and ricotta tart (£5.25) might precede baked whole sea bream with cherry tomatoes, or herb-stuffed chicken breast (both £13.75). Lemon-curd parfait stands out from Italian puddings like Amaretto ice cream (both £4.25). Flag-waving wines from £10.25. Open Sun L and all week D.

Red Chilli   NEW ENTRY

70 Portland Street, Manchester M1 4GU
Tel: (0161) 236 2888
Website: www.redchillirestaurant.co.uk

| Cooking 2 | Chinese | £37 |

'This is the sort of Chinese restaurant that has been sadly missed since Chinatown became fashionable', mused one regular on the scene. What draws such a reaction from an experienced reporter of Chinese food is Red Chilli's simple, unpretentious style and the fact that it offers 'robust, inexpensive stir-fries and casseroles to a largely Chinese student clientele'. More important, it offers an accessible route into corners of Chinese cuisine unfamiliar to most European diners. From the more familiar end of the spectrum, salt and pepper ribs feature tender, good-quality meat, while 'fresh and tasty' gung ho prawns are not overwhelmed by their spicy sauce. Otherwise, the menu largely deals in the likes of beef belly and molly in a clay pot with a 'terrific' gravy, poached sliced duck, stir-fried lily bulb with celery, shredded pig's maw with coriander, braised sea cucumber with shrimp eggs, and even ox tripe in spicy stock. Wines are a fairly straightforward selection, prices starting at £11.50.

Chef: Mr Zhang **Proprietors:** Mr Lui and Mr Yip **Open:** all week 12 to 10.30 (11.30 Fri and Sat) **Meals:** alc (main courses £6.50 to £14). Set D £18 to £26 (min 2) **Service:** not inc **Cards:** Delta, Maestro, MasterCard, Visa **Details:** 90 seats. Vegetarian meals. No smoking. Music. Air-conditioned

---

Restaurant Bar & Grill

14 John Dalton Street, Manchester M2 6JR
Tel: (0161) 839 1999
Website: www.individualrestaurants.com

Cooking 2 | Global | £41

This contemporary brasserie near Albert Square (with siblings in Leeds and Liverpool), is spread over two large floors, both usually bustling with diners. Leather seating, a suspended staircase and lots of marble are features. The menu takes in many global influences, with starters ranging from classic French onion soup with Gruyère, or baked mushrooms with goats' cheese, to fried chilli squid with a Thai noodle salad. Meze plates are available to share and pasta sees the likes of linguine with crab. Main course options take in Thai green chicken curry with coconut rice, grilled ribeye with béarnaise, and roasted halibut with asparagus. All desserts, ice creams and sorbets are made in-house; try chocolate fudge pudding with pistachio ice cream. There's a good selection of liqueurs and wines start at £13.50.

Chefs: Alan Earle and Dave Bright **Proprietor:** Individual Restaurant Company **Open:** all week 12 to 3, 6 to 11 (10.30 Sun) **Closed:** 25 Dec **Meals:** alc (main courses £9.50 to £20). Bar menu available **Service:** not inc **Cards:** Amex, Delta, Diners, Maestro, MasterCard, Visa **Details:** 185 seats. Vegetarian meals. Children's helpings. Smoking in bar only. Wheelchair access (also WC). Music. No mobile phones. Air-conditioned

---

Second Floor

Harvey Nichols, Exchange Square, Manchester M1 1AD
Tel: (0161) 828 8898
Website: www.harveynichols.com

Cooking 4 | Modern European | £47

Clean lines and enormous windows make it feel as if you are floating above the Manchester skyline at this in-store restaurant. The floor is dramatic black marble, while in contrast the tables are set with crisp white linen, accentuating the modish uptown ambience. The compact menu is a modern British affair thanks to Robert Craggs' carefully constructed dishes. Pork and black pudding faggot with Puy lentils and apple appears alongside rare yellowfin tuna niçoise salad for starters, while main courses could be something classical like skate wing with beurre noisette, capers and new potatoes or 'three styles of beef' (fillet, braised oxtail and poached tongue). Vegetarian options might include gorgonzola and globe artichoke risotto. Those with a sweet tooth are well catered for with roasted pineapple, coconut sorbet and lime syrup, or banana tarte Tatin. The wine list is a hefty and far-reaching tome arranged by country and style. House selections start at a reasonable £13.50.

Chef: Robert Craggs **Proprietor:** Harvey Nichols **Open:** all week L 12 to 3 (5 Sun), Tue to Sat D 6 to 10 **Closed:** 25 and 26 Dec, 1 Jan, Easter Sun **Meals:** alc (main courses £11 to £21). Brasserie meals available (main courses £10.50 to £18) **Service:** 10% **Cards:** Amex, Delta, Maestro, MasterCard, Visa **Details:** 92 seats. Vegetarian meals. No smoking. Wheelchair access (also WC). Music.

Simply Heathcotes

Jacksons Row, Deansgate, Manchester M2 5WD
Tel: (0161) 835 3536
Website: www.heathcotes.co.uk

Cooking 2 | Modern British | £42

All the spoils of a modern brasserie are to be had at this city-centre location, and that goes for the other outlets in this successful chain (see also Leeds, Liverpool, and Wrightington). The lively menu may kick off with deep-fried whitebait with smoked paprika and lemon mayonnaise, or crisp Goosnargh duck leg with pickled red cabbage, and follow with grilled Woodall's gammon and glazed belly pork with black pudding, accompanied by pan-haggerty, with a simpler option in the shape of whole grilled plaice with parsley butter and new potatoes. Finish with warm chocolate pudding with cappuccino ice cream. The nifty global wine list is reasonably priced, starting at £13.95 for own-label house wines.

Chef: Eve Worsick **Proprietor:** Paul Heathcote **Open:** all week 12 to 2.30, 6 to 10 (11 Sat, 9 Sun) **Closed:** 25 and 26 Dec, 1 Jan **Meals:** alc (main courses £9.50 to £22). Set L Mon to Sat £12.95 (2 courses), Set D Mon to Sat 6 to 7 £12.95 (2 courses), Set D Mon £15 (inc wine) **Service:** not inc **Cards:** Amex, Delta, Maestro, MasterCard, Visa **Details:** 150 seats. Vegetarian meals. Children's helpings. No smoking. Wheelchair access (also WC). Music. Air-conditioned

---

Stock   AR

4 Norfolk Street, Manchester M2 1DW
Tel: (0161) 839 6644

The Edwardian grandeur of the renovated Manchester Stock Exchange provides a dramatic backdrop to Enzo Mauro's Italian cuisine. The menu covers ever-popular dishes such as a mixed seafood platter for two (£32 per person as a main course) and there's a nice balance between the traditional and the modish: for example, a savoury tartlet of smoked haddock and creamed horseradish (£7.80), home-made black scialatielle with mussels, tomatoes, chillies and garlic (£7.30), and veal escalopes in crab sauce with mustard cream (£17.20). The all-Italian wine list opens at £16.95. Closed Sun.

Tai Pan   AR

Brunswick House, 81–97 Upper Brook Street,
Manchester M13 9TX
Tel: (0161) 273 2798

Occupying the cavernous upstairs floor of a warehouse-like building with an oriental supermarket on the ground floor, this bright, busy Cantonese restaurant always has a lively buzz. The long menu is divided into seafood, chicken, pork, beef and so on – there is even a section of ostrich dishes – taking in everything from sweet-and-sour king prawns (£9.80) to fried duck in yellow-bean sauce (£8.20). There is also a good choice of dim sum (£2.80 to £3.40), Cantonese roast meats such as crunchy belly pork (£8.10), and all-in-one noodle and rice dishes. Open all week.

 This symbol means that accommodation is available at this establishment.

That Café   AR

1031 Stockport Road, Levenshulme,
Manchester M19 2TB
Tel: (0161) 432 4672

A roaring fire greets you in winter as the perfect backdrop to the fulsome menu. Baked goats' cheese tartlet with creamed spinach (£6.95) will start you off, while venison medallions with celeriac and horseradish purée and a game sausage (£15.25), or salmon fillet marinated in herbs served with pesto mash (£15.25) could be among main courses. Finish with chocolate sponge pudding with toffee sauce, or lemon tart with strawberry sauce (each £4.50). Three house wines are £10.25. Live jazz on the first Wed of each month. Open Sun L and Tue to Sat D.

Yang Sing

34 Princess Street, Manchester M1 4JY
Tel: (0161) 236 2200
Website: www.yang-sing.com

Cooking 4 | Cantonese | £41

A Chinatown stalwart since 1977, Yang Sing is marked out by a splendid stone frontage hung with huge red banners. Its long-standing reputation as one of the best Chinese restaurants in the country means it is permanently busy – bringing occasional lapses in standards of service – and usually noisy, but most reporters find waiters friendly and helpful. Chef Harry Yeung claims to have pioneered the concept of the banquet menu, and for those not completely familiar with the more abstruse elements of Chinese cooking it remains one of the best ways to sample the range, 'bringing out an array of dishes one would not find for oneself', including some genuine authentic treats as well as a few more inventive dishes. Thus, scallops with green bean vermicelli and garlic, prawn 'envelopes' with mayonnaise dip, and 'exquisitely sweet' pork stir-fried with French beans and preserved Chinese leaves are served alongside pan-fried ostrich with lemongrass sauce, sizzling chicken in blackcurrant sauce, calamari in cheesy marinade, and asparagus in Szechuan sauce. There is also a comprehensive dim sum menu (before 5pm) and a lengthy carte featuring all the usual favourites. Wines are a better-than-average selection, prices starting under £15.

Chef: Harry Yeung **Proprietors:** Harry and Gerry Yeung **Open:** all week 12 to 10.45 (11.15 Fri and Sat, 9.45 Sun) **Closed:** 25 Dec **Meals:** alc (main courses £8 to £15.50). Set L and D from £27.50 (min 2) **Service:** net prices **Cards:** Amex, Delta, Maestro, MasterCard, Visa **Details:** 230 seats. Vegetarian meals. Wheelchair access (also WC). Occasional music

---

MAP 3 **MARLOW –**
Buckinghamshire

Danesfield House, Oak Room

Henley Road, Marlow SL7 2EY
Tel: (01628) 891010
Website: www.danesfieldhouse.co.uk

| Cooking 7 | Anglo-French | £67 |

For all that it was completely rebuilt around the turn of the twentieth century, Danesfield has a slight hint of Legoland about it. A vast, sparklingly white edifice with ornate red-brick chimneys and battlements and turrets all over the show, it was obviously somebody's idea of imperial magnificence. It opened as a hotel in the early 1990s and offers the full country-house package, complete with an orangery for simpler brasserie dining, and the pale-panelled Oak Room, in which Aiden Byrne gets to spread his wings.

And what wings. Having cooked previously at Tom Aikens (see entry, London), Byrne arrived here in the summer of 2005 and straight away posted his intention to take the place to new culinary heights. The menu descriptions intrigue for their intricacy and imagination, and the cooking delivers. White chocolate and truffle risotto with roast scallops provides food for fascinated thought, as did an inspector's first course of red mullet with a coffee-scented mushroom purée and chopped roast cocoa beans. This made far more sense than a sceptic might have anticipated, with the coffee flavour working brilliantly with the mushroom, and the fish precisely timed in a bain-marie for maximum flavour extraction.

A signature summer main course of loin of lamb appears in small, crisp-crusted slices with a couple of mussels in tow, crumbed sweetbread, a sprinkling of chopped celery and a purée of green olives. The combinations here seemed merely good rather than outstanding, but raw materials are very fine. Slick execution is in evidence in a dessert plate that brings together poached cherries with an astonishingly intense cherry mousse and mint-flecked vanilla ice cream. Mousses seem to be back in, cropping up all over the dessert menu, including a passion-fruit version with sorbet of the same to accompany roast pineapple. Reports suggest that service could withstand a little extra drilling, and as for the silly Muzak in this context, words (nearly) fail us. A wine list to do justice to the food has been compiled. Firmly Franco-centric in orientation, it

nonetheless hauls in a great slew of fine producers (Vernay's Condrieu, Cheysson's Chiroubles, Albrecht in Alsace), as well as good names in Italy and the New World. Prices start at £21.

Chef: Aiden Byrne **Open:** all week 12 to 1.45, 7 to 10 **Meals:** Set L £20 (2 courses), Set D £49. Brasserie menu available **Service:** 12.5% (optional) **Cards:** Amex, Delta, Diners, Maestro, MasterCard, Visa **Details:** 36 seats. 20 seats outside. Car park. Vegetarian meals. Children's helpings. No smoking. Wheelchair access (also WC). Music. No mobile phones. Air-conditioned **Accommodation:** 87 rooms

Hand & Flowers

126 West Street, Marlow SL7 2BP
Tel: (01628) 482277

| Cooking 6 | Modern British | £45 |

A pleasant whitewashed pub with a fence to one side, a boules green at the back and a plethora of low-hanging beams inside is home to the Kerridges' highly polished operation. The place is still a pub, with high stools at the bar and ales on draught for aficionados, but when it comes to the catering side of things it is performing well beyond the pub ethos. The credit for that goes to Tom Kerridge, whose assured, quality-conscious style exudes and inspires confidence. A boudin of ham and parsley with a salad of capers and shallots in a zingy mustard dressing will have you feeling you have been transported across the Channel. Similarly, Suffolk pork tenderloin is treated in Gallic fashion, gaining from Toulouse sausage, Savoy cabbage and truffled artichoke macaroni. In among these offerings, though, come potted Dorset crab with cucumber and dill chutney, potato and horseradish soup with salsa verde, and smoked haddock omelette with Parmesan. The most complex main course might essay a compromise style in honey-roast breast of duck with cauliflower purée, ravioli of foie gras and black pudding, orange confit and caramelised radicchio.

The brio of the cooking idiom is maintained in simpler desserts that might take in rhubarb and apple crumble with vanilla ice cream, or glazed nutmeg tart with banana ice cream. Good wines help to raise the game too, with canny selections from around the world backing up the serviceable house wines, which start at £15.50, or £4 a glass.

Chef: Tom Kerridge **Proprietors:** Tom and Beth Kerridge **Open:** All week 12 to 2.30, all week exc Sun D 7 to 9.30 **Closed:** D 24 Dec to 26 Dec **Meals:** alc (main courses £10 to £21) **Service:** not inc **Cards:** Delta, Maestro, MasterCard, Visa **Details:** 50 seats. 28 seats outside. Car park. Children's helpings. No smoking. Music

Vanilla Pod

31 West Street, Marlow SL7 2LS
Tel: (01628) 898101
Website: www.thevanillapod.co.uk

Cooking 5 | **Modern British** | **£57**

Although it wears the faint look of a tea room on the outside, the Vanilla Pod is a smart neighbourhood restaurant that fits seamlessly into its surroundings in smart Marlow. The tables are fairly close together, but the place is stylishly decorated and the mood of expectation created by Michael Macdonald's cooking. Expect seared scallops to come with a purée of pear poached in the eponymous vanilla (from Tahiti, no less). A complex terrine of ham hock, guinea fowl and shiitake mushrooms is dressed in rosemary and honey vinaigrette, and might be followed by a main course of pan-fried brill with olive and raisin tapenade, or two cuts of lamb with white beans and grain mustard sauce. If the thought of vanilla with sea bass doesn't appeal, wait until dessert stage and enjoy it in a crème brûlée, or opt for apple strudel with cinnamon ice cream. The wine list continues to develop, but is still strongest in France. House Languedoc varietals are £17, or £3.50 for a small glass.

Chef: Michael Macdonald **Proprietors:** Michael and Stephanie Macdonald **Open:** Tue to Sat 12 to 2, 7 to 10.30 **Meals:** Set L £17.50 (2 courses) to £19.50, Set D £40 to £45 **Service:** not inc **Cards:** Amex, Delta, Maestro, MasterCard, Visa **Details:** 42 seats. Vegetarian meals. No smoking in dining room. Wheelchair access (not WC). No music

MAP 8 **MARSDEN –** West Yorkshire

Olive Branch

Manchester Road, Marsden HD7 6LU
Tel: (01484) 844487
Website: www.olivebranch.uk.com

Cooking 4 | **Modern English** | **£41**

This truly rural affair, set in a sheltered valley on the edge of the Marsden Moor Estate, offers informal dining inside and out; they proudly boast a secluded garden out back which catches the afternoon sunshine. The menu is written on blackboards and also on cards pinned on the walls. Paul Kewley puts together an impressive array of dishes which he constantly refines; parfait of chicken

livers, grenadine stewed onions with toasted bread is an example of the way he combines flavours and ideas. Continue with blackened sea bass fillet in a creamy lime sauce, or perhaps steak pie made with diced shin beef, root vegetables and a suet crust. For those with room, dessert options include banana cheesecake with caramel sauce or perhaps a wedge of Cropwell Bishop Stilton. Their wine list opens at £12.95.

Chef: Paul Kewley **Proprietors:** Paul Kewley and John Lister **Open:** Wed to Fri L 12 to 2, Mon to Sat D 6.30 to 9.30, Sun all day 12.30 to 8.30 **Closed:** first 2 weeks Jan **Meals:** alc (main courses £11.50 to £19.50). Light L menu available **Service:** not inc **Cards:** Delta, Maestro, MasterCard, Visa **Details:** 68 seats. Car park. Vegetarian meals. Smoking in bar only. Music **Accommodation:** 3 rooms

MAP 2 **MARSH BENHAM –** Berkshire

Red House   AR

Marsh Benham RG20 8LY
Tel: (01635) 582017

Not far off the M4, this attractive thatched, redbrick pub/restaurant is somewhat off the beaten track in a pretty village. The Anglo-French menu might see a starter of stuffed pig's trotter with braised Puy lentils and port jus (£8.95), followed by spring lamb tournedos with onion carbonara, and asparagus and broad bean fricassee (£19.25), or chargrilled halibut in a pistachio crust with a spicy lemongrass and coconut emulsion (£18.25). Finish with cinnamon- and vanilla-infused rice pudding with caramel sauce (£5.50). Eight house wines are £14, or £3.75 a glass. Closed Sun D.

MAP 9 **MARTON –** North Yorkshire

Appletree

Marton, nr Pickering YO62 6RD
Tel: (01751) 431457
Website: www.appletreeinn.co.uk

Cooking 3 | **Modern British** | **£36**

There have been some changes at the Appletree in the last year. The Drews have found staffing a problem, and their solution has been to reduce the number of covers. Some things remain the same: their refusal to turn over tables during sittings, for example, so every diner is able to relax (booking is essential in the dining room, with tables in the bar and courtyard allocated on a first-come, first-served basis). T.J.'s menu remains in the same modern British style too, with an emphasis on sourcing as much local produce as possible, and he continues to grow vegetables, herbs and fruit. Melanie's front-of-house service is informal and chatty, which adds to the happy ambience. Start with a pork sausage and smoked bacon salad, or minted courgette fritters with sweet chilli sauce and lime mayonnaise, and proceed to roast tenderloin of pork, accompanied by black pudding, sweet potato purée and mustard sauce. A fish option might be plump roast fillet of halibut with smoked bacon, rocket, crushed potatoes and a red wine jus. The half-dozen or so desserts include lemon-curd and meringue parfait, and the Yorkshire cheeseboard (Olde York, Coverdale and Yorkshire Blue) is served with home-made biscuits. The wine list reflects the owners' enthusiasm – a page is devoted to T.J.'s 'favourite Australian wine producer', Brown Brothers, for instance – and casts its net widely in search of plum bottles. Around a dozen are served by the glass, from £3, and ten house wines are £11.

> **Chef:** T.J. Drew **Proprietors:** Melanie and T.J. Drew **Open:** Wed to Sun 12 to 2, 6.30 (7 Sun) to 9 **Closed:** 25 Dec, 2 weeks Jan **Meals:** alc (main courses £10 to £17) **Service:** not inc **Cards:** Delta, Maestro, MasterCard, Visa **Details:** 24 seats. 8 seats outside. Car park. Vegetarian meals. Children's helpings. No smoking in 1 dining room. Wheelchair access (also WC). Music

---

MAP 5   MARTON – Shropshire

Sun Inn

Marton SY21 8JP
Tel: (01938) 561211
Website: www.suninn.biz

Cooking 2 | Modern British | £36

The Sun consists of a traditional bar (with its own menu) and a dining room done out in pale neutral shades, from cream through beige to grey, a colour scheme that creates a calm, contemporary feel. Helen Short, now into her third year here, provides simple, modern cooking that doesn't test diners but seems to satisfy. Start with crayfish and avocado cocktail with lime crème fraîche, or glazed goats' cheese with slow-roast tomatoes and caper berries. Main courses are hearty, with braised lamb shank in a honey and mustard glaze, served with a red

wine sauce and bubble and squeak, offered alongside cod and crab cakes with crab and ginger velouté. Bread and ice cream are made on the premises, as are desserts of vanilla cheesecake with rhubarb compote, or cinnamon syrup pancakes with banana ice cream. The compact wine list opens with white Sicilian at £12.95.

> **Chef:** Helen Short **Proprietors:** J.A. Whateley and Helen Short **Open:** Wed to Sun L 12 to 2, Tue to Sat D 7 to 9.30 **Meals:** alc exc Sun L (main courses £10.50 to £16). Set L Sun £10.50 (2 courses) to £13.50. Bar L menu available Wed to Sat **Service:** not inc **Cards:** Maestro, MasterCard, Visa **Details:** 50 seats. 8 seats outside. Car park. Vegetarian meals. Children's helpings. No smoking. Wheelchair access (not WC). No music

---

MAP 5   MASHAM – North Yorkshire

Swinton Park, Samuel's

Masham HG4 4JH
Tel: (01765) 680900
Website: www.swintonpark.com

Cooking 4 | Modern British | £56

With its tower and turrets, Swinton Park has the look of something a nineteenth-century magnate might have built to proclaim his wealth and power. It's quite a pile, full of majestically large, ornate rooms and surrounded by acres of land (including several acres of walled kitchen gardens), and while there's some emphasis on corporate entertainment, there is a refreshing informality about the place. Andy Burton's menu is an appealing modern British repertoire. For starters, breast of wood pigeon may be accompanied by home-made black pudding, veal sweetbreads and Jerusalem artichokes, while a main course of slow-braised neck of lamb may be teamed with roast shoulder, root vegetables and onion purée, and pan-fried duck breast with duck sausage, hazelnut croquette and a sage and onion jus. Finish with something like peanut and banana iced parfait with a miniature banana Tatin and banana milkshake. House wine is £15.95, with a dozen by the glass from £5.

> **Chef:** Andy Burton **Proprietors:** the Cunliffe-Lister family **Open:** all week 12.30 to 2, 7 to 9.30 (10 Fri and Sat) **Meals:** Set L Mon to Sat £17 (2 courses) to £21.50, Set L Sun £24, Set D £43 to £50. Bar menu available **Service:** not inc **Cards:** Amex, Delta, Diners, Maestro, MasterCard, Visa **Details:** 60 seats. 30 seats outside. Car park. Vegetarian meals. No children under 8 at D. Children's helpings. No smoking. Wheelchair access (also WC). Occasional music **Accommodation:** 30 rooms

Vennell's Restaurant

7 Silver Street, Masham HG4 4DX
Tel: (01765) 689000
Website: www.vennellsrestaurant.co.uk

NEW ENTRY

Cooking 5 | Modern British | £38

The Vennells took over the old Floodlite restaurant in July 2005, gave it a face-lift, and it has come out the other side as a 'sparkling new venture'. A fairly neutral palette of creams and gold gives the impression of quality and comfort – the well-dressed tables aren't too close together, the chairs comfortable – and service is excellent. To these promising surroundings Jon Vennell has weighed in with a classically influenced menu that displays sound technique and some bright ideas. Seared scallops are served with salmon and beetroot tartare and lemon dressing, and potted duck may be presented with nothing more than an apple and orange salad and warm fingers of toast. Rabbit is served in two ways: an upstandingly flavoured sausage of the leg and pan-fried saddle 'done to a T', well matched by Jerusalem artichoke purée and beetroot sauce, while braised lamb comes with a wedge of gratin potatoes and well-judged roast onions and celeriac. A dab hand at pastry work brings on prune, Armagnac and almond tart (with cream cheese ice cream and praline wafers), or there might be a plate of chocolate (fondant, mousse, tart and sorbet). The wine list, organised by style, is a good selection from around the world and keeps prices on a tight leash, opening at £12.95 a bottle, £3.30 a glass.

> Chef: Jon Vennell Proprietors: Jon and Laura Vennell Open: Fri to Sun L 12 to 2, Tue to Sat D 7.15 to 9.15 Closed: first 2 weeks Jan, bank hols Meals: Set L £19.95 (2 courses) to £23.50, Set D £19.95 (2 courses) to £24.90 Service: not inc Cards: Amex, Delta, Maestro, MasterCard, Visa Details: 30 seats. No children under 4 at D. Children's helpings. No smoking. Music. No mobile phones

---

MAP 1   **MAWGAN – Cornwall**

New Yard

Trelowarren, Mawgan TR12 6AF
Tel: (01326) 221595
Website: www.trelowarren.com

Cooking 2 | Modern British | £42

Chef Greg Laskey seems to put vigour and passion into everything he does here, from the determination to source 90 per cent of his ingredients locally

(Menallack farmhouse, the Topponrose dairy and Treleaver farm are just three of his suppliers) to the fact that everything is made on the premises, including ice creams, sorbets and 'superb' bread. The bright and breezy dining room features arched windows, lots of white paint and bouquets of flowers. Wild garlic soup or twice-baked cheese soufflé might start things off, followed by sautéed pigeon breast with parsnip purée and a port and thyme sauce, or sautéed steak and foie gras with spring greens. Try saffron-poached pear with rum and sultana ice cream for dessert, or go for Cornish cheeses. The wine list, split into grape varieties, opens in France at £12.50.

> Chef: Greg Laskey Proprietor: Sir Ferrers Vyvyan Open: Tue to Sun L 12 to 2, Tue to Sat D 7 to 9 Meals: alc (main courses L £4 to £12.50, D £11.50 to £22.50). Set L Tue to Sat £12.50, Set L Sun £12.95 (2 courses) to £14.95 Service: not inc Cards: Maestro, MasterCard, Visa Details: 46 seats. 20 seats outside. Car park. Vegetarian meals. Children's helpings. No-smoking area. Wheelchair access (also WC). Music. No mobile phones

---

MAP 5   **MEDBOURNE – Leicestershire**

Horse & Trumpet

Medbourne LE16 8DX
Tel: (01858) 565000
Website: www.horseandtrumpet.com

NEW CHEF | Modern British | £48

Shortly before the Guide went to press, the Horse & Trumpet's esteemed chef David Lennox moved on to Langshott Manor in Surrey – too late for it to be considered for inclusion, and too late for his successor to be appraised. But new head chef Gary Magnani has been working under Lennox for the past four years as sous-chef and promises to maintain previous standards of quality and consistency. The menus look set to continue in something resembling the inventive, modern style for which the restaurant has become renowned, starters taking in roast scallops with fennel pannacotta and basil, and Cornish crab salad with fennel biscuit, avocado cream and lemon verbena oil, while main courses might feature roast cod cheek with saffron brandade, Tio Pepe and pea shoots, or hickory-smoked Gressingham duck breast with spiced kumquat and macadamia nuts. Finish perhaps with coconut rice pudding with strawberry consommé and ginger and advocaat ice cream. Wine prices start at around £15.

Chef: Gary Magnani Proprietor: BRR (UK) Ltd Open: Tue to Sun L 12 to 1.45 (2.30 Sun), Tue to Sat D 7 to 9.30 Meals: alc exc Sun L (main courses L £9, D £15.50 to £21). Set L Tue to Sat £16 (2 courses) to £20, Set L Sun £17 (2 courses) to £23, Set D £45 Service: not inc Cards: Delta, Diners, Maestro, MasterCard, Visa Details: 45 seats. 20 seats outside. No children under 12 at D. No smoking in 1 dining room. Wheelchair access (also WC). Music Accommodation: 4 rooms

MAP 6 | MELBOURN – Cambridgeshire

Pink Geranium

25 Station Road, Melbourn SG8 6DX
Tel: (01763) 260215
Website: www.pinkgeranium.co.uk

NEW CHEF | Modern British | £59

The Pink Geranium started life as a tea room in the 1940s, catering to servicemen and women, but nowadays this pretty cottage is much less austere, with plenty of pink in the spacious, airy dining room. A new chef is once again in residence, but the carte sees the likes of Tayside smoked salmon with butter-poached langoustines, sevruga caviar and a potato pancake, or ham and parsley risotto with a smoked bacon foam for starters. The main event might be pan-fried sea bass with cauliflower purée, onion bhaji and wild mushrooms, or slow-roast breast of duck with a roast pear, confit potato and pak choi. End with banana tarte fine with tonka bean ice cream and caramel sauce. Wines start at £14.50.

Chef: Gavin Austin Proprietor: Lawrence Champion Open: Tue to Sun L 12 to 2, Tue to Sat D 7 to 9.30 Closed: 25 and 26 Dec, 1 Jan Meals: alc exc Sun L (main courses £16 to £28). Set L Tue to Sat £16.50 (2 courses) to £21.50, Set L Sun £24.50, Set D Tue to Fri £21.50 (2 courses) to £27.50, Set D Tue to Fri £60 Service: 10% (optional) Cards: Amex, Delta, Maestro, MasterCard, Visa Details: 60 seats. Car park. Vegetarian meals. Children's helpings. No smoking. No music

Sheene Mill

Station Road, Melbourn SG8 6DX
Tel: (01763) 261393
Website: www.sheenemill.co.uk

NEW CHEF | Global | £46

Melbourn is an unspoilt village just off the A10 between Cambridge and Royston, with this white-painted hotel sitting just on its edge. It really is a delightful spot with a mill stream, wild flowers and ducks on the pond. Owner Steven Saunders is planning a few changes here and although the food will remain seasonal and regional, with a strong focus on organic produce, he plans to offer more tapas-style sharing dishes in the style of his sister establishment, Steven Saunders in Newmarket (see entry). However, the dinner menu takes in spiced soft shell crab with a sweet chilli dipping sauce, and asparagus salad with marinated goats' cheese to start, while mains include honey-glazed Old Spot pork belly with wilted red chard; and baked salmon fillet with crushed new potatoes and a kalamata olive and tomato ragoût. Dessert sees the likes of lemon posset with poached cherries in Kirsch, or raspberry crème brûlée with shortbread. The wine list is fairly substantial, starting at £14.50 for house French.

Chef: David Morris Proprietor: Steven Saunders Open: all week L 12 to 2.30, Mon to Sat D 7 to 9.30 Closed: 26 Dec, 1 Jan Meals: Set L £15 (2 courses) to £20, Set L Sun £25, Set D £25 (2 courses) to £30 Service: 10% (optional) Cards: Amex, Delta, Maestro, MasterCard, Visa Details: 110 seats. 20 seats outside. Car park. Vegetarian meals. Children's helpings. No smoking. Music. No mobile phones. Air-conditioned Accommodation: 9 rooms

MAP 10 | MELMERBY – Cumbria

Village Bakery

Melmerby CA10 1HE
Tel: (01768) 881811

Now over 30 years since it opened its ecologically sound doors, the Village Bakery remains committed to organic cooking and is certified by the Soil Association. Wholesome, imaginative meals start at breakfast with oak-smoked Inverawe kippers (£4.75), continuing through to snacks such as croissants and open sandwiches (from £4.95) made with bread baked in their wood-fired oven. Main meals might be lamb tagine (£8.75), followed by bread and butter pudding (£3.95). A variety of scones, cakes and biscuits (from £1.10) will also tempt, and there is a gluten-free range. Organic juices, ciders and beers are served along with wines from £10.25. Open all week to 4.30pm.

 This symbol means that smoking is not permitted.

MAP 2 MIDSOMER NORTON – Bath & N.E. Somerset

Moody Goose at the Old Priory [NEW ENTRY]

17–19 Church Square, Midsomer Norton
BA3 2HX
Tel: (01761) 416784
Website: www.theoldpriory.co.uk

Cooking 4 | Modern European | £49

The Shores moved the Moody Goose from the centre of Bath in spring 2005. Its new home, the Old Priory Hotel in the centre of Midsomer Norton, dates from the twelfth century and is a 'warren of a place', all tiny rooms with interestingly shaped windows, mainly neutral décor and a dining room with a floor of the 'biggest flagstones ever'. Stephen Shore is aiming high. His menus are well focused and his cooking is underpinned by solid technical skills, positive flavours and workable combinations, as in starters such as pan-fried pine-kernel-crusted scallops served on parsnip purée ('a very nice dish'), or smoked goose with artichoke pannacotta and beetroot vinaigrette. Good suppliers are evident at every turn: witness supple, accurately timed saddle of lamb layered with braised flageolet beans, truffle oil, and boulangère potatoes, the finishing touch being a little scoop of ratatouille topped with a grilled rasher of pancetta. Dessert at inspection – variations on passion fruit and rhubarb – was not quite on a par with the rest, although it looked convincing. Charming staff serve with cheer, and the wine list offers a broad range of well-chosen wines at restrained prices, with house selections from £14.

Chef: Stephen Shore Proprietors: Stephen and Victoria Shore
Open: Mon to Sat 12 to 1.30, 7 to 9.30 Closed: Christmas, bank hols exc Good Fri Meals: alc D (main courses £17 to £20). Set L £13.50 (2 courses) to £18, Set D £25 Service: not inc Cards: Amex, Delta, Diners, Maestro, MasterCard, Visa Details: 28 seats. 4 seats outside. Car park. Vegetarian meals. Children's helpings. No smoking. Wheelchair access (not WC). Music

MAP 9 MILL BANK – West Yorkshire

Millbank

Mill Bank Road, Mill Bank, nr Sowerby Bridge
HX6 3DY
Tel: (01422) 825588
Website: www.themillbank.com

Cooking 5 | Modern European | £39

Set on a steep slope, the Millbank still functions as a pub but the dining room is the hub of the enterprise. There's nothing to jar the senses here: a wooden floor, low ceilings and closely packed tables work together to create a vibrant yet congenial atmosphere. The modern brasserie-style menu revolves around the best locally sourced produce, with, when necessary, supplies drawn from further afield; Thursday is 'fish night', for example, when Brixham supplies scallops for a salad with orange hollandaise and pistachios, or breaded plaice, which comes with parsley and almond pesto. The well-crafted carte takes centre stage at other times. Lobster risotto with asparagus and herbs makes a luxurious starter, ham hock faggot with cheese mash and grape chutney a gutsier one. Among main courses, braised oxtail with root vegetables and mash, and roast suckling pig with polenta fritters, pak choi, baby onions and a spiced honey sauce with roast almonds are typical of the style. Half a dozen puddings encompass lemongrass crème brûlée with raspberry sorbet, and chocolate fondant with peanut butter ice cream. The annotated wine list is a broad collection of bottles from Europe and the southern hemisphere. Plenty come in under £20, starting at £10.95.

Chef: Glen Futter Proprietor: The Millbank (Halifax) Ltd
Open: Tue to Sun L 12 to 2.30 (4.30 Sun), all week D 6 to 9.30 (10 Fri and Sat, 8 Sun) Closed: first week Jan, first 2 weeks Oct Meals: alc exc Sun (main courses £9 to £19). Set L Tue to Sat and D Mon to Thur and Fri 6 to 7 £11.95 (2 courses), Set L and D Sun £14.95 (2 courses) to £17.95 Service: not inc Cards: Delta, Maestro, MasterCard, Visa Details: 60 seats. 30 seats outside. Vegetarian meals. Children's helpings. No smoking in dining room. Wheelchair access (not WC). Music. Air-conditioned

[NEW ENTRY] This appears after the restaurant's name if the establishment was not a main entry in last year's Guide. Please note, however, it may have been 'also recommended' in the previous edition.

 £5 This symbol means that the restaurant has elected to participate in *The Good Food Guide's* £5 voucher scheme (see 'Using The Good Food Guide' for details).

| MAP 1 | MILTON ABBOT – Devon |

Hotel Endsleigh

NEW ENTRY

Milton Abbot PL19 0PQ
Tel: (01822) 870000
Website: www.hotelendsleigh.com

| Cooking 5 | Modern British | £53 |

After crawling along a twisting single-track drive for more than a mile, taking in stunning views of the Tamar valley, you might expect to find a posh house with formal staff at the end of it. However, Hotel Endsleigh, built in 1812 by the Duke of Bedford as a shooting and fishing lodge, has a simplicity that Olga Polizzi (also of Hotel Tresanton; see entry, St Mawes) has kept, allowing the easy scale of the rooms to influence her own design – a palette of neutral colours offset by some contemporary pieces of art and simple furniture. As a post-modern country-house hotel it works: no frills, no plumped sofas, no pretension, staff are relaxed and half the clientele are in jeans.

Shay Cooper is a talented chef, last seen in the Guide at Talland Bay Hotel in Looe. His unpretentiously written, good-value menu sounds plain ('ham hock tortellini, pea and parsley soup, lemon dressing' is the description of one item), but this only heightens the wow factor when the plate arrives. 'Every element counted' in a main course lemon sole with herb risotto, a soft-boiled quail's egg and roast garlic velouté, while corn-fed guinea fowl with glazed red cabbage, boudin, Jerusalem artichoke purée and Earl Grey jus succeeds due to perfect timing and complementary textures. At inspection, a rich Valrhona chocolate mousse wasn't helped by an equally sweet coconut ice cream and a citrus salad that didn't quite do the job of cutting all that sweetness, but small details like home-made bread and pre-meal nibbles are spot-on. For all this ambition, it is heartening to see that the wine list provides a decent slate of good-value basics from £13.95 before cracking into some canny international choices.

> **Chef:** Shay Cooper **Proprietor:** Olga Polizzi **Open:** all week 12.30 to 2.30, 7 to 10 **Meals:** Set L £21 (2 courses) to £27, Set D £38 **Service:** not inc **Cards:** Amex, Maestro, MasterCard, Visa **Details:** 40 seats. 40 seats outside. Car park. Vegetarian meals. Children's helpings. No smoking. Wheelchair access (also WC). No music **Accommodation:** 16 rooms

| MAP 6 | MILTON ERNEST – Bedfordshire |

Strawberry Tree

3 Radwell Road, Milton Ernest MK44 1RY
Tel: (01234) 823633

| Cooking 6 | Modern European | £48 |

Run with infectious enthusiasm and aplomb by the Bona family, this is a relatively rare feather in Bedfordshire's cap. With two brothers in the kitchen and Mum and Dad heading the place out front, you would expect something of a domestic feel, and you wouldn't be disappointed. A thatched house sitting behind a gravelled drive with potted shrubs, it's every inch the English country house on a human scale.

Jason and Andrew cook a fixed-price dinner menu, with a carte served for lunch three times a week. Dishes don't necessarily make a show of themselves but instead rely on the impact of quality ingredients impeccably sourced and prepared with obvious sensitivity. Start perhaps with a terrine of roast chicken, foie gras and artichoke, served with fig and apple chutney, or a tart of duck confit with potato and onion. There may be an unfashionable preponderance of meat over fish among choices, but the sole fish option on one menu mustered no fewer than four different species – halibut, haddock, grey mullet and monkfish – on the same plate, all sauced with red wine and five-spice. Otherwise, steak and kidney pudding might make an appearance, served with mash and spring greens. The cheering simplicity of it all continues into desserts such as baked meringue with preserved cherries and Greek yoghurt, or caramelised apple tart with vanilla ice cream. House wine starts at £15.

> **Chefs:** Jason and Andrew Bona **Proprietors:** the Bona family **Open:** Wed to Fri L 12 to 1.45, Wed to Sat D 7 to 8.45 **Closed:** Jan, 1 week summer **Meals:** alc L (main courses £14 to £19). Set D Wed to Fri £25 (2 courses) to £32.50, Set D Sat £45 **Service:** not inc **Cards:** Delta, Diners, Maestro, MasterCard, Visa **Details:** 22 seats. Car park. Vegetarian meals. Children's helpings. No smoking. Occasional music

> The price given next to the cooking score is based on the cost of a typical three-course dinner for one person, including coffee, house wine and service.

MAP 3 **MISTLEY – Essex**

Mistley Thorn

High Street, Mistley CO11 1HE
Tel: (01206) 392821
Website: www.mistleythorn.com

Cooking 2 | Modern European | £34

This amiable bistro has a great position just yards away from the quay on the River Stour. There are terracotta floors throughout, with plenty of artwork to interest the eye, and the service is efficient, even when busy. A keen eye for the composition of dishes, combined with the quality and freshness of the produce, makes for a satisfying simplicity. Typical of starters are chicken livers from nearby Sutton Hoo chargrilled on rosemary skewers, accompanied by oak-smoked bacon, sourdough bread, caramelised onions and organic leaves. Marinated Norfolk venison saddle with warm cranberry chutney served with potato latkes and roast root vegetables is a beautifully fresh main course, while honey and whisky semifreddo with hazelnut praline might end a meal. The concise wine list starts at £11.70.

> **Chef:** Sherri Singleton **Proprietors:** Sherri Singleton and David McKay **Open:** all week 12 to 2.30 (3 Sun), 6.30 to 9.15 **Closed:** 25 Dec **Meals:** alc (main courses £9 to £16.50). Set L £10.95 (2 courses) to £13.95 **Service:** not inc **Cards:** Delta, Maestro, MasterCard, Visa **Details:** 75 seats. 12 seats outside. Car park. Vegetarian meals. Children's helpings. No smoking. Wheelchair access (not WC). Occasional music **Accommodation:** 5 rooms

MAP 8 **MITTON – Lancashire**

Three Fishes

Mitton Road, Mitton BB7 9PQ
Tel: (01254) 826888
Website: www.thethreefishes.com

Cooking 5 | Modern British | £32

Plans are afoot to roll out the Three Fishes formula into four neighbouring counties within the next few years, but for the time being the original – a whitewashed pub in a sleepy village – is doing quite well enough on its own. The décor is unstuffy, the walls adorned with framed black and white photographs of local suppliers, like Hollywood publicity shots, and the service

approach is all warmth and charm, if not necessarily unvarying efficiency.

Comforting northern food is David Edward's watchword, and results in dishes such as 'light and fluffy' potato and chive soufflé to start, or stuffed deep-fried pig's trotter, teamed with a salad of golden beet dressed in honey and grain mustard. Variations on fish and chips and Lancashire hotpot push the right buttons at main-course stage, or you might consider slow-cooked shoulder of local mutton with roast root vegetables, barley dumplings and gravy. Leave room if you can for the homely puddings, which include Lancashire curd tart with lemon cream, as well as Bramley apple crumble with custard. Wines are a fairly humdrum selection, starting at £12.50 (or £3 a glass) for Chilean varietals.

> **Chef:** David Edward **Proprietors:** Craig Bancroft and Nigel Howarth **Open:** Mon to Sat 12 to 2, 6 to 9 (9.30 Fri and Sat), Sun 12 to 8.30 **Meals:** alc (main courses £7.50 to £15) **Service:** not inc **Cards:** Amex, Delta, Maestro, MasterCard, Visa **Details:** 120 seats. 60 seats outside. Car park. Vegetarian meals. Children's helpings. No smoking. Wheelchair access (also WC). No music

MAP 6 **MONKS ELEIGH – Suffolk**

Swan Inn

The Street, Monks Eleigh IP7 7AU
Tel: (01449) 741391
Website: www.monkseleigh.com

Cooking 3 | Modern European | £36

In the centre of the village, this thatched and timbered building is effectively a pub with culinary aspirations. There are still real ales in the bar, but the main interest is in the cooking. The surrounding countryside contributes to the kitchen's abundant larder, with game (in season), fruit and vegetables (picked nearby) and fish (delivered from the Suffolk coast) finding their place in Nigel Ramsbottom's modern repertoire. Grilled pigeon breast (served with crispy smoked bacon and a walnut salad) may be followed, for example, by braised lamb knuckle on creamy mashed potatoes with Puy lentil sauce and buttered broad beans, or grilled fillets of plaice on baby spinach with capers and black butter. Puddings continue to fly the flag with summer fruit pavlova and creamy rice pudding, while service proves friendly, observant and efficient. The wine list is sensibly organised and sensibly priced, with eight wines by the glass (from £3 to £5) and house wines at £12.

Chef: Nigel Ramsbottom Proprietors: Nigel and Carol Ramsbottom Open: Wed to Sun 12 to 2, 7 to 9.30 Closed: 25 and 26 Dec, 1 Jan Meals: alc (main courses £9 to £17) Service: not inc Cards: Delta, Maestro, MasterCard, Visa Details: 40 seats. 20 seats outside. Car park. Vegetarian meals. Children's helpings. No smoking. No music

MAP 6 MORSTON – Norfolk

Morston Hall

Morston NR25 7AA
Tel: (01263) 741041
Website: www.morstonhall.com

| Cooking 6 | Modern British | £57 |

The house was originally Jacobean, although much renovated over the centuries, and is less imposing than its name might lead you to fear. Its north Norfolk location makes it an alluring base from which to explore some of the best coastline in England, and the comfortable simplicity of the décor makes it a homely place to return to. Galton Blackiston is an industrious figure, running cookery classes and writing recipe books as well as cooking seven nights a week at the hall (plus Sunday lunch). The format is always a no-choice menu at a single sitting, the dishes assiduously following the seasons. A February menu began with steamed mousse of chicken and Roquefort with béarnaise, before going on to seared monkfish with sautéed artichokes, and then roast pork fillet with boudin noir, buttery mash and Pommery jus. A summer lunch that turned up lobster bisque with samphire, grilled slip sole, and roast beef impressed with its cooking skills, and meals end with either British and French cheeses or a dessert such as cold lemon soufflé with orange ice cream. It is all brought forth with glossy professionalism by well-drilled front-of-house staff.

Immense effort and care have gone into the excellent wine list, which is annotated without pretension and has a fair spread of prices. Trimbach Rieslings from Alsace are one feature, but there is much to seduce, and the arrangement by grape variety is user-friendly. A recommended wine of the month takes the place of conventional house wine, the mark of true enthusiasm.

Chefs: Galton Blackiston and Sam Wegg Proprietors: Galton and Tracy Blackiston Open: Sun L 12.30 for 1 (1 sitting), all week D 7.30 for 8 (1 sitting) Closed: 1 Jan to first week Feb Meals: Set L £30, Set D £44 Service: not inc Cards: Amex, Delta, Diners, Maestro, MasterCard, Visa Details: 40 seats. Car park. Children's helpings. No smoking. Wheelchair access (also WC). No music. No mobile phones Accommodation: 7 rooms

MAP 5 MUNSLOW – Shropshire

Crown

Munslow SY7 9ET
Tel: (01584) 841205
Website: www.crowncountryinn.co.uk

| Cooking 3 | Modern British | £36 |

Set in the picture-postcard surroundings of the Shropshire countryside, this Grade II listed building exudes charm of the olde worlde variety. Richard Arnold and his wife Jane have been running this restaurant for five years now and their menu is updated daily to reflect the available produce, which is almost entirely locally sourced. The dining rooms are cosy, with lots of traditional pub knick-knacks and lacy tablecloths. However, the carefully selected dishes are a cut above for a country pub and even the lunch menu offers some surprises, including beer-battered ginger and chilli risotto cakes, or roast Gressingham duck with fondant potato. Dinner moves up a gear with carpaccio of local Hereford beef served with a red onion and goats' cheese Yorkshire Tatin to start. Breast of Shropshire farm chicken stuffed with mushrooms or roast loin of Ludlow venison with mustard creamed cabbage are satisfying main courses, and all are served with large portions of vegetables. Wait 20 minutes and any remaining gap could be filled by their speciality chocolate fondant. Wines are far reaching with Chilean and French choices from £11.95.

Chefs: Richard Arnold and Alan Lancaster Proprietors: Richard and Jane Arnold Open: Tue to Sun 12 to 2, 6.45 to 9 (6.30 to 7.45 Sun) Closed: Christmas Meals: alc (main courses £10.50 to £17). Set L Sun £13.50 (2 courses) to £16.50, Set D £15. Bar and light L menu available Service: not inc Cards: Amex, Delta, Maestro, MasterCard, Visa Details: 60 seats. 20 seats outside. Car park. Vegetarian meals. Children's helpings. No smoking. Wheelchair access (not WC). Music Accommodation: 3 rooms

MAP 2 NAILSWORTH – Gloucestershire

Mad Hatters
AR

3 Cossack Square, Nailsworth GL6 0DB
Tel: (01453) 832615

This mainly organic restaurant is in a Cotswold town house with oak beams, stone walls and stained-glass windows. Lunch could consist of venison and pork terrine (£5.50), followed by goujons of lemon sole (£11.50), while dinner might entice with lightly spiced grilled mackerel (£5.50), then noisettes of local lamb with braised Puy lentils (£18.50). Both meals could end with bread-and-butter pudding (£5.50). Wines from £12.75. Open Wed to Sun L and Wed to Sat D.

MAP 6   NAYLAND – Suffolk

White Hart

11 High Street, Nayland CO6 4JF
Tel: (01206) 263382
Website: www.whitehart-nayland.co.uk

Cooking 3 | Modern European | £37

This old coaching inn which sits opposite the church in Nayland looks immaculate from the outside and indeed, once inside there's much to be said for the tiled lounge/lobby area, which boasts a bar as well as rows of Michel Roux books. The dining room is simply decorated and the overall feel is relaxed, although the menu offers up some interesting twists, notably some naturally Roux-inspired French touches. Watercress soup with Stilton cream, a warm ham hock salad and tapas are all typical starters, while the main course roast supreme of brill topped with a chicken and sage crust was impressive, served with scented wild mushrooms. Roast duck breast with poached pears in claret, arrived with fondant potatoes and snow peas and was another good combination. Delightful desserts included a chocolate and banana mousse and a 'rounded and delicious' vanilla pannacotta with rhubarb compote. The wine list is split into price category, and is mostly French; their five house choices start at £11.

Chef: Christophe Lemarchand   Proprietor: Michel Roux
Open: Tue to Sun 12 to 2.30, 6.30 to 9.30 (10 Sat, 9 Sun)
Closed: 26 Dec to 9 Jan   Meals: alc (main courses £10 to £17). Set L Mon to Sat £11.50 (2 courses) to £15.50, Set L Sun £16.60 (2 courses) to £21.60   Service: not inc   Cards: Amex, Delta, Diners, Maestro, MasterCard, Visa   Details: 50 seats. 40 seats outside. Car park. Vegetarian meals. Children's helpings. No-smoking area. Music   Accommodation: 6 rooms

 This symbol means that the restaurant has elected to participate in *The Good Food Guide's* £5 voucher scheme (see 'Using The Good Food Guide' for details).

MAP 8   NEAR SAWREY – Cumbria

Ees Wyke

Near Sawrey LA22 0JZ
Tel: (015394) 36393
Website: www.eeswyke.co.uk

Cooking 2 | British | £43

'To say that Ees Wyke is in an Area of Outstanding Natural Beauty is understating it,' noted a reporter of this country-house hotel. The views from the dining room are of meadows, Esthwaite Water and sheep grazing on the fells. The format is classic country-house dining, guests convening in the lounge at 7.30 for pre-dinner drinks, served by congenial hosts Richard and Margaret Lee, before Richard heads back into the kitchen to put the finishing touches to his five-course dinner menu. Starters of perhaps ham hock terrine with parsley wrapped in Savoy cabbage leaves are followed by a no-choice second course: maybe smoked haddock and mushroom pancake. Main course might be a classic such as roast pork loin with crackling, sage and onion stuffing, apple sauce and gravy, or more inventive salmon baked in puff pastry with mint, cucumber and shallots and partnered by creamy saffron sauce. To finish, there might be pear and ginger tarte Tatin, and then a selection of regional farmhouse cheeses. Six house wines at £15.50 open an uncomplicated list.

Chef: Richard Lee   Proprietors: Richard and Margaret Lee
Open: all week D only 7.30 (1 sitting)   Meals: Set D £31
Service: not inc   Cards: Delta, Maestro, MasterCard, Visa
Details: 20 seats. 20 seats outside. Car park. No children under 12. No smoking. Wheelchair access (not WC). No music
Accommodation: 8 rooms

MAP 8   NETHER ALDERLEY – Cheshire

Wizard

Macclesfield Road, Nether Alderley SK10 4UB
Tel: (01625) 584000

Cooking 2 | Modern British | £44

This former pub, on the edge of National Trust parkland, positively brims with character, and old-world charm: three open-plan dining areas, with beamed cottagey ceilings, flagstone floors, and bare wooden tables with raffia table mats. Chef Paul Beattie, who is now into his fourth year here, likes to keep the operation small, with the menu printed on one side of a thick paper sheet. Keeping things simple leaves the door open for plenty of creativity: for instance, starters of carpaccio with wasabi slaw, watercress and beetroot crisps or a tian of crab with guacamole and cherry syrup, followed by grilled fillet of halibut on colcannon with pancetta or Mediterranean vegetable gnocchi with goats' cheese and basil oil. Lemon crème brûlée or caramel apple crumble will sate a sweet tooth. The wine list is surprisingly full-bodied and international, with nine house bottles at £14.50.

Chef: Paul Beattie **Proprietor:** Martin Ainscough **Open:** Tue to Sun L 12 to 1.45, Tue to Sat D 7 to 9.30 **Meals:** alc exc Sun L (main courses £10 to £19). Set L Sun £18.95 (2 courses) to £22.95 **Service:** 10% (optional) **Cards:** Amex, Delta, Maestro, MasterCard, Visa **Details:** 80 seats. 20 seats outside. Car park. Vegetarian meals. Children's helpings. No smoking in 1 dining room. Wheelchair access (also men's WC). Music

---

MAP 2 NETTLEBED – Oxfordshire

White Hart, Number 28

28–30 High Street, Nettlebed RG9 5DD
Tel: (01491) 641245
Website: www.number-28.com

Cooking 4 | Modern British | £48

Outside, it may still resemble the country pub it once was, inside most of the original bar is now a light, modern bistro. Eat here from an appetising-looking menu or make your way to the classy deep-crimson dining room with French windows looking on to a small courtyard garden. The menu here displays an admirable commitment to local produce along with a feel for combining diverse flavours: a starter of scallops, for example, might be served with marinated peppers, chorizo crisps and tomato fondue, while poussin breast and stuffed confit leg are teamed with a 'luxurious, rich, sweet' sweetcorn and foie gras soup. Soup turns up again in a main course, a creamy green sauce enlivened by crisp, barely cooked shreds of lettuce which 'gave a marvellous spring-like feel' to a dish of seared turbot with poached onions and trompettes de mort, while perfectly cooked slices of pork mignon and braised pork belly came with 'heavenly, gluey gravy'. Desserts have included white and dark chocolate pannacotta served with chocolate ice, Black Forest parfait and white chocolate sorbet. Service is polite and well paced, and the clearly presented wine list offers value and flavour

from all over the vinous globe with prices starting at £12.95

Chef: Nick Seckington **Proprietor:** Charlton House **Open:** Restaurant Fri and Sat D only 6.30 to 10; bistro all week 12 to 2.30, 6 to 9.30 **Meals:** Restaurant Set D £35 to £55; Bistro alc (main courses £10 to £15). Set L and D £9.95 (2 courses). Bar menu available. **Service:** not inc **Cards:** Amex, Maestro, MasterCard, Visa **Details:** 30 seats. Car park. Vegetarian meals. Children's helpings. No smoking. Wheelchair access (also WC). Music **Accommodation:** 12 rooms

---

MAP 5 NEWARK – Nottinghamshire

Café Bleu

NEW ENTRY

14 Castle Gate, Newark NG24 1BG
Tel: (01636) 610141
Website: www.cafebleu.co.uk

Cooking 1 | Modern European | £38

Backing on to the River Trent, Café Bleu is a lively fixture in the Newark scene. The French-style décor is striking, with colourful murals of dancing nudes festooning the walls, a mottled yellow ceiling, wooden floorboards and palms. Mark Cheseldine's menu is straightforward, with around half a dozen choices for each course. Start with smoked salmon with Avruga caviar, fennel mousse and a citrus dressing, and follow on with roast Warwickshire sausages with red wine jus and 'beautifully presented' creamed potato with spring onions. Vegetarians could opt for fresh pasta with pesto, pine nuts and Parmesan, and among fish choices could be grilled halibut with roast chicken juices, vanilla-flavoured potatoes, morels, celeriac and spring onions. Tonka bean pannacotta with marinated strawberries makes a satisfying dessert. Extras such as 'really fresh' bread add to the favourable impression, as does a varied, good-value wine list priced from £10.95.

Chefs: Mark Cheseldine and Mark Osborne **Proprietor:** Café Bleu Ltd **Open:** all week L 12 to 2.30 (2 Sat, 3 Sun), Mon to Sat D 7 to 9.30 (6.30 to 10 Sat) **Closed:** 25 and 26 Dec **Meals:** alc (main courses £8.50 to £15) **Service:** not inc **Cards:** Delta, Diners, Maestro, MasterCard, Visa **Details:** 80 seats. 50 seats outside. Vegetarian meals. Children's helpings. No smoking in 1 dining room. Wheelchair access (not WC). Music

MAP 3 NEWBURY PARK – Essex

Curry Special

2 Greengate Parade, Horns Road, Newbury Park
IG2 6BE
Tel: (020) 8518 3005

This modern, yet long-established, North Indian restaurant has canvas paintings, a spiral staircase and a screen downstairs showing Bollywood movies to a mainly young Asian crowd. The menu covers everything from chicken pakora (£5.95) and masala fried fish (£8) to Punjabi prawn curry (£12.50), lamb biryani (£9.95) and murgh tikka masala (£7.50). Parathas are from £2, while vegetable dishes include Bombay aloo (£4.25) and black lentil dhal (£4.80). Wines from £10.95. Open Tue to Fri L and Tue to Sat D.

MAP 10 NEWCASTLE UPON TYNE – Tyne & Wear

Black Door

NEW ENTRY

32 Clayton Street West,
Newcastle upon Tyne NE1 5DZ
Tel: (0191) 261 6295
Website: www.blackdoorrestaurant.co.uk

TYNE & WEAR
OF THE
YEAR
RESTAURANT

| Cooking 6 | Modern European | £54 |

Opening in 2004 in a Georgian terraced house not far from the cathedral, the Black Door is to be found behind (what else?) a shiny black door. Tables are packed into a small dining-room, which enjoys a view over a car park. On chilly evenings, the temperature is boosted by fan heaters. If that sounds a trifle basic, despair not, for it is also home to the seriously talented David Kennedy who cooks in a classic style with enormous flair. Start with just-cooked langoustines on Parmesan gnocchi, dried tomatoes, spinach, and truffled beurre blanc, or perhaps roasted squab on chanterelle risotto, button onions and crisp bacon. Seasoning and attention to timing are admirable, as has been evident in a main course of slow-roasted corn-fed chicken breast with fondant potato, morels, fresh new peas and broad beans. Succulent braised turbot is served on olive oil mash in a generous shellfish broth, while marinated loin of venison comes with crisp polenta, shallot confit and celeriac.

The pre-dessert is light enough to leave you wanting an actual dessert, and it would be foolish to miss out on impeccably crunchy-topped coffee crème brûlée with caramelised walnut ice cream. Stocked in the wine cellar are plenty of classics from both Old and New Worlds, but the list opens with relatively modest French house selections at £13. The team behind the Black Door is also now running a Brasserie operation at Newcastle's Biscuit Factory (see entry below).

Chef: David Kennedy Proprietors: David Ladd and David Kennedy Open: Tue to Sat 12 to 2.30, 7 to 10 Meals: Set L £15 (2 courses) to £16.50, Set D £37 (2 courses) to £39.50 Service: not inc Cards: Amex, Delta, Maestro, Mastercard, Visa Details: 34 seats. Vegetarian meals. No children under 14. No smoking. Music. No mobile phones

Blackfriars Restaurant

Friars Street, Newcastle upon Tyne NE1 4XN
Tel: (0191) 261 5945
Website: www.blackfriarsrestaurant.co.uk

| Cooking 3 | Global | £42 |

The restaurant dates back to 1239 (yes, it really has been a restaurant since then), and is found in a quiet courtyard round the corner from the city's Chinatown district. This tiny enclave is very much at odds with the new architecture in the city but that's what gives it its character. Inside there are old church pews in the bar, wooden tables in the dining area, straw place mats and unusual small concrete blocks with holes for salt and pepper mills. The room is wood panelled and modern-style monastic music adds to the atmosphere. The menu is short with some interesting and eclectic combinations, such as a starter of organic risotto with roast tomato, asparagus and Berwick's Edge cheese. Main course 'posh' fish and chips is labelled so because the batter is made with champagne, while pan-fried local mullet with beetroot crushed new potatoes and cherry balsamic is among similarly inventive options. Pink ginger and Belgian chocolate cake comes with a flavoursome strawberry ice cream. The short global wine list starts at £13.

Chef: Simon Brown Proprietors: Andy and Sam Hook Open: All week L 12 to 2.30, Mon to Sat D 6 to 10 Closed: D 25 and 26 Dec, bank hol Mon Meals: alc (main courses L £11.50 to £18.50, D £11.50 to £24.50). Set L £10.50 (2 courses) to £12.50, Set D before 7pm Mon to Sat £12.50 (2 courses) to £15. Afternoon tea available Service: not inc Cards: Amex, Delta, Maestro, MasterCard, Visa Details: 70 seats. 50 seats outside. Vegetarian meals. Children's helpings. No smoking. Music. Air-conditioned

Brasserie Black Door

Biscuit Factory, Stoddart Street,
Newcastle upon Tyne NE2 1AN
Tel: (0191) 260 5411
Website: www.blackdoorrestaurant.co.uk

 NEW ENTRY

Cooking 4 | Modern European | £45

The setting for this lively brasserie is the ground floor of a refurbished biscuit factory, now an art gallery spread over two floors selling some pricey pieces. Groups of polished dark leather settees create a bar area just inside the entrance, while the dining room has plain white walls broken by bare red-brick sections, and, naturally, artwork for sale is on display. David Kennedy's cooking style offers imaginative twists on French classics but is essentially straightforward. Citrus-cured salmon with an oyster tempura, salt-cod fritters with crisp sage and lemon oil and chicken rillettes with caper berries and bitter leaves display brasserie credentials. Main-course options include crispy duck confit with green beans and sautéed potatoes, and fish is well handled, as in 'beautifully cooked' pan-fried halibut on a bed of mash surrounded by baby clams and tiny cubes of chorizo. Iced apricot and lavender parfait, or milk chocolate mousse with poached pears make for a strong finish. The wine list offers around 40 bins spanning the globe; prices open at £13.50 and around ten are sold by the glass. Related to the Black Door Restaurant; see entry above.

Chef: David Kennedy **Proprietors:** David Ladd and David Kennedy **Open:** Mon to Sat 12 to 2, 7 to 10 **Meals:** alc D (main courses £11 to £15). Set L £15 (2 courses) to £16.50 **Service:** not inc **Cards:** Amex, Delta, Maestro, MasterCard, Visa **Details:** 100 seats. Car park. Vegetarian meals. No smoking. Wheelchair access (also WC). Music. Air-conditioned

Café 21

19–21 Queen Street, Princes Wharf, Quayside,
Newcastle upon Tyne NE1 3UG
Tel: (0191) 222 0755
Website: www.cafetwentyone.co.uk

Cooking 5 | Bistro | £48

For nigh on two decades Terry Laybourne has been cooking at this sassy, modern restaurant set incongruously among imposing Victorian banking buildings close to the quayside and both the Tyne and Millennium bridges. Now it's all change. Later in 2006, after the publication of the Guide, the intention is to move Café 21 further down the quay to larger premises in the Trinity Gardens development. While the details were sketchy as we went to press, devotees can relax, for Terry Laybourne will remain at the helm with head chef Chris Dobson continuing to run the kitchen day to day. The appealing mix of upmarket brasserie dishes, with crowd-pleasers like duck spring rolls with hoisin sauce and fishcakes with buttered spinach, parsley sauce and chips, will continue, served alongside more imaginative offerings, say smoked salmon with blood orange and radish salad, and peppered saddle of venison with creamed celeriac and blue cheese fritter. At dessert stage there may be creamed rice pudding with roasted winter fruits, or farmhouse cheeses, while the soundly chosen, fairly priced wine list starts with house Duboeuf at £13. Reports please.

Chef: Chris Dobson **Proprietor:** Terry Laybourne **Open:** Mon to Sat 12 to 2.30, 6 to 10.30 **Closed:** bank hols **Meals:** alc (main courses £12.50 to £22.50). Set L £14 (2 courses) to £16.50 **Service:** 10% (optional) **Cards:** Amex, Delta, Diners, Maestro, MasterCard, Visa **Details:** 60 seats. Vegetarian meals. Children's helpings. No smoking in 1 dining room. No pipes. Wheelchair access (not WC). Music. Air-conditioned

Fisherman's Lodge

Jesmond Dene, Jesmond, Newcastle upon Tyne
NE7 7BQ
Tel: (0191) 281 3281
Website: www.fishermanslodge.co.uk

Cooking 6 | Seafood/Modern British | £68

'Splendid approach through the dene, with bubbling brook and tumbling waterfalls (we'd only been in the dark previously),' enthused a pair of reporters of this remote Victorian lodge, 'too far to walk from anywhere – yet it's still within the city'. First-class materials are generally impeccably handled, and there is an air of consummate professionalism about the cooking. Known for its fish, options range from light-sounding grilled suprême of halibut with Puy lentils braised with baby onions, and accompanied by pomme purée, to the 'very polished and well-executed' pan-fried turbot served with a cassoulet of white beans, onions and ventrêche bacon tried at inspection, but most dishes operate within a reassuringly classical framework. Roast loin of venison comes with confit cabbage, fondant potato, chestnuts, squash and port jus, for example, and grilled fillet of beef with rösti, seared foie gras, wild mushrooms, caramelised onions and Madeira jus. The repertoire may hold few surprises but certainly doesn't lack interest. A starter of Dorset crab served four ways – with mayonnaise, as a beignet, a spring roll and potted – successfully demonstrates the level of sophistication to which the kitchen aspires, while a 'first-class, classic' chocolate and hazelnut soufflé with hazelnut mousse made a splendid finish. There's little under £20 on the wine list, with £25 just about opening the door to the majority of the otherwise interesting and wide-ranging selection. There's a baker's dozen by the glass, and house wine is £16.

Chef: Jamie Walsh **Proprietor:** Tom's Co. Ltd **Open:** Mon to Sat 12 to 2, 7 to 10 **Closed:** Christmas, bank hols **Meals:** Set L £22.50 to £50, Set D £40 (2 courses) to £50 **Service:** not inc **Cards:** Amex, Delta, Maestro, MasterCard, Visa **Details:** 114 seats. Car park. Vegetarian meals. Children's helpings. No smoking. Wheelchair access (also WC). Music

Jesmond Dene House

Jesmond Dene Road, Newcastle upon Tyne NE2 2EY

NEW ENTRY

Tel: (0191) 212 3000
Website: www.jesomonddenehouse.co.uk

Cooking 4 | Modern British | £56

Formerly home to the industrialist who created Jesmond Dene, this gothic stone mansion has been 'lavishly converted' into a contemporary hotel. Dining takes place amid layers of white napery and muted colours, but for lunch and summer evenings, the conservatory overlooking a wide terrace is the place to be. Jesmond Dene House is the latest addition to Terry Laybourne's stable (see Café 21, Newcastle; and Bistro 21, Durham) and chef Jose Graziosi interprets his simple cooking style admirably well. The refreshing simplicity of a warm salad of Craster kippers with Pink Fir Apple potatoes, soft poached egg and a mustard emulsion has drawn praise, as has the 'happy meeting of flavours' in a beetroot, blood orange, walnut and rocket salad, and main courses of fricassee of spring chicken and lobster with young leeks and truffled noodles, and roast Goosnargh duckling with a Pinot Noir stock reduction. Portions are large so save room for desserts such as crème caramel with fresh strawberries and Grand Marnier. 'Professional, pleasant and efficient' neatly sums up service. The wine list scours the world for interesting bottles and offers a reasonable selection under £25 (with house French at £14), and includes 15 by the glass.

Chef: Jose Graziosi **Proprietor:** Jesmond Dene House Ltd **Open:** all week 12 to 2.30 (4.30 Sun), 7 to 10.30 **Meals:** alc D (main courses £18 to £24). Set L £17.50 (2 courses) to £20.50, Set L Sun £21.50. Bar menu and afternoon tea available **Service:** 10% (optional) **Cards:** Amex, Delta, Maestro, MasterCard, Visa **Details:** 85 seats. 30 seats outside. Car park. Vegetarian meals. Children's helpings. Smoking in bar only. Wheelchair access (also WC). Music **Accommodation:** 40 rooms

Treacle Moon

5–7 The Side, Quayside, Newcastle upon Tyne NE1 3JE
Tel: (0191) 232 5537
Website: www.treaclemoonrestaurant.com

Cooking 4 | Modern British | £55

Tom Maxfield's restaurant has carved a niche as a place for locals to escape the hustle and bustle of the busy Quayside. Bearing that in mind, expect an intimate, and sometimes subdued, dining experience, although the food is first class, well-timed and thoughtfully prepared, with options including a good-value pre-theatre three-course menu, offering two choices per course. The main carte is a tidy, well-balanced affair, and Paul Martin's inventive modern cooking consistently hits the spot. Start with trio of salmon with a chive crème fraîche and jalapeño bagel, or green pea soup with a goats' cheese foam. Main courses include roast rump of lamb with bulgur wheat tabbouleh, pan-seared red mullet with confit fennel or chargrilled ribeye steak with baked field mushrooms. Incidentals, such as the marinated olives and home-made bread have also been praised. End with iced mango parfait with poached mango and lime syrup or maybe set dark chocolate cream with shortbread and marshmallow. Heywood Estate house wines start at £16, or from £4.50 by the glass.

Chef: Paul Martin **Proprietor:** Tom and Jocelyn Maxfield **Open:** Mon to Sat D only 6 to 10.30 **Closed:** 25 Dec, bank hol Mon **Meals:** Set D £30 (2 courses) to £36 **Service:** not inc **Cards:** Amex, Delta, Maestro, MasterCard, Visa **Details:** 24 seats. Vegetarian meals. No smoking. Wheelchair access (not WC). Music. No mobile phones. Air-conditioned

NEW ENTRY	This appears after the restaurant's name if the establishment was not a main entry in last year's Guide. Please note, however, it may have been 'also recommended' in the previous edition.

MAP 6   NEWMARKET – Suffolk

Steven Saunders in Newmarket   NEW ENTRY

4-5 Crown Walk, Newmarket CB8 8NG
Tel: (01635) 665314
Website: www.stevensaunders.com

| Cooking 2 | Modern British | £47 |

Steven Saunders (who splits his time between here and Sheene Mill in Melbourn, see entry) opened this 'confident little operation' in late 2005. The town-centre location may not be the most salubrious but dark wood, dark green walls, and chairs and tables draped in white cut a contemporary edge to match the food. Cooking is inventive, essentially modern British with Asian undertones, but the USP here is the serving of dishes in tapas-sized portions. Examples include tender, finely textured and spiced rare Angus beef salad with wasabi dressing and sushi ginger; a well-made homely, country-style French cassoulet with Toulouse sausage, haricots and bacon; or crispy belly of Old Spot pork, chilli salsa and apple ginger dip, a simple dish that showcases good ingredients. For pudding, try saffron poached pear with organic orange and cardamom parfait. The short, reasonably priced wine list opens with house wines at £12.75.

> **Chef:** Tim Turner   **Proprietor:** Steven Saunders   **Open:** Mon to Sat 12 to 2.30, 6 to 10   **Meals:** alc (main courses 'tapas' £5.50 to £11)   **Service:** 10% (optional)   **Cards:** Amex, Delta, Maestro, Mastercard, Visa   **Details:** 60 seats. Smoking in bar only. Music. No mobile phones

MAP 3   NEWTON LONGVILLE – Buckinghamshire

Crooked Billet

2 Westbrook End, Newton Longville MK17 0DF
Tel: (01908) 373936
Website: www.thebillet.co.uk

| Cooking 2 | Modern British | £43 |

Thatched and 'clearly ancient', the Crooked Billet is now part of a modern residential neighbourhood on the outskirts of the village of Newton Longville. Emma Gilchrist takes care of matters in the kitchen while John Gilchrist holds court in the

compact, open-plan bar and dining room. While the décor suggests that this is the 'village local' – wine-red walls and carpet, plain tables and chairs – the menu and wine list suggest it is much more. Food service, for example, is 'amazingly good, very professional', and seasonal sourcing from a network built up over many years shows in starters like seared scallops with cauliflower purée, slightly overpowered at inspection by English sweet-and-sour sherry vinegar dressing, and in main courses of new season's lamb fillet with fondant potatoes, deep-fried sweetbreads, broad beans, peas, leek and mint cream. At pudding stage chocolate is a favourite theme, while fruity desserts run to pineapple upside-down cake. The wine list bristles with quality and delivers a mix of affordable, intriguing and sought-after bottles from around the world, but is most astute in France. Virtually all are available by the glass. House wines from France and Spain are £12.

> **Chef:** Emma Gilchrist   **Proprietors:** John and Emma Gilchrist   **Open:** Sun L 12 to 2, Mon to Sat D 7 to 9.30   **Meals:** alc (main courses £8 to £25). Set D £45 to £75 (inc wine). Bar L menu available   **Service:** not inc   **Cards:** Amex, Delta, Maestro, MasterCard, Visa   **Details:** 50 seats. 40 seats outside. Car park. Vegetarian meals. Children's helpings. No smoking in dining room. No music

MAP 1   NEWTON POPPLEFORD – Devon

Moores'

6 Greenbank, High Street, Newton Poppleford EX10 0EB
Tel: (01395) 568100
Website: www.mooresrestaurant.co.uk

| Cooking 1 | Modern British | £38 |

A friendly, informal atmosphere prevails at this small restaurant-with-rooms in the centre of a medieval market town. Jonathan Moore cooks, while his wife Kate is a welcoming presence in the dining room, where a light decorative touch complements the bright, modern cooking. The fixed-price menus offer a handful of choices at each course, with perhaps pheasant and celeriac rémoulade, or grilled red mullet with salmon and dill mousse to start, followed by slow-braised belly pork with confit duck leg and rosemary cassoulet, or wild sea bass fillet with sautéed king prawns, a timbale of wild and red rice, and a light shellfish bisque. Interesting desserts might include lavender and poppy seed crème brûlée. Around two dozen wines are priced from £15.

> **Chef:** Jonathan Moore **Proprietors:** Jonathan and Kate Moore **Open:** Tue to Sun L 12 to 2.30, Tue to Sat D 7 to 9.30 **Closed:** 25 Dec, first two weeks Jan **Meals:** Set L Tue to Sat £12.50 (2 courses) to £17, Set L Sun £9.50 (2 courses) to £14, Set D Tue to Thur £15 (2 courses) to £19.50, Set D Fri and Sat £24.50 **Service:** not inc **Cards:** Delta, Diners, Maestro, MasterCard, Visa **Details:** 32 seats. 16 seats outside. Vegetarian meals. Children's helpings. No smoking. Wheelchair access (also WC). Music. No mobile phones **Accommodation:** 3 rooms

MAP 8   **NORDEN –** Greater Manchester

Nutters

Edenfield Road, Norden OL12 7TT
Tel: (01706) 650167

Cooking 3 | Modern British | **£46**

There's something of a quirky character to this eighteenth-century manor house, a feeling enhanced by decorative foibles such as Gothic arches, ornate woodwork, and busy carpets and wallpaper. It provides a cosy bar and several interconnecting dining areas, two of which are in conservatory extensions, and there's a large terrace looking out over six and a half acres of grounds and Ashworth Moor. Andrew Nutter's kitchen deals in ambitious food, turning out, for example, roast cod with a corn kernel fritter, salsa verde and 'designer' sea bass fish fingers, and works with prime materials such as lobster and beef fillet (teamed with a warm salad of roast Mediterranean vegetables). It takes in some regional ingredients along the way, including Goosnargh duck, Bury black pudding (served as won tons with a 'confetti' of vegetables) and, of course, Sandham's Lancashire cheese, but not necessarily the seasons – asparagus in February, for instance. Desserts aim to be as comforting as the rest, judging by a hot chocolate brownie torte with a liquid chocolate centre, while the straightforward wine list focuses on France and the New World. House Australian is £12.95, and there's a reasonable selection of halves.

> **Chef:** Andrew Nutter **Proprietors:** Andrew, Rodney and Jean Nutter **Open:** Tue to Sun 12 to 2 (4 Sun), 6.30 to 9.45 (9 Sun) **Closed:** Christmas, New Year, bank hol Mon **Meals:** alc exc Sun L (main courses L £13.50 to £15.50, D £16.50 to £19). Set L Tue to Sat £12.95 (2 courses) to £15.95, Set L Sun £22, Set D £34 **Service:** not inc **Cards:** Amex, Delta, Maestro, MasterCard, Visa **Details:** 154 seats. Car park. Vegetarian meals. Children's helpings. No smoking in dining room. Wheelchair access (also WC). Music. No mobile phones

MAP 5   **NORTON –** Shropshire

Hundred House Hotel

Bridgnorth Road, Norton TF11 9EE
Tel: (01952) 730353

After two busy decades, the Phillips family continue to juggle the demands of a bar, brasserie, restaurant and hotel with convincing aplomb. Their imaginative, contemporary restaurant menu runs from, say, a salad of smoked eel, black pudding and scallops with pea and mint purée and bacon beurre blanc (£8.95), to roast rack of local lamb with stuffed aubergine, grilled chorizo and rosemary jus (£17.95). Finish with hazelnut meringue with pistachio ice cream and chocolate sauce (£5.95). The bar/brasserie menu offers the likes of Greek salad (£5.95) and steak and kidney pie (£8.95). Wines from £13.95. Accommodation. Open all week.

MAP 6   **NORWICH –** Norfolk

Adlard's

79 Upper St Giles Street, Norwich NR2 1AB
Tel: (01603) 633522
Website: www.adlards.co.uk

Cooking 5 | Modern British | **£56**

It may seem like David Adlard's centrally located restaurant has been around for ever, but that's not to say it's dated. The compact dining room has a wooden floor and a lively array of contemporary art, and seriousness of intent is apparent from the well-spaced tables, good linen and glassware. Roger Hickman's food is modern, but not aggressively so, its backbone of fairly conservative dishes enlivened by a few surprise elements, such as beetroot jelly and mustard ice cream with soused mackerel, and chestnuts and confit turnip with foie gras. Those with simpler tastes might go for baby globe artichoke and potato salad with truffle vinaigrette. Main courses are no less inventive, taking in roast turbot with skate terrine, white beans and broccoli purée, squab pigeon with sarladaise potatoes, samosa and confit cabbage, or braised shin of beef with horseradish mash, braised onion and wilted spinach. To finish, serious temptation is offered in the shape of Tunisian orange cake with iced rhubarb parfait and blood orange foam.

Burgundy is emphatically the main interest of the long wine list. Bordeaux is strong too, complemented by a great range from the Loire and some Rhône heavyweights. Elsewhere, the Antipodes and the USA shine brightest. Four house wines are £16.50.

> **Chef:** Roger Hickman **Proprietor:** David Adlard **Open:** Tue to Sat 12.30 to 1.45, 7.30 (7 Sat) to 10.30 **Meals:** alc (main courses £17.50 to £23). Set L £17 (2 courses) to £21 **Service:** not inc **Cards:** Amex, Delta, Diners, Maestro, MasterCard, Visa **Details:** 40 seats. Vegetarian meals. No smoking. Wheelchair access (not WC). No music. Air-conditioned

Delia's Restaurant and Bar

Norwich City Football Club, Carrow Road, Norwich NR1 1JE
Tel: (01603) 218705

Delia needs no introduction. This contemporary diner is attached to her number one hobby, Norwich City Football Club, and thus her two worlds collide, even if it is just for two nights a week. The menu is compact and set at £29.50 for three courses, which might start with potted Morecambe Bay shrimps served with buttered Irish oatmeal soda bread. Move on to luxury fish pie with rösti caper topping or vegetarian moussaka, ending with old-fashioned custard tart, served with Jersey double cream. The brief wine list opens at £13.35. Open Fri and Sat D only.

Mad Moose Arms, 1 Up Restaurant

2 Warwick Street, Norwich NR2 3LD
Tel: (01603) 627687

Cooking 2 | Modern British | £39

Located in the heart of Norwich's 'golden triangle' this large townhouse, near the University of East Anglia, has established itself as a popular choice. The pub on the ground floor is lively, while the first-floor restaurant is simply decorated with light wooden floors and tables; service is informal and friendly. Eden Derick's menu has broad scope and uses many locally sourced raw materials, including Cromer crab. Chicken liver parfait with saffron pickle courgettes and toasted sour dough is one of ten starter options, while rump of English lamb with braised Puy lentils and truffled Savoy cabbage follows. Fish dishes might include pan-fried cod fillet with creamed white beans and chorizo, while vegetarians can go for asparagus and butternut squash risotto. Desserts with a twist include hazel-

nut parfait with espresso ice cream or dark chocolate 'rumbusco'. Robust wines offer good value, starting at £12.95 for house French.

> **Chef:** Eden Derick **Proprietor:** H.D. Watt **Open:** Sun L 12 to 3, Mon to Sat D 7 to 10 **Meals:** alc (main courses £10 to £14.50). Bar menu available **Service:** not inc **Cards:** Amex, Diners, Maestro, MasterCard, Visa **Details:** 45 seats. Vegetarian meals. Children's helpings. No smoking. Music

Tatlers

21 Tombland, Norwich NR3 1RF
Tel: (01603) 766670
Website: www.tatlers.com

Cooking 2 | Modern British | £43

Tombland is a handsome old street near the cathedral and quite a few of its houses have been turned into restaurants, including this substantial Victorian town house. The three dining rooms occupy the ground floor, each painted a different colour, all with well-spaced wood tables and tended by good-natured, on-the-ball staff. New chef Brendan Ansbro used to work at the Crown and Castle, Orford (see entry), and his cooking is best described as a mix of Mediterranean, Asian and British, with a bit of Caribbean thrown in for good measure. Highlights at inspection were 'tender and fresh' seared scallops with white bean, cumin, lime, coriander and harissa hummus, pomegranate molasses and wild rocket, and 'tender, juicy' pork belly served with crushed new potatoes, baby onions, lardons, sage sauce, pear chutney and sautéed greens. At dessert stage a 'melting' chocolate pudding and rhubarb crumble have been endorsed. House wine is £15.50.

> **Chef:** Brendan Ansbro **Proprietor:** Annelli Clarke **Open:** Mon to Sat 12 to 2, 6.30 to 10 **Closed:** 25 Dec, bank hols **Meals:** alc (main courses £11 to £17). Set L £10 (1 course) to £18 **Service:** not inc **Cards:** Amex, Delta, Maestro, MasterCard, Visa **Details:** 70 seats. Vegetarian meals. Smoking in bar only. Music

> Not a full entry but provisionally recommended. These 'also recommended' establishments are integrated throughout the book.

MAP 5 **NOTTINGHAM –** Nottinghamshire

Geisha

3 The Broadway, Lace Market, Nottingham
NG1 1PR
Tel: (0115) 959 8344

| New Chef | Pan-Asian | £50 |

This lounge bar, located in the Lace Market district, has a style all of its own. In fine Japanese tradition the tables are adorned with flowers, the lighting is low and so is the seating. The Pan-Asian menu takes in everything from large sushi platters to a range of small sharing dishes, including three-way prawns, with the crustaceans in filo parcels, tempura and with prawn, alongside chicken skewers with spicy peanut sauce, and yellowtail sashimi with ginger vinaigrette. 'New style carpaccio' sees the likes of salmon with pickled fennel and chive dressing, or maybe sea scallops with truffle and ponzu. Larger dishes range from black cod with spicy miso, or tempura lobster with creamy curry sauce, to grilled rack of lamb with spinach, mushrooms and chilli soya beans. Wagyu beef, the traditional Japanese marbled meat, also appears pan-fried with oyster mushrooms. End with baked cheese fondant with passion-fruit sauce and papaya sorbet. The plentiful staff are helpful and informed. Saké is available from £2 a glass, while house wines start at £13.50, with eight choices by the glass from £3.50.

Chef: Jacque Ferreira **Proprietors:** Philip Duke and Ashley Walter **Open:** Tue to Sat D only 7 to 10 (6 to 11 Sat) **Closed:** 24 to 30 Dec, 1 to 5 Jan **Meals:** alc (main courses £13.50 to £19). Set D £15 to £45. Bar menu available **Service:** 10% (optional) **Cards:** Amex, Delta, Maestro, MasterCard, Visa **Details:** 50 seats. Vegetarian meals. No children under 16. No smoking. Music. No mobile phones. Air-conditioned

Hart's

1 Standard Court, Park Row, Nottingham
NG1 6GN
Tel: (0115) 911 0666
Website: www.hartsnottingham.co.uk

| Cooking 5 | Modern British | £49 |

A major refurbishment in January 2006 imported a distinctly more intimate and less 'canteeny' feel than this city-centre restaurant has enjoyed hitherto. People still appreciate the 'exemplary' service and the informal brasserie approach, and, best of all, Alan Gleeson's assured, exuberant cooking. An autumn luncher was mightily pleased with what he chose, which spanned the range from confit chicken and foie gras terrine, through pan-fried liver with crispy bacon, shallots and sage, to nougat glace with poached pineapple and passion fruit. There is a nice vein of lightly worn traditionalism running through the expansive menus, resulting in slow-braised belly pork with black pudding fritters and apple sauce, but modernists won't lack for cauliflower purée with their scallops, or saffron and vanilla mash with their sea bass. The sweet of tooth, meanwhile, can round things off with pecan tart and maple syrup or baked figs with honey and whisky ice cream. Wines are set out by style, making navigation and choice easier, and the prices are not at all greedy, given the evident quality of much of the list; prices start at £13.50 for a Chilean Chardonnay.

Chef: Alan Gleeson **Proprietor:** Tim Hart **Open:** all week 12 to 2, 7 to 10.30 (9 Sun) **Closed:** 26 Dec, 1 Jan **Meals:** alc (main courses £13.50 to £22.50). Set L Mon to Sat £12.95 (2 courses) to £15.95, Set L Sun £18, Set D Sun to Thur £21 **Service:** 12% (optional) **Cards:** Amex, Delta, Maestro, MasterCard, Visa **Details:** 80 seats. 20 seats outside. Car park (D only). Vegetarian meals. Children's helpings. No smoking. Wheelchair access (also WC). No music **Accommodation:** 32 rooms

Restaurant Sat Bains

Old Lenton Lane, Nottingham NG7 2SA
Tel: (0115) 986 6566
Website: www.restaurantsatbains.net

| Cooking 7 | Modern European | £62 |

A former farmhouse and outbuildings located on the south-western outskirts of the city (you'll need the sat-nav to find Sat Bains), this restaurant-with-rooms is certainly a distinctive operation. Dining goes on in a stone-floored room and conservatory, with white-gloved waiting staff on hand to explain the menus. They may need some explaining too, as it isn't immediately clear from the layout which are starters and which are mains, and then the descriptions themselves are so determined to intrigue. Try to get your head around Cornish turbot, salsify, Jabugo ham, white beans, fried bread, red wine, Mani olive oil, or perhaps Anjou pigeon, foie gras, turnip, melon, feta, mint, pink grapefruit jus.

At the top end, a tasting menu and a menu surprise allow you to abdicate choice and the kitchen to show its paces. An October version of the latter began with a superb dish of scallops on beetroot purée and rose to that pigeon and foie gras main course, in which the bird appeared with a skewer of its various offals. Otherwise, expect the likes of slow-cooked belly pork with prawns and Granny Smith, followed perhaps by Goosnargh duck with a potato terrine, white cabbage and red wine sauce.

Desserts hit the experimental button again for warm chocolate and polenta biscuit with ginger ice cream, olive cake with a poached peach and almond milk sorbet, or the mysterious banana, caramel, beer. A fine, well-annotated and enthusiastically cosmopolitan wine list accompanies. Wines are grouped by style, from 'Fresh' to 'Concentrated', and the choices – from Mont-Redon's Châteauneuf to pear-scented Arneis from Seghesio in California – are intelligent. A pity, then, that prices are so forbidding. They start at £24, or £5.25 a glass.

Chefs: Sat Bains and John Freeman **Proprietors:** Sat and Amanda Bains **Open:** Tue to Sat D only 7 to 9.30 **Closed:** 2 weeks Jan, 2 weeks summer **Meals:** Set D £40 to £85 **Service:** 12.5% (optional) **Cards:** Amex, Delta, Maestro, MasterCard, Visa **Details:** 38 seats. Car park. No smoking. Music. Air-conditioned **Accommodation:** 8 rooms

---

La Toque

61 Wollaton Road, Beeston, Nottingham
NG9 2NG
Tel: (0115) 922 2268
Website: www.latoqueonline.co.uk

Cooking 3 | **French** | **£35**

La Toque is a 'modest, somewhat cramped' but 'nice little restaurant' where chef Mattias Karlsson shows high ambition in his cooking. Raw materials are good and technique is finely honed, producing starters such as home-cured salmon terrine with Granny Smith apple, or Cornish crab risotto with sauce vierge. Main courses have featured roast Barbary duck with a confit of the leg served with root vegetable pavé and cider vinegar jus, or bouillabaisse, and to finish there might be brioche pain perdu with roast pineapple and pistachios, or vanilla crème brûlée. There's good choice under £20 on the wine list, where France tends to be strongest. House French is £12.

Chef: Mattias Karlsson **Proprietor:** Norman Oley **Open:** Tue to Sun L 11.30 to 2, Mon to Sat D 6 to 10 **Closed:** 26 Dec to 4 Jan, middle 2 weeks Aug **Meals:** alc (main courses £11 to £14). Set L £12.50 (2 courses) to £15.50, Set D £15.50 (2 courses) to £19.50 **Service:** not inc **Cards:** Amex, Delta, Diners, Maestro, MasterCard, Visa **Details:** 34 seats. Vegetarian meals. No children under 8. No smoking. Wheelchair access (also WC). Music. Air-conditioned

---

World Service

Newdigate House, Castle Gate, Nottingham
NG1 6AF
Tel: (0115) 847 5587
Website: www.worldservicerestaurant.com

Cooking 4 | **Modern British** | **£48**

Not a homage to a well-known radio station, the name refers to its Far Eastern ambience: behind the high front wall is a Japanese-style pebbled garden with a paved terrace and potted plants. Inside the building, which was once the Nottingham United Services Club, the bar/lounge is panelled, and there's a striking wood and marble fireplace. The furniture is just as smart, with comfortably upholstered chairs in the dining room, along with dark tables and Indonesian vases. The food is modern British in style, with some exciting combinations, and the kitchen pays good attention to detail. On the set-price lunch could be chicken and artichoke terrine, followed by grilled sea bream with stir-fried vegetables, while the carte might deliver baked local unpasteurised goats' cheese in a caper and raisin crust, followed by roast breast of chicken with oriental rice and an orange and soy dressing. Asian carrot milk pudding with pistachios is an interesting finish. The wine list is a 20-page affair with mostly French and New World bins. Eight come by the glass from £3.75, with bottles from £13.50.

Chefs: Chris Elson and Preston Walker **Proprietors:** Dan Lindsay, Ashley Walker, Chris Elson and Philip Morgan **Open:** all week 12 to 2.15 (2.30 Sun), 7 to 10 (9 Sun) **Closed:** 1 to 6 Jan **Meals:** alc (main courses £13.50 to £19.50). Set L £12 (2 courses) to £16.50 **Service:** 10% (optional) **Cards:** Amex, Delta, Maestro, MasterCard, Visa **Details:** 80 seats. 40 seats outside. Vegetarian meals. Children's helpings. No smoking. Music

---

MAP 5 | **OAKHAM – Rutland**

Lord Nelson's House Hotel, Nick's Restaurant

11 Market Place, Oakham LE15 6DT
Tel: (01572) 723199
Website: www.nelsons-house.com

Cooking 4 | **Anglo-French** | **£44**

Lord Nelson's House is a highly idiosyncratic small hotel, run by a husband-and-wife team, occupying

a medieval timber-framed building on Oakham's marketplace. Its stylishly characterful dining room is brightened up with flowers on bare wooden tables, and relaxed but attentive service helps to create a lively atmosphere. Nick Healey's cooking is as vibrant as the setting, a bright mix of traditional and contemporary ideas. Among starters might be breast of wood pigeon on caramelised onions and wild mushrooms with a port and game jus, and seared scallops with smoked salmon on warm blinis with crème fraîche. Main courses typically feature rack of lamb on pea purée with fondant potatoes and a redcurrant and rosemary sauce, and roast Gressingham duck on celeriac mash with figs and a sweet sherry sauce. Daily specials, mainly fish, extend the range even further. Lemon tart with raspberry coulis, and bread-and-butter pudding with custard are among classic desserts. Up to 20 wines are available by the glass from an interesting list of well-chosen bottles, with plenty under £20, along with a good number of more upmarket bottles in its fine wines section.

Chef: Nick Healey Proprietors: Nick and Amanda Healey Open: Tue to Sat 12 to 2.30, 7 to 9.30 Closed: 2 weeks Christmas, 2 weeks Aug Meals: alc (main courses L £8 to £21, D £14 to £22). Set L £20 (2 courses) to £25, Set D £30 (2 courses) to £35 Service: not inc Cards: Amex, Delta, Maestro, MasterCard, Visa Details: 46 seats. Car park. Vegetarian meals. Children's helpings. No smoking in dining room. Music. No mobile phones Accommodation: 4 rooms

MAP 2 OAKSEY – Wiltshire

Wheatsheaf

Wheatsheaf Lane, Oaksey SN16 9TB
Tel: (01666) 577348

Cooking 1 | Modern British | £39

There's a traditional look to this seventeenth-century grey-stone inn from the outside, but the interior is contrastingly modern, with cream walls, coir matting and spotlights. Assorted jars of preserves on display add a splash of colour. The short menu offers straightforward modern British cooking along the lines of smoked chicken, bacon and black pudding salad with a poached egg, and Cornish crab cake spiced up with chilli and coriander, followed by Barbary duck breast with red cabbage, Parmesan mash and port sauce, and Chinese-spiced bream fillet with sautéed potatoes and herb salad. Finish with a selection from the display of British and French cheeses, or a dessert

such as chocolate torte with pistachio ice cream. Prices on the short wine list start at £12.

Chef: Tony Robson-Burrell Proprietors: Tony and Holly Robson-Burrell Open: Tue to Sun L 12 to 2 (2.30 Sun), Tue to Sat D 6.30 to 9.30 Meals: alc (main courses L £5 to £15, D £8 to £15). Bar L menu available Service: not inc Cards: Delta, Maestro, MasterCard, Visa Details: 48 seats. 16 seats outside. Car park. Vegetarian meals. Children's helpings. No smoking in dining room. Wheelchair access (not WC). Occasional music

MAP 2 ODIHAM – Hampshire

Grapevine   AR

121 High Street, Odiham RG29 1LA
Tel: (01256) 701122

This buzzy bistro favours a distinct Italian/Mediterranean style in cheery and informal surroundings – terracotta and saffron walls, and wooden floors. This is back-to-basics cooking with a choice of set dinners and 'early bird' menus alongside the carte. Bruschetta of pan-fried wild mushrooms in garlic (£5.95), roast poussin with potatoes, Swiss chard and pan juices (£15.95), followed by marmalade sponge with a whiskey custard (£4.95) give a good overview. Wine from £11.95. Closed Sat L and Sun.

MAP 2 OLD BURGHCLERE – Hampshire

Dew Pond

Old Burghclere RG20 9LH
Tel: (01635) 278408
Website: www.dewpond.co.uk

Cooking 4 | Anglo-French | £41

The setting is a great plus, as Dew Pond sits on a narrow lane surrounded by miles of countryside, rising towards the North Downs. A local art dealer keeps the interiors abundantly supplied with the pick of regional talent, and the atmosphere is cool, relaxed and unstuffy. With meats hung to Keith Marshall's specifications and game supplied by a farm that's within sight across the fields, it's clear that this is a kitchen with its eye on the ball. Wine-tasting evenings bring in regulars on the last Thursday of every month, and the fixed-price dinner menus contain a wealth of choice. Thai-spiced mussels, vibrantly replete with chilli, ginger, coconut, coriander and lime, make a stimulating opener to a meal that might proceed to fish of the day, served with a scallop sausage, wilted greens and chive hollandaise, or saddle of local roe deer with crushed root vegetables and a rich reduction of port. Finish with apple and caramel pancakes with Calvados cream, or crème brûlée with seasonal fruits. Wine prices start at £13.50, with a dozen available by the glass from £4.

> Chef: Keith Marshall Proprietors: Keith and Julie Marshall Open: Tue to Sat D only 7 to 9.30 Closed: 2 weeks Christmas to New Year, 2 week early Aug Meals: Set D £28 Service: not inc Cards: Delta, Maestro, MasterCard, Visa Details: 50 seats. Car park. Children's helpings. No smoking. Wheelchair access (not WC). No music

---

MAP 5 OMBERSLEY – Worcestershire

Venture In

Ombersley WR9 0EW
Tel: (01905) 620552

Cooking 3 | **Modern British/French** | **£42**

It's the oldest building in the village, dating from the 1430s; with its half-timbering and distinctive black and yellow striped awning it's certainly not one to miss. Inside, the comfortable surroundings boast an inglenook, coral-coloured sofas, beams and slabs of exposed stone. The food is sometimes old-fashioned and can be complex, but chef/proprietor Toby Fletcher is a sound cook who takes a lot of trouble with his European-inspired cuisine. Start with braised lambs' tongues with mixed mushrooms in puff pastry, and move on to roast breast of guinea fowl accompanied by asparagus, creamed potato and a garlic and thyme sauce, or one of the daily fish specials: perhaps monkfish wrapped in Parma ham on Puy lentils with red wine sauce. Finish with three meringue discs layered with lemon curd and cream. Wines are a mixture of European and New World bottles, with a handful of house selections opening the list at £13.

> Chef/Proprietor: Toby Fletcher Open: Tue to Sun L 12 to 2, Tue to Sat D 7 to 9.45 Closed: 1 week Christmas, 2 weeks Feb, 2 weeks Aug Meals: Set L £17.95 (2 courses) to £21.50, Set D £31.50 Service: not inc Cards: Delta, Maestro, MasterCard, Visa Details: 32 seats. Car park. Vegetarian meals. No children under 12. No smoking in dining room. Music. Air-conditioned

---

MAP 3 ONGAR – Essex

Smith's `AR`

Fyfield Road, Ongar CM5 0AL
Tel: (01277) 365578

This long-running fish restaurant has a menu of classic dishes ranging from French-style fish soup with croûtons, saffron mayonnaise and Gruyère (£5.50) to Dover sole meunière (£21), baked salmon fillet with hollandaise (£13), and whole lobster thermidor (£23). More fashionable ideas include pan-fried sardines with salsa verde (£6.50), and non-fish options feature roast Barbary duck breast with plum sauce (£16.50). To finish, try sticky date and ginger pudding with custard (£5.75). Five house wines are £13 and £13.50. Closed Mon.

MAP 6 ORFORD – Suffolk

Butley-Orford Oysterage `AR`

Market Hill, Orford IP12 2LH
Tel: (01394) 450277

They have grown oysters at Butley Creek since 1950 and this well-known fish restaurant also has its own smokehouse and fishing boats. Go for oyster soup (£4.50) or prawns in garlic oil (£6.80) to start, followed by Butley oysters (£13 for a dozen), or smoked wild Irish salmon (£9.80). Simple main dishes include griddled prawns (£7.90) or sardines (£5.90), and look out for blackboard specials, too. End with lemon syllabub (£3.90). A wide range of wines starts from £12.75. Open all week (exc Sun to Thur D, 31 Oct to 30 March).

Crown and Castle, Trinity

Orford IP12 2LJ
Tel: (01394) 450205
Website: www.crownandcastle.co.uk

Cooking 4 | **Modern British-Plus** | **£42**

With its high-beamed ceiling, polished wooden floors and tables, and large windows letting in plenty of light, the dining room of this Victorian hotel is a bright, airy place. It's all very easy on the eye. An unhurried atmosphere and flexible menus create an unpretentious bistro feel, attracting a crowd for good-value light lunches – dishes like moules marinière, steak frites, or goats' cheese and parsley tortellini – and the evening carte. The kitchen weaves local materials into an ever-changing repertoire, delivering dishes that are simple, fresh and uncluttered, as starters like carpaccio, or home-potted brown shrimps reveal. While warm niçoise-style salad appears as an accompaniment to seared sea bass fillet, and local pheasant is served with red cabbage and celeriac purée, when it comes to dessert a hot bitter chocolate mousse is paired with nothing more than Jersey cream, and rhubarb crumble with 'proper' custard. A reasonably priced, interesting wine list canters across the globe, with house wines from South Africa (white) and Argentina (red) at £13.95 and £14.50 respectively.

Chefs: Ruth Watson and Max Dougal Proprietors: David and Ruth Watson Open: all week 12 to 2.15, 6.45 to 9.30 (10 Sat) Closed: 19 to 21 Dec Meals: alc exc Sat and bank hol D (main courses L £9.50 to £15, D £14 to £19.50). Set L £16.50 to £19.50 (2 courses), Set D Sat and bank hols £35 Service: not inc Cards: Maestro, MasterCard, Visa Details: 50 seats. Car park. Vegetarian meals. No children under 9 at D. Children's helpings. No smoking. Wheelchair access (also WC). No music. No mobile phones Accommodation: 18 rooms

MAP 7 **OSWESTRY** – Shropshire

Sebastians

45 Willow Street, Oswestry SY11 1AQ
Tel: (01691) 655444
Website: www.sebastians-hotel.co.uk

Cooking 3 | French | £46

This sixteenth-century building is bursting with character, from the blue and white exterior, through to the busy dining room with its preponderance of old oak (panels, beams and floorboards). Mark's (aka Sebastian) cooking is resolutely French, and although reports suggest it tends to richness, his technical skills are considerable. There are two menus, an excellent-value no-choice 'menu du marché', which changes weekly, and the monthly changing five-course carte. An inspection meal got off to a good start with a well-balanced potage Crécy (cream of carrot and coriander, with both flavours distinct), and continued with a smoked salmon and sweetcorn terrine. An intermediary Pimm's jelly with lemonade sorbet preceded a main course of first-rate beef fillet, the

meat well-hung and accurately cooked, served with asparagus wrapped in pancetta and an intense Madeira jus. To finish, exemplary home-made ice creams are served in a brandy-snap basket with a light strawberry coulis. The good-value, predominately French wine list is arranged by style but there are some interesting Italian and New World choices, with house French opening the list at £13.50.

Chef: Mark Sebastian Fisher Proprietors: Mark Sebastian and Michelle Fisher Open: Tue to Sat D only 6.30 to 9.30 Meals: Set D £32, Set D Tue to Fri £16.95 Service: not inc Cards: Amex, Delta, Maestro, MasterCard, Visa Details: 35 seats. 20 seats outside. Car park. Vegetarian meals. Children's helpings. No smoking. Wheelchair access (not WC). Music. No mobile phones Accommodation: 7 rooms

MAP 6 **OVINGTON** – Norfolk

Brovey Lair

Carbrooke Road, Ovington IP25 6SD
Tel: (01953) 882706
Website: www.broveylair.com

Cooking 5 | Fusion | £56

Here is a thoroughly singular dining experience in the Norfolk hinterland. Brovey Lair is the Pembertons' home, which they run as a 'café' in the evenings, with a pair of guest rooms thrown in for those who don't fancy the journey home. Dinner is a single sitting, at 7.45, and the four-course menu is whatever Tina has decided to cook that day. A May evening opened with crab cakes, vividly seasoned with chilli, mint and coriander, teamed with stir-fried sesame prawns, as a prelude to a bowl of butternut squash soup with toasted almonds and pumpkin seed oil. Fish is the consistent preference for main course (although meat eaters can be accommodated on request), so prepare for Indian-spiced baked halibut on saffron and cardamom rice, accompanied by roast local asparagus. Dessert might offer a choice of two; then again, it might not. Wheat-free almond cake with strawberries, raspberries and crème fraîche is a possibility, or just relax into the simplicity of French apricots in sweet Muscat with biscotti. A concise wine card has a plethora of Sauvignon and Chardonnay on one side and a gathering of soft, fruity reds on the other. Prices open at £15.95 and come to a gentle halt with Ch. Palmer 1979 at a little under £90.

Chef: Tina Pemberton **Proprietors:** Mike and Tina Pemberton **Open:** all week D only 7.45 (1 sitting). L by arrangement **Closed:** 25 Dec **Meals:** Set D £42.50 **Service:** 10% **Cards:** Amex, Maestro, MasterCard, Visa **Details:** 20 seats. 10 seats outside. Car park. Vegetarian meals. No children under 16. No smoking. Wheelchair access (not WC). Music. Air-conditioned **Accommodation:** 2 rooms

MAP 2   **OXFORD – Oxfordshire**

Al-Shami   AR

25 Walton Crescent, Oxford OX1 2JG
Tel: (01865) 310066

Light and airy Lebanese restaurant offering a convivial atmosphere, lots of white linen and friendly staff. A long list of hot and cold meze (from £1.80 to £4 per item) takes in the likes of tabbouleh, fried broad beans, lamb's brain salad, grilled chicken wings with garlic sauce, fried whitebait and standard favourites such as hummus and falafel. Skewers from the grill (from £6.40) include lamb cubes with onion and garlic or marinated chicken. End with Arabic ice cream (£3). Wines from £11.99. Open all week.

Branca

111 Walton Street, Oxford OX2 6AJ
Tel: (01865) 556111
Website: www.branca-restaurants.com

Cooking 1 | Modern Italian | £39

Good-value lunches and early-supper deals pull in the crowds to this long, light and airy restaurant, where a high glass ceiling, chandeliers and huge wire sculptures add a sense of drama. Modern Italian fare is what's on offer: get things started with smoked chicken and borlotti bean soup, say, or fried calamari with lemon and chilli dressing. Main courses might be king scallop risotto, butternut squash and ricotta ravioli, or roast duck breast with braised lentils. End with rich chocolate torta with pistachio ice cream, or panettone bread-and-butter pudding with apple. The Italian wine list is brief but good value, from £12.25, and all bottles are also served by the glass and 500ml pot.

Chef: Michael MacQuire **Proprietor:** Paul Petrillo **Open:** all week 12 to 11 **Closed:** 24 and 25 Dec **Meals:** alc (main courses £9 to £17). Set L Mon to Fri 12 to 5 £5.95 (1 course, inc wine), Set D Mon to Fri 5 to 7 £10 (2 courses, inc wine) **Service:** not inc **Cards:** Amex, Delta, Diners, Maestro, MasterCard, Visa **Details:** 125 seats. Vegetarian meals. Children's helpings. No smoking at L. No-smoking area. Wheelchair access (also WC). Music. No mobile phones. Air-conditioned

Brasserie Blanc   AR

71–72 Walton Street, Oxford OX2 6AG
Tel: (01865) 510999

The original of Raymond Blanc's group of family-friendly provincial brasseries (formerly known as Le Petit Blanc). The lively, relaxed atmosphere and flexible attitude is a winning format, especially for families. There's a prix-fixe menu at £12 for two courses, a children's menu (£5.95 for 2 courses), and a carte which runs from Thai coconut and lime soup (£4.50) to pappardelle with prawns and chilli (£6.50/£12.50). Finish with pavlova of summer berries and vanilla ice cream (£5.50). Open all week. Branches in Birmingham, Cheltenham, Manchester and Tunbridge Wells (see entries).

Cherwell Boathouse

50 Bardwell Road, Oxford OX2 6ST
Tel: (01865) 552746
Website: www.cherwellboathouse.co.uk

Cooking 1 | Modern English/French | £34

'Simple and unpretentious' was the comment made by a reporter of this bare-boarded bistro-style restaurant. Al fresco dining on the terrace is an added summer attraction – as is the hiring of punts from the boatyard – while the menu offers a mixed bag of Anglo-French ideas. It is not difficult to appreciate the appeal of a well-made terrine of foie gras and Gloucester Old Spot belly pork served with herb salad and apple purée, or a main course of braised ham hock with white-bean casserole, glazed spring carrots and a creamy whole grain mustard sauce, while desserts might feature a banana bavarois with banana ice cream. Service is pleasant and informal. Proprietor Anthony Verdin's background at Morris and Verdin ensures that wines are taken seriously here. The list is arranged according to the major French wine regions with the addition of New World wines of similar character. House wines – all 20 of them – are priced from £11.50 to £25.

Chef: Carson Hill **Proprietors:** the Verdin family **Open:** all week 12 to 2 (2.30 Sat and Sun), 6.30 to 10 **Closed:** 25 to 30 Dec **Meals:** Set L Mon to Fri £12.50 (2 courses) to £21.50, Set L Sat and Sun £21.50, Set D Sun to Wed 6 to 8 £12.95 (2 courses) to £24, Set D Thur to Sat £24 **Service:** not inc **Cards:** Amex, Delta, Maestro, MasterCard, Visa **Details:** 70 seats. 45 seats outside. Car park. Vegetarian meals. Children's helpings. No smoking. Wheelchair access (also WC). No music

Chiang Mai Kitchen

130A High Street, Oxford OX1 4DH
Tel: (01865) 202233

| Cooking 1 | Thai | £39 |

A convivial atmosphere pervades this popular city-centre restaurant, which occupies a beautiful old half-timbered building down a 'Dickensian' alley off the High Street. There are few surprises on the long menu, but straightforward Thai dishes are competently cooked using good-quality ingredients, particularly seafood such as plaa nueng giem buey (succulent steamed trout with tangy, salty preserved plums), and tom yam poh thek (hot-and-sour seafood soup with plump, juicy prawns and mussels) served in a large earthenware pot for two to share. To finish, authentic Thai desserts include steamed sticky rice with cashew nuts and banana. At lunchtime, a short list of meal-in-one rice and noodle dishes supplements the menu. House wines are £12.50.

> **Proprietor** J. & L. Catering Ltd **Open:** all week 12 to 2.30, 6 to 10.30 **Closed:** Christmas, New Year, Easter **Meals:** alc (main courses £7.50 to £12.50) **Service:** not inc **Cards:** Amex, Delta, Maestro, MasterCard, Visa **Details:** 65 seats. Vegetarian meals. No smoking. Wheelchair access (also WC). No music. Air-conditioned

Edamame [AR]

15 Holywell Street, Oxford OX1 3SA
Tel: (01865) 246916

Bustling, informal café named after the popular Japanese snack (green soy beans eaten straight from the pod). The short lunchtime menu majors in stir-fries and noodle dishes (£6 to £8), while the extended evening menu covers everything from deep-fried chicken katsu with a fruity dipping sauce (£6) to pan-fried salmon in butter and Japanese seasoning (£7). Thursday evening is when the sushi menu comes into play, with assorted sushi and sashimi priced by the piece (from £2.50) or by the set (from £6). Drink warm saké by the flask (small £3, large £5), chilled Japanese beer, or house wines (£9). Open Tue to Sun L and Thur to Sat D.

Fishers [AR]

36–37 St Clements Street, Oxford OX4 1AB
Tel: (01865) 243003

There's a welcoming informality here, and the broad nautical touches – yacht sails on the ceiling and a ship's funnel – prove that this seafood restaurant doesn't take itself too seriously. Bouillabaisse with rouille (£5.95) makes a traditional starter, contrasting with something like tempura king prawns with honey and mustard mayonnaise (£6.95). Main courses vary from 'succulent' lemon sole with chilli and coriander butter (£16.50), or kedgeree (£9.95), to plainly baked plaice with parsley butter (£12.50), while sticky toffee pudding (£4.95) is there for those with a sweet tooth. Wines from £10.95. Closed Mon L.

Gee's

61 Banbury Road, Oxford OX2 6PE
Tel: (01865) 553540
Website: www.gees-restaurant.co.uk

| Cooking 2 | Modern British | £48 |

This is very much a 'contemporary' establishment and offers an experience that extends beyond dining. The building itself is an old floristry, and there is plenty of light and space inside. Beyond that, owner Jeremy Mogford has filled the evenings with jazz, the walls with artwork of British painter, Gary Hume, and is prone to describe his waiting staff as 'poets, philosophers and artists'. He also keeps a keen eye on the food. The fish is from his brother, Louis Jackson, in Jersey and you'll often find Gloucestershire pork, Wiltshire bacon and Oxford blue cheese on the menu. Start with seared king scallops followed by confit Aylesbury duck with an orange, fennel and hazelnut salad. Steamed Seville orange marmalade sponge pudding is a typical finish. The wine list offers 60 bins, with 10 by the glass. House choices start at £13.90 for a South African Geo Kinross.

> **Chef:** Michael Wright **Proprietor:** Jeremy Mogford **Open:** Mon to Fri 12 to 2.30, 6.30 to 11.30; Sat 12 to 11.30; Sun 12 to 10.30 **Closed:** 27 and 28 Dec **Meals:** alc (main courses L £10 to £20, D £14 to £20). Set L (exc Sun) £12.95 (2 courses) to £14.95, Set D £22 **Service:** not inc **Cards:** Amex, Delta, Maestro, MasterCard, Visa **Details:** 80 seats. 40 seats outside. Vegetarian meals. Children's helpings. Smoking in bar only. Wheelchair access (also WC). Music. Air-conditioned

Lemon Tree

268 Woodstock Road, Oxford OX2 7NW
Tel: (01865) 311936
Website: www.thelemontreeoxford.co.uk

| Cooking 3 | Mediterranean | £43 |

Mediterranean influences are everywhere thanks to larger-than-life pot plants, enormous gold-framed mirrors and cosy woven chairs. Service is also bright and breezy, matching the buzz when the room is full. Old favourites appear prominently on the well-thought-out menu, including local free-range pork belly with honey-glazed parsnips and apple relish, and steamed Shetland mussels; newer additions might see a steak teriyaki salad for starters, served with a ginger, mirin and soy sauce, while main courses include crispy duck leg with pak choi, red pepper and mangetout, or perhaps whole roasted gilthead bream stuffed with lemon and herbs. Half a dozen dessert choices feature apple tart Tatin with Calvados cream or roasted pineapple and black pepper cooked in Cointreau. The wine list starts at £10.50 for their Australian house.

Chef: Dido Medwin **Proprietor:** Clinton Pugh **Open:** Thur to Sun 12 to 5, all week D 6 to 11 **Closed:** 24 to 27 Dec **Meals:** alc (main courses £9 to £18). Set L £10 (2 courses) **Service:** 12.5% (optional) **Cards:** Amex, Delta, Maestro, MasterCard, Visa **Details:** 90 seats. 40 seats outside. Car park. Vegetarian meals. Children's helpings. Smoking in bar only. Wheelchair access (also WC). Music

Liaison

29 Castle Street, Oxford OX1 1LJ
Tel: (01865) 242944

| Cooking 1 | Chinese | £31 |

Close to County Hall, this Tudor building houses an intimate dining room, and is the setting for an extensive menu that tours the regions and delves into South-east Asia. They offer a takeaway menu, too, which is only a taster of the à la carte. Soup could be anything from won-ton to rainbow bean curd, while appetisers include satay chicken, baked fresh crab and crispy aromatic lamb. Seafood is big here, so go for oyster omelette with chive, or a trio of seafood with green pepper in a black bean sauce. 'Home-made' dishes include five-spice braised beef claypot and pan-fried aubergine with minced prawns. Rice and noodles are also well

represented. The global wine list is short and opens at £9.95.

Chef: Charles Tsang **Proprietor:** Y.K. Tsang **Open:** all week 12 to 3, 6.30 to 11.30 **Meals:** alc (main courses £7 to £20). Set D £15.95 to £19.60 **Service:** 10% (optional) **Cards:** Delta, Maestro, MasterCard, Visa **Details:** 70 seats. No smoking in 1 dining room. Wheelchair access (not WC). Music. Air-conditioned

Sojo Restaurant AR

6–9 Hythe Bridge Street, Oxford OX1 2EW
Tel: (01865) 202888

Shanghai and Szechuan dishes are the specialities of this city-centre restaurant, although Japanese and Thai interlopers also appear on the extensive menu. Lunchtime dim sum are popular, while main courses range from aromatic duck salad (£7) and chilli seafood (£7.50) to king prawns stir-fried in salted duck yolk (£7.50) and teriyaki salmon bento served with miso soup, salad and jasmine rice (£9). Other highlights include a Chinese-style fondue for groups to share, and a Mongolian grill, where you select a choice of ingredients, add sauces and spices and watch the lot being sizzled in a wok by the chef. Wines from £11. Open all week.

MAP 8   OXTON – Merseyside

Fraiche

11 Rose Mount, Oxton CH43 5SG
Tel: (0151) 652 2914
Website: www.restaurantfraiche.com

| Cooking 6 | Modern French | £51 |

In a picturesque conservation village on the fringes of Birkenhead, Marc Wilkinson's stylish restaurant has fairly turned local heads. 'In my opinion, the chef didn't hit *any* wrong notes at all,' reported a reader on behalf of his party of four, who diligently tested the range. The cooking plies a modern French line, drawing on nearby suppliers as well as markets across the Channel for such items as organic asparagus, langoustines and ven-trêche bacon. Those last two ingredients might well crop up alongside each other in a boudin served with Japanese-style shiso salad, giving an indication of the catholicity of the repertoire.

Good reports have come in for smoked haddock soup, and torchon of foie gras with pain d'épice and a compote of pear and Szechuan pepper among first courses. Mains might strike out in inventive directions, offering loin of venison with parsnips two ways, cocoa jelly and truffle jus, or content themselves with a classic and satisfying pairing of sea bream and mussels. A selection of five cheeses is the savoury finishing alternative to three desserts, which have included a fine hazelnut pannacotta with cherry foam. Service has been unsure on whether to address tables as 'ladies and gentlemen' or 'mesdames et messieurs', but that somehow adds to the charm. An exciting wine list offers much to ponder, with highlighted selections from Domaine Drouhin-Larose in Burgundy and Ian Hollick in Coonawarra, South Australia. Good listings of sherry, half-bottles and rosés flesh out a thoroughly sound international spread. House wines from France and Australia start at £17, or £4.50 a glass.

Chef/Proprietor: Marc Wilkinson   Open: Fri and Sat L 12 to 1.30, Tue to Sat D 7 to 9.30   Closed: 25 Dec, 1 to 8 Jan   Meals: Set L £21 to £35, Set D £26 (2 courses) to £45 (whole table only)   Service: not inc   Cards: Delta, Maestro, MasterCard, Visa   Details: 20 seats. Vegetarian meals. No smoking. Wheelchair access (also women's WC). Music. No mobile phones

---

MAP 1   PADSTOW – Cornwall

No. 6

NEW ENTRY

6 Middle Street, Padstow
PL28 8AP
Tel: (01841) 532093
Website: www.number6inpadstow.co.uk

CORNWALL OF THE YEAR RESTAURANT

Cooking 6 | Modern European | £52

Culinary pilgrims who have done Bray and Ludlow on the journey west will eventually end at Padstow, where the thriving restaurant scene still owes much to the genius of Rick Stein. It must have seemed an obvious destination anyway to Paul Ainsworth and partners when they decided to pitch camp here in the autumn of 2005. The setting is a Georgian town house, still in the process of a lengthy period of conversion at the time of writing. It's all light and airy, minimal but elegant, with clean white walls, dark wooden furniture and modern pictures. By the time you read this, a downstairs expansion should have taken place and there will be a lounge for aperitifs among other things.

Paul Ainsworth worked previously at Pétrus (see entry, London), which should set the pulse racing, and indeed the cooking here has started as it means to go on. Outstanding canapés (including aubergine caviar on hemp-seed toast) and home-made breads indicate the attention to detail. Dishes are beautifully presented and offer contrasting textures and well-balanced flavours. Smoked chicken risotto is perfectly cooked, its crowning poached egg spilling forth the deep-yellow yolk of a free-range specimen; creamed corn and shaved Parmesan complete the satisfaction. Duck roulade makes a change from the usual terrine, a central piece of breast meat surrounded by shredded confit wrapped in Parma ham, the flavours pointed up with support from marinated beetroot, seared orange segments, watercress and endive.

This being Padstow, the fish can be relied on: Whitsand Bay sea bream, perhaps, with fennel boulangère and a purée of capers and raisins. At inspection, a main course of pork cheek and belly, voguishly served with seafood (tiny squid) as well as diced chorizo and feta, produced meat of staggering quality, gently counterpointed with a well-made agrodolce sauce. After a palate-cleanser, it's on to desserts. A generous assiette of everything, served for two, might bring forth brightly flavoured lemon doughnuts, butterscotch and pecan ice cream, and caramelised banana with a salted caramel espuma among its tantalising array. When you add in knowledgeable and personable service, it all bids fair to become yet another bright adornment to the North Cornwall scene. Good cocktails front up a concise, modern wine list that opens at £15. Prices are mostly manageable, even for the 'cellar' selections, and there is a catholicity of approach that makes as much room for fine South Africans and New Zealanders as for the great and the good of France.

Chef: Paul Ainsworth   Proprietor: No. 6 (Padstow) Ltd   Open: all week 12 to 2.30, 6.30 to 10   Closed: Jan, 25 and 26 Dec, Mon and Tue Oct to Apr   Meals: alc (main courses L £5 to £11, D £13 to £20). Set L £25, Set D £55   Service: 10% (optional)   Cards: Delta, Maestro, MasterCard, Visa   Details: 60 seats. Vegetarian meals. Children's helpings. No smoking. Wheelchair access (not WC). Music

Rick Stein's Café

10 Middle Street, Padstow PL28 8BQ
Tel: (01841) 532700
Website: www.rickstein.com

Cooking 2 | Seafood | £42

Rick Stein's name ensures there are always plenty of willing diners at this bright and breezy bistro. Situated just a stone's throw away from the quay, the contemporary setting is still pleasant even without the sea views and it's popular with families

(their excellent fish fingers and chips are a favourite). The simple menu is a predominately fishy affair, although there are meat options. Salt and pepper prawns, or mussels with chilli, vie for attention with charcuterie of Serrano ham to start. Mains might be goujons of plaice, chargrilled gurnard or perhaps chicken piri-piri. Finish with pecan tart or Colston Bassett Stilton. Breakfast is available too. The nifty wine list starts with a £22.50 Côtes du Rhône.

Chefs: David Sharland and Paul Harwood **Proprietors:** Rick and Jill Stein **Open:** all week 12 to 3, 7 to 9.30 **Closed:** 24 to 26 Dec, 1 May, D Sun and Mon Nov to Mar **Meals:** alc (main courses £9 to £16). Set D £19.95 **Service:** not inc **Cards:** Delta, Maestro, MasterCard, Visa **Details:** 40 seats. 10 seats outside. Vegetarian meals. Children's helpings. No smoking. Wheelchair access (not WC). Occasional music **Accommodation:** 3 rooms

St Petroc's Bistro

4 New Street, Padstow PL28 8EA
Tel: (01841) 532700
Website: www.rickstein.com

| Cooking 2 | Bistro | £49 |

An early addition to Rick Stein's now bulging portfolio of Padstow ventures, this white-painted hotel just up from the harbour was initially set up as the budget alternative to the Seafood Restaurant (see entry below). It's light and breezy, with lots of wood and colourful modern paintings by local artists, and it continues to offer relatively straight-forward dishes like poached fillet of mackerel with sherry vinegar and mint butter sauce, and main courses of fillet of sea bass with roast fennel and tomato. Outside seafood, the menu might offer hot Toulouse sausage with a tomato, caper and shallot salad, followed by osso buco, while to finish there could be chocolate mousse or Paris-Brest. Staff are friendly, delivering service that's smooth without being stuffy, and a short wine list, concentrating on Europe and the southern hemisphere, starts at £14.50, with a dozen by the glass from £3.55.

Chefs: David Sharland and Alistair Clive **Proprietors:** Rick and Jill Stein **Open:** all week 12 to 2, 7 (6.30 school hols) to 10 **Closed:** 24 to 26 Dec, May Day **Meals:** alc (main courses £14 to £18) **Service:** not inc **Cards:** Delta, Maestro, MasterCard, Visa **Details:** 55 seats. 20 seats outside. Children's helpings. No smoking. Wheelchair access (also WC). Music. Air-conditioned **Accommodation:** 10 rooms

Seafood Restaurant

Riverside, Padstow PL28 8BY
Tel: (01841) 532700
Website: www.rickstein.com

| Cooking 5 | Seafood | £71 |

The big, white double room on the Padstow quay-side benefits from bold, statement-making modern paintings and admirably slick service. It's the place, as if you needed reminding, that put this charm-laden Cornish fishing village on the map, and made its proprietor a star. Fish and shellfish of exemplary freshness are still the main draw, with simpler dishes showing up best. Seared red mullet might begin, with chargrilled Dover sole seasoned with sea salt and lime to follow, or perhaps a classic fish pie with cod, smoked haddock and minty peas.

Considering the fish supplies are practically on the doorstep, prices are certainly energetic. Turbot with hollandaise is £38.50, but comes with just three boiled potatoes and a 'surprisingly bland' sauce. Indian, Spanish, Singaporean and French recipes create a feeling of The World At Once about the menu, with the spicing of the masala sauce accompanying cockles and mussels on the hot side at inspection. A tiny poached pear in reduced red wine syrup makes a tasty finisher, or there might be pannacotta with stewed rhubarb. Wines are a global selection chosen to match the seafood, opening with French Sauvignon Blanc at £18.50.

Chefs: David Sharland and Stéphane Delourme **Proprietors:** Rick and Jill Stein **Open:** all week 12 to 2 (2.30 July and Aug), 7 to 10 **Closed:** 24 to 26 Dec, 1 May **Meals:** alc (main courses £17.50 to £45). Set L and D £65 **Service:** not inc **Cards:** Delta, Maestro, MasterCard, Visa **Details:** 110 seats. Children's helpings; no children under 3. Wheelchair access (not WC). No music. Air-conditioned **Accommodation:** 14 rooms

MAP 5   **PAULERSPURY –**
Northamptonshire

Vine House

100 High Street, Paulerspury NN12 7NA
Tel: (01327) 811267
Website: www.vinehousehotel.com

| Cooking 3 | Modern British | £44 |

Julie and Marcus Springett run this restaurant-with-rooms with a homely charm out front (Julie), and an inspired efficiency in the kitchen (Marcus). Everything is in the detail – noting what type of potato has the best flavour at what time of year – and bread gets top marks. The menu is compact with only three options per course, and the dishes are cooked with conviction. Warm smoked organic Orkney salmon with roasted black pudding and curry oil garnered high praise at inspection, particularly for the salmon, which had been minimally smoked to preserve the delicate flavour. A main-course confit Goosnargh duck with truffle sauce came with a 'super-silky, super-flavourful' potato mash topped with fresh chives, while the meal ended with a home-made saffron and double-cream sorbet topped with carrot and orange wafers in which the flavours complemented each other perfectly. There are just over 70 wines from across the globe, although Bordeaux and Burgundy get a starring role. Four house choices start at £13.95.

Chef: Marcus Springett Proprietors: Marcus and Julie Springett Open: Tue to Sat L 12 to 2, all week D 6.30 to 10 Meals: Set L and D £26.95 (2 courses) to £29.95 Service: 12.5% Cards: Delta, Maestro, MasterCard, Visa Details: 33 seats. 8 seats outside. Car park. Children's helpings. No smoking. Wheelchair access (not WC). No music Accommodation: 6 rooms

MAP 5   PAXFORD – Gloucestershire

Churchill Arms

Paxford GL55 6XH
Tel: (01386) 594000
Website: www.thechurchillarms.com

Cooking 4 | Modern European | £34

This is a tip-top Cotswold setting, just the thing to show off England's heritage: a hamlet of old honey-coloured stone and dry-stone walls. And the Churchill, at the centre, near the church, is as you might expect: simple décor with old floorboards, a low, nicotine-coloured ceiling and walls covered with prints. A glance at the blackboard menu shows a kitchen striving for a degree of local and seasonal input – chicken livers come with spiced butternut purée, roast balsamic onions and pomegranate dressing – but it is the sensible modernist approach that strikes most forcibly. This is down-to-earth cooking, taking in pork and veal terrine, cod fillet with white risotto and roast red peppers, a 'beautifully done and hugely tasty' braised blade of beef en crépinette with mushrooms and thyme, and calf's liver with bacon, shal-

lots and red wine. To follow, choose soft almond meringue with baked figs, or perhaps triple chocolate torte. The short wine list takes a brisk trot around the world, staying mostly below £20, with eight available by the glass from £3 to £5.50.

Chefs: Sonya Brooke-Little and David Toon Proprietors: Sonya and Leo Brooke-Little Open: all week 12 to 2, 7 to 9 Meals: alc (main courses L £8 to £16, D £10.50 to £16) Service: not inc Cards: Delta, Maestro, MasterCard, Visa Details: 60 seats. 40 seats outside. Children's helpings. No-smoking area. Wheelchair access (not WC). No music Accommodation: 4 rooms

MAP 1   PENZANCE – Cornwall

Abbey Restaurant

Abbey Street, Penzance TR18 4AR
Tel: (01736) 330680
Website: www.theabbeyonline.com

Cooking 4 | Modern European | £48

In early 2006 Ben and Kinga Tunnicliffe bought this small restaurant that they have run for the past five years. Not that this is likely to herald any major changes to the operation – after all, if it ain't broke… The downstairs bar retains its striking red colour scheme, while the dining room is decorated in soft, calming colours, creating a peaceful atmosphere. Ben's cooking continues in an eclectic style that has its heart somewhere in southern France but shows wider influences. Among starters, old-fashioned ideas such as twice-baked cheese soufflé are brought up to date with accompaniments of pickled red onions and spiced pears, while main courses range from whole grilled lemon sole with olive oil mash, purple-sprouting broccoli and hollandaise to grilled calf's liver with roast beetroot and cep ravioli. Everything is made in-house, from bread and chutneys through to marmalade and the vanilla ice cream accompanying a dessert of steamed quince and Seville orange pudding. The short, functional wine list includes a Cornish sparkling wine (Camel Valley 2003 at £26 a bottle or £5.95 a glass). House French vins de pays are £14.50.

Chef: Ben Tunnicliffe Proprietors: Ben and Kinga Tunnicliffe Open: Fri to Sun L 12 to 1.30, Tue to Sat D 7 to 9.30 Closed: Tue D Oct to May, Wed D Nov to Feb, Jan Meals: alc D (main courses £16 to £22). Set L £18 (2 courses) to £23 Service: not inc Cards: Amex, MasterCard, Visa Details: 26 seats. Children's helpings. No smoking in dining room. Music. No mobile phones. Air-conditioned

Harris's

46 New Street, Penzance TR18 2LZ
Tel: (01736) 364408
Website: www.harrissrestaurant.co.uk

| Cooking 2 | Anglo-French | £51 |

After 35 years, Roger and Anne Harris have their customers pretty well weighed up, serving a good-value light lunch alongside a generous carte in their centrally located restaurant. Neither old wave nor new, the style is simple, utilising mainly Cornish produce. The kitchen has turned out good crab florentine and hot garlic prawns among starters, and main courses of pan-fried Gressingham duck breast on red cabbage with apple purée and Calvados jus, and grilled Dover sole with chive butter. Desserts might include apple strudel and crème brûlée. From the 40-plus wines listed by country, it should not be hard to find a good match. House wines are £13.50 to £14.95.

Chef: Roger Harris **Proprietors:** Roger and Anne Harris **Open:** Tue to Sat L 12 to 2, Mon to Sat D 7 to 9.30 **Closed:** Mon in winter, 25 and 26 Dec, 1 Jan **Meals:** alc (main courses L £7.50 to £15, D £17 to £25.50) **Service:** 10% **Cards:** Amex, MasterCard, Visa **Details:** 20 seats. No smoking in 1 dining room. Music

Mount Prospect Hotel, Bay Restaurant

Britons Hill, Penzance TR18 3AE
Tel: (01736) 366890
Website: www.bay-penzance.co.uk

| Cooking 3 | Modern British | £42 |

Panoramic views of Mount's Bay add to the appeal of this smart hotel dining room, along with dark wooden floors, marble-topped tables and comfortable wicker chairs. The room doubles as a gallery, and its walls are covered with paintings, while chef Ben Reeve produces his own works of art on the plate, straight from the modern British school. Pan-fried fillets of red mullet and scallops with yellow pepper purée and a fennel dressing is a typically lively and inventive starter, or there might be a rustic terrine with pickled pear salad in a blueberry dressing. Main courses range from grilled fillets of John Dory with a compote of tomatoes and roast red pepper and smoked salmon-flavoured sauce vierge to pan-fried fillet of local beef with truffled crushed potatoes and tarragon hollandaise, and to finish Cornish farmhouse cheeses are an

alternative to desserts such as peach and white wine soup with minted crème fraîche. A short but varied wine list opens with house selections at £13.75.

Chefs: Ben Reeve and Katie Semmens **Proprietors:** Stephen and Yvonne Hill **Open:** Wed to Sun L 11.30 to 1.30, all week D 6.15 to 9 **Closed:** L Oct to Mar **Meals:** alc (main courses £13 to £18) **Service:** not inc **Cards:** Amex (2.5% surcharge), Delta, Maestro, MasterCard, Visa **Details:** 60 seats. 10 seats outside. Car park. Vegetarian meals. Children's helpings. No smoking. Wheelchair access (not WC). Music. No mobile phones. Air-conditioned **Accommodation:** 24 rooms

Summer House

Cornwall Terrace, Penzance TR18 4HL
Tel: (01736) 363744
Website: www.summerhouse-cornwall.com

| Cooking 2 | Mediterranean | £41 |

Tucked away in a narrow lane close to the seafront, the cobalt-blue exterior of this family-run restaurant-with-rooms speaks of sunnier climes, and this is reflected inside, too, where bright colours combine with *trompe l'oeil*, crumbling antique pediments, plaster and gilt frames, and lots of lush plants. The cooking style is rustic rather than refined and very Italian. Ciro Zaino knows that some of the traditional elements of his native cuisine are often the best cornerstones, as can be seen in a starter of linguine with pesto and a main course of baccala livornese (cod with tomatoes, black olives, capers, basil and garlic). The kitchen can also deliver fillet of beef with white wine and rosemary sauce, and rack of lamb with a crust of mustard and aromatic herbs – considered something of a house speciality. To finish, go for warm apple tart with crème Chantilly, or something more exotic like lavender ice cream with spiced figs. The 40-strong wine list is equally Italian, opening at £14.

Chef: Ciro Zaino **Proprietors:** Ciro and Linda Zaino **Open:** Thur to Sun D only 7.30 to 9.30 **Closed:** Nov to Feb **Meals:** Set D £28.50 **Service:** 10% **Cards:** Delta, Maestro, MasterCard, Visa **Details:** 22 seats. 20 seats outside. No children under 8. No smoking. Occasional music **Accommodation:** 5 rooms

 This symbol means that the restaurant has elected to participate in *The Good Food Guide's* £5 voucher scheme (see 'Using The Good Food Guide' for details).

MAP 5 | PERSHORE –
Worcestershire

Belle House

5 Bridge Street, Pershore WR10 1AJ
Tel: (01386) 555055
Website: www.belle-house.co.uk

Cooking 3 | Modern European | £36

This 'rather pretty' restaurant is located in the centre of town, and was once a fire station, thus explaining the enormous arched windows. Stephen Waites's tasteful renovation features exuberant plaster mouldings, oval mirrors and pale wooden floors and tables. Happily, the food matches the ambience. There are only four choices for each course, but timing and consistency are watchwords and good use is made of local produce. Begin with an open raviolo of roast vegetables and confit garlic in a tomato and basil sauce, and follow it with pan-fried fillet of sea bass with prawn and lemon risotto, or perhaps venison casseroled with prunes and tomatoes accompanied by creamed potato. Three desserts round things off, among them perhaps hot orange and chocolate fondant, plus a selection of cheeses. Digestifs are plentiful, and the wine list opens with a Côtes de Gascogne at £11.95.

Chef/Proprietor: Stephen Waites **Open:** Tue to Sat 12 to 2, 7 to 9.30 **Closed:** 25 and 26 Dec, first 2 weeks Jan, 1 week Aug **Meals:** Set L £12 (2 courses) to £18, Set D £24.95 **Service:** not inc **Cards:** Amex, Maestro, MasterCard, Visa **Details:** 80 seats. Vegetarian meals. Children's helpings. No smoking. Wheelchair access (also WC). Music. Air-conditioned

MAP 2 | PETERSFIELD – Hampshire

JSW

1 Heath Road, Petersfield GU31 4JE
Tel: (01730) 262030

Cooking 6 | Modern British | £58

Jake Watkins's modest, uncluttered restaurant off the High Street is described by reporters as 'a neighbourhood restaurant of some class' and 'one of the best regional restaurants I've encountered'. The approach is simple, but of the kind of simplicity that requires a great deal of skill and plenty of culinary good sense. A starter of cep tartlet with

poached duck egg and truffle salad is vibrant with colour and texture, while scallops with fennel are partnered with a 'lovely, light' bouillabaisse sauce.

Main courses layer on flavours in equally impressive fashion, partnering, say, wild monkfish wrapped in bacon with pear purée and bacon velouté, or a slow-cooked suckling pig belly and loin with pea purée, green beans and asparagus tips. Technique is spot on, too: lamb arrives 'perfectly pink' with succulent flavour, and home-smoked beef is 'excellent rare meat with enough flavour to stand up to the smoking'. Meals might finish with cinnamon beignets with apple sorbet and vanilla, or perhaps a lemon parfait, topped by an intense raspberry sorbet. The tasting menu has been described as an 'effortless natural progression of small but perfect creations' and there is a separate vegetarian menu. Wines are a considered mix of classics and modern flavours with broad scope and some serious top-end stuff from California, New Zealand, Italy, Spain and Germany, as well as France. Prices are from £16, but there's not a lot under £20.

Chef/Proprietor: Jake Watkins **Open:** Tue to Sat 12 to 1.30, 7 to 9.30 **Meals:** Set L £23.50 (2 courses) to £35, Set D £34.50 (2 courses) to £45 **Service:** not inc **Cards:** Delta, Maestro, MasterCard, Visa **Details:** 22 seats. Vegetarian meals. No children under 7. No smoking. No music. No mobile phones

MAP 5 | PLUMTREE –
Nottinghamshire

Perkins

Station House, Station Road, Plumtree
NG12 5NA
Tel: (0115) 937 3695
Website: www.perkinsrestaurant.co.uk

Cooking 2 | Modern British/French | £40

This attractive family-run restaurant was once a Victorian railway station, and the single track outside is still used occasionally as a test line. But that's where any relation to the past ends. Inside, it is surprisingly spacious; there is an impressive copper-topped bar, gold-patterned carpet, and an archway decorated with copper pans, while the dining room boasts dark wood tables and pew-type seating. The Perkins have a smokehouse which is used to full effect on fish and poultry. Ham hock and chicken liver terrine is served with an apple and cider chutney for starters, while main courses could be whole boned poached sea bass with asparagus spears and Hollandaise sauce, or a breaded escalope of pork topped with a fried egg, anchovies and capers. End with crème brûlée or chocolate tart. The wine list runs to 50 bins, starting at a reasonable £12.50.

Chef: David Perkins **Proprietors:** Tony, Wendy, Jonathan and David Perkins **Open:** Tue to Sun L 12 to 2 (2.30 Sun), Tue to Sat D 6.45 to 9.45 **Closed:** 25 and 26 Dec, 1 Jan **Meals:** alc (not Sun L; main courses £11 to £18.50). Set L Tue to Sat £11.25 (2 courses), set L Sun £13.50 (2 courses) to £16.95, Set D Tue to Thur £19.50 **Service:** not inc **Cards:** Amex, Delta, Maestro, MasterCard, Visa **Details:** 73 seats. 24 seats outside. Car park. Vegetarian meals. No smoking. Occasional music. Air-conditioned

MAP 1   PLYMOUTH – Devon

Tanners

Prysten House, Finewell Street, Plymouth
PL1 2AE
Tel: (01752) 252001
Website: www.tannersrestaurant.com

Cooking 3 | Modern British | £43

Prysten House, built in 1498, is said to be Plymouth's second oldest house and the fine limestone building with its galleried courtyard is home to the Tanner brothers' restaurant on the ground floor. The olde worlde charm of beamed ceilings, mullioned windows and stone walls and floors is in stark contrast to the modern cooking. James and Christopher Tanner's sensibly short menus with concise descriptions and carefully sourced local and regional ingredients include the likes of seared red mullet with chorizo, pickled cucumber and pea shoots, and seared black bream with a pine-nut crust and red pepper sauce. While fish is a strength, there could be chargrilled lamb rump with ratatouille, fondant potatoes, tomato and olive jus or loin of pork with champ potatoes and apple sauce. Desserts might include white and dark chocolate brandy-snaps, and strawberry shortbread, while six house wines at £12.95 open a list that offers plenty of decent drinking for under £20. This year, however, we've had complaints about poor timing in some dishes, and 'stuffy and distant service'. The brothers have recently opened The Barbican Kitchen in the old Plymouth Gin Distillery in the city.

Chefs/Proprietors: Christopher and James Tanner **Open:** Tue to Sat 12 to 2.30, 7 to 9.30 **Closed:** 25, 26 and 31 Dec, first week Jan **Meals:** Set L £13.50 (2 courses) to £16, Set D £24 (2 courses) to £35 **Service:** not inc **Cards:** Amex, Delta, Maestro, MasterCard, Visa **Details:** 45 seats. 20 seats outside. Vegetarian meals. Children's helpings. Smoking in bar only. Wheelchair access (also WC). Music. No mobile phones

MAP 10   PONTELAND – Northumberland

Café Lowrey

33–35 The Broadway, Darras Hall, Ponteland
NE20 9PW
Tel: (01661) 820357

Cooking 4 | Modern British | £38

A new name follows last year's purchase of Bistro 21 by Ian Lowrey, who had been head chef for the previous five years under Terry Laybourne's ownership, so little else has changed. Talent is obviously at work here. Dishes are straightforward, presentation is uncluttered, and the quality of raw materials is consistently high. The menu shows influences from around the globe, as in starters such as chilli and coriander gravad lax with beetroot pickle, while grilled black pudding with caramelised apples and onion jus has a more Yorkshire ring. Mingled with the modern are old-fashioned favourites: main courses like confit duck with mustard mash, say, or fillet of beef with lardons, baby onions, mushroom and port wine sauce. For dessert, there is crème brûlée or passion-fruit parfait. Service is attentive and the atmosphere relaxed. The compact, fairly priced wine list provides a good choice of easy drinking, kicking off with house Duboeuf at £12.50

Chef: Ian Lowrey **Proprietors:** Ian and Susan Lowrey **Open:** Sat L 12 to 2, Mon to Sat D 5.30 (6 Sat) to 10 **Closed:** 25 and 26 Dec, bank hols **Meals:** alc (main courses £9.50 to £20). Set L £12.50 (2 courses) to £15, Set D 5.30 to 7 £12.50 to £15 **Service:** not inc **Cards:** Amex, Maestro, MasterCard, Visa **Details:** 70 seats. Car park. Vegetarian meals. Children's helpings. No-smoking area. Wheelchair access (also WC). Music. Air-conditioned

The price given next to the cooking score is based on the cost of a typical three-course dinner for one person, including coffee, house wine and service.

MAP 2 **POOLE – Dorset**

Mansion House

Thames Street, Poole BH15 1JN
Tel: (01202) 685666
Website: www.themansionhouse.co.uk

Cooking 3 | Modern British-Plus | £42

Just a stone's throw from the quay, this classy hotel and restaurant has the air of a gentleman's club about it. The dining room features cherry wood panelling and stiff white table linen, but the atmosphere is unstuffy and the service is friendly. An inspector was struck by the confidence of the kitchen, citing its good use of quality produce, particularly local fish, and noted the attention to detail. Pan-fried scallops with diced chorizo on butternut squash purée has been praised, and an alternative starter might be home-cured beef with beetroot chutney and horseradish cream. A main course of beef fillet comes on a bed of aubergine purée with caramelised endive and a well-reduced Madeira and garlic jus, while monkfish is served on a potato cake laced with wasabi, with shiitake mushrooms and 'great flavours combining well' in a rich jus of ginger and chilli. End with 'perfect' caramelised vanilla crème brûlée or rhubarb and custard mille-feuille. The varied and accessible global wine list starts at £13.50.

Chef: Gerry Godden **Proprietors:** Jackie and Gerry Godden **Open:** Sun to Fri L 12 to 2, Mon to Sat D 7 to 9.30 (also open Sun D bank hols) **Meals:** Set L £17.50 (2 courses) to £19.25, Set D £23.95 (2 courses) to £29.95. Bistro menu available **Service:** not inc **Cards:** Amex, Delta, Diners, Maestro, MasterCard, Visa **Details:** 85 seats. Car park. Vegetarian meals. Children's helpings. No smoking in dining room. Occasional music. Air-conditioned **Accommodation:** 32 rooms

MAP 1 **PORTSCATHO – Cornwall**

Driftwood

Rosevine, nr Portscatho TR2 5EW
Tel: (01872) 580644
Website: www.driftwoodhotel.co.uk

Cooking 5 | Modern European | £52

The white hotel may be seen peeping above the brow of a hill overlooking the bay. It's as light and airy within as it looks from outside, with deep windows in the dining room offering panoramic marine views. Seasonal, fixed-price menus with daily specials ply the modern European mode, into which Rory Duncan has settled well over the past couple of years. There is an assurance and a boldness about the cooking, reflected in such dishes as marinated mackerel with crayfish tails, carrots and ginger, or lemon sole fillets with brandade 'lasagne' and leek velouté. While fish may be limited to only a couple of options among main courses, it remains the chief draw: John Dory fillet with mussel fricassee and peas in a shellfish sauce is typical. Meat eaters might go for roast venison loin with confit beetroot and Savoy cabbage sauced with Merlot vinegar. Platters of fruits de mer for two can be arranged at a day's notice. The chocolatey desserts win fans, or there might be old-school rum baba with pineapple and currants in crème anglaise. A well-written wine list opens with a southern French white and a Chilean Merlot at £14, without going into the stratosphere on price at the other end.

Chef: Rory Duncan **Proprietors:** Paul and Fiona Robinson **Open:** all week D only 7 to 9.30 **Closed:** mid-Dec to early Feb **Meals:** Set D £38 **Service:** not inc **Cards:** Amex, Maestro, MasterCard, Visa **Details:** 34 seats. Car park. Vegetarian meals. No babies in dining room. No smoking. Music. No mobile phones **Accommodation:** 15 rooms

MAP 2 **POULTON – Gloucestershire**

Falcon Inn

London Road, Poulton GL7 5HN
Tel: (01285) 850844
Website: www.thefalconpoulton.co.uk

Cooking 4 | European | £39

A pair of the eponymous birds stands guard on either side of the great stone fireplace at this welcoming inn, which is slap-bang in the middle of the village. Subdued lighting has felt a trifle too Stygian for some, but for others it adds to the soothing tone. Home cooking using well-sourced local supplies is the name of the game, manifesting itself in such favoured dishes as crab cakes, homemade burgers with good chips, and ribeye steaks with roast garlic butter. More highfalutin dishes can work well too, as was the case with one reporter's starter of pigeon breast served on a field mushroom with celeriac and bacon, in which all the ingredients pulled together nicely. Less well judged has been a needlessly weighty main course

of battered mackerel with deep-fried diced potatoes and horseradish crème fraîche. Desserts such
as sticky banana and pecan pudding with clotted
cream – a country-pub dish if ever there was – are
a high point: the pannacotta, perhaps served with
poached pear and pear granita, gets the thumbs-up.
A revamped wine list contains plenty of appetising, positive flavours, with wines by the glass from
£3.25, by the bottle from £12.50.

Chefs: Willham Abraham and Jeremy Lockley   Proprietor:
Jeremy Lockley   Open: all week L 12 to 2, Mon to Sat D 7 to 9
Closed: 25 and 26 Dec, 1 Jan   Meals: alc (main courses £9 to
£17). Set L Mon to Fri £12 (2 courses), Set L Sun £15 (2
courses) to £20   Service: not inc   Cards: Maestro,
MasterCard, Visa   Details: 50 seats. Car park. Vegetarian
meals. Children's helpings. No smoking in dining room.
Wheelchair access (also WC). Music

MAP 8   PRESTBURY – Cheshire

White House

The Village, Prestbury SK10 4DG
Tel: (01625) 829376
Website: www.thewhitehouseinprestbury.com

Cooking 3 | Modern British | £47

This part of the world is dominated by Manchester
United, and is a prime venue for celebrity spot-
ting. To the staff's credit no-one seems fazed when
the stars are in but everything about this classy
venue is geared to offering a high level of service
in a relaxed atmosphere. Leather benches and armchairs fill the bar area, which is separated from the
spacious dining room by a glass screen. Linen
tablecloths, exotic flowers and solid cutlery are all
to be expected. Excellent starters have included an
'unusual but light and delicious' méli-mélo of wild
mushrooms, comprising mousse, strudel and fricassee, followed by Cumbrian fell-bred fillet of beef
with pommes frites, and vine-roast tomatoes.
Strozzapreti pasta with roast pumpkin, sage and
feta didn't cut the mustard with one Italian-born
diner, though the sauce had authentic taste and
texture. A mini dessert selection of crème brûlée,
bread-and-butter pudding, sponge and fruit cake
was 'a real treat' for one diner. An interesting wine
list starts with house Chilean at £14.95.

Chef: Dominic Davallou   Proprietor: Shade Down Ltd   Open:
all week L 12 to 2, Mon to Sat D 7 to 10   Closed: 24 to 26
Dec, 1 Jan   Meals: alc (main courses £12 to £27). Set L
£16.95, Set D Mon to Fri £16.95 (2 courses) to £19.45. Bar
menu available   Service: not inc   Cards: Amex, Delta,
MasterCard, Maestro, Visa   Details: 80 seats. 12 seats
outside. Car park. Vegetarian meals. Children's helpings.
Wheelchair access (also WC). Music

MAP 8   PRESTON – Lancashire

Winckley Square Chop House

23 Winckley Square, Preston PR1 3JJ
Tel: (01772) 252732
Website: www.heathcotes.co.uk

Cooking 3 | Modern British | £43

A contemporary feel that takes in the theatre of an
open kitchen and a vibrant menu with a strong
regional thrust makes this Paul Heathcote operation
an understandably popular spot with the Preston
business crowd. While some appreciate the distinctly regional bias in the kitchen – think black
pudding Scotch egg with a salad of baby gems and
home-made salad cream, or warm Lancashire
cheese and leek quiche – there are other influences
too, more broadly European. Roast Goosnargh
duckling is teamed with spiced griottine cherries,
spring greens and red wine, for example, while
seared fillet of sea bream comes with Jerusalem artichokes, wild mushrooms and a rocket and parsley
relish. Finish with Yorkshire curd tart with rhubarb
compote. In the basement is the Olive Press Pizzeria
Bar and Grill, with a rustic feel and a Mediterranean
menu and atmosphere. An upbeat, global wine list
offers decent drinking from £13.95.

Chefs: Thomas Lowe and Andy Parker   Proprietor: Paul
Heathcote   Open: all week 12 to 2.30, 6 to 10 (11 Sat, 9
Sun)   Closed: bank hols   Meals: alc (main courses £9.50 to
£22). Set L Mon to Sat and D Mon to Sat 6 to 7 £12.95 (2
courses, inc wine), Set D Mon £15 (inc wine)   Service: not inc
Cards: Amex, Delta, Maestro, MasterCard, Visa   Details: 90
seats. Vegetarian meals. Children's helpings. No smoking in
dining room. Wheelchair access (also WC). Music.
Air-conditioned

MAP 8   RAMSBOTTOM – Greater Manchester

Ramsons

18 Market Place, Ramsbottom BL0 9HT
Tel: (01706) 825070
Website: www.ramsons.org.uk

Cooking 4 | Italian | £49

Ros Hunter and Chris Johnson's restaurant completed a major refurbishment as we went to press,

too late, unfortunately for a full assessment. It looks very smart, though, and 'wouldn't look out of place in an up-an-coming Milanese suburb', as one regular put it. The basement 'Hideaway' Restaurant is closed for the time being, and the focus is on long-term chefs Abdulla Naseem and Amy Bicknell's Italian-inspired cooking served in the newly improved ground-floor dining room. Passion for British produce permeates the menu. Dinner is a choice of two to five courses, or a seven-course 'tasting' menu, starting with, perhaps, an appetiser of raw Cheshire beef, or grilled fillet of Hawkshead organic trout with barley and truffle risotto. Alternatively, sautéed squid ink risotto or a light lobster and salmon ravioli might be followed by salad or vegetables (served as a middle course). Main courses take in loin of Derbyshire venison, Inglewhite wood pigeon with creamed lentils, and Cornish brill with couscous. Amy's Amalfi lemon trio, or a chocolate mousse teardrop, make for an impressive ending.

The wine list has also undergone a major change; it's a mighty, fully annotated, tour of the Italian wine regions, with detailed notes on producers and colour pictures to boot. Prices start at £14.50 for house wines from the Bergamasca Co-op in Lombardy.

Chefs: Abdulla Naseem and Amy Bicknell **Proprietors:** Ros Hunter and Chris Johnson **Open:** Wed to Sun L 12 to 2.30 (1 to 3.30 Sun), Wed to Sat D 7 to 9.30 **Closed:** 2 weeks May **Meals:** Set L £15 (1 course) to £25. Set L Sun £21 (2 courses) to £28.50. Set D £35 to £50 **Service:** not inc **Cards:** Maestro, MasterCard, Visa **Details:** 32 seats. Vegetarian meals. No smoking. No music. No mobile phones. Air-conditioned

---

MAP 3 RAMSGATE – Kent

Surin

`AR`

30 Harbour Street, Ramsgate CT11 8HA
Tel: (01843) 592001

Tucked away in a narrow street between the town centre and the marina, this small café-like restaurant is run by the lively and friendly Damrong Garbutt. The standard Thai repertoire is extensively covered by a long menu, starters ranging from chicken satay (£4.25) to prawn and coconut soup (£4.95), main courses encompassing roast duck with chilli, garlic, basil and soy (£8.50), fried squid with chilli and basil (£7.95), and pork with ginger (£7.95). A local brewery provides a couple of excellent house beers, and wines start at £11.95. Open Tue to Sun L and all week D; closed all Sun Sept to Apr.

MAP 8 RAMSGILL – North Yorkshire

Yorke Arms

Ramsgill HG3 5RL
Tel: (01423) 755243
Website: www.yorke-arms.co.uk

Cooking 6 | Modern European | £57

The Yorke Arms sits at an angle on the main road through this tiny Yorkshire village, facing a pint-sized triangular green with a little war memorial and a great old oak. Inside is soberly decorated with expanses of dark wood and leather armchairs, but the place is run with a light touch. Frances Atkins leads a kitchen that is proudly aware of its roots. Local potted beef joins ham hock and foie gras in a terrine, which is imaginatively paired not with the usual fruity garnish but with beetroot relish and asparagus velouté. Presentations aim for simplicity but often belie the considered complexity at work in a dish, so a starter serving of quail with a sweet forcemeat appears with hazelnut tartine, black pudding, Yorkshire blue cheese and rhubarb, constituting quite a medley of tastes. Fish is creatively treated too, a pairing of roast sea bass and red mullet arriving with Parma ham, braised gem lettuce, fennel and asparagus. Good Yorkshire beef and lamb are reliable standbys for meat eaters, or there may be guinea fowl, served two ways, with almond and lemon dressing and truffled linguine.

Desserts elicit the 'wow' response with such creations as mango boudin with pineapple tart and passion-fruit sorbet. There are wows aplenty on the wine list too, which is especially good in Burgundy and Australia. Eight variously sourced house wines start at £15.

Chefs: Frances Atkins and Roger Olive **Proprietors:** Gerald and Frances Atkins **Open:** all week L 12 to 2, Mon to Sat D 7 to 9 (residents only Sun D) **Meals:** alc (main courses £14.50 to £24). Set L Mon to Sat £17.50 (2 courses) to £21, Set L Sun £26 (2 courses) to £32, Set D £50 to £80 (inc wine). Bar menu available Mon to Sat L, Mon to Fri D **Service:** not inc **Cards:** Amex, Delta, Diners, Maestro, MasterCard, Visa **Details:** 60 seats. 25 seats outside. Car park. Vegetarian meals. No children under 12. No smoking. Wheelchair access (not WC). Music. No mobile phones **Accommodation:** 14 rooms

---

 This symbol means that the restaurant has elected to participate in *The Good Food Guide's* £5 voucher scheme (see 'Using The Good Food Guide' for details).

MAP 2 READING – Berkshire

Forbury's

NEW ENTRY

1 Forbury Square, Reading RG1 3BB
Tel: (0118) 957 4044
Website: www.forburys.com

Cooking 5 | Modern European | £55

'It's all very elegant, swish and contemporary for Reading,' exclaimed a reporter on encountering Forbury Square, where this restaurant can be found on the ground floor of a striking glass office building. It is very much a modern British urban restaurant. The spacious, off-white dining room, has floor-to-ceiling windows along one side, lots of dark brown leather, blond-wood floorboards and walls covered with large images of French wine labels. In the kitchen, José Cau favours a modern French emphasis, although the materials are among the best our own islands can offer, with Aberdeen Angus beef, fish from Brixham and hand-dived scallops from Scotland. Dishes make a strong visual impact – carpaccio of duck with pan-fried foie gras, foie gras ice cream and liquorice jus, for instance – and classic flavour combinations are implemented with assurance, as in an attractively presented dish of scrambled eggs infused with Périgord truffle. Gressingham duck breast, partnered by duck rillettes, braised Savoy cabbage and lavender jus, has impressed with its interplay of clean, lively flavours, while a light touch and pinpoint timing have made the most of John Dory set on a heap of crushed Jersey potatoes laced with spring onion and a hint of curry. Well-reported desserts have included plum and Armagnac soufflé. Owner Xavier Le-Bellego gives 'presence and personality' to front-of-house, aided by smartly attired staff who are 'attentive, knowledgeable, friendly'. Ten wines by the glass, from £3.50, introduce a list that roams France before heading off elsewhere. Prices start at £15.

Chef: José Cau **Proprietor:** Xavier Le-Bellego **Open:** all week L 12 to 2.15, Mon to Sat D 6.15 to 10 **Closed:** 26 to 28 Dec **Meals:** alc (main courses £14.50 to £26). Set L Mon to Sat £13.95 (2 courses) to £17.95, Set D Mon to Fri £13.95 (2 courses) to £17.95 **Service:** 12.5% (optional) **Cards:** Amex, Delta, Maestro, MasterCard, Visa **Details:** 80 seats. 30 seats outside. Car park. Vegetarian meals. No children under 5. Children's helpings. No smoking. Wheelchair access (also WC). Music. Air-conditioned

To submit a report on any restaurant, please visit *www.which.co.uk/gfgfeedback*.

London Street Brasserie

2–4 London Street, Reading RG1 4SE
Tel: (0118) 950 5036
Website: www.londonstbrasserie.co.uk

Cooking 2 | Modern European | £47

On the River Kennet, this eighteenth-century former tollhouse has been a beer retailer, a chemist's and a hairdresser's, but now it functions as a lively brasserie. The design is simple and uncluttered, featuring bare-brick walls hung with artwork, and a decked terrace overlooking the river. The menu brims with eclectic personality, starters running from white crabmeat and crème fraîche with guacamole and a chilli and tomato salsa to crispy fried ham hock and rocket salad with a poached egg and sauce gribiche. Main courses can be as traditional as calf's liver and bacon with mash, roast shallots and a red wine jus, or deliver a bit of North Africa via a Moroccan meze board with grilled flatbread. Farmhouse British and Irish cheeses make a savoury alternative to desserts such as panettone bread-and-butter pudding. Some good names show up on the wine list. Prices start at £13.95, and around a dozen are served by the glass from £3.95.

Chef: Paul Brotherton **Proprietor:** Paul Clerehugh **Open:** all week 12 to 11 **Meals:** alc (main courses £12 to £20). Set L and D 12 to 7 £13.50 (2 courses) **Service:** not inc **Cards:** Amex, Delta, Diners, Maestro, MasterCard, Visa **Details:** 70 seats. 20 seats outside. Vegetarian meals. No cigars/pipes in dining room. Wheelchair access (also WC). Music. No mobile phones

MAP 3 REIGATE – Surrey

Dining Room

59A High Street, Reigate RH2 9AE
Tel: (01737) 226650
Website: www.tonytobinrestaurants.co.uk

Cooking 3 | Modern British | £54

A mixture of soft colours, smart furnishings and contemporary landscapes enhances the calming feeling of Tony Tobin's now well-established and confident restaurant. Dishes on the fixed-price menu avoid over-elaboration and are reassuringly consistent. Some are robust combinations like a starter of brochette of Indian-spiced marinated lamb with tsatsiki and Indian pastry; others are marked by more subtlety, as in a main course of roast turbot with braised artichokes, peas and lettuce with a light, creamy sauce. There might be calf's liver with black pudding bubble and squeak, or aromatic duck with creamy mustard onions and red wine sauce. Puddings such as baked apple and flapjack pudding with custard and toffee sauce or iced tiramisù make simple and satisfying endings. A dozen well-chosen basics from £15.95, or £4.50 a glass, set the tone for an up-to-date wine list with a 'library' list grouping the smarter, pricier bottles.

Chef/Proprietor: Tony Tobin Open: Mon to Fri L 12 to 2, Sun L 12.30 to 2.30, Mon to Sat D 7 to 10 Closed: Christmas, Easter Sun, bank hols Meals: Set L Mon to Fri £19.50 (2 courses), Set L Sun £28.50, Set D Mon to Thur £28.50 (2 courses) to £42, Set D Fri and Sat £34 to £42 Service: 12.5% (optional) Cards: Amex, Delta, Maestro, MasterCard, Visa Details: 78 seats. Vegetarian meals. Children's helpings. No smoking. Music. Air-conditioned

MAP 3 RICHMOND – Surrey

La Buvette NEW ENTRY

6 Church Walk, Richmond TW9 1SN
Tel: (020) 8940 6264

Cooking 3 | French | £42

The entrance to this bistro in the shadow of St Mary Magdalene Church is through a courtyard, which has tables for al fresco dining. Everything is as smart as you'd expect in this corner of the world, from the cream and red décor to the white-clothed pedestal tables. French country cooking is the order of the day at this sibling of Brula Bistrot in Twickenham (see entry). An 'excellent' starter has been well-timed king scallops nantaise with braised celery and bacon, while a 'brilliant' soufflé of goats' cheese is accompanied by well-dressed apple and walnut salad. Main courses are markedly generous: five slices of tender duck breast with a turnip gratin and green olives, and sea bass with endive aïoli à la grecque. 'Excellent' frites have also been praised. Crème brûlée and chocolate, coffee and cardamom pot are what to expect for dessert. The wine list is Gallic through and through, starting at £12.75, or £3.25 a glass.

Chef: Buck Carter Proprietors: Lawrence Hartley and Bruce Duckett Open: all week 12 to 3, 6 to 11 Closed: 25 and 26 Dec, 1 Jan, Good Fri, Easter Sun Meals: alc exc Sun L (main courses £11.50 to £16.50). Set L Mon to Sat £11.50 (2 courses) to £14, Set L Sun £15.75 Service: 12.5% (optional) Cards: Delta, Maestro, MasterCard, Visa Details: 40 seats. 36 seats outside. Vegetarian meals. Children's helpings. No smoking. Wheelchair access (also WC). No music

Chez Lindsay AR

11 Hill Rise, Richmond TW10 6UQ
Tel: (020) 8948 7473

For authentic Breton cuisine, look no further than Lindsay Wotton's menu. It features a fine array of galettes with various fillings: cheese and ham (£6.15), scallops and leeks (£9.25), or chitterling sausage, onions and mustard sauce (£8.95). 'Les Grands Plats' include fillet of cod with prawns, spinach, potatoes and seafood sauce (£13.75), and cotriade (Breton fish stew; £15.75). Finish with frangipane crêpe and vanilla ice cream (£5.50). French wines (from £13), beers and ciders. Open all week.

Petersham Nurseries Café NEW ENTRY

Church Lane, off Petersham Road, Richmond TW10 7AG
Tel: (020) 8605 3627
Website: www.petershamnurseries.com

Cooking 3 | Modern British | £41

The star attraction here is the possibility of eating al fresco, surrounded by greenery and far from the noise of traffic. The café is in a large greenhouse with little by way of decoration bar garden-style furniture and potted plants; it's at its best on a sunny day, of course, when tables and chairs fill the adjacent courtyard. The menu consists of just four or five choices per course, Skye Gyngell working with fresh, seasonal produce, including herbs, salads and fruit from the walled kitchen garden of Petersham House, to create straightforward, distinctly flavoured dishes. Lightly fried, tender squid comes with sourdough breadcrumbs and aïoli to make a simple starter, and another has been a 'superb' salad of garlicky cubes of toasted Italian bread layered with crisp beef tomatoes, wafers of salami and caramelised red onion, with a variety of leaves ('bursting with flavour'). Among main courses, crisp-skinned, succulent roast wild salmon is coated with salsa verde and accompanied by green, brown and pink Umbrian lentils and braised chard. Finish with 'rich and comforting' chocolate tart with clotted cream. The short wine list opens with Montepulciano d'Abruzzo at £15, but prices soon leap over the £20 barrier.

Chef: Skye Gyngell Proprietors: Gael and Francesco Boglione Open: Wed to Sun L only 12.30 to 3 Meals: alc (main courses £14 to £24) Service: 12.5% (optional) Cards: Delta, Maestro, MasterCard, Visa Details: 80 seats. Car park. Vegetarian meals. No smoking. No music

Restaurant at the Petersham

Petersham Hotel, Nightingale Lane, Richmond TW10 6UZ
Tel: (020) 8940 7471
Website: www.petershamhotel.co.uk

| Cooking 4 | Modern British | £54 |

Built in 1865, this Gothic-looking pile with commanding views of the Thames is in a quiet setting that belies its proximity to London. The interior has been considerably updated over the years but retains a number of original features, and the dining room, which shares those views, has well-spaced tables, comfortable upholstered chairs and mirrors along one wall. Alex Bentley sources top-notch ingredients and imposes on them a broadly British style of cooking that pulls in influences from classic French cuisine. Fish and seafood are strong suits, with seared scallops and smoked eel with cauliflower and celeriac appearing among starters alongside Devon crab voguishly accompanied by ham, fennel salad and lemon couscous. Dishes are well considered, as in a labour-intensive main course of pork en crépinette with foie gras mousseline, beetroot purée and Puy lentils, or grilled dorade with chorizo and pancetta, smoked aubergine and cassoulet 'sauce'. A dab hand at pastry work is evident in desserts along the lines of pineapple tarte Tatin with rum and raisin ice cream. France is the fulcrum of the wine list, although Spain, Italy and the New World are represented too. Prices open at £19.50, £5 by the glass, and half-bottles are bountiful.

Chef: Alex Bentley Proprietors: the Dare family Open: Mon to Sat 12.15 to 2.15, 7 to 9.45, Sun 12.30 to 3.30, 7 to 8.45 Closed: D 24 to 27 Dec Meals: alc exc Sun (main courses £6 to £24). Set L Mon to Sat £18.50 (2 courses) to £25, Set L Sun £29.50, Set D Sun £20 (2 courses) to £25 Service: 10% (optional) Cards: Amex, Diners, MasterCard, Visa Details: 60 seats. Car park. Vegetarian meals. Children's helpings. No smoking. Wheelchair access (also WC). Occasional music. No mobile phones. Air-conditioned Accommodation: 60 rooms

MAP 9 RIDGEWAY – Derbyshire

Old Vicarage

Ridgeway Moor, Ridgeway S12 3XW
Tel: (0114) 247 5814
Website: www.theoldvicarage.co.uk

| Cooking 7 | Modern British-Plus | £65 |

Although not far from Sheffield, the 'gorgeous' rural setting of this country house exudes a sense of calm. But while the grounds and location overlooking the Moss Valley conservation area and the warm welcome within may elicit reporters' praise, Tessa Bramley's food is the star. The cooking is led by local produce, from lamb and beef to partridge and hare, from local cheeses to own-grown fruit and vegetables, which is used to create a simple but sophisticated repertoire of dishes, and high gastronomic expectations are almost invariably met. Luxury materials also find a home – sevruga caviar with lavender-smoked fillet of cod, or pan-fried foie gras with honey-roast squab – but they are deployed sensibly. Roast fillet of loin of spring lamb comes with slow-cooked shoulder as well as sautéed morels and new potatoes, and thyme-roasted fillet of Aberdeen Angus beef is partnered by black pudding, spring herbs, pommes Anna and lavender-smoked sweet peppers. This bright seam of gentle invention runs through much of the menu, producing a cumin-spiced potato cake with chervil sabayon and a poached free-range egg with poppyseed soldiers, and crisp-roast fillet of sea bass on a new potato galette accompanied by a salad of dressed Whitby crab with mango, peas and asparagus, and a minted pea sabayon. Although full of ideas, Tessa Bramley keeps her feet on the ground. Desserts, for example, might take in baked chocolate pudding with chocolate fudge sauce and custard, or a grilled cheese savoury served on walnut bread with devils-on-horseback.

Wines (which include a page of recommendations under £20) don't stint on quality. The full list is a well-rounded international selection arranged by style that turns up a few star names. Two dozen fine wines are offered by the glass from £7 to £20.

Chefs: Tessa Bramley and Nathan Smith Proprietor: Tessa Bramley Open: Tue to Fri L 12.30 to 2.30, Tue to Sat D 6.30 to 9.45 Closed: 26 Dec to 5 Jan, first 2 weeks Aug, bank hol Mon and Tue Meals: Set L £30 to £40, Set D £50 to £60 Service: not inc Cards: Delta, Maestro, MasterCard, Visa Details: 46 seats. 16 seats outside. Car park. Vegetarian meals. Children's helpings. No smoking. Wheelchair access (also WC). Occasional music. No mobile phones

MAP 9   RIPLEY – North Yorkshire

Boar's Head

Ripley HG3 3AY
Tel: (01423) 771888
Website: www.boarsheadripley.co.uk

Cooking 3 | Modern British | £48

Bar, bistro, restaurant, hotel – the Boar's Head, located within the Ripley Castle estate, covers all bases. The bistro is in the old stables, and the menu might run to baked cod fillet topped with rarebit and served with creamed curly kale, and, for dessert, sticky toffee pudding. In the restaurant (ox-blood-red walls, still lifes, plenty of dark wood), a more ambitious carte has seen tempura of sweetbreads with a tower of grilled aubergine, sweet pepper and courgette, for instance, precede a choice of seven or so main courses ranging from poached loin of lamb with an emulsion of hazelnut oil, potato hotpot and braised little gem to pan-fried sea bream with saffron mirepoix and bouillabaisse sauce. Whether you fancy finishing with a traditional rice pudding or something more indulgent, like a trio of Belgian chocolate, the dessert menu can sort you out. A French-led global mix of wines opens with house options at £12.95.

Chef: Marc Guibert   **Proprietors:** Sir Thomas and Lady Ingilby **Open:** all week 12 to 2, 7 to 9 (9.30 Fri and Sat) **Meals:** Bistro: alc (main courses £10 to £16). Restaurant: Set L £16.95 (2 courses) to £19.95, Set D £34 to £40 **Service:** not inc **Cards:** Amex, Diners, Maestro, MasterCard, Visa **Details:** 60 seats. 60 seats outside. Car park. Vegetarian meals. Children's helpings. No smoking. Wheelchair access (also WC). Music. No mobile phones **Accommodation:** 25 rooms

MAP 3   RIPLEY – Surrey

Drake's Restaurant

The Clock House, High Street, Ripley GU23 6AQ
Tel: (01483) 224777
Website: www.drakesrestaurant.co.uk

Cooking 6 | Modern French | £59

A large, solid and imposing three-storey, brick-built Georgian building on the high street, Drake's can't fail to catch the eye, not least on account of the old clock above the entrance. Inside is traditionally decorated, with floral drapes at the tall windows, a green colour scheme and a little garden

at the back, used for summer aperitifs. 'Artisan cooking' is how Steve Drake describes his stock-in-trade, the preparation done in small batches, with dishes cooked to order. Small growers and suppliers furnish the kitchen, but if 'artisan' implies rustic, think again. There is considerable culinary flair in dishes such as a poached egg cleverly infused with creamed peas, served on casseroled ceps with a thin, crisp, mushroom-flavoured biscuit, or sautéed foie gras paired with a purée of beans and apricots.

Quality materials show up in such main courses as John Dory, roasted and partnered by artichokes and a bulb of crisp-baked garlic, all pointed up with a parsley and garlic sauce of high finesse. Desserts seem to have the X-factor too, if the combined intensity of an inspection dish involving rhubarb jelly and basil ice cream, and a layer of shortbread crumble, was anything to go by. It all comes at a fair old price, but the level of accomplishment is powerfully persuasive. Service is professional and attentive. The wine list is predominantly French, with attenuated selections from other countries. Eight reds and whites by the glass range from £4 to £8.

Chef: Steve Drake   **Proprietors:** Steve and Serina Drake **Open:** Tue to Fri L 12 to 1.30, Tue to Sat D 7 to 9.30   **Closed:** Christmas, 2 weeks Aug   **Meals:** Set L £19.50 (2 courses) to £23.50, Set D £36 (2 courses) to £68   **Service:** not inc **Cards:** Delta, Maestro, MasterCard, Visa   **Details:** 34 seats. Vegetarian meals. No children under 12. No smoking. Wheelchair access (not WC). No music

MAP 9   RIPON – North Yorkshire

Old Deanery

Minster Road, Ripon HG4 1QS
Tel: (01765) 600003
Website: www.theolddeanery.co.uk

Cooking 2 | Modern British | £50

This seventeenth-century, Grade-II listed building has a distinctly contemporary interior, although many original features have been retained. Wooden tables, nicely spaced, are set with damask napkins, and the atmosphere is one of happy contentment. In harmony, the menu is suitably up-to-date, and features a separate list for vegetarians: goats' cheese and spinach tart followed by artichoke and pepper strudel, for instance. Evening diners may find chicken liver and foie gras parfait with grape chutney or belly pork slowly roasted with cloves and honey to start, while main courses run to roast monkfish tails with sweet potato and parsley cream or breast of Gressingham duckling accompanied by a compote of star anise, figs and apples. End on a high with white chocolate panna-cotta or pear frangipane tart. Wines are listed by style (for example, 'spicy, peppery, warming'), with the base figure £14.50 and around half a dozen by the glass from £3.65.

> **Chef:** Barrie Higginbotham **Proprietor:** Express Terminals **Open:** all week L 12 to 2, Mon to Sat D 7 to 9.30 **Meals:** alc (main courses L £7 to £10, D £16 to £19.50). Set L £9.50 (2 courses) to £11.75 **Service:** not inc **Cards:** Delta, MasterCard, Visa **Details:** 50 seats. 28 seats outside. Car park. Vegetarian meals. No smoking. Wheelchair access (also WC). Music **Accommodation:** 11 rooms

MAP 8 **RIPPONDEN –** West Yorkshire

Junction

NEW ENTRY

1 Oldham Road, Ripponden HX6 4DN
Tel: (01422) 823070

Cooking 5 | **Modern European** | **£38**

Simon Shaw has been more used to cooking in big, trendy metropolitan places; his CV includes stints at Harvey Nichols (both Leeds and London; see Fifth Floor, London, Fourth Floor, Leeds). Essentially, this is another resurrected country pub, now housing a restaurant and tapas bar, all rough-stone walls and monochrome artworks within, the tables nicely laid with crisp linen, and a front-of-house manager relaxed enough to sit down at the next table while taking your order.

The tapas menu makes all the right Iberian noises, from Manchego with olives and piquillo peppers to Basque-style squid. On the main carte, a serving of flaked salt-cod with a well-timed poached egg, croûtons and tapenade hit the spot for one reporter, offering upstanding flavour without excess saltiness, while good old moules marinière have been a richly satisfying – and generous – object lesson. Main courses wrap monkfish in pancetta, and offer exquisitely tasty bubble and squeak with crisp-skinned duck confit. Unwavering attention to fish timing produces moist and fresh fillet of sea bream with a high-powered accompaniment of creamed Savoy cabbage in a glossy brown mush-room jus, while pastry-based desserts achieve the X-factor with irreproachable chocolate tart, or text-book pear frangipane served slightly warm. Wines are presented in a short, glossy booklet with good notes. There are some ambitious choices – Calera

Chardonnay from California (£30) is a banker – but the lower end is well served too. Spanish house wines are £11.95.

> **Chef:** Simon Shaw **Proprietors:** Chris Williams and Simon Shaw **Open:** Mon, Wed to Fri and Sun L 12 to 2.30 (4.30 Sun), Mon and Wed to Sat D 6.30 to 9.30 (10 Fri and Sat) **Meals:** alc exc Sun L (main courses £13.50 to £14). Set L Sun £12.95 (2 courses) to £16.50. Tapas menu available **Service:** not inc **Cards:** Delta, Diners, Maestro, MasterCard, Visa **Details:** 45 seats. 70 seats outside. Vegetarian meals. Children's helpings. No smoking. Music

MAP 8 **RISHWORTH –** West Yorkshire

Old Bore at Rishworth

Oldham Road, Rishworth HX6 4QU
Tel: (01422) 822291
Website: www.oldbore.co.uk

NEW ENTRY

Cooking 4 | **Modern British** | **£44**

On the outskirts of a village in the Ryburn valley, the Old Bore has, according to one diner, a dining room with 'the feel of a Scottish shooting lodge', with tartan wallpaper, antlers and three drums hanging from the ceiling. The menu embraces tra-ditional British dishes as well as more modern ideas, and seasonal produce from a network of local suppliers is a hallmark (Ryburn lamb, English Parmesan, Dexter beef from Pike End Farm in the village). Bore Benedict – smoked salmon topped with a poached egg and 'excellent' hollandaise on toasted brioche – is a signature starter, or there might be deep-fried haddock and prawn cro-quettes with lemon butter and prawn sauce. Sunday lunch of roast rib of beef with the usual accompaniments had a reporter in raptures – 'the flavour was fantastic; I could go back every Sunday to eat more' – and Gloucester Old Spot pork loin with black pudding and a cider, brandy and apple sauce is a typical main course. Baked double-chocolate liquid-centred brownie, served in a small copper pan, makes a decadent conclusion. A dozen house selections, from £2.45 a glass, £12.95 a bottle, open a fairly priced, varied wine list.

> **Chef/Proprietor:** Scott Hessel **Open:** Tue to Sat 12 to 2.15, 6 to 9.30 (10 Fri and Sat), Sun 12 to 4, 6 to 8 **Closed:** first 2 weeks Jan **Meals:** alc (main courses £10 to £20). Set L Tue to Sat £9.95 (2 courses), Set L Sun £12.95 (2 courses) to £16.95, Set D Tue to Fri and Sun £11.95 (two courses) **Service:** not inc **Cards:** Delta, Maestro, MasterCard, Visa **Details:** 90 seats. 36 seats outside. Car park. Vegetarian meals. No smoking in dining room. Wheelchair access (also WC). Music. Air-conditioned

MAP 5 ROADE –
Northamptonshire

Roade House

16 High Street, Roade NN7 2NW
Tel: (01604) 863372
Website: www.roadehousehotel.co.uk

Cooking 4 | Modern British | £43

Roade House is not only a haven from the M1 but
also handy for Althorp House and the racing at
Towcester. The vividly coloured, beamed dining
room makes quite a visual impact, and there is
much to catch the eye on Chris Kewley's menus
too. Dishes are simply conceived but deliver plenty
of flavour, as was discovered by a couple who dined
on monkfish with a curried mussel sauce, and
walnut-stuffed chicken breast with caramelised
apple and found all to their satisfaction. Contrasts
are handled well, as in Italianate starters like wild
boar prosciutto with mascarpone, Gorgonzola, figs
and pears, and the modern British puddings make
for a fine finish. The latter might encompass
rhubarb trifle made with sweet sherry, or memorable chocolate and ginger cake with orange marmalade sauce and white chocolate ice cream. A
user-friendly wine list, arranged by style, is priced
fairly all the way through, with £12.50 the baseline.

Chefs: Chris Kewley and Debbie Richardson **Proprietors:** Chris
and Sue Kewley **Open:** Mon to Fri L 12 to 1.45, Mon to Sat D
7 to 9.45 **Closed:** 1 week Christmas, bank hol Mon **Meals:**
Set L £20 (2 courses) to £23, Set D £25 (2 courses) to £30
Service: not inc **Cards:** Amex, Delta, Maestro, MasterCard,
Visa **Details:** 50 seats. Car park. Vegetarian meals. Children's
helpings. No smoking. Wheelchair access (also WC). No
music. Air-conditioned **Accommodation:** 10 rooms

MAP 8 ROCHDALE –
Greater Manchester

After Eight

2 Edenfield Road, Rochdale OL11 5AA
Tel: (01706) 646432

Cooking 3 | Modern British | £38

Old-fashioned opulence gives this unpretentious
restaurant the feel of a small country house, with
immaculate antique furniture and *objets d'art* in
abundance. Anne Taylor is a warm and charming
presence front-of-house, while husband Geoff
takes care of business in the kitchen, turning out

an eclectic range of dishes blending modern and
traditional ideas. Thus, starters typically take in
chicken goujons marinated in garlic served on a
Spanish tortilla with pesto, alongside Thai crab
cake on curried cannellini beans and coriander. To
follow, breast of Goosnargh duck is accompanied
by cheese hotpot, sliced flat beans and bacon with
an orange and Cointreau sauce, while brill is
roasted in a brioche and herb crust and served on
spinach and prawn risotto with chive and white
wine sauce. To round off a meal, try individual
ginger pudding with custard. Four house selections at £12.90 open a varied wine list approaching 70 bottles.

Chef: Geoff Taylor **Proprietors:** Anne and Geoff Taylor **Open:**
Sun L 12.30 to 3, Thur to Sat D 7 to 9.30 **Meals:** alc D (main
courses £15 to £18). Set L £14.95 (2 courses) to £17.95
Service: not inc **Cards:** Amex, Delta, Diners, Maestro,
MasterCard, Visa **Details:** 45 seats. Vegetarian meals.
Children's helpings. No smoking in dining room. Wheelchair
access (not WC). Music

MAP 1 ROCKBEARE – Devon

Jack in the Green

Rockbeare EX5 2EE
Tel: (01404) 822240
Website: www.jackinthegreen.uk.com

Cooking 3 | Global | £42

From the outside the Jack exudes a real sense of
tradition. It still functions as a pub, with some good
real ales for those just wanting a drink, plus decent
bar food ranging from braised beef in stout to fish
pie topped with cheesy potatoes. The restaurant
moves things up a notch or two with its cool, contemporary décor and offers a more ambitious
menu in which top-quality local produce is to the
fore, but influences come from all over. Expect
starters such as mutton and caper faggot with
sautéed sweetbreads and kidney, or Lyme Bay crabmeat with avocado, crème fraîche and gingered
cucumber carpaccio. Roast loin of pork with celeriac purée might follow, or seared salmon with
spicy oriental sauce, while to finish go for rice
pudding with apple and Calvados, or a selection of
British farmhouse cheeses. Eight house wines from
£11.95, also available by the glass, introduce an
extensive, reliable list that draws on Europe, the
Americas and Antipodes.

Chefs: Matt Mason and Craig Sampson Proprietor: Paul Parnell Open: Mon to Sat 12 to 2, 6 to 9.30, Sun 12 to 9.30 Closed: 25 Dec to 6 Jan Meals: alc exc Sun (main courses £15.50 to £19.50). Set L and D Sun £17.95 (2 courses) to £23.95. Bar menu available Service: not inc Cards: Maestro, MasterCard, Visa Details: 140 seats. 30 seats outside. Car park. Vegetarian meals. Children's helpings. No smoking in dining room. Wheelchair access (also WC). Music. Air-conditioned

MAP 10   ROMALDKIRK –
Co Durham

Rose and Crown

Romaldkirk DL12 9EB
Tel: (01833) 650213
Website: www.rose-and-crown.co.uk

Cooking 2 | Traditional English | £38

The Rose and Crown's appeal comes from being 'the whole package', wrote one diner, commenting on the charm of the Teesdale village setting, the civilised ambience and the friendly and well-trained staff. The oak-panelled restaurant is formal without being starchy, while the brasserie offers a lighter menu. In the former, dinner might open with Cotherstone cheese soufflé, 'light, airy and delicate', with gazpacho sauce, or chicken liver parfait with jellied strips of Seville orange peel. Pan-fried wood pigeon breasts are served with a parsnip tartlet and juniper berry sauce, and roast monkfish tails with wilted spinach and a red wine and balsamic jus. Chocolate and rum pot is an old fashioned finish. The wine list, arranged varietally, has interesting, useful annotations. Chilean Cabernet Sauvignon and Sauvignon Blanc get things going at £13.95.

Chefs: Christopher Davy and Andrew Lee Proprietors: Christopher and Alison Davy Open: Sun L 12 to 1.30, all week D 7.30 to 9 Closed: 24 to 26 Dec Meals: Set L £17.25, Set D £28. Bar/brasserie menu available Service: not inc Cards: Maestro, MasterCard, Visa Details: 24 seats. 24 seats outside. Car park. Vegetarian meals. No children under 6 in dining room. Children's helpings. No smoking in dining room. Wheelchair access (also WC). No music. No mobile phones Accommodation: 12 rooms

AR	Not a full entry but provisionally recommended. These 'also recommended' establishments are integrated throughout the book.

MAP 2   ROMSEY – Hampshire

Bertie's   `AR`

80 The Hundred, Romsey SO51 8BX
Tel: (01794) 830708

Named after P.G. Wodehouse's Bertie Wooster (the 'B' is everywhere you look), this converted coaching inn is relaxed and elegant. Black pudding, sage and onion faggot with mustard dressing (£5.95), rump of lamb with a mint and walnut pesto, sautéed potatoes, roast onion and green beans (£16.95), and cranberry and almond tart with brandy anglaise (£5.75) all feature. Fixed-price menus Mon to Thur (£12.95/£15.95). Wines from £11.95. Nine guest rooms. Closed Sun.

MAP 2   ROWDE – Wiltshire

George & Dragon   `AR`

High Street, Rowde SN10 2PN
Tel: (01380) 723053

Seafood continues to be at the centre of the action at this convivial, down-to-earth village pub, with 'excellent' supplies from Cornwall. Expect a brochette of chargrilled scallops and black pudding (£8), well-timed roast monkfish with a creamy green peppercorn sauce (£16.50), and whole grilled red snapper with tomato salsa (£14.50). Finish with home-made ice creams or chocolate bread-and-butter pudding (£5.50). Wines from £14. Closed Sun D and Mon.

MAP 8   ROYDHOUSE –
West Yorkshire

Three Acres Inn   `AR`

Roydhouse HD8 8LR
Tel: (01484) 602606

This delightful drovers' inn is not just a restaurant and hotel; there's also a delicatessen selling their own-label preserves and jellies. The menus offer a global view, with everything from crispy Peking duck with pancakes and hoisin sauce (£7.95) to open raviolo of squab pigeon and wild mushrooms served on buttered spring cabbage with lardons of pancetta (£15.95). Fish could be haddock in tomato and basil batter with chips (£14.95), while puddings include traditional sherry trifle with raspberries (£6.50). Wines from £13.95. Closed Sat L.

MAP 3 RYE – East Sussex

Fish Café

17 Tower Street, Rye TN31 7AT
Tel: (01797) 222226
Website: www.thefishcafe.com

| Cooking 4 | Seafood/Modern European | £43 |

The Fish Café is a rather stark, red-brick ware-house conversion on one of the main roads through Rye. There are two parts to the operation: a fairly minimalist ground-floor café serving lunch and weekend dinners, but we focus here on the businesslike, seafood-themed first-floor restaurant, which is open for dinner only. As the name suggests, it's a piscophile's dream, offering a regularly changing menu featuring the likes of lobster, Rye Bay scallops and black bream. But carnivores are catered for too, with perhaps a main course of fillet steak with wild mushrooms, and there are vegetarian alternatives. Flavour combinations can be bold – viz. chargrilled squid with pak choi and scallions stir-fried with sweet soy and tamarind sauce, or a main course of steamed fillets of lemon sole with mussel and Indian spice sauce, cauliflower purée and pan-fried Jerusalem artichoke. Nonetheless, those who like simple things can go for the seafood platter, and end with all the comfort of panettone bread-and-butter pudding. The fairly priced wine list runs to 50-odd bottles, with half a dozen house wines £11.50 to £12.95.

Chef: Paul Webbe Proprietors: Paul and Rebecca Webbe
Open: all week D only 6 to 9.30 Meals: alc (main courses
£10 to £23) Service: not inc Cards: Amex, Maestro,
MasterCard, Visa Details: 62 seats. Vegetarian meals. No
smoking. Music. Air-conditioned

MAP 3 ST ALBANS – Hertfordshire

Darcys   AR

2 Hatfield Road, St Albans AL1 3RP
Tel: (01727) 730777

This smart restaurant is situated close enough to the centre of St Albans to bring in the punters for lunch and dinner. Owner/proprietor Ruth Hurran is Australian, which perhaps explains the kangaroo spring rolls (£6.50) on the menu. Among main courses there might be snapper fillet with smoked chilli jam and pea and broad bean

mash (£14.50), or lamb rump with a juniper berry jus accompanied by red cabbage and lardons (£14.90), and the à la carte menu is supplemented by set-price lunch and early evening deals (£11.50/£14.50). A brief wine list starts at £12.90. Open all week.

MAP 1 ST ERVAN – Cornwall

St Ervan Manor

The Old Rectory, St Ervan PL27 7TA
Tel: (01841) 540255
Website: www.stervanmanor.co.uk

| Cooking 7 | Modern British | £63 |

Hidden among trees off the village road, the former rectory of St Ervan is a peaceful place built of local stone, run with flair by Lorraine and Allan Clarke. The diminutive public rooms may look a little country twee to some, but the sense of relaxation is profoundly welcoming. In Nathan Outlaw, they have a superstar chef too, dedicated entirely to producing a dazzling array of dishes. There will more than likely be a risotto or two, perhaps a lobster version containing flavourful pieces of lobster, enhanced with slivers of orange, strips of basil and a foaming lobster sauce.

The format is a choice of two menus of six courses each, the temptation being for two diners to swap plates halfway through each course. That way, you might start on venison with parsnip and cinnamon, espresso and chestnuts, and then find yourself tasting beef fillet with shallot sauce, chicory and borlotti beans. If there is a moment of doubt, it lies in whether there really is such an obvious gulf in the value of raw materials between the two menus to bridge the £20 gap, but it's hard to cavil when the technique and presentation are sound throughout. A star dish at inspection part-nered new season's asparagus with smoked mayonnaise, watercress and a fried quail's egg, while another featured three soft scallops with Indian-spiced butternut squash purée and roasted squash seeds, and a sublime finale of wafer-thin apple tart came topped with cream-cheese ice cream, surrounded by a vanilla-speckled apple syrup. Canapés are good too, and breads are close to perfect.

There is evidence of passion in the wine department too, with fine selections from Italy and the Rhône, a reasonable spread available by the glass (perhaps the best option with a multi-course menu), and prices that are mostly fair. A glass of Camel Valley Brut (£6.50), made just up the road, makes an appetising way to start. Bottle prices open at £15. As the Guide goes to press news reaches us that St Ervan is for sale.

Chef: Nathan Outlaw **Proprietors:** Allan and Lorraine Clarke **Open:** Wed to Sun D only 7 to 9 **Closed:** 19 Dec to 19 Jan **Meals:** Set D £45 to £65 **Service:** not inc **Cards:** Delta, Maestro, MasterCard, Visa **Details:** 20 seats. Car park. No children under 14. No smoking. Wheelchair access (also WC). Music. No mobile phones **Accommodation:** 6 rooms

---

MAP 1 **ST IVES – Cornwall**

Alba

Old Lifeboat House, Wharf Road, St Ives TR26 1LF
Tel: (01736) 797222
Website: www.alba-restaurant.co.uk

| Cooking 3 | Modern European | £43 |

⊘

If you want to secure the much-desired view over the harbour from this former lifeboat house, ask for a table by the window on the upper floor. The décor throughout is light, bright and minimalist, with white-painted walls and white napery. Dinner starts with an amuse-bouche – maybe creamed cauliflower and Stilton soup served in a tiny tureen – and 'excellent' home-made granary and tomato bread. Mackerel tempura with a sesame and soy dipping sauce 'was an absolute *tour de force*' at inspection, or you could start with terrine of duck with fig chutney. Fish is a strong suit, as in a creamy nage of black bream and scallops infused with star anise, or there might be confit duck leg with braised red cabbage if you want an alternative. Finish with a taster selection of chocolate, including a mould of dark chocolate and orange mousse, and banana and white chocolate ice cream. Plenty of wines are served by the glass from an international list. House Australian is £12.95.

Chef: Grant Nethercott **Proprietor:** The Harbour Kitchen Co. Ltd **Open:** all week 11.30 to 2, 5 to 10 (6 to 9.30 low season) **Closed:** 25 and 26 Dec **Meals:** alc (main courses L £8 to £15, D £14 to £20). Set L and D 5 to 7 £13 (2 courses) to £16 **Service:** not inc **Cards:** Amex, Delta, Maestro, MasterCard, Visa **Details:** 65 seats. Vegetarian meals. Children's helpings. No smoking. Wheelchair access (also WC). Music. Air-conditioned

---

Porthgwidden Beach Café

Porthgwidden Beach, St Ives TR26 1NT
Tel: (01736) 796791　　　　　　AR

Seaside café with great position overlooking the beach and St Ives Bay. Related to the Porthminster Beach Café (see entry below), the lively menu offers simple stuff using the freshest seafood: crisp calamari or moules marinière (both £5.95) to start, perhaps, followed by Porthgwidden fish and chips in herb batter (£9.95), or whole local grilled lemon sole (£10.95). Breakfast and light lunches (baguettes from £5.50). Wines from £10.95. Open all week Apr to Oct.

Porthminster Beach Café

Porthminster Beach, St Ives TR26 2EB
Tel: (01736) 795352
Website: www.porthminstercafe.co.uk

| Cooking 4 | Global/Seafood | £46 |

⊘

The position on Porthminster beach is rather special, with unbeatable and uninterrupted views over the sea. The Art Deco building, right on the beach, was converted to the Beach Café back in 1991, and continues to add a touch of excitement to this ever-gentrifying town. It is closed over winter, so there's no opportunity to enjoy the view over the bay on the stormiest of days, but there's a large terrace for a truly Mediterranean experience in summer. Or should that be an Antipodean experience? Aussie Michael Smith has been chef since 2002, and he now fronts a TV show (Beach Cafe) based on the restaurant on Digital TV. Lunch can be as satisfying as a Cornish crab sandwich or as exotic as crispy fried chilli squid with black spice, Thai salad and citrus white miso. In the evening, Smith pushes the boat out with scallop risotto with piquillo peppers, mascarpone and lemon vodka, followed by twice-cooked Barbary duck on braised salsify with seared foie gras and a gooseberry and Cointreau sauce. Finish with blood orange and Campari posset with a ginger glass biscuit. The sparky wine list kicks off at £11.95.

Chef: Michael Smith **Proprietors:** David Fox, Jim Woolcock, Roger and Tim Symons, and Michael Smith **Open:** all week 12 to 3.45, 6 to 10 **Closed:** Nov to Mar **Meals:** alc (main courses L £7 to £13, D £17 to £20) **Service:** not inc **Cards:** Maestro, MasterCard, Visa **Details:** 57 seats. 70 seats outside. Vegetarian meals. Children's helpings (L only). No smoking. Music. No mobile phones

---

MAP 1 | ST KEYNE – Cornwall

Well House

St Keyne PL14 4RN
Tel: (01579) 342001
Website: www.wellhouse.co.uk

Cooking 3 | Modern British | £52

New owners have taken over this secluded stone-built Victorian mansion overlooking the Looe valley, but otherwise things continue unabated. Glenn Gatland remains at the stoves, delivering menus of a manageable size with straightforward descriptions. There are few surprises in terms of combinations: a plate of roast goats' cheese and Parma ham comes with avocado, tomato and red onion salad, while a meaty main course of fillet of beef might be teamed with wild mushroom and spinach fricassee and horseradish mash, with a fish option along the lines of roast fillet of halibut served with crushed new potatoes and lime beurre blanc. For dessert, there's perhaps rhubarb fool tart with ginger ice cream. Mark-ups on the knowledgeably assembled wine list seem fair, with plenty of choice under £25 and house bottles starting at £13.50.

Chef: Glenn Gatland Proprietors: Richard and Deborah Farrow
Open: all week 12 to 1.30, 7 to 8.30 Meals: alc L (main courses £11 to £15). Set D £37.50 Service: not inc Cards: Delta, Maestro, MasterCard, Visa Details: 36 seats. Car park. Vegetarian meals. No children under 8. No smoking. Wheelchair access (also men's WC). Music. No mobile phones Accommodation: 9 rooms

MAP 3 | ST MARGARET'S AT CLIFFE – Kent

Wallett's Court

Westcliffe, St Margaret's at Cliffe CT15 6EW
Tel: (01304) 852424
Website: www.wallettscourt.com

Cooking 3 | Modern European | £50

Just a mile from the famous White Cliffs, this rural hotel is in the capable hands of the Oakley family. The dining room in their unique seventeenth-century farmhouse is spacious and light, with beams and standing timbers and furniture to match. The Garden of England is well represented on Stephen Harvey's classic menu: Kentish wood

pigeon, Rye Bay scallops, Romney Marsh lamb, and locally landed Dover sole. Those scallops may be pan-fried and served with a rhubarb and ginger compote as a starter, while loin of Battle Forest boar turns up as a main course with roast pear, and celeriac and potato rösti. A fish main course could be seared sea bass with spiced chickpeas, saffron tabbouleh and tahini sauce. Valrhona chocolate and orange tart will sate any sweet cravings, with British and European cheeses with crab apple compote as an alternative. The wine list is an impressive collection from around the world, including Kent. Two house wines come in at £14.95, and there's a decent choice by the glass from £4.25.

Chef: Stephen Harvey Proprietors: Chris and Lea Oakley
Open: Tue to Fri and Sun L 12 to 2, all week D 7 to 9 Closed: Christmas Meals: Set L £17 (2 courses) to £19.50, Set D £35. Bar menu available Service: not inc Cards: Amex, Delta, Diners, Maestro, MasterCard, Visa Details: 70 seats. Car park. Vegetarian meals. Children's helpings. No smoking. Wheelchair access (also WC). Music. No mobile phones Accommodation: 17 rooms

MAP 1 | ST MARTIN'S – Isles of Scilly

St Martin's on the Isle

Lower Town, St Martin's
TR25 0QW
Tel: (01720) 422092
Website: www.stmartinshotel.co.uk

Cooking 6 | Modern European | £58

'The thing which astonishes is that such a wonderful meal is to be had at virtually the end of the kingdom – and that it lives up to the stunning surroundings,' began a reporter, breathless with admiration for the Sykeses' smart, unusual hotel. It was built to look like a row of fishermen's cottages, and overlooks a wild, uninhabited island called Tean, which provides the name of the elegant upstairs dining room. Getting here involves a choice of boat, plane or helicopter.

Whichever you opt for, the reward is John Mijatovic's highly crafted cooking, which tacks to a classical country idiom with no violent shocks, just a high degree of polish, refinement and pleasure. A generous bowl of warm vichyssoise is luxuriously textured and pungent with fresh leekiness. A mosaic terrine looks stunning, comprising quail and foie gras and fine textural range, being earthily offset with celeriac purée. Seafood shows up as well as it ought in the location, so that a main course of flawlessly timed brill comes with a fine risotto of lobster, leek and peas in a green sauce of spinach purée cleverly flavoured with lobster. Meat options have included Gressingham duck – honey-glazed breast and beignets of the leg – with baby turnips in red wine, and vegetarians have a menu to themselves. Desserts deliver a crowd pleasing vanilla rice pudding with raspberry sorbet, crushed praline and raspberries. The sublime listing of West Country cheeses is also worth a look, at the very least. A bistro on the ground floor serves simpler dishes. The wine list kicks off at £17, with around 10 by the glass from £3.

Chef: John Mijatovic **Proprietors:** Peter and Penny Sykes **Open:** all week D only 7 to 9 **Closed:** Nov to Feb **Meals:** Set D £44.50. Bistro menu available **Service:** not inc **Cards:** Amex, Delta, Diners, Maestro, MasterCard, Visa **Details:** 80 seats. Vegetarian meals. No children over 9. Children's helpings. No smoking. Wheelchair access (also WC). No music. No mobile phones **Accommodation:** 30 rooms

MAP 1   **ST MAWES** – Cornwall

Hotel Tresanton

27 Lower Castle Road, St Mawes TR2 5DR
Tel: (01326) 270055
Website: www.tresanton.com

Cooking 4 | Modern European | £55

Olga Polizzi's eye for detail has injected a sense of the Mediterranean into this old Cornish building. The overall effect is contemporary but individual; the blue and cream dining room, with its mosaic floor, leads out on to a terrace, which has views over the sea. Paul Wadham's compact menu is not just about seafood, although, with the abundance of local supplies, seafood might be a natural choice: crab with avocado, egg, tomato and lemon mayonnaise, for example, followed by halibut with mash, broccoli, peas and pancetta. Lobster and oysters require 24 hours' notice; otherwise, start with speck with chicory, Gorgonzola and spring onions, or watercress soup with smoked haddock and white truffle. Main course options like Merrifield duck breast with gratin potatoes, spinach and asparagus, or gnocchi with tomato, goats' cheese and basil, vie for attention amongst the seafood. Finish with tarte Tatin with vanilla ice cream, yoghurt pannacotta with berries, or go for the West Country cheeses with walnut bread and figs. House Pinot Grigio is £18, Pinot Noir £20, each £4 by the glass.

Chef: Paul Wadham **Proprietor:** Olga Polizzi **Open:** all week 12.30 to 2.30, 7 to 9.30 **Meals:** Set L £21 (2 courses) to £28, Set D £38 to £45. Snack L menu available **Service:** not inc **Cards:** Amex, Delta, Maestro, MasterCard, Visa **Details:** 50 seats. 60 seats outside. Car park. Vegetarian meals. Children's helpings. Wheelchair access (not WC). No music **Accommodation:** 29 rooms

Rising Sun

The Square, St Mawes TR2 5DJ
Tel: (01326) 270233
Website: www.risingsunstmawes.com

Cooking 4 | Modern European | £46

Right on the harbour, the Rising Sun is at the heart of the action of this pretty tourist village and successfully combines a role as pub (with a straightforward bar menu) and smart restaurant-with-rooms. Considering that the sea is steps away, seafood is very much in evidence on the menu, although non-fish dishes are also well represented. Expect traditional potted crab, or rabbit terrine with rhubarb chutney, then monkfish flavoured with rosemary and lime, wrapped and cooked in bacon and served with redcurrants, or maybe pink coriander duck breast alongside black cherry compote and red wine sauce. Desserts might include chocolate and cherry terrine with a honey and Muscat parfait, or rhubarb and apple crumble with clotted cream. A modest but interesting wine list starts at £12, with most bottles below £20, and there are a dozen by the glass.

Chef: Ann Long **Proprietor:** John Milan **Open:** Sun L 12 to 2, all week D 7 to 9 **Meals:** Set L £12 (2 courses), Set D £36. Bar menu available **Service:** not inc **Cards:** Maestro, MasterCard, Visa **Details:** 40 seats. Vegetarian meals. No children under 12 exc Sun L. No smoking. Wheelchair access (also WC). No music **Accommodation:** 8 rooms

MAP 1   **ST MERRYN** – Cornwall

Ripley's

St Merryn PL28 8NQ
Tel: (01841) 520179

Cooking 3 | Modern British | £51

If you peek through the window on the left of this cosy-looking yellow cottage you'll see the chefs hard at work. The terrace in a pretty village not far from the north coast is on a small scale, so tables are

close together. The menu contains much of interest in around half a dozen choices at each course. Start with jellied pork knuckle with gooseberry relish, or pan-fried scallops with fennel purée and sauce vierge, then venture on to grilled fillet of turbot with samphire and hollandaise, or roast rump of Cornish lamb with Puy lentils and hasselback potatoes. Whole lemon sole is simply grilled and served with Montpellier butter, and you could end with bread-and-butter pudding. The wine list concentrates on Europe and the southern hemisphere, with six house selections starting proceedings from £14.95.

Chef/Proprietor: Paul Ripley   Open: Tue to Sat D only 7 to 9.30   Closed: Christmas, New Year, Jan   Meals: alc (main courses £14.50 to £19.50)   Service: not inc   Cards: Delta, Maestro, MasterCard, Visa   Details: 32 seats. No young children. No smoking. Music. No mobile phones

---

MAP 8   **SALE –**
          Greater Manchester

Hanni's

4 Brooklands Road, Sale M33 3SQ
Tel: (0161) 973 6606

Cooking 2 | Eastern Mediterranean | £37

The eponymous Hanni is to be found front-of-house at this notable restaurant, which serves up fine eastern Mediterranean and Middle Eastern dishes. Menus open with the usual meze fare, including falafel, hummus and kleftiko, which are all well presented and flavoured. Alternatively, baba ganoush, or lahma bi-ajeen (Lebanese-style pizza with spicy meat toppings) might start, followed by house specialities such as lamb osso buco with tomatoes, peppers and paprika, or mezelica (chicken cooked in garlic butter with white wine and mushrooms). There's a fine array of couscous dishes, plus various tempting kebabs, too. Desserts are a sticky-sweet affair – think rum baba or baklava. Turkish, Greek or Arabic coffee might finish, while the international wine list starts at £12.95 and includes some interesting Greek, Israeli and Lebanese bins.

Chef: Mr Hoonanian   Proprietors: Mohammed Hanni and Jennifer Al-Taraboulsy   Open: Mon to Sat D only 6 to 10.30 (11 Fri/Sat)   Closed: 25 and 26 Dec, 1 Jan, Good Fri, Easter Mon   Meals: alc (main courses £11.50 to £15.50). Set D 6 to 7 £11.95 (2 courses)   Service: not inc   Cards: Amex, Delta, Maestro, MasterCard, Visa   Details: 50 seats. Vegetarian meals. Children's helpings. No smoking area. Wheelchair access (not WC). Music. Air-conditioned

---

MAP 8   **SALFORD –**
          Greater Manchester

Lowry Hotel, River Restaurant

50 Dearmans Place, Chapel Wharf, Salford M3 5LH
Tel: (0161) 827 4041
Website: www.roccofortehotels.com

NEW CHEF | Modern European | £68

The Lowry is on the bank of the River Irwell, and the big-windowed, formally attired River Restaurant continues as the gastronomic hub of the hotel, where a new head chef, Eyck Zimmer, took over the running of the kitchen too late for inspection. However, the style of cooking looks set to continue in a modern European vein, with the carte featuring dishes such as carpaccio with pickled girolles, artichoke and Parmesan, and pressed tomato with Lancashire goats' cheese and shallot dressing to start, while main courses typically range from tuna steak glazed with turmeric and coconut and served with hearts of palm and pak choi to Dover sole accompanied by crisp couscous, watercress, asparagus and a ginger broth. The wine list has been put together with a discerning eye. It's packed with interesting bottles picked up from all over, with around 15 by the glass and own-label wines at £21 and £26.

Chef: Eyck Zimmer   Proprietor: Rocco Forte   Open: Mon to Sat 12 to 2.30, 6 to 10.30, Sun 12.30 to 4, 7 to 10.30   Meals: alc (main courses £15.50 to £34.50). Set L and D £20 (2 courses) to £42   Service: 10% (optional)   Cards: Amex, Delta, Diners, Maestro, MasterCard, Visa   Details: 126 seats. 50 seats outside. Vegetarian meals. Children's helpings. No smoking in dining room. Wheelchair access (also WC). Music. Air-conditioned   Accommodation: 165 rooms

---

MAP 2   **SAPPERTON –**
          Gloucestershire

Bell at Sapperton

Sapperton GL7 6LE
Tel: (01285) 760298
Website: www.foodatthebell.co.uk

Cooking 4 | Modern European | £44

Ivan Reid's adventurous cooking remains the backbone of this attractively converted country inn. The Cotswolds location suggests tradition, but owners Paul Davidson and Patricia Le Jeune have worked hard at elevating the atmosphere of their stone building to something more refined. The monthly-changing menu may kick off in style with potted foie gras with home-made brioche buns, or a baked pigeon faggot on sautéed potatoes with Savoy cabbage. Fish makes the occasional appearance among main courses – perhaps plainly grilled fillet of wild sea bass with hollandaise – but more likely are pure-bred Hereford ribeye with tomatoes, mushrooms and chips. A plate of four West Country cheeses makes an alternative to desserts along the lines of home-made vanilla ice cream with Pedro Ximénez sherry. Three house wines, from £13.50 to £14.75, open the intelligently chosen wine list, which offers some good-quality, fairly priced drinking. Look to the 'Fine Wine' sections for premier-league names.

Chef: Ivan Reid Proprietors: Paul Davidson and Patricia Le Jeune Open: all week 12 to 2, 7 to 9.30 Closed: 25 Dec, 3 to 10 Jan Meals: alc (main courses £12.50 to £18.50) Service: not inc Cards: Delta, Maestro, MasterCard, Visa Details: 70 seats. 40 seats outside. Car park. Vegetarian meals. No children under 10 at D. Children's helpings. No smoking in dining room. Wheelchair access (also WC). No music. No mobile phones

MAP 8 **SAWLEY** – Lancashire

Spread Eagle

Sawley BB7 4NH
Tel: (01200) 441202
Website: www.the-spreadeagle.co.uk

Cooking 4 | Modern British | £32

This charming seventeenth-century building opposite ancient Sawley Abbey evokes an old-world air, but while the bar is traditional the style of food in the dining room, with its views through 'panoramic windows' of the River Ribble, is 'unashamedly modern English with little bits of fusion cooking'. A starter of confit of duck comes with spring onions, beetroot and onions in a pumpkin seed dressing, while pork terrine is accompanied by a soft-boiled egg and a dollop of rhubarb compote. Rare fillet of beef with a creamy sauce of black pepper and brandy served with potato dauphinois has been described as 'classic cooking at its best', while pan-fried chicken breast accompanied by a velouté of wild mushrooms has been simply 'gorgeous'. Vegetables are impressive, and bread is flavoursome and well textured. A trio of raspberry desserts – trifle, parfait and ganache –

and sticky toffee pudding have both been described as 'excellent'. The long and far-reaching wine list is good value, with Georges Duboeuf opening around a dozen house selections at £10.50.

Chef: Greig Barnes Proprietors: Nigel and Ysanne Williams Open: Tue to Sun L 12 to 2, Tue to Sat D 6 to 9 Meals: alc exc Sun L (main courses £9.50 to £16.50). Set L Tue to Sat £9.50 (2 courses) to £12.45, Set L Sun £13.50 (2 courses) to £16.75, Set D Tue to Fri 6 to 7 £10.50 (2 courses) to £13.75, Set D Tue to Fri 7 to 9 £13 (2 courses). Bar L menu available Tue to Sat Service: not inc Cards: Maestro, MasterCard, Visa Details: 80 seats. Car park. Vegetarian meals. Children's helpings. No smoking in dining room. Wheelchair access (also WC). Music

MAP 6 **SAXMUNDHAM** – Suffolk

Bell Hotel

31 High Street, Saxmundham IP17 1AF
Tel: (01728) 602331
Website: www.bellhotel-saxmundham.co.uk

Cooking 4 | Anglo-French | £36

A Grade II listed building, this handsome coaching inn continues to evolve – all the guest bedrooms have been refurbished, for instance – and the dining room is a smart space, though 'not oppressively posh', in which to dine. Andrew Blackburn cooks in a modern Anglo-French style, and our inspector found most dishes on the short menus 'well thought out', and combinations of ingredients 'convincing'. Pan-fried scallops – six of them – are served as a starter on a risotto of butternut squash and herbs, while lambs' sweetbreads with pancetta are given a good contrast of flavour and texture with a pear poached in red wine. Meat is from the top drawer – witness a well-flavoured chunk of loin of lamb attractively presented with cumin-spiced aubergine on sweet potato pancakes – and fish is accurately timed, as in a fillet of crisp-skinned gilthead bream in a pungent sauce of vanilla and cardamom served with roast salsify. Oranges glazed in Cointreau sabayon, accompanied by orange sorbet, is a simple idea well executed. Service is friendly and well paced, and the wine list refrains from heavy mark-ups. Eight house wines, priced from £10.50, are all available by the glass from £2.75 to £4.10.

Chef/Proprietor: Andrew Blackburn Open: Tue to Sat 12 to 2, 6.30 to 9 Closed: 26 Dec, 1 Jan, spring and autumn half-term Meals: alc (main courses £12.50 to £15.50). Set L £11.95 (2 courses) to £14.50, Set D £17.50. Bar menu available Service: not inc Cards: Delta, Maestro, MasterCard, Visa Details: 26 seats. 15 seats outside. Car park. Vegetarian meals. No smoking in dining room. No music Accommodation: 10 rooms

MAP 9 **SCARBOROUGH –**
North Yorkshire

Lanterna

33 Queen Street, Scarborough YO11 1HQ
Tel: (01723) 363616
Website: www.lanterna-ristorante.co.uk

Cooking 3	Italian	£42

Never one to shirk the limelight, Giorgio Alessio is the star of the show at this family-run restaurant. His press cuttings take up wall space along with signed photographs of actors who have appeared at the nearby theatre, and he is happy to leave the stoves for a special dish: he prepares zabaglione classico over a flambé burner at table, the result being a 'deliciously warm, frothy, quite alcoholic, and very, very rich' dessert. Pre-dinner nibbles of small deep-fried herby pastries are equally well received, while the rest of the Piedmont-based menu incorporates local produce in the shape of perhaps spaghetti with mixed fish of the day served 'in bianco', a starter with home-made pasta perfectly al dente, or grilled halibut accompanied by boiled new and deep-fried cubed potatoes, broccoli frittata and peperonata. Truffles are a seasonal speciality, imported from north-west Italy, perhaps accompanying carpaccio, or going into a main course of chicken breast cooked with Italian herbs. Service is prompt and efficient, and particular praise has been lavished on espresso – 'wonderful, very dark and very intense'. The all-Italian wine list is a weighty tome, with pages of classics. House wines are £11.50.

Chef: Giorgio Alessio **Proprietors:** Giorgio and Rachel Alessio **Open:** Mon to Sat D only 7 to 9.30 **Closed:** 25 and 26 Dec, 1 Jan, 2 weeks Oct **Meals:** alc (main courses £14 to £41) **Service:** not inc **Cards:** Delta, Diners, Maestro, MasterCard, Visa **Details:** 30 seats. Vegetarian meals. Children's helpings. No smoking. Wheelchair access (not WC). Music. Air-conditioned

MAP 10 **SEAHAM – Co Durham**

Seaham Hall, White Room

Lord Byron's Walk, Seaham SR7 7AG
Tel: (0191) 516 1400
Website: www.seaham-hall.com

Cooking 5	Modern European	£70

A large spiralling water sculpture stands in front of this historic building where Lord Byron married

in 1815. Inside, the décor is distinctly up to date, with taupe walls, ultra-modern lighting and brown and russet tones to the furniture in the classically proportioned lounge/bar, and a crisp, white look to the formal dining room. Here, Steven Smith's ambitious food makes liberal use of luxury ingredients – a salad of lobster, or champagne-poached turbot, say – but he's not afraid of balancing these with humbler materials. The good-value menu of the day, for example, could produce pan-fried lambs' sweetbreads and braised tongue served with peas and broad beans, and main courses of braised pork cheeks with carrot purée, cavolo nero and pork jus. Poached and stuffed baby chicken comes with gnocchi and morel cream, and Northumberland beef as braised rib with watercress and foie gras, or fillet with its own bouillon and morels. Desserts are properly indulgent, perhaps chocolate tortellini with blood orange and pistachio. The wine list is not short of premier-league players, topped and tailed by a list of fizz including the best from Champagne and a good range of half-bottles. In between you'll find some good drinking in the £20-plus range and around 15 by the glass. House wine is £20.

Chef: Steven Smith **Proprietors:** Tom and Jocelyn Maxfield **Open:** all week 12 to 2.30, 7 to 10 **Meals:** alc (main courses £20 to £34). Set L Mon to Sat £17.50 to £65, Set L Sun £27.50, Set D £30 to £65. Bar L menu available **Service:** not inc **Cards:** Amex, Delta, Maestro, MasterCard, Visa **Details:** 50 seats. 50 seats outside. Car park. Vegetarian meals. No smoking. Wheelchair access (also WC). Music. No mobile phones. Air-conditioned **Accommodation:** 19 rooms

MAP 2 **SEAVIEW – Isle of Wight**

Seaview Hotel

High Street, Seaview PO34 5EX
Tel: (01983) 612711
Website: www.seaviewhotel.co.uk

Cooking 3	Anglo-French	£44

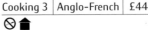

The patio forecourt, bars, small dining room and bright brasserie have a nautical styling that befits the hotel's location just up the street from the sea. A visitor has reported on a buzzy atmosphere and a versatile kitchen 'capable of anything from a sandwich via fish and chips to a three-course lunch and doing it well', while in winter the short, seasonal menu might turn up such comforting starters as oxtail soup with horseradish dumplings, or perhaps sautéed wild mushrooms on butter bread with truffle ice cream and roast tomatoes. Main courses have included roast breast of duck with preserved leg, slow-braised red cabbage and fondant potato, and fillet of local bass with a crab and watercress sauce. The seasonal feel is carried through to enterprising desserts such as mulled poached pear with Stilton crème brûlée, and chocolate soup with doughnuts, sweet parsnip parfait and marshmallows. The short wine list opens with French house wines at £13.95.

Chef: Michael Green Proprietor: Techaid Facilities Ltd Open: all week 12 to 2, 7 to 9.30 Closed: 24 to 26 Dec Meals: alc (main courses £14 to £22). Set L Sun £16.95. Bar menu available Service: not inc Cards: Amex, Delta, Diners, Maestro, MasterCard, Visa Details: 80 seats. 30 seats outside. Car park. Vegetarian meals. No children under 5. Children's helpings. No smoking. Wheelchair access (also WC). No music. No mobile phones. Air-conditioned Accommodation: 17 rooms

MAP 2 SHAFTESBURY – Dorset

La Fleur de Lys AR

Bleke Street, Shaftesbury SP7 8AW
Tel: (01747) 853717

This formal-style dining room – all drapes, linen table covers and soft lighting – offers well-presented Anglo-French cuisine. Dinner could start with a hot soufflé of sole and lobster, and go on to main courses (from £19 to £24) of pan-fried Aberdeen Angus fillet topped with foie gras in a truffle sauce, or chargrilled veal with roast baby leeks. Desserts include poached figs with a lemon mascarpone mousse. Many good wines under £20. Accommodation. Open Wed to Sun L and Mon to Sat D.

Wayfarers

Sherborne Causeway, Shaftesbury SP7 9PX
Tel: (01747) 852821

Cooking 4 | Modern British | £37

Exposed beams, natural stone and a warm welcome await the visitor to this bistro just west of town. The menus are now entirely three-course set-price affairs with choices, but value for money is clearly still a priority. Clare Newton runs front-of-house, and service is efficient and correct. Presentation and attention to detail are strong points of the kitchen's output, where Mark produces complex dishes such as a starter of pan-seared scallops accompanied by lightly curried parsnip fondant, a caper and raisin dressing and parsnip crisps. Main course could be Cornish monkfish on a ricotta and tomato tarte fine with artichokes, crispy ham and an orange and lobster reduction, or roast suprêmes of wild pigeon on sour-and-sweet red cabbage in a truffle reduction accompanied by pommes Anna. Desserts are equally flamboyant: apple and cinnamon sponge comes with a toffee butterscotch sauce and fromage blanc. The wine list favours France but the New World makes a token appearance. Seven house selections are around £13.50.

Chef: Mark Newton Proprietors: Clare and Mark Newton Open: Wed to Fri and Sun L 12 to 1.30, Tue to Sat D 7 to 9 Closed: 3 weeks from 26 Dec, 10 days June to July Meals: Set L Wed to Fri £23 to £35, Set L Sun £24, Set D Tue to Fri £23 to £35, Set D Sat £27 to £35 Service: not inc Cards: Delta, Maestro, MasterCard, Visa Details: 34 seats. 6 seats outside. Car park. Vegetarian meals. No children under 8 at D. Children's helpings. No smoking. Wheelchair access (also women's WC). No music Accommodation: 1 room

MAP 9 SHEFFIELD – South Yorkshire

Artisan and Catch

32-34 Sandygate Road, Crosspool, Sheffield S10 5RY
Tel: (01142) 666096
Website: www.artisanofsheffield.com

Cooking 5 | Mod. British/Mediterranean | £43

Artisan and Catch represents a shift in direction for Richard Smith and his team. Located just off the A57 some way out of the centre of the city, this large corner site was formerly Thyme. There are now two restaurants where there was once one: Catch, a simple seafood café on the first floor dealing in oysters, fish soup, chowders, lobster and chips and omelette Arnold Bennet; and Artisan, a bistrot de luxe, on the ground floor. Here Simon Wild, who headed the Thyme kitchen, is in charge. Early menus yielded appealing brasserie dishes such as jellied ham hock and parsley with Hartington Stilton salad, homemade black pudding and piccalilli, oxtail and black pudding shepherd's pie, and cod roasted with tapenade, sauté of squid, chorizo, potatoes, rocket and red peppers, giving every indication that the refined, imaginative modern approach to cooking, based on classic techniques, will continue. The wine list works well at all levels, from a good basic selection starting at £13 through to a reserve list of considerable depth in Old and New World producers.

Chefs: Richard Smith and Simon Wild **Proprietors:** Richard and Victoria Smith **Open:** all week 12 to 2.30 (3 Sun), 6 to 10 **Meals:** alc (main courses £10 to £26). Set L and D Sat £10 (2 courses) to £15 **Service:** not inc **Cards:** Amex, Delta, Maestro, MasterCard, Visa **Details:** 80 seats. Vegetarian meals. Children's helpings. No smoking. Wheelchair access (also WC). Music. Air conditioned

Blue Room Brasserie

798 Chesterfield Road, Woodseats, Sheffield
S8 0SF
Tel: (0114) 255 2004
Website: www.blueroombrasserie.co.uk

| Cooking 2 | Modern European-Plus | £43 |

The Blue Room, located in an office building to the south of the city, has a very modern approach to the business, both in terms of the smart urban look of the dining room, and what turns up on the plate. Christian Kent's menu is a fusion of global and British ideas with everything from white truffle risotto through to devilled lambs' kidneys in puff pastry. Lobster ravioli with a thermidor sauce, or chicken liver parfait with plum chutney might be followed by smoked haddock rarebit with tomato salad, or aromatic crispy duck pancakes. End with warm chocolate and hazelnut brownie, or perhaps bread and butter pudding with butterscotch sauce. Service is friendly, and they are also accommodating to families. The wine list opens at £11.95.

Chef/Proprietor: Christian Kent **Open:** Tue to Sat D only 6 to 10 **Meals:** alc (main courses £10 to £18) **Service:** not inc **Cards:** Maestro, MasterCard, Visa **Details:** 140 seats. Car park. Vegetarian meals. Children's helpings. No smoking in 1 dining room. Wheelchair access (also WC). Music. Air-conditioned

Greenhead House

84 Burncross Road, Chapeltown, Sheffield
S35 1SF
Tel: (0114) 246 9004

| Cooking 2 | Modern European | £53 |

A little way out of Sheffield, this cottagey restaurant has been run by Neil and Anne Allen for over 20 years. Neil cooks, while Anne cheerfully tends to the front-of-house. There is a lounge for pre-dinner drinks, and the dining room features gold- and red-patterned drapes and wallpaper, white napery and flower arrangements. The four-course dinner menu, which changes frequently, is resolutely euro-centric, so polenta with roast quails and Italian sausage, or pears stuffed with Gorgonzola and walnuts and poached in white wine precede a second course of perhaps lentil soup sprinkled with truffle oil. Main courses follow: saddle of wild boar stuffed with prunes, apricots and pistachio nuts, say, or poached paupiettes of lemon sole with prawn risotto. Among puddings may be vanilla cheesecake with Yorkshire rhubarb compote. Wines have an international flavour, with house selections opening at £15.

Chef: Neil Allen **Proprietors:** Neil and Anne Allen **Open:** Fri L 12 to 1, Wed to Sat D 7 to 8.30 **Closed:** Christmas to New Year, 2 weeks Easter, 2 weeks Aug **Meals:** alc L (main courses £10.50 to £12). Set D £40 to £43 **Service:** not inc **Cards:** Amex, Delta, Maestro, MasterCard, Visa **Details:** 32 seats. 12 seats outside. Car park. Vegetarian meals. Children's helpings. No smoking. Wheelchair access (also WC). No music. No mobile phones

Rafters

220 Oakbrook Road, Nether Green, Sheffield
S11 7ED
Tel: (0114) 230 4819
Website: www.raftersrestaurant.co.uk

| Cooking 3 | Modern European | £48 |

This friendly bistro is a popular neighbourhood haunt, located in a quieter suburb of the city. The décor is bright and breezy, and the tables and upholstered chairs are well spaced. Chef/proprietor Marcus Lane keeps his menu relatively short, with five choices for each course, and changes it every six to eight weeks. Ice creams and breads are prepared daily on the premises, while much produce is sourced from local farms and small growers. Start with grilled fillet of sea bream with orange-glazed endive and marinated artichokes, and move on to roast loin of Derbyshire lamb with cannelloni of aubergine and creamed spinach served on a butter-bean and herb stew. Vegetarians might go for a tart of slow-roast vegetables with warm provençale vinaigrette. End with frosted berries with hot white chocolate sauce and a blood-orange and star anise jelly, or a plate of Yorkshire cheeses. The wine list is a well-thought-through global affair, starting at £12.50 for five French and Chilean house bottles.

Chef: Marcus Lane Proprietors: Marcus Lane and Michael Sabin Open: Mon and Wed to Sat D only 7 to 10 Closed: 25 Dec, bank hols exc Good Fri Meals: alc (main courses £16 to £19.50). Set D £28.95 Service: not inc Cards: Amex, Delta, Maestro, MasterCard, Visa Details: 40 seats. Vegetarian meals. No smoking. Music. No mobile phones. Air-conditioned

MAP 8 **SHELF – West Yorkshire**

Bentley's

12 Wade House Road, Shelf HX3 7PB
Tel: (01274) 690992
Website: www.bentleys-foodandwine.co.uk

Cooking 3 | **Modern British** | **£36**

Bentley's, an unassuming terraced building on a busy road, is made up of a small ground-floor bar and a pair of stone-flagged dining rooms in the basement. The scale may be domestic, but what lifts it beyond the ordinary is the kitchen's attention to detail in the modern bistro-style cooking. Expect good-quality ingredients in starters like deep-fried black pudding with pea purée and a red wine and mushroom jus, or main courses of breast of wild mallard with Indian-spiced swede purée, and fillet of beef with a casserole of bacon, onion, garlic and mushrooms accompanied by a fried potato cake. Desserts have a traditional slant, with ginger sponge served with treacle and custard, and sherry trifle with fresh fruit. Lunch is a bargain but beware supplements, while the style-organised wine list is short and sweet but provides interesting choices from across the world. It kicks off at £10.75, and there are four by the glass from £2.50.

Chefs: Paul Bentley and Anthony Bickers Proprietors: Paul and Pamela Bentley Open: Tue to Fri L 12 to 2, Tue to Sat D 6.30 to 9.30 Closed: Christmas and New Year Meals: alc (main courses £11 to £19). Set L £9.75 (2 courses) to £10.95 Service: not inc Cards: Delta, Maestro, MasterCard, Visa Details: 72 seats. Vegetarian meals. Children's helpings. No-smoking area. Music. Air-conditioned

MAP 2 **SHEPTON MALLET – Somerset**

Blostin's

29–33 Waterloo Road, Shepton Mallet BA4 5HH
Tel: (01749) 343648

Chef-proprietor Nick Reed's restaurant is small but perfectly formed. His practised cooking shows

up on a short set-price menu (£15.95/£17.95) in the shape of grilled Somerset goats' cheese with sun-dried tomatoes and brioche, followed by breast of duck with poached pears and Cassis sauce. Among seasonal specialities could be crab tartlets with sauce grelette (£6.50), then loin of Exmoor venison with smoky bacon and game sauce (£17.50). Round things off with treacle and walnut tart with custard. Four house wines are £12 each. Open Tue to Sat D only.

Charlton House Hotel, Mulberry Restaurant

Shepton Mallet BA4 4PR
Tel: (01749) 342008
Website: www.charltonhouse.com

Cooking 5 | **Modern British** | **£75**

Mulberry may be a name more associated with fashionable suitcases than first-rate modern British cooking, but the restaurant at Charlton House offers another perspective. The setting is a grand country house built in 1608, bought by the luggage tycoon Roger Saul 11 years ago and decorated in idiosyncratic style, with a smart conservatory dining room. Simon Crannage's inventive and elaborate modern British cooking frequently features multiple layers of flavours and textures, giving equal billing to luxury ingredients and humbler items. Thus, starters might feature breast of squab pigeon with cauliflower pannacotta, seared foie gras, chocolate oil and ground coffee, or brill fillet on a casserole of white beans with roast langoustine, crisp Parma ham and parsley essence. Main courses are similarly labour-intensive creations: perhaps soft-poached rabbit partnered with a cannelloni of the leg meat and dates, squash purée and pearl barley ragoût, or roast turbot with black pudding gnocchi, roast salsify, onion purée, and a red wine and bacon dressing. Simpler but no less interesting options might include roast loin of venison with blackberries and liquorice, and to finish there might be an intriguing pairing of honey and cardamom brûlée with parsnip parfait.

The wine list has been compiled with enthusiasm and a fair eye for an interesting bottle. Classic reds appear alongside more innovative choices, grouped by style, and there are 12 wines by the glass. Prices are not cheap, though, with house selections £25.

Chef: Simon Crannage Proprietors: Roger and Monty Saul
Open: all week 12.30 to 2, 7.30 (7 Fri and Sat) to 9.30
Meals: Set L £24 (2 courses) to £28, Set D £52.50 to £65.
Light L menu available Service: not inc Cards: Amex, Delta,
Diners, Maestro, MasterCard, Visa Details: 70 seats. 20 seats
outside. Car park. Vegetarian meals. Children's helpings. No
smoking. Wheelchair access (also WC). Music. No mobile
phones. Air-conditioned Accommodation: 25 rooms

MAP 2 SHERBORNE – Dorset

The Green

The Green, Sherborne DT9 3HY
Tel: (01935) 813821

Cooking 2 | Modern European | £43

Michael and Judith Rust seem on first-name terms with virtually everyone who steps over the threshold at their friendly neighbourhood restaurant. The stylish renovation may be simple, but muted colours and a few large mirrors create a calming ambience. The modern British food is neatly presented, and a lot of energy is spent on finding quality local suppliers. The set-price dinner menu might start with Thai-spiced carpaccio of yellowfin tuna with pickled ginger, lemongrass, lime, coriander and guacamole, or pink-roast breast of wood pigeon with Puy lentils, parsnip crisps and a herb vinaigrette, with main courses of plainly grilled Dover sole with lemon, lime and parsley butter, or roast loin of lamb with pea purée, butternut squash and rosemary jus. Tempting desserts take in iced honey and Amaretto parfait with mangoes and passion fruit, and caramelised lemon tart with raspberries. Prices on the France-tilted wine list start at £14.95.

Chef: Michael Rust Proprietors: Judith and Michael Rust
Open: Tue to Sat 12 to 2, 7 to 9 Closed: 2 weeks Feb, 1 week
June, 1 week Sept, bank hols Meals: alc L (main courses £9 to
£17). Set D £22.50 (2 courses) to £28.95 Service: not inc
Cards: Amex, Delta, Maestro, MasterCard, Visa Details: 50
seats. 10 seats outside. Vegetarian meals. No smoking.
Wheelchair access (not WC). No music

This symbol means that the restaurant has elected to participate in *The Good Food Guide's* £5 voucher scheme (see 'Using The Good Food Guide' for details).

MAP 3 SHERE – Surrey

Kinghams

Gomshall Lane, Shere GU5 9HE
Tel: (01483) 202168
Website: www.kinghams-restaurant.co.uk

Cooking 3 | Modern English | £47

Kinghams is in a seventeenth-century half-timbered building with cottage-style gardens. Inside, the restaurant consists of two small rooms, with low, dark-beamed ceilings, separated by a fireplace; the walls are hung with prints and the tables are dressed in white. This is the setting for some modern English cooking using high-quality materials sourced locally, with fish delivered daily and written on a specials board: perhaps plainly grilled Dover sole with lemon and lime butter, or fillet of halibut glazed with Parmesan and basil on a salad of sun-dried tomatoes, red peppers, and black olives. Convincing starters have included a goats' cheese beignet on tomato jam, and local pigeon breast pan-fried with apples and ceps served on discs of filo with a sticky hazelnut sauce. A meat main course might be pan-fried rump of lamb stuffed with shallots and black pudding. A trio of brûlées, or a more unusual banana and Jersey black butter pudding on sage parfait are satisfying desserts. The balanced wine list holds much of interest. Bottles start at £12.95, and five are served by the glass from £3.50.

Chef/Proprietor: Paul Baker Open: Tue to Sun L 12 to 2, Tue
to Sat D 7 to 9.30 Closed: 25 Dec to 6 Jan Meals: alc exc
Sun L (main courses £11 to £23). Set L Tue to Sat £14.95 (2
courses), Set L Sun £15.95 (2 courses) to £19.95, Set D Tue
to Thur £15.95 (2 courses) Service: not inc Cards: Amex,
Delta, Diners, Maestro, MasterCard, Visa Details: 48 seats.
20 seats outside. Car park. Vegetarian meals. Children's helpings. No smoking. Wheelchair access (not WC). Occasional
music. No mobile phones

MAP 2 SHINFIELD – Berkshire

L'Ortolan

Church Lane, Shinfield RG2 9BY
Tel: (0118) 988 8500
Website: www.lortolan.com

Cooking 6 | Modern French | £78

The old red-brick vicarage of this little biscuit-box village has been a haven of fine dining under various regimes for many a moon. The conservatory might look newish, but the trees on the front lawn are handsomely mature. Service is from a largely well-drilled team, who maintain a tone of gentle formality in keeping with the soft pastoral mood of the setting. Alan Murchison offers a bewildering array of fixed-price menus, with selected wines from a featured producer as one of the options. The cooking aims for the avant-garde stylings of latter times, and it pulls off some neat ideas. A pain d'épice and foie gras sandwich makes an alluring starter, or there might be seared bluefin tuna with salmon confit and marinated scallops making up a comprehensively sea-themed overture.

After that there may well be fashionable John Dory, served with white beans and truffle in a smoked ham and pea velouté, or a tasting plate of various ways with suckling pig, accompanied by sage gnocchi, stuffed Savoy cabbage and a purée of smoked apple. Finish with a gander at the cheese trolley, where British and French items come with walnut and raisin bread, or opt for rhubarb charlotte with a crumble of rhubarb, apple and ginger, and rhubarb sorbet. The assiette of chocolate remains a popular option for two. Prices start at £20 on the wine list, which offers a choice of 15 by the glass from £5.

Chef: Alan Murchison Proprietor: Newfee Ltd Open: Tue to Sat 12 to 2.30, 6.45 to 9.30 (10 Sat) Closed: Christmas Meals: Set L £18 (2 courses) to £60, Set D £49 (2 courses) to £99 (inc wine) Service: 12.5% (optional) Cards: Amex, Delta, Maestro, MasterCard, Visa Details: 60 seats. Car park. Vegetarian meals. Children's helpings. No smoking in dining room. Wheelchair access (also WC). No music. No mobile phones

plenty of modern mixing and combining, and an impressive range of technique. A small fillet of pan-fried Shetland salmon comes with sautéed crayfish, creamed cauliflower and a crayfish butter sauce to make a bright, appetising starter. Main courses cover a range from olive-crusted best end of Cornish lamb with spinach, served agreeably pink with baby leeks and a rosemary sauce, to sea bass with sautéed scallops, teamed with glazed salsify, potatoes braised with onions and thyme, and a hazelnut emulsion.

Desserts to conjure with have included a slice of dreamy dark chocolate and marmalade tart, with milk sorbet and puddles of butterscotch sauce, or there are excellent English cheeses (proudly given their own menu) served in prime condition with walnut bread and chutney. Strong cafetière coffee comes with a line-up of petits fours, to which you will be punctiliously introduced one by one. The wine list is garlanded with familiar wine quotations, and many familiar names. Much of the quality is pretty humdrum for the surroundings. Seven house wines at £25.50 each are tucked away at the back, although it's possible to find something cheaper.

Chef: Kenny Atkinson Proprietor: Von Essen Hotels Open: all week 12 to 2, 7 to 9.30 Meals: Set L £15.50 (2 courses) to £32.50, Set D £32.50 to £65. Bar menu available Service: not inc Cards: Amex, Delta, Maestro, MasterCard, Visa Details: 50 seats. 24 seats outside. Car park. Vegetarian meals. Children's helpings. No smoking. Wheelchair access (not WC). Music. No mobile phones Accommodation: 21 rooms

MAP 2 SHURDINGTON – Gloucestershire

The Greenway

Shurdington GL51 4UG
Tel: (01242) 862352
Website: www.thegreenway.co.uk

Cooking 5 | Modern French | £68

The mellow-hued Elizabethan manor house blends in well with the surrounding Cotswold countryside, as much of its façade is camouflaged with creepers. Inside looks like the better class of interiors magazine, with the dining room done in sober tones of crimson, yellow and cream. Kenny Atkinson cooks a variety of set-price menus, including a vegetarian one and the top-drawer, ten-course, bells-and-whistles version. There is

MAP 9 SINNINGTON – North Yorkshire

Fox and Hounds AR

Sinnington YO62 6SQ
Tel: (01751) 431577

Dating from the eighteenth century, the Fox and Hounds is somewhat off the beaten track, in a small village near Pickering, but is well worth searching out. A light lunch might be crab cakes with red pepper pesto (£5.95), but the dinner menu is the star attraction. As a starter, perhaps smoked salmon blinis with horseradish and shallot cream (£5.95), and for main course slow-cooked shoulder of lamb with roast root vegetables on rosemary and garlic mash (£13.25). Finish with treacle and butterscotch tart (£4.65). Half a dozen house wines are each £11.75. Accommodation. Open all week.

MAP 8   SKIPTON – North Yorkshire

Le Caveau

86 High Street, Skipton BD23 1JJ
Tel: (01756) 794274
Website: www.lecaveau.co.uk

| Cooking 2 | Anglo-French | £39 |

According to its website, this restaurant was once 'a prison for Craven district's felons and sheep rustlers', but fortunately the only thing that rustles nowadays is the sound of unfolding napkins. The interior is notable for a barrel-vaulted ceiling, illuminated by tiny white lights, and stone walls. Service is friendly, while the menu is unlikely to challenge traditionalists: goats' cheese in breadcrumbs with apple and Calvados purée, game terrine, and mushrooms in garlic butter with Stilton and bacon are among starters. Main courses range from half a crisp-roast Gressingham duck with a sour cherry and orange sauce, through breast of guinea fowl stuffed with mushrooms and tarragon to tranche of salmon baked in filo with a shrimp and fennel mousse. Lemon tart or dark chocolate truffle cake might end proceedings. The wine list is strong in the southern hemisphere, although it starts in France with Georges Duboeuf at £11.95.

Chef: Richard Barker **Proprietor:** Brian Womersley and Richard Barker **Open:** Tue to Fri L 12 to 2, Tue to Sat D 7 (5.30 Sat) to 9.30 **Meals:** alc (main courses L £8 to £11, D £10 to £20). Set D Tue to Thur £18.95 **Service:** not inc **Cards:** Amex, Delta, Maestro, MasterCard, Visa **Details:** 28 seats. Vegetarian meals. Children's helpings. No smoking in dining room. Music

MAP 6   SNETTISHAM – Norfolk

Rose and Crown   AR

Old Church Road, Snettisham PE31 7LX
Tel: (01485) 541382

An old pub that has been given a new lease of life thanks to dedicated owners Jeannette and Anthony Goodrich, who have recently renovated the restaurant, bringing in wooden flooring and a splash of gold paint. Favouring local suppliers, chef Andrew Bruce brings together old and new ideas, so leek and potato soup (£4.25) could be followed by Brancaster mussels marinière (£9.25) or Vietnamese-style crispy duck salad (£8.95). There is also a two-course lunch menu (£10) and

a separate children's menu. Wines start at £11.50. Accommodation. Open all week.

MAP 3   SOUTHALL – Greater London

Brilliant

72–76 Western Road, Southall UB2 5DZ
Tel: (020) 8574 1928
Website: www.brilliantrestaurant.com

| Cooking 3 | North Indian | £37 |

'North Indian cooking with a Kenyan touch' is how the Anands bill the cooking at their 'family run restaurant for families', an evergreen of 30 years standing. The dining room, visible behind a long, brightly lit glass frontage, is a wide open space – expanded over the years from relatively humble beginnings – and is frequently thronging with crowds of enthusiastic diners. Consistency is a byword for the cooking, with recent reports highlighting methi chicken in a rich sauce redolent of fenugreek, tender tandoori prawns that were full of prawn flavour, and aloo chollay featuring chickpeas and chunks of potato in a thick spicy sauce. Lower-fat 'healthy options' are now highlighted on the extensive menu – perhaps succulent tandoori chicken on the bone, crisp papri chaat with tamarind chutney, and sizzling tarka dal with garlic and red chillies. Among the wide choice of breads, romali roti stands out, and to finish there is 'devilled chocolate torte', as well as traditional Indian desserts such as rasmalai. Wines from £9 a bottle, or drink Indian beer or lassi.

Chef: Davinder Anand **Proprietor:** Kewal and Davinder Anand **Open:** Tue to Fri L 12 to 2.30, Tue to Sun D 6 to 11.30 **Meals:** alc (main courses £4.50 to £13). Set L and D £17.50 **Service:** not inc **Cards:** Amex, Delta, Diners, Maestro, MasterCard, Visa **Details:** 250 seats. Car park. Vegetarian meals. Children's helpings. No smoking in 1 dining room. Wheelchair access (also WC). Music. Air-conditioned

Gifto's Lahore Karahi   AR

162–164 The Broadway, Southall UB1 1NN
Tel: (020) 8813 8669

With a recent renovation and updated menu this lively canteen is the embodiment of contemporary Pakistani cuisine. Tandoori dishes (from £6.80) and vegetarian dishes (from £4.90), include tandoori jumbo prawn tikka, tarka dal and saag alu. Authenticity comes in the form of Lahore dishes (at £6.90) such as quail cooked in masala sauce, king fish curry and Paya (lamb trotters in thick gravy). Breads and rice dishes are plentiful, while desserts include kulfi (£1.90) and Gajrela (carrot cake; £1.80). Unlicensed but bring your own (no corkage). Open all week.

Madhu's

39 South Road, Southall UB1 1SW
Tel: (020) 8574 1897
Website: www.madhusonline.com

| Cooking 3 | North Indian | £39 |

Sanjay and Sanjeev Anand's catering business is now worth several millions, but the beating heart of their empire is still the restaurant in Southall opened in 1980. It continues to thrive on the virtues of reliable Punjabi home cooking 'with a Kenyan twist', served in comfortable surroundings, and the place is nearly always packed. In the traditional Indian manner, dishes are designed to be shared, with most starters serving two as a minimum: chicken malai tikka, tandoori salmon, and deep-fried prawns in sesame seeds, for example, alongside a wide range of vegetarian options such as pilli pilli boga (crisply fried aubergines, cauliflower, mushrooms, sweetcorn and peppers with garlic and ginger), or pan-fried cassava with cumin and black pepper. Several main courses are available as 'family portions' – perhaps Kerala chicken (cooked with bitter gourd), or boozi bafu (tender lamb chops in a spicy onion and tomato sauce) – while other main-course options include masala tilapia, sag gosht, and makhni chicken. French house wines are £9.

Chef: J.P. Singh Proprietors: Sanjay and Sanjeev Anand Open: Mon and Wed to Fri L 12.30 to 2.30, Wed to Mon D 6 to 11.30 Closed: 25 Dec Meals: alc (main courses £6 to £12). Set L and D £17.50 to £20 Service: not inc Cards: Amex, Maestro, MasterCard, Visa Details: 105 seats. Vegetarian meals. Children's helpings. No smoking in 1 dining room. Wheelchair access (also WC). Music. Air-conditioned

Mehfil

45 The Green, Southall UB2 4AR
Tel: (020) 8606 8811
Website: www.mehfil.co.uk

| Cooking 2 | Indian | £32 |

Although it is located in the Three Tuns Hotel, Mehfil is really a stand-alone restaurant that specialises in North Indian cooking. It is a pleasantly airy dining room, with a modern décor, and even has a dance floor – handy if the food should inspire you to a bit of terpsichorean revelry. The menus offer some dishes that will seem familiar to a Western palate, and others that are more unusual. The tandoor is used to good effect to roast marinated lamb ribs, chicken in cheese and cream, and garlic-marinated fish. Other choices include chicken patiala (a traditional Punjabi curry cooked with eggs), Kashmiri rogan josh, and garlic prawn masala. Finish perhaps with rasmalai or gulab jamun, and drink smooth lassi or something from the short wine list, which has nothing over £20.

Chefs: Bheem Singh Negee and Brijmohan Ne Proprietors: Arun and Kabeer Handa Open: all week 12 to 3, 6 to 11 (12 Fri and Sat) Meals: alc (main courses £4 to £9). Set L £5.95 (1 course) to £6.95 (2 courses), Set D £18 to £20 Service: not inc Cards: Amex, Delta, Maestro, MasterCard, Visa Details: 90 seats. Car park. Vegetarian meals. Children's helpings. No smoking. Wheelchair access (also WC). Music. Air-conditioned

MAP 2 **SOUTHAMPTON –**
Hampshire

White Star Tavern

28 Oxford Street, Southampton SO14 3DJ
Tel: (023) 8082 1990
Website: www.whitestartavern.co.uk

| Cooking 3 | Modern British | £37 |

This renovated former hotel, built for ocean-going passengers, offers the people of Southampton a contemporary venue for wining and dining. The bar area is generally well populated, while the restaurant at the back is thick with panelled wood, sweeping velvet curtains, black leather-look sofas and a chandelier. Gavin Barnes has created a modern menu that is proudly gastropub but put together with confidence and charm. His signature dish is lobster ravioli with minted pea purée, and he uses plenty of local produce, such as Hampshire sausages, New Forest game and fish from Christchurch and Lymington. The menu may start with seared west coast scallops with cauliflower purée and chive vinaigrette, progress to confit shoulder of lamb with cabbage and pommes boulangère, and end with sorbets or prune and cinnamon pudding with butterscotch sauce. The good-value wine list may be short but it treks from France to New Zealand, with prices starting at £13.95.

Chef: Gavin Barnes Proprietors: Matthew Boyle and Mark Dodd Open: Mon to Thur 12 to 2.30, 6.30 to 9.30, Fri and Sat 12 to 3, 6.30 to 10.30, Sun 12 to 9 Closed: 25 and 26 Dec, 1 Jan Meals: alc (main courses L £8 to £15, D £11.50 to £16.50). Bar menu available Service: not inc Cards: Amex, Diners, MasterCard, Visa Details: 75 seats. 25 seats outside. Vegetarian meals. Children's helpings. No smoking in dining room. Wheelchair access (also WC). Music. Air-conditioned

---

MAP 2	SOUTH CADBURY – Somerset

Camelot AR

Chapel Road, South Cadbury BA22 7EX
Tel: (01963) 440448

Owner Jamie Montgomery supplies his restaurant with his own cheeses, including Montgomery Cheddar and Ogle Shield, summing up the truly local approach at this friendly restaurant, which is just a stone's throw from Cadbury Castle. More exotically, there might be starters of tiger prawns in garlic butter on black linguini (£5.95), followed by homespun Somerset pork chops served with baked apples in a Somerset cider and Calvados cream sauce (£13.95), or maybe fillet of sea bass with sautéed truffle potatoes (£12.95). Wines from £11. Open all week.

MAP 8	SOUTH CROSLAND – West Yorkshire

King's Arms

23–25 Midway, South Crosland HD4 7DA
Tel: (01484) 661669

Cooking 4	Modern British	£49

£

The 1930s pub may look a little unprepossessing from the outside, but inside it's a different matter. While there's a pub-like atmosphere in the bar, backed up by friendly and unpretentious service, there's also a contemporary eating area that fits well into the pub ethos – and the mix of leather sofas, wood-burner, comfortable leather dining chairs and soft creams and browns on the walls make for a pleasant environment. Light bites – steak frites, bangers and mash, that sort of thing – supplement the carte, and a sandwich menu is available at lunchtimes. Unflashy elements, such as honey-glazed belly pork with macaroni cheese and a red wine glaze are allowed to shine. Straightforward main courses also bring simple pleasures: glorious plainly roast cod set on a creamy pea and morel concoction, served with crisp pancetta, and succulent pork cutlets with cabbage and black pudding have demonstrated immaculate timing and fine ingredients. Puddings impress too. Poached pear with vanilla ice cream has been described as 'classic and simple but perfectly done'. The well-annotated wine list opens with house wines from Italy and Australia at £11.95 and £13.50 respectively and struggles hard to get above £20.

Chef: Richard Greenway Proprietor: Tracy Lightowlers Open: Tue to Fri and Sun L 12 to 2 (4 Sun), Tue to Sat D 6 to 9 (9.30 Fri and Sat) Meals: alc exc Sun L (main courses £7 to £16). Set L £12 (2 courses) to £15, Set D Tue to Fri £12 (2 courses) to £15. Sandwich L menu available Tue to Fri Service: not inc Cards: Maestro, MasterCard, Visa Details: 42 seats. Car park. Vegetarian meals. Children's helpings. No smoking in dining room. Wheelchair access (also men's WC). Music

---

MAP 9	SOUTH DALTON – East Riding of Yorkshire

Pipe and Glass Inn NEW ENTRY

West End, South Dalton HU17 7PN
Tel: (01430) 810246
Website: www.pipeandglass.co.uk

Cooking 4	Modern British	£36

James Mackenzie, last spotted as head chef at the Star Inn, Harome (see entry), has turned up at this eighteenth-century rural pub and, along with partner Kate Boroughs, has given it a 'total decorative and culinary face-lift'. It still has an attractive oak-beamed, inglenooked bar, but there's also a lounge area with leather chesterfields and two dining rooms done out in brown and cream with well-spaced wooden tables, bare floorboards and candles. Early reports indicate 'knowledgeable and very polite' service and that the chef's pedigree shows in the kitchen's classy output. James's good-value modern British cooking uses top-quality produce (from local suppliers where possible) and delivers oodles of interest and imaginative flavour combinations. Take lobster risotto, or perhaps 'lovely, chunky' salmon fishcakes served in a Cullen skink stew, then agonise over the choice between classic hay-baked chicken with leek and ham hock casserole or tender roe deer stew served with celeriac purée and an 'exceptional' gravy. Ginger burnt cream with rhubarb and sticky toffee pudding have been given the thumbs-up, and the no-nonsense modern wine list is reasonably priced, with house South African opening at £12.95.

Chef: James Mackenzie Proprietors: James Mackenzie and Kate Boroughs Open: Tue to Sun L 12 to 2 (4 Sun), Tue to Sat D 6.30 to 9.30 Closed: 2 weeks Jan Meals: alc (main courses £6 to £16) Service: not inc Cards: Delta, Maestro, MasterCard, Visa Details: 90 seats. 40 seats outside. Car park. Vegetarian meals. Children's helpings. No smoking in dining room. Wheelchair access (not WC). Music

---

MAP 8 SOUTHPORT – Merseyside

Tyndall's   AR

23 Hoghton Street, Southport PR9 0NS
Tel: (01704) 500002

The accent is on French and European cuisine and the atmosphere is informal and friendly, with a separate bar area for pre-dinner drinks. The two-course midweek menu is good value at either £7.95 before 7pm, or £12.50 after, offering crab soup with brandy followed by whole baked seabass on fennel. 'Gourmet dishes' include hot potted shrimps with toast (£5.25) for starters, followed by two roast quail with grape sauce (£14.95). Wines from £12.95. Open Tues to Sat D only.

Warehouse Brasserie

30 West Street, Southport PR8 1QN
Tel: (01704) 544662
Website: www.warehousebrasserie.co.uk

Cooking 3 | Global | £36
 £

A shining star on Southport's culinary map, this bar/brasserie offers an eclectic menu and a buzzy atmosphere in a contemporary setting. The menus have something for everyone, with dishes picked from around the globe, so expect Europe to collide with Asia via the British Isles. Grilled Loch Fyne scallops on curried lentils with a mango and coriander salsa – 'a super combination, and very deftly handled' – appear among starters alongside pan-fried strips of soy-marinated beef with crumbled Gorgonzola in salad leaves. Staples such as cod and chips with mushy peas have also come in for praise, as does Malaysian-style fried halibut with sambal and nasi goreng. The style extends into puddings of ginger and lime crème brûlée with mango sorbet, although the cheeseboard returns to

Europe, with Brie, Lancashire, Stilton and Reblochon among them. The global wine list is split into categories like 'blondes' and 'redheads', opening respectively with Sauvignon Blanc and Merlot, each £13.95.

Chefs: Marc Vérité and Darren Smith Proprietor: Paul Adams Open: Mon to Sat 12 to 2, 5.30 to 10.30 Closed: 25 and 26 Dec Meals: alc (main courses L £7 to £17.50, D £11 to £17.50). Set L £11.95 (2 courses) to £13.95, Set D Mon and Tue to Thur 5.30 to 6.45 £13.95 (2 courses) to £15.95 Service: not inc Cards: Delta, Maestro, MasterCard, Visa Details: 100 seats. Vegetarian meals. Children's helpings. No smoking in dining room. Wheelchair access (also WC). Music. Air-conditioned

---

MAP 2 SOUTHROP – Gloucestershire

Swan at Southrop

Southrop GL7 3NU
Tel: (01367) 850205
Website: www.theswanatsouthrop.co.uk

Cooking 2 | Modern British | £41
£5

Dating from the fourteenth century, this creeper-covered village inn is certainly chocolate box to look at, but there's a lot more to unwrap. The bar remains a local watering hole (the skittle alley survived the revamp), while the dining room is all ceiling beams, a roughly paved or tiled floor, wooden shutters and bare tables, with the owners' modern art on the walls. The lunchtime set-price menu is good value, and the carte deals in good-quality stuff, with most produce locally sourced (the owners plan on breeding Middle White pigs too). Start with, say, confit tuna salad with borlotti beans, chorizo and a poached egg, or guinea fowl and foie gras terrine, and proceed to fillet of bream with a Swiss chard, red pepper and caper risotto, or confit shoulder of lamb with sweetbreads, celeriac purée and peas. Milk chocolate, malt and honeycomb pavé is a well made dessert. The wine list is predominately Old World, with house French £12.50.

Chef: James Parkinson Proprietors: Jerry and Coryn Hibbert, Graham Williams and James Parkinson Open: all week 12 to 2.30 (3 Sat and Sun), 7 to 9.45 Meals: alc (main courses £12.50 to £16). Set L Mon to Fri £12.50 (2 courses) to £16.50 Service: not inc Cards: Amex, Maestro, MasterCard, Visa Details: 60 seats. 12 seats outside. Vegetarian meals. Children's helpings. No smoking in 1 dining room. No music. No mobile phones

---

MAP 2   **SOUTHSEA – Hampshire**

Bistro Montparnasse

103 Palmerston Road, Southsea PO5 3PS
Tel: (023) 9281 6754
Website: www.bistromontparnasse.co.uk

| Cooking 3 | Modern European | £40 |

A relaxed atmosphere prevails at this friendly bistro, which gaudily celebrates its seaside location with tangerine and sea-green walls. Kevin Bingham has been running the kitchen since the restaurant opened in 1999, and for that reason the menu, compact though it may be, is well crafted, and his excellent use of flavours lifts even the simplest dish. Potted rabbit and mustard rillettes is just one of around half a dozen starters, while main courses offer a fish of the day and meat options: perhaps roast rump of lamb with caramelised parsnips or chargrilled Gressingham duck breast with a confit and foie gras ballottine. Apple and toffee parfait with caramel sauce or warm chocolate brownie with toasted pistachio ice cream are both admirable desserts. The 50-strong wine list slightly favours Europe over the New World; house white is £12.95, red £13.95.

> **Chef:** Kevin Bingham   **Proprietors:** John Saunders and Kevin Bingham   **Open:** Tue to Sat 12 to 1.45, 7 to 9.30   **Closed:** 25 and 26 Dec, 1 Jan, 2 weeks Mar, 2 weeks late Sept to early Oct   **Meals:** Set L £14.50 (2 courses) to £17.50, Set D £22.50 (2 courses) to £27.50   **Service:** not inc   **Cards:** Amex, Delta, Maestro, MasterCard, Visa   **Details:** 30 seats. Vegetarian meals. No smoking. Wheelchair access (not WC). Music

MAP 6   **SOUTHWOLD – Suffolk**

Crown Hotel

90 High Street, Southwold IP18 6DP
Tel: (01502) 722275

| Cooking 4 | Modern British-Plus | £39 |

The Crown has been smartened up a little over the years since its eighteenth-century beginnings as a coaching inn. For over two decades it has been the hotel and restaurant arm of Adnams, the wine merchant and brewer of some repute. Eat either in the 'characterful and often crowded' bar or in the more formal restaurant, where a penchant for local and regional supplies drives the menu, which might feature seafood – say, seared king scallops

with warm potato salad and shiso cress – followed by whatever is currently available: maybe potato-crusted wild halibut served with sprouting broccoli and shrimp butter. There might be breast of duck with a wild garlic potato cake and buttered spring cabbage, while desserts include nursery favourites (rhubarb and custard mousse with wild strawberry sorbet) as well as more sophisticated offerings such as dark chocolate ganache tart with milk chocolate sauce and marmalade ice cream. As for service, a 'friendly, open welcome' has been much appreciated. The Crown's jewel – the wine list – is defined by value and diversity. It starts with around 20 varied house wines offered by the glass (from £2.30) and bottle (from £11.50) and moves to an exceptional selection with moderate mark-ups.

> **Chef:** Ian Howell   **Proprietor:** Adnams Brewery plc   **Open:** all week 12 to 2, 6.30 to 9   **Meals:** alc (main courses £9.50 to £16.50). Set D £30. Bar menu available   **Service:** not inc   **Cards:** Delta, Maestro, MasterCard, Visa   **Details:** 80 seats. 12 seats outside. Car park. Vegetarian meals. No children under 5. Children's helpings. No smoking in dining room. Wheelchair access (also WC). No music. No mobile phones   **Accommodation:** 14 rooms

MAP 9   **SOWERBY – West Yorkshire**

Travellers Rest

Steep Lane, Sowerby HX6 1PE
Tel: (01422) 832124

| Cooking 3 | Modern British-Plus | £41 |

This sixteenth-century inn stands alone high on the moors, with views from almost every angle. The bar has some lovely details, such as a stone chimney breast with wood-burning stove and flagstone flooring. Snacks and blackboard specials are available from the bar (think posh steak burger in foccacia with chips, or fish pie). The tidy dining room ups the ante somewhat, offering a menu on which truffled cream of celery soup with poached quail's eggs and pancetta vie for attention with chicken liver and foie gras parfait with toasted brioche and pear chutney. To follow, main courses might be roast rump of spring lamb with creamed Savoy cabbage or seared loin of tuna with aubergine caviar, niçoise garnish and sauce vierge. Traditional desserts such as syrup sponge with custard or berry sherry trifle end. The wine list opens with house choices from £9.75.

Chef: Scott Russon **Proprietor:** Caroline Lumley **Open:** Sat L 12 to 2.30, Sun L 12 to 3.30, Wed to Sun D 5.30 to 9.30 (10 Sat) **Meals:** alc (main courses £12.50 to £19). Set L Sun £13.95 (2 courses) to £17.95. Bar menu available **Service:** not inc **Cards:** Delta, Diners, Maestro, MasterCard, Visa **Details:** 100 seats. 40 seats outside. Car park. Vegetarian meals. Children's helpings. No smoking. Wheelchair access (not WC). Music

MAP 3 | SPELDHURST – Kent

George & Dragon   NEW ENTRY

Speldhurst TN3 0NN
Tel: (01892) 863125

Cooking 2 | Modern British | £39

Dating from the fourteenth century, this black and white timber-framed inn is in the middle of the pretty village of Speldhurst opposite the church. The bar is quintessentially English, with its roaring log fire, heavy beams and flagstone floor, while the informal restaurant is on the first floor. Max Leonard pays great attention to raw materials, with locally sourced produce high on the agenda – Kentish roebuck, Groombridge asparagus and local pigeon breast all make an appearance – and the menu proclaims 'food from a farm, not a factory'. Starters of game terrine with spiced apple chutney, and 'a pretty sensational' oxtail ragoût with pumpkin and spinach gnocchi have been well-executed starters, while main courses of Pata Negra pork chump chop and Ashdown Forest loin of venison have been equally flavoursome, the former infused with smoked paprika and garlic. Vegetables get the thumbs-up, and appetising desserts include saffron burnt vanilla cream with caramelised pears. Ten or so wines are served by the glass, from £2.75, with £12 the baseline for bottles.

Chef: Max Leonard **Proprietor:** Julian Leefe-Griffiths **Open:** all week L 12 to 2.45 (3.15 Sat, 4.30 Sun), Mon to Sat D 7 to 10.30 **Meals:** alc (main courses £8.50 to £17.50). Light L menu available Mon to Sat **Service:** 10% **Cards:** Maestro, MasterCard, Visa **Details:** 120 seats. 140 seats outside. Car park. Vegetarian meals. Children's helpings. No smoking in dining room. Wheelchair access (also WC). Occasional music. No mobile phones

MAP 9 | STADDLEBRIDGE – North Yorkshire

McCoy's at the Tontine   NEW ENTRY

Staddlebridge DL6 3JB
Tel: (01609) 882671
Website: www.mccoysatthetontine.co.uk

Cooking 5 | Modern British | £52

Expect a warm welcome from 'genially eccentric' owners, brothers Eugene and Tom McCoy, at this sturdily built nineteenth-century house with myriad narrow stairwells and inter-connecting rooms, all individually decorated. The dining room features quarry tiling, spindle-backed chairs, candles on white linen-clad tables and an assortment of mirrors, the overall effect 'sumptuous and slightly dotty'.

Seafood stands out among starters, perhaps langoustines, split and lightly grilled, or three perfectly cooked scallops with corals attached, served on a creamy parsley coulis with brandy garlic butter drizzled about. More complex dishes are just as competently and confidently executed, such as a main course rack of lamb with pistachio crust, the meat pink and tender and served with dauphinoise potatoes and an 'inspired' mint and broad bean jus. Vegetables are given a light touch, and to finish, chocolate crème brûlée with raspberry ice cream and shortbread. Service is unrushed and friendly, while the short wine list is an intelligent blend of New and Old World choices, prices starting at £15.95.

Chef: Stuart Hawkins **Proprietors:** Eugene and Tom McCoy **Open:** all week 12 to 2, 6.45 to 9 (9.30 Fri and Sat) **Closed:** 25 and 26 Dec, 1 Jan **Meals:** alc (main courses L £11 to £18, D £16.50 to £24.50). Set L £14.95 (2 courses) to £16.95, Set L Sun £16.95 (2 courses) to £18.95, Set D Sun to Thur before 7.45pm £19.95 (2 courses) to £22 **Service:** not inc **Cards:** Amex, Delta, Diners, Maestro, MasterCard, Visa **Details:** 70 seats. Car park. Vegetarian meals. Children's helpings. No smoking. Music. Air-conditioned **Accommodation:** 6 rooms

NEW ENTRY	This appears after the restaurant's name if the establishment was not a main entry in last year's Guide. Please note, however, it may have been 'also recommended' in the previous edition.

 This symbol means that the wine list is well above the average.

MAP 9 **STAITHES – North Yorkshire**

Endeavour

1 High Street, Staithes TS13 5BH
Tel: (01947) 840825
Website: www.endeavour-restaurant.co.uk

| Cooking 4 | Modern British/Seafood | £37 |

Named after the ship once sailed by Staithes' famous son – Captain James Cook – Endeavour is a cheerful former fisherman's cottage with bright lemon walls, deep blue tablecloths and dark blue curtains. Candles and flowers are on the tables, and fish is the mainstay of the menu. At inspection, seared king scallops set atop a potato and carrot cake and dabbed with chilli jam and crème fraîche made for a good start, and a main course of roast Whitby turbot topped with salmon caviar and surrounded by grain mustard sauce has also been a hit. The token meat dish could be local oxtail braised with Guinness and prunes, or fillet steak with crisped capers and salsa verde. Puddings are perhaps not the kitchen's strongest point, but 'charming and very friendly' service has been reported. A varied and affordable wine list starts with South African or Chilean red and white at £12.50.

> **Chefs/Proprietors:** Charlotte Willoughby and Brian Kay **Open:** Tue to Sat D only 7 to 9; also open bank hol Sun and Mon **Closed:** 25 and 26 Dec, 1 Jan **Meals:** alc (main courses £13 to £16) **Service:** not inc **Cards:** Delta, Maestro, MasterCard, Visa **Details:** 16 seats. Car park (residents only). Vegetarian meals. No smoking. Music. No mobile phones **Accommodation:** 4 rooms

MAP 6 **STANTON – Suffolk**

Leaping Hare

Wyken Vineyards, Stanton IP31 2DW
Tel: (01359) 250287
Website: www.wykenvineyards.co.uk

| Cooking 2 | Modern European | £38 |

'The ideal customer would be a country-loving, artistic foodie,' said a reporter of this picturesque 400-year-old timbered barn that also houses an informal café and country store. The barn and vineyard are on the estate of Wyken Hall, an Elizabethan manor with gardens that are open to the public. The menu is strong on quality ingredients, and dishes are straightforward and full

flavoured. Terrines often start a meal: one of lambs' sweetbreads with tangy chutney and toast, say, or another of wood pigeon and squirrel (truly a taste of the woodland). Otherwise, begin with something light like spiced aubergine with flatbread, and go on to sea trout with al dente asparagus and samphire, or Gorgonzola polenta with caponata and rocket. Successful desserts have included roast pineapple with coconut ice cream, and 'a perfect summer pudding' in the shape of rose and geranium pannacotta. A short wine list features a handful of own-label bottles from £14.50.

> **Chef:** Peter Harrison **Proprietors:** Sir Kenneth and Lady Carlisle **Open:** all week L 12 to 2.30, Fri and Sat D 7 to 9.30 **Closed:** 1 week Christmas **Meals:** alc (main courses £12 to £16). Set L £16.95 (2 courses) to £19.95. Café L menu available **Service:** not inc **Cards:** Delta, Maestro, MasterCard, Visa **Details:** 58 seats. 22 seats outside. Car park. Vegetarian meals. Children's helpings. No smoking. Wheelchair access (also WC). No music. No mobile phones

MAP 2 **STANTON FITZWARREN – Wiltshire**

Stanton House Hotel, Rosemary

The Avenue, Stanton Fitzwarren SN6 7SD
Tel: (08700) 841388
Website: www.stantonhouse.co.uk

| Cooking 3 | Japanese | £44 |

Built of the distinctive local Cotswold stone, this beautiful Elizabethan-style country house retains much of its original character and charm, although Japanese owner Honda – there's a factory down the road – has brought a touch of its homeland to bear on the two restaurants. The Rosemary dining room has a simple, clean minimalist design with blond wooden flooring and pale walls, plenty of greenery to break up the starkness, views across the lake and park, and a menu that offers a fusion of Japanese and European cuisines, with dishes including starters of deep-fried fishcake in seaweed batter, and Carpathian salmon with wasabi mayonnaise, followed by teriyaki-style grilled chicken breast with vegetables, or deep-fried breaded salmon with pomodoro sauce. Mount Fuji (open for dinner only) is pure, authentic Japanese, with low-level tables and cushion seating – and diners are required to remove their shoes on entering. The illustrated, bilingual menu offers everything from agedashi tofu or gyoza dumplings for starters to a wide range of all-in-one bento box main meals, as well as assorted sushi, sashimi, tempura and noodles. A compact, functional wine list opens with three house selections at £11.50.

> **Chef:** Norimichi Mori **Proprietor:** HKC Europe Ltd **Open:** all week 12 to 2, 6 (7 Fri and Sat) to 9.30 **Meals:** alc (main courses £5 to £24) **Service:** not inc **Cards:** Delta, Maestro, MasterCard, Visa **Details:** 80 seats. 40 seats outside. Car park. Vegetarian meals. No smoking. Wheelchair access (also WC). Music. Air-conditioned **Accommodation:** 82 rooms

---

MAP 5 STATHERN – Leicestershire

Red Lion Inn

2 Red Lion Street, Stathern LE14 4HS
Tel: (01949) 860868
Website: www.theredlioninn.co.uk

Cooking 2 | Modern British-Plus | £38

The Red Lion can be described as a true village local, nothing fancy but brimming with atmosphere and abundant in we like to call 'character'. Culinary eclecticism may also be expected, for this is the younger sibling of the Olive Branch in Clipsham (see entry), and the menus (including lunchtime snacks and full-on Sunday lunch) show British tradition with some global gatherings. You could try tempura of squid, scallops and prawn, and go on to sautéed calf's liver with pickled red cabbage, rösti and crispy bacon. Otherwise the Lincolnshire sausages, mash and onion gravy are well reported, and there's lemongrass pannacotta with Yorkshire rhubarb compote for pudding. What makes all this work is decent ingredients, sought locally as much as possible, honestly treated. A broad-minded and commendable wine list opens with French house at £11.50.

> **Chef:** Phil Lowe **Proprietors:** Ben Jones and Sean Hope **Open:** all week L 12 to 2 (4 Sun), Mon to Sat D 7 (6 Sat) to 9.30 **Closed:** D 25 and 26 Dec, 1 Jan **Meals:** alc (main courses £10 to £20). Set L Mon to Sat £12.95 (2 courses) to £15.95, Set L Sun £16.50. Bar L menu available **Service:** not inc **Cards:** Amex, Delta, Maestro, MasterCard, Visa **Details:** 60 seats. 40 seats outside. Car park. Vegetarian meals. Children's helpings. No smoking in dining room. No music

> £ This symbol means that it is possible to have a three-course dinner, including coffee, half a bottle of house wine and service, for £30 or less per person.

MAP 3 STEDHAM – West Sussex

Hamilton Arms   AR

School Lane, Stedham GU29 0NZ
Tel: (01730) 812555

Still reaping the benefits of being one of the first pubs in the country to offer Thai food, the Hamilton Arms also serves real ale and traditional bar snacks. Also available to take away, there's pork dim sum (£4.60), squid salad with a hot-and-sour dressing (£5.60), stir-fried pork with baby aubergines and chillies (£6.25) and favourites such as ped yang (£7.50): roast duck with pickled ginger and cucumber. House wines from £9.50. Closed Mon.

MAP 2 STOCKBRIDGE – Hampshire

Greyhound

31 High Street, Stockbridge SO20 6EY
Tel: (01264) 810833

Cooking 4 | Modern British | £48

Stylish and elegant describe this inn by the River Test, the odd bit of angling paraphernalia hung about the place is a reminder that this is fishing country. There are a few stools at the bar, where a separate menu operates, running from, for instance, eggs Benedict to ribeye with sautéed potatoes and hollandaise, but the carte takes centre stage. Simplicity is the key to the cooking, with a dash of finesse and artistry. The signature fishcake with a poached egg and chive beurre blanc still features as a starter, but there's also pan-fried red mullet with potato and fennel salad. Among the half-dozen or so main courses might be breast of Gressingham duck with sarladaise potatoes, roast beetroot and red onion, and wild sea bass with artichoke purée and roast salsify. Desserts are equally slick, perhaps steamed vanilla sponge with blueberry compote and crème anglaise. The international wine list puts its biggest efforts into France, Italy and Australia, but there is something for most tastes. The weekly-changing house selections start at £15.

> **Chef:** Helene Schoeman **Proprietors:** Mr and Mrs T.C. Fiducia **Open:** all week L 12 to 2 (2.30 Fri, Sat and Sun), Mon to Sat D 7 to 9 (9.30 Fri, Sat and Sun) **Closed:** 25, 26 and 31 Dec, 1 Jan **Meals:** alc (main courses £11.50 to £23). Bar menu available **Service:** 10% (optional) **Cards:** Delta, Maestro, MasterCard, Visa **Details:** 48 seats. 30 seats outside. Car park. Vegetarian meals. Children's helpings. No smoking in 1 dining room. No music **Accommodation:** 8 rooms

MAP 2 **STOCKROSS** – Berkshire

Vineyard at Stockcross

Stockcross RG20 8JU
Tel: (01635) 528770
Website: www.the-vineyard.co.uk

Cooking 7 | Anglo-French | £78

The Vineyard lurks as a low-slung cluster of buildings set amid vast expanses of colour-coordinated gravel off a B-road on the outskirts of Newbury. There are more vast expanses within, as lounge succeeds lounge on the way to the dining room, where a glass frontage affords diverting views of the great pond with its flickering flames. It's all designed to induce gasps in first-timers, and the dining room itself is a relaxing, deep, split-level space, each table dominated by an unfeasibly tall vase of lilies. The observant will note the lighting gently modulating over the course of an evening, from verdant green to sunset yellow and beyond.

John Campbell brings a restlessly ambitious culinary intelligence to the whole scene. An inspection dinner began with a piece of organic salmon, cooked rare and served with a ballottine of foie gras and a small bed of spiced lentils, the whole adding up to an imaginative, finely judged whole. Froths and foams gush forth luxuriantly to add visual intrigue to dishes such as butternut squash risotto with grapefruit and Parmesan froth. Portions are spare, especially at lunchtime, which at least enables you to concentrate on each element of a dish. A spring evening produced decent slow-cooked venison with apposite accompaniments of parsnip purée, choucroute, spinach and some minutely diced pickled pear, all set about with an over-caramelised jus.

Perhaps the most interesting way of sampling the range may be to opt for the tasting menu of ten micro-courses, picking your way from scallop with a chicken biscuit to foie gras with smoked banana. Finish with 'jelly and ice cream', which juxtaposes port and coffee flavours in a rather more adult way than the title promises. The wine list is surely unique in the UK, offering a special journey through the wines of California, guided by the wisdom of Sir Peter Michael. The 'International List' is no slouch either, with a decent number of wines around the £20 mark.

Chef: John Campbell **Proprietor:** Sir Peter Michael **Open:** all week 12 to 2, 7 to 9.30 **Meals:** Set L £22 (2 courses) to £75, Set D £35 to £75 **Service:** not inc **Cards:** Amex, Delta, Diners, Maestro, MasterCard, Visa **Details:** 70 seats. 20 seats outside. Car park. Vegetarian meals. Children's helpings. No smoking in dining room. Wheelchair access (not WC). Occasional music. No mobile phones. Air-conditioned **Accommodation:** 49 rooms

MAP 6 **STOKE HOLY CROSS** – Norfolk

Wildebeest Arms

82–86 Norwich Road, Stoke Holy Cross
NR14 8QJ
Tel: (01508) 492497
Email: wildebeest@animalinns.co.uk

Cooking 2 | Modern European | £42

Just a few miles outside Norwich, this neat and tidy establishment offers some exciting surprises in the form of a large collection of African artefacts, including masks and musical instruments. Brass propeller fans whirl above dark wooden flooring, wicker chairs and dark leather wall seats. There are reasonable set-price deals as well as the carte, which fuses British and French styles. Start with chargrilled rare Scotch beef fillet with Parmesan and rocket and spinach salad, or seared peppered tuna loin with guacamole, charred asparagus and a tarragon dressing, then move on to roast Gressingham duck breast with cocotte potatoes, honey-roast parsnips and truffle-creamed cabbage. End with an assiette of pear comprising vanilla-poached fruit, sorbet and parfait. A page of house wines at £12.95 opens the wine list. White Burgundy is a strength, but bottles from the rest of France and the southern hemisphere have been carefully selected too, and prices across the board seem reasonable.

Chef: Daniel Smith **Proprietor:** Henry Watt **Open:** all week 12 (12.30 Sun) to 2, 7 to 9 **Meals:** alc exc Sun L (main courses £12 to £22). Set L £11.95 (2 courses) to £14.95, Set D Sun to Fri £15 (2 courses) to £18.50 **Service:** not inc **Cards:** Amex, Delta, Diners, Maestro, MasterCard, Visa **Details:** 60 seats. Car park. Vegetarian meals. Children's helpings. No smoking. Music. Air-conditioned

The price given next to the cooking score is based on the cost of a typical three-course dinner for one person, including coffee, house wine and service.

MAP 5 | STOKE PRIOR – Herefordshire

Epicurean Restaurant

68 Hanbury Road, Stoke Prior B60 4DN
Tel: (01527) 871929
Website: www.epicbrasseries.co.uk

NEW ENTRY

Cooking 5 | Modern European | £46

'When you find somewhere cooking as intelligently as this, it really is a breath of fresh air,' wrote an inspector of this former pub, converted into the Epicurean Restaurant and Epic' Brasserie. The restaurant has dark green brickwork, green silk curtains, white voile drapes and a feature fireplace, and a capable chef in Jason Lynas. Service is first-rate, with knowledgeable staff confident to answer questions about the menu. There's a reasonable two- and three-course set lunch menu, while dinner is a three-course affair, starting with an appetiser – a 'simple but effective' pea soup with pancetta and parsnip tortellini – then a starter of seared scallops on a bed of parsley risotto with vanilla cappuccino. Terrine of duck confit and foie gras with Puy lentils and apple and walnut salad is another fine way to begin. Roast squab pigeon breast wrapped in a cabbage leaf features 'beautifully rare' meat and comes on fondant potato with Madeira jus and wild mushroom tortellini. Seafood fricassee with squid ink linguine and bouillabaisse sauce is another winning main course, consisting of wild salmon, red mullet, cod, sea bass and scallops. A pre-dessert of something like vanilla pannacotta whets the appetite for more sweet treats: perhaps hot chocolate fondant with griottine cherries and white chocolate ice cream. Wine prices start at £12.95.

Chef: Jason Lynas Proprietors: Pat and Claire McDonald
Open: Tue to Sat 12 to 2.30, 6.30 to 9.30 Meals: Set L £17.50 (2 courses) to £22.50, Set D £35 Service: not inc
Cards: Amex, Delta, Diners, Maestro, MasterCard, Visa
Details: 90 seats. 30 seats outside. Children's helpings. No smoking. Wheelchair access (also WC). Music

  Not a full entry but provisionally recommended. These 'also recommended' establishments are integrated throughout the book.

MAP 2 | STOKE ROW – Oxfordshire

Crooked Billet **AR**

Newlands Lane, Stoke Row RG9 5PU
Tel: (01491) 681048

Built in 1642, the Crooked Billet, hidden away down a single-track lane (which doesn't deter the crowds), was a hideout of Dick Turpin, who was reputedly romantically involved with the landlord's daughter. Salt and pepper squid with chilli jam (£7), or pan-fried partridge breasts with smoked black pudding and tarragon and mustard sauce (£7.70) are typical of the influences at work, and main courses might include seared tuna and noodle stir-fry with sautéed garlic shrimps (£16.50). End with Belgian chocolate mousse (£5). Around 50 wines from £14.50. Open all week.

MAP 2 | STOKE-SUB-HAMDON – Somerset

Priory House Restaurant

1 High Street, Stoke-sub-Hamdon TA14 6PP
Tel: (01935) 822826
Website: www.theprioryhouserestaurant.co.uk

Cooking 5 | Modern British | £45

An enviable location in the middle of a pretty village populated with houses built of local stone is just one of the many attractions of this charming restaurant. A small terrace provides space for outdoor eating while inside, the dining room has a smart beige and navy blue colour scheme, fruit and flower prints on the walls and posies of flowers on the tables. The place is run by a couple who turned to the business of running a restaurant just a couple of years ago after previous careers in other fields, though Peter Brooks has many years experience in catering. His cooking is executed with care and precision, making the most of well-sourced, high-quality ingredients.

Menus offer around half a dozen options per course, with dishes having broad appeal. Starters may be relatively old-fashioned creations such as seared scallops with smoked bacon and capers, or smoked fish terrine with green peppercorn cream sauce, but a pork and herb terrine is given a decidedly fashion-conscious accompaniment of beetroot chutney. Luxuriant main courses typically feature Somerset beef fillet with confit shallots, seared foie gras and red wine glaze, alongside loin of West Country venison with celeriac rösti and blueberry sauce, and to finish there may be rhubarb brûlée with raspberry sorbet and hazelnut praline. A page of wines by the glass opens a compact but well-chosen list, with house selections from £14.

Chef: Peter Brooks **Proprietors:** Peter and Sonia Brooks **Open:** Sat L 12 to 2, Tue to Sat D 7 to 9.30 **Closed:** first 2 weeks Nov, last week May, first week June, bank hols **Meals:** alc D (main courses £17.50 to £19.50). Set L £15.50 (2 courses) to £19.50 **Service:** not inc **Cards:** Maestro, MasterCard, Visa **Details:** 24 seats. No children under 8. No smoking. Wheelchair access (not WC). Music

---

MAP 5	STOW-ON-THE-WOLD – Gloucestershire

Old Butcher's `NEW ENTRY`

7 Park Street, Stow-on-the-Wold GL54 1AQ
Tel: (01451) 831700
Website: www.theoldbutchers.com

Cooking 3	Modern British	£36

After several successful years at the Kings Arms across town, Peter and Louise Robinson decided to move to smaller, 'more restauranty' premises in August 2005, choosing a former butcher's shop, to which they gave a brasserie-style makeover. The signs are that they have settled in quickly. The modern British menu won't win any prizes for originality, but Peter Robinson's cooking scores highly for the quality of ingredients and his care in timing, key features of an inspector's starter of scallops with sweet chilli sauce and crème fraîche. Other options might include classic steak tartare, or field mushrooms with foie gras on toast. To follow, there might be lamb tagine with couscous and harissa, whole grilled sea bass with pine-nut tarrator, or thick slices of pink-cooked veal rump with soft braised leeks and thinly sliced oyster mushrooms cooked in stock. To finish, try perhaps tender young rhubarb with a crunchy oatmeal crumble topping. Prices on the short wine list start at £12.50.

Chef: Peter Robinson **Proprietors:** Peter and Louise Robinson **Open:** all week 12 to 2.30, 6 to 9.30 (7 to 9 Sun) **Closed:** 1 week May, 1 week Oct **Meals:** alc (main courses £11 to £15) **Service:** not inc **Cards:** Delta, Maestro, MasterCard, Visa **Details:** 45 seats. 12 seats outside. Vegetarian meals. Children's helpings. No-smoking area. Wheelchair access (also WC). Music. Air-conditioned

---

Unicorn Hotel

Sheep Street, Stow-on-the-Wold GL54 1HQ
Tel: (01451) 830257
Website: www.birchhotels.co.uk

Cooking 2	Modern European	£39

This Jacobean Cotswolds inn is homely and intimate, some might say, and décor is traditionally English, with lots of competing colours and patterns from walls, carpet and upholstery in the dining room. The food is simply and honestly prepared by Michael Carr, now in his third year at the stoves, and local sourcing remains a priority: longhorn beef is from Chesterton Farm in Cirencester, for instance, and appears on the menu as ribeye with wild mushrooms and chips. Sunday lunch draws the crowds, while the carte could kick off with shellfish bisque or seared scallops with lemon, chilli and thyme. Main courses could see roast guinea fowl with buttered spring greens and chestnuts, roast potatoes and thyme jus alongside pan-fried red mullet fillet with slow-cooked fennel, roast cherry tomatoes and grilled potatoes. Finish with ginger pudding with butterscotch sauce and cream or perhaps Eton mess. House wines on the compact list are a Chilean Cabernet Sauvignon and Sauvignon Blanc at £15.

Chef: Michael Carr **Proprietor:** Birch Hotels and Inns Ltd **Open:** all week 12 to 1.45, 7 to 8.45 **Meals:** alc (main courses L £8.50 to £13, D £10.50 to £15.50) **Service:** not inc **Cards:** Amex, Delta, Diners, Maestro, MasterCard, Visa **Details:** 40 seats. Vegetarian meals. Children's helpings. No smoking in dining room. Wheelchair access (not WC). Music **Accommodation:** 19 rooms

---

MAP 5	STRATFORD-UPON-AVON – Warwickshire

Malbec `NEW ENTRY`

6 Union Street, Stratford-upon-Avon CV37 6QT
Tel: (01789) 269106
Email: eatmalbec@aol.com

Cooking 2	Modern European	£38

Simon and Rebecca Malin are doing brisk business in their ambitious yet casual bistro, which has found favour with locals. The tall terraced building is just a stone's throw from the busy shopping area; inside, the décor is modern, with cream-painted panelling, spotlights and trendy art for sale on the walls. It makes a smart impression, with a 'clued-up kitchen' working to a contemporary menu that boasts local suppliers, including Lighthorne lamb, perhaps turning up as a main course of roast rack with a mini shepherd's pie along with tomato fondue and rosemary jus. A starter of a warm salad of rabbit and prosciutto comes with orange, beetroot and walnut accompaniments, while pear sorbet – from a trio of home-made sorbets and exotic fruits – has delivered the 'clearest and most intense flavour'. The good-value wine list is grouped by style, and prices start at £12.95.

Chef: Simon Malin **Proprietors:** Simon and Rebecca Malin **Open:** Tue to Sat 12 to 2, 7 to 9.30 **Closed:** 1 week Christmas, 1 week May, 1 week Oct, bank hol Tue **Meals:** Set L £10 (2 courses) to £13, Set D £22 (2 courses) to £26 **Service:** not inc **Cards:** Amex, Delta, Maestro, MasterCard, Visa **Details:** Vegetarian meals. No smoking. Wheelchair access (not WC). Music

MAP 1 STRETE – Devon

Kings Arms

Dartmouth Road, Strete TQ6 0RW
Tel: (01803) 770377

| Cooking 4 | Seafood | £45 |

Its splendid cast-iron balcony overlooking the main road means that this white-painted, eighteenth-century pub is hard to miss. Locals still prop up the bar, but food – particularly seafood – is the main attraction here. The bar and terrace menu features provençale fish soup and treacle-glazed ham with bubble and squeak, while the carte might open with ravioli of Start Bay crab, served with baby spinach and a light saffron cream, or seared dived scallops accompanied by aubergine caviar and star anise syrup. Main courses bring on the likes of wild gilthead bream with candied peel, spicy couscous and burnt orange 'drizzle', or skate wing with cracked pepper, buttered asparagus and a red wine jus. Roast breast of organic duck with Savoy cabbage braised with juniper and bacon and sauced with Cassis is an alternative meat dish, and West Country cheeses make a savoury ending, with prune and Armagnac tart or hot chocolate fondant for dessert. The wine list is an intelligent, and reasonably priced, selection from around the world. Over a dozen bottles, priced from £13.50, are all served by the glass from £3.40.

Chef: Rob Dawson **Proprietors:** Rob Dawson and Virginia Heath **Open:** Tue to Sun L 12 to 2, Tue to Sat D 6.30 to 9.30 **Closed:** last week Jan, first week Feb, first week June **Meals:** alc (main courses £13.50 to £22). Bar L menu available **Service:** not inc **Cards:** Amex, Delta, Diners, Maestro, MasterCard, Visa **Details:** 38 seats. 60 seats outside. Car park. Children's helpings. No smoking in dining room. No music. No mobile phones

Laughing Monk `AR`

Totnes Road, Strete TQ6 0RN
Tel: (01803) 770639

A log fire welcomes visitors in the winter at this former school dating from 1839. The kitchen makes much use of locally sourced produce for starters such as spicy Brixham crab cakes with a baby caper mayonnaise (£6.50), with maybe oxtail braised in red wine (£11.25) or roast breast of Crediton duck with stir-fried vegetables (£14.25) for main courses. A four-course set Sunday lunch menu (£17.25) is also available. The varied wine list starts at £11.95. Open last Sun in month for L and Tue to Sat D.

MAP 2 STUCKTON – Hampshire

Three Lions

Stuckton, Fordingbridge SP6 2HF
Tel: (01425) 652489
Website: www.thethreelionsrestaurant.co.uk

| Cooking 6 | Anglo-French | £50 |

The Womersleys' 'characterful and endearing' restaurant-with-rooms is on a quiet lane on the western edge of the New Forest. A red-brick country inn built in the 1860s, it is decorated in what might politely be described as an assertive style, the throbbing peach and tomato hues of the dining room softening to a warm glow in the evening, when the halogen spots and uplighters supervene.

Jayne Womersley is ably supported in the 'utterly charming poise and grace' of her approach by the amicable cat that mews out a greeting as you arrive. In the decade and more that husband Mike has been at the stoves, he has never been tempted to elaborate on his menu writing. Terse descriptions chalked on the board range from 'asparagus and wild mushrooms' to 'chunky cod, tomato and basil', or 'roast loin of lamb and crispy bits'. What turns up can be a revelation. 'Impeccably fresh' sautéed shrimps and prawns are 'done to absolute perfection', arranged around a mound of wilted spinach and sauced with a creamy bisque. Venison is a signature main course, served with those highly prized wild mushrooms in a flavourful but not over-reduced jus. Vegetables, charged extra, are varied and satisfying, and desserts, despite their dated fruity garnishes, can powerfully impress, as witness 'eye-poppingly good' lime parfait on clear passion-fruit syrup. The wine list is a model of intelligent concision, with many good names packed into a relatively small compass. Prices are demonstrably fair, and there is a good sommelier on hand to dispense advice. House wines start at £12.75, or £2.75 a glass.

> **Chef:** Mike Womersley **Proprietors:** Mike and Jayne Womersley **Open:** Tue to Sun L 12 to 2, Tue to Sat D 7 to 9 (9.30 Sat) **Meals:** alc (main courses £16.50 to £19.50). Set L £16.75 **Service:** not inc **Cards:** Delta, MasterCard, Visa **Details:** 60 seats. Car park. Vegetarian meals. Children's helpings. No smoking. Wheelchair access (also WC). Occasional music. No mobile phones **Accommodation:** 7 rooms

---

MAP 2 **STUDLAND – Dorset**

Shell Bay

AR

Ferry Road, Studland BH19 3BA
Tel: (01929) 450363

Offering superb views of the Purbecks, diners at this well-established seafood restaurant might start with salad of smoked salmon, tuna and halibut (£5.95), followed by whole grey mullet with samphire and almonds (£16.95), or roasted mahi mahi wrapped in banana leaf (£18.95). Those not in the mood for fish could choose fillet steak with onion rings (£18.95). End with cappuccino pannacotta with caramel sauce (£5.25). Wines from £12.50. Closed Sun D.

MAP 2 **STURMINSTER NEWTON – Dorset**

Plumber Manor

Sturminster Newton DT10 2AF
Tel: (01258) 472507
Website: www.plumbermanor.com

Cooking 2 | **Anglo-French** | **£39**

For those who don't already own a country manor, a visit to Plumber Manor is probably the

next best thing. Its lawns shaded by fine trees give a sense of its scale, echoed by a flagged hallway, a sweeping staircase, antiques, and walls lined with family portraits. Yet it feels like a family home – the Prideaux-Brunes have been here since the seventeenth century – and the homeliness is matched by Brian Prideaux-Brune's cooking style, which is not too ambitious, ensuring a high degree of success, from starters of chicken liver parfait with red onion marmalade to the arrival of the dessert trolley laden with goodies like hazelnut roulade and lemon and ginger crunch. In between, there might be roast guinea fowl with black cherries and cinnamon, or roast loin of pork with apricots and a rosemary jus. Service is welcoming and efficient, and wines are mostly French but supplemented by a New World section that's predominantly under £20. House wine is £13.50.

> **Chefs:** Brian Prideaux-Brune and Louis Haskell **Proprietor:** Richard Prideaux-Brune **Open:** Sun L 12 to 1.30, all week D 7.30 to 9.30 **Meals:** Set L Sun £22, Set D £24 (2 courses) to £27 **Service:** not inc **Cards:** Amex, Diners, Maestro, MasterCard, Visa **Details:** 60 seats. Car park. Vegetarian meals. Children's helpings. No smoking. Wheelchair access (also WC). No music **Accommodation:** 16 rooms

---

MAP 1 **SUMMERCOURT – Cornwall**

Viner's Bar and Restaurant

Carvynick, Summercourt TR8 5AF
Tel: (01872) 510544

Cooking 4 | **Modern European** | **£43**

The building is a former farmhouse converted to a pub some 20-odd years ago. In Kevin and Jane Viner's hands, however, the place has benefited from a sense of unflustered cool. With its varnished floorboards, undressed tables and light, airy dining rooms, it feels just right. The kitchen's cooking follows suit, playing to the gallery with a broad modern bistro repertoire that includes some standards like twice-baked cheese soufflé, described as 'perfection', or bread-and-butter pudding with clotted cream, and chocolate tart with coffee and Amaretto ice cream. In between might be roast loin of venison with braised haunch wrapped in pancetta and accompanied by a prune and Armagnac jus, or monkfish chargrilled in chilli and prawn oil served in a light oriental dressing. Main courses come with potatoes and seasonal vegetables – all sourced locally. Service is 'attentive, knowledgeable', and the short, global wine list is cannily chosen and extremely good value. Half a dozen or so house wines are £12.95.

> Chefs: Kevin Viner and Neill Farrelly Proprietors: Jane and Kevin Viner Open: Sun L 12.30 to 3, all week D 6.30 to 9.30 Closed: 4 weeks winter. Possible reduced opening hours winter; phone to enquire Meals: alc D (main courses £16 to £19). Set L £13.95 (2 courses) to £16.95. Bar menu available Service: not inc Cards: Maestro, MasterCard, Visa Details: 90 seats. 40 seats outside. Car park. Vegetarian meals. Children's helpings. No smoking in dining room. Wheelchair access (not WC). Occasional music

---

MAP 3 SURBITON – Surrey

French Table

85 Maple Road, Surbiton KT6 4AW
Tel: (020) 8399 2365
Website: www.thefrenchtable.co.uk

Cooking 4 | French/Mediterranean | £39

Eric and Sarah Guignard have transformed this attractive restaurant into a prime local destination for Mediterranean cooking with a French slant. They offer a short carte that displays plenty of technique, effort and enterprise. Pumpkin soup comes with goats' cheese mousse, and terrine of foie gras with smoked duck magret, apple and Monbazillac jelly and quince chutney. Main courses continue the industrious theme: roast monkfish is served with parsnip purée, smoked vegetables, Bayonne ham and a morel jus, while Pyrenean rack of lamb is teamed with asparagus, roast shallots, crispy spaghetti and lamb sauce. To finish, an assiette gourmand of chocolate vies for attention with hot chestnut soufflé with cognac and raisin ice cream. The set lunch is particularly good value, especially when you consider a marmite of mussels and smoked haddock with lime leaf and saffron, then roast rabbit leg with red wine, spinach and chorizo velouté. Wines are split between France and the rest of the wine-producing world on the helpfully annotated modern list, which opens at £12.50. The Food Room (see entry, London) is under the same ownership.

> Chef: Eric Guignard Proprietors: Eric and Sarah Guignard Open: Tue to Fri and Sun L 12 to 2.30, Tue to Sat D 7 to 10.30 Closed: 25 and 26 Dec, 1 to 10 Jan Meals: alc D (main courses £10.50 to £16.50). Set L Tue to Fri £13.50 (2 courses) to £16.50, Set L Sun £18.50 Service: 12.5% (optional) Cards: Amex, Delta, Maestro, MasterCard, Visa Details: 48 seats. Vegetarian meals. Children's helpings. No smoking. Wheelchair access (not WC). Music. No mobile phones. Air-conditioned

---

MAP 6 SUTTON GAULT – Cambridgeshire

Anchor Inn

Sutton Gault CB6 2BD
Tel: (01353) 778537
Website: www.anchorsuttongault.co.uk

Cooking 2 | Modern British | £41

Although the whitewashed pub in a quiet, rural location 'in the flatness of the Fens' has a small bar, the interior is geared up for eating, with three interlinked rooms casually decked out with chunky solid-pine tables. However, there is nothing casual about the menu, with around six choices for each course supplemented by daily specials. While seriously robust dishes such as grilled dates wrapped in bacon and served with a mild mustard sauce, and fillet of beef with fondant potato, roast cherry tomatoes, beans au lard and a cep jus have been endorsed by reporters, the menu pushes some way beyond that of a typical country pub: for example, wild rabbit and prune pressé with pea and pistachio dressing. Puddings that have received praise have come in the form of a study of oranges – Cointreau pannacotta, orange and rosemary jelly, and blood-orange sorbet – while the wide-ranging wine list has plenty of interest below £20. Eight wines come by the glass from £3.15, with bottle prices starting at £11.75.

> Chefs: Adam Pickup and Greg Thorne Proprietors: Robin and Heather Moore Open: all week 12 to 2, 7 to 9 (6.30 to 9.30 Sat) Meals: alc exc Sun L (main courses £11.50 to £20). Set L Mon to Fri £10.95 (2 courses), Set L Sun £17 (2 courses) to £21 Service: not inc Cards: Amex, Delta, Maestro, MasterCard, Visa Details: 70 seats. 40 seats outside. Car park. Vegetarian meals. Children's helpings. No smoking in dining room. Wheelchair access (also WC). No music. No mobile phones Accommodation: 4 rooms

---

MAP 9 SUTTON-ON-THE-FOREST – North Yorkshire

Rose & Crown   AR

Main Street, Sutton-on-the-Forest YO61 1DP
Tel: (01347) 811333

The Rose & Crown is a village pub that has reinvented itself as a comfortable bistro. The kitchen takes advantage of locally reared beef and lamb, the latter perhaps appearing as loin with pea and mint risotto (£15.95), but the thrust of the menu is on seafood: king scallops with garlic butter and Gruyère to start (£6.50), followed by seared fillets of sea bass with creamed leeks and shrimp butter (£14.50). Finish with dark chocolate pot with orange and polenta biscuits (£4.50). Wines from £12.95. Closed Sun D and Mon.

MAP 6   SWAFFHAM – Norfolk

Strattons

4 Ash Close, Swaffham PE37 7NH
Tel: (01760) 723845
Website: www.strattonshotel.com

| Cooking 3 | Modern European | £51 |

Well hidden down an alleyway off Swaffham's marketplace and surrounded by peaceful lawns and gardens, this attractive red-brick Palladian villa impresses first-time visitors with its flamboyant interior and unusual sculptures and art. It's a highly personal enterprise, everything about it speaking of individualism, in particular the lengths to which the Scotts go in their diligent search for local and regional materials: smoked fish from Cley Smokehouse, cheese and yoghurt from local dairies, Castle Acre beef, and fish and shellfish from the Norfolk coast. Such careful sourcing perhaps helps to explain the pricing, while Vanessa Scott's virtually single-handed approach goes some way to explaining the economical three options at main-course stage. Robust and 'wholesome' mushroom pâté has made a successful starter, followed, perhaps, by a 'mouth-meltingly tender' slow-cooked beef or smoked haddock and griddled courgette lasagne with crispy leeks. Lemon pudding gets high praise, and there may also be a creamy nutmeg cheesecake. Service is knowledgeable, and Les Scott's wine list – organised by style with informative notes – includes bottles from £13 (£4.50 a glass).

Chefs: Vanessa Scott and Maggie Cooper **Proprietors:** Les and Vanessa Scott **Open:** Mon to Sat D only 7 to 8.30 (9 Fri and Sat) (residents only Sun D) **Closed:** 18 to 27 Dec **Meals:** Set D £40 **Service:** not inc **Cards:** Delta, Maestro, MasterCard, Visa **Details:** 20 seats. Car park. Vegetarian meals. Children's helpings. No smoking. Occasional music. No mobile phones **Accommodation:** 10 rooms

---

To submit a report on any restaurant, please visit *www.which.co.uk/gfgfeedback*.

MAP 2   SWANAGE – Dorset

Cauldron Bistro   AR

5 High Street, Swanage BH19 2LN
Tel: (01929) 422671

Terry and Margaret Flenley have been running the Cauldron Bistro for 17 years, and their personal touch is apparent everywhere at their traditional eatery close to the quay. Seared king scallops (£7.50) are a perennial favourite, and wild boar and apple sausages with horseradish sauce (£4.50) might be another starter. Main courses could run from Aberdeen Angus sirloin with red wine gravy (£17.50) to something like roast guinea fowl with bacon, champ and bread sauce (£13.50). Satisfy any sweet cravings with chocolate truffle cake (£4.75). Interesting wines from £11. Open Thur to Sun.

MAP 9   TADCASTER – North Yorkshire

Singers

16 Westgate, Tadcaster LS24 9AB
Tel: (01937) 835121
Website: www.singersrestaurant.co.uk

| Cooking 2 | Modern European | £34 |

The tone of the place is comfortingly old-fashioned, and this old timer packs them in for early-evening deals, but the carte is pretty flexible too. Local ingredients are the mainstay, and the menu is adapted to the daily availability of materials, including seafood: terrine of salmon, crab and king prawn served hot with a lemon and dill essence, say, or ragoût of turbot and scallops with white wine and basil butter. Meat main courses have a familiar ring – pan-fried calf's liver and bacon, perhaps, or chargrilled ribeye with pumpkin and potato mash and caramelised onions – while everyday desserts include Yorkshire curd tart with banana ice cream, and sticky toffee pudding. Thirty or so serviceable wines are sensibly priced, with house Georges Duboeuf £11.95.

Chefs: Adam Hewitt and John Appleyard **Proprietor:** Philip Taylor **Open:** Tue to Sat D only 6 to 9.30 **Closed:** 1 week Christmas **Meals:** Set D Tue to Thur 6 to 7 £14.95 to £22.95, Set D Tue to Thur £18.95 (2 courses) to £22.95, Set D Fri and Sat £22.95 **Service:** not inc **Cards:** Delta, Maestro, MasterCard, Visa **Details:** 38 seats. Vegetarian meals. No smoking in dining room. Wheelchair access (not WC). Music. Air-conditioned

MAP 2 TADPOLE BRIDGE – Oxfordshire

Trout AR

Tadpole Bridge SN7 8RF
Tel: (01367) 870382

Well-situated on the bank of the Thames, the Trout is under new management (reports on the new regime, please), although the kitchen team has stayed the same, as has the focus on good-quality local produce. Seared fillet of gravad lax with a fennel and orange salad (£7.95), or pressed ham hock, ox tongue and fois gras terrine with piccalilli open, followed by roasted veal loin with lyonnaise potatoes (£16.95). A well-chosen wine list starts at £10.95. Closed Sun D.

MAP 3 TANGMERE – West Sussex

Cassons AR

Arundel Road, Tangmere PO18 0DU
Tel: (01243) 773294

This isolated red-brick building is two miles east of Chichester, with a small garden for al fresco dining and a bright yet simply decorated dining room. Chef/proprietor Vivian Casson has put together a varied menu, while husband Cass gives 'super service' out front. Délice of Selsy crab, king prawn and avocado (£8.95) showcases top-class ingredients, and might be followed by cannon of lamb on a minted pea purée (£17.95), with a 'fantasy' of bananas caramel and praline ice cream (£6.95) to finish. Well-chosen global wines from £13.50. Closed all day Mon, L Tue and D Sun.

MAP 3 TAPLOW – Berkshire

Cliveden, Waldo's

Taplow SL6 0JF
Tel: (01628) 668561
Website: www.clivedenhouse.co.uk

Cooking 5 | Modern European | £97

A giant oil portrait of Nancy Astor, whose family once owned Cliveden, hangs in the lounge, while the other woman famously associated with the house, sixties *It Girl* Christine Keeler, turns up on the walls of Waldo's, the basement dining-room. Take time on a visit here to drink in the fabulous grounds, with their mix of woodlands, formal gardens and the exuberant Fountain of Love, sculpted by Thomas Waldo Story – hence the restaurant's name.

This is a place where things are done properly, and the largely French service is spot-on throughout. Daniel Galmiche's first courses offer 'to tantalise and excite', and manage to do so with roasted Orkney king scallops, bedded on pea purée, in a ribbon of light truffle butter, a defiantly old-fangled, but hugely effective, dish. Refined French technique also brings on milk-fed veal carpaccio with pickled girolles, Parmesan and lime oil, and main dishes such as baked Scottish turbot with a ragoût of artichokes, leeks and wild mushrooms in a herb sabayon. Rolled loin of organic Devon lamb retains a thin layer of fat, and is served with potato cream and micro-diced Mediterranean vegetables in a straightforward lemon thyme jus, while herbs and spices give aromatic lift to desserts like pineapple mille-feuille with lemongrass, or apricot Tatin with camomile. Bills include a £1 charge to the National Trust and wines are a splendid collection from around the world, though prices are high, starting just short of £30.

Chef: Daniel Galmiche **Proprietor:** Von Essen Hotels **Open:** Tue to Sat D only 7 to 9.30 **Meals:** Set D £68. Cover £1 **Service:** not inc **Cards:** Amex, Delta, Diners, Maestro, MasterCard, Visa **Details:** 28 seats. Car park. No children under 12. Jacket and tie. No smoking. No music. No mobile phones. Air-conditioned **Accommodation:** 39 rooms

MAP 2 TAUNTON – Somerset

Castle Hotel

Castle Green, Taunton TA1 1NF
Tel: (01823) 272671
Website: www.the-castle-hotel.com

Cooking 7 | Modern British | £46

The magnificent building in the centre of Somerset's county town was once a Norman fortress but has had several centuries' practice in the hospitality trade since, welcoming boarders rather than repelling them. Clad elegantly in wisteria, it is all done up to the nines within, the L-shaped dining room a monumental space with a high, ornately moulded ceiling and a huge stone fireplace. 'The whole atmosphere,' comments a reporter, 'is friendly and welcoming, with attentive but unobtrusive staff.'

The menu begins with as many acknowledgements to suppliers as there might be in an Oscar acceptance speech, from the Brixham fisherman to the Hambridge smokehouse that supplies smoked eel. These ingredients find themselves in the capable hands of Richard Guest, whose style is all about maximising impact with apposite flavours and seasonings. That smoked eel might turn up as accompaniment to scrambled duck egg, while Brixham crab is pointed up with marinated vegetables and avocado. Slow-roasting of duck brings out its character, the dish further gaining from its partnership with roast cranberry compote. Fixed-price lunches are excellent value, as was discovered by a couple who enjoyed a generous serving of home-smoked salmon and then a large, tender organic pork chop with 'pork scratching' risotto (no, really) and apple purée. Desserts sound fun, what with Castle fruit riot, coffee and hazelnut bonfire, and a 'turned-over apple' all making their appearance on a March menu.

A wine list of rare distinction adds to the allure, with a slate of sherries and a page of uniformly well-selected wines by the glass from £4 not the least attractions. The main list is strong in Burgundy, Bordeaux and the Rhône, but there are also good little selections from New Zealand and Italy, and a commendable range of halves.

Chef: Richard Guest **Proprietors:** the Chapman family **Open:** all week L 12.30 to 2, Mon to Sat D 7 to 9.30 **Meals:** Set L and D £20 (2 courses) to £45. Bar L menu available **Service:** 12.5% (optional) **Cards:** Amex, Delta, Diners, Maestro, MasterCard, Visa **Details:** 70 seats. 20 seats outside. Car park. Vegetarian meals. Children's helpings. No smoking. Wheelchair access (also WC). No music. No mobile phones **Accommodation:** 44 rooms

Willow Tree

3 Tower Lane, Taunton TA1 4AR
Tel: (01823) 352835
Website: www.thewillowtreerestaurant.co.uk

Cooking 6 | **Modern British** | **£42**

Darren Sherlock and Rita Rambellas's seventeenth-century town house, in the heart of Taunton, is a model of relaxed restraint, serving stylish, modern British food that manages to avoid fashion clichés. Indeed, the reach of the culinary ambition, and the way in which the kitchen handles the best of local seasonal produce, is the big attraction. Oriental modes, as in marinated tuna tartare with a shoot salad, pickled ginger and wasabi dressing, are mixed with Mediterranean, such as risotto of ham hock and

parsley, and the results seem uniformly engaging. Seared organic salmon with a sesame seed and prawn crust served with noodles, a pea shoot and mange-tout salad and beetroot and soy dressing is an offbeat fish main-course option. Those with simpler tastes might prefer roast breast of corn-fed chicken with Puy lentils and braised root vegetables. Meals conclude with the likes of pear and rhubarb crumble tartlet with crème chiboust ginger ice cream. Service is sharp and engaging, as is the wine list, which covers Europe and the southern hemisphere with brisk aplomb. House Chilean is £13.95.

Chef: Darren Sherlock **Proprietors:** Darren Sherlock and Rita Rambellas **Open:** Tue to Sat D only 6.30 to 10 **Closed:** Jan, Aug **Meals:** Set D Tue and Wed £22.50, Thur to Sat £29.50 **Service:** not inc **Cards:** Delta, Maestro, MasterCard, Visa **Details:** 35 seats. 10 seats outside. Vegetarian meals. No smoking. Wheelchair access (not WC). Music. No mobile phones

MAP 1 **TAVISTOCK – Devon**

Horn of Plenty

Gulworthy, Tavistock PL19 8JD
Tel: (01822) 832528
Website: www.thehornofplenty.co.uk

DEVON OF THE YEAR RESTAURANT

Cooking 6 | **Modern British** | **£57**

The location is everything, with ravishing views along the wooded Tamar valley from the conservatory extension to the dining room. Sitting at the top of a hill always helps, and the gardens are awash with azaleas, camellias and rhododendrons. A welcoming blend of unpretentious hospitality and professionalism provide the setting for Peter Gorton's cooking, which eschews modern spareness without resorting to over-garnished fussiness. These are dishes that are meticulously made, full of interesting juxtapositions, with flavour balances spot-on.

Seared squid is paired with king prawns in a starter with asparagus tempura, while John Dory appears in an arresting combination with fat little tortellini of rough-textured smoked salmon mousse, peppers and spinach, and a white wine reduction flavoured with lime and dill. Main courses feature roast loin of spring lamb with crisply battered artichoke fritters, a mousse of spinach, and a deeply satisfying, traditionally conceived sauce of red wine and black olives, while fish dishes include grilled lemon sole on crushed seasonal Jersey Royals, with asparagus meunière and a saffron sauce. A texturally perfect lemon pannacotta with marinated oranges and properly biting lemon sorbet made a triumphant end to an inspection meal. The French-led wine list offers value and a decent range of flavours. A house selection kicks off at £14 with Spanish white and Argentinian red, which also come by the glass at £3.75.

Chef: Peter Gorton Proprietors: Peter Gorton, and Paul and Andie Roston Open: Tue to Sun 12 to 2, all week D 7 to 9 Closed: 25 and 26 Dec Meals: Set L £25, Set D £42 Service: not inc Cards: Amex, Delta, Maestro, MasterCard, Visa Details: 60 seats. 15 seats outside. Car park. Vegetarian meals. Children's helpings. Smoking in drawing room only. Wheelchair access (also WC). Occasional music. No mobile phones Accommodation: 10 rooms

MAP 12 | TEDDINGTON – Greater London

Wharf

[AR]

22 Manor Road, Teddington TW11 8BG
Tel: (020) 8977 6333

On the Thames, this converted boathouse is a well-frequented venue, with a covered terrace for outside dining. The menu is modern European in style but also draws from Asia, so look out for chilli seafood and noodle salad with kaffir lime leaf, coriander and mango (£8) before, say, rump of Welsh lamb in a herb and mustard crust with cassoulet (£16.50) or seared loin of tuna with garlic confit (£15). Finish with strawberry cheesecake or bread-and-butter pudding (£5). Wines from £14.50. Closed Sun D and Mon.

MAP 2 | TEFFONT EVIAS – Wiltshire

Howard's House

Teffont Evias SP3 5RJ
Tel: (01722) 716392
Website: www.howardshousehotel.co.uk

Cooking 3 | Modern British-Plus | £8

The seventeenth-century dower house is in one of the prettiest villages in Wiltshire, on a lane bounded by a tiny stream, and is surrounded by attractive gardens. It is a relaxed, albeit smart place in which to enjoy Nick Wentworth's contemporary seasonal cooking. Dishes show enterprise and ambition, offering fillet of brill with onion tarte Tatin and wild mushrooms among starters and, perhaps, for main course roast poussin alongside

fondant potato, creamed leeks and a red wine jus. There are some culinary surprises too, such as fillet of sea bass with saffron broth and a pancetta beignet, or a starter of cannon of lamb with aubergine purée and goats' cheese tortellini. Puddings might include passion-fruit-curd soufflé with passion-fruit consommé, or a plate of British cheeses. Seven house wines, available by the bottle (£13.50 to £17.50) and glass (£4.25) point out the best value on the French-dominated wine list, although there are a few well-known names should diners want to push the boat out.

Chef: Nick Wentworth Proprietor: Noele Thompson Open: Tue to Thur and Sun 12.30 to 1.45, all week D 7.30 to 9 Meals: Set L £21.50 (2 courses) to £25, Set D £22.50 (2 courses) to £42 Service: not inc Cards: Amex, Delta, Maestro, MasterCard, Visa Details: 30 seats. 12 seats outside. Car park. Children's helpings. No smoking. Wheelchair access (not WC). No music. No mobile phones Accommodation: 9 rooms

MAP 2 | TETBURY – Gloucestershire

Calcot Manor

Tetbury GL8 8YJ
Tel: (01666) 890391
Website: www.calcotmanor.co.uk

Cooking 3 | Modern British | £52

This elegant manor was once a farmhouse, though you'd be hard pressed to see the signs these days. Its impressive features include a large flat-stoned hall and stately fireplaces, while the outhouses are now guest rooms and a health spa. The décor is modern but doesn't quite erase the country setting, thanks to the low ceilings and small-paned windows. Michael Croft's à la carte menu is succinct yet ambitious with lively combinations. Pumpkin ravioli and sauté wild mushrooms are accompanied by Parmesan and truffle emulsion, while roasted and braised Duchy estate mutton follows for main, and the Royal theme is continued with wood-roasted rack of Balmoral venison, served imaginatively with caramelised salsify and curly kale. Half a dozen desserts include praline crème brûlée or home-made ice cream. The wine list offers few choices under £20. Also on the grounds is the Gumstool Inn; separate from the Conservatory restaurant, it's a family-friendly modern country pub that serves simple bar meals – think fish and chips, or sausage and mash.

Chef: Michael Croft Proprietor: Richard Ball Open: all week 12 to 2, 7 to 9.30 Meals: alc (main courses L £9 to £14, D £16 to £20). Bar meals available Service: not inc Cards: Amex, Delta, Diners, Maestro, MasterCard, Visa Details: 100 seats. 20 seats outside. Car park. Children's helpings. No smoking. Wheelchair access (also WC). Occasional music. No mobile phones. Air-conditioned Accommodation: 30 rooms

Trouble House

Cirencester Road, Tetbury GL8 8SG
Tel: (01666) 502206
Website: www.troublehouse.co.uk

Cooking 5 | Modern European | £41

This unassuming cream-washed stone pub sits on the main Tetbury to Cirencester road, the 'Trouble' referring to some bother during the Civil War. You can call in just for a drink, but most people come to eat, drawn by the unstuffy integrity that permeates the whole operation, from the front-of-house warmth to Michael Bedford's unpretentious approach to food. While the style gives good-quality ingredients the uncluttered space to show their qualities, the short carte features a number of Mediterranean influences that complement modern British dishes such as roast loin of pork with wild mushrooms, ratte potatoes and mushroom cappuccino, or oxtail and ox-cheek bourguignon with horseradish mash. Lemon sole stuffed with Salcombe crab and poached in white wine, cream and caviar, or venison carpaccio with honey and rosemary dressing might be among starters. Puddings range from tiramisù to honey and citrus crème fraîche mousse with spiced fruits, and there's a first-rate selection of British cheeses, too. A wide-ranging list of around 60 wines offers good choice by the glass (from £3.40). House South African Chenin Blanc and Shiraz are £14 and £14.50 respectively.

Chef: Michael Bedford Proprietors: Michael and Sarah Bedford Open: Tue to Sun L 12 to 2.30, Tue to Sat D 7 to 9.30 Closed: Christmas to 3 Jan, bank hols Meals: alc (main courses £15 to £17.50) Service: not inc Cards: Amex, Delta, Maestro, MasterCard, Visa Details: 50 seats. 25 seats outside. Car park. Children's helpings. No children under 14 in bar. Wheelchair access (also WC)

 This symbol means that accommodation is available at this establishment.

MAP 5 TITLEY – Herefordshire

Stagg Inn

Titley, nr Kington HR5 3RL
Tel: (01544) 230221
Website: www.thestagg.co.uk

Cooking 5 | Modern British | £38

Steve and Nicola Reynolds are dedicated to preparing unpretentious food made with quality local produce, including fruit from their own trees, and vegetables and herbs from the adjacent garden. The bar still functions as the village local, while the two separate dining rooms are neat and homely, with bare wooden tables, high-backed faux leather chairs and coir matting. High praise goes to Nicola's efficient front-of-house style, running the show with 'focused simplicity and totally lacking in pretension', while Steve produces classic dishes that are technically spot-on yet straightforward: most plates are left ungarnished, letting the ingredients speak for themselves.

A starter of cod on mustard lentils is accompanied by miniature, crisp chips, while accurate timing is the hallmark of moist and supple rack of spring lamb served with sweetbreads, Jersey Royals and a reduction sauce. A classical training is evident in other main courses of pan-fried John Dory with bouillabaisse sauce, and Herefordshire rump steak with béarnaise. The same attention to detail goes into vegetables – parsnip and carrot wedges and Savoy cabbage with lots of lardons, for example. Standards don't falter at dessert stage: witness a generous portion of caramelised passion-fruit tart, with 'excellent' shortcrust pastry, partnered by mango sorbet. The regional cheeses, served from a double-decker trolley, are also worth noting, among them Ragstone, Stinking Bishop and Hereford Hop. Chilean Merlot and Sauvignon Blanc lead the wine list, at £12.90. An intelligent collection of 50-odd bottles representing most wine-producing regions, at good prices, it concludes with some classy Burgundies and clarets.

Chefs: Steve Reynolds, Grant Powell and Mathew Handley Proprietors: Steve and Nicola Reynolds Open: Tue to Sun L 12 to 2, Tue to Sat D 6.30 to 9.30 Closed: first 2 weeks Nov, 25 to 27 Dec, 1 Jan, Tue following bank hol (exc May Day) Meals: alc exc Sun L (main courses £12.50 to £17). Set L Sun £14.90. Bar menu available Tue to Sat L, Tue to Thur D Service: not inc Cards: Delta, Maestro, MasterCard, Visa Details: 70 seats. 20 seats outside. Car park. Children's helpings. No smoking in dining room. No music Accommodation: 6 rooms

MAP 8 **TODMORDEN –**
West Yorkshire

Old Hall

Hall Street, Todmorden OL14 7AD
Tel: (01706) 815998

Cooking 2 | **Modern British** | **£42**

This Elizabethan manor house is located in the touristy village of Todmorden, and the Hoyles have made their restaurant an attraction in its own right. Many original features remain, including wood panelling and flagstone floors, and Madeleine Hoyle continues to be the most genteel of hostesses. In the kitchen, menus are changed with the seasons and local produce takes centre stage – Goosnargh poultry, black pudding from Bacup, John Penny's meat and fish from Openshaws. Fish specials are noteworthy, perhaps seared sea bass with a shallot and Beaujolais sauce. Orange and sage crusted fillet of pork with roasted parsnips, or pan-fried supreme of halibut in a white wine sauce might follow. Desserts include Yorkshire parkin with gingerbread ice cream and rhubarb sauce. Their global wine list is full-bodied with a good selection from Bordeaux, while house options start reasonably at £12.50.

Chefs: Chris Roberts and Peter Windross **Proprietors:** Nick and Madeleine Hoyle **Open:** Thur, Fri and Sun L 12 to 2 (2.30 Sun), Tue to Sat D 7 to 9 (9.30 Sat) **Closed:** 25 Dec, first week Jan, day after bank hols **Meals:** alc (main courses £14 to £18). Set L Thur and Fri £8.95 (2 courses), Set L Sun £17 **Service:** not inc **Cards:** Delta, Diners, Maestro, MasterCard, Visa **Details:** 70 seats. 20 seats outside. Vegetarian meals. Children's helpings. No smoking. Music

MAP 1 **TORQUAY – Devon**

Elephant

3–4 Beacon Terrace, Torquay TQ1 2BH
Tel: (01803) 200044
Website: www.elephantrestaurant.co.uk

Cooking 4 | **Modern British** | **£46**

Beacon Terrace is, well, a beacon of gastronomy among the chippies and burger bars of Torquay. It's a smart Georgian terrace, all creamy-yellow, with a few tables (not all) enjoying a view over the bay. A mish-mash of East-meets-West interior decorative themes is the setting for Simon Hulstone's ambi-

tious cooking, which calls on an intricate network of local suppliers and scores some palpable hits. Crab tortellini in langoustine and lemongrass cream was a joyous way to begin a spring inspection lunch, and even a pretty straight chicken and bacon Ceasar salad with Parmesan crackers was carefully made. Main courses might feature grey mullet with avocado purée, and chargrilled ribeye with Bloody Mary ketchup. Desserts like chilled Somerset apple pannacotta show up well. A short, serviceable wine list starts at £12.95 for Italian Cortese or Chilean Merlot, and has a fair few by the glass, from £3.50.

Chef: Simon Hulstone **Proprietors:** Peter Morgan and Freidericke Etessami **Open:** Mon to Sat 12.30 to 2.30, 6.30 to 9.30 (bar open all day Fri and Sat) **Closed:** Wed during winter **Meals:** alc (main courses £12.50 to £19.50). Set L £12.50 (2 courses) to £15.50, Set D (Mon to Thur) £16.75 (2 courses) to £20.75. Bar menu available **Service:** not inc **Cards:** Amex, Delta, Maestro, MasterCard, Visa **Details:** 54 seats. Vegetarian meals. Children's helpings. Smoking in bar only. Wheelchair access (also WC). Music. No mobile phones. Air-conditioned

No. 7 Fish Bistro

7 Beacon Terrace, Torquay TQ1 2BH
Tel: (01803) 295055
Website: www.no7-fish.com

Cooking 1 | **Seafood** | **£37**

In a Regency house a hop, skip and jump away from the harbour, this family-run seafood restaurant is a welcoming and friendly place. It hasn't changed much over the years, with its dark wooden floors, seafaring knick-knacks, and practical oilcloths on the tables. Queenie scallops in the half-shell, or Loch Fyne oak-roast salmon are followed by large whole Brixham plaice, Star Point crab, and whole lobster served cold with garlic and lemon. Salmon baked in Moroccan spices, or a selection of fish in tempura accompanied by three dips widen out the choices. Desserts include home-made apple crumble, and the well-priced wine list lifts anchor at £12.

Chefs: Oliver and Paul Stacey **Proprietors:** Graham and Jill Stacey **Open:** Wed to Sat L 12.15 to 1.45, Tue to Sat D 7 to 9.45 (6 to 10.15 summer); also open Mon D June and Oct, Sun and Mon D July to Sept **Closed:** 1 week Nov, Christmas and New Year, 2 weeks Feb **Meals:** alc (main courses £10 to £17.50) **Service:** not inc **Cards:** Amex, Delta, Maestro, MasterCard, Visa **Details:** 38 seats. Vegetarian meals. Children's helpings. Wheelchair access (not WC). Music. No mobile phones. Air-conditioned

MAP 1   TOTNES – Devon

Effings

50 Fore Street, Totnes TQ9 5RP
Tel: (01803) 863435

Cooking 2 | **Modern European** | **£34**

This small restaurant and delicatessen in the heart of Totnes now has a sister branch in Exeter (see entry). The emphasis is on local, seasonal produce backed up by top-quality ingredients from further afield such as Manchego cheese, foie gras and Bayonne ham. Everything is made in-house, including the terrines, tarts and salads for the delicatessen counter (much of which is also on the menu). Blackboard menus offer a couple of daily-changing starters – perhaps salmon terrine with pickled baby cucumbers – followed by a constantly evolving list of main courses that might include wild pigeon breast salad with pickled beetroot, pancetta, pine nuts and fried quail's eggs, a pithiviers of goats' cheese and walnuts, and poached skate with a tomato, caper and parsley butter sauce. Dessert might be pannacotta with rhubarb and vanilla ice cream, and a compact, varied wine list opens with house selections at £13.75.

Chef: Karl Rasmussen   **Proprietors:** Michael Kann and Jacqueline Williams   **Open:** Mon to Sat L only 12 to 2.15 **Closed:** bank hols   **Meals:** alc (main courses £11 to £17) **Service:** net prices   **Cards:** Delta, Maestro, MasterCard, Visa **Details:** 12 seats. Children's helpings. No smoking. Wheelchair access (also WC). No music. No mobile phones. Air-conditioned

Wills

2/3 The Plains, Totnes TQ9 5DR
Tel: (01803) 865192
Website: www.willsrestaurant.co.uk

Cooking 3 | **Modern European** | **£41**

This elegant nineteenth-century terraced house is now less of a shrine to Australian explorer William Wills (whose statue stands opposite) and more a relaxing bistro/café, though you can still see Egyptian frescos on the walls. The dining room upstairs is decorated with paintings and photographs from local artists, tables are laid with white linen and the general effect is spacious and uncluttered. There are daily specials and effort goes into seasonal cooking with locally-sourced produce.

Start, perhaps, with prawn brochette or home-smoked duck breast accompanied by a 'rich and crisp' celeriac rémoulade. Seared squid works well with its onion, chilli lime and lemon juice marinade, while steak Diane has been praised. Finish with something classic like crème brûlée or tiramisù. The global wine list is divided into helpful sections with a good support for local wines, such as Sharpham Dart Valley for £15.25.

Chef: Craig Purkiss   **Proprietors:** Philip Silvester and Jenny Priest   **Open:** all week L 12 to 2.30, Tue to Sat D 7 (6.30 summer) to 9.30   **Meals:** alc (main courses L £10 to £14, D £10 to £18). Set L £9.95 (2 courses)   **Service:** not inc   **Cards:** Amex, Delta, Maestro, MasterCard, Visa   **Details:** 42 seats. Vegetarian meals. Children's helpings. No smoking. Music

MAP 1   TREEN – Cornwall

Gurnard's Head

NEW ENTRY

Treen, nr Zennor TR26 3DE
Tel: (01736) 796928
Website: www.gurnardshead.co.uk

Cooking 3 | **Modern British** | **£35**

Since the Gurnard's Head's makeover, this large pub on the winding coast road to St Ives now has the feel of a contemporary gastro-pub. The Inkin brothers have for a number of years been running the Felin Fach Griffin, Felinfach (see entry, Wales), and they follow the philosophy that simple is best. This shows in everything from the bright yet relaxing décor in the bar, dining room and bedrooms, to the daily changing menus. A wild sea bass salad with vanilla mayonnaise and pink grapefruit was 'moist, light and full of flavour', while whole spider crab claws are well worth the challenge. The ethos of simplicity continues with whole sea bream with roast asparagus and porcini, 'simply cooked to perfection on the bone', while whole lemon sole with a hazelnut crust has also been well executed. Local cheeses are served with a sweet apple jelly and soda bread while the rhubarb brûlée has been an excellent dessert. The good wine selection comes from around the globe, starting at £11.75, with 11 choices by the glass.

Chef: Mathew Williamson   **Proprietors:** Charles and Edmund Inkin   **Open:** all week 12.30 to 2.30, 6.30 to 9.30   **Meals:** alc (main courses L £6.50 to £14.50, D £9 to £16.50)   **Service:** not inc   **Cards:** Delta, Maestro, MasterCard, Switch, Visa **Details:** 50 seats. 40 seats outside. Car park. Vegetarian meals. Children's helpings. Occasional music   **Accommodation:** 7 rooms

MAP 1 TRESCO – Isles of Scilly

Island Hotel AR

Tresco TR24 0PU
Tel: (01720) 422883

Dramatic sea views and a private beach are among the star attractions at this classy hotel. The restaurant was completely refurbished in early 2006 to give it a contemporary look. Refined yet modern ideals are also at the heart of the dinner menu (£38 for three courses), with starters of crisp confit duck leg on baked fig polenta with chocolate oil, or Tresco lobster ravioli with shellfish cream. To follow might be baked sea bass with aubergine dumplings and truffle foam, and dessert choices run to chocolate truffle cake with pistachio ice cream. Wines from £16. Bar menu available. Open all week D only; closed 3 Nov to 1 Mar.

MAP 10 TROUTBECK – Cumbria

Queens Head Hotel AR

Townhead, Troutbeck LA23 1PW
Tel: (015394) 32174

Charming seventeenth century inn on the old coaching route between Windermere and Penrith, with splendid views of the fells. Ambitious dishes include starters such as home-made black pudding on crushed new potatoes with crisp pancetta and pickled walnut jus (£6.50). To follow, perhaps pan-fried sea bass with rösti, green beans and air-dried ham (£15.95) or roast duck breast with duck leg and orange marmalade tortellini, anise and wildflower honey dressing (£14.95), and for dessert, lemon posset with mixed berry compote (£4.95. Locally brewed beers and wines from £12.50 a bottle.

MAP 1 TRURO – Cornwall

Tabb's NEW ENTRY

85 Kenwyn Street, Truro TR1 3BZ
Tel: (01872) 262110
Website: www.tabbs.co.uk

Cooking 4 | Modern British | £44

The former Royal Standard pub has been transformed into the stylish new domain of Melanie and Nigel Tabb. It's in stark contrast to their former

rustic premises in Portreath. Walls painted a fashionable pale lilac, slate floors and cream leather high-backed dining chairs lend the place a contemporary appeal, and the food follows on with innovation and confidence. The Tabbs have long championed local produce – suppliers are credited on the menu – and Nigel conjures up full-blooded flavours: witness a terrine of wild rabbit and chicken with a 'wonderfully gingery' chutney, and 'unbelievably fresh' scallops in a light, creamy sauce with a tang of lime. A broad gastronomic outlook also turns up mains of bream on paprika-flavoured home-made spaghetti with roasted red peppers and herbs. Roast duck with crispy skin and a rich, spicy orange sauce suggests that, even when more involved, the food keeps its feet firmly on the ground. Desserts have included a dark chocolate marquise served alongside a scoop of white chocolate ice cream and a solid chocolate coffee spoon. Very professional service reinforces the comfort factor, and the wine list, starting at £12.95, offers an affordable, global selection.

Chef: Nigel Tabb Proprietors: Nigel and Melanie Tabb Open: Tue to Fri L 12 to 2, Tue to Sat D 6.30 to 9 Meals: alc (main courses L £8 to £11.50, D £12.50 to £20) Service: not inc Cards: Delta, Maestro, Mastercard, Visa Details: 30 seats. Vegetarian meals. Children's helpings. No smoking. Music

MAP 3 TUNBRIDGE WELLS – Kent

Brasserie Blanc AR

5 Lime Hill Road, Tunbridge Wells TN1 1LJ
Tel: (01892) 559170

The newly branded chain, formerly known as Le Petit Blanc (the same goes for the other outlets in Birmingham, Cheltenham, Manchester and Oxford – see entries), continues in the same vein. On offer are good-value set menus, a family atmosphere and brasserie favourites including smoked herrings (£5.50), or Roquefort soufflé (£6.50), followed by hot oak-smoked Loch Duart salmon with beetroot salad (£14), or maybe Cornish lamb rack with pistachio couscous (£17.50). Lemon tart ends. Wines from £12.95. Open all week.

 Not a full entry but provisionally recommended. These 'also recommended' establishments are integrated throughout the book.

Hotel du Vin & Bistro

Crescent Road, Tunbridge Wells TN1 2LY
Tel: (01892) 526455
Website: www.hotelduvin.com

Cooking 4 | **Modern European** | **£45**

The Hotel du Vin is one of the town's historic architectural landmarks, a grade II-listed building, originally created as a private residence back in the eighteenth-century. Now though, it's a bespoke hotel, part of the successful chain that stretches from Bristol to Harrogate (see entries). The dining room features dark wooden tables decorated with candles, and waiting staff who know their stuff. The menu kicks off with half a dozen dishes including pan-fried trout with a vegetable casserole, or seared scallops on a roasted celeriac purée. Main courses see the likes of roast rump of lamb with wilted spinach, and corn-fed chicken breast with foie gras, while 'simple classics' offer up Morecambe Bay potted shrimps and chargrilled ribeye steak with béarnaise sauce. Vegetarians get their own section, and desserts extend from summer pudding with clotted cream to honey roasted figs with goat's cheese ice cream. The cracking wine list opens with own-label house selections from £13.50, continuing with some interesting global vintages.

Chef: Jason Horn **Proprietor:** MWB Plc **Open:** all week 12.30 to 2, 7 to 10 **Meals:** alc (main courses £12.50 to £17.50). Set L Sun £14.50. Bar menu available **Service:** 10% (optional) **Cards:** Amex, Delta, Diners, Maestro, MasterCard, Visa **Details:** 84 seats. 20 seats outside. Car park. Vegetarian meals. Children's helpings. No smoking. Wheelchair access (also WC). No music **Accommodation:** 34 rooms

---

MAP 3 | **TWICKENHAM –**
Greater London

A Cena

418 Richmond Road, Twickenham TW1 2EB
Tel: (020) 8288 0108
Website: www.acena.co.uk

Cooking 2 | **Italian** | **£41**

A friendly neighbourhood restaurant situated in a row of shops. Inside, there are different-sized wooden tables (the smaller ones for two are a squeeze), candles everywhere and an assortment of mirrors. It's authentic, well-flavoured and every-thing, even the basics such as focaccia bread, is carefully executed. The evening menu is a free-form affair; bresaola with pecorino and white truffle oil or pan-fried scallops with anchovy and rosemary sauce are typical starters. Pasta options include penne with aged balsamic, while meat-eaters might be tempted by veal scaloppine milanese with roast cherry tomatoes. End with either chocolate mousse torte, or raspberry and chardonnay jelly. Wines are patriotic and listed by style, with a Merlot Corvina opening the list at £12.95.

Chef: Nicola Parsons **Proprietors:** Tim and Camilla Healy **Open:** Tue to Sun L 12 to 2.30, Tue to Sat D 7 to 10.30 **Meals:** alc (main courses L £8 to £15, D £11.50 to £20). Set L Sun £22.50 **Service:** not inc **Cards:** Amex, Delta, Maestro, MasterCard, Visa **Details:** 55 seats. Vegetarian meals. Children's helpings (no children at D). No pipes/cigars. Wheelchair access (not WC). Music. Air-conditioned

La Brasserie

2 Whitton Road, Twickenham TW1 1BJ
Tel: (020) 8744 9610

Cooking 4 | **French** | **£50**

John McClements appears to have had it with fine dining. As a replacement to his McClements Restaurant, he has opened La Brasserie on the site, and although it's a close relative of his successful Ma Cuisine (next door and in Kew – see entries), it is obviously intended to be more upmarket. It's certainly smarter – polished tables, pleasant plain walls with French-inspired photos – but with an unapologetic flaunting of its French roots it delivers a similarly long menu of hearty classics (terrines, fish soup, calves' sweetbreads and rib of beef with béarnaise), even the same head waiter 'who served me couple of months ago at Ma Cuisine'. At inspection scallops with slow-cooked tomatoes and basil dressing showed a balanced combination of tastes and textures, while free-range chicken with champagne and morel sauce was accurately cooked. To finish, roast pineapple with caramel cardamom sauce with coconut ice cream is refreshing and well prepared, while tarte Tatin may suffer from a surfeit of pastry but the apples are good quality and the Calvados ice cream is 'superb'. France dominates a wine list that yields nothing under £20; a dozen come by the glass from £5.50.

Chef: John McClements **Proprietors:** John McClements and Dominic Séjourné **Open:** Mon to Sat 12 to 2.30, 7 to 10.30 **Closed:** 1 Jan **Meals:** alc (main courses £15 to £25). Set L (exc Sat) £20 **Service:** 10% (optional) **Cards:** Amex, Delta, Diners, Maestro, MasterCard, Visa **Details:** 45 seats. Children's helpings. No smoking. Occasional music. No mobile phones. Air-conditioned

Brula Bistrot

43 Crown Road, St Margaret's, Twickenham
TW1 3EJ
Tel: (020) 8892 0602
Website: www.brulabistrot.com

| Cooking 4 | Modern British | £49 |

Brula is one of those neighbourhood places that feels as if it could have been transplanted directly from France – stained glass, mirrors, dark wood, white tablecloths and olive green banquettes say it all. The menu strays little from the classic bistro repertoire – bouillabaisse is there alongside coq au vin, steak frites and sole meunière. At inspection, intensely-textured skate terrine flecked with capers, chives and chervil revealed solid, fresh flavours, any tendency to blandness saved by a dollop of 'punchy' salsa verde, and a main course fillet of beef served with a forestière sauce was declared 'assured and triumphant', the accompanying chips also excellent. What a pity then, that at this meal, desserts 'were not up to scratch'. Service combines a crisp, even businesslike approach with a welcoming attitude, and the short, mainly French wine list opens at £12.50. La Buvette, Richmond (see entry), is run by the same people.

Chefs: Jamie Russel and Rebecca Muffet **Proprietors:** Lawrence Hartley and Bruce Duckett **Open:** all week 12 to 3, 6 to 10.30 **Closed:** 25 and 26 Dec, 1 Jan, August bank hols **Meals:** alc (main courses £11.50 to £18.50). Set L £11 (2 courses) to £13.50 **Service:** 12.5% (optional) **Cards:** Delta, Maestro, MasterCard, Visa **Details:** 40 seats. 10 seats outside. Vegetarian meals. Children's helpings. No smoking. Wheelchair access (not WC). No music. No mobile phones

Ma Cuisine

6 Whitton Road, Twickenham TW1 1BJ
Tel: (020) 8607 9849

| Cooking 3 | French Regional | £35 |

This is a perfect replica of a classic French bistro: red and white check tablecloths with paper napkins, French popular songs in the background, good humoured, nonchalant staff, and a menu 'straight out of the book of French provincial classics'. Rabbit and ham hock terrine with Chablis jelly and 'a huge dollop of Dijon mustard' is a good way to start, followed perhaps by 'gloriously tasty' belly of pork wrapped in bacon and served with gratin dauphinoise and haricots verts, or a cassoulet that was 'the real thing' – Toulouse sausages, haricots blancs, morteau sausage – and a 'really hearty dish prepared well with good ingredients'. Desserts, at inspection, were not a highlight. The exclusively French wine list is long on inexpensive, reasonably well-chosen bottles with house wine £12.50 and a dozen available by the glass. Run by John McClements, this is a sibling of Ma Cuisine in Kew, and La Brasserie, next door in Whitton Road (see entries).

Chef: John McClements **Proprietors:** John McClements and Dominique Séjourné **Open:** Mon to Sat 12 to 2.30, 6.30 to 10.30 **Closed:** 1 Jan **Meals:** alc (main courses £12.50 to £15). Set L £12.95 (2 courses) to £15.50, Set D (exc Sat) £18.50 **Service:** 10% (optional) **Cards:** Delta, Maestro, MasterCard, Visa **Details:** 80 seats. 10 seats outside. Vegetarian meals. Children's helpings. No smoking. Music

MAP 5 **ULLINGSWICK –**
Herefordshire

Three Crowns

Ullingswick HR1 3JQ
Tel: (01432) 820279
Website: www.threecrownsinn.com

| Cooking 4 | Modern British | £39 |

Despite their reputation for food, Brent Castle and Rachel Baker strive to maintain the pubbiness of their sixteenth-century brick-and-timbered inn. Drinkers and diners mingle in the split bar, where neutral colours, flowers and lots of wood create a rustic, welcoming look; in contrast, the restaurant extension has a more modern feel. Menus tend to be sensibly short with concise descriptions, and carefully sourced ingredients include the likes of Lay and Robson smoked salmon, Cornish crab and Herefordshire beef. Among starters might be a rich fish soup, or Little Hereford Cheddar and spinach soufflé, and to follow casserole of seafood with sea parsley, or crisp belly of pork with 'fantastic' crackling, 'excellent' black pudding, red cabbage and mustard mash. At dessert stage, favourites like chocolate nemesis with vanilla ice cream sit alongside rhubarb compote and strawberry gratin. The fixed-price lunch menu is good value, and the wine list works well at all levels, from a good house selection at £14.50 by bottle or £5.25 by glass to a blackboard list of pricier monthly specials.

> **Chef:** Brent Castle **Proprietor:** Brent Castle and Rachel Baker **Open:** Tue to Sun 12 to 2.30, 7 (6 Sat July and Aug) to 10 **Closed:** L 2 weeks from 24 Dec **Meals:** alc (main courses £14.50). Set L £12.95 (2 courses) to £14.95. Bar menu available **Service:** not inc **Cards:** Maestro, MasterCard, Visa **Details:** 75 seats. 24 seats outside. Car park. Children's helpings. No smoking. Wheelchair access (also WC). No music **Accommodation:** 1 room

MAP 10 ULLSWATER – Cumbria

Sharrow Bay

Ullswater CA10 2LZ
Tel: (01768) 486301
Website: www.sharrowbay.co.uk

Cooking 6 | **English** | **£69**

The place that wrote the book on the country-house hotel format, Sharrow Bay sits in prime Lakeland territory, a white-fronted house gazing serenely out over the sort of landscape that kept Wordsworth living around these parts all his life. Inside is all cultured formality, and the place is run to a level of polish and proficiency that makes most visitors feel privileged to have partaken of it. Old hand Johnnie Martin retired from the kitchen in the summer of 2006, but Colin Akrigg remains to ensure continuity. Meals proceed sedately through several courses, so be sure to have built up an appetite before you get here. A Franco-centric classicism informs the cooking. Soufflé suissesse, quail boudin dressed in honey and balsamic, or crab salad with avocado salsa and roasted asparagus turn up among starters, followed by a choice of soup (such as roast parsnip and chestnut) or fish as an intermediate course, then a sorbet.

Main courses pull out all the stops with intense, harmoniously balanced flavours and precise presentations, whether it be brill fillet with braised Baby Gem and scallop velouté, or Gressingham duck breast with leg confit, sarladaise potatoes and a sauce of apple and Calvados. The unashamedly cosseting desserts shouldn't be missed either. Cappuccino mousse with chocolate biscotti is the kind of thing to expect, with 'Great British cheeses' the savoury alternative. The sizeable wine list offers broad choice with quality high from beginning to end; those without the patience to

plough through the list can turn to the Sharrow Selection. Prices start just short of £20.

> **Chefs:** Mark Teasdale and Colin Akrigg **Proprietor:** Von Essen Hotels **Open:** all week 1, 8 (1 sitting) **Meals:** Set L £39.50, Set D £52.50. Light L menu available **Service:** not inc **Cards:** Amex, Delta, Maestro, MasterCard, Visa **Details:** 60 seats. Car park. Vegetarian meals. No children under 13. No smoking. Wheelchair access (also WC). No music. No mobile phones. Air-conditioned **Accommodation:** 24 rooms

MAP 8 ULVERSTON – Cumbria

Bay Horse

Canal Foot, Ulverston LA12 9EL
Tel: (01229) 583972
Website: www.thebayhorsehotel.co.uk

Cooking 3 | **Country House** | **£51**

In the eighteenth century this comfortable hotel and restaurant was a staging post for coaches crossing Morecambe Bay sands on their way to Lancaster. To this day, the venue retains many original features, and the bar has a nice pubby atmosphere. Robert Lyons produces high-quality cuisine above the pub norm, and his weekly-changing restaurant carte has much of interest. Local potted shrimps with gin and nutmeg, or asparagus tips pan-fried in lemon and balsamic vinegar with Parma ham and shavings of Parmesan can start, followed by the ever-popular Aberdeen Angus rump steak, or medallions of pork fillet, supplied by Woodall's of Waberthwaite, pan-fried with apple, Calvados and cream. Vegetarian options include hazelnut pancakes filled with wild mushrooms, and fish could run to tuna steak grilled with prawns, spring onions and ginger. Round things off with sour apple cream pie or the cheese platter, which comes with soda bread and home-made biscuits. Service is courteous and friendly, and the wine list opens with house selections at £16.

> **Chef:** Robert Lyons **Proprietors:** Robert Lyons and Kris Hogan **Open:** Tue to Sun L 12 to 2, all week D 7.30 for 8 (1 sitting) **Meals:** alc (main courses L £10.50 to £25.50, D £22.50 to £25.50). Set D £30.50. Bar L menu available **Service:** not inc **Cards:** Amex, Delta, Maestro, MasterCard, Visa **Details:** 55 seats. 30 seats outside. Car park. Vegetarian meals. No children under 10. No smoking. Wheelchair access (also WC). Music. No mobile phones **Accommodation:** 9 rooms

MAP 5 UPPER SLAUGHTER – Gloucestershire

Lords of the Manor

Upper Slaughter GL54 2JD
Tel: (01451) 820243
Website: www.lordsofthemanor.com

Cooking 6 | **Modern European** | **£68**

It may be bang in the middle of this much-visited hamlet, but the seventeenth-century former rectory is quite secluded, with eight acres running down to the River Eye. It is an elegant, restful, atmospheric place with décor very much in the country-house hotel mould, and while Les Rennie's food is classy and up-to-date there is nothing here to frighten the horses. The cooking is not formulaic, however, and the starting point is tiptop ingredients – from Gloucester Old Spot pork, via Lincolnshire rabbit to Aberdeen Angus beef – assembled into a tersely described menu that might offer chilli consommé with crab won tons and roast sea bream, crisp belly pork with a roast langoustine and passion fruit, and ballottine of rabbit with prune molasses and celeriac rémoulade. Simplicity is a point in favour, yet dishes involve fine workmanship and good judgement. A main-course red mullet is teamed with roast scallops, focaccia and black olive caramel, or poached breast of guinea fowl with confit leg, couscous and red wine. Those looking for a comforting way to finish might try warm plum tart with hazelnut parfait and golden sultanas, or Valrhona chocolate soufflé with bitter chocolate sorbet and crunchy nut crisps. House red is £19.50, and a dozen wines come by the glass from £4.50.

Chef: Lee Rennie   **Proprietor:** Empire Ventures   **Open:** Tue to Sun L 12 to 2.30, all week D 7 to 9.30 (10 Fri and Sat) **Meals:** Set L £17.50 (2 courses) to £21.50, Set D £40 to £59. Bar/terrace L menu available (exc Sun)   **Service:** 10% (optional)   **Cards:** Amex, Delta, Diners, Maestro, MasterCard, Visa   **Details:** 50 seats. 40 seats outside. Car park. Vegetarian meals. No children under 9. No smoking. No music **Accommodation:** 27 rooms

£5 | This symbol means that the restaurant has elected to participate in *The Good Food Guide's* £5 voucher scheme (see 'Using The Good Food Guide' for details).

MAP 2 UPTON SCUDAMORE – Wiltshire

Angel Inn

Upton Scudamore BA12 0AG
Tel: (01985) 213225
Website: www.theangelinn-wiltshire.co.uk

Cooking 4 | **Modern British** | **£37**

This sixteenth-century coaching inn sits at the heart of a pretty Wiltshire village near Salisbury Plain. Whitewashed and inviting, there is a lovely terraced dining area at the back of the building for those al fresco moments, while inside, the dining room is home to bare tables and yellow walls which are adorned with art for sale. Blackboard specials and fresh fish from Brixham feature, while the lunch menu is just as appealing as the à la carte. Start with steamed Cornish mussels cooked in cider with leeks and cream, or maybe smoked duck breast with ripe melon and raspberry vinaigrette. Roast rack of lamb with a grain mustard and herb crust is a typical main course, as is the grilled fillet of sea bass on Mediterranean couscous with a sweet chilli, spring onion and herb dressing. Vegetarians might go for their creamy pea, asparagus and coriander risotto with Parmesan shavings. End with caramelised orange brûlée or iced chocolate parfait with red fruit sauce and mango sorbet. Global wines from £12.95.

Chef: Paul Suter   **Proprietors:** Carol and Tony Coates   **Open:** all week 12 to 2, 7 to 9.30   **Closed:** 25 and 26 Dec, 1 Jan **Meals:** alc (main courses L £8 to £12, D £12 to £20) **Service:** not inc   **Cards:** Maestro, MasterCard, Visa   **Details:** 60 seats. 40 seats outside. Car park. Vegetarian meals. Children's helpings. Wheelchair access (not WC). Occasional music   **Accommodation:** 10 rooms

MAP 2 VENTNOR – Isle of Wight

Hambrough Hotel   NEW ENTRY

Hambrough Road, Ventnor
PO38 1SQ
Tel: (01983) 856333
Website: www.thehambrough.com

Cooking 4 | **Modern European** | **£50**

A large, imposing town house of Portland grey stone overlooks the bay at Ventnor on the Isle of

Wight's southern fringe. It is now a stylish boutique hotel, with stunning sea views from the minimally decorated, Ocean Restaurant, which has crisp table linen and a marble fireplace. The cooking aims to make an impact, opening with mi-cuit salmon with pickled beets and spiced lentils, or perhaps crisp-fried veal sweetbreads on colourful vegetable julienne, with a jug of garlic and bay leaf velouté. Lively seasonal compositions impressed at inspection, with balance and depth characterising a main course of seared squab on finely shredded creamed cabbage and smoked bacon, with frogs' legs and ripples of dark cherry sauce adding lustre to the dish. Innovative dessert ideas have included a golden-roasted whole peach with a shot glass of peach purée and cinnamon ice cream. The very short wine list is mostly French, but imaginatively chosen, beginning with Delas Frères house wines at £20. The team that runs the Hambrough also owns the Pond Café at Bonchurch, a little way north around the coast.

> **Chef:** Craig Atchinson **Open:** all week 12 to 2, 7 to 9.30 **Service:** not inc **Cards:** Delta, Maestro, MasterCard, Visa **Details:** 30 seats. Vegetarian meals. No children under 10. No smoking. Music. No mobile phones **Accommodation:** 7 rooms

MAP 1 | VIRGINSTOW – Devon

Percy's

Coombeshead Estate, Virginstow EX21 5EA
Tel: (01409) 211236
Website: www.percys.co.uk

Cooking 4 | Modern British | £56

The restaurant website keeps interested parties up to date with news items such as the long-awaited foaling, after a rather protracted gestation, of Madame Percy, one of the team of 15 horses that live here. You've certainly left the big city far behind when you come to Tony and Tina Bricknell-Webb's country estate and hotel. With a wealth of home-reared and home-cured meats to draw on, as well as poultry, eggs, and much organic fresh produce, Percy's is a thriving concern. Tina is responsible for transforming it all into menus that deal in a gentle style of modern country cooking. Expect Cornish squid and scallop salad dressed in mustard, honey and dill, or pork and chicken terrine with avocado vinaigrette to start, followed perhaps by steamed turbot with asparagus in béarnaise. Those home-reared meats are represented by roast rump of rosemary-glazed lamb, or sage-

crumbed pork shoulder steak in juniper gravy. Fine local cheeses might precede a dessert such as caramelised apple tart with cassia bark ice cream and crème fraîche. Organic wines from England, Argentina, Spain and Australia, among others, figure large on the wine list; pricing is fair and starts at £16.

> **Chef:** Tina Bricknell-Webb **Proprietors:** Tony and Tina Bricknell-Webb **Open:** all week D only 6.30 to 9 **Meals:** Set D £40 **Service:** not inc **Cards:** Delta, Maestro, MasterCard, Visa **Details:** 24 seats. Car park. No children under 12. No smoking. Wheelchair access (also WC). No music. No mobile phones **Accommodation:** 8 rooms

MAP 3 | WADHURST – East Sussex

Best Beech Inn | AR

Mayfield Lane, Wadhurst TN5 6JH
Tel: (01892) 782045

Surrounded by beech woods, this tile-hung country inn offers various eating options, with a tapas menu for bar snacks and bistro-style lunches in the dining room (calf's liver and mash £11.50; beef bourguignonne £9.50). Dinner is a more elaborate affair, with starters such as confit duck terrine with red onion marmalade (£5.50), followed perhaps by pan-seared sea bream and tiger prawns with coconut and parsnip purée, spinach and hollandaise (£14.95). A short but varied wine list opens with house selections at £12.95. Accommodation. Closed Sun D.

MAP 9 | WAKEFIELD – West Yorkshire

Brasserie Ninety Nine | AR

Trinity Business Park, Wakefield WF2 8EF
Tel: (01924) 377699

A business park might not be the prettiest setting, but this contemporary brasserie, offering a bold menu, is worth seeking out. Confit of duck pizza with oyster mushrooms and hoisin sauce (£6.95) is followed by loin of venison with a fig tarte Tatin, roast strawberries and vanilla jus (£15.95) or roast sea bass fillet with sautéed scallops and bouillabaisse dressing (£14.25), then triple chocolate terrine with orange sorbet (£4.50). Wines from £11.95. Open Mon to Fri L and Wed to Sat D.

Wolski's

AR

Monarch House, George Street, Wakefield
WF1 1NE
Tel: (01924) 381252

In an impressive Art Deco building, the bar and restaurant takes up three floors of this converted nineteenth-century wine merchant's. Seafood is a speciality here with some supplies coming from their own fishing boat, the Katy-Ann. Lemon-seared squid with a basil herb salad (£4.50), might precede salt-baked sea bass, or escalope of salmon with wilted baby spinach (both £14.50), while for meat eaters there's onion simmered lamb shank on caramelized red cabbage (£10.95). Finish with raspberry pancakes with a Kirsch sabayon (£3.50). More than 60 wines from £11.95. Closed Sun and bank hols exc 25 Dec.

MAP 6 | **WALBERSWICK –**
Suffolk

Anchor Hotel

NEW ENTRY

The Street, Walberswick IP18 6UA
Tel: (01502) 722112

Cooking 2 | **Modern British** | **£30**

Mark and Sophie Dorber have taken over this Adnams-owned 1920s Arts and Crafts pub (she's the chef, he's a beer guru). They haven't broken the bank on interior design – the spartan décor encompasses bare pine tables, a stripped-hardwood floor, greyish-blue colour-washed panelling – but it's a pleasant and informal ambience. The kitchen is clearly focused on the quality and value of the food, using unerringly good local or home-grown raw materials, much of it organic, in a fairly simple repertoire of popular dishes like a salad of seared scallops with artichoke purée and bacon, lamb curry with curried sweet potato and chickpeas ('one of the best pub curries I've tasted in a while'), or salmon fishcakes with creamy leeks. Desserts are all the better for being straightforward: chocolate pudding with vanilla ice cream, for example. The selection of bottled beers is impressive. Otherwise there's Adnams on hand-pump, and a wide-ranging list of wines at fair prices. House French white is £11.25, Spanish red £11.75.

Chef: Sophie Dorber **Proprietors:** Mark and Sophie Dorber **Open:** all week 12 to 3, 6 to 9 **Meals:** alc (main courses £9 to £13) **Service:** not inc **Cards:** none **Details:** 120 seats. 100 seats outside. Vegetarian meals. Children's helpings. No smoking. Wheelchair access (also WC). No music. No mobile phones **Accommodation:** 8 rooms

---

MAP 3 | **WALBERTON –**
West Sussex

Oaks Restaurant

NEW ENTRY

Yapton Lane, Walberton BN18 0LS
Tel: (01243) 552865
Website: www.kencancook.com

Cooking 3 | **Modern British** | **£40**

This 'convivial and classy' restaurant-with-rooms is the setting for Ken and Annabelle Brown's latest venture (Ken is well-known in these parts under the Kencancook moniker). Four rooms open off each other, one a large bar with leather sofas, and all is smart, with lots of polished wood, panelling, soft lights and quality napery. Dishes are well balanced, as in starters of local asparagus with a soft-boiled quail's egg and a gentle Red Leicester mayonnaise, and lightly cooked scallops wrapped in pancetta with a Parmesan and cream sauce. Main courses can be hearty – Aberdeen Angus fillet steak comes with a rib-sticking steamed oxtail suet pudding, horseradish-flavoured dauphinois and Madeira jus – and classic combinations are apparent too: best end of new season's lamb, cooked pink, on minted new potatoes with a rich gravy. Finish with a traditional dessert such as spotted dick, or creamy rice pudding flavoured with lemon. Black-garbed staff are well trained and efficient, and the annotated wine list opens in South-west France at £11.50.

Chefs: Ken Brown and Stuart Taylor **Proprietors:** Ken and Annabelle Brown **Open:** Tue to Sun L 12 to 2.30, Tue to Sat D 7 (6.30 Sat) to 10 **Meals:** alc (main courses £10 to £19.50). Set L Tue to Sat £12 (2 courses) to £15, Set L Sun £16.95 (2 courses) to £20.95 **Service:** not inc **Cards:** Amex, Delta, Maestro, MasterCard, Visa **Details:** 64 seats. 4 seats outside. Car park. Vegetarian meals. Children's helpings. No smoking. Music **Accommodation:** 2 rooms

---

(£) This symbol means that it is possible to have a three-course dinner, including coffee, half a bottle of house wine and service, for £30 or less per person.

MAP 9 WALKINGTON – East Riding of Yorkshire

Manor House `AR`

Northlands, Walkington HU17 8RT
Tel: (01482) 881645

Elegant country-house dining is the draw at this late-nineteenth-century property in three acres of grounds on the edge of the Yorkshire Wolds. Two fixed-price dinner menus (£34.50 and £13.75, plus supplements) provide plentiful choice in an ambitious modern British vein: perhaps North Yorkshire ham hock boudin with home-made piccalilli to start, followed by cured salmon suprême with langoustine broth and foam, or lamb shank with black pudding tempura and squash with potato, and roast figs on brown sugar parfait with port sauce to finish. House wines £13.50. Closed Sat L.

MAP 5 WARWICK – Warwickshire

Findons

7 Old Square, Warwick CV34 4RA
Tel: (01926) 411755
Website: www.findons-restaurant.co.uk

Cooking 2 | Modern European | £45

Situated opposite St Mary's church in Warwick, this traditionally-decorated restaurant is all drapes, mirrors and chandeliers, but the food has more of a modern edge than might be expected in this setting. Bream, scallops and sea bass are delivered daily from Brixham, while vegetables come from Covent Garden. Sautéed garlic prawns or dill-cured salmon with watercress and grain mustard mascarpone are confident starters, while main courses skirt around the Mediterranean offering sea bass on radicchio with olives and caperberries, or calf's liver on wilted spinach with balsamic onions and pancetta. The half-dozen desserts include lemon tart with a berry and Cassis coulis. The compact wine list starts at £14.95, but offers some limited-stock vintage choices from £60.

Chef: Michael Findon **Proprietor:** Findon & Williams Ltd **Open:** Mon to Sat D only 6.30 to 9.30 **Closed:** 31 Dec **Meals:** alc (main courses £15 to £20). Set D Mon to Fri £17 (2 courses) **Service:** not inc **Cards:** Delta, Maestro, MasterCard, Visa **Details:** 42 seats. 20 seats outside. Vegetarian meals. No children under 11. Wheelchair access (not WC). Music

Rose and Crown

30 Market Place, Warwick CV34 4SH
Tel: (01926) 411117
Website: www.peachpubs.com

Cooking 2 | Bistro | £37

As good a 'townie pub' as you'll find, this cosmopolitan venue has a busy bar area and a separate, high-ceilinged dining room with dramatic lighting. The menu is decidedly bistro, while blackboards list the daily specials. You can mix and match from the 'deli board', which includes hummus, chorizo, various cheeses and breads. A beef tomato stuffed with braised oxtail makes an enterprising starter and could be followed by rack of Cornish lamb with lemon and rosemary couscous and Calvados crème fraîche. The 'Either/Or' menu offers seared squid and chicken Caesar salads as both starters and main courses, while dessert might be frozen apricot soufflé or vanilla crème brûlée. The compact wine list kicks off with a Chilean Chardonnay (£11.50) and a Spanish Tempranillo (£12), and most bottles are under £20.

Chef: Nigel Brown **Proprietor:** Lee Cash **Open:** all week 12 to 2.30, 6.30 to 10 (9.30 Sun) **Closed:** 25 Dec **Meals:** alc (main courses £8.50 to £17) **Service:** not inc **Cards:** Amex, Delta, Maestro, MasterCard, Visa **Details:** 70 seats. 40 seats outside. Vegetarian meals. No smoking in dining room. Wheelchair access (also WC). Music **Accommodation:** 5 rooms

MAP 10 WATERMILLOCK – Cumbria

Rampsbeck Country House Hotel

Watermillock, Ullswater CA11 0LP
Tel: (017684) 86442
Website: www.rampsbeck.fsnet.co.uk

Cooking 3 | Anglo-French | £58

This eighteenth-century manor house is in a hard-to-beat location, with stunning views over Ullswater. Inside, the décor is on the conservative side, with high moulded ceilings, candelabra, and plates and portraits peppering the walls. The four-course dinner menu doesn't shy away from bold flavours, perhaps starting with braised and roast pig's cheek with caramelised mango and potato purée with Périgord truffle alongside Loch Fyne bradan rost and cucumber mousse with lobster medallions, toasted dill bread and an Avruga caviar dressing. An intermediate soup, served in tiny cups, might be cream of Jerusalem artichoke. Pan-fried calf's liver with rösti, curried creamed Savoy cabbage and a caraway seed jus, is a likely main course, or there might be steamed fillet of sea bass with noodles and a brochette of langoustines with pimento sauce. Artistic desserts include baked Granny Smith apple and prunes wrapped in sablé biscuit served with prune and Armagnac ice cream and cider syrup. The comprehensive wine list offers good value, and usefully categorises by style. House wines open proceedings at around £12.

Chef: Andrew McGeorge **Proprietors:** Tom and Marion Gibb **Open:** all week 12 to 1, 7 to 8.30 **Closed:** 5 Jan to 10 Feb **Meals:** Set L £28, Set D £39.50 to £47. Bar L menu available **Service:** not inc **Cards:** Delta, Maestro, MasterCard, Visa **Details:** 40 seats. Car park. No children under 7. Children's helpings. No smoking. No music. No mobile phones. **Accommodation:** 19 rooms

MAP 2 **WELLS** – Somerset

Goodfellows

5 Sadler Street, Wells BA5 2RR
Tel: (01749) 673866
Email: goodfellows@btconnect.com

| Cooking 4 | Seafood | £47 |

In the centre of Wells, a minute or so from the cathedral, this tiny venue crams in five tables and an open-plan kitchen in the ground-floor delicatessen-cum-pâtisserie, while a restaurant is reached via a spiral staircase. Adam Fellows delivers a six-course tasting menu, supported by a set-price menu offering three choices per course, and a short carte. Other than a seemingly always-on-the-menu fillet of beef, it's all fish: tuna carpaccio, say, or sea bass with morels, asparagus and broad beans. An inspection dinner turned up some less than successful combinations, but the meal opened with superb home-made bread and included a fine terrine of skate and smoked salmon with a radish and apple salad and citrus dressing, and reports have given the thumbs-up to warm mackerel tart with confit of tomato and tapenade, and fillet of halibut in a citrus and herb crust. Desserts are a selection of pastries from the pâtisserie, perhaps a

'seriously good-looking' peach tart, or there are British farmhouse cheeses. The service has been described as 'attentive, although a tad slow'. The short, global wine list opens at £13, and there are around a dozen by the glass.

Chef: Adam Fellows **Proprietors:** Adam and Martine Fellows **Open:** Tue to Sat L 12 to 2.30, Thur to Sat D 6.30 to 9.30 **Closed:** 25 to 27 Dec, 2 to 18 Jan **Meals:** alc D (main courses £13.50 to £24). Set L £12.50 (2 courses) to £15, Set D £29 to £45. Light L menu available Mon to Sat **Service:** not inc **Cards:** Amex, Delta, Maestro, MasterCard, Visa **Details:** 30 seats. 12 seats outside. Children's helpings. No smoking. Wheelchair access (not WC). Music. No mobile phones. Air-conditioned

MAP 3 **WELWYN GARDEN CITY –** Hertfordshire

Auberge du Lac

Brocket Hall, Welwyn Garden City AL8 7XG
Tel: (01707) 368888
Website: www.brocket-hall.co.uk

| Cooking 5 | Modern French | £75 |

The former eighteenth-century hunting lodge set in the grounds of Brocket Hall was put on the culinary map by Jean Christophe Novelli, but he has departed, and now his former head chef, Phil Thompson, leads the line. The dining area consists of an airy conservatory, with views on to manicured lawns and lake, adjoining a comfortably appointed dining room proper. A third section of the dining room has been converted into a lounge bar. To start there might be cumin-scented scallops with cauliflower, crab and vegetable spring roll, or pepper-coated seared tuna with avocado and lime mousse, salsa verde and a radish salad. Main dishes like pan-seared spiced tournedos of monkfish with baby gem purée, boulangère potatoes and shellfish beurre noisette are approvingly reported. Desserts showed particular technical skills at inspection: witness 'perfect' chocolate orange ravioli served with white chocolate, orange ice cream and walnuts, and port poached pear with prune samosas and bitter chocolate ice cream. Service has been described as 'gracious and well drilled', while the wine list, overseen by sommelier Luca Ravagnati, reveals an enthusiastic approach, broad appreciation and an understanding that not everyone wishes to spend a fortune – there is a good drinking to be had for under £30. House wine is £22.

> Chef: Phil Thompson Proprietor: CCA International Open: Tue to Sun L 12 to 2.30, Tue to Sat D 6.30 to 10 Meals: alc (not Sun L; main courses £21 to £32). Set L Tue to Sat £29.50, Set L Sun £35, Set D £45 (Tue to Fri) to £65 Service: 10% (optional) Cards: Amex, Delta, Diners, Maestro, MasterCard, Visa Details: 60 seats. 50 seats outside. Car park. Vegetarian meals. Children's helpings. No smoking. Music. No mobile phones. Air-conditioned Accommodation: 16 rooms

MAP 2   WEST BAY – Dorset

Riverside Restaurant

West Bay DT6 4EZ
Tel: (01308) 422011
Website: www.thefishrestaurant-westbay.co.uk

Cooking 3 | Seafood | £42

The wooden chalet-style dining room, reached by crossing a walkway, is split over two levels, with views of the sea and the river. The Watsons have been here since 1964 and their approach has changed little over the years. There are daily specials, with fish and shellfish all landed locally and presented in an uncomplicated manner – whole fish is often simply grilled and served with sea salt and lemon. Lobster and crayfish risotto with fresh Parmesan stands out for the freshness of its ingredients, and the same has been true of a simple main course of grilled red mullet fillets with mango, pepper and coriander dressing. Vanilla pannacotta with cherries in grappa syrup might end a meal on a high note. Service is generally friendly although it does get stretched when the restaurant is at capacity. The brief wine list is seafood compatible with some good value choices under £20; house wine by the litre starts at £13.95.

> Chefs: Nic Larcombe and George Marsh Proprietors: Arthur and Janet Watson Open: Tue to Sun L 12 to 2.15, Tue to Sat D 6.30 to 8.30 (open L and D bank hol weekends) Closed: Nov to Feb Meals: alc (main courses £12.50 to £25). Set L Tue to Fri exc Easter and summer £16.50 (2 courses) to £20 Service: not inc Cards: Delta, Maestro, MasterCard, Visa Details: 60 seats. 30 seats outside. Vegetarian meals. Children's helpings. No smoking. Wheelchair access (also women's WC). Occasional music. No mobile phones

> This symbol means that smoking is not permitted.

MAP 3   WESTFIELD – East Sussex

Wild Mushroom   NEW ENTRY

Woodgate House, Westfield Lane, Westfield TN35 4SB
Tel: (01424) 751137
Website: www.wildmushroom.co.uk

Cooking 2 | Modern European | £38

Paul Webbe now devotes his time to the Fish Café in Rye (see entry), and here in Westfield Mathew Drinkwater is turning out some good food in relaxed surroundings. Within the red-brick, late-Victorian farmhouse is a 'genteel bourgeois' dining room with lots of stiff white table linen and tall-backed chairs. Raw materials are first-rate, and everything is carefully made on the premises, from nibbles and walnut bread to ice creams. Pan-fried red mullet with niçoise vegetable salad and saffron dressing – 'a top-class dish, simple and delicious' – might be followed by fillet of Wickham Manor Farm lamb with aubergine confit and a potato cake coated with garlic cream. Finish with coconut pannacotta with pineapple, lime compote and almond macaroon. Uniformed staff are well organised and unstuffy, and house Chilean Chardonnay and Cabernet Sauvignon are £12.75.

> Chefs: Paul Webbe and Mathew Drinkwater Proprietors: Paul and Rebecca Webbe Open: Tue to Fri and Sun L 12 to 2, Tue to Sat D 7 to 9.30 Closed: 2 weeks Christmas, 2 weeks Aug Meals: alc D (main courses £11 to £18). Set L £14.95 (2 courses) to £17.95 Service: not inc Cards: Amex, Delta, Maestro, MasterCard Details: 44 seats. Car park. Vegetarian meals. No children under 12 at D. Children's helpings. No smoking. Wheelchair access (also WC). Music

MAP 9   WESTOW – North Yorkshire

Blacksmiths Inn   AR

Main Street, Westow YO60 7NE
Tel: (01653) 618365

About three or four miles off the A64, this friendly country inn has been taken over by Gary Marshall and his wife Sarah. Imaginative dishes on the daily-changing menus include dressed Whitby crab salad with a Bloody Mary jelly (£8), followed by Ryedale venison pie with wild mushrooms and tarragon and a black truffle cream (£13.50), or fishcakes with chive cream and triple-cooked chips (£10.95). Finish with apple and berry crumble with custard (£5). A page of wines by the glass (from £2.95, or £11.45 a bottle) opens the well-chosen wine list. Open Sun L and Wed to Sat D.

> **Chef:** Geoff Smith **Proprietors:** Geoff and Jan Smith **Open:** Wed to Sun L 12 to 2, Tue to Sat D 6.30 to 9.30 **Meals:** alc (main courses £13.50 to £19) **Service:** not inc **Cards:** Maestro, MasterCard, Visa **Details:** 50 seats. 12 seats outside. Car park. Vegetarian meals. No smoking in 1 dining room. No music. No mobile phones **Accommodation:** 3 rooms

---

MAP 2 **WEST STOKE – West Sussex**

West Stoke House `AR`

Downs Road, West Stoke PO18 9BN
Tel: (01243) 575226

Like something out of a Merchant Ivory film, this wonderfully English country hotel is effortlessly elegant. The three-course set-priced menus (lunch £22.50, dinner £35) meanders around Europe, so expect hand-dived South Coast scallops with pea and mint risotto, followed by roast breast of Anjou guinea fowl with fondant potato, cabbage and bacon, cauliflower purée and morel sauce. End with peanut butter parfait with a matching ice cream and banana foam. Wines from £13.50. Six guest bedrooms. Closed Sun D, Mon and Tue.

MAP 9 **WEST TANFIELD – North Yorkshire**

Bruce Arms

Main Street, West Tanfield HG4 5JJ
Tel: (01677) 470325
Website: www.brucearms.com

| Cooking 4 | Modern English | £40 |

Locally renowned, this pub prepares modern English cuisine in a wholly traditional atmosphere. There's a quaint bar area, stone-flagged floors, horseshoes on the walls and 'lovely leather chairs' from which you can survey the bar and its selection of real ales. The reason why it could be full on a rainy midweek evening is the classy menu, which is displayed on blackboards. Start, perhaps with twice-baked Wensleydale cheese soufflé or smoked haddock with a poached egg, spinach and hollandaise, and move on to a main course of braised lamb shank with parsley mash and red wine gravy, or chargrilled tuna with salsa verde. Round things off with roast pears with chocolate mousse and vanilla ice cream or sablé biscuits with strawberries and syllabub. The spiral-bound wine list offers around 40 bins, starting at £11.95.

MAP 2 **WEYMOUTH – Dorset**

Crab House Café `AR`

Fleet Oyster Farm, Ferryman's Way, Weymouth DT4 9YU
Tel: (01305) 788867

Turning off at the Ferry Bridge Inn towards Chesil beach will bring you to this 'wooden shack' which operates as a café and fish-and-chip shop. French chef Christian Lohez makes good use of local materials – there is an oyster farm next door – in a simple cooking style. 'Nicely timed' scallops in a garlic and cream sauce (£7.50) might be followed by hake fillet with saffron and lemon butter (£15.25), or skate wing with chorizo (£14.25). Caramelized oranges and pineapple with Purbeck champagne sorbet (£4.95) end. Wines from £12.55. Closed Mon and Tue, and D Sun (open all week in summer).

Perry's `AR`

4 Trinity Road, Weymouth DT4 8TJ
Tel: (01305) 785799

This relaxed family-run restaurant has great views over the old harbour. Simply prepared seafood is the main business, much of it local, so expect crab soup with Parmesan (£4.95), followed by baked fillet of Cornish brill with grilled smoked bacon and dauphinois potatoes (£15.95). Meatier dishes include breast of guinea fowl baked in filo pastry with Calvados cream sauce (£13.95). Apple and almond turnover (£4.95) or a selection of cheeses (£5.95) bring things to an end. Good-value wines from £11.95. Open Tue to Fri L and Tue to Sat D.

> `AR` Not a full entry but provisionally recommended. These 'also recommended' establishments are integrated throughout the book.

MAP 9 | WHITBY – North Yorkshire

Greens

NEW ENTRY

13 Bridge Street, Whitby YO22 4BG
Tel: (01947) 600284
Website: www.greensofwhitby.com

Cooking 3 | Modern British | £41

'Probably the town's most sophisticated dining experience' is how one visitor viewed Rob and Emma Green's relaxed restaurant. The décor is moodily dark – brown walls, close-packed rough wooden tables – and everything is done with zeal. The menu sounds appealing, with its emphasis on the freshest of fish – the daily catch from named boats is listed on blackboards – although they do offer meat: say, chargrilled beef sirloin with pickled red onion and Yorkshire Blue salad. Start with Whitby spider crab linguine with parsley and lemon, then move on to grilled turbot with a ragoût of scallops in a Noilly Prat cream sauce. To finish, warm chocolate fondant with chocolate and Amaretto sorbet has drawn praise, as have details like large home-baked rolls. The wine list keeps things simple with its shortish, fairly priced collection of bottles. House wine is £12.50.

> **Chefs:** Rob Green and Ryan Osbourne **Proprietors:** Rob and Emma Green **Open:** Fri to Sun L 12 to 2 (3 Sun), all week D 6.30 to 9.30 (6 to 10 Sat) **Closed:** 25 and 26 Dec, 1 Jan **Meals:** alc (main courses £12.50 to £20) **Service:** not inc **Cards:** Amex, Delta, Maestro, MasterCard, Visa **Details:** 40 seats. Children's helpings. No smoking. Music. No mobile phones. Air-conditioned

Magpie Café

14 Pier Road, Whitby YO21 3PU
Tel: (01947) 602058
Website: www.magpiecafe.co.uk

Cooking 2 | Seafood | £38

'Without doubt, the best fish and chips I have ever had,' exclaimed one happy visitor to this quayside chippie. With such temptations on offer the place is unsurprisingly very popular, so be prepared to queue, especially on bank holidays and weekends. Inside, the friendly staff don't rush you once seated at the closely packed tables so take time to read the lengthy specials board. At inspection, a sautéed soft-shell crab starter was wonderfully fresh, while the main event, haddock and chips, garnered honeyed praise: 'the fish was truly exceptional,

wrapped in the most wonderfully crisp batter – a real joy to eat'. Chips are 'divine' and the 'proper marrowfat' mushy peas are just as they should be. Sticky toffee pudding might end, and while most people eschew alcohol to drink tea, the short, global wine list opens at a good-value £9.95.

> **Chefs:** Ian Robson and Paul Gildroy **Proprietors:** Ian and Alison Robson **Open:** all week 11.30 to 9 **Closed:** 25 and 26 Dec, 1 Jan, 8 Jan to 8 Feb **Meals:** alc (main courses £7 to £19) **Service:** not inc **Cards:** Delta, Maestro, MasterCard, Visa **Details:** 130 seats. Vegetarian meals. Children's helpings. No smoking. Wheelchair access (also WC). Occasional music. Air-conditioned

MAP 8 | WHITEWELL – Lancashire

Inn at Whitewell

AR

Whitewell BB7 3AT
Tel: (01200) 448222

Tucked away in the Forest of Bowland, this upmarket inn offers a welcome break from modern life. The décor may be old-fashioned, but the food skilfully updates traditional dishes. The substantial bar menu includes spicy Cumberland sausages served with champ and a fried egg (£8.20), while the restaurant carte runs from chicken liver pâté (£5.20) to roast breast of wood pigeon with a juniper-flavoured jus, a little game pie and potato purée (£15), and traditional puddings (£4.20). The hefty wine list takes some concentration; house choices start at £9.80. Accommodation. Open all week.

MAP 2 | WHITLEY – Wiltshire

Pear Tree Inn

Top Lane, Whitley, nr Melksham SN12 8QX
Tel: (01225) 709131

Cooking 2 | Modern British-Plus | £40

Martin and Debbie Still ensure that the sourcing of materials continues to be a serious business at their busy pub/restaurant. The food offers as much local produce as the kitchen can muster, and the choice is wide. Starters range from steamed Fowey mussels in a light curry cream to grilled pigeon breast with chorizo, cippolini onions and braised lentils, and main courses encompass everything from home-made pork, apple and herb sausages with bubble and squeak, via pan-fried sea bass with vegetable risotto, to roast rump of lamb served with 'memorably delicious' garlic mash and a generous mound of spinach. Leave room for desserts, which may include home-made banana ice cream, or hot chocolate and fudge fondant. Modest pricing (from £13.50) is a feature of the short wine list, which is arranged by style.

Chef: Marc Robertson Proprietors: Martin and Debbie Still Open: all week 12 to 2.30 (3 Sun), 6.30 to 9.30 (10 Fri and Sat, 9 Sun) Closed: 25, 26 and 31 Dec, 1 Jan Meals: alc (main courses £11.50 to £19). Set L £13.50 (2 courses) to £16 Service: not inc Cards: Maestro, MasterCard, Visa Details: 70 seats. 20 seats outside. Car park. Vegetarian meals. Children's helpings. No smoking in dining room. Wheelchair access (also WC). No music Accommodation: 8 rooms

MAP 3 WHITSTABLE – Kent

JoJo's

209 Tankerton Road, Whitstable CT5 2AT
Tel: (01227) 274591

Cooking 4 | Modern European | £30

Such has been the success of Nikki Billington and Paul Watson's cheerful, informal tapas-style restaurant in the front room of their Victorian terraced house that early in 2006 they closed for a major refit, nearly doubling the seating capacity and upgrading the kitchen in the corner along the way. Now, with its contemporary low-key décor, matching chunky wood tables and swish open-plan kitchen, it's a 'cool setting' for some attractively understated cooking. The menu remains the same, dealing in simple, straightforward ideas (old favourites like thinly sliced lamb cannon with tzatziki, or calamari deep-fried in beer batter with garlic mayo, say) or a seasonally inspired Kentish wild venison that's thinly sliced then seared and served on ciabatta. Sourcing is impeccable, with fish from local day boats and free-range and organic ingredients from local farm shops and farmers' markets. It's a package that appeals, from simple food at realistic prices to smooth service led by Paul Watson. The restaurant is unlicensed, but you can bring your own bottle for a token corkage charge.

Chefs: Nikki Billington and Sarah Hannell Proprietors: Nikki Billington and Paul Watson Open: Wed to Sun L 12.45 to 2.30, Wed to Sat D 6.30 to 10 Meals: alc (main courses £3 to £7.50). Unlicensed; BYO £1 Service: not inc Cards: none Details: 35 seats. 15 seats outside. No smoking. Wheelchair access (not WC). Music. No mobile phones

Sportsman

Faversham Road, Seasalter, Whitstable CT5 4BP
Tel: (01227) 273370

Cooking 4 | Modern European | £37

Head west out of Whitstable along the coast road, past the caravan park and beach-hut shantytown, and soon you will reach this weather-beaten old pub standing in the shelter of the sea wall on the edge of open marshland. An unadorned rusticity prevails inside, with bare floorboards, chunky pine tables and a motley collection of chairs; colourful works by local artists provide interest. The setting might lead you to expect simple pub grub, and terse blackboard menus certainly don't oversell the food. But here it is all about flavour, on which score the food made a big impact at inspection, notably a slab of Seasalter ham terrine containing chunks of home-cured ham from locally raised pigs, set in a subtly herby, spicy jelly and served with a fried egg, cornichons and excellent home-baked bread fried in garlic butter. For main course, there might be poached native lobster with asparagus, new potatoes and a light yet intensely flavoured sauce, or perhaps braised shoulder of flavoursome salt-marsh lamb with mint sauce, while playful desserts include a pairing of burnt cream and rhubarb sorbet sprinkled with popping candy. A handful of wines are listed on a blackboard, priced from around £12 and including a local English wine.

Chefs: Stephen Harris, Dan Flavel, Vicky Harper and David Hart Proprietors: Stephen, Philip and Damian Harris Open: Tue to Sun L 12 to 2 (3 Sun), Tue to Sat D 7 to 9 Meals: alc (main courses £10 to £19) Service: not inc Cards: Delta, Maestro, MasterCard, Visa Details: 50 seats. Car park. Children's helpings. No smoking in 1 dining room. Wheelchair access (not WC). Occasional music

Wheelers Oyster Bar

8 High Street, Whitstable CT5 1BQ
Tel: (01227) 273311

Cooking 2 | Seafood | £31

Much has changed in the lifetime of this tiny restaurant, which reached 150 years in 2006. The famed Whitstable native oysters are now a rare luxury rather than the commonplace item they were in 1856, but they still appear in season on the counter in the front of the shop, along with platters of shellfish and light dishes such as home-smoked salmon with scrambled egg on a toasted muffin.

The main thrust of the kitchen's efforts goes into the menu for the cosy parlour dining room to the rear. Inventive modern British seafood cooking turns up starters of pan-fried crab cake with a pear, chicory and walnut salad, or caramelised scallops on cauliflower and Parmesan risotto with crisp cauliflower beignets, while main courses might feature roast sea bass on braised sauerkraut with dauphinois potatoes and thyme sauce. Booking is essential, and the restaurant is unlicensed, so BYO.

Chefs: Mark Stubbs, Gavin Kember and Sid Phillips **Proprietor:** Delia Fitt **Open:** Thur to Tue 1 to 7.30 (7 Sun) **Meals:** alc (main courses £15 to £18.50). Light menu available **Service:** not inc **Cards:** none **Details:** 16 seats. Children's helpings. No smoking. Wheelchair access (not WC). No music. Air-conditioned

Whitstable Oyster Fishery Co.

Royal Native Oyster Stores, Horsebridge Road, Whitstable CT5 1BU
Tel: (01227) 276856

This large bare-boarded building originally stored oysters and is now a restaurant with blackboard menus and impressive displays of seafood. The straightforward menu starts with half a dozen local rock oysters (£7.50) or perhaps chargrilled sardines (£6.50). Main courses are in similar vein: half a lobster with potato salad (£14.50), grilled halibut with soured cream cheese and chives (£19.50), or whole sea bass roasted with garlic and rosemary (£21). Dessert might be white chocolate cheesecake with raspberry coulis (£4.95). Wines from £12.95. Closed Mon.

Williams & Brown Tapas

48 Harbour Street, Whitstable CT5 1AQ
Tel: (01227) 273373

Cooking 2 | Tapas | £35

The corner site in this now-trendy seaside town exudes a simple charm. Just six plain wooden tables fill the room, with extra seating on bar stools at marble counters running the length of the windows. Although it doesn't have the fiercely regional focus of a typical tapas bar in Spain, Christopher Williams does capture the feel of eating there, and the kitchen shows a real understanding of the Spanish way of cooking. He has identified fishermen, farmers – some local – and

suppliers like Brindisa, who provide materials that honestly reflect their origins. Blackboards list the constantly changing slate of dishes, which could take in roast belly pork with morcilla, meatballs with polenta and ragoût, fish stew with peppers and saffron, and cod, spinach and tomato paella. House wine is £13.50.

Chefs: Christopher Williams and Matt Sibley **Proprietor:** Christopher Williams **Open:** Wed to Mon L 12 to 2 (2.30 Sat, 2.45 Sun), Wed to Sat and Mon D (also Sun June to Aug) 6.30 to 9 (9.30 Fri and Sat) **Closed:** D 24 Dec, 26 and 27 Dec, 1 and 2 Jan **Meals:** alc (main courses £7 to £10) **Service:** 10% (optional) **Cards:** none **Details:** 33 seats. Vegetarian meals. No smoking. Music. No mobile phones. Air-conditioned

MAP 2 | **WHITWAY** – Hampshire

Carnarvon Arms | NEW ENTRY

Winchester Road, Whitway RG20 9EL
Tel: (01635) 278222
Website: www.carnarvonarms.com

Cooking 2 | Modern European | £39

This newly made-over inn – 'big and prosperous looking' – is convenient for Newbury Races and Highclere Castle. Warm natural colours set off by the occasional splash of deep red distinguish both the bar and the 'barn-like' dining room. Menus are reasonably priced and informed by a nicely judged mixture of unpretentious British and modern European dishes, offering risotto of chestnut mushrooms, chives and Parmesan, and fillet of sea bream with lemon and herb crushed potatoes, alongside potted shrimps, steak and ale pie, and calf's liver and bacon. A warm salad of braised duck leg was a hefty starter at inspection, and a main course of sautéed guinea fowl was well timed and served with excellent, buttery fondant potato. At dessert stage pannacotta was let down by poor berry fruits. Wines start at £11.95 on a global list, with most under £25.

Chefs: Robert Clayton and Simon Pitney Baxter **Proprietor:** Merchant Inns **Open:** all week 12 to 3, 6 to 9.30 **Meals:** alc (main courses £12.50 to £19). Set L £9.95 (2 courses) to £14.95. Bar menu available **Service:** not inc **Cards:** Delta, Maestro, MasterCard, Visa **Details:** 60 seats. Car park. Vegetarian meals. No smoking in 1 dining room. Wheelchair access (also WC). Music **Accommodation:** 12 rooms

To submit a report on any restaurant, please visit *www.which.co.uk/gfgfeedback*.

MAP 2   WICKHAM – Hampshire

Old House

The Square, Wickham PO17 5JG
Tel: (01329) 833049
Website: www.oldhousehotel.co.uk

Cooking 1 | Modern British | £48

Though less than five minutes' drive from the M27, the handsome Georgian building is in a tranquil enough setting on Wickham's market square. The entire ground floor is given over to eating and drinking (with bare boards and bare tables), and James Dickson's cooking keeps things relatively straightforward – crab with fennel bread, gem lettuce and mayonnaise, or roast cod and Parmesan crumble with a confit of plum tomatoes, for example – but diversity appears in the shape of Peking duck salad wraps, or chicken and black-bean stir-fry. Chocolate and orange fondant is one way to finish, or there might be iced mixed berries with hot white chocolate sauce; if you can't decide, you can always plump for the assiette of desserts. Wines are a workaday bunch of around 50 bins, with house selections starting at £14.50 and ten or so by the glass.

Chef: James Fairchild Dickson **Proprietors:** Mr and Mrs Paul Scott **Open:** all week L 12 to 2.30, Mon to Sat D 7 to 9.30 **Meals:** alc (main courses L £7.50 to £15, D £12 to £26.50). Set L and D £14.95 (2 courses) to £19.95. Light L menu available Mon to Sat **Service:** not inc **Cards:** Amex, Delta, Maestro, MasterCard, Visa **Details:** 100 seats. 24 seats outside. Car park. Vegetarian meals. Children's helpings. No smoking in dining room. Wheelchair access (not WC). Music **Accommodation:** 15 rooms

MAP 3   WILLIAN – Hertfordshire

Fox   [NEW ENTRY]

Willian SG6 2AE
Tel: (01462) 480233
Website: www.foxatwillian.co.uk

Cooking 2 | Modern British | £39

Opposite the village pond and next to the parish church, the Fox was a 'tired old boozer' before Cliff Nye, also the proprietor of the White Horse in Brancaster Staithe (see entry), took over. The food takes a solid gastro-pub stance, starters taking in escabèche of red mullet with pickled vegetables,

and stir-fried teriyaki beef, and main courses such as roast rump of lamb, rosemary-flavoured mash, and a sauce of lentils and parsley. Among fish options might be herb-crusted fillet of cod, 'laundry-white and very fresh', served with garlicky pea risotto, and crème brûlée is a pleasant way to end. Staff are 'young, bubbly and enthusiastic', and the ambitious wine list is fairly priced, starting off at £10.80 for Georges Duboeuf.

Chefs: Frank Skinner and Hari Kodagoda **Proprietor:** Cliff Nye **Open:** all week L 12 to 2 (2.45 Sun), Mon to Sat D 6.45 to 9.15 **Meals:** alc (main courses L £5 to £16.50, D £10 to £19.50) **Service:** not inc **Cards:** Delta, Maestro, MasterCard, Visa **Details:** 70 seats. 16 seats outside. Car park. Vegetarian meals. Children's helpings. No smoking in dining room. Wheelchair access (also WC). Music. No mobile phones. Air-conditioned

MAP 8   WILMSLOW – Cheshire

Heddy's   [AR]

100–102 Water Lane, Wilmslow SK9 5BB
Tel: (01625) 526855

Offering a taste of the Middle East in the middle of Wilmslow, the eponymous Heddy Ghazizadeh proudly showcases that region's best dishes, with a selection of meze, charcoal-grilled meats and speciality Persian dishes. Falafel (£3.50) or spicy lamb sausages (£3.95) are good openers, while main-course kebabs (meat from £10.95, fish from £13.50) vie for attention among other traditional fare, including lamb couscous (£12.95) or chicken in a yoghurt marinade (£10.95). Canafe or baklava (both £3.50) to finish. Wines from £12.50. Open Tue to Fri L and Mon to Sat D.

MAP 5   WINCHCOMBE – Gloucestershire

5 North Street

5 North Street, Winchcombe GL54 5LH
Tel: (01242) 604566
Email: marcusashenford@yahoo.co.uk

Cooking 6 | Modern European | £50

It all looks the Cotswolds part: a sleepy grey-stone town with a little supermarket and the odd estate agent, and Marcus Ashenford's restaurant squeezed into a building where the upper, half-timbered

storey juts precariously forward. Two little rooms with bare tables and sparsely garnished walls constitute the dining area, where Kate Ashenford makes an assiduous front-of-house operator, describing the dishes with justifiable pride. Fixed-price menus for lunch and dinner, with a separate vegetarian listing, deal in modern European cooking, rendered with a high degree of polish. Baked red mullet in tomato vinaigrette with cuttlefish-ink pasta, langoustine oil and celery leaves makes a diverting way to start, and may be followed by braised ox cheek with creamed celeriac and horseradish in a good strong jus. Intensity of flavour is achieved through accurate cooking and properly complementary sauces and dressings, as when a reduction of grenadine is used to point up a breast and leg of quail with sweet grapes. Richness and intricacy characterise desserts such as caramelised pineapple with coconut rice pudding and a molasses sorbet. Otherwise, opt for cheeses served with chutney, jellies and oat biscuits. The compact wine list is orientated around European classics, with Languedoc Sauvignon and Merlot at £13.50.

Chef: Marcus Ashenford Proprietors: Marcus and Kate Ashenford Open: Wed to Sun L 12.30 to 1.30, Tue to Sat D 7 to 9 Closed: 2 weeks Jan, 1 week Aug Meals: Set L £18.50 (2 courses) to £26, Set D £26 to £50 Service: not inc Cards: Amex, Delta, Maestro, MasterCard, Visa Details: 26 seats. Vegetarian meals. Children's helpings. No smoking. Wheelchair access (not WC). Music. No mobile phones

Wesley House

High Street, Winchcombe GL54 5LJ
Tel: (01242) 602366
Website: www.wesleyhouse.co.uk

Cooking 3 | Modern British | £48

Situated in the narrow, busy high street, this fifteenth-century house is named after its two visits from John Wesley. Original features include wooden beams, while the dining room boasts a wrought iron staircase which is used to hold candles. Meals begin well with home-baked apricot and walnut bread. Daily changing menus might open with chargrilled scallops with a fennel and orange dressing, followed by tender Scottish beef fillet in a peppercorn sauce, or perhaps free-range pork cutlets with 'very good' boulangère potatoes. To finish, dark chocolate tart is accompanied by a tangy grapefruit marmalade. There are over 100 bins on the international wine list, which comes with short notes; house wine starts at £12.50.

Chef: Martin Dunn Proprietor: Matthew Brown Open: all week L 12 to 2, Mon to Sat D 7 to 9.30 Closed: 25 and 26 Dec Meals: alc L (main courses £12.50 to £22.50). Set L £12.50 (2 courses) to £15, Set D £29.50 (2 courses) to £35. Bar L menu available Service: not inc Cards: Amex, Delta, Maestro, MasterCard, Visa Details: 60 seats. Children's helpings. Smoking in bar only. Wheelchair access (not WC). Occasional music. No mobile phones. Air-conditioned Accommodation: 5 rooms

MAP 2   **WINCHESTER –** Hampshire

Chesil Rectory

1 Chesil Street, Winchester SO23 0HU
Tel: (01962) 851555
Website: www.chesilrectory.co.uk

Cooking 6 | Modern French | £64

The half-timbered building dates from the early fifteenth century and is reputedly the oldest building in Winchester (which is saying something). Inside, the décor lets the building do the talking – low dark beams, timbers, dark floorboards and a huge inglenook – but Robert Quéhan's busily inventive menus transcend the period setting. Starters such as foie gras with scallops, wilted baby spinach and foie gras sauce or sweet pea soup with spring morels set the tone and combine exemplary freshness with sound technique. Flavour is built up robustly in main courses, partnering loin of South Downs lamb with confit belly, morels and smoked garlic purée, or fashioning a light, delicate oyster and vanilla foam to accompany well-timed fillets of sea bass (with crisp skin) served with 'more of those sensational morels', spring white truffles and new season's asparagus. There are more traditional dishes too, such as aged fillet of Hampshire beef Rossini served with truffled pomme purée and Madeira sauce. A beautifully crafted trio of rhubarb – soufflé with anglaise, cheesecake, and sorbet – and pear and vanilla tarte Tatin with cinnamon yoghurt ice cream hit just the right note at inspection. Service is 'relaxed, unfussy and attentive'. House wines from £19 open the French-led list.

Chef: Robert Quéhan Proprietors: Carl and Anna Reeve, and Robert and Julia Quéhan Open: Wed to Sat L 12 to 1.30, Tue to Sat D 7 to 9.30 Closed: first 2 weeks Aug Meals: Set L £19 (2 courses) to £23, Set D £45 Service: not inc Cards: Amex, Delta, Diners, Maestro, MasterCard, Visa Details: 45 seats. Vegetarian meals. Children's helpings. No smoking in 1 dining room. Wheelchair access (not WC). Music. No mobile phones

Hotel du Vin & Bistro

Southgate Street, Winchester SO23 9EF
Tel: (01962) 841414
Website: www.hotelduvin.com

Cooking 4 | Modern European | £47

The original of the thriving group, this delightfully lively, informal bistro is within a Georgian town house hotel. The combination of brasserie food and a winning wine list continues: true to the hotel's name, walls team with wine-themed prints and posters, and the mantelpiece is lined with distinguished bottles. Bare floorboards and polished tables and service that's 'youthful, attentive and helpful' create a comfortable and unpretentious feel. Warm goat's cheese set atop a tomato tarte Tatin in a pool of basil pesto, and a generous, accurately timed pea and mint risotto got one meal off to a good start. The quality of the raw materials shone in main courses of tender, pink rump of lamb with 'fabulous lamb jus', which came with sweetbreads, white asparagus and confit cherry tomatoes, and monkfish wrapped in Parma ham and served with shiitake mushrooms and artichokes, while desserts delivered an enjoyable double chocolate soufflé and caramelized pear and almond tart with crème fraîche. Wine buffs can enjoy plenty of top quality bottles from the classic French appellations before moving into the rest of Europe (there's an excellent range of Italians) and the New World. By glass there's some 17 (including champagne) with house wines opening at £12.50 and an excellent selection of half-bottles.

Chef: Matthew Sussex Proprietor: MWB Group plc Open: all week 12 to 1.45, 7 to 9.45 Meals: alc exc Sun L (main courses from £17). Set L Sun £23.50 Service: not inc Cards: Amex, Delta, Diners, Maestro, MasterCard, Visa Details: 63 seats. Car park. Vegetarian meals. Children's helpings. No smoking in 1 dining room. Wheelchair access (not WC). No music. No mobile phones Accommodation: 24 rooms

Wykeham Arms

75 Kingsgate Street, Winchester SO23 9PE
Tel: (01962) 853834

Cooking 3 | International | £36

The Wyk, as it's affectionately known, is tucked away in the oldest part of the city between the cathedral and the college. The pub has been taken over by Fullers brewery, but they know not to mend what isn't broken and, as an inspector said: 'the inn is on song and continues to thrive.' Prop up the bar, stay overnight, or eat in the dining room, which is as full of character as the rest of the building. Traditional food sits alongside the more adventurous, so chicken liver parfait with apple and grape chutney, a 'classic British starter done well', appears with sesame-cured carpaccio, prosciutto and chorizo with pickled beetroot and a balsamic reduction. Main courses range from beef fillet on bubble and squeak with shallots and a Madeira jus ('rich and full of flavour') to crisp-skinned sea bass fillets with saffron-scented seafood risotto, pan-fried calamari and saffron cream. Finish with something like creamy vanilla pannacotta offset by citrus fruits. Most bottles on the global, 90-bin wine list are under £20, with house Côtes du Roussillon £12.50.

Chef: William Spencer Proprietor: Fullers, Smith & Turner Open: all week L 12 to 2.30 (12.15 to 1.45 Sun), Mon to Sat D 6.30 to 8.45 Meals: alc (main courses L £6.50 to £13, D £11 to £20). Set L Sun £15.50 (2 courses) to £19.50 Service: not inc Cards: Amex, Delta, Maestro, MasterCard, Visa Details: 70 seats. 60 seats outside. Car park (residents only). Vegetarian meals. No children under 14. No smoking in dining room. No music. No mobile phones Accommodation: 14 rooms

MAP 2 **WINCHMORE HILL – Buckinghamshire**

Plough

NEW ENTRY

Winchmore Hill HP7 0PA
Tel: (01494) 721001

Cooking 2 | Modern European | £42

'The place is now anything but a traditional village inn' said one diner of this rejuvenated venue which has benefited from a modern makeover. The dining room is spacious with contemporary furnishings and Neil Hayworth's menu fits the bill completely with a straightforward approach that makes the best use of the freshest raw materials. The 'extremely professional' home-baked bread rolls make an immediate impact, before a starter of crisp confit duck with black fig purée. Roasted marinated rump of lamb with cumin green beans was simple but successful at inspection, with well-timed vegetables. The vanilla pannacotta with compote of blackberries is an enjoyable way to end. The bar also offers snacks throughout the day (farmhouse Cheddar and pickle sandwich, or seabass niçoise). The concise wine list is a fairly pricey affair after you get past the house choices which start at £12.95.

Chef: Neil Hayworth **Proprietors:** Paul Smith and Richard Phillips **Open:** all week 12 to 2.30, 6 to 10 **Meals:** alc (main courses £12 to £19.95). Set L £9.50 to £11.50 **Service:** 12.5% (optional) **Cards:** Amex, Delta, Diners, Maestro, MasterCard, Visa **Details:** 80 seats. 32 seats outside. Children's helpings. Wheelchair access (also WC). Music

---

MAP 8 WINDERMERE – Cumbria

Gilpin Lodge

Crook Road, Windermere LA23 3NE
Tel: (015394) 88818
Website: www.gilpinlodge.com

Cooking 6 | Modern British | £58

This well-appointed Victorian Lodge in immaculately tended gardens with woodlands and fells about, is a comfortable place with a homely feel and stylish furnishings. The cooking relies on exceptional ingredients for its impact, with skill and dedication applied to well-sourced materials that might take in sea bream escabèche with tapenade dressing, or crab ravioli with a crab and lemongrass flavoured bisque. Main courses centre on fine-quality meats, from best end of Herdwick lamb (with potato fondant, confit swede, shallot purée and rosemary jus), to loin of Grizedale venison, perhaps with baby Savoy cabbage, parsnips, chestnuts and a cinnamon sauce, while a sense of balance and restraint enables Chris Meredith to bring off some complex dishes like roasted monkfish with salmon gnocchi, ballottine of leeks and a champagne sauce.

Desserts interleave standards of the repertoire – such as tarte Tatin or hot prune and Armagnac soufflé – with a few interesting variants: millefeuille of lemon cream with red wine poached pears, for example. British and Irish cheeses offer a savoury alternative, while the list of soundly chosen wines, with France in the ascendancy, picks off many a fine producer. Fifteen come by the glass (from £5) with house French kicking off at £19.75.

Chef: Chris Meredith **Proprietors:** the Cunliffe family **Open:** all week 12 to 2, 7 to 9 **Meals:** Set L £20 (2 courses) to £25, Set D £42.50. Light L menu available **Service:** not inc **Cards:** Amex, Delta, Diners, Maestro, MasterCard, Visa **Details:** 60 seats. 25 seats outside. Car park. Vegetarian meals. No children under 7. No smoking. Wheelchair access (not WC). No music. No mobile phones **Accommodation:** 20 rooms

---

Holbeck Ghyll

Holbeck Lane, Windermere
LA23 1LU
Tel: (015394) 32375
Website: www.holbeckghyll.com

Cooking 7 | Modern British/French | £70

A warm welcome awaits at the Nicholsons' textbook Lakeland hotel. Kitted out in the classic manner with a log fire in an inglenook, oak panelling and rich furnishings, it's a Victorian former hunting lodge enjoying spectacular views over Windermere and the Langland Fells beyond. David McLaughlin's refined, harmonious and admirably precise cooking is offered on menus that don't bamboozle with way-out experimentalism, but nonetheless have much to recommend them. How about a mini tower of rabbit rillettes on crostini, with a lightly creamy truffle vinaigrette, garnished with anchovies and chopped green beans, as a small but perfectly formed starter? Or there might be a trio of succulent roast scallops on smooth celeriac purée, the dressing a reduced, almost toffee-ish balsamic coulis.

A choice of five main courses follows at dinner, with just one fish among them: perhaps firm yet moist, crisp-skinned roast sea bass with aubergine caviar and a spot-on sauce of red pepper laced with pesto. Meats have included lamb from Kendal Rough Fell, its 'wonderfully sweet flavour' offset by unctuous shallot purée and a rosemary-scented jus. Desserts that impressed readers have included crème brûlée with apple sorbet and a cider sauce, and textbook glazed lemon tart. There are also superb British and French cheeses. Regulars may notice that the menu evolves but slowly, though that only helps to ensure the outstanding level of accomplishment. A 'personal house selection' opens the wine list, providing by-the-glass drinking from £4.75, but the main list is a treasure trove of quality, exerting itself in many other regions as well as France. The centre of gravity feels a little high, though, with not much under £25.

Chef: David McLaughlin **Proprietors:** David and Patricia Nicholson **Open:** all week 12 to 2, 7 to 9.30 **Meals:** Set L £22.50 (2 courses) to £27.50, Set D £49. Light L menu available **Service:** not inc **Cards:** Amex, Delta, Diners, Maestro, MasterCard, Visa **Details:** 50 seats. 30 seats outside. Car park. Vegetarian meals. No children under 8 at D. No smoking in dining room. Wheelchair access (not WC). No music **Accommodation:** 21 rooms

Jerichos

Birch Street, Windermere LA23 1EG
Tel: (015394) 42522
Website: www.jerichos.co.uk

| Cooking 5 | Modern British | £43 |

There's a touch of classic Parisian brasserie styling about the dining room of this town-centre restaurant. Its plum-coloured walls are lined with prints reminiscent of Toulouse-Lautrec, and tables with matching plum-coloured cloths are adorned with tea lights under little Art Deco-style shades. The place is owned and run by husband-and-wife team Chris and Jo Blaydes, with Chris in charge of the kitchen. He cooks confidently in an inventive modern style, with starters taking in confit of corn-fed poussin on roast marinated aubergine and red pepper with mustard sauce, and a salad of poached salmon, feta, cured anchovies and black olives. Main courses feature similarly bold flavour combinations, as in pan-fried cod loin on a salad of sun-dried tomatoes, toasted almonds, new potatoes and green beans, and roast best end of Lune Valley lamb with basil ratatouille, lyonnaise potatoes, caramelised onion and red wine sauce. To finish, there might be pear and ginger frangipane tart with crème anglaise and mascarpone. Wines are arranged in groups according to what food they go with (lamb and duck, beef and game, for example, or fish, chicken and pork) but done in an imaginative way to offer interesting possibilities for adventurous drinkers. Prices start at £13.

Chefs: Chris Blaydes and Tim Dalzell Proprietors: Chris and Jo Blaydes Open: Tue to Sun D only 6.45 to 10 Closed: last 2 weeks Nov, first week Dec, 24 to 26 Dec, 1 Jan Meals: alc (main courses £14.50 to £19.50) Service: not inc Cards: Delta, Maestro, MasterCard, Visa Details: 36 seats. Vegetarian meals. No children under 12. No smoking. Music

Kwela's

NEW ENTRY

4 High Street, Windermere LA23 1AF
Tel: (015394) 44954

| Cooking 3 | African | £33 |

Named after Allan Kwela, the South African jazz musician, this light, airy restaurant occupies the site that was formerly Roger's. It's evidently African from the décor – there's a smattering of African masks and fabrics on the walls – but not laboriously so in the cuisine. Starters range from a 'very rich' Moroccan-influenced chicken and pistachio pastilla, via ostrich pâté, to grilled halloumi wrapped in Woodall's pancetta on wild mushrooms sautéed with chestnuts, thyme and brandy. In addition to South African bobotie, main courses take in well-timed fillet of sea bass served with braised fennel, chickpeas and crispy onion, and roast guinea fowl with steamed spinach and lyonnaise potatoes that was a highlight at inspection. Desserts are of the order of chocolate and pistachio cake with good home-made chocolate ice cream, or South African coconut and apricot tart with an intense coconut ice cream. Service is affable, easy and attentive, while South Africa figures strongly on the wine list, which starts at £11.

Chef: Jess Rossouw Proprietors: Jessica Wright and Jess Rossouw Open: Tue to Sun D only 6.30 (5 mid-July to late Sept) to 9.30 (10 Sat) Closed: 30 Oct to 14 Nov, 24 to 26 Dec Meals: alc (main courses £10 to £16.50) Service: not inc Cards: Maestro, MasterCard, Visa Details: 36 seats. Vegetarian meals. Children's helpings. No smoking in 1 dining room. Wheelchair access (not WC). Music. No mobile phones

Miller Howe

Rayrigg Road, Windermere LA23 1EY
Tel: (015394) 42536
Website: www.millerhowe.com

| Cooking 4 | English Country-House | £61 |

One of the most striking aspects of Miller Howe is its stupendous location perched high on a hillside overlooking Lake Windermere. All the public areas capitalise on the view, but the décor is not to be outdone, dramatically combining antiques with flamboyant touches including innumerable gilded cherubs suspended from the ceilings. Jamie Roberts offers unchallenging but technically sound cooking on both the six-course Menu Gourmand and the à la carte alternatives. A pair of lightly pan-fried scallops set on a bed of creamed potato and topped with crispy onions, capers and tiny slices of black pudding kicked off an inspection lunch. This was followed by poached red mullet served with langoustine foam, parsley gnocchi, artichoke purée and saffron, while meat options have included braised daube of Bleethgill pork with apricot and sage sauce and crisp Waberthwaite ham. A 'perfect' mango soufflé with coconut and rum sorbet finished off that meal; alternatives could be a plate of chocolate desserts. Presentation borders on the over-elaborate while service could be more on the ball at times. House wines are £19 with 10 served by the glass for £4 to £7.

Chef: Jamie Roberts Proprietor: Charles Garside Open: all week L 12.30 to 2, Sun to Fri D 6.45 to 8.45, Sat D 8pm (1 sitting) Meals: alc (main courses L £9, D £18.50). Set L £21.50, Set L Sun £25, Set D £42.50. Light L menu available Service: 10% (optional) Cards: Amex, Delta, Maestro, MasterCard, Visa Details: 65 seats. 20 seats outside. Car park. Vegetarian meals. Children's helpings. No smoking. Wheelchair access (also WC). Music. No mobile phones. Air-conditioned Accommodation: 15 rooms

Samling

Ambleside Road, Windermere LA23 1LR
Tel: (015394) 31922
Website: www.thesamling.com

| Cooking 4 | Modern British | £70 |

For a country house set in 67 acres, the Samling is on a Lilliputian scale, with a small sitting room and dining room. What isn't at all modest is the culinary ambition, which sees dishes like slow-cooked belly of Gloucester Old Spot with langoustines and celeriac purée served alongside more classic combinations such as red mullet and roasted red pepper terrine with basil purée and sauce vierge. While Nigel Mendham draws on regional produce, serving main courses of, say, fillet and braised rib of local beef (with shallot purée and port reduction), or loin of Kendal Rough Fell lamb (with creamed sweetbread tart and wild garlic cream), he also brings luxury items into play in dishes such as roast breast of duck, petits pois à la francaise, foie gras and light duck jus. Blood orange and pink grapefruit terrine with passion fruit sorbet makes a light way to end the meal. Wines are a reasonable selection in both Old and New Worlds with not so reasonable prices – house wine, for example, is £32 – but six are served by the glass from £7.

Chef: Nigel Mendham Proprietor: Tom Maxfield Open: all week 12 to 2.30, 7 to 10 Meals: Set L £48, Set D £48 to £60 Service: not inc Cards: Amex, Maestro, MasterCard, Visa Details: 24 seats. 12 seats outside. Car park. Children's helpings. No smoking. Music. No mobile phones Accommodation: 11 rooms

 This symbol means that accommodation is available at this establishment.

MAP 1   WINSFORD – Somerset

Royal Oak Inn   AR

Winsford TA24 7JE
Tel: (01643) 851455

In the middle of Exmoor National Park, this twelfth-century thatched inn serves lunches in the bar and dinner in the restaurant. In the latter, expect foie gras crème brûlée with butternut squash mousse and poppy-seed 'brick' (£9.95) followed by seared venison with bitter chocolate sauce (£14.95), or roast spring chicken with boudin blanc and tarragon velouté (£11.95). Desserts might include warm chocolate fondant with black cherry chutney and clotted cream (£5.95). Wines from £11.95. Open Wed to Sun D only.

MAP 9   WINTERINGHAM – North Lincolnshire

Winteringham Fields

Winteringham DN15 9PF
Tel: (01724) 733096
Website: www.winteringhamfields.com

| Cooking 9 | Provincial French/Swiss | £95 |

For those who don't know, the little hamlet of Winteringham is on the Humber estuary, north of Scunthorpe, in the boondocks of North Lincolnshire. This is the real 'back of beyond', as more than one reporter reminds us, which is why Winteringham Fields comes as all the more of a surprise. A comfortably furnished country house, it was sold in 2005 by the Schwabs, whose achievements over the years here built the place up into the beacon of quality it is.

To say they would be a hard act to follow seems unavoidable, yet new owners Colin and Rebecca McGurran seem to have hit the ground running. Their smartest move has been to retain the services of Robert Thompson, indeed 'services' seems too small a word for his endeavours. Sourcing of ingredients has always been paramount at Winteringham, with seafood and Aberdeen Angus beef from Scotland, other fish from Grimsby, and local lamb among the mainstays of the menus. In the gentle atmosphere of the spacious dining room, where a dusky salmon-pink hue predominates, the cooking offers one revelation after another. Dishes are elaborate, complex and striking, yet presented with a straightforward absence of lily-gilding, and achieve rare harmony on the palate. 'There isn't a jarring flavour or texture anywhere,' commented our inspector.

A bowl of pasta in broth looks simple enough, but turns out to comprise home-made macaroni stuffed with a farce of black-leg chicken in a consommé of combined veal and chicken stocks, the fragrant and intense liquor scattered with tender chicken oysters and crayfish tails. Juxtapositions of fish and meat might reappear at main course but are consummately handled, as when roast fillet of veal with girolles and asparagus is garnished with langoustines, the whole dish gaining its final lustre from slivers of sensational foie gras.

The high-gloss finish is all the more remarkable when one considers that Thompson is still in his twenties and yet is cooking at the level of some French master with decades under his belt. Alternative temptations might be seared scallops with their corals, accompanied by a pig's trotter and a trio of sauces, followed perhaps by pot-roast quail in apricot and vanilla, served with pilaff rice and sauced with caviar. Nor is there any inclination to let meals down gently with simpler desserts, as many do. Instead, you might be astonished at the quality of a perfect tarte Tatin scented with liquorice, the pastry buttery yet crisp, the accompaniments a jelly of Elysium dessert wine from California and top-notch vanilla ice cream. The trimmings all work brilliantly too, from the appetiser red mullet soup with curry foam to a slice of improbably terrific chocolate and fennel loaf. Staff are attentive without being intrusive, with wine service in particular exemplary for its fairness and impartiality. We did not receive a wine list this year, so cannot comment, but prices start at £22, and ten are available by the glass from £4.50.

Chef: Robert Thompson **Proprietors:** Colin and Rebecca McGurran **Open:** Tue to Sat 12 to 1.30, 7 to 9 **Closed:** 24 Dec to 6 Jan, last week Apr, 2 weeks Aug **Meals:** alc (main courses £22 to £36.50). Set L £31 (2 courses) to £36, Set D £75 **Service:** not inc **Cards:** Amex, Delta, Maestro, MasterCard, Visa **Details:** 52 seats. Car park. Vegetarian meals. No smoking. No music. No mobile phones **Accommodation:** 10 rooms

MAP 8 WISWELL – Lancashire

Freemasons Arms

8 Vicarage Fold, Wiswell BB7 9DF
Tel: (01254) 822218

Ian Martin has moved from the Red Cat at Crank to this new venue. His menus change with the

seasons and might open with seared king scallops with a pineapple and chilli salsa (£7), or a spring dish of English asparagus with a poached egg and shavings of Lancashire cheese (£6.50), and go on to pan-fried sea bass with roast fennel and orange butter (£12.95). End with plum crumble or Eton mess (both £3.95). House wines from around £10 and a long list of fine wines. Closed Mon and Tue. Reports please.

MAP 6 WITCHFORD – Cambridgeshire

Needhams

186 Main Street, Witchford CB6 2HT
Tel: (01353) 661405
Website: www.needhamsrestaurant.co.uk

Cooking 2 | Modern European | £41

Luke and Verity Pearson's restaurant is characterised by their friendly, accommodating approach, with efficient, cheerful service in the neutrally decorated dining room. The menu isn't over-complicated, opening typically with grilled herb brioche and Gruyère-crusted queen scallops with garlic and lemon, followed by, perhaps, whole poussin roasted with fennel or baked cod with ginger and spring onion crab cakes. The house speciality dessert is pain au chocolat and butter pudding with vanilla crème fraîche and coffee syrup, or there might be a trio of chocolate spring rolls with sweet peanut brittle ice cream. The 50-plus wine list is a nicely annotated global affair; house choices start at £11.25.

Chef: Luke Pearson **Proprietors:** Luke and Verity Pearson **Open:** Tue to Sun L 12 to 2, Tue to Sat D 6.30 to 9 (9.30 Sat) **Closed:** 1 to 20 Jan **Meals:** alc (not Sun L; main courses £13 to £20). Set L £17.95 **Service:** not inc **Cards:** Amex, Delta, Maestro, MasterCard, Visa **Details:** 60 seats. Car park. Vegetarian meals. Children's helpings. No smoking. Wheelchair access (also WC). Music

MAP 3 WOBURN – Bedfordshire

Paris House

Woburn, Woburn Park MK17 9QP
Tel: (01525) 290692

Chef/proprietor Peter Chandler takes his French classical cuisine seriously. His dinner menu, at £55 (the three-course midweek lunch is £22), might start with lobster bisque and flambé king prawns in Pernod and garlic butter, followed by fillet of beef with red wine and shallot sauce or veal kidneys in mustard sauce. Hot raspberry soufflé is a good way to end. The wine list is pricey overall, but a handful of house selections are £17 to £19. Closed Sun D and Mon.

MAP 5 | WOLVERHAMPTON – West Midlands

Bilash

2 Cheapside, Wolverhampton WV1 1TU
Tel: (01902) 427762

Opposite the Civic Centre in the middle of town, Bilash is a highly individual upmarket Indian restaurant. Each dish is given a lengthy description on a menu that starts with galouti kebabs (fried minced lamb flavoured with spices and mango powder; £6.90) or diced tiger prawns with red pepper sauce (£7.90), before moving on to black pepper chicken (£12.90), shukno gosht (a dry, spicy lamb dish; £13.90), or maacher jhool (mustard-flavoured pomfret curry; £15.90). Wines from £18.90. Closed Sun.

MAP 6 | WOODBRIDGE – Suffolk

Captain's Table

3 Quay Street, Woodbridge IP12 1BX
Tel: (01394) 383145
Website: www.captainstable.co.uk

| Cooking 3 | Modern European | £35 |

A warm welcome awaits at Jo and Pascal Pommier's restaurant, where three comfortable dining areas are linked by arched open doorways, and there's an outside space for dining al fresco. Jo takes care of customers aided by a young, hard-working team. Local Cromer crab and lobster are perennial favourites, along with twice-baked goats' cheese soufflé and slow-roast duck leg confit. Otherwise expect a platter of smoked fish from Orford with horseradish crème fraîche, or home-made corned beef with sauce gribiche for starters, and move on to local cod fillet baked with an anchovy and red onion crumble, or cassoulet. For dessert there might be home-churned honey-comb ice cream, or dark Belgian chocolate pot

laced with brandy. The brisk wine list opens with vins de pays at £10.95 and rarely strays above £20.

> **Chef:** Pascal Pommier **Proprietors:** Jo and Pascal Pommier **Open:** Tue to Sat 12 to 2, 7 (6.30 Sat) to 9.30; also open bank hol Sun L and D and Aug bank hol L and D **Meals:** alc (main courses L £6 to £12.50, D £9.50 to £18) **Service:** not inc **Cards:** Delta, Maestro, MasterCard, Visa **Details:** 50 seats. 30 seats outside. Car park. Vegetarian meals. Children's helpings. No smoking in dining room. Wheelchair access (not WC). No music

Riverside [AR]

Quayside, Woodbridge IP12 1BH
Tel: (01394) 382587

This contemporary quayside restaurant is part of the oldest cinema in the country. Tapas (£3 to £4 a dish) are served at lunchtime – perhaps mini fish and chips, and tuna carpaccio – while the full menu (main courses between £10 and £20) runs to velouté of haricots blancs, tiger prawns and wild mushrooms drizzled with truffle oil, followed by slow-roast belly of free-range Suffolk pork accompanied by crackling and spiced apples. Finish with basmati rice pudding with apple and butterscotch compote, and then catch a movie. Wines from £12. Closed Sun D.

MAP 5 | WORCESTER – Worcestershire

Brown's [AR]

24 Quay Street, South Quay, Worcester WR1 2JJ
Tel: (01905) 26263

Charmingly located on the Severn, this long-established venue is noted for the reliability of the kitchen's output. A strong lunch menu attracts with home-smoked chicken risotto (£5.95), and slow-braised blade of beef with beetroot and horseradish relish (£14.95), while the set-price dinner menu (two courses £27.50, five £39.50) features pan-seared scallops with cauliflower and cardamom purée, and venison loin with cabbage, bacon and chestnuts with a red wine sauce, rounded off with peanut cheesecake with maple syrup and vanilla cream. A solid wine list opens at £15.95. Closed Sat L, Sun D and Mon.

> The price given next to the cooking score is based on the cost of a typical three-course dinner for one person, including coffee, house wine and service.

MAP 7 WORLESTON – Cheshire

Rookery Hall

Worleston CW5 6DQ
Tel: (01270) 610016
Website: www.handpicked.co.uk/rookeryhall

| Cooking 4 | Modern European | £55 |

Despite the grand looks of this country-house hotel, built in 1816 of mellow sandstone with oak-panelled public rooms, the mood is unstuffy and relaxed. Craig Malone's refined but unpretentious cooking fits in well. Foams and froths and other cheffy touches are common, and luxury items such as foie gras and truffles are abundant, but so are humbler ingredients, as in a starter of Jerusalem artichoke soup with hazelnut milk froth and a crisp duck confit roll. The same goes for main courses of brill fillet with wild mushroom risotto, leek purée, baby vegetables and garlic foam, and Barbary duck breast with sarladaise potatoes, roast salsify and morello cherry jam sauce. Sophisticated dessert options might include vanilla and black-berry pannacotta with warm blueberry pancakes and white chocolate ice cream, although the selection of British and French cheeses from named small producers is a tempting alternative. Wines are one area where opulence prevails, with plenty of high-class bottles and three-figure prices on the substantial list, although there are a few bottles under £20.

Chef: Craig Malone Proprietor: Hand Picked Hotels Open: Sun to Fri L 12 to 2, all week D 7 to 9.30 Meals: alc (main courses £16.50 to £24.50). Set L £15.50 (2 courses) to £19.50, Set D £29.95. Bar menu available Service: not inc Cards: Amex, Delta, Diners, Maestro, MasterCard, Visa Details: 60 seats. 20 seats outside. Car park. Vegetarian meals. Children's helpings. No smoking. Wheelchair access (also WC). Music Accommodation: 45 rooms

MAP 8 WREA GREEN – Lancashire

Ribby Hall   NEW ENTRY

Ribby Road, Wrea Green PR4 2PR
Tel: (01772) 671155
Website: www.ribbyhall.co.uk

| Cooking 3 | Modern Anglo-French | £47 |

The restaurant at Ribby Hall is part of a holiday village, but don't let that put you off. In the restau-rant, with its rather sumptuous décor, chef Nigel Smith offers English/French menus ranging from a carte, through an early-evening deal ('ideal for the family,' as it says) to a market menu. Good quality ingredients are handled with care and delivered with style: seared Oban scallops – 'per-fectly cooked' – are served on celeriac purée with herby tagliatelle and a subtly flavoured langoustine jus, with perhaps a terrine of tomatoes, mozzarella and basil an alternative starter. Goosnargh chicken breast on Puy lentils in a red wine jus has been a well-prepared and attractively presented main course, while cannon of lamb, served pink on Puy lentils with garlicky fondant potato and a port-based gravy has received plaudits. Desserts have 'lots of eye appeal', among them perhaps passion-fruit sorbet and a pyramid of iced nougat. Staff are well trained and smartly turned out, and the rea-sonably priced wine list, starting at £13.25, runs to over 30 bins.

Chef: Nigel Smith Proprietor: Ribby Hall Village Open: Fri and Sun L 12 to 2 (2.30 Sun), Tue to Sun D 5.30 to 9 (9.45 Sat) Meals: alc (main courses £15.50 to £23). Set L Fri £9.95 (1 course), Set L Sun £12.95 (2 courses) to £14.95, Set D 5.30 to 6.45 £11.50 (2 courses) to £13.95, Set D £21.95 (2 courses) to £65 (inc wine) Service: not inc Cards: Amex, Maestro, MasterCard, Visa Details: 120 seats. Car park. Vegetarian meals. Children's helpings. No smoking. Wheelchair access (also WC). Music Accommodation: 37 rooms plus holiday cottages

MAP 8 WRIGHTINGTON – Lancashire

Mulberry Tree

9 Wood Lane, Wrightington Bar, Wrightington WN6 9SE
Tel: (01257) 451400

| Cooking 4 | Modern British | £44 |

This big converted pub on a corner site is a vast, rambling place that incorporates a contemporary-looking bar. Eat here, or make your way to the more formal restaurant; the cooking is fairly similar in each, with many crossover dishes. There's an admirable commitment to local produce, and while Mark Prescott uses plenty of upmarket materials on the carte – chicken liver and foie gras parfait, for example, or lobster with seasonal baby vegetables and a champagne and herb sauce – such ingredients can be balanced by relatively humble ones: witness pea and ham hock soup, or Irish stew with herb dumplings. Elsewhere, there are prawn spring rolls with a sweet chilli and spring onion dipping sauce, then roast breast of chicken with sage and onion mashed potato, pancetta and crispy onion rings. A decent international wine list has reasonable options under £20, starting at £14.25.

Chef: Mark Prescott **Proprietor:** James Moore **Open:** all week 12 to 2, 6 to 9.30 (10 Fri and Sat) **Closed:** 26 Dec, 1 Jan **Meals:** alc exc Sun L (main courses £9.50 to £21.50). Set L Mon to Sat £12.50 (2 courses), Set L Sun £19.50, Set D 6 to 7 £14.50 (2 courses). Bar menu available exc Sat D **Service:** 10% (optional) **Cards:** Maestro, MasterCard, Visa **Details:** 75 seats. 20 seats outside. Car park. Vegetarian meals. Children's helpings. No smoking. Wheelchair access (also WC). Music. Air-conditioned

Simply Heathcotes

Wrightington Hotel, Moss Lane, Wrightington
WN6 9PB
Tel: (01257) 478244
Website: www.heathcotes.co.uk

Cooking 2 | Modern British | £42

Just like the others in the chain (see entries in Leeds, Liverpool and Manchester), this lively brasserie is contemporary and comfortable. Part of a modern hotel complex and approached via an unprepossessing staircase, it has good views over the surrounding countryside. The kitchen showcases local and regional produce in a broadly European accent, turning out brasserie dishes of pea and broad bean risotto, or crisp Goosnargh duck leg with pickled red cabbage. Main courses range from eight dishes of 'Heathcotes comfort' – perhaps pork and leek sausages with champ and onion gravy – to roast monkfish with mussels, curried leeks and pilaff rice. End with caramelised pineapple polenta cake with berries and coconut sorbet, or classic vanilla crème brûlée. Own-label wines get things started at £13.95.

Chef: Michael Noonan **Proprietor:** Paul Heathcote **Open:** all week 12 to 2.30, 6 to 10 (11 Fri and Sat) **Closed:** 27 and 28 Dec, 1 Jan **Meals:** alc (main courses £9.50 to £22). Set L £12.95 (2 courses), Set D Mon to Sat 6 to 7 £12.95 (2 courses), Set D Mon £15 (2 courses, inc wine) **Service:** not inc **Cards:** Amex, Delta, Maestro, MasterCard, Visa **Details:** 81 seats. Car park. Vegetarian meals. Children's helpings. No smoking. Wheelchair access (also WC). Music. Air-conditioned

£	This symbol means that it is possible to have a three-course dinner, including coffee, half a bottle of house wine and service, for £30 or less per person.

MAP 10 **YARM** – Stockton-on-Tees

Chadwick's

104B High Street, Yarm TS15 9AU
Tel: (01642) 788558

Cooking 3 | European-Plus | £38

Chadwick's is a friendly café and restaurant that stands out in slightly olde-worlde Yarm, with its bold, modern exterior contrasting strongly with the more traditional buildings surrounding it. Inside, the contemporary feel continues, with a simple and relaxed take on a Continental café: tables of light wood, walls mostly pale yellow, with one wall completely mirrored. The atmosphere has a general buzz about it, and background music isn't too intrusive. The food melds British and French cuisines, although global influences are at work, too, such as in chicken satay with Indonesian fried rice and peanut sauce. Otherwise, twice-baked cheese soufflé or mussels steamed in white wine are typical starters, while main courses could be seared tuna with provençale vegetables or slow-roast pork rib with black pudding, crushed potatoes and mustard cream. The two-page international wine list is good value, opening with Georges Duboeuf at £11.95.

Chefs: David Brownless and Steven Conyard **Proprietor:** David Brownless **Open:** Mon to Sat 12 to 2.30, 5.30 to 9.30 **Closed:** 24 and 25 Dec, third week Oct, bank hol Mon **Meals:** alc (main courses L £6.50 to £10.50, D £12 to £21.50). **Service:** not inc **Cards:** Amex, Delta, MasterCard, Visa **Details:** 70 seats. Vegetarian meals. Children's helpings. No smoking. Music. No mobile phones. Air-conditioned

MAP 2 **YARMOUTH** – Isle of Wight

George

Quay Street, Yarmouth PO41 0PE
Tel: (01983) 760331
Website: www.thegeorge.co.uk

Cooking 6 | Modern British | £63

The George stands stolidly in the centre of the little coastal town of Yarmouth, hard by the dinky castle. A strong sense of history is invoked by the prints hung about the walls, showing the environs in days gone by. There are two eating options: the

blond-wood Brasserie, with its views over the Solent, and the more formal Restaurant, where crimson wall panels and floor-length tablecloths contribute to the feeling of luxiness.

Kevin Mangeolles oversees the kitchen for both, but it is for the Restaurant that the culinary muscles are most impressively flexed. Crab with seared mackerel and watermelon is a novel presentation of marine flavours, the textures marrying well, the mackerel skin crisp, making an entirely satisfying first course. A dismembered quail comes with crumbed veal sweetbreads and some positively flavoured wedges of oyster mushroom. An inexhaustible striving for innovation distinguishes each course, so that crisped sea bass as a main course arrives crowned with a breaded scallop, the plate dragged with streaks of pea purée and with some minute but delicious sweet gnocchi. Two hungry diners might set about an Aberdeen Angus rib, served absolutely trad with creamed potato. After a pre-dessert, you might light on pistachio mousse with chocolate sorbet, or else go for the decent Anglo-French cheese platter. Taittinger champagnes are featured on a wine list that opens with 13 house wines hearteningly offered at a single price (£14.75). A page of half-bottles does its bit.

Chef: Kevin Mangeolles Proprietors: John Illsley, and Jeremy and Amy Willcock Open: Tue to Sat D only 7 to 10 Meals: Set D £46.50 Service: not inc Cards: Amex, Delta, Maestro, MasterCard, Visa Details: 30 seats. Vegetarian meals. No smoking in dining room. No music. Air-conditioned Accommodation: 17 rooms

---

MAP 5	YARPOLE – Herefordshire

Bell Inn

NEW ENTRY

Green Lane, Yarpole HR6 0BD
Tel: (01568) 780359

Cooking 3 | **Modern British** | **£39**

The Bell represents a branching out for Claude and Claire Bosi (see entry; Hibiscus, Ludlow), although the intention has not been to extend haute cuisine to here, but to offer straightforward country cooking that reflects the building's heritage. Indeed, since taking over this ancient hostelry, the Bosis have changed little, and while the place is now food-focused, it has stayed in

touch with its roots and retains a clutch of local drinkers. The menu isn't too ambitious – it combines pub staples with a few more interesting options – but is quite cumbersome in its division into three: a monthly changing carte, steak-heavy blackboard extras, and bar snacks. Seafood is excellent, notably scallops with a fricassee of lentils and smoked bacon with coconut milk, and cod with a ham, parsley and caper dressing plus caramelized salsify purée, baby spinach and sauté potatoes, while desserts can be impeccably crafted if a simple and well balanced rhubarb and vanilla pannacotta is anything to go by. Service is 'willing rather than knowledgeable', and the wine list is a short, quality offering with some good drinking under £20. House wine is £11.50.

Chef: Mark Jones Proprietors: Claire and Claude Bosi Open: Tue to Sun 12 to 2.30, 6.30 to 9.30 Meals: alc (main courses £9.50 to £17). Snack menu available Service: not inc Cards: Delta, Maestro, Mastercard, Visa Details: 90 seats. 50 seats outside. Vegetarian meals. Children's helpings. No smoking. Occasional music

---

MAP 2	YATTENDON – Berkshire

Royal Oak

The Square, Yattendon RG18 0UG
Tel: (01635) 201325
Website: www.royaloakyattendon.com

Cooking 2 | **Modern British** | **£42**

The sixteenth century red-brick building is as pretty as a picture, with a splendid garden to the rear. Inside are low beams, log fires, old tiled floors and a mix of dark wooden and pine furnishings. The same menu is served in both the smartly appointed restaurant and the more informal brasserie-style area. Duck terrine with Cumberland sauce, and pan-fried scallops with pancetta and rough pea purée were simply executed starters at inspection, while roast venison fillet was the 'best dish of the meal' and came with herby croquette-style potato cakes, celeriac purée and rosemary jus. Other main courses could be pan-fried monkfish with Parmentier potatoes, asparagus and truffle sauce, or penne with goats' cheese, baked tomatoes and herbs, and desserts could bring on vanilla cheesecake with mixed-berry sauce. Six house wines at £15 head up a short international wine list.

> **Chef:** Anton Barbarovic **Proprietors:** William and Janet Boyle **Open:** all week 12 to 2.15, 7 to 10 **Closed:** 1 Jan **Meals:** alc (main courses £13 to £18). Set L Mon to Fri £12 (2 courses) to £15, Set L Sun £23 **Service:** 10% (optional) **Cards:** Amex, Delta, Maestro, MasterCard, Visa **Details:** 65 seats. 30 seats outside. Car park. Vegetarian meals. Children's helpings. No smoking in 1 dining room. Wheelchair access (not WC). No music **Accommodation:** 5 rooms

---

MAP 9 YORK – North Yorkshire

Blue Bicycle

34 Fossgate, York YO1 9TA
Tel: (01904) 673990
Website: www.thebluebicycle.com

Cooking 3 | **Modern European/Seafood** | **£49**

This eclectic bistro, down a cobbled York street, is brimming with homely charm, from the wooden flooring and highly individual furniture to the interesting nooks and crannies filled with eye-catching busts and paintings. There are wide-ranging blackboard specials with an emphasis on fresh fish. Look out for classic moules marinière, fish stew with saffron rice, or fish pie made with parsley mash. New head chef Simon Hirst has been promoted from sous-chef and his modern European menu also features some delicate Asian touches, so you could open with hot-and-sour chicken noodle soup, or tempura prawns on sticky lemon rice. Typical mains include baked sea bass on a crayfish and thyme risotto, or fillet of Yorkshire beef on smoked bacon mash. The half-dozen dessert choices include Yorkshire curd tart with ginger ice cream. The intelligent global wine list offers 19 wines by the glass, from £4.50, while their Italian house opens the list at £17.

> **Chef:** Simon Hirst **Proprietor:** Anthony Stephenson **Open:** all week 12 to 2.30, 6 to 9.30 (9 Sun) **Closed:** 25 and 26 Dec, 1 and 2 Jan **Meals:** alc (main courses L £8.50 to £16.50, D £14.50 to £20). **Service:** 10% (optional) **Cards:** Delta, Maestro, MasterCard, Visa **Details:** 83 seats. Vegetarian meals. No smoking. Wheelchair access (not WC). Music **Accommodation:** 2 rooms

> This symbol means that the restaurant has elected to participate in *The Good Food Guide's* £5 voucher scheme (see 'Using The Good Food Guide' for details).

J. Baker's   NEW ENTRY

7 Fossgate, York YO1 9TA
Tel: (01904) 622688
Website: www.jbakers.co.uk

Cooking 5 | **French/Modern British** | **£36**
£5

J. Baker's Bistro Moderne occupies the site that was once Rish and is the first restaurant venture of Jeff Baker, last seen in the Guide as the head chef at the now-closed Pool Court in Leeds. He's pulled away from haute cuisine – the nibbles, appetiser and petits fours, the truffled luxuries – opting instead for good-value, straightforward dishes along the lines of 'old favourites with a modern twist': Saddleback pork fillet with a handmade Scotch egg, black pudding and Bramley apple, say, or Scott's Galloway rib steak with egg and chips. The commitment to local produce and the quality home-made bread post notice of culinary intent, and inspection showed the kitchen setting a formidable early pace. A good-value grazing menu is offered at lunchtimes – small plates good for sharing or a quick snack with a glass of wine – and this delivered oak-smoked organic salmon served with celeriac rémoulade and quail's eggs, corned beef with spring carrot relish presented in a Kilner jar, and excellent side orders of hand-cut chips, and fine beans with cured bacon and shallots. Desserts are in the same comfort zone, and apple crumble with roast almond ice cream, and jam roly-poly have both received rave reports. Very good service keeps up the cheer, and the enterprising and fairly priced wine list from around the world opens at £10.95.

> **Chefs:** Jeff Baker and Steve Smith **Proprietors:** Jeff Baker and Neil Nugent **Open:** Tue to Sat 12 to 2.30, 6 to 10 (10.30 Fri and Sat) **Meals:** alc L (main courses £4 to £6). Set D £18.95 (2 courses) to £24.50 **Service:** not inc **Cards:** Amex, Delta, Diners, Maestro, MasterCard, Visa **Details:** 60 seats. Vegetarian meals. Children's helpings. No smoking in dining room. Wheelchair access (also WC). Music

Melton's

7 Scarcroft Road, York YO23 1ND
Tel: (01904) 634341
Website: www.meltonsrestaurant.co.uk

Cooking 5 | **Modern European** | **£43**

Melton's has been plying its trade since 1990 in this slightly out-of-the-way corner of York. Inside is fairly snug, the walls decorated with views of the restaurant itself, and the ambience of wooden floors and flickering candles providing something of a bistro feel. The cooking philosophy mobilises influences from all over but in a way that seems determined to avoid preciousness. Starters at inspection lacked sparkle, but then the pace picked up for main courses that included a 'sweet, soft, succulent' piece of roast sirloin with horseradish butter, Yorkshire kale, purple-sprouting broccoli and a full-on red wine reduction. The fish of the day might be pan-fried sea bass, served with a well-made butter sauce and crushed herby new potatoes. Local ingredients command support, as with Holme Farm venison served carpaccio fashion, or seasonal rhubarb that might go into a parfait laced with vodka. A hot mango soufflé with matching sauce was a palpable hit one spring evening. We're delighted to report that Melton's still makes no charge for bottled water or filter coffee. Wines have been imaginatively chosen, the list even finding space for some German Rieslings, which are a rarity nowadays. Reds include Pica Broca, a Coteaux du Languedoc made by a Yorkshireman. House wines are £14.

Chefs: Michael Hjort and Annie Prescott Proprietors: Michael and Lucy Hjort Open: Tue to Sat L 12 to 2, Mon to Sat D 5.30 to 9.45 Closed: 3 weeks Christmas, 1 week Aug Meals: alc (main courses £14.50 to £21.50). Set L and D 5.30 to 6.15 £21 Service: not inc Cards: Delta, Maestro, MasterCard, Visa Details: 42 seats. Vegetarian meals. Children's helpings. No smoking. Wheelchair access (not WC). Music. No mobile phones. Air-conditioned

Melton's Too

25 Walmgate, York YO1 9TX
Tel: (01904) 629222
Website: www.meltonstoo.co.uk

Cooking 2 | Modern European | £30

'Busy, noisy and friendly' was one visitor's take on this informal sibling of Melton's (see entry above), a bare-boarded operation with its bar welcoming those just wanting a drink, and dining rooms spread over two floors. The cooking does not aim to be imaginative or original, but it is both worthy and dependable and the menu has plenty of choice, including all-day breakfast, sandwiches and tapas. While the kitchen keeps tabs on fashionable preparations and presentation, it doesn't lose sight of the importance of good-quality materials, from a barn-raised 'Middleton on the Wolds' chicken breast (served with vegetable tagine) to Whitby smoked haddock croquettes. First courses run from a plain plate of Yorkshire ham, smoked salmon, cheese and chutney, via tapas of deep-fried

squid with chilli sauce, or meatballs, to a leek and blue cheese tart 'that was a highlight of starters'. Desserts have included lemon posset and bread-and-butter pudding. A short list of wines opens with house Italian at £10.95.

Chefs: Karl Smith and Andy Battson Proprietors: Michael and Lucy Hjort Open: all week 10.30 to 10.30 Closed: 25 and 26 Dec, 1 Jan Meals: alc (main courses £7.50 to £13.50) Service: not inc Cards: Delta, Maestro, MasterCard, Visa Details: 120 seats. Vegetarian meals. Children's helpings. No-smoking area. Wheelchair access (also WC). Music. Air-conditioned

Middlethorpe Hall

Bishopthorpe Road, York YO23 2GB
Tel: (01904) 641241
Website: www.middlethorpe.com

Cooking 3 | Modern English | £51

Historical, handsome, comfortable and luxurious, it's one visitor's view that Middlethorpe Hall is 'easily the best dining experience within the York city area'. Given wood panelling, antiques and fine table settings, it is no wonder that the hotel demands smart dress, but the strict jacket and tie rule has now been relaxed. Though it is not a place for cutting-edge cuisine, menus are thoughtful and well balanced, relying on classic treatments for impact. The fixed-price dinner comes as three or four courses, and Lee Heptinstall's daring sleights of hand have produced pan-fried John Dory with herb-crushed potatoes and sun-dried tomato sauce as a starter, main courses of daube of beef with butternut squash, spinach, shallot purée and potato crisps, and a 'cooked just right' chocolate fondant. The atmosphere is one of formal service, and the wine list majors in the French classic regions at fairly brisk prices. There are lashings of halves, though, and the house range starts at £16.50.

Chef: Lee Heptinstall Proprietor: Historic House Hotels Ltd Open: all week 12.30 to 1.30, 7 to 9.45 Meals: Set L £17 (2 courses) to £23, Set D £39 to £55 Service: net prices Cards: Amex, Delta, Maestro, MasterCard, Visa Details: 60 seats. 24 seats outside. Car park. Vegetarian meals. No children under 6. No smoking. Wheelchair access (not WC). No music. No mobile phones Accommodation: 29 rooms

The price given next to the cooking score is based on the cost of a typical three-course dinner for one person, including coffee, house wine and service.

Tasting Room

13 Swinegate Court East, York YO1 8AJ
Tel: (01904) 627879
Website: www.thetastingroom.co.uk

Cooking 3 | **Modern European** | **£42**

On a courtyard in the city's back streets, the Tasting
Room describes itself as a bistro at lunchtimes and
a candlelit restaurant in the evenings. Sandwiches,
salads, beef bourguignonne, and seared calf's liver
with champ, grilled pancetta and red wine gravy
are what to expect at lunchtimes. The kitchen
shows good technique and uses fine ingredients:
witness seared scallops attractively presented on
creamed celeriac with wilted spinach as an evening
starter, or a large bowl of bouillabaisse. Perfectly
timed roast beef fillet, accompanied by dauphinois
potatoes, buttered carrots, fine beans and a red wine
sauce, makes a traditional main course, or seared
hake might be partnered by a salad of fennel, saffron
and black pudding dressed with tapenade. Finish
with brioche bread-and-butter pudding with marmalade ice cream and custard. Service is casual,
friendly and knowledgeable, and the wine list offers
around a dozen by the glass, from £3.50, although
bottle prices are on the high side.

Chef: Russell Johnson **Proprietors:** Sally Robinson, Nigel
Stacey and Mike Staff **Open:** all week L 12 to 2.30, Mon to
Sat D 6 to 10 **Closed:** Sun Jan to Apr, bank hol Mon **Meals:**
alc (main courses L £9.50 to £18, D £13 to £20). Set D Mon
to Thur £17.95 (2 courses) to £20.95. Light L menu available
Mon to Sat **Service:** not inc **Cards:** Delta, Maestro,
MasterCard, Visa **Details:** 38 seats. 20 seats outside.
Vegetarian meals. No children under 4. No smoking.
Wheelchair access (not WC). Music

Scotland

MAP 11 ABERDEEN – Aberdeen

Silver Darling

Pocra Quay, North Pier, Aberdeen AB11 5DQ
Tel: (01224) 576229

Cooking 6 | **Seafood** | **£55**

The rooftop site at the harbour entrance affords
commanding views of the Aberdeen waterfront,
with golfers in the background. For the full dramatic backdrop of changing light, go for a summer
evening booking. Silver darling is a local name for
herring, although these may well be conspicuous
by their absence on the menus. What will be there
is Didier Dejean's acutely honed, intelligent
cooking, which makes the most of the produce of
the sea, as is only proper in the setting.

As always with fish and seafood, timing is all.
'There is a particular preciseness in the steaming of
fish,' noted an observant reporter, 'which produces
a succulence we have not experienced anywhere
else,' added to which the sauces, dressings and
emulsions, while positive in their impact, never
upstage the main ingredient. Squid is marinated
and grilled, sauced with mustard and seaweed, and
accompanied by lobster claw salad. A tricky-
sounding starter of langoustines stuffed with
smoked salmon has been brought off with great
panache, teamed with samphire and shimeji mushrooms. At main course, there may be a choice of
farmed or wild sea bass, dressed with fennel,
piquillos and dill, or a successful presentation of
pepper-dusted monkfish with wilted lettuce and
asparagus. Meat eaters could opt for rosemary-
crusted roast rack of lamb with couscous. Desserts
have disappointed on occasion – an under-par
tarte Tatin, for example – but might impress with
the likes of chocolate pancake roulade with Grand
Marnier mousse and mascarpone ice cream. Wines
are predominantly French, with house selections
starting at £18.50, or £3.95 a glass.

Chef: Didier Dejean **Proprietors:** Didier Dejean and Karen
Murray **Open:** Mon to Fri L 12 to 1.30, Mon to Sat D 7 to
9.30 **Closed:** 2 weeks Christmas to New Year **Meals:** alc
(main courses L £10.50 to £11.50, D £19.50 to £21.50)
Service: not inc, 10% for parties of 10 or more **Cards:** Amex,
Delta, Diners, Maestro, MasterCard, Visa **Details:** 50 seats.
No smoking. Music

MAP 11 ACHILTIBUIE – Highland

Summer Isles Hotel

Achiltibuie IV26 2YG
Tel: (01854) 622282
Website: www.summerisleshotel.co.uk

Cooking 5 | **Modern European** | **£55**

Once you leave the A835 north of Ullapool, the
journey becomes quite an adventure. A single-
track road with passing places runs on for 15 miles
before you reach the hotel, its luxurious but simple
ambience made all the more delightful by the
stunning landscape it inhabits. The approach is
highly commended by visitors – 'unobtrusive,
helpful, absolutely excellent' – as is the way the
service of no-choice dinner menus at a single
sitting is carried out without anyone feeling in the
least bit dragooned. The five courses are often
arranged in surprising order, allowing fine local
seafood to show to its best main-course advantage.
Thus might herbed lobster in champagne butter
sauce be preceded by roast Shetland salmon with
pesto, and then pigeon breast on toasted brioche
with duxelles. Another night might produce a
smoked haddock flan with asparagus, followed by a
fried crab cake with cucumber and dill, and then
saddle of black-faced lamb with potato and courgette rösti and rosemary jus. It is all enthusiastically
approved by reporters, with the seafood perhaps
inevitably getting the palm. A cheese selection
intervenes before the dessert trolley trundles
around, chocolate roulade and bread-and-butter
pudding evoking particular raptures.

Various *cru* Beaujolais and German wines, often unfairly overlooked as food matches, feature on a broad-minded and inspiring list that plumbs France thoroughly before demonstrating equal confidence in the New World. French country wines start at £12.50.

Chef: Chris Firth-Bernard   Proprietors: Mark and Gerry Irvine Open: all week 12.30 to 2, 8 (1 sitting) Closed: 17 Oct to mid-Mar Meals: alc L (main courses £15 to £30). Set D £49. Bar menu available Service: net prices Cards: MasterCard, Visa Details: 30 seats. Car park. No children under 8. Children's helpings. No smoking. Wheelchair access (also WC). No music. No mobile phones Accommodation: 13 rooms

MAP 11   ANNBANK – South Ayrshire

Enterkine House

Annbank KA6 5AL
Tel: (01292) 520580
Website: www.enterkine.com

Cooking 4 | Modern European | £45

An impressive 310 acres of grounds surround this large white 1930s house. The warm welcome and relaxed air is enhanced by fresh flowers, plump sofas and log fires. While taking ideas from further afield, the kitchen draws on excellent local and regional produce and cooks it in a straightforward modern style that is very much in keeping with its surroundings. The set-price menus (with supplements) might open with scallops teamed with saffron risotto and smoked langoustine beurre blanc, or maybe twice-baked goats' cheese soufflé, then take in a sorbet or a soup such as roast parsnip velouté. Next might come saddle of black-faced Castle Douglas lamb with pesto potatoes, ratatouille and rosemary jus, or fillets of halibut and salmon with lobster potatoes, French beans and yellow pepper sauce. Meals end with desserts such as cinnamon parfait with stem ginger ice cream and baby pears. House wines at £18.50 start the bidding on a list that puts the emphasis on France.

Chef: Paul Moffat   Proprietor: Oswald Browne   Open: all week 12.30 to 2 (3 Sun), 7 to 9 Meals: Set L £16.50 (2 courses) to £18.50, Set D Sun to Thur £21.95 (2 courses) to £29.50, Set D Fri and Sat £40 Service: not inc Cards: Amex, Diners, Maestro, MasterCard, Visa Details: 70 seats. Car park. Vegetarian meals. Children's helpings. No smoking. Music. No mobile phones Accommodation: 6 rooms

MAP 11   ANSTRUTHER – Fife

Cellar

24 East Green, Anstruther KY10 3AA
Tel: (01333) 310378

Cooking 6 | Modern Seafood | £49

This long-established venue on the east coast of Fife is housed in a 400-year-old building that has seen sterling service in the cause of Scots gastronomy. Having been a cooperage and then a smokery, it has for the last quarter-century been the setting for Peter Jukes's fastidiously seasonal seafood cookery.

Fixed-price menus keep it simple, and so does the cooking, the better to show off the immaculately fresh marine fare on offer. Start with local crab served only with a few leaves and lemon mayonnaise, or alternatively with a quiche of prawns and smoked sea trout. An intermediate course might bring a bowl of classical gratinated fish soup based on rich shellfish stock.

Regulars return for main courses such as sea bass with chopped black olives and a niçoise dressing, but seared tuna may be treated as meatily as prime fillet steak, arriving with caramelised onions, wild mushrooms, potato gratin and a sauce of crushed black peppercorns. A warming winter pudding in these northern parts is often appreciated, as in date and ginger sponge with toffee pecan sauce and cinnamon ice cream. 'Really enjoyable food, well served,' was the straightforward verdict of one reporter.

Runs of Alsace varietals, premier cru Chablis and New Zealand Sauvignon suit the orientation of the menus, and prices throughout are reasonably fair. A full page of half-bottles allows for more expansive choice. House wines go from £16.50.

Chef: Peter Jukes Proprietors: Peter and Susan Jukes Open: Wed to Sat L 1 to 1.30, Tue to Sat D 7 to 9.30 Closed: 24 to 27 Dec Meals: Set L £17.50 (2 courses) to £21.50, Set D £28.50 (2 courses) to £38.50 Service: not inc Cards: Amex, Delta, Diners, Maestro, MasterCard, Visa Details: 40 seats. No children under 8. No smoking. Occasional music

MAP 11 **ARCHIESTOWN** – Moray

Archiestown Hotel   AR

Archiestown AB38 7QL
Tel: (01340) 810218

In the heart of Speyside, this eighteenth-century hotel is the focal point of the village. The décor is traditional and furnishings are comfortable. The lunch menu has smoked haddock hotpot (£7.50) rubbing shoulders with spicy Thai burger (£8.50). Dinner might start with twice-baked Mull of Kintyre Cheddar soufflé (£7.50), to be followed by fillet steak with haggis in a whisky and mustard sauce (£22.50), or whole roast sea bass with prawns and lime butter (£18). Finish with Eve's pudding with whisky custard (£5.50). House wines are £14. Accommodation. Open all week.

MAP 11 **ARDEONAIG** – Stirling

Ardeonaig Hotel

Ardeonaig FK21 8SU
Tel: (01567) 820400
Website: www.ardeonaighotel.co.uk

Cooking 4 │ South African/Scottish │ £46

'The ultimate escape-from-it-all hotel,' wrote one visitor of this rambling, white-painted building on the shore of Loch Tay. The dining room is classically restrained, with cream curtains and crisp white tablecloths, while South African chef/proprietor Pete Gottgens is happy to spend time chatting to customers about the menu. Produce is locally sourced and presented with a South African slant; pan-fried squid with rocket leaves made 'an amazingly eye-catching display' at inspection, while plump Raven Rock mussels were served in a wine and shallot sauce. Both baked line-caught fillet of turbot, with mash and salad, and loin of venison, in a rich Pinotage-based sauce with rosemary, have been excellent examples of straightforward cooking, 'which impressed because of the respectful treatment of the raw materials'. Vegetables, including baby carrots and turnips, have been praised for their flavour, while homemade seed and raisin bread has been equally well received. Finish with traditional South African malva pudding, a kind of sticky toffee pudding with apricots.

The South African-only wine list is personally annotated, and an 'open bottle policy' operates, so that you pay only for what you drink. Prices start at around £15.

> **Chef:** Pete Gottgens   **Proprietors:** Pete and Sara Gottgens **Open:** all week 12 to 3, 7 to 10 **Meals:** alc (main courses £9.50 to £24). Set L and D £26.50. Bistro menu available **Service:** not inc, 10% for parties of 8 or more **Cards:** Maestro, MasterCard, Visa **Details:** 44 seats. 40 seats outside. Car park. Vegetarian meals. No children under 12 in dining room. No smoking. Occasional music. No mobile phones **Accommodation:** 20 rooms

MAP 11 **AUCHTERARDER** – Perthshire & Kinross

Andrew Fairlie at Gleneagles

Auchterarder PH3 1NF
Tel: (01764) 694267
Website: www.andrewfairlie.com

Cooking 7 │ Modern French │ £85

Andrew Fairlie's restaurant is an autonomous business located in a windowless dining room on the ground floor of the five-star Gleneagles Hotel. Dark-green wood panelling and modern prints of Scottish landscapes create a pleasingly restrained mood, reflected also in the plain white tableware and spray of heather on each table. Only the jazz soundtrack jangles the nerves, especially of non-jazz lovers.

There is plenty of invention going on in the fixed-price menus, which are based on today's preference for modern French-influenced combinations that use classical technique. A velouté of ceps with a truffled poached duck egg might open a meal, and be followed by slow-cooked turbot with clam gratin. For others, it could be home-smoked lobster with herb and lime butter, then twice-cooked Anjou squab with kohlrabi ravioli.

Following the six-course tasting menu, a reporter emerged hugely satisfied with dishes that had included a roasted Skye scallop with pistachio butter and a frothing sauce of champagne and vanilla; an assemblage of herb gnocchi, both types of artichoke, lardons, rocket and Parmesan; and a main course of tenderloin and belly of pork with Savoy cabbage, black pudding and caramelised apple. Apple might also be the foundation of a dessert assiette, or you could opt for the likes of a slow-roasted peach with lemon thyme soufflé and vanilla ice cream. Chocolates with coffee turn out to be filled with cardamom, green tea and rose.

Youthful staff manage to counteract any impression of staidness the opulent surroundings impart. And while you might expect a weighty tome of a wine list in the context, instead there are but two pages of geographical listings. Prices, however, won't confound expectations, starting at £25 before spreading their wings.

> **Chef/Proprietor:** Andrew Fairlie   **Open:** Mon to Sat D only 7 to 10   **Closed:** 24 and 25 Dec, 3 weeks Jan   **Meals:** Set D £60 to £80   **Service:** not inc   **Cards:** Amex, Delta, Diners, Maestro, MasterCard, Visa   **Details:** 40 seats. Car park. Vegetarian meals. No children under 12. No smoking. Wheelchair access (also WC). Music. Air-conditioned

MAP 11   AULDEARN – Highland

Boath House

Auldearn IV12 5TE
Tel: (01667) 454896
Website: www.boath-house.com

Cooking 5 | **Franco-Scottish** | **£63**

'There's a sense of occasion' to dining at this impressive Regency house, noted one visitor, admiring the views over 20 acres of gardens, which include a lake. Don and Wendy Matheson's sympathetic restoration has kept many original features but presents them within a contemporary yet conservative setting, with high ceilings, white-framed sash windows and a full-height portico.

Chef Charles Lockley has been here for 10 years, providing an accomplished five-course dinner menu in which good-quality ingredients are handled inventively. The evening starts promptly at 7pm with an amuse-bouche of maybe foie gras and confit pork rounds in the lounge, moving through to start with a 'beautifully velvety' Jerusalem artichoke velouté with morels, or two sweet Uist dived scallops with crushed peas and Parma ham. At inspection, a main course of saddle of Shetland lamb was attractively presented with an aubergine, tomato and courgette galette, while 'fresh and bouncy' fillet of halibut was accompanied by a crab, fennel and orange salad. Small chunks of Scottish cheese precede dessert of, perhaps, vanilla rice pudding with an intriguing but successful sweet beetroot yoghurt and orange sorbet.

Service is pleasant, although sometimes overformal, while Mr Matheson makes his chatty pres-

ence known. Wines are mostly French, starting at £15-£18 for a handful of house choices. After that there's not much under £30 but it is an intelligent list that will cater to most.

> **Chef:** Charles Lockley   **Proprietors:** Don and Wendy Matheson   **Open:** Thur to Sun L 12.30 to 1.15, all week D 7 to 8.15   **Closed:** 1 week at Christmas   **Meals:** Set L £32.50, Set D £45   **Service:** not inc   **Cards:** Amex, Maestro, MasterCard, Visa   **Details:** 28 seats. Car park. Children's helpings. No smoking. Wheelchair access (also WC). Occasional music. No mobile phones   **Accommodation:** 6 rooms

MAP 11   BALLANTRAE – South Ayrshire

Glenapp Castle

Ballantrae KA26 0NZ
Tel: (01465) 831212
Website: www.glenappcastle.com

Cooking 6 | **French** | **£74**

Built in the nineteenth century, Glenapp Castle is a magnificent sight. Now a luxury retreat about a mile from Ballantrae (there is a distinct lack of signposting from the village), it is all panelled halls, opulent lounges and dining rooms, grand staircases, moulded ceilings, chandeliers, antiques and paintings. Matt Weedon rises to the stately occasion with no-choice, daily-changing five-course dinner menus that combine classical French technique with today's more exploratory culinary mode. Reports attest that the cooking is achieving heights of dizzying refinement of late, apparent as soon as the appetiser arrives, perhaps the velvety asparagus velouté with truffle oil that impressed at inspection. The standard thus set, subsequent dishes manage to maintain the pace. A starter of chicken and foie gras mousse with morels, broad beans and a foaming Gewurztraminer sauce has been a triumph of gentle strength, as is pan-fried red mullet with squat lobster, saffron risotto and bouillabaisse jus. Soft textures, bold seasoning and rich sauces define dishes such as a traditional fillet of beef in a red wine sauce, served with potato gratin and braised onions.

The quality of even the simplest preparations shines forth, so that a quenelle of Dunsyre Blue is expertly rendered, well matched by a lovely Pinot Noir jelly and good apple purée, as is a more complex nougatine dome filled with an intense strawberry sorbet and set on a 'well-nigh perfect' vanilla parfait in a pool of iced raspberry soup.

While the atmosphere is properly formal, it is far from intimidating.

The wine list shows a preference for France, especially Burgundy and Bordeaux, although some good, modern choices turn up elsewhere. Mark-ups don't give much quarter, with prices opening at £25 for New Zealand Sauvignon Blanc and Pinot Noir.

Chef: Matt Weedon **Proprietors:** Graham and Fay Cowan **Open:** all week D only 7 to 9 **Closed:** 1 Dec to 1 Apr **Meals:** Set D £55. Light L menu available **Service:** not inc **Cards:** Amex, Delta, Maestro, MasterCard, Visa **Details:** 34 seats. Car park. No children under 5 in dining room. Children's helpings. No smoking. Wheelchair access (also WC). No music. No mobile phones **Accommodation:** 17 rooms

---

MAP 11 BALLATER –
Aberdeenshire

Balgonie Country House

Braemar Place, Ballater AB35 5NQ
Tel: (013397) 55482
Website: www.balgonie-hotel.co.uk

Cooking 4 | **Modern Scottish** | **£56**

An air of tranquillity suffuses this smart, comfortably furnished Edwardian house, whose lofty windows give views across 'immaculate' gardens towards Glen Muick and Lochnagar. Good raw materials are at the heart of the daily-changing menus, with fish, meat and game sourced from local suppliers. Results extend from the relatively familiar (fillet of beef with roast potatoes, red onion confit and a red wine reduction), via a comforting caramelised French onion soup, to a more enterprising fillet of sea bass with butternut squash risotto, wilted spinach, roast cherry tomatoes and Pernod cream. Profiteroles show the style of the puddings, or you may end a meal with a selection of Scottish and Irish cheeses. Service has been described as 'first-class', and the wine list provides for most eventualities, although the majority now tip the scales at £20 or more.

Chef/Proprietor: John Finnie **Open:** all week 12.30 to 2 (reservations only), 7 to 9 **Closed:** 6 Jan to 31 Mar **Meals:** Set L £20, Set D £40 **Service:** not inc **Cards:** Amex, Delta, Diners, Maestro, MasterCard, Visa **Details:** 30 seats. Car park. Children's helpings. No smoking. Wheelchair access (also WC). No music **Accommodation:** 9 rooms

Darroch Learg

Braemar Road, Ballater AB35 5UX
Tel: (013397) 55443
Website: www.darrochlearg.co.uk

Cooking 6 | **Modern Scottish** | **£50**

A substantial-looking late-Victorian mansion just to the west of Ballater, Darroch Learg is full of large-windowed, spacious rooms with dark panelling, the Scottish baronial manner done with admirable confidence and taste. At its heart, David Mutter's kitchen operation conscientiously sources the prime ingredients on which his modern Scottish cooking is based.

Deeside lamb, beef and venison, fish from the Aberdeen catch, and Loch Fyne seafood are all present and correct, and many of the staples are produced in-house, including breads, pasta and shortbread. The culinary style keeps to a country-house idiom, and satisfies mightily as it does so. Dinner might begin simply with a smoked haddock tart with Parmesan and chives, or with roast monkfish and mussels in an Indian-spiced velouté, before offering best Aberdeen beef fillet as a main course, served with crushed butter beans, wild mushrooms and a sauce spiked with thyme. Raw materials are handled with zest and respect, as when a main course of sea trout arrives with truffled potatoes, asparagus and peas, and desserts are a roll-call of favourites, encompassing cheesecake with berries, warm chocolate brownie with crème fraîche, and classic lemon tart. The six-course tasting menu elicits plaudits, and staff are commended for their knowledge and warmth.

A large wine list zips about the vinous globe with great brio, taking time, though, to find the star producers and describe each listing exhaustively. A list of fine sherries kicks things off, and the imaginatively chosen house selections start at £23.

Chef: David Mutter **Proprietors:** the Franks family **Open:** Sun L 12.30 to 2, all week D 7 to 9 **Closed:** Christmas, last 3 weeks Jan **Meals:** Set L £22, Set D £40 to £45 **Service:** net prices **Cards:** Amex, Delta, Diners, Maestro, MasterCard, Visa **Details:** 48 seats. 8 seats outside. Car park. Children's helpings. No smoking. Wheelchair access (also men's WC). No music **Accommodation:** 17 rooms

Green Inn

9 Victoria Road, Ballater AB35 5QQ
Tel: (013397) 55701
Website: www.green-inn.com

| Cooking 4 | Modern Scottish/French | £51 |

Improvements abound at this solid-stone inn, with the addition of a conservatory dining room this year. Chef Chris O'Halloran is the owners' son and, supported by his parents' efficient and friendly front-of-house service, he keeps his menus small but perfectly formed. A separate vegetarian menu might start with ravioli of quail's eggs, spinach and wild mushrooms flavoured with truffle and Parmesan beurre blanc, and go on to a warm salad of globe artichokes with pommes Anna and a dressing of Cabernet Sauvignon and walnut oil. The main menu offers four choices per course. Warm venison salad croustillant with Cumberland sauce and game jus, and grilled red snapper with fennel fondue and bouillabaisse cappuccino are typically inventive starters. Main courses are well presented, as in roast partridge with crépinettes, caramelised apples and pears, roast baby onions, foie gras and a wild mushroom sausage in roasting juices, or steamed fillet of sole with langoustine ravioli, julienne of vegetables, and shellfish cream. Desserts are no less accomplished: witness a banana soufflé with rum and banana ice cream and caramel sauce. There are useful descriptions on the wine list, which opens with half a dozen house recommendations from France and the southern hemisphere at £16.95 and £17.95.

Chef: Chris O'Halloran Proprietors: Trevor and Evelyn O'Halloran Open: Mon to Sat D only 7 to 9 Meals: Set D £29.50 (2 courses) to £35 Service: not inc Cards: Delta, Maestro, MasterCard, Visa Details: 30 seats. Vegetarian meals. No smoking. Wheelchair access (not WC). Music Accommodation: 3 rooms

 This symbol means that the restaurant has elected to participate in *The Good Food Guide's* £5 voucher scheme (see 'Using The Good Food Guide' for details).

 MAP 11 BALQUHIDDER – Stirling

Monachyle Mhor

Balquhidder FK19 8PQ
Tel: (01877) 384622
Website: www.monachylemhor.com

| Cooking 5 | Modern Scottish | £57 |

This secluded country house, in a hauntingly lovely glen, enjoys plenty of peace and quiet, which might well be down to the condition of the road you take to reach it: with few passing places, it is narrow enough to deter casual visitors. The view of Lochs Viol and Doine from the conservatory dining room may emphasise the isolation, but the place has a contemporary feel and the kitchen is serious. Tom Lewis is justly proud of his commitment to quality Scottish produce – lamb and game come from the estate, there's own-grown organic produce – and he takes a lively approach to whatever comes his way, turning out a starter of vanilla-cured gravad lax with a tian of white crabmeat, a demi-tasse of onion soup with balsamic onion topping, or a simple salad of tartare of beef with a caper and white truffle oil vinaigrette. Combinations are interesting without being outlandish: witness fillet of pork and a breast of wood pigeon with port- and orange-braised red cabbage and a ginger and game jus. To finish, there's quince poached in Earl Grey, topped with walnut and teamed with lemon and ginger pannacotta, or lemon and passion-fruit crème brûlée. Six house selections at £16 (white) and £18 (red) are the only offerings under £20 on the varietally organised wine list.

Chef/Proprietor: Tom Lewis Open: all week 12 to 1.45, 7 to 8.45 Closed: 5 Jan to 1 Feb Meals: alc L (main courses £15 to £17). Set L £29, Set D £44. Snack L menu available Service: not inc Cards: Maestro, MasterCard, Visa Details: 40 seats. 16 seats outside. Car park. No children under 12. Children's helpings. No smoking. Wheelchair access (also WC). Occasional music Accommodation: 13 rooms

MAP 11 **BLAIRGOWRIE –** Perthshire & Kinross

Kinloch House Hotel

Blairgowrie PH10 6SG
Tel: (01250) 884237
Website: www.kinlochhouse.com

Cooking 5 | Scottish | £57

Kinloch House is a creeper-clad, early Victorian stone manor on a human scale, with much dark oak beaming and panelling, and views over lush green pastures and grazing cattle. Andrew May has stepped up from sous-chef, and is intent on maintaining the relaxed, country-house style of cooking for which the hotel has been renowned. Terrine of lamb confit is appositely teamed with apricot chutney and marinated sultanas, or you might prefer to start with red mullet escabèche and puréed herbs. Limited fish options might include monkfish with leek risotto and a mussel and basil sauce, but meats are the business. A lunch dish of cold, sliced roast ribeye had impeccable flavour, and the kitchen has the confidence to send it out with just potato salad and leaves for company. In the evenings, expect the likes of loin of venison with red cabbage and dauphinois, braised celeriac and port.

Desserts range from treacle-dark date pudding with vanilla ice cream and butterscotch sauce to more-contemporary pannacotta with summer berry compote. Well-judged, unintrusive service is commended. Burgundy is the wine list's strongest suit, with gem after gem, from Corton-Perrières to Meursault-Blagny, to tempt those heedless of thrift. Elsewhere, it is sound rather than exciting, but house selections from £18, and wines by the glass from £6, offer encouraging variety.

Chef: Andrew May **Proprietors:** the Allen family **Open:** all week 12 to 2, 7 to 9 **Meals:** Set L £17.50 to £23.50. Set D £39.50. Light bar L menu available **Service:** not inc **Cards:** Amex, Maestro, MasterCard, Visa **Details:** 50 seats. Car park. Children's helpings. No children under 7 at D. Jacket. No smoking. Wheelchair access (also men's WC). No music. No mobile phones **Accommodation:** 18 rooms

 This symbol means that the wine list is well above the average.

MAP 11 **CAIRNDOW** – Argyll & Bute

Loch Fyne Oyster Bar

Clachan, Cairndow PA26 8BL
Tel: (01499) 600236
Website: www.lochfyne.com

Cooking 2 | Seafood | £41

The crowds flock to this unpretentious restaurant in search of the fresh seafood that is the kitchen's strength: sweet, succulent oysters, a pair of Loch Fyne kippers, or the *pièce de résistance*: a grand seafood platter, preceded, perhaps, by fish soup. A different vein is tapped in a first course of Kinglas fillet of smoked salmon, served sashimi-style with wasabi and soy sauce, while Arctic char (from Loch Duart) baked with herbs admirably demonstrates the restaurant's simple formula: to cook the freshest of fish (and meat) without any frills via a philosophy of total sustainability. To this end they farm their own oysters and mussels, source salmon from small independent producers and shellfish from local fishermen, and this intelligent response to the environment and circumstances extends to local meat such as venison and beef. Service is good, and the 20 or so reasonably priced wines (from £11.95) include a fair proportion by the glass and half-bottle.

Chef: Tracy Wyatt **Proprietor:** Loch Fyne Oysters Ltd **Open:** all week 9 to 9 (may close earlier Nov to Mar) **Closed:** 25 and 26 Dec, 1 and 2 Jan **Meals:** alc (main courses £6 to £29.50) **Service:** not inc **Cards:** Amex, Maestro, MasterCard, Visa **Details:** 150 seats. Car park. Vegetarian meals. Children's helpings. No smoking. Wheelchair access (also WC). Occasional music. No mobile phones

MAP 11 **CARRADALE –** Argyll & Bute

Dunvalanree Hotel

Port Righ Bay, Carradale PA28 6SE
Tel: (01583) 431226
Website: www.dunvalanree.com

Cooking 2 | Modern British | £34

This stylish cream and brown three-storey building, which dates from the thirties, has been thoughtfully refurbished, with Alyson and Alan Milstead offering a warm and personal welcome.

403

It's in a lovely spot, perched on a cliff above Port Righ Bay, with magnificent views of Arran, so it's fitting that the hands-on couple have a 'green' philosophy – they rear their own chickens and source local produce, including Carradale shellfish, smoked fish from Campbeltown and lamb from Ifferdale. It's Alyson who works the stoves and her style is straightforward and simple, starting perhaps with Campbeltown haggis with neeps and whisky cream, while to follow there might be rack of Saddell lamb with well-timed and 'deliciously sweet' carrots and leeks. To finish, hot cross bun and butter pudding has been a well-received seasonal novelty. The minimalist global wine list starts at £11.95, but they offer over 50 malt whiskies and Arran beer.

> **Chef/Proprietor:** Alyson Milstead **Open:** all week D only 7.30 (1 sitting) **Meals:** Set D £21 (2 courses) to £24 **Service:** not inc **Cards:** Amex, Delta, Maestro, MasterCard, Visa **Details:** 24 seats. Car park. Vegetarian meals. Children's helpings. No smoking. Music **Accommodation:** 5 rooms

MAP 11 | CLACHAN-SEIL – Argyll & Bute

Willowburn Hotel

Clachan-Seil, by Oban PA34 4TJ
Tel: (01852) 300276
Website: www.willowburn.co.uk

Cooking 3 | Modern Scottish/French | £47

On the island of Seil, reached by a humpback bridge, this long, whitewashed building has views over Clachan Sound and the hills beyond, with a telescope in the lounge for guests to use. Chris Wolfe 'shows a total commitment to sourcing the best and freshest local produce', as one reader put it, and the garden supplies herbs, soft fruit and vegetables. Canapés – perhaps a pastry case of light pâté – get the four-course dinners off to a fine start. Turbot mousseline with lobster and lemon sauce, or roast quail salad with a bittersweet beer jelly might begin, followed by a sorbet or soup: perhaps well-balanced asparagus and mushroom. The main course might be 'pink and tender' rack of lamb with sun-dried tomato and pine-nut risotto and a 'sharp, refreshing' kiwi-fruit and mint chutney, or medallions of roast venison on potato scones with a juniper sauce, with perhaps fillet of turbot the fish alternative. High praise has gone to a 'lovely, light' orange soufflé with chocolate and Cointreau sorbet. The annotated wine list is international in scope, with even Thailand represented. A number of bottles are below £20, and four house wines are £13.50.

> **Chef:** Chris Wolfe **Proprietors:** Chris and Jan Wolfe **Open:** all week D only 7 (1 sitting) **Closed:** mid-Nov to mid-Mar **Meals:** Set D £36 **Service:** not inc **Cards:** Delta, Maestro, MasterCard, Visa **Details:** 20 seats. Car park. Vegetarian meals. No children under 8. No smoking. Music. No mobile phones **Accommodation:** 7 rooms

MAP 11 | COLBOST – Highland

Three Chimneys

Colbost, Dunvegan, Isle of Skye IV55 8ZT
Tel: (01470) 511258
Website: www.threechimneys.co.uk

Cooking 5 | Modern Scottish | £65

The Spears' ultra-refined restaurant-with-rooms, on a single-track loch-side road that cuts through the Skye moorland, is a haven of relaxed civility. Over 20 years of service to Scottish catering have smoothed the front-of-house operation to a burnished gleam, and the kitchen under Michael Smith is as dedicated to fine Highland produce as it ever was.

The menus evolve at a stately pace, making no sudden movements but aiming to show off prime materials at their simple best. Bracadale crab forms the generous topping for a light, crisp tart, accompanied by well-judged lemon-balm butter, while local lobster might appear with new potatoes in a fresh and appetising salad starter. It may well prove equally hard to resist choosing seafood for a main course when there might be top-notch turbot with tiger prawns in a shellfish sauce on offer. If you do decide to resist, however, it will likely be because Highland venison fillet with skirlie potato cakes, baby neeps, braised red cabbage and a game jus flavoured with blueberries and juniper has caught your eye. Desserts such as chocolate pudding with boozy black cherries have drawn plaudits. 'Nan's lemon trickle cake' is the partner for lemon posset, or there are good Scottish cheeses with home-made oatcakes.

The thoughtfully chosen wine list embraces all the major countries, with plenty of half-bottles and good notes. Highlights include Rolly-Gassmann's Alsace Gewürztraminer, Hans Zenner's Sicilian Nero d'Avola red, and Henschke's Julius Riesling from the Eden Valley,

South Australia. Prices start at £17.95 for red and white Vins de Pays des Côtes de Thongue.

Chef: Michael Smith Proprietors: Eddie and Shirley Spear
Open: Mon to Sat L 12.30 to 2, all week D 6.30 to 9.30
Closed: L Nov to Mar, 3 weeks Jan Meals: Set L £21 (2 courses) to £27, Set D £47.50 to £55 Service: not inc
Cards: Amex, Delta, Maestro, MasterCard, Visa Details: 32 seats. 6 seats outside. Car park. Vegetarian meals. No children under 8. Children's helpings. No smoking. Wheelchair access (not WC). No music Accommodation: 6 rooms

MAP 11 COLONSAY – Argyll & Bute

Isle of Colonsay Hotel

NEW ENTRY

Colonsay PA61 7YP
Tel: (01951) 200316
Website: www.thecolonsay.com

Cooking 2 | Modern Scottish | £32

Colonsay is a remote, sparsely populated island rich in wildlife and archaeological remains – just the place to get away from it all. So for one visitor, it was quite a surprise 'to find a spanking new boutique hotel just 100 metres from the ferry'. With the bar serving as the island's social hub (and the place for light lunches and supper), and the airy, contemporary dining room the setting for dinner, the transformation of this eighteenth-century inn by 'the island laird and others' is to be applauded. The kitchen's approach is focused on island produce, some from its own garden, and there's a strong accent on fish from local boats. Robust flavours in a game terrine, and red deer served with red cabbage, broccoli and pepper sauce were highlights at an inspection dinner, as were home-made bread rolls and deliciously fresh scallops with green split peas, carrot salad and herb oil. Service is 'really committed' and the brief wine list covers most bases, opening with house selections from £11.50.

Chefs: Annabel Taylor and Simon Wallwork Proprietors: Alex and June Howard, Dan Jago, Mark Matza, and Hugo Arnold Open: all week D only 6 to 9 Meals: alc (main courses £8.50 to £14). Bar meals available L and D Service: not inc Cards: Maestro, MasterCard, Visa Details: 30 seats. Car park. Children's helpings. No smoking. Wheelchair access (not WC). Music Accommodation: 9 rooms

MAP 11 CRINAN – Argyll & Bute

Crinan Hotel, Westward Restaurant

Crinan PA31 8SR
Tel: (01546) 830261
Website: www.crinanhotel.com

Cooking 4 | Modern European | £60

A soothing sense of seclusion surrounds this substantial white-painted loch-side hotel, which stands at the end of a narrow country road with views across the Crinan Canal basin towards Jura and Islay. Picture windows in the spacious dining room allow diners to soak up the full majesty of the setting, while enjoying some accomplished modern country-house cooking. There are never more than four choices at each stage on the four-course dinner menu, but no shortage of appealing dishes, starting perhaps with ravioli of West Coast crab with roast courgette and langoustine velouté, or roast saddle of rabbit with Stornoway black pudding, roast fennel and garlic cream. A no-choice intermediate fish course typically produces langoustine bisque before the main event, which might be roast rack of Argyll lamb and kidney with Maxim potatoes, roast baby carrots and leeks, and a redcurrant jus, or pan-seared Islay monkfish on tagliatelle with braised chicory and herb glaçage. Poached pear sabayon, or caramelised white chocolate tart with raspberry ice cream might round off the meal, with a savoury alternative of perhaps Stilton and avocado salad. A pair of varietal house wines from Chile at £19.50 open a varied international list.

Chef: Scott Kennedy Proprietors: Nicolas and Frances Ryan Open: all week D only 7 to 8.30 (9 summer) Closed: Christmas Meals: Set D £45. Bar menu available Service: not inc Cards: Delta, MasterCard, Visa Details: 40 seats. 20 seats outside. Car park. Children's helpings. No smoking. Wheelchair access (also WC). No music Accommodation: 20 rooms

 This symbol means that accommodation is available at this establishment.

MAP 11 CROSSMICHAEL – Dumfries & Galloway

Plumed Horse

Main Street, Crossmichael DG7 3AU
Tel: (01556) 670333
Website: www.plumedhorse.co.uk

Cooking 6 | Modern European | £52

Since he opened it in 1998, Tony Borthwick's small, unpretentious restaurant next to the pub in the middle of a snoozy village has been making discreet but powerful waves. The humble yellow dining room contains no extraneous décor to distract from the seriously classy cooking, which is naturally centred on impeccable Scottish meats, seafood, and locally grown organic vegetables, together with pedigree poultry from France.

All this comes together in dishes that speak boldly and eloquently for themselves in many tongues. 'There is no suggestion of *sotto voce* in this cooking,' commented a reporter, who sang the praises of a main course of duck leg confit on spiced beetroot and red cabbage, served with the salt-strewn breast and a slice of seared foie gras on a mound of Castellino lentils, a dish of muscular but harmonious flavours. Complexity marks fish preparations too, so that roast halibut might arrive with saffron and crab mashed potato, asparagus, a sautéed scallop, and a sauce of smoked salmon and Avruga butter.

Choices are kept to four at each course, which makes sense when there is so much going on in each plate. Loch Arthur Cheddar, for example, might be worked into a twice-baked soufflé, which comes – as soufflés will – with an ice cream, this one made of roast onions and port. Salting is more assertive than is quite the fashion nowadays, but not usually to the detriment of a dish, and its impact on the palate will later be gentled by finely wrought desserts. Passion-fruit délices turns out to be a sort of cheesecake, with a thin layer of jelly on top, served with a richly rewarding white chocolate ice cream. Down-to-earth, chatty staff help to relax diners, even if their knowledge of the menu may easily be found wanting. Clarets ascending to 1996 Latour form the backbone of a list that does a brisk, efficient job in a few countries. Prices start at £15.

STOP PRESS: Tony Borthwick is moving the Plumed Horse to 54 Henderson Street, Leith, Edinburgh. See the restaurant's website for details.

Chefs: Tony Borthwick and Malcolm Kirkpatrick Proprietor: Tony Borthwick Open: Tue to Fri L 12.30 to 1, Tue to Sat D 7 to 9; also open one Sun L per month Closed: 25 and 26 Dec, 1 and 2 Jan, 2 weeks Jan, 2 weeks Sept Meals: alc exc Sun L (main courses £19 to £21). Set L Tue to Fri £23, Set L Sun £25 Service: not inc Cards: Delta, Maestro, MasterCard, Visa Details: 28 seats. No smoking. Wheelchair access (also WC). Occasional music. No mobile phones. Air-conditioned

MAP 11 CUPAR – Fife

Ostlers Close

25 Bonnygate, Cupar KY15 4BU
Tel: (01334) 655574
Website: www.ostlersclose.co.uk

Cooking 5 | Modern Scottish | £48

Ostlers Close has become a hive of industry, largely centred on the burgeoning kitchen garden. Fruit, vegetables and unusual varieties of herbs can thus be used in the kitchen within half an hour of their being picked, with bilberries looking set fair to be this year's cranberries in the fashion stakes. Other local produce naturally features strongly in Jimmy Graham's cooking, which is presented in the homely format of handwritten menus in a comfortable red dining room.

Roast fillet of monkfish makes a robust starter, topped as it is with pine nuts and sultanas and served in a sherry-laced potato soup. If you've started with something meaty such as pigeon breast with black pudding, haricots and beetroot and port sauce, you might then opt for the main-course selection of Pittenweem market seafood, lavishly sauced with champagne. That fondness for boosting sauces with alcohol, in preference to dairy fats, is about emphasising natural flavour rather than aiming for extraneous richness. In any case, you can get as rich as you like at dessert stage, when there might be pear tarte Tatin with ice cream and butterscotch sauce to go at. Wines start at £16.

Chef: Jimmy Graham Proprietors: Jimmy and Amanda Graham Open: Sat L 12.15 to 1.30, Tue to Sat D 7 to 9.30 Closed: 25 and 26 Dec, 1 and 2 Jan, 2 weeks Easter, 2 weeks Oct Meals: alc (main courses L £10.50 to £15, D £18 to £19.50) Service: not inc Cards: Amex, Delta, Maestro, MasterCard, Visa Details: 26 seats. Vegetarian meals. No children under 6 at D. Children's helpings. No smoking. Wheelchair access (not WC). No music. No mobile phones

MAP 11 DALRY – North Ayrshire

Braidwoods

Drumastle Mill Cottage, Dalry KA24 4LN
Tel: (01294) 833544
Website: www.braidwoods.co.uk

| Cooking 6 | Modern Scottish | £45 |

The whitewashed building in the midst of rolling countryside retains its cottagey character outside but has been well renovated within. A pair of dining areas has the dark beams and bare-stone walls of old, but there are modern pictures, smart napery, and a civilised, informal approach.

Keith and Nicola Braidwood have taken local sourcing to new levels, calling on their immediate neighbour for beef and lamb. Sourcing throughout is of a high order, though, with Gressingham duck, Arbroath smokies, and scallops from Wester Ross among the lures. The menus are kept within reasonable limits, and there is much to commend. An inspection visit kicked off robustly with crisp duck confit, brilliantly rendered and served on intense Puy lentils in a duck stock reduction. A soup or salad then intervenes, the former perhaps a judiciously textured curried prawn cream.

Precise timing brings lustre to a main course of grilled sea bass on langoustine and pea risotto, while squab pigeon might appear two ways, the breast roasted, the legs slowly cooked, bedded on crunchy chopped leeks scattered with mustard seeds that popped on the tongue. Strong, complementary flavours distinguish desserts such as caramelised lime and lemon cream with a compote of champagne rhubarb, or pecan parfait with a sharp coulis of raspberries and tayberries. Iain Mellis supplies pedigree British farmhouse cheeses.

Not only is the food informed by the seasons but wines are too, with a page of house recommendations evolving as the year goes by. The house wines themselves open with de Wetshof Chardonnay from South Africa at £15.95, and the main list gives equal billing to the newer winemaking countries as to Europe, with plenty of quality all the way through.

> **Chefs/Proprietors:** Keith and Nicola Braidwood **Open:** Wed to Sun L 12 to 1.30 (Sun L Sept to Apr only), Tue to Sat D 7 to 9 **Closed:** 25 and 26 Dec, first 3 weeks Jan, first 2 weeks Sept **Meals:** Set L Wed to Sat £17 (2 courses) to £20, Set L Sun £25, Set D £33 to £38 **Service:** not inc **Cards:** Amex, Delta, Diners, Maestro, MasterCard, Visa **Details:** 24 seats. Car park. No children under 12 at D. No smoking. No music. No mobile phones

MAP 11 DORNOCH – Highland

Quail

Castle Street, Dornoch IV25 3SN
Tel: (01862) 811811
Website: www.2quail.com

| Cooking 4 | Modern European–Plus | £48 |

'Excellent materials, well handled and well timed' was the verdict from one diner at this unassuming restaurant with just three rooms. Michael and Kerensa Carr are hands-on and hospitable. In fact, the home-from-home atmosphere pervades throughout as the book-lined lounge is cosy, while the dining room, also home to many books, is as pleasant as Kerensa's super-efficient service. With just a dozen covers you can be sure of the personal touch and Michael's four-course menu makes the most of local produce, treating high-quality raw materials with respect and imagination.

At inspection, the four-course no-choice menu opened with Spanish air-dried ham, well matched with Parmesan shavings and fennel; followed by 'beautifully fresh and delicate' supreme of halibut with asparagus mousse. For main course, well-hung beef fillet was accompanied by an intensely flavoured stock and wine jus, and vegetables including carefully cooked French beans. And for dessert, fresh raspberries bursting with flavour accompanied caramelised raspberry tart with Drambuie ice cream. The 70-bin wine list, from £14, looks mostly to France.

> **Chef:** Michael Carr **Proprietors:** Michael and Kerensa Carr **Open:** Tue to Sat D only 7.30 to 9.30 **Closed:** 1 week at Christmas, 2 weeks Feb/Mar **Meals:** Set D £37 **Service:** not inc **Cards:** Amex, Delta, Maestro, MasterCard, Visa **Details:** 12 seats. No smoking. Wheelchair access (not WC). Occasional music. No mobile phones **Accommodation:** 3 rooms

MAP 11 DUFFTOWN – Moray

La Faisanderie

2 Balvenie Street, Dufftown AB55 4AD
Tel: (01340) 821273
Website: www.dufftown.co.uk/lafaisanderie.htm

| Cooking 3 | Franco-Scottish | £36 |

Once a greengrocer and fish-and-chip shop, La Faisanderie occupies a granite corner building near the clock tower on the main square. The split-level dining room has the atmosphere of a French bistro, thanks to a plain wooden floor, rural artefacts and music. Amanda Bestwick is calmly efficient front-of-house, while Eric Obry cooks in a largely French style using fine Scottish produce, especially seasonal game. Wild boar and chestnut terrine with red cabbage relish, or a roast parcel of hot-smoked salmon with caper vinaigrette showcase the merging of two countries. Among main courses, seared breast of mallard in an orange and sage glaze may be partnered by pumpkin gratin, and noisette of lamb with swede purée, haggis croquettes and a whisky and mustard sauce. Quince and apple tarte Tatin or prune and Armagnac crème brûlée are fine notes to end on, and there's always the Scottish and French cheeseboard, served with oatcakes. The reasonable French wine list opens at £9.90.

Chef: Eric Obry Proprietors: Amanda Bestwick and Eric Obry Open: Thur to Mon L 12 to 1.30, Wed to Mon D 6 to 8.30 (7 to 9 Fri and Sat) Closed: Wed D Nov to Mar, 3 weeks Nov, 25, 26 and 31 Dec, 1 and 2 Jan Meals: alc (main courses £9.50 to £17.50). Set L £13.50 (2 courses) to £16.80, Set D £25 Service: not inc Cards: Delta, Maestro, MasterCard, Visa Details: 26 seats. Children's helpings. No smoking. Wheelchair access (also WC). Music

MAP 11 DUMFRIES – Dumfries & Galloway

Linen Room NEW ENTRY

53 St Michael Street, Dumfries DG1 2QB
Tel: (01387) 255689
Website: www.linenroom.com

Cooking 4 | **Modern European** | **£43**

The Linen Room is in an unassuming street of shops, but, inside, an attempt has been made to create a suave, sophisticated look by painting walls black or white, setting properly dressed tables well apart to give a 'private feeling' and taking care with the service, which is charming and enthusiastic. But what distinguishes this restaurant is the singular quality of Russell Robertson's cooking. While it currently scores hits and misses as it tries to cover a number of culinary bases, an inspector was impressed by the level of ambition. Enterprising and successful dishes, based largely on local ingredients, have included scallops with carrot, toasted sesame and smoked bacon froth, halibut with black linguine on a bed of pak choi with hot tomato jelly, and lamb in a herb crust with roast Jerusalem

artichokes, pea purée and a boudin of lamb's liver. The timing of fish and meat seems never less than pinpoint-accurate, and understanding of flavour is such that when it comes off the dish is 'delicious and memorable'.

An exotically spicy dessert combining mango and anise could bring a meal to an end. France is the main focus of the wine list, with global support. There are bottles aplenty for big spenders, but the interest and value in the lower reaches impress more. House wine is £16, and there are around a dozen by the glass.

Chef: Russell Robertson Proprietors: Peter and David Byrne, and Russell Robertson Open: Tue to Sun 12.30 to 2.30, 7 to 9.30 Closed: 2 weeks Jan, 2 weeks Oct Meals: alc D (main courses £13 to £18), Set L £14.95 to £15.95, Set D £39.50 to £45 Service: not inc Cards: Amex, Delta, Maestro, MasterCard, Visa Details: 32 seats. Car park. Vegetarian meals. No smoking. Wheelchair access (also WC). Occasional music. No mobile phones

MAP 11 DUNDEE – Dundee

Dil Se AR

101 Perth Road, Dundee DD1 4JA
Tel: (01382) 221501

This Bangladeshi-run restaurant has a sister restaurant in St Andrews called Balaka, where vegetables and herbs are grown for both establishments in a large kitchen garden. Dil Se has a modern glass frontage, and a menu that takes in many familiar curries alongside more unusual dishes such as mas Ecosse (£12.95), where Scottish trout is substituted for the traditional koy, and keema aloo (£8.95), prepared with minced Scottish lamb. Service is polite and efficient. Open all week.

MAP 11 DUNKELD – Perthshire & Kinross

Kinnaird

Kinnaird Estate, by Dunkeld PH8 0LB
Tel: (01796) 482440
Website: www.kinnairdestate.com

Cooking 6 | **Modern European** | **£73**

An enterprising reporter on a Scottish gastronomic odyssey emerged from Kinnaird a thoroughly satisfied customer. 'First-class food, some delightful extras, and friendly, attentive service – one of the best,' was how he summed it all up. Situated on an estate near Dunkeld, it's a majestic hotel with just a handful of guest rooms, the interiors done in traditional, country-house taste, and with seductive daylight views over the Tay valley from the dining room.

Trevor Brooks still draws some fresh supplies from the estate's own kitchen garden, with the balance coming from Rungis Market in Paris each week. Lunch and dinner are offered seven days a week, and yet the enthusiasm and brio of the cooking don't appear to flag. Dinner might begin with an intricately worked terrine of poultry, ham hock and artichoke, served with rhubarb chutney and brioche, or there might be a fanciful mini take on osso buco, made with pork and accompanied by a spring roll of crab and pig's trotter. Main courses are equally split between fish and meat, the former including perhaps pot-roast John Dory with braised salsify, Chinese mushrooms and a red wine sauce, while the latter could be an assiette of veal, with caper and mustard mash and ceps, in a Madeira sauce. Finish with a gander at the cheese trolley, or maybe with pistachio parfait served with a chutney of physalis and thyme, passion fruit and coffee ice. Wines are a sound international selection, taking in all the major producing countries, prefaced with house suggestions, from £22, and four by the glass at £6.

Chef: Trevor Brooks **Proprietor:** Constance Ward **Open:** all week 12.30 to 1.45, 7 to 9.30 **Meals:** Set L £15 (2 courses) to £30, Set D £55. Light L menu available **Service:** not inc **Cards:** Amex, Maestro, MasterCard, Visa **Details:** 36 seats. Car park. No children under 12. Jacket. No smoking. No music. No mobile phones **Accommodation:** 9 rooms

MAP 11 EDINBURGH – Edinburgh

Atrium

10 Cambridge Street, Edinburgh EH1 2ED
Tel: (0131) 228 8882
Website: www.atriumrestaurant.co.uk

Cooking 1 | Modern European | £53

Atrium is in the heart of the city, adjacent to the Traverse and Lyceum Theatres. The interior may be looking its age, but the menu is lively and modern and the kitchen sources ingredients from local artisan producers and changes the menu daily. Start perhaps with smoked fillet of Perthshire eel with a daikon, radish and apple salad, or seared

Campbeltown scallops with onion purée and mango salsa, and move on to fillet of organic Shetland salmon with black beans, or herb-crusted loin of Perthshire lamb accompanied by braised Puy lentils and haricots verts. Finish with passion-fruit pannacotta with crème anglaise and fresh coconut. The international wine list is extensive, and all bottles are also served by the glass (from £4.75). Prices open at £17.

Chefs: Neil Forbes and Fabrice Bouteloup **Proprietors:** Andrew and Lisa Radford **Open:** Mon to Fri L 12 to 2, Mon to Sat D 6 to 10 (all week L and D during Festival) **Closed:** 25 and 26 Dec, 1 and 2 Jan **Meals:** alc (main courses £18 to £22). Set L £13.50 (2 courses) to £17.50, Set D £27 **Service:** not inc **Cards:** Amex, Delta, Diners, Maestro, MasterCard, Visa **Details:** 80 seats. Vegetarian meals. Children's helpings. No smoking. Wheelchair access (also WC). No music. Air-conditioned

Balmoral, Number One

1 Princes Street, Edinburgh EH2 2EQ
Tel: (0131) 556 2414
Website: www.roccofortehotels.com

Cooking 6 | Modern European | £69

Number One by name, and intent on living up to its own billing, the restaurant in the basement of Rocco Forte's unashamedly luxurious city-centre hotel shows no shortage of ambition. The setting is sleek and sophisticated, with smart banquette seating, subtle lighting, lots of watercolours on the walls, and mirrors to convey a sense of space. Smartly dressed, generously sized tables are set widely apart, and the mood is formal but not stuffy.

Dinner is very much the full-on fine dining experience, padded out with a complement of appetisers, pre-desserts and so on. But there's no sense of Jeff Bland being prone to razzle-dazzle gimmickry, with prime materials being the cornerstone of a confident yet sensible cooking style. Starters of mille-feuille of crab with asparagus and a soft-boiled quail's egg, or pistachio-crusted quail breast with confit leg tortellini, morels and broad beans may sound complex but make good culinary sense and are typically handled with aplomb.

Likewise main courses of poached beef sirloin with horseradish gratin, gnocchi and a mushroom emulsion, corn-fed duck with creamed celeriac, beetroot fondant and plum chutney, or wild salmon with white asparagus, fennel, herb noodles and lemongrass vinaigrette. To finish, standards are maintained by passion-fruit soufflé with a matching jelly and coconut parfait, or pineapple tarte Tatin with sorbet and pineapple carpaccio.

France takes centre stage on the wine list, with big names from Bordeaux and Burgundy much in evidence. Fashionable selections from the New World provide well for those looking to spend under £40, although few bottles will give change from £25.

Chef: Jeff Bland Proprietor: Sir Rocco Forte Open: Wed to Fri L 12 to 2, all week D 6.30 to 10 Closed: first 2 weeks Jan Meals: alc D (main courses £25.50 to £27). Set L £24 (2 courses) to £28, Set D £65 Service: not inc Cards: Amex, Delta, Diners, Maestro, MasterCard, Visa Details: 50 seats. Vegetarian meals. No smoking. Wheelchair access (also WC). Music. No mobile phones. Air-conditioned Accommodation: 188 rooms

blue

10 Cambridge Street, Edinburgh EH1 2ED
Tel: (0131) 221 1222

Its location above the Traverse Theatre, near the Usher Hall and the Lyceum, means that this bright and contemporary café/brasserie attracts an arty crowd. The menu is what you might expect, given the style and décor: starting with, for example, tuna niçoise (£6.75), or goats' cheese tart with red pepper coulis (£6.25), main courses of whole sea bass with plum tomatoes, roast fennel and beurre blanc (£15.50), or chargrilled Aberdeen Angus ribeye with horseradish mash (£15), and puddings such as orange tart with lime sorbet (£4.95). The intelligently chosen, modern wine list kicks off at £12.95. Closed Sun.

The Bonham

35 Drumsheugh Gardens, Edinburgh EH3 7RN
Tel: (0131) 274 7444
Website: www.thebonham.com

Cooking 3 | Modern European | £46

Part of the draw of this restaurant in a modish West End hotel is the prospect of meal in 'an elegant pair of rooms'. The tastefully turned out dining room is portioned into two, the back overlooking gardens, and is the setting for Michel Bouyer's well-judged food. The menu tends to the Mediterranean-inspired end of modern European cooking – red mullet with vegetable escabèche, for example – and is kept short, with five choices per course. The repertoire moves along gently with plenty of orig-

inal ideas and novel presentations, such as white asparagus risotto with blood orange juice, but the focus is on sound culinary principles and traditional cooking methods, backed up by well-sourced ingredients, as in main courses of seared Shetland sea trout with fresh green peas, purple potato gnocchi and gravad lax dressing or veal osso bucco with lemon and red onion fettucine, and classic dark chocolate tart and vanilla ice cream for dessert. Wine prices start at around £15.

Chef: Michel Bouyer Proprietor: Peter Taylor Open: all week 12 to 2.30 (12.30 to 3 Sun), 6.30 to 10 Meals: alc D (main courses £13 to £22.50). Set L Sat and Sun £65 for 4 people (inc wine) Service: not inc Cards: Amex, Delta, Diners, Maestro, MasterCard, Visa Details: 75 seats. Car park. Vegetarian meals. No smoking. Wheelchair access (also WC). Music Accommodation: 48 rooms

Café St Honoré

34 NW Thistle Street Lane, Edinburgh EH2 1EA
Tel: (0131) 226 2211
Website: www.cafesthonore.com

Cooking 3 | Modern Bistro | £42

Well established on the Edinburgh scene, this modish bistro belies its location, creating a definite sense of Gallic identity: think rickety wooden tables and lots of mirrors. The menus take the best of Scottish produce to create some bistro favourites, including chicken fricassee, boeuf bourguignonne and steak frites. Otherwise, open with baked oysters with shrimps, tiger prawns and Gruyère, and go on to saddle of venison with lentils, spinach and boudin noir, or pan-fried swordfish with tapenade, clams and sun-blush tomatoes. Those with room could try pear and Brazil nut steamed pudding with cinnamon ice cream and custard. Wines are mostly from France and the New World, with prices starting at £12.45 for half a dozen house selections.

Chefs: Chris Colverson and Bob Cairns Proprietors: Chris and Gill Colverson Open: all week 12 to 2.15, 5.30 (6 Sat and Sun) to 10 Closed: 3 days Christmas, 3 days New Year Meals: alc (main courses L £9 to £15, D £16 to £20.50). Set D Mon to Fri 5.30 to 6.45, Sun 6 to 7.15 £14.95 (2 courses) to £19.95 Service: not inc Cards: Amex, Delta, Diners, Maestro, MasterCard, Visa Details: 45 seats. Vegetarian meals. Children's helpings. No smoking. Music

Channings

15 South Learmonth Gardens, Edinburgh
EH4 1EZ
Tel: (0131) 315 2225
Website: www.channings.co.uk

Cooking 5 | Modern Scottish | **£39**

Close to the city centre, yet in a comparatively quiet cobbled street overlooking private gardens, Channings is part of a small group of luxury hotels (see the Bonham above). The kitchen is headed by Hubert Lamort, who brings a sound culinary intelligence and produces some fine workmanship. He sets out an appealing menu that might take in scallops with cauliflower pannacotta, shiso cress, wasabi cream and Granny Smith, or roast sesame-crusted Crottin de Chavignol with beetroot and orange salad. Timing and production are impressive, and the handling of fine raw materials is assured. There is no needless experimentation, no attempt at shock effects, just a succession of fine ingredients that work together harmoniously. Thrice-cooked chips and onion fondue are teamed with beef fillet, roast rib of free-range organic pork with braised belly, and organic salmon served with chestnuts, artichokes, fennel and leeks with vinaigrette. The simplicity of desserts is another plus, judging by a winter fruit salad with vanilla syrup and passion-fruit sorbet, or leche frita with cinnamon ice cream and poached pear. Wines are grouped by grape variety on the 70-plus list, starting with ten house wines from £14 to £18.

Chef: Hubert Lamort **Proprietor:** Peter Taylor **Open:** all week 12 (12.30 Sat and Sun) to 3, 6 to 10 (11 Fri and Sat) **Meals:** alc D (main courses £11.50 to £24). Set L £12 (2 courses) to £15 **Service:** not inc **Cards:** Amex, Delta, Diners, Maestro, MasterCard, Visa **Details:** 40 seats. Vegetarian meals. No smoking. Music **Accommodation:** 41 rooms

David Bann

56–58 St Mary's Street, Edinburgh EH1 1SX
Tel: (0131) 556 5888
Website: www.davidbann.co.uk

Cooking 2 | Vegetarian | **£29**

David Bann's intention is to bring vegetarian food to a mainstream audience. His restaurant is contemporary in style, with two rooms separated by three steps, wooden floors throughout and bare tables. The imaginative menu states that everything is 'traditionally cooked from fresh ingredients – no microwave', and it clearly marks vegan dishes. Thai fritters, grilled Parmesan and basil polenta with tapenade and beetroot salad, or a tartlet of blue cheese and slow-dried tomato showcase the Asian and Mediterranean influences that run throughout. Main courses continue in the same vein: crêpe provençale, which is packed with roast aubergine, courgette, red onion, peppers, tomato, basil and Parmesan, appears alongside vegetable curry dosai. Amaretto cheesecake with raspberry coulis ends things on a high note. All but a handful of bottles on the compact wine list are under £20, with prices starting at £10.80 (£2.70 a glass).

Chef/Proprietor: David Bann **Open:** all week 11 to 10 (10.30 Fri and Sat) **Closed:** 25 and 26 Dec, 1 and 2 Jan **Meals:** alc (main courses £7.50 to £12) **Service:** not inc **Cards:** Amex, Delta, Maestro, MasterCard, Visa **Details:** 86 seats. Children's helpings. No smoking. Wheelchair access (not WC). Music. Air-conditioned

Fishers

1 Shore, Leith, Edinburgh EH6 6QW
Tel: (0131) 554 5666

With an attractive location overlooking the Leith waterfront, this long-established seafood bistro knows what it does best. There's a dazzling array of fish on their daily-changing menu, starting with hot smoked salmon with vodka, blueberry, raspberry and thyme compote (£6.75), followed by grilled baby turbot with crab bisque and truffle oil (£17.25) or Arbroath smokie with black pudding and béarnaise (£12.95), while meat-eaters should be happy with pan-fried poussin with apple compote and a red wine and date jus (£12.75). End with mixed berry cheesecake (£4.75). House wine £11.95. Open all week. Related to Fishers in the City (see entry below).

Fishers in the City

58 Thistle Street, Edinburgh EH2 1EN
Tel: (0131) 225 5109
Website: www.fishersbistros.co.uk

Cooking 2 | Seafood | **£38**

This Edinburgh institution thrives on its pleasant atmosphere and a modern menu that offers the freshest of fish and seafood; favourites include steamed West Coast mussels, Loch Fyne oysters

and chilled seafood platter. A good-value two-course lunch has been added to the repertoire, while the à la carte might start with fillet of gurnard on confit garlic mash, followed by roast monkfish tail on sautéed spinach with braised Puy lentils and chorizo. If you must, there is pan-fried sirloin steak. Dessert might be chocolate and banana iced parfait with banana sauce. The good-value, extensive wine list is divided up by country, starting at £12.95 for house French, with many decent bottles under £20. Related to Fisher's Bistro in Leith (see entry above).

Chefs: Rhys Phillips and John Newton Proprietors: James Millar and Graeme Lumsden Open: all week 12 to 10.30 Meals: alc (main courses £9 to £24). Set L £10.95 (2 courses) Service: not inc Cards: Amex, Delta, Maestro, MasterCard, Visa Details: 85 seats. Vegetarian meals. Children's helpings. No smoking. Wheelchair access (also WC). Music. No mobile phones. Air-conditioned

---

Forth Floor

Harvey Nichols, 30–34 St Andrews Square, Edinburgh EH2 2AD
Tel: (0131) 524 8350
Website: www.harveynichols.co.uk

Cooking 3 | Modern British | £45

Offering outstanding views over the city from its roof terrace, the Forth Floor restaurant is part of the Harvey Nichols chain, and when the sun is shining, as one reader put it, you 'really imagine yourself to be somewhere in Europe' (well, you know what they mean). Prices are on the high side, the set lunch bumped up by supplements and a fixed service charge, leading to high expectations. Unfortunately, the kitchen sometimes fails to meet the level of its ambition, though raw materials are well-sourced and recent high points have included 'perfectly cooked, very sweet and delicious' scallops with pancetta, and well-timed sea bass in a red pepper sauce with roasted fennel. Coconut and white chocolate pannacotta complemented by thin slices of pineapple has proved a good way to finish. Petits fours are praised, as is the service, which if anything is over-attentive. Harvey Nichols's own-label French wines at £13.50 open the extensive international list.

Chef: Stuart Muir Proprietor: Harvey Nichols Open: all week L 12 to 3 (3.30 Sat and Sun), Tue to Sat D 6 to 10 Meals: alc D (main courses £15 to £20). Set L Mon to Sat £24.50 (2 courses) to £29.50, Set brunch Sun £13.50. Brasserie and bar menus available Service: 10% Cards: Amex, Delta, Diners, Maestro, MasterCard, Visa Details: 90 seats. Children's helpings. No smoking. Wheelchair access (also WC). Music. Air-conditioned

---

La Garrigue AR

31 Jeffrey Street, Edinburgh EH1 1DH
Tel: (0131) 557 3032

Transporting you straight to the lush vineyard setting of Languedoc, owner and chef Jean-Michel Gauffre has spent six years building a strong prix fixe (£19.50/£24.50) that offers solid bistro fare. Expect smoked ham terrine with gherkins, braised lamb shank with Puy lentils and Toulouse sausage, or his classic cassoulet from Castelnaudary with a walnut salad. Desserts include rich chocolate mousse with chestnut liquor and the obligatory crème brûlée flavoured with lavender. Wines are indigenous but good value. Closed Sun, exc during Festival.

Haldanes

13B Dundas Street, Edinburgh EH3 6QG
Tel: (0131) 556 8407
Website: www.haldanesrestaurant.com

Cooking 3 | Modern Scottish | £48

After ten years occupying the basement below a hotel in Albany Street, Haldanes has moved to new premises, also in a basement, about half a mile away. It is similar to the old site in other respects, spread over a series of labyrinthine small rooms, its bare-stone walls lined with Jack Vettriano prints. And in the kitchen chef/proprietor George Kelso continues to turn out accomplished modern cooking with a Scottish character.

Game and shellfish feature strongly, the latter typically including a starter of Shetland crab tart with avocado, while a baked filo parcel of haggis with roast turnip and whisky sauce states the restaurant's identity even more emphatically. A main course of 'the best venison I have ever eaten' wowed a seasoned inspector, the tender, flavoursome meat served with an intense wine and stock reduction and 'fantastic' dauphinois potatoes. To finish, a chocolatey trio of mousse, marquise with cherries and white chocolate crème brûlée will suit those with a sweet tooth.

Notable bottles from South Africa and California pepper the international wine list, but it is the French regions that receive best coverage in terms of depth, quality and value. Twenty wines by the glass, from £3.50, encourage experimentation.

Chef: George Kelso **Proprietors:** George and Michelle Kelso
Open: Mon to Fri L 12 to 1.45, all week D 5.30 to 10 **Closed:**
25 and 26 Dec **Meals:** alc D (main courses £17 to £26). Set
L and D 5.30 to 6.30 £15 (2 courses). Light L menu available
Service: not inc **Cards:** Amex, Delta, Diners, Maestro,
MasterCard, Visa **Details:** 60 seats. Vegetarian meals.
Children's helpings. No smoking. Occasional music

Kalpna

2–3 St Patrick Square, Edinburgh EH8 9EZ
Tel: (0131) 667 9890

| Cooking 3 | Indian Vegetarian | £30 |

'You don't have to eat meat to be strong and wise,'
says Ajay Bhartdwaj, and who are we to argue
when his strictly vegetarian city-centre restaurant
has been a fixture on the Edinburgh dining scene
for 25 years? Gujarati cuisine is the main thrust of
the menu, extended by a handful of Rajasthani and
South Indian dishes. House specialities include
saam savera (spinach stuffed with paneer, saffron,
ginger and nuts, served with a pink mughlai gravy)
and dam aloo Kashmiri (baked potatoes stuffed
with tomatoes, honey and ginger, served with a
creamy almond and saffron sauce). There are also
various dosais filled with spiced vegetables and
lentils, served with sambhar and coconut chutney,
and, to finish, traditional Indian desserts such as
gulab jamun and mango kulfi. Mango lassi is the
thing to drink here, but there are also wines from
£10.75, including three from India.

Chef/Proprietor: Ajay Bhartdwaj **Open:** Mon to Sat 12 to 2,
5.30 to 10.30 (11 Sat); also open Sun D 6 to 10 Apr to Sept
Closed: 25 and 26 Dec, 1 Jan **Meals:** alc (main courses £5.50
to £12.50). Set L £6, Set D £12.95 to £16.95 **Service:** 10%
Cards: MasterCard, Visa **Details:** 65 seats. No smoking.
Wheelchair access (not WC). Occasional music

Off the Wall

105 High Street, Edinburgh EH1 1SG
Tel: (0131) 558 1497
Website: www.off-the-wall.co.uk

| Cooking 2 | Modern Scottish | £53 |

Reasonably spacious and very brown, David
Anderson's first-floor restaurant looks out over the
overtly touristy part of Edinburgh's Royal Mile,
taking in lots of tartan and kilt merchandisers. His
cooking has a broad sweep, with an eye for native
produce in the shape of fillet of Scottish beef with
a red wine and shallot jus, and saddle of venison
(served with baby spinach, a ragoût of carrots,
dauphinois potatoes and port sauce), while starters
might take the form of squab breast and ham hock
with bone-marrow sauce, or smoked haddock
risotto with parsley dressing. To finish, caramelised
pineapple with mincemeat, rum ice cream and a
pineapple and mint salsa sounds a lively idea, but
there are traditional desserts too, including
meringue with raspberries, cream and mango, and
toffee and date pudding. Good-value drinking
adds to the appeal: Argentinian white and Chilean
red are £13.95 and £14.95 respectively.

Chef: David Anderson **Proprietors:** David Anderson and Aileen
Wilson **Open:** Tue to Sat 12 to 2, 7 to 10 (all week 12 to 2,
5.30 to 11 during Festival) **Closed:** 24 to 26 Dec, 2 Jan
Meals: alc D (main courses £20 to £22). Set L £16.50 (2
courses) to £19.95 **Service:** not inc **Cards:** Amex, Delta,
Maestro, MasterCard, Visa **Details:** 44 seats. No smoking. No
music

Prestonfield, Rhubarb

Priestfield Road, Edinburgh EH16 5UT
Tel: (0131) 225 1333
Website: www.prestonfield.com

| NEW CHEF | Modern European | £56 |

Lavishly extravagant décor – the result of a £2
million refurbishment in 2003 – complements the
grand baroque style of the former home of
Edinburgh's Lord Provost, built in 1687. Highly
attentive service adds to the feeling of indulgence
and luxury, and the opulence is trowelled on
nowhere thicker than in the Rhubarb dining
room.

News of a personnel change in the kitchen
reached the Guide too late for inspection, but new
chef Laurence Robertson has picked up where his
predecessor left off, with a menu of refined and
elaborate, French-accented modern cooking that
makes good use of top-quality native produce.
Red mullet barigoule with rocket, spinach and
crisp pear salad appears among starters, while main
courses encompass rack of black-faced lamb with
celeriac dauphinois and red pepper and basil
purée, and turbot with butternut squash tortellini,
braised fennel and lobster nage. To finish, there
might be mille-feuille of raspberry and white
chocolate with raspberry sorbet and jelly.

Quality is high throughout the extensive wine
list, although choice at the bottom end of the price

scale is rather limited. That said, house French selections open the bidding at a not unreasonable £16 a bottle, £4.50 a glass.

Chef: Laurence Robertson **Proprietor:** James Thomson **Open:** all week 12 to 3, 6 to 10.30 (11 Fri and Sat) **Meals:** alc (main courses £16 to £28). Set L and D 6 to 7 and 10 to 10.30 (11 Fri and Sat) £16.95 (2 courses). Bar menu available **Service:** not inc **Cards:** Amex, Delta, Diners, Maestro, MasterCard, Visa **Details:** 100 seats. 20 seats outside. Car park. Vegetarian meals. No children under 12 after 7pm. No smoking. Wheelchair access (also WC). Music **Accommodation:** 22 rooms

Restaurant Martin Wishart

54 The Shore, Leith, Edinburgh EH6 6RA
Tel: (0131) 553 3557
Website: www.martin-wishart.co.uk

| Cooking 8 | Modern French | £72 |

Martin Wishart continues on his mission of cooking some of the most challenging and engaging food in the Scottish capital. The context in which it takes place is a mix of the understated and the elegant. The proprietor's name appears above the corner door of a plain white building, while inside, dark wood panels, huge full-length mirrors and generously sized tables all contribute to an impression of grown-up civility.

The menu formats are simple: a fixed price for lunch and dinner, with the option of a more-expensive tasting menu (with vegetarian version, too). Something of the surprises in store might be hinted at when the appetiser arrives. Be gone, little cups of soup, for here are monkfish livers sautéed in orange butter. Many were the further highlights of an inspection visit. Cured foie gras and pork knuckle topped with grain-mustard ice cream made a majestic opener, its richness offset with white radish slices smeared with wasabi and crisp deep-fried langoustine beignets. Another starter juxtaposed Shetland smoked salmon with scallops seared to just-golden, with a fromage frais and truffled honey dressed salad.

Fashionable land and sea pairings are exploited to the full, as in monkfish grenobloise with pork liver, or poached Anjou pigeon and oysters, with Puy lentils and Savoy cabbage ('a whole orchestra of tastes and textures'), but more traditional preparations excel, too. Beef might appear as the braised cheek and short rib, the meat 'unctuously rich and flavoursome, some of it softly frondy', served with veal sweetbreads and wild mushroom ravioli. Dessert creations impress quite as powerfully, with the likes of chocolate soufflé served with a ball of

pistachio cream, or mango purée topped with lemongrass jelly and explosively concentrated strawberry sorbet. Service begins confidently enough, but can lose its way towards the end of a busy session.

Wines are grouped by country in the old-fashioned way, and the un-annotated list assumes a certain amount of knowledge on the part of the consumer, as to both styles and vintages. That said, quality is good to very good and, although there is plenty of high-end drinking, there is much in the £20-£30 bracket. Wines by the glass start at £4.50.

Chef/Proprietor: Martin Wishart **Open:** Tue to Fri L 12 to 2, Tue to Sat D 6.45 to 9.30 **Meals:** Set L £22.50, Set D £50 to £60 **Service:** not inc **Cards:** Amex, Delta, Maestro, MasterCard, Visa **Details:** 50 seats. Vegetarian meals. No smoking. Wheelchair access (also WC). Music. No mobile phones

Skippers

1A Dock Place, Leith, Edinburgh EH6 6LU
Tel: (0131) 554 1018
Website: www.skippers.co.uk

| Cooking 1 | Seafood | £38 |

This ambitious seafood restaurant on the Leith waterfront offers the visitor a hearty welcome. The décor is warm, with deep burgundy walls, dark wooden panelling to match the tables, and quirky marine artefacts. The menu, which changes twice daily, focuses on the fruit of the sea: West Coast mussels marinière, or potted crab with crayfish tails to start, then maybe baked mackerel fillet wrapped in Serrano ham on Savoy cabbage and garlic, finnan haddie with Brie, asparagus and pine kernels, or whole grilled Dover sole with garlic and tarragon butter. A couple of meat options might run to duck confit with dauphinois potatoes, and lavender crème brûlée or sticky toffee pudding could bring things to an end. Wine prices start at £10.95 for Georges Duboeuf.

Chef: Mary Walker **Proprietor:** Skippers of Leith Ltd **Open:** all week 12.30 to 2, 6 to 10 **Closed:** 25 and 26 Dec, 1 Jan **Meals:** alc (main courses L £7.50 to £16, D £12 to £22.50). Set L £8.45 (2 courses) to £11.45, Set D Sun to Fri £19.95 **Service:** not inc **Cards:** Amex, Delta, Maestro, MasterCard, Visa **Details:** 60 seats. 12 seats outside. Vegetarian meals. Children's helpings. No smoking. Wheelchair access (also WC). Music

Suruchi Too [AR]

121 Constitution Street, Leith, Edinburgh
EH6 7AE
Tel: (0131) 554 3268

Vegetable haggis fritter is among the specialities of this unusual hybrid restaurant that offers 'the brawest Indian food, music an atmosphere' with a distinctly Scottish twist. The menu – written in a style Burns would be proud of – is divided into two parts: in one, popular curry-house standards; in the other, less commonly sighted authentic regional Indian specialities such as simla chaat ('a cantie mix o chickpeas, tatties, cucumber, coriander and bannannies, tappet wi a tangy sauce and spices') and gosht Malabar ('tender lamb cookit wi garam masal in coconut mulk'). House Chilean is £10.50. Open all week.

Valvona & Crolla Caffè Bar

19 Elm Row, Edinburgh EH7 4AA
Tel: (0131) 556 6066
Website: www.valvonacrolla.com

Cooking 3 | Italian | £33

The Contini family continue to serve the people of Edinburgh the best of regional Italian dishes. Customers flood through the doors throughout the day, with lunch a big draw. The Continis source some of their food from Italy but also showcase Scottish producers, bringing all the ingredients together in a stylish and traditional manner. Breads such as focaccia and bruschetta with prosciutto and rocket whet the appetite before antipasti of buffalo mozzarella with tomatoes and basil, or a selection of cured meats, followed perhaps by savoury pancakes stuffed with ricotta and spinach in a cheese and tomato sauce, or spaghetti with queen scallops. Bigger plates might include chargrilled tiger prawns, or Aberdeen Angus ribeye with truffle butter. Finish with crumbly lemon polenta cake, or treacle tart. The short wine list starts at £10, but for £5 corkage you can drink anything you might fancy in the shop.

> **Chef:** Mary Contini **Proprietors:** Philip and Mary Contini **Open:** Mon to Sat 8 to 6, Sun 10.30 to 4.30 (L served 11.45 to 3.30). Also open Thur to Sat D during Festival **Closed:** 25 and 26 Dec, 1 and 2 Jan **Meals:** alc (main courses L £9 to £15, D £9 to £19.50) **Service:** not inc **Cards:** Amex, Delta, Maestro, MasterCard, Visa **Details:** 80 seats. Vegetarian meals. Children's helpings. No smoking. Wheelchair access (also WC). Music. Air-conditioned

Valvona & Crolla Vincaffè [NEW ENTRY]

11 Multrees Walk, Edinburgh EH1 3DQ
Tel: (0131) 557 0088
Website: www.valvonacrolla.com

Cooking 2 | Italian | £40

The Contini family have spread their wings with this sister restaurant to the long-established institution in Elm Row (see entry above). Enter the glass-fronted building, in Edinburgh's exclusive shopping centre, and go left to the bar if you are after a snack; otherwise take the stairs to the restaurant. Here, dark wooden furniture is offset by big windows, giving the place a light and airy appeal. Crostini and olives start things off, followed by antipasti: vitello tonnato, say, or grilled fillets of red mullet with tapenade. Farfalle with peas, grated courgettes and cream has been a successful pasta dish, and more substantial offerings run from deep-fried breadcrumbed monkfish with roast potatoes and tartare sauce to griddled lamb chops with mash, sautéed greens and mint sauce. Pannacotta flavoured with Drambuie makes an appropriate dessert. Italy is the main thrust of the wine list. Plenty are served by the glass, and own-label bottles are £14.

> **Chefs/Proprietors:** the Contini family **Open:** all week L 12 to 3.30, Mon to Sat D 5 to 9.30 (10.30 Thur to Sat) **Closed:** 25 and 26 Dec, 1 Jan **Meals:** alc (main courses £9 to £19.50) **Service:** not inc **Cards:** Amex, Delta, Diners, Maestro, MasterCard, Visa **Details:** 140 seats. 28 seats outside. Vegetarian meals. Children's helpings. No smoking. Wheelchair access (also WC). Music. Air-conditioned

Vintners Rooms

The Vaults, 87 Giles Street, Leith, Edinburgh
EH6 6BZ
Tel: (0131) 554 6767
Website: www.thevintnersrooms.com

Cooking 4 | French | £50

Elegance is still the order of the day at this atmospheric old wine merchants' building. The dining room is split into two distinct sections, the smaller illuminated by candlelight, and showcases high ceilings and intricate plasterwork, while the front bar area boasts a large selection of bottles stored above the bar. Locally sourced food retains its

Scottish accent but mixes in some Mediterranean flavours. West Coast oysters or cod carpaccio with blood oranges and salsa verde have been among the half-dozen starters, while main courses take the high road from fillet of Highland beef with sauce bordelaise to roast loin of Perthshire lamb with an olive jus. A speciality of the house is roast côte de boeuf, which is prepared for two people, served rare and accompanied by béarnaise. Desserts could bring on crème brûlée with prunes and Armagnac. The wine list is joyfully comprehensive. House selections start at £15, but there are many special-occasion bottles in the £40 to £50 range, going up to a spectacular £850 for a Ch. Le Pin Pomerol 1985.

Chef: Patrice Ginestrière **Proprietor:** The Vintners Rooms Ltd **Open:** Tue to Sat 12 to 2, 7 to 10 **Meals:** alc (main courses £16 to £22). Set L £15.50 (2 courses) to £19 **Service:** 10% (optional) **Cards:** Amex, Delta, Maestro, MasterCard, Visa **Details:** 60 seats. No smoking. Wheelchair access (not WC). Music

Witchery by the Castle

Castlehill, Royal Mile, Edinburgh EH1 2NF
Tel: (0131) 225 5613
Website: www.thewitchery.com

Cooking 3 | Modern Scottish | £54

The Witchery, by the gates of Edinburgh Castle, was originally built for a wealthy merchant in 1595 but is now a haven for the great and the good of the twenty-first century, drawn by the theatrical atmosphere, seven luxury suites and fine dining. The décor in both dining rooms is dark, opulent and atmospheric, with antiques by the dozen, magnificent candelabra, flagged floors, dark oak panelling, tapestries and painted ceiling panels in the Secret Garden. The food, however, is contemporary. Fish soup comes with a Gruyère croûton, flaked Buckie crab and rouille, while roast loin of Perthshire roe deer is imaginatively served with braised red cabbage, grilled Stornoway black pudding and chocolate sauce. Among fish main courses could be organic Shetland salmon and crayfish ravioli. A light touch is given to desserts, which might be raspberry and pistachio pannacotta or glazed Italian lemon tart. Isle of Mull Cheddar appears on the cheeseboard. The wine cellar runs to around 1,000 bins, catering to all tastes and price ranges, though house choices start at £15.95.

Chef: Douglas Roberts **Proprietor:** James Thomson **Open:** all week 12 to 4, 5.30 to 11.30 **Closed:** 25 and 26 Dec **Meals:** alc (main courses £14 to £50). Set L £12.50 (2 courses), Set D 5.30 to 6.30 and 10.30 to 11 £12.50 (2 courses) **Service:** not inc **Cards:** Amex, Delta, Diners, Maestro, MasterCard, Visa **Details:** 90 seats. 20 seats outside. Vegetarian meals. No smoking. Music **Accommodation:** 7 rooms

MAP 11 EDNAM – Borders

Edenwater House

Ednam TD5 7QL
Tel: (01573) 224070
Website: www.edenwaterhouse.co.uk

Cooking 4 | Modern British | £50

Edenwater is a large converted manse in a small hamlet surrounded by 'magical landscape', with a trout stream running through the flower garden and a meadow beyond. Jacqui and Jeff Kelly make visitors feel at home, serving drinks before dinner, and coffee after, in the sitting room. Jacqui creates the four-course menu single-handedly. Langoustines served with raw spinach and celery leaves, mushrooms and foie gras has been 'a fabulous dish', according to one diner. A soup – perhaps tomato broth with herbs – might follow the starter before a main course of Eyemouth halibut en papillote with tarragon and chive sauce, or rack of Border lamb, served pink, in a mustard crust with redcurrant jus. A 'truly delicious' bitter chocolate tart with ginger and avocado ice cream was a star dish at inspection. The wine list is Jeff's hobby and is full of interesting and unusual bottles. Prices start at £12.50.

Chef: Jacqui Kelly **Proprietors:** Jacqui and Jeff Kelly **Open:** Wed to Sat D only 8pm (1 sitting) **Closed:** first 2 weeks Jan **Meals:** Set D £37.50 **Service:** not inc **Cards:** Delta, Maestro, MasterCard, Visa **Details:** 16 seats. Car park. No children under 10. Children's helpings. No smoking. No music. No mobile phones **Accommodation:** 4 rooms

	This symbol means that accommodation is available at this establishment.

MAP 11 ELIE – Fife

Sangster's

51 High Street, Elie KY9 1BZ
Tel: (01333) 331001
Website: www.sangsters.co.uk

Cooking 4 | Modern British | **£41**

A small-scale restaurant with big ideas, Sangster's stands on the main street through this handsome village. It has a domestic feel, although a light and airy modern-style décor gives it a cosmopolitan edge, and this is reflected in Bruce Sangster's inventive and artistically presented cooking. High-quality native ingredients are at the core of a culinary philosophy that draws inspiration from far and wide to come up with starters of crispy 'bonbon' of duck confit and foie gras on wilted cucumber with oriental dressing, or roast scallops in coconut broth with spring onions and coriander. At dinner, an intermediary course of perhaps crusted croquettes of Arbroath smokies precedes main courses such as seared monkfish tail with a pancetta wafer on crushed potatoes and ratatouille with an orange and cardamom reduction, or venison loin in a mushroom and herb crust with red cabbage and apple compote, celeriac gratin and a morel and red wine sauce. And to finish there might be sticky toffee pudding, or pannacotta with mango, pineapple and passion-fruit soup. Five house wines carefully chosen to suit the food open the list at £15 a bottle, £4 a glass. The rest of the list is a varied selection of easy-drinking bottles at reasonable prices.

Chef: Bruce Sangster **Proprietors:** Bruce and Jacqueline Sangster **Open:** Wed to Fri and Sun L 12.30 to 1.45, Tue to Sat D 7 to 9.30 **Closed:** 25 and 26 Dec, first 3 weeks Jan **Meals:** Set L £16.75 (2 courses) to £18.75, Set D £25 (2 courses) to £32.50 **Service:** not inc **Cards:** Delta, Diners, Maestro, MasterCard, Visa **Details:** 28 seats. No children under 12. No smoking. Wheelchair access (also woman's WC). No music. No mobile phones

MAP 11 ERISKA – Argyll & Bute

Isle of Eriska

Ledaig, Eriska PA37 1SD
Tel: (01631) 720371
Website: www.eriska-hotel.co.uk

Cooking 4 | Scottish | **£49**

The Buchanan-Smith family have been running their majestic Victorian pile on its own private

island – don't worry; you drive over a wooden bridge – for 33 years, while their chef, Robert MacPherson, has clocked up a decade. His menus change daily, and seafood typically appears in some form: a starter of open ravioli of Loch Creran mussels at one meal, local langoustines accompanying a main course of roast turbot at another. The six-course dinner format also takes in a no-choice intermediate soup – perhaps cauliflower with lemon and thyme dumplings – and there's normally a couple of meat options at main-course stage: say, roast haunch of venison with juniper jelly, or corn-fed guinea fowl with salsify confit, morel velouté, creamed cabbage and cider fondant. Dessert choices have included a Valrhona chocolate tower with mango sorbet and blood oranges, and pineapple soufflé with iced coconut parfait and stem ginger syrup.

The wine list takes its Bordeaux and Burgundies seriously, but other French regions and the rest of the world are briefly covered. There's plenty of choice under £20, and a good selection of halves, while house wines from France and Argentina are £12.50.

Chef: Robert MacPherson **Proprietors:** the Buchanan-Smith family **Open:** all week D only 8 to 9 (L residents only) **Closed:** Jan **Meals:** Set D £38.50 **Service:** not inc **Cards:** Amex, Delta, Maestro, MasterCard, Visa **Details:** 44 seats. Car park. Vegetarian meals. No smoking. Wheelchair access (also WC). No music. No mobile phones. Air-conditioned **Accommodation:** 22 rooms

MAP 11 FAIRLIE – North Ayrshire

Fins

Fencefoot Farm, Fairlie KA29 0EG
Tel: (01475) 568989
Website: www.fencebay.co.uk

Cooking 2 | Seafood | **£44**

With its own smokehouse, plus on-site sea water tanks for locally caught lobsters and crab, there's no denying the main business of this cottagey restaurant: fish and shellfish, some of it caught from Bernard Thain's own boat. The dining room is split between a conservatory and a square room with thick stone walls, chunky wooden furniture and some seafaring prints. Daily specials are chalked on a blackboard, and the service is informal. Local Cumbrae oysters or Fencebay cold- or hot-smoked salmon get things started, while lemon sole fillets with a citrus herb crust, or halibut fillet with squat lobster tails and langoustine with a Chardonnay sauce are typical main courses. Arran

Cheddar with oatcakes is alongside classic desserts such as crème brûlée. The short wine list is understandably stronger in whites, France opening at £12.40.

> **Chefs:** Jane Burns, Gary Brown and Paul Harvey **Proprietors:** Jill and Bernard Thain **Open:** Tue to Sun L 12 to 2.30, Tue to Sat D 6.30 to 9 **Closed:** 25 and 26 Dec, 1 Jan **Meals:** alc (main courses £10.50 to £28). Set L Tue to Thur £12 (2 courses) to £15, Set D Tue to Thur £15 (2 courses) to £17 **Service:** not inc **Cards:** Delta, Maestro, MasterCard, Visa **Details:** 34 seats. 24 seats outside. Car park. No children under 7 at D. Children's helpings. No smoking. Wheelchair access (also WC). Music

MAP 11 FORT WILLIAM – Highland

Crannog

Town Pier, Fort William PH33 6PD
Tel: (01397) 705589
Website: www.crannog.net

Cooking 2 | Seafood | £42

Now back at their original premises after suffering extensive storm damage in 2005, fisherman Finlay Finlayson and new chef Gary Dobbie can once again offer cosy surroundings as well as freshly caught fish. The restaurant, established to allow fisherman to be more involved in the marketing of their catch, is honest and confident in its endeavours. Razor clams are steamed in lemon, parsley and garlic; rainbow trout comes with ceps, garlic and pancetta; while Loch Nevis mussels might be served as a light Thai curry. Specialities include Loch Linnhe langoustines, and the grand seafood platter, which bursts forth with eight different seafoods, including Highland oysters, squat lobsters, whole crab and queenie scallops. Desserts include Belgian dark chocolate pot or Scottish cheeses such as Isle of Mull cheddar. Wines from £14.50.

> **Chef:** Gary Dobbie **Proprietor:** Finlay Finlayson **Open:** all week 12 to 2.30, 6 to 9 (10 Apr to Oct) **Closed:** D 24 Dec, 25 and 26 Dec, D 31 Dec, 1 Jan **Meals:** alc (main courses £12 to £29) **Service:** not inc **Cards:** Delta, Maestro, MasterCard, Visa **Details:** 66 seats. Vegetarian meals. Children's helpings. No smoking. Wheelchair access (also WC). Music

> To submit a report on any restaurant, please visit *www.which.co.uk/gfgfeedback.*

Inverlochy Castle

Torlundy, Fort William PH33 6SN
Tel: (01397) 702177
Website: www.inverlochycastlehotel.com

Cooking 6 | Modern European | £80

It is the hotel that you want, not the castle itself, which is just nearby but has rather gone to rack and ruin since the thirteenth century. The hotel, on the other hand, is a Relais et Châteaux magnificence, all dolled up in best shootin' and fishin' style. There is a vast lounge replete with fireside reading matter, and a dining room, run on scrupulously full-dress lines in the evenings, that has commanding daytime views over the lake in the grounds.

The kitchen is most at ease with the country-house manner, gilding seared brill with caviar and truffle, and partnering roast fillet of veal with morels and artichoke. That said, there is no trepidation about venturing into more contemporary avenues, so a late-winter first course might juxtapose roast monkfish with braised pork cheek, next to a portion of saffron risotto. An appreciable level of care is taken over main ingredients, with seasoning subtle but effective, and cooking times judged to perfection. The main drill is a four-course dinner menu, with a soup such as butternut squash with spätzli after the starter, but there is also a tasting menu for the adventurous, seven courses that extend into two desserts and then cheese. With desserts like chocolate truffle beignet with champagne butter sorbet and pineapple compote in the offing, you won't lack for stimulation.

The wine list is quite a tome, with attractive illustrations, painstaking notes and obvious strength in depth. France is a roll-call of the fine and the very fine, but a dab hand is in evidence throughout. Prices start at £30, and after that the sky's the limit.

> **Chef:** Matthew Gray **Proprietor:** Inverlochy Castle Ltd **Open:** all week 12.30 to 1.15, 6.30 to 10 **Meals:** Set L £28.50 (2 courses) to £35, Set D £58. Light L menu available **Service:** not inc **Cards:** Amex, Delta, Maestro, MasterCard, Visa **Details:** 50 seats. Car park. Vegetarian meals. Children's helpings. Jacket and tie at D. No smoking. Wheelchair access (not WC). No music. No mobile phones **Accommodation:** 17 rooms

MAP 11 | GLASGOW – Glasgow

Brian Maule at Chardon d'Or

176 West Regent Street, Glasgow G2 4RL
Tel: (0141) 248 3801
Website: www.brianmaule.com

Cooking 3 | French/Mediterranean | £52

The entrance to this grand city-centre house is through a glass lobby, where an enthusiastic maître d' greets visitors – beware of the outward-opening door. This leads to a smart bar area, which is flanked by high-ceilinged dining rooms, plainly decorated save for some ornate cornicing and a few abstract prints, and furnished with black leather banquettes and well-spaced white-clothed tables set with vases of lilies, all to very pleasant effect.

The menus point to the aspirations of an ambitious chef/proprietor who has previous experience at such high-ranking addresses as the Gavroche (see entry, London), with an unsurprising leaning towards classic French style. To start, smoked haddock is topped with a poached egg and 'glazed' with a creamy herb and white wine sauce, while a well-made filo tart is filled with a tangy, soft mousse of leek and mozzarella and served with a salad of sun-blush tomato in truffle dressing. Among main courses, grilled sea bass has impressed, served inventively atop a mixture of parsnips and shallot confit with wild mushrooms scattered about. Walnut mousse with honeycomb ice cream makes an unusual but successful way to finish.

The wine list offers good global coverage, with bottles to suit all pockets and value particularly good at the top end. French 'vin du maison' gets the ball rolling at £18.90.

Chef/Proprietor: Brian Maule Open: Mon to Fri L 12 to 2.30, Mon to Sat D 6 to 10 Closed: first 2 weeks Jan, last week July, first week Aug, bank hols Meals: alc (main courses £19.50 to £22.50). Set L and D 6 to 7 £15.50 (2 courses) to £18.50, Set D £48.50 Service: not inc Cards: Amex, Delta, Maestro, MasterCard, Visa Details: 110 seats. Vegetarian meals. Children's helpings. No smoking. Music. Air-conditioned

This symbol means that the restaurant has elected to participate in *The Good Food Guide's* £5 voucher scheme (see 'Using The Good Food Guide' for details).

Buttery

652 Argyle Street, Glasgow G3 8UF
Tel: (0141) 221 8188

Cooking 5 | Modern Scottish | £54

A change of décor has brought a markedly different style to this old Glasgow stager. Gone are the chintzy ornaments and the saucy French prints in the lavatories, and in come modern lighting, muted carpets and stargazer lilies. In, too, comes Christopher Watson, with a mission to cook in the modern Scottish idiom overlaid with a patina of the lightest Gallic.

Start with a pair of briefly fried, springy West Coast scallops and a few meaty mussels in a winey fish bouillon sprinkled with chives. That made for considerable happiness at inspection, as did a dish-of-the-day daube of succulent beef with turnips and mash. More experimental dishes might see brill fashioned into a roulade and served with romescu sauce and a mussel and leek ragoût, followed by chestnut-crusted Dunkeld lamb in a lovage-scented red wine reduction. Desserts should spark the imagination, as with vanilla steamed pudding with spiced treacle sauce and 'excellent' russet apple ice cream. A carefully annotated modern wine list ascends in price from a glass of Pinot Grigio at £4 to a bottle of Gevrey-Chambertin aux Combottes 2000 from Domaine Dujac at £125.

Chef: Christopher Watson Proprietor: Ian Fleming Open: Tue to Fri L 12 to 2, Tue to Sat D 6 to 10 Closed: 26 Dec, 1 and 2 Jan Meals: Set L £16 (2 courses) to £22, Set D £34 (2 courses) to £38 Service: not inc Cards: Amex, Delta, Maestro, MasterCard, Visa Details: 60 seats. Car park. Vegetarian meals. Children's helpings. No smoking. Wheelchair access (also men's WC). Music. No mobile phones. Air-conditioned

étain

The Glass House, Springfield Court, Glasgow G1 3JX
Tel: (0141) 225 5630

NEW CHEF | Modern Scottish | £50

A glass frontage (as you'd expect, given the address), a series of tall mirrors, discreet lighting and a small lounge area for drinks, all add up to produce an elegant restaurant. No longer part of the Conran empire, there is also a new chef: Neil

Clark has taken over the stoves from Geoffrey Smeddle (who has taken over the renowned Peat Inn in Fife). Expect to start with glazed Loch Fyne oysters with tarragon and parsley, or braised pig's cheek with a carrot and ginger purée. Peterhead halibut on poached slices of celery and mussels is served with a light velouté of garlic and butter as a main course, while Gressingham duck breast comes with a satisfying white-bean casserole. Desserts might include rhubarb crumble tart with a ginger granita and a scoop of clotted cream. The wine list starts the ball rolling at £20.

Chef: Neil Clark   **Proprietor:** Zinc Bar/Grill Ltd   **Open:** Sun to Fri L 12 to 2.30 (3 Sun), Mon to Sat D 5.30 to 10 (10.30 Sat) **Closed:** 25 Dec, 1 Jan   **Meals:** Set L £16 (2 courses) to £29, Set D £26 (2 courses) to £39   **Service:** 12.5% (optional) **Cards:** Amex, Delta, Maestro, MasterCard, Visa   **Details:** 60 seats. Vegetarian meals. No smoking. Wheelchair access (also WC). Music. Air-conditioned

Gamba

225A West George Street, Glasgow G2 2ND
Tel: (0141) 572 0899
Website: www.gamba.co.uk

Cooking 3	Seafood	£59

Shored by a good local reputation, Gamba is best known for serving seafood dishes in a Mediterranean-style environment. Although there are non-fish options, it's the seafood that holds all the cards, from simple presentations to dishes with more Asian influences. Prices are on the high side, particularly as what comes on the plate doesn't always hit the heights, but there are some interesting ideas. Mussel and onion stew with saffron and red pepper, or hummus with smoked salmon, cottage cheese and toasted onion bread are examples of the fusion techniques. Main courses follow the lead with simply grilled lemon sole one option, while among more complex dishes could be whole roast sea bream with Chinese cabbage, chilli oil, scarlet prawns and ginger. End with warm banana sponge with vanilla ice cream and maple syrup or lemon and blueberry crème brûlée. The expansive wine list is pricey but global, with house choices starting at £15.95 for a South African Chenin Blanc.

Chefs: Derek Marshall and John Gillespie   **Proprietors:** Alan Tomkins and Derek Marshall   **Open:** Mon to Sat 12 to 2.30, 5 to 10.30   **Closed:** 25 and 26 Dec, 1 and 2 Jan   **Meals:** alc (main courses £11 to £24). Set L and D 5 to 6 £15.95 (2 courses) to £17.95   **Service:** not inc   **Cards:** Amex, Delta, Maestro, MasterCard, Visa   **Details:** 66 seats. Vegetarian meals. Music. No mobile phones. Air-conditioned

Michael Caines at ABode Glasgow

The Arthouse, 129 Bath Street, Glasgow G2 2SZ
Tel: (0141) 572 6011
Website: www.michaelcaines.com

Cooking 5	Modern European	£53

The fashionable greens and browns of this latest opening from Michael Caines and Andrew Brownsword's ABode Group (see Royal Clarence Hotel, Exeter) hardly redeem the bleak view on to a faceless modern building opposite, but the prize draw is Martin Donnelly's dazzling culinary talent, evidenced from canapés to petits fours. He translates the restrained cuisine of Michael Caines with considerable panache, focusing largely on fresh Scottish raw materials and allying French technique to modern British sensibility, teaming pan-fried red mullet with smoked aubergine purée, tomato, courgette and fennel cream sauce, or serving a main-course saddle of venison with red cabbage, fondant potato, celeriac purée and redcurrant and tea sauce. Elsewhere, 'voluptuously smooth' roast pumpkin and Parmesan soup is poured on to a spoonful of pumpkin oil and a heap of 'delectably earthy' wild mushrooms, and a fine piece of halibut is teamed with a risotto of fennel, sun-blush tomatoes, basil and Parmesan.

Desserts maintain the pace with a light cranachan soufflé served with a flavour-packed raspberry sorbet, and a classic tarte Tatin, the latter with buttery 'croustillant' pastry. Vegetarian menus offer good choice, and the wine list is varietally organised and offers much of interest for those with little over £20 to spend. As well as a short fine wine section and bin-ends, there are eight house wines starting at £16.50.

Chef: Martin Donnelly   **Proprietor:** ABode Glasgow   **Open:** Mon to Sat 12 to 2.30, 7 (6.30 Fri and Sat) to 10   **Meals:** alc D (main courses £16 to £23). Set L £12.50 (2 courses) to £17.50, Set D £55   **Service:** not inc   **Cards:** Amex, Delta, Diners, Maestro, MasterCard, Visa   **Details:** 45 seats. Vegetarian meals. No smoking. Wheelchair access (also WC). No music. No mobile phones. Air-conditioned **Accommodation:** 60 rooms

No. Sixteen

16 Byres Road, Glasgow G11 5JY
Tel: (0141) 339 2544

Cooking 2 | **Modern British** | **£39**

Fitting the bill perfectly as a handy neighbourhood restaurant, this compact venue may not win any prizes for comfort but more than compensates with its honest, good-value food – as the crowds who fill it every night will testify. Lamb fillet with herb couscous and tsatsiki has stood out among main-course options on the dinner menu, but there might also be pan-roast chicken breast with haricot and green beans, gazpacho and guacamole. Meals might be book-ended with a pan-fried fishcake with lime yoghurt and sweet chilli sauce, or perhaps a terrine of confit duck, pistachios, apricots and coriander with pear syrup, and a dessert of pecan tart with chocolate and coconut parfait. Wines are sensibly chosen from around the world with an eye for good drinking at affordable prices, house selections getting the ball rolling at £15.45.

Chef: Grant Neil **Proprietors:** Margaret and Ronnie Campbell **Open:** all week 12 to 2.30, 5.30 to 9.45 (9 Sun) **Meals:** alc (main courses £12.50 to £17). Set L and D 5.30 to 6.30 Mon to Fri £11.50 (2 courses) to £13.50 **Service:** not inc **Cards:** Amex, Delta, Diners, Maestro, MasterCard, Visa **Details:** 40 seats. Vegetarian meals. No smoking. No music. No mobile phones

Rococo

202 West George Street, Glasgow G2 2NR
Tel: (0141) 221 5004
Website: www.restaurantrococo.co.uk

Cooking 3 | **Modern European** | **£59**

The outside belies the swish interior of this basement restaurant. White-tiled floors, dark brown leather upholstery, reproduction classical paintings and a mass of tiny ceiling lights give the venue a distinctly stylish edge. Mark Tamburrini's cooking style suits the setting, demonstrating real flair and a light touch. The menus offer the likes of pan-seared fillet of mackerel with pesto aïoli potatoes, or Thai chicken soup, while main courses might be roast fillet of John Dory in a foie gras froth with wild mushroom and broad bean risotto and glazed asparagus, or grilled chump of Pentland lamb with nutmeg-flavoured dauphinois potatoes, petits pois, mint hollandaise and a veal reduction. Traditional desserts with a twist include profiteroles filled with

praline cream, or lemon bread-and-butter pudding. Service is sharp, and incidentals such as bread and petits fours all add to the experience. The wine list gives a lot of room to France, but the rest of Europe and the New World are well represented too, with some classy names showing up. List prices start at £22.

Chef: Mark Tamburrini **Proprietors:** Alan and Audrey Brown **Open:** all week 12 to 3, 5 to 10 (10.30 Fri and Sat) **Closed:** 1 Jan **Meals:** alc L 12 to 2.30 and D 5 to 6.30 (6 Fri and Sat) (main courses £10 to £19). Set L 12 to 2.30 £18.95, Set L 12 to 3 £22.95, Set D 5 to 6.30 (6 Fri and Sat) £22.95, Set D £31 (2 courses) to £39.50 **Service:** not inc **Cards:** Amex, Delta, Diners, Maestro, MasterCard, Visa **Details:** 70 seats. Vegetarian meals. Children's helpings. No smoking. Music. Air-conditioned

Rogano

11 Exchange Place, Glasgow G1 3AN
Tel: (0141) 248 4055
Website: www.rogano.co.uk

Cooking 3 | **Seafood** | **£53**

Artistic, elegant and reputedly Glasgow's oldest restaurant, Rogano has a splendid Art Deco interior dating from 1935. Some of the classic seafood dishes on the menu are of similar vintage, or older: fish soup with rouille and croûtons, lemon sole meunière, bouillabaisse, and lobster thermidor, for example. But more up-to-date ideas are also evident in the shape of pan-seared scallops with black pudding, warm bacon and shallot vierge, grilled sea bass with fennel and beetroot, lime and coriander oil, and seared salmon with crayfish gazpacho. Non-fish eaters might choose grilled pigeon breast with green lentil broth to start, followed by pan-fried venison cutlets with smoked venison haggis and game jus, and there is a separate vegetarian menu. Finish with, perhaps, lemon sponge with coconut ice cream. Wines are predominantly white, as you'd expect, with a couple of house selections at £16.50. The restaurant is for sale as we go to press.

Chef: Andrew Cumming **Proprietor:** Punch Brewery **Open:** all week 12 to 2.30, 6.30 to 10.30 **Closed:** 25 Dec, 1 Jan **Meals:** alc (main courses £18.50 to £35). Set L £17.50. Bar and café menus available **Service:** 12.5% (optional) **Cards:** Amex, Delta, Diners, Maestro, MasterCard, Visa **Details:** 140 seats. 20 seats outside. Vegetarian meals. No children. No smoking. Music. No mobile phones. Air-conditioned

78 St Vincent

78 St Vincent Street, Glasgow G2 5UB
Tel: (0141) 248 7878
Website: www.78stvincent.com

NEW CHEF | Modern Scottish | £43

There's more than a hint of glamorous Parisian *belle époque* style about this big city-centre venue – fitting enough for a building that dates from 1914. News of a change in kitchen personnel reached the Guide too late for inspection, but the menus look set to continue in a global modern brasserie style. Starters typically feature haggis gâteau with whole-grain mustard cream, alongside a salad of pan-fried tiger prawns, scallops and asparagus with chilli and lime butter, while main courses show similarly broad scope, ranging from pork fillet with sage-scented caramelised apples and a port and shallot jus to seared turbot in a parsley, smoked Cheddar and lemon crust on pasta with a caviar butter sauce. Finish perhaps with pear and almond tart with Calvados cream. A choice of eight wines by the glass opens a diverse international list arranged by nationality. Prices start at £13.95.

Chefs: Martin Furlong and Craig Ferguson **Proprietors:** Julie and Frederick Williams **Open:** all week 12 to 3, 5 to 10 (10.30 Fri and Sat) **Meals:** alc exc Sat D (main courses L £7 to £11, D £14.50 to £23). Set L and D 5 to 7 £12.50 (2 courses) to £15.50, Set D Sat £24.95 (2 courses) to £29.95 **Service:** not inc **Cards:** Amex, Delta, Diners, Maestro, MasterCard, Visa **Details:** 120 seats. Vegetarian meals. Children's helpings. No smoking. Wheelchair access (also WC). No music

Stravaigin

28 Gibson Street, Glasgow G12 8NX
Tel: (0141) 334 2665
Website: www.stravaigin.com

Cooking 2 | Global | £45

An ever-popular basement restaurant and bar in the student district, Stravaigin remains one of the best options for interesting and good-value food in lively, informal surroundings. To call the menu eclectic barely does it justice, the global fusion cooking turning up starters ranging from Thai-style salmon ceviche with coconut and chilli-toasted peanuts to roast cashew and vegetable korma pie with saffron-roast cauliflower and a spinach and yoghurt salad. Main courses are simi-larly varied, taking in Cadaquès-style rabbit with belly pork and mustard estofado and boulangère potatoes, alongside roast cod fillet with rosemary-infused root vegetables and a dark Belgian chocolate and red wine sauce. The inventive streak runs through to desserts such as vanilla-roast baby pineapple with coconut crème fraîche ice cream. A well-chosen wine list offers a varied modern selection of bottles from £13.95.

Chef: Daniel Blencowe **Proprietor:** Colin Clydesdale **Open:** all week 12 to 5, 5 to 11 **Closed:** 25 Dec, 1 Jan **Meals:** alc (main courses £12 to £24). Set L and D 5 to 7 (6.30 Sat) £11.95 (2 courses) to £13.50. Café/bar menu available **Service:** not inc **Cards:** Amex, Delta, Diners, Maestro, MasterCard, Visa **Details:** 70 seats. Vegetarian meals. Children's helpings. No smoking. Music. Air-conditioned

Stravaigin 2

8 Ruthven Lane, Glasgow G12 9BG
Tel: (0141) 334 7165
Website: www.stravaigin.com

Cooking 2 | Global | £45

The second of Colin Clydesdale's restaurant duo (see entry above) comes with comfortable dark leather banquettes and modish light wooden tables. It owes its lively, relaxed atmosphere in part to an eclectic university crowd and also to the kitchen's broad-minded modern cooking. Haggis, neeps and tatties tip their bonnet to the Scottish larder, but there's much more besides. Try Thai fishcakes, vongole nero, or Persian chicken breast with lemon-dressed fatoush and taboulleh salad, and white miso soup with pork and chicken dumplings and soba noodles. Otherwise, the global menu promises everything from vegetarian and salad dishes to kaffir lime leaf mascarpone panna-cotta with berry compote. House wines from France and Australia are £13.45.

Chef: Andrew Mitchell **Proprietor:** Colin Clydesdale **Open:** all week 12 (11 Sat and Sun) to 11 **Closed:** 25 Dec, 1 Jan **Meals:** alc (main courses £10 to £20). Set L and D 5 to 7 (6 Sat) £11.95 (2 courses) to £13.95 **Service:** not inc **Cards:** Amex, Delta, Diners, Maestro, MasterCard, Visa **Details:** 74 seats. 10 seats outside. Vegetarian meals. Children's helpings. No smoking. Wheelchair access (also WC). Music. Air-conditioned

Ubiquitous Chip

12 Ashton Lane, Glasgow G12 8SJ
Tel: (0141) 334 5007
Website: www.ubiquitouschip.co.uk

___

Cooking 4 | **Scottish** | **£51**

Here since 1971, the Chip is something of an old stager on the Glasgow eating scene, so you might think that tradition is the name of the game. Not so. The menu has always been noted as much for its speculative culinary approach as it has for its fine Scottish produce. While the kitchen seems to relish interesting combinations, with Scotch Bonnet chillies flavouring a cauliflower crème caramel, for example, you can always opt for a plate of hot langoustines with garlic butter if this all seems an ingredient too far. But the vein of unusual ingredients enlivens main courses too, with lunch delivering free-range chicken roasted in lemon, with spinach, a Crowdie cheese and potato cake, and lemon-curd tartlet, while dinner sees bitter chocolate sauce and roast cherry tomatoes accompanying loin of hare with basil and water chestnut stovies. Inspection, however, revealed some inconsistencies, and, while service does its best, there are reports of lapses. The long, international wine list is strong in both classic and modern styles. Interesting bottles in the £20 to £30 range include selections from the Loire, South Africa, California and Australia. House wines are £14.95.

___

Chef: Ian Brown **Proprietor:** Ronnie Clydesdale **Open:** all week 12 to 2.30 (12.30 to 3 Sun), 5.30 (6.30 Sun) to 11 **Closed:** 25 Dec, 1 Jan **Meals:** Set L Mon to Sat £22.80 (2 courses) to £28.65, Set L Sun £17.95 (inc wine), Set D £33.80 (2 courses) to £38.95. Bar and brasserie menus available **Service:** not inc **Cards:** Amex, Delta, Diners, Maestro, MasterCard, Visa **Details:** 180 seats. Vegetarian meals. Children's helpings. No smoking. Wheelchair access (also WC). No music. Air-conditioned

Urban Grill

NEW ENTRY

61 Kilmarnock Road, Shawlands, Glasgow
G41 3YR
Tel: (0141) 649 2745
Website: www.urbangrill.co.uk

___

Cooking 1 | **European** | **£34**

Urban Grill is the latest venture by Alan Tomkins and Derek Marshall, who also own the city's Gamba (see entry). The stylish restaurant, a magnet for young professionals, has dark wood and dark furnishings in a sort of retro 1950s style and a short menu that is long on familiarity, although some unusual elements appear, such as fish soup with prawn dumplings and ginger. Spanish ham with pears, rocket and Parmesan, and mussel, onion and tomato stew are typical starters, while main courses run from smoked haddock and salmon fishcake with well-flavoured creamed leeks and a creamy mustard sauce to ribeye with chips, or Italian sausages with pesto mash and red pepper gravy. Milk chocolate crème brûlée and sticky toffee pudding might end a meal. The short, reasonably priced wine list opens at £12.95 for house French.

___

Chef: Michael Macaree **Proprietors:** Alan Tomkins and Derek Marshall **Open:** all week 12 to 10.30 (10 Sun to Wed) **Closed:** 25 and 26 Dec, 1 and 2 Jan **Meals:** alc (main courses L £5 to £9, D £8 to £19) **Service:** not inc **Cards:** Amex, Delta, Maestro, MasterCard, Visa **Details:** 140 seats. Vegetarian meals. Children's helpings. No smoking. Wheelchair access (also WC). Music. No mobile phones. Air-conditioned

MAP 11 GLENLIVET – Moray

Minmore House

AR

Glenlivet AB37 9DB
Tel: (01807) 590378

___

Victor and Lynne Janssen run their elegant nine-bedroom hotel, surrounded by the beauty of the Glenlivet Crown Estate, with hands-on efficiency. Set-price dinner (£37.50) could start with game terrine with Cumberland sauce or seared West Coast scallops, and proceed to tournedos of Highland venison with rösti and redcurrants or roast fillet of pork with morels. Hot chocolate fondant is one way to finish. Wines from £15.95. Open all week.

___

£ This symbol means that it is possible to have a three-course dinner, including coffee, half a bottle of house wine and service, for £30 or less per person.

MAP 11 **GULLANE** – East Lothian

Greywalls Hotel

Muirfield, Gullane EH31 2EF
Tel: (01620) 842144
Website: www.greywalls.co.uk

Cooking 3 | Modern British | £60

This tremendous building of golden, not grey stone, was designed by Edwardian architect Sir Edwin Lutyens, as a 'dignified holiday home', and that it is, although not just for the chosen few. The gardens are also impeccable and that's the theme that runs throughout, from the formally attired staff, to the attention to detail in the restaurant; wine is poured regularly and crumbs are fastidiously brushed from your tablecloth. David Williams has injected some modern twists into their monthly changing four course à la carte menu; over the last year he has added a six-course tasting menu and more than doubled their suppliers. Look out for langoustine ravioli in a langoustine and brandy bisque, or perhaps seared dived scallops in a curry velouté to start, followed by Scottish salmon, buttered lobster and pommes mousseline. Meat eaters might be tempted by black-faced Scottish lamb rump with gratin potatoes. End with a selection of cheeses or perhaps their cranachan parfait with a chilled raspberry soup and raspberry sorbet. Thirteen choices of house wine start at £18.50.

Chef: David Williams **Proprietor:** Giles Weaver **Open:** all week 12 to 2, 7.30 to 9 **Closed:** Nov to Mar incl **Meals:** Set L £20 (2 courses) to £25, Set D £45 **Service:** not inc **Cards:** Amex, Delta, Maestro, MasterCard, Visa **Details:** 50 seats. Car park. Vegetarian meals. No smoking. Wheelchair access (also WC). No music **Accommodation:** 23 rooms

La Potinière

34 Main Street, Gullane EH31 2AA
Tel: (01620) 843214
Website: www.la-potiniere.co.uk

Cooking 6 | Modern British | £51

It is easy to drive past La Potinière, as signposting is discreet and the grey-stone terrace is in a part of town where houses seem to outnumber commercial properties. Inside, the small dining room is elegant in a restrained way, with a pleasantly down-

to-earth atmosphere aided, in no small part, by unflaggingly polite and charming service. Keith Marley and Mary Runciman's cooking is led by local produce, which is used to create a simple yet sophisticated repertoire of dishes with a predominantly modern British flavour. Reporters are unanimously impressed. The four-course fixed-price dinner offers a couple of choices per course and might feature grilled goats' cheese with honey and cardamom on a red onion, pepper and cranberry tart, then go on to cream of fennel soup with crab and orange cream. Main courses are similarly varied, taking in, for example, roast loin and slow-cooked haunch of venison with celeriac dauphinois and a morel and cep sauce, or steamed fillet of lemon sole stuffed with its own mousse and served on a smoked haddock, leek and parsley mash with a light grainy mustard sauce.

Desserts tend to stick to a theme: almond, pistachio, apple and apricot sponge comes with Amaretto pannacotta, apricot coulis and apricot sorbet, and passion-fruit mousse with a coconut and mango tart, pineapple granita and tropical fruit coulis. Lunch is in a similar vein, but is offered at two or three courses and is very good value. The concise and sound wine list opens with Spanish white and Argentinian red at £16.

Chefs: Mary Runciman and Keith Marley **Proprietor:** Mary Runciman **Open:** Wed to Sun 12.30 to 1.30, 7 to 8.30 **Closed:** Sun D Oct to Apr, last 2 weeks Jan **Meals:** Set L £17 (2 courses) to £20, Set D £38 **Service:** not inc **Cards:** Maestro, MasterCard, Visa **Details:** 30 seats. Car park. Children's helpings. No smoking. Wheelchair access (also WC). No music. No mobile phones

MAP 11 **INVERKEILOR** – Angus

Gordon's

32 Main Street, Inverkeilor DD11 5RN
Tel: (01241) 830364
Website: www.gordonsrestaurant.co.uk

Cooking 5 | Modern Scottish | £48

This unremarkable looking building in the tiny village of Inverkeilor is certainly a find. Inside, a calm atmosphere pervades thanks to Maria and Gordon Watson's efficient management. The décor is in keeping with the Scottish location, with exposed beams, a real fire, and various interesting artefacts to catch the eye.

The food is delicately presented and confidently made by Gordon and his son Garry. Breakfast is always a treat, and the three-course lunch menu impresses, offering perhaps a tian of white crabmeat and ginger followed by roast monkfish tail, but it's the stylish evening menu that really hits the spot, with a convincing blend of the traditional and modern. A pressed terrine of smoked fish may start off proceedings, with an intermediate course to follow of perhaps a lightly curried parsnip velouté with crab dumplings. Sautéed loin of Perthshire venison with sweet potato and goats' cheese dauphinois could be a main-course choice, while open ravioli of halibut and John Dory shows a lighter touch. For those with room to spare, try the farmhouse cheeses with quince and walnut bread; a sweet option could be lemon and ginger pudding. Coffee and home-made petits fours finish things off nicely. The global wine list, with its good descriptive notes, starts off at £11.95 for the house choices, and a number of other bottles are under £20.

> **Chefs:** Gordon and Garry Watson **Proprietors:** Maria and Gordon Watson **Open:** Wed to Fri and Sun L 12 to 1.45, Tue to Sat D 7 to 9 **Meals:** Set L £25, Set D £38 **Service:** not inc **Cards:** Delta, Maestro, MasterCard, Visa **Details:** 24 seats. Car park. Vegetarian meals. No children under 12. Children's helpings. No smoking. Wheelchair access (not WC). No music. No mobile phones **Accommodation:** 3 rooms

MAP 11 **INVERNESS** – **Highland**

Culloden House Hotel, Adams Dining Room

Culloden, Inverness IV2 7BZ
Tel: (01463) 790461
Website: www.cullodenhouse.co.uk

Cooking 2	International	£53

Part of the Culloden House Hotel, this proudly traditional restaurant (the waiters wear tartan) is the sort that requires a special occasion to be truly appreciated. The menus bear four impressive courses, the kitchen's bias towards Scottish produce producing starters of a parcel of spiced Orkney crab and smoked salmon with lemon and truffle oil, or carpaccio of Highland venison with a dressing made with shallots and juniper berries. An intermediate course follows – perhaps cream of smoked haddock soup, or strawberry and lime granita – while main dishes weigh in with Scottish beef fillet topped with pâté and coated in a wild mushroom bordelaise, or grilled salmon in a

mussel and monkfish broth with a ginger and leek potato cake. Hot caramelised pear with ginger pudding will fill any gap. The wine list offers decent enough choice and some premier producers for those who can afford its prices, which open at £25. Around half a dozen are served by the glass from £3.25.

> **Chef:** Michael Simpson **Proprietor:** Romantic Places **Open:** all week 12.30 to 2, 7 to 9 **Closed:** 24 to 27 Dec **Meals:** alc (main courses £14.50 to £24). Light L menu available **Service:** 10% (optional) **Cards:** Amex, MasterCard, Visa **Details:** 60 seats. Car park. Vegetarian meals. No children under 10. Children's helpings. No smoking. No music. No mobile phones **Accommodation:** 28 rooms

Glenmoriston Town House, Abstract Restaurant

20 Ness Bank, Inverness IV2 4SF
Tel: (01463) 223777
Website: www.abstractrestaurant.co.uk

Cooking 4	Modern French	£61

The restaurant and bar occupy the ground floor of a solidly dignified three-storey grey-stone house on the east bank of the river Ness, where minimal décor and non-figurative artwork are perhaps the inspiration behind the restaurant's name – Abstract. Loic Lefebvre's pairing of unusual flavours is clearly a passion and has seen a starter of roast scallops matched with braised pork and endive compote as well as orange sauce, while a main course of roast wild duck breast combines the leg served in a pastilla with plum confit and orange and star anise sauce. The kitchen can also deliver Aberdeen Angus beef with a terrine of potato and shin, and balsamic and beetroot sauce. Desserts may feature crispy poached pear with gingerbread ice cream and salpicon in a vanilla jelly. The 'impressive' tasting menu can offer a foie gras duo (poached in a Thai bouillon and a terrine glazed with orange and saffron jelly), roast lobster with large macaroni, and breast of wood pigeon with creamy quinoa and curry sauce. Wines kick off at £18, and there are eight by the glass, but deeper pockets are indulged with the rest of the French-dominated list.

> **Chef:** Loic Lefebvre **Proprietor:** Barry Larsen **Open:** Tue to Sun 12 to 2, 7 to 9.30 **Meals:** Set L £14 (2 courses) to £18, Set D £34 (2 courses) to £67 (inc wine) **Service:** not inc **Cards:** Amex, Delta, Diners, Maestro, MasterCard, Visa **Details:** 55 seats. Car park. Vegetarian meals. Children's helpings. No smoking. Music. No mobile phones. Air-conditioned **Accommodation:** 30 rooms

Rocpool Rendezvous

1 Ness Walk, Inverness IV3 5NE
Tel: (01463) 717274

Cooking 2 | Modern European | £41

There's a relaxed bistro feel to this long, narrow restaurant close to Inverness's main shopping centre. Our inspector found perfectly competent renditions of modern European cooking, classics such as chicken liver parfait with fresh mango chutney, and roast loin of venison served with bacon and black pudding, creamed parsnip and garlic mash, but not quite the sparkle for which the place was once celebrated, causing him to wonder if the organisation has been stretched with the January 2006 opening of a boutique hotel, restaurant and bar in Culduthel Road. On a more ambitious night there might be Italian meatballs with smoked bacon and pine nuts, and roast chump of lamb with lyonnaise potatoes, and there are simpler, fixed-price lunch and early-evening menus. Service has been described as 'more caff than restaurant', while the wine list has fair choice below £20, with house French £13.50 a bottle

Chef: Steven Devlin **Proprietors:** Steven Devlin and Adrian Pieraccini **Open:** Mon to Sat 12 to 2.30, 5.45 to 10; also open Sun D Mar to Oct **Meals:** alc (main courses £9 to £18.50). Set L £8.95 (2 courses), Set D 5.45 to 6.45 £10.95 (2 courses) **Service:** not inc **Cards:** Amex, Delta, Diners, Maestro, MasterCard, Visa **Details:** 55 seats. Vegetarian meals. Children's helpings. No smoking. Wheelchair access (also WC). Music. No mobile phones. Air-conditioned

---

MAP 11 KILLIECRANKIE – Perthshire & Kinross

Killiecrankie House Hotel

Killiecrankie PH16 5LG
Tel: (01796) 473220
Website: www.killiecrankiehotel.co.uk

Cooking 3 | Modern European | £43

Killiecrankie, midway between Pitlochry and Blair Atholl, was the site of the 1689 battle when the Jacobites vanquished the English. Nowadays, the nearby hotel is something of a country retreat, noted for its unpretentious décor and a modern repertoire that surprises and delights. Combinations are not outlandish, however:

chicken livers are served in a puff pastry case with smoked bacon, shallots and a brandy cream sauce, and goats' cheese brûlée with salad leaves and chive oil. Roasting is a favoured cooking method, applied to main courses such as Gressingham duck breast with mange-tout, lyonnaise potatoes and an orange and Drambuie glaze, or fillet of venison with spring onion mash and a date and port jus, and at dessert stage, teaming roast rhubarb with a stem ginger cheesecake, and serving slow-roast peaches with a pistachio, caramel and orange glaze. Tim Waters' wine trade experience has gone into an inspirational list that covers Old and New Worlds roughly equally. Although there are pricey bottles (mostly claret), there is also good choice at the cheaper end. Prices start at £14.90 for a French Merlot, and there are eight wines by the glass from £3.85.

Chef: Mark Easton **Proprietors:** Tim and Maillie Waters **Open:** all week D only 7 to 8.15 **Closed:** Jan to Mar **Meals:** Set D £22 (2 courses) to £34. Bar L and D menu available **Service:** not inc **Cards:** Delta, Maestro, MasterCard, Visa **Details:** 34 seats. Car park. Vegetarian meals. No children under 9. No smoking. Wheelchair access (not WC). No music. No mobile phones **Accommodation:** 10 rooms

---

MAP 11 KINGUSSIE – Highland

The Cross

Tweed Mill Brae, Ardbroilach Road, Kingussie
PH21 1LB
Tel: (01540) 661166
Website: www.thecross.co.uk

Cooking 5 | Modern British | £55

Refurbishment at this comfortable restaurant-with-rooms has seen the back of 'stuffy' white tablecloths, and now plain wooden tables are adorned simply with Scottish slate place mats and plain Riedel glassware. It is part of a process of 'de-formalisation', creating a more relaxed mood, although fans of David Young's classy modern British cooking will be pleased to hear that changes in that department have been confined to minor tweaks. Meals start with an appetiser – perhaps line-caught mackerel with rhubarb salsa – and the menu runs to two or three choices per course. Among winter starters might be venison boudin with beetroot and apple chutney, Puy lentils and rocket salad, while spring choices could include a simple dish of Perthshire asparagus with sauce mousseline, or seared scallops with a broth of peas and pancetta. Main courses continue in similar vein: perhaps rack of black-faced lamb with ratatouille, wilted spinach and dauphinois potatoes, wild sea bass with sauce vierge, baby leeks and crushed ratte potatoes, or breast of Gressingham duck with apple and shallot compote and chive mash. To finish, there's classic lemon tart with raspberries, or, for the more adventurous, hot chocolate fondant with chilli ice cream. The wine list aims to strike a balance between high quality and fair prices, which it achieves admirably with a wide choice of carefully chosen bottles from top growers around the world. Choice in the £25 to £40 bracket is outstanding, but there is also a decent handful of wines under £20.

Chefs: Becca Henderson and David Young Proprietors: David and Katie Young Open: Tue to Sat D only 7 to 8.30 (8.45 Sat) Closed: Christmas, 2 Jan to mid-Feb Meals: Set D £37 to £47 Service: net prices Cards: Amex, Delta, Maestro, MasterCard, Visa Details: 24 seats. Car park. No children under 10. No smoking. Wheelchair access (also WC). No music. No mobile phones Accommodation: 8 rooms

MAP 11 LARGOWARD – Fife

Inn at Lathones

By Largoward, St Andrews KY9 1JE
Tel: (01334) 840494
Website: www.theinn.co.uk

Cooking 2 | Modern European | £51

The oldest part of this luxuriously appointed former coaching inn is the bar, built in 1603 as stables and supposedly haunted by a 'grey lady'. The restaurant, in the slightly less ancient front house, is where to go for high-flown French-accented cooking along the lines of pan-fried smoked pigeon breast with Puy lentils, roast beetroot and parsnip crisps, followed by roast rack of lamb with dauphinois potatoes, or loin of codling with mussel, scallop and leek velouté. Seafood platters are a highlight, made with caught-that-day shellfish. 'Trilogies' are another, as in a beef dish comprising pan-fried fillet, a miniature cottage pie and an onion stuffed with braised oxtail. There is even a trilogy menu, with tripartite dishes at each course, finishing perhaps with milk chocolate délices, dark chocolate ganache and white chocolate sorbet. The democratic wine list offers good drinking at every price point from £12.95, with a wide choice of highly quaffable bottles under £25. Some interesting and unusual

names have been chosen for those with an adventurous streak. Around half a dozen wines are available by the glass.

Chef: Martin Avey Proprietors: Nick and Jocelyn White Open: all week 12 to 2.30, 6 to 9.30 Closed: 2 weeks Jan Meals: alc (main courses £17.50 to £28.50). Set L £14.50 to £19 Service: not inc Cards: Amex, Delta, Diners, Maestro, MasterCard, Visa Details: 90 seats. Car park. Vegetarian meals. Children's helpings. No smoking. Wheelchair access (not WC). Music. No mobile phones Accommodation: 13 rooms

MAP 11 LOCHINVER – Highland

Albannach

Baddidarrach, Lochinver IV27 4LP
Tel: (01571) 844407
Website: www.thealbannach.co.uk

Cooking 6 | Modern Scottish | £57

Way up on the north-west Highland coast, Colin Craig and Lesley Crosfield's long-established restaurant, a Victorian house built around the shell of a much older cottage, is a beacon of regional class. The favoured culinary inflections may be French, but they are brought to bear on the proudest and best of Scottish produce, with all the right boxes ticked – free-range, local, organic and wild. Set menus of five courses plus coffee, served in the evenings at a single sitting, change daily, and the cooking aims for lightness and balance, matching ingredients in apposite combinations rather than striving for shock value.

Diners settling in one Wednesday evening in late July were presented with a bowl of seafood broth combining lobster and langoustine, as a curtain-raiser to an intermediate course of guinea fowl breast on juniper chard with roast shallots and a wild mushroom jus. Star of the show was turbot, caught locally, served on a bed of greens with braised fennel and grandly sauced with champagne. A brace of cheeses – Wigmore from Berkshire and Ireland's Ardrahan – were served as intermission before the dessert, a tartlet of caramelised apple with Calvados ice cream and apple crisps. Great home-made breads and sympathetic service enhance the overall appeal.

Also worthy of note is an eye-catching wine list with a backbone of fine French bottles, but with some engaging selections from Spain and the New World too. A plethora of half-bottles will tempt the abstemious, and the imaginative house selections, at £13, are a Picpoul de Pinet white and a quality Languedoc Merlot.

Chefs/Proprietors: Colin Craig and Lesley Crosfield **Open:** Tue to Sun D only 8 (1 sitting) **Closed:** Nov to Mar **Meals:** Set D £45 **Service:** not inc **Cards:** MasterCard, Visa **Details:** 18 seats. Car park. No children under 12. No smoking. No music. No mobile phones **Accommodation:** 6 rooms

---

MAP 11 MELROSE – Borders

Burt's Hotel

AR

Market Square, Melrose TD6 9PL
Tel: (01896) 822285

Built in 1722, this comfortable hotel on the market square has been run for the past 37 years by the Henderson family. Seasonally focused menus (lunch £24.75, dinner £31.75 for three courses) might feature starters of smoked chicken breast with citrus couscous and red pepper coulis, or chilli- and soy-marinated monkfish with mango salsa, while main courses typically include roast sea bass on saffron risotto with charred asparagus, and seared lamb rump on potato and apple rösti with rosemary jus. To finish, go for perhaps layered chocolate gâteau with white chocolate ice cream and pistachio crème anglaise. House wines £12.95. Simpler bar meals also available. Open all week.

MAP 11 MILNGAVIE – East Dunbartonshire

Wild Bergamot

NEW ENTRY

1 Hillhead Street, Milngavie G62 8AF
Tel: (0141) 956 6515

Cooking 2 | Modern Scottish | £45

Two small, comfortable rooms are the setting for the cooking of former army chef Alan Burns, who puts his all into his craft from a tiny kitchen. There's a lounge with black leather sofas from which to peruse the menu, which, with just three or four items at each course, lists the kitchen's suppliers: meat is from the Aberfoyle Butcher, fish from Fish People and so on. A salad of white crabmeat with a crab biscuit, horseradish mousse and avocado ice cream, or ravioli of pigeon, hazelnuts and mushrooms showcase the bold style. Fish is well timed, as in a fillet of sea bass, served on a light

scallop and smoked potato broth and enhanced by a silky tortellini of scallop and langoustine. Otherwise there might be basil-braised shin and roast fillet of Aberdeen Angus beef, accompanied by mustard-infused Anna potatoes, 'lovely, creamy' celeriac purée, and béarnaise. End with bitter chocolate tart with cocoa and coffee bean crunch and Earl Grey ice cream, or rhubarb mousse and sorbet with frozen walnut custard. Interesting notes accompany the wine list, which starts at £15 and is arranged varietally.

Chef/Proprietor: Alan Burns **Open:** Fri and Sat L 12.30 to 1.45, Wed to Sun D 7 to 9.30 **Meals:** Set L £14.50 (2 courses) to £45, Set D £30 to £45 **Service:** not inc **Cards:** Amex, Delta, Maestro, MasterCard, Visa **Details:** 24 seats. No children under 14. No smoking. Music. No mobile phones

---

MAP 11 MOFFAT – Dumfries & Galloway

Limetree

High Street, Moffat DG10 9HG
Tel: (01683) 221654
Website: www.limetree-restaurant.co.uk

Cooking 2 | Modern British | £36

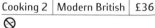

A philosophy of simple food, cooked well, using fresh local ingredients has served the Limetree well since it opened in 2001, and this converted house on the high street of the busy small town of Moffat continues to thrive. The menus are short but cover plenty of ground, starters ranging from lamb and mint sausage with spiced tabbouleh and mint yoghurt to Creole-style prawns with basil butter. Among main courses might be haunch of venison with mushroom and potato gratin, roast celeriac and green peppercorn sauce, alongside honey-roast duck breast with curried parsnips in coconut milk, basmati rice and coriander, followed by poached plums with apple crumble ice cream, or warm ginger cake with toffee sauce. A compact wine list includes six by the glass and house French, from Corney & Barrow, at £12.50.

Chef: Matt Seddon **Proprietors:** Matt and Artemis Seddon **Open:** Sun L 12.30 to 2.30, Tue to Sat D 6.30 to 9 **Closed:** 2 weeks Oct **Meals:** Set L £14.75 (2 courses) to £18.50, Set D £18.50 (2 courses) to £23.50 **Service:** not inc **Cards:** Delta, Maestro, MasterCard, Visa **Details:** 26 seats. Children's helpings. No smoking. Wheelchair access (not WC). Music. No mobile phones

---

Well View

Ballplay Road, Moffat DG10 9JU
Tel: (01683) 220184
Website: www.wellview.co.uk

Cooking 4 | Franco-Scottish | £39

Well View, a small Victorian restaurant-with-rooms, is a sedate affair, located in the old spa town in Scotland's border country. Eating is communal, with guests sitting at one long table in the florally decorated dining room, while the menu is compact, offering just once choice for each course, completed by three desserts. Dinner starts with an amuse-bouche, to be followed by, for instance, a salad of melon, avocado and Parma ham with strawberry vinaigrette. Roast breast of guinea fowl might be the main event, served on sautéed baby potatoes with woodland mushrooms, sun-blush tomatoes and a tarragon cream sauce, and dessert could be chocolate heather cream pot, or lemon yoghurt cream. As Well View is no longer licensed, complimentary wine is served with meals.

Chefs: Janet and Lina Schuckardt Proprietors: Janet and John Schuckardt Open: Sun L 12.30 (1 sitting), all week D 7.30 (1 sitting) Meals: Set L £19, Set D £35 Service: none Cards: Amex, Delta, Maestro, MasterCard, Visa Details: 12 seats. Car park. No children under 6. No smoking. No music. No mobile phones Accommodation: 3 rooms

MAP 11 **MUIR OF ORD** – Highland

Dower House

Highfield, Muir of Ord IV6 7XN
Tel: (01463) 870090
Website: www.thedowerhouse.co.uk

Cooking 2 | Modern British | £51

This quaint Highland cottage is run with hands-on enthusiasm by Robyn and Mena Aitchison. After an extensive kitchen renovation, Robyn can be found working the stoves, creating a set-price menu of three courses, while Mena offers drinks in the drawing room, which has a well-worn comfort about it. The food is contemporary yet simple; the bread is home-made and seasoning is spot-on throughout. Marinated red mullet salad, followed by loin of lamb with tapenade, then prune and Armagnac tart comprised the no-choice, daily-changing menu one evening in autumn; another

evening might see braised breast of wood pigeon, then fillet of local beef with a port and anchovy sauce, rounded off by lemon and rum tart. Dinner ends with coffee and home-made truffles. The well-rounded wine list opens at £16.

Chef: Robyn Aitchison Proprietors: Robyn and Mena Aitchison Open: all week D only 8 (1 sitting) Closed: Christmas Meals: Set D £38 Service: not inc Cards: MasterCard, Visa Details: 15 seats. Car park. No children under 6. Children's helpings. No smoking. Wheelchair access (also WC). No music. No mobile phones Accommodation: 4 rooms

MAP 11 **NEWTON STEWART** – Dumfries & Galloway

Kirroughtree House AR

Newton Stewart DG8 6AN
Tel: (01671) 402141

Built in 1719, with Victorian additions, Kirroughtree is a grand country-house hotel in the Scottish baronial style. Dinner (£32.50 for three courses) is a suitably refined affair, making good use of the area's bountiful natural larder, starting perhaps with breast of partridge on chive risotto with Madeira sauce, main courses typically including sea bass fillet with steamed potatoes, spring onions and Noilly Prat sauce, or breast of Gressingham duck with fondant potato and cranberry sauce. Finish with a plate of Scottish cheeses or something like nougatine glace with melba sauce. Three house wines are £15.75. Open all week.

MAP 11 **Oban** – Argyll & Bute

Ee-Usk

North Pier, Oban PA34 5QD
Tel: (01631) 565666
Website: www.eeusk.com

Cooking 1 | Seafood | £37

'Bang on the waterfront: what more could you ask for?' declares a reporter after visiting this unusual outfit at the end of Oban pier. Given its location, seafood is an understandable preoccupation, taking in anything from 'perfect freshly dressed' crab, and

Lismore oysters, via sweet creel-caught langoustine, to fish-of-the-day specials – perhaps 'fantastic' baked turbot with a leek and cream sauce and deep-fried potatoes – and good old haddock and chips from the printed menu. To sum up, they 'take it out of the sea, cook it and put it on a plate'. Desserts might run to clootie dumpling or lemon cheesecake, service is charming, and a straightforward, roving wine list stays mostly under £20 and starts with a French white and Chilean red at £11.95.

Chef: Marianne MacDonald Proprietors: the Macleod family Open: all week 12 to 3, 6 to 9.30 (9 in winter) Closed: 25 and 26 Dec, 1 Jan Meals: alc (main courses £9 to £29.50) Service: not inc Cards: Delta, MasterCard, Visa Details: 110 seats. 24 seats outside. No children under 10 at D. Children's helpings. No smoking. Wheelchair access (also WC). Music. No mobile phones. Air-conditioned

Waterfront   AR

1 The Railway Pier, Oban PA34 4LW
Tel: (01631) 563110

New owners have signalled a new era at this waterside restaurant located on the Calmac Ferry pier – they now boast a seafood bar downstairs selling locally smoked and fresh shellfish and seafood and also own two fishing boats. Chef Alex Needham is also the new manager but still works the stoves. Look out for seared scallops with crab spring rolls (£8.50), halibut fillet with red onion and sage mash (£16.95), or Waterfront fish pie (£9.50), a lunchtime special. Steamed chocolate pudding (£4.25) ends. Wines to complement the fish start at £12.99. Open all week. Reports please.

MAP 11 PEEBLES – Borders

Cringletie House   NEW ENTRY

Peebles EH45 8PL
Tel: (01721) 725750
Website: www.cringletie.com

Cooking 4 | Franco-Scottish | £51

Set amid 28 acres of park and woodland in the rolling Borders hills, this Victorian shooting lodge has been given a £2 million refurbishment to create a light, modern and cosmopolitan look and feel. The Sutherland dining room has a spectacular painted ceiling and an appealing menu in which local ingredients are to the fore – including produce from the hotel's seventeenth century walled kitchen garden.

Chef Paul Hart's classical French training is apparent in starters such as wood pigeon and foie gras pithiviers with date and orange sauce, or a hot faggot of hare with crushed sprouts, roasted chestnut and caramelised apple. To follow, pan-fried saddle of venison with pumpkin, mulled pears and cinnamon lines up next to herb-crusted turbot with black kale, smoked eel, bacon lardons, ratte potatoes and a soubise sauce, while desserts are refined takes on nursery favourites, such as baked toasted rice and quince pudding with rice pudding ice cream. Lunch is lighter and simpler, with hot smoked salmon on spiced lentils followed perhaps by poached chicken with a light truffle sauce. Five well-chosen house wines at £18 a bottle, £4.75 a glass, open a respectable list that packs in a good range of interesting New World wines to go with the classy Bordeaux and Burgundies.

Chef: Paul Hart Proprietors: Jacob and Johahna Houdt Open: all week 12 (12.30 Sun) to 2, 7 to 9 Closed: early Jan to early Feb Meals: Set L £15 (2 courses) to £19.50, Set D £37.50 to £50 Service: not inc Cards: Amex, Delta, Maestro, MasterCard, Visa Details: 35 seats. Car park. Vegetarian meals. Children's helpings. No smoking. Music. No mobile phones Accommodation: 13 rooms

MAP 11 PERTH – Perthshire & Kinross

63 Tay Street

63 Tay Street, Perth PH2 8NN
Tel: (01738) 441451
Website: www.63taystreet.co.uk

Cooking 4 | Modern Scottish | £37

The Wares' aim is to focus on seasonal local produce, delivered in an informal environment, and served in a relaxed and friendly manner; judging by the bustle on a Thursday night, they clearly succeed in their intention. The décor is restrained but contemporary, working well within a small space. Fillet of Scottish beef and seared Skye scallops, served perhaps with a tomato and cucumber salsa and crispy onion 'grass', both make regular appearances on the menu, and Jeremy Wares' unfussy yet imaginative approach works well. Crab spaghetti with chilli, ginger and coriander, or chicken liver and foie gras parfait with onion chutney and toasted brioche are impressive starters, and main courses are equally varied: ox faggot with mash, Savoy cabbage and onion jus might appear alongside seared sea bream with leek risotto in a red wine reduction, or a trio of pork with provençale vegetables, crispy potato cubes and apple sauce. Finish with rhubarb crème brûlée, or steamed ginger pudding with crème anglaise.

The wine list has been revamped and is now a substantial global affair, arranged by style. A dozen half-bottles and eight by the glass encourage mixing and matching. The house selections start at £11.25, and the list culminates in a handful of fine reds.

Chef: Jeremy Wares Proprietors: Shona and Jeremy Wares Open: Tue to Sat 12 to 2, 6.30 to 9 Meals: Set L £12.95 (2 courses) to £15.50, Set D £20.95 (2 courses) to £27.95 Service: not inc Cards: Amex, Delta, Maestro, MasterCard, Visa Details: 32 seats. Vegetarian meals. No smoking. Wheelchair access (also WC). No music

MAP 11 PLOCKTON – Highland

Plockton Inn

AR

Innes Street, Plockton IV52 8TW
Tel: (01599) 544222

An unassuming inn near the harbour is the setting for some good seafood. Locally caught prawns with garlic butter (£6.50) are among starters, with baked sea bass with rosemary and balsamic butter (£13.95) perhaps one of the main courses. Meat eaters could opt for chicken liver pâté (£3.95), then pork loin steak stuffed with walnuts and ginger accompanied by apple and cider sauce (£8.75). Finish with cranachan ice cream (£3.50) or Scottish cheeses with Orkney oatcakes (£4.25). Three house wines are £10 each. Accommodation. Open all week.

MAP 11 PORT APPIN – Argyll & Bute

Airds Hotel

Port Appin PA38 4DF
Tel: (01631) 730236
Website: www.airds-hotel.com

Cooking 5 | Modern Scottish | £63

The hotel is a long, low, white building on a virtually single-track road off the main Oban to Fort William route. It feels good and remote, all the better to enjoy the comfortable interiors, where, despite the odd stag's head, the tone is reassuringly domestic. The dining room, newly redecorated, boasts serene views over Loch Linnhe. In these agreeable surroundings, Paul Burns's cooking establishes a refined but unpretentious tone. A carte now operates at lunchtime, with the four-course fixed-price formula remaining in place for evenings. A soup such as red pepper and tomato intervenes between starters – perhaps seared sea bass with sun-dried tomatoes, red onion and black olive – and main courses that showcase quality local produce. Two fish and one meat is the weighting, with shellfish-sauced turbot or sautéed sea bream with broad beans and wild mushrooms holding the line against roast venison loin with celeriac purée and red cabbage at an early-spring dinner. Finish with prune and Armagnac soufflé or a four-fruited crumble with crème anglaise. Service is efficient and personable, and a page of well-chosen house wines, from £16 to £27, heads up a classically minded list that does France thoroughly before lighting out for points south.

Chef: Paul Burns Proprietors: Shaun and Jenny McKivragan Open: all week 12.30 to 1.45, 7.30 to 9 Closed: 2 days each week Dec to Jan, 5 to 22 Jan Meals: alc L (main courses £11 to £17.50). Set D £47.50. Light L menu available Service: not inc Cards: Delta, Maestro, MasterCard, Visa Details: 32 seats. Car park. Vegetarian meals. Children's helpings. No children under 8 at D. No smoking. No music. No mobile phones Accommodation: 12 rooms

MAP 11 PORTPATRICK – Dumfries & Galloway

Knockinaam Lodge

Portpatrick DG9 9AD
Tel: (01776) 810471
Website: www.knockinaamlodge.com

Cooking 5 | Modern European | £63

'Reaching this hotel after a long trek along a single-track road full of potholes feels like reaching the end of the world. The waves of the Atlantic lap on the private beach, and Northern Ireland can be seen in the distance on a clear day.' So secluded is this Victorian hunting lodge, indeed, that Churchill met General Eisenhower here in secrecy during the war. Once inside, the thrilling bleakness of the setting melds into the 'golden, natural, classical, mellow' interiors and the relaxed, easy-going approach of the staff.

The formula is a set menu at lunch and dinner, with a choice of dessert or cheese. Tony Pierce cleaves to a fairly traditional country-house style, showing great precision in timings and seasoning, maintaining a sense of balance throughout. A

February dinner proceeded from a chicken and tarragon sausage with Bayonne ham and shiitake mushrooms, to a main dish of baked potato-crusted fillet of halibut with spinach and beurre noisette, via an intermediate salad course involving dried tomatoes, globe artichoke and French beans with a truffle oil dressing. A due sense of occasion at Sunday lunch brings forth superb roast Angus sirloin, powerful horseradish dressing, buttered root vegetables, exemplary Yorkshire pudding and a sweetly rich Madeira gravy. Old-fashioned desserts show up well, as is the case with rhubarb and pear crumble surrounded by a moat of vanilla-speckled custard.

'Welcome to the wonderful world of wine!' begins the list, and wonderful is a pretty fair summation of the contents. There are many pages of French classics, but good to very good choices elsewhere. Australia looks great, and there is even a handful of quality German wines. House wines start at £18 for a crisp Spanish white from Rueda.

Chef: Tony Pierce **Proprietors:** David and Sian Ibbotson **Open:** all week 12 to 1.30, 7 to 9 **Closed:** 24 to 26 Dec **Meals:** Set L Mon to Sat £37.50, Set L Sun £25, Set D £47.50. Bar L menu available **Service:** not inc **Cards:** Amex, Delta, Maestro, MasterCard, Visa **Details:** 20 seats. Car park. Vegetarian meals. No children under 12 at D. Children's helpings at L . No smoking. Wheelchair access (also WC). Music **Accommodation:** 9 rooms

---

 MAP 11 ST ANDREWS – Fife

Seafood Restaurant

The Scores, Bruce Embankment, St Andrews KY16 9AB
Tel: (01334) 479475
Website: www.theseafoodrestaurant.com

Cooking 4 | **Seafood** | **£62**

This dramatic construction of glass, metal and wood perched on the sea wall looking on to the water is alluring even from a distance. Inside, too, it is modern and just as sleek. The main draw is 'really excellent' fish of unbeatable freshness, treated with a light touch. A starter of escabèche of red mullet with cherry tomato and chilli fondue and beetroot syrup adds spice to some fine Scottish ingredients, and a main course of grilled fillet of turbot with a polenta cake, leek ragoût and sauce vierge looks to mainland Europe for inspiration. Other main courses have included grilled fillet of cod served with crevette and spring onion colcannon,

anchovy butter and fish fumet, and breast of duck has come with dauphinois potatoes and red onion marmalade. A selection of mature cheeses (served with pickled figs, quince and oatcakes) is the savoury alternative to desserts such as pannacotta with summer berries and lime consommé, or dark chocolate mousse with kumquat compote and white chocolate ice cream. The wine list offers a rewardingly broad range of good choices at reasonable prices, starting at £17, with a decent choice by the glass and half-bottle. A sister restaurant is located in nearby St Monans.

Chefs: Craig Millar, Neil Clarke and Scott Miller **Proprietors:** Craig Millar and Tim Butler **Open:** all week 12 to 2.30 (12.30 to 3 Sun), 6.30 to 10 **Closed:** 25 and 26 Dec, 1 Jan **Meals:** Set L £21 (2 courses) to £25, Set D £45 **Service:** not inc **Cards:** Amex, Delta, Maestro, MasterCard, Visa **Details:** 60 seats. 25 seats outside. No children under 12 at D. Children's helpings. No smoking. Wheelchair access (also WC). No music. No mobile phones. Air-conditioned

---

MAP 11 ST MARGARET'S HOPE – Orkney

The Creel

Front Road, St Margaret's Hope KW17 2SL
Tel: (01856) 831311
Website: www.thecreel.co.uk

Cooking 7 | **Seafood/Modern Scottish** | **£50**

A cream-painted house in a little Orcadian community on South Ronaldsay has been home to the Craigies' restaurant-with-rooms for over 20 years. Backing on to a narrow pavement on one side, the place overlooks the bay on the other. Everything is as authentically local as it gets, from the furniture and artwork to the plate of bannocks on each table, baked on a griddle from local barley and bursting with wholesome, natural flavour.

Alan Craigie specialises in fish and seafood, of course, and delights in introducing guests to unusual species. Steamed sea witch might make an appearance, paired with seared scallops in a main course, dressed in basil and red pepper pesto, while megrim and tusk could be the partners in the signature chunky fish soup. This may well be the place, too, for monkfish livers, lightly poached and served with an avocado and fennel salsa. There is as much of a fondness for chutneys and dressings as for traditional sauces, which keeps things moving with the times, and there is always one meat main course: perhaps seaweed-fed lamb slow-cooked in barley broth.

The menus may not change quite rapidly enough for those staying here to feel they have seen enough variety, but the freshness and quiet, unwavering commitment to quality shine through in most people's experience. At dessert stage, glazed lemon tart comes in for repeated plaudits, as does its accompanying marmalade ice cream, or there may be variations on a theme such as rhubarb, comprising crumble, a baked custard, and ice cream. Joyce Craigie handles front-of-house with laudable professionalism. House wine starts at £15.

Chef: Alan Craigie **Proprietors:** Joyce and Alan Craigie **Open:** Apr to Oct D only 7 to 8.45 **Closed:** Mon June, July and Aug; Mon and Tue April, May and Sept **Meals:** alc (main courses £18 to £24) **Service:** not inc **Cards:** MasterCard, Visa **Details:** 36 seats. Car park. Children's helpings. No smoking. Wheelchair access (also WC). No music **Accommodation:** 3 rooms

MAP 11 **ST MONANS** – Fife

Seafood Restaurant

16 West End, St Monans KY10 2BX
Tel: (01333) 730327
Website: www.theseafoodrestaurant.com

Cooking 5 | Seafood | £50

Views out over the harbour towards the Bass Rock and Edinburgh are part of the appeal of this smart, popular restaurant. Although it's fronted by an informal pubby bar, this elder brother to the Seafood Restaurant, St Andrews (see entry), offers a degree of sophistication in the dining room, where white-clad tables, Rennie Mackintosh-style chairs and smartly dressed staff set the scene. The piscatorial choice on offer is of unimpeachable freshness, as befits the location, and there is an appealing mix of traditional simplicity and the influence of foreign climes. Thus, half a dozen Kilbrandon oysters, or warm home-cured gravad lax with cucumber relish and lemon oil might preface a main course such as grilled fillet of halibut with pomme purée, ratatouille and tomato butter sauce, or steamed fillets of lemon sole with sesame-dressed pak choi and an aromatic broth. As to the one token meat dish, there could be collops of beef for lunch, roast loin of venison with fondant potato, braised cabbage and jus for dinner. Puddings are as rich as they come, with rhubarb custard and Calvados ice cream served with a spiced apple financier, and lavender ice cream teamed with white chocolate and honey

crème brûlée. A good-value, fish-friendly international collection of wines kicks off at £16 and comes with eight half-bottles, the same number by the glass, and with some notably fine bottles adding extra polish.

Chefs: Craig Millar and Andrew Simpson **Proprietors:** Craig Millar and Tim Butler **Open:** Wed to Sun 12 to 2.30 (12.30 to 3 Sun), 6.30 to 9.30 **Closed:** 25 and 26 Dec, first 2 weeks Jan **Meals:** Set L £20 (2 courses) to £25, Set D £30 (2 courses) to £40 **Service:** not inc **Cards:** Amex, Delta, Maestro, MasterCard, Visa **Details:** 40 seats. 30 seats outside. No children under 12 at D. Children's helpings. No smoking. Wheelchair access (also WC). No music. No mobile phones

MAP 11 **SHIELDAIG** – Highland

Tigh an Eilean Hotel

Shieldaig IV54 8XN
Tel: (01520) 755251
Email: tighaneileanhotel@shieldaig.fsnet.co.uk

Cooking 3 | Modern Scottish | £53

The name literally means 'the house opposite the island' and this white-washed pub has great views over Loch Torridon. A relaxed bar leads to the dining room, which is decorated to bring the outside in, with shades of blue-grey and green. The menu thinks local when it comes to sourcing yet global in its culinary philosophy; local fishing boats bring their catch straight to the kitchen door every day, and Gloucester Old Spot comes from a small croft across the loch. Local lobster or perhaps hand-dived Hebridean scallops with Serrano ham and a coriander beurre blanc might start, followed by medallions of saddle of Highland estate venison or perhaps fillet of Kinlochbervie lemon sole with grapes and a Gewürztraminer velouté. End with spiced apple crêpe flamed in calvados or perhaps a hot chocolate fondant. The wine list is a short but reasonable global affair, starting at £13.50.

Chef: Christopher Field **Proprietors:** Christopher and Cathryn Field **Open:** all week D only 7 to 8.30 **Closed:** end Oct to mid-Mar **Meals:** Set D £41. Bar menu available **Service:** not inc **Cards:** Amex, Delta, Maestro, MasterCard, Visa **Details:** 28 seats. Vegetarian meals. Children's helpings. No smoking. Wheelchair access (not WC). No music. No mobile phones **Accommodation:** 11 rooms

MAP 11 STEIN – Highland

Loch Bay [AR]

1–2 Macleod Terrace, Stein, Isle of Skye
IV55 8GA
Tel: (01470) 592235

This seafood restaurant offers only the best of the local harvest, confidently presented and well timed. Blackboard specials, changed daily, could include Cullen skink (£4.50) or wild Esk salmon (£15.95), while the dinner menu boasts half a dozen grilled oysters with Parmesan and herbs (£8.70), followed by Loch Bay king prawns grilled in garlic butter (£19.90). End with raspberry meringue roulade (£4.80). House wines £12.75. Closed Sat L and Sun.

MAP 11 STONEHAVEN – Aberdeenshire

Tolbooth [AR]

Old Pier, Stonehaven AB39 2JU
Tel: (01569) 762287

Floor-to-ceiling windows frame the harbour view from this friendly seafood restaurant, which gets a large percentage of its produce on a daily basis from local fishing boats. Crab, lobster and squid all appear; otherwise, expect starters of seared scallops with chorizo and a caramelised shallot emulsion (£7.95), and main courses of monkfish with udon noodles and a lemongrass and coconut milk froth (£15.95), or poached halibut with wild red rice and chive sauce (£16.50). Meat eaters are not overlooked, and desserts could include lemon meringue pie with orange sorbet (£5.95). House wines are £13.95. Closed Sun and Mon.

[AR]	Not a full entry but provisionally recommended. These 'also recommended' establishments are integrated throughout the book.

MAP 11 STRATHYRE – Stirling

Creagan House

Strathyre FK18 8ND
Tel: (01877) 384638
Website: www.creaganhouse.co.uk

Cooking 4 | French/Scottish | **£38**

⊘ £5 🏠

The journey to Creagan House is itself a treat, with the Highland views of Glen Ample best appreciated when the sun is low in the sky. Gordon and Cherry Gunn pour their heart and soul into making sure that their seventeenth-century farmhouse lives up to expectation. The baronial dining room is home to an impressive fireplace, and privacy is assured thanks to the generous space between tables. Gordon runs the kitchen, and much of his produce is grown specifically for the restaurant in local smallholdings. Dishes receive a classical French treatment but with strong Scottish flavours, so among starters could be 'smokie in a pokie' or breast of pigeon on pearl barley risotto with chasseur sauce. Saddle of Glen Artney venison is a classical-style main course, while fillet of Aberdeen Angus is served 'in your favourite way'. Desserts might include iced raspberry shortbread torte with mixed berry compote, while Scottish cheeses are also offered. Eight house wines, from £10.90, kick off the global wine list, and at least 20 bins come by the half-bottle.

Chef: Gordon Gunn **Proprietors:** Gordon and Cherry Gunn **Open:** Fri to Wed (Fri to Mon from 24 Nov to 24 Dec) D only 7.30 (1 sitting) **Closed:** 5 to 23 Nov, 21 Jan to 9 Mar **Meals:** Set D £22.50 to £29.50 **Service:** not inc **Cards:** Maestro, MasterCard, Visa **Details:** 14 seats. Car park. No children under 10. Children's helpings. No smoking. Wheelchair access (not WC). No music. No mobile phones **Accommodation:** 5 rooms

MAP 11 STROMNESS – Orkney

Hamnavoe [AR]

35 Graham Place, Stromness KW16 3BY
Tel: (01856) 850606

Neil and Sarah Taylor generate a homely atmosphere at their friendly bistro in the harbour town of Stromness. An open coal fire welcomes visitors, while the kitchen deals in fresh local produce, including Orkney beef, lamb and cheeses. The no-fuss food might be local oysters with Polish vodka and horseradish (£6.50) to start, followed by haddock and lobster parcel in puff pastry with a leek and ginger butter (£15.50) or roast duck breast in a port and chocolate sauce (£16.95). Dessert might be lemon and ginger cheesecake (£4.50). A personal, well-chosen wine list starts at £9.85. Open Tue to Sun D only (weekends only Nov, Jan and Feb).

MAP 11 **STRONTIAN – Highland**

Kilcamb Lodge

Strontian PH36 4HY
Tel: (01967) 402257
Website: www.kilcamblodge.co.uk

Cooking 4 | French/Scottish | £57

The Ruthven Foxes' small-scale country-house hotel looks like a solid Victorian vicarage and is run with characteristic care and attention to detail. The countryside in which it stands is especially wild and beautiful, with views on to Loch Sunart – in such a setting it is hardly surprising that local produce dominates the menu. Meals might start with a warm fluffy oatcake with braised mixed mushroom ragoût, or Inverawe smoked salmon and dill bavarois with flaky smoked salmon rémoulade, cucumber relish and herb crème fraîche dressing. A soup, such as velouté of smoked haddock and mustard with a poached quail's egg, intervenes before the main course, which may be fillet of Mallaig halibut with a Loch Fyne oyster beignet and shellfish velouté sauce, or a gutsy dish of roast Aberdeen Angus beef fillet served with oxtail suet roly-poly, ox heart faggot, creamed celeriac, Savoy cabbage, and Montpellier butter and red wine jus. Among tempting dessert options might be lemon and lime tart with frothy lemon sorbet. Wines, arranged stylistically, are an attractive mixture of bottles mainly from France and the New World, with prices starting at £15.80.

Chefs: Neil Mellis and Shaun Vernon Hall **Proprietors:** Sally and David Ruthven Fox **Open:** Tue to Sun L 12.30 to 2.30, all week D 7.30 to 9 **Closed:** Jan **Meals:** alc L (main courses £9.50 to £18.50). Set D £42. Snack menu available **Service:** not inc **Cards:** Maestro, MasterCard, Visa **Details:** 24 seats. 8 seats outside. Car park. Vegetarian meals. No children under 12. No smoking. Music. No mobile phones **Accommodation:** 10 rooms

MAP 11 **SWINTON – Borders**

Wheatsheaf

Main Street, Swinton TD11 3JJ
Tel: (01890) 860257
Website: www.wheatsheaf-swinton.co.uk

Cooking 3 | Modern Scottish | £40

Overlooking the grassy village square, the Wheatsheaf is driven by John Keir's dedication to gathering Scottish produce and translating it into a conservative yet well-considered menu. Membership of the Scotch Beef Club ensures that he uses traceable prime cuts, while fresh seafood travels the short distance from Eyemouth harbour. Breast of wood pigeon on black pudding and celeriac, or a smoked haddock, salmon and dill fishcake with lime and tomato salsa make classic starters, while daily specials are displayed on a blackboard. Sorbets still make an appearance – passion-fruit, perhaps – before perhaps roast loin of wild Highland venison on braised red cabbage, or medallions of Scottish beef fillet on a mushroom and roast shallot sauce with truffle oil. Fish might appear as a main course of seared salmon with a poached egg and watercress dressing. Finish with hot sticky ginger and pear pudding with fudge sauce. The good-value 150-bottle wine list is a far-ranging affair, starting with ten house selections from £11.95 to £18.95, or £2.95 to £4.75 a glass.

Chef: John Keir **Proprietors:** Chris and Jan Winson **Open:** all week 12 to 2, 6 to 9 (8 Sun) **Closed:** Sun D Dec to Feb, 25 to 27 Dec **Meals:** alc (main courses L £8.50 to £13, D £14.50 to £19) **Service:** not inc **Cards:** Maestro, MasterCard, Visa **Details:** 45 seats. Car park. Vegetarian meals. No children under 6 after 7pm. Children's helpings. No smoking. Wheelchair access (also WC). Music. No mobile phones **Accommodation:** 10 rooms

MAP 11 **TROON – South Ayrshire**

MacCallums Oyster Bar

The Harbour, Troon KA10 6DH
Tel: (01292) 319339

Cooking 3 | Seafood | £42

There's no doubt that this is a classic spot for an oyster bar: right on Troon harbour just yards from where the fishing boats are tied up, and near the

Seacat terminal. The white-painted brick walls inside are covered in memorabilia relating to Sir Thomas Lipton's racing yachts, and the kitchen can be glimpsed through a hatch at the end of the dining room. Fresh seafood is naturally the order of the day – the owners have a wet-fish shop in Glasgow – so half a dozen oysters or mussels marinière might start, while roast monkfish, grilled lobster or baked salmon with Thai ginger, basil, pak choi and a light curry cream might be among the interesting main-course selections. There is also a catch of the day on the board. Desserts could be a chocolate and Cointreau tart, sticky toffee pudding or maybe raspberry crème brûlée with shortbread. The compact, annotated wine list opens at £11.60.

Chefs: Ewan McAllister and Adele Wylie Proprietors: John and James MacCallum Open: Tue to Sun L 12 to 2.30 (3.30 Sun), Tue to Sat D 6.30 to 9.30 Meals: alc (main courses £8.50 to £22.50) Service: not inc Cards: Delta, Maestro, MasterCard, Visa Details: 43 seats. Car park. No children under 14 after 8pm. No smoking. Wheelchair access (not WC). Music

leeks, tagliatelle and mussels. Raspberry pavlova with toffee sauce has proved an enjoyable way to finish. The wine list offers some good-value bottles from the New World, with house selections at £12.75.

Chef/Proprietor: Craig Wilson Open: Wed to Fri and Sun L 12 to 1.45, Wed to Sun D 6.30 to 9 Closed: first 2 weeks Jan Meals: alc (main courses £13 to £19). Snack L menu available Service: not inc Cards: Delta, Maestro, MasterCard, Visa Details: 65 seats. Car park. Vegetarian meals. Children's helpings. No smoking. Wheelchair access (not WC). Music

To submit a report on any restaurant, please visit *www.which.co.uk/gfgfeedback*.

MAP 11 UDNY GREEN – Aberdeenshire

Eat on the Green NEW ENTRY

Udny Green AB41 7RS
Tel: (01651) 842337
Website: www.eatonthegreen.co.uk

Cooking 2 | Modern British | £41

Formerly a pub, this two-storey grey-stone building overlooking the village green now functions as an ambitious modern restaurant. And very popular it is too, despite a somewhat remote location. The menus confidently blend traditional and contemporary ideas, with starters typically taking in a 'light and refreshing' pea and mint soup alongside confit duck with orange salad and cider dressing. These might be followed by 'tender and sweetly flavoured' herb-crusted loin of lamb with garlic mash and a prune and mustard reduction, or steamed halibut, sea bass and scallops with creamed

Wales

MAP 4 ABERAERON – Ceredigion

Harbourmaster Hotel

2 Pen Cei, Aberaeron SA46 0BA
Tel: (01545) 570755
Website: www.harbour-master.com

| Cooking 3 | Modern Welsh | £43 |

Much has been made of the sympathetic renovation done to this ex-harbourmaster's residence by Glyn and Menna Heulyn. The bar serves a selection of Welsh ales, while the restaurant is decorated with paintings of beach scenes and metal fish sculptures. The daily-changing menus, written in Welsh and English, have a good selection of seafood (a local fisherman comes by with live shellfish), while European influences account for the appearance of chargrilled chorizo with roast polenta and red pesto. Smoked Gower cod served with a poached egg and beurre blanc is a typical starter, followed perhaps by fillet of plaice meunière, or honey-glazed rack of Ceredigion lamb with dauphinois potatoes and a red wine and thyme jus. Finish patriotically with bara brith fruit pudding with crème anglaise or a selection of Welsh cheeses, among them Snowdonia Cheddar and Gorwydd Caerphilly. The wine list opens at around £11.50, or try a local white at £15.

Chef: Stephen Evans **Proprietors:** Glyn and Menna Heulyn **Open:** Tue to Sun L 12 to 2, Mon to Sat D 6.30 to 9 **Closed:** 24 Dec to 11 Jan **Meals:** alc (main courses L £10.50 to £18.50, D £14.50 to £19.50). Set L Oct to Mar £12.50 (2 courses) to £16.50. Bar menu available **Service:** not inc, 10% for parties of 8 or more **Cards:** Maestro, MasterCard, Visa **Details:** 40 seats. Car park. Vegetarian meals. No smoking in dining room. Wheelchair access (also WC). Music **Accommodation:** 9 rooms

 This symbol means that the wine list is well above the average.

MAP 7 ABERDARON – Gwynedd

Ship Inn

AR

Aberdaron LL53 8BE
Tel: (01758) 760204

As the Guide went to press, chefs Matthew Vernan and Carol Jones were due to marry. Their partnership works just as well in the kitchen, producing food that combines good appreciation of local produce and excellent value. Freshly dressed Aberdaron crab (£5.95), or spicy chicken wings with barbecue sauce (£4.95) both start, while local pork and leek sausages with mustard mash (£7.50), or Welsh fillet steak (£14.95) follow. Welsh cheeses with home-made chutney and bara brith butter and whisky pudding are both £3.60. Nine rooms. Open all week during summer, kitchen closed Jan, and Mon and Tues during winter.

MAP 7 ABERDOVEY – Gwynedd

Penhelig Arms Hotel

Terrace Road, Aberdovey LL35 0LT
Tel: (01654) 767215
Website: www.penheligarms.com

| Cooking 2 | British | £38 |

Overlooking the sea in a delightful small resort in Snowdonia National Park, this small hotel and restaurant might struggle to live up to its setting if it weren't such a charming, well-run and stylish establishment. 'Friendly and competent' service is the norm, and reports endorse the restaurant's reputation for super-fresh, carefully cooked seafood, with praise for Moroccan-spiced black sea bream, whole sea bass with rosemary, olive oil and Anglesey sea salt, and loin of cod with king prawns, chilli and mint. Among starters, 'rich, creamy' fennel and apple soup, and grilled mackerel with spicy tomato and chilli sauce have also rated well, while successful desserts have included vanilla and lemon cheesecake. If the food and setting are not enough of a draw, the wine list should be, with over 300 well-chosen bottles. Plantagenet 2004 Riesling from Mount Barker, Western Australia, for example, is a bargain at £16 and a great match for seafood to boot – and there are plenty more choices of similar quality under £20. No fewer than 30 wines are available by the glass.

> **Chefs:** Bronwen Shaw and Jason Griffiths **Proprietors:** Robert and Sally Hughes **Open:** all week 12 to 2.30, 6.30 to 9.30 **Closed:** 25 and 26 Dec **Meals:** alc L (main courses £8 to £16). Set L Sun £17, Set D £27. Bar menu available **Service:** not inc **Cards:** Delta, Maestro, MasterCard, Visa **Details:** 36 seats. 30 seats outside. Car park. Vegetarian meals. Children's helpings. No smoking in dining room. No music. No mobile phones. Air-conditioned **Accommodation:** 16 rooms

MAP 5 **ABERGAVENNY –** Monmouthshire

The Hardwick

 NEW ENTRY

Old Raglan Road, Abergavenny
NP7 9AA
Tel: (01873) 854220
Website: www.thehardwick.co.uk

WALES OF THE YEAR NEWCOMER

Cooking 4 | Modern British | £39

In the middle of nowhere (a couple of miles south of Abergavenny, in fact), the Hardwick is a foursquare-looking, pebbledash pub with a slate roof and a garden to one side. The interior doesn't aspire to country-pub flounce but offers instead a modest ambience of red-tiled floor, dim lighting and bare wooden tables.

If all this sounds a trifle basic, be of good cheer, for in the kitchen is an accomplished team led by the redoubtable Stephen Terry, youthful veteran of many smart London addresses. This is his first proprietorial venture, and the bold and direct cooking in evidence at inspection suggests that ambition will be the name of the game here. Start with crisp, breadcrumbed Old Spot belly pork with fennel, rocket, lemon and capers, a perfect modern pub dish at a steal of a price, founded on crusty slabs of fat, tasty meat. An alternative might be a smoked haddock risotto cake with a poached egg and curried spinach, again an essay in crowd-pleasing, big, bright flavours. Pan-fried mackerel fillets with roast beetroot, smoked bacon and horseradish cream is a good main-course idea that suffered a little from uneven timing at inspection, but there is

also free-range chicken breast filled with mozzarella and Parma ham, served with fried courgette strips, and classic grilled ribeye with roast tomato, field mushrooms, chips and béarnaise. Chocolate brownie ice is the highlight of an ice cream selection, and other sweet temptations encompass Seville orange cheesecake, and apple and raisin crumble. 'Friendly, cheery, smiley' service is a credit to the place. House wine is £11.50.

> **Chefs:** Stephen Terry and Leigh Allmond **Proprietor:** The Hardwick Company Ltd **Open:** Tue to Sun L 12 to 3, Tue to Sat D 6.30 to 10 **Closed:** 25 Dec, D 26 Dec **Meals:** alc exc Sun L (main courses £9.50 to £17). Set L Sun £15.50 (2 courses) to £18.50 **Service:** not inc **Cards:** Delta, Maestro, MasterCard, Visa **Details:** 70 seats. 20 seats outside. Car park. Vegetarian meals. Children's helpings. No smoking. Music. No mobile phones

MAP 7 **ABERSOCH –** Gwynedd

Porth Tocyn Hotel

Bwlchtocyn, Abersoch LL53 7BU
Tel: (01758) 713303
Website: www.porth-tocyn-hotel.co.uk

Cooking 4 | Modern European | £50

'Our team evolves. Only one new face who was not here last year', writes Nick Fletcher-Brewer. This is exactly what regulars to this family-run hotel, on a headland of the Lleyn Peninsula, like to hear. It is run as it was when first opened by Nick Fletcher-Brewer's grandparents, with an understanding, family-centred approach and the kind of personal touch that creates a comfortable, unpretentious atmosphere. Good food is at the heart of the appeal, care is taken in the sourcing of ingredients, and the fixed-price four-course dinner menu changes daily. Fish shows up well, whether in a starter of sautéed herring milts on a tomato and tarragon blini with lemon and celeriac salad and warm honey and herb dressing, or in a fine main course of baked sea bass with olive crushed potatoes, confit fennel, aubergine caviar and sauce vierge. But there's also roast venison with fondant potato, and braised lamb shank with Madeira and thyme. At dessert stage, buck rarebit offers an alternative to lemon mousse and sticky toffee pudding. House wines from South Africa and Chile are £14.

Chefs: Louise Fletcher-Brewer and Anthony Cowley **Proprietors:** the Fletcher-Brewer family **Open:** Sun L 12.15 to 2, all week D 7.15 to 9 (9.30 high season) **Closed:** early Nov to 2 weeks before Easter **Meals:** Buffet L Sun £22, Set D £38.50. Light L menu available Mon to Sat **Service:** not inc **Cards:** Maestro, MasterCard, Visa **Details:** 60 seats. 30 seats outside. Car park. Vegetarian meals. No very young children at D. Children's helpings. No smoking. No music. No mobile phones **Accommodation:** 17 rooms

MAP 4 ABERYSTWYTH – Ceredigion

Le Vignoble

31 Eastgate Street, Aberystwyth SY23 2AR
Tel: (01970) 630800

Modern British cooking with a hint of a French accent is what to expect at this Aberystwyth newcomer. The food is simple and well-sourced (beef comes from their own herd of Welsh Blacks), while the surroundings are smart, in an understated way. Lunch is a fixed-price menu (£12.50-£16), while dinner is à la carte and offers a few more options, perhaps starting with crab cakes with citrus cream (£5.80), followed by baked pork cutlet with pistachio and apricot mousse (£16.50), ending with dark chocolate and raspberry tart with raspberry sorbet (£5). Wines from £10.95. Closed Sun and Mon, and L Tue.

MAP 4 BASSALEG – Newport

Junction 28

Station Approach, Bassaleg NP10 8LD
Tel: (01633) 891891
Website: www.junction28.com

Cooking 2 | Modern European | £44

The name refers to the nearest M4 junction, and the restaurant can sometimes be as busy as a bank holiday motorway, but service is slick and a professional air pervades. Food is cut from the modern European cloth, and the carte has a something-for-everyone attitude, so curried eggs on toast with flaked smoked haddock, or salt and chilli pepper king prawns may start, followed by fillet of lemon sole with lobster and creamed potato served on lobster bisque, or perhaps best end of Welsh lamb on a crab, ginger and leek tartlet in a spiced sabayon with rosemary lamb sauce. The eight

dessert options are at the same time exotic and classic, so expect liquorice-scented baked Alaska, or apple and raspberry crumble with crème anglaise. The international wine list is well priced from £12.50.

Chef: Jonathan West **Proprietor:** Richard Wallace **Open:** all week L 12 to 2, Mon to Sat D 5.30 to 9.45 **Closed:** 24 July to 8 Aug **Meals:** alc exc Sun L (main courses £7 to £17). Set L Mon to Sat £10.95 (2 courses) to £12.45, Set D 5.30 to 7 £14.95, Set D £17.95 **Service:** not inc **Cards:** Amex, Delta, Diners, Maestro, MasterCard, Visa **Details:** 160 seats. Car park. Vegetarian meals. Children's helpings. No smoking in dining room. Wheelchair access (also WC). Music. Air-conditioned

MAP 7 BEAUMARIS – Isle of Anglesey

Café Neptune

First Floor, 27 Castle Street, Beaumaris LL58 4AP
Tel: (01248) 812990

Cooking 4 | Seafood | £38

Located above a top-notch fish-and-chip shop, this contemporary café scoops up ideas from the Far East, adding that extra twist to the appealing roster of predominantly seafood dishes. The décor is black, white and grey, with some striking leather curtains and classical-style statuettes – not for the faint-hearted but fun all the same. The menu makes pointed reference to Anglesey sea salt and Conwy mustard, and the fish specials are usually what was caught that day. Hot buttered Arbroath smokies, and Vietnamese-style poached chicken with mint and coriander salad and coconut jelly both make the cut to start, while a main course of cod comes with minted pea purée, chunky chips and béarnaise. Meat eaters might try fillet of Welsh beef with sweet onion confit, rösti and horseradish butter. Treacle tart with clotted cream and roast plum compote makes a sweet ending, and for something savoury there's a choice of locally sourced farmhouse cheeses. Wines are nicely annotated, and prices start at £12.95.

Chef: Ernst Van Halderan **Proprietors:** Andrew and Christine Pulford **Open:** Mon to Sat 12 to 2.30, 6 to 9, Sun 12 to 9 **Closed:** 25 and 26 Dec **Meals:** alc (main courses £8.50 to £18). Light L menu available **Service:** not inc **Cards:** Amex, Delta, Maestro, MasterCard, Visa **Details:** 48 seats. Vegetarian meals. Children's helpings. No smoking. Music. Air-conditioned

Ye Olde Bulls Head

Castle Street, Beaumaris LL58 8AP
Tel: (01248) 810329
Website: www.bullsheadinn.co.uk

Cooking 6 | Modern European | £51

Steeped in history, the Grade II listed building dates from the fifteenth century, although the Loft Restaurant – upstairs in the eaves of the oldest part – has been made over to create an elegant, contemporary feel. Native Welsh ingredients are to the fore in the modern European cooking, in which chef Keith Rothwell shows great flair allied to finely honed technique and a fondness for multi-component dishes. Pressed terrine of local skate with salad potatoes, Dijon mustard, capers and gherkins is typical of starters, as is a parcel of wild rabbit with white asparagus, Parma ham, prune purée, baby onions and rabbit jus. To follow, Anglesey beef fillet is served in classic style with spinach, shallots in red wine, fondant potato, pancetta and a Madeira jus, while Menai sea bass is partnered by sautéed potatoes, batons of salsify, wild garlic oil, roast ceps and beurre blanc. The level of industry doesn't let up at dessert stage, with options typically including an assiette of chocolate comprising a pecan and milk chocolate bourbon biscuit, white chocolate ice cream and a shot of hot dark chocolate. The major French regions are the focal point of the wine list, with quality in abundance throughout. Smaller but equally well chosen selections from elsewhere add variety. Four house wines are £16.75 a bottle, £4.35 a glass.

Chef: Keith Rothwell **Proprietor:** Rothwell & Robertson Ltd
Open: Mon to Sat D only 7 to 9.30; also open Sun L bank hols
Closed: 25 and 26 Dec, 1 Jan **Meals:** Set D £35. Brasserie menu available L and D **Service:** not inc **Cards:** Amex, Delta, Maestro, MasterCard, Visa **Details:** 45 seats. Car park. Vegetarian meals. No children under 7. No smoking. No music. No mobile phones **Accommodation:** 13 rooms

---

MAP 7 **BETWS-Y-COED** – Conwy

Ty Gwyn Hotel

 AR

Betws-y-coed LL24 0SG
Tel: (01690) 710383

In the vale of Conway, the dramatic backdrop draws in the crowds to this sixteenth-century coaching inn. The menu combines British and ori-ental styles, with starters as diverse as Thai-style marinated julienne fillet steak (£5.50) or chicken liver terrine (£4.25). Main courses could be baked Welsh lamb fillet Wellington (£13.95) or aromatic Thai duck stir-fry (£13.95). Vegetarians are also well catered for, with Thai vegetable curry and aromatic rice (£6.95) an option. Wines from £10. Accommodation. Open all week.

MAP 4 **BRECON** – Powys

Barn at Brynich

AR

Brynich, Brecon LD3 7SH
Tel: (01874) 623480

Dating from the seventeenth century, this converted hay barn has fine views of the Brecon Beacons. Local produce features prominently in the kitchen's output, with Welsh black beef steak and Breconshire ale pie (£8) and crisp Llangynidr duck breast with a roast fig and black cherry jus (£14) among main courses. Starters take in sautéed garlic mushrooms with lemon mayonnaise (£4) and oak-smoked salmon with scrambled eggs (£6), and daily-changing fish dishes are on a specials board: perhaps sea bass fillet with baby leeks and a cockle and laverbread beurre blanc (£13). Good-value wines from £8.95. Open all week exc Mon Nov to Feb.

Tipple 'n' Tiffin

AR

Theatr Brycheiniog, Brecon LD3 7EW
Tel: (01874) 611866

'Plates and bowls to share' states the menu at this relaxed venue in the Brecon Theatre. All the dishes (between £5 and £9) are tapas-style, although a flexible approach means that diners with more time can eat a more conventional meal. Lightly battered chicken goujons, much-admired slow-roast ribs of Tamworth pork marinated in hoisin, game sausages on root mash, and a ragoût of Mediterranean vegetables are all here. 'Our organic salads are famous,' writes the co-proprietor. The short wine list starts at around £11. Closed Sun.

 AR | Not a full entry but provisionally recommended. These 'also recommended' establishments are integrated throughout the book.

MAP 4   BROAD HAVEN – Pembrokeshire

Druidstone

Druidston Haven, Broad Haven SA62 3NE
Tel: (01437) 781221
Website: www.druidstone.co.uk

Cooking 1 | **Global** | **£36**

Now in its thirty-fifth year, this family-run hotel is perched on a clifftop overlooking the rugged seascape of Druidston Haven. The dining room has bare floorboards, an open fire, interesting paintings on the walls and an upright piano. All produce, some organic, is sourced locally, and the menu changes daily. Gravad lax with a dill and Dijon dressing, or avocado with toasted nut and herb salad might start, while St Brides' sea bass with pesto on chorizo and basil mash, or best end of Welsh lamb with swede dauphinois and red wine gravy could follow. Vegetarian options might include blackened aubergine stuffed with cheese, tomatoes and pesto, and puddings are of the traditional sort: banoffi pie or coffee and walnut gâteau, say. House wines, from France and Spain, are £9.90.

> **Chefs:** Chris Fenn, Guy Morris, Jon Woodhouse and Angus Bell **Proprietors:** Rod, Jane and Angus Bell **Open:** Sun L 12.30 to 2.30, all week D 7.15 to 9.30 **Meals:** alc (main courses £11.50 to £19). Bar menu available **Service:** not inc **Cards:** Amex, Delta, Maestro, MasterCard, Visa **Details:** 50 seats. 50 seats outside. Car park. Vegetarian meals. Children's helpings. No smoking in dining room. Wheelchair access (not WC). Occasional music **Accommodation:** 11 rooms

MAP 7   CAPEL GARMON – Conwy

Tan-y-Foel

Capel Garmon, nr Betws-y-coed LL26 0RE
Tel: (01690) 710507
Website: www.tyfhotel.co.uk

Cooking 6 | **Modern British** | **£57**

The Pitmans' small hotel, a seventeenth-century farmhouse on a hill peering down into the Conwy valley, combines country tranquillity with modern elegance. Coffee and cream décor is easy on the eye, as is the dining room's subtle lighting and bamboo floor. The highly personal design style is

mirrored in the way the place is run, with calm efficiency and a minimum of standing on ceremony.

Janet Pitman offers five dinner menus a week, changing every day for the benefit of residents but limiting the options to a pair of alternatives at each of the three courses, so as to keep things manageable. Results can be stupendous, with the best dishes achieving a balance of natural flavours, textures and seasonings that continues to impress. Start with local grey mullet exotically dressed in mint, coriander, tomato and roast cumin seeds, or maybe with seared pigeon breast teamed with its own boudin, griddled leeks, pancetta and Cumberland sauce. Main-course options might involve choosing between turbot and wild boar, the former in the company of smoked salmon and spring cabbage, the latter sauced with cider and thyme and joined by caramelised apple and onions and sweet potato purée. Welsh cheeses add a third choice to the desserts, themselves sorely tempting in a hazelnut meringue with framboise cream sort of way.

A treasure trove of international wines adds lustre to the occasion, with many imaginative selections including Torino Torrontés from Argentina, Janodet's benchmark Moulin-à-Vent and Italian varietals from Californian pioneer Seghesio. The base price is £19.

> **Chef:** Janet Pitman **Proprietors:** Mr P.K. and Mrs J.C. Pitman **Open:** Wed to Sun D only 7.30 to 8.15 **Closed:** 1 Dec to 14 Jan **Meals:** Set D £39 **Service:** not inc **Cards:** Maestro, MasterCard, Visa **Details:** 12 seats. Car park. No children under 7. No smoking. No music. No mobile phones **Accommodation:** 6 rooms

MAP 4   CARDIFF – Cardiff

Armless Dragon

97–99 Wyeverne Road, Cathays, Cardiff
CF24 4BG
Tel: (029) 2038 2357

Cooking 2 | **Modern Welsh** | **£35**

There is a strong Welsh identity to this bright, modern bistro-style restaurant in Cardiff's student quarter (students should note the value of the set lunch). Chef/proprietor Paul Lane diligently seeks out the best local produce and uses it to good effect, not least in a starter 'Taste of Wales' platter. This comprises five small items based around a theme, such as 'Sea' (featuring Pembrokeshire spider crab tart and sewin pancakes with dill) or

'Earth' (incorporating a laver ball with ginger-pickled vegetables, and smoked Glamorgan sausages with piccalilli). Main courses, meanwhile, might include best end of Brecon lamb with a faggot, lamb and rosemary cake and spring greens, or skate wing with a cockle and leek sauce and Pembrokeshire new potatoes. For dessert, bara brith bread-and-butter pudding is a suitably patriotic option. There's a compact list of easy-drinking wines from just about everywhere, including Wales, prices starting at £8.90.

> **Chef/Proprietor:** Paul Lane **Open:** Tue to Fri L 12 to 2, Tue to Sat D 7 to 9 (9.30 Fri and Sat) **Closed:** 1 week Christmas, 1 week Easter, 1 week Aug **Meals:** alc (main courses £12 to £18). Set L £12 (2 courses) to £14 **Service:** not inc **Cards:** Amex, Delta, Diners, Maestro, MasterCard, Visa **Details:** 45 seats. Vegetarian meals. Children's helpings. No smoking in 1 dining room. Wheelchair access (not WC). Music. No mobile phones

Da Castaldo

5 Romilly Crescent, Canton, Cardiff CF11 9NP
Tel: (029) 2022 1905
Website: www.dacastaldo.com

Cooking 2 | **Modern Italian** | **£38**

There's a lively atmosphere at this contemporary family-run Italian bistro. The décor is easy on the eye, with bare tables, wooden floors and blue-upholstered banquettes. Complementing the setting is the hearty Italian food. Antipasti include Neapolitan sausages with caramelised red onion and sage jus, fagottini of smoked salmon and crab-meat with pesto, plus the usual plate of salami and prosciutto. Pasta is a speciality, ranging from lasagne to seafood risotto, and among main courses are saltimbocca alla romana, medallions of beef accompanied by a wild mushroom and port sauce, and chicken breast stuffed with asparagus and pancetta in a creamy saffron sauce. Welsh and Italian cheeses vie for attention among desserts of cassata, or warm almond tart laced with grapefruit. The flag-waving wine list opens with Sicilian red and white at £11.50.

> **Chefs:** Antonio Castaldo and Rodrigo Gonzalez **Proprietors:** Antonio and Cheryl Castaldo **Open:** Tue to Sat 12 to 1.45, 7 to 9.45 **Closed:** 24 to 26 and 31 Dec **Meals:** alc (main courses £8 to £16). Set L £13.50 **Service:** not inc **Cards:** Delta, Maestro, MasterCard, Visa **Details:** 40 seats. Vegetarian meals. Children's helpings. No smoking. Wheelchair access (not WC). Music. Air-conditioned

Le Gallois

6–10 Romilly Crescent, Canton, Cardiff CF11 9NR
Tel: (029) 2034 1264
Website: www.legallois-ycymro.com

Cooking 5 | **Modern French-Plus** | **£50**

'Le Gallois' in French, 'Y Cymro' in Welsh: either way, the name means 'the Welshman' and refers of course to its presiding spirit, Cardiff-born Padrig Jones. Not far from the city centre, this is an unpretentious, informal place. The split-level dining area has pale wooden flooring, ceramic uplighters and displays of flowers, and staff cope admirably even when stretched by the press of business the place reliably enjoys.

The cooking is modern by anyone's definition of the term, serving braised shoulder of lamb with chestnut mash, quince jelly, roast turnips and puréed kiwi. An inspection visit began in fine style with a slice of chunky oxtail terrine, sharpened with horseradish cream and a dandelion salad, and proceeded to perfectly timed olive-crusted sea bass with boulangère potatoes, baby fennel and herb-flecked sauce vierge. Dishes are brought off with confidence and a high degree of technical flair, which extends into desserts such as luxurious hot chocolate fondant with pistachio ice cream and orange crème anglaise, or pear frangipane tart with honey ice cream and lime syrup. The wine list kicks off each section with a listing of vins de pays before heading into the classic French regions, backing them up with cursory selections from elsewhere. Prices start at £14.95, or £3.75 a glass.

> **Chef:** Padrig Jones **Proprietors:** the Jones and Dupuy families **Open:** Mon to Sat 12 to 2.30, 6.30 to 10.30 **Closed:** 23 Dec to 4 Jan **Meals:** Set L £16.95 (2 courses) to £19.95, Set D £30 (2 courses) to £35 **Service:** not inc **Cards:** Maestro, MasterCard, Visa **Details:** 60 seats. Car park. Vegetarian meals. Children's helpings. No smoking in dining room. Wheelchair access (also WC). Occasional music. Air-conditioned

Gilby's

Old Port Road, Culverhouse Cross, Cardiff
CF5 6DN
Tel: (029) 2067 0800
Website: www.gilbysrestaurant.co.uk

Cooking 2 | **Modern European** | **£45**

An eighteenth-century tithe barn has been converted into a spacious dining room with high rafters and a lounge with banquettes, easy chairs and large windows giving good views. Chef/proprietor Anthony Armelin continues to source his meats locally, with fish coming from Brixham and from Cardiff market. The lunchtime and early-evening menus are good value and take in much of interest: omelette Arnold Bennett, say, followed by pavé of rump of beef with bubble and squeak, crisp parsnips and red wine sauce, or battered fish and chips. Diners choosing from the carte might work their way through caramelised hand-dived scallops with ginger, garlic and foaming parsley butter, pink-roast saddle of Goodrich Estate venison with baby vegetables and a sauce of blackberries, juniper and chocolate, or sea bass with salsa verde, then brioche bread-and-butter pudding. The short wine list, opening at £12.95, gives a decent choice of good-value bottles under £20.

Chefs: Anthony Armelin and Michael Jones **Proprietor:** Anthony Armelin **Open:** Tue to Sun L 12 to 2.30 (3.30 Sun), Tue to Sat D 5.45 to 10 **Closed:** 10 days Christmas, 1 week Whitsun, 2 weeks Sept **Meals:** alc exc Sun L (main courses £13 to £20). Set L Tue to Sat £14.50 (2 courses), Set D 5.45 to 7.15 (6.30 Sat) £18.50 **Service:** not inc **Cards:** Amex, Maestro, MasterCard, Visa **Details:** 100 seats. 30 seats outside. Car park. Vegetarian meals. No children under 8. No smoking in dining room. Wheelchair access (also WC). Music. No mobile phones

Le Monde `AR`

60–62 St Mary's Street, Cardiff CF10 1FE
Tel: (029) 2038 7376

Just turn up to eat (they don't take bookings) at this lively eatery, which features large fish and meat displays, plus a salad bar, and find a free table. Start with deep-fried whitebait (£4.25) or shell-on shrimps with garlic butter (£4.55), and for a main course try Scottish beef fillet (£15.95), red snapper (£12.95), or halibut. All but a few items – among them sea bass baked in rock salt, and deep-fried hake cutlet – are chargrilled. House white is £13.95, red £14.95. Closed Sun. There's a branch at The Pavilion, Triangle West, Clifton, Bristol, tel: (0117) 934 0999.

 This symbol means that smoking is not permitted.

Woods Brasserie

The Pilotage Building, Stuart Street, Cardiff CF10 5BW
Tel: (029) 2049 2400
Website: www.woods-brasserie.com

Cooking 2	Modern European	£45

With views of the harbour walk, this old pilotage, which overlooks Cardiff Bay, is an immediately thrilling venue; the original stonework has been retained, while inside an open-plan kitchen adds drama and the large, modern glass extension boasts a patio for summer eating. Sean Murphy's menu seeks inspiration from many places; start with twice-baked Roquefort soufflé with red wine poached pear, followed by roasted fillet of red snapper with provençale vegetables or maybe garlic marinated lamb rump on rösti with a tomato and olive jus. End with apple and sultana pie with cinnamon ice cream. The global wine list offers 18 choices by the glass (from £3.85), while bottle prices start at £15.95 for house French.

Chef: Sean Murphy **Proprietor:** Choice Produce Ltd **Open:** all week L 12 to 2 (3 Sun), Mon to Sat D 7 to 10 **Closed:** 24 to 27 Dec **Meals:** alc (main courses £10 to £20). Set L £12.50 (2 courses) to £15.95, Set pre-theatre D 5.30 to 7pm £16.95 (2 courses) to £19.95, Set D £32.50 (min 6) **Service:** not inc **Cards:** Amex, Diners, Maestro, MasterCard, Visa **Details:** 100 seats. 60 seats outside. Vegetarian meals. Children's helpings. Smoking in bar only. Wheelchair access (also WC). Music. Air-conditioned

MAP 4 CASTLEMORRIS – Pembrokeshire

Tides `AR`

Llangloffan Farm, Castlemorris SA62 5ET
Tel: (01348) 891383

Chef/proprietor Emma Lewis runs this small venture on the farm owned by her cheese-maker parents. To that end, Llangloffan cheese and real ale pickle baguette (£4) makes a lunchtime snack, while at dinner starters could be seared scallops with watercress and chilli sauce (£7.95), or chick-pea salad (£5.95). Locally reared beef with caramelised onions and a Madeira and wild mushroom sauce (£17.95) and organic chicken breast stuffed with cream cheese, garlic and herbs and wrapped in Parma ham (£14.95) may turn up among main courses. Finish with champagne and passion-fruit sorbet (£4.95). Wines from £12. Open Apr to Oct Tue to Sat L and Wed to Sat D; Nov to Mar Sat and Sun L and Fri and Sat D.

MAP 4   CLYTHA – Monmouthshire

Clytha Arms

Clytha NP7 9BW
Tel: (01873) 840206
Website: www.clytha-arms.com

Cooking 3 | Modern Welsh | £42

The Clytha Arms remains an attractive proposition for locals looking for bar snacks and interesting ales, while simultaneously appealing to those in search of something special. Just up the road from Abergavenny, on the way to Raglan Castle, it's a converted dower house surrounded by lawns. The dining room is intimate, but tables are nicely spaced, and smartly set. Ingredients are locally sourced: lamb is from the farm over the road and butter is from the Forest of Dean, while fish travels a little further (from Pembrokeshire, Dorset and Cornwall, to be precise). The modern yet patriotic menu might offer wild mushroom risotto or oysters with garlic and herbs, followed by venison in Rioja with chorizo and ceps, or roast duck with butternut squash and orange brûlée. A savoury such as Y-fenni rarebit on walnut bread, and a selection of Welsh cheeses might appear alongside the list of desserts, such as treacle pudding with custard. A well-thought-out international wine list has plenty of choice under £20, and opens at £12.95.

Chefs: Andrew and Sarah Canning   **Proprietors:** Andrew and Beverley Canning   **Open:** Tue to Sun L 12.30 to 2.15, Tue to Sat D 7 to 9.30   **Closed:** 25 Dec   **Meals:** alc exc Sun L (main courses £12 to £20). Set L and D Tue to Sat £16.95 (2 courses) to £19.95, Set L Sun £14.95 (2 courses) to £17.95. Bar menu available exc Sat D, Sun L   **Service:** not inc   **Cards:** Amex, Delta, Diners, Maestro, MasterCard, Visa   **Details:** 60 seats. 40 seats outside. Car park. Vegetarian meals. Children's helpings. No smoking in dining room. No music   **Accommodation:** 4 rooms

---

 This symbol means that the restaurant has elected to participate in *The Good Food Guide's* £5 voucher scheme (see 'Using The Good Food Guide' for details).

MAP 7   CONWY – Conwy

Castle Hotel, Shakespeare's Restaurant

High Street, Conwy LL32 8DB
Tel: (01492) 582800
Website: www.castlewales.co.uk

Cooking 3 | Modern Welsh | £38

Behind this tastefully revamped coaching inn's imposing Victorian façade is a smart restaurant that takes its name from the Shakespearian scenes that adorn its walls. Here Graham Tinsley manages a skilled team producing carefully constructed dishes. His modern Welsh cuisine, which seeks to support local suppliers, is highlighted in starters such as millefeuille of Conwy mussels, or a main course of parsley and horseradish-crusted beef fillet teamed with buttered salsify and mushroom purée. Other culinary influences show in roasted cod fillet with spiced lentils, or an open lasagne of chicken with a watercress cream sauce. Winter desserts have encompassed roasted plum compote with treacle tart, and warm dark chocolate and pecan brownie with dark chocolate sauce and vanilla pod ice cream. A global wine list of some 50 bins opens with house French at £11.95.

Chefs: Graham Tinsley and Gareth Dwyer   **Proprietor:** Castle Hotel Conwy Ltd   **Open:** Sun to Fri L 12.30 to 2, all week D 7 to 9.30   **Closed:** 25 Dec D, 26 Dec   **Meals:** alc D (main courses £17 to £20). Set L £12.95 (2 courses) to £15.95. Bar menu available   **Service:** 10% (optional)   **Cards:** Amex, Delta, Maestro, MasterCard, Visa   **Details:** 100 seats. 20 seats outside. Car park. Vegetarian meals. Children's helpings. Smoking in bar only. Wheelchair access (also WC). Music   **Accommodation:** 28 rooms

---

MAP 4   CRICKHOWELL – Powys

Bear Hotel

High Street, Crickhowell NP8 1BW
Tel: (01873) 810408
Website: www.bearhotel.co.uk

NEW CHEF | Modern Welsh | £40

The old coaching route that passes by the front door of this fifteenth-century inn has over the course of time grown into the busy A40, but the pace of change is somewhat slower in the downstairs bar and cavernous upstairs dining room, with

rough-stone walls and dark panelling giving a genuinely ancient look. This is not to say that nothing changes. Indeed, a new chef was due to be appointed as the Guide went to press, too late for inspection. New menus were not available, but an ambitious modern cooking style has previously been the norm: pan-seared scallops with cauliflower purée, garlic coulis and a cucumber emulsion to start, followed perhaps by local venison on a parsnip purée tart with pears poached in red wine, sherry sauce and red onion marmalade, with strawberry crème brûlée to finish. House wines are £10.50.

Proprietors: Stephen and Judy Hindmarsh **Open:** Sun L 12 to 2, Tue to Sat D 7 to 9.30 **Meals:** alc exc Sun L (main courses £12.50 to £21). Bar menu available **Service:** not inc **Cards:** Amex, Delta, Maestro, MasterCard, Visa **Details:** 80 seats. 40 seats outside. Car park. Children's helpings. No smoking in dining room. Wheelchair access (also WC). Music **Accommodation:** 35 rooms

Nantyffin Cider Mill Inn

Brecon Road, Crickhowell NP8 1SG
Tel: (01873) 810775
Website: www.cidermill.co.uk

Cooking 2 | Modern Welsh-Plus | £41

'Nantyffin' means 'the brook by the border', and this pink-painted building was originally a sixteenth-century drovers' inn. Chef Sean Gerrard and partners Glyn and Jess Bridgeman continue to work in harmony to promote the great British pub: staunchly traditional but done with warmth and generosity, and successfully marrying contemporary design with original features. Locally sourced raw materials appear as, perhaps, loin of wild rabbit wrapped in home-cured ham with porcini risotto, or Welsh goats' cheese baked with honey and apple, and meat is reared on their nearby family farm. Baked minced lamb filo parcels with winter root vegetables and garlic sauce could open, followed by sturdy main courses of 21-day aged ribeye with hand-cut chips, or roast loin of Old Spot pork with bubble and squeak and red wine sauce. A well-known roster of desserts includes treacle tart, crème brûlée and baked apple with cinnamon and mascarpone. The wine list gives decent choice under £20, starting at £13.25.

	This symbol means that the wine list is well above the average.

Chef: Sean Gerrard **Proprietors:** Sean Gerrard, and Glyn and Jess Bridgeman **Open:** all week 12 to 2.30, 6.30 to 9.30 **Closed:** Sun D, Mon L and D Sept to Mar **Meals:** alc (main courses £7.50 to £17). Set L Mon to Fri £12.95 (2 courses) to £16.95, Set D Mon to Thur £12.95 (2 courses) to £16.95 **Service:** not inc **Cards:** Amex, Delta, Maestro, MasterCard, Visa **Details:** 100 seats. 45 seats outside. Car park. Vegetarian meals. Children's helpings. No smoking. Wheelchair access (also WC). No music

---

MAP 4   CWMBACH – Powys

Drawing Room

Cwmbach LD2 3RT
Tel: (01982) 552493

Colin and Melanie Dawson's elegant country restaurant-with-rooms has a 'chef's table', where diners can watch their meals being prepared in close proximity. There's a good sense of location woven into the menu, which sources great Welsh produce to go into dishes such as set Parmesan custard with crispy Carmarthen ham and rocket salad (£8.25), followed by peppered loin of Brecon venison with herb roasted vegetables (£17.50), and lemon sabayon tart with a pine-nut crust (£6.50) to finish. Wines from £13.95. Closed Sun and Mon.

MAP 7   DOLGELLAU – Gwynedd

Dylanwad Da

2 Ffôs-y-Felin, Dolgellau LL40 1BS
Tel: (01341) 422870
Website: www.dylanwad.co.uk

Cooking 2 | Bistro | £34

A culinary bright spot in this part of the world, Dylanwad Da is basically a front and back parlour in a terraced building. Inside, the stylish blond wooden tables, decorated with single flowers, are invariably all taken, but relaxed and friendly staff never rush people. Dylan Rowlands' short but assured menu can seem traditional – two steak dishes out of six main courses, for instance – but the food is well prepared and carefully cooked. A reporter found a main course of braised lamb in red wine, thyme and onion sauce to be 'melt in the mouth good'. This was preceded by mussel, leek and saffron soup of 'velvety texture'. Alternatives might be avocado, bacon and pumpkin seed salad, followed by Mediterranean fish stew. Standards are maintained into puddings of chocolate and ginger truffle cake ('superb') and rhubarb fool. The fully annotated wine list is an interesting collection, reflecting the proprietor's tastes. All four house selections are £12, or £3 a glass.

Chef/Proprietor: Dylan Rowlands Open: Thur to Sat D only 7 to 9; also open Tue, Wed and bank hol Sun D in high season. Open for coffee and cakes 10 to 3 Closed: Feb Meals: alc (main courses £11.50 to £15). Set D £18.50 Service: not inc Cards: Maestro, MasterCard, Visa Details: 28 seats. Vegetarian meals. Children's helpings. No smoking. Wheelchair access (not WC). Music. No mobile phones

---

MAP 7 EGLWYSFACH – Powys

Ynyshir Hall

Eglwysfach SY20 8TA
Tel: (01654) 781209
Website: www.ynyshir-hall.co.uk

Cooking 8 | Modern British | £82

The whitewashed manor house dates from the six-teenth century, although it was face-lifted exten-sively in the Georgian period. Then along came Queen Victoria, who spruced up the gardens a bit. Add in the tranquil Dyfi estuary and an RSPB bird sanctuary, and there isn't much more you could want in a country retreat, except perhaps 14 acres of exultantly colourful gardens. And it has those as well.

It also has Adam Simmonds, who aims to match his culinary style to the vibrant modern touches in Ynyshir's interior styling. Gathering wild herbs and garlic, wood sorrel and samphire is one aspect of his kitchen's assiduous striving for quality, which is also reflected in the sourcing of pedigree meats and fish. A first course of red mullet counter-pointed with spiced lentils, melon and foie gras is indicative of the care taken; likewise beautifully timed veal sweetbreads with cinnamon-scented apple purée. Intensity of flavour is impressively combined with an overall lightness in a main course of crisp-skinned sea bass with a courgette flower stuffed with a vigorous scallop mousse, and a streak of vanilla-scented fennel purée; or tender roasted squab pigeon with mango and celeriac, the plate sparingly streaked with coffee oil.

Extras abound. A pre-dessert of three types of fruit jelly was preceded by a pre-pre-dessert at inspection of green tea under lime jelly with

ginger froth on top. If you make it through to another whole course, expect something like a world-beating pistachio soufflé with a wholly suc-cessful savoury foie gras ice cream plunged in, or consider the cheeses, an irreproachably fine Franco-Celtic selection, served with celery sorbet, Stinking Bishop soufflé and a glass of port. The Reens run the place with a firm hand each on the tiller, and their staff are well-briefed on what is going on in the kitchen. Wines are extremely classy, a geographical listing of legions of quality growers from France to New Zealand via the best of Italy, Austria and the rest. Prices are highish (bottles start at £19), but there are squadrons of half-bottles to inspect. Glass prices start at £3.50.

Chef: Adam Simmonds Proprietors: Rob and Joan Reen Open: all week 12.30 to 1.30, 7 to 9 Closed: 3 to 31 Jan Meals: Set L £21 (2 courses) to £32, Set D £62 to £72. Light L menu available Service: not inc Cards: Amex, Delta, Diners, Maestro, MasterCard, Visa Details: 28 seats. Car park. Vegetarian meals. No children under 9. No smoking. Wheelchair access (also WC). Music. No mobile phones Accommodation: 9 rooms

---

MAP 4 FELINFACH – Powys

Felin Fach Griffin

Felinfach LD3 0UB
Tel: (01874) 620111
Website: www.eatdrinksleep.ltd.uk

Cooking 3 | Modern British | £45

The solidly built farmhouse of rough painted stone is the picture of an inn of today, with a relaxed, informal atmosphere, a smart rural look and cooking that aims to impress without showi-ness. The kitchen focuses squarely on quality local ingredients and on seasonality – organically grown fruit and vegetables from the Inkins' own kitchen garden, for example – all backed up with some precise cooking. Roast diver-caught scallops (with cep marmalade and black pepper butter) or roast plum tomato and basil soup might be followed by loin of lamb with braised white haricot beans and potato dauphinois, or duck breast with green pep-percorn sauce, although lunch sees more tradi-tional sausage and mash, or plaice fillets and chips. Traditional favourites like sticky toffee pudding or rhubarb and vanilla fool appear at dessert stage, but you may want to look to the well-chosen wine list for something to accompany the impressive selec-tion of Welsh cheeses. House wines from £12.75

head the list. During 2006 the Gurnard's Head in far away Cornwall joined the stable.

> **Chef:** Ricardo van Ede **Proprietors:** Charles and Edmund Inkin **Open:** Tue to Sun L 12.30 to 2.30, all week D 6.30 to 9.30 **Closed:** 24 to 26 Dec **Meals:** alc (main courses L £8 to £10, D £16 to £17). Set D £27.90 **Service:** not inc **Cards:** Delta, Maestro, MasterCard, Visa **Details:** 60 seats. 50 seats outside. Car park. Vegetarian meals. Children's helpings. No smoking. Wheelchair access (also WC). Occasional music **Accommodation:** 7 rooms

MAP 7 GLANWYDDEN – Conwy

Queen's Head   `AR`

Glanwydden LL31 9JP
Tel: (01492) 546570

This pretty white-painted inn in an idyllic village offers traditional values of a warm welcome and nourishing meals. Menus offer plenty of choice, starters taking in everything from deep-fried Brie (£5.50) to smoked goose breast with spiced plum compote (£5.25). Among 'hearty mains' might be Welsh lamb shank with red wine and rosemary jus (£12.50), while 'from the sea' comes monkfish and prawn kebab with creamy coconut sauce (£13.50). There are also grills and steaks, pasta and salads, plus daily blackboard specials, and desserts including crème brûlée or sticky toffee pudding. Accommodation in nearby Storehouse Cottage. Open all week.

MAP 7 HARLECH – Gwynedd

Castle Cottage

Y Llech, Harlech LL46 2YL
Tel: (01766) 780479
Website: www.castlecottageharlech.co.uk

Cooking 2 | **Modern Welsh** | **£43**

Glyn and Jacqueline Roberts have recently renovated their characterful 400-year-old restaurant-with-rooms near the castle. The three-course menu, however, still bears Glyn's stamp: honest, well-prepared food, with good sourcing and timing. Canapés in the bar are followed by perhaps aromatic lamb pancakes with hoisin sauce or duck liver and Cointreau parfait with a fruit chutney and toasted brioche. Main courses, always good, might consist of free-range Shropshire chicken breast with a creamy wild mushroom and Madeira sauce, or a duet of Welsh beef – grilled fillet

mignon and a steak, kidney and mushroom suet pudding with red wine sauce. Follow that with grilled prunes wrapped in bacon on toast or more traditional treacle tart with nutmeg ice cream. Pudding wines and port are plentiful, with the reasonable wine list starting at £14.

> **Chefs:** Glyn Roberts and Ryan Britland **Proprietors:** Glyn and Jacqueline Roberts **Open:** all week D only 7 to 9.30 **Meals:** Set D £29 **Service:** not inc **Cards:** Delta, Maestro, MasterCard, Visa **Details:** 40 seats. Car park. Vegetarian meals. Children's helpings. No smoking. Wheelchair access (not WC). Occasional music. No mobile phones **Accommodation:** 7 rooms

Maes-y-Neuadd

Talsarnau, Harlech LL47 6YA
Tel: (01766) 780200
Website: www.neuadd.com

Cooking 4 | **Modern Welsh** | **£44**

A stroll through the well-managed gardens of this solid granite mansion rewards with sweeping views across Snowdonia National Park, but if the setting is rural the food is a shade more cosmopolitan. Peter Jackson is proud of his top-quality materials, provided by a well-established network of suppliers, and of his home-grown fruit, vegetables and herbs, which might show up at lunchtime as home-made pickle and red cabbage with a deep-fried smoked duck and ginger parcel, and garden herbs alongside breaded escalope of chicken with cured ham and cheese. Dinner can run to five courses, and the modern country-house style of cooking produces Pantysgawn and olive mousse with tomato and onion salad, then breast of chicken stuffed with chilli sausage and herbs, or fillet of beef with rösti, caramelised onions and pickled walnut sauce. Desserts might include bread-and-butter pudding served with ginger custard, and a warm compote of pineapple, kiwi and pear; alternatively, choose Welsh cheeses, served in peak condition. The wine list centres on France but also offers a varied range of styles from the rest of the world, and Wales gets an entry. There's a page of bottles under £16, and the house selection starts at £13.95.

> **Chefs:** Peter Jackson and John Jones **Proprietors:** Peter and Lynn Jackson, and Peter Payne **Open:** all week 12 to 1.45, 7 to 8.45 **Meals:** alc L Mon to Sat (main courses £7 to £12). Set L Thur £12.50 (2 courses, inc wine), Set L Sun £15.75, Set D £33 to £37 **Service:** not inc **Cards:** Amex, Maestro, MasterCard, Visa **Details:** 60 seats. 20 seats outside. Car park. Vegetarian meals. No children under 8. Children's helpings. No smoking. Wheelchair access (also WC). Occasional music. No mobile phones **Accommodation:** 16 rooms

MAP 7   **HAWARDEN** – Flintshire

Hawarden Brasserie

68 The Highway, Hawarden CH5 3DH
Tel: (01244) 536353
Website: www.brasserie1016.com/hawarden

Cooking 2 | Modern European | £35

Partners Neal Bates and Mark Jones are the duo behind this village concern, delivering a confident and lively menu of contemporary British dishes that take inspiration from France and Italy. Expect starters of grilled trout fillet on a salad of new potatoes, grapes and sun-blush tomatoes, or smoked chicken and chorizo Caesar salad, followed by fillet of beef with Stilton dauphinois potatoes and a wild mushroom, leek and pancetta gratin, or grilled sea bass with crab won ton, preserved lemon, new potatoes baked with rosemary and salt, and sorrel cream sauce. The good-value two-course menu might offer a baked prawn and chive tart, followed by roast loin of pork with a chorizo and cider sauce. End with Cheshire Farm ice creams or green apple pannacotta with cinnamon ice cream. The short wine list covers a variety of styles, and prices, from £9.95, are fair. Related to Brasserie 10/16 in Chester (see entry).

> **Chefs:** Mark Jones and Shaun Last   **Proprietors:** Neal Bates and Mark Jones   **Open:** Sun to Fri L 12 to 2, all week D 6 to 9.30   **Meals:** alc (main courses £10 to £18). Set L and D Sun to Fri £11.95 (2 courses). Light L menu available   **Service:** not inc   **Cards:** Amex, Delta, Maestro, MasterCard, Visa   **Details:** 70 seats. Vegetarian meals. Children's helpings. No smoking. Music. Air-conditioned

 This symbol means that accommodation is available at this establishment.

MAP 7   **HENDRERWYDD** – Denbighshire

White Horse Inn

Hendrerwydd LL16 4LL
Tel: (01824) 790218
Website: www.white-horse-inn.co.uk

Cooking 2 | Modern European | £35

Despite its quiet rural location in the Clwyd valley, this old stone-built inn attracts good crowds of enthusiastic diners, who appreciate the stylish modern look of the dining room and its unstuffy atmosphere. On the food front, portion sizes are satisfyingly uncompromising, although the cooking is not lacking refinement, with starters taking in smoked goose breast with fig and orange salad and cranberry, pear and crystallised ginger chutney, pan-seared scallops with sherry vinegar and Parma ham, or 'outstanding' Conwy mussels marinière. Main courses feature 'extra-mature' fillet or ribeye steak alongside sea bass with slow-cooked fennel and tomatoes, and roast poussin with potato and bacon rösti and herb butter. And to finish, a selection of top-notch Welsh farmhouse cheeses makes an appealing alternative to desserts of sticky toffee pudding or Eton Mess. Wines are a varied and well-chosen international bunch priced from £11.95.

> **Chefs:** Ruth Vintr, Chris Hurst and Graham Ryder   **Proprietors:** Ruth and Vit Vintr   **Open:** Tue to Sun L 12 to 2.30, Tue to Sat D 6 to 9.15   **Closed:** 31 Dec, bank hols   **Meals:** alc (main courses £12 to £20). Bar menu available   **Service:** not inc   **Cards:** Delta, Diners, Maestro, MasterCard, Visa   **Details:** 85 seats. 80 seats outside. Car park. Vegetarian meals. Children's helpings. No smoking in dining room. Wheelchair access (not WC). No music

MAP 4   **LAUGHARNE** – Carmarthenshire

Cors

Newbridge Road, Laugharne SA33 4SH
Tel: (01994) 427219
Website: www.the-cors.co.uk

Cooking 3 | Modern Welsh | £38

'An eye for quality and contemporary cuisine not often seen in the country,' said one happy visitor of this delightful Victorian residence set in a few acres out of town; al fresco diners overlook the garden and stream, while inside the preserved period features are the attraction. The romantic setting is perfectly complemented by the cooking, which combines the best local and seasonal produce, including rack of Welsh spring lamb, grilled Loath smoked salmon and sewin. Dinner might start with new season's asparagus on walnut toast with Parmesan shavings, or Nick Priestland's signature haddock 'crème brûlée'. A main course of tournedos of Pembrokeshire beef fillet with green peppercorns and red wine jus might be followed by home-made ice creams or a wedge of chocolate torte. The 24-bin wine list is a lively European affair, starting at £11.50 for house French.

> **Chef/Proprietor:** Nick Priestland **Open:** Thur to Sat D only 7 to 9.30 **Closed:** Nov, 25 and 26 Dec **Meals:** alc (main courses £14.50 to £19.50) **Service:** not inc **Cards:** none **Details:** 24 seats. 12 seats outside. Car park. Vegetarian meals. No children under 8. No smoking in 1 dining room. Wheelchair access (not WC). Music **Accommodation:** 2 rooms

MAP 4 | LETTERSTON – Pembrokeshire

Something's Cooking AR

The Square, Letterston SA62 5SB
Tel: (01348) 840621

For a traditional plate of cod, chips and home-made mushy peas (£5.25), this friendly establishment is just the ticket. It's a popular sit-down chippy and take-away, offering Pembrokeshire crab cakes (£7.25), served with sweet chilli sauce, line-caught haddock (£6.25), or plaice fillet (£6.95), all served with home-made tartare sauce. You could start with marinated herrings or potted shrimps (£3.45). Roast chicken (£6.50) and barbecued spare ribs (£7.95) will keep meat eaters happy. Finish with pineapple fritters (£3.35). Wines from £10.95. Open Tue to Sat.

> | £ | This symbol means that it is possible to have a three-course dinner, including coffee, half a bottle of house wine and service, for £30 or less per person. |

MAP 7 | LLANARMON DYFFRYN CEIRIOG – Wrexham

West Arms

Llanarmon Dyffryn Ceiriog LL20 7LD
Tel: (01691) 600665
Website: www.thewestarms.co.uk

Cooking 3 | Anglo-French | £47

You have to venture a long way off the beaten track to find this white gabled building, but once inside, the slate-floored village inn doesn't disappoint. There are several rooms making up the bar and dining rooms, which all feature low black beams, plenty of antiques, gleaming horse brasses and fireplaces. The menu runs the gamut from ploughman's lunches at the bar to the French-inspired dinner menu, with local ingredients featuring heavily. Start with poached asparagus wrapped in Parma ham, or mussel and crevette tart with a chervil and parsley butter sauce, and follow on with aromatic duck breast roasted with pear and fresh thyme, or medallions of Welsh beef. Only three dessert choices make the dinner menu, perhaps strawberry and white chocolate terrine with confit of orange, or lemon and vanilla cheesecake. An international wine list will suit most purses with house wines starting at £14.95.

> **Chef:** Grant Williams **Proprietors:** Grant Williams, Lee and Sian Finch **Open:** Sun L 12 to 2, all week D 7 to 9 **Meals:** alc L (main courses £9 to £17). Set D £32.90. Bar menu available **Service:** 10% **Cards:** Delta, Maestro, MasterCard, Visa **Details:** 50 seats. 40 seats outside. Car park. Children's helpings. No smoking. Music **Accommodation:** 16 rooms

MAP 7 | LLANBERIS – Gwynedd

Y Bistro

43–45 High Street, Llanberis LL55 4EU
Tel: (01286) 871278
Website: www.ybistro.co.uk

Cooking 2 | Modern Welsh | £42
£5

With 28 years' experience at the helm of their comfortable, unpretentious bistro, Danny and Nerys Roberts can justifiably claim to have got the business of running a restaurant well and truly sussed. It may not be cutting-edge gastronomy, but

Nerys's cooking continues to be successful year after year because she gets the fundamentals right, with fine local produce at the heart of many dishes. Well-balanced starters might be as simple as white mushroom and tarragon soup and are rarely more complex than melted goats' cheese on beetroot and haricot beans with elderflower dressing. To follow, best end of Welsh lamb is roasted with a herb crust and served on rösti with thyme and Rioja sauce, while more inventive options might include cod fillet baked with a Welsh rarebit topping accompanied by tempura prawns, leeks and roast cherry tomatoes. Finish with perhaps bara brith bread-and-butter pudding. There are even a couple of Welsh bottles on the short wine list, with house selections £11.50.

> Chef: Nerys Roberts **Proprietors:** Danny and Nerys Roberts **Open:** Tue to Sat D 7.30 to 9.45 **Closed:** first 2 weeks Jan **Meals:** alc (main courses £14.50 to £21) **Service:** not inc **Cards:** Delta, Maestro, MasterCard, Visa **Details:** 38 seats. Vegetarian meals. Children's helpings. No smoking in 1 dining room. Wheelchair access (not WC). No music

MAP 4 LLANDEWI SKIRRID – Monmouthshire

Walnut Tree Inn

Llandewi Skirrid NP7 8AW
Tel: (01873) 852797
Website: www.thewalnuttreeinn.com

Cooking 3 | Mediterranean/Italian | £50

The interior and décor have undergone fairly radical change since Franco Taruschio's day. Standards can be rather inconsistent, not helped by a lengthy menu, but the restaurant still has plenty to offer, with combinations working more often than not. Great pride is taken in the sourcing of materials – Welsh lamb and beef, English Channel oysters, cheese from McBlain's of Usk – and Spencer Ralph balances the distinctly Italian bias of the kitchen with a more broadly European influence. Roast rabbit may be accompanied by black pudding and Waldorf salad, game terrine comes with red onion jam, and cod is wrapped in Parma ham and served with Jerusalem artichokes and chestnuts. At dessert there might be a 'professionally made' hazelnut soufflé with cacao ice cream, or duck egg crème brûlée with rhubarb. Francesco Mattioli runs front-of-house in a 'courteous', very hands-on manner, around a dozen

wines are offered by the glass (from £3.50) and house wine is £13.50.

> Chef: Spencer Ralph **Proprietor:** Francesco Mattioli **Open:** Tue to Sun L 12 to 2.30, Tue to Sat D 7 to 9.30 **Meals:** alc (main courses £16.50 to £20.50) **Service:** not inc **Cards:** Maestro, MasterCard, Visa **Details:** 60 seats. 20 seats outside. Car park. Vegetarian meals. Children's helpings. No smoking. Wheelchair access (not WC). Music. Air-conditioned

MAP 7 LLANDRILLO – Denbighshire

Tyddyn Llan

Llandrillo LL21 0ST
Tel: (01490) 440264
Website: www.tyddynllan.co.uk

WALES OF THE YEAR RESTAURANT

Cooking 7 | Modern British | £56

On the outskirts of a tiny village, somewhere along a B-road that meanders along the River Dee until it reaches Lake Bala, Tyddyn Llan is in as rural a spot as it's possible to find. The building looks more like an extended rustic Welsh farmhouse than anything else, all in rough grey stone, and inside is done in varying shades of blue, with plenty of windows giving views on to a verandah and over the garden.

The Webbs feel that they have properly settled in here now, following their move a few years ago from London. A solid local following has been built up, and Bryan's cooking makes the most of what is regionally and seasonally available. The small-format menus are user-friendly, not larded with technicalities, and dishes reliably add up to more than the sum of their essentially simple parts in the eating.

Thus it was with a starter of grilled red mullet, served with unctuously smooth aubergine purée, and subtle yet clear spicing from chilli and garlic oil, cumin and coriander seeds, 'a hugely successful dish'. Soups, perhaps of butternut squash or wild mushroom, show great concentration of flavour, while creamy truffle risotto has been an object lesson in texture.

Pink-roast duck on a bed of potato and leek has made a stunning main course, the meat bursting with true flavour, while spring lamb in May offered four fabulous cutlets, with some lightly minted peas and broad beans, earthy sliced artichoke and a thin, tomato-based jus.

To finish, there are fine British and Irish cheeses from Neal's Yard, or if you've a sweeter tooth the desserts are pretty impressive too. Pannacotta at one visit was pronounced 'the best ever', its texture properly deliquescent, its accompanying segments of blood orange in grappa a resonantly good idea. Ice creams and sorbets in an array of flavours look tempting too, or you might opt for the bracing simplicity of a slice of lemon tart.

The wine list is a joy and is as easy to understand as the menu (although there's rather more of it). Arranged in style categories, with helpful notes, it has much to recommend it, not least the fine list of wines by the glass from £3.50 (or £14 a bottle). Growers are superb all the way through, and there are plenty of half-bottles.

Chef: Bryan Webb **Proprietors:** Susan and Bryan Webb **Open:** Fri to Sun L 12.45 to 2 (2.30 Sun), all week D 7 to 9 (9.30 summer) **Closed:** last 2 weeks Jan **Meals:** Set L Fri and Sat £19.50 (2 courses) to £25, Set L Sun £21.50, Set D £35 (2 courses) to £55 **Service:** not inc **Cards:** MasterCard, Visa **Details:** 40 seats. 10 seats outside. Car park. Vegetarian meals. Children's helpings. No smoking. Wheelchair access (also WC). No music. No mobile phones **Accommodation:** 13 rooms

---

MAP 7 LLANDUDNO – Conwy

Bodysgallen Hall

Llandudno LL30 1RS
Tel: (01492) 584466
Website: www.bodysgallen.com

Cooking 4 | Modern British | £52

The impressive seventeenth-century building (with thirteenth-century roots, apparently) sits in 200 acres of parkland with views of Snowdonia and Conwy Castle. Inside is all antiques, oak panelling, oil paintings and open fires; a traditional environment for John Williams's modern British cooking. His menus are short but imaginative. Starters might bring a good, accurately made confit of duck with sweet-and-sour red cabbage, and carpaccio served with a dollop of goats' cheese fondant, while among main courses succulent, tender, slow-cooked belly pork has been a hit. What stands out above all else is the high quality of ingredients throughout, including bass (served with smoked haddock and potato brandade wrapped in piquillo peppers and a haricot bean broth), and roast rump of lamb (with Umbrian lentils, aubergine purée and home-made white pudding).

Desserts proved the highlight for one couple, who ate a precisely made vanilla pannacotta with caramelised figs, and iced espresso parfait with white chocolate ice cream and a dark chocolate sauce. On that occasion, however, service proved 'rather offhand' for such a 'genteel' hotel. A classically styled and well-chosen wine list concentrates on Bordeaux and Burgundy before venturing to other French regions, the rest of Europe and the New World. House bottles start at £15.50.

Chef: John Williams **Proprietor:** Historic House Hotels Ltd **Open:** all week 12.30 to 1.45, 7 to 9.30 **Meals:** Set L £17.50 (2 courses) to £19.50, Set D £40. Bar L menu available **Service:** net prices **Cards:** Amex, Delta, Maestro, MasterCard, Visa **Details:** 50 seats. Car park. Vegetarian meals. No children under 6. No smoking. Wheelchair access (also WC). Occasional music. No mobile phones. Air-conditioned **Accommodation:** 34 rooms

St Tudno Hotel, Terrace

Promenade, Llandudno LL30 2LP
Tel: (01492) 874411
Website: www.st-tudno.co.uk

Cooking 6 | Modern European | £54

The hotel is the jewel in Llandudno's seafront crown, occupying pride of place on the promenade, facing the pier and gardens and sheltering under the hulk of the Great Orme. In a world of steel and stripped-pine minimalism, the Terrace restaurant comes as a pleasant surprise. Situated on the ground floor, it is decorated with a mural of Lake Como, extending over two walls, while in the centre of the room a water feature with lions' heads softly tinkles forth.

It all makes a diverting background for the cooking of new head chef Andrew Williams, appointed in April 2006, to live up to. First indications suggest a kitchen motoring in top gear already, with cooking that grafts French techniques on to sound Welsh ingredients and shows a keenness to source well. A signature soup of seafood features mussels, cockles, oysters, sole and salmon in a liaison of anise and wild garlic, the last ingredient picked fresh each morning in the mountains. Fixed-price menus include a vegetarian version as well as the *de rigueur* Tasting Menu. Dishes that shone at inspection included a stunning opener that involved a single, barely cooked scallop with a pannacotta of butternut squash, smoked haddock froth, tortellini of scallop mousse and smoked caviar. Sea bass came Sri Lankan style, with a saffron, potato and coconut broth, while salt-marsh lamb was as impressive as one hopes for in Wales, the superb meat cooked to a light char on the outside but still pink within. Nor are vegetarians let down, as is shown by the delicacy and fine judgement in evidence in a main course of 'creamy, savoury and delicious' asparagus and Parmesan risotto, with lightly battered courgette fritters and herbed oil.

Welsh cheeses are served in fine fettle, or you might opt for one of the admirably creative desserts, such as a spin on crème brûlée that flavours it with caramelised apple and bourbon, offsetting the fairly sweet central component with a sharp apple sorbet. Well-trained staff deliver it all with amiable proficiency.

A page of Hidalgo sherries introduces an elegant, serious wine list that makes features of individual producers such as Forrest Estate in New Zealand, Lebanon's Ch. Musar and Australia's d'Arenberg. There are legions of half-bottles, and wines by the glass from £3.50. Prices, from £14.50, seem demonstrably fair throughout.

> **Chef:** Andrew Williams **Proprietor:** Martin Bland **Open:** all week 12.30 to 1.45, 7 to 9.30 (9 Sun) **Meals:** Set L Mon to Sat £15 (2 courses) to £18, Set L Sun £22.50, Set D £31 (2 courses) to £49.50. Bar menu available **Service:** not inc **Cards:** Amex, Delta, Diners, Maestro, MasterCard, Visa **Details:** 60 seats. Car park. Vegetarian meals. No children under 5 at D. Children's helpings. No smoking. Wheelchair access (not WC). Occasional music. No mobile phones. Air-conditioned **Accommodation:** 18 rooms

---

MAP 7 LLANFYLLIN – Powys

Seeds `AR`

5 Penybryn Cottages, Llanfyllin SY22 5AP
Tel: (01691) 648604

The atmosphere at this unassuming restaurant is relaxed, with background jazz, original works of art on the walls and even books and puzzles for those who need extra non-edible stimulation. Dinner is fixed price (two courses £21.50, three £23.75), and the page-long menus are solidly enterprising, with good basics such as a soup of the day or sun-dried tomato risotto for starters. Main courses might take in roast rack of Welsh lamb with a herb and Dijon mustard crust or grilled haddock fillet on a bed of Mediterranean vegetables. End with treacle tart. Wines from £13. Open Thur to Sun L and Thur to Sat D, plus bank hol Sun D and Mon L and D.

MAP 4 LLANGAMMARCH WELLS – Powys

Lake Country House

Llangammarch Wells LD4 4BS
Tel: (01591) 620202
Email: info@lakecountryhouse.co.uk

Cooking 4 | Modern British | £56

Half-timbered and with a verandah, this Victorian country lodge peers out over the Irfon valley, with the river flowing beyond its manicured lawns. Inside, staff are courteous and efficient, while the dining room is elegant, with large draped windows and lofty ceilings. Sean Cullingford is now in his ninth year as chef, and his modish menu might kick off with something as complicated as whole roast local squab with roast fig sauce, parsnip ravioli, gaufrette potato, and Thai asparagus salad with truffle foam and cep oil, or as plain as terrine of venison with mushroom salad and Cumberland sauce. Take a breath before multi-component main courses: perhaps cinnamon-roast breast of duck with a tartlet of creamed lentils and confit, served with macaire potatoes and a tarragon vinegar jus. A more straightforward dish could be monkfish tail wrapped in Carmarthen ham on a purée of anchovies and potatoes with a roast fish, red wine and shallot reduction. Lovers of puddings would enjoy hot passion-fruit soufflé served with orange and cardamom ice cream and passion-fruit sauce. The wine list, which starts at £17.50, is equally weighty, with accents on southern France.

> **Chef:** Sean Cullingford **Proprietor:** J.P. Mifsud **Open:** all week 12.30 to 2, 7.15 to 9 **Meals:** Set L £24.50, Set D £39.50. Light L menu available **Service:** not inc **Cards:** Amex, Diners, Maestro, MasterCard, Visa **Details:** 50 seats. 12 seats outside. Car park. Vegetarian meals. No children under 8. Children's helpings. No smoking. Wheelchair access (also women's WC). No music. No mobile phones **Accommodation:** 30 rooms

---

NEW ENTRY	This appears after the restaurant's name if the establishment was not a main entry in last year's Guide. Please note, however, it may have been 'also recommended' in the previous edition.

MAP 4   **LLANRHIDIAN – Swansea**

Welcome to Town

Llanrhidian SA3 1EH
Tel: (01792) 390015
Website: www.thewelcometotown.co.uk

| Cooking 3 | Classical/Modern Welsh | £46 |

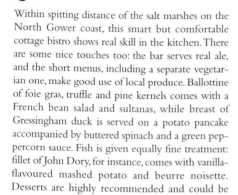

Within spitting distance of the salt marshes on the North Gower coast, this smart but comfortable cottage bistro shows real skill in the kitchen. There are some nice touches too: the bar serves real ale, and the short menus, including a separate vegetarian one, make good use of local produce. Ballottine of foie gras, truffle and pine kernels comes with a French bean salad and sultanas, while breast of Gressingham duck is served on a potato pancake accompanied by buttered spinach and a green peppercorn sauce. Fish is given equally fine treatment: fillet of John Dory, for instance, comes with vanilla-flavoured mashed potato and beurre noisette. Desserts are highly recommended and could be anything from rhubarb fool with sablé biscuits to passion-fruit délices with an oriental-style orange salad. The international wine list is helpfully annotated, opening at £12.50 for house choices.

Chefs: Ian Bennett and Nigel Bissett **Proprietors:** Ian and Jay Bennett **Open:** Tue to Sun L 12 to 2, Tue to Sat D 7 to 9.30; also open Mon July and Aug **Closed:** last 2 weeks Feb, last week Oct **Meals:** Set L Tue to Sat £13.50 (2 courses) to £15.95, Set L Sun £14.95 (2 courses) to £19.95, Set D £27 (2 courses) to £32.50 **Service:** not inc **Cards:** MasterCard, Visa **Details:** 40 seats. 20 seats outside. Car park. Vegetarian meals. Children's helpings. No smoking. Wheelchair access (not WC). Music

MAP 4   **LLANWRTYD WELLS – Powys**

Carlton House

Dol-y-coed Road, Llanwrtyd Wells LD5 4RA
Tel: (01591) 610248
Website: www.carltonrestaurant.co.uk

| Cooking 6 | Modern Welsh | £48 |

The three-storey Victorian town house, its façade painted an unmissable deep red, is filled with a collection of prints, paintings and ornaments that give testimony to a much-travelled past. Here for 16 years now, the Gilchrists' description of a 'restau-

rant-with-rooms' gives a clear indication of their culinary priorities. The menus make a virtue of simplicity and are sensibly short, with three choices for each course. Mary Ann Gilchrist is proud of her top-quality materials provided by a well-established network of suppliers, which might show up as a straightforward dish of locally smoked salmon with a dollop of crème fraîche and caviar, or a thick cream of celeriac soup. The choice at main course might be between fillet of Welsh black beef with Parmesan mash, tapenade, wilted spinach, roast tomatoes and red wine and oxtail jus ('the best ever eaten'), or roast cannon of Welsh lamb served atop minted pea purée, with crushed new potatoes and béarnaise, and a strong mustard and cheese sauce acting 'as a kind of fondue dip' for cauliflower florets. Soft textures and gently rich flavours characterise the dessert repertoire, epitomised at inspection by a bread-and-butter pudding that was 'comfort food at its sophisticated best'. More unusual is raspberry and sloe gin jelly teamed with a red fruit sorbet in a sugar basket, creamy elderflower syllabub, and red fruit coulis.

Efficient, good-humoured service from Alan Gilchrist augments a thoroughly classy operation, which extends to a wine list noted for good value, with plenty of choice from across the New and Old Worlds (and Wales) for under £20.

Chef: Mary Ann Gilchrist **Proprietors:** Alan and Mary Ann Gilchrist **Open:** Mon to Sat D only 7 to 8.30 (L bookings only) **Closed:** 6 to 30 Dec **Meals:** alc (main courses £22 to £26). Set D Mon to Thur £25 **Service:** not inc **Cards:** Delta, Maestro, MasterCard, Visa **Details:** 16 seats. No smoking. Wheelchair access (not WC). Occasional music **Accommodation:** 6 rooms

Lasswade Country House   NEW ENTRY

Station Road, Llanwrtyd Wells LD5 4RW
Tel: (01591) 610515
Website: www.lasswadehotel.co.uk

| Cooking 2 | Modern British | £36 |

This welcoming and unpretentious Edwardian house is the setting for the Stevens's double act, Emma conducting business out front, Roger cooking in a typically confident, controlled and down-to-earth way – an approach that's also framed by the view that organic produce is best. Dinner offers a sensibly limited three or four items per course, and dishes turn up with appealing combinations: watercress pesto with a raviolo of smoked salmon and crème fraîche, or black truffle oil and smoked bacon lardons with a warm salad of woodland mushrooms. Main courses typically include a fish dish, maybe roast monkfish with chilli jam, lemon couscous and chilli oil, while a trademark reduction of port and blackberries accompanies seared saddle of wild venison with bubble and squeak, which was a hit at inspection. Finish with a filo basket of sautéed fruits, or a 'lovely, creamy, custardy' cognac crème brûlée, and drink from a good-value wine list from Tanners which starts at £9.95.

Chef: Roger Stevens   Proprietors: Roger and Emma Stevens   Open: all week D only 7.30 to 9   Meals: Set D £28   Service: not inc   Cards: Amex, Delta, Maestro, MasterCard, Visa   Details: 20 seats. Car park. Vegetarian meals. No children under 10. Music. No mobile phones   Accommodation: 8 rooms

 MAP 7   MACHYNLLETH – Powys

Wynnstay

Maengwyn Street, Machynlleth SY20 8AE
Tel: (01654) 702941
Website: www.wynnstay-hotel.com

Cooking 2 | Modern Welsh | £35

The Georgian coaching inn – near Machynlleth's Clock Tower – succeeds in the difficult task of being simultaneously a relaxed restaurant, a bustling bar, a pizzeria, and a place to lay your head. The pizzeria has its own chef and is in a separate wing, while the menu offered in the red-painted bar and the plain but comfortable restaurant is a seamless blend of Welsh and Italian ideas, both classic and contemporary. Raw materials are sound, with local supplies taken seriously, and the repertoire covers the likes of terrine of local game, gurnard in a spicy, aromatic fish broth, and brill with a cockle and laverbread cream. Main courses might run to roast pollack with preserved lemon dressing, breast of local pheasant with lentils and foie gras, or tagliata of salmon with lettuce sauce. Welsh buttermilk cake with poached berries and vanilla ice cream makes a good finish. The mostly Italian wine list opens with four house wines at £13.95.

Chef: Gareth Johns   Proprietors: Charles Dark and Sheila Simpson   Open: all week 12 to 2, 6.30 to 8.45   Meals: alc exc Sun L (main courses £9 to £16), Set L Sun £10.95 (2 courses) to £12.95, Set D £25   Service: not inc   Cards: Delta, Maestro, MasterCard, Visa   Details: 80 seats. 40 seats outside. Car park. Vegetarian meals. Children's helpings. No smoking. Wheelchair access (also WC). Occasional music. No mobile phones   Accommodation: 23 rooms

MAP 7   MOLD – Flintshire

56 High Street   NEW ENTRY

56 High Street, Mold CH7 1BD
Tel: (01352) 759225

Cooking 3 | Seafood | £35

'Quite a find,' wrote a happy diner of this little restaurant in a row of shops opposite a thirteenth-century church. It opened its doors in May 2005 and is already locally popular. The minimalist interior – mushroom-coloured walls, small square black tables, 1930s-style dining chairs – is broken up by large mirrors and contemporary artwork on the walls. Seafood is the main business, with supplies sourced locally or from Menai Bridge, and Karl Mitchell hand-picks fish twice a week from Manchester's Smithfield market. Oysters Rockefeller, scallops St-Jacques and mussels any which way are among starters, and main courses range from lobster thermidor, through bouillabaisse, to tilapia and king prawns in an oriental-style sauce served with rice.

The highlight of an inspection meal was a mixed grill of no fewer than nine specimens of fish and shellfish, each perfectly cooked. Meat eaters are not overlooked and have plenty of choice, from smoked chicken and sweet potato salad with pesto to lamb braised on the bone and partnered by mash and a rosemary jus. Desserts such as kiwi sorbet in a brandy-snap basket with vanilla ice cream have also received plaudits. The wine list starts in France at £10.95.

Chefs: Karl Mitchell, Kirsten Robb and Martin Fawcett   Proprietors: Karl Mitchell and Kirsten Robb   Open: Tue to Sat 12 to 3, 6 to 10 (10.30 Fri and Sat)   Closed: bank hols   Meals: alc (main courses £8 to £20)   Service: not inc   Cards: Amex, Delta, Diners, Maestro, MasterCard, Visa   Details: 52 seats. Vegetarian meals. Children's helpings. No smoking. Wheelchair access (also WC). Music. No mobile phones. Air-conditioned

MAP 4 | NANTGAREDIG – Carmarthenshire

Y Polyn

Nantgaredig SA32 7LH
Tel: (01267) 290000
Website: www.ypolyn.com

Cooking 3 | Modern British | £39

Don't be fooled by the modest outward appearance of this 200-year-old mock-Tudor building. A display in the foyer of menus from renowned restaurants is the first hint that the current owners take a serious approach to food, and the cosy but stylish dining room has a bookcase full of cookery books, along with bare pine tables, and paintings by local artists on the white-painted stone walls. The cooking leans towards modern interpretations of classic French and British dishes, with good-quality native Welsh produce at the heart of everything, from rillettes of Carmarthenshire organic pork served with peach and apricot chutney to Pembrokeshire black fillet steak with béarnaise. Traditionalists might opt to start with potted shrimps on toast followed by fish pie and dessert of warm treacle tart with vanilla ice cream, while those with more modern tastes might prefer walnut-crusted goats' cheese with thyme-scented beetroot salad before honey-roast belly pork with pea and spring onion mash, with a plate of artisan Welsh cheeses to finish. The short but varied wine list focuses on value, with plentiful choice under £20, opening with house French red and white at £13.50.

Chefs: Susan Manson and Maryann Wright **Proprietors:** Mark and Susan Manson, and Simon and Maryann Wright **Open:** Tue to Fri and Sun L 12 to 2, Tue to Sat D 7 to 9 **Meals:** alc L exc Sun (main courses £8.50 to £11.50). Set L Sun £15.50 (2 courses) to £19.50, Set D £20.50 (2 courses) to £26.50 **Service:** not inc **Cards:** Amex, Delta, Maestro, MasterCard, Visa **Details:** 40 seats. Car park. Vegetarian meals. Children's helpings. No smoking in dining room. Wheelchair access (also WC). Music

MAP 2 | NANT-Y-DERRY – Monmouthshire

Foxhunter

Nant-y-derry NP7 9DN
Tel: (01873) 881101
Website: www.thefoxhunter.com

Cooking 4 | Modern European | £48

The Foxhunter has been through many incarnations – it has been a stationmaster's house, a tea room and a country pub – and thanks to Matt and Lisa Tebbutt's tasteful renovation it continues to thrive as the latter in this tiny village a few miles from Usk. Flagstone floors and log-burning stoves are features, as are watercolours from local artists. Service is polite and relaxed, and the cooking has much to be commended, from home-made breads to the truffles that accompany coffee. Seafood is a favoured starter: bourride with rouille and garlic toast has impressed, with prawns sautéed with parsley, lemon and horseradish among alternatives. For main course, 'very generous' chargrilled longhorn ribeye comes well timed and tender, accompanied by crisp chips, and monkfish with curried leeks and steamed mussels has also won praise, while the accompanying Jersey mash was creamy and flavoursome. Finish with something like lightly spiced apple sponge pudding with butterscotch sauce and clotted cream. The wine list skips around the globe with much to please, starting with four house selections at £13.50, or £3.50 a glass. A newly acquired self-contained cottage is 'rolling distance' from the pub.

Chef: Matt Tebbutt **Proprietors:** Matt and Lisa Tebbutt **Open:** Tue to Sat 12.30 to 2.30, 7 to 9.30 **Closed:** Christmas, 2 weeks Feb **Meals:** alc (main courses £12 to £20). Set L £17 (2 courses) to £21 **Service:** not inc **Cards:** Delta, Maestro, MasterCard, Visa **Details:** 50 seats. 12 seats outside. Car park. Vegetarian meals. Children's helpings. No smoking. Wheelchair access (also WC). Music

 This symbol means that it is possible to have a three-course dinner, including coffee, half a bottle of house wine and service, for £30 or less per person.

 This symbol means that the restaurant has elected to participate in *The Good Food Guide's* £5 voucher scheme (see 'Using The Good Food Guide' for details).

MAP 4 | NEWPORT – Newport

Celtic Manor, Owens

NEW ENTRY

Coldra Woods, Usk Valley, Newport NP18 1HQ
Tel: (01633) 413000
Website: www.celtic-manor.com

Cooking 4 | Modern European | £60

Named as the host venue for the 2010 Ryder Cup, this 'five-star resort at the gateway to Wales' (in other words, a modern 400-bedroom hotel in 1,400 acres close to junction 24 of the M4) is equipped with all the conference and leisure facilities the twenty-first-century traveller could dream of. There are four restaurants, of which the star of the show is Owens, a spacious ground-floor room done out in pale shades with modern prints on cream walls, plenty of plants and flowers, and smart table settings. Service is friendly, well-drilled and highly attentive, and the ambitious cooking aims to match the grandeur of the setting.

Elaborate, multi-layered constructions are the norm, often breathing new life into classic flavour combinations, such as an inventive starter of cassoulet terrine, comprising various meats, sausages, white beans and vegetables lightly bound in aspic, or a visually high-impact main course of tender honey-glazed belly pork with langoustines and cep 'cannelloni' (a square of pasta with a cep topping), apple purée and langoustine foam, the carefully crafted components arranged separately in a line on a long, narrow plate. Desserts have been a high point, typically a generous helping of vanilla pannacotta topped with a clear rhubarb jelly, accompanied by a small scoop of rhubarb sorbet and fragrant madeleines. To sample the kitchen's full range, try the eight-course tasting menu, which optionally comes with wines suggested by the Austrian sommelier, whose preference for the wines of his own country has been noted. The full list, however, covers all the world's major regions, with prices starting at around the £20 mark for house varietals and rising into the stratosphere for the likes of Ch. d'Yquem.

Chef: Nick Evans **Proprietor:** Sir Terence Matthews **Open:** Tue to Sat D only 7 to 10 **Meals:** Set D £45 to £60 **Service:** not inc **Cards:** Amex, Delta, Diners, Maestro, MasterCard, Visa **Details:** 45 seats. Car park. Vegetarian meals. No smoking in dining room. Wheelchair access (also WC). Music. No mobile phones. Air-conditioned **Accommodation:** 400 rooms

Chandlery

77–78 Lower Dock Street, Newport NP20 1EH
Tel: (01633) 256622
Website: www.thechandleryrestaurant.com

Cooking 4 | Modern European | £41

This smart double-fronted Georgian building on the edge of the centre looks rather posh by Newport standards, blending original period features with contemporary styling. The welcome is warm, and service is friendly and well informed, overseen by an 'enthusiastic' manager. Quality native produce is the cornerstone of everything the kitchen turns out, although culinary inspiration is much broader, taking in starters of tomato and buffalo mozzarella tart, roast wood pigeon with lentil salsa, and Thai fishcakes with mango and papaya salad. Main courses cover a similarly broad range, from Welsh black beef sirloin with polenta, Portobello mushrooms and tomatoes with peppercorn sauce through to grilled turbot with spring vegetable risotto, and roast monkfish with smoked bacon, bubble and squeak and green pepper butter. Desserts might include griottine cherry and frangipane tart, or carpaccio of pineapple with coconut bavarois and ginger chilli syrup. A straightforward list of 30-plus varied wines opens with half a dozen house selections from £11.95 a bottle, £2.90 a glass.

Chefs: Simon Newcombe and Carl Hamett **Proprietors:** Simon and Jane Newcombe **Open:** Tue to Fri L 12 to 2, Tue to Sat D 7 to 10 **Closed:** 1 week Christmas to New Year **Meals:** alc D (main courses £9.50 to £18). Set L £9.95 (2 courses) to £12.95. Light L menu available **Service:** not inc **Cards:** Amex, Delta, Diners, Maestro, MasterCard, Visa **Details:** 80 seats. Car park. Vegetarian meals. Children's helpings. No-smoking area. Wheelchair access (also WC). Music. Air-conditioned

MAP 4 | NEWPORT – Pembrokeshire

Cnapan

East Street, Newport SA42 0SY
Tel: (01239) 820575
Website: www.cnapan.co.uk

Cooking 2 | Modern British | £38

This 'homely' restaurant-with-rooms, where the Cooper and Lloyd families deliver 'professional'

service and cooking of 'individual quality', is considered good value by reporters. At lunchtime, simple dishes dominate: perhaps spicy salmon fishcakes, or honey- and cinnamon-baked ham. The evening menu has a few more bells and whistles, producing a starter of smoked eel served with a smoked salmon and laverbread timbale and an anchovy and olive tapenade, and main courses of marinated fish kebab featuring monkfish, tuna and crevette, or roast pork and pancetta parcel with apricots and coriander and leek and pea purée. Puddings are of the baked orange and marmalade sponge, and apricot and almond tart variety. An unassuming wine list includes a couple of organics. Prices start at £10.75.

Chef: Judith Cooper **Proprietors:** Eluned and John Lloyd, and Michael and Judith Cooper **Open:** Wed to Sat and Mon L 12 to 2, Wed to Mon D 6.45 to 8.45 **Closed:** Christmas, Jan to mid-Mar **Meals:** alc L (main courses £7.50 to £12.50). Set D £22 (2 courses) to £27.50 **Service:** not inc **Cards:** Delta, Maestro, MasterCard, Visa **Details:** 35 seats. 30 seats outside. Car park. Vegetarian meals. Children's helpings. No smoking. Music. No mobile phones **Accommodation:** 5 rooms

---

MAP 4 **PEMBROKE –**
Pembrokeshire

Old Kings Arms   AR

13 Main Street, Pembroke SA71 4JS
Tel: (01646) 683611

This esteemed hostelry remains the town's focal point. The dining room is comfortable, with wooden tables and china on the dresser. Produce is locally sourced, and fish specials change daily: perhaps grilled bass stuffed with herbs, and monkfish in garlic and parsley butter (both £15.50). There's also leg of duckling on juniper cabbage (£5.95) to start, followed by seared Welsh lamb fillet on wilted greens with port and redcurrant sauce (£15.95). The compact but reasonable wine list opens at £8.75. Accommodation. Open all week.

AR	Not a full entry but provisionally recommended. These 'also recommended' establishments are integrated throughout the book.

MAP 4 **PENDOYLAN –**
Vale of Glamorgan

Red Lion   NEW ENTRY

Pendoylan CF71 7UJ
Tel: (01446) 760332
Email: kamisoroush@compuserve.com

Cooking 2 | Modern European | £34

Next to the Norman church of St Cadoc in a tiny village surrounded by rolling countryside, the Red Lion is an attractive and traditional-looking stone-built country inn. Inside, it is all original stonework and wooden beams, with a cream and burgundy colour scheme throughout. There's a pleasant lounge and a spacious bar area for informal drinks, but the accent is very much on the restaurant side of the business. The menus offer straightforward modern cooking, broadly European in scope, with starters typically featuring tagliatelle in a basil-scented creamy sauce with wild mushrooms and Parmesan, and bacon-wrapped king prawns with mustard in a salad dressed in sesame oil. To follow, there might be tender baked chicken breast with a sweet-and-sour combination of aubergine, tomato, port and balsamic, or lamb shank given a zingy lift with a sauce containing sun-dried lime, tomato and chickpeas, and to finish perhaps a light but richly flavoured orange crème brûlée. Wines are split between Europe and the southern hemisphere, with four house selections, all French, at £10.80.

Chefs: Kamran Soroush, Graham Burgess and Sharon Escott **Proprietors:** Kamran and Azita Soroush **Open:** Tue to Sun L 12 to 2.30 (3 Sun), Tue to Sat D 6 to 9.30 **Meals:** alc (main courses £9 to £16.50). Set L Tue to Sat £9 (two courses), Set D Tue to Fri 6 to 7 £12.50 (2 courses) to £14.50 **Service:** not inc **Cards:** Amex, Delta, Maestro, MasterCard, Visa **Details:** 70 seats. 50 seats outside. Car park. Vegetarian meals. Children's helpings. No smoking in dining room. Music

---

NEW ENTRY	This appears after the restaurant's name if the establishment was not a main entry in last year's Guide. Please note, however, it may have been 'also recommended' in the previous edition.

MAP 7 **PENMAENPOOL –**
Gwynedd

Penmaenuchaf Hall

Penmaenpool LL40 1YB
Tel: (01341) 422129
Website: www.penhall.co.uk

Cooking 2 | **Modern British** | **£53**

Beside the spectacular views of the Mawddach estuary, service that strikes the right balance, and the comfort afforded by open fires on a winter's day, the elegant, Victorian Penmaenuchaf Hall delivers uniformly good cooking. Start with perhaps braised pig's cheek with tomato risotto, or seared chilli tuna with an avocado and lime smoothie. Moving on, red snapper is teamed with braised fennel, dauphinois potatoes and tomato sauce, breast of Gressingham duck with confit peppers, Jerusalem artichoke and a honey sauce, and escalope of veal with sweet potato purée and Madeira sauce. Finish with chargrilled fruit kebabs with basil sorbet, or an assiette of orange (sorbet, terrine and tart). Wines are a line-up from passionate winemakers around the world, presented with great enthusiasm and offering good drinking at all price levels from £15.50.

> **Chefs:** Justin Pilkington and Tim Reeve **Proprietors:** Lorraine Fielding and Mark Watson **Open:** all week 12 to 2, 7 to 9.30 (9 Sun) **Closed:** 2 to 10 Jan **Meals:** alc D (main courses £20 to £24.50). Set L £15.95 (2 courses) to £17.95, Set D £35. Light L menu available Mon to Sat **Service:** not inc **Cards:** Delta, Diners, Maestro, MasterCard, Visa **Details:** 34 seats. 8 seats outside. Car park. Vegetarian meals. No children under 6. Children's helpings. No smoking. Wheelchair access (also WC). Music **Accommodation:** 14 rooms

MAP 7 **PWLLHELI – Gwynedd**

Plas Bodegroes

Nefyn Road, Pwllheli LL53 5TH
Tel: (01758) 612363
Website: www.bodegroes.co.uk

Cooking 6 | **Modern Welsh** | **£55**

A white Georgian manor house set in delicious gardens – all rhododendrons, wisteria and roses – Plas Bodegroes is a classy restaurant-with-rooms on the Llyn peninsula. The dining room was somewhat ahead of the crowd in going for a blond-

wood brasserie look quite some time ago, and has a bustly, uninhibited atmosphere. Walls are crowded with paintings, in a kind of Green-Park-railings jostle of art.

There is a speculative edge to Chris Chown's cooking these days. Welsh mountain lamb is anchovy-crusted, while different pork components may come with langoustines, but traditionalists will also welcome the simplicity of whole Dover sole sauced with lemon, butter and parsley. Starters aim for impact straight away, with a tart of smoked haddock, mussels and saffron with sorrel salad, or a spin on Thai green curry involving monkfish and prawns. Not all was well at inspection this time. A sinewy piece of ribeye wholly submerged under mushroom foam didn't impress, and the small portions, even at main courses, will irk many on a £40 menu. At the peripheries though, things were much better, with creamy cappuccino brûlée and whisky ice cream showing up well in separate desserts, while the mini-quiche and burger canapés are superb.

Good wines open with a broad house selection from £14.50. Judicious listings from the southern hemisphere supplement the big French names, and there are also a couple of Welsh wines.

> **Chef:** Chris Chown **Proprietors:** Chris and Gunna Chown **Open:** Sun L 12.30 to 2, Tue to Sat D 7 to 9 (9.30 summer) **Closed:** Dec to Feb **Meals:** Set L £17.50, Set D £40 **Service:** not inc **Cards:** MasterCard, Visa **Details:** 40 seats. Car park. No smoking. Wheelchair access (also WC). Occasional music. No mobile phones **Accommodation:** 11 rooms

MAP 4 **REYNOLDSTON – Swansea**

Fairyhill

Reynoldston SA3 1BS
Tel: (01792) 390139
Website: www.fairyhill.net

Cooking 4 | **Modern Welsh** | **£53**

An eighteenth-century, ivy-covered house is the setting for this unpretentious restaurant in 24 acres of woodland with a stream and lake. An air of 'discreet luxury' pervades the place; the décor is in country-house style, with a dash of Regency, and the restaurant overlooks the grounds. The dining room is comfortable, and the team takes pride in an efficient but understated service. For chef Paul Davies, simplicity is the order of the day, with the focus on quality, and local and organic produce seemingly ever-present. Praise has been lavished on first courses: ham hock terrine, accompanied by sharp yet sweet piccalilli, and courgette fritters with a poached duck egg. A main course of roast loin of Welsh lamb is nicely offset by a faggot, mashed potatoes and cawl, and fish might feature as grilled Dover sole with saffron potatoes and a caper, lemon and butter sauce. Finish with something like blackberry parfait, 'full of fruit flavour'. The wine list is a full-bodied tome but recommendations are listed on the menu. You can skip from Alsace to New Zealand, with a number of bottles under £20 and around a dozen by the glass from £3.75.

Chef: Paul Davies Proprietors: Paul Davies and Andrew Hetherington Open: Tue to Sun L 12.30 to 2, Mon to Sat D 7.30 to 9 Closed: first 2 to 3 weeks Jan Meals: alc L (main courses £14 to £19.50). Set L £15.95 (2 courses) to £19.95, Set D £29.50 (2 courses) to £37.50 Service: not inc Cards: Delta, Maestro, MasterCard, Visa Details: 60 seats. 20 seats outside. Car park. Vegetarian meals. No children under 8 at D. Children's helpings. No smoking in dining room. Wheelchair access (not WC). Music Accommodation: 8 rooms

MAP 5 ROCKFIELD – Monmouthshire

Stone Mill

Rockfield NP25 5SW |AR|
Tel: (01600) 716273

Near the Wye Valley and not far from the Forest of Dean, this converted mill dates from the sixteenth century. Seared loin of rabbit with chestnuts and herb salad (£7.95) could start a meal, followed by fillet of local longhorn beef with port-glazed shallots, braised oxtail and parsley cream (£18.50), or black bream steamed over seaweed served with fennel butter (£16.75). A page headed 'the grand finale' lists such items as chocolate truffle torte (£5.50). House wines £11.95. Accommodation in self-catering cottages. Closed Sun D and Mon.

 This symbol means that the restaurant has elected to participate in *The Good Food Guide's* £5 voucher scheme (see 'Using The Good Food Guide' for details).

MAP 4 ST DAVID'S – Pembrokeshire

Lawtons at No 16 NEW ENTRY

16 Nun Street, St David's SA62 6NS
Tel: (01437) 729220
Website: www.lawtonsatno16.co.uk

Cooking 2 | Modern Welsh | £44

Occupying a pair of knocked-through terraced houses, No 16 has big windows to let in the light and give views of the picturesque cathedral city of St David's. Inside, a stylish decorative scheme of Mediterranean blue and white with colourful paintings and pottery gives the place a bright and breezy, modern feel, enhanced by a 'warm and professional welcome'.

Prime Pembrokeshire seafood takes centre stage on the menu, with highlights including a starter of large, juicy scallops done tempura-style in a light, honeyed batter, with fried leek and a tangy sweet-sour chilli sauce, and a main course of succulent steamed halibut with coriander, lemongrass and a lime and ginger sauce. Alternatively, meat options might include duck confit with haricot bean casserole, followed by 'substantial and flavoursome' Welsh black beef fillet served on a satisfying horseradish suet pudding with a rich red wine gravy. Finish perhaps with brioche summer fruit pudding. Three house selections at £15.80 open a straightforward list of value-conscious wines.

Chef: Stephen Lawton Proprietors: Stephen and Kim Lawton Open: Mon to Sat D only 5.30 to 9.30 Closed: Nov, 5 Jan to 1 Mar Service: not inc Cards: Delta, Maestro, MasterCard, Visa Details: 36 seats. Vegetarian meals. Children's helpings. No smoking. Wheelchair access (not WC). Music. No mobile phones

MAP 4 ST FAGANS – Cardiff

Old Post Office

Greenwood Lane, St Fagans CF5 6EL
Tel: (029) 2056 5400
Website: www.old-post-office.com

Cooking 3 | Modern European | £50

The former post office may be old but the dining room is in a comfortable, modern conservatory extension to the rear, with terracotta-coloured

459

walls and white linen-clothed tables. Chef/proprietor Wesley Hammond's efforts in the kitchen might be summed up as refined country cooking, taking relatively humble ingredients and presenting them in occasionally fairly elaborate form, such as a starter of warm pigeon salad with matchstick potatoes, quail's eggs and hazelnut oil, or a 'trio' of fish comprising roast scallops, dill-marinated salmon and a jellied langoustine consommé. Similarly, for a main course, slow-braised pig's cheeks are set on truffled mash with a sausage of ham hock and sage, while simpler options might include pan-fried salmon on sarladaise potatoes with glazed carrot ribbons and green beans, or sautéed cod fillet with bubble and squeak, pancetta jus and a poached egg. Desserts typically feature raspberry and vanilla teardrop with apricot sorbet, and port- and cinnamon-poached pear with a sablé biscuit and raspberry sorbet. There's plenty of choice under £20 on the compact wine list, starting with a French house red at £13.95.

> **Chefs:** Wesley Hammond and David Hamer **Proprietors:** Wesley Hammond and Kevin Tarr **Open:** Thur to Sun L 12 to 2, Wed to Sat D 7 to 9 **Meals:** Set L £10 (2 courses) to £15, Set D £28.95 (2 courses) to £35 **Service:** 10% (optional) **Cards:** Amex, Delta, Maestro, MasterCard, Visa **Details:** 30 seats. Car park. Children's helpings. No-smoking area. Wheelchair access (also WC). Music. Air-conditioned **Accommodation:** 6 rooms

---

MAP 4   SALEM – Carmarthenshire

Angel

Salem, nr Llandeilo SA19 7LY
Tel: (01558) 823394

Cooking 4 | **Modern British** | **£42**

A crowd-pleasing blend of generous and reliable food coupled with a relaxed atmosphere proves a winning formula at this smart country pub. Liz Smith and her staff contribute to the warm welcome, while Rod Peterson's short menu draws on mainly Welsh ingredients but reveals a fairly cosmopolitan influence. He's an imaginative chef, producing parfait of Pant ys Gawn cheese and basil, and teaming fennel salad and crayfish vinaigrette with smoked salmon for starters; while mains bring roast breast of guinea fowl with rillettes made of the leg, and a fricassee of leeks; and roast saddle of venison with red cabbage and apple beignet. For dessert, rose jelly with lemon ice cream and rhubarb gratin might appeal, while more conventional puddings such as apple crème

brûlée with rum and raisin ice cream are also on offer. House wine is £12.95, with three options by the glass.

> **Chef** Rod Peterson **Proprietors:** Rod Peterson and Liz Smith **Open:** Wed to Sat L 12 to 2, Tue to Sat D 7 to 9 **Closed:** 2 weeks Jan **Meals:** alc (main courses L £8 to £14, D £15 to £19) **Service:** not inc **Cards:** Delta, Maestro, MasterCard, Visa **Details:** 70 seats, 30 seats outside. Car park. Vegetarian meals. Children's helpings. No smoking. Wheelchair access (not WC). Music. No mobile phones

---

MAP 2   SKENFRITH – Monmouthshire

Bell at Skenfrith

Skenfrith NP7 8UH
Tel: (01600) 750235
Website: www.skenfrith.co.uk

Cooking 1 | **Modern British** | **£39**

Charmingly located on the River Monnow, this seventeenth-century coaching inn faces the ruins of Skenfrith Castle, while, inside, the flagstone flooring, beams and antiques tick all the right boxes. The sourcing of local supplies is much heralded, and the Hutchings have also established an organic kitchen garden to supply the restaurant's needs all year. Pre-dinner nibbles have included salmon sushi nori, which was followed by a starter of seared sea bream with 'properly made' lemon and herb risotto. A main course fillet of Welsh beef, well seared but pink, came with rösti and red wine jus. Marmalade soufflé with liquorice ice cream, with 'a good strong flavour', is a good way to finish. Service is friendly, and the wine list is, as ever, strong in Bordeaux, with prices reflecting some great vintages. Other regions are not overlooked, Australia given a recent boost with the addition of bins from the Henschke estate in Eden Valley. Half-bottles are plentiful, as are cognacs (another self-confessed 'unhealthy interest' of William Hutchings). Prices start at £13.

> **Chef:** David Hill **Proprietors:** Janet and William Hutchings **Open:** all week 12 to 2.30, 7 to 9.30 (9 Sun) **Meals:** alc exc Sun L (main courses L £13 to £16, D £14 to £18). Set L Sun £18.50 (2 courses) to £21.50 **Service:** not inc **Cards:** Amex, Delta, Maestro, MasterCard, Visa **Details:** 80 seats. 20 seats outside. Car park. Vegetarian meals. No children under 8 at D. Children's helpings. No smoking. Wheelchair access (also WC). Music **Accommodation:** 8 rooms

MAP 4 **SOLVA – Pembrokeshire**

Old Pharmacy

5 Main Street, Solva SA62 6UU
Tel: (01437) 720005
Website: www.theoldpharmacy.co.uk

Cooking 2 | Modern Welsh-Plus | £43

Pembrokeshire's finest produce is celebrated on the Old Pharmacy's menu. The restaurant is on the main street of a harbour village, and it meets its location head-on, as a large percentage of the food on offer is drawn from the sea: from sweet and succulent Solva lobster, through fillets of Milford Haven plaice rolled around crabmeat accompanied by Noilly Prat sauce, to roast hake steak in a nut and herb crust. That's not to say that meat is anything but first class, coming as it does from organic butchers in Haverfordwest and Carmarthen. Pork fillet may turn up as an oriental-style starter, stir-fried with finely shredded vegetables accompanied by a dipping sauce of soy and sesame, and Welsh black beef fillet steak may be chargrilled and served as a main course with red pepper purée, roast shallots and garlic, and a drizzle of treacle. Those with room could try baked banana bread sponge with custard and vanilla ice cream. The wine list is compact but good value, with five house bottles £12.90, or £3.70 a glass.

Chefs: Matthew Ricketts and Tom Phillips Proprietor: Martin Lawton Open: all week D only 5.30 to 9.30 Closed: 24, 25 and 26 Dec Meals: alc (main courses £12 to £24) Service: not inc Cards: Maestro, MasterCard, Visa Details: 60 seats. 12 seats outside. Vegetarian meals. Children's helpings. No smoking. Wheelchair access (also WC). Music. No mobile phones

MAP 4 **SOUTHERNDOWN – Vale of Glamorgan**

Frolics

52 Beach Road, Southerndown CF32 0RP
Tel: (01656) 880127

Cooking 1 | Modern European | £41

Originally a small corner shop, this popular ground-floor conversion is a valuable asset to the area, boasting views over fields and the Bristol Channel. Chef/proprietor Doug Windsor has managed to create a stylishly simple menu that matches the laid-back ambience. He makes the most of exemplary local supplies ('we let the ingredients do the talking'), so look out for Welsh black beef, Courtfield Farm venison, and mallard, pigeons and pheasants from Ewenny. The carte might kick off with crisp Pembroke crab pasties, or duck liver, Madeira and cep parfait with beetroot relish, and go on to roast monkfish 'osso buco', or rump of lamb with porcini polenta and a sweet shallot sauce. Proceedings are brought to an end with warm roast fig and almond tart with cinnamon ice cream. Italian house wines are £11.95.

Chef/Proprietor: Doug Windsor Open: Tue to Sun L 12 to 2.30, Tue to Sat D 6.30 to 9.30 Closed: 24 and 26 Dec, 1 Jan Meals: alc exc Sun L (main courses £10 to £17). Set L Tue to Sat £10.95 (2 courses) to £13.95, Set L Sun £12.95 (2 courses) to £14.95, Set D Tue to Fri £13.95 (2 courses) to £16.95 Service: not inc Cards: Delta, Maestro, MasterCard, Visa Details: 50 seats. 6 seats outside. Car park. Vegetarian meals. Children's helpings. No smoking. Occasional music

MAP 4 **SWANSEA – Swansea**

La Braseria

28 Wind Street, Swansea SA1 1DZ
Tel: (01792) 469683
Website: www.labraseria.com

Cooking 1 | Spanish | £38

Bright floral displays in window boxes and hanging baskets set against whitewashed walls evoke an authentic Spanishness at this bodega-style restaurant and wine bar in a thriving quarter of the city. Inside the vast dining room, the mood is lively and informal, with counters heaving under the weight of assorted seafood, steaks, kebabs, burgers and so on. There might be garlic prawns, sardines, spare ribs or 'diablo' chicken livers to start, with suckling pig, rump steak, red mullet, halibut Mornay, and pheasant in mushroom sauce among main courses. While the place has a reputation as something of a carnivore's emporium, vegetarians are not entirely neglected, with options including stuffed aubergine or vegetable stir-fry. To finish, choose something from the display of gâteaux, cheesecakes and trifles. Good-value wines start at

£11.95, and there's a decent selection of vintage clarets for big spenders.

Chef: Paul Vaughan Proprietor: D. Tercero Open: Mon to Sat 12 to 2.30, 7 to 11.30 Closed: 24, 25 and 31 Dec, 1 Jan Meals: alc (main courses £9 to £17). Set L £8.50 (2 courses). Tapas menu available Service: not inc Cards: Amex, Delta, Diners, Maestro, MasterCard, Visa Details: 250 seats. Vegetarian meals. Wheelchair access (also WC). Music. Air-conditioned

Didier & Stephanie

56 St Helens Road, Swansea SA1 4BE
Tel: (01792) 655603

Cooking 4 | French | £38

This authentic taste of France continues to be great news for the people of Swansea. The restaurant is close to the city centre, and its presence in a Victorian house is accentuated by a large green awning over the first-floor bay window. Inside, the décor is slightly muted but relaxed, with cream walls, dark green tablecloths and stripped-pine floors. Stephanie can be found front-of-house and is happy to answer any questions about the food, which she also helps prepare. This 'joyfully Gallic experience' might start with chicken liver salad with beetroot or maybe a mini omelette with prawns and herbs. Boeuf bourguignonne or rabbit braised with Dijon mustard are staples among main courses, while fish dishes may include smoked haddock fillet with parsley and garlic cream. Vegetarian options might run to pasta with basil, pine nuts and asparagus. Chestnut tart with custard cream or pistachio and almond cake make a fine finish. The flag-waving French wine list, with just a nod to the rest of the world, starts at £10.90.

Chefs/Proprietors: Didier Suvé and Stephanie Danvel Open: Tue to Sat 12 to 1.30, 7 to 9 Meals: alc D (main courses £14 to £17). Set L £9.90 (1 course) to £14.90 Service: not inc Cards: Delta, Maestro, MasterCard, Visa Details: 28 seats. No smoking. Music. Air-conditioned

Mermaid [AR]

686 Mumbles Road, Swansea SA3 4EE
Tel: (01792) 367744

A busy café and restaurant, the Mermaid takes full advantage of its position on the seafront, and customers can fully appreciate the views over Swansea Bay from the tables outside. Tapas (from £1.95)

have recently been introduced and range from tortilla, via sardines in garlic butter, to stuffed mushrooms, while the full restaurant menu has a good showing of seafood (crab and cockle gratin with laverbread, then red mullet in a crust of crayfish and Welsh rarebit) in among quail stuffed with chicken mousse (£4.95), followed by fillets of Welsh beef with faggots and a jus of red onions, bacon and mustard (£15.95). End with classic citrus tart with glazed peaches and raspberry purée (£4.45). Wines from £10.95. Open all week.

P.A.'s [AR]

95 Newton Road, Mumbles, Swansea SA3 4BN
Tel: (01792) 367723

Sourcing all their ingredients from Swansea market, Kate and Steve Maloney have successfully carved out a good reputation for themselves. Their daily changing menus offer fennel and orange soup (£3.95), while mains could be one of their fish specials including baked fillet of hake wrapped in Parma ham (£13.95) or simple whole grilled lemon sole (£16.95). Meat options include rack of Welsh lamb (£14.95) but there is also a separate vegetarian menu. Affordable wines from £9.95. Closed Sun D.

The Restaurant @ Pilot House Wharf

Pilot House Wharf, Trawler Road, Swansea SA1 1UN
Tel: (01792) 466200

Cooking 3 | Modern British/Seafood | £37

If ever a restaurant was in the right place it's this one at the far end of Swansea marina where the trawlers dock. Formerly Hanson's (Andrew Hanson has moved to new premises in St Mary Street), former co-owner Helen Tennant has kept things along the same lines. New chef Craig Gammon has a refreshing attitude: on the day of our inspection he'd just bought a large turbot and was still deciding what to do with it, stating 'you can have anything you want, the menus are just suggestions'. Given that freedom, this newly refurbished room has a relaxed air, with a small bar for pre-dinner drinks. Deep-fried squid is presented in an attractively presented tower with a delicate home-made chilli jam, while crisp, non-greasy hand-rolled fishcakes are dipped in the lightest whipped batter. Whole lemon sole is served simply in a 'clean and fresh' butter sauce, while a thick chunk of perfectly roasted hake comes with new season asparagus and a blob of hollandaise. To finish, try Tia Maria crème brûlée. Service is 'proper and interested', while the wine list offers around 40 seafood-friendly bins from £10.95.

MAP 4 **TREDUNNOCK –**
Monmouthshire

Newbridge Inn

AR

Tredunnock NP15 1LY
Tel: (01633) 451000

This substantial inn stands in an idyllic rural location by a bridge over the River Usk. Completely refurbished in 2000, it has a stylish modern look and a menu to match. Starters of seared scallops and mesclun salad with rhubarb vinaigrette (£8.50) or warm new potato and black pudding salad with a soft-poached egg (£5.50) might be followed by Welsh beef fillet with oyster mushrooms, blistered cherry tomatoes and a red wine jus (£19.50), Gloucester Old Spot pork loin with a potato cake and buttery tarragon jus (£16.50), or one of the daily fish specials listed on a blackboard. An interesting wine list opens at £12.50 for French Merlot and Sauvignon Blanc. Accommodation. Open all week.

MAP 4 **WELSH HOOK –**
Pembrokeshire

Stone Hall

AR

Welsh Hook SA62 5NS
Tel: (01348) 840212

A 600-year-old manor house is the setting for Marion Evans' French country cuisine, and her approach is governed by simplicity and tradition: escargots in garlic butter (£6.95), or home-made pasta filled with chicken mousseline, spinach and mushrooms (£7.10) open proceedings, followed

by pan-fried duck breast with onion marmalade (£17.85), or fillet of Welsh beef in Madeira sauce (£17.95). Finish with profiteroles (£6.95), or hazelnut meringue with raspberry coulis (£6.60). House wines are £15.50. Four guest rooms. Open Tue to Sat D only.

MAP 4 **WHITEBROOK –**
Monmouthshire

Crown at Whitebrook

Whitebrook NP25 4TX
Tel: (01600) 860254
Website: www.crownatwhitebrook.co.uk

Cooking 4 | Modern European | £53

Calling itself 'the original restaurant-with-rooms', this long white building is in three acres of gardens a mile from the River Wye. The emphasis is on relaxation and comfort, so guests are invited to take a pre-dinner drink in the lounge before making their way to the dining room for three-course lunch or dinner, which are punctuated by incidentals, including a sorbet. Starters of pan-fried wild sea bass with a sweet onion quiche, beetroot purée and vanilla aïoli, and poached rabbit cannelloni with butternut squash velouté and Parmesan emulsion show how complex some of the dishes can be. Main courses continue along the same line, perhaps roast saddle of Welsh lamb with truffle and potato ravioli and aubergine caviar in a rich truffle jus, or roast crown of poussin accompanied by peppered cabbage, sweet potato Anna and smoked olive sauce. 'We ate extremely well,' noted a couple, who found that desserts maintained the quality: a 'delicious' ginger soufflé with hazelnut ice cream, and rhubarb pannacotta. The global wine list, arranged by style, has a number of interesting bottles around £25. Ten come by glass from £4.75, and there are plenty of half-bottles.

Channel Islands

 MAP 1   **BEAUMONT** – Jersey

Bistro Soleil

La Route de la Haule, Beaumont, St Peter
JE3 7BA
Tel: (01534) 720249

| Cooking 4 | Bistro/Seafood | £40 |

Large windows afford beguiling views over the beach and the sea, the maritime scene enhanced by the bright, fresh, sunny décor of this bistro. Outdoor tables are arranged in a small courtyard to make the most of the Jersey climate. Ian Jones cooks an unpretentious menu orientated around good home cooking. Navarin of lamb with carrot and swede purée might vie with battered cod and mushy peas, but there is also crispy duck with noodles in a spring onion and coriander broth for the adventurous. The food of sunny climes makes sense in the surroundings, bringing on a starter of goats' cheese with aubergine caviar, sun-dried tomato bruschetta, rocket and pesto. Side orders of garlic bread will keep punters happy, as will puddings such as treacle tart with vanilla ice cream and sauce anglaise. The wine list is short and to the point, with house wines from Italy (£11.95) and France (£12.75).

Chef: Ian Jones Proprietor: Chris Power Open: all week L 12.15 to 2 (2.30 Sun), Mon to Sat D 6.45 to 9.30 Closed: Mon Nov to Apr, bank hols Meals: alc exc Sun L (main courses £13 to £18). Set L Sun £14.85, Set D £25.85 summer, £15 winter. Terrace L menu available in summer Service: not inc Cards: Amex, Delta, Maestro, MasterCard, Visa Details: 55 seats. 40 seats outside. Car park. Vegetarian meals. Children's helpings. No smoking. Wheelchair access (not WC). Music. No mobile phones. Air-conditioned

 This symbol means that the restaurant has elected to participate in *The Good Food Guide's* £5 voucher scheme (see 'Using The Good Food Guide' for details).

MAP 1   **GOREY** – Jersey

Jersey Pottery, Garden Restaurant

Gorey Village, JE3 9EP
Tel: (01534) 850850
Website: www.jerseypottery.com

| Cooking 4 | Modern British | £49 |

Set in a huge conservatory at the rear of the Jersey Pottery complex (which one reporter thought 'has come to resemble a small theme park'), the Garden Restaurant has 'gargantuan' vines, planted when the place opened, covering most of the ceiling. It's a tasteful and attractive place in which to lunch, with lots of natural light, generously spaced tables, and staff who do a good job. The Italian-leaning, modern British menu lists simple, logical combinations with an emphasis on local raw materials, especially fish and seafood: a 'rather good' wild mushroom risotto with grilled asparagus and wild rocket salad with white truffle pesto, perhaps, with a main course of roast fillet of Jersey sea bass (replaced by a 'large, fresh' fillet of brill at inspection) served with crushed Jersey Royals, spring onion salad and an excellent crab and lemon beurre blanc. The short globetrotting wine list offers some excellent bottles at reasonable prices, plus a good selection by the glass. House wine is £13.50.

Chefs: Tony Dorris and Andy Robson Proprietors: the Jones family Open: Tue to Sun and bank hol Mon L only 12 to 2.30 Closed: Jan and Feb Meals: alc (main courses £11 to £32.50). Set L £15.50 (2 courses) to £19.50 Service: net prices Cards: Delta, Diners, Maestro, MasterCard, Visa Details: 280 seats. 50 seats outside. Car park. Vegetarian meals. Children's helpings. No smoking. Wheelchair access (also WC). Music

Suma's

Gorey Hill, St Martin, Gorey JE3 6ET
Tel: (01534) 853291

Cooking 5 | Modern European | £41

The view from the terrace at Suma's could be straight from the Jersey tourist board's brochure; there's the ancient stone-walled harbour filled with yachts and fishing boats, the twelfth-century castle, and brightly painted waterfront cottages. Suma's wedge-shaped building isn't quite as pretty, but its reputation positively glows. Inside, the dining room is modern, with 'bright blue chairs and plain white everything else'. There are good-value set lunches and dinners, while Daniel Ward's imaginative cooking is big on visual impact: stacks, drizzles, and assorted slicks abound. Combinations are initially surprising as he draws from Europe and Africa to create his dishes, so Moroccan spices, turlu turlu and more straightforward options all appear. Roast langoustines with braised lambs' tongues, a potato tuile and lightly curried mussels impressed an inspector, arriving as a 'leaning tower of Pisa'. Local line-caught sea bass with aubergine caviar, truffled pomme purée, samphire and a 'fabulous' bouillabaisse sauce is a successful main course, the fish well timed, its flesh 'firm and juicy'. To finish, an unusual white chocolate fondant with Drambuie ice cream hits the spot. Service is polite, attentive and chatty, and the well-assembled wine list offers around 50 bins from around the world. House Chilean red is £10.75, French white £11.50, and around ten are served by the glass from £2.75.

Chef: Daniel Ward Proprietors: Malcolm Lewis and Sue Dufty Open: all week 12 to 2.30, 6.15 to 9.30 Closed: Christmas, early Jan Meals: alc exc Sun L (main courses £14 to £25). Set L Mon to Sat £12.50 (2 courses) to £15, Set L Sun £20, Set D Mon to Sat 6.15 to 6.45 £12.50 (2 courses) to £15, Set D Sun to Thur £30 Service: net prices Cards: Amex, Delta, Diners, Maestro, MasterCard, Visa Details: 40 seats. 16 seats outside. Vegetarian meals. Children's helpings. No smoking in dining room. Music. No mobile phones. Air-conditioned

NEW ENTRY	This appears after the restaurant's name if the establishment was not a main entry in last year's Guide. Please note, however, it may have been 'also recommended' in the previous edition.

MAP 1 ST HELIER – Jersey

Bohemia

NEW ENTRY

Green Street, St Helier
JE2 4UH
Tel: (01534) 880588
Website: www.bohemiajersey.com

Cooking 7 | Modern European | £61

Jersey does money like nowhere else. Plumb in the middle of Finance Central, rubbing shoulders with global investment institutions and expensive law firms, Bohemia is in opulent company. It has to be said that first sight of the building – 'a cubic hunk of granite with large dark-tinted windows' – might make you wonder if the name isn't a bit of a misnomer, but the interior is more the part. Rich upholstery and classy tableware lend lustre to the dining room, while the piped music brings you Air and Massive Attack rather than another dose of Ella Fitzgerald.

'I've no doubt,' commented a reporter, 'that this is the best restaurant Jersey has ever had.' That puts down some sort of marker for Shaun Rankin's classically based but unmistakably modern cooking, which does its bit for local suppliers and seasonality, not to mention stimulating the imaginations of Jersey's well-to-do. The standard format of top-end restaurants is followed, with the alternatives of a three-course fixed-price menu or a tasting menu with optional wine selections, and every available interval filled in with something – an array of canapés, a choice of five breads, a shot glass of jelly with foam on top, a pre-dessert, and petits fours with coffee. You could shear away all of that, though, and this would still be an outstanding restaurant. An inspection dinner began with a tower fashioned from white crabmeat, a piece of lobster tail, a scallop and a raviolo of scallop, the whole construction moated with a buttercup-yellow sauce of sweetcorn, more crabmeat and clouds of crab-flavoured froth. 'Unusual treatments, inspired flavours and textural combinations', allied to near-perfect execution, distinguish many dishes, including a main-course line-up of confit belly pork on wilted spinach with langoustines, a piece of roast foie gras on slow-cooked apple, and a serving of majestically good braised pork cheek on a buttery pastry base.

Appealing variations on established themes might see Angus beef carpaccio and tartare served with a horseradish bavarois. The dessert menu might look a trifle understated in the context, but just wait until the plate arrives. Another three-way dish might combine Valrhona chocolate délices with nougat ice cream and a mandarin sabayon. A lemon soufflé comes with milk chocolate semifreddo, or there is the option of properly mature farmhouse cheeses. Wine provision is a matter of a two-page listing of carefully chosen, well known names and small producers. Around a dozen are sold by the glass, from £3.75 for Languedoc varietals, while bottle prices start at £14.75.

Chef: Shaun Rankin **Proprietor:** Lawrence Huggler **Open:** Mon to Fri L 12 to 2.30, Mon to Sat D 6.30 to 10 **Meals:** Set L £16.50 (2 courses) to £45, Set D £45 to £95 (inc wine). Bar menu available Mon to Fri **Service:** 10% **Cards:** Amex, Delta, Diners, Maestro, MasterCard, Visa **Details:** 36 seats. Car park. No children under 10 at D. No smoking. Wheelchair access (also WC). Music. No mobile phones. Air-conditioned **Accommodation:** 46 rooms

---

MAP 1 ST MARTIN'S – Guernsey

Auberge

Jerbourg Road, St Martin's GY4 6BH
Tel: (01481) 238485
Website: www.theauberge.gg

Cooking 5 | **Modern British-Plus** | **£42**

The Auberge is a contemporary, stylish restaurant a few miles out of St Peter Port. The redesign of a few years ago has given the place a cosmopolitan feel: a smart long bar, blond wooden tables and a deck that overlooks the sea. Daniel Green, who joined in 2005, works to a lively and imaginative menu and uses lots of locally sourced produce, particularly fish, which is delivered daily. Fois gras parfait comes with home-made peach chutney, goats' cheese and a dressing of pomegranate and balsamic, while king prawns in garlic mayonnaise are served with avocado ice cream and Thai-spiced crab cakes. Interesting combinations are found among main courses too: poached medallions of monkfish are accompanied by prawn mousse, shiitake mushrooms, and crisp Parma ham, and roast pork fillet is partnered by honey-roast belly and served with shallot mash, apple and sage compote, and a sauce of chicken livers. Desserts are true to form: chilled rhubarb and orange soup with deepfried white chocolate spring rolls, for example. The wine list is compact but wide-ranging, with plenty of choice under £20. House selections are £13.95.

Chef: Daniel Green **Proprietor:** Ian Irving-Walker **Open:** all week 12 to 2, 6.45 to 9.30 **Closed:** 25 Dec, 1 Jan **Meals:** alc (main courses £12.50 to £16) **Service:** not inc **Cards:** Amex, Delta, Diners, Maestro, MasterCard, Visa **Details:** 70 seats. 50 seats outside. Car park. Vegetarian meals. Children's helpings. No smoking. Wheelchair access (also WC). Music. Air-conditioned

---

MAP 1 ST PETER PORT – Guernsey

Da Nello

46 Pollet Street, St Peter Port GY1 1WF
Tel: (01481) 721552

In a fifteenth-century granite building, this robust Italian eatery makes the best use of local fish and shellfish and the island's veal and dairy produce, with spring lamb brought over from Sark. Signature dishes include a starter of roast sweet balsamic baby onions with Parma ham, mozzarella and tomatoes (£6.75), main-course medallions of beef with a Barolo sauce (£13.95), and ginger and mascarpone cheesecake (£4.50). Italian wines stand out among a short international list from £11.50. Open all week.

La Frégate

Les Cotils, St Peter Port GY1 1UT
Tel: (01481) 724624
Website: www.lafregatehotel.com

Cooking 4 | **Modern European** | **£44**

Castle Cornet, an 800-year-old fortress, dominates the St Peter Port skyline, but after 25 years in business this smart hotel and restaurant has become a landmark of equal renown. The light, airy dining room has contemporary styling and picture windows giving unrivalled views of the castle and the bay, while the menus showcase the best of Guernsey produce, notably fish and seafood. As well as straightforward platters of Herm oysters, or lobster with herb mayonnaise, starters run to sashimi-style seared tuna with a spicy oriental salad and pineapple crisp, or seared scallops on a warm tian of crab with chive butter sauce. To follow, there might be brill fillet on champ topped with crabmeat and hollandaise, while a handful of meat options could include pink-cooked peppered duck breast with honey-roast root vegetables and foie gras sauce. Mandarin cheesecake with lemon and basil sorbet makes an unusual alternative to something like crêpes suzette for dessert. There are some hefty *grand cru* clarets and Burgundies on the wine list, plus plenty of regional French and New World bottles for under £25, including house selections at £13.50.

ples from Bordeaux and Burgundy to exciting New World offerings. There is good drinking across the board, starting with house vins de pays at £19, and an excellent choice of over 20 are served by the glass.

Chef: Neil Maginnis   Proprietor: Guernsey Summer Holiday Ltd   Open: all week 12 to 1.30, 7 to 9.30   Meals: alc (main courses £11 to £18.50). Set L £15 (2 courses) to £17.95, Set D £22.75 (2 courses) to £26.50   Service: not inc   Cards: Amex, Delta, Diners, Maestro, MasterCard, Visa   Details: 80 seats. 20 seats outside. Car park. Vegetarian meals. No smoking. No music. Air-conditioned   Accommodation: 22 rooms

Chef: Andrew Baird   Proprietor: Malcolm Lewis   Open: all week 12.30 to 2, 7 to 9.30   Meals: alc (main courses £28 to £30). Set L £12.50 (2 courses) to £15, Set L Sun £27.50. Set D £55 to £95 (inc wine). Light menu available   Service: net prices   Cards: Amex, Delta, Diners, Maestro, MasterCard, Visa   Details: 70 seats. 40 seats outside. Car park. Vegetarian meals. Children's helpings. No smoking in 1 dining room. Wheelchair access (not WC). No music. No mobile phones   Accommodation: 31 rooms

MAP 1 | ST SAVIOUR – Jersey

Longueville Manor

St Saviour JE2 7WF
Tel: (01534) 725501
Website: www.longuevillemanor.com

Cooking 5 | Modern European | £65

Longueville is a small-scale country-house hotel with an upmarket feel, and in its two dining rooms the ambitious cooking matches the surroundings both in its luxurious style and its accomplished execution. The menus make the best of an abundance of local seafood as well as produce from the manor's own kitchen gardens. A highly wrought starter of poached lobster tail on vanilla- and tomato-scented jelly with lobster and Malibu foam demonstrates the kind of heights the kitchen is aiming for, while sautéed foie gras with pickled aubergine, quince purée, poached rhubarb and coconut foam shows a willingness to experiment with flavour combinations. But there are also a few more straightforward, classically minded options, such as a main course of grilled fillet of Aberdeen Angus beef with seared foie gras, lyonnaise onions and ceps, although even this is finished with a beef jelly, while pot-roast squab pigeon comes with tagliolini, glazed lime curd, beetroot, carrot and caviar. Desserts are no less elaborate or inventive, taking in an 'assiette of pineapple and coffee', and Valrhona chocolate fondant with white chocolate and ginger ganache and lemongrass and coconut sorbet. The wine list boasts '400 perfectly conditioned wines', ranging from famous, classic exam-

Northern Ireland

MAP 16   BELFAST – Co Antrim

Aldens

229 Upper Newtownards Road, Belfast BT4 3LW
Tel: (028) 9065 0079
Website: www.aldensrestaurant.com

Cooking 2 | Modern Irish | £40

Adding a touch of sophistication to an unglamorous location, this stylish restaurant has a relaxed, unfussy feel. It's as accommodating as can be, offering a straightforward menu, whether you're just popping in for a light lunch, a weightier dinner, or sometimes the other way round. The range extends from steamed mussels with spicy tomato and beer, via beetroot risotto with pancetta, to roast rack of lamb provençale. On the way it takes in lunch specials like spicy meatballs with mash and onion gravy, and a good-value set dinner offering the likes of chicken liver pâté, then crisp duck confit with red cabbage and mushroom cream. A prodigious list of desserts, including orange marmalade cheesecake, and violet sherbet, rounds things off. The solid, fairly priced wine list opens with a page of house wines from £13.95.

> **Chef:** Denise Hockey **Proprietor:** Jonathan Davis **Open:** Mon to Fri L 12 to 2.30, Mon to Sat D 6 to 10 (11 Fri and Sat) **Closed:** 2 weeks July, bank hols **Meals:** alc (main courses L £6 to £16, D £8 to £19). Set D (exc Fri after 7 and Sat) £18.95 (2 courses) to £21.95 **Service:** not inc **Cards:** Amex, Delta, Maestro, MasterCard, Visa **Details:** 70 seats. Vegetarian meals. Children's helpings. No-smoking area. Wheelchair access (also WC). No music. Air-conditioned

> This symbol means that it is possible to have a three-course dinner, including coffee, half a bottle of house wine and service, for £30 or less per person.

Cayenne

7 Ascot House, Shaftesbury Square, Belfast BT2 7DB
Tel: (028) 9033 1532
Website: www.rankingroup.co.uk

Cooking 4 | Fusion | £48

This smart and fashionable city-centre restaurant is a welcoming place. That it appeals to a wide-ranging clientele is due to a crowd-pleasing menu that recognises no boundaries. But while the style can be described as fusion, it occurs mostly across the menu rather than within the dish. Pork and ginger pot stickers with a spicy soy dipping sauce might get the ball rolling, while among main courses have been Korean-spiced loin of lamb with kim-chee and crispy spiced potatoes, and roast skate wing with steamed Asian greens, new potatoes, yuzu, and cockle and soy vinaigrette. Quirkier touches include Asian-style fish 'n' chips with spiced lentils and Thai mayonnaise, while among desserts have been a Bounty parfait with passion-fruit jelly, and kaffir lime leaf pannacotta with mango salad and a citrus cookie. The varietally arranged wine list sweeps from a range of easy-going gluggers under £20 to some smart bottles, taking in along the way astute choices from all over. Paul and Jeanne Rankin also run Rain City and Roscoff Brasserie (see entries below).

> **Chef:** Danny Millar **Proprietors:** Paul and Jeanne Rankin **Open:** Mon to Fri L 12 to 2.15, all week D 6 (5 Sun) to 10.15 (11.15 Fri and Sat, 8.45 Sun) **Closed:** 25 and 26 Dec, 1 Jan, 12 July **Meals:** alc (main courses L £10.50 to £15, D £14.50 to £20). Set L £12 (2 courses) to £15.50, Set D Sun to Thur £15.50 to £19.50 **Service:** not inc **Cards:** Amex, Delta, Diners, Maestro, MasterCard, Visa **Details:** 120 seats. Vegetarian meals. Children's helpings. No-smoking area. Wheelchair access (also WC). Music. Air-conditioned

James Street South

21 James Street South, Belfast BT2 7GA
Tel: (028) 9043 4310
Website: www.jamesstreetsouth.co.uk

| Cooking 5 | Modern European | £47 |

There's a feel of a modern art gallery to this popular city-centre restaurant, its stark white walls lined with displays of abstract contemporary paintings, and during the day light floods in through large windows. Add to the equation large, well-spaced tables with white cloths and the overall effect is refreshingly bright and airy. This impression is re-created in the food, starters partnering smoked salmon with caperberries and a poached quail's egg, or cutting the richness of roast wood pigeon with an apricot and orange marmalade. Chef Niall McKenna shows accomplished technique and an inventive way with fish and seafood to come up with main dishes of sautéed sea trout with tiger prawn and pearl barley risotto and lemon foam, or roast halibut with artichoke and foie gras foam. Meat and game are equally well used in finely balanced combinations such as roast loin of Finnebrogue venison with golden raisins, parsnip purée and Valrhona chocolate jus. Finish perhaps with vanilla pannacotta with spiced plums and coconut tuiles, or chocolate fondant with almond praline and warm white chocolate sauce. The wine list includes some fairly grand bottles as well as plenty of more modest options, with house selections from £16.

Chef: Niall McKenna Proprietors: Niall and Joanne McKenna Open: Mon to Sat L 12 to 2.45, all week D 5.45 to 10.45 (9.30 Sun) Closed: 25 and 26 Dec, 1 Jan, 12 and 13 July Meals: alc (main courses £12.50 to £18.50). Set L £13.50 (2 courses) to £15.50, pre-theatre Set D Mon to Thur £15.50 (2 courses) to £17.50. Bar menu available Service: not inc Cards: Amex, Delta, Maestro, MasterCard, Visa Details: 75 seats. Vegetarian meals. Children's helpings. No-smoking area. Wheelchair access (also WC). Music. Air-conditioned

Metro Brasserie

13 Lower Crescent, Belfast BT7 1NR
Tel: (028) 9032 3349

Near the university, this modern brasserie is located within the Crescent Townhouse Hotel. The globe-trotting menu might start with baked fig and goats' cheese galette with vanilla-poached pear and honey (£5.75), before main courses of Glenarm salmon baked with lavender (£12.95), or dry-aged Irish sirloin with Gorgonzola butter and chips (£17.50). End with dark chocolate and caramel cheesecake

with cherry sorbet (£4.95). Wines from £13. Open Wed to Sat L and all week D.

Nick's Warehouse

35 Hill Street, Belfast BT1 2LB
Tel: (028) 9043 9690
Website: www.nickswarehouse.co.uk

| Cooking 3 | Modern Irish | £40 |

⊗ ⓔ

This warehouse conversion has built up a solid following. Lunch is a popular affair in the buzzy downstairs wine bar – sandwiches, salads and hot dishes such as roast loin of pork with mash and casseroled vegetables and lentils – while dining upstairs is a more formal experience. Nick and Kathy Price's emphasis is on sourcing materials from small local producers; Finnebrogue venison, rare-breed pork, and cheeses such as Glebe Brethan all make appearances, while a yearly Slow Food Fair is held where producers can promote their wares. Pork and prawn dumplings in a Thai noodle broth or pan-fried pigeon with pommes Anna might be followed by duck breast on parsnip purée with a honey and ginger sauce, or perhaps chargrilled swordfish with a pineapple and red pepper salsa. End on a sweet note with dark chocolate and nut terrine with a white chocolate sauce. The global wine list has a page of fine wines and makes a feature of Spain. Chilean house white is £12.95, red £14.50.

Chefs: Nick Price, Sean Craig and Danny Monaghan Proprietors: Nick and Kathy Price Open: Mon to Fri L 12 to 3, Tue to Sat D 6 to 9.30 (10 Fri and Sat) Closed: 24 to 26 Dec, 1 Jan, Easter Mon and Tue, 7 May, 12 July Meals: alc (main courses L £7.50 to £18, D £9.50 to £18.50) Service: not inc Cards: Amex, Delta, Diners, Maestro, MasterCard, Visa Details: 185 seats. Vegetarian meals. Children's helpings. No smoking. Wheelchair access (also WC). Music. Air-conditioned

Rain City

33–35 Malone Road, Belfast BT9 6RU
Tel: (028) 9068 2929
Website: www.rankingroup.co.uk

| Cooking 3 | International | £35 |

ⓔ

Rain City is an American-style diner owned by Paul and Jeanne Rankin (see also Cayenne and Roscoff Brasserie). It sprawls over two ground-floor rooms with a distinct retro vibe, and presents menus that span mix-and-match dishes to allow diners to snack or create a three-course meal, with a number of items served in medium-sized and larger portions. Seafood chowder, pesto toast, and slow-roast Texan barbecue ribs could start a meal, while main courses encompass anything from chicken and wild mushroom bolognese, through New England-style crab cakes with fennel salad, chilli jam, and coriander mayonnaise, to venison burger with Roquefort, red onion marmalade and fries. The weekend brunch menu brings forth smoked salmon bagel, eggs Benedict, and buttermilk pancakes with maple syrup and blueberry compote, and children have their own menu. End with cheesecake with a seasonal fruit compote, or chocolate truffle cake. The short wine list is competitively priced, with most bins under £20, starting at £15.50.

Chef: Gerry McCann **Proprietors:** Paul and Jeanne Rankin **Open:** all week 12 (10 Sat and Sun) to 5, 5 to 10.30 **Closed:** 25 Dec **Meals:** alc (main courses £6 to £14.50) **Service:** not inc **Cards:** Amex, Delta, Diners, Maestro, MasterCard, Visa **Details:** 90 seats. 25 seats outside. Vegetarian meals. Children's helpings. No-smoking area. Wheelchair access (also WC). Music. Air-conditioned

Restaurant Michael Deane

36–40 Howard Street, Belfast BT1 6PF
Tel: (028) 9033 1134
Website: www.michaeldeane.co.uk

Cooking 5 | **Modern European-Plus** | **£63**

Michael Deane's cooking comes in two parts. Tuck into comfort-zone dishes like French onion soup, ribeye with chips and béarnaise, or duck breast with creamed parsnip, juniper and cranberry in the buzzy ground-floor brasserie, or ascend the Hollywood-style sweeping staircase for some 'serious eating' in the 'hushed and respectful atmosphere' of the first-floor restaurant. An amuse-bouche of velvety parsnip cream, and good bread impressed at inspection, followed by stuffed rabbit saddle, with sweet pepper couscous, aubergine, cocoa beans and Pommery mustard. Not all dishes seem to match their menu specifications, thus undermining overall performance. A chocolate plate (baby doughnut filled with milk chocolate ganache, dark mousse, a shot glass of ice cream, tiramisù, chocolate cream with dipping strawberries) is an accomplished dessert, though, made with good chocolate and full of considered, balanced flavours. Staff are polite, and there's a formal, old-fashioned touch to the service. Many bottles on the wine list are pitched at big spenders, but close scrutiny reveals numerous interesting options

under and around £25 from less mainstream regions. The sommelier's choice of nine bottles opens at £23, £5.50 a glass.

Chefs: Michael Deane and Derek Creagh **Proprietor:** Michael Deane **Open:** Wed to Sat D only 7.30 to 9; brasserie Mon to Sat 12 to 3, 5.30 to 10 (11 Fri and Sat) **Meals:** Set D £35 (2 courses) to £62; brasserie menu available **Service:** not inc **Cards:** Amex, Delta, Maestro, MasterCard, Visa **Details:** 35 seats. Children's helpings. No smoking in dining room. Music. No mobile phones. Air-conditioned

Roscoff Brasserie

7–11 Linenhall Street, Belfast BT2 8AA
Tel: (028) 9031 1150
Website: www.rankingroup.co.uk

Cooking 5 | **Modern European** | **£50**

The Rankins' city-centre brasserie opened in 2004 to loud acclaim. Just behind the City Hall, it is a relaxed, stylishly decorated place, with curved, blue-grey banquettes, good modern artwork and soft, recessed lighting. What's more, the welcome is full of Irish warmth, and service is well attuned to the task in hand.

The menus deal in Paul Rankin's signature style of up-to-the-minute, inventive but heartening cooking. This is food you want to eat. You might start with something as simple as French onion soup with Gruyère and croûtons, or more richly with sweetbreads accompanied by crisp shallots and lentils cooked in sherry. Main courses aim for the umami factor, partnering roast monkfish with braised oxtail, root vegetables and gremolada, or adding pancetta, pommes Anna, Savoy cabbage and a green peppercorn sauce to properly crisped-up duck confit. Veal meatballs with buttered noodles might make a hearty winter dish, served with artichokes, green olives and sage. The wealth of choice continues into appealing desserts that range from spiced roast plum mille-feuille with orange mascarpone to white chocolate mousse with espresso ice cream and a cardamom tuile. Wines by the glass from £3.95 head up a concise brasserie list that does the business and has enough under £20 to give the budget-conscious a fair choice.

Chef: Connor MacCann **Proprietors:** Paul and Jeanne Rankin **Open:** Mon to Fri L 12 to 2.15, Mon to Sat D 6 to 10.15 (11.15 Sat) **Closed:** 25 and 26 Dec, 1 Jan, 12 July **Meals:** alc (main courses £14 to £25). Set L £15.25 (2 courses) to £19.50, Set D Mon to Thur £21.50 (2 courses) to £27 **Service:** not inc **Cards:** Amex, Delta, Diners, Maestro, MasterCard, Visa **Details:** 86 seats. Vegetarian meals. Children's helpings. No-smoking area. Wheelchair access (also WC). Music. Air-conditioned

Ta Tu

AR

701 Lisburn Road, Belfast BT9 7GU
Tel: (028) 9038 0818

A cosmopolitan bar and grill that serves the south side of Belfast very well indeed with menus ranging from tapas (from £2.50), a children's menu (£4.95), and a modern European carte. Start with chilli salt squid with a mango and mint salad (£5.95), and move on to pan-fried fillet of salmon with prawn and chive potato cake and sauce vierge (£14.95), or grilled sirloin with dauphinois potatoes and sauce chasseur (£15.95). Conclude with baked chocolate and orange tart (£4.95). House Chilean is £11.95, and there's a decent showing by the glass. Open all week.

MAP 16   KIRCUBBIN – Co Down

Paul Arthurs

66 Main Street, Kircubbin BT22 2SP
Tel: (028) 4273 8192
Website: www.paularthurs.com

Cooking 3 | Seafood/Modern European | £40

Not the most inspiring of locations for a fine-dining restaurant – above a fish and chip shop and amusement arcade – but the inventive, upmarket cooking rises above the setting. Paul Arthur has trained in the kitchens of some of Northern Ireland's finest and it shows in dishes such as seared foie gras crostini with crispy onions and port jus, or a simple grilled sirloin of beef with classic béarnaise sauce. Tortellini of ricotta combines wild mushrooms, mascarpone and Parmesan, while a main course of peppered haunch of venison may come with glazed red onions and champ. Finish with something like sticky toffee pudding. The wine list is short but takes in reasonably priced selections from around the globe. Six house wines are £10.95.

> **Chef/Proprietor:** Paul Arthurs   **Open:** Sun L 12 to 2.30, Tue to Sat D 5 to 9   **Closed:** Jan   **Meals:** alc (main courses £13.50 to £25)   **Service:** not inc   **Cards:** Amex, Delta, Diners, Maestro, MasterCard, Visa   **Details:** 45 seats. 20 seats outside. Vegetarian meals. Children's helpings. Occasional music. Air-conditioned

> To submit a report on any restaurant, please visit *www.which.co.uk/gfgfeedback*.

Index